Gun Digest®

1999 / 53rd Annual Edition

Edited by Ken Warner

Manuscripts, contributions and inquiries, including first class return postage, should be sent to the GUN DIGEST Editorial Offices, Krause Publications, 700 E. State Street, Iola, WI 54990-0001. All materials received will receive reasonable care, but we will not be responsible for their safe return. Material accepted is subject to our requirements for editing and revisions. Author payment covers all rights and title to the accepted material, including photos, drawings and other illustrations. Payment is at our current rates.

CAUTION: Technical data presented here, particularly technical data on handloading and on firearms adjustment and alteration, inevitably reflects individual experience with particular equipment and components under specific circumstances the reader cannot duplicate exactly. Such data presentations therefore should be used for guidance only and with caution. Krause Publications, Inc., accepts no responsibility for results obtained using this data.

Published by

krause
publications

700 E. State Street • Iola, WI 54990-0001
Telephone: 715/445-2214

Please call or write for our free catalog.

Our toll-free number to place an order or obtain a free catalog is 800-258-0929 or please use our regular business telephone 715-445-2214 for editorial comment and further information.

Library of Congress Catalog Number: 44-32588

ISBN: 0-87349-203-X

About our Covers

Nikon has been manufacturing superb optical products since the introduction of the first Nikon binocular in 1917, over 80 years ago. (Interestingly, this binocular pre-dated Nikon cameras by 31 years.) Since then, Nikon binoculars, spotting scopes and riflescopes have gained a well-earned reputation for dependability, ruggedness, and unmatched optical quality. Nothing epitomizes this long-standing reputation for quality like the Nikon Monarch® UCC® line of riflescopes.

Monarch riflescopes were introduced to hunters and shooters in 1996 and have earned a reputation as quality instruments that are at home on the finest firearms.

Nikon Monarch lenses are precisely ground on some of the world's most advanced equipment, then meticulously polished to remove even the slightest surface aberrations. The Nikon Ultra Clear Coat® optical system combines these lenses with an advanced anti-reflection multicoating technology that provides scratch resistance and boosts light transmission to a full 95%. This is an especially useful advantage at dawn and dusk, or on the overcast days that often accompany hunting.

The entire Nikon Monarch UCC line is built on one-inch diameter, one-piece main body tubes milled by CNC machinery from aircraft-grade aluminum tubestock. They feature 1/4-minute steel-to-brass positive click windage and elevation adjustments (1/8-minute on 6.5-20x44 models), assuring repeatability and adjustment precision.

All Nikon Monarch scopes are purged of air, filled with dry nitrogen and O-ring sealed to provide waterproof, fogproof and shockproof integrity. This allows them to perform under grueling hunting conditions and stand up to rifle and handgun recoil.

The rifle on the front cover is a 280 Ackley Improved built on a customized pre-64 Winchester Model 70 in a commissioned project planned and coordinated by stockmaker Kent Bowerly of Camp Sherman, Oregon. It wears the highly popular Nikon Monarch 3-9x40 matte.

The metalwork on this fine rifle was completed by Jim Wisner of P.M. Enterprises and features a 23" Shilen match grade barrel contoured to Bowerly's instructions, installed on the externally and internally polished action. In addition, there is extensive engraving and French greying with platinum and gold wildlife scenes on the floorplate and grip cap. This work is accented with modest gold highlights all by Bob Evans, engraver, of Oregon City, Oregon. Bowerly then jewelled both the bolt and magazine follower.

The stockwork is Bowerly's, and features an exhibition grade blank of California English Walnut with an extraordinary dark "Marble-Cake" figure. The stock design is American Classic, and integrates 24 LPI checkering with Bowerly's unique Fleur-de-lis pattern and ebony forend tip.

The matched pair of rifles on the back cover are also by Kent Bowerly. There rifles are built on consecutively serial numbered Dakota Safari actions chambered in 7mm Remington Magnum and 338 Winchester Magnum. They wear 4x40 and 2-7x32 Nikon Monarchs, respectively. Both rifles feature drop box magazines, Shilen match grade barrels, quarter ribs with express sights, Talley rings and barrel band swivel studs. The metalwork is by Jim Wisner.

These unique rifles utilize matching blanks of Circassian walnut, and hand-rubbed oil finishes for conservative, elegant looks. Identical 24 LPI checkering patterns are set off by Bowerly's masterful scribe cut borders.

Both rifles are complemented by engraver Bob Evans' English scroll and fine gold borders.

For information on these rifles contact Kent Bowerly, 26247 Metolius Meadows Dr., Camp Sherman, Oregon 97730. (541) 595-6028.

For more information on Nikon Monarch UCC riflescopes, plus information on Nikon's full line of Riflescopes, Binoculars and Spotting Scopes, write: Nikon Sport Optics, 1300 Walt Whitman Rd., Melville, NY 11747-3064 or call 1-800-248-6846. www.nikonusa.com

Photos by John Hanusin

— GUN DIGEST STAFF —

EDITOR-IN-CHIEF
Ken Warner

SENIOR STAFF EDITORS
Ken Ramage
Harold A. Murtz

ASSOCIATE EDITOR
Kevin Michalowski

CONTRIBUTING EDITORS
Bob Bell

Holt Bodinson

Raymond Caranta

Doc Carlson

John Malloy

Layne Simpson

Larry S. Sterett

Hal Swiggett

Don Zutz

Editorial Comments and Suggestions

We're always looking for feedback on our books. Please let us know what you like about this edition. If you have suggestions for articles you'd like to see in future editions, please contact

Ken Ramage/Gun Digest
700 East State St.
Iola, WI 54990
email: ramagek@krause.com

CONTENTS

Another Modest Proposal

From Ken Warner

IN THE FULLNESS of time, readers of GUN DI-GEST may become accustomed to seeing an editorial idea displayed right here. It will take longer than that, of course, before anyone pays attention, but we have to start somewhere.

Limiting the number of cartridges a hunter might carry in the interests of better sport was a good idea we tried on a couple of years ago. This time, we move into the political arena.

In quaint old Switzerland, at least in certain voting districts of certain cantons, voters still parade to the polls on Election Day as did their ancestors—under arms. In those old days, it was no doubt unsafe to go anywhere unarmed; today, the carrying of swords, or pikes, or assault rifles or a wide variety of other instruments is the celebration of the Schwyzer's established *right to be armed.*

It is a charming custom, and photos of the quaint little rich people en route to vote, guns slung or swords belted, have graced all the better travel publications for decades. It's one of those things—after money— that make the Schwyzers *Swiss.*

And now and here we ask: Why should this elegant rite of biennial passage be confined to the Swiss? Why not us? Where is the state legislature with the strength to decree that only U.S. citizens under arms may vote in their state! It is NOT a stretch; no one can deny we won our right to vote with a contest at arms.

Think of it. We are unlikely, of course, to see much four-color art in travel magazines of quaint American citizens strolling to the polls, fowling pieces politely broken over arms. There would be, at first, a *lot* of press coverage, nonetheless. By the time the 20th state leg-islature trussed up its guts and went for it, however, this idea would be ho-hum, just another thing we do.

And we would be left with the political reality of the armed citizen firmly and publicly mortared into our fundamental law. And there would be a few specific advantages, all of them clear gain.

The two most important rights a U.S. felon loses, or at least the two that generally are cited, are the right to vote and the right to be armed. So the two—the right to vote and the right to be armed—are already connected. This, the 1999 Idea, could formalize that relationship.

No doubt there are felons voting all the time. We do not, after all, *brand* them. And, of course, there are a *lot* more felons who go armed, unfortunately and illegally. However, the idea that a felon would wear a sword or tote a shotgun to a polling place is ludicrous. Felons, by definition, do dumb stuff, but not usually *that* dumb.

Besides, it is not our intent that this be an empty parade of *images* of arms. If that were so, you could arm at Toys'R'Us. Part of any genuine Armed Voter Law would have to be the requirement that the arms be real. That is, the swords be sharp, the bows strung, the guns accompanied by cartridges, though perhaps not loaded. Indeed, it should be law that every other 25th or 50th weapon should be tested—the swords used to cut, the guns and bows shot—right then and there. We need no *symbolically* armed citizens.

As a consequence, of course, we will see the creation of "voter's arms." Nice 22 rifles and 410 shotguns for the elderly or infirm; red-white-and-blue pistols for the particularly patriotic; just anything off their own racks for sportsmen and sportswomen.

Voting, we must in our hearts admit, is in a sad state in these United States. Not many of us—not a majority—do it, in fact. It is our contention here that an Armed Voter Law would give the process new dignity, new merit, new *symbolic* importance. And those things could lead to new *real* importance.

Indeed, the right to vote could become, as it should be, a rite of passage. At 18, a citizen—one who is not a felon or otherwise legally barred from either voting or being armed—could be *invested* by the family or the neighbors with a suitable arm and thus be *recognized* as a citizen.

Of course, the whole neighborhood would know. That would go on, this being America even today, in all sorts of neighborhoods, with all sorts of people, none of them felons, and very probably, all sorts of guns. That's *very* American.

There would probably be a bit of peer pressure going on, too. There doesn't seem to be much of that about *voting*, but the right to carry, and the rite of carrying, a weapon is substantively different. Its effect is not remote; it's right *there*, like on Main Street. And absolutely, explicitly central to the idea: No felon can do it, not legally, not in public.

Further, this is not a right spoiled by being gender-related. Young women would take their rightful places made, both symbolically and actually, equal in this one thing, regardless of other circumstance, regardless of other argument.

This is to its author—that is me—an altogether charming idea. Not the least of its charms is the fact that

Chortling over the opportunities before him, Warner displays his 18th Gun Digest.

it would affect every voter in the land and it would not cost anything. That's not only charming, but almost impossible.

The event would not be, most places, illegal either. That is, it would be unnecessary to adjust other laws. In any number of states, for instance, firearms—not to mention bows, pole arms and swords—may be carried openly by statute. In the main, this is discussed in terms of the handgun openly on the belt, the shotgun in the window rack and so forth, but it would doubtless apply on Election Day.

Some early legislatures may have intended something like this, or perhaps intended that all citizens be armed whenever they chose that happy state. In some of those states, where open carry is permitted, it is disallowed in schools and banks and establishments which serve liquor, but states that ban arms at the polls are few in number.

There does not seem from here, in short, to be any obstacle at all. Some legislature *can* do it. Any legislature *should* do it. How about yours?

Galco International's "Trail Boss" outfit — the cartridge belt is a money belt, the six-gun is a stainless steel *Vaquero*.

COWBOY SHOOTING NOW

BY JERRY BURKE

As TV Westerns were replaced by situation comedies in the '60s, quick draw faded from general public notice. Traditional bullseye target shooting remained, and innovators like Jeff Cooper emerged to present the handgun as a real life combat weapon and a practical hunting tool.

As American handgunning thus evolved, and perhaps over-evolved, competitors could be seen seeking ways to alter equipment (and maybe bend the rules) in all sorts of new courses of fire. Some shooting sports came to replicate all the expense and frantic competitiveness of the work-a-day world, the very thing most people try to avoid in recreational pursuits.

It came to pass that a few Californians grew tired of working so hard just to have gun-fun. With full-blown pioneering spirit, they formed "The Wild Bunch," based on a simple credo... have competitive fun with 19th century-style firearms while paying homage to America's Western heritage. For them, competition served primarily as an excuse to get together and shoot.

Shooters ready to compete at the Winter Range. The cute little wagons carry their equipment.

Cowboy Action Shooting events emphasize safety first — shooters often cock with the off hand.

Anything that went then goes now. This trio is walking Vendor's Row.

That was in 1983, and that original Wild Bunch has grown into an affiliation of more than 135 clubs across the U.S. and around the world. At this writing, more than 15,000 card-carrying, alias-approved members pay modest annual dues to maintain their good standing status with the Single Action Shooting Society. Considering the original rebirth of cowboyism in the 1950s and '60s less than satisfying, I couldn't help but wonder how this newfangled, old-fashioned Cowboy Action Shooting business compared to the real Old West.

These shooters, I found, each assume a unique "alias" ... the persona of a specific individual or profession from the original Wild West era or a fantasy character from those old B-movie or now-classic Western television shows. Each alias accepted for registration is truly unique, and an SASS member's pseudonym is limited only by his or her imagination. Many are great names, like Gila Slim, Hipshot, K.C. Jack, Lone Star Ranger; others employ words like Deadeye, Buckaroo, even Bucolic.

The Old West of reality is usually defined as the period between the end of the War Between The States (1865) and the end of the century.

The Wild West covered an incredible amount of real estate to be settled in such a short period of time. We're talking vast expanses of unknown and uncharted land as strange as the back side of the moon. The West on any map was everything "from the Mississippi River all the way to the Pacific coastline; from the Canadian border south to the Rio Grande.

California, over the period, sported a modicum of high society and suspiciously civilized behavior be-

fore the dust settled in the rest of the West, but it was plenty raucous in its own right. Many of today's cowboy action shooters are found on the same pieces of real estate as the pioneers of the Old West.

It was the promise of free land and the freedom to succeed or fail on their own merits which enticed eager settlers to the early American West, impatient to grab their portion of Manifest Destiny. European interest in the Old West was still strong in 1944, when Nazi-controlled German newspapers announced that Rangers were part of the landing force in occupied France. Erroneously, they reported it was the Texas Rangers who'd hit the beaches and stormed the cliffs.

For those original Westerners, hazards were everywhere, both on the open prairies and in ill-conceived shanty towns and tent cities. If the Injuns or outlaws didn't assault settlers and drovers in the virtually unprotected hinterlands, the unpredictable weather or tainted water supply could prove just as deadly. Law and order was a sometimes thing on the frontier; often, the presence of celebrating cowboys from Texas and elsewhere was too much for local gendarmes to control at least in story and film.

The original settlers of America's Wild West certainly weren't immune to fashion. However, a cowboy who saw the laced hat brim of another might decide to duplicate that look on his next trip into town, without realizing it was the sign of a cheap hat that wouldn't hold its shape. Keeping fashionable thoughts in the forefront were drummers, local merchants and limited-circulation Old West newspapers, tempting both ladies and gents with what was or had

lately been in vogue in Paris and New York.

Many settlers wore homemade items and most men braved the West in a simple shirt of cotton or wool, with only a spare in reserve. Same for pants, held in place by braces (suspenders), plus a coat, probably of canvas duck. Boots were daily wear for those working outdoors, with more pronounced heels if you found yourself routinely swinging into a saddle.

For town and city folks, hightop shoes were standard footgear, but respectable women had to have their ankles covered. A banker would wear a suit; so would a professional gambler, but his likely something more garish, with maybe a lacy silk shirt for good measure. Saloon and pleasure-palace working girls dressed a little differently than the rest of the female population, with pleasing the itinerant male population more important than considerations of modesty; exposed ankles were the least of their decorum infractions.

Now, a totally new clothing and accessory industry has emerged to support every wardrobe whim of today's cowboy action folks. Any and all forms of attire which graced the backs of Old West citizens is being replicated today, right down to men's drawers and ladies' pantaloons. Most SASS members have considerably more disposable income than did the pioneers of old. Get-ups vary from the simplest garb of the dirt-poor cowhand to lavish period gowns for ladies fit for any Governor's Ball, then or now.

Someone new to Cowboy Action Shooting might get started with hardware and clothing already on-hand - a flannel shirt, non-designer

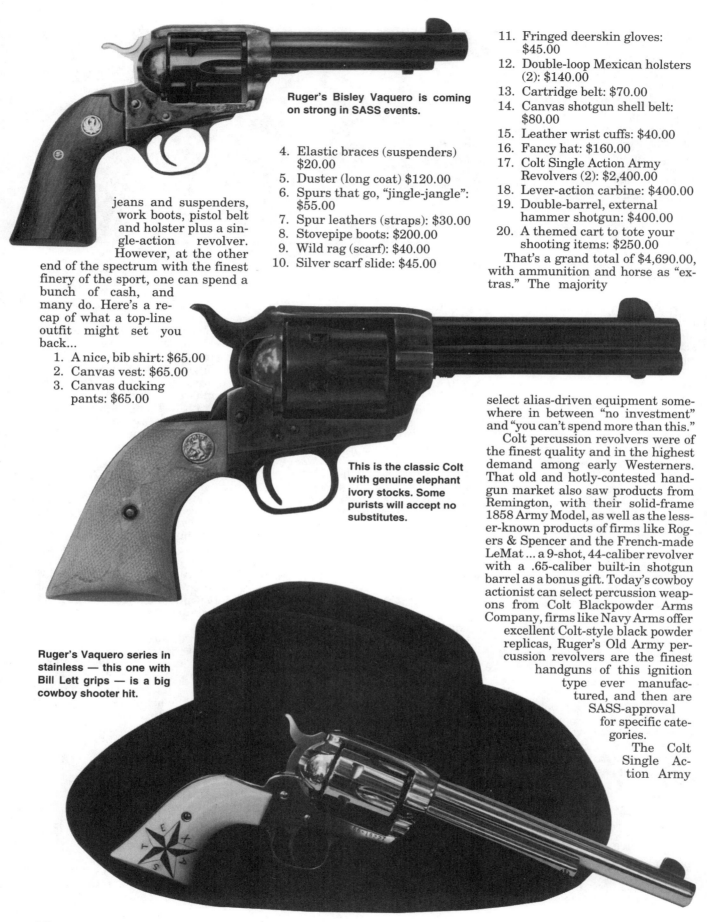

Ruger's Bisley Vaquero is coming on strong in SASS events.

jeans and suspenders, work boots, pistol belt and holster plus a single-action revolver. However, at the other end of the spectrum with the finest finery of the sport, one can spend a bunch of cash, and many do. Here's a recap of what a top-line outfit might set you back...

1. A nice, bib shirt: $65.00
2. Canvas vest: $65.00
3. Canvas ducking pants: $65.00

4. Elastic braces (suspenders) $20.00
5. Duster (long coat) $120.00
6. Spurs that go, "jingle-jangle": $55.00
7. Spur leathers (straps): $30.00
8. Stovepipe boots: $200.00
9. Wild rag (scarf): $40.00
10. Silver scarf slide: $45.00

11. Fringed deerskin gloves: $45.00
12. Double-loop Mexican holsters (2): $140.00
13. Cartridge belt: $70.00
14. Canvas shotgun shell belt: $80.00
15. Leather wrist cuffs: $40.00
16. Fancy hat: $160.00
17. Colt Single Action Army Revolvers (2): $2,400.00
18. Lever-action carbine: $400.00
19. Double-barrel, external hammer shotgun: $400.00
20. A themed cart to tote your shooting items: $250.00

That's a grand total of $4,690.00, with ammunition and horse as "extras." The majority

This is the classic Colt with genuine elephant ivory stocks. Some purists will accept no substitutes.

Ruger's Vaquero series in stainless — this one with Bill Lett grips — is a big cowboy shooter hit.

select alias-driven equipment somewhere in between "no investment" and "you can't spend more than this."

Colt percussion revolvers were of the finest quality and in the highest demand among early Westerners. That old and hotly-contested handgun market also saw products from Remington, with their solid-frame 1858 Army Model, as well as the lesser-known products of firms like Rogers & Spencer and the French-made LeMat ... a 9-shot, 44-caliber revolver with a .65-caliber built-in shotgun barrel as a bonus gift. Today's cowboy actionist can select percussion weapons from Colt Blackpowder Arms Company, firms like Navy Arms offer excellent Colt-style black powder replicas, Ruger's Old Army percussion revolvers are the finest handguns of this ignition type ever manufactured, and then are SASS-approval for specific categories.

The Colt Single Action Army

revolver in 45 Long Colt caliber was decidedly the most popular cartridge handgun of the Old West. A look at hundreds of authentic photos or a stroll through any major Western museum will confirm that; so will written records and reports filed by lawmen of the times. Handle a Colt SAA and the products of its original competitors and you'll know why. Nothing was or is as quick handling as the product developed for the U.S. Army after Colonel Colt's death. However, back then, that Colt cost the equivalent of a month's pay to a working cowboy; there were less expensive alternatives for those needing protection, but not expecting to live by the gun.

Regardless of the firearm they might have desired, pioneers often faced a limited selection. Whatever was available for sale at the hardware

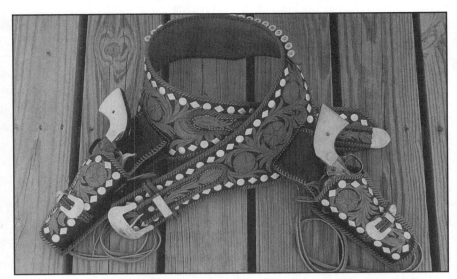

Shooters may take aliases of B-movie heroes or TV series buckaroos, then get into double buscadero rig — like this by El Paso Saddlery.

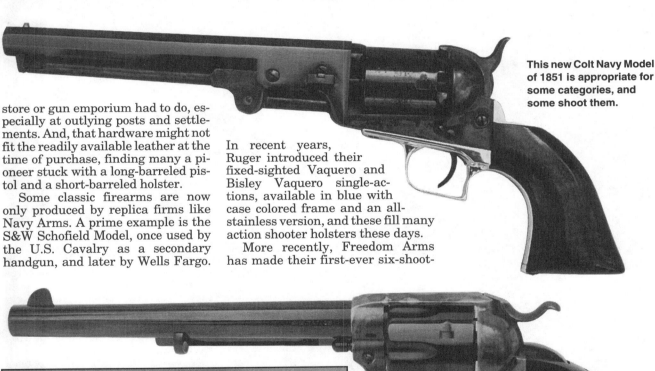

This new Colt Navy Model of 1851 is appropriate for some categories, and some shoot them.

store or gun emporium had to do, especially at outlying posts and settlements. And, that hardware might not fit the readily available leather at the time of purchase, finding many a pioneer stuck with a long-barreled pistol and a short-barreled holster.

Some classic firearms are now only produced by replica firms like Navy Arms. A prime example is the S&W Schofield Model, once used by the U.S. Cavalry as a secondary handgun, and later by Wells Fargo.

In recent years, Ruger introduced their fixed-sighted Vaquero and Bisley Vaquero single-actions, available in blue with case colored frame and an all-stainless version, and these fill many action shooter holsters these days.

More recently, Freedom Arms has made their first-ever six-shoot-

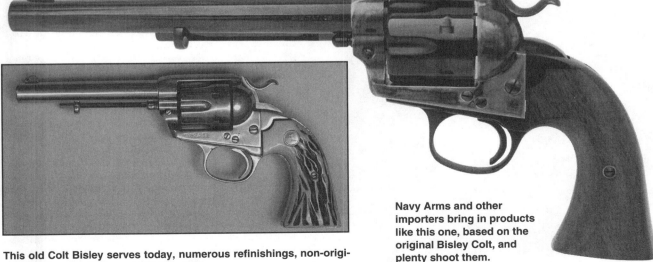

This old Colt Bisley serves today, numerous refinishings, non-original barrel and cylinder notwithstanding.

Navy Arms and other importers bring in products like this one, based on the original Bisley Colt, and plenty shoot them.

Both shooters and the event staff wear authentic garb at cowboy events. Virtually every Old West character, male and female, is represented.

For SASS, "get-ups" and hardware have to be authentic Old West. This shooter has a couple of spares belted while blazing away with a Navy Arms Schofield.

Cowboy shooting participants spend much time researching the lives and times of the characters they represent.

er, crafted to the same standards as their heavy-duty five-shooters. This Freedom Arms sixgun fits the same holsters as a Colt SAA of identical barrel length. And speaking of Colt in the present tense, that firm's long-awaited "Colt Cowboy" has finally become a reality. The "Cowboy" is slightly smaller than the original historic SAA still created in Colt's Custom Shop, and features half-cock loading, frame-mounted firing pin and transfer bar safety system. The frame is color cased, sights are fixed and grip panels are adorned with the traditional rearing Colt trademark.

For every handgun sold, way back then, many more rifles and carbines were retailed. Winchesters and Marlins were the most respected in the Old West, but there's no need to tote originals to SASS-sanctioned events. Marlin looked deep into their history to develop the current line of Marlin 1894 Cowboy rifles of yesteryear, these finely-crafted Marlins are available in 45 Colt, 44-40, 357 Magnum and 44 Magnum.

Rossi's Model 92 rifles and carbines are available in a variety of styles and just as many chamberings. My favorite is the all-stainless steel Rossi Model 92 in 45 Colt. Navy

Arms offers relevant lever-actions, including iron and brass-framed Henry replicas, plus reproduction Winchester Models '66, '73 and '92. And, if you need a reincarnated U.S. Springfield cavalry carbine or infantry rifle, Navy Arms has 'em.

Shotguns of yore had big bores and short barrels; external hammers were usual. Pump and lever-action shotguns were also available. In greatest demand were scatterguns by Westley Richards, Lefever, Burgess, Winchester and even Colt. Probably most used at today's SASS-sanctioned shooting events are original Model '97 Winchester pumps, with exposed hammer. However, Stoeger imports the IGA doubles and Tri-Star offers a double-barrel with Greener-style action, while the used market offers plenty of Rossi Coach guns yet.

When the self-contained metallic cartridge arrived on the scene, quality control wasn't always under control, and problems plagued the concept through most of the era. This kept some professional gunmen, like Wild Bill Hickok, packing percussion Colt revolvers on a daily basis well after cartridge guns became available. The raw material used for shell casings varied from good to not-so-hot.

Although nothing short of a pinpoint air strike would have likely altered the final outcome, flimsy shell casings jammed the U.S. Springfield carbines of General Custer's troops on the Little Big Horn. The substandard shell casings stuck in the chambers of hot gun barrels; then, when troopers tried to reload, extractors simply ripped off the cartridge case heads, presenting a fatal combat situation.

In addition to production irregularities, transportation and storage of ammunition was primitive as a privy in the Old West. Supplies of all kind moved by waterways, train and freight wagon as far as St. Louis and other stepping-off points. And along the way, protection from the elements was haphazard. From Mississippi River distribution points westward, cartridge shipments took even more primitive conveyances. Finally, general stores, hardware emporiums, gun shops and even feed stores took delivery of whatever ammunition they thought their customers might require, although the goods might become shopworn before anyone asked to trade for any. There weren't the choices in bullet types we're accustomed to today — you got lead.

Those who can do it on horseback. World Champion Beth Shotwell (aka Cassie Redwine) of Galco International is getting up on one.

Since the cowboyist is interested in recreating those days-of-old, ammunition manufacturers like Black Hills and Winchester offer cartridges specifically designed for the sport, with special attention paid to bullet type and "legal" velocity. For example, Black Hills currently offers CAS-approved ammunition in 45 Colt, 44-40, 44 Special, 44 Russian, 44 Colt, 38-40, 45 S&W Schofield, 357 Magnum, 38 Special, 38 Long Colt and 32-20. That 44 Colt, originally designed for Colt conversion revolvers (and now, today's replicas of those) is a Black Hills exclusive.

Leathergoods were also an important part of every iron packer's life in the Old West. Cowboys, gamblers, sod busters and frontier lawmen all needed to carry handguns on their person, and long guns on their horses. Holsters and gunbelts, then as now, varied in quality from lightweight construction to beautifully-crafted first-rate workmanship, the former decidedly more prominent.

Once he's up and going, no one will know about the hay bale.

Today, there's an endless variety of top-quality leather products; everything from wrist cuffs to gunbelts which double as money belts. Old-line custom makers like El Paso Saddlery continue to make stunning products from original 19th century patterns. John Bianchi is again of-

Galco employee Beth Shotwell ain't just for show — she's also the SASS's champion horseback shooter.

alike the experiences of some of the action their forefathers faced in taming the West, but all in the name of fun. Shooting competitions are conducted by "stages," and just about any Old West situation you can think of is represented, each cleverly orchestrated with the emphasis on safety.

The largest gathering of shooters is found at End of Trail, for which Colt Manufacturing Company is a Master Sponsor; Winter Range, also a major SASS-sanctioned event, is sponsored by Sturm, Ruger & Company. Both events attract many hundreds of competitors and thousands-upon-thousands of spectators.

Shooters may find themselves engaging targets from inside an open-door privy or from atop a rocking horse. The action might start with a shooter blazing away first with one handgun and then another from behind the cover of an old wooden wagon. Next, the shooter might be required to shift to a store front, collect a lever-action carbine and engage additional targets. The stage could end with a chance to pepper yet more stationary targets with a classic-style shotgun.

Specific requirements for SASS-approved firearms used in competition, and how to sign-up, can be reviewed on the world wide web, at: http://www.sassnet.com. For mail, the address is, SASS, 1938 N. Batavia Street, Orange, California 92865. You'll also discover details on the competitive categories available, including Modern, Traditional, Frontier Cartridge (black powder), Duelist and

Gail Davis, Hollywooded up as TV's Annie Oakley shot double-action revolvers — not quite the SASS image.

Frontiersman. Some matches also include specific events for women, juniors (at least 12 years-of-age) and seniors; there is literally something to interest everyone. Side matches add additional variety to Cowboy Action Shooting events by permitting the safe use of pocket pistols and derringers, long range rifles and more.

Targets at SASS events are metal plates, sometimes bearing the likeness of an Old West bad guy, and either go down or clang when hit. Scoring at each shooting stage is based on a combination of the number of targets successfully engaged and the time it took to complete the stage; miss a target and seconds will

fering custom leather goods, this time for today's Westerners, under the brand name, "John Bianchi's Frontier Gunleather." Galco International, of Phoenix, Arizona, is another purveyor of authentic leather products unequaled in the Old West.

And what sort of shooting scrapes did citizens of the Old West get themselves into? Hunting for food was the most practiced use for firearms in the Old West. A certain amount of target shooting seems to always have been part of Americana. Most talked about and written about are firearms used as weapons. Whether on the defense or offense, settlers, cowmen, lawmen, Indians, hotel and saloon employees, the U.S. Army and workers hired by telegraph companies and the railroads all counted on firearms to survive, if not to prosper. So did the killers, robbers and conmen of the day. There, as now, trouble could make an appearance anytime at any place. You had to be prepared to take care of yourself, whatever your role in the grand New West scheme. By the time Sam Bass and his gang screwed-up big time during a visit to Round Rock, Texas, in July of 1878, civilian concealed carry of weapons was prohibited within incorporated areas of Texas, but 1878 was by no means the end of the Old West's violent time.

Today, cowboy action shooting offers participants and spectators

Purveyors of Old West equipment are in evidence at every major event. They work pretty hard at the authentic thing themselves.

George Montgomery, once a real cowboy, once married to Dinah Shore, played in Lone Ranger films, looked rightous.

Hoot Gibson was a world champion cowboy, big-ticket shoot-em-up star, died broke, but looked good, looked right.

Rodeo star Sunset Carson toured with Tom Mix, played on the big screen, was a horse opera host on TV — slick but OK look.

be added to your elapsed time. Since stages vary at each event, a specific SASS-wide "perfect score" doesn't exist; scoring also depends on the expertise of shooters participating at any given event. Finally, an aggregate score is developed for each competitor from the individual stages, and the lowest score wins.

In the Old West, nearly every man, woman and youngster found it necessary to have some measure of horse sense; that's the way most everyone and everything motivated before the infernal horseless carriage. Today's population is only peppered with individuals possessing true

equine expertise, but at SASS Mounted Shooting events you get the impression they're all assembled in that one location.

Riders traverse a carefully laid-out courses with barrel racing-style turns and thundering straight aways and engage inflated balloons with their sixguns along the way. All ammunition for these sanctioned mounted events is provided by the sponsoring organization. The caliber is 45 Colt, and the "projectiles" are common cornmeal. These mounted shooting events have their own special requirements beyond being able to stay in

Jim Garner in his all-purpose Maverick suit — not far out of line at all for an Old West townie.

There's plenty of support from manufacturers of firearms, ammunition, leathergoods and period clothng. These are Ruger's digs at the 1997 Winter Range.

Glenn Ford looks right in gambler clothes — the cigar and the Marlin are pretty good.

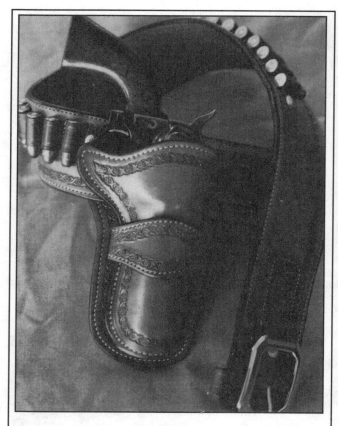

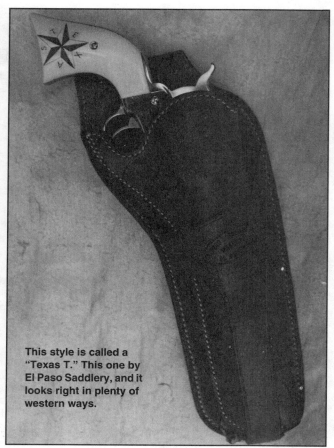

This style is called a "Texas T." This one by El Paso Saddlery, and it looks right in plenty of western ways.

Single loop (above) or double loop (below), long barrel or short, John Bianchi is back with what it takes to suit (literally) today's cowboy shooter.

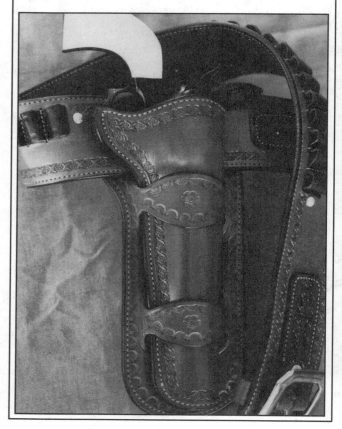

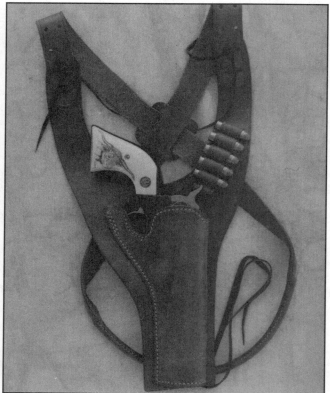

This Vaquero sits in a shoulder holster pattern originally designed for killer John Wesley Hardin.

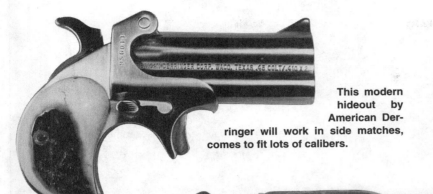

Action shooting perfection — Navy Arms' replica Model '73 carbine, chambered for the classic 44-40. It looks right, and righteous, too.

This modern hideout by American Derringer will work in side matches, comes to fit lots of calibers.

Navy Sheriff's Model has a birdshead grip, which didn't exist in the true Old West, but who cares? It's neat.

and shoot from the saddle. You'd better have a well-trained broomtail who knows the ropes and doesn't mind the sound of gunfire (commonly, ear plugs are fitted to competing horses).

And what was the real level of shooting prowess in the Old West? Despite the movies and TV shows depicting those Westerners of old as crack shots, there weren't that many accomplished gunmen in the old days; far more were, out of necessity, accomplished non-human game hunters. If nothing else, it took a lot of shooting then as today to become and remain fully proficient with any firearm; the cost of ammunition alone was a deterrent to most from becoming too handy with any form of shootin' iron.

Except for those real gunfighters who roamed the West in limited numbers, even the murderers and general cutthroats weren't especially skilled marksmen. They were bullies or maniacs, if not both, willing to kill. Distances were usually short, so close losers clothing was set on fire by muzzle flash. Most victims were set upon from cowardly ambush or other

advantageous positioning, not in those imaginative high noon face-offs on Main Street.

At least two famous examples of high volume poor shooting in the Old West are widely recognized. The first is the Gunfight at the O.K. Corral. Most people have some knowledge about this infamous encounter between the Earps and their buddies and another group of violence-prone malcontents also in the saloon and gambling business. Carnage certainly made its appearance that fateful day, but enough lead was exchanged to kill most everyone in the county. The aforementioned destruction of the Sam Bass gang in Round Rock, Texas, in 1878, took 68 seconds by my best calculations during which 45 or more shots were fired from Colt revolvers and Winchester lever-guns. A handful of bad guys and only a slightly larger number of lawmen and plucky civilians were involved. One lawman was killed at point-blank range during the initial outbreak of hostilities; another lost a lung almost immediately thereafter, also at close range. Bass took a hit in the hand as he ran down the street, and later, a shot that hit him while mounting his horse would eventually prove fatal. Another Bass gang member had his

head burst like a melon while gaining his horse, and that's it. Plenty of red-hot, spinning lead was propelled through the air that day by accomplished professionals on both sides, but most were misses.

You see a lot more hits than misses at modern cowboy shooting events. Cowboy action shooting targets are stationary, of generous size and placed at moderate distances from the shooters to encourage successful shooting, and they never shoot back. For example, the suggested target size is 16 inches x 16 inches; revolver shooting ranges run from 20 to 30 feet. Don't think you can't miss at that range until you've tried it! This shooting is fun for all levels of competitors, from novice to consummate expert. SASS leaders design events based on the premise that the satisfaction of making regular hits on steel targets encourages repeat shooters in large numbers. They want enthusiasm for return visits.

With all that, it's easy to see the good ol' days of the Wild West are now, and there's certainly no end in sight for this well-organized, fun-driven bunch of Old West paper tigers. Shooters and spectators alike leave Cowboy Action Shooting events with welcome memories—targets hit and costuming fun—the consummate twin joys of shooting well and looking good. •

Some competitors use genuine Colt Lightning or Thunderer DA revolvers like this one in side matches.

Cheap, thin leather couldn't hold up to quality hand tooling. However, plenty of such gun leather was worn in the Old West, especially by the non-professionals. *(John Bianchi photo)*

COWBOY SHOOTING THEN

BY

JERRY BURKE

A GALLERY

Original Colt Sheriff's Model and a matching late 19th century single-loop holster — the way they did it then.

The famous Jersey Lilly Saloon of Judge Roy Bean of Law West of The Pecos in a look at the look of the late 19th century. *(U.T. Institute of Texan Cultures photo)*

An original shoulder holster from the 1880's. Such items help both holster makers and cowboy action shooters achieve authenticity for the sport.

This is Creed Taylor, Injun-fighting Texas Ranger of the 1870's in a nicely cleaned up and restored photo.

Rancher John Cotulla (left) with Texas Ranger Jim Wright in a rare late 1800's photo. Note holster sewn onto the Ranger's chaps, a practice followed by some Rangers into the 1950's. *(U.T. Institute of Texan Cultures photo)*

A true lady of the Old West, Ms. Topperwein was a famous exhibition shooter in modest times. Today, many female cowboy shooters compete in jeans. *(U.T. Institute of Texan Cultures photo)*

The Elfego Baca Story — Also the Real West

By Art Reid

A brash 19-year-old Latino wannabee lawman pinned on a mail-order tin star to arrest a drunken troublemaker shooting up the town with a Colt sixgun. What followed is still regarded as the longest sustained volley of gunfire ever directed at a single human being in the West. The side effects were bizarre.

The young target was Elfego Baca, born in Socorro, New Mexico, in 1865. His father, Francisco, was a vaquero who hired out to ranchers when and where he could find work. His highly respected reputation as a crack shot with both rifle and sixgun were especially sought by stockmen when troublesome Apache Indians were raiding ranches, and later when Texas outlaws invaded west central New Mexico Territory.

The region was also beginning to fill with Anglo cowmen, most of them from nearby Texas. As ranchers usually brought cowboys with them, or sent for fellow Texans, work for Francisco became sporadic at best, much of the time nonexistent.

Most hard-bitten Texans not only did not like Mexicans, often referring to them as "greasers", but many of them regarded Mexicans as targets to be gunned down with little to no provocation and less remorse for having done so. Notorious gunman John Wesley Hardin, who killed at least 11 men and probably more, expressed the prevailing attitude of Texans when he said of his victims, "I never counted greasers."

So as big cattlemen from Texas bought out lesser ranch owners in New Mexico, native vaqueros found themselves in dire straits for steady employment. Francisco Baca moved his family to Kansas.

Dodge City was destined to become an important terminal for immense cattle drives throughout the

southwest, particularly from Texas and New Mexico's cattle country. Although Francisco failed to prosper in Kansas he managed to keep food on the table and a roof over his family long enough for Elfego to become a teenager. Then, for reason or reasons history fails to reveal, the Baca family, with one of the of the oldest names in New Mexico, returned to the Territory.

For generations the name Baca and New Mexico were synonymous. In 1869, when Ulysses S. Grant was elected president, Saturnino Baca was a member of the territorial legislature. He was, in fact, credited with proposing a new county, which would be named Lincoln, honoring Abraham Lincoln, in what was then massive Socorro County.

Within Lincoln County and the village by the same name would be the primary battle ground in the infamous "Lincoln County War" of 1878. And in that bloody confrontation triggered by greed and power, another Baca, this one a Probate

Texas Ranger "Blackie" Blackwell got it all on for this turn-of-the-century picture. He was headed somewhere important.

George Washington Saunders of San Antonio, Texas, seen here late in life, moved herds of longhorn cattle to northern markets in the 1870's and '80's. *(U.T. Institute of Texan Cultures photo)*

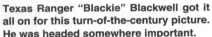

... 4,000 shots ...

Judge, was instrumental in hearing some of the charges and counter charges by participants.

But it was in Socorro in 1882 when Elfego's father became involved in a shootout which left two ranch hands dead as stale beer in the dusty street. Once again it was the timeless animosity between Hispanics and Anglos which, fueled by too much mind-altering booze, caused bold, senseless threats to be made, followed by guns being carelessly jerked from holsters at the wrong time. Francisco Baca drilled both cowboys so thoroughly that the court refused to believe that he had not, with premeditation, created the lethal situation by drawing first. He was given a lengthy prison sentence.

With his father in prison, young Baca's evaluation of life and himself gradually changed. Although he idolized his father, he had not, until now, regarded him as a fierce gunman, a case-hardened killer who could calmly and deliberately shoot not one but two antagonists. Elfego decided that he wanted to be like his father, but on the side of law and order.

So even as Elfego worked at many odd jobs, he started an intensive practice routine with his father's Colt 45 Single Action six guns, discovering that he was indeed a natural chip-off-the-old-block marksman. Gifted with excellent eyesight and youthful coordination coupled with determination to succeed, Elfego soon was satiated with confidence that he could be a formidable opponent for anyone.

His less than average stature would be offset by his innate fearlessness and deadly marksmanship.

Wearing the cheap mail-order lawman's star wouldn't hurt the scenario, either.

The stage was set for a fateful occurrence in October, 1884, in the small village of Frisco a few miles from Socorro. A cowboy named McCarty, who rode for the huge Tom Slaughter outfit, was harassing the Mexican population by shooting at everyone he could identify through a drunken haze. Baca, who happened to be in Frisco, quickly pinned on his shiny tin star and with drawn Colt six-shooters audaciously confronted McCarty.

Advising the cowboy he was under arrest the pseudo-lawman herded him to the town plaza where he intended to sit out the night and take his prisoner to the nearest jail in Socorro the next morning. But Mc-

The Texas border was still plenty wild when these Texas Rangers rode the Big Bend. It took a trip to town to bring out a bow tie.

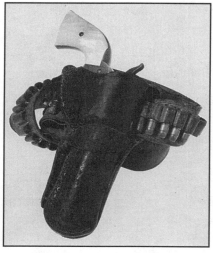

This is genuine Texas-made gun leather of the 1880's, with pearl-handled Colt Single Action Army Revolver, worn by a famous Old West lawman. *(John Bianchi photo)*

Carty's friends, with whom he had shared elbow room at the bar, streamed from the saloon with other ideas.

At the approach of the mean-spirited knot of surly cow-punchers, Baca sternly told them to leave town before he finished counting to three. As they scoffed, he counted and then opened fire. One of the astonished Slaughter men went down with a 45-caliber bullet in his leg while another's horse killed its rider by falling on him. The remaining cowboys scattered to find shelter from Baca's deadly guns.

Soon after sunup, townsmen, concerned with the consequences of all those guns displayed by angry men from the Slaughter ranch, convinced Baca that in all likelihood he would not reach Soccoro alive with his prisoner. Would he avoid this real risk, and also negate the probability of having the village shot to smith-

ereens, by taking McCarty to the local justice of the peace? Baca would and did.

Reasonably sober now, but no doubt suffering a horrendous temple-throbbing headache, McCarty reluctantly paid the five-dollar fine levied by the judge. Five dollars for shooting at people seems today like a paltry sum; in 1884 it was an especially stiff penalty, the equivalent of a full week's work. McCarty was fortunate to have the cash in his pocket and was released to become part of the menacing gang waiting on the outside for Baca.

As the young man stepped out the door he was astounded to see wall-to-wall enemies. They had a single purpose—to kill the upstart greaser. The army of 80 mounted cowboys waited for someone to fire the first shot. One did, and it went wide as Baca wheeled around and raced for a nearby alley.

In the alley, Baca reached the first available shelter, a small shed-like building called a *jacal* by Mexicans. This one contained a terrified woman and two frightened children who, without explanation, were ordered outside by Baca. With the innocent noncombatants safely out of harm's way, an unprecedented siege began.

The awesome array of muzzles aligned at Baca's flimsy shelter included, but were not limited to at least two Sharps buffalo rifles, one known as the "Big 50." This heavy bullet was powerful enough to punch fist-size exit holes in the thin facade of Baca's scrawny jacal. The other Sharps was a 44-90 Creedmore; also in use was a 50-caliber single shot Ballard and a Remington rolling block in 44, similar to the rifle once owned by George Armstrong Custer.

The majority of rifles, however, were more contemporary Winchester lever actions, carbines, in fact. Each was capable of throwing an extraordinary amount of lead, which often replaced a singular lack of marksmanship by average cowboys who were not overly skilled gun hands.

Nor did it require skilled marksmen to hit a building just a few yards distant. So there were handguns, mostly Colt Single Action Army models in 45 and 44 calibers. There was at least one S & W No. 3, an extra fine piece in 44 caliber, and a S & W 45 1st Model Schofield. Perhaps the most unusual firearm on the scene that day in New Mexico country was a Colt Single Action with a 16-inch barrel equipped with a detachable rifle stock.

When shooting began in earnest, the first to fall was Jim Herne. He foolishly rushed the shed shooting his rifle on the run. Baca waiting until Herne was in deadly handgun range, then killed him with two shots. Baca allowed the body of Herne to be carried from the field by his companions. Then, they cascaded literally volley after volley of bullets into the shed.

Within minutes Baca should have been riddled to a state of unsightly hamburger. Instead, the disbelieving cowboys were being picked off one by one by the unruffled teenager's withering fire. At one point, Baca's count of wounded rose so fast that the ranchmen strung their lassos between buildings and flung blankets over them, forming a shield from Baca's view. The cowboys scampered from position to position behind blankets.

Meanwhile, an especially courageous cowhand located a better cover of midnight darkness one man cautiously skulked to dynamite-tossing distance.

Although under the stressful circumstances his aim was commendable it was far from perfect. The explosion shattered only half the building. Satisfied the blast had killed their adversary, the cowboys would wait until daylight to look for body parts. They slept fitfully on saddle blankets thrown on the ground, their guns cool for the first time in 16 hazardous hours.

If, in the collective opinion of the Tom Slaughter ranch hands, the opening hours of the deadly confrontation had been preposterous, the daylight scene had them truly aghast. Amid cheers from a large gathering of his Mexican booster club, totally untroubled Elfego Baca was serenely cooking breakfast!

So the bombardment resumed. With the same result. The cowboys lost more companions carried from the battle zone with ugly bullet wounds, and Elfego remained unbloodied.

boys had been killed with more than a dozen seriously wounded. Townsfolk counted nearly 360 bullet holes *in the door* of the shed and a conservative estimate is that more than 4,000 bullets had been fired at Baca.

Eventually the young man struck a deal with the deputy and cowboys. He would accompany them to Socorro to be charged with murder, but only if he remained armed with his six-guns. So a very strange procession entered Socorro. Riding in a buckboard, Baca sat behind the drive, his guns in hand and aimed at the cowboys riding ahead.

He was tried twice for murder. Both juries found him not guilty.

News of young Elfego's "Miracle of the Jacal" spread like a wind-driven prairie fire. When acquitted of the charges against him, he took advantage of his growing reputation by entering politics. He would eventually become a real law officer.

Baca also was a county clerk, school superintendent, mayor of Socorro, deputy sheriff and county sheriff. He would become a lawyer,

.. from wannabee kid to real sheriff, real hero ...

shield. It was part of an old cast iron stove. The strategy of getting close to Baca quickly fell through the cracks, however, when a bullet sliced the skin on the cowboy's head, knocking him temporarily senseless.

It was uncanny! The frustrated attackers were convinced that Baca should have been dead hours ago. By dark, however, the amazing number of bullets pumped into the shed, apparently, had no effect whatsoever. Even when crude poles supporting the roof were blasted into splinters and it tumbled down, partially burying Baca beneath the rubble, he hung on with the tenacity of a pit bull, dug himself out and continued to return fire.

The cowboy's final solution came as a single stick of dynamite complete with fuse and blasting cap. Gloating over the prospective devastation, the crowd had no doubt that this little puppy would bring the embarrassing fiasco to a halt. Under

Finally, a real lawman with bonafide deputy sheriff credentials arrived on the unlikely scene. Accompanied by the Frisco justice of the peace—the same man who had fined McCarty five dollars for making Mexicans dance—the deputy approached the mangled shack. Shaking his head with disbelief, he was astounded at how Elfego survived.

Carefully picking his way around the rubble, the deputy stepped in and down to the floor of the shack. The operative word here is "down." The jacal floor was about 18 inches below the outside ground level. When the shooting started, Baca simply flattened out on his stomach while bullets passed harmlessly over him.

When the stick of dynamite went off Baca was, fortunately, on the far side of the building. The explosion happened to go up rather than spreading out.

When Baca walked away from the ruined shed, he had been under relentless attack for 33 hours. Four cow-

be elected district attorney, but he lost races to be district judge and governor of New Mexico.

Perhaps one of Baca's shrewdest achievements as Sheriff of Socorro County was pulled off successfully in 1919. Fully aware of the number and names of outlaws living in his bailiwick, the sheriff concocted a clever plan to reach all of them. Instead of chasing them down one by one. Baca mailed letters to the outlaws. He advised them to surrender quickly and peacefully. Refusal would bring unpleasant consequences.

Several of these fugitives gave themselves up.

That audacious teenager who barricaded himself in an untenable shack, defying the accuracy of dozens of sixguns and rifles, the same brash youngster who was given only seconds to live in 1884, died in 1945 in Albuquerque, New Mexico at the age of eighty. How many of his opponents made it that far is not recorded.

•

JAMES PARIS LEE

AND HIS SEARCH FOR A REALLY MODERN RIFLE

by John Wallace

British shooters think of James Paris Lee's British military action as his crowning achievement. The agreement specified a total payment of $250,000, which the British government has frequently spent on worse things than the preservation of Western civilization. But fewer know of Lee's work with Sharps, Remington and Winchester, or the rifle he must have thought of as far more advanced.

The inventor was born James Paris Lees in Hawick in Scotland, in 1834. When he was five, the family emigrated to Canada, where they changed their name to Lee, and James was apprenticed to a watchmaker. It is chastening to think that, like most of the men who perfected what Jeff Cooper terms the Queen of Weapons, he must at one time have managed very well with muzzle-loaders, although at the age of sixteen he shot himself in the heel, and carried five pellets until their removal in 1899. He moved to the U.S. in the 1850s, but is first described as a U.S. citizen in 1888. A portrait still owned by his family suggests that he resembled Rider Haggard's Allan Quatermain in his old age. But then, people with that kind of beard usually do.

He soon drifted into firearms development. Besides various rifles, and a surgical appliance which one would prefer to believe was veterinary, he patented a concave primer for safe use of round-nosed bullets in tube magazines. A matching pimple around the firing-pin would have been advisable, making it unusable in falling-block weapons, and a conventionally-primed round could have been detonated by this pimple before the breech was locked. So it is not surprising that Lee's primer was never produced.

After an early association with Remington, Lee's interest in repeaters seems to have been aroused by

overtures from Sharps. A Lee Arms Company, apparently almost synonymous with Sharps, was formed in May, 1879, and Lee's major U.S. patent, No. 221,328, followed on the 4th of November. Their first U.S. naval contract, for three hundred 45-70 rifles, was interrupted by the Sharps bankruptcy in 1880, when Remington took over contract, tooling, and their association with Lee. The Navy receivers were apparently begun by Sharps, but completed by Remington, and like all Remington-Lees they have the square Remington rolling-block receiver thread. Seven hundred more 1879 Lees were later bought from stock by the U.S. Navy, and 3,956 of the 1885 improvement.

There was nothing particularly original in the bolt of Lee's action - except, of course, for seeing that the military rifle of the future had to have one, a fact which eluded some people. It bears comparison with an entire generation of tube-magazine military rifles, among them the M71/84 Mauser, Kropatschek and Winchester-Hotchkiss, which were saddled with slow loading, flat-pointed bullets, and shifting balance. Lee's great invention was the detachable box-magazine, upon which almost all current military firearms are based. In 1896, Lee sued Mauser for infringement, and lost (under German law) on the basis of prior British and American box-magazine patents. But these do not show effective magazine lips, and Mauser never disputed that magazine detachability was Lee's.

Lee's earliest magazines had very short lips, with a tendency for the cartridge to cock upward or fall out. To avoid this, Lee had the topmost cartridge slide forward slightly, to lodge in a protruding "nose", and no use was made of a patent by Hugo Borchardt, to use an internal ledge in-

stead. A notch on the bolt, as it moves rearward, engages with the rim and drags the cartridge out of this nose, provoking an abrupt upward tilt which is halted by an extension of the receiver ring. The nose was soon eliminated by the sliding cartridge-stop of the Lee-Cook magazine, and later by lengthening the lips.

But the concave guiding surface initially used merges into an internal web, which reduces the interior of the receiver ring to around case-rim diameter. This resembles the strengthening stop-ring later used in most Mannlichers and the Mauser 98, which may well have been inspired by the Lee. During the First World War, American propagandists made much of how a Herr Mauser worked in the Remington plant, observed the Lee action, and decamped to Germany with his pirated design. This is not entirely baseless, for Franz Mauser, an elder brother of Paul and Wilhelm, did work there, and may have facilitated the interchange of ideas which characterizes this industry. But there was nothing secret about the identity of Franz, who remained with Remington until his death in 1893, a highly esteemed citizen. His brothers had made bolt actions comparable with Lee's, apart from the magazine, since the early seventies. It would have been easier to buy a copy of Lee's German patent, as they no doubt did.

The story of the M1882 and M1885 Lees is mostly one of detail improvements and small to medium orders, but failure to win large ones, while Lee's personal success in Britain produced no business for Remington beyond the 300 trials rifles. Apparently following Mannlicher's lead of the previous year, Lee shifted the M1882's bolt lever to the rear of the action, and turned it down in just the way we would wish for a scoped rifle, although he never used a solid receiver bridge. Eight or ten thousand M1882 rifles were sold to China, and 3,956 M1885 to the U.S. Navy. Lugs says 25,000 M1882 rifles and 15,000 carbines were sold to Mexico, although Myszkowski does not confirm this, and would seem to contradict it by saying that the Chinese contract was E. Remington and Sons' largest for the Lee.

In 1885, for U.S. Army trials, the Lee successfully endured rigorous and well-conceived testing, during which Lee himself fired fifty unaimed shots in a minute. Then, 750 each of the three leading contenders were issued to 149 companies, and the Lee was found decisively superior to the

sounding defeat on a much larger force of Foreign Legion and Marines. As Lee had anticipated, the tube-magazine Kropatscheks of the French Marines functioned as single-shots in continuous action. Despite offering several wholesome lessons at once, Long Son was ignored by the French, not least by adopting the tube-magazine Lebel the following year.

Five hundred M1885 rifles were withdrawn, with some acrimony, by New Zealand, after a history of case separations and breech explosions. This seems to have been caused by the cases, unstamped but probably U.M.C., which may have been supplied by a local contractor, and were loaded with powder from a manufac-

rather neatly sporterized, which suggests faith in their soundness with better ammunition.

It is widely known that the British Lee was criticized as old-fashioned, on its adoption in 1888. Elderly generals must have remembered the brief period in the fifties when the Mini rifle-bullet enabled the infantry to outrange field artillery, and most authorities thought something similar was happening again, with musketry becoming a precision weapon for use at extreme ranges. For this, a fairly resilient rear-locking action was far from ideal. Almost accidentally, though, the British government had adopted an ergonomically superb design, and an almost unjammable firearm when it

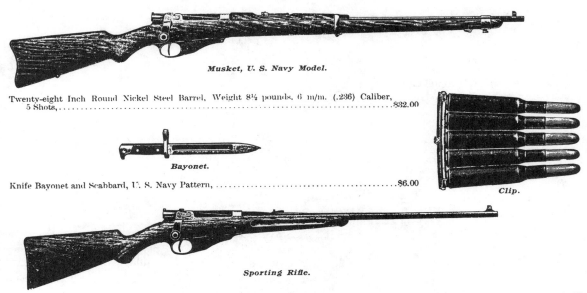

The Lee Straight Pull Rifle.

Made For 6 m/m. (.236) Cartridges.

Musket, U. S. Navy Model.

Twenty-eight Inch Round Nickel Steel Barrel, Weight 8¼ pounds, 6 m/m. (.236) Caliber, 5 Shots,...$32.00

Bayonet.

Knife Bayonet and Scabbard, U. S. Navy Pattern,.....................................$6.00

Clip.

Sporting Rifle.

Twenty-four Inch Round Nickel Steel Barrel, Weight 7½ pounds, 6 m/m. (.236) Caliber, 5 Shots,...$32.00

In 1899, Winchester cataloged their Lee this way.

Winchester-Hotchkiss and Chaffee-Rice rifles, each with a tube magazine in the butt, but far less popular than the trapdoor Springfield. Anybody who believes that fighting soldiers nine years after the Little Bighorn believed that will very likely believe anything. Perhaps the company commanders were asked whether they were for the Springfield or against the Army. The Board decided that as the Army was so splendidly equipped already, it could afford to await further developments.

In the defense of Long Son on the Tonkin border in 1885, during a French incursion in pursuit of pirates who were playing Pancho Villa's frontier game, the Chinese inflicted a re-

turer more used to blasting powder. Few bolt-action rifles of the eighties would have handled massive case rupture better than the Lee, and the blame may lie partly with the New Zealand government, which, in the improbable belief that Russia was about to attack New Zealand, ordered the rifles in too much haste to find out whether the caliber was to be 450 or 400, and may have paid inadequate attention to cartridge quality. In fact it was 43 Spanish Remington, an excellent black powder cartridge which seems to have been Lee's favorite when given the choice. A refund was negotiated, but some of the withdrawn rifles still exist in New Zealand, having been sold off and

was to matter most, in the conditions of trench warfare. Unlike the Mauser, its shorter bolt movement allows an uninterrupted view of the target, for there is no need to move head or buttplate, to avoid being poked in the eye.

To make Lee's magazines loadable on the rifle, they were slit so that the lips might be sprung over the cartridges, and the same applied to the Lee-Metford and clip-loading M1889 Mauser. So the double-column magazine which the British developed for the Lee-Enfield of 1895 was a significant improvement, being reliable and easy to load, with a ten-round capacity. But although the British had bought an interchangeable-magazine system, it became no more than a maintenance measure, for they never used it to facilitate loading, during some seventy years of first-line service, extended to around a century by the sniper 7.62mm. They had undertaken to pay around the

sample Remington-Lees being presented to the Small Arms Committee in the U.K.

The British took a year to select and improve what was basically the Swiss Colonel Rubin's cartridge. They had, in fact, had the enormous good judg-

The U.S. Army trials had been concluded sixteen months earlier, at a time when Vieille's work on smokeless powder was the deepest of military secrets in France, and Geronimo was a more compelling intelligence target than the chancellories of Europe. So

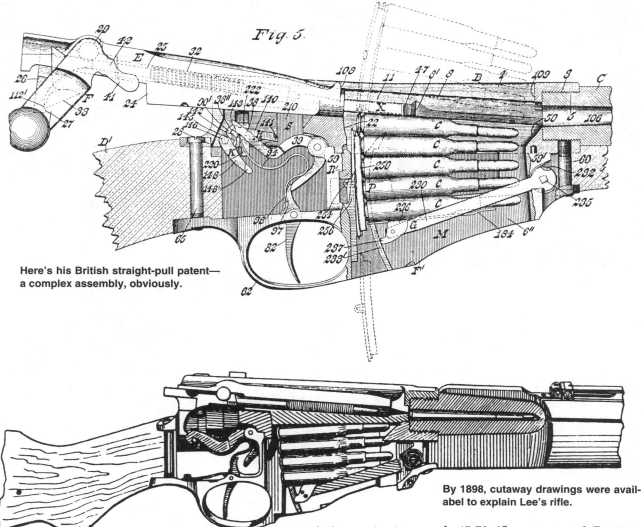

Here's his British straight-pull patent—a complex assembly, obviously.

By 1898, cutaway drawings were availabel to explain Lee's rifle.

full retail price, in a London gunshop, of 10,000 Lee-Enfields, for little but the right to put cartridges one on top of another, and the Lee versus Mauser judgment presumably caused some embarrassment. Perhaps the fact that $200,000 of that quarter-million was to be paid on the basis of 500 per magazine had something to do with it, but neither did they adopt Mauser-style charger-loading, before experiencing its superiority the hard way in South Africa. Charger-loading, in a form intended for the Lee, had been patented by Remington's L.P. Diss in 1887, within a few days of the

ment to waste two years introducing and shelving minor ballistic improvements to the black powder Martini, before considering magazine rifles at all. This delayed a decision until, as the 1887 "Treatise of Small Arms" shows, they were aware of "chemical powder" having been adopted in France. So although the first version, the Lee-Metford, used a pellet of compressed black powder, and had Metford's non-angular rifling to shed fouling, the prospect of smokeless powder was surely a consideration. With the adoption of cordite, the Metford rifling was found to erode quickly, and was replaced by five-groove concentric rifling in the Lee-Enfield of 1895.

only 45-70 rifles were tested. But it is interesting to speculate on what might have happened if the U.S. Army had adopted the Lee. The unity (which could be different from the union) of the English-speaking peoples was a live political issue at the time. So it is far from impossible that the smallbore military Lee, either deliberately or by accident, might have become a transatlantic project.

In 1886 Remington had followed Sharps into bankruptcy, occasioned mainly by losing the enormous Turkish army contract to the tube-magazine Mauser. (Ironically, this contract was itself curtailed in 1890, in favor of a box-magazine Mauser of the type Lee sued over.) Following receivership the company was part-owned from 1888 to 1896 by Winchester, who at that time were predominantly a sporting arms manufacturer, and did not attempt to emulate Remington's innovative pursuit of specifically military developments. Perhaps Mauser's defense against the infringement charge had created doubts as to whether the magazine patents could be defended outside the U.S. So production of the front-locking M1899, essentially an in-house development of the Lee by Remington's Roswell Cook, did not begin until all the major powers already had their first-generation smokeless rifle, and formidable competitors were vying for non-aligned or

always a dubious exercise, but it may be that the paper independence of Lee Arms was meant to create a sort of redoubt in which the former Sharps management could take refuge from absorption or dismissal by Remington. After the Remington bankruptcy, Lee probably thought he had done enough for middle-men whom he had helped when their need was greater, but who had no claim upon his latest piece of intellectual property. So on its adoption by the Navy, Lee's straight-pull rifle became the M1895 Winchester-Lee. It is the rifle carved on his gravestone in Hartford, and deservedly so, although there is an argument for the Lee-Enfield.

Adapted to Maynard Rifles.

Cartridges	per 1,000, $13.00
Primed Shells	" 9.00
Bullets (45 grs pure lead)	" 2.50

Powder .... 8 grains.
Cartridges packed 2,000 in a case.

Smokeless Powder, Full Copper Jacketed Or Soft Point Bullet.
Adapted to Lee Straight Pull Rifle adopted by U. S. Navy.

Cartridges, Loose	per 1,000, $50.00
" in Clips	" 58.00
Primed Shells	" 20.00
Bullets	" 15.00

Powder, Smokeless.
Bullets, Full Copper Jacketed
or Soft Point..........112 grains.
Cartridges packed 1,000 in a case.

The cartridge was a pretty modern design, perhaps even well before its time.

private purchasers.

This delay cost Lee his last chance to become an armorer to the world, on the scale of Mauser, Mannlicher and Maxim. But he had been working on a straight-pull design, which was insufficiently prepared for the 1892-93 Army trials, and was rejected in favor of the Krag, due to reliability problems. During the Navy Board trials of 1894 and 1895, something rather odd seems to have happened. Remington submitted turnbolt precursors of the 1899 Lee, and the Lee Arms Company submitted a rifle which the Board described as practically a Mauser. But James Paris Lee, as an individual, submitted an improved version of his straight-pull design.

There had been a dispute over rights between Lee and the Lee Arms Company, of which the secretary, E.G. Westcott, was the former president of Sharps. Reading between the lines is

There is a truism that a rifle designer ought to start with the cartridge. Lee, apart from his primer, showed an extreme lack of interest in cartridge innovation, and the 6mm. U.S. Navy round was developed by Winchester and the Navy, inspired largely by a 6.5x53R Mannlicher imported for evaluation by Colt. Fremantle claims that the bullet weight had to be reduced to 112 gr. to avoid excessive pressures, producing a slightly lower sectional density than most military rifles of the period. So the original may have been the little-used 135-grain load, which is the only one catalogued by D.W.M. in 1904, and works out as a scaling-down in diameter but not length of the 6.5x53R Dutch and Rumanian military bullet. An extremely rare rimmed version may have been intended by Winchester for their 1885 Single Shot, but is no longer cataloged in 1899, and probably never was.

Service and sporting loads for the 236 or 6mm Navy/cartridge, with a 112 gr. round-nosed bullet, gave 2,550 fps/at a time when the 30-40 Krag and 303 were in the 2,000 fps class. Although the cartridge is often called the 236 Navy, this is the land diameter of the six-groove segmental rifling, and bullet diameter is .243-in., just like modern 6mm rifles. The 7-8-in. twist seems fast, now that this caliber is usually a light-bullet one, but it is identical in angle, or when expressed in calibers, to the 10-in. twist of the Krag, and would therefore stabilize bullets an identical number of calibers in length. This seems a more likely explanation for its choice than the rather similar metric twist of almost all 6.5mm Mannlichers, and as it seems slow, though most likely adequate, for the 135 gr. bullet, it may have been altered for the 112-gr.

Mannlichers would not be rimless for several years, so the only prior 6.5mm. rimless round in this head size was the unfairly-maligned 6.5x52mm Mannlicher-Carcano, which as one would very naturally expect of the work of an Italian named Luigi Douglas Scotti, deserved a better rifle and loadings than it received, The Lee closely resembles a slightly longer and thinner 243 Winchester, and the chief difference from the semi-rimless 220 Swift, its only commercial descendant, appears to lie in the longer, wider neck. The Swift was altered to semi-rimless purely to increase case strength, as its narrow rim is not intended for headspacing. The Navy Winchester-Lee saw no major conflicts, although it apparently served the U.S. Marines well in Peking, in the Boxer Rebellion of 1900. Fremantle, by 1901, claims that it was a failure, and already replaced by the Krag. This must have been a disappointment to Lee, who died in 1904, but of course, he had used their cartridge.

I have not attempted to shoot my Winchester-Lee, but R.C.B.S. dies, although a special-order item, are not unduly expensive or slow. I feel 30-40 Krag might be better brass than the often-recommended Swift, since the latter leaves the neck over 1/10-in. short, and 240 Weatherby or Bertram 242 Holland and Holland cases are probably too thin in the neck. The Krag would require to be swaged on a powerful press, and have its solid base turned about .007" smaller, and you must section a case or two to check that there is no thinning near the head, because we are at the outside limit for treating in this way. The

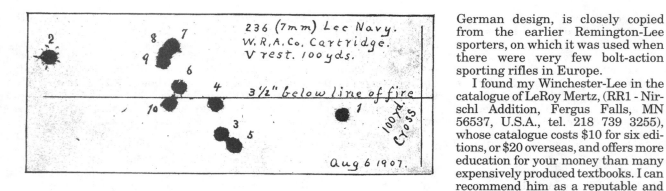

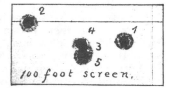

236 (7mm) Lee Navy. W.R.A.Co. Cartridge. V rest. 100 yds.

3½" below line of fire

100 yd. Cross

Aug 6 1907.

100 foot screen.

100 foot.

Not bad stuff for the turn of the century—two wide over and then eight in a cluster.

German design, is closely copied from the earlier Remington-Lee sporters, on which it was used when there were very few bolt-action sporting rifles in Europe.

I found my Winchester-Lee in the catalogue of LeRoy Mertz, (RR1 - Nirschl Addition, Fergus Falls, MN 56537, U.S.A., tel. 218 739 3255), whose catalogue costs $10 for six editions, or $20 overseas, and offers more education for your money than many expensively produced textbooks. I can recommend him as a reputable and helpful supplier, and although a dealer is no doubt more expensive than private purchase or auction, one mistake can cost you far more than paying for reliable cataloging. Another source is "Gun Journal", made up almost exclusively of small ads for gun collectors, of 8009 34th Avenue S. #1391, Minneapolis, MN 55425, U.S.A.

rim will have to be altered, on a lathe arbor made with a stud to fit the primer pocket, and secured by a screw through the flash-hole. A lathe owner could probably anneal an unplated Swift die and enlarge the neck with an engineer's reamer. But it really is essential that you know exactly how to check and if necessary modify the headspace given by such a die, by either grinding a little off the bottom, or adjusting it a little high in the press. Use a tightly-locking adjusting-ring in the latter case, even if you have to cannibalize it from something else. Some rimless rifles will fire excessively short rounds in relative safety - relative - because the extractor holds the case-head against the bolt. But the Lee has a sliding extractor which will not do this.

Lee's futuristic straight-pull action may have been a response to the criticisms of the British Lee. One imagines his new-found wealth paying for some extremely advanced prototype engineering, for the Winchester-Lee exhibits a higher order of machining and mechanical vision than any of Lee's previous work. The barrel threads, at 1-3/32in. by 16 T.P.I., had the largest diameter of any production Winchester rifle, and probably still do, so perhaps chamber swelling was a problem in early development, although the nickel steel used in production rifles would have cured this equally well. The slim action and single-column magazine make for a graceful and rigid stock, comparable with many rimfires, and smaller barrel threads could have made it even slimmer and lighter without loss of strength. But

Component Parts Of The
Lee Straight Pull Rifle.

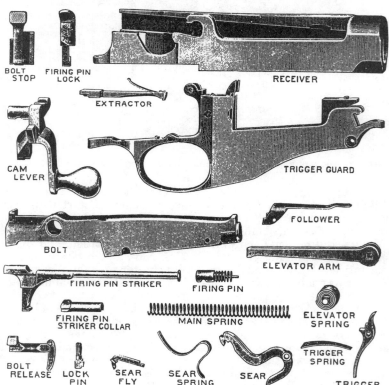

Very complex for today, the Lee was nonetheless simple to operate and easy to shoot well.

if a more heavily-recoiling round had been used, the lack of an effective recoil lug would surely have produced the stock cracking which is common in the Winchester-Hotchkiss. Interestingly, the schnabel-tipped splinter forearm, often assumed to be a

My rifle is Winchester's own sporting version, and cost less than many more widely-collected lever-actions in comparable condition, though at $32 it was nearly double the price when new, and is now one of the rarest Winchesters of all. The barrel is of an unusual contour which I rather like, tapering to only .550in. diameter at the muzzle, but considerably thicker than a modern lightweight sporter in the area, just before the chamber swelling, where barrel vibration and heating are complicated by forearm and fingers. So its 7-1/2-lb. weight is extremely central. The backsight, unfortunately, is the ordinary ratchet-elevator buckhorn of the lever-actions.

It is well-worn, though with no deep pitting, and the bore seems too dark to give useful accuracy, although rifles sometimes surprise in this regard. The operating tabs were broken off the bolt-stop and safety, and so far I have replaced only the

these were the military musket, which was also cataloged for private purchase. Sporter production, in the same number series, commenced only upon completion of the naval order, and was a fraction of the 6,439 not explicitly known to be military. I have seen it quoted as anything between 1,400 and 1,700 rifles, averaging under 100 per annum, and total Winchester-Lee sales failed to make three figures in about half of its twentieth-century years, which we might surmise were "civilian-only". While most metal parts, probably including the barrel contour, are identical, the sporter is far from a crude conversion. The military-sling swivel hole in the

Unlike the Mannlicher, its ingenious clip released its cartridges on insertion and fell out during firing. So clips were not essential, and allowed single-shot use or topping-up of the magazine. We cannot take sheet metal entirely on trust, and I was unable to obtain any clips for testing, but they look simple and durable in catalog illustrations.

The 6mm. Lee was probably the flattest-shooting and most penetrative round available at the time, and Winchester's 1899 catalog quotes penetration of 1/2-in. steel plate at five feet, or 7/16-in. at a hundred feet, which must have been highly relevant to naval boarding parties. Note that if you care to try this, the five-foot shot was surely not hand-held and you must wear safety glasses even at much longer ranges. Dr. Mann bought three apparently unused rifles as surplus in 1907, and had a barrel lapped by H.M. Pope before inserting it in his concentric breech and V-rest. Excellent accuracy considering the period and military ammunition, was obtained from this long, thin barrel, but the first two shots are wild. The British, with the very first experimental 303 ammunition, attributed a similar effect to core-melting before bullet friction was reduced by fouling, and they eliminated it by thickening the jacket. Dr. Mann seems to have shown little interest in the complete Winchester-Lee rifle. For that most tireless of researchers, practical shooting meant a lead-bullet Pope-Ballard and woodchucks.

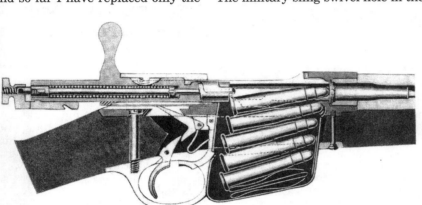

This is the original 1879 Lee bolt action although in fact the actual barrels were threaded.

latter by silver-soldering, which appears very satisfactory. The sear fly appears to be a replacement, and slightly too short, allowing the bolt to rise slightly under mainspring tension. The downward prong of the sear fly is broken off, rendering the bolt release inoperable, so that the rifle cannot be uncocked without firing. Another should be easily made. The Lee safety is difficult to apply, but appears positive, durable and passably quiet, with a tiny hardened roller which engages with the striker. But the bolt cannot be cycled without some mechanical noise. The lockwork seems unnecessarily delicate and complex, and a separate firing-pin, which appears in the Krag and Springfield but not in Lee's patent drawings, was presumably a military requirement.

Madis lists 16,439 Winchester-Lees made between 1896 and 1916, although you may find serials up to 21,173, as a block of over 4,000 numbers were not used. The original naval order for 10,000 was completed in 1898, and occasional peaks in production suggest naval topping-up or naval militia orders. Probably all of

front of the magazine has either never been drilled, or cut away and probably reblued afterwards.

Straight-pull actions were not new, but the earliest Mannlichers move a hinged locking-block, and most others induce rotation of a conventional bolt or bolt-head. The Lee is a less conventional mechanism, and arguably neither a true bolt-action nor truly straight-pull. It was often criticized for the uncomfortable direction of bolt movement, but I found that this followed a path close to the natural hand movement of a prone rifleman, whose forearm rotates around the elbow. Initial lever movement cams the bolt upward, disengaging it from a shoulder in the receiver, rather like an inverted Savage 1899 lever-action. Thereafter the bolt, mostly rectangular in section, slides back and upward at a considerable angle to the bore axis.

The magazine is fixed, resembling the Mannlicher type, and has the unusual distinction of having no magazine lips whatever. Their function is fulfilled by the extractor, a system which appears to work, but may depend upon one small spring.

Various studies have shown that a small bullet can have disproportionate wounding effect, but this undoubtedly varies with circumstances. The 1904 "Textbook of Small Arms" quotes a Surgeon-Colonel Stevenson as saying that the dramatic effects observed in cadaver tests are a notoriously unreliable guide to what happens with living targets. He makes a distinction, which is clearly borne out by Boer War memoirs, between close-range explosive effect (of tissues, not the bullet itself), and the ability to incapacitate at extreme ranges. With round-nosed military bullets, explosive effect depended almost entirely on striking bone.

One imagines Stevenson, if he remained active another twenty years or so, having little difficulty getting onto the radio. For the distinction he draws must have been of some significance to the future Lord Reith of the British Broadcasting Corporation, who was shot through the head and shoulder by a German sniper in 1915, the bullet shattering his cheekbone high enough to leave the teeth intact, but wrote reassuring notes to his family on the spot, walked half a mile to the dressing station, and three weeks later went to see "The Birth of a Nation", which he enjoyed tremendously, Soon afterwards he was running the British inspectorate at the Remington Arms factory in Eddystone, where he may have inspected my P14.

The decline in wounding effect must have been even greater for the

even the nation's finest riflemen, apparently, believed that anything forbidden must be good. By the late Thirties, U.S. military rifle powders incorporated powdered tin for the same purpose. It is interesting, therefore, that the Winchester-Lee used tin-plated copper bullets in both military and soft-point forms. It is doubtful whether the Army, in the Twenties, knew this, or whether Winchester and the Navy meant to prevent anything but verdigris. But it probably had the same effect on foul-

smokeless powders to specification without dangerous inconsistency. Modern handloaders, dependent on what label and loading manual tell us, have to pay the powder-makers to do a great deal of testing, and they may reclassify or remanufacture powders which do not measure up. Commercial loaders, however, still buy powder in very large batches and tailor their loads to its power, and they must have had to make much wider adjustments to charges around the turn of the century. The

The Lee-Metford—a lean, clean machine— proved the system.

Lee than for the 303 "smallbores" Stevenson had in mind. Nonetheless, modern powders, slower rifling and a 90-gr. pointed bullet, which could have a ballistic coefficient of around 45, should give 2,900 ft./sec. with considerably lower than 243 Winchester pressures. Recoil velocity, according to my ballistics programs, would then be around two-thirds of the 308's, with a greater disparity in recoil energy. (It is my belief that velocity is the better index of discomfort, though how much the muzzle climbs may be more truly related to energy.) U.S. Army studies in the twenties found that explosive effect was most readily achieved with a marginally-stabilized 256-inch spitzer, which yawed on impact, though unless this means after impact, it would greatly reduce penetration of armor or obstacles.

General Hatcher describes how Colonel Townsend Whelen, in the Twenties, remembered the French artillery practice of using tinfoil strips in the powder to reduce metallic fouling from the copper driving-band. Cupro-nickel fouling having proven particularly troublesome at Springfield velocities, he experimented with tin-plated bullets. Tin eliminated fouling, but produced greatly increased bullet pull, which appeared harmless under normal circumstances, and compatible with exceptional accuracy. This development was used only in the National Match ammunition of 1921, as it was found to produce dangerous pressures when combined with grease lubrication of bullets, and

ing - and, potentially, on grease enthusiasts - as Colonel Whelen's plating.

The 6mm Lee was inconvenient for handloading, which Winchester, in their February, 1 899 catalog, advised against for all smokeless rounds, though they sold the components. They cited the mysterious deterioration of cases which we now know to result from mercuric primers, undiluted by black powder fouling. Actually this was no mystery to the Ordnance Department, for although Winchester quotes copiously from their report of 1896, they make no mention of the 1897 report which identified the problem, or the government arsenals' change to non-mercuric chlorate primers for Krag cartridges in 1898. The civilian shooter was not out of the woods when these primers reached the market, for potassium chlorate attacked steel instead of brass, and the need to flush out with water was not appreciated for many years. The Lee's caliber and twist made it peculiarly difficult to clean, and vulnerable to corrosion. Many have badly pitted bores, although thanks to the limited availability of ammunition during much of their lives, fewer are worn out.

This does not mean that Winchester's warning was entirely misplaced. We may wonder why writers often attribute the Lee's demise to the lack of suitable propellants, and yet proceed to list perfectly good loads which they have worked up with commonplace thirty-caliber powders. Greener, in 1910, claims that no manufacturer could make

handloader of the time would have been on even more dangerous ground if he had attempted the high loading densities which characterize the 243 Winchester today, and we all know people who cannot bear to see wasted space.

Neither the Winchester-Lee nor the M1899 Remington-Lee (using, among others, the same cartridge) were popular sporting weapons, and probably only the obligation to stock military parts kept the sporter in production so long. To American hunters, any bolt action was an unfamiliar device, and the 6mm was a bizarre and expensive expedient, probably with unreliably expanding bullets, which was justifiable only by the military's need for long range and portability of ammunition. A scope or receiver sight, which are necessary to obtain some real benefit in return for the inconvenience of the Lee, would be difficult to fit, and I know of no Winchester-Lee with either the relatively precise open sights which were catalogued as options for other rifles, or the Lyman cocking-piece sight which was common on Remington-Lee sporters. A necked-up version, though eminently logical, never materialized. To us today, a 19th century 243 is most of what excites us about the Lee. But Winchester's greatest mistakes lay in keeping it a one-cartridge rifle, and fitting sights which left it on a par with handier and cheaper lever-actions. The rimmed version would surely have been worth keeping in the 1885 single-shot, which was routinely fitted with the best triggers and sighting equipment the industry knew.

As to whether all this justifies the early demise of the military 6mm., I do not believe it does, and I think the Winchester-Lee round could, to some advantage, replace any military smallarm round we know today. Ironically, although the 30-06 Springfield was a splendidly-executed and popular weapon, the U.S. Army would surely have been as well served, in their only large bolt-action war, by a Lee or clip-loading adaptation of the Krag, pending a change to a small-bore semi-automatic or selective-fire weapon. By 1918, the B.A.R. and other light machine-guns had ushered in a successful revolution in infantry tactics; the Pedersen Device semiautomatic accessory for the Springfield had concentrated a few minds; and the first Bergman submachine-guns had proven formidable close-range weapons. So a good many people must have remembered how, before the war, both American and British authorities had recognized the automatic infantry rifle as the weapon of the future, whenever it could be made reliable and compact.

This would surely have been more easily realized in 6mm than in 30-06, and could still have owed much to the Winchester-Lee, for patent protection of his shoulder-locking, tipping bolt does not appear to have been limited to manually-operated weapons, and it much resembles the system later used in the extremely successful

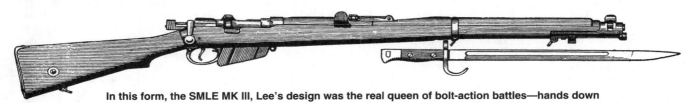

In this form, the SMLE MK III, Lee's design was the real queen of bolt-action battles—hands down

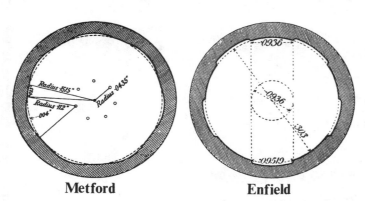

Metford **Enfield**

The Medford rifling was easy to clean, but smokeless loads gave it fits, so..... enter the Enfield mode.

Fabrique Nationale F.A.L. Like the 7mm. round of the abandoned British EM2, the right sort of 6mm Lee assault rifle should have been controllable in fully-automatic fire, and yet a far better long-range weapon than the 5.56mm. As with so much else of Lee's history, those, of course, are might-have-beens. •

BIBLIOGRAPHY

Barnes, Frank C.
Cartridges of the World
DBI Books, Northfield Illinois, 6th Ed. 1989

Deutsche Waffen und Munitionsfabriken (D.W.M.)
Munitions-Katalog,
Karlsruhe, 1904

Donnelly, John J.
Handloader's Guide to Cartridge Conversions, Stoeger, South Hackensack New Jersey, 1987

Fremantle, the Rt. Hon. T.F. (Later Lord Cottesloe)
The Book of the Rifle London, 1901 (Reprinted by W.S Curtis, Newport Pagnall, U.K., 1988)

Greener, W.W.
The Gun and its Development, 9th edition of 1910 (Reprinted by Arms and Armour Press, London)

Hayes, Col. Thomas J., and McFarland, Col. Earl

Elements of Ordnance: A Textbook for Use of Cadets of the United States Military Academy, John Wiley and Sons, New York and Chapman and Hall, London, 1938

Hatcher, Major General Julian S., U.S.A. retd.
Hatcher's Notebook, Stackpole, Harrisburg PA, 3rd Ed. 1966

Hebler, Professor Friedrich Wilhelm
Das kleinste Kaliber, oder das zukiinftige Infanterie-gewehr, Zurich and Leipzig, 1890

Lugs, Jaroslav
Firearms Past and Present, Prague, 1956 (English edition Greville Publishing, London, 1973)

Madis, George
Winchester Dates of Manufacture, Art and Reference House, Brownsboro, Texas, 1981

Mann, Dr. Franklin W.
The Bullet's Flight from

Powder to Target, 1909 (reprinted by Wolfe Publishing Company, Prescott AZ, 1980)

Myszkowski, Eugene
The Remington-Lee Rifle, Excalibur Publications, Latham NY, 1994

Reitz, Denys
Commando: A Boer Journal of the Boer War, 1929 (reprinted in the **Trilogy of Deneys Reitz,** Wolfe Publishing Company, Prescott AZ, 1994)

The War Office
Treatise of Small Arms, London, 1887

The War Office
Textbook of Small Arms, various editions, London, 1904-1929

Winchester Repeating Arms Company
Winchester Catalogue of 1899, (reprinted by Wolfe Publishing Company, Prescott, AZ, 199

BEFORE THE SELF-CONTAINED metallic cartridge made them practical, there were many attempts to produce machineguns. Virtually all were guns with many barrels—some with twenty or more. One of these examples was the Chambers Swivel Gun. It fired 175 shots in one long salvo through only seven barrels.

Joseph Chambers of West Middleton in Washington County in Western Pennsylvania patented his gun in 1813, and in 1814 the U.S. Navy ordered twenty. They issued two of them as part of ship's complements of six swivel guns, and no less famous a ship than the U.S.S. Constitution had a pair.

One description states: "Upon her capstan the Constitution mounted a piece resembling seven musket bar-

by KONRAD F. SCHREIER, JR.

rels. These were fixed together with iron bands. It was discharged with a (flint) lock. Each barrel threw twenty-five balls, within a few seconds of each other, making 175 balls that were shot from the piece within two minutes." (James Durand [journal of], New Haven, 1926.)

The only surviving Chambers Swivel Gun is in the great Musee d'Armes, Liege, Belgium. It is caliber 80, measures about 6 feet long, and has 60-inch barrels. Its barrels are very heavy, and the entire gun weighs about 100 pounds.

Its barrels are heavy because the gun is fired by a system adopted from a popular form of fireworks known

as a "Roman Candle," which fires a series of colored pyrotechnic balls out of a tube. Each of the barrels of the Chambers swivel gun was loaded like a Roman Candle with twenty-five superposed loads, one on top of the next, contrived to fire in succession. This was accomplished by using a load consisting of a layer of slow-burning blackpowder—low in saltpeter and high in charcoal—then a charge of regular blackpowder, and then the ball. The twenty-five loads filled about half of the barrel.

Upon ignition, the top load nearest the muzzle fired first and ignited the slow-burning composition, which burned past the ball behind it to the

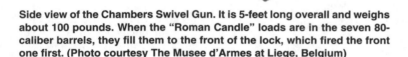

Side view of the Chambers Swivel Gun. It is 5-feet long overall and weighs about 100 pounds. When the "Roman Candle" loads are in the seven 80-caliber barrels, they fill them to the front of the lock, which fired the front one first. (Photo courtesy The Musee d'Armes at Liege, Belgium)

THE CHAMBERS SWIVEL GUN:

It shot—in 1815—175 times in one long burst!

The loading ramrod is shown in the middle of the seven barrels. The ramrod is marked with grooves to show the proper position of each of the twenty-five loads in each of the barrels. Note the barrels are smoothbore and much heavier than musket barrels of the same period, so they can withstand the powerful "Roman Candle" loads. *(Photo courtesy The Musee d'Armes at Liege, Belgium)*

next load, firing it. This effect was repeated until all twenty-five loads in the barrel had fired.

The trouble with such a gun is that it takes great care and caution to load it properly, and it probably took the better part of a day to load one salvo. Contemporary descriptions say the gun was kept loaded with moisture-proof packing in its flashhole and on top of the charges to keep the powder dry. This was removed before firing, of course.

The crew manning a ship's two Chambers Swivel Guns could fire just two salvos in a battle—first one gun, then the second. Then the guns had to be laid aside until there was time to reload them. In naval actions of the time, of course, two such salvos laid into close-packed enemy boarders could be very useful, if not decisive.

Although the gun undoubtedly worked and was one of the few early "machineguns" used in action, it was not truly practical. The U.S. Navy had discarded them by the 1830s, and today the Chambers Swivel Gun is a nearly forgotten step in the evolution of the machinegun. ●

EASY TO CONCEAL.
EASY TO FIRE. EASY TO ACQUIRE.
HARD TO BEAT.

Cougar F, available in 9mm, .40 and .45 ACP

Cougar D, available in 9mm, .40 and .45 ACP

New Cougar Mini, in F and D, available in 9mm and .40 cal.– Extended magazine optional

Beretta Cougar pistols set a tough new standard, making heavy firepower easy to handle. The *compact contoured frame* with rounded edges makes it easy to *conceal, draw and hold.* The patented Cam-Loc locked-breech *rotating barrel system absorbs recoil energy*, improving accuracy and *fast second shot recovery.*

You get a lot *more for your money,* too.

Like cold hammer forged barrels. *Hard-chromed bore.* Quick read 3 dot sights. Automatic visual firing pin block. *Tough corrosion resistant mil-spec Bruniton® finish.* 9mm, .40 or .45 cal. firepower with single/double action "F" and double action only "D" operating systems. *In new more concealable* *Mini Cougar* or standard Compact. Be sure to explore the full line of *Beretta Sport clothing and accessories* at your Beretta dealer today.

The ergonomically-designed contoured frame takes advantage of anatomy and instinctive hold for greater comfort and accuracy.

The patented Cam-Loc rotating barrel system absorbs recoil energy for remarkably low felt recoil.

For best results, use Beretta Gun Oil.

BERETTA

A tradition of excellence since 1526

Beretta U.S.A. Corp., 17601 Beretta Dr., Accokeek, MD 20607, www.beretta.com. For a Beretta Worldwide Catalog of firearms & Beretta Sport clothing and accessories, call 1-800-528-7453 ($3.00 shipping). Visit The Beretta Gallery in New York and Dallas.

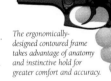

You can pay more.
You just can't get more.

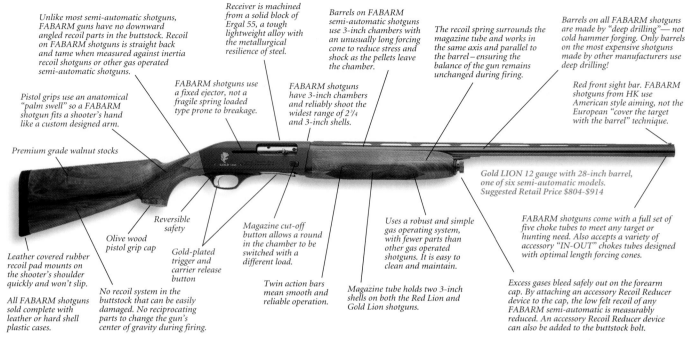

Unlike most semi-automatic shotguns, FABARM guns have no downward angled recoil parts in the buttstock. Recoil on FABARM shotguns is straight back and tame when measured against inertia recoil shotguns or other gas operated semi-automatic shotguns.

Receiver is machined from a solid block of Ergal 55, a tough lightweight alloy with the metallurgical resilience of steel.

Barrels on FABARM semi-automatic shotguns use 3-inch chambers with an unusually long forcing cone to reduce stress and shock as the pellets leave the chamber.

The recoil spring surrounds the magazine tube and works in the same axis and parallel to the barrel—ensuring the balance of the gun remains unchanged during firing.

Barrels on all FABARM shotguns are made by "deep drilling"— not cold hammer forging. Only barrels on the most expensive shotguns made by other manufacturers use deep drilling!

Pistol grips use an anatomical "palm swell" so a FABARM shotgun fits a shooter's hand like a custom designed arm.

FABARM shotguns use a fixed ejector, not a fragile spring loaded type prone to breakage.

FABARM shotguns have 3-inch chambers and reliably shoot the widest range of 2³/₄ and 3-inch shells.

Red front sight bar. FABARM shotguns from HK use American style aiming, not the European "cover the target with the barrel" technique.

Premium grade walnut stocks

Gold LION 12 gauge with 28-inch barrel, one of six semi-automatic models. Suggested Retail Price $804-$914

Reversible safety

Olive wood pistol grip cap

Magazine cut-off button allows a round in the chamber to be switched with a different load.

Uses a robust and simple gas operating system, with fewer parts than other gas operated shotguns. It is easy to clean and maintain.

FABARM shotguns come with a full set of five choke tubes to meet any target or hunting need. Also accepts a variety of accessory "IN-OUT" chokes tubes designed with optimal length forcing cones.

Leather covered rubber recoil pad mounts on the shooter's shoulder quickly and won't slip.

Gold-plated trigger and carrier release button

Twin action bars mean smooth and reliable operation.

Magazine tube holds two 3-inch shells on both the Red Lion and Gold Lion shotguns.

Excess gases bleed safely out on the forearm cap. By attaching an accessory Recoil Reducer device to the cap, the low felt recoil of any FABARM semi-automatic is measurably reduced. An accessory Recoil Reducer device can also be added to the buttstock bolt.

All FABARM shotguns sold complete with leather or hard shell plastic cases.

No recoil system in the buttstock that can be easily damaged. No reciprocating parts to change the gun's center of gravity during firing.

FABARM shotguns

Feature for feature, premium grade semi-automatic shotguns from Italian gun maker Fabbrica Bresciana Armi (FABARM) are unsurpassed. Deep-drilled barrels. Forged double action bars. Rugged and simple design. Straight-back low recoil. All translate into the finest autoloading shotguns made.

Plus HK/FABARM has a full line of quality shotguns, including over-&-unders, side-by-sides, and a pump action utility gun—all designed and manufactured with a synthesis of old world craftsmanship and advanced engineering.

HK/FABARM shotguns are made for any and every shooting need you have...sporting clays, trap, skeet, waterfowl, upland bird, turkey, and personal security.

Best of all, HK/FABARM shotguns are covered by a lifetime warranty— the only shotgun with such a guarantee.

MAX LION 12 gauge with 28-inch barrels, one of eight over-and-under models. Suggested Retail Price $1,053-$1,807

Classic Lion Grade II 12 gauge with 26-inch barrels, one of two side-by-side models. Suggested Retail Price $1,488-$2,110

FP6 12 gauge pump action with 20-inch barrel. Suggested Retail Price $472

Exclusively from
HECKLER & KOCH, INC.
21480 Pacific Boulevard
Sterling, Virginia 20166 U.S.A.

FABARM • Fabbrica Bresciana Armi

by: Jim Foral

For nearly 80 years, we have had those..... Russian "Sporters"

Hurry-up replicated Russian sporter—just like the guns our grandads tinkered.

It lay on the dealer's table like a mongrel in the midst of a litter of fit purebreds. It was the wormy mutt of the rifle world, a pitiful specimen of the Russian Mosin-Nagant, stripped of its handguard, its forearm and barrel amputated, assaulted with saws and sandpaper, the poor thing looked undignified and anorexic. If rifles could blush, this one had every reason.

"Mind if I take a close look at your Nagant?", I inquired. "You'd be the only one", the owner sighed. "That thing doesn't seem to attract too much attention. It probably came home in a duffle bag after the War."

"If this gun could talk, I don't believe that it would be telling any war stories", I interrupted. "Butchering Mosin-Nagants was a popular pastime way before the war. I wondered when I'd see one. What do you gotta have for it?"

"Sixty bucks" he piped up, "and you'd best get it today. That thing will bring a hundred dollars come fall"

"That may be", I allowed," but I'll pass for now, if I may."

Cruising the rest of the show, I encountered another sad Russian. Picking it up, I proceeded to give it the once-over.

"Got ammo for that", blurted its owner, without making eye contact.

"Is that so?" I responded, affording him the same courtesy.

Originally a Russian service rifle, this gun was now a chopped up, battered and reblued wreck. Military sights were still on the barrel. The replacement stock, a scandalous clubby affair, was a badly fit Bishop. Gaping behind the tang was a cavernous crack. One of those awful black plastic forearm tips was separated from the wood by a once fashionable fake ivory spacer. This one was now homely in the extreme. By all indications, this bleak-looking Nagant was cobbled up by some rascal in the 1950s, long after the 1925-34 heyday of surplus Russian sporterization.

"Eighty five bucks and I can wrap that up for you", the dealer pressured, finally looking in my direction.

"Not just yet", I answered, "I'm gonna look around a bit more if you don't mind."

How a glut of Russian military rifles got into general circulation in America requires a brief explanation.

With an entire continent at war in 1914, the Imperial Russian Government felt compelled to seek additional weapons and turned to the U.S.

Winchester signed contracts to deliver almost a third of a million Model 1895 lever guns in 7.62 x 54mm. And New England Westinghouse and Remington Arms agreed to tool up to put the Russian Mosin-Nagant into mass production.

When manufacturing was at its peak, Remington and an overly picky crew of Russian inspectors passed 5,000 rifles per day. In combination, the two plants fabricated almost one and a half million rifles from 1915 to 1917.

When the Bolsheviks seized power in Russia in 1917, all agreements with foreign contractors were effectively voided. The upset had a devastating and immediate effect in Bridgeport. Production of Mosin-Nagants slammed to a halt and thousands of wage earners clocked out permanently. Remington executives despaired and hundreds of thousands of undeliverable Nagants were put in storage.

At the same time, the ill prepared U.S. armed forces officials assessed the severity of the desperate international state of affairs. The future required solvent suppliers of rifles and ammunition. Uncle Sam thereupon bailed out Remington-UMC by purchasing 280,000 of those Russian rifles, reducing the company's losses to a manageable level.

Many of these guns were shipped overseas to arm the White Russian Army, which opposed the Bolsheviks. Some saw active duty and combat in the hands of the joint American/British North American Expeditionary Force in 1918-20.

Surplus Russian turn bolts were also to have been distributed to America's "fourth line of defense", the National Guard and home guard units. And so, in the July 27,1918 ARMS AND THE MAN, American rifle cranks were exposed to the Mosin-Nagant. Writer Steven Trask walked readers through a mostly objective familiarizing look at the Russian, titled somewhat irreverently," The Bolshevik Fusee". Trask detailed the rifle's physical characteristics and functions from the buttplate to the front sight.

He skirted any thoroughly disparaging labels when he chose the words "rangy divvil" and "homely brute' to describe the look of the Nagant.

After Armistice, our government decided to dispose of the surplus Russian Nagants by making them accessible to NRA members through the Director of Civilian Marksmanship channels. In late 1921, ARMS AND THE MAN announced the price of a new unfired rifle at ten dollars. Cartridges sold for eight dollars per thousand. A decent Krag could be bought for $10.00. Ten bucks went a long ways towards the purchase of a more respectable deer rifle—a Winchester, Marlin, or Savage. So, there were few takers.

The Russian rifles had aliases during this period. Informally, they were called "Rooshins" or "91s", from the year of their adoption. The endearing designation "Three Line" was a purely American invention; *lini* was a now-obsolete Russian unit of measurement equal to .1 inch. The most common nickname was the most obvious—"Russian".

In the June 1, 1923 issue, AMERICAN RIFLEMAN announced that the Russian's price was now $3.34, including packing. Cartridges were now $4.00 per thousand, and the supply was seemingly inexhaustible. Included with the rifle was a cleaning rod, screw driver, wooden front sight cover, and what was known technically as the sling strap, useful in carrying, but not shooting, the rifle.

The vast majority of American riflemen still managed to restrain themselves. It appears that there was a reluctance to embrace the Bolshevik battle rifle for aesthetic reasons. Cheap was only worth so much. The

rifleman of the early 1920s was underwhelmed.

There was something fundamentally objectionable about the Russian. Magazine writers who evaluated products for the shooting consumer made clear their impressions. To an individual, the journalists described the foreigner negatively. It was pronounced "ugly".

"Ugly" is a comprehensive term. The fraternity of riflemen got specific, too. The stubby bolt handle stuck right out there and totally destroyed the symmetry of the weapon. Particularly offensive was the dangling magazine. Up-to-date, presentable rifles had flush magazines. The grossly oversized cocking knob was "as prominent and as pleasing as a facial boil on a bucktooth woman."

At the same time, a small and scattered group of gun cranks detected a sporting rifle concealed beneath the handguard and the cosmoline. There was a minor effort in certain localities to remodel this Russian novelty.

In the beginning, there was a certain stigma attached to the Russian. Showing up at the range with a U.S. Krag kitchen table sporter was OK but uncasing a Russian in any form was socially risky.

Some kind words were needed if the rifles were to sell, the assurance and approval of authorities would be helpful. That era's gunwriters did what they could.

Townsend Whelen made public his opinion concerning the crude and clumsy Russian about 1924. He wrote, "It has in it the makings of a most excellent weapon."

Whether or not Whelen owned a Three Line is not recorded. He was quite devoted to the Krag and his beloved Springfield 1903 action. Whelen and the Russian sporter were not strangers though.

"I have seen dozens of Russian rifles slightly remodeled by NRA members that were perfectly splendid sporting rifles and very fair target rifles", the rifle crank's crank said.

During the 1930s, F.C. Ness ran the Dope Bag in *American Rifleman*. Before that he wrote for others. In a 1929 number of OUTDOOR LIFE, Ness described his personal Russian sporter. He had performed some basic stock slenderizing procedures, cut the barrel back to 24 inches, installed a Springfield front sight and fitted a King 6-R leaf rear sight on the receiver ring. He bent his bolt handle downward, but didn't think that added anything. A decent sling completed the job. The finished rifle weighed six and a half pounds, and set its converter back nine bucks, when the cost of the gun, sights and sling were totalled.

C.G. Williams, who edited the Arms and Ammunition column for OUTDOOR LIFE for a time in the early '20s, insisted the fundamental metal work necessary to put the military Russian into sporting shape was easily seen, and its accomplishment simple and straightforward. Among OL subscribers, some scratched their heads about the steps needed to get the stock to look like something.

"Thin it down to resemble a shotgun stock", Williams offered, and explained that remodeling the issue stock was perfectly acceptable.

"The straight grip is good and looks especially racy and clean."

The hesitant may have felt reassured when Williams admitted in

Me and the raw material —an uncobbled Russian ready for the rasp and also the saw.

print: "I have remodeled two of these on these lines, and they were especially fine looking rifles."

William's statement, published in October of 1922, undoubtedly vitalized sales of the slow- moving Nagants, and the movement to carve up the Russian rifle.

Springfields and Krags had been readily available for a number of years, and sportrizing them was fairly popular. In the 91's case, there was no terrific or widespread rush to do so.

There was a certain attraction to the Russian, especially the cheap cost of owning and shooting it. Against that, further, there was an unmistakable distain— the outlook of those who bought them seemed to be; "If I ravage this thing, what have I ruined?"

These two factors in combination resulted in an unexampled movement to buy the ugly battle rifle. As the availability of surplus Nagants became more and more publicized, and this model's suitability as a sporting weapon made better known, interest in and demand for the cheap Three Line grew exponentially. And, the practice of sporterizing the Russian at home gained momentum from coast to coast.

A crowd of entrepreneurs now emerged and stood ready to offer products and services to folks who had fallen for the rifles for as long as the Russian fad lasted. Gunsmiths and stockmakers of varying levels of skill placed ads in the AMERICAN RIFLEMAN and other publications, trolling for Russian-owning customers. S.J. Fryer would cut the barrel, and reshape a military Russian stock into sporting type for $6.50. A father and son team by the name of Warner made a specialty of Russian remodeling in the Twenties. They would add a pistol grip, raise the comb, apply a buttplate and refinish the stock, all for six bucks.

In the August 1923 issue of OUTDOOR LIFE, would-be guncraftsman E.H. Osborn described his Russian conversion. This day and a half project demonstrates his ingenuity and it represents a typical good example of a Russian makeover accomplished with limited financial resources.

Osborn gathered the "few tools in his possession" and tackled the ponderous woodwork, sawing the forearm off ahead of the front band, pretty much a standard operation among Russian sporterizers. The sling guards were removed and discarded. Surplus wood was removed by shaving down the stock with a broken piece of glass. Osborn used his shotgun as a pattern, and continued until the two buttstocks began to look similar. With only coarse and very fine sandpaper, he hurried through the sanding stage and selected a stock finish from his limited bag of tricks—a few fingerfulls of Winchester gun grease. Unsightly sling strap holes were filled with hot black roofing asphalt, finished flush with the surface. Stray screw holes got the asphalt, too.

Shortening the barrel constituted the entire metal-working segment of Osborn's Americanizing. Presumably because he lacked a hacksaw, Mr. Osborn carefully amputated six and a half inches of excess length with a three cornered file. He squared up the muzzle as best he could, and crowned it with a piece of emery paper.

Osborn retained the arsenal rear sight. The new front sight was set in a common band, its blade fashioned from a slug of brass, into which a hole was bored to accommodate a piece of chalk in lieu of ivory.

The finished rifle weighed eight pounds, reportedly with perfect balance. A range test showed the rifle was capable of grouping into "a small circle with no wild shots" at 800 yards. Osborn considered removing more wood, but changed his mind.

"I like mine just as it is, and will let good enough alone" he explained to his fellow OUTDOOR LIFE readers.

Ornamenting done-over Russians, came through inspiration and a deep wellspring of creativity. Many objected strongly to the useless holes left in the buttstock by the abandonment of the sling swivels and devised some novel plugs. Coins were sometimes inletted into the wood— a silver dollar covered nicely. Compasses also found their way into these orifices, as did plugs of bone, pieces of amber, colored glass, and genuine elephant ivory.

Garish diamond-shaped inlays of various materials were very fashionable and, in the eyes of some beholders, very decorative. These gun cranks had bakelite, hard rubber, some stuff known as rosepearl, and a few others. One citizen sawed a black buttplate from an automobile battery. There was a synthetic amber called of amberoid. In the classier stock jobs, irregularly shaped patches of matching walnut camouflaged those dreadful holes.

Anyone who wanted a pistol grip had to restock or add one. Most took the latter course. This involved attaching a block of wood and shaping the assembly to the individual taste. Some such jobs were better executed than others, of course. Untrained attempts at coarse checkering helped to distract critical eyes from bad joints and other indicators of a botched job.

This grafting was practiced on the Mosin-Nagant just as on the Springfield and Krag rifles. Trendy schnabel tips were added in the same manner, and a cheekpiece or two; sometimes a shooter bought a lace-on cheekpiece.

Other changes to the issue stock might include discarding the steel buttplate and installing a recoil pad.

Some couldn't justify a $1.50 Hawkins or Jostam Anti-Flinch Pad on a $3.00 gun, and a no-cost option was to tack on a section of worn-out automobile tire, trimmed to fit. The smooth original buttplate did slip off the shoulder, so you'll find some "checkered", with a file, which helped. Stippling with a punch was another way. The '91's buttplate was pitched at a contrary angle, so a number of cranks bent it straighter than it was, and ground it to reduce weight and mass. While at the grinder, some ground the head off the striker knob or reduced it to a neater size.

By the late 1920s, surplus Russians had become unexpectedly popular. The membership rolls of the NRA swelled as people signed up just for the privilege of buying a three-dollar rifle and cheap ammunition. As the Three Lines were being distributed, the demand for expert guidance in remodeling increased correspondingly.

For twenty years, NRA publications had printed tips on sporterizing the U.S. Krag and Springfield rifles, and the membership was familiar with most of the fundamental techniques. Growing numbers of Russian purchasers now wanted to know what could be done. The NRA's response was to recruit Alvin Linden, the talented all-around gunsmith from Wisconsin. By 1927, Linden had made over a fair number of Mosin-Nagants for his Langlade County, Wisconsin neighbors. With the publication of Linden's wordy how-to essay in the December, 1927 issue of AMERICAN RIFLEMAN, do-it-yourselfers were provided with enough knowledge to make twenty-dollar sporters out of their mail-order Russians.

Cutting the 31-inch barrel was a simple matter, and squaring up the muzzle and crowning were not tricky either if Linden's instructions were read and followed. Linden shed light on the attachment of the Springfield or Lyman front sight band, explained how to prepare metal surfaces, and taught a two-sentence lesson on tinning barrel and sight.

Lyman's #36 receiver sight was the only rear sight worth considering, in Linden's estimation. It could be fixed to the Russian receiver by drilling and tapping. If a person wanted a jarproof installation, he could sweat the Lyman prior to tightening the screws.

The gunsmith-author walked his readers through bending the bolt handle to a more agreeable length and position. And he detailed a novel method of lengthening the bolt handle using the barrel stub. How to form and reshape a new knob was also made clear. The only tools Linden required were a hacksaw, file and a torch.

When Linden turned the reader's attention to dolling up the beastly arsenal stock, he untangled the procedures to plane and rasp away unnecessary poundage, told him from where to trim the fat, and which tools to use. Some tips on finishing the wood were furnished, too.

Linden's article was published in two parts. The second, in January, 1928, focused entirely on whittling a sporting style stock from a walnut blank. I believe this specialized subject matter was certainly beyond the interest or capabilities of most NRA members. Nonetheless, Linden spelled out the complex procedures of laying out and inletting the peculiar Russian barrelled action for any who might want to try their hand at stockmaking. There was much fine measuring and marking, checking and double-checking to be done.

A lot of people who might have seriously considered such a project were very likely discouraged or intimidated by Linden's persistent cautions to be careful, and his reminders of the consequences of failing to do so. Deterring several more was the need for the exacting determination of dimensions and painstaking fitting. Those able to follow directions may have doubted their personal proficiency with gouges, chisels, and draw knives.

Presumably, at least some neophyte woodworkers gathered up a slab of walnut and the required patience. With their copy of the January, 1928 AMERICAN RIFLEMAN in front of them, they proceeded as directed by Alvin Linden. Hopeful of a $40 looking rifle, they made the attempt at stockmaking their own Russians. Their success varied in degree.

Frustrated, the disadvantaged majority of America's riflemen accepted the sad fact that their pitiful Russian sporters could never measure up to Linden's work, and that they would be forever reduced to dragging an embarrassment into the woods. This didn't bother everybody, but it bothered some. Legions blushed when, in the late 1920s, a disgraceful expression came into use: the cruel term "Russian peasant rifles" was popularly used to refer to the humble bare-bones home shop conversions of Russian rifles.

In January of 1932, Minnesotan Algot Lidholm gave these men hope. He showed them what could be accomplished by a man armed with a knife, a knack and a double measure of desire, when he published a step by step "here's how I did it" type of article in AMERICAN RIFLEMAN.

The first order of business was to remove the issue stock. Lidholm then fired up a gasoline blowtorch, attacked the eyesore rear sight, and filed off the sight pad. He sawed a half-foot of excess barrel length off and crowned the muzzle. He then hand-forged a ramp sight with an integral band. The Lyman #36 was chosen to mount over the receiver.

Cosmetic work was next. Lidholm wasn't enamored by the Russian right angle bolt handle, and reworked the thing to satisfy himself. Careful to avoid overheating the bolt body, he heated the bolt knob and drew it out to the approximate diameter of the shank and gave the knob a slight bend upward. The handle was finished with alternating horn and fiber washers were applied to it's bottom, finished smooth.

A hard blank of black walnut was selected for the stock. Lidholm persisted in the cutting, scraping, and gouging ritual until a graceful, pleasing stock, fitted to his wiry physique, ultimately took its final shape. A forearm tip was fashioned from horn and doweled to the stock, and an elaborately inlaid pistol grip cap, also of horn, was installed. A hand rubbed oil finish was the next unhurried step. Not one to waste words, all Lidholm had to say about the process was: "I was at it for six weeks."

He next undertook checkering the finished stock and eventually succeeded in completing an intricate and ornate design he modestly described as "a little unusual." Obviously, patience was among Lidholm's virtues, and he was rewarded for his endurance with an impressive, professional-looking job executed to perfection, a stunning example of what could be done with a lot of time and a homemade checkering tool.

The final treatment of the project was to reblue the steel parts using the Townsend-recommended Hoffman bluing solution.

Two good, sharp, attention-producing photographs illustrated Lidholm's information saturated-article, and many eyes grew wider upon noticing them. Without doubt, reader reaction to Lidholm's report would have been mixed, but those considering personalizing a Nagant

must have gawked and daydreamed. Admirers of any form of good workmanship who happened to take notice would have agreed, most likely.

Certainly, some held steadfastly to the belief that Lidholm's expenditure of time and effort did little to dignify an otherwise unworthy gun. The "misspent" ability should have been lavished upon a U.S. rifle, a Springfield or a Krag, these felt.

E.J. Witzel, a dentist and amateur stocker put together a Russian after Lidholm's example. His was stylishly stocked with a wonderful chunk of circassian walnut. A brief write-up accompanied a photo in the February, 1934 AMERICAN RIFLEMAN. The clean, well proportioned lines of Dr. Witzel's stock provided a refreshing change from the standard photos of pared-down military stocks. A nice swept-back bolt handle added to the visual appeal of this particular gun. Further, this example served to reinforce and re-emphasize the notion that a finished '91 didn't have to be ugly.

Remarkably, not every adult U.S. male of that generation possessed such elemental knowledge or expertise. An already modified '91 could be had from Benicia Arsenal out in California. The inept needed only to mail $7.30, a copy of his NRA membership card, together with the shipping charge of $7.62 to Benicia. A clean sawed-off Mosin-Nagant would arrive at his door a few days later.

The details of the Benicia conversion are not all clear. There was the customary barrel and forend shortening. Some back and front sight switching was involved, too.

During the height of the Russian sporter craze, the New York City firm of Stoeger's marketed a remodeled 1891, the Peerless model as a standard catalog item. For $24, a sportsman could purchase an eight-pound,

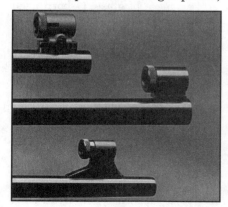

Lyman's #17 front sights, favorites in the '20's, are still around—ask Lyman.

reblued number with a shortened barrel and a stylish, no frills walnut stock. The Peerless came supplied with the excellent Pacific Model R-1 adjustable bolt peep at the rear; the hooded ramp front looks like another Pacific Gunsight product. For the money, the Stoeger's Peerless was a presentable deer gun and a terrific value. The word was that they were good shooters, too.

There was the Philadelphia firm of R.F. Sedgley, Inc, which turned out custom rifles based on the Springfield action on a semi-production basis. Sedgley was the acknowledged leader in this branch of the gun trade. Some insist Sedgley also gussied up the Russians making a decent lightweight sporter. Self-declared Sedgley experts, however, dispute this claim. The Great Depression was at hand and outfits such as Sedgley's were known to stray from their specialties in the struggle to remain solvent.

Not everyone was afraid to spend real money on his Russian. I have heard of two conversions that some-one went to the trouble and expense to engrave.

The generous supply of Mosin-Nagants brought about another sort of entrepreneur. In the late 1920s, New York City surplus dealer Francis Bannerman bought a quantity of Russians and reworked them to shoot the 30-06 cartridge. Dwindling inventories of surplus 7.62 Russian ammunition coupled with the attractive '06 chambering, lured buyers to the .30 caliber hybrid. Bannerman called it the "Russian-

Lidholm's Russian as shown in the American Rifleman, January, '32—definitely respectable to 30s' eyes.

Springfield front band and blade, the favorite of converters. It cost $1.35, and could be ordered the same time as the rifle.

The Lyman #36, shown here with the sight arm swung to the rear, was the upscale darling in Russian sporter sights.

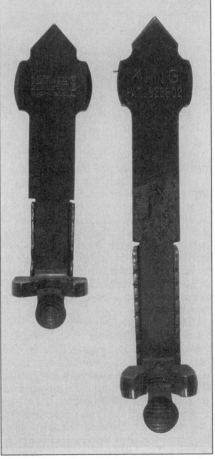

Typical of buckhorns used by 1920's Russian butcher: Marble's at left, and a vintage King at the right.

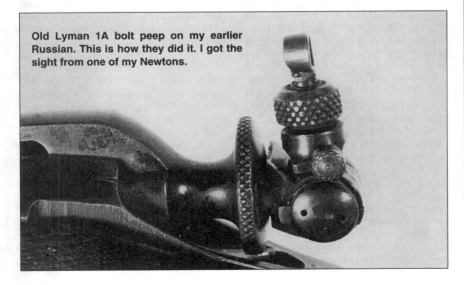

Old Lyman 1A bolt peep on my earlier Russian. This is how they did it. I got the sight from one of my Newtons.

Springfield". Workmanship varied considerably. Some had their barrels set back properly, bolt faces and extractors adapted to the '06 case head dimensions; on others, a 30-06 reamer was run into the Russian chamber to about the correct depth, with little concern that the resultant chamber was too large at the breech end, and left a scary amount of cartridge case unsupported. When the trigger was pulled on a high intensity handload or overly soft G.I. ball cartridge, the poorest of these half breed rifles often let go. Reports of these things coming apart ahead of a shooter's face during the Depression were not highly unusual.

Townsend Whelen got the word out about these deathtraps, repeatedly cautioning the unsophisticated poor folks not to invest in them. He told tales of a score of complaints and several serious accidents. Whelen wrote that Bannerman's Russian-Springfield was "distinctly unsafe". Use reduced loads or mid-range handloads if the gun must be fired, but

and slide assembly. Rearward bolt travel was controlled by twin helical guides straddling the top of the receiver. On the whole, this gimmick was a cumbersome failure.

The safety mechanism on the Three Line was a source of universal irritation seventy years ago. Engaging the safety required a deliberate series of motions and an unnaturally firm hold on the rifle. It didn't lend itself to speedy manipulation. There was a rearward pull on the cocking knob against the resistance of an inordinately strong mainspring, followed by a turn to the left. This was not a normal American impulse.

Releasing the safety required a similar amount of effort. The routine was such a slow, disrupting nuisance that some folks expecting a snap-shooting situation dispensed with the Russian safety altogether. Others elected to use a partly-opened bolt as a speedier equivalent. The rifle would unlock and could not be fired if the bolt handle was raised an inch or so. Pushing the handle down when

ing piece and sear. The bolt stop is a small lug formed at the top of the trigger. The direct interaction of these two parts produced a practical and simple set up, but their relationship made it difficult to improve upon the system. A good release wasn't obtainable by the usual method of polishing contact points. As a military trigger, the Russian was tolerable, but Americans grumbled. A number of cures for the '91s trigger pull were contrived.

Reducing the thickness on the underside of the sear spring was the easiest way to lighten the pull. Filing a tapered swale near the spring's center, about half its thickness in depth, seemed to work well. This resulted in a crisp and snappy pull and minimized creep. Some annoying sloppiness could be taken out with a V-spring fashioned from a short length of piano wire. A coil was formed in the center and looped around the trigger pin. One end then bore on the sear spring, the other on the front of the trigger itself, and re-

My Russian restocked with the help of The Great American stock folks—I still like it.

"never under any circumstances use modern commercial loads."

The adage "you get what you pay for" had an application. In 1928, one could also buy from Bannerman a genuine Springfield rifle "assembled and refinished" for just twice the price of the born again Mosin-Nagant. Whelen recommended people in the market for a high-power rifle to save their nickels until they had accumulated the purchase price of a "real rifle."

These Russian-Springfields still surface from time to time, and continue to give all ugly rifles a bad name. If ever there was a gun that needed to be planted in a garden or thrown over a bridge, Bannerman's Russian-Springfield was it.

Just about everyone was able to resist an early '30's aftermarket contraption sold by the Nimrod Tool Co. of Long Island, New York. This device converted the Nagant into a straight-pull rifle. This was accomplished by replacing the Russian bolt handle with a bulkier handle

game was sighted was a lot easier and quicker, but most of us would agree the practice was not safe.

J.L. Collins shared his better idea with AMERICAN RIFLEMAN readers in a 1931 issue. Collins devised a sliding trigger block which could be "made and installed by anyone" and could be disengaged while the rifle was being shouldered. The chief component was a thin, flat, spring-loaded L-shaped piece of steel, filed to shape and held to the stock with a wire nail. Releasing a button mounted ahead of the trigger swung the locking piece out of the way, unlocking the trigger. Collin's button came from an old harness strap.

The Russian trigger mechanism is the essence of simplicity. The number and complexity of components was absolutely minimal, and then they were forced to serve multiple functions. The sear, a stiff thin bar screwed to the underside of the receiver, doubles as its own spring and passes through a slot in the trigger to limit engagement of the cock-

moved most of the slack. Almost anyone could do this.

Fred Warner described a more elaborate modification in the June, 1931 AMERICAN RIFLEMAN. Warner brazed a steel block to the rear of the trigger and sandwiched a coil spring between the base of this block and the bottom of the sear. The sear spring was hinged just behind the attachment screwhole, which allowed the spring to pivot up and down. This modification permitted full engagement of the sear block, an important safety consideration. In addition, it was far stronger than the filed sear spring arrangement. Reportedly, Warner's layout gave his Russian military trigger the pull of a tuned sporting trigger, but copying it was beyond the ability or need of the average Mosin-Nagant shooter.

Commercial ammo manufacturers realized the supply of surplussed Russian hardball was finite, and that the rifles would outlast the ammunition. After it was gone, people would still need something to shoot in their cheap Russian rifles. When the leaves began to fall, deer hunters in the early '20's looked for domestic 7.62mm Russian sporting loads with proper expanding bullets. Thus, early in 1924, the U.S. Cartridge Co. provided a loading with their standard .30 caliber 145 grain Copper Tube bullet starting at a velocity of 2,900fps. Remington-UMC's competitive cartridge was topped with their new 150-grain Bronze Point bullet. Which came first is debatable poin, but is safe to presume they arrived within weeks of each other.

These cartridges were not cheap by 1920s standards. They retailed at around $8.50 per hundred rounds. The rather high cost of humane deer hunting cartridges was the only drawback to an otherwise cheap and effective rifle. No doubt the velocity of the commercial ammunition was taken with the uncut 31-inch barrel of a military rifle, which accounts for the unexpectedly high muzzle speed which actually surpassed the 2,700 fps mark of the Springfield cartridge.

results from war rifles which don't agree at all with what we would expect theoretically", he wrote in January of 1926.

Owners of rifles with slightly oversized bores, up to .311-312", could benefit from using either the 190 grain 303 Savage bullet, or the 215-grain 303 British projectile, or the special Western Tool and Copper Works bullets for these calibers. High speed varmint loads for these barrels could be assembled using the 115-grain 32- 20 bullet. A properly sized lead alloy bullet could fit the loosest of grooves, of course.

In terms of accuracy, the average Russian would shoot as well as the average Krag. Townsend Whelen proved this rather conclusively when he wrote in 1931 that a well-sighted Three Line would place its shots in groups around 2 7/8"-3 1/2". These were ten consecutive 100 yard groups of ten shots each, from a fair sampling of unselected rifles. It was said that the immense sight radius of the Russian contributed to its per-

of matches on the program. Those who arrived at the firing line with a Russian usually found the competition adjusting the sling or fiddling with the sights of a Krag, a National Match Springfield, or a well-tuned Model 54 Winchester. The surplus ammunition wasn't match grade, but in the hands of a skilled hard holder, it was competitive.

A special three-position, 30-shot, 200-yard "Krag-Russian" match generally attracted a surprising number of entries. Competitors' equipment was restricted to either of these two models with iron sights only. The stock Mosin-Nagants were not sneered at on the range. By all accounts, they were as accurate as the Springfield or the Krag, some say slightly more so.

It appears the Krag-Russian competitions lasted up into the mid-'30s, and were reasonably popular during this period. Results were posted in AMERICAN RIFLEMAN bulletins.

In the main, people weren't satisfied with the wheel- barrow-shaped

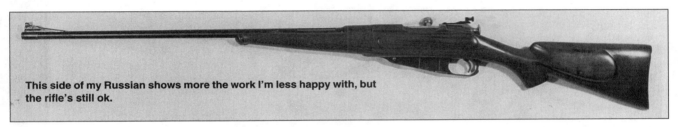

This side of my Russian shows more the work I'm less happy with, but the rifle's still ok.

Since the Russian Nagants were built with wartime tolerances and originated in a number of foreign arsenals and two U.S. arms plants, it wasn't unexpected that reports of a startling range of bore dimensions should land on the desks of the Question and Answer specialists of the outdoor magazines. The accounts stated that groove diameters ran from the standard .308 in. to as much as the measured maximum of .315in. Those not interested or concerned with this generally shot factory cartridges or their supply of D.C.M. 7.62mm hardpoints. Gun cranks sophisticated enough to detect the effects and consequences of using undersized bullets wrote to gun editors for guidance.

Townsend Whelen speared these questions repeatedly. His stock response was to fit the bullet to the bore as closely as possible. Exhaust the possibility that commercial .30 caliber bullets or the surplus 150 grain 30-06 service bullets wouldn't give satisfactory results first, he advised. "Sometimes one gets practical

formance on the range. Fred Ness' testing, combined with input from dozens of Nagant shooters, enabled him to arrive at almost the same conclusion Whelen did. Handloads with properly fitting bullets made it possible for a lot of riflemen to achieve accuracy in the inch-and-a-half to two-inch range.

Despite all the printer's ink devoted to individualizing the discounted Russian, some citizens had no inclination to be followers of fashion. These people were interested in a three-dollar deer killing tool and an everlasting supply of cartridges for a few dollars more. For these, the as-issued Russian wasn't too long, too heavy, or too ugly. Just as they were received from the arsenals, more than a few '91s were slung over shoulders for the annual sashay through the woods.

Other NRA members ordered a Russian to be used as a competitive arm. The NRA conducted a series of summertime rifle and pistol outdoor matches which a Russian shooter could enter. Any center-fire rifle with metallic sights was legal in a number

military rear sight on their Russian. Belittled in the press as a "useless monstrosity", it was not worth fooling with. The magazine authorities advised that the new Russian purchaser would be time, ammunition, and aggravation ahead if they just took someone's word for it, rather than finding out the hard way. These NRA members were putting together custom rifles that might set them back five or six dollars, after all, and they weren't about to botch the project by using the issue barrel sight.

Among the back sight's faults was that there was no windage. Adjustment was made by knocking the front sight back and forth, a practice recommended by no one. The concensus was the barleycorn front made a passable battle sight, but it was absolutely hopeless for a sporting rifle.

The rear sight was solidly sweated onto a dovetail pad formed as part of the barrel. A blowtorch was required to get it off. A fair number of cranks weren't aware the sight was soldered on until they read about it in the RIFLEMAN, and actually

The five-shot group (below) is with Norma factory loads in the rifle I restocked; the six-shot cluster (left) is military ammo out of less prestigious Russian.

tried to chisel the whole thing off. Others tried to remove the sight pad with the same torch. One guy applied a pipe wrench to the unit. He succeeded in starting the barrel, but failed to move the sight or its base.

Gunwriter Wesley King sifted the aftermarket rear sights for the '91 in a nicely done feature in the May, 1928 issue of HUNTER-TRADER-TRAPPER. A popular 1920s peep sight option was the Lyman 1A cocking piece sight, or its windage adjustable version, the #103. The 1926 Lyman catalog lists them at $8 and $12 respectively. This now-obsolete sight dovetailed into the cocking knob of the Springfield or Krag rifle, and the stem could be folded back on its base, if one wished to use an auxiliary sight. The Lyman 1A was, in effect, a bolt-mounted variation of the tang sight William Lyman had pioneered in the late 1880's.

The cocking piece sight afforded an extraordinarily long sight radius, up to 40 inches with an uncut issue Russian barrel. It's chief merit was that it put the aperture as close to the shooter's eye as was practical, and was very fast to the target. The principal disadvantage of the Lyman bolt peep was that it interfered with the manipulation of the Russian rotating safety when upright. This kept the 1A from being considered by some riflemen. The necessary dovetail slot discouraged a number of folks, too, although some do-it-yourselfers cut their own slots in the soft Russian cocking piece with a three-cornered file as Lyman suggested. Others entrusted the job to a gunsmith or other mechanic.

Pacific Gun Sight Co. put out a very practical and rigid bolt peep sight for the Russian. The Model R1 was introduced in the late 1920s in

Russian ammunition—two commercials loads and a military cartridge—is pretty hot stuff, well into the 30-06 class.

response to a cry for a cheap adjustable bolt peep sight for a cheap bolt action rifle. In 1929, it retailed for four dollars. The sight mounted on the rear of the cocking piece by means of a collar. Dovetailing, soldering, or drilling and tapping were not required. All it took to mount the R1 was a screwdriver, and Pacific even provided that. This appealed to those with two handfuls of thumbs.

Due to the Mosin-Nagant's split bridge, there was only one traditional receiver sight ideally suited to the rifle—the Lyman #36 receiver sight. Townsend Whelen, a powerful influence in those days, convinced the Lyman GunSight Corporation to provide a quality receiver sight for the Russian '91. This involved a simple alteration of the base of a currently cataloged model, the time-tried Model #36, which fit the Mannlicher-Haenel and Mannlicher Schoenauer, both of which had split bridge receivers. In profile, the Russian #36 was very similar to any other receiver sight in the Lyman line. Unlike all the other Lymans, the sight arm of the #36 was not rigid. Rather, it was hinged, allowing the crossarm to swing to one side when the rearward moving bolt handle made contact. When the bolt was pushed forward, the cross arm returned automatically. In principle, it worked like a swinging door with a spring hinge. The sight was adjustable for both windage and elevation.

This was the best Russian sight on the market, but its location prevented the safety from being engaged. The price of the #36 was commensurate with its quality, and a lot of rifle shooters balked at buying one since "putting a ten-dollar sight on a three-dollar rifle" was the height of foolishness. In some circles, the cheap Russian was considered unworthy, and Townsend Whelen had a few words for these people: "The Lyman is the best sight for the Russian. Only when the Lyman #36 is fitted to it can accurate aim be taken."

Frugal Three Line shooters got away with fitting the Lyman #33 Krag sight positioned near the center of the receiver. Since the crossarms on these cheaper models didn't swing, the sights were mounted just forward of where the bolt handle lifted. Those who opted for the second-best five-dollar system seemed to be contented with the arrangement, and noted that a receiver sight located in this fashion placed the aperture almost the same distance from the eye as that of the Lyman #48 on the Springfield rifle.

The ordinary barrel-situated open sight was the sort this era's hunters were accustomed to, and a fair percentage of Russian buyers opted for this style when they discovered that every negative thing ever written about the Bolshevik battle sight was absolutely accurate. Open rear sights were still very much in vogue. Marbles and King were the primary manufacturers of these basic utility sighting devices at the time, units sold at retail affordably in the two-dollar range. Double-step elevators were used on both lines to adjust for elevation. Adjusting for windage was accomplished by drifting the sight left or right in its dovetail. Oftentimes a decent buckhorn or flat-top open rear sight was cannibalized from some other rifle, such as a relative's Winchester or Savage, and jury-rigged to the Russian.

The flat receiver of the Westinghouse and Remington-made guns provided a nice bed for a leaf sight base, and a number of sight makers' goods used it. The standard Lyman #6 was sometimes used in combination with a receiver or cocking piece sight. Their alignment could be checked with the #6 crotch, and the "U" notch leaf sight folded neatly and conveniently flat when not in use. According to Mr. King, most 7.62 Russian users who preferred such a sight wanted a "U" notch folding leaf. For the others King marketed an aperture folding rear with an aperture disc. This arrangement sat on the flat receiver ring in a separate base. A large adjustable peep sight which folded flat was the result. Placing a peep sight on the front of the receiver put it some six inches from the shooter's eye, which was a little too far forward for most people to use effectively.

AMERICAN RIFLEMAN readers were notified in August, 1931 that the stock of Russian rifles at Benicia Arsenal, the Ordnance Department's entire remaining supply, had been exhausted. Inventories of surplus 7.62 Russian cartridges had reportedly all been sold at some point in 1928. And the once-vibrant fad died a natural death.

Some individuals got tired of their made-over Russian rifles and put them up for sale in the AMERICAN RIFLEMAN classified section. Representative examples of an economy grade sporter would often be advertised by their fickle owners, "sacrificing" them for $10-20 each. Up into the mid-1930's, unaltered guns could still be found for five to ten dollars each.

After the Great Depression ran its course, the attractiveness of a cheap, ugly, foreign military gun wore off, and the Russian sporterizing craze shriveled up and the shooting public's attention was redirected to a number of other areas. Those rifle enthusiasts whose creative impulses hadn't been satisfied busied themselves hacksawing, filing, and rasping on a thoroughly American gun with a renewed zeal-the 1917 Enfield. Alvin Linden stepped forward and showed them again how to do it properly through the columns of AMERICAN RIFLEMAN in the Spring of '33.

Those who had wanted or needed to try out the Russian had done so. Those who passed couldn't say that they lacked ample opportunity. Very few could have truthfully said that owning and shooting a Mosin-Nagant sporter had been financially out of reach.

Some families kept a Russian around, as a rainy day rifle, a loaner or a spare for when Junior got old enough. The fate met by untold thousands of other '91s was to languish in neglected and forgotten attics, closets and barns. Remodeled Russians never achieved heirloom status, were unlikely to be hung over an American fireplace mantel, and became the least likely of Grandpa's firearms to be squabbled over by the grieving when the estate was parceled out.

Temporarily caught up in nostalgia over this little known fad, I decided to replicate a do-it-yourself Russian conversion. I shopped until I located a decent American-made Mosin-Nagant at a gun show. It was a good one; Westinghouse made it in 1915. Mechanically, it was flawless; A Hoppe's #9 saturated patch run through the bore came out clean, and this particular gun may never have been fired. The stock was filthy, deeply scarred, and banged up. Aside from a couple of petty dings, metal finish was pretty nice.

With a propane torch, I dislodged the military rear sight. The tinned sight pad didn't particularly offend me, and I left it alone. Cutting the barrel to 26 inches and recrowning was the extent of the metal work. My meager stock alterations were no more extensive than the typical hobbyist seventy years ago was willing to devote to their '91s. I sawed off the excess wood a couple inches ahead of the rear band, and rasped the squared end to a reasonably rounded form. The reshaped tip was then stained to come close to matching the patina the Westinghouse had acquired during its years in storage. After tightening the barrel band, I called it a job. I didn't spend a lot of time at it.

Only original style sights would do for this project. The 1903 Springfield band sight, the favored sight of my economy minded 1920's predecessors, was fastened up front. Next, I turned up a spare Russian cocking piece, filed a dovetail slot in the end of it, and slid in a Lyman 1A bolt peep sight I'd pilfered from a rifle in my collection.

This replicated Three Line Sporter handled and shot reasonably well, but it was no particular source of pride. Sunday afternoon regulars at the range shared this assessment. The Russian and I drew patronizing stares from the ultra accuracy crowd, silently manifesting their collective "only accurate rifles are interesting" mentality. Ordinarily good company, they can be a bit overbearing at times.

Maybe I'm paranoid, but I'm sure I detected a certain uncharacteristic coolness in those I regard as my peers, the serious shooters of the hunting and varmint rifle class. I accepted, in the end, that my minimally made-over Russian wasn't exactly the image of classic riflecrafting. Aesthetically, it had severe short comings, much too Bolshevicky for my taste. Nostalgia only counts for so much. Sixty-odd years hasn't made a difference—ugly is still ugly.

There is no longer any excuse to own a really miserable Mosin-Nagant. Today's marketplace offers alternatives that didn't exist in the early '30s, including stocking options. I found precisely one ready-made stock offered for the Model 1891 Russian in the Reinhart Fajen, Inc. catalog, this being a fully inletted and finished stock of American hardwood that many among us would find attractive and serviceable at around fifty dollars. You could simply drop in the barreled receiver, snap in the trigger guard/magazine assembly, tighten a couple screws and head for the range.

But what I had personally envisioned was a dark walnut stock, traditionally styled after the pre-war European influence and Fajen didn't quite fill that bill. My restocked Russian would have a schnabel forearm tip, a cheekpiece, and, if I could arrange it, raised side panels.

Folks at Great American Gun-stock Co. in Yuba City, California, were able to set me up. To begin with, their wood is available in various stages of completion. I ordered what is known as a "pre-fit", which means that the tough part - the inletting - has already been entirely and carefully done by machine. The barrel channel has been fully and tightly grooved out for an issue barrel. I got a moderately figured stock of black walnut with a classy old world shadow line cheekpiece. As specified, the stock was sufficiently oversized on the front end to allow whatever refinement I might attempt. A Niedner-type checkered steel buttplate was shop-fitted.

Given this headstart right out of the shipping box, I went to work. After rasping out a surprisingly symmetrical schnable, I shaved wood from the forearm to give it a trimmer appearance. Using an original Mauser sporter as a pattern, I laid out side panels and, with a linoleum knife, removed surplus wood until

to blend, which I did by eye. Carving a scallop ahead of the magazine box solved the problem of tapering the forearm too sharply, and added a nice Teutonic touch, I thought.

The endless sanding ritual and the application of an oil finish finally completed this project, my first serious attempt at stockworking. I spent a lot of time at it, and I think, cost and purpose considered, it is entirely acceptable. The total investment in the wood, incidentally, was roughly equivalent to the price of an average Mosin-Nagant rifle—a good deal less than a hundred bucks.

It seems to me this approach beats whatever a person could do to alter or improve an issue Mosin-Nagant stock by a considerable margin. Any multiple-thumbed knothead can operate a rasp and piece of sandpaper. Your correspondent is living proof.

"There's something you don't see everyday," summarized the reaction at the range. A few shooters were stirred to wander over to my

both obstacles. There are two commercial mounts on the market. If one chooses the mount made by B-Square, one will have to leave the base of the Bolshevik battle sight on his gun. B-Square's mount attaches to this awful appendage, and this won't appeal to everyone, particularly those with freshly remodeled rifles. Williams offers a side mount with two styles of rings. One type, which requires a serious modification to the bolt handle, positions the scope centrally over the bore. The second style offsets the scope on the left side of the receiver. For most of us, this arrangement would take some getting used to. The general concensus is that neither mounting system would win any beauty prizes.

Each rifle type has an appropriate niche. Few would disagree that the Russian's field of usefulness is as a moderate range deer rifle and centerfire plinker. For these purposes, those who elect to equip their '91's with iron sights are operating under no serious disadvantage.

I'm sold on the idea of a peep sight mounted at the rear of the bolt, and if it could be arranged, I intended to have one. If one couldn't be bought, perhaps one could be devised, and I turned the full and frightful power of my imagination to this little matter.

Williams Gunsight Co. puts out the most extensive and varied line of metallic sights, so I studied their catalog thoroughly.

Williams makes no sights that strap on or dovetail to the cocking knob, so we looked at another location. It seemed to me the top of the cocking piece extension was a perfect platform. Williams—we were on the phone now—stocked an aluminum alloy sight in their WGOS series, the W92, intended for a Weatherby model rifle, with a mounting base and its insert, to which the aperture is fitted. Installing the entire assembly atop the cocking piece the aperture uncomfortably close to the eye, but you can discard the base and use only the insert, installing it with a couple of screws. Like the cocking-piece sights of yore, this device moves with the cocking piece, is compact lightweight, and rigid. It gets in the way of nothing, including operation of the safety. It is adjustable for windage and elevation, and affords a familiar sight picture.

There is a useful assortment of open or barrel sights from U.S.

When Graham Foral can grin like this over a $25 junker Russian, we know there will be yet another generation.

the panels were an eighth of an inch high all-around. A steel straight that thick served as a guide. The sharp panel edges were tediously rounded off with file and scraper and sandpaper. I may be overly critical, but my side panels didn't turn out exactly right, though they eventually passed my inspection.

After the panels were finished the forearm required more slimming

bench and take a closer look, even a couple of the benchrest brethren. The silence that followed expressed a courteous indifference.

For those who insist upon a scope mount for their Three Line sporters, there is some good news and some bad news. The Russian split bridge and straight handle combine to complicate scope mounting, but Yankee ingenuity has overcome makers. The Willaims flat-based WGOS fits nicely on the receiver flat and fitted with a peep aperture, though most will find this too far from the eye to be feasible. Filling an identical niche is Marble's #20 Universal rear sight. This adjustable sight is exactly the same width and length as the receiver flat, giving the blued steel sight a classy custom look. The Marbles can be supplied with a variety of uprights. Lyman still furnishes their #16 folding leaf sight. This windage and elevation adjustable sight slides into a #25 base, which is fixed to the barrel. Marble's will sell you their version of the Lyman #16, the #69, which also requires a base to mount to the '91's barrel.

I put a #69 on my Russian, an inch ahead of the receiver. Someday I may have a need for an auxiliary sight. Like the old Lyman #6, it can be used to check alignment of the rear aperture. For throwbacks and traditionalists, sturdy buckhorn rear sights are still sold and used. We have to look in the Marble's catalog for these.

All manner of obsolete rear sights clutter up the junk boxes of gun show dealers. In just such a treasure chest, I rooted out a simple peep sight from an unidentified and forsaken 22 rifle dismantled long ago. It adjusts for windage and elevation by loosening and repositioning the eyepiece, and is as simple as can be. It could be mounted on top of the Russian cocking piece extension.

Common ramp front sights are available from each of the major domestic manufacturers. Lyman still sells the #17, for those who prefer a globe target front sight. And, the nostalgic Springfield band and blade are still to be found at any sizeable gunshow and work just as well now as seven decades ago.

A late 1920's vintage Mosin-Nagant no-frills sporter recently came my way, a standard U.S.-made rifle, unprofessionally remodeled with all the fashionable Depression refinements: The stock is a shaved-down issue, grossly oversanded and thickly finished with the spar varnish of the day, evidently applied with a coarse bristle brush. The customary barrel band apparently didn't appeal and it is missing. Together with a black composition spacer of some sort, a period Jostam

recoil pad has been poorly fitted to the butt. Inlays of bone have been inletted into the sling holes. A Redfield ramp sight, contemporary to the rest of the outfit, sits up front, ahead of the military rear sight.

Still discolored from the heat, the bolt handle has been bent downward without increasing its length. The barrel was whacked off at 20 1/2 inches, with an unnecessarily deep crown cut uniformly into the muzzle. Judging by the file marks on the trigger spring, the trigger has been worked over by the AMERICAN RIFLEMAN prescription, resulting in a noticeable improvement in the pull. Finally, someone did an especially nice job of cold bluing all metal surfaces.

The roots of this particular gun can be traced to Southern Michigan, where it was used to dispatch the annual venison by two generations of whitetail chasers. Ultimately, this Russian migrated to Nebraska, and it was in the cards that I wind up with it. In certain regions of New York and Pennsylvania, a significant numbers of these leftover '91 cutdowns remain in service as deer rifles yet. They and their operators continue to dispatch whitetails each fall.

As the years roll by, more and more of these veterans are being retired, though. The high cost of soft-point cartridges has caused long-time Russian shooters to desert their Mosin-Nagants for rifles that shoot cheaper shells. Norma distributes the only commercially loaded 7.62 Russian ammunition with expanding bullets. At $1.50 a pop, this ammo is not for plinking. The load is no slouch, by the way. Propelling a 180 grain projectile at 2,575 fps, the 7.62mm Russian is nearly the ballistic duplicate of the 308 Winchester with the same weight bullet. The factory stuff shoots very well in my restocked rifle. Using the bolt peep sight, I don't have any trouble getting inch and a half five-shot groups at 100 yards.

The sale of the final D.C.M. Russian rifle hardly represented the last gasp of the Three Line in the United States. Tremendous quantities of surplus Russian, Chinese, and Finnish Mosin-Nagants have infiltrated the U.S. gun marketplace, and they are here to stay. A lot of American-made Russians are

still around. A shootable standard example can be bought at any gun show of size for around sixty to eighty dollars. Advertisers in Gun List or Shotgun News can also supply serviceable Russian rifles.

Priced at 12-25 cents per cartridge, foreign surplus ammunition is very abundant, much of it corrosive primed. Because of the cost factor, shooting the '91 is gaining in popularity these days. The lion's share of modern day Russian buyers are preferring to own and shoot an original military issue specimen. At the same time, a noticeable increase in the numbers of people remodeling their Mosin- Nagants is occurring. Most of them are unaware that they are re- inventing the wheel.

Some guns are diamonds, some guns are stones. Some rifles are a joy to own, others just get you by. These sporterized Russians fall somewhere in the middle. Like the twelve year old truck, the forkhorn deer, and the sub-trophy brother-in-law, made-over Nagants are tolerable once you get used to them and shine as medium range deer rifles. If you get an invitation to join the partners in your law firm or fellow oil company executives on their South Texas deer lease, you might want to arrive with a Weatherby or a Dakota. Almost anywhere else you go a Three Line sporter would fit right in, and makes a good, worthy companion in the woods.

The 1920s craze to sporterize the Russian was one of the most extraordinarily positive episodes in the history of American arms and ammunition. Everyone concerned benefitted. The press' coverage seems to have been worth the paper, ink and space. The government exhausted vast stores of unneeded orphan rifles. Would-be guncraftsmen were loosed to practice widespread evildoing without fear of destroying something precious. And, the man with the lean purse was handed something to shoot in desperate economic times. The chance to buy a three dollar high power rifle from the DCM meant a significant migration of new members into the fold of the NRA. More than a few stayed in it for the long haul. •

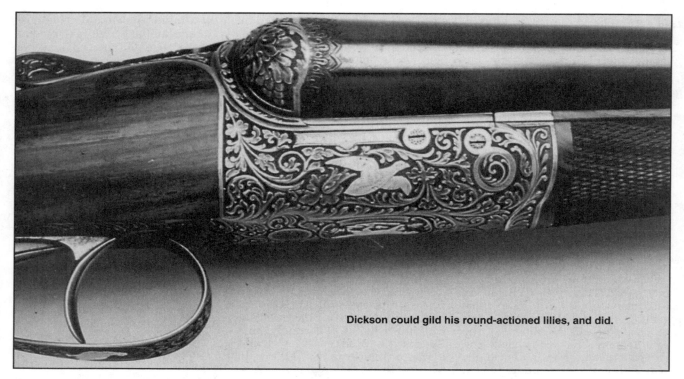

Dickson could gild his round-actioned lilies, and did.

The Dickson Guns

by GEOFFREY BOOTHROYD

John Dickson & Son is the oldest Scottish gunmaker firm still in business and, in the opinion of many, the most deservedly famous. The reasons for the latter claim are many and will be dealt with later, but, first of all, let us have look at their history.

John Dickson, the founder of the firm, was born in April, 1794, one of two children of John Dickson, a wine importer and Margaret Somerville. John, did not follow in his father's footsteps, as was usual in those days, but instead was apprenticed to the Edinburgh gunmaker, James Wallace.

James Wallace had served his time with the Innes gunmakers of Edinburgh and he set up in 1875, with a member of the Innes family as Innes & Wallace at 45 North Bridge, Edinburgh. The firm changed its name to Wallace & Agnew and moved to 63 Princes Street. In 1849, Wallace had ceased to trade and in 1849 Dickson moved into the premises at No. 63, probably buying the stock of his old Master when Wallace ceased to trade.

The indentures signed on behalf of young John have survived, and from these we learn, that his father "obliges himself to provide and maintain the said John Dickson Jnr, in bed and board and all manner of proper apparel, both linen and woollen, suitable for his use and station and in washing and mending during the pace of these indentures."

The said "James Wallace, his heirs and successors, shall by the best means he can, teach and instruct or cause to be taught and instructed, the said John Dickson, in the whole art and practice and branches of the Gunmaker Craft and use his utmost skill to cause him to understand the same, in all manner and reason thereof, in so far as he knows."

Young John served his time "and having faithfully completed his part of the indenture, James Wallace do hereby discharge him." The date of the discharge is 1813.

John had married Margaret Henderson in 1811 when he was 17 years old; his bride was 30! There

were five children of this, his first marriage. John Dickson II was born in 1820. There is some evidence that having completed his apprenticeship, he entered into a partnership with Wallace but, by 1840, John was in business in his own right. It was a bold step, since Edinburgh in the mid-19th century was an important center of gunmaking and competition must have been fierce.

The founder died on June 2nd, 1880 at his home, following a stroke.

The record of Dickson guns built commences with No. 1590, sold in 1854. By this time, the firm was trading under the style of John Dickson & Son, John Dickson II having served the customary seven years, presumably at the bench of his father's workshop.

Young John was to outlive his father by a mere five years, and his son, John Dickson III, born in 1843, must also have served his time with his father. No indentures of his apprenticeship have survived.

Celebrated World-Wide For Good Reason

Dickson's lion shows clearly, on an old trade label.

Another old trade label used when Dickson's premises were in Princes Street.

The Dickson's shop on Frederick Street, where it's been since 1937.

John Dickson, The founder... "a truly splendid figure of a Victorian gunmaker."

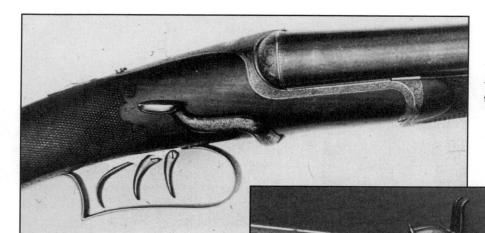

You can't see it, but this is a Dickson three-barrel — a side by side by side.

This muzzleloader, with grip safety, is No. 1570, sold prior to 1854.

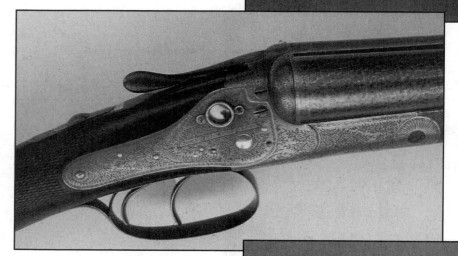

This Dickson was built on a Scott action in 1881 with back-action locks and the Scott "window" to check cocking.

This 20-bore percussion double was sold to eccentric Charles Ferrier Gordon in 1893.

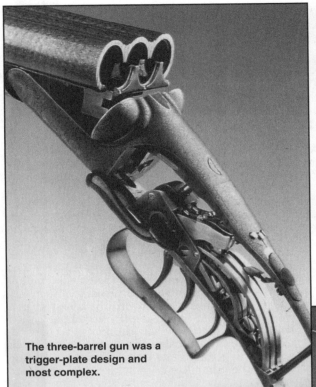

The three-barrel gun was a trigger-plate design and most complex.

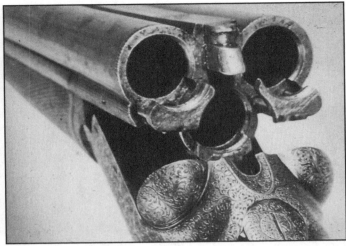

This Dickson three-barrel has the middle tube below the other two.

This pinfire Dickson, No. 2410, was sold in 1863.

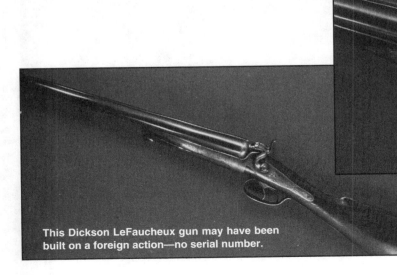

This Dickson LeFaucheux gun may have been built on a foreign action—no serial number.

Dickson built boxlocks, Anson & Deeley's, and this one has both fine Damascus barrels and fine engraving.

This third John Dickson had a brother Peter, also a gunmaker. He died on a voyage to Australia in 1892; the ship, the Ashbank, was reported as missing and there were no survivors. Why Peter set off for Australia we shall now never know.

The third John Dickson married in 1886; there were no sons and John died in 1927. By this time he had sold the business and the family connection with the firm ceased.

As previously mentioned, by 1849 we find the firm established at No. 63 Princes Street, Edinburgh. The address gives us some indication of the stature of Dickson's at this time, since Princes Street was the most famous thoroughfare in the Scottish capital and they remained here until 1929. The shop became quite famous because in the window there was a full-sized stuffed lion! I was told that children demanded to be taken along Princes Street to see the lion and the lion was featured in the literature published by the firm and was

also a trademark of the cartridges which Dicksons sold.

A move took place in 1929 to Hanover Street, where the firm remained until they moved to their present premises at 21 Frederick Street in 1937.

Many famous people were attracted to Dickson's: Duelling pistols were supplied to Lord Byron; Lord Nelson bought a blunderbuss and Queen Victoria purchased a stalking rifle for her servant, John Brown. The importance of the firm rested not only on their prestigious address and the undoubted quality of the product, but also on the collective inventive genius available to the firm.

The first patent taken out in the name of the firm was No. 294 of 1880 to protect a self-cocking sidelock hammerless action. Few of this type of hammerless Dickson shotgun appear to have survived, the main feature of which was the provision of a flat bar inside the bar of the action which, when the gun was opened, was pushed rearwards by a piece on the forend iron. The rear end of the bar acted against the tumbler and so cocked the hammer. From information which has survived these early

This is a recent Dickson Round Action gun—the best of the firm's many designs.

An unusual 500 Black Powder Express double delivered to the remarkable Gordon in 1990.

Dickson built three-barrels one up and two down — look at all those holes!

Around the side of the Frederick St. premises, Dickson dignity still prevails.

Dickson hammerless actions were fitted with back action locks.

This patent was followed in 1882 by No. 873, which covered their ideas for three barrelled shotguns and which, no doubt, also laid the foundation for the later famous Round Action. As you can see from the patent illustration (Fig 1) the chief feature of the three barrelled gun, apart from the three barrels, was the adoption of a trigger plate lock mechanism. Instead of the lock being mounted on side plates, as in a sidelock, or built into the action body, as with the boxlock, in the Dickson system the locks are mounted on an enlarged trigger plate. Guns built on this type of action had the barrels arranged so that their axes are in the same plane, but Dickson also built three barrelled guns where one barrel was above the other two and also where one barrel was below the other two. Guns were built with either rotary under-lever or a side-lever.

The benefit of the trigger plate action is obvious when one has to deal with three locks, since they can be mounted with ease, side-by-side. The alternatives to this system which other gunmakers used were complex and not entirely satisfactory. Other British gunmakers built guns with three barrels, Boss, Westley Richards and Greener among them. None ever built three-barrel guns with the three variations of barrel configuration as did Dickson.

In 1887, patent No. 9399 protected ejector systems for what was to develop eventually into the Round Action. The ejector system depended on two small levers, inlet into the flats of the bar of the action. When the barrels are closed, these levers are depressed and force back two rods in the bar of the action and they also compress the ejector springs. When the gun is fired, the hammers fall and the rear end of the ejector rods are disengaged so that as the gun is opened, the fired cases are ejected. Later in the same year, Patent 10, 621 saw the final design of the Round Action perfected. A comparison of the drawings of the action in Fig. 1 and Fig. 2, show how, in the later patent, the hammers are pivoted nearer to the body of the gun which allows for the use of shorter firing pins. These are now carried almost entirely within the body of the action, unlike the firing pins shown in the earlier patent which are quite lengthy. Modifications were also made at this time to the arrangement of the ejector sys-

21,681. **Dickson, J.**, and **Morrison, W.** Sept. 19.

Single-trigger mechanisms. — Consists in mechanism for preventing double discharge. The hammers A, B, Figs. 1 and 2, have respectively sears a^1, b^1 kept in bent by springs c, c^1, the hammers being actuated by springs e. The right-hand sear b^1 is operated directly from the trigger, and the left-hand sear through the medium of mechanism which allows for the involuntary pull and comprises a floating bar F, Figs. 4 and 4^a, having a spindle f^1 and a spring f^8 which normally impels the bar forwards, and a rear forked portion f. The left-hand side of the bar has a projection f^2, the right-hand side a cam f^3, the under edge a tooth f^4, and the top edge carries a pivoted lever f^5 which is forked at the rear end, one side of the fork carrying a projection f^6 and the other side a rounded end f^7. The trigger blade D has a projection d^1, Fig. 5^a, on the right to operate the sear b^1, and a cam d on the left which operates with the cam f^3 on the bar F. An opening d^2, Fig. 9^a, is also formed in the trigger-blade to receive the part g^1 of the trigger-spring g, the part g^1 also operating with a catch h which is pivoted at h^3 and at the end h^2, Fig. 7, engages the catch f^4 on the bar F. A spring j normally holds the catch in engagement with the tooth f^4. In operation, the first pull of the trigger fires the right-hand barrel and simultaneously the end h^2 of the lever h is depressed and thereby disengaged from the tooth f^4 of the bar F. The spring f^8 draws the bar F forwards until the cam f^3 thereon engages the cam d on the trigger-blade, and in this position of the bar F the projection f^2 is over the projection a^1, Fig. 8, on the left-hand sear a^1, an involuntary or other pull on the trigger being thereby rendered ineffective. As the firearm recoils, the bar F is driven backwards to its initial position; the subsequent release of the trigger allows the cam d to pass beneath the cam f^3, and the spring f^8 then pulls the bar F to its extreme forward position in which the cam d comes beneath the part f^7 of the lever f^5, and

the part f^6 beneath the projection a^2, Fig. 8. The second voluntary pull of the trigger raises the lever f^5 and consequently the sear a^1 to discharge the left-hand barrel. The mechanism is re-set, when the gun is broken down for loading, by means of a pivoted lever k, Fig. 1, and a slotted lever K^1. A safety-catch k^2 engages the trigger when set to prevent firing, this catch being automatically put on by the lever K^1 when the gun is broken down. The catch k^2, when released by hand before firing, moves the levers K^1 and k into position to permit the bar F to operate.

Reference has been directed by the Comptroller to Specifications 5404/97, 4156/98, 6456/99, 7930/99, 2650/00, 6584/01, 22,946/07, 7889/08, *and* 13,742/08.

Figure 1: Patent No. 1873, from 1887, protected the three-barrel action and was a basis for the Round Action development, Boothroyd believes.

tem. Then in 1910, Patent No. 21,681 protected further modifications to the Round Action, (Fig 3) intended to prevent the possibility of an accidental double discharge and this patent also protected the Dickson Single Trigger mechanism, few examples of which appear to have been made.

Certainly, by 1887, the distinctive outline of what was to become the famous Round Action had already appeared. The rounded shape of the action body, so comfortable when the gun was to be carried over the forearm in the field, and the slender outlines of the gun, the graceful appearance of which made the Round Action unique and quite appealing. So, let us now have a look at some of the guns which have survived and upon which the fame of the firm depended. The firm did build flintlocks, a pair of flintlock pistols are known which were built for their most famous customer, Charles Gordon but because of the

10,621. **Dickson, J.** Aug. 2.

Breech actions, drop-down barrel.— Consists of improvements on the invention described in Specification No. 9399, A.D. 1887. The hammers S are pivoted nearer the body of the gun, so that shorter firing-pins y are required, and are carried entirely in the body of the action. The bars E, for operating the ejectors, are formed as springs the tendency of which is to press the hooks on their rear ends into engagement with the edges of the nipples F. The rods E are released, as the barrels fall, by the projections t on the hammers. The bars E may be replaced by jointed rods, or by rods acted on by springs which depress their rear ends S.

Figure 2: This, No. 10,621 is nearly the perfected Round Action patent — shorter pins and hammer throws — also 1887.

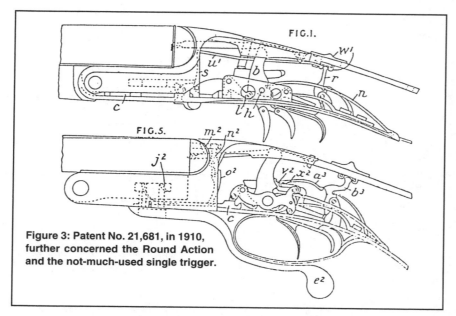

Figure 3: Patent No. 21,681, in 1910, further concerned the Round Action and the not-much-used single trigger.

eccentric nature of Gordon, these pistols would have been made especially for him well after the flintlock era. The earliest percussion muzzle loader I have been able to photograph is No. 1570 which was sold prior to 1854, before the existing records, the earlier records having been lost. This gun is in 12 bore and it has seen a great deal of use. The interesting feature is the provision of a grip safety which can be seen just behind the trigger guard.

Then we come to another percussion muzzle loader. This gun was made for Dickson's eccentric customer, Charles Ferrier Gordon of Halmyre. Gordon collected a large arsenal of sporting guns, many from Dicksons and the pristine condition of many of the guns which have survived is due to the fact that Gordon never fired any of them! He would take an unloaded gun into the field and, when a bird rose, he would shout "bang"!

The gun illustrated, a 20-gauge percussion double muzzle loader is in mint condition and was bought by Gordon in 1893, well into the breech loading period. It was unusual in that it was fitted with detachable noses to the hammers.

Dicksons also built pin-fire breech loaders. The one illustrated is No. 2410 which was sold in August 1863. The gun weighs 7 1/4, lbs and was regulated to fire 1 oz. of shot ahead of 2 3/4, drams of black powder.

One of the earliest of the breech loading designs was based on patents taken out by Casimir Lefaucheux. Dickson built a double central-fire shotgun on the Lefaucheux action. This gun bears no serial number and may have been built on a foreign sourced action. As you can see the operating lever lies along the forend. Lacking a serial number, we have no date for this gun.

A more conventional double hammer gun was sold in 1880 to the Earl of Roseberry. This gun, No. 3559, has a top lever, conventional back action hammer sidelocks and splendid damascus barrels. The unusual feature is that it is of a type known as "bar in the wood" for as you can see the action is wood covered.

An early hammerless double shotgun No. 3622, was built on a Scott action in 1881. This gun has back action lockwork and the famous Scott "window" to show whether the gun is cocked or not can be clearly seen.

Dickson's also built guns based on the Anson & Deeley boxlock action. The example illustrated is of particularly high quality with top quality engraving and very fine damascus barrels.

In the closing years of the 19th century a number of gunmakers built three-barrelled shotguns. Boss built guns with the three barrels in line, Westley Richards used the configuration with one barrel above the other two. As we have already seen, Dicksons built such guns with the barrels in line, with one barrel above the other two and with one barrel below the other two. Examples of all three exist to-day. In order to simplify the lock mechanism to fire three barrels Dicksons placed the lockwork on an enlarged trigger plate. Viewed from the side, the three barrel gun with the barrels in line has a delightfully slim outline,

the only clue that here is something different are the three triggers. With the stock removed, the complexity of the design can be seen and also you can see how the locks are mounted on the trigger plate. One of the problems of the three barrel guns was the ejector system. This can be seen in the illustration of a three-barrel Dickson, with one barrel below the other two. The third type has one barrel above the other two and a splendid example is shown in the open position. The three-barrel trigger plate action guns laid the foundations for the most famous of all the Dickson shotguns, the Round Action. A recent example of the Round Action is illustrated from which you can appreciate the fine lines of this gun. The Round Action was made with a conventional top lever and it was also offered with a side lever. For the man who sought something different Dicksons also built the Round Action with side panels. The gun could also be had with special engraving and example with gold inlay as shown in the illustration. Dicksons also built over-under shotguns but, as one might expect from their past history, they were unlike most other over-under guns, for the Dickson opened to the side. This was to the right hand side, so that the ejected cases were flung clear of the shooter. The over-under was, in effect, the Round Action turned through 45 degrees. I remember being loaned one of these guns for a shoot, the problem was that I could scarcely get to use the gun because the other members of the shoot wanted to handle it. Dicksons also built double rifles and magazine rifles. Here is an illustration of a double 500 Black Powder Express hammer rifle built for that remarkable man, Charles Gordon in 1890. Note the lack of checkering on the grip and forends. This rifle is unused!

Today, the Round Action is still being built, the barrels, action, and the lockwork done by specialist outworkers to the trade. All other work, except for engraving, is carried out on the premises in Edinburgh. Today Dickson builds only the Round Action. To end, here is a photograph of the founder, a truly splendid figure of a Victorian gunmaker. I also illustrate two examples of the trade labels that Dicksons used, the first, showing a view of Princes Street, Edinburgh and the second, still at Princes Street address, showing the Dickson "Lion".

The Story of a gun built for airplane drivers....

The first Ultra pistol developed by Walther around 1940— combines P38 and PP features.

Germany's
ULTRA PISTOLS

by Gene Gangarosa, Jr.

In the late 1930s, Germany's resurgent *Luftwaffe* wanted a new pistol for aviators. *Luftwaffe* weapons experts regarded the standard German service pistol at the time, the 9mm Parabellum caliber P08 or Luger, as heavy and bulky for aviation use and expensive to produce, while criticizing the 7.65mm (32 ACP) caliber pistols popular in police work as portable enough but underpowered. What was sought, then, was a relatively small and light pistol, since space is at a premium in a cramped airplane cockpit, but with a power level approaching that of the 9mm Parabellum round used in the P08.

Working together, the Gustave Genschow ammunition company, better known as GeCo, and the Carl Walther gun company developed a joint ammunition/pistol project known as Ultra in an attempt to meet the military requirement. Work was underway by 1939 and ceased around 1941.

The original Ultra round used a 9mm bullet weighing 7 grams (108 grains), with a cartridge case length of 18.5mm, and having a muzzle velocity of 300 meters (984 feet) per second. These performance figures split the difference between the 7.65mm police pistol round and the 9mm Parabellum pistol round favored by the military. The 9mm Ultra round also represented an advance in power over the previous two rounds widely regarded as the best available in unlocked breech (blowback) pistols, the 9mm Browning Long and the 9mm Browning Short (380 ACP).

The pistol developed by Walther for this project combined features of the company's successful PP and P38 designs. The Ultra pistol's slide and frame construction, and the lockwork and safety systems, clearly derived from the PP popular in police work, while the barrel and the presence of an external slide stop showed the larger military P38's influence. Reflecting the tentative nature of the design, Walther used wooden grips in the Ultra pistol prototypes, rather than go through the trouble and expense of developing machinery to make plastic grips for a pistol which might not win a military contract.

Ultra ammunition designers wanted the most powerful round suitable for blowback pistols. From left to right: 9mm Parabellum, 9x18mm Makarov, 9mm Police, and 380 ACP.

Walther's tentative approach proved well-founded. By the time the Ultra project had a handful of pistols and 20,000 rounds of ammunition available for testing, World War Two was well underway and the air force had more serious matters to attend to than pistol armament for its aircrew. The *Luftwaffe* therefore made a decision to standardize on 7.65mm pistols for its aviators (though the aviators also had recourse to smaller numbers of 25 ACP and 380 ACP pistols), and paratroopers and other combat branches under air force control used mostly 9mm Parabellum pistols. Thus, the Ultra idea was stalled. It was not, it proved, stillborn.

In the immediate aftermath of World War Two, the Russians took possession of the former Walther factory in the eastern part of Germa-ny. And thereby gained the details of Walther's Ultra project. During World War Two, the Russians had become impressed with double-action German pistol designs. Having never been particularly pleased with their standard wartime handgun, the single-action Tokarev TT-33, the Soviet armed forces were quick to call for a new handgun, and by 1945 the first of several new prototypes was being made.

Although Feodor Tokarev, creator of the previous TT-30/33 service pistol, was still alive, he did not submit a candidate pistol to the postwar pistol trials. However, many of the other major Soviet arms design teams eventually sent sample pistols to the Red Army for testing and possible adoption as the next Soviet service pistol.

Between 1945 and 1951 the Red Army tested a number of double-action pistols chambering a new 9x18mm cartridge similar in size and performance to those of the Walther/Geco wartime German Ultra prototype. Candidate pistols, which were submitted by Baryshev, Makarov, Korovin, Simonov, Stechkin and Voyevodin, all showed the recent influence of German pistolmaking skills. Walther's Model PP inspired all the Soviet prototypes to a greater or lesser extent, although Baryshev's candidate pistol more strongly resembled the similar Mauser HSc. All of the guns except Simonov's entry used a magazine release mounted on the bottom rear, or heel, of the grip. With one notable exception, all of the candidate pistols were small and handy, convenient and suitable both for open carry on a belt holster or for concealed carry. Stechkin's prototype pistol was considerably larger than any of the others, and served as the prototype for his service pistol described below.

All the Russian designs were impressive, but the one submitted by Nikolai Makarov stood out. Slightly larger than the Walther PP to accommodate the bigger Ultra-inspired 9x18mm cartridge, the Makarov entry became Soviet service standard by 1951 as the *Pistolet Makarova* or PM, though many in the West simply call it the Makarov The Makarov represented a considerable improvement over the Tokarev-designed TT-33 in handling, owing to its slightly smaller size, handier shape, double-action trigger and hammer-decocking manual safety (the TT-30/TT-33 series pistols had had no manual safety at all!).

Despite the comments of some Western firearms experts, notably Ian Hogg and Edward Ezell, the Makarov pistol is by no means a slavish copy of the Walther PP. Compared to the PP, the Makarov is considerably simpler in design and stronger, using fewer parts. In its simple, sturdy construction, the Makarov reminds this writer of the Beretta Mo. 1934 service pistol, of which the Russians were also painfully aware from World War Two, it having been used against them by Italian, Romanian, and Finnish troops.

The Makarov quickly caught on in Soviet service. Production of the older TT-33 ceased entirely in Russia by 1954 in favor of the new pistol, and by the mid-1950s Makarov pistols were becoming widespread in Soviet Bloc countries as well as in the Soviet Union itself. Although the Soviets later developed a new military pistol, the smaller 5.45mm PSM, to partially supplant it, the Makarov remains in widespread military and police service around the world, especially in Eastern European and Asian countries, and in some Third World countries, notably in Africa and South America, and especially those with Soviet or communist leanings.

While the small 8-shot Makarov went into issue in the Soviet Union as the general service pistol, a larger, more specialized weapon developed by Igor Stechkin also went into production at about the same time. Called the APS in Russia and the Stechkin in the West, this much bigger pistol resembled an overgrown Makarov and was made in the same factory as the PM, but had a selec-

The Makarov is well-made and accurate. This 5 shot, 1.9-inch group was fired offhand at 25 feet.

tive-fire capability, with a cyclic rate of around 700 rounds per minute, and a large 20-round magazine.

Though slightly larger even than the high-capacity 9mm service pistols now popular in the West, the Stechkin was still of a manageable size. The Ultra-inspired 9x18mm (9mm Makarov) cartridge it also used along with the smaller Makarov pistol made the Stechkin a passable machine pistol, though of course accuracy was much reduced when the shooter used the weapon in fully-automatic fire. Like the early machine pistols first developed around the turn of the century, the Stechkin came with a shoulder stock which doubled as the pistol's holster. The rear end of the Stechkin pistol's frame had a slot cut into it to accommodate the shoulder stock. Use of the stock allowed a shooter to fire with accuracy in semiautomatic mode on targets as much as 150 yards distant; when using the fully-automatic rate of fire or without the shoulder stock attached, the accuracy was considerably less, of course.

Originally intended for general issue to Soviet combat troops, including noncommissioned officers, the Stechkin soon came under criticism for its size and bulk. Eventually Soviet military doctrine called for soldiers who did not carry the standard AK-47 (later AKM and AK-74) assault rifle to carry the light, handy Makarov, and the Stechkin became relegated to special forces units. The development of the radically-shortened AKSU-74 assault-rifle/submachine gun in the early 1980s removed even this specialized niche from the Stechkin. Never produced in the huge quantities of the Makarov, the Stechkin has been largely supplanted in Russian service, though some were exported (notably to Libya) and may still show up from time to time, especially in the hands of terrorists.

Both the Makarov and the Stechkin have appeared in specialized variants as well as in their standard configurations. The *Pistolet Byezshumniy* or PB is a silenced version of the Makarov: *Byezshumniy* means "without noise" in Russian. The PB uses both a built-in integral silencing unit placed around the modified barrel and a separate silencer attachment which can be attached to the pistol's muzzle for greater sound suppression, though it also adds considerably to the pistol's overall length and bulk. While not as sophisticated as some Western silenced pistols, the PB is highly effi-

This Makarov is an East German model with a typical European military and police-issue holster.

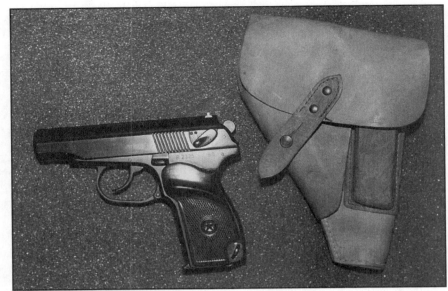

The communist Chinese also made the Makarov as the Model 59 pistol. Between 1989 and 1995, China Sports, marked CSI on the slide in this view, imported the Type 59 here.

cient. Its production, issue and use have necessarily been limited compared to those of the standard Makarov pistols, but PBs are known to have seen combat use in the Middle East and in Afghanistan. The APB, similarly, is a silenced version of the Stechkin, modified by lengthening the barrel so that the muzzle extends several inches beyond the end of the slide, to which the shooter then clamps a large cylindrical sound suppressor. A collapsible wire stock replaces the bulky wooden or plastic combination shoulder stock/holster of the original Stechkin. The most notorious use of the APB occurred in December 1978, when Soviet *Spetznatz* (special forces)

troops armed with them invaded the palace of the President of Afghanistan and murdered him preparatory to the Soviet invasion of that country and the long war which followed.

Issue of the Makarov pistol in the Soviet Union from 1951 onward led to the pistol's subsequent adoption by numerous Soviet satellites and client states. Eventually most of the Warsaw Pact countries of Eastern Europe, with the notable exception of Czechoslovakia, adopted the Makarov pistol, as did many Asian communist countries. Factories in East Germany and Bulgaria tooled up to produce the Makarov for their own armed forces and for export. The communist Chinese, with Soviet help, also set up a factory to produce Makarov pistols; called the "Type 59" in Red Chinese service, and the Makarov has become the standard service weapon in that large country and is also exported. Type 59 pistols saw use in Vietnam, for example.

Seeing the success of the Makarov, several Eastern European countries then decided to apply Ultra technology to their own designs. In Hungary, FEG had already made several clones of the Walther Model PP shortly after the end of World War Two. The first near-copy appeared in 1948 in 380 and 32 calibers. A decade later, FEG unveiled a much more ambitious Walther derivative, the smaller PPK-sized RK59. The RK59, in 9mm Makarov caliber, used an aluminum-alloy frame for light weight. Somewhat unusually, the frame remained "in the white," that is, having the unanodized aluminum left in its natural silvery color, while the slide received the traditional deep blue, giving the gun a two-tone effect unusual in a service pistol. FEG also reshaped the frame, raising and rounding the grip tang at the rear, to avoid the problems of the hammer or slide pinching the shooter's hand which many people encounter when firing small Walther-made pistols. Despite its unconventional appearance, the RK59 was an efficient little handgun with good power for its small size and light weight, thanks to its use of the 9mm Makarov round. Like the 380 caliber PPK, the most powerful version of that famous pistol, the RK59 held six shots in its magazine. The magazine release, as in the PPK, was a pushbutton type placed on the frame just beneath the slide.

A slightly improved version, the R61, appeared two years later, in 1961. The only difference between this model and the RK59 was that the R61's frame had added reinforcement in the trigger area. The RK59 and R61 served for thirty years as armament for high-ranking officers and for the Hungarian secret police. A slightly larger, PP-sized version, the PA-63, went to Hungarian armed forces units. All three of these guns have appeared in Western surplus-arms markets since the collapse of communism in Eastern Europe in the early Nineties.

Poland also developed 9x18mm Makarov caliber pistols to a great extent. First came the P-64 in 1964. This PPK-inspired pistol was very similar to the contemporary Hungarian-made R61, except that it used a bottom-mounted, heel-type magazine re-

lease like the Soviet Makarov. The P-64 was a serviceable enough design, but the Polish army decided that they wanted a slightly larger, more robust pistol and so in 1983 the P-83 appeared. This is, in features and performance, essentially a Polish-built version of the Russian Makarov, holding eight shots in its magazine. It uses a stamped sheet steel triggerguard and, unlike the P-64, has a lanyard loop and an external slide release control. The grips use longitudinal grooving like those found on World War Two-vintage Walther P38s.

Another, and far more exotic Polish development was the wz.63 (wz. being an abbreviation for *wzor* [pronounced "vzor"], the Polish word for "model"). The wz.63, a selective-fire weapon with a cyclic rate of fire of 600 rounds per minute, is a large machine pistol. It is one of the few weapons in 9x18mm Makarov caliber which is not descended from the Walther PP. Instead, the wz.63 has a barrel with raised locking lugs machined into its bottom rear. These lugs fit into corresponding grooves machined into the frame, in the manner of the Colt Pocket Model pistol of 1903 designed by John Browning.

To fire, the shooter first inserts a magazine into the pistol grip and then draws back the slide until it locks open. The slide remains fully

back until the shooter presses the trigger, wherupon the slide springs foward, stripping a cartridge from the magazine, chambering and firing it, and then repeating the cycle until the shooter releases the trigger or ammunition is exhausted. A 25-round magazine which fits into the pistol's grip is standard, and a 40-round magazine, which protrudes prominently from the bottom of the grip, is also available when having a large ammunition supply is more important than concealing the weapon.

Though similar in concept to the Stechkin, the wz.63 is somewhat larger, and has several features which make it more controllable in fully-automatic fire than its Soviet counterpart. The wz.63's controllability-enhancing features include a rate reducer to make the rate of fire manageable and so reduce recoil, the typical bane of machine pistols. Another useful feature is a folding front handgrip which positions the shooter's support hand below the muzzle as an aid to reducing muzzle rise upon firing. Still another useful feature is a sliding metal buttstock with which the shooter can brace the weapon against his shoulder. For times when portability and/or concealability are paramount, both the front handgrip and the buttstock lie compactly alongside the receiver when not in use.

FÉG has 9x18mm Makarov guns, such as the PA-63 model shown here. Hungarian PP-style double-action pistols like the R61, PA-63, and SMC's have heavy trigger pulls—note the flyer here.

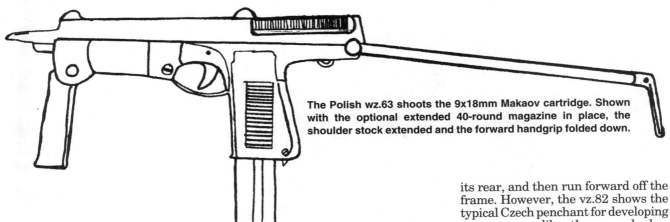

The Polish wz.63 shoots the 9x18mm Makaov cartridge. Shown with the optional extended 40-round magazine in place, the shoulder stock extended and the forward handgrip folded down.

The Poles originally developed the wz.63 to arm military vehicle crewmen and paratroopers, but at a folded length of just under 23 inches and an unloaded weight of just under four pounds, the wz.63 is capable of being carried concealed under a loose-fitting overcoat or in a briefcase. The wz.63's concealment characteristics have also endeared it to airplane hijackers and other terrorists, so it shows up from time to time in terrorist incidents. Though not especially accurate, since it fires from an open bolt, the wz.63 is capable of rapid and deadly fire at close quarters.

Czechoslovakia, the most independent-minded of the Warsaw Pact countries when it came to arming its troops, was slow to adopt the 9mm Makarov round. Only with the apperance of the vz.82 in 1982 did the Czechs switch over to this round (as in Polish, vz. means *vzor* or model in Czech, too). The vz.82 is a medium-frame automatic pistol. An amalgam of Walther and Makarov influences with some uniquely Czech features, the vz.82 uses the Walther method of disassembly wherein one hinges the triggerguard down to allow the slide to be pulled backwards, tipped up at

its rear, and then run forward off the frame. However, the vz.82 shows the typical Czech penchant for developing a weapon unlike those used elsewhere, yet one which is undeniably efficient in its own right. Unlike either the PP or the Makarov pistol, the vz.82 has a high-capacity magazine holding an impressive twelve rounds stacked in a double column, an ambidextrous magazine release button conveniently mounted on the triggerguard, a firing-pin lock deactivated only by pulling the trigger all the way through, and an ambidextrous manual safety lever which allows the shooter to cock the pistol and then apply the safety. In contrast, in both the Walther and Makarov pistols, applying the safety (which is suited for right-handed use only) automatically decocks the hammer. To suit the vz.82 pistol to cold-

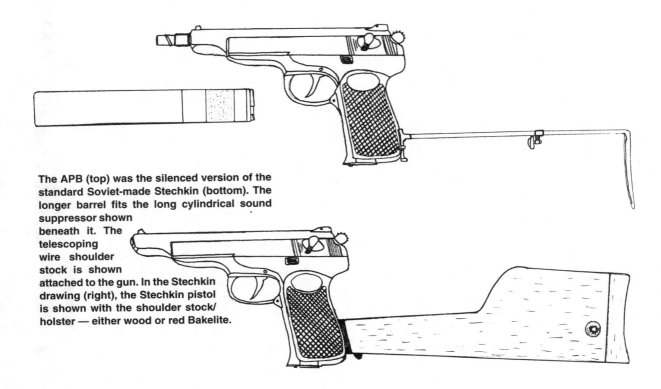

The APB (top) was the silenced version of the standard Soviet-made Stechkin (bottom). The longer barrel fits the long cylindrical sound suppressor shown beneath it. The telescoping wire shoulder stock is shown attached to the gun. In the Stechkin drawing (right), the Stechkin pistol is shown with the shoulder stock/holster — either wood or red Bakelite.

(above) The FEG SMC-918 (bottom), is appreciably smaller and lighter than the ubiquitous Makarov (top), but offers considerably greater recoil.

(right) The FEG SMC-918's prominent thumbrest gives it sufficient points for legal importation here. This series of pistols are said to be the smallest pistols to come into the country since passage of the Gun Control Act in 1968.

creased, first with the importation of new-manufacture Type 59s from China, followed by surplus East German pistols, and later on new guns of Bulgarian and Russian manufacture. Other pistols in the same caliber came into the United States from Hungary during the same period. While importation has greatly decreased since 1995, many of these guns remain available to the shooter and collector.

With the increased availability of Makarov-caliber pistols came a tre-

weather use, or for use in a chemical-warfare environment, a favorite feature of Cold War-era Warsaw Pact tactics, the Czechs extended the front of the triggerguard well forward of the usual location, allowing the pistol to be fired even by a shooter wearing heavy gloves.

After initial issue to Czech military forces, the vz.82 also appeared in 12-shot 380 ACP and 15-shot 32 ACP caliber civilian versions as the "CZ Model 83." This is one of the best pistols made in either of the three calibers, as it is highly accurate, has a large ammunition capacity, and is easy to use, while still being reasonably compact.

In 1965 the Czechs also experimented with a version of their vz.62 Skorpion machine pistol, usually made in 32 ACP, in 9mm Makarov caliber. Intermediate in size between the Soviet Stechkin and the Polish wz.63, the Skorpion is another darling of terrorists. Upgunning the Skorpion to 9mm Makarov caliber, however, involved enlarging the weapon, and its recoil also increased. While the weapon still remained reasonably portable and controllable, customers overwhelmingly preferred the original 32

caliber version to such an extent that Ceska Zbrojovka, the company that created the Skorpion, soon discontinued manufacture of the 9mm Makarov vz.65 to concentrate on production of the original .32 ACP vz.62.

In America and in Western Europe the Ultra pistol/cartridge combination went neglected for decades. While the Makarov pistol's existence was known to Western intelligence analysts, a lack of specimens to analyze caused an unfortunate tendency to underrate the Soviet/Eastern European developments in creating small but relatively powerful pistols. Not until the Vietnam War did American soldiers, based on firsthand encounters, begin to realize the Makarov's capabilities. Makarov pistols became one of the most desired working handguns in Vietnam and one of the most desirable war trophies from that conflict.

Between the late Sixties and the late Eighties very few Makarov pistols, mostly Vietnam-era Type 59s made in China, were available in the United States, and these pistols were expensive collector's items. From 1989 on, however, the supply of Makarov pistols greatly in-

mendous improvement in ammunition development. Prior to 1989, the only genuine 9x18mm Makarov ammunition in the United States was Chinese-made military ball ammunition with corrosive primers. Although the Makarov pistol can in a pinch fire either 9mm Police (see below) or 380 ACP ammunition, feeding reliability and accuracy is problematic with both rounds, as the bullets are undersized for the Makarov's .362-inch (9.2mm) bore. As the supply of Makarov-caliber pistols grew, however, American ammunition manufacturers developed a number of useful rounds to make the most of the Makarov cartridge. These included jacketed hollowpoints from Hornady, frangible ammunition from MagSafe, aluminum-cased Blazer ammunition from CCI, and high-velocity hollowpoints from Cor-Bon. The supply of military-surplus ammunition also increased, and several Eastern European commercial ammunition manufacturers, as well as the Norinco company of China, contributed additional variety to the ammunition supply.

In Western Europe the Ultra project took a slightly different direction. In early 1973, responding to calls for a new West German police handgun to replace the aging Model PP, Walther introduced a new model called the PP Super, firing a newly-developed round called the 9mm Ultra or 9mm Police round. The 9mm Ultra/Police round used a cartridge casing 18mm in length, just like the 9mm Makarov, but the 9mm Ultra/Police round's bullet was a true 9mm, being .355 inch in diameter. Thus the pistols made for 9mm Ultra/Police caliber would not safely fire the 9mm Makarov round, as the bullets were slightly too wide for the bore. The 9mm Ultra/Police round, as originally issued by the Hirtenberger ammunition company of Austria, fired a 94-grain bullet at about 1083 feet (330 meters) per second. Later Fiocchi of Italy added a 100-grain bullet to its line in this caliber, and this is the most common 9mm Police round today.

The PP Super, basically an enlarged PP, showed some Makarov in-

way in which the PP Super differed from the Makarov pistol was in its safety arrangements. In the Makarov, applying the safety both decocks the hammer and locks the hammer and slide, and the shooter must manually reset the safety to its fire setting before the pistol will operate. However, the PP Super's manual safety control is actually just a decocking lever. Applying it only lowers the hammer, after which, if the pistol is loaded, merely pressing the trigger will fire it. When the pistol is carried loaded, an ingenious passive safety system is at work at all times, in which a small spring continually pushes the firing pin down into a recess in the slide where the hammer, even if it should accidentally fall or be struck so as to hit the slide, cannot reach the firing pin. Only at the last moment of a deliberate trigger pull does the firing pin rise out of its recess into the path of the falling hammer to allow the pistol to fire. This is an excellent safety

ested in the idea of a compact handgun in the more powerful 9mm Parabellum military caliber, a goal they realized in 1978-79 with the introduction of Walther's P5, SIG's P225 (P6) and Heckler & Koch's PSP (P7). Walther's introduction of the PP Super on the commercial market in 1975 was only modestly successful, as the 9mm Police round got off to a slow start. Even the introduction of a 380 caliber version of the PP Super failed to attract much interest, as the gun was large for this caliber; ultimately the Walther company made only a thousand of this variant. With official sales ended and civilian sales sluggish, Walther discontinued PP Super production in 1981. By 1984 the PP Super was surplused out of West German service.

Despite the PP Super's poor showing, the 9mm Police round has enjoyed some success in Western Europe, notably in Italy and in Switzerland. In 1980 the Italian company Renato Gamba introduced the R.G.P. 80, a copy of the Mauser HSc with an enlarged frame holding a high-capacity magazine, in 9mm Police caliber. In 1982 Benelli introduced the B82, a 9mm Police version of their popular B76 pistol. In 1984 Tanfoglio introduced the TA-18, a compact version of their CZ-75 clone, in 9mm Police caliber. While none of these guns sold in huge numbers, they were successful enough to prompt Italy's most respected ammunition manufacturer, Fiocchi, to keep the 9mm Police round in production, and Fiocchi 9mm Police ammunition remains in production at this writing. In Switzerland, SIG offered its P230 pistol in 9mm Police caliber beginning in 1976, and ITM/Sphinx offered the AT-380, ordinarily in 380 ACP caliber, in 9mm Police caliber on special order. While none of these Italian or Swiss designs has seriously challenged the Makarov in terms of numbers produced or distribution, they have at least kept the 9mm Police, which is the only Western European descendant of the wartime Ultra project, alive.

Because of the original intended police mission for this round, the major ammunition manufacturers that have carried the 9mm Police round have not offered it with a hollowpoint bullet. The limitations of a full metal jacketed bullet in a relatively small diameter have limited the appeal of the 9mm Police round for civilian self-defense.

The Czech-made vz.82 is scarce here, but almost identical, except for caliber, finish and markings, to the popular Model 83 in 380 ACP.

fluences, as well as some notable differences from the Soviet design. Like the Soviet-designed Makarov, the PP Super had an external slide stop. The PP Super's triggerguard was also extended at the front to facilitate handling with a gloved trigger finger. However, the PP Super differed from the Makarov pistol in a few respects. The PP Super was heavier than the Makarov, and had a larger, fuller grip. These changes made the PP Super a more comfortable gun for the shooter than the Makarov, since the PP Super recoils very little while the Makarov has a sharper recoil. The most significant

system for military and police use, as it allows the gun to be carried loaded without the fear of an accidental discharge in the event one drops the gun, yet leaves the gun instantly ready for action. Walther has since used this same system on several subsequent pistol designs with great success.

The PP Super itself, however, was a failure in the marketplace. After the West German national border police and the police in the West German state of Bavaria bought several thousand PP Supers in 1973, official interest in the 9mm Police waned. The police then became more inter-

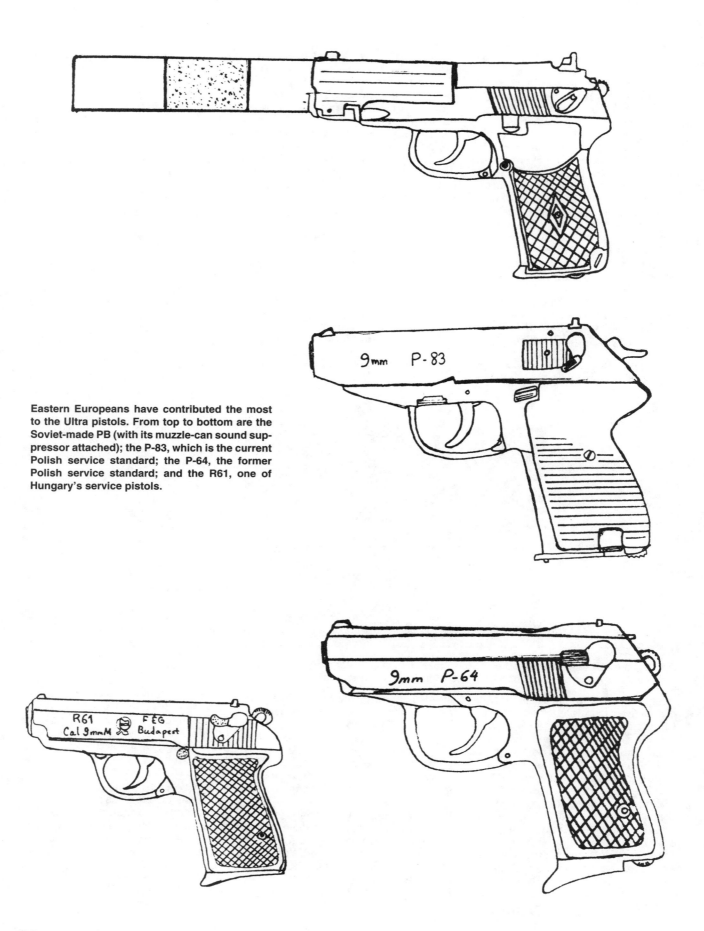

Eastern Europeans have contributed the most to the Ultra pistols. From top to bottom are the Soviet-made PB (with its muzzle-can sound suppressor attached); the P-83, which is the current Polish service standard; the P-64, the former Polish service standard; and the R61, one of Hungary's service pistols.

Ironically, with the changes in Europe brought about by the collapse of communism in Eastern Europe, interest in the 9mm Makarov round has now begun to soar in Germany and other Western European countries where the 9mm Police has had a small foothold. Today one can buy various Hungarian, Czech and even Russian pistols in Germany in 9mm Makarov caliber, with the Makarov pistol itself and the Czech vz.82 being especially well-received. Whether the 9mm Police round can survive this competition remains to be seen. For the moment, the 9mm Police is surviving, but barely.

The Makarov, the most successful of the Ultra pistols, remains in production. The current commercial Baikal IJ-70 comes from the same Izhevsk plant which once made Makarov and Stechkin pistols for the Soviet military during the Cold War. The only major differences between the IJ-70 and the Makarov PMs of the Cold War era is that the IJ-70 has a prominent adjustable rear sight and a matte blued finish, whereas older Makarov pistols had a small fixed rear sight and a polished blued finish.

FÉG reintroduced its 9mm Makarov caliber R61 for commercial sale in 1992 as the SMC-380 in 380 caliber, in 1995 as the SMC-918 in 9mm Makarov caliber, and in 1996 as the SMC-22 in 22 Long Rifle caliber. These well-made pistols differ from the Cold War-era Hungarian service pistols only in having their lightweight alloy frames anodized black to closely match the blued slide. Surplus ex-military and police issue Hungarian pistols are no longer available from the importer, but do show up used from time to time.

The Clinton Administration in 1994 banned further importation of Chinese-made firearms, including the 9mm Makarov Type 59 pistol. These well-made guns sometimes also still show up used, however.

A useful and prolific class of handguns, the Ultra pistols still offer today what Nazi Germany's air force sought nearly sixty years ago: a lightweight, compact and inexpensive pistol with good power for its size. These guns are both mechanically straightforward and easy to use. The reliability and accuracy of most models ranges from very good to excellent. Though not up to the power of traditional American favorites like the 357 Magnum and 45 ACP, the success of the Makarov, in particular, is causing shooters even in the United States to take a closer and more respectful look at the interesting Ultra pistols •

Bibliography

Buxton, Warren H. *The P.38 Pistol, Volume Three* Los Alamos, NM Ucross Books, 1990.

Ezell, Edward C. *Small Arms of the World, 12th Edition*. Harrisburg, PA: Stackpole Books, 1983.

Hogg, Ian and John Weeks. *Military Small Arms of the 20th Century, 6th Edition*. DBI/Krause Publications Iola, WI.

Pistols of the World, 12th Edition. DBI/Krause Publications Iola, WI.

Markham, George. *Guns of the Elite: Special Forces Firearms, 1940 to the Present* London, England Arms and Armour Press, 1991.

Zhuk, Aleksandr B., translated by Nikolai N. Bobrov. *The Illustrated Encyclopedia of Handguns: Pistols and Revolvers of the World, 1870 to the Present* London, England Greenhill Books, 1995.

The PP Super (bottom) is slightly larger and heavier than the Makarov (top), which makes it more pleasant to shoot, since the two pistols are using ammunition closely comparable in size and power.

The latest commercial Makarov-type pistol, the IJ-70 (top) made for importation into the United States, has a prominent adjustable rear sight, whereas Makarovs made for military and police service, like the East German Pistole M (bottom) have a low-profile fixed rear sight.

The original Model 1100 was a fast-moving, accurate-pointing gun on far-flushing game such as this Hungarian partridge.

Ah........ There Was an
AUTOLOADER

by Don Zutz

They were unbelievable words, words I'd never expected to see in the best-selling British shooting magazine, <u>Sporting Gun.</u> I did a double-take and read them again. Yup, there in the pages of the July, 1996, issue were the hyphenated adjectives "lightning-fast" and "much-loved" describing the original Remington Model 1100 autoloader. How dare anyone loyal to the Union Jack and Her Majesty print that in the land of Purdey, Holland & Holland, Boss, Powell, Churchill, Watson, Greener, Lancaster, and the rest of those great builders of classic, side-by-side, game guns?

If one followed international clay shooting, he wouldn't bother to ask.. For although Americans almost au-tomatically equate British shooting with the handmade doubles for which they are justly famous, rank and file clay shooters of the U.K. long ago learned that over-unders and semiautos scored better in competition; and while the side-by-side is still the traditional hunting piece, they have openly and unabashedly accepted the semiauto as a totally legitimate shotgun. In the course of things, the Remington Model 1100 came on strong, having generated a popular following well before Beretta's Model A-303 came along and attracted some attention of its own, especially in sporting clays.

Any number of outstanding British clay shooters used the original Model 1100 Remington for skeet, both English and ISU style. Moreover, Englishman Duncan Lawton twice won the world's FITASC sporting championship with the same work-worn Model 1100, and in this writer's opinion there is no clay target contest that's more demanding of gun handling speed and ease than FITASC (which is the international form of sporting clays). And so it went in other parts of the world. I remember one world cup match when Belgian skeetmen surprised everyone by showing up with 1100's.

The fact is that, in its original form with fixed-choke barrels, the Model 1100 had superb handling qualities, was a natural pointer, and swung as smooth as silk. Its detractors claimed it dirtied up too fast, but

I'll gladly clean a gun more frequently if it has qualities which win. And win the M1100 did, undoubtedly claiming the most important skeet and trap trophies of any semiauto. Unfortunately, the original M1100 was being altered and phased out when sporting clays began to catch on in the U.S. or it could have been a champion in that discipline, too. But let's start at the beginning...

Although the M-1 Garand of WWII proved that gas-operated shoulder guns could function reliably, it was 1958/59 before American-made, gas-operated, autoloading shotguns appeared. One was the J.C. Higgins Model 60 as made by High Standard but offered solely by Sears, Roebuck & Co.; the other was Remington's Model 58. The Higgins followed the M-1 Garand's piston concept, having its spring/piston assembly wrapped about the magazine tube, whereas Remington tucked the spring-piston stuff into the magazine tube. This left the M58 a bit trimmer through the forearm, while the M60 had a radically deep forearm for its day.

The Remington M58 had superb pointing qualities, but, alas, it also had mechanical woes such as snapped action bars, receiver wear in the raceways, and bolt cracking. It also experienced carbon fouling in the magazine tube which necessitated arduous cleaning. And when one went from heavy loads to light ones, or vice versa, he had to adjust the indexing magazine cap for gas capture or relief. This need for a mechanical load adjustment was quickly eliminated in a little-known Remington, the Model 878, which came out in 1959 and lasted into 1962. Profiled like the M58, and still possessed of a piston/spring assembly inside the magazine tube, the M878 had a self-compensating pressure valve which handled both the lighter and heavier shotshells of its day interchangeably sans adjustments or barrel changes. Exactly why that self-compensating device wasn't carried forward immediately into the then-building Model 1100 has never been explained.

Remington began filling the pipeline with Model 1100s in 1963. The

Model 58 and 878 were history, although I still have a fond spot in my ticker for the M58 because one day I managed 250x250 to win my state's 12-gauge skeet championship. While sitting in a duck blind one lazy day, thereafter, I looked down to see that the M58's bolt had cracked, and that, along with severe wear elsewhere, brought me quickly to the newfangled Model 1100.

A main difference was that the M1100's piston assembly now encircled the magazine tube a'la the Garand and M60 Higgins. Powder gases were sealed by a neoprene O-ring. This change in the location of the piston assembly necessitated a new forearm concept which aped the Higgins gun's depth. The sporting world not only forgave Remington, but soon began to praise the M1100 for its effective pointing qualities. Either by luck or design, the M1100's pistol grip placed the shooter's trigger hand on the same basic plane as his front hand, thereby producing the desirable hands-in-line accommodation for optimum coordination. Indeed, it is very difficult, if not impossible, to find a repeater that works better with a shooter's hand-to-eye attributes than the original M1100 with fixed-choke barrel.

Another virtue of the M1100 is its relatively shallow receiver. The 12 gauges on my rack show a receiver depth of just 2.55 in. at the leading edge and 2.42 in. at the rear of the loading gate. These figures mean nothing by themselves, of course, but they're in the same category as popular over-unders. I've measured more than a few hot-selling stackbarrels at 2.50 in. and even more through the standing breech. In reality, the M1100's receiver depth isn't significantly different than that of the Browning 12-gauge Superposed and Citori. Even the Berettas, which are considered to be shallow-profiled, come to about 2.43 in. at the standing breech in 12 bore.

The first M1100s were made in 12, 16, and 20 gauge. All used the same receiver, and only the interior parts and barrel were adjusted for the gauge. Skeet shooters soon learned that if they put a steel Cutts Compensator on the early 20-bore M1100s they'd have the same weight as the 12. The 16 gauge was no bargain, though, as the hunter carried a 12-gauge framework with a smaller barrel. No big deal. Things like this helped to kill the public's interest in the 16 gauge.

Its also worked fine on close-in shots such as this ruffed grouse in thicker cover.

At the same time, the M1100 became one of the winningest skeet guns of all time, as it also was in American-style trapshooting.

Initially, Model 1100s had somewhat lower combs than they eventually acquired. Remington had used a 1-5/8 in. comb drop on many prior shotguns, but clay shooters in particular found the first M1100 combs too low. I remember discussing this with the late Ed. C. Scherer, oft-times All-American skeetman, and we opted for trap-grade M1100s for their slightly higher combs; we merely changed barrels for the shorter skeet tubes and had the longer trap stocks shortened.

The stock dimensions changed after the M1100 had been on the market for a short time. I recall Jim Martin, who retired from the Remington R&D department, telling me that in finalizing the newer stock dimensions he kept taking samples into the shop and having virtually everyone mount the gun and give an

opinion. He wasn't satisfied until the fit was practically universal. Since then, the M1100 has fit a high percentage of all who handle it.

Remington began making the M1100 in 28 gauge and 410 bore in 1969. Skeet shooters of the day leaped upon them with glad cries, and some high averages were posted. The company also devised a set of weights for inclusion on the target-grade smallbores for smoother swings.

In 1971, Remington scaled down the receiver of the 20 gauge and introduced it as the Model 1100 20-gauge Lightweight at 6'4-6 lbs. It had a mahogany stock. Later, this variant was dropped and the slenderized M1100 20 was given walnut rather than mahogany. A 3 in. 20-gauge M1100 Lightweight Magnum was also introduced and remains in the line, now also available with synthetic stock and forend. I spent a full bird season with the 20-gauge Lightweight M1100 beginning with the 26 in. IC barrel and 1-oz. handloads for ruffed grouse and pheasants. My results weren't satisfying, though, and I soon traded the 26 in. barrel for a 28 in. unit with modified choke.

I felt that I had been poking and whipping with the lightgun/shortbarrel tandem, and the 28 in. barrel seemed to smoothen

In 1984, there was a short barreled, Special M1100 with a straight-gripped stock to catch the upland hunter's attention. It did, and this one caught a few woodcocks.

In 1987, the great ol' M1100 was discontinued in favor of the heavier Model 11-87, which was subsequently and necessarily lightened by reducing the forearm length, as illustrated here by the M11-87 Sporting Clays gun.

things. Despite the slightly tighter pattern, my bird shooting improved.

Through the intervening years, Remington has made a series of commemorative Model 1100s. It had the distinction of being the first Ducks Unlimited commemorative in 1973, and other DU projects followed. These included a 20-gauge "Special," and a pair of 12-gauge magnums in "The Chesapeake" and "The Atlantic" which paid tribute to major flyways. The Atlantic was the only 12-gauge magnum M1100 made with a 32 in. barrel.

The M1100 sold well during the 1970s despite an economic glitch at mid-decade when an oil embargo caused an upheaval. Another economic event found all gunmakers foundering in the early 1980s as the Federal Reserve tried to bring down inflation by increasing interest rates, a monetary move that brought many businesses to a standstill

What do you do when everyone already has a M1100? You make variants, such as this "SP" waterfowler.

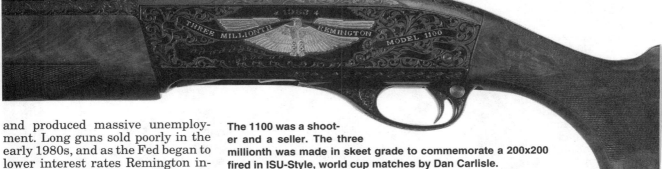

The 1100 was a shooter and a seller. The three millionth was made in skeet grade to commemorate a 200x200 fired in ISU-Style, world cup matches by Dan Carlisle.

and produced massive unemployment. Long guns sold poorly in the early 1980s, and as the Fed began to lower interest rates Remington introduced a stumpy version of the M1100 labeled the "Special Field." It had but a 21 in. barrel, fixed chokes, a shortened forearm, and a straight grip. And it did attract new sales.

I used a Special Field for two woodcock seasons and didn't miss a bird. It had the pointing and handling qualities of a double with 26 in. barrels. But overall it was a poke-and-hope gun, since it didn't have the length required for smoothness of swing on the longer shots or fast crossers. It failed on skeet and had enough muzzle blast to knock the ears off a brass monkey. Eventually, Remington put a 23 in. barrel on the Special Field for an improvement of sorts. But then other problems swept in. . .

In the late 1980s, Remington shot the M1100 in its proverbial foot by introducing a screw-in choke system — the Rem-Choke — which was nested in a heavily-walled barrel that gave the gun a different, weight-forward sag. This totally de-

stroyed what the British magazine writer termed the M1100's "lightning-fast" quality and turned it into a field piece that was dull and dead in one's hands. To worsen matters, Remington ceased production of fixed-choke barrels which balanced off the M1100 so nicely. Fortunately, the gun still had good stock fit; a lot of hunters could pull it up and find it working to their eye.

But the coming of Rem-Choked barrels deprived M1100s of their original balance and liveliness. Fortunately, I had some plain, fixed-choke barrels lying around, and I didn't have to lug the new ponderous pipes. One such barrel was a 26 in. plain tube given a screw-in choke by the late Ralph T. Walker, noted gunsmith of Selma, AL, and I use it for a lot of my hunting with the 12-gauge M1100. That barrel is still quick to a game bird; however, those who bought the Rem-Choked

M1100s don't know the true handling dynamics of the great ol' Eleven Hundred!

Nor did they find it in Remington's 1987 introduction, the Model 11-87. Pushed by marketing forces (either real or imagined), Remington brought forth a semiauto which looked almost like the M1100 in profile but which had a self-metering pressure valve built into the barrel loop to enhance versatility. Unlike the M1100 which required a special barrel with downsized bleeder valve for 3" magnum loads, the M11-87's self-metering valve al-lowed instant interchangeability of all legitimate commercial loads, target and dove through 3 in. magnums, without any need for barrel changing or mechanical adjustments. The concept initiated in the Model 878 Automaster was finally coming of age. This in itself wasn't a bad marketing move.

But the M11-87 was oh, so heavy. My consignment sample had a 26 in. barrel, and I carried (dragged, actually) it for one full afternoon of pheasant hunting. Remington finally adjusted the M11-87's undue frontal heft by taking about 6-8 ozs. off the barrel in a so-called "Light Contour" manner which gave the barrel thick walls at the muzzle and chamber segments while trimming it in hour-glass fashion about the middle. The M11-87 carries and swings better now, but it's still not the original M1100.

By 1994, the market began to grumble about the absence of low-priced semiautos. Much hunter trade was now enjoyed by the various "marts," which liked to keep goods readily affordable. Re-enter now the newest variant of the M1100. Like the Remington Model 870 Express pumpgun, the mart-styled M1100 came back as a 12-gauge gun with black synthetic stock and forearm plus the matte finish and painted trigger guard that had permitted a price reduction. Additional production tricks learned on the M870 Express project helped keep the mart-styled M1100 12 bore within range of most typical hunters.

Although just a limited, special-order deal for gun merchants in 1995, the 12-gauge M1100 was made a bona fide catalog piece again in 1996, available to all gun deal-

ers and buyers of the various mart systems. But, alas and alack, this was just a marketing venture to satisfy a price point rather than to bring back the late, great, original gun in all its glory. Fortunately, this mart-styled M1100 does retain much of the old pointing quality, although it is obviously schnozz-heavy and hardly as graceful on the swing as the old-timers. Indeed, returning to fixed-choke barrels could improve the resurrected M1100's

weight/balance condition, as it could make a better gun of the M11-87. And leaving the ventilated rib off said guns would improve things even more, since no hunter ever needed a rib!

Thus, I'm certain the Brits won't ooze glorious adjectives over the born-again Eleven Hundred. It's not the same ol' gun, but it's back in 12 bore, perhaps for as long as we'll have This-mart and That-mart. And when it was in its heyday, ah-h — there was an auto-loader!

The born-again mart-styled Model 1100 just ain't the same. Made to sell at a lower price point on today's market, it still has those great pointing qualities.

The Model 1100 was initially designed to balance best with a 28" barrel, which is what was used to fold this decoying mallard.

All Weather, All Purpose, All World...
All GLOCK!

It's A Big World...
...and big worlds demand superior performance.

With 10 + 1 round capacity in 10 mm or .45 Auto, it's easy to see how the new GLOCK models 29 and 30 are once again setting the world-wide standard for compact automatic pistols. And, as with all GLOCK pistols, out-of-the-box accuracy and reliability assure that you'll put each and every shot where you need it - *ON TARGET.*

It's A Small World...
...and small worlds have exacting limitations.

Compact, concealable, and packed with GLOCK features, the G29 and G30 can go where other 10's and .45's can't. Both come equipped with GLOCK's recoil-taming, light-weight polymer frame construction, finger gripped front strap and ambidextrous thumb rests to make these new compacts more ergonomic than ever before. GLOCK's corrosion resistant Tenifer finish leaves them diamond hard and ready for anything. And, these diminutive heavy hitters accept the standard size magazines of their larger counterparts – a big selling point for law enforcement officers and citizens alike.

Introducing the compact **GLOCK 29** and **GLOCK 30**

GLOCK ®

PERFECTION

Contact your local GLOCK Stocking Dealer today, pick one up, and see for yourself how GLOCK Perfection makes a small world so big.

.50 A.E. DESERT EAGLE PISTOL
SCOPED, WITH BRUSHED
CHROME FINISH

.30-06 LONE EAGLE PISTOL
SCOPED, WITH MUZZLE BRAKE
AND MATTE CHROME FINISH

Power tools for hunters.

The Desert Eagle™ Pistol and the Lone Eagle™ Pistol get the job done with accuracy and style. The renowned Desert Eagle is a handgun hunter's dream in three Magnum calibers. With barreled actions in 15 calibers, the Lone Eagle is the best single-shot pistol available – and the best value.

See your dealer. Call for brochures. Or visit our handy Web site.

Magnum Research, Inc.

1-800-772-6168
612-574-1868
www.magnumresearch.com

IF YOU WANT THE MOST ACCURATE PRODUCTION RIFLE MADE, YOU HAVE TWO CHOICES:

THE

A-Bolt II

OR THE

A-Bolt II

WITH THE BOSS.

A-Bolt II Stainless Stalker $708.25 (suggested retail)

A-Bolt II Medallion w/ BOSS $697.95 (suggested retail)
(scope not included)

Compare quality. Compare price. Compare targets. In an independent test by Popular Mechanics magazine, the A-Bolt II soundly beat the competition, and the A-Bolt II with BOSS blew them away.

Experts and thousands of A-Bolt owners prove the A-Bolt II is one of the finest rifles made. Now it's even better because all BOSS-equipped rifles include both the muzzle brake BOSS and the BOSS-CR (conventional recoil). Both systems offer the same simplicity and accuracy with any quality load.

The decision to buy an A-Bolt is easy. The hard part is choosing one of the 162 options. Your Browning dealer can help you. See him, today.

CALL FOR YOUR FREE VIDEO AND HUNTING CATALOG TODAY.

Call 1-800-333-3504 to receive a free BOSS video. Also, ask for our 100-page hunting catalog with the latest in Browning firearms and accessories. www.browning.com

THE BEST THERE IS.

Warning: The BOSS™ with muzzle brake provides substantial increased noise (muzzle blast). Always wear hearing protection to prevent hearing loss or damage.

T/C 1968 ad for the Contender. The 45 Colt-410 combination barrel was made only briefly because of objections by the U.S. Dept. of the Treasury. Later barrels were offered in 44 Magnum-44 Hot Shot as described in the article. In more recent years the Treasury reversed itself and the 45-410 barrels are again being sold. (T/C photo)

MY 30 T/C YEARS

BY WILLIAM HOVEY SMITH

Counter-culture obstinacy took me to the new Thompson/Center Contender pistol in 1968. I had fired almost every model of hand-held and crew-served gun used in Korea and Vietnam, and my interest in military guns had dimmed. I still shot the 45, but I liked trying to shoot a better score than my last with single-shot pistols.

There were three 22-caliber single shots in my life at the time, a German falling block, a Remington rolling block, and a Smith & Wesson Olympic model. When I read about the Contender in the 1968 *Gun Digest*, the opportunity to purchase a modern single-shot pistol with interchangeable barrels that would shoot center-fire pistol cartridges was too appealing to resist.

In time I received number 1618, cased with 22 LR, 357 Magnum, and 22 Remington Jet barrels. I returned the 22 LR octagon barrel with a crooked front sight; it was quickly replaced.

This early gun came with small target grips raked at an angle that felt very comfortable with 22 LR and reduced velocity 357s loaded with wadcutters, but was punishing when fired with factory 357 loads. Recoil was even more bothersome when I later acquired a 44-Magnum-44 Hot Shot barrel. A few factory 44-Magnum loads was all I cared to shoot at one session. When barrels were replaced on this frame, the gun had to be re-zeroed.

Elmer Keith had written for years about shooting big game with large-caliber pistols, but the idea of hunting big game with a powerful single-shot pistol took some time to seem practical to the hunting public. Was there room in the market until then for a single-shot pistol that was mostly going to be used for informal target shooting, plinking, and small game? Ken Thompson and Warren Center thought so.

By 1964, Thompson had relocated his company from Long Island to Rochester, New Hampshire. He was manufacturing investment casting molds and parts for the firearms industry when he was approached by Warren Center with a single-shot pistol design. Thompson needed a product that he could manufacture to help even out production cycles between parts contracts, and Center needed someone to build his gun. Thompson/Center Arms Co. was founded in 1965 to satisfy these needs.

Center had established his reputation as a gun designer while working at Army Ordnance and later with Iver Johnson and Harrington & Richardson. Already employed at Thompson/Center were Red Ronayne and Joe Behre who would later become vice presidents of the company. Robert Gustafson, now President, was also already working at the company.

The first Contender was produced in 1967. Through 1974, the classic Contender with its back-swept grips, 8-3/8 and 10-inch tapered octagon barrels was manufactured with few changes other than additional calibers. By 1974, 22 chamberings were catalogued including the 17-K Hornet, 222 Remington, 357/44 B & D, 256 Winchester, 9 mm Parabellum, and 44 Magnum.

I worked in Montana during much of the '70s and killed several grouse and a number of rattlers with the 44 Hot-Shot cartridge, a 44 Magnum case loaded with a shot capsule. The cartridge had ballistics similar to the 2-1/2-inch 410. The T/C 44 Magnum barrel was fitted with a screw-on choke with parallel interior rifling to help straighten out the shot charge.

This combination worked with shot charges at 20 yards and less, and did well with the 44 Magnum ball out to 75 yards. I still had reservations about the gun and I wrote Thompson/Center about the uncomfortable nature of the recoil with this load and grip design.

A reply from Tim Pancurak was received in March, 1977. He acknowledged the problem, and informed me, "The Contender pistol grip was changed to a much more comfortable design over four years ago...The new grips can be installed on the older Contenders without any modifications. It is a simple remove and replace installation."

In the same letter I had asked if Thompson/Center would consider chambering the 45-70 in their pistol. Pancurak's comment was, "A few test 45-70 barrels were made up for the Contender. The recoil and muzzle blast were too severe for efficient shooting. The combination was quite ineffective due to the short 10-inch barrel and the medium rate powders used in factory ammo."

He recommended the 30 Herrett and the 357 Herrett as cartridges which "far surpass the 44 mag."

Warren Center began to look at other gun production possibilities where Thompson/Center could define its

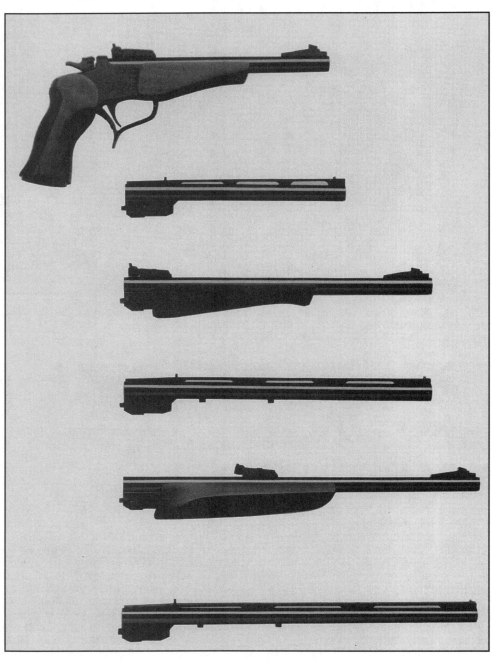

This late production gun illustrates the range of bull barrels in 10, 14, and 16-inch lengths. The gun has a walnut grip with a rubber cushion insert. Increasing the weight of the gun and redesigning the grips to decrease felt recoil were two steps that allowed the shooter to more comfortably use Contenders chambered for cartridges like the 30-30 Winchester and 35 Remington. (T/C photo)

The author's Patriot pistol with a 25-yard target. Although regular production is now discontinued, the pistol is still available through Fox Ridge Outfitters.

own market segment. In the late 1960s there was a revival of interest in muzzle-loading firearms, a sustained interest in muzzle-loaders continued. Soon original guns became too valuable to use, and Center saw a demand for a quality American-made muzzle-loader made form investment cast parts. Ken Thompson concurred, and Center developed a modified Hawken rifle, with a medium-weight octagon barrel, set-triggers, walnut stock, and brass furnishings as his initial offering. These guns earned a reputation for reliable performance on the range and as excellent hunting guns.

The Hawken was introduced in 1970. Only two years later a newly designed pistol, the Patriot, began to be sold. The Patriot used a smaller lock than the Hawken rifle and also had walnut stocks and investment-cast parts. Otherwise, there was little similarity.

Offered in 36 and 45 calibers, the Patriot had reverse set triggers and a modified saw-handle stock with a finger grip trigger guard. I bought one of the 45s at a shoot near Blackshear,

As were many Thompson/Center guns, the Patriot was also offered as a kit, but difficult stuff like neatly installing a bult cap was already accomlished.

Georgia, and I have used it successfully for years. Mine likes 20 grains of FFFg, corn meal filler, and saliva-lubricated patched .445 round balls.

While the Patriot could be used for potting late season rabbits in the briars, its forte is off-hand target shooting at 25 and 50 yards. Accuracy is aided by an excellent set of reverse-levered set triggers. In the usual set-trigger design the rear trigger is "set" by pulling on the front trigger. In the Patriot, the front trigger does the setting, and the rear fires the gun. My

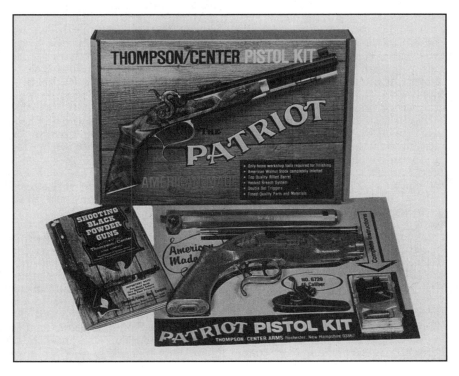

The stainless steel Contender Hunter shown in this version is scope mounted, with synthetic stock, muzzle brake, and sling. Hunter models are offered in 12 and 14-inch barrel lengths and in calibers including 223 Remington, 35 Remington, 375 Winchester, and 45-70. (T/C photo)

complaint was that the finger spur on the trigger guard was extraneous. I shot more consistent groups by holding the grip with four fingers.

The Patriot is still available through Thompson-Centers Custom Shop, and it is sold exclusively through Fox Ridge Outfitters, the company's sales store at the Rochester plant. Fox Ridge offers specialized products produced by the company's custom shop, round-ball twist barrels, and hunting accessories. Most of Fox Ridge's sales are through mail order, and a catalogue has been available on request.

Larger-capacity cases using rifle powders pushed Thompson Center into breaking its 10-inch barreled custom when the Super-14 Contender was introduced in 1978. The Super-14 utilized the same frame as other Contenders, but had a longer bull barrel. The new barrel required a special forend that was screw-attached to the barrel, and a redesigned finger-grooved grip was also introduced with this pistol. The style of shooting had changed to the use of both hands, big game hunting with pistols demanded more powerful cartridges, and Thompson/Center successfully adapted its gun to these changing market conditions.

Increasing the gun's weight from 44 to 56 ounces made it more man-

ageable in the 30-30 Winchester and 35 Remington loads. And the 44 Magnum became pleasant to shoot. The 10-inch barrel length could be carried comfortably on a belt holster, but the longer 14-inch version had to be carried in-hand, slung over the shoulder, or in a shoulder holster, a minor drawback.

More powerful calibers, longer barrels, and redesigned grips led the way to the Super-16 which in 1993 was also available in stainless. This gun has a number of options including synthetic or wood stocks, and currently is sold in eight chamberings including the 45-70, 30-30 Winchester, 35 Remington, and the 45 Colt 410 gauge (3-inch) combination. A muzzle brake is offered to further reduce recoil.

The design limits of the modified Contender design had been reached. The frame was not strong enough to safely handle the 50,000 psi pressures generated by standard rifle cartridges such as the 30-06. Thompson Center made a carbine chambered for pistol and low-pressure rifle cartridges based on the Contender action to expand sales and potentials. The carbine is equipped with a buttstock and 16-1/4 and 21-inch barrels. Except for offering different construction and materials, barrel lengths, sights, and chamber-

ings, the Contender pistol could not be developed further.

Thompson/Center Arms Co. had grown from one foundry building to a complex of six buildings containing over 65,000 square feet and had become one of the largest employers in the Rochester area. Thompson died in 1978, but he left a viable company, an able partner, and a cadre of employees who were to become future company officers. New people had been added during his tenure, and included among them was Ken French who later became the Director of Research and Development and had an instrumental part in developing the companys recent products.

Vital aspects of the company's culture and business policies were retained. Among these was Thompson/Center's unwavering commitment to a lifetime guarantee to the original purchaser. My No. 1618 became increasingly stiff to the point where the gun would open only with extreme difficulty. I returned it to the company, and was advised the gun was non-repairable. As the gun had collector's value, they would either return the frame to me or replace it with another from current production. I chose the second option and received a new frame.

Differences between No. 1618 and the new one were mostly inter-

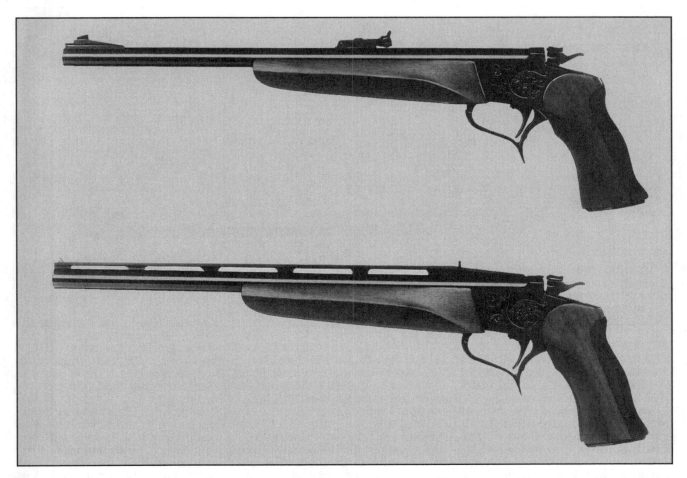

The Super 16 Contender in blued steel with bull and ventilated rib barrels. The latter is chambered for 45 Colt and the three-inch 410. These bigger T/C's are lots easier to shoot well. (T/C photo)

nal. The new gun used the "Easy Open" internal parts as well as a lever on top of the hammer to change between rim-fire and center-fire ignition. The trigger mechanism was as crisp, and all my old barrels fit without modification. I later purchased new grips and a Super-14 44 Magnum barrel and forend. I carried the gun only on wet-weather days when I did not trust my flint-lock guns, so it was several years before I killed something with it.

With the Contender and its variants paving the way, the idea emerged at Thompson/Center that there were people who would prefer to hunt with a muzzle-loading pistol if one could be developed that was powerful enough. Percussion revolvers, including the Colt Walker, were on the feeble side; and only a few replica single-shot pistols, such as the Harper's Ferry 58-caliber model 1855, generated sufficient energy to take deer consistently.

Some states, like Georgia, required a pistol to have a retained muzzle energy of 500 foot pounds at 100 yards. Few muzzle loading pistols could achieve this energy level without exceeding factory recommended loadings. This was another market that Ken French felt Thompson/Center could fill and development of a new muzzleloading pistol began in the late 1980s. Having seen the desirability of easily interchangeable and/or removable barrels in both their Contender and black-powder guns, this feature was retained.

Black powder fouling is unavoidable in a muzzleloading pistol, so the decision was made to produce a new design made with a few simple components. Side-lock mechanisms, as on the Patriot, were rejected because of the need to contain greater pressures and the added expense of making a complex stock.

With sufficient production capacity available, it was possible to introduce the Scout in both carbine and pistol versions in 1990. A Scout rifle with a 24-inch barrel was introduced in 1995. The Scout pistol is now available in 50 and 54 calibers, and the 45-caliber version has been discontinued. The 12-inch barreled Scout weighs about 70 ounces and is the heaviest Thompson/Center handgun.

Hal Swiggett was among the first to field test a 50-caliber Scout, and his report appeared in the 1991 issue of Gun Digest. Swiggett used 370-grain Maxi-balls pushed by charges of 80, 90, and 100 grains of FFg. He reported shooting clover-leaf groups with each charge at 25-yards while posting velocities of 1055, 1119, 1187 fps.

For shooting small Georgia deer at 40 yards and less, I chose to drive the 370-grain bullet with 75 grains of FFg for a velocity of about 1000 fps and a muzzle energy of about 1000 ft. lbs. This load was a good trade-off between recoil and the need to meet the state's retained energy requirement. This load killed a deer on Georgia's Cumberland Island with one shot last year. On consecutive days I shot two deer, the first with the Scout and the second with the 44 Magnum Super-14. The deer were about the same size

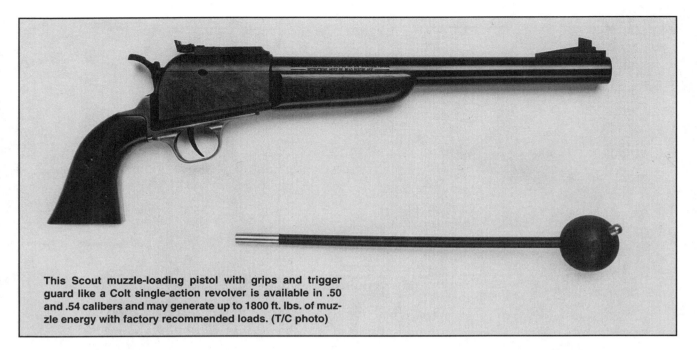

This Scout muzzle-loading pistol with grips and trigger guard like a Colt single-action revolver is available in .50 and .54 calibers and may generate up to 1800 ft. lbs. of muzzle energy with factory recommended loads. (T/C photo)

and shot placement was almost identical. The Scout-killed deer fell where it was shot, and the Super-14 deer ran 30 yards and expired — no real difference in apparent effectiveness.

With the early-production Scouts, cap fragments would occasionally fall into the mechanism and prevent the gun from firing. This was solved by fitting a spring steel cap shield to the hammer that moved horizontally back and forth in the frame. A cosmetic change made here lately was color case hardening the pistol frame.

The Colt-style grips cause the fired gun to rotate in the hand to help dissipate recoil energy rather than absorbing the full shock of the load. These grips were comfortable for my smallish hands and the Scout is easier to thumb-cock than the Contender. Also distinctive to the Scout is a novel in-line ignition system which results in faster ignition than the conventional nipple-drum arrangement.

When I first spoke to Thompson/Center's Eric Brooker about this piece, he mentioned there would be a new pistol called the Encore which would be chambered for 30-06 power rifle cartridges. Arrangements were made for me to get some information about it and a test gun when they were available in late 1996.

The Encore looks and operates something like the Contender but was designed from the start with heavier components to take higher pressures. Parts and barrels are not interchangeable between the Encore and the Contender. Another change was that the must-open-before-re-

cocking feature of the Contender has been dropped so that Encore can be recocking without the necessity of reopening and closing the gun — a worthwhile improvement in a hunting gun, I think.

Originally, the Encore was to be produced with 10 and 15-inch barrels and a weight of 64 ounces with the longer barrel. Initial production calibers are 7mm-08 Remington, 7mm Bench Rest, and 44 Remington Magnum offered in the 10-inch barrel length. In 15-inch barrels the calibers

offered are 223 Remington, 22-250 Remington, 7mm-08 Remington, 7mm Bench Rest, 308 Winchester, 30-06 Springfield and 44 Remington Magnum.

Ad pictures of the first bench-built gun showed a slick-barreled pistol mounted with a Thompson/Center pistol scope. Production models will have adjustable sights. Being sensitive to muzzle blast and recoil, I requested a scope-mounted 15-inch barreled version in 30-06. To gain maximum use of these calibers, long

A Scout-killed deer taken on Cumberland Island, Georgia, in 1995 during the coldest winter in 17 years. The following day the author killed a similar-sized doe with a Super-14 in .44 Magnum. There was little differences in the results.

barrels and scope sights appeared to me to be the best options.

If I were to use a single word to describe the Encore pistol that word would be "robust." The Encore frame is 3/8ths of an inch longer than the Contender, has sidewalls a full 1/4-inch thick, and measures 1 3/8-inches at the rear. The newly designed hammer does not have the lever to operate dual firing pins as the Encore is not available in rimfire chamberings.

The 15-inch barrel of the 30-06 measures an inch at the breech and tapers to 11/16-inch at the muzzle. The muzzle is countersunk, a useful improvement. The sight radius is 13 7/8-inches and a useful addition to the rear sight are "up" and "right" markings.

In my teens, a bolt-action Springfield was the first 30-06 I ever fired. I remembered the recoil from that rifle as being stout. A few years later I was an ROTC cadet. I had grown during the interim and the recoil was not as severe as I remembered. With these past experiences in mind it was with some trepidation that I shot the first few rounds from a 30-06 pistol.

Recoil with 150-grain military ammunition was stout, but not unmanageable. It was a step up from shooting the 44 Magnum in the Super-14. Using a Weaver stance, I had to remember to keep my left hand two fingers lower than my right to avoid painful raps to my left index finger. I changed my hold and used my left hand to support the forend and avoided this problem. The one-hand-on-pistolgrip, one-hand-on-forend method also provided for steadier aim. This alternate stance is definitely preferred with the Encore.

There have been no failures to fire or function attributable to the gun. Some of the 36-year-old ammunition even failed to fire in my Springfield rifle. Moving to Federal 150-grained Premium ammunition, function was flawless and reasonable off-hand groups were obtained at 25 yards. I was making sight adjustments at the time, but none of the shots would have missed the vital area of a deer. This is not an unrealistic personal parameter for an iron-sighted handgun since most of my deer are shot at ranges of less than 40 yards.

Restricting the use of a 30-06 handgun to ranges of 50 yards is like running a speedboat dragging its anchor. The Encore in this caliber needed a scope to express its full potential.

A handload with a 150-grain Nosler Partition bullet seems to me to be an optimum deer load for the pistol.

With iron sights, I found the Encore would fit into my Scout holster if the flap was removed, but when mounted with the Thompson/Center 2.6-7 Recoil Proof Pistol scope the handiest way of carrying the pistol was in the crook of the left arm like a light-weight carbine. Then it would be instantly ready without having to be drawn from a holster.

The Encore is a shootable pistol, the troublesome must-break-open-to-recock feature has been eliminated, and it is certainly powerful enough to use for 100-yard shots on deer-size game. If I were living back in Arizona, this would definitely be my preference for a hunting handgun — particularly when used with a scope. Of all available chamberings, the 7mm-08 Remington would be the most appealing to me in balancing recoil and performance characteristics for deer and antelope-sized game.

And maybe I'll get one anyway. It's been 30 years and my T/C's haven't disappointed me yet. I might as well stick with them. •

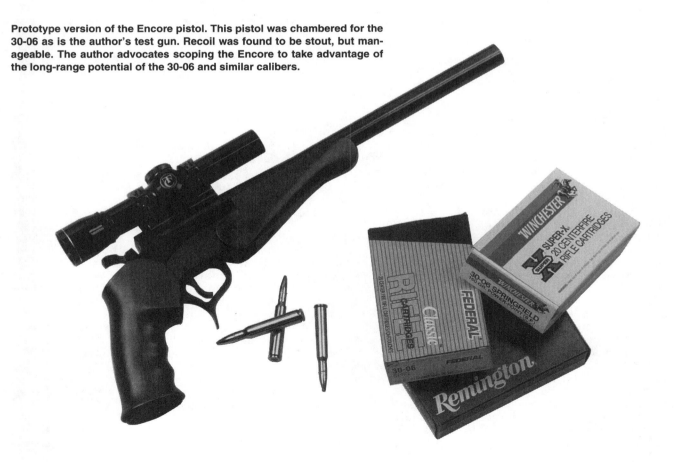

Prototype version of the Encore pistol. This pistol was chambered for the 30-06 as is the author's test gun. Recoil was found to be stout, but manageable. The author advocates scoping the Encore to take advantage of the long-range potential of the 30-06 and similar calibers.

Luckier than most, My First Rifle was:

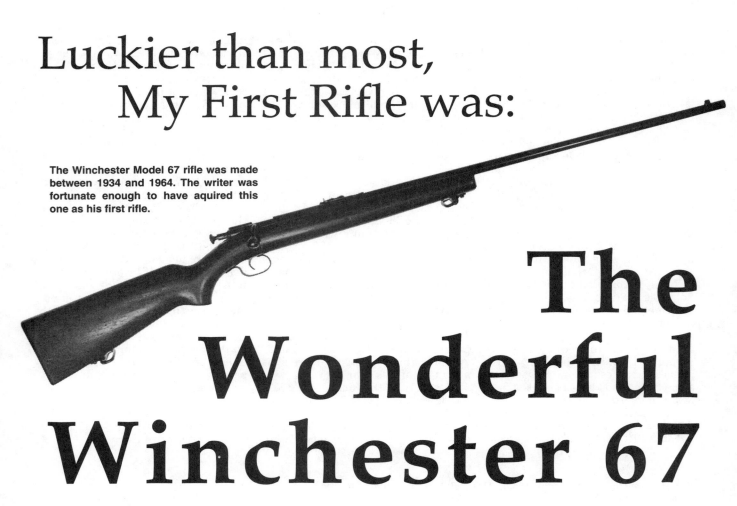

The Winchester Model 67 rifle was made between 1934 and 1964. The writer was fortunate enough to have aquired this one as his first rifle.

The Wonderful Winchester 67

by John Malloy

My first rifle was a Winchester 67, s simple manually-cocked single-shot 22. It turned out to be a wonderful rifle.

When I got it, I didn't have any real idea of its history. Later, I learned that the rifle might be considered an outgrowth of John M. Browning's sense of humor.

In the late 1800s, the Winchester company was buying every design that Browning invented. Even if the company did not plan to produce them, they did not want competitors to produce them either.

During the 1890s, Browning designed five simple single-shot 22s. There is some reason to believe he did it as a humorous attempt to see how few parts would make a shooting rifle. Four were crude but ingenious designs in which the hammer, trigger and breechblock were all one piece. The fifth was a small, simple bolt action.

We might well believe that Winchester was reluctant to buy the

first four, knowing they could never market such contraptions under the prestigious Winchester name. However they could not afford to let another company produce them, so they bought all five designs, shelved the first four, and considered the bolt action.

Introduced as the Winchester Model 1900, the little bolt-action was the last Browning design marketed by Winchester. It was the basis for the later Models 02 and 04, and the unusual thumb-trigger Model 99. The design eventually was modified into the Model 58, then enlarged into the Model 59 and 60. The Model 60 was further improved, and in 1934 the Model 67 was introduced.

The Model 67 was the high point of Winchester's manually-cocked single-shot line of rifles.

There were other variations: The Model 68 was the same rifle with a peep sight; the 677 had a scope

sight; a shorter version with a 20-inch barrel was at different times cataloged as the 67 Junior or the 67 Boy's Rifle.

Still, the mainstay of the line was the standard Model 67, with its wonderful 27-inch barrel, a longer barrel than that found on any other 22 of the time except a few target rifles. (Editor's Note: Long ago, a salesman at Von Lengerke & Antoine told me the gun companies believed consumers, when shopping for guns, picked up the longest barreled example first. K.W.)

Introduced in 1943, in the depths of the Great Depression, it stayed in production until the entire Winchester line was changed in 1964. By then, almost 1 1/2 million of the Winchester single-shot 22s based on the Browning design had been made, with close to half a million of them the Model 67 and its variants.

I acquired my 67 in 1948, at age 11. In those postwar years, there was a tremendous surge of interest in shooting, and I just had to have a 22. The 67 was one of the first 22 rifles Winchester put back into postwar production. I wanted a Model 67.

The price of a new one climbed to $16.10 after the war. Too much. I scraped together $9 of my lawn-mowing money and bought a second-hand 67 from a friend.

At five pounds, that little rifle was light enough for a kid, but it

bounding firing pin and additional thumb safety—locked securely into the receiver at the root of the bolt handle. In a slot in the bottom of the receiver beneath the bolt was a single piece. It served as extractor, ejector, sear and bolt stop—a real tribute to Browning's genius for getting one part to do several different things. A single screw held the barrel and action into the walnut stock. Over the years, several stock designs were

A group of friends and I joined an NRA Junior Rifle Club and began working on the 50-foot Qualification Awards. At that time, the awards were available only to Junior shooters. No target rifles were available, so we shot what we had, and I had the 67. My father helped me install swivels and a sling, and I was a target shooter.

The 67 shot like a dream. I had to wear glasses, even back then, but

Not quite as skinny now, the writer has hunted with his Winchester Model 67 for about half a century, and the rifle is still capable of tumbling a squirrel out of a tree every time. The writer is capable of doing it every now and then, also.

was a full-size rifle that a youngster could grow into. The short receiver allowed the full 27 inches of barrel without being overly long. The operation was simple: open the bolt, put in a cartridge, and close the bolt. When ready to fire, the cocking piece was pulled back. Until cocked manually in this manner, the rifle was on "safe" and would not fire.

The barrel and receiver were machined as one. The simple bolt—manually cocked, but with a re-

used, but mine was the type with the semi-beavertail forearm.

Back then, when I got the 67, no one thought there was anything wrong with a kid with a 22 rifle being in the woods by himself or with a few friends. Over the years, my 67 accounted for innumerable plinking targets and an assortment of slow or unlucky small game. The locale was Florida palmetto county, and the little rifle also dispatched some rattlesnakes.

I could see well enough to get a consistent sight picture with the open sights, and that was all the 67 needed. The nice semi-beavertail forearm made it feel like a target rifle; it took the hint and shot like one. I worked my way through Pro-Marksman, Marksman, Marksman First Class, and most of the Sharpshooter bars with the 67. Perhaps it could not have carried me through the Expert and Distinguished stages, but by then, I was on a school

A bolt; a barrel and receiver unit; a part in the bottom of the receiver unit; a part in the bottom of the receiver that serves as extractor, ejector, bolt stop and sear; and a stock with the trigger pinned in. Not much to go wrong with a 67.

rifle team and used a real target rifle to complete the course.

In the summer of 1956, at age 18, I took a job running the shooting program at a Boy Scout summer camp. Just before the camp opened, there was a break-in, and the camp rifles were stolen. Something was needed until replacements arrived. The camp director and the caretaker each had a bolt-action 22. I added my 67, and ran the program with those three rifles for the first week.

Somewhere along the line, I began to be aware of the other gender. What better way to entertain a young lady, I reasoned, that to take her shooting? The 67 was light and safe as a firearm could be. Strangely, not all girls seemed to be interested, but some were. Scattered among my old snap shots of the period are a number of young ladies posing with my 67.

As the years went by, I became involved in other Boy Scout shooting programs, including an Explorer Scout Marksmanship Specialty Post. The indestructible Model 67

was always there, available for an extra boy who needed an accurate rifle.

When we first met, my wife shot it. When they arrived, my two boys started with it. Now, they have rifles of their own. I, too, have a number of other rifles now. To tell the truth, the 67 doesn't get as much use as it did in times past.

But, every once in a while I pick it up, become fascinated all over again by the ingenious simplicity of the action, and just have to take it out and shoot it a bit.

I'm glad I got the Model 67 as my first rifle. I'm sure countless other boys also got their start in shooting with a 67. I'll bet they are glad, too. ●

The Winchester 67 doesn't show up very well in this grainy old snapshot, but the large Florida diamondback it dispatched does. In his teens then, the somewhat skinny writer was already over six feet tall, which gives some scale to the size of the snake.

The Winchester 67
Family Tree

by John Malloy

The history of the Winchester Model 67, its predecessors, and its variations, spans a period of 63 years. From its introduction in 1900, the Browning single-shot 22 rifle design underwent a gradual evolution that produced what was arguably the best manually-cocked 22 bolt-action ever made. The Winchester Model 67 itself stayed in production from its introduction in 1934 through 1963, when the complete reorganization of Winchester's product line took place. Well over 1-1/2 million of Winchester's manually-cocked 22s had been made, and almost half a million were the Model 67 and its variants. The firearms industry went through tremendous changes during these 63 years, but few people paid much attention to the simple single-shot 22s. Without much fanfare, they became the introduction to the shooting sports for many people. Their story should be better known.

Winchester Model 1900

The simple manually-cocked single-shot was based on John M. Browning's 1899 patent. It was Browning's last design for Winchester. It was also Winchester's first entry into the low-priced field, and was made by simple production methods. The barrel and receiver were made of a single piece of steel, and the straight-grip stock had no buttplate. It was the first Winchester firearm that was not serial numbered. Made for only two years, the little rifle proved a good seller, and over 100,000 were made. The 1900 handled 22 Short and 22 Long (22 S & L) interchangeably. Winchester made a few experimental pistols using the 1900 action.

Model 1900

Winchester Model 1902

A slight redesign of the 1900, the Model 1902 also had an 18-inch barrel and weighed only slightly more. A buttplate had been added, and the new trigger guard curved back to form a pistol grip. Originally chambered for 22 S & L, it was later available in 22 Extra Long (22 XL) then later in 22 Long Rifle (22 LR.) The 1902 was very popular. Winchester featured it as a suitable rifle for the Junior Rifle Corps shooting program the company had initiated. About 640,000 were made, and the model stayed in production until 1931. Winchester's interesting Model 36 9mm shotgun was a modified 1902.

Model 1902

Winchester Thumb Trigger (Model 99)

A simplified 1902-style rifle aimed at the low-priced market, the interesting Thumb Trigger rifle used the same basic action parts as the 1902. The sear was extended to the rear so that it could be pressed by the shooter's thumb. The rifle featured a new rebounding firing pin, and was chambered for 22 S & L, later 22 XL. In 1920, it was given the arbitrary model number 99. Not a big seller in America, it was reportedly very popular in Australia, and over 75,000 were made before it was discontinued in 1923.

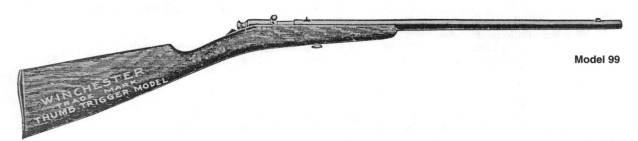

Model 99

Winchester Model 1904

The Model 1904 was produced to appeal to those wanting a somewhat larger and more graceful-looking 22 rifle. With its heavier 21-inch barrel, and larger schnabel-forearm stock, it was still just a bit over a yard long and weighed only 4 pounds. A larger trigger guard curved back to form an attractive 1902-style pistol grip. The 1904 featured an adjustable rear sight and a rebounding firing pin. The extra weight and adjustable sight made it suitable for junior target shooting, and the 1904 was also offered to the Junior Rifle Corps. It was chambered first for 22 S & L, then 22 XL, later 22 LR. It stayed in production until 1931, and over 300,00 were made.

Model 1904

Winchester Model 36

In 1920, Winchester added three low-priced shotguns to their line, one of which was the Model 36. This little gun was chambered for the 9mm rimfire shot cartridge, and was based on a modified Model 1902 action. It can be quickly distinguished from the 1902 by its large bore and lack of a rear sight. It was not particularly popular in America, and was discontinued in 1927. Total made was probably about 20,000 to 25,000, most to foreign sales.

Model 1936

Winchester Model 58

About 1928, Winchester brought out the Model 58 to once again meet low-priced competition in the 22 rifle market. Returning to the concept of the original Model 1900, it was made as inexpensively as possible and sold at a low price. The stock was sawed from 1-inch gumwood boards, then the corners were edged; no buttplate was provided. The Model 58 used a 1904-type action with rebounding firing pin. Its 18-inch barrel carried a non-adjustable rear sight and was chambered for 22 S, L, & LR, interchangeably. It stayed in the line into 1930. About 40,000 of the little rifles were made.

Model 58

Winchester Model 59

The Model 59 superseded the Model 58 in May, 1930. The action was the same, retaining the 1904-style bolt with its small straight bolt handle, but the new offering was a full-sized rifle, with a 23-inch barrel, adjustable sights and a larger stock. The Winchester Junior Rifle Corps had been absorbed into the National Rifle Association in 1925. With the new NRA Junior Division program offered to youth nationwide, Winchester may have felt they needed to have a larger 22 single-shot in their line. The stock was still gumwood, but was well-shaped, and provided the first true pistol-grip stock on a Winchester single-shot bolt-action 22. The Model 59 had a very short production run -- 1930 only -- for Winchester soon had a replacement in the works. About 10,000 Model 59 rifles were made.

Model 59

Winchester Model 60

Introduced in 1930 to replace the Model 59, the new Model 60 was similar in size and weight. With the Model 60, the bolt-action single-shot rifles had walnut stocks as standard for the first time. Perhaps the most notable change was the bolt, which now had a larger curved handle with a sizable gripping knob. Barrel length was 23 inches, changed to 27 inches in 1933. At that same time a variant, the Model 60A Target, was introduced, also with a 27-inch barrel. The standard Model 60 stayed in production for another year, until 1934, when it was replaced by the Model 67. About 166,000 were produced.

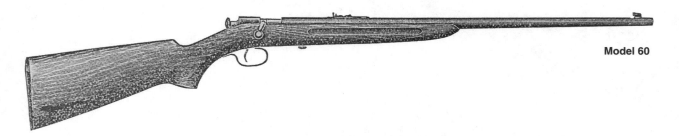

Model 60

Winchester Model 60A Target

A variant of the Model 60 action, the 60A Target was introduced in 1933. It used the new long 27-inch barrel mated to a heavier stock. The new stock was furnished with a front barrel band and sling swivels. Sights were a blade front sight and a Lyman 55 receiver sight. The 60A Target stayed in production until 1939, and about 6000 were made.

Model 60A Target

Winchester Model 67 (early production)

In April 1934, the Model 67 was introduced, the first of over 380,000 that would bear that number. Similar to the Model 60, it featured the improved turning thumbpiece safety. This safety was the last major mechanical modification made to the manually-cocked single-shot Winchesters. They continued in this basic form, with only stock, sight and barrel-length changes to mark the variants. Early production stocks had finger grooves. Barrel length was 27 inches, offered first in 22 S, L & LR. Within a few years, 22 Winchester Rim Fire (22 WRF) and 22 smoothbore variants had been introduced.

Model 67 (early production)

Winchester Model 68

Identical to the Model 67 except for sights, the Model 68 was introduced in 1934 also. It featured a ramp front sight with detachable hood, and a new Winchester 96A peep sight. The sight, mounted at the rear of the barrel, was adjustable for windage and elevation. Theoretically, this position is too far forward for a peep sight, but in actual practice, it worked very well. Chambering was 22 S, L, LR, with some made in 22 WRF. The 68 went out of production during WWII, but a cleanup of parts after the war pushed production to over 100,000 in 1946. Some sights were left, and the standard Model 67 was advertised as being available with such sights into the early 1950s.

Model 68

Winchester Model 677

Scope sights had been offered on Winchester's 22 rifles before 1937. In that year, however, Winchester offered the Model 677, a variant of the Model 67, equipped with only either a 2-3/4- or 5-power scope sight. The primary difference defining it from the 67 was the lack of iron sights and no sight cuts in the barrel. The prices for a 677 or for a 67 with a scope were exactly the same. Possibly, prospective buyers preferred to get the "free" iron sights by buying a scoped 67. The 677 stayed in production only 2 years, and fewer than 2300 were sold.

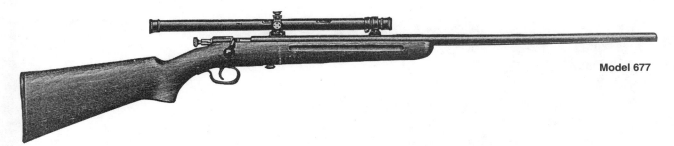

Model 677

Winchester Model 67 Junior

The 67 was a great success, but some felt it had outgrown the young shooters that had been well served by some of the previous smaller models. In 1937, three years after the 67's introduction, the Model 67 Junior was authorized. It had a 20-inch barrel, and the length of pull had been reduced from 13-1/2 to 12-3/16 inches. Weight went down from 5 pounds to 4-1/4. Standard chambering was 22 S, L, LR, although a few were made in 22 WRF. A small number of early-production Juniors were made with early finger-groove stocks, but most have intermediate-production stocks.

Model 67 Junior

Winchester Model 67 (intermediate production)

About 1938, the original finger-groove stocks had been replaced by a new design with a semibeavertail forearm. The front of the forearm had a squared appearance that easily distinguished it from the earlier version. Other features remained about the same. The 67 had begun to gain a reputation for accuracy. Firearms writer Philip B. Sharpe was only one of those who commented on the "remarkable groups" fired by Model 67s. Production of the Model 67 was apparently curtailed during WWII (although it has been speculated that some were made for clandestine operations.) Probably because of its simplicity, the 67 was one of the first of Winchester's sporting arms to resume production after the end of the war. The intermediate-production 67 was the variant produced through the end of the 1940s.

Model 67 (intermediate production)

Winchester Model 67 (late production)

The final variation of the basic Model 67, phased in during the 1950s, used a heavier, thicker stock. The forearm was lengthened, and was round in cross-section. There was more wood in the grip, and the comb was higher and thicker. The bolt, trigger, and trigger guard were chrome plated. The trigger was grooved. Many other, more "modern" postwar 22s were being offered, but the short action allowed the 67 to retain its 27-inch barrel and be no longer than competing designs with shorter barrels. The full-size 67 with its 27-inch barrel was listed for the last time in Winchester's 1962 catalog.

Model 67 (late production)

Winchester Model 67 Boy's Rifle

Not really a model change, but more a name change, the Model 67 Boys Rifle replaced the Model 67 Junior after about 1950. It retained the same 20-inch barrel, but added the grooved trigger and chromed parts of the later full-size 67. All late-production short 67s, with their thicker stocks and round forearms, were listed as Boy's Rifles. The Model 67 Boy's Rifle was destined to be the last of the Browning-origin bolt-action single-shots. Winchester changed its entire product line in the early 1960s. The 1963 catalog carried only one bolt-action sporting 22, the Model 67 Boy's Rifle. The 27-inch standard model had been dropped the year before. The story of Winchester's manually-cocked single-shot 22s, begun over six decades and well over 1-1/2 million rifles before, had come to an end.

Model 67 (Boy's Rifle)

Model 60A Adds Mechanical Safety

A significant feature of the Model 60A was the incorporation of a mechanical safety in addition to the manual cocking feature. Earlier Winchester single-shots had simply relied on leaving the rifle uncocked until ready to shoot. The cocking piece of the new bolt could be rotated to place the firing pin in either "fire" or "safe" position. The bolt body had a port that allowed the shooter to see the position of the striker, which was marked, first with letters, then with words, to indicate "safe" or "fire."

New, Improved Safety in the Model 67

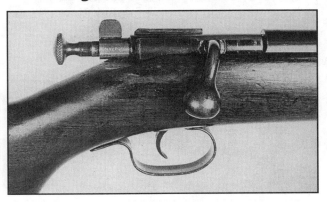

The Model 67 was very similar to the Model 60 it replaced, but had a new and very effective manual safety in addition to its rebounding firing pin. When the rifle had been manually cocked, a turning thumbpiece could be rotated counterclockwise to lock the firing pin. In this locked position, the thumbpiece protruded into the shooter's line of sight, indicating that the safety was engaged. To prepare the rifle to fire, the thumbpiece was turned off to the right. This operation was similar to that of Winchester's centerfire bolt-action, the Model 54, which was in production at the time.

Winchester Manually-Cocked
Single-Shot Bolt-Action 22 Rifles

Model	Dates of Manufacture	Production (approx)	Barrel Length	OAL	Weight (lbs)	Remarks
1900	1900-1902	105,000	18	33-1/4	2-3/4	1st low-price 22
1902	1902-1930	640,000	18	33-1/2	3	used for Junior Rifle Corps
Thumb Trigger	1904-1923	75,000	18	33-5/8	3	No conventional trigger
1904	1904-1931	300,000	21	36-3/4	4	used for Junior Rifle Corps
36	1920-1927	25,000	18	33-1/2	3	9mm shotgun based on 1902
58	1928-1931	40,000	18	33-1/4	3	Low-priced 22
59	1930 only	10,000	23	38-3/4	4-1/2	full-size 22
60	1930-1934	166,000	23, 27	38-3/4	4-1/4	1st curved bolt handle
60A Target	1933-1939	6,000	27	42-3/4	5-1/2	manual safety
67	1934-1962	380,000	27	42-3/4	5	turning thumb safety
68	1934-1946	100,000	27	42-3/4	5	peep sight
677	1937-1939	2,300	27	42-3/4	5-3/4	scope sight only
67 Junior/Boy's Rifle	1937-1963	included w/67	20	34-1/2	4-1/4	name changed after 1950

Note: None of the Winchester manually-cocked single-shot bolt-action 22 rifles were serial numbered, and the exact numbers of certain models are in some doubt. Production totals from different authorities differ somewhat. To provide comparison, the best figures available were rounded off for use in this table.

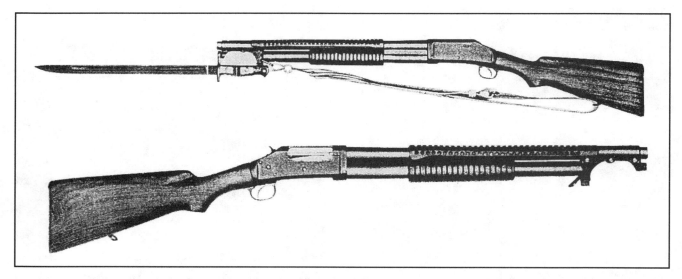

The much used World War II Winchester Model 1897 combat riot shotgun. Although this model was classified "limited standard" in World War II it saw extensive use during that conflict and was still a US Armed Forces item of issue thirty years later.

U.S. WORLD WAR II COMBAT RIOT SHOTGUNS

by Konrad F. Schreier, Jr.

IN 1777, the infant U.S. Army issued ammunition regulations authorizing the preparation and use of buckshot paper cartridges for use in its smoothbore muzzle loading flintlock muskets. At that time shooting buckshot from muskets was a common compensation for the poor accuracy of those smoothbores. The U.S. Army used buckshot loads in smoothbore muzzle loaders until they were replaced by rifles in the Civil War.

When breech-loading shotguns came into general use about the end of the Civil War, the U.S. Army began using them, particularly on our frontiers, to forage for game to supplement their rations. The U.S. Army procured a few shotguns for this use.

In the 1860s and 1870s shotgun shells had to be hand-loaded because moisture caused them to deteriorate quickly. Moisture-resistant shotgun shells and magazine-loading repeating shotguns became available in the 1880s, and the U.S. Army began using both. By this time, shotguns were employed for guard duty as well as for foraging.

In the 1880s civilian express messengers escorting valuable shipments such as gold and silver widely used sawed-off shotguns with shortened barrels as "guard guns". Never officially authorized by the U.S. Army, such guns were procured for use by the guards of its own valuable shipments such as cash payrolls.

When U.S. Armed Forces became involved in the Philippines in the early 1900s, insurgent tribesmen became a serious problem because of their suicide attacks on sentries, guards and outpost. The Army procured sawed-off shotguns to guard against this, and one type which proved very successful was the commercial Winchester Model 1897 pump action 12 gauge "riot" gun. In the Philippines two-man sentry posts had one rifle and one shotgun. They were provided for most outposts and patrol attachments. In many cases, these shotguns stopped attackers when no other weapon did.

By the time World War I began in 1914, the riot gun had become widely used in the U.S. Army although no standard model had been adopted. However, the one soldiers liked best was the six-shot 12-gauge Winchester '97 and the Army procured a substantial number of them.

By this time, the Army authorized issue of two riot shotguns per company, though these shotguns were issued only when the unit commander requested them. That remained true through World War II. The shotguns were issued as unit property, and were issued to soldiers who knew how to use them when, as and if they were required.

When the U.S. went to France in 1917 to fight World War I, units which had them took their riot guns along. Since no other armies used them, these shotguns came as a surprise to friends and foes. Such were even more surprised when they were taken "up front" and used in trench warfare, where the guns quickly proved very effective in this kind of close-quarters combat.

The Imperial German Army was outraged when they encountered American soldiers using riot shotguns

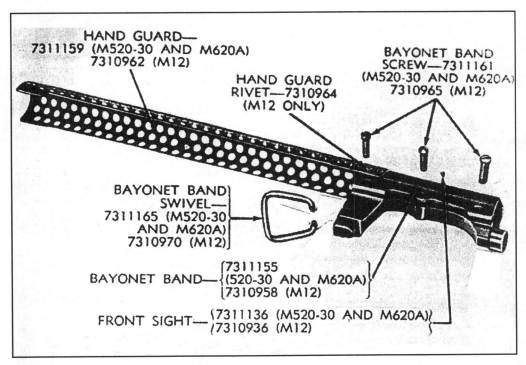

HAND GUARD—
7311159 (M520-30 AND M620A)
7310962 (M12)

HAND GUARD
RIVET—7310964
(M12 ONLY)

BAYONET BAND
SCREW—7311161
(M520-30 AND M620A)
7310965 (M12)

BAYONET BAND
SWIVEL—
7311165 (M520-30
AND M620A)
7310970 (M12)

BAYONET BAND—{ 7311155
(520-30 AND M620A)
7310958 (M12)

FRONT SIGHT—{ 7311136 (M520-30 AND M620A)
7310936 (M12)

This "Bayonet Band Assembly" made the US Army World War II combat riot shotgun unique. There were two standard World War II models of this assembly: The "Type W" (FSN 731097) which was used on the Winchester Model 1897 and Model 12 combat riot shotguns and the "Type S" (FSN 7311175) which was used on the Stevens Models 520-30, 620 and 620A combat riot shotguns. Experimental Bayonet Band Assemblies for the Ithaca Model 37 and Remington Model 31 combat riot shotguns were designed in World War II, but they were only produced in very limited numbers. All these Bayonet Band Assemblies used the standard bayonet for the US cal. .30 Rifle M1917, the "Enfield" bolt action rifle.

in combat. In the summer of 1918, German government sent a protest through the neutral Swiss government threatening to execute any American soldier captured armed with a shotgun. The Germans claimed shotguns violated the Geneva Convention regulating "civilized warfare". The U.S. Government replied that poison gas the Germans had introduced in World War I violated the Geneva Convention and if the Germans executed any American soldiers for using a shotgun they would respond by executing a German soldier. Besides they announced anybody who knew about the U.S. Army knew it had used the shotgun as a part of its armament long before World War I. That ended the German protest.

During World War I, U.S. forces not only used riot shotguns in combat, but also to guard prisoners, and to arm all manner of guards, sentries and outposts. To better adapt

the riot gun for military use, the pump action type in 12-gauge was made standard and several military use modifications were added. It was decided to make these "trench guns," as they were unofficially called, from available commercial shotguns.

Thus, the U.S. Army riot gun got its perforated sheet metal handguard with a mount for the standard bayonet used with the U.S. cal. .30 rifle Model of 1917, the Enfield. It was also equipped with swivels for a standard U.S. military rifle sling. In World War I, the U.S. Army designated these special model pump guns as the 12-gauge Riot Shotgun, Model of 1917.

ter Model 1897 pump gun, and this hammer shotgun proved excellent for military use. The rest were about equally divided between the hammerless Remington Model 1910 and Winchester Model 1912 pump guns. When World War II began in 1939 the U.S. Army still had stocks of all three models on hand.

World War I established the 12-gauge Model of 1917 as standard U.S. Army, Marine Corps

and Navy weapon. During the years between World War I and II, several could be found in every unit's armory available for issue when, as and if required. Army and Marine Corps post guard houses had as many as a dozen of them each for use by prisoner guards and anything else they were suitable for. They were used to guard supplies, equipment and troop movements, and on a few occasions by troops ordered out on riot duty during civil disturbances. They were used by U.S. soldiers and Marines who guarded railway mail cars from the outbreak of train robberies in the period. Every ship in the U.S. Navy carried them as a part of the small arms issue.

During the World War I, over 30,000 Model of 1917 riot shotguns were procured based on three commercial model pump shotguns. About 19,200 of these were based on the rugged, reliable Winches-

The Winchester Model 12 combat riot shotgun which was "standard" in World War II and for many years more. This and the Winchester 97 were the most used types in the US Armed Forces in combat in World War II.

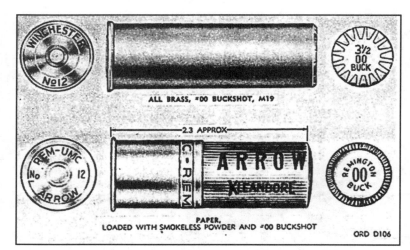

ALL BRASS, #00 BUCKSHOT, M19

2.3 APPROX

ARROW KLEANBORE

PAPER,
LOADED WITH SMOKELESS POWDER AND #00 BUCKSHOT

ORD D106

The 12-gage "00" buckshot load was the only combat riot shotgun shell authorized for combat use in World War II. the top M19 brass shell is the US Army standardized version of the commercial brass case load, the bottom is the standard commercial "high base" paper case load. Brass case shells were procured for their water proofness wanted in rainey tropical areas in the Pacific Theater.

Despite this wide use and availability throughout the forces, there was little or no official training in their care and use. Fortunately, shotgun hunting and skeet and trap shooting were popular sports in the era, so very few troops needed to learn how to handle shotguns.

Before World War II, and to some extent during it, the shotgun manufacturers parts list and use and care publications were widely used in the U.S. Armed Forces. As often as not, when spare parts were needed they were purchased either from the local sporting goods stores or ordered direct from the manufacturer since this was much more efficient than trying to procure them through the U.S. Army Ordnance Department. However, the 12-gauge buckshot-loaded shells were a standard "item of issue" as were the guns.

When the U.S. Army began preparing for World War II in the late 1930s, there was a sudden demand for shotguns for military use. Riot guns were required for new units as they were formed, and for reserve and National guard units called to active duty. Most of this demand was supplied from the existing stocks of World War I riot shotguns in war reserve storage.

During World War I it had been observed that good shooting aircraft pilots and gunners were often also good shotgun shots. In 1939, the U.S. Army, Navy and Marine Corps began using trap and skeet shooting as part of the gunnery training for these aviators, and by 1940 large numbers of commercial shotguns were being procured for this training. By the end of World War II, it was estimated that over 60,000 commercial skeet and trap shotguns had been procured for this use, and some 11,000 of these were procured from the used shotgun market.

At the same time, U.S. Army Ordnance began procuring commercial riot shotguns to arm guards hired to protect factories, depots and many other installations involved in the rearmament program. By the end of World War II, an estimated 50,000 such shotguns, which did not have the military perforated sheet metal handguards, bayonet provisions or sling swivels were procured for this use. Most, if not all, of the self-loading semiautomatic shotguns procured in World War II fell into this class.

In 1940, the Ordnance Department knew the existing stock of World War I combat riot shotguns would not meet the requirements for them, and placed an order for 1,500 Winchester Model 1897s. These were to be exactly like the Model of 1917 version with the perforated metal handguard, bayonet provisions and sling swivels. Since Winchester had not only the original tooling for the military parts but also a stock left over from the World War I production, this was no problem.

Thus, 13,405 combat riot shotguns were delivered in 1942, and when their production was stopped in 1944 with the requirements for them filled, a total of about 75,800 had been delivered. The exact numbers by make and model delivered will never be known. The U.S. Army Ordnance Department purchased shotguns of all types for the entire World War II US Armed Forces under "blanket contracts" which included skeet, trap and all other types. All these shotguns were "com-

This photo of a US Marine Corps "mop up" detachment shows, left to right, a man with a flame thrower, a man with a combat riot shotgun and a man with a M1 Garand rifle. Photos of American GI's or Marines are very unusual, and this one was taken in the Pacific Theater in late 1943.

This photo shows a civilian instructor demonstrating a US Army Air Force shooter in the use of a shotgun equipped with a Lyman-Cutts Compensator muzzle brake. Combat riot shotguns were never used for training aircrew gunners, but this was a very important US Armed Forces use of shotguns in World War II.

mercial standard items procured for military use". In addition, commercial riot guns and military riot shotguns were not separated in procurement records, and spare military shotguns perforated metal handguards with bayonet provisions were used to rebuild and/or modify shotguns to the combat riot gun model at several Ordnance facilities.

The Winchester Model 1897, and their Model 12 which was also procured, were considered the best combat riot guns. An estimated 25,000 of each model were procured. Although the Winchester Model 97 was old-fashioned, with an exposed hammer, and was rated "limited standard" by the U.S. Army, it was a rugged, reliable weapon which saw a great deal of

combat use. The Winchester Model 12 was a hammerless gun classified "standard" by the US Army, and this excellent model also saw a great deal of combat use. Both these Winchester combat riot shotguns were used by the US Armed Forces for decades after World War II.

To fill the requirements for combat riot shotguns the U.S. Army also classified the Stevens Models 520-30, 620 and 620A "standard" when they had 20-inch barrels, the perforated metal hand guard with bayo-

net provisions and sling swivels. A substantial number of these Stevens combat riot shotguns were procured. They were not as well liked at the Winchesters, and they were primarily used by troops stationed in places where they were less likely to engage in combat operations.

The World War I stocks of the Remington Model 1910 riot shotguns were exhausted by 1942, and the few remaining were then withdrawn from combat unit use. The Model 1910 has been discontinued in 1928, and spare parts were not readily available.

Both were classified "standard", but neither the Remington Model 31 or the Ithaca Model 37 combat riot shotguns were placed in production in World War II. Their manufacturers both had other high priority war production contracts to produce other much-needed weapons.

In 1942, the Army published the first, and only, shotgun manuals for World War II, and they remained in use long after the war. TM 9-285, SHOTGUNS, ALL TYPES, September, 1942 included the basic mechanical information troops required to disassemble, assemble and maintain them.
TM 9-1285, SHOT-

This illustration of the World War I Model 1917 combat riot shotguns appeared in the 1918 US Army Ordnance Handbook. The top gun is the Winchester Model 97 practically identical to the World War II model, the bottom the Remington Model 10 which was obsolescent by the time of World War II.

GUNS, ALL TYPES, November, 1942 included the necessary information for ordnance maintenance, repair and overhaul.

Manuals to instruct and/or train soldiers in the use of shotguns in combat were practically non-existent. There was no manual of arms for carrying them, and most troops handled them the way they were taught to handle the BAR Browning Automatic Rifle—always carried at "sling arms". Combat riot shotguns were

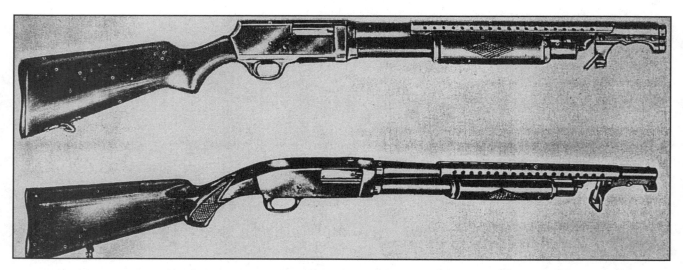

The World War II Remington Model 31 combat riot shotgun. Although this was a "standard" model Remington's involvment in more essential war production prevented its procurment or use by combat units.

seldom, if ever, carried by troops in any parade, review or other formal military formation because they were considered to look "unmilitary".

Since there were no training regulations or manuals for the combat riot shotgun, units had to do it on their own initiative. This required a great deal of ingenuity on the part of their training officers and non-coms. Shotgun hunters in units were called in to help, and they sometimes became soldiers who carried riot guns into combat. Outdoor magazines were often consulted, and so were the shotgun care and use publications of the shotgun manufacturers. These publications did include a few useful hints on using shotguns in combat.

The National Rifle Association's American Rifleman magazine published one of the few "manuals" there was: "The ABC of Practical Riot Gun Instruction" by FBI Agent T. Frank Baughman, in the December, 1942, and January, 1943, issues. It was widely circulated throughout the U.S. Armed Forces, and was the basis for some of the "provisional" combat riot manuals used in many units.

This described a nine-hour shotgun training course with four basic parts: 1. Suitable Guns and Ammunition; 2. Organizing the School; 3.

Conducting the School, and 4. Mechanical Characteristics of the guns to be used. It also included two one-hour sessions of live firing practice. Unfortunately, the number of GI's and Marines who used riot shotguns in combat who received this kind of comprehensive training was never as high as it should have been.

The issue and use of combat riot shotguns was, at best, sketchy and never as well-regulated as it should have been. The long-standing order authorizing issue of two combat riot shotguns per company when requested permitted many units to have them. Some units, particularly in the Pacific Theater, used as many as two per platoon!

Among the few units with combat riot shotguns as a part of their T.O.&E., Table of Organization and Equipment, issue weapons were military police battalions. They were authorized from 34 to as many as 136 depending on their mission. In 1942, the U.S. Marine Corps authorized the issue of 100 combat riot shotguns to infantry regiments as "additional weapons for special operations"! These were part of the Marine regiment's headquarters stock of special ordnance and they were issued as and when required to Marines selected, and possibly trained, to use them. Post-war reviews of the use of weapons in combat indicate that combat riot shotguns were much more used by units in the Pacific Theater than those

in the European Theater, but they were in action both places.

Those weapons-use reviews all comment that the 12-gauge combat riot shotgun was both intimidating and effective when it was used properly. Its three-quarter-inch bore was very impressive. It was an unfamiliar and menacing weapon, particularly with its bayonet fixed. However, World War II records indicate that, like rifle bayonets, shotgun bayonets were not much used in combat.

The standard nine 00 size, .34-inch lead buckshot load used in combat was devastating at 50 yards range, and effective to 75 yards range. This limited range capability made the combat riot shotgun very useful for jungle fighting as it was done in the Pacific Theater. It was also effectively employed in street fighting in cities and towns, and in the "hedgerow" farm country encountered in the European Theater.

At the time World War II began, the 12-gauge buckshot loads issued for combat riot shotguns were all commercial standard ammunition, packed like all commercial shotgun ammunition in 25-shell paperboard shell boxes in wooden cases of 25 boxes. The U.S. Army specification called for special tin-lined wooden boxes for overseas shipments. The

Above is the Stevens Model 520-30 combat riot shotgun and below is the Stevens Model 620A combat riot shotgun, both "standard" in World War II but not much used by combat troops. The Stevens Model 620 was practically identical to the Model 620A. The above shotguns remained US Armed Forces models long after the war.

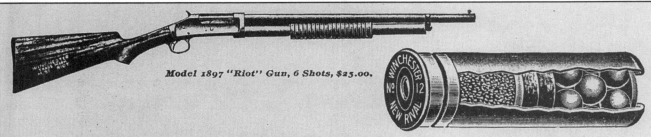

Model 1897 "Riot" Gun, 6 Shots, $25.00.

Buckshot Cartridge.

The Winchester Model 1897 "Riot" gun is made with a 20 inch rolled steel cylinder bore barrel, bored expressly to shoot buckshot. These guns are used by sentries in the U. S. Army, express messengers, watchmen, prison guards, train hands, and by many people for home defense. They are far superior to a revolver for shooting in the dark, where aim is uncertain, as a buckshot cartridge contains nine bullets to one contained by a revolver cartridge. The "Riot" gun has the same action as the regular model 1897. The magazine holds five cartridges, which, with one in the chamber, makes a total of six at the command of the shooter. Price, $25.00.

This ad for the 12-gauge Winchester Model 1897 riot shotgun appeared about 1905. Note it refers to their use "by sentries in the U.S. army". The buckshot shell shown is the paper "low base" type.

preferred load had the standard "high base" waxed paper case; however, a limited amount of brass-case shells were procured for issue in tropical climates in places like Panama and the Philippines.

Early in World War II it was found

The Ithaca Model 37 riot shotgun was "limited standard" and few, if any, were procured with the sheet metal handguard and bayonet provisions for combat use although the version shown was used in non-combat rear areas.

that wet conditions, particularly in the Pacific Theater, was causing paper shot shells in the hands of troops to swell so they would not function properly. The first measure taken to correct this problem was to have the 25 round boxes coated with or covered with a wax paper to make them moisture resistant. In 1944, manufacturers were ordered to pack all 12-gauge buckshot loads in a specified wax-impregnated 25-round moisture-resistant box. This was soon revised with instructions to

pack them in 10-round boxes, 60 boxes to the case, a much more suitable packing for combat issue.

In 1944, the U.S. Army Ordnance Department finally got around to ordering brass case 12-gauge buckshot loads when the shortages of brass to make them lifted. These were made to a specification designated as 12-gauge Shotgun Shell, All Brass, No. 00 Buck, M19, and they were to be packed in ten-round boxes. This became the "standard" shell for use in combat riot shotguns, and it was moisture proof.

Surprisingly no dummy 12-gauge shotgun ammunition for training and ordnance repair shop testing was provided. Such 12-gauge dummies were commercially available, and U.S. Army regulations required the use of

dummies for training and repair shop use. Blank cartridges, which would also have been useful for training, were another type never procured. The lack of these special purpose shells is another indication of the orphan status of World War II U.S. armed forces shotguns.

Despite the lack of training regulations, standardized military models, and regular issue allotments 12-gauge combat shotguns were widely and effectively used by the U.S. Armed Forces in World War II. The shotgun was exclusively a U.S. Armed Forces weapon, never available to the Allies although practically any and every other U.S. weapon was. Few were even provided to Allied units like the Free French who were otherwise completely armed with U.S. arms and equipment. ●

NOTE:

All the information in this article is from official and semi-official U.S. Armed Forces publications, reports and other related documents.

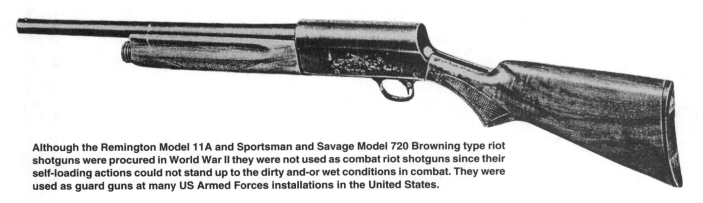

Although the Remington Model 11A and Sportsman and Savage Model 720 Browning type riot shotguns were procured in World War II they were not used as combat riot shotguns since their self-loading actions could not stand up to the dirty and-or wet conditions in combat. They were used as guard guns at many US Armed Forces installations in the United States.

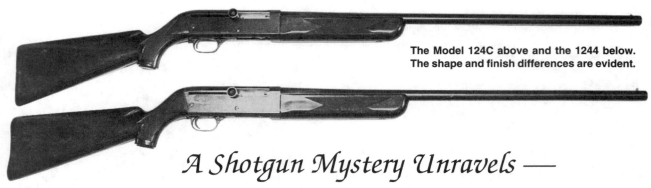

The Model 124C above and the 1244 below. The shape and finish differences are evident.

A Shotgun Mystery Unravels —
The Truth About...

THE SAVAGE CROSS-BOLT

by Larry Sterett

FOUR DIFFERENT books of used gun values in print and two of them refer to the Stevens 124 as either an autoloader or semi-automatic, while one doesn't list it, although this volume does list many other lower-priced single barrel Stevens shotguns. The fourth volume calls it a cross bolt repeater. Which book lists this shotgun correctly, or do any of them? One thing is for sure—some have it wrong.

Historically speaking, THE SHOOTERS BIBLE used to be just that. Most of the various gun descriptions were lifted directly from manufacturer's catalogs. One of the older rumors regarding the value of the "Bible" concerned Army Intelligence having to refer to Stoeger's 1939 edition to determine exactly what they had when the Walther P-38s were first captured in World War II. This edition listed the Walther HP, which was the forerunner of the P-38, for commercial sale in the U.S.; how many, if any, actually reached these shores before the war is not known.

The Model 124 is not listed in the 1953 (No. 44) SHOOTER'S BIBLE, but it is listed in the 1952 edition with a price of $37.50. So at least two of the gun value books have the last production date close to correct. All the "Bible" editions checked had the same coverage for the Model 124, as follows:

STEVENS REPEATING SHOT-
GUN MODEL 124 12 GAUGE
The New-Low Cost
Repeating Shotgun
Now you can be the proud owner of a modern, fast handling, 12 gauge repeating shotgun at a sensationally

low price! Model 124 is the result of Savage determination to produce a "repeater" at a cost low enough for every shooter to afford—without sacrificing either the Savage quality or performance. Savage engineering skill and the most modern methods of precision firearms manufacture made it possible. Perfectly balanced, beautifully streamlined, its **cross bolt action** *is an entirely new departure in repeating shotgun design—simple to operate, lightning fast, smoothly efficient. Latest in a long line of Savage pioneered "Firsts" Model 124 is a new and essentially different repeating shotgun combining outstanding utility, service, and value.*

The new "Stevens 124" is featured by a compactly efficient, fast, simple to operate, CROSS BOLT ACTION that's new in repeating shotgun design. This action is opened by pulling cross bolt out and back...closed by pushing bolt forward and in. Opening stroke of bolt ejects fired shell...closing stroke moved loaded shell from magazine to chamber. FIRING PIN REMAINS LOCKED UNTIL ACTION IS COMPLETELY CLOSED. To open when in firing position, a release is provided at the lower left of receiver. SAFETY— Push button type at forward end of trigger guard. BARREL—Special alloy gun barrel steel, 28" only, modified or full choke. Chambered for 12 gauge 2-3/4" shells. RECEIVER-- Polished and blued. Solid frame, side ejection. Tubular magazine—2 shot capacity—with one shell in chamber making 3 shot repeater.

STOCK and FOREARM--of durable, service-proven, beautiful TEN-ITE. Fine checkering...capped full pistol grip...attractive paneling, fluting and handsome burling give stock custom-built features and appearance. WEIGHT—about 7 lbs. Price $32.45.

Nowhere in that description is there any mention of semi-automatic or autoloading. It is a manually-operated bolt action, and a not turn-bolt, but a modified straight-pull bolt. It may even have been based on the Savage Models 6 and 7, and Stevens Models 57, 85 and 87 rim-fire autoloading rifles. Those rifles had actions which could be used as single shots, bolt action repeaters or as semi-automatic repeaters. When operated manually the bolt was moved forward and pushed to the left to lock into a port in the left receiver wall. Following firing, the bolt knob was pulled straight out to the right, than rearward to eject the fired shell, pushed forward again to chamber a fresh round, and pushed to the left. The Model 124 shotgun functions exactly the same way, except it has no recoil spring and cannot function as an autoloader. The rifle design was introduced around 1938, prior to World War II, and the Model 124 shotgun was not introduced until 1947.

Several Model 124 shotguns have been examined, and all have been similar, but not identical. The two used in this report did not even have the same model designation, although both were marked **STE-VENS**, with the same manufacturers

> **STEVENS Model 124:** autoloader, solid frame, hammerless, 12-ga. only, 28" barrel; improved, modified, full chokes; 2-rd. tube magazine; checkered Tenite plastic stock, forearm. Introduced in 1947; dropped, 1952. Used value, $75 to $85.
>
> That description appeared in a recent edition of a rather large volume of modern gun values. A different publisher of such books doesn't even list it, under either Savage or Stevens, while a third has the following to say:
>
> **Stevens Model 124 Cross Bolt Repeater...$125** Hammerless. Solid frame. 12 gauge only. 2-shot tubular magazine. 28-inch barrel; improved cylinder, modified or full choke. Weight: about 7 pounds. Tenite stock and forearm. Made from 1947 to 1952.
>
> A fourth large tome, stressing identification and values, stated it a bit differently, as follows:
>
> **Stevens Model No. 124**
> **Gauge:** 12
> **Action:** Semi-automatic; side ejection; hammerless
> **Magazine** 2-shot tubular
> **Barrel:** 28" improved cylinder, modified, or full choke
> **Finish:** Blued; checkered plastic, pistol grip stock and forearm
> **Approximate wt:** 7 lbs.
> **Comments:** Manufactured from late 1940's until mid 1950's.
> **Estimated Value: Excellent:** $110.00 **Very Good:** $85.00

name and address, on the left side of the barrel:

Savage Arms Corporation
Chicopee Falls, Mass. USA

Following the name and address, one shotgun was stamped **Model 124C**, while the other one was stamped **Model 1244**. On the right side of the barrel, both shotguns were stamped the same:

Prooftested—12 Gauge
—2-3/4 inch Chamber—

Each shotgun had slightly different features. The Model 124C weighed 7-1/4 pounds, measured 47-3/8 inches in overall length and had a barrel length of 28-1/16 inches. The barrel and receiver both had a blued finish, as did the cocking or charging handle, while the breech bolt had a bright finish. The magazine tube, concealed within the forearm, was also blued, as was the magazine follower, while the lifter in the action was bright.

The Model 1244 weighed 6-3/4 pounds, measured 47-1/4 inches overall, and had a barrel length of 27-7/8 inches. The barrel on this model had a blued finish, but the receiver was color case-hardened finish, just as did some of the receivers on the Model 24 over/under (.22/.410) combination guns. The magazine tube on this model was in the white, with blued follower, while the lifter had a matte black finish. On top the barrel, just forward of the receiver a small

letter **P** was stamped; this letter did not appear on the barrel of the 124C.

The trigger guards on the two shotguns were of a non-ferrous alloy, with a black enamel finish. On the 1244, the blued trigger had a finger-fitting curve to it, while on the 124C the blued trigger as short and quite straight.

The buttstocks and forearms on both shotguns were of TENITE, an *Eastman* plastic, produced by Tennessee Eastman Corporation (Subsidiary of Eastman Kodak Company), Kingsport, Tennessee, and introduced on Stevens shotguns prior to World War II. TENITE was originally introduced on the Stevens No. 530-M double barrel shotgun in 12, 16, 20 Gauge and 410 Bore, the No. 240 over/under 410 Bore shotgun, prior to World War II. Following the War TENITE was used to stock the Stevens Model 124, Stevens Models 311 (double barrel) and 94 (single barrel) shotguns, and the Stevens Model 22-410 over/under, plus the Noble Model 33 slide action rimfire rifle.

The forearms on the two shotguns were nearly identical, U-shaped in cross section, with a round tip, the sides amply covered with excellent integral checkering at 22 lines-per-inch. The buttstocks were different, a feature rather unusual on a lowprice shotgun which apparently had limited production. On the 1244, the length of pull measured 13-3/4 inches, with drops at the comb and heel of 1-5/8 and

2-1/2 inches, respectively, and zero pitch. On the 124C the length of pull was 13-13/16 inches, with drops at the comb and heel of 1-7/16 and 2-15/16 inches, respectively, and with 2-1/8 inches downpitch. The black grip caps were identical, but the black buttplate on the 1244 had a flat surface with horizonally grooved, curved center portion, and smooth toe and butt areas. The buttplate on the 124C had a slightly convex surface, completely covered with checkering. The sides of the pistol grip on both stocks had panels of checkering at 22 lines-per inch, and the black plastic caps graced the based of both grips. Except for the buttplate on the M124C, all checkered surfaces had a two-line border.

The Stevens Model 124, in its various forms, was a good-looking, streamlined—it does have the *appearance* of an autoloader—bolt action repeater. It has twin extractors. It cannot be fired unless the cross bolt/charging handle is securely locked into the left receiver wall, and once locked the breech bolt cannot be retracted unless the bolt release, on the lower left part of the receiver breech, by the trigger guard, is pushed upward. (The bolt release is similar to the same feature found on modern slide action shotguns, such as the old Winchester Model 12, the Mossberg Model 500, etc.) There's a cross bolt safety on the forward bow of the trigger guard; right to "on" and left to "off" or the "fire" postition.

The Stevens Model 124C above, Model 1244 below. Note the difference in the shape of the triggers, and the position of the screw head below the charging knob.

During conversations with Roe Clark, non-resident Savage-Stevens historian, he confirmed there was at least four variations in the overall production of 75,000 Model 124 Cross Bolt Action Shotguns. These included a 124 and 124B, in addition to the 124C and 1244. (The 1950 *Component Parts Price List For SAVAGE, STEVENS, FOX Shotguns and Rifles* lists Model 124, 124A and 124B shotguns, but the 1951 Component Parts....issued November 1, 1951, lists Stevens Models 124 - 124B - 124C 12 Gauge Repeating Cross Bolt Action Tubular Magazine Shotguns.) Reason? Whenever a change was made, a letter was added so if repair parts were ordered later, the correct ones could be provided. In those days, shotguns were not required to have serial numbers, and most of the lower priced models did not.

The 1244 was apparently a special version for a large retailer, back before house brand names, such as Hawthorn, J.C. Higgins, Ranger, Revelation, and Western Field became popular. There have always been house brand names, but some of the above are post World War II.

Mr. Clark also stated the Model 124 was not listed in the February 1948 issue Savage catalog, or in the 1952 catalog. However, if the shotgun was introduced in late 1948, it might not have appeared in the February, 1948 catalog. The fact that it is mentioned in the 1952 publications is probably due to the fact that most annuals, such as the GUN DIGEST and SHOOTER'S BIBLE are

pre-dated; the 1995 edition is assembled and printed in 1994, at which time the Model 124 was still in production. It would not have appeared in 1953 editions, printed in 1952, because it was no longer in production.

Thus, the Model 124 and its variants can safely be assumed to have been in production from 1948 to sometime in 1951. An added clincher is the following from the 4th edition of the GUN DIGEST (1949) printed in 1948:

STEVENS MODEL 124 CROSS BOLT ACTION REPEATING SHOTGUN

This cross bolt action is new (1948) in repeating shotgun design. Opened by pulling cross bolt out and back—closed by pushing forward and in. Opening stroke of bolt ejects fired shell, closing stroke moves loaded shell from magazine to chamber. Firing pin remains locked until action is completely closed. Push button type of safety at forward end of trigger guard. Special alloy gun barrels 28" only, modified or full choke. Chambered for 2-3/4" shells in 12 gauge only. Solid frame, side ejection. Tubular magazine—2 shot capacity with one shell in chamber making 3 shot repeater. Checkered tenite stock and forearm. Capped full pistol grip. Weight about 7 lbs.

Note that no mention is made above of improved cylinder being available as a choke choice. However, the 5th edition of the GUN DIGEST (1951), published in 1950,

states under the Stevens Model 124 Cross Bolt Repeating heading:

Barrel: Alloy steel, 28" only, Imp. Cyl., Mod. or Full

The first edition of the OFFICIAL GUN BOOK, published in 1950, had this listing:

STEVENS MODEL 124
Gauge: 12 only

Action: Cross bolt repeater. Hammerless. Chambered for 2-3/4" shells. Tubular magazine has 2-shot capacity, with one shell in chamber making 3-shot. Opened by pulling cross bolt out and back, closed by pushing bolt forward and in. Opening stroke of bolt ejects fired shell, closing moves loaded shell from magazine to chamber. Side ejection. Push button safety at forward end of trigger guard.

Stock: 13-3/4" x 1-1/2" x 2-3/4". Tenite. Checkered, capped, full pistol grip. Fluted comb. Checkered forearm.

Barrel: 28" improved cylinder, modified, or full choke.

Other Data: Solid frame. Overall length 48". Weight about 7 lbs. About $32.

History: First manufactured in 1947.

Neither of the two shotguns examined for this article had an indication of the degree of choke marked on the barrel, although the 124 was advertised as being available in improved cylinder, modified and full choke. Checking the bore diameters revealed the 1244 to measure 0.725-inch, with 8 points of constriction, while the 124C had a bore diameter of 0.727-inch, with 32 points of con-

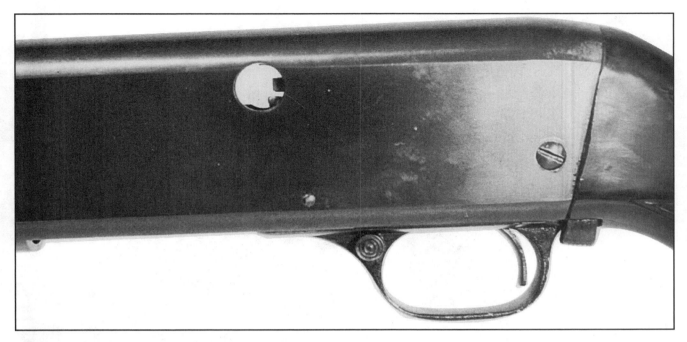

Left side of the 124C with the breech bolt withdrawn. Again, note the crossbolt safety—this end is actually painted red, the shape of the trigger, and the breech bolt release.

striction. This would make them improved cylinder and full choke, respectively, although a bit light.

Another discovery, which seemed a bit unusual, was a 1/2-pound difference in weight, for what appeared to be minor design modifications. Nothing visible could account for this weight difference. In the center of the buttplate of each of the TENITE stocks is a large slotted head steel plug to allow access to the stock bolt. Unscrewing the plugs revealed the 1244 stock to be entirely hollow, while the 124C stock was partially filled with a large hardwood block, held in position by an integral internal rib; since the buttplates are chemically welded to the stock butt, the

hardwood block had to be inserted at the factory.

The 1244 stock did not have any integral internal rib to hold a block in position.

Based on Savage/Stevens literature, pertinent firearms literature of the era, conversations with Mr. Clark, and personal observation, it appears this non-autoloading Stevens shotgun was manufactured in five slightly different forms. Included were the Models 124, 124A, 124B, 124C, and 1244. Other than the already noted differences in the buttstocks, trigger shapes, safety, receiver, lifter and magazine tube finishes, and charging handle knob grooves (actually the cross bolt knob

or the locking bolt knob) there were others, less noticeable. Internally, the cartridge stop, release lever and release lever spring, mainspring and mainspring plunger, and the hammer were slightly different, depending on the model designation.

Since the 124C and 1244 shotguns examined did not have choke designations stamped on the barrels, it was decided to pattern them at 40 yards. Locating shotshells manufactured in the late 1940s and early 1950s was out of the question; the next logical choice was to use some paper-cased Federal Extra-Lite Trap loads containing 1-1/8 ounces of size 7-1/2 lead shot, or an average of 433 pellets per shell by

The 124C with the breech bolt drawn to the rear, a shell caught by the extractors ready to load.

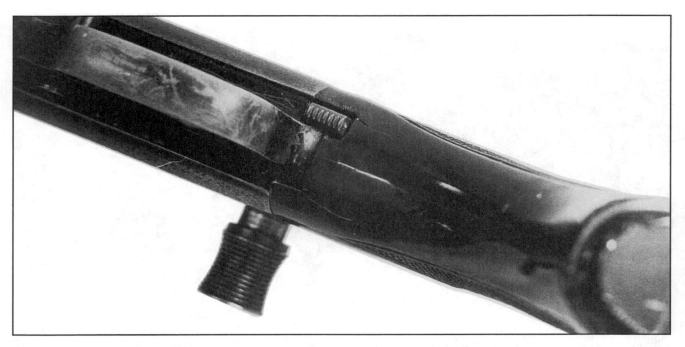

Most of the 124 shotguns examined have had one or more cracks on the underside of the tenite stock at the junction of the buttstock/receiver, as shown here on the 1244. The tenite did not prove to be quite as durable as Eastman Kodak had thought.

actual count. (Plastic-tubed shotshells were still a decade-plus in the future when the Stevens 124 shotguns were introduced; only paper-cased or metal-cased shells were available for shotgun use.) The other catch was the plastic wad column in current shells; such wads with integral shotcup were not available during the time the Stevens 124 was manufactured. The introduction of the plastic shotcup sometimes increased the choke designation of a shotgun one entire designation, or one-quarter choke, such as from 3/4-choke to full choke, or from modified choke to full choke.

The 124C was patterned first at 40 yards, using the Federal load, with five shots being fired to obtain an average. This barrel had 32 points of constriction, which should have made it a light full choke, or possibly even tight improved modified choke. It actually produced patterns averaging 76.2 percent, with 40.0 percent of this total in the four center fields of the 16-field patterning target. The patterns were centered just over an inch below and slightly less than 3-1/2 inches to the left of the point-of-aim.

The 1244 was patterned second, following the same procedure. This barrel, which had 8 points of constriction, placing it in the improved cylinder range, actually produced patterns averaging 73.9 percent, of which 37.2 percent of the pellets were in the center fields. These patterns were centered slightly less than 1-3/4 inches below and just under 1-1/2 inches to the left of the point-of-aim. The plastic wad column definitely exerted an influence on these patterns.

The Stevens 124 single barrel shotguns were not autoloaders, but cross bolt repeaters. The design was reliable, with a number of unusual features for a bolt action shotgun, and our two shotguns produces good, sound patterns. The major problem with the entire series seems to have been the tenite buttstock cracking at the buttstock/receiver junction; cold weather apparently added to the problem. The Model 530-M and 311 doubles may also have had this problem, and to a lesser degree the 22-410. With a hardwood stock and forearm, the Model 124 and its variants might have lasted another couple of decades, but regardless, it is a bolt-action repeater, not an autoloader. ●

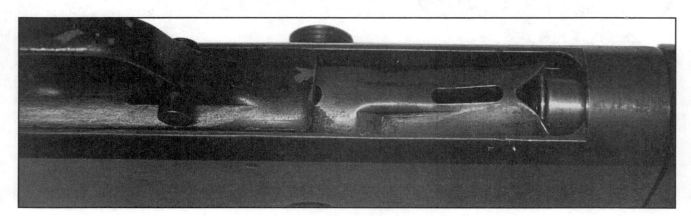

The underside of the 124C, a shell ready to slide onto the lifter later. The shotgun is locked at this point.

MY HI-POWER ISN'T.....

.....but for what I want to to, what a lot of hunters want, it will do fine.

By. B.R. Hughes

Back in those halcyon days when the current century was young, smokeless powder was a new and exciting—if mysterious—element on the hunting fields of the world. Cartridges such as the 25-35, 6.5 Mannichler-Schoenauer, 7x57 Mauser, 30-40 Krag, *et al* were quickly replacing previously popular black powder hulls like the 40-60 Winchester, 44-60 Sharps. and 45-75 Winchester.

Not only did the increased velocities made possible by smokeless powder make it easier to hit game targets at ranges exceeding 100 yards, the recoil was less and the absence of a cloud of smoke made follow-up shots, should they be needed, a stronger probability. Perhaps even more impressive, animals struck with properly placed bullets traveling in the neighborhood of 2000 feet per second, or even faster, seemed to go down very quickly.

Because of this, it occurred to some that the key to quick, clean kills was not bullet diameter or bullet weight, but velocity. It was into this atmosphere that Arthur W. Savage formed the Savage Repeating Arms Co. on April 5, 1894, and the firm's first rifle, the Model 1895, was introduced shortly thereafter. It was initially chambered in 303 Savage, which was a decidedly different cartridge than the 303 British. The Savage entry featured a 190 grain bullet leaving the muzzle at an advertised 1890 fps. It was clearly designed to compete with Winchester's new 30-30, also introduced in 1898, which shoved a 160 grain slug at a muzzle velocity of somewhat less than 2000 fps.

This form of 99 is very comfy in the woods.

The Savage 1895 was a hit! Modern in design even by today's standards, this hammerless lever-action possessed a rotary magazine, a cartridge counter which allowed the user to keep count of how many shells remained in the magazines, and a reputation for reliability and accuracy. A slight modification was made in 1899, and thus was born one of the genuine legends of American shooting circles—the Savage 99. Quickly, the company added four Winchester cartridges to the chamberings for which the M1899 was available: 25-35, 30-30, 32-40 and 38-55. But none of these were in any sense of the word truly revolutionary, even in the early 1900s.

In 1912, Charles Newton, a cartridge designer, took the 25-35 case, sized the neck down to .228 inch, and with a 70 grain bullet he was able to achieve velocities of an announced 2800 fps, which meant that in order to arrive at 200 yards, the slug only had to achieve a mid-range trajectory of three inches! This was pretty hot stuff in those days! Arthur Savage quickly made his 99 for it, and the combination became a hit. The new cartridge was dubbed the 22 Savage Hi-Power, and the peculiar spelling of "high" is the version preferred by Savage.

Rather quickly, the new offering became known as the 22 Imp, but I have been unable to come up with the source of this name. Originally offered as the Model 1899-H, a lightweight, takedown model with a 20 inch barrel, it was obviously made with hunters in mind, not accuracy buffs. Later, the Hi-Power was offered in other versions of the Savage lever-action, including the M99-E, a solid-frame lightweight model; the M99-G, a deluxe takedown rifle with a checkered pistol-grip stock; the M99-EG, similar to the M99-G, but with a solid frame; and the M99-T solid frame featherweight with a semi-beavertail-type forearm.

Kissin' cousins! From left to right, the 30-30 Winchester, the 25-35 Winchester, and the 22 Savage Hi-Power, all based on the 25-35 case, which was first introduced in 1894, a year before the 30-30 and 18 years before the Savage.

The cartridge was not noted for accuracy. Some reported obtaining groups that ran from five to six inches at 100 yards, while others, perhaps luckier or simply better shots, wrote that their Imps shot into three inches or so, all of this performed with the aid of iron sights. Some have suggested that the takedown feature was responsible for the lack of tackhole accuracy, but I have shot several takedown M99's over the years, and without excep-

tion, they would all stay around three to four inches at 100 yards, without benefit of a scope.

Intended for game up to pronghorn antelope and whitetail deer, human nature being what it was and is, it wasn't long before the Hi-Power was used on much larger game, and it quickly developed an avid following in Alaska and Canada. Many of those who were successful in dumping game such as bear, elk and moose with the 22 Savage wrote glowing letters of praise, many of which were published in the shooting journals of that day. I remember reading many years ago of a missionary who served in Asia between the World Wars, and who, armed with a 22 Imp, shot and killed a man-eating tiger. It was obvious the missionary knew little or nothing about guns, because he saw nothing of a remarkable nature regarding that shot. Another writer indicated that while he had used a 405, 35 WCF, 30-06 and 40-82, never had he enjoyed so much satisfaction as he did when hunting with a 22 Savage Hi-Power!

As for most hunters this writer's age, a scope really helps.

It was correspondence of this type that ultimately gave the Imp a bad name, because there simply is no magic in a .228-inch 70 grain slug driven at 2800 fps! Of course the manufacturer certainly did nothing to temper such enthusiasm, as may be noted from this excerpt from Savage's 1914 catalog pertaining to the 22 Hi-Power: "Greater velocity, accuracy, penetration and actual killing power than any other rifle made in the United States...Penetrates 1/2 inch steel boiler plate."

In the meantime, Newton quickly realized that he could do better and in 1913, he developed one of the truly great centerfire cartridges of this century—the 250-3000. But the Hi-Power continued to sell and to be overmatched by optimistic hunters; gradually its popularity waned. Savage had dropped the Imp in all versions from production by 1941, but cartridges continued to be loaded in this country until 1959.

No American-made 22 Hi-Power other than those bearing the Savage label were made, although the

Some previous owner, who took very good care of the 22 Imp now in the author's possession, had this small compass inletted into the stock.

There are at least a couple of current sources for 22 Hi-Power reloading dies. Hughes' were made by Hornady, and they work just fine!

round did appear occasionally in European combination guns; on the Continent it was known as the 5.6x52R. Indeed, the round became popular enough in Europe to encourage Norma to load ammunition for it for a number of years. In this country, at one time or another, it was loaded by Peters, Remington, Savage, and Winchester. The last over-the-counter ammo commercially produced was made by Canadian Industries Limited, and CIL fodder was available for approximately a decade after it was dropped by the American firms.

Should you have a good 22 Savage Hi-Power, ammunition need be no problem. Dies are available from at least two sources, and mine were made by Hornady. This same firm still offers a suitable bullet in the form of a .227 inch spire point with a sectional density of .194. Not brisk sellers, these slugs *are* available, although your dealer may have to order them for you. Yes, the original 22 Imp projectiles were .228 inch but the missing thousandth does not seem to be a critical loss.

My Savage Model H shoots handloads of the Hornady bullet somewhat more accurately than it does CIL factory loads and the traditional .228 inch slugs. I might add that my supply of CIL ammo was bought at a gun show at collector prices, and it grieves me to touch one off at two bucks per pop! In a pinch, readily-available .224 inch bullets can be used in the 22 Hi-Power, although I do note a slight decrease in accuracy.

When it comes to cases, you can do what Charles Newton did over 80 years ago—neck down 25-35 Winchester cases. As these lines are written, such cases are still plentiful, but if you find a supply, I suggest you stock up, because I don't believe they'll be available much longer. If you use 30-30 cases you should run them through a 25-35 sizing die before squeezing them down to 22 inch to prevent "wrinkles" in the shoulder of the case.

When I first set out to work up a good load, I got lucky. One of the first I tried was 25.0 grains of IMR 3031 powder behind the 70-grain Hornady bullet. It didn't seem to matter if I used CCI or Winchester primers, because this load regularly plunked three slugs into slightly less than three inches at 100 yards, shooting off a bench. Occasionally, when everything is working just right, I get groups that hover around two inches.

Some previous owner of my rifle did me a favor when he or she had it drilled and tapped for scope bases. Had this M1899 been undrilled when I purchased it, I wouldn't have been brazen enough to alter it, but the modification made it a simple task indeed to mount an elderly K4 Weaver on it. Too, the presence of those four holes in the receiver knocked about two hundred bucks off the price I paid. My load, incidentally, comes very close to original factory ballistics.

Should you try it, I urge you to begin at 23.0 grains of IMR 3031 and work up carefully a half-grain at a time, backing off a full grain at the first signs of excess pressure. This load is perfectly safe in my rifle, but it may not be in yours. Since the 70 grain bullet wasn't the only load provided by the factories, and Hornady's .227 inch slug is the only one

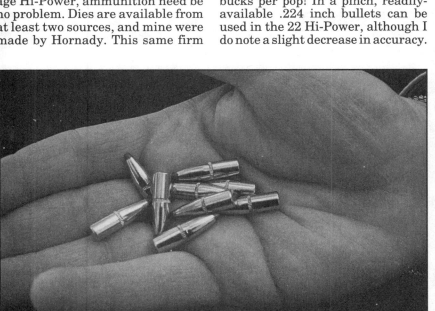

The most practical bullet for reloading the Hi-Power at the present time is the Hornady 70 grain .227" slug, shown here.

The original rear sight on the Model-H is adjustable for both elevation and windage, and it bears Savage markings. The scope mount hole is not original.

This serrated button on the underside of the forearm is the takedown device. When it is pushed, and the action open, the barrel can be rotated a quarter-turn and removed.

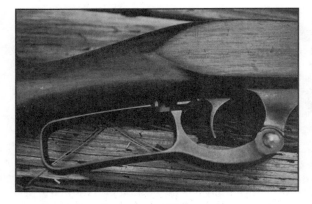

The lever is a bit squarish in shape, and the absence of a pistol-grip is a common finding on early Savages. Note that the safety is capable of locking the lever when in the "on" position.

readily available today, there simply isn't a lot of variety in shooting a 22 Imp.

The only alteration on my Savage other than the holes for the scope mount was the inletting of a small compass in the stock, which I find a bit appealing, because it indicates a real person took this rifle hunting, and provided very good care of it in the process. I'll try to give it proper attention too, and I hope that some future owner will be appropriately appreciative.

Will I take it hunting? Probably. On the land where I generally hunt whitetails, there is a stand in heavy cover where it is virtually impossible to see more than 100 yards or so in any direction. I am of the opinion that the 70-grain Hornady will promptly dispatch even a large buck with a properly placed shot at this distance. Too, it should be nearly ideal for javelinas, which seldom weigh more than 50 pounds or so. I won't ask more of it than that and, truth be known, if this is all anyone had ever asked of the 22 Savage Hi-Power, it would probably still be on the current production list!   •

Many of the early Savage lever actions were fitted by the factory with tang sights. Shown here is a Model G with a Lyman version.

BROWNING Gold.
THE SEMI-AUTO SHOTGUN FOR THE NEXT 100 YEARS.

NEW Stalker Gold Shotgun
$735 (suggested retail)

BETTER MAGAZINE CAPACITY. BETTER BALANCE. BETTER HANDLING. BETTER HURRY.

On February 8, 1900, John M. Browning filed for a patent on the world's first semi-automatic shotgun — the Auto-5. It has taken nearly 100 years to produce its equal. The Browning Gold.

You will find a well-proportioned, lightweight aluminum receiver gives the Gold better between-the-hands balance and a more natural swing compared to shorter, steel receivers.

The Gold's one-of-a-kind gas system uses no complicated O-ring systems or intricate linkages. And superior engineering houses that simple, self-cleaning gas system beneath a sleek forearm without hampering magazine capacity like some autoloaders.

A shorter piston throw and a self-lubricating composite slide reduce wear and contribute to the Gold's reliability and longevity.

With the bolt locked back, its speed loading feature automatically sends the first shell thumbed into the magazine directly to the chamber where it is ready to be fired.

Best of all, it's as easy on your shoulder as it is your wallet.

Available in the following models: 20 gauge Hunter, 12 gauge 3" and 3 1/2" magnum Hunter and Stalker, Deer Special and Sporting Clays.

CALL FOR YOUR FREE CATALOG TODAY.

Call 1-800-333-3504 to receive our 100-page catalog full of the latest in firearms and accessories.

BROWNING
THE BEST THERE IS.

The Most Powerful .50 cal. Muzzleloader in the World!
(no disc required)

240 Grain XTP™ Bullets with T/C Mag Express™ Sabots

ENCORE 209x50 MAGNUM ™

The Encore 209 x 50 Magnum Muzzleloader is the most reliable, accurate, long range muzzleloader ever produced.

- It's a "minute of angle" muzzleloader based on a proven single shot break open action.

- 26" barrel of 4140 rifle grade steel, button rifled with a 1 in 28" twist.

- Designed to handle magnum loads of up to 150 grains of FFG Black Powder or the Pyrodex® equivalent. Also handles 3 of the new 50 grain Pyrodex® Pellets with impressive results...

  - **Muzzle velocity of 2203 feet per second**
    (using 240 grain XTP™ Bullet and T/C Mag Express Sabot)
  - **Muzzle energy equal to a 7mm Rem. Mag.**
  - **Lethal at 200 yards!**

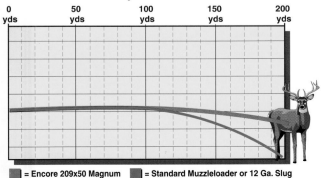

= Encore 209x50 Magnum   = Standard Muzzleloader or 12 Ga. Slug

- Closed breech design and 209 shotgun primer ignition assures firing in the most adverse conditions.

- "Universal Breech Plug" allows for quick, reliable ignition with both loose powder or Pyrodex® Pellets.

- The easiest cleaning muzzleloader on the market today. There is no striker or breech area to clean. Because of the sealed ignition chamber, all fouling is contained in the barrel.

- With T/C's Patented QLA™ Muzzle System (#9,639,981) loading is a snap. Exact bullet alignment, shot after shot produces greater accuracy.

- An exposed hammer with an automatic hammer block (Pat. Pend.) makes it the most "user friendly" muzzleloader you can buy, and one of the fastest to get into action.

And, if that's not enough, when the special season is over, it only takes a few seconds to remove the .50 caliber muzzleloader barrel and install your favorite centerfire rifle barrel. Same frame, same feel, same confidence.

No other company gives you this much versatility, and no other company can provide you with a muzzleloader that you'd swear was a centerfire rifle... and it can be, by merely switching barrels.

T/C is #1 In Muzzleloading

THOMPSON/CENTER
One Shot...No Room For Compromise

Rochester, New Hampshire 03866
603-332-2333 • http://www.tcarms.com

The Variety in Airgun Projectiles

much more than BBs...

by J.I. Galan

The Air Power Sabot Cannon could shoot special steel darts, ball bearings and even a load of buckshot.

Ask the vast majority of folks out there what an airgun is and chances are, about eight out of ten times, the response will be: "a BB gun." The other respondents may go so far as to say "A pellet gun." I am willing to bet a case of your favorite holy water that no one will say "Dart gun."

This is hardly surprising. Most of us grew up with the omnipresent BB gun as our passport to imaginary adventures battling all sorts of bad guys and/or ferocious beasts. In the process, in most cases, we managed to acquire a modicum of prowess in marksmanship and shooting safety procedures that served us well as we moved on to "real" guns. Copper-colored steel BBs and diabolo-style lead pellets symbolize our concept of airgun ammo.

In our real world, however, the ubiquitous airgun BBs and lead pellets were developed less than a hundred years ago. Long before them, darts and other projectiles were the norm for airguns.

One of the earliest reliable written records dealing with an airgun and its projectiles is that of the so-called "Magdeburg Air Rifle" developed by a German named Otto von Guericke near the mid-1600s. A period illustration of von Guericke's precharged pneumatic gun shows a device that looks more like a light artillery piece, than a shoulder-fired gun. A version of this early airgun reportedly could shoot iron balls weighing four pounds with enough oomph to penetrate thick wooden boards at 400 yards.

Going much farther back, there are chronicles regarding certain Greek inventors who may have applied pneumatic boosters to some of the huge crossbow-like siege machines of the time. One such lad was named Ctesibius (or Ctesiphus) and lived in Alexandria, Egypt, around 100 B.C. Although not an airgun in the literal sense of the term, Ctesibius' pneumatic-assisted catapult was apparently able to hurl large stones with great power. Thus, stones sort of qualify as airgun projectiles as well.

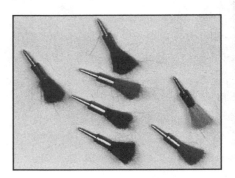

Modern airgun darts are not much different from those employed in bellows airguns of the past.

The first shoulder-fired airguns we know of originated in Central Europe sometime between the 15th and 16th centuries. Some of the early European airguns utilized a bellows power plant and shot carefully crafted darts with extreme accuracy. Bellows airguns and their darts were employed mostly in indoor target shooting by the upper classes. By the 17th century, bellows airguns had reached a very high level of sophistication, rivaling many of today's world-class match air rifles in quality and precision. Bellows guns and their darts were produced by highly specialized craftsmen in a wide assortment of calibers, generally between 4.5 mm (.177 in.) and 6.33 mm (.25 in.).

In contemporary times, however, airgun darts have been relegated to a relatively minor role in the overall realm of airgun ammunition. Although they are still produced by several companies, most of today's mass-produced darts come in .177 caliber and are intended for low-power, budget-priced smoothbore airguns. Since most modern airgun darts have steel bodies, they must never be used in rifled bores. In addition, their rather steep cost vis-à-vis BBs and pellets makes them less desirable for practically all shooting pursuits.

One clever solution to the problem of using steel darts in rifled bores is the so-called "ballistic bolt." This flechette-like .177 in. steel dart has a plastic rear half that rides the rifling, allowing its use in a wide variety of rifled airguns. Instead of the traditional fiber tufts used for tails or bases, ballistic bolts have four arrow-like vanes. Keep in mind that

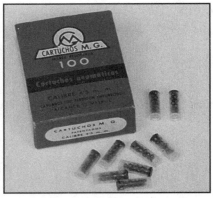

These 177-caliber plastic shotshells worked in standard airguns. Maximum effective range on small targets was perhaps to 10 yards.

regular airgun darts are normally shot out of low-power airguns only. Ballistic bolts, on the other hand, can be shot in many higher power air rifles and air pistols, making their recovery and reuse a very difficult proposition in the best of cases, given their needle-like points and awesome penetrative capabilities.

A very different and highly specialized type of dart used in airguns in recent times is the "capture" dart. As its name implies, this projectile finds use in situations involving mostly the capture of wildlife, although it can also be employed most satisfactorily to subdue a variety of specimens belonging to the human race. Airgun capture darts are comparatively large and are, in reality, flying syringes with a thick hypodermic needle that enables the tranquilizing drug in the dart to be injected quickly.

Most capture airgun darts have ranged in caliber from .25 in. all the way up to .68 in. or so. The guns employed have been primarily standard production CO_2 or pneumatic models modified by a specialist company by adding a smoothbore barrel of the desired caliber. Interestingly,

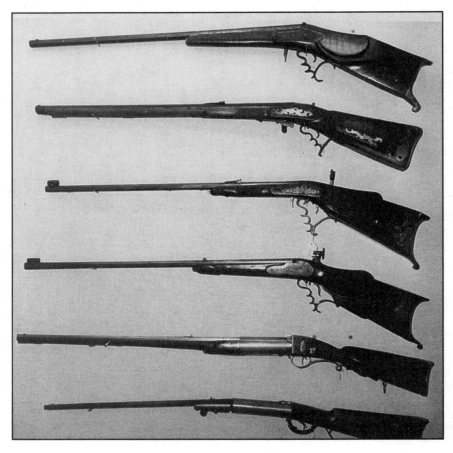

The top four specimens are tyical examples of European bellows airguns from centuries gone by. They shot special darts with a high level of precision.

Benjamin Sheridan introduced three 50-caliber capture dart airguns—one pistol and two long guns—in 1997.

Although those highly accurate and exquisitely crafted bellows airguns with their expensive precision darts played an important part in the dawn of European airgunning, it was the potent precharged pneumatic gun that put airguns onto a new and far deadlier plateau. By the early 1700s the production of powerful precharged pneumatic guns was rather widespread throughout Central Europe and England. Airgun lore is chock-full of accurate information on those powerful guns. Most of them shot musket-type lead balls ranging in size from around 30 to over 50-caliber. There is ample proof that these pneumatic rifles were potent enough to kill deer and wild boar. Landgrave Ludwig VIII of Hesse in what is now Germany was a dedicated airgun enthusiast and by 1750 had taken quite an array of large game animals with his big-bore pneumatic guns.

In war, too, the wind-powered musket ball left its trail of bodies. The powerful pneumatic rifles developed by Batholomeo Girandoni during the closing years of the 18th century were employed by a special troop of Austrian sharpshooters with great effect against Napoleon Bonaparte's troops. These 51-caliber precharged pneumatic rifles had magazines with capacity for 20 lead balls and an effective range of approximately 150 yards.

The SABO was a thoroughly unconventional airgun pellet (or bullet) produced in England during the 1980's.

Following well over one hundred years of hibernation, the concept of a truly powerful airgun that can shoot heavy projectiles capable of taking deer-size game animals began to make a comeback during the 1980s. In 1989, the AirrowA-8S Stealth was introduced, produced by Swivel Machine Works in Milford, CT. The A-8S had a fairly close outward resemblance to the Colt AR-15 rifle and was designed to shoot broadhead-tipped hunting arrows at muzzle velocities

This pistol version of the Mega-Dart shot 38 caliber blowgun darts with impressive power.

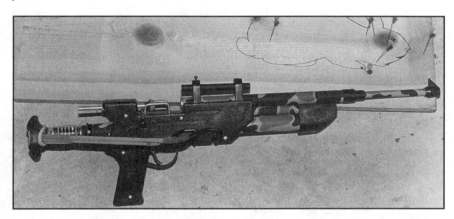

(above) The Mega-Dart MX-7 could shoot blowgun-type steel darts at velocities exceeding 500 fps.

(left) Another unusual airgun projectile from England in the 1980s was the Prometheus, with a zinc head and synthetic skirt.

(below) This one-of-a-kind experimental CO_2 gun from the 1980s shot special crossbow-type bolts and was intended as a hunting weapon.

The Airrow A-8S Stealth is powered by CO2 or compressed air and can shoot a heavy hunting arrow with lots of power and precision.

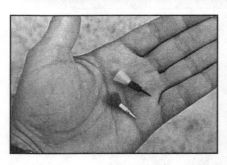

Steel airgun darts have been produced by a variety of manufacturers in a variety of popular calibers. Shown: a 177 and a 22.

The ever-popular Crosman 1100 CO2 shotgun can also shoot a variety of 38 caliber projectiles rather effectively.

approaching 500 fps, propelled by either CO_2 or compressed air. Different versions of the basic Stealth gun were produced, some designed for line-throwing in marine environments. Then, the Model A-8SRB (Stealth Rifled Barrel) could shoot bullet-like projectiles in a variety of popular calibers. Still, the original arrow-shooting Stealth remained the most popular model, taking a respectable number of deer, boar and wild turkey in recent years.

Besides hunting-type arrows, certain airguns in recent years have been designed to shoot blowgun darts, as well as other less conventional projectiles. One such gun, produced in Texas during the mid-1980s, was the Mega-Dart. This un-

There's no doubt that the A-8S Stealth is capable of taking a variety of game animals. (Photo: Swivel Machine Works.)

usual gun employed a rubber band-driven piston as the power plant that propelled modern 38-caliber steel blowgun darts at rather fearsome velocities.

A few years after the Mega-Dart came along, the Air Power Sabot Cannon was introduced. This pre-charged pneumatic bazooka-like contraption could shoot a variety of unusual projectiles, including a heavy blunt-tipped steel dart, ball bearings, paintballs and even a sizable load of bird shot. The Air Power Sabot Cannon, while not a commercial success—it remained in production less than two years—did nevertheless illustrate in a most dramatic fashion that all sorts of projectiles, other than BBs and diabolo pellets, are still being shot out of a variety of airguns.

The Selector pistol offered a selection of special-purpose defense projectiles.

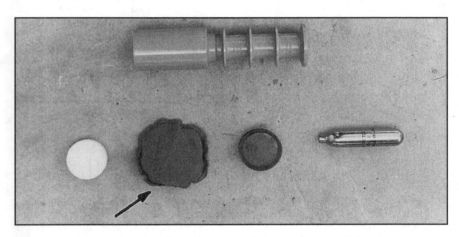

The Prowler-Fouler's beanbag weighed nearly seven ounces and could flatten a fully grown two-legged predator with a solid hit.

Incidentally, firing a load of shot from an airgun, shotgun style, has been around for a very long time as well. Even now there are rather powerful CO_2 and pneumatic shotguns produced in such diverse places as South Korea and England. One of them, called the Farco, has also been used successfully to kill deer and wild boar employing a saboted .433 in. caliber lead ball. The U.S. is no stranger to pneumo scatterguns, either, with such classics as the Paul 420, Vincent, Plainsman 28-S and the 1960s vintage Crosman 1100. All of these were capable of firing a fairly respectable load of shot with a creditable pattern at 20 to 30 yards, and with enough power to bring down doves and small birds.

In the realm of self-defense applications, airguns with highly specialized projectiles have also been produced in recent years. Beginning in the late 1960s, a variety of mostly CO_2-powered devices have been

marketed that shot all sorts of projectiles such as blunt impact, chemical agents and even exploding munitions. One of these was called the Selecter, a 72-caliber smooth-bore pistol powered by CO_2. Another rather impressive personal defense CO_2 device from the early 1970s was the Prowler-Fouler. Shaped rather like a fat flashlight, the Prowler-Fouler could shoot a 3-inch-diameter "beanbag" projectile weighing nearly seven ounces with

enough force to flatten even a grown man.

Undoubtedly, the most unusual of all the projectiles shot from airguns throughout history have been huge artillery shells. One of the most incredible examples of the above involves the large pneumatic guns, also called "dynamite guns," aboard the USS Vesuvius, a light cruiser which saw action during the Spanish-American War of 1898-1902. Using compressed air, the guns of the Vesuvius reportedly could deliver 14-3/4-inch-diameter shells measuring approximately 7 feet in length at a range of roughly 1ness of those huge air-propelled shells with their 250-pound warhead of high explosives was not apparently significant in deciding the outcome of any battle, their existance sure shows most vividly the variety of air-powered projectiles used throughout history. ●

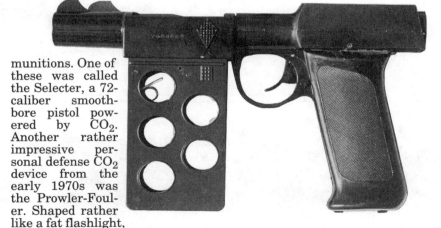

A "noise/confusion" exploding shell from the Selecter could get people's attention or even ruin a perpetrator's day.

The Last Mannlicher

Hungary's 35M came very late to the world's bolt-action party

by Paul S. Scarlata

Private Lajos Grosz's only concern was to try and keep up with his comrades. In spite of the entreaties and threats of their officers, the column of dispirited troops just kept moving west as fast as their frozen, blistered feet could take them. What in hell were they doing in Russia anyhow? They had all complained (out of the hearing of their officers, of course) that it was madness to let the Germans bully Hungary into supplying the Carpathian Army Corps for this crazy war against Stalin. What business was it of theirs if the Nazis and Soviets wanted to tear each other to pieces? The Hungarian 2nd Army had experienced over 70% casualties so far and had little to show for their sacrifice. So on they trudged westward that January of 1943, away from the frozen Don River, in the faint hope that they might escape from the Russian tanks and Cossacks. Unlike many of his comrades, Lajos still carried his 35.M rifle and ammunition. The damn thing was galling his shoulder, but he had a feeling it might come in handy if anyone, Soviet or German, tried to stop them from making their way out of this frozen death trap.

The Hungarian 35.M rifle was the last Mannlicher military rifle to be officially adopted as standard issue by the armed forces of any nation. While the Mannlicher-type magazine and bolt were excellent designs for their day, it was obvious that they were obsolete by the time the Hungarians adopted the 35.M. The M98 Mauser bolt action and the Mauser charger-loaded, staggered-column magazine were so inherently superior that the Hungarians-decision to stay with the Mannlicher design is difficult to understand.

Hungary became a separate nation in 1918, after being part of the Austro-Hungarian empire since 1687. After a bloody period of Soviet rule and counter-revolution, the nation stabilized under the benevolent dictatorship of Admiral Miklos Horthy. The new Hungarian army continued to use the same weapons it had while part of the Dual Monarchy, with the basic infantry rifle being the straight pull M95 Mannlicher in 8x50R. These had been manufactured locally at the Hungarian national armory, Femaru Fegyver es Gepgyar, in Budapest from 1897 until 1918.

The M95 rifle was Herr Ferdinand von Mannlicher's most successful military design. It used a straight pull bolt (as did most early Mannlicher rifles) with dual frontal locking lugs that are rotated in and out of engagement by the action of two lugs bearing on helical grooves cut into the bolt head cylinder. But Mannlicher's magazine generated much more enthusiasm than his straight pull bolt action. Perfected in the early 1880s, it was the first really practical method of rapidly recharging a rifle's magazine. The heart of the design was a metal clip or packet that held five cartridges and was inserted into, and became part of, the rifle's magazine. A spring loaded follower, integral with the magazine body, pushed cartridges up into feeding position. After the five rounds had been fired, the empty clip fell out of a small hole in the bottom of the magazine housing or was pushed out when the next full clip was inserted. But there were three shortcomings to this system that were never overcome. The most glaring deficiency is that without the metal clips the rifle is reduced to a single shot weapon. Nor can it be "topped off" with loose rounds. Lastly, the clip ejection opening allowed debris to enter the action. In spite of these faults, the Mannlicher magazine was very successful and rifles utilizing it were

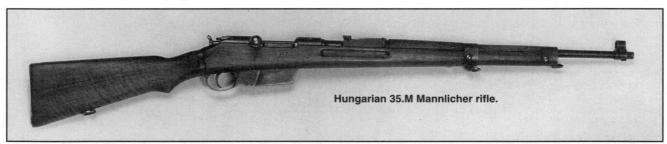

Hungarian 35.M Mannlicher rifle.

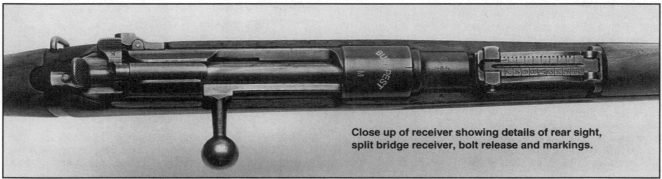

Close up of receiver showing details of rear sight, split bridge receiver, bolt release and markings.

adopted by the armies of Austria-Hungary, Italy, Holland, Rumania, China, Germany, Greece, Turkey, Chile, Siam and Bulgaria. In spite of this, in 1914 Austria-Hungary had planned to adopt a M98 type Mauser, but the Great War intervened and the M95 remained in production until 1919 or so.

To retrogress for a moment, we must discuss another aspect of the 35.M's background. In 1888 the German army adopted their first smokeless powder rifle, the Gew 1888. The M1888 Commission rifle (as it was also called) used a modified Mannlicher en-bloc magazine system, without the benefit of a license. As a result of winning the soon-to-follow patent infringe-

ment lawsuit, Mannlicher's patent holder, the Osterreichische Waffenfabriks-Gesellschaft of Steyr, obtained permission to manufacture the Gew 1888. The Gew 1888's bolt was based on the designs of the German engineer Louis Schlegelmilch. It featured a tubular split bridge receiver with a two piece bolt that cocked on opening. The bolt handle passed through and turned down in front of the split bridge receiver and acted as a safety lug. The separate non-rotating bolt head contained both the extractor and ejector. It was locked by two frontal lugs positioned on the bolt body directly behind the bolt head. The Schlegelmilch bolt was easier to manufacture and just as strong, if not stronger, than Mannlicher's M95 pattern and became the basis for other rifles such as the Mannlicher-Schoenauer and Mauser-Vergueiro.

After World War I, both Austria and Hungary continued to issue M95 Mannlicher rifles to their respective armed forces. Both nation's rifles were chambered for the old 8x50R Mannlicher, an 1890s style cartridge with a short, fat rimmed case that pushed a

244 gr. (16g) round nosed FMJ bullet to barely 2040 FPS (623m/s). The cartridge had never been updated with a spitzer-type bullet as most military rounds had been in the early 20th century. Austria and Hungary jointly began work on a new cartridge in the late 1920s. The necessity of using it in modified M95 rifles limited their choices. The resulting cartridge, known variously as the 8x56R Mannlicher, 8mm Model 30 (Austria), 8mm Model 31 or 8mm cart 31M (Hungary), still used a fat, rimmed case, but it was longer with greater powder capacity and was loaded with a lighter 206 gr. (13.3g) spitzer bullet at a velocity of 2420 FPS (737m/s). Tens of thousands of old M95 rifles and carbines were modified to use the new cartridge. In Austria, converted weapons were stamped on the chamber with a large "S" (for Spitze-

schoss - "pointed bullet"). Hungarian M95s were similarly marked, but with a large "H."

Not completely satisfied with the modified M95 rifles, the Hungarian army began looking about for a more modern rifle in the early 1930s. As I said earlier, the decision to stay with the Mannlicher system at this late date was a bit hard to fathom. My personal opinion (for whatever it is worth) is that it was probably a matter of national pride, that great bugaboo of firearms designers down through the ages. One must realize that the Mannlicher system, while obsolete by the mid-1890s, was the development of a "local boy" and thus held in higher esteem in Central Europe than elsewhere. The engineers at Femaru Fegyver es Gepgyar designed a new 8x56R rifle that combined characteristics of the M95 Mannlicher, Gew 1888, Lee-Enfield, Mannlicher-Schoenauer and the Kar 98k Mauser along with a few novel ideas. It was adopted by the Hungar-

ian army in 1935 as the Huzagol 35.M.

The Huzagol 35.M was a modern appearing rifle for its time. It was 43.7 inches (1110mm) long with a 23.6 inch (600mm) barrel and weighed 8.9 pounds (4.02kg). Its most distinguishing feature is a two-piece stock similar in appearance, but of a different design, to the English Lee-Enfield. The buttstock is a separate piece of wood attached to the receiver by a through bolt. Unlike the Lee-Enfield, the 35.M's butt socket is not integral with the receiver. It is fitted between the receiver tang and the end of the triggerguard and held in place by the rear guard screw. The top and bottom of the butt socket are milled out to fit tightly over the tang end of the triggerguard to prevent it from rotating. Hooks at the top and bottom of the butt socket also engage grooves in the tang and triggerguard to further secure it in place. Un-

like the Lee-Enfield, the forend is tenoned into the butt socket making for a stronger and more rigid design. The bolt is similar to the Gew 1888 and Mannlicher-Schoenauer with a heavy-duty extractor mmortised into the separate, non-rotating bolt head. The ejector is mounted on the left side of the bolt and is also similar to that used on the M's. Two frontal locking lugs are positioned behind the bolt head. An integral guide rib runs most of the length of the bolt. The straight bolt handle (there are reports of some 35.Ms with turned down bolt handles) is part of this rib and features a rather prominent grasping ball. The bolt handle/guide rib turns down in front of, and bears on, the split bridge receiver to provide additional locking surface. There is a M95-style thumb piece that allows manual recocking or lowering of the firing pin. The thumb safety is of Mauser-style and can be applied whether the bolt is cocked or not. While a very strong design, the 35.M

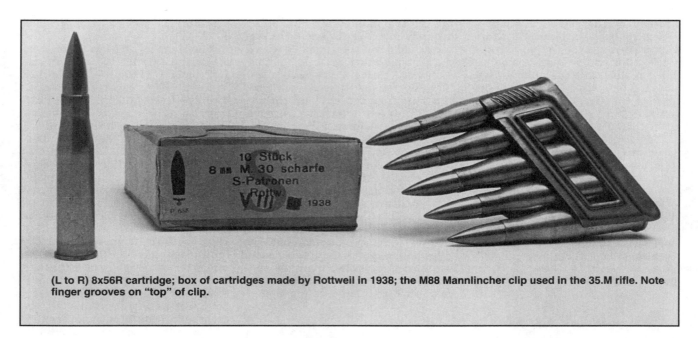

(L to R) 8x56R cartridge; box of cartridges made by Rottweil in 1938; the M88 Mannlincher clip used in the 35.M rifle. Note finger grooves on "top" of clip.

suffers from one of the Mannlicher's chronic faults—the bolt can be assembled and the rifle fired without the bolt head in place. This is partially rectified by the fact that unless the bolt head is in place the bolt stop must be manually depressed before it can be inserted into the receiver. While some feel the bolt handle is too far forward for easy manipulation, the bolt has the Mannlicher's inherent smoothness of operation. There is a single gas escape hole in the bolt that directs gases from a ruptured case or pierced primer down the

round clip is inserted into the magazine, the tail of the follower sticks out of the clip ejection opening. Whether this was meant as a way of showing the magazine was fully loaded or not, I couldn't say. The rear sight is a Mauser-style tangent with a V-notch adjustable from 100 to 2000 meters, while the front sight is a hooded inverted V-blade. The handguard runs from the rear sight base to the muzzle band. The single barrel band and muzzle band are held in place by screws through the stock. There are two sets of sling swivels allowing it to be used

over a projecting stud on the muzzle band. But their most unique feature is that the cavalry model bayonets have an auxiliary front sight, adjustable for windage, mounted on top of the muzzle ring. This is used to compensate for the change in point of impact from the bayonet's weight. This idea was no doubt copied from the earlier M95 Mannlicher "Stutzen" carbine, which had a similar sight arrangement on the bayonet muzzle ring. I cannot fathom why the Hungarian army felt it was only necessary for their cavalry, and not infantry, to

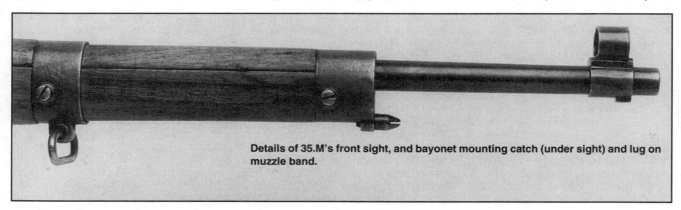

Details of 35.M's front sight, and bayonet mounting catch (under sight) and lug on muzzle band.

left locking lug raceway where it is vented out the thumb clearance cutout in the left side of the receiver.

The 35.M's magazine is pure M95 Mannlicher style and even uses the original M1888 Mannlicher clip that can only be inserted into the magazine one way (note the finger grooves on the "top" of the clip so that the shooter could tell if he was inserting it properly, even in the dark). When a five

by either infantry or mounted troops.

There are four versions of the 35.M bayonet (two each, infantry and cavalry models) and they are even more fascinating than the rifle itself. All feature a 13 inch (330mm) double edged blade and mount via a thumbbox catch on the left sides the muzzle ring that mates with a stud under the front sight band, a system similar to the French Lebel. The bayonet's hilt fits

have this auxiliary sight on their bayonets? The bayonet photographed for this article also has what appears to be a "sling swivel" or loop mounted at the base of the grip. According to Jerry Janzen's excellent book on bayonets, this indicates that this is a Cavalry NCO's bayonet and the loop was used to attach a small pennant to the rifle to indicate the NCO's position when the troops were in parade formation.

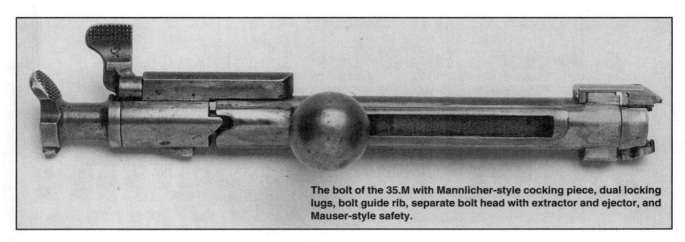

The bolt of the 35.M with Mannlicher-style cocking piece, dual locking lugs, bolt guide rib, separate bolt head with extractor and ejector, and Mauser-style safety.

The 35.M was manufactured in Budapest from 1936 to 1942 and was the standard rifle to the Hungarian armed forces, although it never completely replaced all of the older M95 Mannlichers, especially after Hungary began expanding its armed forces during WW2. The 35.M was used by Hungarian troops taking part in Operation Barbarossa, the German invasion of the Soviet Union, and also by those assisting the Germans in anti-partisan operations in Central Europe and the Balkans. It proved to be a sturdy, reliable rifle. So much so, in fact, that a modified version was adopted by the German army to supplement their Kar98K Mausers in the rapidly expanding Wehrmacht. The German version, known as the Gew.98/40 was chambered for the 8x57 and can be recognized by its charger loaded Mauser

Hungarian government switched production of the 43.M between 1947 and 1950, but this ended when the Hungarians switched over to Soviet pattern weaponry.

My good friend Al Castle of Austin, Texas, lent me a 35.M complete with an NCO bayonet from his extensive collection to test fire and photograph for this article. It was made in 1940 and is in extremely nice condition with a very good bore. Workmanship and quality of materials appear to be excellent. Mr. Steve Kehaya of Century International Arms (PO Box 714, St. Albans, VT 05478. Tel 800-258-8879) kindly provided me with a supply of 8x56R ammunition that was made in Germany by Rottweil in 1938. It came in 10-round boxes already loaded in the correct M1888 Mannlicher clips.

sights were easy to use and gave a very good sight picture. The rifle had a very comfortable fitting stock which, along with the hefty weight, reduced the effect of recoil considerably. The 35.M has one of the smoothest operating bolts I've ever worked. The cock on closing feature is also so smooth it is hardly noticeable. And I cannot agree with those who claim the forward position of the bolt handle is a detriment. The first round out of the clip required a hefty shove, but after that the other four fed effortlessly and it ejected empty cases very positively. Empty clips fell out as soon as the fifth round was chambered. It was a very fine shooting rifle. Most of my five shot groups are around 2.5 to 3 inches (64 to 76mm) and well centered, with my best measuring 2 1/8 inches (54mm). With the rear sight set on 100 meters it tended

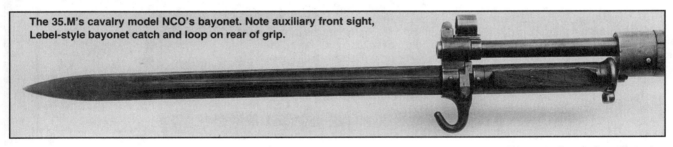

The 35.M's cavalry model NCO's bayonet. Note auxiliary front sight, Lebel-style bayonet catch and loop on rear of grip.

style magazine, Kar 98k style side mounted sling and bayonet. Many thousands were manufactured and it became one of the most common non-Mauser rifles used by German forces in World War 2. In 1943, under pressure from the Germans to standardize arms and simplify supply, the Hungarians adopted the 8x57 cartridge. A new rifle, the Huzagol 43.M was adopted, being little more that the Gew.98/40 using Hungarian style stock fittings and bayonet. Production began in 1944, but only a few thousand were produced before the war ended. It has been reported that the post-war

The boxes, and each round of ammo, were marked with the Nazi eagle. I test fired the 35.M at 100 yards (91.4m) from a benchrest using standard bulls-eye targets. Loading a rifle with Mannlicher clips is without a doubt the fastest way to charge a rifle magazine.

Saying that, I realize I can now expect to hear choruses of protest from all the Mauser fans out there. But calm down folks, I'm not saying the Mannlicher type magazine is superior to the Mauser, just faster to reload. The trigger was the typical two-stage military type, but had a fairly crisp let off. The

to print about 3 inches below the point of aim. I forgot to bring the bayonet with me, so did not get a chance to see how it shot with the auxiliary sight.

My impression of the 35.M? To be perfectly frank, I can find little bad to say about it. It's a fine handling, accurate rifle that deserves a better reputation than Mannlichers usually receive (I sometimes think the firearms press is controlled by a secret clique of Mauser lovers.) I believe it compares very favorably with its contemporaries such as the Kar 98k Mauser or M1903 Springfield and would have served any soldier carrying it very well. I like it. ●

It's a candidate for best elk rifle ever, but....

What happened to the 8MM Magnum?

by B.R. Hughes

It had a lot going for it. Introduced in 1977, when American nimrods by the drove were going to Africa, it could drive a 200 grain slug somewhat faster than the surprisingly successful Winchester 338. Too, the incredible popularity of Remington's 7 mm Magnum weighed in, too.

So what went wrong? Less than 20 years into its history, it has all but disappeared. The only readily available rifle so-chambered in this land today is Remington's high dollar Safari Grade, Model 700. Factory production figures aren't available, but I can assure you that they're not exactly selling like hot cakes! Try to find a box of 8mm Magnum fodder on your local dealer's shelf, or, better still, try to find someone who has a set of reloading dies in stock.

The success that Remington had enjoyed with their metric 6mm and 7mm cartridges was doubtless a powerful factor in their decision to introduce an 8mm. The surprising thing was they opted for the full-length H&H case as the basis for this new cartridge. Winchester had shortened this same hull to get their 264, 300, 338, and 458 magnum line, which have, with the exception of the first, all proven good sellers. In 1977, with the unshortened case, Remington obtained a powder capacity almost as great as the legendary 340 Weatherby.

In my mind, it seems clear Remington had been motivated to some degree by the non-belted 8x68, which originated in Germany in 1940, very probably the work of E. A. Von Hofe, the noted cartridge designer. World War II was consuming all of Europe, and it was no time for a sporting cartridge to win a wide audience, but the 8x68 refused to die. After hostilities ended, Germany was soon turning out quality sporting guns and ammunition, and there was, in 1960, a Mannlicher-Schoenauer magnum rifle chambered for the 8x68. This 8x68mm shoved a 186 grain H-mantel bullet at an announced 3280 feet per second. In case you're interested, this computes to 4463 foot pounds of energy. It was said to be just the ticket for game such as bear, elk, and moose, and judging from those statistics, which are doubtless inflated, there seems little question of that.

Another Teutonic ancestor of Remington's ill-fated magnum was the 8x64 Brenneke, which was introduced around 1912 and provided a 185 grain DWM bullet at an announced muzzle velocity of 2890 fps—which figures out to 3420 foot pounds of energy. Wildcatters will quickly note that the once-popular 8 mm/06 can approach these figures, which may have a little hot air in them!

Remington offered two 8mm factory loadings: a 185-grain slug shoved along at 3080 fps, and a 220-grain bullet propelled at 2830 fps. The former churns up 3896 fps and the latter 3912. Those stats are right there in the ballpark with such lusty performers as Winchester's 338. Incidentally, it didn't take long for

folks to complain about the severe recoil of the 8 Magnum, and some of those horror stories were pretty grim. Actually, when I tested one of these rifles in 1977, I found it more comfortable to shoot than the 338; indeed, if a nimrod can handle a 300 magnum, he or she should have no problem with the 8 mm.

One drawback of the 8mm's introduction was the lack of appropriate bullets for reloading. There were plenty of projectiles of .323 in. diameter around, but these were made for

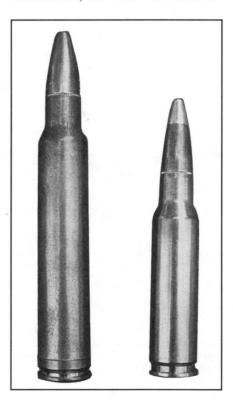

The 8mm Remington Magnum with the 308 Winchester. The 8mm is based on the full-length 375 case.

the 8x57mm Mausers brought home by GI's after WWII. For the most part, they were 150 and 170-grain slugs, and they were designed to expand at the 8x57's modest velocities of around 2400 fps.

In the spacious 8mm Magnum case, it was possible to dump a lot of slow-burning powder, such as H4831, IMR-4831, 11450, Norma MRP, and the like, and it was no trick at all to drive a 150-grain bullet out the muzzle at 3400 fps or so. Talk about flat trajectory! Zero this slug three inches high at 100 yards, and you're on the money at 300!

Of course, lacking sectional density, the velocity dropped off pretty quickly after that, but this is slightly flatter than a garden variety 270 shooting a 130-grain bullet. And then the 150 grain .323" slug was not made with such velocities in mind. Hit the shoulder bone of something no tougher than a mule deer at 100 yards, just for example, and there was a distinct possibility that the projectile would simply go to pieces without driving into a vital area.

Hornady, Nosler, and Speer soon introduced bullets designed for the velocities of the 8mm Magnum, but none of these companies offered anything heavier than Hornady's 220 grain projectile. We'll never know for sure but, to my dying day, I will believe that had someone introduced a suitable bullet weighing in the neighborhood of 235 to 250 grains, it might have saved the day. After all, 220 grains is a heavy bullet only in terms of a 30 caliber bore, and many authorities suggest that if you take a 30-06 or 300 magnum in quest of bear or elk, you should load it with good 220 grain slugs. With the larger .323 in. bore of the 8mm Magnum, it stands to reason that a heavier bullet would have made it more attractive to hunters of really big game.

Be that as it may, the most accurate load I have ever used in any of the three 8 mm magnums I have ever owned over the years is the 150 grain Hornady bullet in front of 85.0 grains of H-4831, ignited by the CCI magnum primer. This load has proven perfectly safe in my three M700's but, should you try it, back off about five grains of powder and work up carefully a half grain at a time, easing off a full grain at the first signs of excessive pressure. More often than not, this load will place three shots in less than an inch shooting at 100 yards from a solid bench rest. Occasionally, when I yank the trigger properly, the group may shrink to three-quarters of an inch. Recoil is not at all excessive, and one of these days I just may use that load on a pronghorn hunt. Why not?

After asking around a bit, I finally located a fellow in Colorado who had used an 8mm Remington almost since its inception for elk and mule deer. He admitted to having taken eight bull elk with the 220-grain factory load, and he was staunch in his conviction that there was never a better elk rifle made on these shores. Prior to his purchase of the M700 8mm, he had used a 300 Winchester Magnum for about 15 years. The noted writer Col. Charles Askins, Jr., a long-time admirer of the 8 mm bore, used a wildcat version of the 8 mm Remington for several years prior to its introduction and seemed well-satisfied with it.

There's an 8 mm Remington Magnum 700BDL standing in my gun rack as these lines are typed and I have no intention of getting rid of it, although I've taken only one head of game with this cartridge--a so-so whitetail buck shot at perhaps 125 yards using the factory 185 grain load, and did it ever go down. I feel that it may be the ultimate elk rifle, which means that it would be great for such game as kudu and sable. Unless you're a reloader, I wouldn't suggest that you rush out to buy an 8mm, because I have a hunch that factory ammo won't be available much longer. It is a cartridge deserving a better fate. Its ballistics were never inflated; if anything, a canny handloader can improve on factory performance. Do you suppose that if they had dubbed it the 323 Remington Magnum, it would have had a better life. ●

Writer Hughes shoots his 8mm Magnums off the bench, can handle the recoil.

It could be 200 k. to the next house in the Nicaragua back country, Schmidt says.

Tropical Pistolas

by Carlos Schmidt

El Bailerín was one of the last guerrillas still running loose in the northern mountains of Nicaragua long after the Contra War had ended in 1990. The guerillas under El Chacal (The Jackal) had disbanded in 1994; the more recalcitrant guerrilla El Charro had been blown up with a booby-trapped walkie-talkie in 1996. But in the spring of 1997, I had the bad luck to round a bend on a remote stretch of the Coco River that divides Nicaragua and Honduras and run straight into El Bailerín (which roughly translates as "Fancy Dancer"; his character is much more like the Larry McMurtry character known as Blue Duck). Le Bailerín's first reaction was to tell me and my traveling companions in the dugout canoe that he was going to shoot us. Luckily, one of my friends was a former Contra Commandante Javier—in civilian life now Dr. Antonio Ortega—the chief medical officer of the Contra war who set up the emergency hospitals on the Honduras side of the Coco River.

This is all the gun Schmidt wants for real needs in the woods. Gunfights are not on his agenda.

The pleasant fellow on the right with the M16A2 is El Bailerin, killer, rapist, thief, freedom fighter; Schmidt at center, 45 out of sight; on the left, the esteemed Dr. Ortega — a scary moment just went by.

During the 1980s he had at least seven hospitals bombed out by the Sandinistas and treated hundreds of wounded Contra. One of those wounded that Ortega treated years ago was El Bailerín.

When Commandante Javier spoke, El Bailerín recognized him and we were instantly friends. We took a few pictures, talked about old times, and continued on our way down the Coco River, the longest river in Central America and still one of the wildest, with several hundred kilometers accessible only by canoe.

I was traveling the river with Dr. Ortega and Miguel Angel de la Trinidad, chief hostage negotiator for the OAS peacekeeping force that had done so much since 1990 to keep the uneasy peace between the Sandinista army and the demobilized Contra forces. Ortega and de la Trinidad were going down the Coco to find out about the progress of the establishment of local government in remote, northern Nicaragua. I went along to look for archaeological remains reported in the area 150 years ago by an American named Ephraim Squier, and to pursue my interest in botany and look for various

species of rare orchids that may exist in the mountains of the Coco River.

We travelled light and fast down the river; our biggest cargo the 60 gallons of gas we needed to get back to Wiwilí, where we put in. Our destination was a small village 200 km down the Coco and 15 km up the fabled Bocay River. From Wiwilí to where the Coco empties into the Caribbean, 500 km downstream, there are no gas stations. We had only one backpack of personal effects for the trip. Under my vest in an Uncle Mike's shoulder holster, I packed my favorite jungle pistola, a Ruger stainless steel Blackhawk in 45 Colt caliber.

Many might blanch at the idea of taking a single action revolver into an area with known guerrillas and "bad guys" running around free. Some would want the latest in defensive or concealed carry thinking — a Glock or Sigarm or Smith & Wesson. Others would not think of entering such unknown waters without first getting practiced up in the latest IPSC techniques. Still others would not go to such a place under any circumstances.

As soon as we embarked on the Coco River at Wiwilí we left the zone

of Nicaragua where there is civil authority. With Ortega and de la Trinidad I entered that area that had (and still has) absolutely no civil authority for thousands of square kilometers. I gave more thought to getting the correct type of film for my cameras and what type of food to take than armaments. Along with the Blackhawk, which always travels with me where there are no roads, I took the shoulder holster, 20 rounds of my standard load for the 45 Colt and 20 rounds of shot cartridges, mainly for the fer-de-lance, one moderately common snake that really is dangerous.

I have long felt that the best defense weapon is the brain, not any object. In rural Nicaragua, anyone with any sort of command of Spanish can still buy a selective fire AK-47 for about $100. Thus, most folks have an AK or two around the house, and know how to use them. In the two or three instances that I have run into guerrilla bands, they have numbered between 10 and 20 persons and included all sorts of weapons, usually including FALs and G3s along with AKs, an occasional Soviet heavy machine gun, and the ubiquitous RPG 7. Fat chance I would have trying to shoot it out in that remote jungle against an armed band. The slickest Glock or IPSC racegun that ever lived couldn't cut it. You simply have to think ahead of your guns and not rely on them as the solution to all imminent problems.

As an example, coming back to Wiwilí at the end of the trip, we ran into a guerrilla band led by another free spirit known as El Cobra. He was in a bad mood as he was having his tooth pulled. jungle style, with a pair of pliers. One of his soldiers had a Doberman attack dog on a leash, and a new Glock. It seems that a rich coffee farmer got the self-defense religion and began practicing to protect himself against kidnapping, which is now fairly common among some folks as a means of raising money quite rapidly. El Cobra's band of merry cutthroats knew about the rich farmer's defensive activities and waited until they could surround his pickup and put an FAL down his nose. He happily handed over both his Glock and his Doberman attack dog. So much for the latest personal combat training as meaningful response to rural banditry.

Any thought about acquiring a handgun should include a realistic approach to how it will be actually used. Actual use is the acid test of reality. With Nicaragua's rather reasonable laws in the matter of concealed weapons, and the complete lack of police authority where the roads end, the major consideration for a handgun is that it fits its use perfectly and that the possessor be completely comfortable with the piece. Thus, I can carry just about any sort of handgun in just about any kind of holster; the only person that must be satisfied is me.

I use handguns to collect mammalian specimens for my biologist amigos or to shoot small game for the cooking pot—some of the tropical gamebirds and medium-sized mammals make fine table fare. In order to do that job, there are a few minimum requirements that bear mention. First, the handgun and load must be capable, consistently, of groups of two inches or less at 25 yards. I shoot a lot of animalitos, including the iguana and its close cousin, the "garrobo" or *Psentosaura similis,* in the tree tops and pinpoint accuracy is absolutely essential. A second characteristic is that the bullet must not blow up the body of the ani-

mal—just punch a clean hole through and leave the rest for skinning and preservation and eating. The cartridge casing must be big enough to hold a lot of small bird shot, both for collecting small lizards, and also for the occasional nasty snake (which really is quite rare).

Since I travel to areas that are true rain forests or close to it, I also need a handgun that will not rust. That means either a stainless steel pistola or one covered with an effective barrier between humid air and steel. And lastly, the holster should allow easy access but maintain the handgun securely, no matter the activity or circumstance. I have no plans to shoot anyone and so a semiautomatic pistola with a double-column magazine in a lightning fast bikini holster is of little use to me. Most of the animals I shoot at only allow one shot before they rapidly leave the area, and five or six rounds in a cylinder are enough.

My hands-down choice for a tropical pistola is the stainless steel Ruger Blackhawk in 45 Colt. My experience with that revolver goes back almost 20 years, when I obtained a Blackhawk Convertible 45 Colt- .45 ACP with a 4-3/4 inch barrel. It shot very high for my eyes, even with the sights turned down all the way; it had a very heavy trigger pull; and it wouldn't shoot any 0.452-

inch bullets worth beans. It took some time, but I gradually discovered an unsized .45 caliber 255-grain Keith bullet from an RCBS mold—it measured between 0.454 and 0.455-in.—would give me two-inch groups or less at 25 yards every time. I had a friend silver-solder a piece of steel 0.10-in. thick on top of the Ruger front sight and got the point of impact dead on at 25 yards with my favorite load of 9.5 grains of Unique. With a little voodoo I got the trigger pull down to around three pounds and with little creep.

Then I had a really useful revolver that went on many trips and took a lot of small game. I found the Keith semi-wadcutter bullet punched 45-caliber holes through anything I hit and destroyed no meat. Once, on an elk hunt by the headwaters of the Yellowstone, I shot five ruffed grouse with that gun and load. The other hunters and I ate the grouse and only noticed a hole punched by the bullet with no blood shot meat. I also killed some beeves for slaughter and found that, as Elmer Keith had written in the first half of this century, the hard cast semi-wadcutter bullet punched though the cow's head every time. I had enough power to spare when the need arose. And that load of 9.5 or 10 grains of Unique shot flat enough for me to be able to hit small targets easily out to

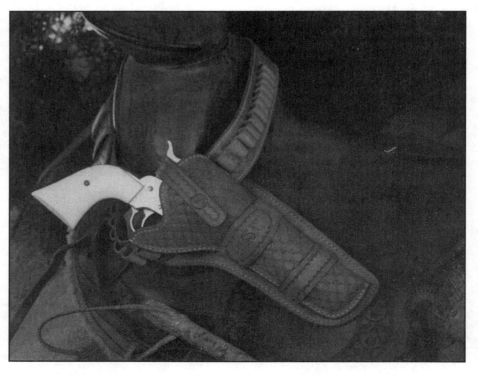

Leather work by the Sozas family suits Schmidt, except where it is very wet.

75 yards. I was pleased with that Ruger and that load!

A couple of years ago, I lucked onto the possibility of obtaining another Ruger Blackhawk, this time in stainless steel and in 45 Colt and quickly snapped it up. I found, as I had with my first Ruger, that the trigger pull was creepy and heavy and that the Blackhawk shot very high at 25 yards. This time I had a new sight installed that shot low, so a little filing and sight adjusting got it hitting dead on at 25 yards. I measured the cylinder mouths and found them .454-inches in diameter, the real secret to accuracy with the 45 Colt. My unsized cast bullets from an RCBS mold make a tight fit in the cylinder mouths and shoot within the same two inches my old Ruger did years ago, with many groups approaching one inch at the 25 yard range. The trigger got slicked up a bit and now the stainless steel Ruger goes with me almost everywhere, loaded with Mr. Keith's hard-cast, unsized bullet in front of a appropriate charge of Winchester 231, a stand-in until I can get some Unique in Central America.

The hard-cast semi-wadcutter bullet starting out around 1,000 feet per second is just the ticket for trop-ical use. I can eat right up to the bullet hold on big iguanas and garrobos and find no bloodshot meat. Ditto with the tasty chachalaca, a tropical bird that resembles nothing so much as the domestic chicken. The largest mammal in Central America is the Baird's tapir, which can weigh in at 300 pounds and is related to, and tastes like, the domestic horse. The choicest morsel is the snout, which is prehensile and quite tasty roasted in the coals of an open campfire. But the tapir is now on the restricted CITES list and protected, so the largest allowable game is the familiar whitetail deer, which seldom goes over 100 pounds. The Keith bullet, placed through the shoulders, allows the deer to be taken with little or no tissue damage. There is no question I could load heavier loads in the 45 Colt, perhaps 44 Magnum power. I still have a cache of Bulgarian Ball powder that burns quite similar to H 110 and could propel the hard-case bullet much faster. But I have no need or interest in loading the 45 Colt any heavier when I have pinpoint accuracy and sufficient power for all my hunting needs.

A major consideration is how to carry the piece in the countryside.

Leather work in Nicaragua is good and inexpensive, so I have had the opportunity to experiment with various designs of holsters and saddles. The Soza Saddlery in Mas-aya, not far from Managua, the capital of Nicaragua, made a first rate replica of my old Du Hamel single-rigged Californio saddle, made in Rapid City, South Dakota around the time of the First World War. I had them put a Mexican-style horn on the saddle tree and slim the front swell to something more like a slick fork, and copy everything else, down to the leather tooling. Old man Soza did a fine job and that saddle has taken me over a lot of northern Nicaragua. His nephew does the small jobs and so I started taking him my pistols to make holsters. He has made me crossdraw holsters, Mexican double loop holsters, and various gunbelts, complete with cartridge loops (when I wanted them) and my choice of tooling. He takes about a week, when I have to leave my pistola with him, and he costs about $20, regardless of design or the amount of tooling. He always produces a holster that could grace the catalog of any of the American holster companies.

The one holster I have not had him copy is my favorite holster for horseback and usage in the jungle, the El Paso Saddlery M1917 half flap. Sheriff Jim Wilson once defined a good holster as one that would maintain the pistola while you do a cartwheel. The El Paso holster will do that plus keep dirt out. I recently had the involuntary opportunity to test out the pistola-retaining capability of that holster. In early 1997, a prestigious American museum asked me to take a group into the northern jungles to the crash site of a B-26 bomber that had disappeared during the Bay of Pigs invasions in 1961. While making that trip I got to talking with one of the wranglers who told me about some unexplored limestone caves located north of the crash site. We found the crash site and I decided to return to those mountains during the next dry season to find those rumored caves.

In March of 1998 I returned to the small village of San José de Bocay, found my wrangler, and set out on mule back to the unknown caves located 20 km east of the banks of the Bocay River. The ride was scenic and there was not 100 yards of level ground in those 20 km. About half way there, my saddle loosened and went forward over the withers of the mule, which

This one's from State-side—an El Paso Saddlery 1917 half-flap Schmidt says is the best travel rig.

A compass, either a 45 or a 22 revolver, some spurs, a Loveless belt knife, good glasses and a GPS — Nicaraguan travelers' aids.

caused the mule to buck. I am a bit too old for rodeoing and so I jumped off that mule, down a 15-foot coulee. I broke the fall by grabbing a banana tree, which I snapped off, and rolled to the bottom of the gulley, still holding onto the top half of the tree. My wrangler friend thought I was a pretty funny gringo, as did the other gringo on the trip. Both chuckled as I crawled back up to the mules. Through it all, my El Paso M 1917 holster retained my Blackhawk, and except for a few scratches where I slid over a boulder, the holster was fine. I recently took my saddle back to Señor Soza and had him put on the buckle for attaching a crupper to keep the saddle from sliding forward again, and I made it to the caves and pulled out some pre-Columbian pottery, now in the possession of the Nicaraguan Ministry of Culture.

My only objection to the half-flap holster is that it is made of leather. It works fine in the dry season, when I do most of my wandering. When it is necessary to venture into the rain forest during the rainy season, a mighty rare and unpleasant experience, I leave the leather holster at home and take along one of Uncle Mike's nylon shoulder holsters for the Blackhawk. On last year's trip down the Coco River the rains were just ending, which means it was still raining, just not very hard. After a day or two everything got either wet or damp and leather items start to mold up. No matter, my nylon holster retained the Blackhawk, did not mold, and allowed me easy access to my favorite jungle pistola whenever it was needed.

A couple of other pistolas have utility in the jungle. Undoubtedly any 22 revolver or pistol will find its niche as a game getter. Either of two 22s go with me when I want something a little lighter and less bulky than the Blackhawk. For example, when I shotgun the spot-bellied bob-white quail, old *Colinus leucopogon,* I always take along a Ruger stainless steel semi-auto, in case my pointer finds a rattlesnake. And hunting some of the highly populated coffee farms for the agouti, a rabbit-sized member of the rat family that is spotted like a fawn and tastes like suckling pig, is not the place to take along the 45 Colt with its big bullet to bounce around and potentially hurt someone, so I take an old Smith and Wesson K-22 with a 6-inch barrel.

That old Smith was confiscated by the Sandinistas in 1979 and tossed onto a cement floor in a poorly maintained armory. It lay there until 1990, when I talked the local commandante into letting me trade some gunsmithing for some old wrecks and rusted-up guns. I got the pick of a big wooden box of old pistolas and immediately picked out that Smith and Wesson, among others. Back when I shot NRA bullseye matches in my youth I began with my brother's Smith & Wesson K-22 in that same barrel length and shot it until I saved up enough to buy a Smith and Wesson M 41. When I picked that rusty K-22 up the cylinder would not revolve and the wood grips were rotted away on one side where the gun butt lay against the cement floor. And when the gun was confiscated, someone threw it on the floor and smashed the adjustable rear sight.

It took some doing, but I got the action working and the cylinder revolving. The original bluing was long gone but the barrel inside was in good shape and none of the cylinder chambers was pitted. It took two years to get a rear sight, but finally I got that K-22 shooting. With no outer finish, the pistola literally rusted red while I carried it in the field. I finally resolved that with Brownell's Teflon spray finish. Baked in my wife's oven, the teflon finish somewhat resembles a glass bead finish and is completely impervious to moisture. I have refinished a Smith & Wesson M 39 and Ruger 10/22 and am tempted to finish all of my remaining carbon steel weapons. It is that good.

Nowadays things are getting back to being peaceful in the northern mountains. I wander the Cordillera de Dipilto or the Isabelia Mountains and occasionally do a bit of gold panning, look for rare orchids, or scatterings of potsherds along the Coco River drainage. Next dry season I plan to go back to the little-known tributary of the Bocay River to look again for those same ruins that old Ephraim Squier, the first United States ambassador to Nicaragua, found sometime between 1849 and 1855 and that I did not find in 1997. That area is home to the Sumo Indians, now called the Mayagna by the politically correct, and there is located the Bosawas National Reserve, the size of the country of El Salvador, and the largest tract of relatively untouched rain forest left between the United States and Amazonas. There is much archaeology and botany to do there and no one has compiled a mammalian inventory since 1902. I believe the Blackhawk will make up for some of that lack of knowledge and assist in the identification of some of the mammalian inhabitants of that huge forest reserve.

Going with me will be some of Mr. Keith's semi-wadcutters loaded with way he loaded them, some shot cartridges, maps, a compass, a GPS, surveying equipment, a waterproof notebook, (my invaluable Loveless knife) and enough salt and preservative to keep the specimens and tissues stable until I can get back out of that wilderness. I will almost certainly see no other gringos or Canadians or Europeans, and relatively few Indians. But I will have Mr. Ruger's Blackhawk with me as my favorite tropical pistolas and I will be contented hombre, ready for any one eventuality. And that's the way it should be.

With graph paper and diligence you can find the simple rules of...

The Interior Ballistics of
MUZZLE LOADERS

by Marshall R. Williams

45 cal.
28" BBL

TEST GUN .... UNIVERSAL
Barrel Length: .... 28"
Rate of Twist: .... 1 IN 66"
Bore: .... 0.453"
Groove: .... 0.472"

PROJECTILE: .... R. B.
Diameter: .... 0.445"
Weight: .... 133 Grs.
Lube: .... Crisco
Patch: .... 0.015"

BARREL NUMBER: ..12

IGNITION: .... Cap
Brand: .... Navy Arms
Size: .... No. 11

PROPELLANT:
Brand: .... G-O
Granulation: ...... FFg

Charge (Grs.)	Velocity (FPS)	Pressure (LUP/CUP)		Muzzle Energy (Ft./lbs.)	Energy at 100 yds. (Ft./lbs.)
30	1144	3,510	LUP	386	N/A
40	1291	4,840	LUP	492	N/A
50	1438	6,170	LUP	610	N/A
60	1585	7,500	LUP	741	245
70	1670	8,300	LUP	822	260
80	1755	9,100	LUP	908	278
90	1882	12,100	CUP	1045	305
100	2008	15,100	CUP	1189	335

PROJECTILE: .... R. B.
Diameter: .... 0.445"
Weight: .... 133 Grs.
Lube: .... Crisco
Patch: .... 0.015"

BARREL NUMBER: ..12

IGNITION: .... Cap
Brand: .... Navy Arms
Size: .... No. 11

PROPELLANT:
Brand: .... G-O
Granulation: ..... FFFg

Charge (Grs.)	Velocity (FPS)	Pressure (LUP/CUP)		Muzzle Energy (Ft./lbs.)	Energy at 100 yds. (Ft./lbs.)
25	948	1,335	LUP	265	N/A
30	1089	2,810	LUP	349	N/A
35	1230	4,285	LUP	446	N/A
40	1370	5,760	LUP	553	N/A
45	1511	7,235	LUP	673	N/A
50	1651	8,710	LUP	803	257
55	1792	10,185	CUP	947	287
60	1932	11,660	CUP	1100	317
65	1963	12,670	CUP	1136	325
70	1994	13,680	CUP	1172	332
75	2025	14,690	CUP	1209	341

This is the writer's source, reprinted here with Lyman's permission.

Shooters have used black powder as a propellant in muzzle-loading guns since the fourteenth century. As a result of 600 years of trial and error, black powder's practical applications are well known. However, if anyone has ever published rules of internal ballistics of muzzle loading small arms, I have not been able to find them.

The probable reason for this lack of scientific data is that cartridge guns and smokeless powder replaced muzzle loaders and black powder at about the same time that pressure and velocity measuring equipment became available. As a result, the internal ballistics of smokeless powder cartridge guns are now well established, while the internal ballistics of black powder remain in the realm of folklore.

The "Lyman Black Powder Handbook," (Lyman, Middlefield, Cònn., 1975) contains tabulated data from a comprehensive program to determine pressure and velocities in black powder guns. Using the information in that book, I was able to determine that the internal ballistics of black powder follow the simple rules set out below.

To develop their data, Lyman researchers adapted a crusher breech to a muzzle-loading barrel and measured the chamber pressure when they fired a shot. At the same time, they used a chronograph to measure the velocity obtained. Starting with barrels 43 inches long, the researchers tested a series of powder charges for concurrent velocities and chamber pressures. Tests stopped when pressures reached a level of 15,000 copper units of pressure (CUP). Then, the researchers cut the barrels to shorter lengths and repeated the tests.

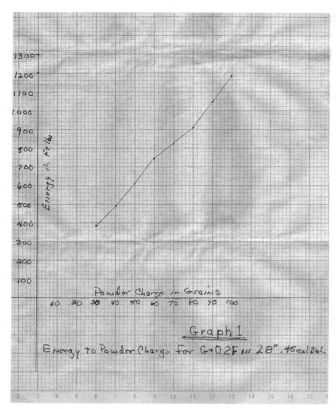

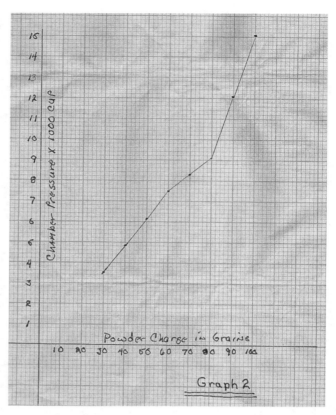

Graph 1: These simple rules did not spring out at me merely from reading Lyman's book. Instead, they result from many hours of study and analysis on my part, stumbling along with two pocket calculators and graph paper. Eventually, I graphed every table in the book which permitted a comparison with any other table. No doubt the time and effort would have been less if I had been trained as a scientist and knew how to operate a computer. I will point out that I can find tables which appear at variance with one or another of these rules, but I believe they fall within the realm of allowable statistical variation.

Graph 2: Some definitions may be required. "Direct proportion" means things increase or decrease by simple counting, one, two, three, four. "Geometric proportion" means things increase or decrease by squares, one, two, four, nine. "Energy" is "kinetic energy," or the energy of mass in motion. The term "efficiency" refers to the amount of energy to be gotten from the amount of powder burned. Fifty grains of 3F will give more energy than fifty grains of 2F; therefore, 3F is more efficient than 2F.

The researchers repeated the procedure for a number of different calibers and charted the information by caliber, barrel length, powder type, and bullet type. Illustration 1 is an example of the two charts on page 97 of Lyman's book. Lyman's charts easily permit graphing for direct comparison. Most of the accompanying graphs are taken from the two charts on page 97.

Lyman's researchers used Gearhart-Owens (G&O) powders for most of their testing, but also used some Curtis & Harvey (C&H) black powders. There is not enough information to determine whether the rules applicable to G&O powders also apply to C&H powders. There is no information about any other powders.

Thus, the following rules apply primarily to G&O black powder

performance at pressure levels up to 15,000 CUP:

1. Muzzle energy varies in direct proportion to powder charges.
2. Chamber pressure varies in direct proportion to powder charge.
3. Any given level of muzzle energy will be achieved at the same chamber pressure without regard to the caliber of the gun or granulation of the powder, whether 2F or 3F, used to obtain the given level of energy.
4. Muzzle energy varies in direct proportion to barrel length, but at one-half the rate.

Rule 1 states that muzzle energy varies in direct proportion to powder charges. This means that a 20% increase in powder charge results in a 20% increase in muzzle energy.

Rule 1 is illustrated by Graph 1. Graph 1 shows the energy in foot pounds (ft. lbs.) on the vertical and the powder charge in grains on the horizontal for G&O 2F powder when using a round ball in a .45 caliber barrel 28 inches long. As is apparent, each increase in powder charge resulted in a corresponding increase in energy. The line is roughly straight and, if extended downward, would point to zero values on both axes. The straight line of the graph tells us that muzzle energy is in direct proportion to powder charges. Graphs for all of Lyman's charts are similar, regardless of caliber or powder granulation. However, the angle of the line varies somewhat according to the efficiency of the powder.

Rule 2 states that chamber pressure varies in direct proportion to powder charge. This means that a 20% increase in powder charge re-

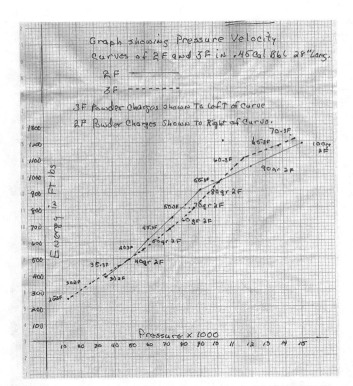

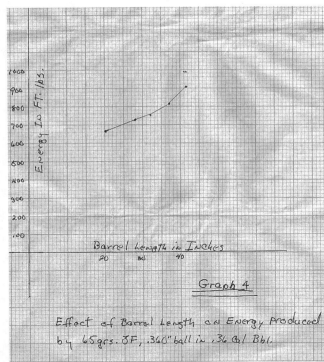

Graph showing Pressure Velocity Curves of 2F and 3F in .45 Cal BBl 28" Long.

2F ―――
3F ------
3F Powder Charges Shown To Left of Curve
2F Powder Charges Shown To Right of Curve

Graph 4

Effect of Barrel Length on Energy Produced by 65grs. 3F, .360" ball in .36 Cal Bbl.

Graph 3: Lyman data stop at a pressure level of 15,000 CUP. Because 56% of the products of black powder combustion are solids, pressures may increase faster with slower burning powders as powder charges increase to the point that this part of the ejecter becomes significant.

Graph 4: This was the most difficult thing to determine working from Lyman's information because there were more variations in performance from barrel to barrel, but having graphed the increase for other bore sizes, this is representative. The same holds true with conical bullets, but is less definite. From my calculations, it appears that the percentage increase in energy is equal to one-half the percentage increase in barrel length. With round balls the 43" barrels gave an average of 25% more energy than the 28" barrels. With conical bullets, it varied from 2% up to 25%.

sults in a 20% increase in chamber pressure.

Rule 2 is illustrated by Graph 2. Graph 2 shows the chamber pressures corresponding to the same increases in powder charges as in Graph 1. Again, each increase in powder charge results in a corresponding increase in pressure. The similarity between Graphs 1 and 2 is striking. Again, graphs for all of Lyman's charts are similar, regardless of caliber or powder granulation. Also again, the angle of the line varies somewhat according to the efficiency of the powder.

As a corollary of rules 1 and 2, at least with G&O black powder, muzzle energy and chamber pressure are directly tied to each other and rule 3 gives a somewhat startling view of this.

Rule 3 states that any given level of energy will be achieved at the same pressure without regard to the caliber of the gun or the granulation of the powder used to obtain the given level of energy. Thus, a gun which is loaded to develop 500 ft. lbs. of muzzle energy will have the same chamber pressure, no matter whether 2F or 3F powder was used.

This is dramatically illustrated by Graph 3. The two lines, chart the energy/pressure curve for 2F and 3F in a 28 inch .45 caliber barrel. They virtually overlay each other. (Note, however, that due to 2F's lower efficiency, a larger charge of 2F than of 3F will always be required for any energy/pressure level.)

This rule startled me. Six hundred years of folklore and tradition say we should use fine grain powder in small bores and coarse grained powders in large bores, and, as a rule of thumb, the transition between 3F and 2F lay about .45 caliber. Rule 3 says it makes no difference, provided you adjust the powder charge to equalize performance.

Lest one hastily jump to the conclusion that the caliber of the gun is coincidentally responsible for Rule 3, I assure you the situation is the same in Lyman's tables for .50 and .54 calibers.

Rule 4 states that muzzle energy varies in direct proportion to barrel length, but at one-half the rate. This means that a 20% increase in barrel length should result in 10% increase in muzzle energy from a given powder charge.

Rule 4 is illustrated by Graph 4. This graph shows the increase in energy for 65 grains of 3F in a .36 caliber barrel of various lengths from 20" to 43". An increase in barrel length from 28" to 43" is very nearly a 50% increase. The energy developed in the 28" barrel with 65 grains of 3F powder was 733 foot pounds (ft. lbs.); the energy developed in the 43" barrel was 906 ft. lbs. This is 24% more than the 733 ft lbs. developed in the 28" barrel using the same powder charge. As in Graphs 1 and 2, the result is a nearly straight line indicating a direct proportional relationship between barrel length and energy.

I would hope that rules help to dispel some of the folklore surrounding black powder. ●

For many decades, the world's armed forces have relied upon rifles and pistols firing 22-caliber rimfire ammunition to supplement their full-caliber firearms. These rimfire pieces have primarily served for training, although some, particularly handguns, have also seen more belligerent service. In fact, rimfire pistols are used for a wide range of official duties, spanning the gamut from the most mundane training command to competitive shooting to exotic covert operations.

The disadvantages of rimfire ammunition are well known and include its low power. The rimmed configuration of the 22 cartridge and its dirtiness also conspire to lead to unreliable feeding in many self-loading firearms designs.

What is not so well known is that from a military standpoint the advantages of rimfire ammunition often outweigh its disadvantages. For one thing, rimfire ammunition is much less expensive than centerfire ammunition, making training with it far less costly. This means that a shooter of rimfires is often an expert shot. The comparatively low power level of rimfire ammunition also makes it easier to build suitable ranges and training facilities, which do not require such extensive grounds as ranges for more powerful centerfire arms. Rimfire ammunition is also inherently quieter than high-powered centerfire cartridges and, moreover, is easier to suppress still further with integral or add-on silencing units. The degree of sound suppression possible with a rimfire weapon is astounding. Moreover, an effective sound suppressor or silencer for a rimfire handgun is typically far less bulky than that required to suppress a more powerful centerfire gun.

This unique combination of disadvantages and advantages means that military rimfire pistols are at the same time both controversial and extraordinarily useful and versatile. Let us consider some of the major types in use:

Walther

Germany's Carl Walther Waffenfabrik has long been involved in the production of rimfire pistols that armed forces the world over have added to their inventories in considerable numbers. Most Walther rimfires in military service are variations of the Model PP family, though a few of the more exotic target-shooting models are also retained for competition.

Walther rimfire service models in widespread use include the PP itself, the smaller PPK and PPK/S and, most recently, the ultra-compact Model TPH. The PP-type pistols'; double-action lockwork allows a first shot with the hammer in its uncocked position simply by pulling through the trigger to cock and then release the hammer. The PP was the first commercially viable automatic pistol to offer this double-action trigger feature.

Although the PP is primarily regarded as a centerfire pistol, rimfire variants of it appeared within a year after its 1929 introduction. The same situation existed with the PPK at its introduction in 1931. Originally Walther offered both PPs and PPKs in a choice of four calibers: 22 LR, 6.35mm (25 ACP), 7.65mm (32 ACP) and 9mm Short (380 ACP). The 25 caliber variants died out quickly. The 380 had relatively limited production until after the war while the 32 became service standard in Germany and most other countries. Perhaps surprisingly, the rimfire variations were remarkably successful and popular, so much so that Walther maintained a limited production of 22 LR PPs and PPKs to the very end of World War II in 1945. When the French corporation Manurhin resumed Walther pistol production under license in 1952, they picked up the 22 LR variants with as much gusto as they did the 32 and 380 models. Interarms continues to sell the 22 caliber PP in the United States.

The much smaller TPH dates from mid-1968 and its import was barred here because of its size. Basically a downsized Model PP, the TPH was virtually unavailable in the United States for nearly twenty years. Walther eventually licensed its manufacture to Interarms, who now builds it at the Ranger factory in Alabama.

Walther rimfire pistols have long been popular with military and police forces as training pistols. They are also well suited to the clandestine uses of espionage and assassination - the use of a PPK by the fictional character James Bond has plenty of historical precedent.

Depending upon the mission, Walther pistols in official use are sometimes fitted with suppressors. Owing to the Walther pistol's design, in which the slide encloses virtually the entire barrel, suppressors for these pistols usually take the form of a cylindrical attachment screwed onto the front of an extended barrel which is threaded at the muzzle. Often the barrel from the next-larger Walther pistol can be fitted to a smaller gun, with the resulting protruding portion threaded for the suppressor.

This type of silencer, attached to the front of the barrel, is sometimes called a "muzzle can." Muzzle cans can be easily adapted to a variety of firearms, and a number of manufacturers make them. For instance,

Martial Rimfire Handguns

by Gene Gangarosa, Jr.

AWC Systems Technology makes the tiny Warp III suppressor for Walther pistols. Small enough to fit on a keychain, the AWC Warp III suppressor allied with a stainless steel Walther TPH is an excellent combination for clandestine purposes and has seen use with the U.S. Navy SEALs, among others.

During World War II, Walther made a 22 LR prototype of their P-38 service pistol and offered it to the German armed forces as a training pistol. Although this gun did not go into series production during the Nazi era, after the war Walther again pursued this idea with more success. From 1970 until the late 1980s, Walther made a 22 LR caliber P-38. In addition, beginning about 1960, Walther for many years marketed conversion kits so that owners of 9mm or 7.65mm P-38s could also shoot 22 LR ammunition by changing the barrel, slide and magazine. Production of these dedicated rimfire pistols and conversion units was never extensive, since they cost about as much as a standard pistol. However, they did see police and military use and are today highly coveted by collectors.

In general, it can be said of the Walther military rimfire handguns that they are solid, reliable and consistent performers. Their high price usually limits their sales, though the tiny TPH in particular is an outstanding handgun and is very popular.

Beretta

Italy's Pietro Beretta Co., like Walther, is a respected firearms manufacturer with extensive experience in building rimfire handguns. Although best known for their larger military-caliber pistols like the World War II era Model 1934 and the current Model 92, Beretta also makes several excellent rimfire pistols which are popular for clandestine use. As early as 1948 Beretta made a rimfire version of the Model 1934, and today rimfire pistols account for a significant portion of Beretta's business.

Beretta rimfire pistols of importance today include the tiny Model 950 "Minx" which is, interestingly enough, chambered in 22 *Short*, and the larger (Walther PP-sized) Model 70. The Model 70, a single-action pistol, is very highly regarded and has been used by Israel's elite *Mossad* counterterrorist organization, among others.

During the mid-to-late 1970s, the Model 70 gained worldwide fame and notoriety as *Mossad* operatives using them hunted down the leaders of the Palestinian organization "Black Sep-

tember," who had masterminded the deadly attack on Israeli athletes at the 1972 Olympics. The *Mossad*'s tactics were simple and fatally effective: several agents would surround their target and quickly shoot him in the head, a dozen or more times, at point-blank range. The smooth trigger and rapid cyclic rate of the Model 70 was well suited to this type of shooting and well-practiced *Mossad* agents could empty a Model 70's eight-shot magazine in less than three seconds. The *Mossad* spent the better part of a decade killing all of the Black September leadership - many with 22s - who had been involved in planning the Olympic attack.

Both the Model 950 and the Model 70 are single-action designs. The Model 950 remains in production, while Beretta dropped the Model 70 in the late 1980s. Beretta has since the late 1960s also developed several innovative double-action rimfire pistols as well, some of which have found their way into official service. These include the Models 21, 87 and 89. The Model 21 is only slightly larger than the Walther TPH and, like that pistol, is too small for importation into the United States. Beretta licensed its U.S. subsidiary, Beretta U.S.A., to make this pistol and it has proven to be an enormous

Ruger's Mark II Government Model (top) and Walther's Model TPH (bottom) are two of the most popular rimfire pistols currently in military service.

Ruger's Mark II, fitted with an AWC Amphibian integral silencer, is a popular choice for clandestine service with elite forces like the Navy SEALS (Photo courtesy of AWC System Technologies).

success.

Just under 5 inches long and weighing only 12 ounces fully loaded, the Model 21 is a good backup or undercover pistol and has proven to be very popular with police forces.

The larger Model 87 or "Cheetah" is one of the world's finest 22 LR handguns. Essentially a miniaturized version of the Model 92 service pistol, the Model 87 is the ideal trainer for shooters who will be issued double-action military pistols. Because the Model 87 has a thumb safety which can lock the hammer in its cocked position, it is also a good training pistol for a shooter who will be using a single-action pistol like the M1911A1 or FN Hi-Power. The versatile Model 87 can also serve as an excellent training tool for a shooter who will transition to a double-action pistol with the cocked and locked carry option, such as the CZ-75.

In addition to its use as a training pistol, the Model 87 is known to have been used in espionage and counter-terrorism by *Mossad*. For them the Model 87 is the logical replacement for the out-of-production Model 70, being about the same size. Interestingly, *Mossad* seems to prefer the competition version of the Model 87, which has the same grip frame as the standard version but also has a longer, 6-inch barrel.

Beretta's Model 89 belongs in a class by itself. A single-action design, the Model 89 is unquestionably a target and competition piece primarily. Still, there is no doubt Beretta intended it to have a military training capability as well. Its arrangement of operating controls and slab-sided appearance are clearly features intended to appeal to military organizations seeking a training pistol.

All Beretta pistols have a well-deserved reputation for nearly flawless reliability, a real accomplishment when a rimfire round must be coupled with a semi-automatic mechanism.

Beretta's Model 70 has been for decades one of the top pistols for clandestine use. The .22LR version shown here sports AWC's Archangel suppressor (Photo courtesy of AWC System Technologies).

Walther Model PP-series pistols, often in .22LR caliber, have long been favored by military organizations for clandestine uses. Here a Model PPK/S with Pachmayr grips is fitted with the excellent AWC Warp III suppressor (Photo courtesy of AWC System Technologies).

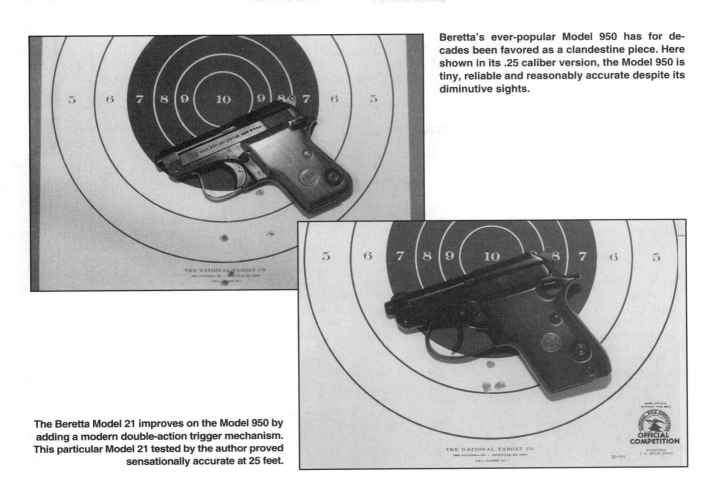

Beretta's ever-popular Model 950 has for decades been favored as a clandestine piece. Here shown in its .25 caliber version, the Model 950 is tiny, reliable and reasonably accurate despite its diminutive sights.

The Beretta Model 21 improves on the Model 950 by adding a modern double-action trigger mechanism. This particular Model 21 tested by the author proved sensationally accurate at 25 feet.

Colt

European companies don't hold a monopoly on rimfire handguns suited for military use. American manufacturers have long produced some of the world's top rimfire pistols. During World War II a variety of Colt Woodsman pistols saw service, including models used as trainers and suppressor-equipped versions for clandestine use.

With their long, thin, exposed barrel, Colt Woodsman pistols were well set up for installation of an integral suppressor completely surrounding the barrel, which was then drilled through with extra holes to reduce the bullet's velocity. Although it is more difficult to manufacture because of the extra work involved in modifying the barrel, an integral suppressor is generally a more efficient silencing arrangement than a muzzle can.

Perhaps the most interesting Colt rimfire pistols placed into military service were the Ace and Service Ace pistols based on the Model 1911. Colt envisaged these two models as training pistols when introducing them in 1931 and 1937 respectively. While the

Ace simply married a lightweight slide to a standard M1911A1 frame, the more sophisticated Service Ace added a floating firing chamber to closely duplicate the recoil of a full-bore 45 caliber M1911A1. This feature made the Service Ace a most useful and valuable training tool. Colt also briefly marketed, from 1938 on, a

22 caliber conversion unit, with which an owner of a 45 caliber M1911-type pistol could modify the gun to use 22 Long Rifle ammunition. Production continued during the war but ended soon afterwards, though the U.S. armed forces still list Colt Service Aces in their inventory. M1911A1s converted to fire 22 Long Rifle ammunition are still a delight to shoot, but original rimfire Colts are getting scarce and are now highly valued as collectors' items.

High Standard

High Standard pistols also saw extensive use by the U.S. military in World War II and

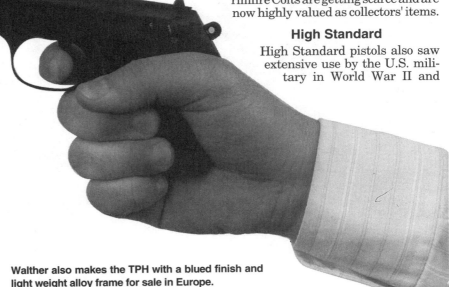

Walther also makes the TPH with a blued finish and light weight alloy frame for sale in Europe.

have remained in service in considerable quantities ever since. Slightly more durable than the slender-barreled Woodsman, several of the various High Standard models are well suited for clandestine use. Francis Gary Powers, the U2 pilot shot down over the Soviet Union in 1960, carried a silenced High Standard Model HD on that fateful mission. Suppressor-equipped High Standard pistols also saw extensive service in the Vietnam War.

As a training pistol, the High Standard excelled in various forms, particularly the Supermatic Trophy and Citation. High Standard modeled the stocks or grips of these pistols to approximate as closely as possible the handling of the M1911A1.

Although High Standard went out of business in early 1985, new companies have been gradually resuming production of High Standard pistols, successfully rebuilding virtually the entire High Standard line. The new High Standard pistols are reported excellent in functional quality and workmanship and faithful to the original guns, although most are built in stainless steel.

Ruger

Sturm, Ruger's famous Standard pistol, their first firearm introduced back in 1949, and the later Mark II version of the same pistol introduced in 1982, have also seen considerable official use. Ruger rimfire pistols have been especially popular in the United States, where their use has spanned the most humble training command to the feared Tunnel Rats of the Vietnam War, but Ruger rimfire pistols have also seen use in Canada, Israel, and other countries. The current version of the Ruger Mark II in use by the United States government is, appropriately enough, called the Mark II Government Model. It has a 6 7/8-inch barrel and is made both in blued and stainless steel.

AWC makes an excellent suppressor system for the Mark II, called the Amphibian. This, unlike the Warp III, is an integral unit and fits around the Ruger's long, slim barrel. Though it gives the pistol a bull-barreled appearance it adds no length to the gun. The Ruger Mark II equipped with the Amphibian suppressor system has also seen clandestine use, including SEAL Team service.

Ruger pistols, compared to competitors from Smith & Wesson, Colt and High Standard, are considerably less expensive. Making extensive and innovative use of low-cost manufacturing techniques such as investment casting, Ruger offers a pistol comparable in quality, workmanship and performance to guns costing far more. The Mark II's one weak point is its relatively complicated disassembly procedure.

Smith & Wesson

Smith & Wesson joined the military rimfire pistol collection in the late 1950s with the superb Model 41 and a lower-priced version, the Model 46. The Model 41, an excellent and accurate pistol, remains popular with military shooting teams, However, because its barrel is surrounded almost entirely by the slide, the Model 41 is not well suited to the installation of a sound suppressor. It is also a very expensive firearm.

Smith & Wesson K-frame 22 LR rimfire revolvers have proven popular with military and police forces as sub-caliber training pistols for the 38 caliber Model 10 and similar revolvers; current Smith & Wesson designations for these rimfire revolvers are Models 17 and 18.

Rimfire Conversions

A number of military pistols in addition to the Colt M1911A1 and Walther P-38 are capable of being fitted with rimfire conversion kits. For instance, the Peter Stahl com-

With excellent sights and a smooth trigger pull, the Beretta Model 87 is capable of fast accurate fire as demonstrated by this 5-shot offhand group fired from a distance of 25 feet.

The arrangement of manual safety, slide top, and magazine release of the Beretta Model 87 (bottom) are identical to those of the Browning High Power shown above it, making the Model 87 an inexpensive training adjunct to the larger service pistol.

Walther's Model P38, a full-sized 9mm service pistol, can be fitted with a conversion kit featuring a slide light enough to cycle with the weaker .22LR rimfire round, a special barrel or (as here) a barrel insert for .22 cartridges, and a special magazine.

pany of Germany has made 22 LR conversion kits, consisting of slide, barrel and magazine, to fit the Colt M1911A1 or Commander, SIG P-210, FN Hi-Power, Smith & Wesson Model 39, Star Models 28/30 and CZ-75. These kits function well, with accuracy often as good as, or better than, that of the original pistols. They feature numerous thoughtful touches, notably excellent adjustable sights to allow the shooter to compensate for the difference in point of impact between the rimfire ammunition and the centerfire ammunition of the standard unconverted pistol. However, the Peters Stahl rimfire conversion kits do not mimic the recoil of the guns in their service caliber, usually 9mm, thus reducing their realism in training; hence their popularity among military services is slight. In addition, these kits are extremely expensive, in many cases costing as much or even more than the full-

sized pistol, and so are doubly unlikely to see widespread use.

Considerably less expensive is the kit made by the Jonathan Arthur Ceiner Company for the M1911 pistol. Ceiner makes 22 conversion kits for several long arms as well as the M1911. Like the Peters Stahl units, each Ceiner kit attaches to a centerfire gun supplied by the cutomer and is considerably less expensive than a complete rimfire gun would be. The chief drawback of the Ceiner is that, like most rimfire setups, they tend to be sensitive to the type of ammunition being used.

In 1993, Action Arms announced that CZ would begin offering a 22LR top half (barrel and slide), as well as a new magazine, to allow owners of a 9mm CZ-75 to convert their gun to rimfire operation. According to inital reports, this kit would cost only about half as much as a new pistol. However, it has existed only in prototype form for more than a year, with

a U.S. introduction date not yet announced as of this writing.

SIG offers a factory rimfire conversion kit for their Model P-210 pistol, but like everything else associated with that classic handgun, it is very expensive. Heckler & Koch also makes a 22 caliber conversion kit for its 32 or 380 caliber P7K3 pistol. Again, like SIG, this is expensive, but both units have seen military and police service in Europe as training guns. The rimfire's high initial cost is quickly offset by the price differential between rimfire and centerfire ammunition, and the SIG and H&K conversions are also extraordinarily accurate.

Rimfire handguns have served the world's armed forces very capably in a variety of specialized roles. Military rimfires offer an interesting field either for the collector or for the casual shooter who wants an historic and interesting firearm that is both enjoyable and economical to shoot.   ●

Colt pistols of the Woodsman type have seen U.S. military service since World War II, both for pistol training and for clandestine operations. The Woodsman's long, exposed barrel is ideal for the fitting of an integral suppressor for situations where silence is golden.

How To Shoot A Boat Anchor

by Jon Love

Pistol shooters are like marathon runners: appearances are deceiving. You can't tell by how a competitor looks at the starting line how well he's going to place at the finish. I know this; I don't have to be told; still, I couldn't help but be surprised watching that old man at the firearms class.

It was a firearms certification class for private investigator and security types that would qualify them to carry a handgun while on duty. There were about 25 students, most of them in their 20s and 30s. and all had their handguns on the desk in front of them, waiting as the instructor inspected each weapon for safety. Most students carried one of the new combat-style semi-automatics in either 9mm or 40 caliber. The lone exception was a weathered man who was well into his 60s.

"Haven't seen one of these in a long time," the instructor said, stopping at the old man's desk. He picked up the man's short barreled Colt revolver, closed the cylinder and worked the action.

"While it can be done," the instructor said, raising his voice and holding the revolver up so everyone could see, "we don't recommend trying to qualify on this course with a snub-nosed revolver. They don't have the accuracy."

The old man looked pained. "It's all I brought," he said.

The instructor peered down at him, noticing for the first time the day-old whiskers, worn-out boots and jeans; short, scrawny frame; and overall smell of tobacco. The picture reminded him of the country-western song lyrics about an old man who "had to drink a beer to keep his Levis on his hips."

The instructor shrugged, put the gun down and went on to the next student. "Not my worry," he mumbled.

Besides trying to qualify with a two-inch, the old fool was using a Colt. Even in the days before automatics, when everyone carried revolvers, there weren't many who used the Colt. Most shooters agreed it had a more primitive action than the Smith

The geezer at left shoots the belly gun better than either of them look to a range master.

& Wesson. Those who did use it did so for no rational reason. Pinned to the wall they'd usually come up saying something like they "carried the damn Colt because they liked it."

The old man's Colt was the Python model, a 357 with a 2-1/2 inch barrel. Colt brought these out in the '50s, advertising them in the *American Rifleman* alongside a picture of a '55 Cadillac, touting the Python as the Cadillac of the firearms world, with a list price of $125.

No matter how well the action was polished, and it was smooth as glass, Colt couldn't hide the fact the design hadn't been changed since they brought out their Army Special model in 1908. In the '60s, shooters in the know were going with Smith & Wesson. In Los Angeles, both the P.D. and the Sheriff's Department issued Smith Combat Masterpieces to their troops.

"There's nothing wrong with the Colt," one range master said. "They make a great boat anchor."

Still, some used their own money to buy a Colt. These guys, the ones who used Colt revolvers, were usually the same guys who in the '50s had run flat-head Fords in their coupes when they could just as easily have dropped in a small block Chevy; or who passed on the panhead Harley to go with a late '30s Indian Chief.

The Colt, like the flat-head Ford and the Indian, was just a more down-to-earth machine, built closer to the ground, so to speak. Perhaps mastering it was more of a challenge, and victory with it somehow sweeter.

They understood the Smith might be a better machine, the design more refined, the piece manufactured with closer tolerances. They chose the Colt for no other reason than they liked the feel of the thing, liked the way it handled.

When the lecture part of the class was finished, the instructor had the students move to an indoor range to fire the qualification course. And the first ten students lined up at the firing points and listened to instructions from an ex-cop range master.

"The command to commence firing and cease fire will be this whistle," the range master said, and demonstrated by blowing the whistle he carried on a string around his neck.

The old man sidled up to him: "Listen," he told the range master in a low voice, I could see you blow that thing, but I couldn't hear it worth a damn."

The range master stared at him, dumbfounded.

"If you gotta get my attention," the old man said, "just kick me in the butt."

The range master nodded and rolled his eyes. And he appeared nervous as he watched the old man load six rounds for the first string of fire.

"Commence firing," the range master yelled and blew the whistle he knew the old man couldn't hear.

Bringing his revolver onto target, the old man moved slowly and didn't appear hurried, yet got his rounds off well before any of the others. Three automatic pistols jammed and the line waited while these shooters cleared their weapons and finished firing the string.

The range master had everyone run their targets back to check them. He stood behind the old man's firing point to see how he'd done. Five rounds were in the ten ring with one nine, just out at six o'clock. The range master shook his head, then checked on the other shooters who were mostly all over the target.

The rest of the course went much the same and at the end of the day, after all 25 students had fired and scored their targets, only one shooter had a score higher than the old man's.

"You're a pretty good shot," the range master told him. "How come you use that old two-inch Colt?"

"Hell, I don't know," the old man said. "I guess 'cause I like it." ●

Ducros in full flow — ideas in birth.

THE CLEAN
NEW LINE
is the

daily goal of

CHRISTIAN DUCROS —
The Temperament

Radical and rational at the same time, Ducros' reshaping pares the cylinder.

From the working side, the cylinder is entirely functional, but a lot lighter.

# of an Artist

by Raymond Caranta

Living at Pont-Saint-Esprit, along the Rhone river, in the South-East of France, where gold nuggets were found in 1964, Christian Ducros has become the most innovating of the current French custom gunmakers. His guns are remarkable.

Pont-Saint-Esprit has never been a traditional gunsmithing center, but it is at the verge of the Ardeche Trail and famous for boar hunting since the oldest Gallic times. Even when there is no iron ore in the area, enthusiastic hunters form another sort of nucleus required for the founding of a dynamic gunsmithing workshop. At first, Ducros worked in the repair and restructuring of loved family guns; and then, moved into the styling of bold custom rifles and shotguns.

Now just over 30, Christian Ducros started in working life on a milling machine, 15 years ago. Then, he learned the skill of fitting in the old-fashioned "window shop" of Mr. Chariot, an exacting craftsman born in Saint-Etienne. Chariot highly appreciated Ducros' integrity and temper, and led him into the custom gun world, opening to him the most hidden doors of the French gunmakers' Mecca.

Irresistibly attracted by gun steel, Ducros moved later to Saint-Etienne, 80 miles northwards and attended the Saint-Etienne gunsmithing school. However, it was in the shops of then-numerous craftsmen that he became a complete gunsmith, skilled at the making of fine actions, barrels, ejectors, locks, shaped blade springs and stocks.

The French proofhouse agrees — Ducros' remodeling doesn't hurt this S&W.

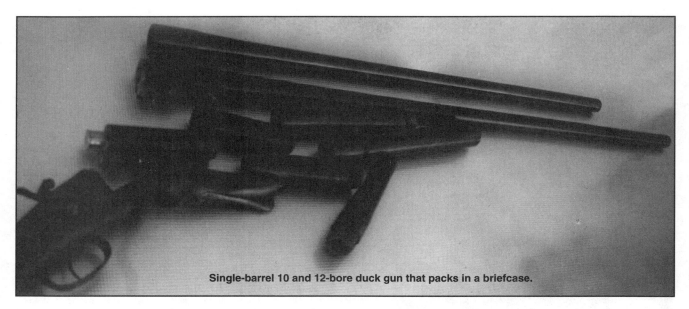

Single-barrel 10 and 12-bore duck gun that packs in a briefcase.

When he felt he was ready, he went back to his native Ardeche and opened a modest gun repair shop, slowly making a name and hiring two seasoned specialists. At this stage, Ducros made several side-by-side shotguns of the first generation from vintage Holland & Holland action forgings. He considers the Holland and Holland system supreme, and

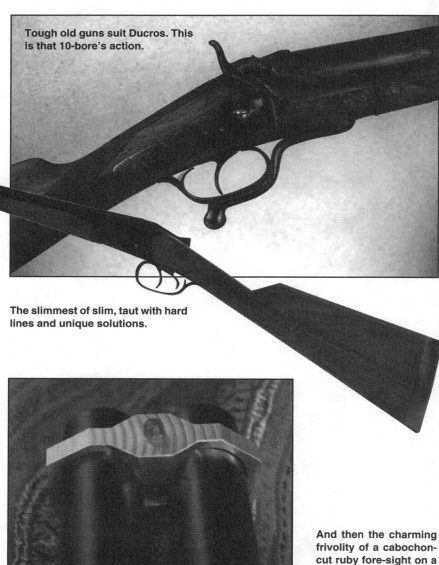

Tough old guns suit Ducros. This is that 10-bore's action.

The slimmest of slim, taut with hard lines and unique solutions.

demonstrated he could produce an entire gun.

The game at which Christian Ducros is a master, however, is remodeling and rebuilding, in which he artistically converts old actions of the best quality, into futurist creations.

For instance, Ducros has in his armory a huge single-shot duck gun he built from an old "Desagart in Saint-Etienne" hammer folding action locked under the trigger guard, with a crazy 10-gauge Magnum (3.5-inch chambering) 1.45-inch diameter barrel, which is 51-inches long, but can be taken apart in five sections for carrying in a suitcase! Of course, the barrel length can be varied as required, if used as a cylinder bore and the choked muzzle fitting is interchangeable. And there's a spare 12-gauge (3-inch chambering) barrel, 38 inches long.

During our visit, our stylist was fitting a rich Lefaucheux side-by-side double hammer action, with ultra-modern Kevlar barrels and a faceted stock. He was also working on a "restructured" Holland & Hol-

And then the charming frivolity of a cabochon-cut ruby fore-sight on a platform.

No-nonsense moorings for the regulated barrels of an over-under combination gun mount and front sight as well.

land Royal first-type shotgun and a Holland & Holland-style side-by-side action with Purdey locks and improved ejectors, made by Auguste Lebeau, founder of the famous Belgian Lebeau-Courally company.

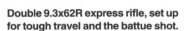

Double 9.3x62R express rifle, set up for tough travel and the battue shot.

The Lebeau 12-gauge shotgun was fitted with the faceted stock designed by Ducros and two pair of barrels for woods and for country hunting.

Ducros is very fond of his rebuilding job, as he claims that it saves both time and money. According to him,

This combination is a side-by-side fitted for battue's close-range snap shots with a Leupold pistol scope.

the customer can get for $2000 a superb handmade action of yesteryear, which would cost a fortune to make nowadays.

Ducros is now preparing a new generation of double shotguns. He has in stock 200 Holland & Holland style action forgings, 50 pair of first-quality old French barrels and 50 blanks of outstanding red burl-walnut. According to our Ducros, such forgings should be stored for at least fifty years before fitting, in order to achieve a proper stabilization of steel. Ducros can work on every conventional action, but his favorite trick is fitting Anson & Deeley barrels to Holland & Holland triple-lock actions, using what he calls his "B" closure which, he claims, efficiently combines the helix sturdiness with Purdey-style refinement.

Of course, in this particular field of activity, cost efficiency is only a remote criterion. As far as workmanship is concerned, the goal of Ducros is "to challenge by

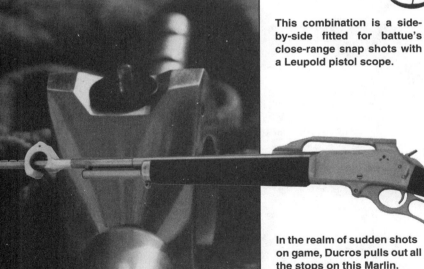

In the realm of sudden shots on game, Ducros pulls out all the stops on this Marlin.

In the split-second work of the forest battue this is a sight for hunters' eyes!

hand the machine, in terms of precision and cleverness". His dream would be to restore the Versailles manufactory.

In this connection, Ducros believes the basic step in fine gunmaking is the quality of fitting. His actions are so closely fitted to the barrels they do not fall when at-

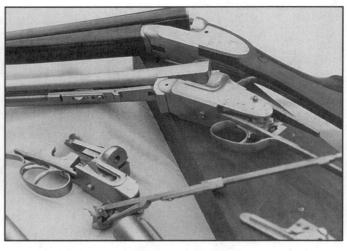

The trick is to put the impressive sharp and clean edges where the shooter's hand isn't.

Nothing extra on a Ducros' remodelization job.

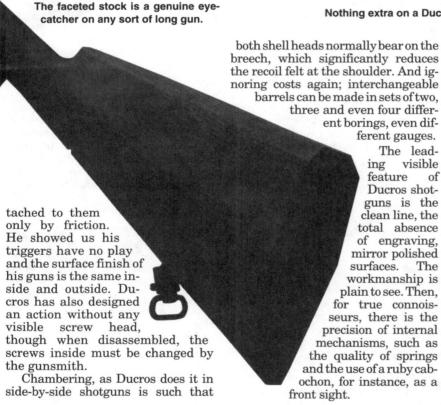

The faceted stock is a genuine eye-catcher on any sort of long gun.

tached to them only by friction. He showed us his triggers have no play and the surface finish of his guns is the same inside and outside. Ducros has also designed an action without any visible screw head, though when disassembled, the screws inside must be changed by the gunsmith.

Chambering, as Ducros does it in side-by-side shotguns is such that both shell heads normally bear on the breech, which significantly reduces the recoil felt at the shoulder. And ignoring costs again; interchangeable barrels can be made in sets of two, three and even four different borings, even different gauges.

The leading visible feature of Ducros shotguns is the clean line, the total absence of engraving, mirror polished surfaces. The workmanship is plain to see. Then, for true connoisseurs, there is the precision of internal mechanisms, such as the quality of springs and the use of a ruby cabochon, for instance, as a front sight.

Currently, double shotguns chambered in 410 bore or 28 gauge can be delivered within one year with up to three pairs of interchangeable barrels. This lead time is also applicable for Holland & Holland style shotguns of other calibers, provided the customer requirements match the existing stock of forgings and stock blanks. Otherwise, customers have to wait three to five years.

Among other paradoxes, Ducros is full of admiration for the work of Russian and Czech gunmakers, in spite of their imperfections, because he feels they still are among the last working the old way. Therefore, he is converting — for about $2000 base price — Russian Baikal shotguns supplied by the customer. And he is negotiating now to make a batch of fifty such guns.

Beside this custom work, Ducros has developed a slide-action conversion—with fast spring return of the slider—for self-loading rifles requiring a gun licence in France, such as the Remington 7400. He can also easily adapt any slide action gun to this fast spring forearm return design. He has also invented a clever device for regulating double express over-under rifle barrels. It properly sets the upper barrel, using an adjustable clamp. He is very proud of his untasselled faceted stock.

These are, Ducros says, just practical achievements. Custom guns are, for Ducros, the materialization of an ideal, beyond the outstanding sporting implements they are intended to be. They faithfully reflect the personality of their creator and the appreciation of his customer. More simply, Christian Ducros makes dream guns. •

More hard edges and innovative shapes.

Still America's Original

THE MOSSBERG® MODEL 500®

Model 500
1970

Model 500
1998

Over four generations, the MOSSBERG family has produced affordable firearms, made in America for the American sportsman. MOSSBERG has continued to set the standards for reliability and durability, previously unheard of in production shotguns. Why?...Because firearms is our business and we proudly put our name on every one.

The MOSSBERG Model 500 continues to improve over time and still has the steel-to-steel lock up, dual cartridge stops, twin extractors and an ambidextrous top-tang safety, that was a first on any pump shotgun. In addition, MOSSBERG is still the only American made shotgun to meet U.S. government military specifications. New challenges have led to further innovation. **Many Model 500 barrels are factory ported** and feature a wide assortment of specialized choke tubes, stocks and finishes.

With models available in 12 ga., 20 ga. and .410, plus adult and youth versions, it's easy to see why the MOSSBERG Model 500 continues to be America's favorite pump shotgun.

12 ga. Model 500 Camo #52193

MOSSBERG

Shotguns
Heard Around the World

*Safety and safe firearms handling
is everyone's responsibility.*

O.F. Mossberg & Sons, Inc. • 7 Grasso Avenue • P.O. Box 497 • North Haven, CT 06473-9844
An ISO 9001 registered company
Visit our website at: www.mossberg.com

The Colt® Magnum Carry™

The Colt® Magnum Carry™ shown actual size - Actual weight 21 ounces

Six Rounds of Practical - Tactical .357 Magnum Power

When Colt® announced the Detective Special® revolver in 1927 we didn't know that this revolver would become the benchmark for all concealed carry revolvers yet to come.

The new Colt® Magnum Carry™ revolver will carve its own niche in shooting history.

Chambered for six rounds of .357 Magnum, the stainless steel Colt® Magnum Carry™ revolver is the world's most practical - tactical self defense revolver.

IF IT ISN'T A COLT . . . . . . IT'S JUST A COPY™

To speak to the authorized Colt® dealer nearest you, call 1-888-818-2658 ext. 6226

Colt's Manufacturing Company, Inc., P.O. Box 1868, Hartford, CT 06144-1868

The Best Resources

for every firearm enthusiast

1998 Standard Catalog of

FIREARMS

THE COLLECTOR'S PRICE & REFERENCE GUIDE

8TH EDITION

NEW EDITION

ALL NEW 11th EDITION

HANDGUNS '99

Handgun Tests
Self-Defense
Gun Law Update
Concealed Carry
Etiquette
Ammunition & Reloading
Gunsmithing
Hunting
Collecting
Complete Catalog of
Handguns and
Accessories

Edited by
RAY ORDORICA

NEW EDITION

EXPANDED! New Chapter • Many Revisions • More Photos

FLAYDERMAN'S GUIDE TO ANTIQUE AMERICAN FIREARMS ...and their values

7TH EDITION
By Norm Flayderman

FULLY UPDATED

NEW EDITION

COLT MEMORABILIA PRICE GUIDE

MORE THAN 1,500 COLOR PHOTOS AND PRICES

FEATURE KNIVES, BUCKLES, OFFICE SUPPLIES, PATCHES, JEWELRY AND MORE

HIGHLIGHTS COLLECTIBLES FROM SAM COLT'S MANY BUSINESS VENTURES

JOHN OGLE

Colt .45 "Peacemaker"

NEW

Krause Publications
700 E. State St., Iola, WI 54990-0001

For a free copy of our catalog *please call* 800-258-0929
Dept. FDB1 or visit our web site at www.krause.com

since 1952

Standard Catalog of Firearms
8th Edition
by Ned Schwing
The firearms enthusiast's best source for current values, technical specifications and history now boasts 1,200 pages with more than 4,000 photos. That's 100 more pages of text with 25,000 updated prices and 1,400 new photos when compared to the seventh edition! There are expanded sections for Savage, Sauer, Ithaca, Sturm and many others.
Softcover • 8-1/2 x 11 • 1,200 pages • 4,000 b&w photos • **GG08** • **$29.95**

Handguns '99
11th Edition
Edited by Ray Ordorica
Information on ammunition and reloading, self-defense, ballistics, collecting, competition, customizing, military and law enforcement, hunting and accessories. More than 1,000 handguns currently manufactured in or imported to the U.S., including full specifications and retail prices. Coverage of metallic sights and handgun scopes and mounts, a list of periodical publications and arms associations, the handgunner's library and a comprehensive directory of the trade.
Softcover • 8-1/4 x 10-11/16 • 352 pages
• 1,800+ b&w photos • **H99** • **$22.95** • **Avail. 8/98**

Flayderman's Guide to Antique American Firearms & Their Values
7th Edition
by Norm Flayderman
More than 3,600 models and variants are extensively described. Includes 2,800 individually priced firearms with full information on how to assess values based on demand, rarity and condition. More than 1,700 photos accompany model descriptions for convenient identification. Histories of the makers are described with dates and locations of manufacture and quantities manufactured. Softcover • 8-1/4 x 10-11/16 • 656 pages • 1,700 b&w photos • **FLA7** • **$32.95**

Colt Memorabilia Price Guide
by John Ogle
The Colt Memorabilia Price Guide is the first book compiled about the vast array of non-gun merchandise produced by Sam Colt's companies, and other companies using the Colt name. More than 1,500 color photos help the reader identify a wide range of objects from knives, buckles, and badges to office supplies, decals, glassware and coasters. Realistic market prices, prepare the reader to begin their own collection or evaluate the collectibles they already own. If you have been collecting Colt for years, or are just beginning, this must-have book is simply the best source of information available.
Softcover • 8-1/2 x 11 • 256 pages • 1,500 color photos • **CCOL** • **$29.95**

CREDIT CARD CALLS TOLL-FREE
800-258-0929
Dept. FDB1

Mon.-Fri., 7 a.m. - 8 p.m. • Sat. 8 a.m. - 2 p.m., CST

Visit and order from our secure web site at:
www.krause.com

A New Look at the

Webley Mark IV .38

by Gene Gangarosa, Jr

History has often harshly treated a good handgun, the Webley Mark IV 38 revolver. It's a fine-handling, accurate revolver which deserves a better break than it has received from most commentators. This article represents that new perspective because I maintain the Webley 38 was far better than it is usually believed to be.

The Webley company developed the Mark IV 38 revolver beginning in 1923. The British were re-evaluating their military handgun needs based on their experiences in World War One. They had decided the 455-caliber Webley Mark VI, which had served very well in that war, was too heavy and bulky and produced excessive recoil for the average recruit (who was not likely to be a gun enthusiast) So the British Army purchased samples of a revolver being developed for police use by the Webley company. Webley based this new design on a smaller version of the Mark VI firing a 38-caliber bullet weighing 200 grains. This round, originally called the "38 Web-ley Special" and later the "38/200," had a muzzle velocity of about 600 feet per second, slower than the original 455 Webley cartridge.

Satisfied in principle with the Webley design, the Royal Army became dissatisfied with the company's slow progress in getting the prototype into series production. Therefore, in 1926, they directed the Royal Small Arms Factory at Enfield Lock (RSAF Enfield) to create its own design, based on the Webley but incorporating changes they wanted made to the trigger mechanism and lockwork. The resulting revolver, the No. 2, went into service with the Royal Army in 1932, and they were well satisfied with it.

In 1938, the British armed forces dropped the original 200-grain lead bullet in favor of a 178-grain jacketed bullet which, it was thought, would produce less painful and more survivable wounds in keeping with international agreements on military small-arms ammunition. Using this lighter bullet also raised the muzzle velocity to about 650 feet per second, and most of these revolvers today will be found to be sighted in with this ammunition.

Meanwhile, Webley continued to promote its own design, which the company finally introduced as a private venture in 1929. The company was modestly successful selling its well-made 38-caliber revolver (along with a 22 rim fire training version, plus target and pocket models) to police forces in Great Britain and in foreign countries prior to World War Two.

When war broke out in 1939, Britain was desperately short of modern firearms with which to equip its troops. Consequently, in 1940 the government ordered 100,000 Webley revolvers as the Mk. IV 38. Deliveries began in 1942 and continued until 1945.

Early wartime Webleys were soon preferred to the Arsenal-made Enfields.

Ironically, British troops held the Webley Mk. IV 38 in higher esteem than the official Enfield revolver derived from it. The Webley company had enjoyed a decades-long association with the British armed forces and the Mk.IV 38 was invariably better made and finished than its Enfield rival. For all that, the Mk. IV 38 got a reputation of being a poor antipersonnel handgun, and was frequently derided, particularly by elite troops, such as Commandos, who placed heavy emphasis on handgun use.

The Mk. IV 38 served well throughout the war and beyond. The Army did not declare the type obsolete until 1956. However, some continued to serve British police forces and Commonwealth countries for many more years after that, and some probably still remain in service in areas where British influence was strong.

Although the British government quit buying Mark IV 38 revolvers for its armed forces in 1945, commercial production continued after the war, albeit at a reduced level. Postwar production consisted of the standard full-sized service model, which had a four or five-inch barrel, a pocket model with smaller grip and three-inch barrel, and two target models, in either 22 or 38 calibers, with adjustable sights and six-inch barrels. Production of this revolver line finally stopped in 1979, at which time the Webley company discontinued all firearms production to concentrate on air gun manufacture instead.

The Mk. IV 38, while obviously less powerful than the company's legendary Mk.VI of World War One fame, is easy to handle and fire and is very accurate. The Webley and British Army personnel who had input into the revolver's design clearly succeeded in regard to making it an easy gun to handle and shoot.

The very light recoil and comparatively low noise level associated with the 38 cartridge are highly conducive to accurate shooting. The Royal Army realized, a long time ago, that a small hit is better than a large miss. There are other factors besides the low power which give the Mk. IV 38 such exemplary handling.

It is, in fact, an impressively ergonomic design and represents in many ways the zenith of military revolver design and manufacture.

The Mk. IV 38 has comfortable and attractive grips that are far superior to those found on any contemporary Smith & Wesson revolver. The grips are checkered black bakelite plastic with Webley logo at the top. They have slight palm swells in their center section and flare slightly at the bottom to give a firm and steady grip with either hand. A lanyard loop, which is a highly valuable accessory for the military shooter who might otherwise lose a gun in action, is well-located at the bottom of the frame, in a position where it will not interfere with the left-handed shooter's grip on the pistol. The Mk. IV 38's lanyard loop also rotates to the desired position, unlike the fixed loop found on so many other military pistols and which can interfere with the gun's handling.

The Mk. IV 38's top-break mechanism is faster and more reliable for unloading than that used on any modern revolver. The cylinder latch, located on the left side of the frame, can be reached easily without the (right-handed) shooter breaking his grip on the revolver, yet is far enough out of the way of the thumb so as to make it unlikely to be activated unintentionally. The reloading process itself is easily accomplished and requires only the type of gross motor skills that are not lost when a person is under an adrenaline rush in combat.

Once the gun is shot empty, one presses the thumb latch forward while at the same time pushing down at the front of the barrel. The action, which is hinged at the front of the frame just ahead of the trigger guard, then begins to break open. As the shooter opens the action to its fullest extent, the extractor star lifts out the spent cartridge casings, emptying the cylinder charge holes. Depending on how vigorously the shooter opens the action, the spent brass can be ejected mildly or thrown several feet clear.

With the empty casings out, the shooter can then insert fresh ammunition round by round. During World War One, the British had a speed loader, called the Prideaux, for use with their 455-caliber Webley Mark VI. I do not know if such a device was ever made for the smaller Mk. IV 38, but it would

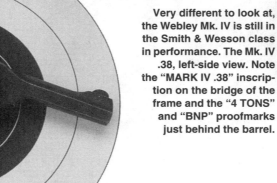

Very different to look at, the Webley Mk. IV is still in the Smith & Wesson class in performance. The Mk. IV .38, left-side view. Note the "MARK IV .38" inscription on the bridge of the frame and the "4 TONS" and "BNP" proofmarks just behind the barrel.

The Mk. IV 38's close-range provided by this rapid-fire 5-shot, all double-action offhand group measuring just 1.5 inches across.

surely have come in handy. Reloading a revolver cartridge by cartridge while under fire at close range does not appeal to me! Still, one has to unload a revolver before he can reload it, and the reloading procedure of the Mk. IV 38 is a great deal easier and therefore better than that used on any of the more modern revolvers of Colt or Smith & Wesson configuration, with their small cylinder latches and cylinders which swing out from the frame. While such modern revolvers can be reloaded from widely-available speed loaders, there

This simultaneous-ejection feature, popularized in the late 1800s, is much more efficient at unloading a revolver's chambers than the "improved" swing-out chamber.

are simply too many things which can go wrong with such revolvers in the unloading cycle. In contrast, the unloading cycle of the Mk. IV 38 is virtually foolproof.

Both the single-action and double-action trigger pulls are excellent for a military weapon—not so light as to be dangerous in the hands of nervous troops, but very smooth and easy to pull all the way through.

The sights are very good, too. The front sight, though unfortunately semicircular in profile like that of many obsolete handguns of early Twentieth Century design, is wide enough to show up well. The rear sight is a massive affair, as it is located on the sturdy cylinder latch. The resulting sight picture is prominent enough to make it quite suitable for rapid fire at close ranges, and is also precise enough for precise aimed fire at greater distances. Few if any other service-type handguns of the period, whether automatic pistols or revolvers, boast such a good sighting arrangement.

I found the Mk. IV 38 to shoot just as well as it handled. In fact, it is as impressive on the firing range as most modern handguns. For instance, I succeeded in obtaining a rapid-fire five-shot offhand group just 1.5 inches across from a distance of 25 feet. This is good shooting for me, especially as I fired all

shots using the heavier double-action trigger pull.

To see what kind of group I could fire with the Mk. IV 38 from a distance of fifty feet, I cocked the hammer before each shot to allow easier single-action shooting, reasoning that the extended range would make cocking the hammer both feasible and sensible even in a combat situation, as distance translates into time. The best resulting five-shot group measured just 2.3 inches across. This kind of accuracy is competitive with that of many guns built decades later and costing much more.

The chief criticism leveled at the Mk. IV 38 concerns its ammunition. This criticism is valid only if one assumes that some handgun ammunition is truly powerful and offers reliable one-shot stops. However, the assumption is questionable, even today with the improved modern hollow point and armor-piercing ammunition now available, and is certainly invalid with military ball ammunition even in that most overrated of handgun calibers, the 45 ACP. The fact is that no handgun ammunition of the period was a totally reliable man stopper, absent a direct hit in the brain or spinal column, and given such a direct hit, even the much-derided rounds used by the Mk. IV 38 would do the job. While not terribly powerful, the Mk. IV's .38 caliber round certainly surpasses the 32 ACP in most instances and is nearly as powerful as the 380 automatic pistols so popular in Europe during the Mark IV 38's heyday. What's more, the Mk. IV 38 revolver is more reliable than the 32- and 380-caliber medium-frame pistols.

Currently, the availability of ammunition for the Webley Mark IV 38 is quite good, since it can use surplus 38/200 or 38/178 service ammunition or even commercial 38 S&W rounds, which have a 145- or 146- grain lead round-nosed bullet. Century International Arms, the occasional importer of these revolvers, sometimes also stocks appropriate surplus British military or commercial ammunition. Commercial 38 S&W (NOT 38 Special) is also plentiful in many gun stores and works fine. Just bear in mind that

While the Walther P38 is generally considered more desirable, the Mk. IV 38 has better sights and a smoother and easier double-action trigger pull, making it a more accurate handgun.

the modern commercial 146-grain bullet, with its higher velocity of around 685 feet per second, will shoot slightly above point of aim in this fixed-sight revolver, which was originally sighted in for the Model 1938 178-grain bullet. However, as the accompanying photographs of targets show, the difference in impact is hardly enough to matter at sensible military handgun distances, which range only from a few inches out to perhaps fifty feet at most.

The British Mark IV 38 revolver is a far better handgun that its many critics suggest. It has excellent handling and, while low-powered as military handguns go, is not utterly hopeless, even today, as a self-defense weapon. Accurate shot placement is essential, to be sure, but such is the case with any handgun, and this particular revolver certainly possesses enough intrinsic accuracy to make pinpoint accuracy a feasible proposition at close ranges. What's more, as Mark IV 38 revolvers are generally held in low esteem by collectors and military buffs, their prices tend to be low. These are well-made, interesting and potentially useful handguns. •

The Other British 38s
by Gene Gangarosa

The Webley Mark IV 38 was not the only 38-caliber revolver in British service. The Enfield No. 2, which first went into service with the Royal Army in 1932, was the chief British revolver of the World War Two period and beyond until being replaced by the L9 (FN High Power) automatic pistol from 1957 on. Similar in appearance to the Webley from which it was derived, The No. 2 revolver differed mainly in some details of the lock work.

The No. 2 revolver appeared in three major variations. The No. 2 Mark I was the first. Adopted on June 2, 1932, this revolver had a prominent hammer spur which allowed cocking by the thumb for single-action shooting if desired; it could also, of course, be fired double-action.

While the No. 2 Mark I was a solid, serviceable revolver, the exposed hammer spur let to complaints from some users, notably the Royal Tank Regiment. Tank crewmen found that the hammer tended to snag in the enclosed spaces within armored vehicles, and asked that a hammerless version of the revolver be developed for them. This was done, and the resulting No. 2 Mark I* was officially adopted on June 22, 1938. In addition to removing the hammer spur, Enfield removed the single-action notch from the inside of the hammer; thus the revolver was capable only of double-action fire. To compensate for the loss of the light and accurate single-action mode, the Enfield technicians also lightened the No. 2 Mark I*'s mainspring so that the double-action trigger pull was appreciably easier than the No. 2 Mark I's had been. The grips were reshaped, too, with grooves along their upper surface for the shooter's thumb. Most No. 2 Mark I revolvers were converted to No.2 Mark I* standard, making the No.2 Mark I* by far the most common variation of this famous revolver.

During the war the Enfield factory, looking for ways to speed up production, redesigned the No. 2 Mark I*'s lockwork to create the No. 2 Mark I**. Officially accepted for British service on July 29, 1942, the No. 2 Mark I**'s chief omission was the elimination of the hammer safety stop that had been part of the mechanism of all earlier No.2 revolvers. While the elimination of this feature made the No. 2 Mark I** appreciably easier to manufacture it proved an altogether false economy, since it gave the revolver an alarming tendency to fire accidentally if dropped, which happens all too frequently in military service. As a result of its notorious lack of safety, the No. 2 Mark I** revolvers were mostly recalled and converted back to No. 2 Mark I* standard by the reintroduction of the hammer safety stop as soon as more leisurely conditions prevailed in the postwar period.

In addition to its production at RSAF Enfield between 1932 and 1957, production of complete No. 2 Mark I* revolvers also took place at Albion Motors Ltd. in Glasgow, Scotland. Albion-made No. 2 Mark I* revolvers will be seen with ALBION marked on the right side of the frame. Albion Motors made approximately 24,000 revolvers between June 1941 and November 1943. The Singer Sewing Machine Company of Clydebank also made components which it then sent to Enfield for assembly into its revolvers. These parts, marked SM or SSM, frequently appear on No. 2 Mark I* revolvers from the mid-war period.

The standard barrel length of the No. 2 revolver was five inches. However, in an apparent attempt to make it a more concealable firearm, the No. 2 revolver will occasionally be seen with the barrel cut down to two or three inches. This barrel shortening was apparently done unofficially or perhaps at armories or repair depots rather than at the factory.

Like the Webley Mark IV 38, the No. 2 revolver served British and Commonwealth police forces for decades after the war. Some remain in service with such organizations in out-of-the-way places. The No. 2 revolver had all the good points of the Webley product covered in our article, although Enfield's manufacturing standards were not as high as Webley's Altogether an estimated one million or so No. 2 revolvers were made.

Smith & Wesson, the United States revolver manufacturer, also made revolvers in 38/200 caliber for British and Commonwealth service during and after the war. Smith & Wesson began making a 38/200 caliber version of its famous Military & Police revolver in 1940, after the company's 9mm Light rifle proved a dismal failure. The British advanced Smith & Wesson one million dollars to develop the Light Rifle, but when this ill-conceived weapon proved unable to withstand the rigors of firing full power 9mm ammunition of European manufacture, the British demanded a refund. Having spent most of the advance, Smith & Wesson instead offered to repay the British by building them a million dollars' worth of Military & Police revolvers—in 38/200 caliber, rather than the usual 38

Special, the better to suit British logistics. Desperate for modern firearms, the British agreed to the Smith & Wesson proposal. Production of this model began on March 11, 1940 and from September 1940 until the end of February 1941 Smith & Wesson built the British service revolver exclusively.

The 38/200 Military & Police gained an excellent reputation in British service as a well-made and accurate revolver. Smith & Wesson built Military & Police revolvers for the British in 4-inch, 5-inch, and 6-inch barrel lengths. Early production revolvers had a polished blue finish and checkered wooden grips complete with the company's distinctive S&W medallion. Smith & Wesson then switched to a military blue finish, with plain smooth wooden grips, in December 1941. In May, 1942, the company

important adjunct to the company's revolver production for U.S. forces. By March 1945, the company had produced 568,204 revolvers for British service. Following the war, demand continued from Commonwealth countries for a Smith & Wesson-type revolver in 38/200 caliber, so Smith & Wesson reintroduced the type in February 1947. It remained in production into the 1960s, being known from 1958 on, when Smith & Wesson assigned model numbers to its products, as the Model 11.

Although the British 38-caliber revolvers never gained the reputation for stopping power enjoyed by the earlier 455-caliber Webleys, these later, smaller guns served well in World War Two and afterwards. Certainly they saw much greater production and wider use

The Mk. IV 38 held its own with the Smith and Wesson Model 13 shown below it. Both were popular service weapons with police forces around the world.

switched to a parkerized finish to lower costs even further and thus to allow faster production. Revolvers built from this point on also came from the factory only in the 5-inch barrel length, although some may have been modified "in the field" to use a shorter barrel.

Smith & Wesson's Military & Police production for the British was an

than any previous revolver in British service. For instance, production of each of the three chief 38-caliber British service revolvers: the Webley Mark IV 38, the Enfield No. 2, and the Smith & Wesson Military & Police model—far exceeded that of the legendary Webley Mk. VI of World War One fame, only 300,000 of which were ever built. •

Biannually, my friend Ted Walter and I left behind the grind of sporadically attending college, working odd jobs and riding motorcycles. We needed the break. So we took two long hunts. One trip was bow-and-arrow only. The other was rifle only. The longest run was a full month in the mountains with naught but archery tackle and what gear we could backpack. We felt guilty about our adventures and knew that we'd never amount to much if we kept doing them, but looking back, those survival hunts, as we called them, were worth every step taken, every camp made, every meal cooked over hardwood coals.

Selecting bows and arrows was always easy. Ted and I had matched recurves. But the survival rifle—that was something else. When deer or javelina were open season, we had to worry about legal big game cartridges. When big game seasons were closed, living off the land meant taking cottontails and other small edibles with a 22 rimfire. When everything was open season, we never knew what rifle to carry into the lonely backcountry.

Those survival hunts ended, but the concept of a specific survival rifle burned on, luring me toward that one perfect firearm for the job. The Basic Question: Who needs a survival rifle, anyway? The Basic Answer: Nobody, really, except perhaps a military man challenged to make it in unknown territory. On the other hand, who needs a 222 Remington or a 300 Winchester Magnum? Nobody, really. An American sportsman can get by with two rifles: a 22 rimfire and a 30-06 Springfield. Know what? That'd be as boring as watching reruns of *Gilligan's Island* twice daily for the next decade.

IN SEARCH OF
THE SURVIVAL RIFLE

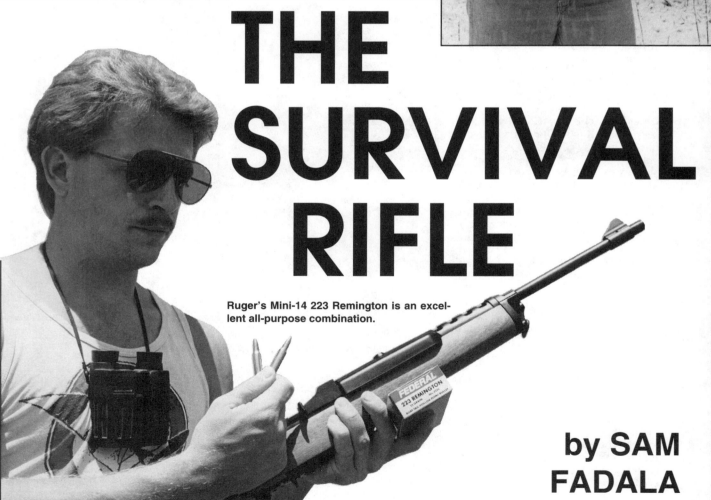

Ruger's Mini-14 223 Remington is an excellent all-purpose combination.

by SAM FADALA

The rugged Model 94 Winchester 30-30 is high on the list.

Marlin Model 25M rifle chambered for the 22 WMR cartridge will go a long way, but maybe not all the way, in survival.

Wild meat in camp can be provided by any rifle, of course, but Fadala thinks his choice is best anywhere.

Rifle lovers love to talk about practicality and ballistic matchup, but manufacturers know they can sell new guns and ammo because practicality and ballistic matchup, important as they may be, are mundane as white toast. So the quest for one rifle/cartridge good for "living off the land for a little while" stayed ever-fresh.

The best survival rifle must be a semi-automatic capable of spewing out plenty of lead when the chips are down. Wait a minute. This isn't a war we're talking about. Our survival rifle is for hunters heading into the outback. These guys don't need a semi-auto rifle. Although that style would do all right, a bolt-action would work as well. Or how about a single shot? A single shot fits the spirit of the hunt just right. But so does a lever-action. Yes, a levergun would be excellent, unless you prefer a slide-action. No, the survival rifle hardly depends on the rifle's system. Semi-auto, pump, bolt, single shot— any will do.

Maybe we should be looking at ammo instead. The 22 rimfire is a fruitful cartridge, a real producer. People shoot 22 rifles well, because there's little noise and even less felt recoil. It's wrong, but deer-sized game has been laid low with a 22 rifle. I watched it happen in Old Mex-

ico when Don Gustavo sneaked within twenty paces of a buck and dropped the animal with one shot from a broken 22 Stevens rifle that had to be single-loaded because it wouldn't feed rounds from the magazine. Furthermore, I was thinking about the Louisiana Man the other day. He taught me how to hunt when I was a lad living in Yuma, Arizona. I met him through his son. Mr. Mullens had one reason to hunt: food. If you couldn't eat it, you didn't shoot it, and if you did shoot it, you ate it.

His boy and I were two-legged bird dogs for the man with the Remington rolling block single shot 22 rimfire rifle that never saw a Long Rifle round. Big medicine in that tiny rifle was a 22 Short with one well-directed bullet. Everything was headshot. Bullfrogs sank rock-like to the bottom of the drainage canal, where we plucked them out of the muck on the bottom for Mrs. Louisiana Man to cook up floured and fried in butter. In deference to what that old-time hunter could do with a 22 rimfire, it might be just the ticket for surviving. After all, small game tastes good and is good for you, and you don't get a hernia packing a cottontail out of the woods back to your cookfire.

But the 22 rimfire is plumb illegal in many places for anything much larger than rabbit. You can't even hunt javelina with a 22 rimfire in Arizona, where I used to go on my annual survival treks. However, there is the 22 Winchester Magnum Rimfire. A cool shot can drop a lot of game with the 22 WMR, and you don't have to look for the spent case because you can't reload it anyway, which is a plus when you're having fun shooting and hunting. If I were making a temporary living in an area that had cottontails, tree squirrels, wild hogs and turkeys, that little 22 WMR might be just right. All the 22 Magnum ammo I ever tried was super: Winchester's solids or hollowpoints, Federal's excellent 50-grain bullet, RWS's hot stuff with 40-grain soft-nose hollowpoint at over 2100 feet per second—all first-rate.

The 22 WMR is a good round, but if you were turned loose to live a fall and winter in the north woods, would you opt for it as your sole survival-rifle cartridge? Maybe I've read Rowland's book *Cache Lake Country* too many times. The old title is soul food for the fellow who thinks he'd like to thrive in the backwoods for a while, perhaps in a hand-hewn cabin like the author's. That could be a real survival hunt, lasting several months, running all the way from cottontail to moose seasons, and would also take in varmints and furbearers. It would be nice, on that sort of hunt, to forget the mythical survival rifle and pack in two firearms: a 22 rimfire for small stuff and, hmmm, what about a 30-30 for everything else? Forget the rimfire. A handloader could get by with one 30-30 for everything on that six-month-long survival hunt.

He would handload a 110-grain bullet for small game, maybe a 150-grain bullet for deer, and if he knew how to hunt right and get close to elk or moose, he might load a few 190-grain Silvertips extracted from Winchester 303 Savage ammo. These heavy-for-the-30-30 bullets penetrate well. So the 30-30 might be an ideal cartridge for the survival rifle. But if the 30-30 is good, the 308 Winchester is better, with its terrific accuracy potential and good power in a compact rifle, not to mention versatile loads. I have one that goes with me more and more. Mine is a Model 77 Ruger International with 18.5-inch barrel. It's topped off with a Bushnell 2.5-8x scope, because I learned how effective higher magnification was on that little rifle for putting a bullet perfectly on the mark at 200 yards, especially from a field rest.

But if the 308 Winchester is about right, isn't the 30-06 Springfield even more correct for a true survival rifle? No. This is *my* fantasy, and I say the line has been drawn. A hunter needs nothing with greater authority than the 308 Winchester as a survival cartridge, with bullets up to 200 grains weight at about 2400 fps. So the 30-06 and all its kin are out. Magnums we won't even waste ink on.

Something *is* missing. We left something out. What was it? Oh yes, the 22 centerfire. After all, an accu-

The AR-7, assembled and shooting, is a specialized tool with its own niche.

rate 22 centerfire from Hornet to Swift could, indeed, do it all. In the hands of a good shot, the 220 Swift, for example, is deadly as two rattlers on a field mouse. But wait a minute. Who needs the noise? And what about small game? You don't need, or want, a blow-up varmint round for small game. I did my duty mentioning the 22 centerfire, and we'll leave it there in the imagination, where it belongs.

We need a survival rifle cartridge that will perform at close to medium range. We do not need long-range authority. If you're in a live-off-the-land situation, then you have time to hunt, which means stalking close enough for that one sure shot. Get close enough, and medium power is the same as high power at long

Fadala's quest brought him to a rifle he already owned, a Ruger Model 77 International. Rebedded, with new forend cap of ebony, and a Black-T finish, it stands up to any kind of weather.

range. Accuracy? Yes, the survival rifle must be accurate enough to get the job done, but this isn't a benchrest contest. A couple-inch group at a hundred is sufficient, but we can do a lot better. Noise? The noise factor is a moot point. In the middle of nowhere, one big boom does not permanently disturb game. But my partner and I never did like big boomers in the back country. There seemed to be something wrong about a stick of dynamite going off in paradise.

A reliable, reasonably accurate rifle chambered for a versatile cartridge—that sums up the concept of the survival rifle, for it is only a concept. Nobody needs one, as admitted earlier. But can you picture yours anyway? I finally saw mine. It was under my nose all the time. I already owned my "perfect" survival rifle.

You see, the process was the product in my search. The process of thinking about, and looking for, that ideal survival rifle taught me what I needed to know about that nobody-really-needs-one-anyway survival rifle. I grabbed my little Model 77 Ruger International 308 Winchester and rushed off to my gunsmith. "Dale," I said, "I want you to change the forend cap on this rifle for a piece of ebony, rebedding the barrel in the process. I want you to rebed the ac-

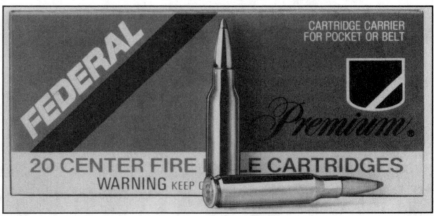

Handloads make the 308 Winchester extremely versatile, and there are a multitude of good factory loads.

tion in glass, too, and slick up the trigger for me. Then I want the rifle mailed off for a Black T finish." Dale didn't blink, so I continued. "It's going to be my survival rifle."

I started to explain, "Well, suppose I'm on my way to see an old aunt up north, and the plane develops engine trouble, but the pilot manages to land us in a remote region? We all live, but the radio is damaged, and somebody forgot to put in the electronic locater before takeoff. Furthermore, a storm blew us way off route, and they're looking for the airplane where it isn't. Now I get into the hold of the plane and pull out my 308 survival rifle, along with squib loads for small game, full-power loads for big game, and I go hunting. We're kept alive until they find us, and not only that, but we eat like

kings. That's what my survival rifle is all about."

"It all makes sense to me," Dale replied, proving there's a lot more to enjoying guns than logic. "I'll get to work on it right away."

When he said that, I knew why I liked that guy. My efficient, livable, trustworthy, versatile, easy-storing, easy-travelin', light-carrying survival rifle that nobody needs became a reality. It shoots groups smaller than hoped for, and handloads tailored for my rifle show about 2900 fps for a 150-grain bullet, 2000 with a 110-grain, and 2400 with a 200-grain. My survival rifle is not entirely ideal for any particular game—small, medium or large—but sufficient for just about everything. I guess we knew that in the first place.   •

The Ljungmann AG42B was

the 1940's.....

SECOND-BEST SEMI-AUTO.....

and it's still a good rifle for a shooter.

By Charles W. Karwan

Most people believe Switzerland managed to avoid invasion by the Nazis during World War Two (WWII) because she was well armed and well prepared militarily and Hitler was not willing to pay the heavy price in men and equipment necessary to defeat her. Much the same also held true for Sweden. In the years just preceding WWII and throughout that war, Sweden undertook a massive military buildup in an effort to maintain her neutrality by making an invasion too costly.

A big problem was that Sweden's traditional outside sources of small arms supply, particularly for automatic weapons, were Belgium and Germany, neither of which were available once the war broke out. An effort to procure ZB26 light machine guns from Czechoslovakia was also short lived due to Hitler's occupation of that country.

It became all too clear Sweden would have to arm itself to accomplish a buildup of her military capabilities. Part of that buildup involved the development, adoption, and production of a truly excellent semi-automatic rifle that was probably second in performance only to the M1 Garand among the semi-automatic rifles developed during WWII. This rifle was designated the Automatiskgevar (automatic rifle) 42 or Ag42. It is also commonly known by the name of one of its designers, Ljungmann (the j is pronounced like a y).

The Ljungmann rifle was significant in a number of ways, not least that it was the first autoloading rifle to use the direct gas impingement system later so successful in the French MAS 44, 49, and 49/56, the Armalite AR-10, and the U. S. M-16. The remarkable thing, particularly considering the excellence of the results, was that the Ag42 was conceived, prototyped, tested, and put into production all within one year. Much credit for this remarkable feat went to one of Sweden's foremost engineers at the time, Eric Eklund.

Early in their war, Finland supplied Sweden with captured examples of the Russian Tokarev semi-automatic rifle. The Swedes were impressed enough with it that they felt that a semi-automatic rifle should be developed and adopted as soon as possible as a means to increase the firepower and effectiveness of the Swedish Army. To simplify development of the Ag42, the Swedes used a variation of the excellent bolt and bolt carrier locking system of the Tokarev rifle. This same tilting bolt system was eventually also used in the Soviet SKS, the FN SAFN M1949, the French MAS 49 series, and the superb FN FAL rifle series.

While the Ljungmann was an extremely important and significant rifle, it is often ignored in the firearms literature, likely because Sweden was not a combatant. Nevertheless, the Ljungmann was very much the inspiration for many significant arms that came later. And for a different reason the Ljungmann is significant today: it and its spin-off brother, the Egyptian Hakim, are excellent semi-automatic rifles readily available at quite moderate prices, particularly the Hakim. Thus, even a shooter on a tight budget can outfit himself with a high-powered semi-automatic rifle of excellent quality and performance at a very moderate price.

The Ag42 was designed and built for the superb 6.5X55mm rifle cartridge, standard chambering for Sweden's Mauser rifles, and most of her light and medium machine guns. The 6.5X55mm cartridge is notable for its low recoil, high accuracy, and excellent down range performance. The original military load — a 156-grain round nosed bullet at about 2300 fps — was replaced with a modernized loading in the '40s, a 139-grain spitzer boattail bullet that would do 2460 fps out of the Ag42. This might seem quite moderate, but a high ballistic coefficient meant it retained velocity extremely well. Out at 300 yards, this load delivered about the same velocity as the 7.62mm NATO at the same distance; beyond that, it actually has more velocity and a flatter trajectory. The 6.5X55mm was no slouch, and had the further advantage of non-corrosive priming, something our 30-06 and the German 7.92X57mm never had during the war.

The Ag42 stayed in production, but it was never made in large enough quantities to replace the standard Swedish Mauser rifles that had been in service in Sweden since the mid-1890s. Ag42 rifles

The Ljungmann Ag42B on the bottom, the Hakim above it, and Rashid on the top. The Rashid is about the same length as the common SKS; the Ljungmann and Hakim are about 4 inches longer than an M1 Garand.

were typically issued at a rate of two to four per infantry squad.

The clever Ljungmann gas system eliminates the gas cylinder, gas piston, and operating rod. It is a simple gas tube that taps into the barrel several inches behind the muzzle. After the fired bullet passes this gas port a portion of the gas shoots backward through the gas tube to deliver a hammer blow directly to the bolt carrier. The bolt carrier moves to the rear a short distance unlocking the bolt from the receiver and then the bolt carrier and bolt continue to the rear together extracting and ejecting the fired case and recocking the hammer. Once they have completed their rearward travel they return forward under pressure of the recoil spring, stripping the next round out of the magazine and chambering it. When the round is chambered the bolt carrier continues forward camming the bolt into the locked position and the cycle is ready to be repeated.

This direct gas impingement system simplified the rifle's construction and operation and, with possible effect on accuracy, the barrel does not have a bunch of parts hanging on it moving back and forth to create undesirable vibrations. It is common for Ljungmann rifles to shoot sub-two inch groups at one hundred yards with high grade ammunition. Many of these rifles will approach minute of angle accuracy quite closely.

Not surprisingly, a number of areas of improvement were identified for this rifle after ten years of service. The major complaints were that ejection was excessively violent, the gas tube would sometimes clog up with corrosion, the rifle would not function with lightly loaded ammunition, and ejected cases were often too damaged to be reloaded, which the Swedes did with practice ammunition.

So, about 1953, an upgrading program resulted in the Ag42B. There were minor changes to the sights and magazine, a strengthened extractor and trigger mechanism, a stainless steel gas tube, and a rubber buffer at the ejection port to prevent damage to ejected cases. Modified rifles have a B added after their serial number and virtually all the Ljungmann rifles imported into the U. S. have these modifications.

A number of gas tube modifications were tried to deal with the violent ejection and inability to function semi-automatically with ammunition loaded to lower pressure levels. One included a longer gas tube that wrapped around the rifle's barrel. Another used an expansion chamber in the middle of the gas tube while yet another put an adjustable valve in the middle of the gas tube. Since the violent ejection was only a problem with weak brass and the Swedish ammunition was of such uniformly high quality it was determined unnecessary to adopt any of them, so the original tube was simply made from stainless steel so it would not corrode. Later, that adjustable gas valve was used in the Egyptian Hakim.

The Madsen company of Denmark worked extensively with the Ljungmann after the war, and it would probably have been adopted by Denmark. However, USA supplied the Danes with large quantities of M1 Garand rifles. In 1954, the Egyptian government was in the market for a semi-automatic rifle they could manufacture at home. Egypt purchased the tooling and en-

Pro-Somali rebels rallying in support of Somalia's war with Ethiopia circa 1977. Among the wide selection of arms being held aloft are Italian Carcanos, a Beretta SMG, a German Stg44, a couple of Czeck Vz52 carbines, an M14, a Mauser rifle, and two Egyptian Hakim rifles (one right behind the Beretta in front and one well to the rear.) The Hakim was not a front line rifle anywhere by then, but it was obviously still seeing action. Photo credit- U.S. Army SOCOM

Action view of the Ag42B. Note the lack of a cocking handle and the rubber buffer on the bolt cover designed to keep brass from being damaged. Also note the extremely secure double magazine release with a catch in the rear of the magazine and another in the front of the magazine.

Action view of the Hakim. The loop on the bolt cover can be used as a handle to push the bolt cover forward to retract the bolt. Note the lever extension on the magazine release shown here in the secure position. This keeps the magazine from being accidentally released but slows down magazine changes. Normally, reloading would be via stripper clips from the top.

Action view of the Rashid. Note the conventional cocking handle that is used to retract the bolt. Also note the detachable 10 round magazine, with the protected magazine release.

gineering expertise from Sweden to produce the rifle in a modified version. Called the Hakim, they put it into production in 1955 chambered for the 7.92X57mm cartridge that was their standard.

The Hakim differs from the Ljungmann in minor details, chambering aside, and many parts are interchangeable including even the magazines, though they are not identical. The Hakim has a heavier and bulkier stock; a separate muzzle brake, not an integral one; a tangent rear sight instead of the drum type; no cleaning rod; and a different, though similar, bayonet. The most significant difference is that the Hakim has an adjustable valve with eight settings in the gas tube to allow for the use of ammunition of varying power and bullet weights. One setting completely blocks gas flow so the rifle must be operated manually. The quality of manufacturing and materials used in the Hakim is uniformly excellent,

though fit and finish of the Swedish version is a bit better. Like its parent, the Hakim is an accurate rifle with good ammunition.

The gas tube valve is located in the top handguard. There is a combination tool designed to turn the valve adjustment, but smooth-jawed pliers work. The adjustment is an important feature because 7.92X57mm ammunition comes in such a wide variety of pressure levels and bullet weights. The accepted technique is to keep closing down the valve adjustment until the rifle will no longer eject reliably, then open it back up one click for practice and two clicks for duty. This saves wear and tear on the gun.

The management of these guns is quite unconventional and puts off some people. At the rear of the receiver, a lever swings right and left. This is the weapon's manual safety and it also serves as a takedown lever and a hold open latch. When the lever is

to the right the safety is engaged as is the bolt hold open. When it is to the left, the rifle is in the firing mode and the hold open is disengaged.

There is no bolt handle or cocking handle in evidence. To retract the bolt, you must first push the bolt cover all the way forward until it clicks. Then retract the bolt cover and the bolt will move with it. If the safety is in the fire position, when you pull the bolt and bolt cover all the way to the rear the bolt will be released. If there is no magazine in place or there is a loaded magazine in place, the bolt will go forward, chambering a round if one is there. If an empty magazine is in place, then the bolt will stay to the rear .

If the safety is engaged (to the right) when the bolt cover and bolt are retracted, the bolt will stay to the rear regardless of the magazine situation. To release the bolt, just wing the safety to the left and pull back on the bolt cover.

What drives people nuts is how to get the bolt to go forward if there is an unloaded magazine in place, without removing the magazine. It is quite simple if you know how, but few do and none of the books are much help. Assuming the magazine is empty and the safety is to the left in the firing position, when retracted, the bolt will be held to the rear by a bolt hold-open latch activated by the magazine follower. To close the bolt without removing the magazine, push the bolt cover forward a short distance until you hear a click. Then push the magazine follower down, and a very slight rearward pull (too much and the bolt slams on whatever is depressing the follower) will allow the hold open latch to drop and then you push the bolt cover forward. The bolt will go forward as well. Now push the cover release lever at the rear end of the cover and ease the cover to the rear. It sounds complicated but it is quite simple and easy and only takes a couple of seconds. If you have problems with the bolt closing on the finger or thumb depressing the follower do the procedure with the safety engaged.

Considering the superb engineering evidenced in the Ljungmann rifle's design, it is unclear why its designers resorted to a reciprocating bolt cover as a means to manually operate the rifle's bolt. I suspect that it was chosen so there were no slots or openings in the action for a cocking handle as found on the M1 Garand. The lack of such openings would help keep snow and dirt out of the rifle's action. The Ljungmann proved to be remarkably reliable in the Swedish field trials that understandably emphasized operating in severe cold and snow.

Some sources criticize the Ljungmann and Hakim for being dirt-sensitive, but my experience and research, particularly with the latter, does not support that position. One of my best friends has shot a Hakim extensively in desert conditions with considerable exposure to blowing sand and dust. He reports excellent reliability as long as a few simple precautions are taken. First, the ammunition should be powerful military loads and not the extremely low powered U. S. commercial 8mm Mauser loads. Second, the gas selector valve should be opened up a notch or two more than normal. Third, the rifle should be appropriately lubricated, preferably with a dry lubricant or at least with the bare minimum of a conventional lubricant. Finally, care must be taken to keep the rifle's action closed at all times. This is all pretty much standard procedure with any semi-automatic or automatic weapon in dusty conditions.

The Ljungmann saga continued after the Hakim. Shortly after the Hakim was put into production, the Soviets began to supply Egypt with SKS rifles chambered for the 7.62X39mm cartridge. Evidently Egypt was favorably impressed with this rifle and cartridge and that about 1959 the Egyptian State Factory at Port Said (later renamed Maadi) reengineered the Hakim into an SKS configuration and put it into production in 7.62X39mm as the Rashid.

The Rashid is about the same length and size as the SKS and like the latter it has a folding blade bayonet and a 10-round magazine capacity. It also uses a more conventional cocking handle to cycle the bolt rather than the reciprocating bolt cover system of the Ljungmann and Hakim. In several ways, the Rashid is actually superior to the SKS and in a couple it is inferior. On the superior side it has the more versatile adjustable gas system of the Hakim, an excellent fully detachable magazine, and, typically, superior accuracy. On the inferior side it does not have a chrome lined bore and it tends to weigh more than the SKS depending on the wood on each.

Total production of the Rashid was relatively small with some estimates as few as 5,000. The reason was primarily because Russian-supplied SKSs were cheaper and the Egyptians soon tooled up with Soviet help to make AKM assault rifles instead. Regardless, the Rashid is a sweet-shooting little carbine.

As with the Ljungmann and Hakim rifles, I strongly recommend against shooting corrosively primed ammunition in Rashids to help prevent corrosion damage to the gas system which is difficult to clean. Much of the cheap Chinese and other 7.62X39mm ammunition on the market is corrosively primed.

Hakim in recoil after firing. Note the lack of muzzle jump brought about—it's a very comfortable, accurate rifle.

Ljungmann-System Rifle Specs

	Ag42B	Hakim	Rashid
Chambering (mm)	6.5X55	7.92X57	7.62X39
Operation	direct gas impingement with tilting bolt		
Feed Mechanism	10 round box magazine		
Weight Empty (lbs.)	10.25	10.7	8.25
Length Overall (in)	47.8	47.9	40
Barrel length (in)	25.3 w/comp 23.5 rifled	25.5 w/comp 23.25 rifled	20.5
Sights, front	post with round cover		
Sights, rear	screw adjustable for windage		
(100 meters)	drum (1-7)	ramp (1-10)	ramp (1-10)
Furniture	wood		
Finish	blue black		
Accessories	rod extension bayonet w/ scab sling	combo tool bayonet integ.sling	combo tool bayonet w/ scab sling night sights
Manufacturer	Carl Gustaf Husqvarna	Maadi	Maadi
Status	Obsolete no longer in service, on the used gun market.		
T&E Summary	Accurate, reliable, soft shooting, easy field strip, excessively long (except Rashid), excessively heavy, excellent value—particularly the Hakim— interesting and historically significant collectible.		

The Rashid was one final evolution of the Ljungmann system. That bayonet in the folded position is very SKS-like.

It is only natural to compare the Ljungmann and Hakim with the M1 Garand. Many believe the detachable ten-round magazines of these rifles are superior to the eight-round clip of the M1. Field stripping of the Ljungmann series is much easier; and unlike the M1 the bore of these rifles can be cleaned from the rear. And average accuracy of Ljungmann and Hakim rifles is better than that of the service grade M1.

On the M1's side, it is faster to reload, it has far better sights, it is probably somewhat more durable and reliable under adverse conditions, it is chambered for a more common cartridge, and spare parts and gunsmithing are more readily attainable.

Another major advantage of the M1 is that its receiver is substantially shorter than the Ljungmann receiver. That combined with the fact that the M1 is not saddled with a muzzle compensator makes the M1 over four inches shorter overall and much handier. I find the muzzle compensators of the Ag42 and Hakim to be more annoyances than assets but neither rifle has significant recoil or muzzle flip. The bottom line is that I would prefer the M1 every time, but I would still feel well armed with the Swedish or Egyptian rifles. Certainly the Ljungmann is more durable, more reliable, less complicated, and more accurate than the German G43 or the Russian M40 Tokarev rifles, the only other significant WWII-era semiauto rifle contenders. Thus I would rate the Ljungmann Ag42 second only to the M1 Garand among the period semi-automatic military rifles.

A decent M1 will cost you $450 or more and a good semiauto M1A, G-3, or FAL will set you back twice that to well over $1,000. I often see Ljungmann rifles for sale for $350 or less and Hakim rifles for under

$200. After-market magazines that fit either rifle and hold 30 rounds are readily available in the gun trade papers at reasonable prices. Surplus German MG13 30-round magazines, which are available for as little as $10 to $15, work perfectly in the Hakim with only minor modification. Thus the Ljungmann and especially the Hakim offer somewhat heavy and long tactical equivalents of one of the 7.62mm NATO semi-automatic battle rifles at a fraction of the cost.

Actually, these fine rifles can serve a number of roles quite well. I know one fellow who keeps a Hakim handy with a loaded magazine, empty chamber, and safety engaged as a rural home defense weapon. He feels the proprietary way the rifle is put into action helps keep it from being fired by unauthorized persons. I feel that the Hakim would also be a good gun to keep handy in rural areas that have the big bears. The 8mm cartridge has more energy and penetration than any of the standard 308 loads if you use the hot Norma sporting ammunition. American-loaded 8mm Mauser ammunition is severely underloaded and should be avoided for this role.

Both the Ljungmann and Hakim rifles have extremely low recoil and muzzle jump and consequently are excellent for use against moving targets like running coyotes and such. Any police officer could do far worse than to carry one of these rifles in the trunk of his car for use in road block situations where a car or truck may have to be stopped with small arms fire or for barricaded shooter situations.

With full metal jacket ammunition, either rifle offers tremendous penetration. Both rifles are excellent big bore backups to .223 or 7.62X39mm rifles or carbines. Ammunition is readily available, though the Hakim has the advantage when it comes to military surplus ammunition. Please note that some 6.5X55mm ammunition on the market, made in Yugoslavia, is not loaded to sufficient pressures to cycle an Ag42B reliably.

The Ljungmann introduced the direct gas impingement system into self loading small arms. Its development in so short a time was a remarkable accomplishment. Many believe it helped keep Sweden out of war during a trying time in her history. It and its spin-offs are good rifles.   •

FIELD STRIPPING

The Ljungmann System

Field stripping the Ag42, Hakim, or Rashid is extremely simple; starting with an unloaded rifle without a magazine in place, simply push the bolt cover forward a couple of inches. Holding it in that position, turn the safety until it is positioned straight to the rear and then lift the entire safety block out of the receiver. Next slide the bolt cover with recoil spring, bolt carrier, and bolt off the rifle to the rear. You now have complete access to the rifle's bore from the rear. Most field maintenance of the bore and bolt face can be carried out without further disassembly.

However, if further disassembly is necessary, the bolt can be removed from the bolt carrier. Turn the entire assembly upside down; put your thumb on the rear of the bolt and fore finger on the front of the bolt. While gently lifting the rear of the bolt up and to the rear, give the bolt a slight counter clockwise turn and lift it out of the bolt carrier.

An option for disassembly for the Ag42 and Hakim (but not the Rashid) is to start by pushing the bolt cover all the way forward until it locks the bolt cover and bolt carrier together. Then when the safety block is removed, the bolt cover, recoil spring, bolt carrier, and bolt can all be removed as an assembly and replaced as an assembly. This is handy for situations where the shooter just wants to inspect the bore or work on the barrel or chamber.

When the above procedure is used, the bolt carrier is attached to the bolt cover under the spring tension of the recoil spring so be careful separating the two if you need to. While firmly holding the bolt cover put strong thumb pressure against the front of the bolt carrier and then push the bolt carrier latch at the rear of the bolt cover and then ease apart the bolt carrier, bolt cover, and recoil spring. Optionally hold the bolt cover down against a non-marring surface like a folded newspaper with the rear faced upward. Hanging on to the bolt cover firmly, press the bolt carrier latch, releasing the bolt carrier. Ease the parts apart.

Reassembly is straight forward and just the reverse of disassembly. About the only difference is that you will have to push the cocked hammer down out of the way to slide the bolt carrier and bolt back into the receiver.

No further disassembly is normally necessary or recommended in the field. As you can see, field stripping of the Ljungmann, Hakim, and Rashid is far simpler than that of the M1 Garand or M14, ranking right up there in simplicity and ease with the best such as the FN FAL and AR-15/M-16 series.   •

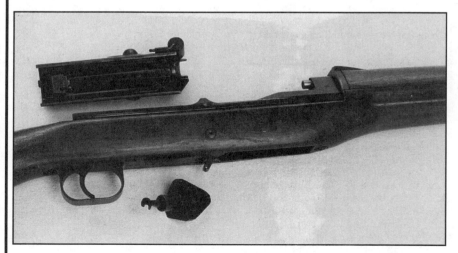

Field stripping the Ljungmann and Hakim, but not the Rashid, can be accomplished with the bolt, bolt carrier, bolt cover, and recoil spring all locked together as shown. This is extremely convenient if all that is needed is to work on or inspect the bore or chamber. The rifle can then be quickly reassembled with those parts still locked together.

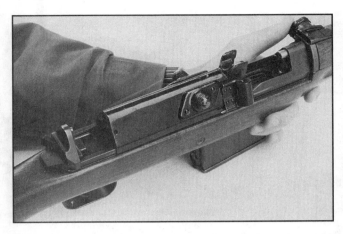

1. Starting with an unloaded rifle, push the bolt cover forward a couple of inches and hold it there.

2. Put the safety lever in the center position and lift the entire safety block out of the receiver.

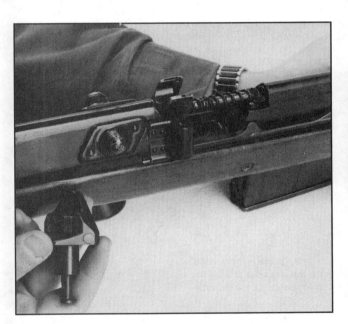

3. Carefully release the bolt cover and let it slide to the rear.

4. Slide the bolt cover and recoil spring off the receiver to the rear and do the same with the bolt carrier and bolt.

5. The Ag42B field stripped for routine maintenance. The bolt can be easily separated from the bolt carrier as described in the text.

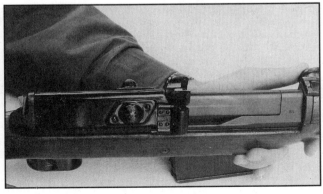

6. To retract the bolt from the forward position as shown, push the bolt cover all the way forward. Then, pulling the bolt cover all the way to the rear the bolt will also go to the rear. (Once all the way to the rear, the bolt will snap forward and chamber a round if one is in position.)

ARE 22 POCKET PISTOLS
PRACTICAL?

by Warren Peters

Wilkinson Sherry can disappear in your hand—has 138 bulk factor.

More than half of these United States now permit honest citizens to carry concealed weapons. With this privilege— which many of us think is a right— comes a need for discretion. Many people and some police take offense at behavior they perceive to be culturally incorrect. In winter, handguns of all sizes may be easily shielded from nervous eyes, but summer in the south and west challenges concealment. A couple strolling in a city in muscle shirts, walking shorts, and thongs must have pocket pistols if they are to be armed.

In that context, I visualize pocket pistols as **barely**, **marginally**, and **readily concealable**. These classes encompass many current and discontinued handgun models.

Barely concealable are snubnose 38 Special revolvers of the type made by Smith & Wesson, Rossi, and Taurus, and most 380 autoloading pistols.

Marginally concealable are the smaller 380s such as the Grendel and AMT Backup, and 22 autos of similar size. Some marginally concealable 22s are available in larger calibers.

Readily concealable are tiny 25 autos like the Baby Browning and its clones, plus a few 22 autos (some available in 25, even 32) and 22 revolvers of like size.

To compare all these, I have coined the term **Bulk Factor**, which is the product of a handgun's length, height, and width (to the nearest 1/10") and weight (to the nearest 1/2 oz, fully loaded). Weight is an important concealability element because of sag. The **Bulk Factor** of a number of pocket pistols appears in the included table. The boundaries between my concealability classes cannot be fixed rigidly because other factors apply, such as shape of the gun, its carrier's size, and garment fashions.

This report focuses on the marginally and readily concealable 22 autoloaders because of their surging popularity, in spite of their questionable defensive capability and functional reliability. I don't condemn the choice of others merely because I prefer something a little heavier. Practice is an essential factor in defense, and the 22 undeniably is the least expensive route to extensive shooting. All references herein to the 22 are directed to the **22 Long Rifle** cartridge, unless otherwise indicated.

To get this going, I acquired one of each gun discussed below, along with assorted brands of 22 ammunition. Velocities spanned hyper, high, standard, some target and subsonic. The shooting was conducted over the course of more than a year. I broke in all new pistols with at least 100 rounds, mostly with high-velocity ammo. Then, unless otherwise noted, in each gun I fired four full magazines, plus a round in the chamber, of each ammo variety on hand. I stopped after two loadings if a particular ammo variety clearly wasn't working, and I formally tested the subsonic only in the smallest pistols, one load only. Initially I had an elaborate table to show each gun's performance with all loads, but this system broke down from sheer volume.

Few of the pistols worked reliably with hyper or standard ammo, and most expressed preferences among varieties of high-velocity ammo. Hyper velocities are achieved with a light bullet, subsonic 22s did not open slides enough to eject the hulls from any of the small pistols, which have relatively light slides and stiff recoil springs; one must suppose that the fabled assassins' silenced pistols are specifically regulated. Accuracy was not a performance criterion for those belly guns; however, they all did a heavy number on the seven-yard combat target, despite generally miserable sights. No key holing was observed at this short range, but from a few guns it did appear at 25 yards.

.22 AUTO NINE

FLT (Old Model) Auto Nine: left thumb releases safety; fair shooter. John Malloy photo.

BARELY CONCEALABLE GUNS

Barely concealable 22s available to me were the Smith & Wesson Model 2214 (short version of S&W's slabsided 22 auto), Smith & Wesson 61 (ancestor of the 2214), Llama XV (a miniature of Colt's 1911), AMT 22 Backup, and Heckler & Koch HK4.

All performed well with various high-velocity and standard-velocity loads. Because of their size and their availability (except for the Smiths) in 380 (Llama also in 32, and H&K in 32 and 25, as well as in 380), I did not break them in and test them as thoroughly as I did the smaller pistols. The 2214 was the only test pistol in this or any category that functioned well with hyper-velocity ammo. Others tended to smokestack with hyper, although the H&K did this only once. The 2214 ejected subsonic loads, but did not feed them satisfactorily; I did not try those loads in the others. If I had to settle for this size 22, then smooth performance, price and current availability would propel me toward the S&W 2214.

MARGINALLY CONCEALABLE

Marginally concealable pistols I tested were the Galesi 9, Walther TPH, Iver Johnson TP22 (some were sold under the "American" label), and the Phoenix HP22. All but Walther come in 25, as well.

The Galesi, no longer imported (a few came in 22 Long), exhibits the best quality, and mine has a good trigger. However, its magazine will not feed if loaded with more than five rounds (the bullets tip downwards), and its weak firing-pin spring occasionally fails to light the fire. All high-velocity rounds and two standard-velocity brands cycled perfectly when they did ignite.

The Walther TPH, basically a scaled-down PPK made in brilliant stainless steel by Interarms in the USA, was a $325 disappointment. In addition to its difficult safety and mushy trigger, my TPH could not be persuaded to perform reliably with any ammo. An assortment of maladies, including feeding, extraction and ejection, defied analysis. This model was discontinued for a while and recently re-introduced; I've not tested a later sample. The European version is made with a duraluminum frame, which might drop it into the readily concealable category. I cannot comment on that version's performance because it doesn't meet BATF's thoughtful import points minimum.

Iver Johnson, also a PPK copy (this one by Erma) has a fair single-action trigger pull, but double-action (first round) is gargantuan. However, my TP22 works well with all high-velocity ammo.

The Phoenix HP22, which like the TP22 sells for a bit over $100, is a racy design with two (count 'em-two!) safeties; one on the slide and one frame-mounted. This belt and suspenders arrangement prevents not only firing, but also slide retraction, cocking, and magazine removal. I had to use my bowscale to weigh its single-action trigger pull: 17 pounds! The Phoenix has a rear sight that is adjustable for windage only. During break-in, hardly any ammo worked, but afterwards my

Sterling 302: easiest slide to jack, good shooter—bulk points up to 252.

Jennings J-22: crude finish but author's favorite autoloader. Bulk factor: 213

Beretta 21A: legendary quality, disappointing performance. Bulk factor: 262

HP22 functioned perfectly even with target loads. Moral: don't give up too quickly.

READILY CONCEALABLE

Readily concealable 22 pistols tested were the Lorcin L22, Jennings J-22, Sterling 302, SEDCO SP-22 (all of which cost less than $100), Beretta 21-A, Norton TP-70, FTL Auto Nine (old model), and Wilkinson Sherry (new model Auto Nine).

Lorcin may offer the cheapest 22 pistol, a totally pot-metal production. Compactness is compromised by a magazine extension I am tempted to grind off. Esthetics aside, the

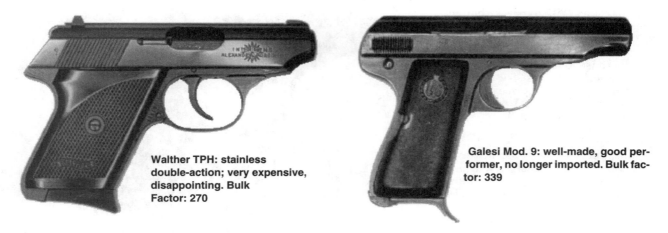

Walther TPH: stainless double-action; very expensive, disappointing. Bulk Factor: 270

Galesi Mod. 9: well-made, good performer, no longer imported. Bulk factor: 339

L22 flawlessly digested all high-velocity ammo offered it.

The Jennings has a gritty trigger and the least expensive appearance, with chrome mottling and alloy casting bubbles. It appears fragile, but no parts failed during the test. Despite this, my J-22 welcomed both high-velocity and standard-velocity ammo. It has a thin, serrated sliding safety that is easier to manipulate than it appears to be.

Sterling is the sturdiest looking. Its trigger pull is aggravated by a sear angle that retracts the cocked striker an additional 1/16" before letoff. My 302, representing one-quarter of Sterling's blue/stainless 22/25 family, did well with most, but not all, high-velocity ammo.

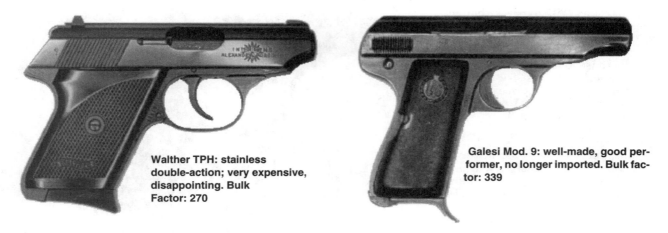

North American Arms: author's best 22 choice. Bulk Factor very low: 37.

The SEDCO, of neatly painted non-ferrous alloy, is the sleekest of the lot, with smoothly beveled corners and edges. Unfortunately, I couldn't get any ammo to work reliably in my SP-22. Usually a fired case remained in the chamber, indicating a problem.

The American-made double-action Beretta 21-A is the single-action 22 Shot Minx / 25 Jetfire on steroids. Available also in 32, it compares very well in apparent quality with its Italian cousins. I did not test an identical model made by Taurus. Trigger action in both double-action and single-action modes is smooth and light, although in double action it is difficult to keep the finger from rubbing on the bottom of the trigger guard. First round must be loaded in the tip-up barrel; attempts to jack a round into the chamber from the magazine resulted in unintentional field stripping. Sharp edges on the slide are guaranteed to lacerate the shooter's hand. My specific 21-A had major feeding problems not cured by a new magazine and feed-ramp recontouring, very disappointing for a $150 gun.

At this point I should say that all gun manufacturers appear anxious to help shooters keep their guns safe and reliable. Invariably, they will do whatever they can to correct a problem in a new gun, never at more expense to the owner than shipping the gun to the factory. You needn't go through a dealer for this, by the way.

The Norton TP-22 is one of the reincarnations of the Budischowsky, all of which now are discontinued $200-plus collectors' items. Several pieces of mine broke during its test, prompting my gunsmith to comment, "It's not what it appears to be." One of the smallest 22s (also made in 25) and possessing all the bells and whistles of the double-action wonder nines, the attractive TP-22 might have been my top choice. Unhappily, mine would not extract some ammo brands at all, had numerous misfires, and was altogether unreliable.

The two Auto Nines are nothing alike, mechanically. The old model (FTL) was inspired by the striker-fired Baby Browning, with fine alloy frame, steel side, and twist-barrel takedown. Trigger pull originally was atrocious. Upon disassembly, the sear protrudes above the frame and the mating striker falls into your hand. A little honing on both surfaces produced an excellent pull. The FTL performed well with only two brands of high-velocity ammo. The new model (Wilkinson Sherry) is of similar quality and materials, but is a concealed hammer design that employs an entirely different pinned breechblock takedown, rather like that of the AMT Backup. With a much better trigger, the Sherry likewise performed well with only two ammo brands, but not the same brands as the FTL. Both guns are in the $150 range.

ALTERNATIVES

Double derringers were not considered because of their two-round limitation. Some 38 derringers are as light as their 22 counterparts because of their larger bores. The market offers a couple of relatively cheap four-shot derringers I felt were beyond the scope of this test.

The little five-shot North American Arms and similar Freedom Arms stainless revolvers offer, in my opinion, a reasonable alternative to the 22 pistol. Aside from limited ca-

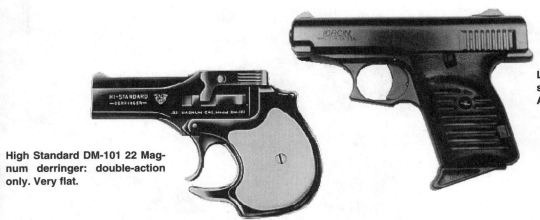

High Standard DM-101 22 Magnum derringer: double-action only. Very flat.

Lorcin L22: tiny safety, still easy to release. Author photo.

pacity, the main drawback is the single-action-only firing mode. Fumble-cocking and relatively severe recoil through their tiny bird's-head grips hamper target recovery. On my North American Arms revolver, the cocked hammer's firing pin obscures the rudimentary sights. These revolvers also are available in 22 Short (why bother?) and 22 Magnum. The Magnum would appear to be the better choice, but its greater length and fierce recoil disqualify it for me.

The upside is that both derringer and revolvers are essentially 100% reliable with all 22 ammunition.

CONCLUSIONS AND RECOMMENDATIONS

Even large-caliber, centerfire autoloading pistols are limited to a relatively narrow range of ammunition for reliable function. The variety of available 22 rimfire ammo is much broader than that. All 22 pistols, even large ones, tend to be ammo-sensitive, being regulated for either high-velocity or target ammo, seldom both. Small pistols are more finicky because of their smaller mass. Limp-wrist shooting may disable the best of them, because the frame is recoiling along with the slide, which then can't open correctly. It should be clear that price has nothing to do with performance. Generally, size is a better indicator of reliability.

A professional trigger job should be contemplated. This might cost half as much as the pistol did, but it could help achieve the multiple 22 hits that may be required, which is the main advantage of the auto-loading pistol. Make sure your pistol works when it is clean, because that's the way you probably will be carrying it. Check the bore occasionally for lint and other obstructions picked up from your pocket.

All owner's manuals recommend carrying the pistol with an empty chamber. However, jacking a round into the chamber is one of the most dependable ways to jam one of these little guns. Some of their safeties are very difficult to work, and even more difficult to trust. For liability reasons, I offer NO carry-mode recommendations.

I cannot recommend any particular brand of gun or ammo, nor did I intend to do that when I undertook this project. Your gun, which may appear identical to mine, almost surely will behave differently. So what is the point of all this? It is to convince you that you must not buy one of these little guns, load it with something off your ammo shelf, drop it into your pocket, and feel protected.

Try out your gun like I did. Find a load that is reliable (hopefully a high-velocity hollow point) and buy a couple of bricks of it to practice with, shoot them a lot, and *then* trust the gun. Of all the options there are in pocket pistols, this is the only one you must select. •

Author's Concealment Specs

Gun	Bulk Factor
North American 22	37
Baby Browning 25	112
FTL Auto-Nine 22	126
Wilkinson Sherry 22	138
Sedco SP-22—22	181
Norton TP70—22	187
Beretta Minx 225	189
Jennings J-22—22	213
Sterling 302—22	252
Beretta 21—22	262
S&W 61—22	263
Walther TPH22—22	270
AMT Backup-380	285
Iver Johnson TP-22—22	316
Galezi 9—22	339
Grevdel P-10-380	443
Lorcin L-22—22	445
Phoenix HP22—22	482
S&W 2214—22	648
Liama XV-22	825
S&W Chief's Special-38	8420

Percy, left, holds a pair of elk antlers, alongside Elmer, center, and Turner, right, with his wheellock.

They hunted together 40 years ago.
Turner Kirkland was....
The Last Man Standing

by H. Lea Lawrence

The mountain cabin at the Smothers camp where Turner, Percy and Elmer stayed for two weeks.

"When I think of that long ago hunt," Turner Kirkland said, "there are two words that come to mind - 'chipmunk stew!'"

He laughed, leaned back in his chair, and for a moment his eyes had a far-away look. When he looked back at me, he was still chuckling.

"That's something that deserves an explanation, because it was never said in the field. It's a joke Elmer Keith thought up, and in the years that followed, every time we met at shows and conventions, he'd ask if I recalled that particular dish."

Turner was in the process of telling me about a muzzleloading elk hunt he and a friend made in Idaho with Keith in 1955, only a couple years after Turner founded the now-famous Dixie Gun Works at Union City, Tennessee. His hunting part-

ner was Percy Haynes, an oil distributor from Columbia, Tennessee. Both were black powder shooters, gun traders and collectors. In later years, Percy also went into the gun business in Nashville, but only on a small scale compared to Turner's massive operation.

"The trip came about in an unusual way," he said. "Percy knew I wanted to go on an elk hunt, and because he and Elmer were already acquainted by being together at gun shows, he knew his soft spot. Percy offered Elmer a fine Colt 3rd Model Dragoon if he'd take us on a hunt, and Elmer quickly accepted."

"It was a good deal for Elmer, since Percy's Dragoon was probably worth about $2500.00. Even then, you couldn't get a good one for less than $1500.00.

Getting ready to make the six-mile pack trip back to Elmer's place on the Salmon River.

Elmer, left, and Turner with his antlers and Wheelock rifle.

"This was to be strictly a black-powder hunt, of course, and my choice of rifles was a .60-caliber German wheelock, a nine pound gun with a 34-inch barrel that was made about 1650. It was in fine condition, with a perfect lock and a rifled barrel with one turn in 50 inches. Just because the gun was old didn't mean that it wouldn't shoot hard. It developed a muzzle velocity of about 1500 feet per second when using 130 grains of 3F black powder. Along with the special 950 grain slugs I cast, it developed shocking power that would be nearly suitable for elephants.

"Percy preferred to use a less overwhelming weapon, choosing a

Elmer and his wife, Lorraine, at their home on the Salmon River.

.47-caliber R. Southgate flintlock that developed upwards of 2200 feet per second muzzle velocity. As it turned out, Elmer decided to hunt with a .58-caliber Civil War musket.

"We flew to Idaho, then went to Elmer's home on the Salmon River to prepare for the journey into the back-country for the two-week hunt. We departed one morning with a 13-horse pack train for the six-hour ride into the elk camp operated on the western side of the Continental Divide by Ralph Smothers and his wife, Rae."

He chuckled again, then resumed.

"You see, I'd never been on a horse before, and not long after we started, my foot caught in a limb and I pitched over the head of the horse and almost took a 400-foot drop off a precipice. I made the rest of the trip with my heart in my throat!

"As Elmer had predicted, we encountered all kinds of weather, some fair, and plenty of snow at other times, the latter of which is death to early firearms, as any black powder enthusiast knows. We had to devise all kinds of ways to try to prevent misfires, the best of which was working animal tallow into the cracks and crevices above and below the flash pans, between the barrel and the forearm, and around the pan cover.

"In the meantime, we were surrounded by some of the most beautiful country I've ever been privileged to visit, and the amount of wildlife was spectacular. We saw blacktail deer, mountain lions, big horn sheep, mountain goats, and plenty

of elk. There was no hurry to bag our animals and, besides, Elmer wanted us to have nice sets of antlers to take home.

"There was more to remember: the great food prepared by the Smotherses, including elk liver roasted over a campfire; the days of zero weather; puffing up and down mountainsides; Elmer and his tall tales of earlier years; nights around the campfire, and the many other incidents that are a part of a primitive mountain hunt.

"All of us took nice elk, and my wheellock performed perfectly, as did Percy's and Elmer's black powder guns. Yet when we departed, I had the sense this was one of those hunts that would never happen again. It didn't, and now with Percy and Elmer long gone, I'm the last man standing."

And the last to remember chipmunk stew! •

Sad to tell, but Turner Kirkland passed on July 26, 1997, so now there is no man standing except in our memories.

Ken Warner

A Swede Makes Good in Holland

Here's all it takes in the hardware line — the clamp-like object is a sight tool — for a satisfactory quarter-century.

This is the story of a military target rifle. To make the story live, I must first give some background of shooting in my home country, The Netherlands. This is a small country with a large population. As far as shooting sports is concerned, hunting is not the main pastime. Most people that want to shoot fire at targets. One of these target games is what we call Military Rifle Match. It is fired at 100 meters (about 110 yards) with unaltered military rifles. This means that the rifle has to be standard issue in some military force somewhere in the world. Experimental rifles are permitted (to make the use of the many AR10s possible) but in case of doubt the shooter has to have documentation of its use in tests. Bolt action rifles are permitted if they are from before 1945. A separate and related match form is the Veterans Rifle Match, in which only bolt action rifles from before 1945 are allowed—participants need not be veterans, the rifles must be.

About 1983 I decided to start shooting the Veterans Rifle Match. For this I needed a rifle and I had decided to buy a Schmidt-Rubin K31 straight pull rifle. For the military match, I was already using a Swiss SIG 510-4 rifle and the also-Swiss K31 seemed a logical extension of that. A friend had a superb example of such a rifle for sale and we started negotiations. He had a large amount of Swiss ammo with it and that made the rifle rather expensive for the student that I was then. To make a long story short we just could not get to an agreement. We parted friends but I still did not have a suitable rifle.

Shortly after that I found a perfect substitute for the K31 in a long established gun store in Amsterdam. It was a factory new Swedish Mauser M96 made in 1912 by the Carl Gustavs Stadts Gevarsfactori (Carl Gustavs City Rifle Factory). In the Netherlands, we call

these rifles "Carl Gustavs" for that reason. The caliber was 6.5 Swedish Mauser (properly called 6.5x55 Mauser). It had never been used and was sitting there waiting for me. It cost me a quarter of the highest bid I made on the K31 for just the rifle without the ammunition.

The stock was rough and unfinished or nearly so. I sanded it and gave it a good rub of True-Oil to make prettier and to seal the wood against the humid weather we get here. After this I went to the range to fire it for the first time. I had loaded some 144-gr. Lapua Match bullets in front of a very mild load of Belgian-made (PRB) ball powder. The first target I fired at after zeroing gave 94 points. I had never got a result like that from a military rifle before, and that with open sights! The ten ring of the tar-

get is 1.34 inches, the nine is 2.68 inches. I stopped experimenting with loads before I had started and never changed. That result gave me an unlimited confidence in the rifle. The certain knowledge that if I did my part of the work right it would result in a ten or maybe a nine sometimes. Now this may not seem much but a consistent score of 90 points or more would put you in the top of any military or veterans rifle match at that time.

Then the 1985 National Championships came up. I had had more results like that first score and so I entered the match with some confidence. With the highest score of the competitors before me in my head, I counted the points I had shot whilst firing. It went well, the first two targets (of three) ended well above the 90. The beginning of

the third target was not so good and upon counting before my last shot I realized that it had to be a ten to win. Behind me, several other shooters were watching through a telescope to see what would happen. They had noticed that I was up to something and the tension was tangible. That is not conducive to good shooting. Nevertheless, the shot landed in the ten ring and for me the match was over. In that series, I was the last one to fire. The rifle and I both like to take our time and the spectators came up to tell me that the highest score up to that moment was one point higher than I thought. I had overlooked one score! To say that was a disappointment is to put it mildly. Fortunately, the guys who were in the pit to tend the targets came to us and gave me my results and I had miscounted one

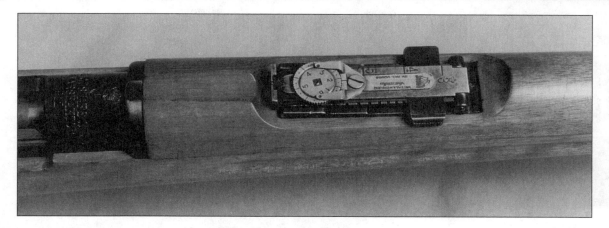

The Swedish military sights are open sights, but lack nothing in precision.

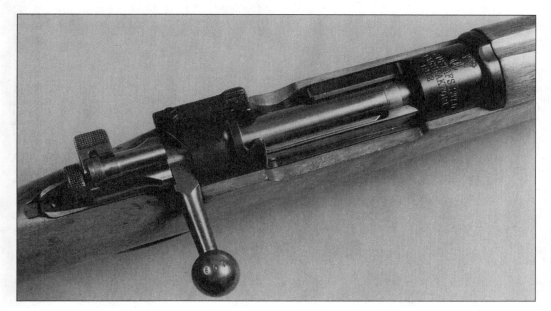

Straight and clean, it's a military rifle of another time now, but Carl Gustaf can still take pride.

point during the match. I was the champion for that year.

The next year the championship ended the other way round and I came in second. Again with one point of difference, behind the man who was second in the previous year. That is one of the worst things that can happen. When Bill Jordan gave the title "No Second Place Winner" to his book about gunfighting he could also have been talking about target competition, as he does in the beginning of his last chapter.

Two years later I ended up first in the National Championship Veterans rifle. After that I started with contact lenses and for me that was the end of good shooting with open sights for the time being. In the last few years I am back with older eyes,

spectacles and shooting again. Not as good as before but still having fun and now and then winning minor matches.

I said I never experimented with ammunition for this rifle and to a certain extent this is not true. I changed from the 144 gr. Lapua Match bullet to the 140 gr. HPBT Sierra or Hornady dependent on availability of either. It made little or no difference to the results. And I used Lapua Match ammo when I could afford it or needed new cases.

Three years ago some surplus Swedish Sniper ammunition came on the Dutch market. Now if the Swedes put the term "Prickskytte" (=sniper) on ammunition and have it manufactured by Norma you can blindly count on quality. I

bought a large number of rounds even though it is Berdan primed and thus not practicable to reload. In a training session I got the result shown in the picture, 98 points in a group of 3x3 cm (1,2x1.2") with two called flyers. Unfortunately, this Swedish ammo burns a lot of powder and this makes the rifle very hot during a 30-shot match (plus 10 sighters). This results in mirage above the front end of the barrel which disturbs the sight picture. Furthermore it can lead to a shifting point of impact after a number of rounds. In the 40 minutes a match lasts it is just not possible to cool the rifle down enough. So the ammo is now used for practice (at a slower pace) and my old load is used for matches.

Incidentally, I eventually bought the K31 I mentioned in the beginning some years later and shot it in practice too. I never could get the results out of it that I get out of the Carl Gustav so I was forced to make a good choice in the beginning. Only in rapid fire is it better due to the straight pull action but the matches described are slow fire only.

This is my one good gun. Although I have collected a rack full of rifles, some by the world's best makers like Holland & Holland and Purdey this is the rifle I will keep to the last and this is the rifle I use most often.

—*Paul Leoff*

Swamp Child by Ruger

Kimber just didn't suit kayak life in the swamp.

After forty years of searching, I have mine, a Ruger 10/22 laminated stocked International. It is close to minute of angle accurate with many types of ammo. Even more important, the first shot from a cold barrel is to point of aim, not a common occurrence with 22 rimfires. The rifle will even shoot CCI CB Longs accurately to 35 yards. It is extremely reliable having jammed only twice in 10,000 rounds fired. It is light, compact, and weather resistant which are definite requirements for a Northwest Florida kayak gun. The stock modifications make the rifle more attractive, at least to my eyes, unique, and well balanced. So my search is over. Getting here was frustrating, expensive and tiring. And FUN.

It all started back in 1958 just after I turned twelve. I had received a Mossberg bolt action 22 carbine for my eighth birthday four years earlier and it had fulfilled all my requirements up to this time. But then I started hanging out with my cousin's husband, Richard. I picked up two bad habits from him which would lead to my 40-year quest. Richard was an accuracy nut and an amateur gunsmith. He had built a beautiful custom 30-06 from a surplus Springfield rifle. It had all the custom touches of the day; reshaped bolt handle, fancy black walnut stock, custom barrel, shiny blue and custom trigger. Made my Mossberg look pretty mundane.

Richard then took me to my first gun show. At almost every table, the traders would ask to see his rifle. Richard would explain his work on the gun and show them targets with three-shot groups all clustered within an inch. The traders would inquire if a trade was possible and upon a negative reply, return the rifle with the comment "Sure is a beautiful rifle." Richard would smile, say "Thank you", and just kind of glow.

That was it for me. The exact moment in time I changed from a casual rifle user into a certified Gun Nut. I now wanted to customize rifles into accurate and beautiful pieces of art that others would covet.

I started immediately. The Mossberg stock got refinished and a Mossberg 4X scope mounted. My first disappointments were forthcoming. The groups were not any better than what I attained with the factory peep sights and no one at the next gun show seemed interested in it.

My friends were now getting their first 22s and all of them were fast firing repeaters, pumps, levers and autoloaders. Not only could they shoot faster than I, but the Marlin lever gun shot better groups than my Mossberg, so I started my search for something better.

I built a decent rifle range out in our woods, confiscating the family picnic table for a shooting bench. I shot all my friends' rifles for groups, read all the firearms publications I could get my hands on and searched the local gun stores for new examples of the art. On one of my

very few trips to the big city, I saw a 22 that would leave a lasting impression. I cannot remember the name of the gun shop, but the rifle was a Steyr Mannlicher-stocked bolt action. I was really taken by that stock. Having seen my interest in that high class 22, the owner also showed me a Grade III Browning Auto. My senses were overloaded. Which would I choose? Actually I had no choice. Both rifles were over $100, more than twice what I had earned working on a pig farm all summer.

Beaten and disheartened, I now felt denied my dreams. How could I ever hope to buy or build anything as beautiful as those two shining examples of rimfire art? However, I did not give up. A short time later in our local gun shop, I was telling the proprietor about the two rifles I had seen. He went in the back and returned with a used Grade I Browning Auto. This was his personal rifle he had used for some time, which he needed to sell to help pay for another 22 rifle he had purchased recently. He said he could give me a good price on it. The stock finish was flaking and the blueing was

worn in places from handling, but there was no rust or major damage evident. And the price was right. I would even have enough left over to buy a Weaver J2.5X scope. The refinishing of the stock, touch-up bluing, and recutting the checkering would give me the satisfaction of customizing my own rifle. That was what I needed. I had my one good 22.

On my way out, as an afterthought, I asked the owner what kind of new 22 he had bought that was worth selling a Browning for. From under the counter, he withdrew a Winchester Model 52C Sporter. It was decent enough, but to my eyes not as striking as either the Steyr, with its Mannlicher stock or the Browning Grade III with its engraving and fancy walnut. Then the owner showed me some targets. All the groups could be covered with a dime. WOW!! That was accuracy. Those groups would haunt my search in the years to come, causing the rejection of many rifles. But for now the Browning was good enough.

After completely refinishing the Browning, adding a sling,

The swamp rifle is best because it hits—first pop every time.

and the Weaver scope, I felt I had put my mark on it. I used it almost daily and it performed well. The barrel joint would loosen occasionally, spreading my groups, but a quick adjustment would put all back to normal. Though its accuracy was not near as good as the Winchester 52 Sporter, it was good enough for the squirrels, rabbits and other small game I hunted. My interests changed to girls and motorcycles for the next few years, temporarily suspending any further searches. But soon enough, fate would again push me down that road less traveled.

In 1966, my final tour in the Air Force landed my new bride and I in Bittburg, Germany. My parents had moved from the country to a condominium, giving away my Mossberg and Browning in the process. It was time for a new rifle.

Between the Rod and Gun Club on base and the German gun stores, I now had a very large assortment to choose from. My favorite was an Anschutz bolt action with a full Mannlicher stock (much later imported into the U.S. as the 1418 Sporter). The factory test target showed 10 shots into a tiny cluster of about 1/2 inch at 50 meters. This was some kind of rifle! The bad news was the price —about three of my E-4 paychecks. The search would go on.

The Rod and Gun Club had just received a new shipment of Ruger 10/22s, including the Mannlicher stocked International. I liked it, but what would my new wife think of spending half a month's pay on a 22? I soon found out. Under our small Christmas tree, there it was. My bride purchased the Ruger for our first married Christmas together. What a wife— choosing her as a bride was the best first-time choice of my life.

The 10/22 International was a good look-ing rifle. I stripped the factory finish off the stock which revealed some decent walnut underneath. I polished all the moving parts, worked on the trigger, and cleaned all the packing grease from the barrel. At the range, the groups proved disappointing. I mounted a scope. The groups tightened up some. I took the rifle completely apart and discovered loose barrel anchor bolts. After tightening, the groups shrank some more. I was beginning to learn about accuracy.

The next 30 years would be in pursuit of 22 rimfire rifle accuracy. There would be short lapses into other areas. Pistol target shooting cost me the Ruger in a trade for a Browning Medalist. I delved into rebuilding old single shot Ballards, Winchesters, Stevens and others for a while. But I always came back to 22 rifles. Accuracy was my Pot of Gold at the end of the Rainbow! I would spend another 15 years before I found out what accuracy really was for a hunting, plinking and informal target shooting rifle. I could write a book on what I discovered and how I discovered it.

I found out that heavy bull barrels with match chambers would shoot wonderfully small groups, but often fail to deliver that first shot from a cold, fouled barrel on a squirrel's head. That action type in a 22 was much less important to accuracy than expected. That chamber dimensions and ammunition were very important. I experimented with all the action types. I ruled out single shots after accidentally running into some dope growers out in the woods. Luckily, my bull-barreled Stevens 44 looked impressive enough to allow me to extricate myself from the situation. A Savage Model 29 pump that I rebarreled was wonderfully accurate but difficult to shoot offhand because of the moving forearm.

A Browning BL 22 lever gun also shot decent groups after a rebarrel but pointed out three more lessons to me. The tubular magazine plunger slipped from my grasp during reloading and launched itself over the side of my canoe into ten feet of black water. My rifle then became a very inefficient single shot. Loading a round directly into the chamber was impossible and trying to load one via the under-barrel magazine without a plunger caused a jam that required the complete disassembly of the rifle—not a job that could be done in a canoe.

I learned hard lessons on point of impact changes caused by weather, poor quality scopes, inadequate stock bedding and even in how the rifle was held. So now small groups were only

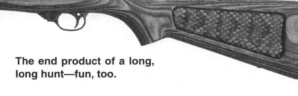

The end product of a long, long hunt—fun, too.

A little off here, just a touch there—and all of a sudden it's obvious.

1/3 of my accuracy equation. First round shots had to be to point of aim, and the point of aim had to remain consistent, irrespective of the weather, the firing position, or the bumps and jarring a rifle would receive in a hunting situation. The rifle had to disassemble easily, allow for single loading, and most importantly possess a trigger pull and stock fit that would allow me to shoot my best.

I came back to the Ruger 10/22 in the late '80s after helping friend Bill clean his. I asked him what he thought of it and he replied that the Ruger had always worked for him the past 15 years until just recently. The gun would not feed reliably with the after-market high capacity magazines. I looked at one of the magazines and found the feed lips were mangled. I got the magazine from a Ruger 77/22 I owned and proceeded to fire 10 rounds without a hitch. I showed Bill how to disassemble and clean the rifle. There was enough powder fouling inside the gun to fill a tablespoon. Asked when the last time the rifle was cleaned, Bill replied, "never."

I was impressed. Not with Bill's gun cleaning habits, but that the rifle could still function under such adverse conditions. I had worked with an accurized Browning auto several years before. After facing off the breech enough to shorten the sporting chamber to match specifications, it would shoot like a target rifle. But the Browning could only go about 200 rounds before cleaning was necessary. Also the extra pressure and bolt speed caused by the tight chamber would wreck some internal part about every 2000 to 3000 rounds. I had given up on semiautos, but I decided maybe to give the Ruger a try.

Shortly thereafter, Wal-Mart started selling the 10/22 with a laminated stock and a stainless steel barrel. I got one. I didn't waste any time on the stock barrel. The bore was as crooked as a live oak limb. I ordered a Volquartsen barrel from Brownells, worked on the trigger, slimmed the stock and coated everything with water proof epoxy and polyurethane. It shot well, it looked good, it resisted the hazards of hunting from a kayak, it was fairly light and it was short. I was almost there.

The first shot from a cold fouled barrel was iffy. The barrel joint attachment seemed to lead to a wandering zero occasionally. And the aesthetics did not completely satisfy me. But I was close, closer than ever before.

By the summer of '93 I had worked with one more Wal-Mart Ruger 10/22. The factory barrel was much better this time. By counterboring the receiver. 100 inch and facing the barrel breech an equal amount, I ended up with a decent chamber, a more secure barrel/receiver joint, in a lighter rifle. The laminated wood (after receiving a real waterproof coating in and on the wood) held up much better to our abusive climate and swamps than the walnuts I had been using. By creating a cutout in the buttstock, the weight and balance were enhanced. And I discovered that by counterboring the muzzle with a .22 chamber reamer, group size decreased and first shot hit probability increased. I wished now I had never traded my original 10/22 International. A streamlined, accurate International would be the best. My wife, hearing of my wish for that first 10/22 of so long ago, said "I told you not to trade it."

I shut up and shot my carbine. And I would still be shooting it today, but on Christmas Eve, 1994, there sat a black laminated stocked 10/22 International under the tree. What a wife!!

I immediately went to work on the modifications needed to enhance accuracy and handling. The barrel setback and receiver counterbore worked once again, rendering consistent 50 yard groups close to 1/2 inch with Federal Ultra Match and 5/8 to 3/4 inches with CCI Green Tag, Winchester T-22s, and even Federal Lightning. The trigger tuning went as planned. The trigger released crisply at three pounds. Overtravel was limited by the longer trigger return spring plunger I made. Once cut and tried, this method of eliminating overtravel, though not adjustable, is very reliable. Anything adjustable might someday unadjust. The bedding proved to be O.K. the way it came from the factory, allowing removal and reinstallation of the barreled action without affecting the scope zero. The accuracy enhancements completed, it was now time for the handling and visual modifications.

The stock modification, to most, would determine whether my creation was viewed as just another butcher job or a truly well executed process to enhance the handling and visual aspects of the rifle. I started on the forearm with my sandpaper and sanding block. By sight and touch, wood was removed until the forearm more resembled that of a M1903 Mannlicher-Schoenauer, a series of shallow, concave, complex curves culminating at the nose cap. In the process about 2/10ths of an inch was removed from the bottom front of the receiver and magazine, allowing the forearm taper to start at the triggerguard.

The modifications on the buttstock did not happen all at once. At first I just cut out the center of the butt to eliminate some excess weight and to move the balance point forward to the magazine. A month later, the rubber butt pad was cast aside and replaced with skateboard tape. I have always shot better with a shorter stock plus the rubber pad always hung up on my shirt. About a year later, one of my non-shooting coworkers was looking at a picture of the rifle and wanted to know why I left such a big lump on the buttstock. He meant the pistol grip cap, and he was correct - it did look not quite right. The pistol grip was very long, so I removed the cap and reshaped it somewhat. I was left with a hole in the grip from the cap anchor screw, so I plugged it with a sling swivel stud, intending to install a metal cap later. After actually using the sling anchored at the pistol grip for awhile, I liked this arrangement. Sling carry either muzzle up or down seemed more comfortable and secure.

The last modification was the butt stock inlay. Though the cutout served its purpose, it left an unfinished appearance to the rifle. Out of the blue, I decided to fill it with something. I shaped a chunk of polyester foam to fit and covered it with rattlesnake hide. The hide was stained darker to match the stock, and a few compact emergency tools fabricated which fit within. The results, I think, are not half bad. Not something I would do to a $300 piece of walnut, but appropriate enough here.

And my perfect .22 rifle emerged. My custom rifle. It still would be out of place with the truly custom rifles displayed in the Gun Digest, just as out of place as those custom rifles would be in the bottom of my kayak gliding around Yellow River Swamp. It is composed only of factory standard parts, just moderately modified to suit my needs, it is "my" custom rifle. And I was the 'smith.

After almost three years of constant use, I have only become more certain of my final choice. I can shoot this rifle from any position as well as any I have ever fired. The rifle does get noticed, from the rattlesnake hide in the buttstock cutout to the slimmed lines of the receiver bottom and forearm. I now have a rifle that can compare to Richard's. A little anyway.

The good Lord and the government willing, I'll have another forty years to enjoy my one good gun. But it would be nice to have one good small 22 pistol as a companion piece, one good pocket binocular, one good sheath knife, maybe a larger kayak to accommodate the grandchildren, one good....

—Mike Lyle

The snakeskin fills a hole, holds some tools, and looks good—all at once.

TESTFIRE TESTFIRE TESTFIRE

Stealth Shadow

The Stealth Shadow pistol, right view. A safety lever on each side allows ambidextrous use of the safety.

The Stealth Shadow is one of a new breed of 9mm pistols that has appeared within the past few years, introduced early in 1996 by Heritage Manufacturing, Inc. The small pistol measures just a bit over six inches long and 4 inches high, and has a "legal-limit" 10-round magazine.

Such small, relatively large-capacity pistols came into being as the result of two major factors. The move to permit legal concealed carry by law-abiding citizens had grown to include 31 states, and all those newly-licensed people created a market for more compact pistols. The Crime Bill of September 1994 restricted all pistols to a magazine capacity of 10 rounds, making 9mm pistols designed for 17 or more rounds seem overly large for the new restricted magazine capacity.

Thus, smaller 9mm pistols, with a magazine capacity at or close to the legal limit of 10,

came into demand. The first Stealth pistol offered by Heritage was given model number C-1000 and was available with a stainless-steel slide and a black polymer frame. By early 1997, the Stealth Shadow, Model C-2000, was available. The Shadow still has a stainless-steel slide, but it is black chrome plated to match the black frame. This was the version tested.

The black finish on the slide is a good match to the polymer frame, giving the pistol a uniform black finish. In bright letters, the right side of the slide reads: "Stealth Shadow C-2000." On the left appears this legend in script: "Heritage Manufacturing, Inc., Opa Locka, FL." Opa Locka, Florida? Yes, Florida is becoming ever more important in the firearms world, and the South Florida town of

Opa Locka is the origin of the Stealth Shadow.

Caliber is 9mm Parabellum, or 9mm Luger. The steel magazine is of double-column type and holds 10 rounds.

The pistol itself weighs about 20 ounces unloaded. Length is about 6 1/4 inches and height is about 4 1/4 inches, a size that allows the pistol to be almost hidden beneath a common 4x6 index card. This size places the pistol into what has come to be called the small, or subcompact, class. The finger-rest magazine adds about 1/2 inch of height, but provides a good grip for the pinky finger. Width of the pistol is a bit over one inch, being widest at the ambidextrous safety levers.

The pistol has an interesting delayed-blowback action. A gas piston is fastened to the lower front end of the slide and travels with the slide, within a

cylinder under the barrel. A small gas tap hole in the barrel forward of the chamber enters this cylinder at its rear. Thus, when a cartridge is fired and the bullet enters the rifling, powder gas enters the gas cylinder and acts on the piston to resist the rearward movement of the slide.

The slide itself weighs 9 1/2 ounces, almost half the weight of the pistol, and the inertia of the slide has an effect on retarding the opening of the action. A rather strong recoil spring is also used, positioned around the barrel.

The Stealth is striker-fired. The mechanism is of the general type by Glock known as "Safe Action." It is neither single-action nor double-action. The movement of the slide brings the striker to a "half-cock" position; pressure on the trigger then draws the striker farther back and releases it.

The interesting design allows for a barrel just shy of four

In half-cock position, the rear end of the Stealth's striker protrudes slightly.

inches in a pistol just over six inches long. The barrel is fixed to the frame and does not move. It is rifled with eight lands and grooves, right-handed twist.

The manufacturer claims a number of safety features. The most noticeable are the magazine safety, which prevents the trigger's being pulled when the magazine is removed, and the manual thumb safety. The thumb safety lever covers a red dot when engaged; the dot is exposed when ready to fire. There is a lever on both the left and right side of the pistol. The thumb safety simply prevents movement of the trigger. This arrangement seems perfectly adequate, since the pistol is actually not cocked until the trigger is pressed.

The trigger is black polymer, about 5/8 inch wide at the top and tapering to less than 1/2 inch at the bottom. It has a long travel, about 1/4 inch, but a fairly light pull. Literature with the pistol lists the pull at approximately 4 pounds; my scale showed something over 4 1/2, still a fairly light and smooth pull.

The sights are a fixed front blade integral with the slide, and a square-notch rear sight, drift-adjustable for windage. The sights have vertical white bars to aid in alignment in low light.

Takedown of the unloaded Stealth is accomplished by pressing in on two take-down

The firm two-hand hold works best with the Stealth Shadow.

buttons at the rear of the frame with the strong hand. With the other hand, the slide is moved rearward about an inch. Then the rear of the slide is lifted off the frame. At this point, the rear portion of the slide can be eased, against the pressure of the recoil spring, up over the chamber end of the barrel, then forward off the barrel.

The position at which the slide is released is not marked, and the first takedown, when one does not know what to expect, is a bit tricky. Once you see how everything fits together, it is much easier. A new owner could become familiar with the takedown by taking out the recoil spring, then practicing disassembly and reassembly without spring pressure.

Range sessions with the Stealth Shadow showed that the gas-retard system works very well. Felt recoil was moderate with all loads tried. Indeed, although it is a subjective

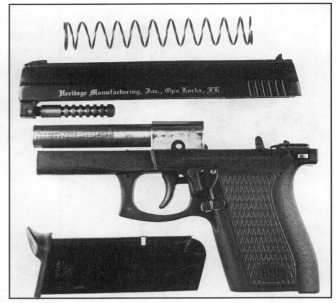

The Stealth Shadow, stripped to its major components, shows the gas piston, attached to the lower front end of the slide, that rides in a gas cylinder under the fixed barrel. Gas pressue retards the rearward movement of the slide when the pistol is fired.

evaluation, the recoil from moderate and full loads seemed about the same.

Initial 10-yard groups fired from a bedroll rest indicated that the pistol shot slightly to the right. Tapping the rear sight to the left centered the groups, which formed just above the point of aim. Five-shot groups fired with several different factory loads all centered just over the front sight.

Because most buyers will acquire a Stealth Shadow for short-range protection, shooting at Bianchi Cup tombstone targets at 10 yards from a two-handed standing position seemed appropriate. A number of different factory loads and moderate reloads were tried. Five-shot groups averaged a little over two inches, with 1 5/8 inch being the smallest and 3 1/4 inch the largest. All groups were within the 4-inch center of the target. Getting used to the long trigger pull proved easy - just roll it back the same way for every shot.

Encouraged by the accuracy demonstrated at 10 yards, I

tried the Stealth at the 25-yard range. The sight adjustment achieved at 10 yards worked also at 25. Groups were centered and formed just above point of aim. Best 5-shot group was 4 1/2 inches, within the 5 1/2 inch black aiming bull of a standard 25-yard target.

Bullseye target shooting is perhaps the pistol sport most dependent on precise trigger control. The Stealth Shadow's long trigger pull, which had felt strange to me at first, had become familiar. I was curious as to how well it would do under Bullseye shooting condition.

I tried several 10-shot groups from the traditional one-hand bullseye shooter's stance, on the 25-yard timed-fire target. All my scores were in the 80s. Not too bad. True, such scores will not get you to Camp Perry. They do, however, show that the Stealth Shadow is an eminently shootable pistol that has defense capabilities to at least 25 yards.

About a hundred rounds were fired. These included several different types of factory loads with metal-case and hollow-point bullets, and some moderate reloads. There were no malfunctions with any type of ammunition.

The Stealth Shadow seems to have the satisfactory accuracy and reliability to appeal to those who are considering a small 9mm pistol for personal protection.

John Malloy

Stealth Shadow C-2000

All the controls work easily and well, right or lefthanded.

TESTFIRE TESTFIRE TESTFIRE

Phoenix's HP 22

Woodrow Wilson's Vice President, Thomas Riley Marshall, likely never found that "good five cent cigar" he felt the country needed. Many shooters have been on a similar quest for a good, reliable 22 LR pocket pistol for plinking and personal defense-one that did not cost an arm and a leg.

For those desiring a small carry gun, the 25 ACP has been the standard for one basic reason—reliability. Until recently the 25 could be fed only a fifty-grain FMJ bullet at 820 fps. New lightweights from CCI at 35 grains will clock 900 fps, and even expand a bit in tissue. The big problem with the 25 has and will always be ammunition cost—around $16 for fifty FMJ, $9 for twenty 35-grain hollow-points, and about $8 for fifty aluminum-case practice rounds.

Everybody thought it would be nice if those little autoloaders could be made to handle long rifles which, on sale, are a buck a box. Almost every manufacturer's effort in this direction ended in failure—guns that constantly jammed. The why of this problem lay in the fact the long rifle cartridge is one of the worst designs for functioning through autoloading actions. It's rimmed, long in proportion to its diameter, has a soft case and exposed soft bullet with a weak heel-crimp joint between bullet and case. Such a cartridge catches and bends on the rough trip through the standard 25 type of action.

To make a small, reliable, 22 autoloader would seem to require one with the tolerances of a Swiss watch. Walther did exactly this with their TPH and the one I examined functioned perfectly. It also came with a Rolex price tag—nearly $500.

The good nickel cigar proposition was not lost on designer Dave Brazeau. While at the Raven plant, making small inexpensive 25s that worked reasonably well and 22s that didn't, Brazeau began work on a pistol with the TPH's reliability that would sell at about one fifth the price. This was in 1992. When the Raven plant burned, out of the ashes arose Phoenix Arms. The first production pistols were finished in 1993. The HP22 is 1/8" longer than the TPH and six ounces heavier. It boasts a three inch barrel and ten shot magazine compared to the Walther's 2 1/4" barrel and six-shot magazine.

In this writer's estimation, Brazeau's pistol lives up to all his expectations. The Phoenix first received good press in GUN TESTS magazine when it blew away competition from Lorcin and Jennings. The finish of the Phoenix—matte nickel or black—was so good GT thought it was an all-steel gun. Herein lies a clue to the pistol's high quality and low price—smart engineering. Frame and slide are die-cast zinc alloy. Steel is used in the barrel, slide core, magazine and all working parts except the trigger. The frame and barrel housing (expensive parts to machine) are precision cast and polished. The black-oxide finish is a proprietary process tougher

Field stripping requires no tools, but is a bit tricky. Follow the instructions <u>exactly</u>.

than most blueing and is done in a hot oil bath. Cold blue touch-up preparations will not work on this finish.

The rifling is microgroove style with a fast 1-8 in. RH twist, buttoned for a slick surface and good grip on bullets. According to Brazeau, factory tests of 6000+ rounds have been run. A small crack developed in the slide below the extractor, but did not affect functioning. The slide has since been strengthened at this point.

Our test gun came with a black finish that did look like steel. Functioning was perfection itself with eight domestic and one foreign type of ammunition. Over the first 200 rounds, the only hangup was on a first round fed manually without a full pull of the slide. The function test included 32-grain Stingers, 42-grain Super Silhouette and both standard and high velocity ammunition. Additional hurdles were added by use of rough, oxide-crusted Winchester Leader cartridges from the early 1950s and some heavily greased Remington SV from WWII -- no problems! The grip was rated good by both the male and female shooter. Trigger pull was 5.5 lbs. on our Chatillon gauge, and creepy. After the testfire this creep was eliminated by having a gunsmith square up the hammer notch. DO NOT TRY THIS AT HOME! The sights are large and clear yet smooth -- designed not to catch on clothing. The rear is easily adjusted for windage. No adjustment was needed on our test gun.

Accuracy was first tested by firing five-shot groups at seven yards (no. this is not a target gun) from a rest, yielding the following results.

WW Super Silhouette 0.9"
WW Power Point HP 2.1"
WW Leader Std Vel 1.5"
WW T-22 Std Vel 1.6"
Rem Std Vel 1.4"
Rem Yellow Jacket HP 2.0"
CCI Mini Mag HP 1.4"
CCI Stinger HP 2.4"
Fiocchi Pistol Match 2.5"

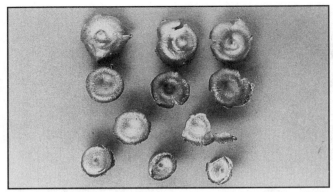

Hollowpoint bullets gave good expansion. Remington Yellow Jackets (top row) were consistently the best followed by CCI Mini Mag (second row) and Winchester Power Point (third row). CCI Stingers (bottom) gave poor expansion in the 3" barrel.

Rapid-fire groups (unsupported) at the same range yielded the following.

WW Power Point 4.0"
WW Super Silhouette 4.5"
CCI Mini Mag HP 7.5"
Rem Std 3.3"

The Mini Mag HP and Super Silhouette were tried at longer ranges (slow-fire unsupported).

CCI Mini Mag HP 5.1"
   (20 yards)
WW Super Silhouette
   6.0" (25 yards)

Both shooters felt unsupported groups would have been better if the creep was eliminated from the trigger. As a benchmark a second HP22 was tested by a third shooter. At seven yards, two groups fired with CCI Blazer HV ammunition produced a 2.5" ten-shot group slow fire and 3.75" rapid fire group at this range. There were no function problems.

Phoenix offers a conversion kit featuring a 5 inch barrel and a magazine with an extra finger grip. Neither shooter was particularly fond of the extended grip. The longer barrel yielded the following results at twenty yards. It did not turn the HP22 into a target pistol.

WW Super Silhouette 2.8"
Rem Std Vel 3.7"
CCI Mini Mag HP 5.9"

Since a pistol of this type is carried as a kit/camp/protection arm, velocity and expansion are factors for consideration. Chronographed velocities were taken in seventy-degree weather with an Oehler 35P on selected ammunition. Results are for five-shot groups with the 3" barrel:+ highest velocity; - lowest velocity - E-extreme spread; M-mean vel; S-standard deviation.
CCI Mini Mag HP: 0933+; 0912-; 0021E; 0923M; 0007S.
WW Power Point HP: 0916+; 0848-; 0068E; 0876M; 0027S.
WW Super Silhouette: 0896+; 0857-; 0039E; 0881M; 0014S.
Expansion tests were made by shooting into water at close range. As could be expected, none of the solids expanded. Results with the hollow points, however, were rather good. All expanded to some degree. The best performance was by the Yellow Jacket to nearly 45 caliber. The CCI Mini Mag came in a close second at between 35 and 44 caliber, about the same as the Winchester Power Point. The CCI Stinger with only one round expanding to 32 caliber was the poorest performer. This is

not surprising since the Stinger with its slower-burning powder is designed as a rifle cartridge, though it does fairly well in long-barreled hand guns.

Field-stripping the Phoenix is a bit tricky. While takedown is fairly simple, reassembly presents more of a problem. Fortunately the pistol comes with a good set of illustrated instructions. No tools are required, but all the steps must be followed exactly in the proper order. The only point in reassembly that could be made clearer is the final repositioning of the barrel in the frame. The instructions are clear about placing the barrel in the frame and "allowing the slide to go forward." We were super careful about holding the slide and easing it forward. This failed to lock the barrel in place. However, allowing the slide to snap forward, with the barrel in place, popped it right where it belonged. Since cleaning can be done by locking back the slide, I would advise against field stripping for this purpose. Why risk damaging or losing a small part?

The HP22 comes with a lifetime warranty for the original owner. Worn finish can be restored at the factory. If you get a gun second hand be sure to get the instruction sheet as this is not one of those you can simply "figure out." Instructions are free by writing Phoenix Arms 1420 South Archibald Ave. Ontario, CA 91761.

Two tips from the designer are not to dry fire the pistol and to use standard velocity ammunition for practice since this will put less wear and tear on the mechanism. We rate this one of the best small-frame 22 autoloaders we have encountered under $100. It has a performance record equaling the very best.

C. Rodney James

An extra set of guide lugs on the front of the magazine insure that cartridges are fed straight into the chamber.

The Phoenix is larger than most 25's, but offers a 3" barrel, larger grip and two more shots in the magazine.

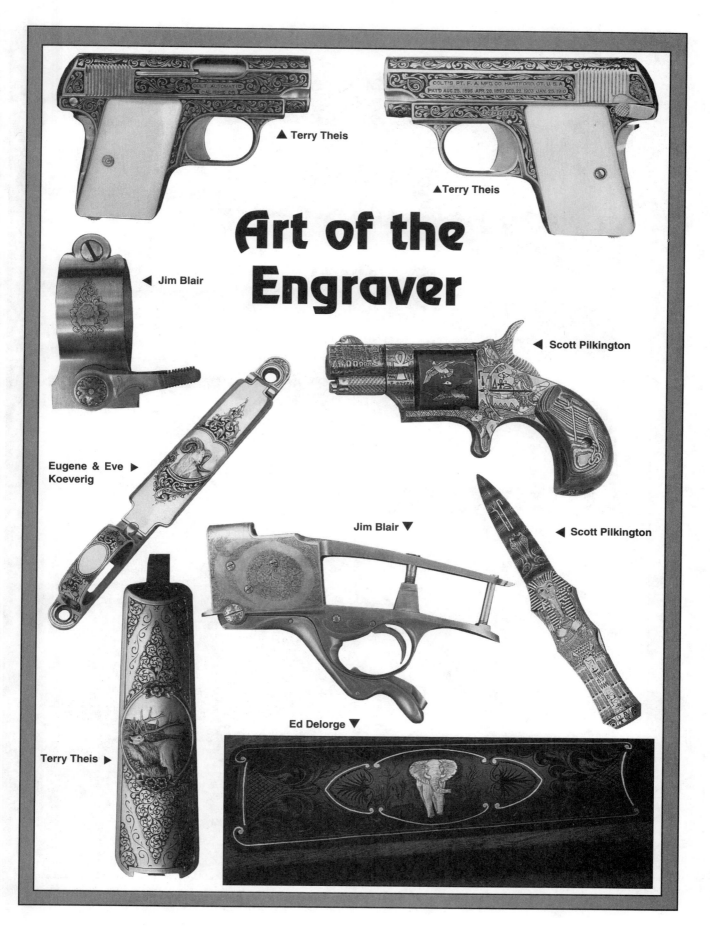

▲ Terry Theis

▲ Terry Theis

◄ Jim Blair

Art of the Engraver

◄ Scott Pilkington

Eugene & Eve ►
Koeverig

Jim Blair ▼

◄ Scott Pilkington

Terry Theis ►

Ed Delorge ▼

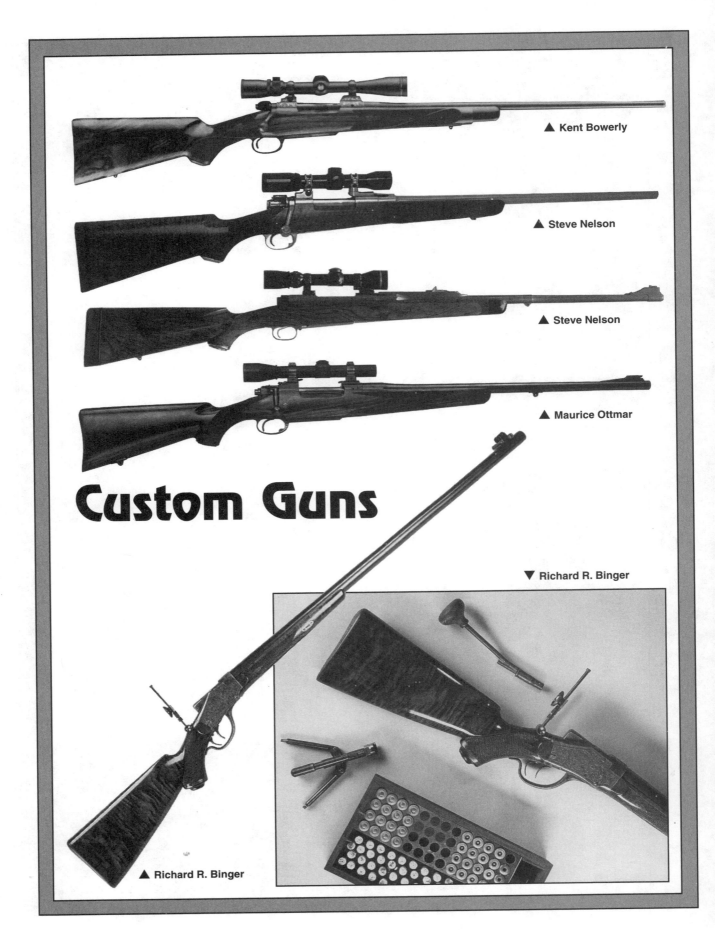

▲ Kent Bowerly

▲ Steve Nelson

▲ Steve Nelson

▲ Maurice Ottmar

Custom Guns

▼ Richard R. Binger

▲ Richard R. Binger

Custom Guns

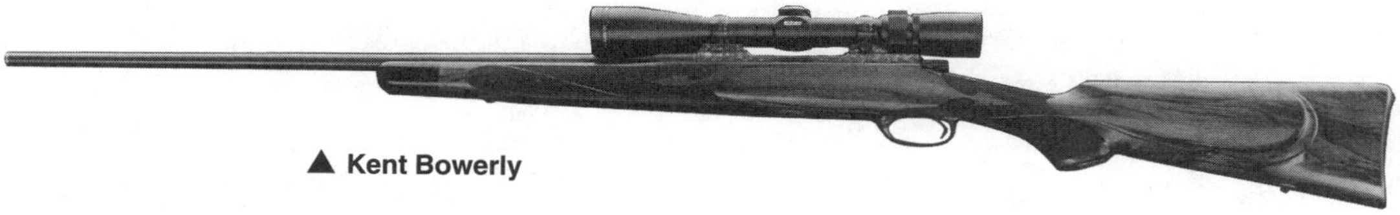

▲ Kent Bowerly

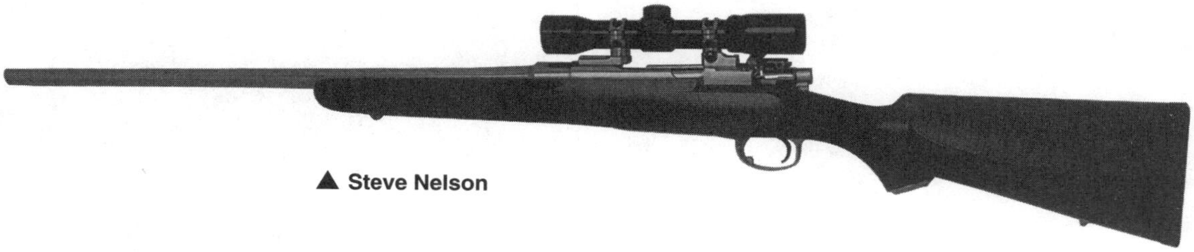

▲ Steve Nelson

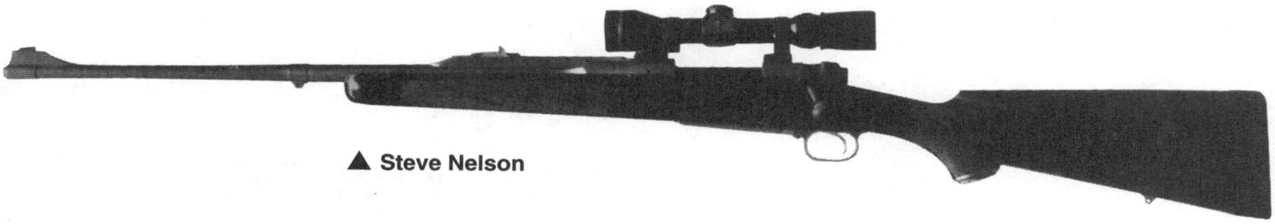

▲ Steve Nelson

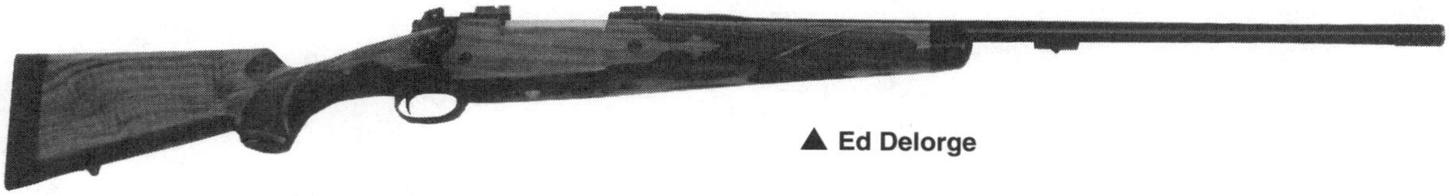

▲ Ed Delorge

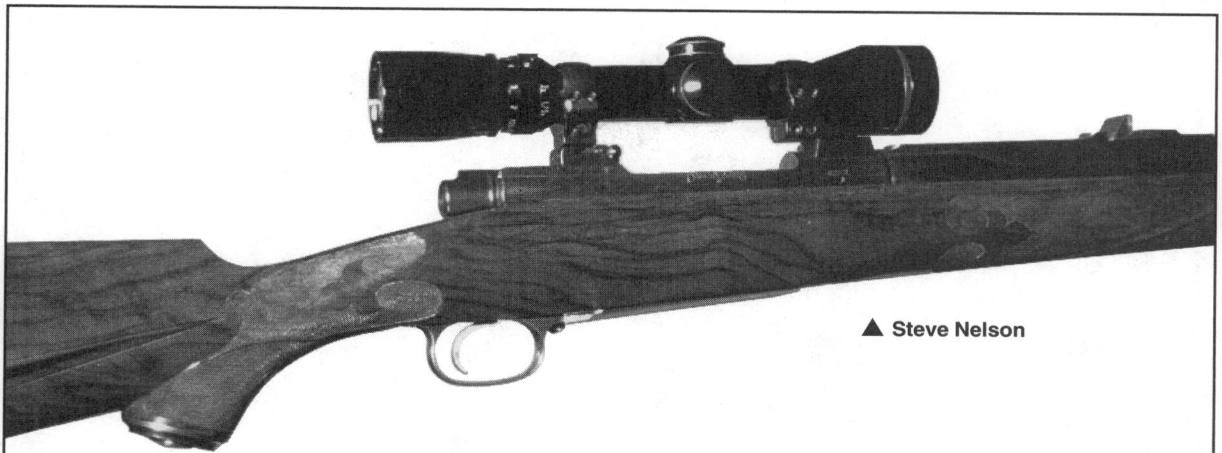

▲ Steve Nelson

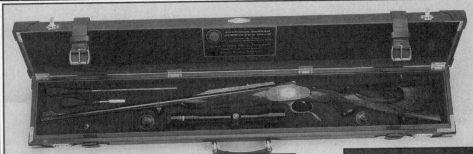

This is the John Amber Commemorative Rifle, raffled in 1996. Built by Bartz, Cromwell, Silver, stocked by Corpe, engraved by Boucher, it's a single shot on a Hagn action. (Bilal photo) ◄

This is the 100th Anniversary Mauser 98 by Jim Johnston, Tucher, Sterch, Hands—all the Teutonic touches are there. ▲

The Parker, engraved by Ruchel Ward, other work by Turnbull, Leeds, Moeller. ▲

American Custom Gun Guild: Special Guns By Special People

The finished Winchester by Blair, Moeller, Turnbull, Leeds—a splendid 1892 rifle. ▲

The ACGG Gent's Sporting Collection—a three-gun battery here in the white—Winchester and Colt 44-40's and a Parker 12. ▼

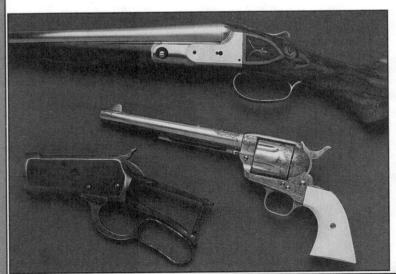

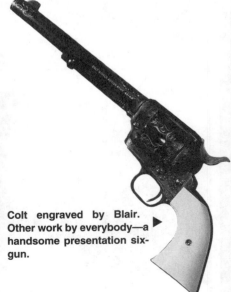

Colt engraved by Blair. Other work by everybody—a handsome presentation six-gun. ►

by LAYNE SIMPSON

RIFLE REVIEW

The year 1999 holds great promise for we lovers of the rifle, even though most of what is new amounts to variations of what we already had. There is, however, a new bullpup-style rifle and this time it is designed for hunters rather than soldiers. Another rifle, called Scout, gets my vote as the most interesting for this year, but if you are convinced that rifle evolution should have stopped with the adoption of wood and steel, you probably won't enjoy reading about it--or looking at it. An old wildcat with plenty of punch on both ends has now found a permanent home while a new variant of an old woods rifle is sure to gladden the hearts of those who drown worms in bear country. Here then, are those and other things that will keep me excited during the entire upcoming year. And here's hoping they do the same for you.

Browning

Browning's new Low Wall Traditional Hunter; a Japanese-made reproduction of the Winchester Model 1885, has a 24-inch half-round/half-octagon barrel in 30-30, 38-55 or 45-70 Government. A very nice little rifle, indeed. Also new for 1998 is the 45-90 chambering in the BPCR.

Cimarron

Want to own a 1874 Sharps like the one "buffler" hunter Billy Dixon allegedly used to bump off a redskin at extremely long range? If so, Cimarron offers just that in a variety of chamberings, including 40-65, 40-70

enteen into a 220 Swift. On several occasions I have gone through 400 rounds of ammo without cleaning the Lilja barrel and it still averaged less than half-minute-of angle for five shots, a feat made possible by the use of moly-coated bullets.

Incidentally, I am now using what I consider to be the world's best portable benchrest on all my prairie dog shoots. Made by Red Cornett of Cornett Machine, Inc. (who also builds high-performance Ford and Chevy racing engines), it is the most stable rig of its kind I have found and its top surface is long and wide enough to hold an adjustable front rifle rest, rear sandbag and an ammo box. Its four legs adjust for levelling on uneven terrain and

The Scout from Steyr utilized the forward-mounted scope position and has integral folding bipod, good feel and strange looks.

and 45-70. It is made in Italy, as is Cimarron's Model 1873 Winchester reproduction in 32-30 WCF.

Cooper Arms

Among other rifles, I used one of Dan Cooper's Varmint Extremes in 17 Remington on several prairie dog shoots during 1997 and was impressed by its performance. It has a gorgeous English walnut stock with a semi-beavertail-style forearm and a heavy Lilja stainless steel barrel. The little rifle wears a Burris 6-24X Signature scope with the mil-dot reticle. My favorite load for that rifle consists of the Remington case, No. 7-1/2 primer, and enough W760 to push Walt Berger's 30-grain moly-coated hollowpoint along at 4000 feet per second. As far as trajectory and wind-bucking go, that bullet basically transforms Remington's Sweet Sev-

since the seat along with the table top swivel 360 degrees, no varmint in any direction is safe.

Dakota

Dakota has introduced the Model '97, a slightly less expensive version of its Model 76 woodstock rifle with a black synthetic stock and available in 13 chamberings ranging from the 25-06 to the 375 H&H Magnum. Its list of credentials include a cylindrical-shaped receiver, match-grade barrel, Mauser-style extractor and a three-position safety. Also new is the 14-pound Longbow Tactical Engagement Rifle replete with half-minute-of-angle accuracy guarantee, Mauser-style claw extractor and 28 inch barrel in a variety of magnum chamberings including 300 Winchester, 338 Lapua and 300 Dakota.

While hunting in New Mexico during the '97 season I was

lucky enough to bag a pronghorn antelope that missed the B&C record book by only a couple of points. The outfit I used was a Dakota Model 10 single shot in 270 WCF with a Leupold 2.5-8X Vari-X-III scope. It might as well have been a one-shot hunt since that's all the Winchester 130-grain Ballistic Silvertip ammunition I used. Nice rifle and darned good ammo.

Dixie Gun Works

Back when I was young and foolish and traded guns at the drop of a hat, I owned a genuine trapdoor Springfield carbine in 45-70 Government. It was in near-mint condition and I shot it a lot—before foolishly trading it away. I'm saying all of this to say that I'll probably have to have one of the carbines now available from Dixie. Even though this one is made in Italy rather than Springfield Armory like the one I used to own was, it looks, feels, handles and shoots the same. A rifle version with 32-1/2 inch barrel is also available.

Fajen

I don't know about you but there are times when I grow a bit bored with rifles made of plastic and stainless steel. Now don't take what I just said in the wrong vein; there will always be a place in the big-game hunting scheme of things for weather-proof rifles and I am reminded of this each time I hunt in southeastern Alaska but the occasions when I actually need such a rifle are outnumbered by the times when I don't.

When it comes down to pride of ownership and the pure enjoyment of just holding a rifle in your hands, blued steel and Mother Nature's walnut still can't be beat. It was with this thought in mind that I first sent a Winchester Model 70 action to Doug Shilen for the installation of one of his match-grade, chrome moly barrels in 7mm STW. Leaving the barreled action in the white, Doug then forwarded it to the Fajen custom

shop for the installation of a stock carved of extra-fancy grade English walnut. In addition to that, the specifications I sent to Fajen included a wrap-around checkering pattern in the fleur-de-lis style, Model 70 Super Grade-style quick-detach sling swivels, ebony forearm tip, checkered steel grip cap, Pachmayr Old English recoil pad and several other goodies as well. After inletting the stock, Fajen returned the barreled action to Shilen for a very attractive satin-finished blue job. The barreled action then went back to Fajen where the outfit was final prepped before being shipped to me.

The result of all that effort on the part of a very talented group of craftsmen is one of the very finest rifles I have ever owned. Shoots quite accurately too, and

averages just under an inch for three shots at 100 yards with any good 140-grain bullet seated atop a maximum charge of Reloader 22. Soon after receiving the rifle, I received a few boxes of Federal's new 7mm STW factory loads with the 150-grain Trophy Bonded and 160-grain Sierra bullets. The Trophy Bonded load proved be so accurate that I decided to use it on a south Texas whitetail hunt and it worked quite well. After making myself comfortable in a tower stand overlooking a long sendero, I used the excellent Bushnell YardagePro 800 laser rangefinder to range various natural objects in the landscape so when a buck stepped out at 340 yards I immediately knew that a dead-on hold to its shoulder would do the trick. And it did.

Kimber

Last time we got together I mentioned that Kimber's Model 770 bolt gun was in production. While that's exactly what I had been led to believe at the time, such was not the case. Next time I mention it here you can bet I'll have a production rifle

sitting beside me. My apologies for the false alarm.

LakeLander

The LakeLander Model 389 bolt-action rifle is being imported from Sweden by Lakelander USA and is available in 6.5 Swede, 270, 308 and 30-06. Some of its design details bear a close resemblance to the Kongsberg Model 393, with its magazine being a good example. Other features include

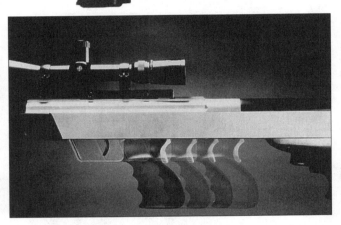

The bolt of this bullpup from Germany is manually cycled by pulling and pushing on the pistol grip.

dovetail grooves on the receiver for scope mounting, fully adjustable trigger and three-position, side-mounted safety.

Lazzeroni

In addition to building a line of high-quality rifles around his own action, John Lazzeroni is now offering a less expensive rifle built on the Remington Model 700 action. Available in all Lazzeroni chamberings except the 375 Saturn and 416 Meteor, it has a synthetic stock with aluminum receiver pillars and a 26-inch, match-grade barrel. Also new is a short action version of the Lazzeroni rifle chambered for Lazzeroni's own magnum-velocity cartridges of various calibers.

Layne was glad he had his Rifle, Inc. rifle in 257 STW when it came time to take this coues buck at 290 yards.

Marlin

During 1998 Marlin is producing the Model 1897 Annie Oakley, a dressed-up version of the Model 39A. It has an 18-1/2 inch tapered octagon barrel and its Marble adjustable sights include consist a semi-buckhorn at the rear and a brass bead up front. Other features include a roll-engraved, blued receiver replete with a replica of "Little Sure Shot's" signature in gold fill. The American walnut buttstock and forearm have cut checkering, a blued-steel forearm cap and a hard rubber buttplate.

Moving on to bigger things, the Model 1895G "Guide Gun" is an abbreviated version of the standard 1895 with a 18-1/2 inch barrel in 45-70 Government. Ballard-type (in lieu of Micro-Groove) rifling inside the barrel is sure to shoot both cast and jacketed bullets with equal accuracy while gas ports at its

(top) Marlin's Model 1897 Annie Oakley has an octagon barrel and engraving on its receiver, and fancy wood in its butt

(bottom) The Model 15N is a new 22 Rimfire youth rifle from Marlin, built for small people.

muzzle should reduce muzzle jump a bit and make lots of noise. There's also a ventilated recoil pad (which should be solid), straight grip and squared finger lever (which I like very much), and cut-checkered American walnut beneath a Mar-Shield coat. A nice and handy handful of bear repellant, this 1895G.

Latest version of Marlin's 22 rimfire bolt gun is the Model 81TS replete with a black synthetic stock and a 17-round tubular magazine hanging beneath its 22-inch Micro-Groove barrel. Other bolt gun news from North Haven in-cludes the Model 15YN with its 16-1/4 inch barrel and shortened length of pull aimed squarely at the youth gun market. Marlin will also offer a stock of standard dimensions for that gun to have on hand when that young guy or gal outgrows the short one. The Model 60 autoloading family continues to grow as well, with the latest additions being the Models 60SB and 60SSK, both in stainless steel but the former with a birch stock and the latter wrapped in black synthetic. Fiber optic sights called Fire Sights are new options on Marlin's Model 882SS bolt gun and the Model 512DL slug gun.

Remington

Lots of new stuff from Remington this year. In the centerfire bolt gun category, we have the custom shop's 40-XB with a thumbhole-style laminated wood stock. I shot one in 260

Remington and despite the fact that through the years I have tried hard to like that style of stock, I still don't. That same rifle is now available in 7mm STW, as are four other custom shop variations of the Model 700-AWR (Alaskan Wilderness Rifle), Custom KS Mountain Rifle (with left- or right-hand action) and the Custom KS Stainless. That same chambering is also available in two standard-production variations, the Model 700 Sendero SF and Model 700 BDL Stainless.

(Incidentally, we now have four 7mm STW factory loads 140-grain Pointed Core-Lokt and Swift A-Frame of the same weight from Remington, 150-grain Trophy Bonded Bear Claw and 160-grain Sierra Spitzer boattail from Federal, and 145-grain Grand Slam in the Speer Nitrex lineup.)

For the benefit of those who keep up with such things, I'll mention that the series of limited-edition Model 700 Classic rifles began with the 7x57mm mauser in 1981. Then came the 257 Roberts, 300 H&H Magnum,

This South Texas whitetail fell to the author, his Fajen/Shilen custom Model 70 and Federal's new 7mm STW factory load.

250-3000 Savage, 350 Remington Magnum, 264 Winchester Magnum, 338 Winchester Magnum, 35 Whelen, 300 Weatherby Magnum, 25-06, 7mm Weatherby Magnum, 220 Swift, 222 Remington, 6.5x55mm Swedish, 300 Winchester Magnum, 375 H&H Magnum, 280 Remington, and for 1998 it's the 8mm Remington Magnum. Also new for that cartridge is Remington's new loading of the 200-grain Swift A-Frame bullet. What's left to do? Well, the 270 Winchester and 300 Savage are far more classical than some chamberings Remington has done in the past and when they along with the 17 Remington, 8mm Mauser and 35 Remington have seen their day in the sun, the picking and choosing will become mighty tough.

tom Shop has also gotten into this same act by introducing its new Custom Target and Custom Target Magnum version of the Model 597, both with heavy, free-floated barrels, minimum-dimension target chamber, fine-tuned trigger and laminated wood stock.

Rifles, Inc.

Since introducing the 7mm Shooting Times Westerner (STW) as a wildcat in 1988, I have received numerous letters from readers urging me to develop other calibers on the same case. And of all the calibers requested, the 257 got asked for the most often. Considering that 25-caliber cartridges enjoy

inch barrel. When finally getting a shot at a nice little buck, I didn't have time to even think about how far away it was. The deer was walking briskly uphill and to my left so I simply aimed where I figured it was about to be and squeezed the trigger. As luck would have it, the miniature whitetail stumbled on for a couple of steps and then piled up in a boil of dust. After my shot, when we found time for such things, the Leica Geovid laser rangefinder indicated 293 yards from me to where the buck lay dead.

I also had the pleasure of wringing out several of Webernick's custom varmint rifles in 223, 22-250, 6mm-285 and 257

el 75 action. Among other things, I recommended a stock of laminated wood with a forearm wide enough to be easily stabilized by a sandbag. I also asked for a barrel length of 26 inches for the 22-250 and 220 Swift. As it turned out, I didn't get the stock material I had asked for but I did get the style of stock. Carved from European walnut, it is quite nicely shaped for shooting over sandbags. As I write this, even Paasikivi is not certain what chamberings will be available but my guess is we will at least see the 223, 22-250 and 243 in time for the '98 varmint season.

You may have noticed that Sako management likes to test the waters with a new chambering by first offering it in the TRG-S and if it sells well in that rifle, it is added to the list of options for Sako's other rifle. That's exactly what happened with the 7mm STW a couple of years ago; initially offered only in the TRG, it quickly became available in the Sako Model 75 as well. now the same thing is starting to happen with the 30-378 Weatherby Magnum. This year it is available in the TRG-S rifle. Next year?

Sako describes the new Tikka Sporter in 223, 22-250 and 308 as "well suited for competition shooting and hunting". While I have yet to think of any type of competitive shooting or hunting I would want to use it for, its heavy barrel and the adjustable cheekpiece and buttplate on its stock make it an excellent candidate for shooting prairie dogs. It should certainly be accurate enough for that job.

Accuracy packages, big-time are now on offer with Springfield Armory's M/A.

The new Tikka Sporter is not a bad varmint rifle—enough said.

For the first time since the Model 700 has been in production, it is now available in a "youth" version with a 13-inch length of pull and the 243 for little kids and the 308 for bigger or perhaps tougher kids. A new chambering, the 260 Remington, has also been added to the list of options for the Model Seven Youth.

Slide action rifles have long been popular where hunters want plenty of firepower but can't hunt with autoloaders (like Pennsylvania) and those who hunt come rain or shine will surely like the Model 7600 synthetic in 243, 270, 280, 308 and 30-06. And for those who can hunt with an autoloader, there's the new Model 7400 synthetic. Apply a good rust-resistant metal finish such as Teflon or electroless nickel to one of these and along with its enclosed receiver and water proof stock it would not be a bad rig for rainy weather hunting.

New variants of the Model 597 autoloader include the SS (Stainless Synthetic), the Sporter (blued steel and hardwood stock), and the Magnum LS (laminated wood stock and blued steel). Remington's Cus-

no more than mild popularity among today's hunters and shooters, I was really surprised by this. Be that as it may, I did what I was asked to do and simply necked down the 7mm STW case for 25-caliber bullets to create the 257 STW. Lex Webernick of Rifles, Inc. built the first rifles and I have worked with two, both on Remington 700 actions and both wearing Shilen barrels. One is his standard-weight rifle with a McMillan synthetic stock, the other is a flyweight job with his own synthetic stock.

When outfitted with a new Leica 3.5-10X scope, the lightweight rifle weighed six pounds, two ounces. I liked the rifle so well that in late December of '97 I decided to use it for hunting Coues deer in the state of Sonora, down in old Old Mexico. Those who were born before the last shot of World War II was fired might find it interesting to know that I hunted only a few miles from where Jack O'Connor camped on a hunt during which he was inspired to write a story called "We Shot The Tamales". At any rate, the .257 STW handload I used consisted of the Nosler 100-grain Ballistic Tip and a maximum charge of Reloder 22 for just over 3700 fps in a 26-

Weatherby Magnum on a prairie dog shootout. The use of a Leica Geovid laser rangefinder made the outing even more fun and no pasture poodle within 400 yards of the muzzles of the 6mm and 25 were safe. I nailed a couple beyond 700 yards but missed far more than I hit beyond 500. At those ranges, missing close is almost as much fun as hitting.

Robar

New from Robar is the QR2-F, a tactical rifle that should do quite well in law enforcement circles. Built around either a Remington 700 or Ruger 77 action, it has a 19-inch Shilen barrel, McMillan fiberglass stock and is available on in 308 Winchester. Options include Harris folding bipod, various tactical-style telescopic sights and a conversion that allows high-capacity detachable M1A magazines (made by Springfield, Inc.) to be used.

Sako

In early 1997, Henry Paasikivi who is the president of Sako, called me from Finland to get my ideas on a stock for the company's upcoming heavy-barrel varmint rifle; it would be built around the excellent Mod-

Savage

Biggest news from Westfield is the introduction of a short action version of the Model 110/112 action in both single shot and repeater versions. The new variations are too great in number to describe in detail here, but they range from the Model 12BVSS with its stainless steel barreled action and laminated wood stock to a youth version with a blued steel barreled action and a shortened birch stock. Most of the important short cartridges are there, including the 223, 22-250, 243 and 308 but no 7mm-08 for now.

In the plinking, small game hunting and close-range varminting departments, Savage is now offering its Model 93FVSS Magnum with synthetic stock and a 21 inch

Its short stock makes Savage's new Model 10GY a good choice for a youngster—they left the barrel full length.

The Savage 93FVSS is a stainless steel 22 magnum Varminter with synthetic stock and 21-inch barrel.

This is Weatherby's Mark V carbine in standard cartridges only.

heavy barrel in 22 WMR. Then there's the Model 93F with its blued steel, synthetic stock and standard-weight barrel in the same chambering. The 22 Long Rifle cartridge is also receiving plenty of attention from Savage. Wearing a black synthetic stock, the Model 64VF autoloader is what the company describes as a rifle of the 1990s. Factory-install an economygrade 4x scope on the Model 64VF and you have the Model 64FXP. New 22 rimfire bolt guns include the Mark FV with a 21-inch heavy barrel, the same rifle with a standardweight barrel (Mark II-F) and that rifle with a 4x scope (Mark-FXP).

Now for the bad news. Let's all gather 'round the campfire and shed a tear for the Model 99 lever action, a grand old American tradition that you won't see in the 1998 Savage catalog. Which brings up an interesting question: Since USRAC is now producing 10 variations of its Model 94 lever action in eight different calibers, why is Savage not manufacturing at least one version of the Model 99 in 250-3000 caliber?

SIGARMS

The new SHR-970 bolt gun from SIGARMS has a blued steel barreled action in a synthetic stock and weights a nominal 7.2 pounds. It's a switchbarrel gun which would be a moot point to most hunters since its only two chambering options for now are 270 and 30-06. Its

other features include a detachable box magazine, 65-degree bolt rotation and three-position side safety. A hard carrying case is included in the price.

Sommer Ockenfus GmbH

Bullpup-style rifles have been around for a long time and while the design has enjoyed some acceptance in military circles it has yet to win the hearts of big-game hunters and varmint shooters. Whether or not such a rifle now being imported from Germany by Wilcox Distributors of Portsmouth, NY will change that remains to be seen. Labeled with the less than dignified name of "Shorty", this particular bullpuppy is manufactured by the German firm of Sommer Ockenfus GmbH (hope I got that right) and has a pullback-type action. To operate the action, simply pull back on the pistol grip of the stock. The grip safety is reminiscent of the one on John Browning's 1911 pistol. Even though Shorty has quickswitch 25.5 inch barrels, it overall length is only 33.5 inches. Nominal weight is 9.5 pounds which will increase to about 10.5 pounds when a scope is added. Available chamberings run from 6mm BR Remington to the 416 Remington Magnum. A number of options are available, including blued or stainless steel and walnut or polymer. As the helmeted character on an old TV show called Laugh In used to be fond of saying; vellyintellesting.

Springfield, Inc.

Springfield's "Reload" program for its M1A rifle works like this: Each rifle will be shipped with over $300 worth of accessories and upgrades, including three pre-Clinton 20-round magazines, one post-Clinton five-round magazine, National Match trigger, National Match flash suppressor and one "Reload" coupon which authorizes the new owner of the rifle to purchase other items such as Springfield's new 6x40 scope and National Match stainless steel barrel upgrade, all at drastically reduced prices. As I have mentioned before, my M1A Super Match has all the accuracy upgrades offered by Springfield, including a Heavy stainless steel barrel made by Hart and it averages half an inch for five shots at 100 yards with a number of loads.

Steyr

Years ago, Redfield and possibly other manufacturers offered extended eye relief rifle scopes designed to be mounted out on the barrel of the Winchester Model 94. This was during the Pre-Angle-Eject days when a deer hunter who wanted a glass sight on his old 94 had no choice but to use a side mount. Those forward-mounted scopes never caught on, mainly because field of view was quite cramped and the extra weight out front didn't do a lot for the balance of the rifle. Years later, Jeff Cooper started to promote that same idea on

the "Scout" rifle as he called it, and as far as I know he is the only firearms writer to have done so. As I understand the concept, Cooper feels that the fact that a forward-mounted scopes leaves the magazine of a top-loaded bolt gun more accessible than a scope mounted on its receiver outweighs the disadvantage I mentioned earlier.

Steyr has introduced a short-barreled bolt-action carbine which is being endorsed by Cooper and while it is indeed an interesting firearm, one wonders why it was designed to use a forward-mounted scope. According to Steyr's promotional literature, the up-front scope makes loading the rifle easier when, in fact, it has a detachable box magazine in its belly.

Available only in 308 Winchester at present, the Scout has a futuristic-style stock made of a synthetic material called Zytel, a 19-inch hammerforged barrel with lightening flutes, adjustable trigger (3.50 to 4.00 pounds), flush-mounted, quick-detachable sling swivel sockets, flip-up aperture rear sight and a Picatinny-style rail system that allows a scope be mounted over the receiver or out on the barrel. Removable spacers beneath the recoil pad allow length of trigger pull to be adjusted for the individual shooter. The Scout's detachable magazine holds five rounds although a 10-rounder is available; a spare magazine can be stored in the buttstock. Nominal weight is said to be 6.3 pounds with two empty magazines.

I have examined the Scout and will have to admit that its balance and feel are not half bad. Of its many features, the two I like best were its three-position tang safety and a bipod that, when folded up, appears to be an integral part of the stock.

Sturm, Ruger

Following the success of the Model 96/44 lever action rifle in 44 Magnum comes a bolt action of the same caliber. One thing is certain, Ruger is getting maximum mileage out of its Model 77/22 action. First introduced in 22 Long Rifle, the 22 WMR came next and it was followed by the 22 Hornet. Ruger's in-line muzzleloader is built on a modified version of the 77/22 action, as is the new bolt gun in 44 Magnum. Called the Model 77/44RS, it has a blued steel barreled action, walnut stock, 18-1/2 inch barrel and an integral scope mounting base atop its receiver. Its detachable rotary magazine holds four of those big, fat, .44 caliber cartridges. I have not shot one of these but the Model 96/44 lever action I worked with was considerably more accurate with 44 Special ammo from Federal and Black Hills than with any 44 Magnum factory load I tried and the shorter cartridge worked fine in its rotary magazine.

The only other long gun news from Ruger is the addition of the 9x19mm Luger chambering in its autoloading carbine. The PC9 has regular open sights while the PC9GR has an aperture-style sight attached to its receiver.

Taconic Arms

The Ultimate Mountain Hunter, as Taconic officials call it, is a lightweight rifle with a '98 Mauser-style action carved from a block of titanium alloy. It is presently available only with a short action in short chamberings such as 243, 7mm-08, 308 and 284 Winchester.

USRAC

U.S. Repeating Arms Company has a number of new Winchester rifle variations. One is a made-in-Japan reproduction of the Winchester Model 1886 lever action in 45-70 Government. It has a 26-inch full octagon barrel, full-length eight-round magazine, crescent steel buttplate, steel forearm nose-cap and walnut buttstock and forearm. The High Grade, of which only 1000 will be built, has all that plus cut-checkered semi-fancy walnut and engraving on its receiver.

Moving on to the less conservative, who would have ever thought the Model 94 would be available with a black synthetic stock and forearm? Well, it certainly is and USRAC calls it the Black Shadow. The "BS" has a half magazine and a 24-inch barrel chambered for the 30-30, 44 Magnum and 444 Marlin, the latter a first for USRAC. Also new in the Model 94 woods rifle lineup is the Ranger Compact, an economy-grade youngster's version of the old Trapper model with birch wood, 16-inch barrel and an abbreviated 12-1/2 inch pull. Last but certainly not least in this department, cowpoke action shooters should be pleased to see the 44-40 chambering available in the Model 94 Trail's End and deer hunters who like to poke big holes through things are sure to go for the Model 94 Big Bore in its new 444 Marlin chambering.

USRAC's family of Model 9422 rifles keeps growing as well. New additions include the Legacy with a curved grip and cut-checkered walnut, the Large Loop & Walnut with a Chuck Conner-style finger loop and walnut stock, and the High Grade Series II with its high grade walnut, cut checkering and dogs and squirrels engraved on its receiver.

As Model 70 bolt guns go, the new Classic Compact in 244, 7mm-08 and 308 has a 20 inch barrel and a 12-1/2 inch pull for short arms while the Camo Stainless has a stainless steel barreled action and synthetic stock, the latter finished with Mossy Oak's Treestand pattern. Switch the plastic stock for one made of laminated wood and you have the Model 70 Laminated Stainless. Two other new variations to the Model 70 line are the Laredo LRH (Long Range Hunter) with its heavy fluted barrel and the economy-grade Black Shadow.

Weatherby

Sometime back I mentioned that after several years of trying, I finally convinced Ed Weatherby that the time had come for him to introduce the 30-378 Magnum chambering to his line of Mark V rifles. To make a short story even more so, the number of rifles sold in that caliber far exceeded Ed's wildest dreams (as well as mine). Ed is following up that cartridge with the 33-378, sort of a super 340 Weatherby Magnum if you will. Through the years I have worked several rifles in that caliber and while I have not shot a Mark V so chambered, I'm sure its performance will be up to par. Both rifles and ammo loaded for Weatherby by Norma should be available by the time you read this. Also new is the Mark V Accumark Lightweight, a six-pound, synthetic-stocked rifle with a 24-inch barrel in 243, 240 Weatherby Magnum, 25-06, 270, 7mm-08, 280 and 30-06. A carbine version of that same rifle has a 20-inch barrel and is called the Mark V Lightweight Stainless. ●

The new Sako Model 75 varmint rifle has a heavy barrel, semi-beavertail style forearm and (right) detachable magazine box in various varmint calibers.

by BOB BELL

SCOPES AND MOUNTS

It amazes me when I think of how much the scope field has changed over the years. In the late '30s when I started using one, 2 1/2x was an almost universal choice for big game, with 4x occasionally chosen for long range, open country use. Even after World War II, 6x scopes were thought of primarily as varmint scopes. I remember trading a then-new Weaver K6 to a friend who wanted it for his chuck and crow rifle—a Model 70 220 Swift. He thought he had the world by the tail when he got that scope. Maybe he did, for he killed countless critters with it, but I'll bet there isn't one guy in the county today who would choose a 6x scope for that kind of shooting with a Swift.

It's pretty much the same with big game scopes. Commenting on the 6x Zeiss *Zielsechs* and 8x *Zielacht*, Elmer Keith once said they permitted a view of the Promised Land, but were too damn big and clumsy to put on a hunting rifle. For him, the 4x *Zielvier* was as big as he wanted to go, and the smaller 2 1/2x Lyman Alaskan was better. And I doubt if anyone knew more about North America big game hunting than Ol' Elmer.

Of course, when the young Elmer went hunting, he hunted. A saddle horse might take him back of beyond, but after he got there and made camp, he hunted afoot. From before dawn till he got back to his tent maybe hours after dark, cold, often wet, always hungry. Often in snow or rain. And then at the next dawn he was out there again, for weeks on end. Does anyone hunt that way now? Maybe a few--I hope--but there aren't many.

Nowadays, a big game hunt is almost a fly-in, bash-'em-quick, get-out affair, if it's up Alaska way; a drive-in, home-for-supper whitetail hunt that never gets 300 yards from the road; or a 4WD back-country, dirt-road cruise for mulies. Carrying a big-scoped rifle in a Jeep is no problem, and brain-washing advertising being what it is, many have succumbed and mounted 4-12x hunting scopes or, lately, even larger action-mounted target scopes. They reason that the bottom power of a big variable will let them pop critters in open woods and they always have 16x or so if they need it.

I'll tell you something, flat out: a big game hunter doesn't need 16x. Not a pronghorn hunter, not a sheep hunter, not an ibex hunter, no one. None of us has any moral right to be shooting at big game so far away that a 16x scope is needed to aim. That magnification permits aim at a distance where no shoulder-fired cartridge is efficient, and none of us is so good a shot that he can guarantee, even if he manages a hit, that it will be in a vital area. So most of the time, a hit is gonna re-sult in a wounded animal that will escape, probably to die miserably.

It might be argued that ultra-long range shooters like the 1000-yard/benchrest competitors qualify for such shooting. They certainly have the rigs to shoot at long range and many have accurate military or laser rangefinders to solve the distance problem. That still leaves the windage factor, though, and if you don't think that can be important, shoot in the Wimbledon at Camp Perry next year. And I can't forget a story that the late Al Hoyer, one of the founders of the 1000-Yard Bench Shoot above Williamsport, happened to tell a couple of us when we asked him for information about hunting mulies in Wyoming's sage country around Baggs. This was 25 or 30 years ago. Seems that one day he had his portable bench set up and was glassing when he found a deer that the rangefinder indicated was about 1300 yards out yonder. Conditions were such that Al decided to shoot. He was using a heavy 30-338, as I recall, though I'm not positive about that. I'm sure it was a 30-cal. magnum of some kind.

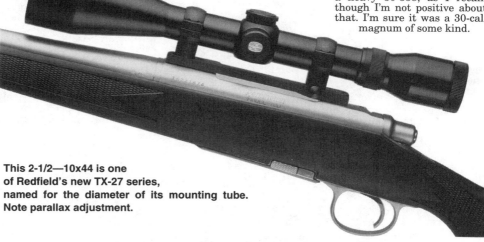

This 2-1/2—10x44 is one of Redfield's new TX-27 series, named for the diameter of its mounting tube. Note parallax adjustment.

The long and the short of it—Redfield's new 40x for benchresters and their 2x Scout for deer jumpers.

Anyway, over a period of some time, Al said he fired over two dozen shots at that critter, and finally it either collapsed or lay down. At least, it was dead when he got to it. And maybe if you told someone you'd killed a deer at 1300 yards it would sound impressive. But when cleaned and skinned, that critter had 13 holes through its body, small, pinpoint holes, because the bullets didn't expand at all at that range.

Admittedly, bullets suitable for long-range hunting have improved a lot in the last couple of decades. But I still can't help wondering what would have happened had that deer wandered off in the sage after the first one or two bullets went through its chest. Actually, I know, and so do you, it would have been coyote food.

I'm not criticizing such long-range shooters. Undoubtedly they lose less cripples than brush hunters. There are probably only a few hundred long-rangers in the whole country, and that number is insignificant when you consider the millions of guys who go deer hunting. But having a high-power scope immediately available can tempt a hunter to take shots beyond his normal range -not necessarily 1000-yard stuff, where he wouldn't hit anything anyway, but 500-yard shots, where he might scatch one in.

And you don't actually need a 16x for normal shooting. I'd bet that 99+ percent of the shots

fired at big game are under 300 yards. A 3-9x will easily handle this and a 2-7x would be even better, everything considered. In Montana last year, my hunting buddy Bob Wise wrapped up in his military sling, lay down in eight inches of snow, and put a 250-grain Grand Slam into the near shoulder and out the far one of a 6x5 elk. The bull was on the other side of a high-country meadow, broadside, a strong 300 yards away, just the way we all dream of seeing one. And it didn't move a step after the shot.

When they went up, the young wrangler who was doubling as a sort of guide was amazed that the bullet had exited. "What kind of gun is that?" he asked. "I never saw that happen before."

"What caliber do guys use around here?" Bob asked.

"Most of 'em have 270s or '06s.

"This is a 338, and it usually goes through on broadside shots."

"You put the bullet right where it's supposed to go, too. What kinda scope is that, a 3-9x?"

"No, it's a 4x Zeiss. That's plenty of magnification for elk. It's given me 4-inch groups at 300 yards all summer."

"Jeez, I thought you hadda have 3-9 or bigger. Most of the out-of-state guys who come in here seem to have them. Some even have folding rests on the forend. I never saw anyone use

a sling before, except to carry their rifle."

"Bipods like that are okay on varmint rifles, but they're pretty much a nuisance in country like this. A sling does it all if you practice a little."

Maybe that incident gave the young fellow something to think about and, I hope, profit from. Admittedly times and hunting methods have changed from when ol' Wisey and I were young, but change doesn't always mean progress. Sometimes the earlier ways were best. A good 4x scope is unbeatable for the vast majority of big game hunting, and the Zeiss is better than good. It's not normally available in this country anymoreq—undoubtedly because it didn't sell like the big variables--but Bob and I have ours (in fact, he has two), so we're satisfied.

Admittedly, since hunters have become willing to accept large heavy scopes, scopemakers have been able to incorporate advanced features, so

Using a parallax adjustment that shifts the erector system (left) allows the same size objective lens in a smaller tube than an AO permits.

nowadays we have many scopes with great properties to choose from, and that is progress. Anyway, here's this year's new stuff:

Redfield has a number of new scopes this year, including a 40x40 for the benchresters (yep, that's 40 power, which means its exit pupil is just 1mm, which might be a problem when light is dim), a new series of five scopes called the TX-27, and a new Scout scope, for the fans of Jeff Cooper. They've also updated the Trackers and have new Torx screws for simplifying solid mounting.

The TX-27 series takes its name from the diameter of the mounting section of the tube, 27mm. This sort of splits the difference between the long-popular American diameter of one inch (25.4mm) and the comparatively recent move by various makers to 30mm. The larger sizes make possible thicker tubes or larger lenses or more room for adjustment

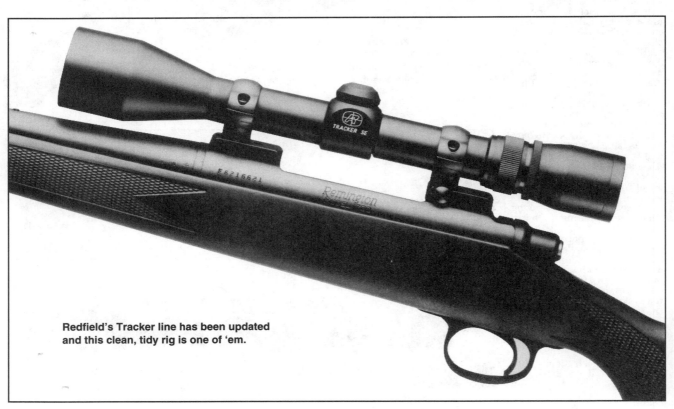

Redfield's Tracker line has been updated and this clean, tidy rig is one of 'em.

The Simmons 44 Mag now has a Smart Reticle.

This 3—9x32 with adjustable objective has been added to Simmons' rimfire line.

for mounting ahead of the action, so it has an eye relief of 9 1/2-20 inches. Field is only 24 feet, which is small for this power, but when using a Scout rifle the shooter's left eye is normally looking along the left side of the scope, giving a view along the outside of the tube, so field is essentially unlimited. Since the scope's power is low, there is little disparity between the magnified and non-magnified views.

Leica has long been world renowned for their cameras and binoculars—thirty-five years ago I got one of each from the widow of a hunter, and I can't imagine parting with either—and like numerous other shooters I've long wondered why they didn't also make scopes. Well, now they do.

New this year are three Leica Ultravid riflescopes. There's a 1.75-6x32 for general big game hunting, 3.5-10x42 for those who often get long shots, and 4.5-14x42F (focusing objective) for those whose shooting is almost always on the long side. These are built in the U.S. Tubes are machined from a block of aircraft grade aluminum and are matte finished. The mounting sections of the tubes are 30mm, with 1/4-moa finger adjustments, and eyepieces have rapid adjusting diopter control, and lenses are multicoated, of course. Eye relief is long, 3.6 inches minimum, weights are 14,16, and 18 oz., and plex reticles are standard, though dots, crosshairs, and European-style posts are available through Leica's service center.

Bausch & Lomb's Elite 4000 line extends from the 1 1/2-6x, which has served perfectly on my 7mm Remington Magnum pronghorn popper, to a straight power 36x, so there's not much need for more magnifications here, but they have added one scope to the Elite 3000 line, a 5-15x with 50mm objective. This is the highest power yet offered in this series. Like most of the other 3000s, it has quarter-minute audible finger-adjustable clicks, multicoating and an extra lens to improve resolution and color correction. Its objective unit moves through 270 degrees to adjust precisely for range, thus eliminating parallax, of course. Its power spread makes it suitable for open country big game hunting or varmints of any kind, though at 24 oz. plus mount, I'd rather use it for sit-and-look shooting than carry it in rough country. As expected from B&L, optics are great.

Bushnell, which I suppose can be thought of as half of a Siamese-twin relationship with B&L, has added a couple

mechanisms, or whatever. Redfield's basic claim is that their new size is stronger than a one-inch tube, lighter than a 30mm, and that seems self-evident.

There are five TX-27 scopes, 4x40, 2 1/2-10x44, 3 1/2-14x40, 3 1/2-14x50, and 5-20x44. All have 1/4-moa clicks except the two largest, which have 1/8. Housing for adjustment knobs are machined, not screwed, in place, to eliminate a potential leak path, and eyepieces are quickly and easily focused. Eye relief is long at 3 1/2 inches, for use with magnums. Parallax adjustment is on the left side of the turret on sev-

eral models, allowing adjustment for range without moving the objective unit.

The TX-27 scopes have four layers of high-tech multicoating, which "allows an amazing 99.5% light transmission per lens surface," to quote the catalog. If you read it quickly, that suggests almost 100% of the light which enters the front end of the scope comes out of the back end and enters the eye. Maybe I'm a nitpicker, but I wish the guy who wrote that copy would also have told us how many lens surfaces there are in a scope. And does it mean

only the glass/air surfaces or the interfaces where two lenses nestle together. Or what? These things all make a difference.

I'm sure light transmission in the TX-27s is very high and, strictly speaking, the claim is true but it doesn't actually answer the question a prospective buyer asks: what percentage of entering light actually comes out of the exit pupil? Doubtless, any of Redfield's optical engineers could tell us this--without sounding like a political speech-writer.

The Scout scope is a short, straight objective 2x intended

of 3-9x models to their Sport-view line.

They also have Trophy, Banner, and Buckhorn lines, each with numerous models, plus the HOLOsight, so anyone oughta be able to find a Bushnell to suit his needs.

Anyway, one of the new 3-9s has a 40mm objective, the other 50mm. The latter transmits a bit more light, if your normal hunting conditions are dim, but the former sits lower on the gun, so would be my choice.

The HOLOsight isn't a scope but certainly deserves mention. About half the length and weight of a hunting scope, it uses holographic technology to display an illuminated reticle ahead of the shooter. Well, a virtual image, if that makes any difference to the shooter. This image is in exact focus with the target and eye alignment is not critical. The HOLOsight, which has been available for several years, does not magnify the target; this is of no importance when mounted on a shotgun or handgun, but when put on a rifle some power would be useful. So, new this year, is a 2x attachment. It adds only 2 1/2 oz. and should be useful on big game in the woods. Numerous reticle designs are available and easily interchanged; their brightness

levels are adjustable. Zeroing is via click adjustments, and it's powered by two Type N 1 1/2-volt batteries. It's installed on a Weaver-type base.

Nikon has joined with Buckmasters, a leading whitetail deer hunting organization, to produce a line of scopes called-- surprisingly--Buckmasters. Their retail price is considerably below that of Nikon's Monarch UCC line. At present, Buckmasters come in 4x40, 3-9x40, and 3-9x50. They have deep steel-to-brass 1/4-moa adjustments, plex reticles, hardened aluminum tubes.

Nikon's Monarch UCC series consists of seven scopes running in power from a little 2x20 EER for handguns up to 6.5-20x44, made with either fine crosshairs or Nikoplex reticle, depending if your use is on varmints or ultra-longrange big game. I've used one for years on a heavy M700 223 for chucks and prairie dogs, with complete satisfaction. There's a 4x in the line too, which pleases me, as I feel that's the most satisfactory power for normal big game hunting. Well, maybe a 1 1/2-4 1/2x or 2-7x32, if you like variables, and Nikon makes the latter. The "UCC," incidentally, stands for Ultra ClearCoat,

which refers to the high grade optical system of these scopes.

Leupold, for the first time, I believe, is offering red dot sights for handgun action shooters. Obviously, they can also be mounted on muzzleloaders, shotguns—even bows, if they're your hunting tool. Two models are made, the LG-1 on a one-inch tube, which has a 45-foot field, and the LG-35 on a 35mm octagonal tube. This one has a 70-foot field. The former has a 2-moa dot, the latter either a 4- or 8-moa. Dot intensity in both is variable. The designation "LG" derives from the initials of Leupold and Gilmore. Riley Gilmore is a champion shooter and is regarded by many as the dean of red dot sight engineering. These sights come with lens covers and mounting rings to fit cross-slot bases.

Four scopes have been added to the Vari-X III series, all built on 30mm tubes and all having Leupold's new side-focus feature. With this system, instead of screwing the objective unit in or out to focus for range and thus eliminate parallax, there is an adjustment on the left side of the turret which can be rotated while looking through the scope; this is more

convenient for the shooter than lowering the gun to get at an adjustable objective.

Called the Long Range Target models, these come in 3 1/2-10x40, 4 1/2-14x50, 8 1/2-25x50, and 6 1/2-20x50 powers. The first two of these are actually tactical scopes intended primarily for military or police use. The 3 1/2-10x features Bullet Drop Compensating dials matching the trajectory of standard loads for either the 5.56, 308, 30-06, or 300 Winchester Magnum. The large tubes allow greater than normal adjustment ranges and add strength. Leupold now has nine tactical scopes, five of which are variables, ranging from 6x to 16x.

Swarovski has added a pair of scopes to its extensive line called the American Hunting Series. Built on one-inch, one-piece alloy tubes in 3-10x42 and 4-12x50 magnifications, they have fully multicoated lenses from Austria and are waterproof even with the turret caps removed. Ocular units are slimmer than usual, permitting low mounting, and eyepieces are fast focusing. Optical quality, of course, is excellent.

Swarovski, incidentally, was the first and I believe the only manufacturer so far to produce a riflescope having an integrated laser rangefinder. I've written about it before, but its uniqueness deserves another mention. A 3-12x50 with a boxy appearance that doesn't look normal to an American, it's big and heavy (15 1/2 in. and 40 1/2 oz.) and it's expensive, but there are many times when it would be nice to have an accurate rangefinder right in the scope. Accuracy is to within two meters at 600, which should take in all shooting a hunter takes at anything.

Talley Engineering is the business name for Dave Talley's mount-making venture out in Wyoming, and countless hunters have learned how good his Quick Detach Rings & Bases are. Now Swarovski has entered into an agreement with Dave to supply a special version of his mount to Swarovski for sale through authorized dealers. The Talley/Swaroski rings will utilize that standard Talley base system with quick detach rings in 30mm and 1 inch, with bases to fit all popular receivers. Rings will be made with levers or hex screws for solid mounting.

Tasco supplies a lot of scopes in all normal sizes and magifications, but their latest entry has to be the smallest and lightest of all. Technically, it's not a scope at all, but we've been mentioning various makes of this class of sights for many years, so here's Tasco's newest,

The tiny Tasco Optima 2000 ProPoint.
It weighs 1/2 oz.

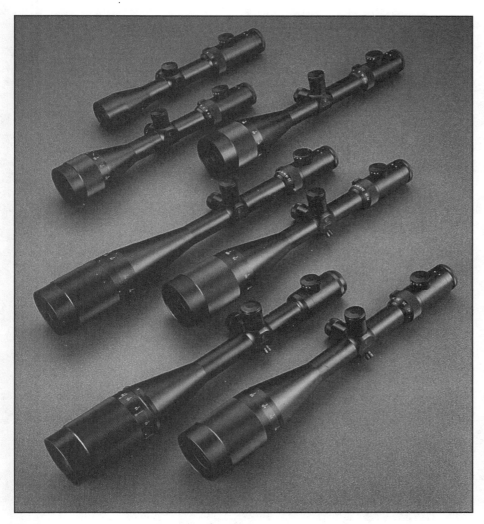

Nightforce scopes are big and heavy—but oh what optics!

guns they fit, and says there are more they didn't bother to include. So it's a lot, no matter how you slice it. I believe ol' John Amber, longtime GD editor, was the first to describe Conetrols as "sleek," and the word still fits. The split rings are projectionless, secured by a perfectly blended-in cap on top and locked in place by screws at the bottom. Currently they're made in 25.4mm (one inch), 26, 26 1/2, and 30 millimeters, and I expect they'll soon be made in 27mm to fit Redfield's new scopes, and they can be had in the three common heights plus an extra-high version, though these are a horizontally split design. There are also bases to fit actions having intergral mounting systems, such as Sako's tapered dovetails, which has always seemed to me the most solid way to attach a scope to a gun. When you write to them, ask about their "NRA Percent" discount.

Pentax has added the Zero-X/V SG Plus to its Lightseeker line. Intended primarily for turkey hunting, this scope's actual magnification can be varied from natural or unit size, commonly called 1x, to 4x. It has Comp-Plex reticle, which is essentially a plex with an open circle at the intersection of the crosshairs. This circle subtends 2-1/2 to 5 inches at forty yards, depending on scope magnification. The one-inch tube is slightly enlarged at the front end to contain a 27mm objective, field is 54-15 feet, and eye relief is 3 1/2-7 inches. Length is less than 10 inches, weight 10.3 oz., matte finish only. The earlier 2 1/2x Lightseeker is now offered in Mossy Oak camo.

the Optima 2000 ProPoint. Other ProPoints have been around for years and they're simplest to think of as electronic red dot sights, chosen by many handgun action shooters. The Optima 2000 is notable for its small size and light weight--0.5 oz. Yeah, that's right, one half of a whole ounce. It mounts on the rear of an autoloading pistol's slide, of course, but can be used on a shotgun, rifle, or whatever. Its lens is thick, durable plastic.

Swift, too, has followed today's trend to larger objectives by adding a 3-9x50 to their line. It's called the Model 871M. They have for some time provided 3-9s with 32 and 40mm objectives, so the user has a good choice. The 40mm scope has a wide angle eyepiece, incidentally, which is round rather than TV-screen shape. Swift also has a short (5 1/2-inch)/red dot scope called the Fire Fly. It comes with 30mm rings that fit Weaver-style bases. Its unlimited eye relief makes it fast to

use in thick, gloomy deer woods. Other Swift scopes cover all hunting needs.

Simmons has added what they call a Smart Reticle to their popular 44 Mag scope, which varies from 3.8-12x. This is a cut-glass, range calculating reticle in the first focal plane, so relative to the target it is the same at all powers. This means that when used as a rangefinder, it is consistent, so there is less for the shooter to remember. There is a 6-moa diamond in the center of the Smart Reticle, and each vertical and horizontal segment of it has a specified value as well. Instructions for its use are included with each scope.

Simmons also has added the 1022T rimfire model to their extensive line. A 3-9x32 AO, it's obviously suited to both hunting and plinking. Other 22 Mag models are factory set parallax free at 50 yards, but this ones adjustable objective can be set wherever the user wants.

Conetrol claims to manufacture the world's most extensive line of mounts for high power rifles, and I know I won't dispute that. Their literature lists four pages (small type) of

Burris' biggest news this year is their 3-12x50 Black Diamond scope, the only one in their line that's made on a 30mm tube. It's almost 14 inches long and weighs 25 oz., which

Warne's new Maxima mount is available with either QD levers, shown, or screws for solid installation.

Built on one-inch tubes for easy mounting here, these are the Sarovaki 3-1.x42 and 4-12x50 in their American Series hunting scopes.

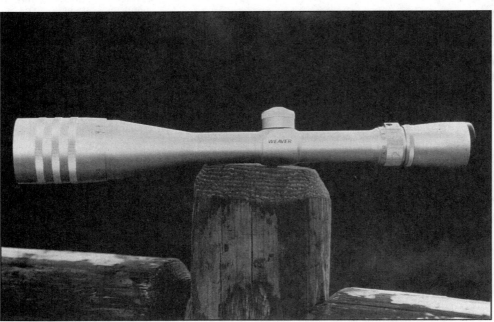

Weaver V16 is great for varmints if the mirage isn't bad; works well on the bench too.

Rear view of the focus adjustment features on one of Leupold's Vari-X III Long Range scopes.

is on the big side for some types of hunting, but as always with Burris scopes it has wonderful optics. Clicks are 1/4-moa with resettable dial and it has 110 inches of internal adjustment; the eyepiece is fast focusing and there's 3 1/2-4 inches of eye relief. Reticles available include Plex, Mil-dot, German #1 (3 posts, the bottom one pointed), and German #4 (3 flat-ended posts with crosshairs). The Mil-dot, which was designed for military sniping, is becoming more popular all the time with numerous scopemakers; it's basically a plex with a series of dots on the horizontal and vertical crosshairs, 1 1/4 mil on centers. The dots are oval shaped (don't ask me why, only the military knows), in the long dimension and 3/4 mil between adjacent dots. One mil equals 3.6 inches at 100 yards at highest scope magnification. The term "mil" means milliradian, incidentally, not military, as many assume. If the approximate size of the target is known, this reticle is useful for range estimation and holding off for wind, and can be used for long distance hunting as well as sniping.

Burris supplies about a dozen reticle styles, though not every one in all scopes. They range from traditional crosshairs or post through several thicknesses of Plex, a Peep Plex, Circle Plex, the two German styles mentioned, Target Dot, Mil-dot, and Electro-Dot.

There are also a new line of low-power shotgun/muzzleloader scopes, 3-9x and 4-12x

Rimfire scopes which can be focused down to 75 feet, and Double Dovetail bases for extra solid mounting. These can be used with the Pos-Align Offset Inserts, which fit around the scope and inside Signature rings. Because their thickness varies like a cam, they can be rotated to align the scope in any direction to keep the optics centered and relieve stress.

Warne has been offering its top line of scope mounts, the Premier Series, for about eight years now for one-inch, 26 or 30mm scopes. A pair of neat streamlined rings, they can be quick detachable double-lever design or permanently attached by a pair of hex screws in each ring. A cross-bolt in the bottom prevents fore-and-aft movement in either Warne bases or the long-familiar Weaver type.

Now a less expensive Maxima Steel Series has been added. This is manufactured by the sintered steel process, which is the one used by Porsche and BMW to manufacture connecting rods for their high performance engines; it allows very complex shapes to be manufactured at reasonable cost. These are also available in solid stainless steel (not nickelplated regular steel), or hardened aluminum. Some have thumb knob attachment rather than levers, or all can be permanently installed.

Nightforce scopes are made in eight models—six variables and two straight powers. The variables range from a 1.7-6x42 for conventional big game shooting through a 12-42x56 for stuff at the longest distance. The straight powers come in 26x and 36x. The combination of high magnification and large objective leads to the highest twilight factors I can think of, 48.5 in the case of the 12-42x56. (TF = square root of scope magnification x objective diameter in millimeters.) This was a rating developed in Europe long ago; it intends to suggest that the higher the number, the more detail a scope reveals in dim light. This seems correct to me as long as the scope's exit pupil equals the eye's entrance pupil—on other words, supplies all the light the eye can absorb. I'm not sure if a TF rating holds up when the scope's exit pupil is smaller, despite the image's larger size. Experience with high grade American target scopes, such as a 2-inch 20x Unertl, which has a TF of 31+ but an exit pupil of only 2.5, suggests otherwise. The image is larger but dimmer than, say, an 8x56 scope, which provides an exit pupil equal to the diameter of a fully distended eye pupil.

But I'm only quibbling here; mebbe the results you get are

The 3-9x40 is one of three less expensive Nikon Buckmasters scopes

different from mine. I have used a Nightforce scope a little, and want to tell you that this is an extremely high grade instrument—big and heavy (up to 38 oz. plus mounts), but if your kind of shooting isn't bothered by that, a Nightforce could be for you. Their catalog quotes barrelmaker Dan Lilja as seeing 50-cal. bullet holes at 1000 yards, which is something I've never been able to do with anything optical, so you can get an idea of their efficiency from that. (Or maybe Dan lucked into better atmospheric conditions than I've ever had at that range.)

Weaver scopes are available in almost two dozen models, if I count correctly—four straight powers, seven variables, five target, four handgun, two rimfire, and one shotgun design. Magnification ranges from the 1x setting of the little V3 to the 36x of the biggest target model, most with 1/4-moa clicks although the H2 2x handgun model is 3/4 minute, the H4 is 15/16, and some of the target models are 1/8 minute. Unless you're trying to hit a chicken egg at 500 yards, I don't know why such a fine adjustment is necessary, but at least it's there if you need it.

The T-Series (target models) all have the reliable Micro-Trac adjusment system, which features four tiny carbide balls as contact points with internal erector tube. This for years has been recognized by benchresters and others as unusually accurate and repeatable.

It's nice to know that although the Weaver line now includes big scopes such as the T-Series and the 6-24x42, the K2.5, K4, and K6 are still available. These were introduced just after WWII, the first American hunting scopes, I believe, built on one-inch tubes. The response to them was incredible; in fact, the K4 was claimed for many years to be the biggest selling big game scope made. Maybe it still is, though I wouldn't be surprised to learn that some 3-9x has taken over.

After all, "if it's bigger, it's better," is the American motto.

Zeiss is now making the Diavari ZM/Z 2 1/2-10x48 available in North America. Formerly, it could be had only in Europe. This scope is intended specifically for low-light conditions, so in addition to its large objective unit it has an illuminated reticle. A knob on the left side of the adjustment turret is an on/off switch and also controls reticle brightness, which is lithium-battery powered. The Diavari 2 1/2-10x48 has Zeiss's well known T* multicoating.

One of several reticles can be chosen. In all ZM/Z-type scopes except the 1 1/4-4x, the reticle is in the first focal plane, thus appears larger when magnification is increased. It varies directly with magnifications, of course, so subtends the same amount at all powers. Some hunters prefer the American approach, in which the reticle varies inversely--subtension goes down as power goes up--as it's then easy to use top magni-fication on small targets such as varmints. But the European style has an advantage of easier rangefinding. Also, the point of impact never wanders from apparent reticle movement when power is changed, as sometimes happened with old American variables. As in all Z-series scopes, adjustment clicks are 1cm/100m, or approximately 1/3moa. All Diavari scopes are built on 30mm tubes.

The 3-9x36 MC, which Zeiss announced awhile back as being assembled in this country, is going well. Some shooters apparently appreciated the involvment of American workers with a European maker of worldwide reputation. At a bit over $600, this scope is approximately in the price range of some U.S.-made models. While no one would say that's inexpensive, it's less than half the cost of most models made by Zeiss. Incidentally, this scope is built on a 1-inch tube to take common mounts, and can be had with Z-Plex or crosshair reticle.

A number of other Zeiss scopes can be had here, including their recent Diavari-ZM/Z 1 1/4-4x. I particularly like this size. It sits low on the gun and has a very wide field (96-30 feet). And don't think that bottom power isn't useful. I had a recent run of 22 consecutive kills with the scope set at 1-1/2x. ●

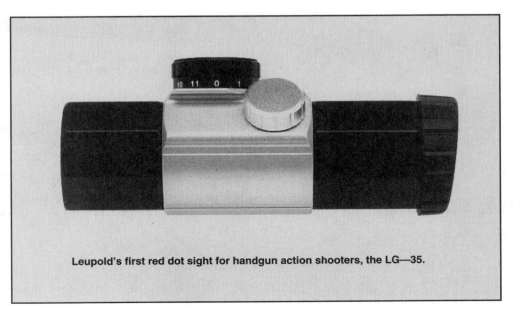

Leupold's first red dot sight for handgun action shooters, the LG—35.

by DOC CARLSON

BLACKPOWDER REVIEW

Way back when elephants had long hair and curved tusks and I was getting started shooting black powder, there was very little choice in either guns or accessories to be bought. Guns were originals and you made most everything else. With other beginning shooters, I would have mortgaged the home place for a chance at a tenth of today's black powder products. And every year brings more.

Last year marked the first foray into this market by one of the old names in the firearms industry. **Remington** introduced their modified Model 700 muzzleloader and created quite a stir. Not to be outdone, **Ruger** brought out their Model 77 muzzleloader late last year. Both guns quickly proved popular with front-loader hunters.

The Ruger 77/50 is an inline muzzle loader with the look and

tact the breech plug if it is not fully seated to stop the bolt from reaching the closed position. This eliminates any chance of a slam-fire when the bolt is closed on a primed nipple. The bolt has two locking lugs that rotate into recesses in the rear of the receiver. The safety swings, with three positions—locked, striker-locked, fire.

The Ruger is a 50 caliber with a 22 inch barrel, rifled with 8 lands and grooves, the grooves narrower than the lands which facilitates loading in a fouled bore. Twist is 1 in 28 inches, a slug and sabot gun.

Remington has not rested on their laurels. They have added a redesigned and lightened version of their 700ML. the pull on this one is an inch shorter; there's a 20 inch barrel. They offer it in

the original 50 caliber; it's intended for smaller stature shooters and hunters.

Remington, for a long time, was the only source for percussion caps, back in the dark ages of muzzleloading rebirth. The company has now redesigned their tried-and-true caps for 40% hotter flame and dimensioned them to fit nipples better. They will continue to be available in both #10 and #11 sizes.

CCI, and another major cap supplier, are also out with a better cap that they are calling a #11 Magnum. They have added aluminum to the priming mix for a much hotter flame. It would appear misfires will be on the decline.

Traditions Performance Muzzleloading has added a new model to their bolt action inline guns. Called the Lightning, there's a stainless steel fluted barrel and action with a muzzle brake installed. In 50 caliber, the rifle allows two choices of ignition. A standard #11 cap can be used or an interchangeable Lightning Fire System can be installed that uses musket caps for much hotter ignition. The company recommends a load of three 50gr. Pyrodex pellets with a sabotted bullet such as Nosler's new 250-gr. Partition along with the LFS musket cap system. They claim velocities over 2100 feet per second using this loading. Pretty impressive for a muzzleloader!

The Traditions guns are all equipped with Tru Glo hunting sights with fiber optic inserts so three illuminated dots are seen by the shooter. This is one of the better sighting systems that I

have seen recently, extremely visible in all types of light conditions and very helpful to those of us who tend to shoot from memory with open sights due to over-40 eyes.

Connecticut Valley Arms continues to expand their line of guns. Now there's an in-line rifle priced under $135.00 Called the Stag Horn, it has the same barrel as the more expensive CVA guns, but is strictly no-frills with no options. There's a synthetic stock and a manual notch safety system. The 24" barrel can be had in either 50 or 54 caliber.

If your taste runs more to the traditional side-hammer type of muzzleloader, **October Country** is marketing an English-style half-stock rifle with a very large bore and slow twist. The browned half-octagon, half-round 28 inch barrel is called a "14-bore," an English designation that refers to "gauge." The 69-caliber barrel is rifled 1 turn in 104 inches and sight narrow lands with wide grooves. The caliber and barrel specifications match those recommended by Lt. James Forsyth, a 19th century hunter who advocated large round balls in slow twist barrels for large game. The percussion rifle has an English-style stock of American walnut with pistol grip and shotgun style butt. All furniture is browned.

The gun is fairly hefty, weighting 10 pounds, but, given the large caliber, it needs to be. The recommended maximum load is 210gr. black powder heind the big 500 gr. round ball. Velocity with the loading exceeds

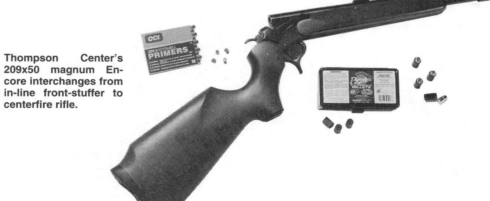

Ruger's 77/50 RSO is as slick a looker as a muzzleloader as it is as a centerfire or rimfire in other 77's.

feel of the widely used M-77 center fire rifles. The rifle is light and trim at 7 pounds and 41 1/2 inches overall. It reminds one of the M77/22, Ruger's very popular 22 rifle.

While the gun appears to be a converted M77, the action is completely redesigned for its intended use. The recoil lug has been moved to the rear to make room for a lengthy ramrod. And that makes loading and cleaning easier as there is enough rod to allow a good hold. The bolt/striker assembly has a projection on the front that will con-

Thompson Center's 209x50 magnum Encore interchanges from in-line front-stuffer to centerfire rifle.

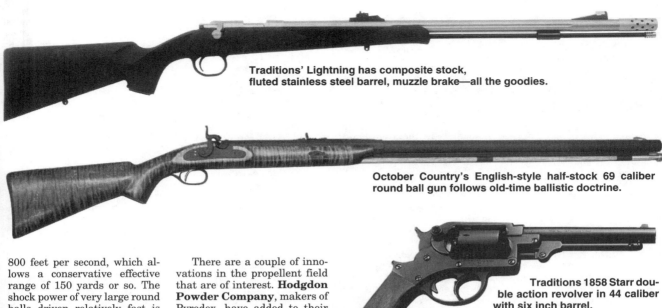

Traditions' Lightning has composite stock, fluted stainless steel barrel, muzzle brake—all the goodies.

October Country's English-style half-stock 69 caliber round ball gun follows old-time ballistic doctrine.

Traditions 1858 Starr double action revolver in 44 caliber with six inch barrel.

800 feet per second, which allows a conservative effective range of 150 yards or so. The shock power of very large round balls driven relatively fast is awesome. If one is serious about hunting large game, and prefers the traditional style of gun, this one certainly deserves a look.

October Country also carries the Cureton Powder Horn, well-known among traditional style shooters. These horns are made from select grade horns, nicely finished with traditional style plugs, strap grooves and an antique, dark stain that gives the horns an old look. The look of the horns is unique. These make a nice addition to the shooting equipment of the historically oriented shooter and hunter.

Another very traditional type of firearm to be seen on dealers shelves, hopefully, is a made in the Czech Republic. Two of the guns I have handled were a 1795 US Musket and a wheellock rifle. Both show very nice workmanship and the wheellock is certainly unique. Hopefully one of the importing companies will bring these well-made guns into the US and make them available to traditional type shooters.

Among ancillary products for the muzzle loader is one old friend with a new form. Ox Yoke Originals Wonder Lube, which has been used on patches and as a bore grease by many, is now available as a liquid that comes in a spray dispenser for ease of application to either shooting or cleaning patches. if you use the stuff on metal and wood parts of your rifle, as I do, this should be a easy way to apply it--much easier then wiping it on as a grease. The Ox Yoke folks tell me that it is the same product, just in a different form. Sounds like a winner.

There are a couple of innovations in the propellent field that are of interest. **Hodgdon Powder Company**, makers of Pyrodex, have added to their Pyrodex pellets. These handy loading pellets are now available in both 50 grain and 30 grain size. This will allow a much wider range of loadings by combining the two different weights. They are 50 caliber only at present, but Hodgdon is planning to bring them out in other calibers, once they catch up with demand for the 50s. The pellets can be used in inline or side hammer guns but work with more uniformity in inline style guns.

Speaking of Pyrodex, **Mountain States Muzzleloadig** has added a Pyrodex measure to their popular black powder measure line. The new measure has larger metering cavities to handle the bigger grains of Pyrodex as opposed to black powder. This is a welcome move. Their black powder measure has been very popular with black powder cartridge reloaders but it wouldn't handle Pyrodex very well.

Traditions Performance Muzzleloading has brought out a plastic dispenser to hold 18 Pyrodex 50 gr. pellets and dispense two of them each time you push the button. The unit fits easily in pocket or pouch and I suspect hunters will be very interested in this well designed accessory.

A new replica black powder is coming into the marketplace. Called **Clean Shot Powder**, it is an ascorbic acid-based product that seems to have handled the problems that this type powder has had in the past. The older products were hygroscopic; that is, they attracted water; and their granulations were very uneven, giving variable ve-locities. The older powders were very dependent upon heavy seating pressures that tended to deform bullets and contributed to erratic accuracy. The new Clear Shot appears to have solved those troubles and we may well have another replica black powder. While more expensive than black powder at present, prices should come down as more is produced. Shipping is much easier than black powder as Clear Shot is classified as a smokeless powder and is under the same shipping regulations as Pyrodex. We will, no doubt, be hearing more.

The Traditions folks have also taken an old product and updated it, a quick reloader for muzzleloaders called the EC Loader. The shooter can carry three fast reloads using powder, Pyrodex pellets, patched round ball, slugs or sabot type bullets. This one comes with inserts that will allow you to fit about any muzzleloader on the market today in either 50 or 54 caliber; a belt pouch is included.

Most bullet makers now make some form of bullet for muzzleloaders, either sabot type or slub. Check your dealer for all the new designs from folds like Hornady, Lyman, Buffalo Bullet, Nosler and many others, There's a bullet for most any use or purpose. The vast array allows one to tailor his load for his particular rifle and game.

In-line rifles are certainly one of the major areas of growth in black powder shooting, black powder cartridge firearms are not far behind with the greatly increased interest in cowboy shooting. Long-range buffalo gun matches have also spawned a wide range of guns and accessories. **Dixie Gun Works** and **Navy Arms Company** both have the copy of the popular Winchester High Wall single shot rifle in production. These guns have been coming for a couple of years and are now a reality. Chambered in 45-70 with 40-65 to be available soon, these replicas are well made and of high quality. They have 30 inch octagon barrels and case-hardened receivers. you can get buckhorn open sights or target tang sights combined with a hooded front using interchangeable inserts.

Both Dixie and Navy also carry a wide range of other black powder cartridge type guns such as Sharps, Remington Rolling Block, Springfield 1873 Trapdoors and wide range of Winchester lever action models. All are available with variations of sighting equipment and custom options such as engraving. Combined with the wide selection of Old West cartridge revolvers and leather accessories like holsters, belts and scabbards, they can supply most anything that the 1870s period shooter could want.

Another single shot black powder rifle that has had birthing problems over the past few years now appears to be on the road to reality. The **Ballard Rifle and Cartridge Company** is under new ownership, managed by well-known shooter Steve Garby. The company is reproducing a full line of rifles based on the Ballard single shot action. Delivery will run a maximum of six months and they are in production as you read this. The receivers are milled from solid stock and color case hardened using real packed case hardening. Barrels are rust-blued and the guns are offered in a wide range of black powder calibers from 32-40 to 50-90. They can be ordered with either standard or gai twist barrels.

The company also sells black powder cartridge barrels in various contours and either standard or gain twist. They are a good source for most of the obsolete cartridge brass. This includes brass shotgun cases of various gauges, many obsolete metric cartridge cases, and American and British cases from 22 Winchester to 700 Nitro Express and 8 Bore Rifle.

Cimarron Firearms Co. is a well-known name among the cowboy action shooters. They have been leaders in the field of Old West type firearms for some time. New this year is a short-barrel version of the popular Schofield revolver, available in 45 Colt, 45 S&W Schofield, or 44-40 calibers. the early problems with production of this line of guns have been largely worked out.

Cimarron is also bringing out a Richards Conversion of the 1860 Colt, making the cap and ball Army into a cartridge revolver. These should be available in late 1998.

Cimarron now offers—on all their guns—an "Antique" version. The guns look like they have ridden many miles in a puncher's holster. It is not merely a "beat up" appearance. It really duplicates the patina that normally takes years to develop. Have your dealer look into this. It can be had on most any of their guns on special order and the price is very reasonable.

Traditions Precision Muzzleloading is another company that has added the cartridge conversion cap and ball revolvers to their line. They will offer the Colt 1860 Army, 1851 Navy and 1861 Navy in 38 Special caliber. These guns were probably more common in the Early West than most any other gun due to their low cost compared to the newer Smith and Wessons and Colts. Many original guns were converted by cowboys who owned the cap and ball revolver and wanted to take advantage of the handier cartridge but liked the heft and feel of their familiar 1860 or 1851.

Traditions is also importing a nicely made replica of the 1858 Starr double action percussion revolver. This adds another unique replica to the list that is available to Civil War Reenactors, Cowboy Action Shooters and others who would like to own a cap and ball revolver that is different from what is generally seen. The gun is available with the original six-inch barrel length in blued finish. Caliber is 44.

More good news for the black powder cartridge shoot is the fact that **Green Mountain Rifle Barrel Co.** is now making black powder cartridge barrel blanks. The blanks are 34 inches long and available in 1 1/8 inch round, 1 inch round, and 1 1/8 inch octagon. Calibers are 32 with 1 in 14 twist, 38 with a 1 in 14 twist, 40 with 1 in 16 twist and 45 with a 1 in 18 twist. This will cover most of the more popular calibers. The Green Mountain barrels are well known and this addition to their line should be really well received. Barrel blanks for black powder calibers are in short supply, as a general rule, so those wishing to rebarrel should be very happy with this.

In the interesting accessory line, I ran on to a company that makes traditional Swedish axes. **Gransfors Bruks Inc.** makes a rather complete line of Swedish style axes. These axes have a very authentic Early American look. There is evidence that both the log cabin and many of our ax styles were brought to this country by early Swedish immigrants, which would explain this similarity. The line includes felling axes, a hunters ax, broad axes, hewing axes and others that would look right at home at a 1700s rendezvous. All are made of famous Swedish steel and not only look good, but they are serious tools. If you are into the rendezvous scene or just like good tools that have an old time look, these are worth checking into. Have your local dealer check into carrying this fine line of cutting tools.

The products out there for the black powder enthusiast continue to amaze me. It also continues to grow, year by year. It's a great time to be involved. ●

Addresses that are not already listed in GD

Grasfors-Bruks
PO Box 818
Summerville, SC 29484

Clean Shot Technologies
21218 St. Andrews Blvd.
Suite 504
Boca Raton, FL 33433

Ballard Rifle And Cartridge Co., L.L.C.
113 W. Yellowstone
Cody, WY 82414

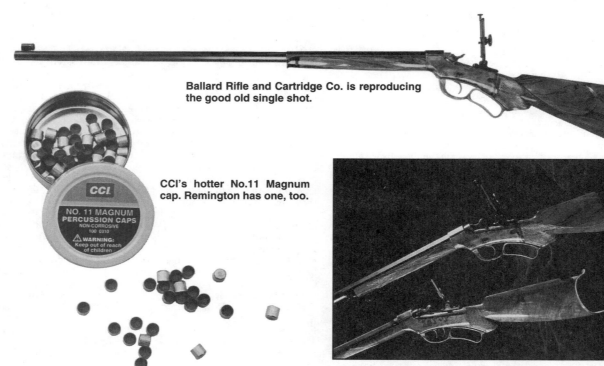

Ballard Rifle and Cartridge Co. is reproducing the good old single shot.

CCI's hotter No.11 Magnum cap. Remington has one, too.

Rifle Styles that are available through Ballard Rifle and Cart. Co.

by HAL SWIGGETT

HANDGUNS TODAY:

SIXGUNS AND OTHERS

January 7, 1998

Savage "STRIKER" .308 Win.
Burris 2X scope

This 3 shot group, at 100 yards, was fired an hour or so before the Striker was packed for return to Savage.

Savage "STRIKER' Hal tested is topped with a Burris 2X scope. This one chambered .308 Winchester.

A lot to talk over in this department, single-action and double-action in revolvers plus five short rifles, as some folks like to call them. I, and this is MY pulpit, prefer thinking of them as long — make that read "mighty long"— range pistols

Let's start with them: In alphabetical order for three that are production line — manufactured, then two built ONLY on order, meaning check in hand before production begins.

REMINGTON

Remington has revived their XP-100R. This one was introduced and manufactured two years, then production was stopped in 1995. "R" simply means repeater. Originally, XP-100s were single shot.

Those first two years, "R"s were built in Remington's very excellent Custom Shop. This reintroduction comes from "R"s production line. Barrel length is 14

1/2-inches. Chamberings are: 223 Remington, 22-250 Remington, 260 Remington and 35 Remington Barrels are drilled and tapped for metallic sights, as are receivers for scope mounting. These "R" pistols have a "blind" magazines, meaning they are loaded through the top. The rear-handle stock is one-piece composite fiberglass.

SAVAGE

Rumors have been circulating that Savage was working on a hunting handgun. As the old Indian Chief said, "Where there is smoke, there is fire" -- quoting Carl B. Hildebrandt, Senior Product Engineer of Savage Arms.

The Striker pistol sent for this review was made up for their booth in the Las Vegas SHOT Show, so it was a very few days in my hands. It wore Burris' 2X scope in a 3-ring mount. Barrel length, including the manufacturers "adjustable muzzle brake", is 14 1/4-inches. Its grooved trigger required only 4 1/4 lbs of pressure to fire.

The ambidextrous black synthetic stock wears

sling swivel studs fore and aft, and this example came with a bipod mounted up front. Chamberings are to be 22-250 Remington, 243 Winchester and 308 Winchester. The one in hand was chambered 308 Winchester. Shooting Winchester's new load, featuring their 150-grain "Ballistic Silvertip" bullet I soon caught on that the two were made for each other, for lack of any better way to say it. All shooting was at 100 yards. Bullet holes stayed close together. Some would say, "Mighty close together".

Their "on/off" muzzle brake — you can take this to your bank — does its job well. "ON" the pistol was really comfortable to shoot. "OFF" it bucked ferociously!

A feature that really got my attention was its lefthand bolt with right-side ejection. It is a three-shooter when one cartridge is chambered. The composite stock is described as mid-grip ambidextrous with a wide bottom swell.

The day I had to send it back I felt it important to go shoot it five (5) more times. That's ALL the ammo I took with me. Shot number two actually touched that first hole. Number three did not touch but was less than half-bullet diameter to the left. I stopped shooting. I DO believe you would have done the same thing.

WEATHERBY

California-based Weatherby has brought back their centerfire pistol called Mark V CFP chambered 22-250 Remington, 243 Winchester, 7mm-08 Remington and 308 Winchester.

The pistol in hand a very few days (it, too, was scheduled for the SHOT Show) was chambered 308 Winchester and topped with a Burris 1.5X-4X scope. Over-all length, stainless steel barrel and action, measured 25 3/4-inches. It's 15-inch barrel was fluted. Weight, as described, was a thin line under 6 lbs. Trigger pull, with absolutely NO movement, let off at 3 3/4 pounds. And so designed that the trigger, on this test pistol, was all but invisible. Its stock is one-piece, multi-layer laminates, rear-grip with trigger guard included. And so designed that the trigger was all but invisible but with sufficient surface to allow let-off with absolutely NO problem.

How did it shoot? As you might expect a Weatherby to perform. Weather was from horrible to worse, yet groups consistently printed under 1 1/4-inches. Again, weather was the culprit. This one I would like to have been able to keep longer than the five days allowed. I know it would do better.

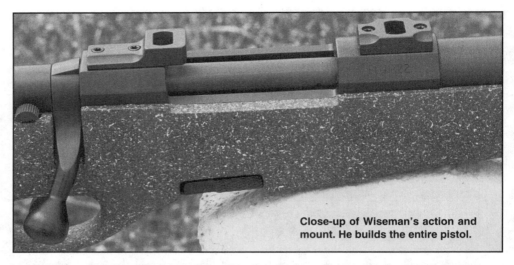

Close-up of Wiseman's action and mount. He builds the entire pistol.

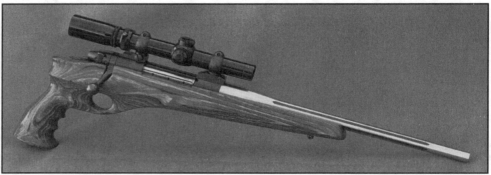

Weatherby's Mark V CFP wearing a Burris 1.5X-4X scope. It is mighty good looking and shot up to that appearance.

ULTRA LIGHT ARMS

Melvin Forbes builds/manufactures personally every firearm shipped from his West Virginia shop. These are done ONLY on order. His catalog includes most anything a customer might dream up. He builds his own actions, left or right hand, scope mounts and any combination thereof — meaning left side bolt with right ejection or right bolt — left ejection should the customer desire.

Likewise for chambering. You name the cartridge and Melvin WILL build a pistol (or rifle) around it.

I was invited on a groundhog shoot with Melvin and some of

his cronies. They with l-o-n-g range rifles and yours truly with a pistol. All shots 300 yards or less were mine. At the end of five days, I was given credit for the most kills. A few of their "misses" were so far away I couldn't even see their targets. Mine was a 22-250; I have no idea what they were shooting.

Ultra Lights are fitted with ULA's patented two-position, three-function safety and weigh less than six pounds scoped for rifles, pistols even less.

BILL WISEMAN

Texas-based, Wiseman is a retired United States Marine.

While serving, he spent a lot of his time building their competition firearms. As a civilian he continues that same line of work in that he builds his own short, right-hand actions, scope mounts and barrels, along with pistol and rifle barrels for several other manufacturers of

those firearms. Plus Bill manufactures both pressure and velocity barrels for other companies in that line of work.

Wiseman mounts his bolt action pistols in a mighty handsome rear-grip synthetic stock. And yes — Bill Wiseman works closely with the Alcohol Tobac-

Wiseman's muzzle brake and fluting is standard, but it doesn't look it.

Melvin Forbes' Ultra Light pistol, in Hal's hands, knocked this woodchuck over at a bit more than 250 yards.

Phillips and Rodgers multi-cartridge revolver. It handles easily 357 Magnum, 38 Special, 9mm or 380 Auto.

co and Firearms Bureau— as will be pointed out in my review of this next firearm.

Phillips & Rodgers

This one has been around several years, as Medusa, but never got a running start. Now in production and using the company name— stamped on the revolver frame's left side. Same side of the slab-sided barrel reads 38/357/9mm cal. P&R is truly black-finished, handsomely black, I'd best add. It is a six-shot, double action, with a five-inch barrel. The grip is checkered rubber-like with finger grooves.

Sights? Front blade with a red dot centered, rear square-notched adjustable for both windage and elevation. Weight, unloaded—on my postal scale— 43 ounces. P&Rs grooved trigger pulls very comfortably at a fraction over four pounds. In fact, the only "improvement" I can offer is a slightly wider rear sight. That's how good this one feels to me.

About those multi-chamberings: rimmed cartridges cham-ber in the normal way. Those designed for autoloaders use a spring-loaded projection on the ejector that protrudes a bit less than 1/10". This catches in the groove of autoloading 380 ACP or 9mm cartridges. This makes them a bit slower to load but gets those empties out *muy pronto*.

About Bill Wiseman's connec-tion: AFT came to him and asked, make that read "told", him to de-sign a rifling that could/would identify this revolver specifically, because of its multi-cartridge ca-pability. Normal rifling is, so I've been told, either four or five lands - grooves. Phillips & Rodgers re-volver has nine (9) — making it totally different than any other revolver or pistol manufactured and so easy to identify

How did it shoot?

Five-shot groups (average of two) at 7 yards, off hand and dou-ble action: 1 3/4 inches to 3 1/2 inches. So far as this writer is concerned, that's good shooting.

CIMARRON

This Texas-based distributor of early-day firearms offers a complete line of well-manufac-tured cowboy guns. One that caught my attention was their 1851 Richards Conversion. It's available in 5 or 7-inch and chambered 38 Special or 38 Colt. Along with this one Cimaron also catalogs the 1861 Richards Con-version with 5 or 7-inch barrel and chambered as above. Their third, in this line, is a 1860 Rich-ards Conversion in 5 or 7-inch and chambered 44 Colt. Finish, all three, can be blue with case hardened frames or nickel.

COLT

Their catalog lists DS-II 38 Special, stainless steel, 6-shot, 2 or 4-inch barrel; King Cobra 357 Magnum, stainless 6-shot, 4 or 6-inch/ Anaconda 44 Rem-ington Magnum, stainless 4, 6 or 8-inch and 45 Colt, S/S, 6 or 7 3/4-inches.

Colt's Python Elite is offered in two versions: stainless matte blue and chambered 357 Mag-num (6 rounds) or 45 ACP (7 rounds). Barrel lengths are 5 and 6 inches.

Colt's Single Action Army is chambered 45 Colt with barrel lengths of 4 3/4 or 5 1/2-inches in blue with color case or nickel.

Colt's Blackpowder Division offers their A-COMPANY No. 1 and COLT CUSTER - 1861 Navy General Custer. You real-ly need these catalogs, which are beautifully done.

DAN WESSON

Dan Wesson Firearms is, again, back manufacturing re-volvers we are told. I've not seen one but on the word of Robert W. Serva, President of New York International and Dan Wesson Firearms, I am giving you this information. Usually addresses are in the back of GD but in this case, and our editor approving, you can find out more by writing to New York In-ternational Corp., Dan Wesson Firearms Co., 119 Kemper Lane, Norwich, NY 13815 -- or call them at 607-336-1174 of FAX 607-336-2730.

FREEDOM ARMS

New in this Wyoming-based manufacturers line is a 41 Rem-ington Magnum Model 654 large frame of five-shot configu-ration. They are also offering a six-shot 357 Magnum with fixed or adjustable sights and yes— for you really tough single action shooters— their Model 555 chambers the 50 A.E. round, along with, of course, their real-ly great 454 Casull, 44 Reming-ton Magnum, 357 Magnum. There is also a really fine jewel, the Model 252 in 22 Long Rifle.

M.O.A. MAXIMUM

Richard Mertz' falling block single shot pistol has been around a long time and won a good many silhouette matches. Once, in South Africa, in the hands of Dr. Richard Rogers, I saw a beautiful one-shot kill on a magnificent gemsbok made with one.

Mine has accounted for more prairie dogs than I would have ever thought possible, mostly in western Kansas and eastern Colorado. Richard's chambered 350 Remington Magnum; mine is a 250 Savage.

Mertz has changed his grip a bit, is now fluting barrels and adding muzzle brakes, but it is the same old, reliable, falling block action that has served so well for so many years.

MAGNUM RESEARCH

Remember D-MAX, manu-factured by Darvin and Maxine

This close up photo reveals Phillip's and Rodger's secret. The small spring-loaded extractors built into the ejector star.

Cimarron's 1851 Richards Conversion is available 5 or 7- inch, chambered 38 Special or 38 Colt.

Carda? Their truly great single action has found a new home. Magnum Research has taken over sales and distribution. Their original 410/45 Colt (long cylinder) with 7 1/2-inch barrel has grown to a 10-inch version chambered 45-70 or 444 Marlin and called MAXINE.

The standard cylinder model is chambered 454 Casull with 6 1/2, 7 1/2 or 10-inch barrel, 45 Colt with 6 1/2-inch barrel and 22 Hornet or 50 AE with 7 1/2-inch barrel. This one is called/named LITTLE MAX and offered with standard wood or optional pearl grip.

Accessories include Hogue grips, Ruger scope base and rings, muzzle brake and holsters (shoulder or hip). and MR's LONE EAGLE is alive and well, chambered to accept 15 cartridges from 22 Hornet to 444 Marlin.

NAVY ARMS

The right side barrel lug is stamped "SCHOFIELD PATS JUNE 20th 71 APR 22nd 73." Left side simply "CAL 45 L.C." Left side barrel lug reads "NA-VY ARMS CO. RIDGEFIELD N.J.", then under that "A. UBERTI MADE IN ITALY". Left side grip reads "1877" with scrolled initials in an oblong circle near its bottom. Right side grip simply has other scrolled initials in an oblong circle.

There is a V notch full length in the barrel rib. It is six-shot, with the firing pin on its hammer face. Overall length is 13-inches including the 7-inch barrel. Trigger pull is 6 1/2 lbs and it weighs, unloaded, 2 lbs 11 oz.

"To Open the Arm without ejecting the cartridges— Break open the revolver while simultaneously depressing the rear of the ejector-pawl located in front of the trigger guard. This will disengage the ejector and prevent the cartridges from being expelled." Those are their printed instructions.

Admittedly I fell in love with this 45 Colt Schofield on opening its box, and felt even more so after shooting it. Loaded with five (no live cartridge under its hammer) CCI BLAZER 255-grain lead cartridges, all shooting was at 25 yards and over sandbags. One group printed three of its five in 1 1/8-inches, center to center. Another printed three in 5/8-inch. My best group was 3 5/8-inches for all five, center to center. Overall, five groups of five each, averaged 4 5/8-inches. Not at all bad for not overly good sights and 76-year old shooter.

ROSSI

Imported by Interarms, CYCLOPS is chambered 357 Magnum, offered with 6 or 8-inch ported heavy barrel. The deal includes B-SQUARE scope mounts and rings.

This company's M971 VRC 357 Magnum is ported, with a choice of three barrel lengths, 2 1/2, 4 or 6-inches, stainless and with rubber grips. And their M851 is chambered 38 Special, stainless steel, 6 shot and with 4-inch barrel. The Model M971 357 Magnum is available in five versions with 2 1/2 to 6-inches of barrel and choice of blue or stainless.

SMITH & WESSON

The one that caught my eye was Model 317 AirLite, an 8-shot 22 with 2-inch barrel, weighing only 9.9 ounces. Two other two-inchers, both hammerless and stainless steel, are 357 Magnum and 9mm Parabellum.

This gun writer also likes the all-stainless Model 617 10-shot 22 revolver.

Obviously, I am 22 rimfire-oriented: one more of my favor-

Magnum Research has acquired the distribution of these big multi-caliber single actions. This one is called MAXINE and digests 3-inch 410/45 Colt. Others shoot 45-70 or 444 Marlin.

M.O.A.'s handsome Falling Block pistols can be built to chamber most any cartridge you feel up to shooting.

Navy Arms Schofield is 13 inches over all with a barrel length of 7 inches; it's chambered 45 Colt.

S&W's Model 317 Airlite 2 inch is an eight shot 22—little cutie.

ites is their Model 651 stainless steel 22 Winchester Magnum Rimfire with its 4-inch barrel. This one is a six-shooter and weighs 26.5 ounces.

STURM, RUGER

Ruger's Bisley is now cataloged in 22 LR, 6 1/2-inch; 357 Magnum, 44 Magnum or 45 Colt with 7 1/2-inch barrel, all blue-finished. Their Vaquero and Bisley Vaquero is now available in 22 LR and 44 Magnum, in blue only. They STILL want your elderly Super Bearcat for updating.

TAURUS

Taurus' 454 Casull five-shooter with its 6 1/2 or 8 3/8-inch ported barrel is offered in blue or stainless steel. Not only is it ported but also includes Taurus' exclusive security system. The grip is soft black rubber with recoil-absorbing insert.

S&W's two-inch stainless steel 357 Magnum is hammerless.

There's a S&W Model 940, in 9mm as well.

Taurus' Model 85 stainless steel 38 Special is 5-shot.....

.....comes with a great security system. Depress that protrusion and it cannot be fired.

From the right angle, the Taurus model 85 is mighty vicious looking, capable of handling any close situation.

Another interesting Taurus is their Model 617, a 7-round 357 Magnum with 2-inch barrel offered in blue or stainless. You can have concealed or visible hammer and a key lock, too.

THOMPSON/CENTER

Still the biggest news from Rochester, NH, is their EN-CORE pistol. Same format as Contender — just heavier built for more potent cartridges. Barrels are 10 and 15-inch with adjustable sights and those same lengths in ventilated rib, bead front sight, chambered 45/410. There are a lot of chamberings.

T/C now offers the ENCORE Hunter's Package. It includes a 15-inch barrel, Weaver Style base and rings 2.5X - 7X variable Recoil Proof Pistol Scope; and a rugged soft carrying case that also houses extra barrels. Frame and barrels are blued, grip and forend are rugged black composite. Caliber choices for this one are 22-250, 270, and 308.

I have used this ENCORE rather extensively. I took a very unusual antlered whitetail in Texas, then an unusual antlered mule deer in Wyoming along with an antelope.

Caliber? I started with prototype Z 2 in 308, so stuck with that chambering when the first production pistols were delivered.

My extra barrel? Over many years of shooting, I long ago settled on 22-250 for lesser game and varmints. Both barrels wear T/C's 2.5X-7X scope. •

Thompson/Center's Encore with 308 Winchester barrel ready for action and the 22-250 Remington waiting to serve. Both topped with T/C's 2.5X-&X scope.

Trapper Gun 44-40 made from a 357 Ruger Blackhawk just for Hal.

by JOHN MALLOY

HANDGUNS TODAY:

AUTOLOADERS

Mag, who died in 1996. Caliber will be the original 44 AMP (44 Auto Mag Pistol).

ANGEL ARMS

This new California company created quite a stir at the 1998 SHOW Show with two unconventional semiautomatic pistol designs.

The original type, called "Gun One" by inventor Raphial Morgado, is a 45-caliber personal-defense pistol. The position of the grip is such that the recoil comes back in a straight line to the forearm to eliminate muzzle rise. The cartridges are carried in a special carrier above the barrel; after firing, cases are ejected downward through the grip. The cartridge is listed as "45 Light Magnum," reportedly pushing a light 100-grain bullet to about 1500 fps. This would seem to be similar to

the Danish Schouboe cartridge which was tested by the U.S. Army in 1912, but no Angel Arms cartridges were available for observation.

The second variant is a smaller, concealed-carry pistol designated QT 427. It uses a caseless round of .427-inch diameter, called the Integrated Case Projectile (ICP). The cartridge is reminiscent of the old Volcanic cartridge of the 1850s—the powder is contained in a hollow projectile with a priming device at the base—but modern materials have brought the concept into modern times. The light, hollow copper-alloy projectiles reportedly achieve high velocities, and separate loads are listed for 250, 350 and 500 foot-pounds of energy at the muzzle. Five cartridges are carried in a short tubular

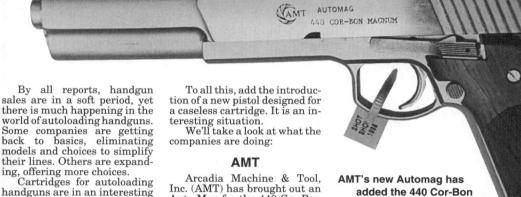

AMT's new Automag has added the 440 Cor-Bon chambering.

By all reports, handgun sales are in a soft period, yet there is much happening in the world of autoloading handguns. Some companies are getting back to basics, eliminating models and choices to simplify their lines. Others are expanding, offering more choices.

Cartridges for autoloading handguns are in an interesting state. The 9mm Parabellum (Luger) cartridge, which seemed to be king of the hill for sometime, has now filled most of its possible niches. This year, the 45 ACP cartridge is again prominent, with a number of companies producing pistols only in that caliber and two long-time manufacturers are now making their first 45s. Two new 45-caliber cartridges have also been recently developed.

The current trend seems to be toward packing more power into a semiauto handgun through large bullet diameter or increased powder capacity or higher-pressure loadings. Colt's 9x23 and the two larger-bore high-velocity cartridges introduced by Cor-Bon have been well received, and even the 44 Auto Mag is being revived.

In contrast, though, there is a renewal of interest in the old 32 ACP, considered a dead duck in the U.S. until recently. The 32 S&W long revolver cartridge also is getting new attention here as a cartridge for autoloading target pistols. Of course, the 22 rimfire gets little fanfare, but sells a lot of pistols.

To all this, add the introduction of a new pistol designed for a caseless cartridge. It is an interesting situation.

We'll take a look at what the companies are doing:

AMT

Arcadia Machine & Tool, Inc. (AMT) has brought out an Auto Mag for the 440 Cor-Bon Magnum cartridge. This is the second pistol chambered for this powerful new cartridge; last year there was the Desert Eagle. The case is essentially the 50 Action Express (50 AE) necked down to 44 caliber. AMT believes the wide selection of 44 bullets for handloading and the flatter trajectory will make the 440 a good alternative to the 50 AE. A 240-grain 44 bullet going a reported 1850 feet per second (fps) is pretty impressive.

Also new in the AMT line of 1911-style pistols are the Commando, a 4-inch-barrel compact 40 S&W, and the Accelerator. The Accelerator is a 7-inch-barrel, 46-ounce pistol chambered for the 400 Cor-Bon, which is basically a 45 ACP necked down to 40 caliber. Reported velocity— 1590 fps with a 135-grain bullet — is pretty fast. At 10.5 x 5.25 inches, this is a large pistol.

Fans of the original Auto Mag pistol will be interested in the limited production run of original-design 44 Auto Mag pistols. One thousand will be made to commemorate Harry Sanford, the creator of the Auto

Wayne Strong of Gart Sports examines an original Auto Mag; 1000 will now be made by AMT to commemorate designer Harry Sanford.

To make full use of the 400 Cor-Bon cartridge, AMT's new Accelerator has adjustable sights and a 7-inch barrel.

The original Pit Bull has been reintroduced by Auto Ordnance; the compensated version dropped.

AMT's new compact 1911-style pistol is named the Commando. It is available in 40 S&W.

magazine above the 3.5-inch barrel. The pistol uses a rocking breechblock similar to the "Gun One." This smaller pistol *folds* for concealment or when not in use, and is on "safe" when folded.

Angel Arms scheduled the QT 427 for summer 1998 availability. The Gun One was scheduled for 1999, and may be later redesigned for a caseless cartridge.

AUTO-ORDNANCE

The Auto-Ordnance handgun line is being streamlined. All the "smaller" calibers have dropped out of the line, and Auto-Ordnance pistols are available now only in 45 ACP. The line of 1911-type pistols is available in blue, parkerized, or a new high-polish blue finish. Stainless steel is a possibility for the future.

The compensated Pit Bull, introduced last year, has bowed out and the standard short-barrel Pit Bull has been reintroduced with its original 3.5-inch barrel. The compensated barrel is still available as a parts item for those who missed last year's production and want to make their own compensated Pit Bull.

BENELLI

Some years ago, Benelli match pistols were imported by EAA. Then, for several years, they were not available in the United States. Now, they are imported again in calibers 22 Long Rifle and 32 S&W Long (with wad cutter bullet only). The MP 95 S is the company's world-class, top-of-the-line target pistol. The lower priced MP 95 E, intended to compete in price with more conventional target pistols, is mechanically the same except for trigger and grip.

BERETTA

Beretta's big news is a Cougar in 45 ACP. This is the first 45-caliber pistol Beretta ever produced. The rotating-barrel 45 is available in a full-size Cougar version as the Model 8045. At 7.2 x 5.5 inches, the pistol can be considered a small full-size or a large compact. A "mini" version with short grip has been scheduled for availability later in 1998. The Cougar 45 is available in both F and D styles, that is, conventional double action (DA) or double action only (DOA).

In addition, the Model 92 Compact 9mm, not available for a while, has been reintroduced. It has a slimmer, flatter grip that holds an 8-round single-column magazine. And a 92/96 Combo is now offered for those who can't make up their minds whether they would rather have a 9mm or a 40. The combination package has two barrel/slide assemblies with the necessary parts to switch from one caliber back to the other, at the owner's choice.

There's an M9 package which consists of a military-specification 9mm M9 pistol (with a legal 15-round magazine) and a military-type holster and accessories.

BROLIN

Brolin has acquired Mitchell Arms. The acquisition has allowed an expansion of the Brolin line beyond their standard 1911-style Legend 45-caliber pistols. Brolin pistols now are available in full-size (5-inch barrels) and compact size (4-inch barrels). Lighter models with recessed slides and slimmer grips are now offered.

Perhaps the most noticeable additions are double-actions from FEG in Hungary. These

are available in three styles: TAC (full-size) in 9, 40 or 45; Compact, with a 4-inch barrel and with a 10-round frame, in 9 or 40; and Bantam, with a short barrel, a shortened 6-round grip frame, in 9 and 40. Brolin also handles Mauser firearms now. The Mauser Parabellum pistol, in original P08 configuration, is thus now available through Brolin.

BUL TRANSMARK

Conversion from one caliber to another is apparently of interest to a number of shooters. The BUL M5, an Israeli-made 1911-type pistol with a wide-body polymer frame, is now available in a multicaliber conversion kit. The same pistol can be a 9mm, a 40 or a 45, as the owner chooses.

Another new variant is a compact 4-inch-barrel model. As introduced, the short-barrel new BUL has a standard grip frame. Later production will have a shortened grip frame. BUL magazines hold 14 to 18 rounds, depending on caliber, but 10-round magazines are available for U.S. shooters. BUL pistols are available in 9mm, 9x21, 9x23, 38 Super, 40 S&W and 45 ACP.

The Angel Arms display of caseless-cartridge autoloaders generated a lot of interest at the 1998 SHOT Show. Inventor Rahial Morgado explains his concepts.

play specimen had a full-size slide and barrel mounted on a compact polymer frame. A grip extension boot on the full-size magazine essentially turned it into a full-size pistol. One would think these options might well be offered in the near future. Although the polymer Witness is available now only as a 45, conversion kits are available to turn it into a 9mm or a 40. The redesigned Star PD that was announced last year never reached production and will not be available.

FIREARMS INTERNATIONAL

The Firearms International name has been resurrected from several decades ago. The new use is a renaming of the Houston company known last year as Israel Arms International, and before that as J. O. Arms. FI is the marketing agent for the Israeli manufacturer.

The pistols offered by this company have also been renamed. Those 45-caliber pistols patterned after the 1911 design are Model 5000. The 9mm and 40 guns based on the Browning High Power design were originally introduced some years ago as the

CHARLES DALY

The Charles Daly name was resurrected by KBI last year for shotguns, and at the 1998 SHOT Show, a new 1911-style pistol was introduced under that name. The new pistol is the first handgun ever to wear the Charles Daly name, which has been used on other firearms since about 1875.

KBI's Michael Kassnar said that the new pistol has most of the features most shooters want, at a very competitive price. Among the niceties, each pistol comes with a Sprinco recoil reducer, a full-length recoil-spring guide with an extra buffer spring. The Charles Daly 1911-A1 P is available in one style, with a 5-inch barrel, in 45 ACP.

COLT

Colt has introduced three "enhanced" models, all variants of the 45-caliber 1911 pistol. All are updated with features that seem to be in vogue at the present, such a redesigned grip safety, extended thumb safety, a light trigger, and Hogue grips.

The models with these features are the Combat Commander (4 1/4-inch barrel), Concealed Carry Officer (3 1/4-inch barrel), and the brand-new smaller Defender (3-inch barrel). This latter pistol is a very small 45.

The Colt Pony, the DAO locked-breech 380 introduced last year, is now also available with an alloy frame as the Pony Pocketlite.

COONAN

Coonan Arms, the designer of the original 1911-style pistol to

handle the 357 Magnum revolver cartridge, has added a new caliber. Displayed for the first time at the 1998 SHOT Show, a Coonan pistol chambered for the 41 Magnum revolver cartridge has been added to the line. The new 41 is available with a five-inch barrel and can be had with a variety of sights and grips.

CZ

The Czech Republic gunmakers have introduced a new full-sized 45-caliber pistol, the CZ 97 B. This is the first pistol ever made by CZ in 45 ACP caliber. Serial number 001 was on display at the 1998 SHOT Show. The pistol is a tilting-barrel locked-breech design, with conventional DA mechanism. It resembles an enlarged CZ 75, but the frame extends to the front of the slide. Capacity is 10+1.

A new alloy-frame compact 9mm was also displayed. A variant of the CZ 75 line, the new lightweight is available in 9mm only at this time.

ENTERPRISE

Enterprise Arms has introduced a new full-size variant of their widebody 1911 series. The new "Boxer" is a bull-barrel 45 ACP. It has a redesigned bushingless slide.

Another new addition to the line is the Tactical P325 Plus, which as essentially all the standard and enhanced features that the company provides, in a small package.

This is a prototype of a low-cost "Plinker" field pistol that High Standard plans to introduce soon. It is based on the Duramatic/Plinker design popular several decades ago.

Recall that a "325" model designation at Enterprise means the pistol has a 3.25-inch barrel.

EAA

European American Armory (EAA) has its polymer-frame Witness pistol from Tanfoglio now in production, and available in 45 ACP in compact from (3.75-inch barrel) only. At the 1998 SHOT Show, a dis-

Kareen, and are now cataloged as Model 1500.

The 45s are all Commander-size, with 4-1/4-inch barrels. The forged frames and slides are made from different grades of stainless steel. Several finishes are available, and a number of currently-desired features are standard.

GLOCK

Glock frames have been changed. 1998 and later pistols will have finger grooves on the front strap of the frame, and the interesting little "thumb rests" on both sides. Frames of subcompact versions will stay the same, as they already have these features.

Five new models were introduced at the 1998 SHOT Show. Three are Glocks chambering the 357 SIG cartridge. The Model 31 ("standard") Model 32 (compact) and Model 33 (subcompact) are essentially the same as the earlier 40-caliber counterparts, but handle the 357 SIG round, which reportedly can equal 357 Magnum revolver ballistics.

Also new are the Practical/Tactical models 34 (9mm) and 35 (40 S&W). These pistols meet IPSC specifications for competition in the Standard/Limited categories. Barrels are 5.3 inches long, and the pistols have competition trigger pulls of 3.5 pounds. An extended slide stop, an extended magazine catch and accessory rails complete the package.

GRIFFON

Continental Weapons, the South African company, has made improvements and expanded their line of Griffon pistols since their introduction last year: The 45-caliber Griffon 1911A1 Combat, based rather obviously on the 1911 Colt/Browning design, is now available with a 5-inch barrel, as well as the 4 1/4-inch version originally introduced. Niceties such as a full-length recoil spring guide, grooved frame, adjustable trigger and enlarged ejection port have been added. Ported versions are now available. The Griffon CW 11, a 9mm

The Charles Daly name goes back to 1875, but KBI is using it on a handgun for the first time.

pistol based on the Tokarev design, is now available with red dot sights.

HECKLER & KOCH

H&K has tried to leave no gap unfilled in its USP pistol line. The latest entry is the USP 45 Tactical Pistol. Available in 45 ACP only, it is basically a USP with micrometer target sights and a protruding barrel threaded at the muzzle. Thus, it shares some features with the USP, and USP Match and the Mark 23. An interesting feature is the rubber O-ring that positions the barrel in the slide when the action is closed. HK claims a significant effect on accuracy and a life span of over 20,000 rounds for the easily replaceable O-ring.

HERITAGE

The 40 S&W version of Heritage Manufacturing's Stealth pistol is now in production. In fact, the first shipment of the new C-4000 was made the week before the 1998 SHOT Show. This 40-caliber Stealth

Coonan Arms, the 357 auto people, has added a 41 Magnum pistol to their line.

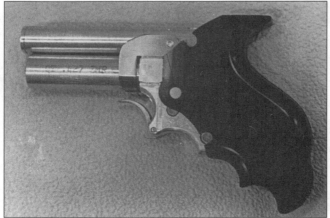

The Angel Arms QT 427 uses caseless cartridges, fed from the tube over the barrel. The design directs recoil straight back to the forearm to control muzzle rise.

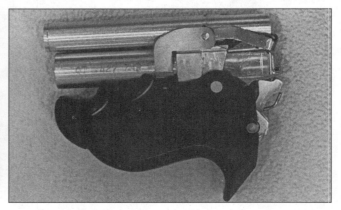

The Angel Arms QT 427 can be folded for pocket carry. When folded, pistol is on "safe."

CZ has introduced the big new Model 97 B, the firm's first.

New ported Griffon pistols are available from the South African manufacturer, as are longer barrel versions.

is the same size and the same weight as the original 9mm version, and the 40 magazine retains the full 10-shot capacity. Each pistol will come with a Pachmyr slip-on grip.

HIGH STANDARD

High Standard has updated the handy pistol made during the '50s and '60s which was called at various times the Duramatic or the Plinker. An unfinished prototype for the new pistol was not on display, but your writer was able to get a look at it during the 1998 SHOT Show. The new 22 pistol, to be introduced soon as the Plinker, will add an inexpensive field pistol to High Standard's line of 22 target pistols. Plans are for the new Plinker to be marketed by Crusader Gun Company, which will also offer a revolver in the near future.

To round out their line, and to equip conventional bullseye pistol shooters with guns for 22, Centerfire and 45 matches, High Standard has plans to bring out 1911-type pistols in 38 Super Mid-Range and 45 ACP calibers. The new guns were scheduled for late 1998 introduction.

Shooters of the older "slant-grip" High Standard pistols may be interested to know that the company is now producing magazines for those earlier models.

HI-POINT

The compensated 9mm Hi-Point, introduced on these pages in prototype form, is now a production item. Cataloged as the 9mm Comp Gun, the next fixed-barrel blowback 9mm has a 4-inch barrel, adjustable sights and a muzzle break compensator. Slots allow mounting a laser sight or flashlight. Capacity is 10+1.

INTERARMS

The 32 ACP chambering has slipped quietly back into

the Walther line imported by Interarms. The 32 was considered dead in the U.S., killed off by the 380, but the recent appearance of several 25-sized 32s has apparently revived interest in the 32-caliber cartridge. At the 1998 SHOT Show, the Walther PP and PPK/S were reintroduced in 32 ACP.

INTER ORDNANCE

This North Carolina company, Inter Ordnance of America, is another with a new 32 ACP pistol. Made in Romania, their Model 96 is made on the Walther PP design and comes with a 3.4-inch barrel and 8+1 capacity. A similar Model 95 is chambered for the 380 cartridge. Inter Ordnance also offers surplus Steyr 1912 pistols and C-96 "Broomhandle" Mauser pistols.

KAHR

Kahr's biggest news was the downsizing of their already small K9 9mm pistol. The new model, designated MK9, is shortened a half inch in both directions. With a 3-inch barrel, it measures just 4 x 5.5 inches, and hides easily beneath a 4 x 6 note card. The shorter grip reduces the magazine capacity to six with a flush baseplate. However, each MK9 also comes with an additional extended magazine that boosts the pistol's capacity up to 7+1. And the K40 is due for a similar miniaturization process. The smaller 40-caliber pistol was scheduled for June 1998 availability.

The standard K9 and K10 will be available in new two-tone variants customized by Wilson's Gun Shop. These guns will be marked "Wilson Custom," and only a limited number will be made. For Kahr collectors who want even more variants, the basic K9, MK9 and K40 were also to be made in "Elite 98" versions, with polished stainless slides and a special combat trigger. The Elite 98

Kahr's new MK9 is miniaturized version of the company's 9mm K9 pistol.

guns were scheduled for limited quantity production beginning in April, 1998.

KEL TEC

Kel Tec's new 40 S&W version is now in production. The larger-caliber Kel Tec is just 5/32-inch longer than the original 9mm pistol. It weighs only two ounces more, bringing it up from 14 to 16 ounces. At an just one pound, the new Kel Tec is a very light 40.

KIMBER

Several new Kimber pistols were announced at the 1998 SHOT Show. All are 45 ACP, on the basic 1911 design.

Perhaps the greatest departure is that Kimber has added compact pistols to its line. The compacts have 4-inch barrels, fitted directly to the front of the slide, eliminating the barrel bushing. The grip frame is .400-inch shorter than that of the full-size pistol, but the magazine still holds seven rounds. Matte black and stainless versions are available

now, with a 28-ounce aluminum-frame version scheduled for mid-1998.

It might have seemed that the introduction of a high-capacity pistol would be a chancy thing after the federal magazine ban. Kimber, however, has come up with a quantity of pre-ban 14-round magazines, and is offering widebody pistols with polymer frames. Because of the lighter weight of the polymer frame, the loaded weights of 14-shot and 7-shot pistols are within one ounce of each other.

The Stainless Gold Match is Kimber's new top-of-the-line hand-fitted target pistol for those who want one of stainless steel. All Kimber pistols are in 45 ACP, but there have been rumors that a sub compact 40 S&W may be in the works.

LAR

The makers of the big Grizzly pistols have been holding aside the first 50 guns produced. These original Grizzlies have been sitting in a vault for

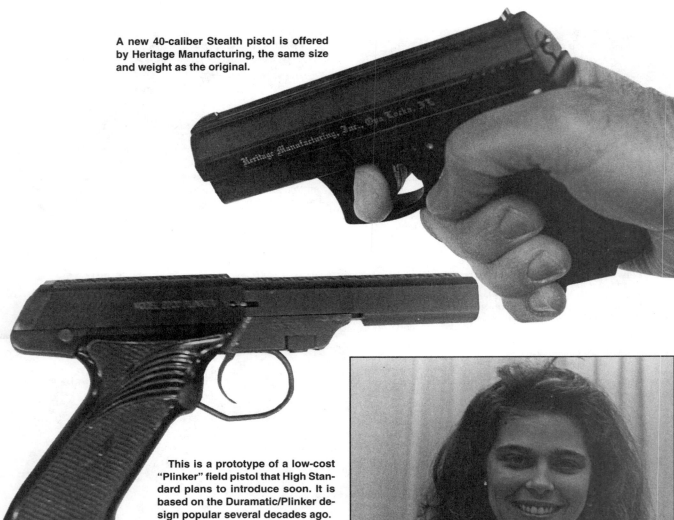

A new 40-caliber Stealth pistol is offered by Heritage Manufacturing, the same size and weight as the original.

This is a prototype of a low-cost "Plinker" field pistol that High Standard plans to introduce soon. It is based on the Duramatic/Plinker design popular several decades ago.

years. Now, these 50 pistols have been made into a series commemorating the fifty states, with one pistol representing each state. Serial numbers represent the order in which each state entered the union. The blued guns are engraved and inlaid with gold, and come in a wood-and-glass display case. Grizzly pistols are now offered in 45 Win. Mag., 45 ACP, 357 Mag., 357/45 Grizzly Win. Mag., 10mm, 44 Mag. and 50 AE.

MAGNUM RESEARCH

The Desert Eagle line is now manufactured in the U.S. as the Mark XIX, but the last of the Mark VII pistols, made in Israel, are being offered for sale now. Collectors who are assembling complete sets of Desert Eagle variants should take note. Magnum Research plans to continue to offer parts and accessories for the Mark VII pistols. The U.S.-made

Desert Eagle pistols are now available in 357 Magnum, 44 Magnum, 440 Cor-Bon and 50 AE.

The line of Swiss-made OnePro pistols, introduced last year in 45 ACP and 400 Cor-Bon, now includes a new subcompact 10-shot 9mm pistol. The small new addition is named OnePro9.

MILTEX

This Maryland company imports pistols from two major Bulgarian manufacturers, Arcus and Arsenal. New pistols were displayed for the first time at the 1998 SHOT Show.

The Arcus-94 is modeled after the Browning 1935 design, and looks a bit like a squared-off High Power. Some parts, including magazines, will interchange. In 9mm only, it features a 10-round magazine, an ambidextrous safety and finger-groove rubber grips. Several finishes are available, and a

The 32 Automatic seems to be making something of a comeback. Johanna Randolph displays an Inter Ordnance Model 96, a 32 made in Romania.

Top-of-the-line target pistol from Kimber is the new Stainless Gold Match. Caliber is 45 ACP.

The OnePro45, a Swiss pistol, was introduced in the U.S. by Magnum Research. It is also available in 400 Cor-Bon.

40-caliber version may be offered in the future.

The Arsenal company manufactures the Bulgarian Makarov pistol, and Miltex is offering it in the original 9x18 Makarov caliber, as the Makarov "Special Edition." Trigger guard is squared off, a modified magazine base provides a longer curved finger grip, and finishes are high polish. Extended barrels and compensators may become available, pending BATF approval.

MOROVIA

Lots of full-size 9mm pistols are being made today. However, not many really big new 9mm pistols are being introduced today, the trend being to smaller and smaller 9s. Arms Morovia in the Czech Republic, has, however, brought out its PS 97, a full-size pistol available only in 9mm. With a barrel length of 4.5 inches, the pistol measures 8.25 x 5.5 inches, and weighs 40 ounces. The new pistol is a conventional DA with tilting-barrel locking system. The magazine release is thumb-operated, on the left side only.

MOSSBERG

Mossberg's UZI Eagle pistols are now available in full-size and compact models, including polymer-frame compacts. Calibers are 9mm and 40 S&W. The 45 ACP version, although it has been advertised, had not yet made its appearance at the 1998 SHOT Show. Anticipated availability of the 45 was Spring 1998.

Recall that UZI America is a subsidiary of Mossberg, handling the sale of IMI firearms, and providing parts and service. New developments are expected, but no word was available during the SHOT Show.

NORTH AMERICAN ARMS

The North American Guardian, a little 25-sized 32 pistol,

reached production by the beginning of 1998, in a stainless-steel version. Another variant, black over stainless, was scheduled for summer 1998 availability. North American is well-known for their diminutive 22-caliber revolvers, and the Guardian, their first semiauto pistol, fits nearly into their product line.

PARA-ORDNANCE

Para-Ordnance, the Canadian firm that began by introducing high-capacity frames and magazines for 1911-type 45 pistols, then graduated to making complete pistols, recognizes the lure of large capacity. The company still has a significant quantity of "pre-ban" high-capacity magazines, and is now offering them as standard equipment with new high-capacity pistols. They will also include a certificate with each pistol to allow the buyer to legally acquire up to two additional high-capacity magazines.

REPUBLIC ARMS (U.S.)

Republic Arms, Inc., of Chino, California, introduced its

20-ounce 45 ACP pistol last year, and is shipping production pistols now. The current version has a black polymer frame and stainless-steel slide. An additional all-black version was scheduled for tentative introduction by mid-1998.

REPUBLIC ARMS (SOUTH AFRICA)

Displayed for the first time at the 1998 SHOT Show was a new South African pistol, the RAP-440. It is offered in 40 S&W and is a variant of the RAP-401, a 9mm which was

A new subcompact 9mm is the Swiss OnePro9, also handled by Magnum Research, with a new-baby look.

Miltex offers a squared-off High Power-style pistol, the Arcus-94, made in Bulgaria.

Not many big new full-size 9mm pistols are introduced these days, but the Morovia PS 97, made in the Czech Republic, is one.

adopted as the official South African government pistol.

The RAP-440 is a conventional DA. It measures 6.5 x 4.75-inch, comes with a 3.5-inch barrel, and has a steel frame. Weight is about 31 ounces. The single-column magazine holds seven rounds. The Republic Arms pistol is sold in the U.S. by TSF of Fairfax, VA. Shipments reportedly began in January 1998.

ROCK RIVER ARMS

The Armalite 45 pistol displayed last year had been built by Rock River Arms, of Cleveland, IL. Now, new pistols have been introduced under the Rock River name. Rock River offers seven different variations, predominantly designed for different types of competition shooting. These are full-size guns, with 5-inch barrels, based on the 1911 design. Standard caliber is 45 ACP, but 40 S&W, 38 Super, 9x23 and 9x19 versions are also available. A "Commander" size compact is said to be in the works.

RUGER

No big splash for Ruger this year, but new things sometimes slip into the Ruger catalog with little fanfare, as Ruger collectors are aware. This year, several blued semiautomatics have quietly slipped into Ruger's centerfire pistol lineup. The large-bore Ruger autoloader line had been dominated by stainless steel of late, but the blued versions will sell for less and make the guns more affordable.

SAFARI ARMS

Safari Arms is a subsidiary of Olympic Arms, and Safari's Matchmaster and Enforcer pistols are easily recognized by the large single finger grip on the front strap of the frame. Now, Safari is expanding its line with three new variants, all with the more conventional straight grip frame. The Cohort is a 4-inch model, the Carrier is a full-size with a 5-inch bull barrel, and the European sports a 6-inch barrel. Caliber for all models is 45 ACP.

SIGARMS

Two new variations of SIG's popular P 229 have been introduced. The nickel finish pistol is available in 9mm, 357 SIG and 40 S&W. The P 229 S (Sport) pistol is all stainless steel with a vented compensator and adjustable sights. The Sport is available in 357 SIG only. The P 232 S (Sport) pistol is all stainless steel with a vented compensator and adjustable sights. The Sport is available in 357 SIG only. The P 232, introduced last year, already has a new variant. It is a stainless steel pistol with night sights and Hogue grips.

SIGARMS handles the Hammerli line of target firearms, and have introduced a new Hammerli pistol. The SP 20 is one of the breed of magazine-forward, low-in-the-hand target pistols. Sights can be adjusted for width as well as elevation and windage. Available in 22 Long Rifle or 32 S&W Long (wadcutter only), the same pistol can be changed from one caliber to another, if desired, with a factory kit sold separately.

SMITH & WESSON

S&W's Performance Center introduced two new 45-caliber pistols at the 1998 SHOT Show. the Model 45 RECON is a compact pistol with a 3.75-inch ported barrel. Capacity is 7+1. The Model 845, also called the Model of 1998, is a limited-edition full-size stainless-steel 45 set up for competition shooting. It features a match-grade barrel and adjustable sights. Capacity is 8+1.

STRAYER-VOIGT

Strayer-Voigt is now making their Infinity line of high-capacity 1911-style pistols with a detachable breechface insert in the slide. This device allows caliber changes with a single slide. Also, if the breechface

North American Arms' little 25-sized 32, the Guardian, is now in production.

The SIG-Sauer P229S (Sport) pistol has adjustable sights and comes in 357 SIG caliber only.

The SIG-Sauer P232 is now available with night sights and Hoque grips.

should ever become worn (some people really do a lot of shooting, you know) a new breechface can be installed.

The breechface is held in place with a hollow screw in the firing pin channel. the installation tool simply goes through the firing pin hole. All Infinity guns will have this feature from now on.

Choice of calibers is probably extensive enough to please most shooters. It includes 9mm, 9x21, 9x23, 9x25, 38 Super, 357 SIG, 10mm, 40 S&W, 400 Cor-Bon and 45 ACP.

TRUVELO

Truvelo Armoury of South Africa is marketing the ADP line of small lightweight gas-delayed pistols. The ADP pistols are not sold in the U.S. due to an arrangement with Heritage Manufacturing, of Opa Locka, Florida. That American company offers pistols based on the South African design.

The ADP pistols are offered elsewhere in the world in 380, 9mm and 40 S&W. Designer Alex Du Plessis has recently added a fourth caliber to the line — the 45 ADP. The case is 3mm shorter than the 45 ACP case, and the bullets are seated to give an overall length no longer than that of the 9mm. Thus, the new 45 cartridge can be handled through many of the same general mechanisms as the small rounds.

VALTRO

Displayed for the first time at the 1998 SHOT Show, the Valtro 1998 A1 is a full-size pistol based on the 1911 design. Valtro is an Italian company, founded in 1962. In 1997, the firm decided to expand by producing shotguns and pistols for the American market. The pistol they offer, in 45 ACP only, is designed as an accurate competition pistol. Most of the features currently in vogue with American shooters seem to be included.

WILSON

Wilson Combat is celebrating their 20th Anniversary. The company has provided predominantly full-size 1911-type pistols, with a lesser call for Commander-size pistols. At the 1998 SHOT Show, a prototype was shown of a new smaller gun with a 3 1/2-inch barrel and 6+1 capacity. Wilson called this the Sentinel, and planned to put it into production in early 1998.

WOLF

Wolf competition pistols, made in Austria, were formerly Ultramatic pistols, manufactured by a company named Ultramatic. Last year, the company remained Ultramatic, but the pistols were marketed under the Wolf name. Now, the company name has also been changed, to Wolf Sporting Pistols. Wolf pistols are handled in the U.S. by Hangunner Custom Gunshop in Pennsylvania. Calibers available are 9mm, 9x21, 9x23, 38 Super, 40 S&W and 45 ACP.

POSTSCRIPT

What would an autoloading pistol be without a magazine? A single-shot? In some cases, a nonfunctioning group of parts. It is hard to overemphasize just how important a proper maga-

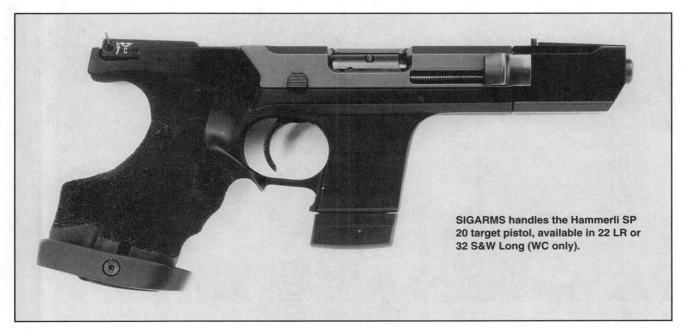

SIGARMS handles the Hammerli SP 20 target pistol, available in 22 LR or 32 S&W Long (WC only).

zine is to the function and feeding of a semiautomatic pistol. Yet, manufacture of precision magazines has become so good that we tend to take these critical parts for granted.

The recent U.S. magazine ban has made some shooters look at magazines more closely. Shooters in some of the shooting sports gain an advantage through larger-capacity magazines. From the standpoint of personal defense, it seems absurd to force people to carry only ten rounds if they own a pistol capable of holding more. At any rate, large magazine capacity is important to many shooters, and several companies, such as Kimber, Para-Ordnance and even Beretta, have responded by offering some of their stock of "pre-ban" magazines as standard equipment with the purchase of some of their new pistols.

We are interested in the new offerings in the world of autoloading handguns, but we like to see the older ones keep shooting, too. It is reassuring that a company such as High Standard is reintroducing magazines for early "slant-grip" models.

There are a number of companies that offer magazines for earlier pistols. One company that really stands out is Triple K Manufacturing Company, of California. Need a magazine for your Frommer, Jo-Lo-Ar, Nambu or Walther Model 6? Triple K's available magazine listings go from AAA to Zehna, literally from A to Z in the world of autoloading handguns. ●

Beretta's big news is a Cougar in 45 ACP, the first 45 pistol ever made by that company.

Using a new shortened cartridge, Truvelo's 45 ADP pistol offers a light pocket pistol of 45 caliber.

S&W's 45 RECON is a 45 ACP and features a ported barrel and all the neat stuff.

Mossberg's UZI Eagle line is available in 9mm and 40 S&W, with a 45 ACP version, Malloy shoots a 9mm here.

by DON ZUTZ

SHOTGUN REVIEW

When I sat down to start this 1998 review of shotguns, I did a short preface lamenting the paucity of anything brilliantly new. After I finished I threw that initial preface away! Things aren't as bad as I thought.

There certainly are not tons of spanking new shotgun designs out there, but some fresh air was wafted in. A relatively new American organization, Connecticut Shotgun Manufactur-

ing Co., is making what must be the finest O/U ever built on these shores, the Galazan. The accuracy of slug guns keeps improving, and apparently the 3-1/2" 12-gauge magnum is generating enough market share to induce gunmakers to add the chambering and new models therefore.

Importers keep things lively, too. An old name, Charles Daly, is back with an expanded line of SxS and O/U shotguns bearing the great old Daly names: Superior, Empire, Diamond and Diamond Regent grades. Tristar Arms branched out into a line of Italian-made O/Us plus a hori-

zontal double, while Sigarms had begun receiving 20-gauge versions of its dynamic O/U bird gun, the SA 3 and SA 5. Nor is Bill Hanus being shut down by confusion at Ugartechea of Spain; Hanus has hooked up with AYA, which is considered the premier gunmaker of Spain, for shipments of doubles built to his specs for re-

sponsiveness and natural pointing. And there's more...

For all practical purposes, then, the current shotgun scene is bright and lively despite the paucity of totally new designs. The variations of existing themes are quite interesting; they take each piece into new areas of specialization for enhanced results. Thus, it should be a pretty good year for shotgunners, which is why I had to redo this preface.

BENELLI

Benelli and its original importer, Heckler & Koch, have

split, with Benelli going its own way as Benelli USA. Based on the ingenious Montefeltro semi-auto system, the Benellis have a few wrinkles for '98.

One of these is the Benelli Sport, which is the normal Bennelli bedecked by interesting accessories. There are spacers to regulate length of pull as well as comb drop. It has the longer competition-style forend. A true innovation is the pair of interchangeable vent ribs, one a high, stepped rib and the other a low, wide rib. They're easily removed and reset.

Benelli's new Legacy line is an attempt to give the hunter an upgraded gun at less cost than the Executive models. Finally, the 20-gauge Montefeltro is being made with a Realtree camo finish overall.

BERETTA

Adjustable stocks are now available on Beretta Model S682 Gold trap guns. The range of adjustment includes both height and cast. Ventilated ribs offer shooters the choice of flat international styling or the American high, stepped rib.

Beretta's Model 390 semiauto is being decked out in Advantage camo, a woodland pattern placed on fiberglass-reinforced stock and forearm. Turkey hunters can get a 24 inch camo barrel, while 28 inch is the basic upland and water flowing length.

Beretta's other semiauto, the Pintail, which is built like the Benelli Montefeltro, is now being turned out in slug persuasion with a rifled barrel. Beretta argues that the solid barrel-

to-receiver assembly, along with the one-piece receiver enhances accuracy.

BROWNING

Shotgunners have had their emotions twinged by Browning's sudden announcement that the grand ol' Auto-5 has been discontinued. With patents dating back to 1900, the Auto-5 has been in almost consistent production (except for the war years) for nearly a century. A doff of our pot hats to the venerable klanker.

After lots of different designs, Browning finally seems to have settled on a semiauto which will also have longevity in spades, the Gold series. Especially notewor-

thy is the new 3-1/2 inch-chambered 12-gauge Gold Hunter. With a catalog weight of less than 8 pounds, the gun handles nicely for a true magnum and, as gas-operated autoloaders do, reduces the sharpness of that 3-1/2 inch shotshell's recoil. The Gold 3-1/2 1/2 inch Hunter wears a solid wooden stock and forearm, while the Stalker model has a black synthetic stock/forend tandem. The gun handles all loads interchangeably from 1-oz. field fodder to the massively long 2-1/4-oz. 3-1/2 inch turkey magnums. Available barrels are Invector - equipped in 26 inch, 28 inch, and 30 inch lengths and are also over-bored.

The standard Gold 12-gauge field gun is also being given Stalker synthetic stock/forearm accoutrements for '98, and a rifled Deer Hunter barrel (or one made with smooth bore plus 5 inch Invector rifled choke tube) is being offered with cantilever mount. The cantilever mounting system is also being made for Browning's BPS pumpgun.

The 3-1/2 inch 12-gauge Browning PBS was built on the BPS 10-gauge frame, leaving the magnum 12 ponderous and slow to mount. For '98, Browning's boys trimmed the 3-1/2 inch 12-gauge BPS by about a full pound through the use of the standard 12-bore receiver, which tests have shown is totally capable of handling the high-pressure 3-1/2 inch maggies. This makes up into about an 8-1/4 to 8-1/2 lb. piece.

In O/Us, the very popular Lighting series of Citoris has been given a silver nitride receiver, while the basic Citori

has been fashioned into a new concept called the Citori Sporting Hunter, a gun which has features which give good field performance plus adaptability to serious sporting clays.

CHARLES DALY

Guess who's back in town! Well, maybe it's not Chas. himself, but rather KBI, Inc. which is using his moniker--after it has changed ownership something like a half dozen times since 1919.

The new Daly line is quite extensive and looks appealing. Prices range from about $700.00 for a field-grade O/U to a full six grand for the classic Diamond Grade SxS. There are lots of Dalys between those figures, including a much less expensive

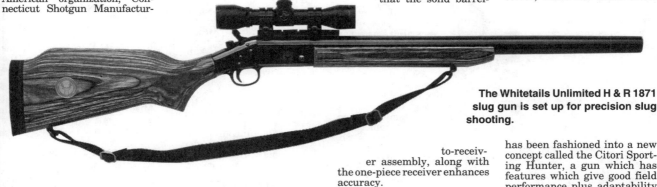

The Whitetails Unlimited H & R 1871 slug gun is set up for precision slug shooting.

set of horizontal doubles know as the Field Hunter and Superior Hunter with retail listings form $749.00 to nearly $1,000. The gauges range from 410 to a whopping 10-bore.

EUROPEAN AMERICAN ARMORY

Better known for its pistols and cowboy stuff, EAA is importing a Turkish-made semiauto at very modest retail prices. The Bunda autoloader is available in 12-gauge only but with either Turkish walnut or black synthetic stock/forearm treatment. Barrels are in 19, 26, 28, and 30 inches with four choke tubes each.

Also from EAA is the Scirocco, an O/U by Lu-Mar of Italy. It's an upland piece, quite sporty at just 7 pounds, and possessed of European walnut woodwork. Barrels can be 26 or 28 inches; both have screw-in tubes.

And if you're the "slap leather" cowboy sort, EAA also plays into your hands with an exposed hammers SxS, the Bounty Hunter SG. The EAA literature shows lots of variations and barrel lengths.

FABARM

When Benelli went its own way, Heckler & Koch, Inc. was left without a shotgun line. It scrambled, coming up with the FABARM smoothbores from Italy, which includes gas-operated autoloaders, both SxS and O/U doubles, and, if you're into SWAT stuff, a pump that has no esthetics but has been battle-proven in Bosnia and is the choice of the French national police.

Dynamic SA3 field gun from Sigarms now comes in 20-bore.

The FABARM O/Us are modern and well-balanced, running from hunting grades to sporting clays designs. The side-by-sides have screw-in chokes, and there is a side plated gun as well as a sturdy, but lively, boxlock. All the FABARM doubles are in 12 and 20 gauge.

FABARM semiautos are gasurged and quite light for their breed, catalog listings ranging from 6.9 to 7.2 pounds. Those I've handled had responsive upland hunting qualities.

GALAZAN

Galazan is a division of Connecticut Shotgun Manufacturing Co., which makes the reproduction A.H. Fox doubles. The main thrust of Galazan is its American-made O/U with Boss features. Galazan also provides Winchester Model 21 parts, having bought tooling from Winchester. It services M21s and can build them on special order through Winchester (USRAC) dealers. These are gorgeous, but expensive, shotguns; the Galazan in undoubtedly the finest sidelocked O/U ever made in America.

HANUS AYA BIRDGUNS

One of the few gun sellers who truly understands the fine points of classic SxS birdguns is Bill Hanus. The guns he had made by Ugartechea of Spain were natural pointers at moderate prices.

Some of these are still in inventory; however, problems are Ugartechea closed that pipeline, and Bill Hanus had to look elsewhere.

Sometimes things work in one's favor, and Hanus is now with AYA, a respected gunmaker. Bill's 1998 offering from AYA are again to his specs, namely 27-inch barrels with concave rib, auto ejectors, skeet 1&2 chokes, upgraded walnut and checkered butt. They're in 16, 20, and 28 gauge, but 12s and 410s are made on special order. Pricing is still below two grand, and the guns are both responsively and classically profiled.

HARRINGTON & RICHARDSON, 1871

Harrington & Richardson put most of its effort into hot-selling break-action rifles this year, but the sole shotgun introduction meets with my approval. It's a 12-gauge Youth gun under the New England Firearms "Pardner" label. I've always argued that beginners should be given as much gun and load as they can

handle, and the 12-bore makes it possible for a beginner to use loads with greater pattern density afield while switching to the light-recoil 7/8 and 1-ounce (24 and 28-gram) 12-gauge loads now catching on. The 12-bore Youth model has a 22 inch barrel, 3 inches chambering, and could easily serve as a turkey gun.

In connection with Whitetails Unlimited, H&R is producing its first limited edition of the ULTRA Slug Hunter. The stock is a black/gray laminate, and it has a Monte Carlo comb for use with its scopes. The bull barrel is 24 inches long, and the guns feature laser engraving of the WTU logo. For every sale of this slug gun, H&R makes a cash donation to Whitetails Unlimited.

ITHACA

Ithaca's comeback in new hands seems solid and positive. The company isn't attempting to set production records. It employs but fourteen men, all experts at their phase of assembly. The result is high-quality pumpguns based on the proved Model 37 nucleus.

For '98, Ithaca offers a new Waterfowler bedecked with Advantage Wetlands camo; the Classic 37, a traditional form with corncob forearm and sunburst recoil pad plus 3 inch chambering; and a 20-gauge Turkeyslayer with 28 inch barrel and extended turkey-tight choke tube. Other 20-gauge tubes can interchange with the turkey tube. Ithaca also entered the Information Age by announcing hunter/shooter capability of ordering replacement parts via the internet (www.ithacagun.com)

KRIEGHOFF

The mounting popularity of the 20-gauge in both skeet and sporting clays has brought Krieghoff to make 30 inch 20-gauge barrels for the current 12-gauge frame. The big news, however, is that Krieghoff is planning a new 20-gauge O/U for 1999 with the receiver sized to the gauge. Wait 'till next year, as they say in sports.

MARLIN

Marlin has decked out its Model 512DL Slugmaster with high-visibility, fiber-optic open sights called "Fire Sights." The

gun is twisted 1:28 for optimum accuracy with sabots. It's an effective combo for early morning and late evening hunts.

MAROCCHI & CLASSIC DOUBLES

In Europe and the U.K., some target-grade O/Us by Marocchi are known as Classic Doubles. There's a lot of gun here, and the current listings by the U.S. importer (Precision Sales International, Inc.) don't show prices that are out of line.

The newest Marocchi/Classic, for example, is the Model 92 Classic Doubles in sporting clays configuration at just a stateside suggested retail or $1,598.00. The gun has been winning in the U.K. for years but only recently came to America. It has muzzle porting, back boring, long forcing cones, chrome-lined bores, 3 inch chambers, and adjustable trigger position. I've handled these, and they're responsive while still being disciplined and smooth.

MOSSBERG

Time certainly flies, doesn't it? The 3-1/2 inch 12-gauge magnum has been around for a full decade; and Mossberg, the primary leader in this category, is celebrating with a new version of it--the Ulti-Mag 835 "Special Hunter." Finished in what Mossberg terms "Stealth" black synthetics, the 385 SH has a Parkerized metal exterior. Its 26 or 28 inch barrel is ported to quell muzzle jump. Otherwise, the original M835 is being made with Mossy Oak Shadowgrass fore and aft as a '98 innovation.

NAVY ARMS

Hardly a major player in scatterguns, Navy Arms nevertheless has something to interest black powder shooters who'd like to keep using soot-belchers on waterfowl. This is a SxS percussion gun with chromed bores for steel compatibility. It's 10-gauge with both barrels open cylinder. I must observe that steel shot has a different pressure and flow than lead, and hunters must try to learn more about these interior ballistics before merely substituting steel for lead shot.

PERAZZI

For the first time in its history, Perazzi is making a 16-

Continuing the comeback, Ithaca announces it's new M37 Waterfowler, finished in Advantage Wetlands camouflage.

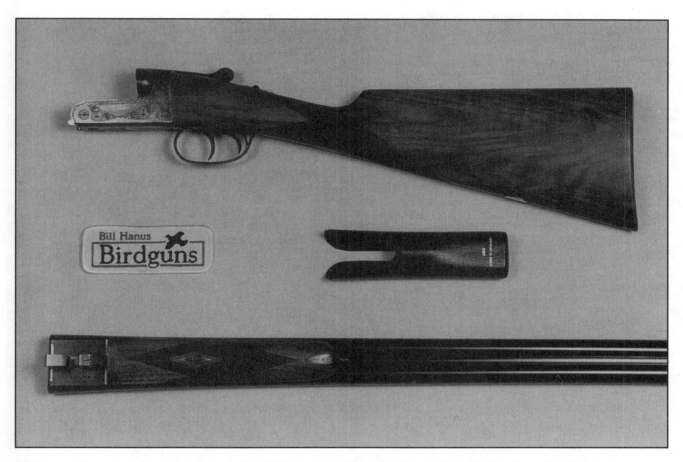

Bill Hanus sells a proper barrel handguard with his Birdguns to encourage proper out-on-the barrels gun handling.

gauge gun. It's listed as the MX16 and is designed as a field gun. As with most Perazzis, it has excellent handling qualities. But the supply is limited as Perazzi tests the market waters. That might not be a big problem, since most of us don't hunt with $8,000 16s, anyway.

REMINGTON

It seems the 3 1/2 inch 12-gauge magnum is here to stay. Not only have more and more loads for it come on line, but now the Model 870 pumpgun is chambered for it. Built on the 12-gauge Express frame, the gun handles much like the basic 12-gauge M870. The addition of the 3-1/2 inch chamber was accomplished via a telescoping breech bolt which retains the strength and smoothness of the original system. Hunters are going to like this one, which will be made with wooden stock/forearm combos or with black synthetics. To each his own!

Otherwise, Remington has put some time into the 20 gauges. Both the M1100 and M870 20s now have elegant fineline scroll engraving (Wingmaster only in M870 line, not Express 20s) on their receivers in field grades. There is also a M1100 20-gauge Sporting 20 with certain features for sporting clays. With a 28 inch barrel for discipline and smoothness, the Sporting 20 comes with the extra-length choke tubes now in vogue.

Remington's stylish M11-87 Premier Sporting Clays gun with nickel plating is being packed with the 28 inch barrel for '98, whereas the originals had only the 30 inch option which everyone didn't want. Soft-shooting and with pointing qualities akin to those of the great M1100, the 12-bore M11-87 sporters are underrated by stateside clay shooters. The fact is that these do a perfect job on skeet, too, as well as on some upland game like doves. ●

by RAYMOND CARANTA

THE GUNS OF EUROPE

The Modern European Revolver

It was unquestionably Samuel Colt who pioneered, during the first five years of the 1830s, the manufacture of the factory-made percussion revolver with a mechanically-rotated cylinder. However, flintlock, manually-rotated designs had been experimented with in Europe from the turn of the XVIIth century.

Much later in Great Britain, Elisha Haydon Collier patented, in 1818, such a mechanism, originally with a spring-rotated cylinder and shooting single action, like the Colt. Some of these guns were subsequently converted to percussion, and manual rotation.

As soon as the Colt revolver found acceptance in Europe, it had to face strong competition from the British Adams self-cocking revolver first, in 1851 and, then in 1854 on, from many French Lefaucheux pin-fire designs shooting single, double or treble action (the hammer could be cocked by hand, by the trigger, set in that configuration

and released, at will, in single action.)

During the 1870s, with the advent of the center fire, the European revolver industry became flourishing and culminated with such famous designs as those from Chamelot-Del-vigne, Louis Nagant, Rast-und-Gasser, Webley & Scott, Nicolas Pieper, Rudolf Schmidt, and the French Service swing-out revolver Model 1892.

Mauser, Luger and Browning automatic pistols, in just a few years, put a sharp end to that glorious period. From the close of World War I to the Sixties, with the exception of the Spaniards who managed to export their low-cost production to Central and South America, European revolver manufacturers had a hard time. They survived with small government orders at a discount.

Then, the revolver became fashionable again, under the American influence for police and defense work, and in accordance with the ISU (International Shooting Union) regulations, for the "Sport pistol" ISU event.

These modern designs were accompanied by a strong revival of the American Western tradition, instigating the rise of the replica industry, followed, more recently, by cowboy action shooting. However, fortune changed once more, several years ago, and nobody can live since then, with only six shots in a cylinder...so long to reload!

Thus, replicas are going as strong as ever in the hands of blackpowder addicts, but modern designs are slowly relegated to basic ISU training, home defense, plinking and, only in France, police use. *Sic transit gloria mundi.*

Revolver production is still going, nonetheless, mostly in the Czech Republic, France, Germany, Italy, Yugoslavia, Russia and Spain.

As far as handguns are concerned, the best-known of modern Czech designs is certainly the CZ-75 15-shot 9mm piston, but the most famous in the circles of ISU Sport pistol competition, the "ZKR 551" revolver, was designed in 1956 by the Koucky brothers and manufac-

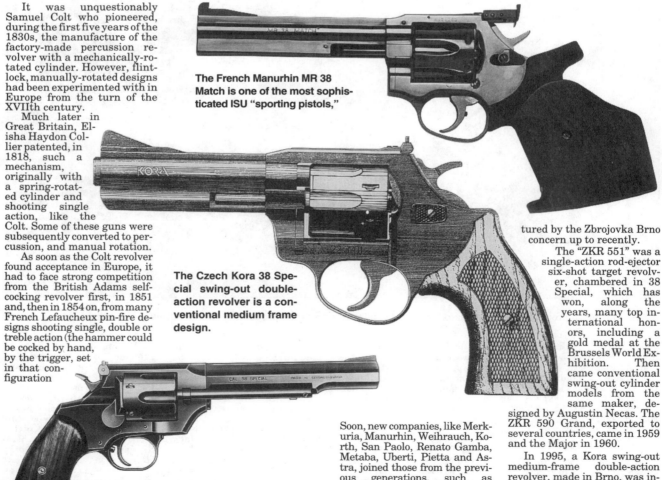

The French Manurhin MR 38 Match is one of the most sophisticated ISU "sporting pistols,"

The Czech Kora 38 Special swing-out double-action revolver is a conventional medium frame design.

The Czech ZKR 551, 38 Special solid frame single action revolver was one of the most accurate in the world.

tured by the Zbrojovka Brno concern up to recently.

The "ZKR 551" was a single-action rod-ejector six-shot target revolver, chambered in 38 Special, which has won, along the years, many top international honors, including a gold medal at the Brussels World Exhibition. Then came conventional swing-out cylinder models from the same maker, designed by Augustin Necas. The ZKR 590 Grand, exported to several countries, came in 1959 and the Major in 1960.

In 1995, a Kora swing-out medium-frame double-action revolver, made in Brno, was introduced at the IWA Exhibition in Germany. It was an eight-shot in 22 Long Rifle and in 38 Special held six rounds. Three

Soon, new companies, like Merkuria, Manurhin, Weihrauch, Korth, San Paolo, Renato Gamba, Metaba, Uberti, Pietta and Astra, joined those from the previous generations, such as Bernardelli, Gabilondo and the Soviet arsenals, while Webley & Scott abandoned the field, victim of the fall of the British empire.

The brand new MR 96 Manurhin, with combat grip and six-inch ventilated rib barrel.

Manurhin MR Silhouette 357 Magnum D.A. revolver, with 10-3/4 inch barrel. A 3-oz counterweight can be fitted in the grip.

versions are offered: the short-barrel Detective with fixed sights; the four-inch barrel Sport; and the six-inch Sport Special, with adjustable micrometer sights.

In France target shooters and veterans of the services, lived since World War I with nostalgia for the now-obsolete Model 1892 revolver. Starting in the mid-Fifties, Smith & Wesson revolvers met with a strong acceptance in these circles, in spite of the high price they commanded during that period—a Smith & Wesson K38 Masterpiece was worth a month's salary for an aircraft engineer, circa 1960. Later, when the French police decided to replace their 32 auto 9-shot pistols with 38 special and 357 Magnum me-

dium-frame revolvers, a need arose for domestic production.

The company in charge of this task was Manurhin, basically a large manufacturer of machine tools, producing Walther PP and PPK automatic pistols since 1955. Their first design was the expensive MR-73, marketed in 1973, featuring lockwork similar to that of the American Military & Police, but with the rebound slide actuated

by a second leaf spring, providing an exceptionally smooth double action pull.

MR-73 target versions were highly successful on their domestic market, but the police soon required a better price for their service handguns and, in 1980, Manurhin offered first, in co-operation

The modular MR 93 Manurhin revolver, a middle of the road success.

with Ruger, a derivative of the Speed-Six called the RMR Special Police. Two years after, further to a dramatic increase of the US dollar rate, Manurhin introduced a new service model, the MR Special Police F1, with an improved grip, a side plate and a reinforced cylinder yoke. This gun is still in service.

Based on their previous experience, Manurhin developed then, in 1993, the progressive MR 93, featuring four interchangeable barrels, three grips and six different sets of adjustable sights. In 1996, this model

was further improved, and as the MR 96 is now in full production.

In Germany, besides the infamous Saturday Night specials marketed by minor companies, production of revolvers is essentially limited to Hermann Weihrauch, under the "Arminius" trade mark, and to Korth.

Herman Weihrauch has made since the '50s a highly appreciated line of air guns in direct competition with Diana, alarm-guns and inexpensive revolvers chambered in 22 Long Rifle, 22 Winchester Magnum, 32 S&W Long, 38 Special and 357 Magnum. Their Western Six-Shooter is a derivative of the Colt Single-Action Army and the Arminius are swing-out double action revolvers, mounted with coil springs. These revolvers are very sturdy and, in spite of some crudeness, extremely accurate.

The Korth guns are entirely different propositions. The intent of their maker is to reach mechanical perfection. And to do this at any price, we would be tempted to say.

As a matter of fact, Korth revolvers are practically custom guns of the very best quality, now sold on the French market, from $4,500.00 for the Combat and Sport models up to $5,500.00 for the Match. They are swing-out double-action guns with heavy barrels, featuring an original cylinder lock.

The oldest Italian revolver manufacturer is Bernardelli, a Beretta competitor since 1860. Bernadelli made the 1889 service model for the government before World War II. Bernadelli Tiro and Tascabile revolvers, still listed in their catalog, are straight replicas of the old Smith

Two popular Arminius D.A. revolvers—(above) the eight-shot HW7, chambered in 22 Magnum; (left) the six-shot HW357 in 357 Magnum.

& Wesson Kit gun and 32 Hand Ejector, available in 22 Long Rifle, 22 Winchester Magnum, and 32 S&W Long with fixed or adjustable sights and various barrel lengths. They are very well made, as all Bernardelli products, but quite expensive.

Then, in the late '50s, came the new generation of Colt and Remington blackpowder replicas, made by Euroarms, Fratelli Pietta, Armi San Marco, San Paolo and, above all of them, Aldo Uberti. New models, such as the "Rogers & Spencer 1855", miscellaneous Confederate percussion revolvers, the prestigious Le Mat and, even, the Smith & Wesson Schofield have come along. Some of these replicas are cheap, but others, mostly from Aldo Uberti, are true masterpieces of modern technology. Renato Gamba made, in the 1980s, his small Trident 38 Special six-shot pocket revolver, strongly inspired from the Colt Detective Special. This gun seems to have gone out of production. It displayed beautiful workmanship.

In this connection, mention must be made of the San Paolo line of swing-out double-action six-shot revolvers, chambered in 22 Long Rifle and 38 Special calibers, manufactured under German Sauer & Sohn license agreement.

Aldo Uberti, too, beside his famous production of replicas, lists in his catalog a line of 38 Special six-shot revolvers, modeled after the Colt small frame designs.

However, in spite of the tens of thousands of Civil War and Western replicas engineered in Gardone (VT) every year, the Mecca of the Italian revolver is not there, but in the small Pavia

The Hermann Weihrauch Western Six-shooter S.A.A. revolver—the Western tradition in 45 caliber.

Main components of the MR 93 revolver—designed to assemble.

German Korth 357 Magnum Sport revolver, with four-inch barrel.

Mateba workshop, where il Signor Ghisoni, a genuine wheelgun aficionado, has put his heart and soul, since 1983, into the design of some of the most ingenious creations of the modern period.

The first-generation Metaba revolvers were eight-shot and 12-shot inside hammer affairs, chambered in 38 Special, or 357 Magnum, with automatic pistol-type grips, extremely low sights, and unfluted cylinders located in front of the triggerguard. The hammers could be thumb-cocked, using a side lever.

Later, in 1986, Ghisoni changed his styling, with the external hammer and inter-changeable barrel six-shot "MTRR 6", featuring a centrally located swing-up cylinder, shooting from the lower cham-

and shoots both 38 Special and 357 Magnum ammunition, without any adjustment. The trigger pull is four pounds in single action and twelve in double action.

Up to the Bosnian Civil War, Zastava was manufacturing a swing-out six-shot police style M1983 revolver for export, chambered in 357 Magnum, or 9mm Luger. The lockwork was entirely mounted on coil and wire springs.

In Russia, during the '50s, conventional Nagant seven-shot service revolvers, chambered in 7.62mm, were commonly customized and used for target shooting, in accordance with ISU regulations. Then, a

Smith & Wesson swing-out revolvers chambered in all classical calibers for small and medium frame models. Their "Ruby Extra" and "Llama" trade marks are still at work. Along the years, their workmanship has considerably varied, from excellent to fair. For instance, when this writer shifted from the

ber. Two years after, Mateba issued a "M 2006" revolver, featuring a choice of new grips and a sliding trigger, instead of the conventional rotating one.

The year 1989 was that of the light and compact seven-shot fixed barrel "2007 S", with a special small-diameter cylinder fitted backwards in the Ergal frame, so as to reduce length as much as possible.

Finally, at IWA 97, in Germany, Mateba disclosed their most recent achievement, the "Unica 6 Autorevolver," chambered in 357 Magnum, with a six-shot capacity. The Unica 6 is, in fact, an "automatic revolver", in line with the British Webley-Fosbery designed in 1895 and continually perfected up to the death of the inventor, in 1907.

In the Mateba design, the hammer can be thumb-cocked, or cocked by pulling the trigger for the first shot, the gun being recoil operated, shooting single action thereafter. The Mateba Unica 6 is said to be much more reliable than its British ancestor

Weihrauch's six-shot Vindicator 357 Magnum heavy barrel revolver, marketed in 1993.

special competition revolver, the TOZ 49, chambered in the same 7.62mm Nagant caliber, featuring a six-shot cylinder, micrometer sights, an adjustable sight radius from 7.3 to 7.7 inch target grips and a trigger fully adjustable from 3 to 4 pounds, with a .02" to .06" travel, was developed. This excellent target revolver is still made and exported by Techmash export, under the TOZ 96 nomenclature, in 32 S&W Long.

The two current Spanish revolver manufacturers are Llama-Gabilondo, located in Vitoria and Astra-Unceta y Cia, from Guernica. The Gabilondo company never stopped making derivatives of

P-08 Luger to 38 Special revolvers, forty years ago, for shooting ISU Sport pistol, he started with a six-inch Ruby Extra, costing then, one-third of the "K-38 Masterpiece" price and practically as accurate, but, of course, not as sumptuously finished.

Astra revolvers use the conventional Smith & Wesson double cylinder lock, but the mainspring is of the coil type,

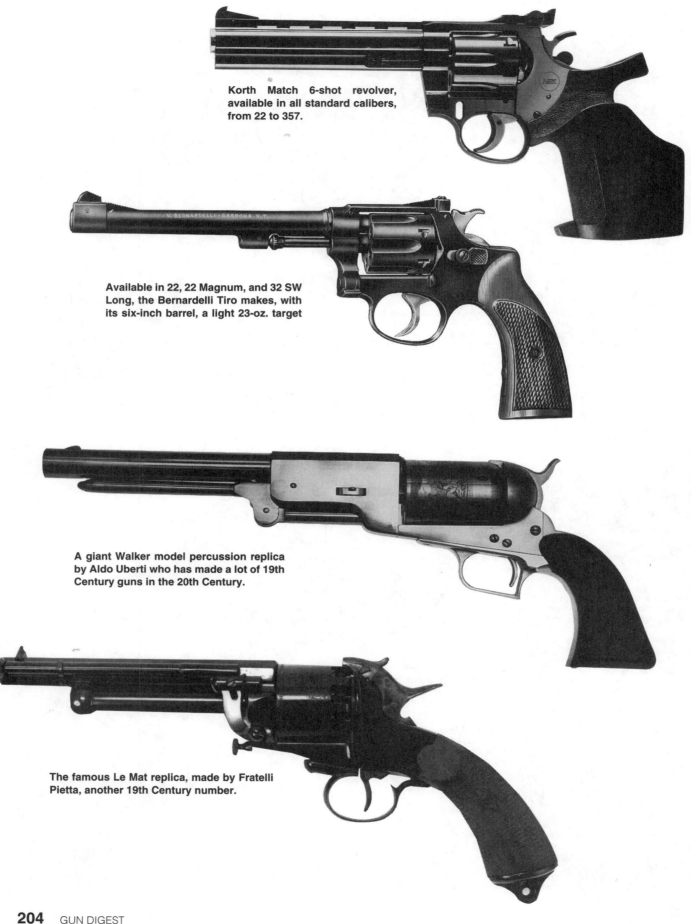

Korth Match 6-shot revolver, available in all standard calibers, from 22 to 357.

Available in 22, 22 Magnum, and 32 SW Long, the Bernardelli Tiro makes, with its six-inch barrel, a light 23-oz. target

A giant Walker model percussion replica by Aldo Uberti who has made a lot of 19th Century guns in the 20th Century.

The famous Le Mat replica, made by Fratelli Pietta, another 19th Century number.

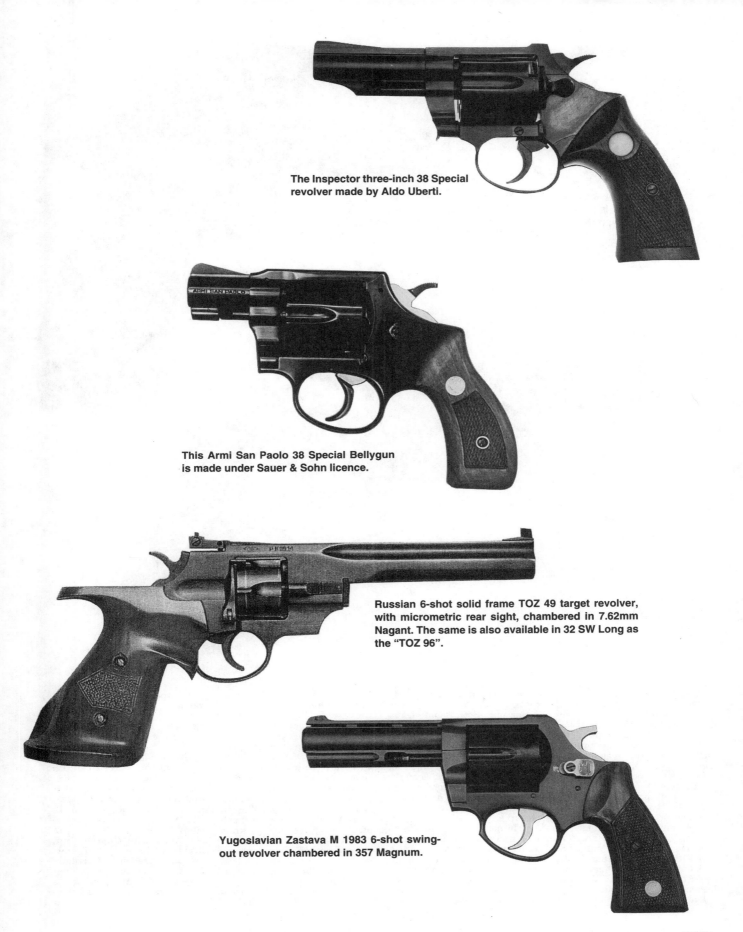

The Inspector three-inch 38 Special revolver made by Aldo Uberti.

This Armi San Paolo 38 Special Bellygun is made under Sauer & Sohn licence.

Russian 6-shot solid frame TOZ 49 target revolver, with micrometric rear sight, chambered in 7.62mm Nagant. The same is also available in 32 SW Long as the "TOZ 96".

Yugoslavian Zastava M 1983 6-shot swing-out revolver chambered in 357 Magnum.

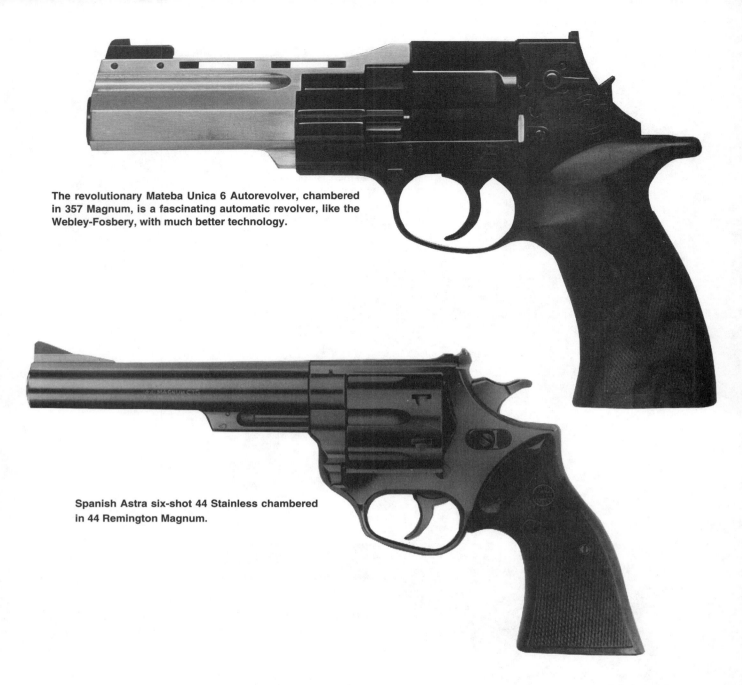

The revolutionary Mateba Unica 6 Autorevolver, chambered in 357 Magnum, is a fascinating automatic revolver, like the Webley-Fosbery, with much better technology.

Spanish Astra six-shot 44 Stainless chambered in 44 Remington Magnum.

fitted in a grip ring featuring several countersunk recesses of different depth so the mainspring compression can be varied to improve trigger pull. This is very clever and, according to my experience, it enables an easy trigger adjustment. These Astra swing-out revolvers are chambered in all classical calibers, from the 22 Long Rifle to the 44 Remington Magnum, and exported the world over.

As far as styles and mechanisms for the future are concerned, the Kora, Manurhin MR 73, Bernardelli, San Paolo, Zastava, Astra and Llama can be considered as mere variations of the basic Smith & Wesson system, principally intend-

ed to reduce the manufacturing costs, or to improve the double action pull. Both Renato Gamba's Trident and Aldo Uberti's Inspector are similar attempts, based on Colt competitive models.

Such a trend results not from a lack of inventive spirit, but from the customer's approach, requiring a classical gun at a better price, or with a smoother pull.

The double-action Arminius has more personality, while starting also from the Smith & Wesson lock, because it involves as much technical simplification as possible, without any consideration to the appearance, in order to produce a

low cost reliable and accurate gun. In this connection, both the Czech ZKR 551 and the Russian TOZ 49, are meritorious and successful designs, intended to produce original competition revolvers in accordance with the ISU applicable regulations, at a good price.

The Manurhin MR 93 and MR 96 new designs, and follow some of the late Dan Wesson concepts with, perhaps, a touch of improved technology, while the MR 38 and Korth Match, are probably the most sophisticated (and expensive) modern target revolvers intended for ISU sport competition.

And now, how are they comparing with their American

counterparts? Not so bad, we would say, but certainly not better, as the revolver technology is bottoming, on both sides of the ocean, for quite many years.

It is obvious, from this survey, that the Mateba Unica 6 is, by far, the most original European design on the market and the first, since the courageous efforts of William B. Ruger and Dan Wesson, twenty-five years ago, to bring in something truly different. But, beside the technological prowess, what need does it actually answer? The answer to that question doubtless describes the future of the European revolver. ●

by **LARRY S. STERETT**

HANDLOADING UPDATE

Midway's Deluxe Front Rest helps out on the bench.

Handloading continues to grow and it would be difficult to determine between shotshell or metallics which is growing faster. Cowboy Action Shooting has given a spurt to handloading for older handgun calibers, such as 38-40, 44-40, and 45 Colt, while Sporting Clays has definitely given a boost to shotshell reloading. Equipment continues to improve, and for computer literates, more and more programs are becoming available.

BLOUNT/RCBS always has something special for handloaders and this year is no exception. Five new three-way cutters, 6mm, 25, 6.5mm, 270 and 7mm, are available for the RCBS Trim Pro trimmers, power or manual, and there are seven new X-Sizer dies in calibers from 22-250 Remington to 308 Winchester. These X-Sizer dies replace standard full-length sizing dies in said calibers and are designed to permit repeated full length resizing of the case without shortening it or causing metal build-up in the neck. Only rifle calibers are now available. Full length, neck and trim dies for the 260 Remington have been added to the Group A line of RCBS dies, and there's a new mould (#82087) to cast bullets for the 50 Action Express cartridge. Casting a 340-grain SWC bullet, this mould can probably also be used to cast bullets for the 500 Lindbaugh cartridge.

RCBS has a new RC-130 Mechanical Scale that features a precision-machined aluminum beam and steel-on-steel pivots. Capable of weighing to 130 grains +0.1 grain, the RC-130 has an ABS polymer base and index bar, plus a newly-designed non-static powder pan with integral hanger. The PowderMaster Electronic Powder Dispenser is now available in a 220 VAC version with both it and the 120 VAC model requiring the use of a RCBS Powder Pro Electronic Scale.

The really big news is the RCBS.LOAD Reloading Software, which requires a 486DX 66Mz PC with 16mb RAM and at least a Windows 95 operating system. Required hard drive space is 5mb with up to 14mb if all optional libraries are purchased, and a color monitor with 1024x768 pixel resolution is recommended. RCBS.LOAD has a database of some 269 different cartridges. Electronic versions of the Speer Reloading Manual #12, RCBS Cast Bullet Manual, and Accurate Loading Guide #1 are including in the system, and an index is provided to show sources for data on over 450 standard and wildcat cartridges. Other features include a kinetic energy calculator, minimum rate of twist chart, powder burning rate chart and a pressure assignments list.

DILLON PRECISION PRODUCTS always seems to have a few new items for handloaders, with their biggest news being the SL 900 Shotshell Reloader. Actually being shipped now, the SL 900 features a 25-pound capacity shot hopper and electronic case feeding system, to mention only a few of the features. Other new items include RL 450 Upgrade Kits that allow any owner of a Dillon RL 450 press to upgrade it to RL 550B status, including the detachable toolhead feature, for about half the cost of a new reloader. The upgrade can be done at one time, or in stages. There are also Machine Maintenance Kits that can be obtained strictly for cleaning and lubing, or with spare parts kits, to keep the

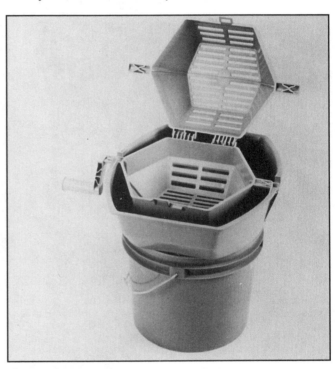

The Midway Rotary Sifter cleans up the problems of brass polishing, simply and quickly.

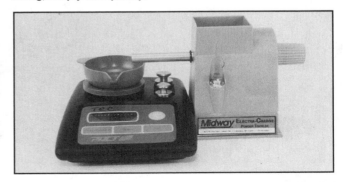

Running off AA batteries, this Midway powder trickler can be used with all types of smokeless powders, starts and stops instantly.

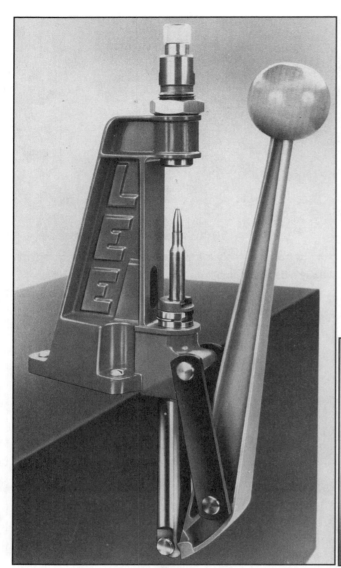

new rifle die sets, plus a 58-piece Outfitter's Sports Utility Tool Set that could be handy for adjustments on loading equipment. The bullet moulds are for the 38-55, 43 Mauser, 44 Russian and the 69 Musket cartridges and all turn out flat base bullets. The rifle die sets include a two-die set for the 260 Remington cartridge, while the others are three-die sets for the 45-90, 44 Russian, and 45 Schofield. The latter two have carbide sizing dies.

Handloaders never seem to have enough loading manuals available, and there are several new ones available. Dealers handling HODGDON powders should have copies of Hodgdon's new 2nd edition Cowboy Action Data with suggested smokeless and Pyrodex loads for popular cowboy calibers, including shotshells. Hodgdon also has a separate Pyrodex data booklet, and a Basic Reloaders Manual 1998, with loading data on popular rifle, handgun, and shotgun car-

the Loading Guide from Accurate Arms for $12.95, but it is good. VIHTAVUORI has a new Reloading Guide For Rifle And Handguns 1-98, which replaces all rifle and handgun loading data in previous guides 1-6. This guide is almost as thick as the old Ideal handbooks of the 1930's and '40's, and definitely covers more cartridges. It even has some data for Cowboy Action cartridges. One great feature of this guide is the Burning Rate Chart just inside the front cover; it covers 107 powders.

Vectan powders by NOBELSPORT of France are now available through ADCO dealers. Two small data booklets are available - Reloading for 12 gauge shotshells, and IPSC SP2 Practical Reloading Charges for handgun cartridges. Cartridges for which SP2 loading data is provided range from the 7.63mm Mauser to the 45 ACP, including the 7.65mm French Long and the 357 SIG. There is also a Nobel Sport Handloading Manual, which is much larger and complete. Costing less than a double sawbuck, it provides loading data for rifles cartridges from the 22 Hornet to the 460 Weatherby Magnum and the 32 ACP to the 50 Action Express, each with a dimensioned drawing. There are chapters covering a variety of handloading topics, such as powders, equipment, wildcats, case forming, available die sets including Hornady, Lee, Lyman, Outils Lynx, RCBS, Redding, and Simplex, sources for obsolete cartridge cases, and a host of other useful information for handloaders.

S.D. MEACHAM TOOL & HARDWARE out in Idaho manufactures Pope-style re/decappers for cartridges in calibers from 22 to 45. Designed mainly for the older cartridges used in single shot rifles of yesteryear, such as the 25-20 Single Shot or the 40-72 Winchester, the re/decappers can be built for more modern calibers, if needed. Using RCBS shell holders and interchangable decapping rods, the tools are polished, with a color casehardened finish.

MIDWAY, just a few miles from the University of Missouri, has supplied handloaders for

To celebrate their 40th Anniversary, Lee Precision is providing a free Lee Reloader Press to purchasers of Modern Reloading by Richard Lee. It's a great deal.

loaders in factory-new condition. Strong Mounts to raise Dillon loaders to new heights, and Toolhead Stands are available, and there is a new electronic scale, the D-Terminator. The D-Terminator weighs in grains or grams, with a capacity of 1,200 grains, and the weights are displayed out to 0.1 grain, in large, easy to see digits.

FORSTER PRODUCTS case trimmer has been one of the best on the market for many years, and two new models have been introduced. Designed for large cases, the new models include the Classic 50 which will handle such cases as the 416 Rigby, 500 Nitro Express, and a host of the big bore black powder cartridges, and the 50 BMG Trimmer to handle the really big bore. Collets and pilots for the Classic 50 trimmer are available separately, but the 50

BMG trimmer comes complete with a pilot and an integrated rim holding device.

LEE PRECISION is celebrating its 40th Anniversary, and has an Anniversary Pack. The customer can purchase a copy of Modern Reloading, by Richard Lee, and receive a Lee Reloader Press FREE. It doesn't get much better than that. The Classic Lee Loader, which Richard Lee starting turning out in his garage 40 years ago, is available in nearly three dozen rifle and handgun calibers, but unfortunately not for any shotshells as was the original. The current version is a bit fancier, and comes in a plastic case in place of a cardboard carton, but it still can turn out a good handload at a decent price.

LYMAN PRODUCTS has four new bullet moulds and four

tridges. ACCURATE arms dealers should have copies of The Accurate Solution for Reloading 1998, with data on many popular rifle and handgun cartridges, plus shotshells. It doesn't contain nearly as much data or information as

For handloaders with a 1292 Thumbler, Midway has a Moly Ultra-Coat Deluxe pack; there's also a kit that includes the 1292.

more than two decades, but recently they have increased the number of items bearing the Midway label. Among the several new items, we like the Midway LoadMAP for the 45 ACP cartridges. Featuring 46 different bullets ranging in weight from 185 to 260 grains with up to ten different powders this LoadMAP provides loading data in a logical manner. Pressure differences between bullets having the same weight, but different configurations varied up to 11 percent when using the same powder charges. Printed in full color, the LoadMAP has 475 easy-to-read graphs, and is a worthwhile investment for anyone reloading the 45 ACP. A LoadMAP for the 9mm Parabellum (Luger) may be available by the time you read this.

Moly-coated bullets are the 'in' thing now. Not exactly new, such bullets seem to have made the first serious commercial appearance at the 1997 SHOT Show. Now Midway has a kit available so handloaders can coat their own bullets easily. The Moly Ultra-Coat Ultimate consists of a Model 1292 Midway Thumber, two extra bowls, and 8-oz. of Molybdenum Disulfide.

Molybdenum is an element discovered in 1778, but not actively mined until nearly a century later. Looking somewhat like lead, which explains the name from the Greek "Molybdos" meaning lead-like, it has a high melting point - 4,730 degrees Fahrenheit. Various grades of the refined moly are added as alloying agents in steels and a host of other items, including paints, synthetic rubber, inks, lubricants and even in computer chips. Molybdenum Disulfide is a lubricant with a high degree of lubricity and a high melting point. Applied to bullets it forms a friction-reducing, protective coating which reduces barrel wear and bore fouling. The result is more consistent velocities and increased accuracy!

For reloaders who own a 1292 tumbler, Midway has the Moly Ultra-Coat Deluxe pack which includes only the two extra bowls and eight ounces of Moly.

Midway recommends a different bowl be used for each type of bullet coated.

Every handloader needs a powder trickler if much reloading of metallics is done, and most of us started with a small finger-operated model. Midway has a new Electra-Charge Powder Trickler that runs off a set of AA batteries. Push-button operated, the Trickler is gear-driven, comes with a wide, stable, removable base, and is suitable for all smokeless powders. The unit can also be operated manually, if desired.

Any reloader who uses a case tumbler to polish brass cases knows the problem of sorting out

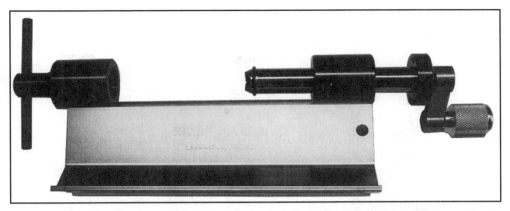

Forster Products has two "Big 50" case trimmers. This is the Classic 50 suitable for big bore rifle calibers such as the 416 Rigby, and 500 Nitro Express. The second is specific to teh 50 BMG cartridge.

the polished product. It can be done with a pan-type sifter, but Midway has a new Rotary Sifter that is a gem. Constructed of heavy duty polymer, the Sifter comes with a special funnel-type adapter than permits attachment to any 3 1/2 or 5 gallon bucket. The Sifter is locked into special cradles on the sides of the adapter, and the cases and media poured directly into it. The halves of the Sifter are secured and the unit rotated, causing the media to fall into the bucket, leaving the polished cases in the hopper. It's simple to use, fast to operate, and the media can be left in the bucket. Available with or without a 3 1/2 gallon bucket, the Midway Rotary Sifter comes with the bucket adapter, 8-oz. of Midway Brass Polish, and 7 pounds of corn medium.

MULTI-SCALE CHARGE LTD. has been producing Universal Charge bars for MEC shotshell loaders for nearly 25 years and they've just made an excellent product even better by providing a Free Powder Baffle with each charge bar purchase. Two models, the C/CS for single stage MEC loaders and the D/DS for the progressive loaders, and either will handle both lead and steel shot. Capable of handling all gauges, the Multi-Scale bar replaces 42 powder bushings and 23 standard charge bars. Powder capacity is from 12 to 55 grains, and shot capacity from 1/2-ounce to 2 1/4 ounces of lead or 1 1/2 ounces of steel shot. For those handloaders having most of the powder bushings, a 'shuttle charge bar' is available which is adjustable for the shot charges, but accepts the regular MEC-type bushings.

SHOOTING CHRONY INC. turns out a line of economical chronographs that will measure velocities from 30 to 7,000 feet/second. Capable of being ready to measure in approximately two minutes or less, the Chrony comes in at least a dozen versions, all upgradable at slight additional cost if desired. There are even models for measuring

The RCBS.LOAD Reloading Software is one of the most extensive such programs available today. Optional libraries can to prchase to add, with the Speer Reloading Manual #12, RCBS Cast Bullet Manual, and Accurate Loading Guide #1 already included.

paintballs and arrows; the paintball version comes with a fold-down splatguard and gun cradle. The latest feature is a Ballistic Chrony Printer that will fit the Alpha, Beta, and Gamma Shooting Chrony models, plus the Master Chrony models. Featuring a 14-foot interface cable, the printer runs on

four AA batteries, and will print low, high and average velocities, extreme spread and standard deviation. It will print as you shoot, or by retrieving afterwards from memory. All Chrony models will mount on a camera tripod, or can be placed on a table or bench, and come with a five year limited warranty.

Three-way cutters for the RCBS Trim Pro are now available in five additional calibers from 6mm to 7mm.

shooting ranges, and smaller firms that want to get into commercial loading of metallic handgun and rifle cartridges. Reamers, rollers, and boxing machines, and now a Pistol Brass Separation Machine. Available in two production rates, up to 20,000 cases per hour, the machines funnel the cases into eight 5-gallon buckets. Everything smaller than 380 Auto, and that includes 22 rimfire, dirt, etc., goes into one bucket, while the other seven collect cases up to the 45 Colt.

at least a couple of European manufacturers of such loading equipment was exhibiting at the 1998 SHOT Show in Las Vegas. Available ready to load shotshells in 12, 16, 20, 24, 28, or 32 gauges, plus 410-bore, or 8mm or 9mm on special order, the machines by BSN INTERNATIONAL S.R.L. of Brescia, Italy, can be obtained to produce the entire case or to load pre-primed hulls. The complete set-up to produce empty shotshell hulls can turn out 6,000 finished hulls per hour, while the two loading machines can turn out 4,000 (Futura 95) or 2,500 (Jolly) loaded shells per hour using pre-primed cases. For a large gun club wanting to turn out loaded shotshells in volume, or a small specialty shotshell loader, the Jolly model would be ideal. Self-contained, with built-in

RCBS X-Sizer dies, shown here as a cut-away, are designed to permit repeated full length resizing without causing metal build up or shortening.

Shooting Chrony has a Bullet Ballistics Program hand-loading PC owners might find useful. Available in two versions, one for DOS and one for Windows, the program has reloading data for hundreds of cartridges, with bullet and powder selections, ballistic tables and graphs, coefficients, diagrams, and more. It does require an IBM 486 with 4mb RAM and 10mb hard disk free space.

NECO has a slightly different method for application of Molybdenum Disulfide (MOS2, if you remember your chemistry.) to bullets. Designed for use on the bullets in already loaded cartridges, commercial or handloads, it provides the same advantages as with bullets treated prior to loading, reduced metal and bore fouling, longer barrel life, etc. Called Bullet-Slide, the NECO process consists of inserting the bullet of the loaded round, rimfire or centerfire, into the center of the Bullet-Slide applicator and twisting it around enough to leave a thin film on the bullet. (A minimal amount of "Moly" is required to produce big results.) Bullet-Slide consists of 1.2 ounces of laboratory grade MOS2 paste with an applicator as the BS-30, or with a anodized aluminum base as the BS-60. The only difference is the base, as the paste and applicator are the same in both versions.

REDDING RELOADING has a new Competition Model 10X-Pistol Powder Measure that surpasses the renowned 3BR and BR-30 Match Grade Measures. Designed to meter charges from 1 to 25 grains with extreme precision, the 10-X has a reduced diameter metering cavity with

hemispherical shape, zero backlash micrometer, and adjustable powder baffle. It can be mounted on many progressive reloading presses, and the drum is reversible. Also new from the Redding/Saeco firm is the Type S bushing-style full length sizing die for 48 popular cartridges. Coupled with Competition Shellholders, the new die can provide increased accurate adjustment. (The Com...Shellholders come five to a set in 0.002-inch increments.) For 338/340 reloaders, there's a new 338 carbide sizing button to reduce button drag.

SCHARCH MFG., INC. produces equipment for commercial ammunition companies, law enforcement agencies,

(223 Remington cases will drop in with the 380 Auto, if such cases are in the batch being sorted.) The sorter operates on 110 volts, and efficiency is approximately 90 percent, with a relatively low noise level, according to the manufacturer.

Shotshell manufacuers, or rather loaders of shotshells are becoming more common, and

checking indicators, the Jolly is automatic in all cycles, with one loaded shell produced with each stroke of the machine. It can be fitted with printer and packer machines, if desired.

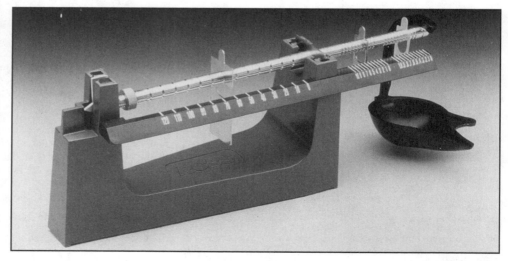

RCBS RC-130 Mechanical Scale has a capacity of 130 grains 0.1 grain. The base is an ABS polymer.

French-produced Vectan powders for handloaders can be put to use with data from the new New Sport Handloading Manual.

lubricants tend to hold any dust which settle on them, and wiping it away doesn't always do the job. One of the best lubricants this handloader has used is the new White Lightning by LEISURE INOVATIONS INC. Available as Outdoor Gear Lube and Gun Lube, White Lightning is waterproof when dry and self-cleaning, which means dirt literally falls off items lubed with it. Parts need cleaned with a degreaser prior to coating with White Lightning, and Gun Lube is better than Gear Lube to use on press rams, due to being slightly lighter-bodied. Invented for use on racing bike chains, which get really dirty, White Lightning should be applied warm, but instructions come with each bottle.

Handloaders needing data on some of the obsolete British cartridges may be able to purchase a Rifle Chamber and Cartridge Sizes chart from dealers handling Kynoch ammunition. A reproduction of the 1913 Gun Trade standardising chart, it covers British Sporting Rifle cartridges from the 600 Nitro Express down to the 375/303, plus the 22 rimfire dimensions. There is also a set of two charts providing an illustration and description of the cartridges, along with other ballistic data. The dimension chart and the ammunition set did cost a sawbuck each, but well worth it.

JANE'S AMMUNITION HANDBOOK, 6th Edition, provides information of military small arms cartridges from the 4.5x39mm Russian to the 15.2mm Steyr AMR, but no reloading data. Basic dimensions are listed, along with specifications, development and description information. Headstamps coverage and a listing of manufacturers is included. The volume is expensive, and the data on cannon, field artillery, coastal guns, and mortars is not needed by handloaders, but the small arms ammunition is useful.

Handloading devotees continue to increase in number, as does new equipment and information. Tong tools are not much in evidence, and dippers for powders are seldom used, as technology provides better equipment to load more cartridges at a faster rate. It's a great time to be a handloader. ●

The Futura 95 is larger, requiring more floor space, but it can produce up to 1,500 additional loaded shells per hour. Considering the Jolly can produce 20,000 loaded shells per eight hours, assuming no problems and the hoppers are kept filled, it would be ideal for a small business.

SIERRA, 'The Bulletsmiths,' now have the 4th edition of their reloading manuals on CD-ROM. The rifle and handgun volumes are both included on one CD, and the cost is less than that of the two printed volumes. It does require a 486 PC or higher, 8mb of RAM, a CD-ROM Drive (2x), audio board, 256-color or better display (640 x 480 VGA), headphones or speaker, mouse or compatible pointing device, and access to the Internet is recommended. Also included in the program is the Burris Varminter shooting game.

The OLD WESTERN SCROUNGER has a new edition of Wiederladen, the German-language reloading manual. Although the text is in German, the loading data is provided in grams and grains, and the bullet brands include Hornady, RWS, Geco, H & N, Sierra, Speer, and Remington, depending on the caliber. Data is provided for rifle calibers from the 17 Remington to the 460 Weatherby Magnum, handgun calibers from the 221 Fireball to the 45 Colt, and 12, 16, 20, 28 gauge and 410-bore shotshells. Illustrated with both black and white and full color photographs, Wiederladen is an excellent data source if you have access to German powders.

The rams on loading presses sometimes gall, and keeping dust and grime off the moving parts can be a problem. Regular

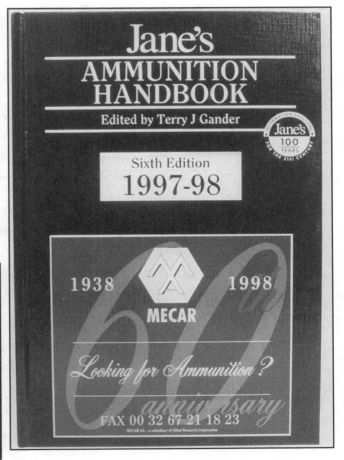

Not a loading manual, but a good source of information on many military cartridges is Jane's Ammunition Handbook, now available in the 6th edition.

Midway's new LoadMAP features 476 different load combinations for the 45 ACP cartridge, stays flat when opened.

by HOLT BODINSON

AMMUNITION, BALLISTICS AND COMPONENTS

AGUILA

In Mexico, the Aguila brand of shotshells, centerfire and rimfire is dominant and, through an aggressive R&D and export effort, the company (partially owned by Remington) plans on making inroads in sporting ammunition circles far beyond their traditional domestic market. Imported into the U.S. by Centurion Ordnance of San Antonio, Aguila is offering some unique items this year-- the 22 SSS, a super heavy 60-grain 22 LR load at 960 fps; the 22 Super Magnum LR, generating 1750 fps with a 30-grain HP bullet; and the 45 ACP High Power cartridge propelling a 117grain HP alloy bullet at 1450 fps. The latter is designed to both give superior penetration against hard surfaces and yet break into 3 or 4 separate projectiles when encountering soft targets. The 22 LR loads are assembled using the latest Eley technology and machin-

ery. Should be great and refreshingly new rimfire ammo.

ALLIANT

Extending their successful RELODER powder series, Alliant is announcing the introduction of Reloder 25, a very slow burning, temperature insensitive, heavy magnum rifle powder designed for the likes of the Weatherby 30-378, and Lazzeroni magnums. Not to be outdone in shotshell propellants, the company is fielding a new STEEL shotgun powder especially formulated to provide superior velocity and pressure ratios for steel shot loads in the 10 and 12-gauges. And, if you cruise the Internet, Alliant offers an interactive web site at http://reloading.atk.com.

AMMO DEPOT

If you enjoy fussing with odd-ball calibers, Ammo Depot is a great place to find both loaded cartridges and components at very attractive prices. Their latest catalog lists gems like moly-coated bullets for the 43 Spanish and 8mm Nambu and custom loads for the 7.5 MAS, 351 SL and 455 Webley. How cheap? Twenty rounds of impossible-to-find 8x54 Krag-Jorgensen will run you $23. That's cheap.

A-SQUARE

A-Square's indomitable Art Alphin always keeps the cartridge world a'humming. This year, A-Square has made a run of 405 Winchester service and proof ammunition in anticipation that someone, somewhere, will shortly be reviving the Winchester Model 1895 in that much sought-after, historic caliber. No gun, yet, so if you're the lucky owner of an original

The new year witnesses an increasing number of strategic alliances between the major ammunition manufacturers and the larger bullet-making specialty houses. Olin-Winchester and Nosler have been particularly aggressive in the development of their Partition handgun bullet line as well as improved Partition Gold and Ballistic Silvertip rifle bullets. Remington has integrated Hornady and Swift bullets into its lines. Federal is drawing upon Sierra, Nosler, Woodleigh and Trophy Bonded for bullets.

"Not invented here" is no longer heard in the engineering and design departments of the majors. Bullet coatings designed to reduce fouling and bullet deformation have become the rage across the whole industry. Molybdenum disulfide is in the driver's seat for the moment, but that may change given the amount of research now underway.

The down-the-road future for small arms ammunition is getting intriguing. The U.S. military seems intent on developing shoulder-fired 20mm "smart" ammunition for its next generation of combination 5.56/20mm rifles. "Smart" means that if an adversary were hunkered down in back of a stone wall, a GI could measure the distance to the wall with his laser sight and with the push of a button, fuse the 20mm projectile to deliver an air burst when it reaches the other side of the wall. Velocities for the new 20mm ammunition could exceed 4000 fps. The cost? Ah, well, but it only takes one round, not 100,000, to account for one of the enemy or so the argument goes. Stay tuned.

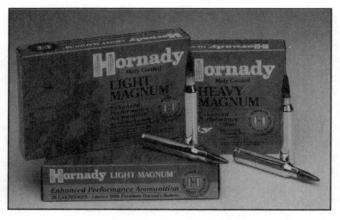

Moly ammunition from Hornady—they're enhancing the enhanced.

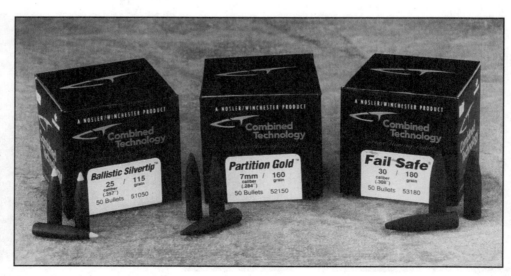

Combining technological assets, Nosler and Winchester will be offering Ballistic Silvertip, Partition Gold, and FailSafe in loaded ammunition and as component bullets.

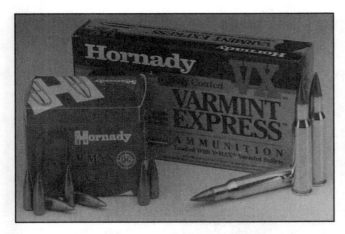

Moly-coated Red Tip V-Max bullets and VX Varmint Express by Hornady makes life tougher on the smaller critters.

Black Hills is now offering the Hornady V-Max bullet in its varmint ammunition, as if Hornady wasn't doing enough.

More Match stuff—this from Hornady in the Red Box line, molycoated.

PMC and Sierra are teaming up—here it's with Match King bullets in 223 and 303.

1895, A-Square has loads of ammo and unprimed brass just sitting there.

The voluminous 300 Pegasus cartridge is up and flying. It consumes 125-grains-plus of powder at each sitting, but it promises to generate 3450-3500 fps with a 180-grain bullet. And that's flying.

As a member of SAAMI, A-Square has successfully promoted the industry-wide standardization of a number of interesting cartridges recently, including the 6.5-08 A-Square, 6.5-06 A-Square, 7mm STW, 338-06 A-Square, 358 Shooting Times A-Square, 405 Winchester, 470 Capstick and 500 A-Square. And on a nostalgic note, A-Square has made a run of 400 Whelen brass designed to be headspaced off the mouth of the case for initial fire-forming.

BARNES

The X-Bullet finally got a coat. The new XLC coating is reported to reduce normal X-Bullet fouling by 40%, heat buildup

by 50% and provide 10% greater accuracy.

BELL BRASS/MAST TECHNOLOGY

What began as a trickle between major production runs is now becoming a stream of hard-to-find component brass from Jim Bell's Mast Technology. Available this year are 404 Jeffrey formed or cylindrical brass with blank heads to make cases like the Imperial, Jamison and G&A designs; 416 Rigby formed or cylindrical brass; 45-90, 45-3 1/4, 45-120, 50-70 and 50-90 formed cases; Weatherby 378 formed or cylindrical brass for the Weatherby and A-Square magnum calibers; H&H cylindrical brass for such numbers as the 458 Lott, 358 STA, and 475 OKH; and fully formed cases for the 470 NE, 500 NE, 43 Mauser; and 338 Lapua. Their website address is: www.bell-lammo.com.

BERGER BULLETS

Building on its extensive line of benchrest and varmint bullets, Berger is introducing a new line of 7mm and 30-caliber big game hunting bullets and is offering small-batch molycoating services to shooters who want to try the process on their current brand of bullets. Other new bullet introductions include 30- and 35-grain 224-caliber Hornets; 115-grain 257caliber VLD; 140-grain 6.5mm; and 168-grain 7mm. A point of interest is Berger's recommendation that shooters use KROIL and USP Bore Paste to clean moly-fouled bores.

BIG BORE BULLETS OF ALASKA

A radical new design coming out of the state that hosts those big Kodiak bears is a heavy copper-jacketed, 375- or 458 caliber bonded core bullet that features a series of serrations around the circumference of the ogive. According to its design-

er, these cuts initiate expansion just behind the tip keeping the nose of the bullet intact to further drive open the expanding body.

BLACK HILLS AMMUNITION

Black Hills continues to take advantage of specialized niche markets by providing highly accurate ammunition at very competitive prices. In the absence of a local stocking dealer, the company will sell and ship case lots at retail prices. Added this year to its cowboy action shooting line are the 115-grain 32-20 and 230-grain 44 Colt loads-the latter being historically correct for reproductions of early percussion conversion revolvers. Still popular but seldom seen on dealers' shelves, the 32 H&R Magnum is getting a boost this year with the company loading of an 85-grain Hornady XTP at 1100 fps.

There are a number of new handgun and match rifle offerings but possibly the most interesting development is that Norma has contracted with Black Hills Ammunition to produce a line of moly-coated ammunition for them in the U.S. Initial Norma loadings offered will include the 223, 22-250, 308 as well as 9mm, 40- and 45caliber pistol rounds. See them on the web at www.blackhills.com

BLOUNT

Blount International, parent of CCI and Speer, announced the acquisition of Federal Cartridge. For the immediate future, Blount indicates that the three ammunition units will continue to be managed and operated as separate entities.

CCI

With the appearance of sporting magnum cases holding 100 plus grains of powder, the

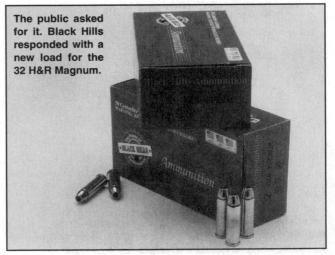

The public asked for it. Black Hills responded with a new load for the 32 H&R Magnum.

folks who brought us the first magnum primer, the CCI 250, felt it was time to go upscale with a super magnum primer. They're calling it the 251-MAG-X. It should be quite a sparkplug.

CORBON

When it comes to high performance defensive and hunting handgun ammunition, CorBon continues to be a leader to watch. Matching bonded-core bullets tailored to each caliber loaded with powders generating the highest possible velocity, CEO Peter Pi continues to surprise the competition. New offerings this year include six new loadings for the 454 Casull ranging from flat shooting 265grain pills at 1800 fps to 320- and 360-grain "Penetrator" slugs that carry a heavy full copper jacket over a linotype hard lead core and seem quite effective on Cape buffalo and other macho species. In fact, "Penetrator" bullets are now loaded across the-board in Cor-Bon's 44 Magnum, 45 Colt Magnum +P, and 357 Magnum offerings.

The 45 Colt Magnum +P, designed for Ruger, Freedom Arms, Colt Anaconda and T/C guns only, really performs with 265-grain bonded bullets at 1350 fps. A new cartridge, the 440 CorBon Magnum, combines the excellent ballistic coefficient of the 44 caliber bullets with the case capacity of the 50AE--like a 260-grain bonded core bullet at 1700 fps. For the single shot pistol hunter, Cor-Bon is introducing hot performing, bonded-core loads, packed ten to a blister pack, for the 7-30 Waters, 30-30, 35 Rem., 45-70, 30-06, 308 and 7mm-08. Finally the busy bees at CorBon are marketing another new product-the BeeSafe-a self-defense, frangible bullet load that contains shot behind a penetrating lead nose slug.

Swift A-Frame™ bullets mushroom quickly in a controlled manner, with maximum expansion, and 95%+ weight retention.

ELDORADO-PMC

Getting into the swing of cowboy action shooting, PMC is introducing seven cowboy action loads featuring hard cast lead bullets at standard velocities. In addition to the popular handgun calibers, PMC has added the 30-30 with a 170-grain LFP bullet at 1500 fps and the 45-70, sporting a 405-grain LFP at 1250 fps. Two new match loads are making a debut featuring Sierra MatchKing bullets—the venerable 303 British and the 223. In its 12-gauge shotshell line, PMC is

Just right for the 7.62 Tokarev, 30 Mauser, and 30 Luger: Sierra's 30-caliber 85-grain soft points.

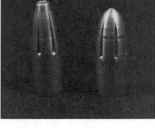

Big Bore Bullets of Alaska serrates the ogive of their bonded core bullets.

Now there's a 25-caliber 100 grain HPBT MatchKing to suit loyal 25 caliber shooters.

adding a 3-3/4 dram, 1-1/4 oz, Heavy Field Load and a one-ounce #7-1/2 and #8 Lite Clay Target. And in response to the growing popularity of compact handguns chambered for the 32 ACP, the company is fielding a new 68-grain JHP loading at 880 fps.

FEDERAL

With the first waterfowl season permitting the use of Federal's Tungsten-Iron behind it, Federal is launching a new Tungsten-Polymer, 12-gauge shot load in #4's and 6's. Designed to be safe in any shot-gun bore, the Tungsten-Polymer shot is designed for 20-50 yard shots on waterfowl and upland game species while the 30-70 yard Tungsten-Iron waterfowl loads were restricted to bores approved for steel shot. Canada has already approved the new shot for waterfowling and the U.S. is expected to follow.

On the upland trail, a new Tungsten-Iron 12 gauge 3-inch turkey load will be fielded featuring 1- 3/8 oz. of #4s. Particularly impressive this year is Federal's further integration of Trophy Bonded and Woodleigh

(top) The 100-grain Nosler 6.5 mm spitzer was bound to come and here it is.

Weldcore brand premium bullets into its rifle lines with some real surprises like a 55-grain Trophy Bonded Bear Claw pill in the 22-250 and 220 Swift, a 140-grainer in the 6.5x55 and a 150-grainer in the 7mmSTW. Two interesting additions to Federal's High Energy line include a 300-grain Trophy Bonded Bear Claw souped up to 2700 fps in the 375 H&H, and a 180-grain Bear Claw in the 303 British clocking 2590 fps.

Casting about for a superior projectile for 12-gauge rifled slug guns, Federal and Barnes cooperated in the development of a saboted 1 oz., solid copper HP slug that, according to Federal, shows greater expansion and weight retention than any slug on the market. Low-recoil slug and #2 pellet shotgun loads have been added to the personal "defense" line. And being of modern mind, Federal has installed a great interactive web site and catalog at: www.federalcartridge.com.

GARRETT

If you ever want to win a "my bullet will penetrate further than yours" bet, be sure to load up with Randy Garrett's factory 44 Magnum or 45-70 ammunition. You'll win the bet. This past year I sent some of Garrett's 310-grain, super hard cast bullet loads to a prominent ammunition maker which was making some distinct claims for the superior penetrating quality of their latest 44 Magnum bullet. You guessed it. Garrett's hard lead bettered their high-tech jacketed bullet by quite a margin. Loading his 310-grain 44 ammo to 1320 fps and his 415-grain 4570 ammo to 1730, Garrett produced two, very superior hunting combinations.

HAWK

Noted for producing an excellent hunting bullet in odd calibers, Hawk offers a dead-soft

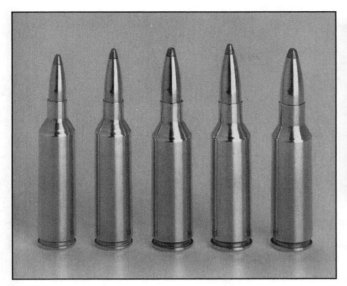

The 40/44 Woodwalker and the 40/454 JDJ — determined to increase range and whomp.

J.D. Jones newest creations include (L-R) 6.5 Mini Dreadnought, 280 JKJ, 30-06 JDJ, 338-06 JDJ, and 375-06 JDJ.

Lazzeroni's hot new line of short, beltless magnums in 243, 264, 7mm, 308, and 338-calibers are designed for compact, light mountain rifles.

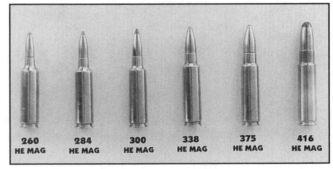

260 HE MAG **284** HE MAG **300** HE MAG **338** HE MAG **375** HE MAG **416** HE MAG

Heavy Magnum Express is introducing a new family of non-belted, short magnums derived from the 348 case.

copper jacket and a pure lead core that expands fully while retaining its integrity. Hawk has now added some more of those impossible-to-find calibers, notably the 43 Spanish, 43 Mauser, 10.75mm, 577/450 Martini-Henry, 11.2mm, 11.4mm, 500/465 N.E., and a 475-caliber bullet for the Wildey.

HEAVY MAGNUM EXPRESS

Here's another new series of non-belted, short action magnum cartridges in 264-, 284-, 300-, 338-, 350-, 375-, 416-, and 450-caliber. The parent case is derived from modified and blown-out 348 Winchester cases with the rims turned down to .532-inch and a 40-degree shoulder. This case lets the laddies who like short actions and light rifles to achieve regular magnum performance from compact, powder-conservative cartridges. The velocity data looks great. No information is provided about working pressures.

HODGDON

The powder masters have been busy this season making major improvements in the chemistry and grain characteristics of their entire extruded rifle powder line plus adding two new formulas. "Hodgdon Extreme" is the label given the improvements which consist of reducing drastically the temperature sensitivity of their extruded rifle powders while reducing the grain size to insure easy measuring on the reloading bench, particularly when progressive presses are being used. Contained in their new pamphlet, "Hodgdon Ex-

treme", are some eye-opening comparative velocity and pressure tests of competitive brands of powder when the temperature variable ranges from 125 F. to 0 F. The two new powders this year are "Titewad"-- a spherical 12-gauge powder for 7/8-1 1/8 oz. loads featuring low charge weights, mild muzzle report, minimum recoil and reduced residue—and "Titegroup" --a powder for straight-walled pistol cases that ignites well regardless of where the powder is in the case. New age cowboys should love it.

HORNADY

Expanding on the success of their polymer-tipped V-Max bullet, Hornady has carried over the concept to a new big game bullet--the SST--standing for "Super Shock Tipped." Featuring a red polymer point that drives into the cavity beneath it upon impact, the new bullet is designed to provide a streamlined ballistic profile and controlled expansion. An interesting departure for Hornady this year is the introduction of a 12 gauge jacketed HP slug that draws upon the XTP engineering concepts of their handgun bullet line. The slug will be loaded by the factory and marketed in five-round boxes. Moly-coating gets a big boost in 1998-99 with the coating being applied to VMax and Match component bullets as well as to Light and Heavy Magnum, Varmint Express and Match ammunition. And recreating an historical method of adding penetration to muzzleloading round balls, Hornady is bringing out a line of hardened balls. Wouldn't you know it - they're called

HardBalls. Check out their web site at: www.hornady.com

HUNTINGTON

This is my favorite one-stop shopping place for reloading components of any brand, shape or flavor. Recently I needed some 6.5 (.266) bullets for the Italian Carcano, 310 Martini bullets and 33 Winchester brass. Huntington had everything in stock. My order was placed over the Internet, and these hard-to-find components were in my hands in two days. Great service. Great online catalog. Reach them at: www.huntingtons.com.

IMR

No new powders this year, but a lot of great information on their web site including a complete copy of their "Handloader's Guide," powder profiles, news and technical assistance. The address is: www.imrpowder.com.

KENG'S FIREARMS SPECIALITY

Keng's, distributor of the Lapua ammunition and component lines, is the source of sev-

eral new Finnish innovations. Lapua is loading a new, CNC-machined, solid bullet named the Forex. The Forex is designed for brush hunting and features a deep hollow cavity in the base that throws the center of gravity forward insuring better stability through the bushes—much like a Foster shotgun slug. Rotating bands have been cut into the body of the bullet to engage the rifling and reduce pressure. The new bullet is available in 308-, 338-, and 9.3-calibers. Long a source for match quality 22 LR ammunition, Lapua has produced an improved match cartridge, the Midas, that will be furnished in two diameters and a new hunting/target load, the Scoremax, that features a heavy 49-grain bullet at approximately 1033 fps.

KYNOCH

Distributed in the U.S. by Zanders Sporting Goods, there are over 50 different loadings available today with the 505 Gibbs, 240 H&H Belted, 375-2 1/2", 700 N.E., 9.5 MS, 475 N.E., and 455 Webley being added this year. For more data, the web site is:www.gzanders.com.

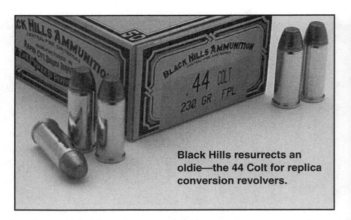

Black Hills resurrects an oldie—the 44 Colt for replica conversion revolvers.

PMC reaches for the Cowboy Action with six new loads—38 Special to 45-70.

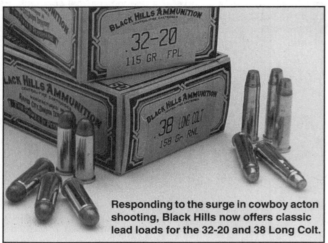

Responding to the surge in cowboy acton shooting, Black Hills now offers classic lead loads for the 32-20 and 38 Long Colt.

LAZZERONI ARMS COMPANY

Lazzeroni has succeeded in packaging magnum performance in a refreshing new line of non-belted short magnum cases that represent a perfect match for the light, short actioned mountain rifles so beloved by the big game fraternity. In typical fashion, Lazzeroni launched not one, not two, but five different calibers in the series-243, 264, 284, 308 and 338. The cartridge names are rather racy, too—the Spitfire, Phantom, Tomahawk, Patriot, and Galaxy. Brass is being drawn by MAST, and independent pressure testing is provided by the H.P. White Laboratories. These efficient cases use less powder than standard belted magnums to achieve comparable velocities, so recoil is reduced accordingly. During the recent deer season, I used the 308 Patriot with a 150-grain Nosler Partition at 3300 fps in a handy little, 6 3/4 lb. Lazzeroni rifle on Mule deer and Coues deer. One shot, one buck; both bucks were over 200 yards away. Couldn't ask for more in terms of performance, portability and reduced recoil. Informative web site at www.lazzeroni.com.

LIGHTNING PERFORMANCE INNOVATIONS

Here is a small custom bullet maker that specializes entirely in 338-caliber bullets--heavy ones, light ones, bonded, non-bonded, spitzers, hollow points. On the unusual side, two frangible varmint bullets are offered in weights from 125-to160-grains. The "Lightning Twister" consists of 8 strands of aluminum or copper wire swaged within the jacket. The "Lightning Duster" consists of a prefragmented core containing #12, #9 or #6 shot. The maker indicates he has achieved 3600+fps with a 125-grain Twister. No comment on accuracy achieved. This is one you're going to want to try.

LYMAN

When it comes to cast bullets, no outfit has more experience than Lyman. Who is in a better position to market a new line of cowboy action bullets sized to today's cylinder throats and having the crimping groove correctly located to ensure proper overall length in both rifles and pistols? Lyman, and the name of the new line is "Silver Star Bullets." The Silver Stars are available in 38/

357-, 44/40-, 44 Spec/44 Magnum 45 Colt calibers. Also added to the "Shoker Series" of prelubed muzzleloading bullets this year are a 420-grain 50-caliber and a 445-grain, 54 caliber--real bone crunching heavyweights.

MAGNUM PERFORMANCE BALLISTICS (MPB) / POLYWAD

This new division of Polywad is offering some very creative products. First is the reintroduction of Quik-Shok 22 LR ammunition which features a 32-grain, pre-stressed, HP bullet at 1550 fps. Designed to fragment into three separate projectiles upon impact in a fluid-based target, the Quik-Shok bullet is designed to dump as much energy as possible over the largest possible area. The new Quik-Shok is manufactured by Blount using Stinger cases and a Stinger bullet profile. Accuracy? Blount's tests indicate average group sizes of 3.23" at 100 yards.

Similar in concept is MPB's factory loaded Quik-Shok 12-gauge Sabot Slug that weighs 1 1/8oz., has a velocity of 1500 fps, and breaks into 3 projectiles at distances up to 150 yards. The 20-gauge and 16-gauge loads will follow. Tests indicate excellent accuracy in both rifled and smoothbores. MPB is also fielding a 12-gauge Polymag shotshell designed to fill out the fringe areas of a pattern with either 1 1/4 oz. of #7 lead shot or 1 1/2 oz. of nickel-plated shot for longer shots up to 60 yards. And for that touch of nostalgia, the company is importing the full line of paper-hulled British Gamebore shotshells.

NATIONAL RELOADING MANUFACTURERS ASSOCIATION

The NRMA has launched an impressive web site that provides basic reloading instructions and a complete roster of all the member companies with hot links to their own web sites. Find it at www.reload-nr-ma.com.

NAVAL ORDNANCE WORKS

While proprietor L.E. Hull can provide cast and jacketed bullets in calibers from 228 thru 700, he is most known for his creations at the larger end of the spectrum including 2000 gr. 4-bore projectiles. If you're into such cannons, you'll find his catalog a virtual gold mine of esoterica.

NECO

One of the early sources for moly-coating materials, NECO is now offering "Bullet-Slide"--a jar of 60% molybdenum disulfide paste into which a shooter can dip loaded ammunition (rimfire or centerfire) to coat the bullet with a thin film of moly.

NORTHERN PRECISION

This small custom bullet house stretches the bounds when it comes to big bore "Varmint" bullets. If you want to get some off-season practice with your 375-, 416-, or 458-caliber magnums, check this source out. How about a hollow point, 215grain 416-caliber bullet in which the nose is cut into six, sharp teeth!. It's called a "Sabre Star" and, varmints, it looks ever so much like a death star to me.

Federal's non-toxic Tungsten-Polymer load is gentle on the old barrels.

The classic 12-gauge, pigeon load is being revived by Winchester featuring 3-1/4.

Federal's 12-gauge 3' Tungsten-Iron Turkey load carries 1-3/8 oz of #4's

NOSLER

Through a strategic alliance with Olin-Winchester, Nosler has developed a series of improved and new partition jacketed bullets. The Partition-HG is a new line of handgun bullets that include a 180-grain 357 caliber, 250-grain 44-caliber and 260-grain 45-caliber. I used the 44-caliber Partition-HG's in a Ruger 44 Magnum carbine this past season and they produced massive wound channels and so much penetration that no slugs were recovered, even from 200 - pound wild hogs. The Partition-HG's are also being loaded in sabots for 50- and 54-caliber muzzleloaders and should prove highly effective. Nolser is introducing two new bullets in its Partition line--a 100-grain 6.5mm missile that should help boost the flagging popularity of the 260 Rem, and a 286-grain 9.3mm for the overseas trade. Ballistic Tip varmint bullets and a number of regular handgun bullets will be available this year in 250 round bulk packs.

OLD WESTERN SCROUNGER

If you have an old 1903 Winchester in 22 Winchester loafing around, take heart-the Old Western Scrounger is bringing back this great little round. The fifty-round boxes will picture the Winchester rifle while the 10-box brick will depict Ad Topperwein sitting atop 72,500 wooden cubes he drilled with his little 1903. The Scrounger indicates that if there if sufficient interest voiced by the shooting community, he will reintroduce the 25 Stevens Long, 41 Remington loaded with black powder, 41 Long Colt and 41 Swiss. Now in stock are 60 calibers of newly loaded obsolete ammunition; 8, 10, 12, 16, and 20-gauge black powder shotshells; and 8-bore smokeless loads. See them on the net at www.snowcrest.net/old-west/index.htm

OREGON TRAIL

Home of the "Lazer-Cast Silver Bullets," Oregon Trail has gained the reputation of producing some of the most accurate—and prettiest—cast bullets in the country. Their complex virgin casting alloy contains, yep, SILVER, copper, tin, bismuth, antimony, arsenic and lead. Available in 35 different rifle and pistol designs in calibers from 30-to-45, these silver bullets can be seen at www.laser-cast.com.

PRECISION AMUNITION AND SHOOTING SUPPLIES

This general mail order supply house for brass and bullets offers one custom touch that sets it apart. It will sort a variety of rifle brass by weight to +/- 0.3 grains in batches of 20 to 100 cases.

RCBS

RCBS has just released a brilliant piece of software called RCBS.LOAD. The program combines the latest in ballistic technology with a impressive data base manager. Based on Windows 95, you can graph, plot, compute, review stored loading data, drag up 260 cartridge drawings, compare multiple cartridges on the same screen. If you get my drift and like working with a computer, get this program. It comes loaded with all the data from the Speer #12 Reloading Manual, the RCBS Cast Bullet Manual, and Accurate Arms #1 Guide. Diskettes containing additional manuals from Speer and other sources are readily available from RCBS as well.

REMINGTON

Big Green restructured its Premier centerfire rifle ammunition line into three specialty segments: Premier Boat Tail, Premier Safari Grade and Premier Varmint. The Premier Boat Tail line replaces the recent "Extended Range" line. Two new big game cartridges have added to Safari Grade--the 7mmSTW 140-grain and the 8mm Rem. Mag. 200-grain both loads feature the Swift A-Frame.

In 12 gauge their 3-3/4—1-1/4 load pushes 4, 5, 6 or 7-1/2 shot to 1330 fps.

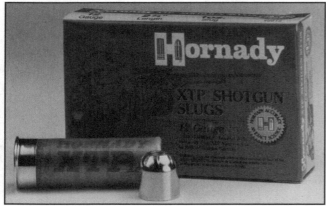

Hornady's XTP Shotgun Slug is designed to expand reliably at all velocities.

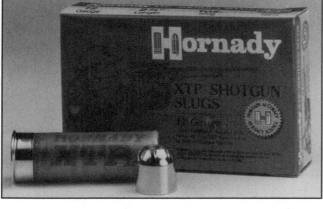

Improving its Premium line, Federal is now loading the Barnes Expander slug to get even more expanison.

SELLIER & BELLOT, USA

Ideally positioned to begin supplying metric sporting ammunition for all those surplus firearms, S&B is doing just that with a 180-grain softpoint load for the 7.62x54R at 2624 fps, a 140-grain softpoint loading for the 6.5x55 at 2671, and a 139-grain FMJ in the 9mm Luger at the subsonic level of 1033 fps. Lots of new brass and shotshell components as well this year.

SIERRA

Two new bullets from the Bulletsmiths--a 25-caliber 100 grain HPBT MatchKing bullet and an 30-caliber 85-grain round nose handgun bullet for the 7.62x25 Tokarev, 30 Mauser and 30 Luger. Sierra continues its high-tech presence with their complete reloading manuals being offered on CD-Rom and an informative web site at: www.sierrabullets.com.

SSK

The irrepressible J.D.Jones has come up with three new proprietary cartridges for the T/C Encore. The 6.5 Mini Dreadnought utilizes a blown out 220 Swift case with a 60 degree shoulder to generate 2800 fps with a 120-grain bullet in a 15 inch barrel. Similar in design is the 30-06 JDJ that generates 2800 fps with a 150-qrain bullet, again in a 15 inch barrel. Necking the 454 Casull case to 40-caliber, J.D. has produced the 40/454 JDJ which produces 2550 fps with a 200-grain bullet in a 12.5 inch barrel. And finally, the 40/44 Woodswalker, a 44 Magnum case necked to 40-caliber, that churns up 2000 fps with a 200-grain bullet in a standard 10 inch Contender barrel.

SWIFT

The popular A-Frame series has been expanded to include 120 and 140-grain pills for the 6.5mm, and 140, 160, and 175-grain bullets for the 7mm. A whole new family of A-Frame handgun bullets has been released that includes the 44-caliber in 240, 280, and 300-grain weights and the 45-caliber at 300 grains.

TRITON

Triton is licensed to make Quik-Shok handgun and rifle ammunition and is introducing a complete menu of loads for the most popular calibers featuring pre-stressed, jacketed HP bullets, that separate into three parts when impacting with soft targets. Its regular line of Hi-vel, jacketed HP handgun ammunition offers loads specifically tailored to short barreled handguns and well as a complete selection of loads for the 45 Super.

VIHTAVUORI

No new powders this year, but for cowboys and cowgirls, VihtaVuori has compiled rather complete loading data for those low velocity action shooting combinations. It's available for the asking.

WEATHERBY

Taming yet another wildcat based on the Weatherby cases, Weatherby is domesticating the 338-378 Weatherby. Ballistics look impressive, especially with a 200-grain Nosler Ballistic Tip at 3350 fps. In fact, Nosler Ballistic Tips are now factory loaded across the complete Weatherby line.

WEST COAST BULLETS

Using sintered iron, West Coast Bullets is introducing the "Powder Bullet" in most handgun calibers and the 223, 308, and 7.62x39 rifle calibers. It's a totally frangible and lead-free bullet somewhat reminiscent of Remington's sintered 22 Short Rocket bullet of the late '50s.

WINCHESTER

The "combined technology" alliance between Winchester and Nosler is generating some sensational new bullets. The traditional Nosler Partition rifle bullet has been improved by adding a steel insert that surrounds the lead in the rear core thereby strengthening the shank, reducing bulging upon impact and improving penetration. Coated with molybdenum disulfide, it's called the Partition Gold Rifle and will be loaded this year in the 270 Winchester 7mm Remington Magnum, 308 Winchester, 30-06, 300 Winchester Magnum and 338 Winchester Magnum.

At the handgun level, a similar new bullet, named the Gold Partition Handgun, is available in 357,44 and 45-calibers. Component bullets for handloaders will be available from Nosler. Another interesting addition to Winchester's handgun ammunition line is a lead-free bullet consisting of a solid tin core surrounded by a copper alloy jacket. As loaded with lead-free primers in the 9mm Luger, 38 Special, 40 S&W, 10mm Auto, and 45 Auto, it will be known as SuperClean NT.

Speaking of non-toxic ammunition, Winchester is giving the complete Bismuth shotshell line a promotional push this year. offering the heaviest shot payloads available (actual pellet counts), Bismuth shotshells produce greater pattern densities than steel or tungsten alloy alternatives. New, too, in Winchester's shotshell line, are high velocity 12-gauge turkey loads featuring #4 shot in either 3 inch or 3-1/2 inch hulls; a 12-gauge, 2-3/4 inch, a AA Super Pigeon load providing 3 1/4-drami equivalent with 1-1/4 oz. of hard copper plated shot; and a low recoil OO buck load. ●

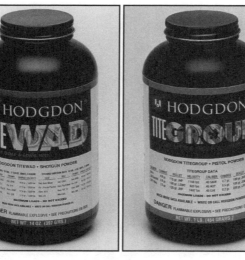

Hodgdon's Titewad for 12-bore target loads, Tite Group for handguns.

Caliber	Bullet Weight Grams	VELOCITY (fps)					ENERGY (ft. lbs.)					TRAJ. (in.)				Approx. Price per box
		Muzzle	100 yds.	200 yds.	300 yds.	400 yds.	Muzzle	100 yds.	200 yds.	300 yds.	400 yds.	100 yds.	200 yds.	300 yds.	400 yds.	
17 Remington	25	4040	3284	2644	2086	1606	906	599	388	242	143	+2.0	+1.7	-4.0	-17.0	$17
221 Fireball	50	2800	2137	1580	1180	988	870	507	277	155	109	0.0	-7.0	-28.0	NA	$14
22 Hornet	45	2690	2042	1502	1128	948	723	417	225	127	90	0.0	-7.7	-31.0	NA	$27**
218 Bee	46	2760	2102	1550	1155	961	788	451	245	136	94	0.0	-7.2	-29.0	NA	$46**
222 Remington	40	3600	3117	2673	2269	1911	1151	863	634	457	324	+1.07	0.0	-6.13	-18.9	NA
222 Remington	50	3140	2602	2123	1700	1350	1094	752	500	321	202	+2.0	-0.4	-11.0	-33.0	$11
222 Remington	55	3020	2562	2147	1773	1451	1114	801	563	384	257	+2.0	-0.4	-11.0	-33.0	$12
22 PPC	52	3400	2930	2510	2130	NA	1335	990	730	525	NA	+2.0	1.4	-5.0	NA	NA
223 Remington	40	3650	3010	2450	1950	1530	1185	805	535	340	265	+2.0	+1.0	-6.0	-22.0	$14
223 Remington	52/53	3330	2882	2477	2106	1770	1305	978	722	522	369	+2.0	+0.6	-6.5	-21.5	$14
223 Remington	55	3240	2748	2305	1906	1556	1282	922	649	444	296	+2.0	-0.2	-9.0	-27.0	$12
223 Remington	60	3100	2712	2355	2026	1726	1280	979	739	547	397	+2.0	+0.2	-8.0	-24.7	$16
223 Remington	64	3020	2621	2256	1920	1619	1296	977	723	524	373	+2.0	-0.2	-9.3	-23.0	$14
223 Remington	69	3000	2720	2460	2210	1980	1380	1135	925	750	600	+2.0	+0.8	-5.8	-17.5	$15
222 Rem. Mag.	55	3240	2748	2305	1906	1556	1282	922	649	444	296	+2.0	-0.2	-9.0	-27.0	$14
225 Winchester	55	3570	3066	2616	2208	1838	1556	1148	836	595	412	+2.0	+1.0	-5.0	-20.0	$19
224 Wea. Mag.	55	3650	3192	2780	2403	2057	1627	1244	943	705	516	+2.0	+1.2	-4.0	-17.0	$32
22-250 Rem.	40	4000	3320	2720	2200	1740	1420	980	660	430	265	+2.0	+1.8	-3.0	-16.0	$14
22-250 Rem.	52/55	3680	3137	2656	2222	1832	1654	1201	861	603	410	+2.0	+1.3	-4.0	-17.0	$13
22-250 Rem.	60	3600	3195	2826	2485	2169	1727	1360	1064	823	627	+2.0	+2.0	-2.4	-12.3	$19
220 Swift	40	4200	3678	3190	2739	2329	1566	1201	904	666	482	+0.51	0.0	-4.0	-12.9	NA
220 Swift	50	3780	3158	2617	2135	1710	1586	1107	760	506	325	+2.0	+1.4	-4.4	-17.9	$20
220 Swift	55	3650	3194	2772	2384	2035	1627	1246	939	694	506	+2.0	+2.0	-2.6	-13.4	$19
220 Swift	60	3600	3199	2824	2475	2156	1727	1364	1063	816	619	+2.0	+1.6	-4.1	-13.1	$19
22 Savage H.P.	71	2790	2340	1930	1570	1280	1225	860	585	390	190	+2.0	-1.0	-10.4	-35.7	NA
6mm BR Rem.	100	2550	2310	2083	1870	1671	1444	1185	963	776	620	+2.0	-0.6	-11.8	NA	$22
6mm Norma BR	107	2822	2667	2517	2372	2229	1893	1690	1506	1337	1181	+1.73	0.0	-7.24	-20.6	NA
6mm PPC	70	3140	2750	2400	2070	NA	1535	1175	895	665	NA	+2.0	+1.4	-5.0	NA	NA
243 Winchester	55	4025	3597	3209	2853	2525	1978	1579	1257	994	779	+0.6	0.00	-4.0	-12.2	NA
243 Winchester	60	3600	3110	2660	2260	1890	1725	1285	945	680	475	+2.0	+1.8	-3.3	-15.5	$17
243 Winchester	75/80	3350	2955	2593	2259	1951	1993	1551	1194	906	676	+2.0	+0.9	-5.0	-19.0	$16
243 Winchester	85	3320	3070	2830	2600	2380	2080	1770	1510	1280	1070	+2.0	+1.2	-4.0	-14.0	$18
243 Winchester*	100	2960	2697	2449	2215	1993	1945	1615	1332	1089	882	+2.5	+1.2	-6.0	-20.0	$16
243 Winchester	105	2920	2689	2470	2261	2062	1988	1686	1422	1192	992	+2.5	+1.6	-5.0	-18.4	$21
243 Light Mag.	100	3100	2839	2592	2358	2138	2133	1790	1491	1235	1014	+1.5	0.0	-6.8	-19.8	NA
6mm Remington	80	3470	3064	2694	2352	2036	2139	1667	1289	982	736	+2.0	+1.1	-5.0	-17.0	$16
6mm Remington	100	3100	2829	2573	2332	2104	2133	1777	1470	1207	983	+2.5	+1.6	-5.0	-17.0	$16
6mm Remington	105	3060	2822	2596	2381	2177	2105	1788	1512	1270	1059	+2.5	+1.1	-3.3	-15.0	$21
6.17(.243) Spitfire	100	3350	3122	2905	2698	2501	2493	2164	1874	1617	1389	2.4	3.20	0	-8	
240 Wea. Mag.	87	3500	3202	2924	2663	2416	2366	1980	1651	1370	1127	+2.0	+2.0	-2.0	-12.0	$32
240 Wea. Mag.	100	3395	3106	2835	2581	2339	2559	2142	1785	1478	1215	+2.5	+2.8	-2.0	-11.0	$43
25-20 Win.	86	1460	1194	1030	931	858	407	272	203	165	141	0.0	-23.5	NA	NA	$32**
25-35 Win.	117	2230	1866	1545	1282	1097	1292	904	620	427	313	+2.5	-4.2	-26.0	NA	$24
250 Savage	100	2820	2504	2210	1936	1684	1765	1392	1084	832	630	+2.5	+0.4	-9.0	-28.0	$17
257 Roberts	100	2980	2661	2363	2085	1827	1972	1572	1240	965	741	+2.5	-0.8	-5.2	-21.6	$20
257 Roberts+P	117	2780	2411	2071	1761	1488	2009	1511	1115	806	576	+2.5	-0.2	-10.2	-32.6	$18
257 Roberts+P	120	2780	2560	2360	2160	1970	2060	1750	1480	1240	1030	+2.5	+1.2	-6.4	-23.6	$22
257 Roberts	122	2600	2331	2078	1842	1625	1831	1472	1169	919	715	+2.5	0.0	-10.6	-31.4	$21
257 Light Mag.	117	2940	2694	2460	2240	2031	2245	1885	1572	1303	1071	+1.7	0.0	-7.6	-21.8	NA
25-06 Rem.	87	3440	2995	2591	2222	1884	2286	1733	1297	954	686	+2.0	+1.1	-2.5	-14.4	$17
25-06 Rem.	90	3440	3043	2680	2344	2034	2364	1850	1435	1098	827	+2.0	+1.8	-3.3	-15.6	$17
25-06 Rem.	100	3230	2893	2580	2287	2014	2316	1858	1478	1161	901	+2.0	+0.8	-5.7	-18.9	$17
25-06 Rem.	117	2990	2770	2570	2370	2190	2320	2000	1715	1465	1246	+2.5	+1.0	-7.9	-26.6	$19
25-06 Rem.*	120	2990	2730	2484	2252	2032	2382	1985	1644	1351	1100	+2.5	+1.2	-5.3	-19.6	$17
25-06 Rem.	122	2930	2706	2492	2289	2095	2325	1983	1683	1419	1189	+2.5	+1.8	-4.5	-17.5	$23
257 Wea. Mag.	87	3825	3456	3118	2805	2513	2826	2308	1870	1520	1220	+2.0	+2.7	-0.3	-7.6	$32
257 Wea. Mag.	100	3555	3237	2941	2665	2404	2806	2326	1920	1576	1283	+2.5	+3.2	0.0	-8.0	$32
257 Scramjet	100	3745	3450	3173	2912	2666	3114	2643	2235	1883	1578	+2.1	+2.77	0.0	-6.93	NA
6.5x50mm Jap.	139	2360	2160	1970	1790	1620	1720	1440	1195	985	810	+2.5	-1.0	-13.5	NA	NA
6.5x50mm Jap.	156	2070	1830	1610	1430	1260	1475	1155	900	695	550	+2.5	-4.0	-23.8	NA	NA
6.5x52mm Car.	139	2580	2360	2160	1970	1790	2045	1725	1440	1195	985	+2.5	0.0	-9.9	-29.0	NA
6.5x52mm Car.	156	2430	2170	1930	1700	1500	2045	1630	1285	1005	780	+2.5	-1.0	-13.9	NA	NA
6.5x55mm Light Mag.	129	2750	2549	2355	2171	1994	2166	1860	1589	1350	1139	+2.0	0.0	-8.2	-23.9	NA
6.5x55mm Swe.	140	2550	NA	NA	NA	NA	2020	NA	NA	NA	NA	NA	NA	NA	NA	$18
6.5x55mm Swe.*	139/140	2850	2640	2440	2250	2070	2525	2170	1855	1575	1330	+2.5	+1.6	-5.4	-18.9	$18
6.5x55mm Swe.	156	2650	2370	2110	1870	1650	2425	1950	1550	1215	945	+2.5	0.0	-10.3	-30.6	NA
260 Remington	140	2750	2544	2347	2158	1979	2351	2011	1712	1448	1217	+2.2	0.0	-8.6	-24.6	NA
6.71 (264) Phantom	120	3150	2929	2718	2517	2325	2645	2286	1969	1698	1440	+1.3	0.0	-6.0	-17.5	NA
6.5 Rem. Mag.	120	3210	2905	2621	2353	2102	2745	2248	1830	1475	1177	+2.5	+1.7	-4.1	-16.3	Disc.
264 Win. Mag.	140	3030	2782	2548	2326	2114	2854	2406	2018	1682	1389	+2.5	+1.4	-5.1	-18.0	$24
6.71 (264) Blackbird	140	3480	3261	3053	2855	2665	3766	3307	2899	2534	2208	+2.4	+3.1	0.0	-7.4	NA
270 Winchester	100	3430	3021	2649	2305	1988	2612	2027	1557	1179	877	+2.0	+1.0	-4.9	-17.5	$17
270 Winchester	130	3060	2776	2510	2259	2022	2702	2225	1818	1472	1180	+2.5	+1.4	-5.3	-18.2	$17
270 Winchester	135	3000	2780	2570	2369	2178	2697	2315	1979	1682	1421	+2.5	+1.4	-6.0	-17.6	$20
270 Winchester*	140	2940	2700	2480	2260	2060	2685	2270	1905	1590	1315	+2.5	+1.8	-4.6	-17.9	$20
270 Win. Light Mag.	140	3100	2894	2697	2508	2327	2987	2604	2261	1955	1684	+1.37	0.0	-6.32	-18.3	NA
270 Winchester*	150	2850	2585	2336	2100	1879	2705	2226	1817	1468	1175	+2.5	+1.2	-6.5	-22.0	$17
270 Wea. Mag.	100	3760	3380	3033	2712	2412	3139	2537	2042	1633	1292	+2.0	+2.4	-1.2	-10.1	$32
270 Wea. Mag.	130	3375	3119	2878	2649	2432	3287	2808	2390	2026	1707	+2.5	-2.9	-0.9	-9.9	$32
270 Wea. Mag.*	150	3245	3036	2837	2647	2465	3507	3070	2681	2334	2023	+2.5	+2.6	-1.8	-11.4	$47

Caliber	Bullet Weight Grams	VELOCITY (fps)					ENERGY (ft. lbs.)					TRAJ. (in.)				Approx. Price per box
		Muzzle	100 yds.	200 yds.	300 yds.	400 yds.	Muzzle	100 yds.	200 yds.	300 yds.	400 yds.	100 yds.	200 yds.	300 yds.	400 yds.	
7mm BR	140	2215	2012	1821	1643	1481	1525	1259	1031	839	681	+2.0	-3.7	-20.0	NA	$23
7mm Mauser*	139/140	2660	2435	2221	2018	1827	2199	1843	1533	1266	1037	+2.5	0.0	-9.6	-27.7	$17
7mm Mauser	145	2690	2442	2206	1985	1777	2334	1920	1568	1268	1017	+2.5	+0.1	-9.6	-28.3	$18
7mm Mauser	154	2690	2490	2300	2120	1940	2475	2120	1810	1530	1285	+2.5	+0.8	-7.5	-23.5	$17
7mm Mauser	175	2440	2137	1857	1603	1382	2313	1774	1340	998	742	+2.5	-1.7	-16.1	NA	$17
7x57 Light Mag.	139	2970	2730	2503	2287	2082	2722	2301	1933	1614	1337	+1.6	0.0	-7.2	-21.0	NA
7x30 Waters	120	2700	2300	1930	1600	1330	1940	1405	990	685	470	+2.5	-0.2	-12.3	NA	$18
7mm-08 Rem.	120	3000	2725	2467	2223	1992	2398	1979	1621	1316	1058	+2.0	0.0	-7.6	-22.3	$18
7mm-08 Rem.*	140	2860	2625	2402	2189	1988	2542	2142	1793	1490	1228	+2.5	+0.8	-6.9	-21.9	$18
7mm-08 Rem.	154	2715	2510	2315	2128	1950	2520	2155	1832	1548	1300	+2.5	+1.0	-7.0	-22.7	$23
7mm-08 Light Mag.	139	3000	2790	2590	2399	2216	2777	2403	2071	1776	1515	+1.5	0.0	-6.7	-19.4	NA
7x64mm Bren.	140						Not Yet Announced									$17
7x64mm Bren.	154	2820	2610	2420	2230	2050	2720	2335	1995	1695	1430	+2.5	+1.4	-5.7	-19.9	NA
7x64mm Bren.*	160	2850	2669	2495	2327	2166	2885	2530	2211	1924	1667	+2.5	+1.6	-4.8	-17.8	$24
7x64mm Bren.	175						Not Yet Announced									$17
284 Winchester	150	2860	2595	2344	2108	1886	2724	2243	1830	1480	1185	+2.5	+0.8	-7.3	-23.2	$24
280 Remington	120	3150	2866	2599	2348	2110	2643	2188	1800	1468	1186	+2.0	+0.6	-6.0	-17.9	$17
280 Remington	140	3000	2758	2528	2309	2102	2797	2363	1986	1657	1373	+2.5	+1.4	-5.2	-18.3	$17
280 Remington*	150	2890	2624	2373	2135	1912	2781	2293	1875	1518	1217	+2.5	+0.8	-7.1	-22.6	$17
280 Remington	160	2840	2637	2442	2556	2078	2866	2471	2120	1809	1535	+2.5	+0.8	-6.7	-21.0	$20
280 Remington	165	2820	2510	2220	1950	1701	2913	2308	1805	1393	1060	+2.5	+0.4	-8.8	-26.5	$17
7x61mm S&H Sup.	154	3060	2720	2400	2100	1820	3200	2520	1965	1505	1135	+2.5	+1.8	-5.0	-19.8	NA
7mm Dakota	160	3200	3001	2811	2630	2455	3637	3200	2808	2456	2140	+2.1	+1.9	-2.8	-12.5	NA
7mm Rem. Mag.*	139/140	3150	2930	2710	2510	2320	3085	2660	2290	1960	1670	+2.5	+2.4	-2.4	-12.7	$21
7mm Rem. Mag.*	150/154	3110	2830	2085	2320	2085	3221	2667	2196	1792	1448	+2.5	+1.6	-4.6	-16.5	$21
7mm Rem. Mag.*	160/162	2950	2730	2520	2320	2120	3090	2650	2250	1910	1600	+2.5	+1.8	-4.4	-17.8	$34
7mm Rem. Mag.	165	2900	2699	2507	2324	2147	3081	2669	2303	1978	1689	+2.5	+1.2	-5.9	-19.0	$28
7mm Rem Mag.	175	2860	2645	2440	2244	2057	3178	2718	2313	1956	1644	+2.5	+1.0	-6.5	-20.7	$21
7mm Wea. Mag.	140	3225	2970	2729	2501	2283	3233	2741	2315	1943	1621	+2.5	+2.0	-3.2	-14.0	$35
7mm Wea. Mag.	154	3260	3023	2799	2586	2382	3539	3044	2609	2227	1890	+2.5	+2.8	-1.5	-10.8	$32
7mm Wea. Mag.*	160	3200	3004	2816	2637	2464	3637	3205	2817	2469	2156	+2.5	+2.7	-1.5	-10.6	$47
7mm Wea. Mag.	165	2950	2747	2553	2367	2189	3188	2765	2388	2053	1756	+2.5	+1.8	-4.2	-16.4	$43
7mm Wea. Mag.	175	2910	2693	2486	2288	2098	3293	2818	2401	2033	1711	+2.5	+1.2	-5.9	-19.4	$35
7.21(.284) Tomahawk	140	3300	3118	2943	2774	2612	3386	3022	2693	2393	2122	2.3	3.20	0	-7.7	
7mm STW	140	3325	3064	2818	2585	2364	3436	2918	2468	2077	1737	+2.3	+1.8	-3.0	-13.1	NA
7mm STW	160	3250	3087	2930	2778	2631	3752	3385	3049	2741	2460	+2.78	+3.4	0.0	-7.97	NA
7mm Firehawk	140	3625	3373	3135	2909	2695	4084	3536	3054	2631	2258	+2.2	+2.9	0.0	-7.03	NA
30 Carbine	110	1990	1567	1236	1035	923	977	600	373	262	208	0.0	-13.5	NA	NA	$28**
303 Savage	190	1890	1612	1327	1183	1055	1507	1096	794	591	469	+2.5	-7.6	NA	NA	$24
30 Remington	170	2120	1822	1555	1328	1153	1696	1253	913	666	502	+2.5	-4.7	-26.3	NA	$20
30-30 Win.	55	3400	2693	2085	1570	1187	1412	886	521	301	172	+2.0	0.0	-10.2	-35.0	$18
30-30 Win.	125	2570	2090	1660	1320	1080	1830	1210	770	480	320	-2.0	-2.6	-19.9	NA	$13
30-30 Win.	150	2390	1973	1605	1303	1095	1902	1296	858	565	399	+2.5	-3.2	-22.5	NA	$13
30-30 Win.	160	2300	1997	1719	1473	1268	1879	1416	1050	771	571	+2.5	-2.9	-20.2	NA	$18
30-30 Win.*	170	2200	1895	1619	1381	1191	1827	1355	989	720	535	+2.5	-5.8	-23.6	NA	$13
300 Savage	150	2630	2354	2094	1853	1631	2303	1845	1462	1143	886	+2.5	-0.4	-10.1	-30.7	$17
300 Savage	180	2350	2137	1935	1754	1570	2207	1825	1496	1217	985	+2.5	-1.6	-15.2	NA	$17
30-40 Krag	180	2430	2213	2007	1813	1632	2360	1957	1610	1314	1064	+2.5	-1.4	-13.8	NA	$18
7.65x53mm Arg.	180	2590	2390	2200	2010	1830	2685	2280	1925	1615	1345	+2.5	0.0	-27.6	NA	NA
307 Winchester	150	2760	2321	1924	1575	1289	2530	1795	1233	826	554	+2.5	-1.5	-13.6	NA	Disc.
307 Winchester	180	2510	2179	1874	1599	1362	2519	1898	1404	1022	742	+2.5	-1.6	-15.6	NA	$20
7.5x55 Swiss	180	2650	2450	2250	2060	1880	2805	2390	2020	1700	1415	+2.5	+0.6	-8.1	-24.9	NA
308 Winchester	55	3770	3215	2726	2286	1888	1735	1262	907	638	435	-2.0	+1.4	-3.8	-15.8	$22
308 Winchester	150	2820	2533	2263	2009	1774	2648	2137	1705	1344	1048	+2.5	+0.4	-8.5	-26.1	$17
308 Winchester	165	2700	2440	2194	1963	1748	2670	2180	1763	1411	1199	+2.5	0.0	-9.7	-28.5	$20
308 Winchester	168	2680	2493	2314	2143	1979	2678	2318	1998	1713	1460	+2.5	0.0	-8.9	-25.3	$18
308 Winchester	178	2620	2415	2220	2034	1857	2713	2306	1948	1635	1363	+2.5	0.0	-9.6	-27.6	$23
308 Winchester*	180	2620	2393	2178	1974	1782	2743	2288	1896	1557	1269	+2.5	-0.2	-10.2	-28.5	$17
308 Light Mag.*	150	2980	2703	2442	2195	1964	2959	2433	1986	1606	1285	+1.6	0.0	-7.5	-22.2	NA
308 Light Mag.	165	2870	2658	2456	2263	2078	3019	2589	2211	1877	1583	+1.7	0.0	-7.5	-21.8	NA
308 High Energy	165	2870	2600	2350	2120	1890	3020	2485	2030	1640	1310	+1.8	0.0	-8.2	-24.0	NA
308 Light Mag.	168	2870	2658	2456	2263	2078	3019	2589	2211	1877	1583	+1.7	0.0	-7.5	-21.8	NA
308 High Energy	180	2740	2550	2370	2200	2030	3000	2600	2245	1925	1645	+1.9	0.0	-802	-23.5	NA
30-06 Spfd.	55	4080	3485	2965	2502	2083	2033	1483	1074	764	530	+2.0	+1.9	-2.1	-11.7	$22
30-06 Spfd.	125	3140	2780	2447	2138	1853	2736	2145	1662	1279	953	+2.0	+1.0	-6.2	-21.0	$17
30-06 Spfd.	150	2910	2617	2342	2083	1853	2820	2281	1827	1445	1135	+2.5	+0.8	-7.2	-23.4	$17
30-06 Spfd.	152	2910	2654	2413	2184	1968	2858	2378	1965	1610	1307	+2.5	+1.0	-6.6	-21.3	$23
30-06 Spfd.*	165	2800	2534	2283	2047	1825	2872	2352	1909	1534	1220	+2.5	+0.4	-8.4	-25.5	$17
30-06 Spfd.	168	2710	2522	2346	2169	2003	2739	2372	2045	1754	1497	+2.5	+0.4	-8.0	-23.5	$18
30-06 Spfd.	178	2720	2511	2311	2121	1939	2924	2491	2111	1777	1486	+2.5	+0.4	-8.2	-24.6	$23
30-06 Spfd.*	180	2700	2469	2250	2042	1846	2913	2436	2023	1666	1362	-2.5	0.0	-9.3	-27.0	$17
30-06 Spfd.	220	2410	2130	1870	1632	1422	2837	2216	1708	1301	988	+2.5	-1.7	-18.0	NA	$17
30-06 Light Mag.	150	3100	2815	2548	2295	2058	3200	2639	2161	1755	1410	+1.4	0.0	-6.8	-20.3	NA
30-06 Light Mag.	180	2880	2676	2480	2293	2114	3316	2862	2459	2102	1786	+1.7	0.0	-7.3	-21.3	NA
30-06 High Energy	180	2880	2690	2500	2320	2150	3315	2880	2495	2150	1845	+1.7	0.0	-7.2	-21.0	NA
7.82 (308) Patriot	150	3250	2999	2762	2537	2323	3519	2997	2542	2145	1798	+1.2	0.0	-5.8	-16.9	NA
308 Norma Mag.	180	3020	2820	2630	2440	2270	3645	3175	2755	2385	2050	+2.5	+2.0	-3.5	-14.8	Na
300 Dakota	200	3000	2824	2656	2493	2336	3996	3542	3131	2760	2423	+2.2	+1.5	-4.0	-15.2	NA
300 H&H Magnum*	180	2880	2640	2412	2196	1990	3315	2785	2325	1927	1583	+2.5	+0.8	-6.8	-21.7	$24
300 H&H Magnum	220	2550	2267	2002	1757	NA	3167	2510	1958	1508	NA	-2.5	-0.4	-12.0	NA	NA
300 Peterson	180	3500	3319	3145	2978	2817	4896	4401	3953	3544	3172	+2.3	+2.9	0.0	-6.8	NA
300 Win. Mag.	150	3290	2951	2636	2342	2068	3605	2900	2314	1827	1424	+2.5	+1.9	-3.8	-15.8	$22
300 Win. Mag.	165	3100	2877	2665	2462	2269	3522	3033	2603	2221	1897	+2.5	+2.4	-3.0	-16.9	$24

CAUTION: PRICES SHOWN ARE SUPPLIED BY THE MANUFACTURER OR IMPORTER. CHECK YOUR LOCAL GUNSHOP.

Caliber	Bullet Weight Grains	VELOCITY (fps)					ENERGY (ft. lbs.)					TRAJ. (in.)				Approx. Price per box
		Muzzle	100 yds.	200 yds.	300 yds.	400 yds.	Muzzle	100 yds.	200 yds.	300 yds.	400 yds.	100 yds.	200 yds.	300 yds.	400 yds.	
300 Win. Mag.	178	2900	2760	2568	2375	2191	3509	3030	2606	2230	1897	+2.5	+1.4	-5.0	-17.6	$29
300 Win. Mag.*	180	2960	2745	2540	2344	2157	3501	3011	2578	2196	1859	+2.5	+1.2	-5.5	-18.5	$22
300 W.M. High Energy	180	3100	2830	2580	2340	2110	3840	3205	2660	2190	1790	+1.4	0.0	-6.6	-19.7	NA
300 W.M. Light Mag.	180	3100	2879	2668	2467	2275	3840	3313	2845	2431	2068	+1.39	0.0	-6.45	-18.7	NA
300 Win. Mag.	190	2885	1691	2506	2327	2156	3511	3055	2648	2285	1961	+2.5	+1.2	-5.7	-19.0	$26
300 W.M. High Energy	200	2930	2740	2550	2370	2200	3810	3325	2885	2495	2145	+1.6	0.0	-6.9	-20.1	NA
300 Win. Mag.*	200	2825	2595	2376	2167	1970	3545	2991	2508	2086	1742	-2.5	+1.6	-4.7	-17.2	$36
300 Win. Mag.	220	2680	2448	2228	2020	1823	3508	2927	2424	1993	1623	+2.5	0.0	-9.5	-27.5	$23
300 Wea. Mag.	100	3900	3441	3038	2652	2305	3714	2891	2239	1717	1297	+2.0	+2.6	-0.6	-8.7	$32
300 Wea. Mag.	150	3600	3307	3033	2776	2533	4316	3642	3064	2566	2137	+2.5	+3.2	0.0	-8.1	$32
300 Wea. Mag.	165	3450	3210	3000	2792	2593	4360	3796	3297	2855	2464	+2.5	+3.2	0.0	-7.8	NA
300 Wea. Mag.	178	3120	2902	2695	2497	2308	3847	3329	2870	2464	2104	+2.5	-1.7	-3.6	-14.7	$43
300 Wea. Mag.	180	3330	3110	2910	2710	2520	4430	3875	3375	2935	2540	+1.0	0.0	-5.2	-15.1	NA
300 Wea. Mag.	190	3030	2830	2638	2455	2279	3873	3378	2936	2542	2190	+2.5	+1.6	-4.3	-16.0	$38
300 Wea. Mag.	220	2850	2541	2283	1964	1736	3967	3155	2480	1922	1471	+2.5	+0.4	-8.5	-26.4	$35
300 Warbird	180	3400	3180	2971	2772	2582	4620	4042	3528	3071	2664	+2.59	+3.25	0.0	-7.95	NA
300 Pegasus	180	3500	3319	3145	2978	2817	4896	4401	3953	3544	3172	+2.28	+2.89	0.0	-6.79	NA
32-20 Win.	100	1210	1021	913	834	769	325	231	185	154	131	0.0	-32.3	NA	NA	$23**
303 British	150	2685	2441	2210	1992	1787	2401	1984	1627	1321	1064	+2.5	+0.6	-8.4	-26.2	$18
303 British	180	2460	2124	1817	1542	1311	2418	1803	1319	950	687	+2.5	-1.8	-16.8	NA	$18
303 Light Mag.	150	2830	2570	2325	2094	1884	2667	2199	1800	1461	1185	+2.0	0.0	-8.4	-24.6	NA
7.62x39mm Rus.	123/125	2300	2030	1780	1550	1350	1445	1125	860	655	500	+2.5	-2.0	-17.5	NA	$13
7.62x54mm Rus.	146	2950	2730	2520	2320	NA	2820	2415	2055	1740	NA	+2.5	+2.0	-4.4	-17.7	NA
7.62x54mm Rus.	180	2580	2370	2180	2000	1820	2650	2250	1900	1590	1100	+2.5	0.0	-9.8	-28.5	NA
7.7x58mm Jap.	180	2500	2300	2100	1920	1750	2490	2105	1770	1475	1225	+2.5	0.0	-10.4	-30.2	NA
8x57mm JS Mau.	165	2850	2520	2210	1930	1670	2965	2330	1795	1360	1015	+2.5	+1.0	-7.7	NA	NA
32 Win. Special	170	2250	1921	1626	1372	1175	1911	1393	998	710	521	+2.5	-3.5	-22.9	NA	$14
8mm Mauser	170	2360	1969	1622	1333	1123	2102	1464	993	671	476	+2.5	-3.1	-22.2	NA	$18
8mm Rem. Mag.	185	3080	2761	2464	2186	1927	3896	3131	2494	1963	1525	+2.5	+1.4	-5.5	-19.7	$30
8mm Rem. Mag.	220	2830	2581	2346	2123	1913	3912	3254	2688	2201	1787	+2.5	+0.6	-7.6	-23.5	Disc.
338-06	200	2750	2553	2364	2184	2011	3358	2894	2482	2118	1796	+1.9	0.0	-8.22	-23.6	NA
330 Dakota	250	2900	2719	2545	2378	2217	4668	4103	3595	3138	2727	+2.3	+1.3	-5.0	-17.5	NA
338 Lapua	250	2963	2795	2640	2493	NA	4842	4341	3881	3458	NA	+1.9	0.0	-7.9	NA	NA
338 Win. Mag.	200	2960	2658	2375	2110	1862	3890	3137	2505	1977	1539	+2.5	+1.0	-6.7	-22.3	$27
338 Win. Mag.*	210	2830	2590	2370	2150	1940	3735	3130	2610	2155	1760	+2.5	+1.4	-6.0	-20.9	$33
338 Win. Mag.*	225	2785	2517	2266	2029	1808	3871	3165	2565	2057	1633	+2.5	+0.4	-8.5	-25.9	$27
338 W.M. Heavy Mag.	225	2920	2678	2449	2232	2027	4259	3583	2996	2489	2053	+1.75	0.0	-7.65	-22.0	NA
338 W.M. High Energy	225	2940	2690	2450	2230	2010	4320	3610	3000	2475	2025	+1.7	0.0	-7.5	-22.0	NA
338 Win. Mag.	230	2780	2573	2375	2186	2005	3948	3382	2881	2441	2054	+2.5	+1.2	-6.3	-21.0	$40
338 Win. Mag.*	250	2660	2456	2261	2075	1898	3927	3348	2837	2389	1999	+2.5	+0.2	-9.0	-26.2	$27
338 W.M. High Energy	250	2800	2610	2420	2250	2080	4350	3775	3260	2805	2395	+1.8	0.0	-7.8	-22.5	NA
8.59(.338) Galaxy	200	3100	2899	2707	2524	2347	4269	3734	3256	2829	2446	3	3.80	0	-9.3	
340 Wea. Mag.*	210	3250	2991	2746	2515	2295	4924	4170	3516	2948	2455	+2.5	+1.9	-1.8	-11.8	$56
340 Wea. Mag.*	250	3000	2806	2621	2443	2272	4995	4371	3812	3311	2864	+2.5	+2.0	-3.5	-14.8	$56
338 A-Square	250	3120	2799	2500	2220	1958	5403	4348	3469	2736	2128	+2.5	+2.7	-1.5	-10.5	NA
338-378 Wea. Mag.	225	3180	2974	2778	2591	2410	5052	4420	3856	3353	2902	3.1	3.80	0	-8.9	NA
338 Titan	225	3230	3010	2800	2600	2409	5211	4524	3916	3377	2898	+3.07	+3.80	0.0	-8.95	NA
338 Excalibur	200	3600	3361	3134	2920	2715	5755	5015	4363	3785	3274	+2.23	+2.87	0.0	-6.99	NA
338 Excalibur	250	3250	2922	2618	2333	2066	5863	4740	3804	3021	2370	+1.3	0.0	-6.35	-19.2	NA
348 Winchester	200	2520	2215	1931	1672	1443	2820	2178	1656	1241	925	+2.5	-1.4	-14.7	NA	$42
357 Magnum	158	1830	1427	1138	980	883	1175	715	454	337	274	0.0	-16.2	-33.1	NA	$25**
35 Remington	150	2300	1874	1506	1218	1039	1762	1169	755	494	359	+2.5	-4.1	-26.3	NA	$16
35 Remington	200	2080	1698	1376	1140	1001	19*21	1280	841	577	445	+2.5	-6.3	-17.1	-33.6	$16
356 Winchester	200	2460	2114	1797	1517	1284	2688	1985	1434	1022	732	+2.5	-1.8	-17.1	NA	$31
356 Winchester	250	2160	1911	1682	1476	1299	2591	2028	1571	1210	937	+2.5	-3.7	-22.2	NA	$31
358 Winchester	200	2490	2171	1876	1619	1379	2753	2093	1563	1151	844	+2.5	-1.6	-15.6	NA	$31
358 STA	275	2850	2562	2292	2039	NA	4958	4009	3208	2539	NA	+1.9	0.0	-8.6	NA	NA
350 Rem. Mag.	200	2710	2410	2130	1870	1631	3261	2579	2014	1553	1181	+2.5	-0.2	-10.0	-30.1	$33
35 Whelen	200	2675	2378	2100	1842	1606	3177	2510	1958	1506	1145	+2.5	-0.2	-10.3	-31.1	$20
35 Whelen	225	2500	2300	2110	1930	1770	3120	2650	2235	1870	1560	+2.6	0.0	-10.2	-29.9	NA
35 Whelen	250	2400	2197	2005	1823	1652	3197	2680	2230	1844	1515	+2.5	-1.2	-13.7	NA	$20
358 Norma Mag.	250	2800	2510	2230	1970	1730	4350	3480	2750	2145	1655	+2.5	+1.0	-7.6	-25.2	NA
358 STA	275	2850	2562	229*2	2039	1764	4959	4009	3208	2539	1899	+1.9	0.0	-8.58	-26.1	NA
9.3x57mm Mau.	286	2070	1810	1590	1390	1110	2710	2090	1600	1220	955	+2.5	-2.6	-22.5	NA	NA
9.3x62mm Mau.	286	2360	2089	1844	1623	NA	3538	2771	2157	1670	1260	+2.5	-1.6	-21.0	NA	NA
9.3x64mm	286	2700	2505	2318	2139	1968	4629	3984	3411	2906	2460	+2.5	+2.7	-4.5	-19.2	NA
9.3x74Rmm	286	2360	2089	1844	1623	NA	3538	2771	2157	1670	NA	+2.5	-2.0	-11.0	NA	NA
38-55 Win.	255	1320	1190	1091	1018	963	987	802	674	587	525	0.0	-23.4	NA	NA	$25
375 Winchester	200	2200	1841	1526	1268	1089	2150	1506	1034	714	527	+2.5	-4.0	-26.2	NA	$27
375 Winchester	250	1900	1647	1424	1239	1103	2005	1506	1126	852	676	+2.5	-6.9	-33.3	NA	$27
375 Dakota	300	2600	2316	2051	1804	1579	4502	3573	2800	2167	1661	+2.4	0.0	-11.0	-32.7	NA
375 N.E. 2-1/2"	270	2000	1740	1507	1310	NA	2398	1815	1362	1026	NA	+2.5	-6.0	-30.0	NA	NA
375 Flanged	300	2450	2150	1886	1640	NA	3998	3102	2369	1790	NA	+2.5	-2.4	-17.0	NA	NA
375 H&H Magnum	250	2670	2450	2240	2040	1850	3955	3335	2790	2315	1905	+2.5	-0.4	-10.2	-28.4	NA
375 H&H Magnum	270	2690	2420	2166	1928	1707	4337	3510	2812	2228	1747	+2.5	0.0	-10.0	-29.4	$28
375 H&H Magnum*	300	2530	2245	1979	1733	1512	4263	3357	2608	2001	1523	+2.5	-1.0	-10.5	-33.6	$28
375 H&H Hvy. Mag.	270	2870	2628	2399	2182	1976	4937	4141	3451	2150	1845	+1.7	0.0	-7.2	-21.0	NA
375 H&H Hvy. Mag.	300	2705	2386	2090	1816	1568	4873	3793	2908	2195	1637	+2.3	0.0	-10.4	-31.4	NA
375 Wea. Mag.	300	2700	2420	2157	1911	1685	4856	3901	3100	2432	1891	+2.5	-.04	-10.7	-	NA
378 Wea. Mag.	270	3180	2976	2781	2594	2415	6062	5308	4635	4034	3495	+2.5	+2.6	-1.8	-11.3	$71
378 Wea. Mag.	300	2929	2576	2252	1952	1680	5698	4419	3379	2538	1881	+2.5	+1.2	-7.0	-24.5	$77
375 A-Square	300	2920	2626	2351	2093	1850	5679	4594	3681	2917	2281	+2.5	+1.4	-6.0	-21.0	NA
38-40 Win.	180	1160	999	901	827	764	538	399	324	273	233	0.0	-33.9	NA	NA	$42**

Caliber	Bullet Weight Grams	VELOCITY (fps)					ENERGY (ft. lbs.)					TRAJ. (in.)				Approx. Price per box
		Muzzle	100 yds.	200 yds.	300 yds.	400 yds.	Muzzle	100 yds.	200 yds.	300 yds.	400 yds.	100 yds.	200 yds.	300 yds.	400 yds.	
450/400-3"	400	2150	1932	1730	1545	1379	4105	3316	2659	2119	1689	+2.5	-4.0	-9.5	-30.3	NA
416 Dakota	400	2450	2294	2143	1998	1859	5330	4671	4077	3544	3068	+2.5	-0.2	-10.5	-29.4	NA
416 Taylor	400	2350	2117	1896	1693	NA	4905	3980	3194	2547	NA	+2.5	-1.2	15.0	NA	NA
416 Hoffman	400	2380	2145	1923	1718	1529	5031	4087	3285	2620	2077	+2.5	-1.0	-14.1	NA	NA
416 Rigby	350	2600	2449	2303	2162	2026	5253	4661	4122	3632	3189	+2.5	-1.8	-10.2	-26.0	NA
416 Rigby	400	2370	2210	2050	1900	NA	4990	4315	3720	3185	NA	+2.5	-0.7	-12.1	NA	NA
416 Rigby	410	2370	2110	1870	1640	NA	5115	4050	3165	2455	NA	+2.5	-2.4	-17.3	NA	$110
416 Rem. Mag.*	350	2520	2270	2034	1814	1611	4935	4004	3216	2557	2017	+2.5	-0.8	-12.6	-35.0	$82
416 Rem. Mag.*	400	2400	2175	1962	1763	1579	5115	4201	3419	2760	2214	+2.5	-1.5	-14.6	NA	$80
416 Wea. Mag.*	400	2700	2397	2115	1852	1613	6474	5104	3971	3047	2310	+2.5	0.0	-10.1	-30.4	$96
10.57 (416) Meteor	400	2730	2532	2342	2161	1987	6621	5695	4874	4147	3508	+1.9	0.0	-8.3	-24.0	NA
404 Jeffrey	400	2150	1924	1716	1525	NA	4105	3289	2614	2064	NA	+2.5	-4.0	-22.1	NA	NA
425 Express	400	2400	2160	1934	1725	NA	5115	4145	3322	2641	NA	+2.5	-1.0	-14.0	NA	NA
44-40 Win.	200	1190	1006	900	822	756	629	449	360	300	254	0.0	-33.3	NA	NA	$36**
44 Rem. Mag.	210	1920	1477	1155	982	880	1719	1017	622	450	361	0.0	-17.6	NA	NA	$14
44 Rem. Mag.	240	1760	1380	1114	970	878	1650	1015	661	501	411	0.0	-17.6	NA	NA	$13
444 Marlin	240	2350	1815	1377	1087	941	2942	1753	1001	630	472	+2.5	-15.1	-31.0	NA	$22
444 Marlin	265	2120	1733	1405	1160	1012	2644	1768	1162	791	603	+2.5	-6.0	-32.2	NA	Disc.
45-70 Govt.	300	1810	1497	1244	1073	969	2182	1492	1031	767	625	0.0	-14.8	NA	NA	$21
45-70 Govt.	405	1330	1168	1055	977	918	1590	1227	1001	858	758	0.0	-24.6	NA	NA	$21
458 Win. Magnum	350	2470	1990	1570	1250	1060	4740	3065	1915	1205	870	+2.5	-2.5	-21.6	NA	$43
458 Win. Magnum	400	2380	2170	1960	1770	NA	5030	4165	3415	2785	NA	+2.5	-0.4	-13.4	NA	$73
458 Win. Magnum	465	2220	1999	1791	1601	NA	5088	4127	3312	2646	NA	+2.5	-2.0	-17.7	NA	NA
458 Win. Magnum	500	2040	1823	1623	1442	1237	4620	3689	2924	2308	1839	+2.5	-3.5	-22.0	NA	$61
458 Win. Magnum	510	2040	1770	1527	1319	1157	4712	3547	2640	1970	1516	+2.5	-4.1	-25.0	NA	$41
450 Dakota	500	2450	2235	2030	1838	1658	6663	5544	4576	3748	3051	+2.5	-0.6	-12.0	-33.8	NA
450 N.E. 3-1/4"	465	2190	1970	1765	1577	NA	4952	4009	3216	2567	NA	+2.5	-3.0	-20.0	NA	NA
450 N.E. 3-1/4"	500	2150	1920	1708	1514	NA	5132	4093	3238	2544	NA	+2.5	-4.0	-22.9	NA	NA
450 No. 2	465	2190	1970	1765	1577	NA	4952	4009	3216	2567	NA	+2.5	-3.0	-20.0	NA	NA
450 No. 2	500	2150	1920	1708	1514	NA	5132	4093	3238	2544	NA	+2.5	-4.0	-22.9	NA	NA
458 Lott	465	2380	2150	1932	1730	NA	5848	4773	3855	3091	NA	+2.5	-1.0	-14.0	NA	NA
458 Lott	500	2300	2062	1838	1633	NA	5873	4719	3748	2960	NA	+2.5	-1.6	-16.4	NA	NA
450 Ackley Mag.	465	2400	2169	1950	1747	NA	5947	4857	3927	3150	NA	+2.5	-1.0	-13.7	NA	NA
450 Ackley Mag.	500	2320	2081	1855	1649	NA	5975	4085	3820	3018	NA	+2.5	-1.2	-15.0	NA	NA
460 Short A-Sq.	500	2420	2175	1943	1729	NA	6501	5250	4193	3319	NA	+2.5	-0.8	-12.8	-	NA
460 Wea. Mag.	500	2700	2404	2128	1869	1635	8092	6416	5026	3878	2969	+2.5	+0.6	-8.9	-28.0	$72
500/465 N.E.	480	2150	1917	1703	1507	NA	4926	3917	3089	2419	NA	+2.5	-4.0	-22.2	-	NA
470 Rigby	500	2150	1940	1740	1560	NA	5130	4170	3360	2695	NA	+2.5	-2.8	-19.4	NA	NA
470 Nitro Ex.	480	2190	1954	1735	1536	NA	5111	4070	3210	2515	NA	+2.5	-3.5	-20.8	NA	NA
470 Nitro Ex.	500	2150	1890	1650	1440	1270	5130	3965	3040	2310	1790	+2.5	-4.3	-24.0	NA	$177
475 No. 2	500	2200	1955	1728	1522	NA	5375	4243	3316	2573	NA	+2.5	-3.2	-20.9	NA	NA
505 Gibbs	525	2300	2063	1840	1637	NA	6166	4922	3948	3122	NA	+2.5	-3.0	-18.0	NA	NA
500 N.E.-3"	570	2150	1928	1722	1533	NA	5850	4703	3752	2975	NA	+2.5	-3.7	-22.0	NA	NA
500 N.E.-3"	600	2150	1927	1721	1531	NA	6158	4947	3944	3124	NA	+2.5	-4.0	-22.0	NA	NA\
495 A-Square	570	2350	2117	1896	1693	NA	5850	4703	3752	2975	NA	+2.5	-1.0	-14.5	NA	NA
495 A-Square	600	2280	2050	1833	1635	NA	6925	5598	4478	3562	NA	+2.5	-2.0	-17.0	NA	NA
500 A-Square	600	2380	2144	1922	1766	NA	7546	6126	4920	3922	NA	+2.5	-3.0	-17.0	NA	NA
500 A-Square	707	2250	2040	1841	1567	NA	7947	6530	5318	4311	NA	+2.5	-2.0	-17.0	NA	NA
500 BMG PMC	660	3080	2854	2639	2444	2248	13688		500 yd. zero			+3.1	+3.90	+4.7	+2.8	NA
577 Nitro Ex.	750	2050	1793	1562	1360	NA	6990	5356	4065	3079	NA	+2.5	-5.0	-26.0	NA	NA
577 Tyrannosaur	750	2400	2141	1898	1675	NA	9591	7633	5996	4671	NA	+3.0	0.0	-12.9	NA	NA
600 N.E.	900	1950	1680	1452	NA	NA	7596	5634	4212	NA	NA	+5.6	0.0	NA	NA	NA
700 N.E.	1200	1900	1676	1472	NA	NA	9618	7480	5774	NA	NA	+5.7	0.0	NA	NA	NA

= Weatherby Magnum. Spfd. = Springfield. A-A-Sq. = A-Square. N.E.=Nitro Express. Many manufacturers do not supply suggested retail prices. Others did not get their pricing to us before press time. All pricing can vary dependent on the exact brand and style of ammo selected and/or the retail outlet from which you make your purchase. Pricing has been rounded to the nearest dollar and represents our best estimate of average pricing. An * after the bullet weight means these loads are available with Nosler Partition or Swift A-Frame bullets. Listed pricing may or may not reflect this bullet type. ** = these are packed 50 to box, all others are 20 to box.

CENTERFIRE HANDGUN CARTRIDGES—BALLISTICS AND PRICES

Caliber	Bullet Wgt. Grs.	VELOCITY (fps)			ENERGY (ft. lbs.)			Mid-Range Traj. (in.)		Bbl. Lgth. (in).	Est. Price/ box
		MV	50 yds.	100 yds.	ME	50 yds.	100 yds.	50 yds.	100 yds.		
221 Rem. Fireball	50	2650	2380	2130	780	630	505	0.2	0.8	10.5"	$15
25 Automatic	35	900	813	742	63	51	43	NA	NA	2"	$18
25 Automatic	45	815	730	655	65	55	40	1.8	7.7	2"	$21
25 Automatic	50	760	705	660	65	55	50	2.0	8.7	2"	$17
7.5mm Swiss	107	1010	NA	NA	240	NA	NA	NA	NA	NA	NEW
7.62mmTokarev	87	1390	NA	NA	365	NA	NA	0.6	NA	4.5"	NA
7.62 Nagant	97	1080	NA	NA	350	NA	NA	NA	NA	NA	NEW
7.63 Mauser	88	1440	NA	NA	405	NA	NA	NA	NA	NA	NEW
30 Luger	93†	1220	1110	1040	305	255	225	0.9	3.5	4.5"	$34
30 Carbine	110	1790	1600	1430	785	625	500	0.4	1.7	10"	$28
32 S&W	88	680	645	610	90	80	75	2.5	10.5	3"	$17
32 S&W Long	98	705	670	635	115	100	90	2.3	10.5	4"	$17
32 Short Colt	80	745	665	590	100	80	60	2.2	9.9	4"	$19
32 H&R Magnum	85	1100	1020	930	230	195	165	1.0	4.3	4.5"	$21
32 H&R Magnum	95	1030	940	900	225	190	170	1.1	4.7	4.5"	$19
32 Automatic	60	970	895	835	125	105	95	1.3	5.4	4"	$22
32 Automatic	65	950	890	830	130	115	100	1.3	5.6	NA	NA
32 Automatic	71	905	855	810	130	115	95	1.4	5.8	4"	$19
8mm Lebel Pistol	111	850	NA	NA	180	NA	NA	NA	NA	NA	NEW
8mm Steyr	112	1080	NA	NA	290	NA	NA	NA	NA	NA	NEW
8mm Gasser	126	850	NA	NA	200	NA	NA	NA	NA	NA	NEW
380 Automatic	60	1130	960	NA	170	120	NA	1.0	NA	NA	NA
380 Automatic	85/88	990	920	870	190	165	145	1.2	5.1	4"	$20
380 Automatic	90	1000	890	800	200	160	130	1.2	5.5	3.75"	$10
380 Automatic	95/100	955	865	785	190	160	130	1.4	5.9	4"	$20
38 Super Auto +P	115	1300	1145	1040	430	335	275	0.7	3.3	5"	$26
38 Super Auto +P	125/130	1215	1100	1015	425	350	300	0.8	3.6	5"	$26
38 Super Auto +P	147	1100	1050	1000	395	355	325	0.9	4.0	5"	NA
9x18mm Makarov	95	1000	NA	NA	NA	NA	NA	NA	NA	NA	NEW
9x18mm Ultra	100	1050	NA	NA	240	NA	NA	NA	NA	NA	NEW
9x23mm Largo	124	1190	1055	966	390	306	257	0.7	3.7	4"	NA
9x23mm Win.	125	1450	1249	1103	583	433	338	0.6	2.8	NA	NA
9mm Steyr	115	1180	NA	NA	350	NA	NA	NA	NA	NA	NEW
9mm Luger	88	1500	1190	1010	440	275	200	0.6	3.1	4"	$24
9mm Luger	90	1360	1112	978	370	247	191	NA	NA	4"	$26
9mm Luger	95	1300	1140	1010	350	275	215	0.8	3.4	4"	NA
9mm Luger	100	1180	1080	NA	305	255	NA	0.9	NA	4"	NA
9mm Luger	115	1155	1045	970	340	280	240	0.9	3.9	4"	$21
9mm Luger	123/125	1110	1030	970	340	290	260	1.0	4.0	4"	$23
9mm Luger	140	935	890	850	270	245	225	1.3	5.5	4"	$23
9mm Luger	147	990	940	900	320	290	265	1.1	4.9	4"	$26
9mm Luger +P	90	1475	NA	NA	437	NA	NA	NA	NA	NA	NA
9mm Luger +P	115	1250	1113	1019	399	316	265	0.8	3.5	4"	$27
9mm Federal	115	1280	1130	1040	420	330	280	0.7	3.3	4"V	$24
9mm Luger Vector	115	1155	1047	971	341	280	241	NA	NA	4"	NA
9mm Luger +P	124	1180	1089	1021	384	327	287	0.8	3.8	4"	NA
38 S&W	146	685	650	620	150	135	125	2.4	10.0	4"	$19
38 Short Colt	125	730	685	645	150	130	115	2.2	9.4	6"	$19
39 Special	100	950	900	NA	200	180	NA	1.3	NA	4"V	NA
38 Special	110	945	895	850	220	195	175	1.3	5.4	4"V	$23
38 Special	130	775	745	710	175	160	120	1.9	7.9	4"V	$22
38 (Multi-Ball)	140	830	730	505	215	130	80	2.0	10.6	4"V	$10**
38 Special	148	710	635	565	165	130	105	2.4	10.6	4"V	$17
38 Special	158	755	725	690	200	185	170	2.0	8.3	4"V	$18
38 Special +P	95	1175	1045	960	290	230	195	0.9	3.9	4"V	$23
38 Special +P	110	995	925	870	240	210	185	1.2	5.1	4"V	$23
38 Special +P	125	975	929	885	264	238	218	1	5.2	4"	NA
38 Special +P	125	945	900	860	250	225	205	1.3	5.4	4"V	#23
38 Special +P	129	945	910	870	255	235	215	1.3	5.3	4"V	$11
38 Special +P	130	925	887	852	247	227	210	1.3	5.50	4"V	NA
38 Special +P	147/150(c)	884	NA	NA	264	NA	NA	NA	NA	4"V	$27
38 Special +P	158	890	855	825	280	255	240	1.4	6.0	4"V	$20
357 SIG	115	1520	NA	NA	593	NA	NA	NA	NA	NA	NA
357 SIG	124	1450	NA	NA	578	NA	NA	NA	NA	NA	NA
357 SIG	125	1350	1190	1080	510	395	325	0.7	3.1	4"	NA
357 SIG	150	1130	1030	970	420	355	310	0.9	4.0	NA	NA
356 TSW	115	1520	NA	NA	593	NA	NA	NA	NA	NA	NA
356 TSW	124	1450	NA	NA	578	NA	NA	NA	NA	NA	NA
356 TSW	135	1280	1120	1010	490	375	310	0.8	3.50	NA	NA
356 TSW	147	1220	1120	1040	485	410	355	0.8	3.5	5"	NA
357 Magnum	110	1295	1095	975	410	290	230	0.8	3.5	4"V	$25
357 (Med.Vel.)	125	1220	1075	985	415	315	270	0.8	3.7	4"V	$25
357 Magnum	125	1450	1240	1090	585	425	330	0.6	2.8	4"V	$25
357 (Multi-Ball)	140	1155	830	665	420	215	135	1.2	6.4	4"V	$11**
357 Magnum	140	1360	1195	1075	575	445	360	0.7	3.0	4"V	$25
357 Magnum	145	1290	1155	1060	535	430	360	0.8	3.5	4"V	$26
357 Magnum	150/158	1235	1105	1015	535	430	360	0.8	3.5	4"V	$25
357 Magnum	165	1290	1189	1108	610	518	450	0.7	3.1	8-3/8"	NA
357 Magnum	180	1145	1055	985	525	445	390	0.9	3.9	4"V	$25
357 Magnum	180	1180	1088	1020	557	473	416	0.8	3.6	8"V	NA
357 Rem. Maximum	158	1825	1590	1380	1170	885	670	0.4	1.7	10.5"	$14**
40 S&W	135	1140	1070	NA	390	345	NA	0.9	NA	4"	NA
40 S&W	155	1140	1026	958	447	362	309	0.9	4.1	4"	$14***
40 S&W	165	1150	NA	NA	485	NA	NA	NA	NA	4"	$18***
40 S&W	180	985	936	893	388	350	319	1.4	5.0	4"	$14***
40 S&W	180	1015	960	914	412	368	334	1.3	4.5	4"	NA
400 Cor-Bon	135	1450	NA	NA	630	NA	NA	NA	NA	5"	NA
10mm Automatic	155	1125	1046	986	436	377	335	0.9	3.9	5"	$26
10mm Automatic	170	1340	1165	1145	680	510	415	0.7	3.2	5"	$31
10mm Automatic	175	1290	1140	1035	650	505	420	0.7	3.3	5.5"	$11**
10mm Auto. (FBI)	180	950	905	865	361	327	299	1.5	5.4	4"	$16**
10mm Automatic	180	1030	970	920	425	375	340	1.1	4.7	5"	$16**
10mm Auto H.V.	180†	1240	1124	1037	618	504	430	0.8	3.4	5"	$27
10mm Automatic	200	1160	1070	1010	495	510	430	0.9	3.8	5"	$14**
10.4mm Italian	177	950	NA	NA	360	NA	NA	NA	NA	NA	NEW
41 Action Exp.	180	1000	947	903	400	359	326	0.5	4.2	5"	$13**
41 Rem. Magnum	170	1420	1165	1015	760	515	390	0.7	3.2	4"V	$33
41 Rem. Magnum	175	1250	1120	1030	605	490	410	0.8	3.4	4"V	$14**
41 (Med. Vel.)	210	965	900	840	435	375	330	1.3	5.4	4"V	$30
41 Rem. Magnum	210	1300	1160	1060	790	630	535	0.7	3.2	4"V	$33
44 S&W Russian	247	780	NA	NA	335	NA	NA	NA	NA	NA	NA
44 S&W Special	180	980	NA	NA	383	NA	NA	NA	NA	6.5"	NA
44 S&W Special	180	1000	935	882	400	350	311	NA	NA	7.5"V	NA
44 S&W Special	200†	875	825	780	340	302	270	1.2	6.0	6"	$13**
44 S&W Special	200	1035	940	865	475	390	335	1.1	4.9	6.5"	$13**
44 S&W Special	240/246	755	725	695	310	285	265	2.0	8.3	6.5"	$26
44 Rem. Magnum	180	1610	1365	1175	1035	745	550	0.5	2.3	4"V	$18**
44 Rem. Magnum	200	1400	1192	1053	870	630	492	0.6	NA	6.5"	$20
44 Rem. Magnum	210	1495	1310	1165	1040	805	635	0.6	2.5	6.5"	$18**
44 (Med. Vel.)	240	1000	945	900	535	475	435	1.1	4.8	6.5"	$17
44 R.M. (Jacketed)	240	1180	1080	1010	740	625	545	0.9	3.7	4"V	$18**
44 R.M. (Lead)	240	1350	1185	1070	970	750	610	0.7	3.1	4"V	$29
44 Rem. Magnum	250	1180	1100	1040	775	670	600	0.8	3.6	6.5"V	$21
44 Rem. Magnum	250	1230	1132	1057	840	711	620	0.8	2.9	6.5"V	NA
44 Rem. Magnum	275	1235	1142	1070	931	797	699	0.8	3.3	6.5"	NA
44 Rem. Magnum	300	1200	1100	1026	959	806	702	NA	NA	7.5"	$17
440 CorBon	260	1700	1544	1403	1669	1377	1136	1.58	NA	10	NA
450 Short Colt	226	830	NA	NA	350	NA	NA	NA	NA	NA	NEW
45 Automatic	165	1030	930	NA	385	315	NA	1.2	NA	5"	NA
45 Automatic	185	1000	940	890	410	360	325	1.1	4.9	5"	$28
45 Auto. (Match)	185	770	705	650	245	204	175	2.0	8.7	5"	$28
45 Auto. (Match)	200	940	890	840	392	352	312	2.0	8.6	5"	$20
45 Automatic	200	975	917	860	421	372	328	1.4	5.0	5"	$18
45 Automatic	230	830	800	675	355	325	300	1.6	6.8	5"	$27
45 Automatic	230	880	846	816	396	366	340	1.5	6.1	5"	NA
45 Automatic +P	165	1250	NA	NA	573	NA	NA	NA	NA	NA	NA
45 Automatic +P	185	1140	1040	970	535	445	385	0.9	4.0	5"	$31
45 Automatic +P	200	1055	982	925	494	428	380	NA	NA	5"	NA
45 Super	185	1300	1190	1108	694	582	504	NA	NA	5"	NA
45 Win. Magnum	230	1400	1230	1105	1000	775	635	0.6	2.8	5"	$14**
45 Win. Magnum	260	1250	1137	1053	902	746	640	0.8	3.3	5"	$16**
455 Webley MKII	262	850	NA	NA	420	NA	NA	NA	NA	NA	NA
45 Colt	200	1000	938	889	444	391	351	1.3	4.8	5.5"	$21
45 Colt	225	960	890	830	460	395	345	1.3	5.5	5.5"	$22
45 Colt	250/255	860	820	780	410	375	340	1.6	6.6	5.5"	$27
454 Casull	260	1800	1577	1381	1871	1436	1101	0.4	1.8	7.5"V	NA
454 Casull	300	1625	1451	1308	1759	1413	1141	0.5	2.0	7.5"V	NA
50 Action Exp.	325	1400	1209	1075	1414	1055	835	0.2	2.3	6"	$24**

Notes: Blanks are available in 32 S&W, 38 S&W, and 38 Special. V after barrel length indictes test barrel was vented to produce ballistics similar to a revolver with a normal barrel-to-cylinder gap. Ammo prices are per 50 rounds except when marked with an ** which signifies a 20 round box; *** signifies a 25-round box. Not all loads are available from all ammo manufacturers. Listed loads are those made by Remington, Winchester, Federal, and others. DISC. is a discontinued load. Prices are rounded to nearest whole dollar and will vary with brand and retail outlet. † = new bullet weight this year; "c" indicates a change in data.

RIMFIRE AMMUNITION—BALLISTICS AND PRICES

Cartridge Type	Bullet Wt. Grs.	Velocity (fps) 22-1/2" Bbl.		Energy (ft. lbs.) 22-1/2" Bbl.		Mid-Range Traj. (in.)	Muzzle Velocity
		Muzzle	100 yds.	Muzzle	100 yds.	100 yds.	6" Bbl.
22 Short Blank	—	—	—	—	—	—	—
22 Short CB	29	727	610	33	24	NA	706
22 Short Target	29	830	695	44	31	6.8	786
22 Short HP	27	1164	920	81	50	4.3	1077
22 Long CB	29	727	610	33	24	NA	706
22 Long HV	29	1180	946	90	57	4.1	1031
22 LR Ballistician	25	1100	760	65	30	NA	NA
22 LR Pistol Match	40	1070	890	100	70	4.6	940
22 LR Sub Sonic HP	38	1050	901	93	69	4.7	NA
22 LR Standard Velocity	40	1070	890	100	70	4.6	940
22 LR HV	40	1255	1016	140	92	3.6	1060
22 LR Silhoutte	42	1220	1003	139	94	3.6	1025
22 LR HV HP	40	1280	1001	146	89	3.5	1085
22 LR Hyper HP	32/33/34	1500	1075	165	85	2.8	NA
22 LR Stinger HP	32	1640	1132	191	91	2.6	1395
22 LR Shot #12	31	950	NA	NA	NA	NA	NA
22 Win. Mag.	30	2200	1373	322	127	1.4	1610
22 Win. Mag. JHP	34	2120	1435	338	155	1.4	NA
22 Win. Mag. JHP	40	1910	1326	324	156	1.7	1480
22 Win. Mag. FMJ	40	1910	1326	324	156	1.7	1480
22 Win. Mag. JHP	50	1650	1280	300	180	1.3	NA
22 Win. Mag. Shot #11	52	1000	—	NA	—	—	NA

Note: The actual ballistics obtained with your firearm can vary considerably from the advertised ballistics. Also, ballistics can vary from lot to lot with the same brand and type load.

CAUTION: PRICES SHOWN ARE SUPPLIED BY THE MANUFACTURER OR IMPORTER. CHECK YOUR LOCAL GUNSHOP.

SHOTSHELL LOADS AND PRICES

Dram Equiv.	Shot Ozs.	Load Style	Shot Sizes	Brands	Avg. Nom. Price/box	Velocity (fps)
10 Gauge 3-1/2" Magnum						
4-1/2	2-1/4	premium	BB, 2,4,5,6	Win., Fed., Rem.	$33	1205
4-1/4	2	high velocity	BB, 2, 4	Rem.	$22	1210
4-1/2	2-1/4	duples	4x6	Rem.	$14*	1205
Max	18 pellets	premium	00 buck	Fed., Win.	$7**	1100
Max	1-7/8	Bismuth	BB, 2, 4	Win., Bis.	NA	1225
4-1/4	1-3/4	steel	TT, T, BBB, BB, 1, 2, 3	Win., Rem.	$27	1260
Mag	1-5/8	steel	T, BBB	Win.	$27	1285
4-5/8	1-5/8	steel	F, T, BBB	Fed.	$26	1350
Max	1-3/8	steel	T, BBB, BB, 2	Fed., Win.	NA	1450
Max	1-3/4	slug, rifled	slug	Fed.	NA	1280
12 Gauge 3-1/2" Magnum						
Max	2/14	premium	4, 5, 6	Fed., Rem., Win.	$13*	1150
Max	18 pellets	premium	00 buck	Fed., Win., Rem.	$7**	1100
Max	1-7/8	Bismuth	BB, 2, 4	Win., Bis.	NA	1225
4 -1/8	1-9/16	steel	TT, F, T, BBB, BB, 1, 2	Rem., Win., Fed.	$22	1335
Max	1-3/8	steel	T, BBB, BB, 2, 4	Fed., Win.	NA	1450
Max	1-3/8	Tungsten - Iron	BB, 2, 4	Fed.	NA	1450
12 Gauge 3" Magnum						
4	2	premium	BB, 2, 4, 5, 6	Win., Fed., Rem.	$9*	1175
4	2	duplex	4x6	Rem.	$10	1175
4	1-7/8	premium	BB, 2, 4, 6	Win., Fed., Rem.	$19	1210
4	1-7/8	duple	4x6	Rem., Fio.	$9*	1210
Max	1-3/4	turkey	4, 5, 6	Fio., Win.	NA	1300
4-1/2	1-3/4	duplex	2x4, 4x6	Fio.	NA	1150
4	1-5/8	premium	2, 4, 5, 6	Win., Fed., Rem.	$18	1290
Max	1-5/8	Bismuth	BB, 2, 4, 5, 6	Win., Bis.	NA	1250
4	24 pellets	buffered	1 buck	Win., Fed., Rem.	$5**	1040
4	15 pellets	buffered	00 buck	Win., Fed., Rem.	$6**	1210
4	10 pellets	buffered	000 buck	Win., Fed., Rem.	$6**	1225
4	41 pellets	buffered	4 buck	Win., Fed., Rem.	$6**	1210
Max	1-3/8	Tungsten - Polymer	4, 6	Fed.	NA	1330
Max	1-3/8	slug	slug	Bren.	NA	1476
Max	1-1/4	slug, rifled	slug	Fed.	NA	1600
Max	1-3/16	saboted slug	copper clug	Rem.	NA	1500
Max	1-1/8	Tungsten -Iron	BB, 2, 4	Fed.	NA	1400
Max	1	slug, rifled	slug, magnum	Win., Rem.	$5**	1760
Max	1	saboted slug	slug	Win., Fed.	$10**	1550
3-5/8	1-3/8	steel	TT, F, T, BBB, BB, 1, 2, 3, 4	Win., Fed., Rem.	$19	1275
Max	1-1/8	steel	T, BBB, BB, 2, 4, 5, 6	Fed., Win.	NA	1450
Max	1-1/8	steel	BB, 2	Fed.	NA	1400
4	1-1/4	steel	TT, F, T, BBB, BB, 1, 2, 3, 4, 6	Win., Fed., Rem.	$18	1375
12 gauge 2-3/4"						
Max	1-5/8	magnum	4, 5, 6	Win., Fed.	$8*	1250
Max	1-3/8	turkey	4, 5, 6	Fio.	NA	1250
Max	1-3/8	duplex	2x4, 4x6	Fio.	NA	1200
Max	1-3/8	Bismuth	BB, 2, 4, 5, 6	Win., Bis.	NA	1280
3-3/4	1-1/2	magnum	BB, 2, 4, 5, 6	Win., Fed., Rem.	$16	1260
3-3/4	1-1/2	duplex	BBx4, 2x4, 4x6	Rem., Fio.	$9*	1260
3-3/4	1-1/4	high velocity	BB, 2, 4, 5, 6, 7-1/2, 8, 9	win., Fed., Rem., Fio.	$13	1330
Max	1-1/4	Tungsten - Polymer	4, 6	Fed.	NA	1330
3-1/2	1-1/4	mid velocity	7, 8, 9	Win.	Disc.	1275
3-1/4	1-1/4	standard velocity	6, 7-1/2, 8, 9	Win., Fed., Rem., Fio.	$11	1220
3-1/4	1-1/8	standard velocity	4, 6, 7-1/2, 8, 9	Win., Fed., Rem., Fio.	$9	1255
Max	1	steel	BB, 2	Fed.	NA	1450
Max	1	Tungsten - Iron	BB, 2, 4	Fed.	NA	1450
3-1/4	1	standard velocity	6, 7-1/2, 8	Rem., Fed., Fio., Win.	$6	1290
3-1/4	1-1/4	target	7-1/2, 8, 9	Win., Fed., Rem.	$10	1220
3	1-1/8	spreader	7-1/2, 8, 8-1/2, 9	Fio.	NA	1200
3	1-1/8	duplex target	7-1/2x8	Rem.	NA	1200
3	1-1/8	target	7-1/2, 8, 9, 7-1/2x8	Win., Fed., Rem.	$7	1200
3	1-1/8	duplex clays	7-1/2x8-1/2	Rem.	NA	1200
2-3/4	1-1/8	target	7-1/2, 8, 8-1/2, 9, 7-1/2x8	Win., Fed., Rem., Fio.	$7	1145
2-3/4	1-1/8	duplex target	7-1/2x8	Rem.	NA	1145
2-3/4	1-1/8	low recoil	7-1/2, 8	Rem.	NA	1145
2-1/2	26 grams	low recoil	8	Win.	NA	980
2-1/4	1-1/8	target	7-1/2, 8, 8-1/2, 9	Rem., Fed.	$7	1080
Max	1	spreader	7-1/2, 8, 8-1/2, 9	Fio.	NA	1300
3-1/4	28 grams (1 oz)	target	7-1/2, 8, 9	Win., Fed., Rem., Fio.	$8	1290
3	1	target	7-1/2, 8, 8-1/2, 9	Win., Fio.	NA	1235
2-3/4	1	target	7-1/2, 8, 8-1/2, 9	Fed., Rem., Fio.	NA	1180
3-1/4	24 grams	target	7-1/2, 8, 9	Fed., Win., Fio.	NA	1325
3	7/8	light	8	Fio.	NA	1200

Dram Equiv.	Shot Ozs.	Load Style	Shot Sizes	Brands	Avg. Nom. Price/box	Velocity (fps)
3-3/4	8 pellets	buffered	000 buck	Win., Fed., Rem.	$4**	1325
4	12 pellets	premium	00 buck	Win., Fed., Rem.	$5**	1290
3-3/4	9 pellets	buffered	00 buck	Win., Fed., Rem., Fio.	$19	1325
3-3/4	12 pellets	buffered	0 buck	Win., Fed., Rem.	$4**	1275
4	20 pellets	buffered	1 buck	Win., Fed., Rem.	$4**	1075
3-3/4	16 pellets	buffered	1 buck	Win., Fed., Rem.	$4**	1250
4	34 pellets	premium	4 buck	Fed., Rem.	$5**	1250
3-3/4	27 pellets	buffered	4 buck	Win., Fed., Rem., Fio.	$4**	1325
Max	1	saboted slug	slug	Win., Fed., Rem.	$10**	1450
Max	1-1/4	slug, rifled	slug	Fed.	NA	1520
Max	1	slug, rifled	slug, magnum	Rem., Fio.	$5**	1680
Max	1	slug, rifled	slug	Win., Fed.	$4**	1610
3	1-1/8	steel target	6-1/2, 7	Rem.	NA	1200
2-3/4	1-1/8	steel target	7, 8	Rem.	NA	1145
3	1#	steel	7	Win.	$11	1235
3-1/2	1-1/4	steel	T, BBB, BB, 1, 2, 3, 4, 5, 6	Win., Fed., Rem.	$18	1275
3-3/4	1-1/8	steel	BB, 1, 2, 3, 4, 5, 6	Win., Fed., Rem., Fio.	$16	1365
3-3/4	1	steel	2, 3, 4, 5, 6, 7	Win., Fed., Rem., Fio.	$13	1390
Max	7/8	steel	7	Fio.	NA	1440
16 Gauge 2-3/4"						
3-1/4	1-1/4	magnum	2, 4, 6	Fed., Rem.	$16	1260
3-1/4	1-1/8	high velocity	4, 6, 7-1/2	Win., Fed., Rem., Fio.	$12	1295
Max	1-1/8	Bismuth	4, 5	Win., Bis.	NA	1200
2-3/4	1-1/8	standard velocity	6, 7-1/2, 8	Fed., Rem., Fio.	$9	1185
2-1/2	1	dove	6, 7-1/2, 8, 9	Fio., Win.	NA	1165
2-3/4	1		6, 7-1/2, 8	Fio.	NA	1200
Max	15/16	steel	2, 4	Fed., Rem.	NA	1300
Max	7/8	steel	2, 4	Win.	$16	1300
3	12 pellets	buffered	1 buck	Win., Fed., Rem.	$4**	1225
Max	4/5	slug, rifled	slug	Win., Fed., Rem.	$4**	1570
20 Gauge 3" Magnum						
3	1-1/4	premium	2, 4, 5, 6, 7-1/2	Win., Fed., Rem.	$15	1185
3	1-1/4	turkey	4, 6	Fio.	NA	1200
Max	18 pellets	buck shot	2 buck	Fed.	NA	1200
Max	24 pellets	buffered	3 buck	Win.	$5**	1150
2-3/4	20 pellets	buck	3 buck	Rem.	$4**	1200
3-1/4	1	steel	1, 2, 3, 4, 5, 6	Win., Fed., Rem.	$15	1330
Max	7/8	Tungsten - Iron	2, 4	Fed.	NA	1375
Mag	5/8	saboted slug	275 gr.	Fed.	NA	1450
20 Gauge 2-3/4"						
2-3/4	1-1/8	magnum	4, 6, 7-1/2	Win., Fed., Rem.	$14	1175
2-3/4	1	high velocity	4, 5, 6, 7-1/2, 8, 9	Win., Fed., Rem., Fio.	$12	1220
Max	1	Bismuth	4, 6	Win., Bis.	NA	1200
2-1/2	1	standard velocity	6, 7-1/2, 8	Win., Rem., Fed., Fio.	$6	1165
2-1/2	7/8	clays	8	Rem.	NA	1200
2-1/2	7/8	promotional	6, 7-1/2, 8	Win., Rem., Fio.	$6	1210
2-1/2	1#	target	8, 9	Win., Rem.	$8	1165
2-1/2	7/8	target	8, 9	Win., Fed., Rem.	$8	1200
Max	20 pellets	buffered	3 buck	Win., Fed.	$4	1200
Max	5/8	slug, saboted	slug	Win.,	$9**	1400
2-3/4	5/8	slug, rifled	slug	Rem.	$4**	1580
Max	3/4	saboted slug	copper slug	Rem.	NA	1450
Max	3/4	slug, rifled	slug	Win., Fed., Rem., Fio.	$4**	1570
Max	3/4	steel	2, 3, 4, 6	Win., Fed., Rem.	$14	1425
28 Gauge 2-3/4"						
2	1	high velocity	6, 7-1/2, 8	Win.	$12	1125
2-1/4	3/4	high velocity	6, 7-1/2, 8, 9	Win., Fed., Rem., Fio.	$11	1295
2	3/4	target	8, 9	Win., Fed., Rem.	$9	1200
Max	5/8	Bismuth	4, 6, 7	Win., Bis.	NA	1250
410 Bore 3"						
Max	11/16	high velocity	4, 5, 6, 7-1/2, 8, 9	Win., Fed., Rem.	$10	1135
Max	9/16	Bismuth	4, 6, 7	Win., Bis.	NA	1175
410 Bore 2-1/2"						
Max	1/2	high velocity	4, 6, 7-1/2	Win., Fed., Rem.	$9	1245
Max	1/5	slug, rifled	slug	Win., Fed., Rem.	$4**	1815
1-1/2	1/2	target	8, 8-1/2, 9	Win., Fed., Rem., Fio.	$8	1200

NOTES: * = 10 rounds per box. ** = 5 rounds per box. Pricing variations and number of rounds per box can occur with type and brand of ammunition. Listed pricing is the average nominal cost for load style and box quantity shown. Not every brand is available in all shot size variations. Some manufacturers do not provide suggested list prices. All prices rounded to nearest whole dollar. The price you pay will vary dependent upon outlet of purchase. # = new load spec this year; "C" indicates a change in data.

NEW 80MM SPOTTING SCOPE

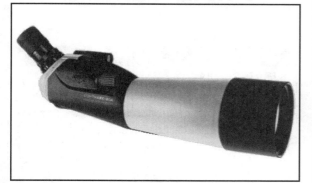

The Model 849U Nighthawk from Swift Instruments is geared for the hunter and nature photographer. Measuring 350mm in length without the eyepiece, this compact, lightweight spotting scope is virtually free from chromatic aberration or distortion and offers excellent depth of field and resolving power. The rubber-armored main body housing features a 1.8x optical finder and a retractable hood to protect the objective lens from direct exposure to sunlight and dew. Accessories include interchangeable eyepieces, 19x, 25x, 31x, 50x, 75x; a zoom eyepiece, 20-60x; a soft carrying case; and telephotographic equipment. All optics are multi-coated and eyepieces feature a bayonet-type mounting for quick lens attachment. Also available as a straight viewing scope (Model 849). Both come attractively gift-boxed.

SWIFT INSTRUMENTS, INC.

NEW HUNTING BINOCULARS

Swift Instrument's 817 Trilyte 8x42mm all-purpose, all-weather binocular is ideal for use in virtually all field conditions. Weighing only 20.4 ounces, the 817 is light, compact and, with its rubber-armored exterior, is waterproof. All air-to-glass surfaces are fully coated, with multi-coating applied to both the ocular lens and objective lens. The camphered roof prisms help the high resolving power of the optical system deliver clear, crisp images afield. The retractable rubber eye cups provide comfortable and protected viewing. The 817 Trilyte comes complete with handsome case and woven neck strap and is attractively gift boxed.

For more information, write or call
Swift Instruments.

SWIFT INSTRUMENTS, INC.

BUILD A GATLING GUN

Complete plans for the 22-caliber Long Rifle Gatling are now available and have been fully adapted to incorporate obtainable materials and makeable parts. No castings are required.

The to-scale blueprints are fully dimensioned and toleranced. A 40-page instruction booklet lists materials and explains each part and how it is made.

The package includes drawings and instructions for making rifled barrels, wooden spoked wheels and all internal parts. The finished piece has 10 rifled barrels and is 3 feet long by 2 feet high. The plan package is $58.57; priority postage within the U.S. included. Overseas air add $14.00. Materials, kits and finished parts also available. Major credit cards, check or money order accepted.

RH MACHINE AND CONSULTING, INC.

TOP-QUALITY BULLET LUBE

Rooster Laboratories offers consistently high performance, professional high-melt cannelure bullet lubricants in a choice of two hardnesses. Both are available in 2″x 6″ sticks for the commercial reloader, and 1″x 4″ hollow and solid sticks.

With a 230°F melting point, both are ideal for indoor and outdoor shooting. Both bond securely to the bullet, remaining intact during shooting.

Zambini is a hard, tough lubricant designed primarily for pistols. HVR is softer, but still firm. Designed primarily for high-velocity rifles, HVR is easier to apply, and also excellent for pistols. Application requires the lubesizer be heated.

Prices: 2″x 6″ sticks $4.00; 1″x 4″ sticks $135.00 per 100. Contact Rooster for more information.

ROOSTER LABORATORIES

REVOLVER LASER SIGHTS

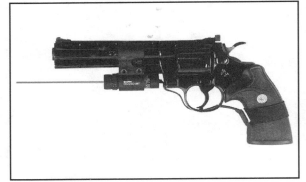

Specifically designed for the demands of revolver shooting, Beamshot Professional Laser Sighting Systems are constructed of high-grade, lightweight aluminum and will maintain accuracy in extreme conditions.

Available in black or silver, the Beamshot 1000 and 3000 series have various ranges from 670nm/300 yards to 635nm/800 yards. There's even a special Beamshot 780nm, visible only when viewed through night vision equipment.

All Beamshots are battery powered to provide continuous "on" operation for 20+ hours. Beamshot laser sights come with a 1 year warranty and are easily mounted to virtually any handgun.

For more information, write or call Quarton USA.

QUARTON USA, LTD. CO.

LONG LASTING LASER SIGHTS

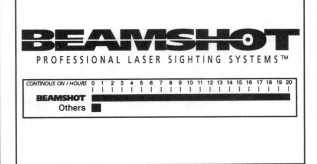

Quarton USA's family of Beamshot Laser Sights have a continuous "on" usage of over 20 hours. That is up to 25 times the life of other laser sights.

Designed and built much better than the average laser sight, the Beamshot laser costs the consumer less initially as well as in battery usage over the long run.

The most important feature of any laser sight is its mounting system; a laser sight that won't mount securely to your weapon is useless. Some manufacturers would have you believe their lasers will mount to "any" weapon, but Beamshot produces the widest variety of mounts available...and they're all in stock. It is not likely there is a weapon that Beamshot can't be easily mounted to. For more information, write or call Quarton USA.

QUARTON USA, LTD. CO.

SEMI-AUTO LASER SIGHTS

Designed specifically for the harsh use and extreme conditions associated with pistols, Beamshot Professional Laser Sighting Systems are constructed to take a beating, yet maintain superior operation and accuracy.

Available in black or silver, the Beamshot 1000 and 3000 series have various ranges from 670nm/300 yards to 635nm/800 yards. There's even a special Beamshot 780nm, visible only when viewed through night vision equipment.

All Beamshots are constructed of lightweight, high-grade aluminum and are battery powered to provide continuous "on" operation for 20+ hours. Beamshot laser sights come with a 1 year warranty and are easily mounted to virtually any handgun. For more information, write or call Quarton USA.

QUARTON USA, LTD. CO.

LONG GUN LASER SIGHTS

Beamshot Professional Laser Sighting Systems are designed for use on rifles and shotguns.

Available in black or silver, the Beamshot 1000 and 3000 series have various ranges from 670nm/300 yards to 635nm/800 yards. The 1001U laser sight projects a precise 1.5″ laser dot at a range of 100 yards. There's even a special Beamshot 780nm, visible only when viewed through night vision equipment.

All Beamshots are constructed of lightweight, high-grade aluminum and are battery powered to provide continuous "on" operation for 20+ hours. Beamshot laser sights come with a 1 year warranty and are easily mounted to virtually all rifles, shotguns or scopes. For more information, write or call Quarton USA.

QUARTON USA, LTD. CO.

FOLDING BIPODS

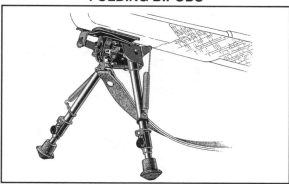

Harris Bipods clamp securely to most stud-equipped bolt-action rifles and are quick-detachable. With adapters, they will fit some other guns. On all models except the Model LM, folding legs have completely adjustable spring-return extensions. The sling swivel attaches to the clamp. This time-proven design is manufactured with heat-treated steel and hard alloys and has a black anodized finish.

Series S Bipods rotate 35° for instant leveling on uneven ground. Hinged base has tension adjustment and buffer springs to eliminate tremor or looseness in crotch area of bipod. They are otherwise similar to non-rotating Series 1A2.

Thirteen models are available from Harris Engineering; literature is free.

HARRIS ENGINEERING INC.

NEW PASTE LUBE FOR SLIDING SURFACES

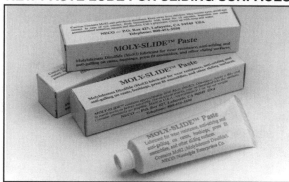

NECO announces the introduction of Moly-Slide™, a new moly-based paste lubricant designed specifically for firearms. Used for many years in industrial applications, Molybdenum disulfide is highly regarded as an effective means for reducing friction between sliding metal-to-metal surfaces. Moly-Slide is ideal for moving components on semi-auto pistols/rifles, pistol slides, bolt-action components, most trigger components and firearm locking lugs. It's available in one-ounce plastic tubes and has the consistency of thick toothpaste. The formulation contains approximately 60% laboratory-grade, extremely small, micron-sized Moly with no graphite. It has a wide working temperature range with minimal evaporative loss. Price per tube is $7.10; $144.84 per case of 24.

NECO (NOSTALGIA ENTERPRISES COMPANY)

RIFLE ACCESSORIES

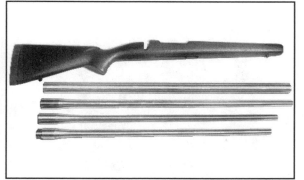

B. Perazone-Gunsmith offers a full range of rifle accessories and services for sporterizing Mauser 93 through 98 rifles from pre-threaded and chambered barrels to synthetic stocks, adjustable triggers, low-swing safeties and scope mounts. Barrels and accessories are also available for the Ruger 10/22 and 77/22 rifles from heavy barrels and synthetic stocks to scope mounts. Perazone also offers: Wilson Arms match-grade barrels; Dayton Traister triggers and safeties; Choate, Butler Creek and Bell & Carlson stocks; Boyd's triggers and stocks; PM Enterprises scope mounts, safeties and speed locks; and Power Custom titanium parts for Ruger 10/22 rifles. Also, special sale items and closeouts. Their catalog is free with order or send $3.00. Dealer inquiries welcome; send a copy of your F.F.L.

BRIAN PERAZONE—GUNSMITH

QUALITY GUNSTOCK BLANKS

Cali'co Hardwoods has been cutting superior-quality shotgun and rifle blanks for more than 31 years. Cali'co supplies blanks to many of the major manufacturers—Browning, Weatherby, Ruger, Holland & Holland, to name a few—as well as custom gunsmiths the world over.

Profiled rifle blanks are available, ready for inletting and sanding. Cali'co sells superior California hardwoods in Claro walnut, French walnut, Bastogne, maple and myrtle.

Cali'co offers good, serviceable blanks and some of the finest exhibition blanks available. Satisfaction guaranteed.

Color catalog, retail and dealer price list (FFL required) free upon request.

CALI'CO HARDWOODS, INC.

10/22 TARGET HAMMER

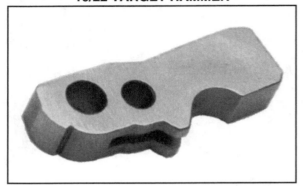

This new target hammer with replacement hammer spring from Volquartsen Custom is designed to give the stock Ruger 10/22 a superb "trigger job" by simply installing it in place of the factory hammer. No stoning or fitting is required to the sear or springs.

This hammer may appear similar to the production hammer, but is geometrically advanced in the sear engagement area. The hammers are heat-treated to achieve 60-61 Rc, then sapphire-honed for ultra smooth RMS. Trigger pull is reduced to 1-1/3 pounds to 1-3/4 pounds, depending on the gun.

The target hammer sells for $35.00 plus $5.00 shipping and handling, satisfaction guaranteed. To receive a catalog, send $5.00; mention *Shooter's Marketplace* and that catalog is yours for just $4.00.

VOLQUARTSEN CUSTOM LTD.

PRECISION RIFLE REST

Bald Eagle Precision Machine Co. offers a rifle rest perfect for the serious benchrester or the dedicated varminter.

The rest is constructed of aircraft-quality aluminum and weighs 7 pounds, 12 ounces. It's finished with three coats of Imron Clear. Height adjustments are made with a rack and pinion and a mariner wheel. A fourth leg allows lateral movement on the bench.

Bald Eagle offers approximately 56 rest models to choose from, including windage adjustable, right or left hand, cast aluminum or cast iron. The Standard Rest with rifle stop and bag is pictured above.

Prices: $99.95 to $260.00. For more information or a free brochure, contact Bald Eagle.

BALD EAGLE PRECISION MACHINE CO.

RIMFIRE CARTRIDGE GAGE

The Rimfire Cartridge Gage from Bald Eagle Precision Machine Co. can improve overall group size up to 25% by sorting rimfire ammo into uniform rim-thickness lots.

The more consistent the rim thickness, the more consistent the ignition of the primer and powder charge, and the firing pin travel remains uniform from shot-to-shot.

The Cartridge Gage is a snap to use—grab a box or two of rimfire ammo and start sorting. It is ideal for BR-50 benchrest competitors and serious small game hunters.

Normally $80.00, mention *Shooter's Marketplace* and it's only $74.95. Write Bald Eagle for a free brochure.

BALD EAGLE PRECISION MACHINE CO.

FREE CHRONOGRAPH CATALOG

Oehler Research, Inc. offers shooters and reloaders their encyclopedic catalog of ballistic test equipment free of charge. This 40-page catalog describes and illustrates Oehler's family of ballistic testing equipment, from reliable chronographs for handloaders to their personal ballistics laboratory, a computer-based system that calculates and integrates chamber pressure, muzzle and downrange velocity and acoustic target measurements. Used by industry and military laboratories, Oehler's ballistic laboratory is invaluable for serious load development and costs little more than a good factory rifle with scope. For the serious handloader and hunter, Oehler offers their Ballistic Explorer exterior ballistics software. Available for both DOS and Windows, the programs have established a reputation for both ease of use and technical accuracy.

OEHLER RESEARCH, INC.

H&R, WTU OFFER COMMEMORATIVE RIFLE

Harrington and Richardson has once again teamed with Whitetails Unlimited to benefit deer and their habitat. A portion of the sale of each new commemorative rifle will benefit Whitetails Unlimited.

The newest rifle, in 30-30 Win, is built around an investment-cast steel frame with a highly polished blue action and barrel. A stock of fine American black walnut has been carefully finished, hand-checkered and laser-engraved and a pewter-finished Whitetails Unlimited medallion inletted into the stock.

The barrel is 22 inches long with fully adjustable sights and is drilled and tapped for a scope base. All Harrington and Richardson rifles use the patented Transfer Bar System that virtually eliminates the possibility of an unplanned discharge due to a blow to the hammer or a dropped hammer during cocking.

HARRISON AND RICHARDSON

HANDI-RIFLE GOES SYNTHETIC

To make one of the toughest rifles on the market even tougher, New England Firearms has added synthetic stocks and forends to its line of Handi-Rifles. The newest version of this rifle will carry a black synthetic forend and Monte Carlo stock and will sport a factory-installed scope base and an offset hammer extension. The Monte Carlo version will be available in 223 REM, 243 WIN, 270 WIN, 280 REM and 30-06 SPRG. The stocks include a recoil pad and sling swivel studs and the rifles retain all the great NEF features, including the patented transfer bar system which virtually eliminates the possibility of an accidental discharge from a blow to the hammer or from a dropped hammer during cocking. Like all NEF Handi-Rifles, a wide range of additional rifle and shotgun barrels are available for factory retrofitting.

NEW ENGLAND FIREARMS

ULTRA VARMINT 243

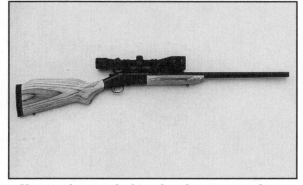

Varmint hunters looking for a heavier round to use against predators will be happy to see Harrington and Richardson's new offering: the Ultra Varmint Rifle in 243 WIN. The original UVR in 223 REM has made its mark as a solid performer at a reasonable price. The new 243 WIN model offers the same performance, but adds range and bullet weight options not available with the 223 REM.

The new 243 WIN Ultra Varmint Rifle is equipped with a heavy 24-inch barrel, which features a deeply rebated muzzle to protect the rifling. A simple and efficient single-stage trigger mechanism offers crisp pulls with virtually no creep. Safety is assured with the patented Transfer Bar Mechanism and the stock and forend are carved from select laminated wood. A recoil pad and sling swivel studs are included.

HARRINGTON AND RICHARDSON

YOUTH MODEL GROWS WITH SHOOTERS

The New England Firearms Handi-Rifle has a well-earned reputation for accuracy at a fair price. Now the rifle is offered in a configuration that's perfect for young shooters. The youth version of the Superlight Handi-Rifle in 223 REM is made lighter with a quick-handling 20-inch barrel and a special youth-sized synthetic stock and forend. The semi-matte black finish features a non-slip finish and includes sling swivel studs. The barrel includes fully adjustable rifle sights and is drilled and tapped for a scope mount. As the young shooter grows, New England Firearms offers an accessory adult-sized stock and a variety of rifle and shotgun barrels for factory retrofitting. Like all NEF products, the youth rifle features the patented Transfer Bar System that virtually eliminates the possibility of an accidental discharge.

NEW ENGLAND FIREARMS

BOLT ACTION 50 CAL BMG RIFLE

Built for the serious big-bore rifle shooter, the RHM&C bolt-action 50 cal. is suited for left-and right-handed shooters. Weighing in at 24 pounds with an overall length of 44 inches, recoil is similar to 12-gauge shotgun. The rifle is easily disassembled with two takedown pins. A bipod and scope base are installed at the factory. This rifle is ready for rugged use with Parkerized steel surfaces and aluminum surfaces covered with black teflon. A carbide version is available as are drag bags in green and black. A semi-auto version is under development. Made in U.S.

Caliber: 50 CAL BMG. **Barrel:** 36". **Weight:** 24 lbs. **Length:** 44" overall. **Stock:** Textured aluminum. **Sights:** Optional folding or scope. **Price:** $2,500.

RH MACHINE AND CONSULTING INC.

SLIP-ON GRIP FOR COMPACT AUTOS

The Pachmayr Division of Lyman Products is first again to expand the slip-on grip market by offering a model for compact pistols like the Glock model 26/27/33 and the Beretta Mini-Cougar. The Model 5 offers a comfortable hollow finger groove design and assures ergonomic positioning of the finger groove. Made of the same high quality rubber that feels great and is easy to install, this new grip is sure to be a winner. No more cutting down a larger grip to fit.

For more information, please contact: Carl Cupp, Pachmayr, Ltd.

PACHMAYR, DIV. OF LYMAN PRODUCTS

MID-RANGE RIFLE FOR SERIOUS SHOOTERS

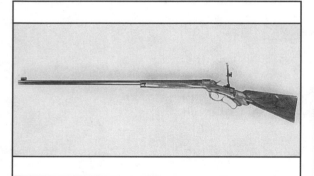

The Ballard rifle was the choice of discerning riflemen in the late 1800s. Its reputation was established all across America. The Ballard Rifle and Cartridge Company has made a commitment to keep that reputation alive by creating faithful reproductions based on the original patent. The entire product line is based on original production models.

The newest edition is the No. 41/2 "Mid-Range" Model. The gun is ideal for black powder cartridge silhouette shooting and features a standard or heavy half-octagon barrel of 30 or 32 inches. It offers single or double set triggers, a pistol grip and a shotgun buttstock. It is available in 32-40, 38-55, 40-65 Win., 40-75 SS and 45-70 Gov. For more information contact Ballard Rifle and Cartridge Co. LLC.

BALLARD RIFLE & CARTRIDGE CO., LLC

GHILLIE SUIT FOR TOTAL CONCEALMENT

You can almost become part of the terrain with a ghillie suit by Custom Concealment, Inc. Designed primarily for military and law enforcement use, the suits have full hoods with face veils, and are designed to be lightweight and cool, even in tropical or desert conditions. The burlap outer layer is hand-brushed, dyed to match the applicable environment and treated with DuPont fire retardant and AquaSeal Water Repellent. Equipment covers, for everything from shotguns to tactical surveillance equipment are also available. Ghillie suits from Custom Concealment, Inc. include extra padding and are designed to allow the wearer to crawl over, around and through obstacles and brush without having the suit tangle in the obstacles.

For more information contact Custom Concealment.

CUSTOM CONCEALMENT

HAR-15A2 IS UP TO THE JOB

Built with parts that adhere to strict military specifications, the Hesse HAR-15A2 is as close as you can get to the original military model. Available in five configurations; the Standard Rifle, National Match, Bull Gun, Dispatcher and Carbine, the HAR-15A2 is ready for the demands you'll place on it. Choose your caliber from 17 Rem, 223 Rem, 6mm PPC, 6mmx223, 300 Fireball, 7.69x39 and 9mm. Each rifle comes with a heavy barrel, dry film lube, a Hesse muzzle brake, a standard magazine, sling, manual and a hard case. For more information contact Hesse Arms.

HESSE ARMS

FAL-H READY FOR ACTION

Built on the well-known Belgian "Fusil Automatique Leger" design, the Hesse FAL-H is an American-made faithful re-creation of one of the world's most proven battle rifles. The Hesse FAL-H is available in 308 Win., 243 Win. and 22-250 with either black polymer or original wood stocks. The adjustable gas system offers superior reliability even under the most severe conditions. Sometimes called "the Free World's right arm," the FAL design delivers potent ammunition accurately and reliably. With barrel lengths from 16 to 26 inches, the FAL-H weighs between 9.5 and 13.3 pounds and has fully adjustable sights. For more information contact Hesse Arms.

HESSE ARMS

H-22 FOR SERIOUS RIMFIRE SHOOTERS

Serious rimfire shooters reach for their Hesse H-22 when they want to put rounds right on target. A lengthy poll of rimfire shooters produced the H-22 Tigershark with its distinctive stock design and free-floating forend that hangs under a fluted, heavy stainless steel barrel for the ultimate in accuracy. The H22 Competition Rifle goes easily from the range to the field and comes complete with a thumbhole stock for greater control. The H22 Wildcat and H22 Standard Rifle also feature heavy barrels and Hesse's stainless steel receiver. The Wildcat features a screwed-in barrel while the Standard Rifle is perfect for those just getting into competition shooting or varmint hunting. For more information contact Hesse Arms.

HESSE ARMS

RIFLE AND PISTOL MAGAZINES

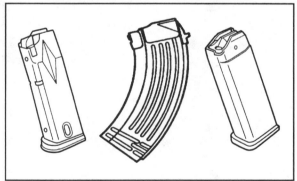

Forrest Inc. offers shooters one of the largest selections of standard and extended high-capacity magazines in the United States. Whether you're looking for a few spare magazines for that obsolete 22 rifle or pistol, or wish to replace a reduced-capacity ten-shot magazine with the higher-capacity pre-ban original, all are available from this California firm. They offer competitive pricing especially for dealers wanting to buy in quantity.

Forrest Inc. also stocks parts and accessories for the Colt 1911 45 Auto pistol, the SKS and MAK-90 rifles as well as many U.S. military rifles. One of their specialty parts is firing pins for obsolete weapons.

Call or write Forrest Inc. for more information and a free brochure. Be sure and mention *Shooter's Marketplace*.

FORREST INC.

NEW LIGHT WEIGHT WATERPROOF BINOCULARS

The Waterproof and armored SWIFT 825R Eaglet 7x36 is Swift Instrument's newest light weight (22 oz.) roof prism binocular. The 825R Eaglet will focus from 4.9 feet to infinity, making the glass ideal for the hunter, hiker or shooter. Its four lens ocular system and three objective lenses eliminate spherical aberration and reduce astigmatism, which results in especially high resolving power. Multi-coating on the ocular and objective lenses, plus full coated optics, give an especially bright image in fair or foul weather. Its high eyepoint of 16mm provides a full field of view for eyeglass wearers. The SWIFT 825R EAGLET is an all weather waterproof binocular and comes complete with a black vinyl case and Swift broad woven neck strap. For more information call or write Swift Instruments.

SWIFT INSTRUMENTS, INC.

"COWBOY DEFENDER" DERRINGER

The "Cowboy Defender" is a double-barrel derringer specifically designed for cowboy action shooting. Features include heat-treated stainless steel construction, spring-loaded extractor, blade front and fixed rear sights, rebounding hammer, retracting firing pin, crossbolt safety, laminated black ash or rosewood grip and interchangeable barrels. Choice of calibers include Colt/410 shot shell, 357 Magnum/38 Spl., 9mm Para., 45 ACP and 44 Mag/44 Spl. 32 H&R Mag. For further information, contact: Lyndol Askew at Bond Arms, Inc.

BOND ARMS, INC.

RANGE FINDING SCOPE

Shepherd Scope offers a German-designed Speed Focus eyepiece that provides razor sharp images with a twist of the rear ring.

The eyepiece remains rock solid throughout focusing and zooming.

Also available is a adjustable objective lens housing which will accept Shepherd Scope's sunshade. The scopes have a scratch-resistant 340 hard matte finish.

All scopes have Shepherd's patented dual reticle system that provides one-shot zeroing, instant range finding, bullet drop and contant visual verification of the original zero.

Call, write or fax Shepherd Scope direct for a free brochure.

SHEPHERD SCOPE LTD.

CASPIAN ARMS LTD

For those who realize that custom guns come only from professional pistolsmiths, Caspian Arms offers a complete array of high precision 1911 components. Custom Caspians have shot their way into the winners circle of world and national IPSC competitions, the world speed shooting championships, and NRA action championships. Whether it's for race, duty or personal protection let Caspian help you build your next gun from the ground up, to your specs, to the industry's closest tolerances.

CASPIAN ARMS LTD

CUSTOM 1911 PISTOLS AND PARTS

Les Baer Custom manufacturers superior quality 1911 custom pistols at America's most competitive prices.

More than twenty high performance models are available for defense, law enforcement and competition. All pistols are custom built and hand fitted by Baer's custom gunsmiths. Match-grade accuracy is guaranteed. All models are built on Baer's own American made, NM forged frames, slides and barrels. Government, reduced size "Commanche" and Six-Inch sizes available; stainless steel and aluminum models also available.

Also available: Baer Custom's forged steel, stainless steel and aluminum frames and slides and Baer NM barrels plus a complete line of precision machined custom 1911 parts and accessories.

LES BAER CUSTOM, INC.

PRECISION EQUIPMENT

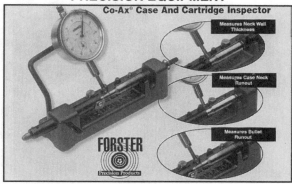

Forster Products has been providing quality conscious shooters and reloaders with precision equipment since 1939. During its 60th Anniversary year, Forster has introduced the "Big 50s", two new case trimmers for 50 cal. enthusiasts. Also new for '98: Forster's triple-purpose Co-Ax® Case & Cartridge Inspector. For optimum rifle accuracy, Forster's Bench Rest© seater and sizing dies and Ultra© micrometer bullet seater dies, plus Forster's quality case trimmers are all industry leaders. Forster gunsmithing tools set the standard of quality for the world's most particular gunsmiths, and Forster's muzzleloading tools are favorites among blackpowder enthusiasts.

FORSTER PRODUCTS

QUIK-SHOK

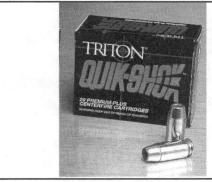

Triton's new Quik-Shok ammunition delivers the highest level of stopping power. During penetration, the bullet expands rapidly and then splits into three segments which continue to penetrate in three directions over an ever-widening area within the target. This dynamic new round surpasses the performance of exotic fragmentary ammo at one-third the price. Quik-Shok comes in a full 20-round box as opposed to a six-round blister pack. Available in all popular calibers.

TRITON OPTIMUM PERFORMANCE AMMUNITION

HI-VEL

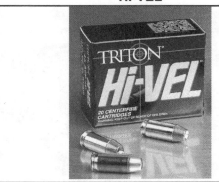

Triton's Hi-Vel offers high performance in conventional hollow point ammunition. Whether you rely on the Hi-Vel .380 ACP+P or the powerhouse 45 Super, you can rest assured that you are carrying the finest comercial ammunition made...all at a price you can live with.

TRITON OPTIMUM PERFORMANCE AMMUNITION

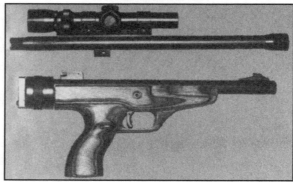

AMERICAN CUSTOM GUNMAKERS GUILD

American Custom Gunmakers Guild

Leading the custom gunmaking craft by the example of high quality and ethics, ACGG Members complete custom metal and stockwork, restoration, engraving and associated accessories on fine custom firearms.

Dedicated to the exchange of ideas, techniques, promotion of public awareness, and the advancement of custom gunmaking as an accepted art form, the ACGG publishes a quarterly journal, directory, videotapes, and produces an annual exhibition of Members' work.

Associate affiliation in the ACGG is open to any person or firm interested. Contact for information or sent $5 for Directory of Custom Gunmaking Services.

AMERICAN CUSTOM GUNMAKERS GUILD

10-22 HAMMER AND SEAR PAC

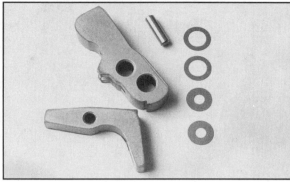

Power Custom introduces a new Ruger 10-22® Matched Hammer & Sear to reduce the trigger pull weight for your 10-22®. This allows for a 2 factured by the E.D.M. process out of carbon steel and heat treated to a 56-58 Rc and precision ground with honed engagement surfaces. Kit includes Extra Power Hammer & Sear Disconnector Spring, 2 Precision Trigger Shims, 2 Precision Hammer Shims, and a Replacement Trigger return spring. Price $55.95.

10-22® is a registered trademark of Strum, Ruger & Co. Inc.

POWER CUSTOM, INC.

HIGH PERFORMANCE AMMO, RIGLES

Heavy Express, Inc., with a new line of short, non-belted, very high velocity magnum cartridges known as "HE MAG", also markets two bolt-action hunting rifles, built on Ruger Model 77 Mk II and Winchester Model 70 Classic FWT short and standard actions. These guns are chambered in 8 HE MAG calibers. Options include choices of barrels, contours, weights, and finishes, with stocks of factory walnut, laminates, or various composites, and laser engraving. Heavy Express rifles are sold with 100 HE MAG brass cases, Hornady loading dies, HE MAG loading booklet, and Hoppes' hard-sided lockable gun safe. Heavy Express also offers a custom Ruger #1 chambered in rimmed versions of several HE MAG calibers. Orders must be placed with Heavy Express, Inc

HEAVY EXPRESS INC.

BALLISTIC CHRONY PRINTER

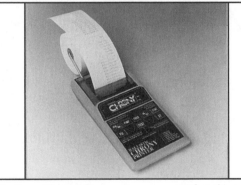

Works with regular paper, comes with 14' interface cable and runs on 4 batteries (AA included). For Alpha, Beta and Gamma Shooting Chrony and respective Master Chronys.

Prints velocities as you shoot, and/or afterwards, when retrieving from memory. When done, push the button and the Printer gives statistics, such as LO, HI and Average Velocity, Extreme Spread and Standard Deviation. Attach the printout to target or file. Weight 1 lb; 1.75" x 4" x 7.5" high. Suggested retail $89.95. Ask your dealer or call 1-800-385-3161.

SHOOTING CHRONY INC.

CUSTOM RESTORATION/CASE COLORING

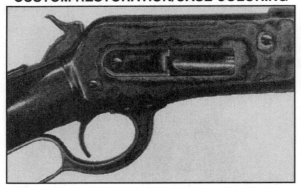

Doug Turnbull Restoration continues to offer bone charcoal case hardening work, matching the original case colors produced by Winchester, Colt, Marlin, Parker, L.C. Smith, Fox and other manufacturers. Also available is charcoal blue, known as Carbona or machine blue, a pre-war finish used by most makers. Currently doing work for Remington (Rolling Block, color case), Colt (125th anniversary, color and blue), Dakota Arms (color case), CSM-Fox (color case hardening-charcoal, carbona blue), Lone Star Rifle Co. (color case) U S Firearms (Armory blue, bone case) "Specializing in the accurate re-creation of historical metal finishes on period firearms, from polishing to final finishing. Including Bone Charcoal Color Case Hardening, Charcoal Bluing, Rust Blue, and Nitre Blue".

DOUG TURNBULL RESTORATION

DELUXE LEATHER ENGLISH STYLE TRUNK CASE WITH MATCHING CARTRIDGE CASE!!

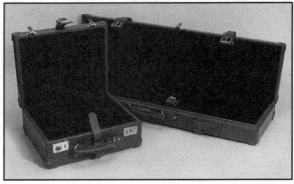

• Constructed of heavy duty calf skin leather with harness type trim • Hand stitched leather corners • Leather trunk straps • Padded wood interior with accessory compartments for snap caps, oil bottles and much more! • Brass locks. • Will hold barrels up to 30" • For SxS or O/U's.

Suggested retail for the two pieces. $589.95
Reduced for a limited time to $339.95
Shipping & handling $15.00
Cases individually priced
Deluxe leather shot gun case only $299.95
Deluxe leather cartridge case only. $149.95
Largest supplier of cases in the USA. Please send $2.00 for current full line catalogue. Prices subject to change.

CAPE OUTFITTERS

FULL CUSTOM COWBOY GUNS

From the originator of the full custom Cowboy series, Gary Reeder Custom Guns. Home of the original Ultimate Vaquero, as seen in GUNS MAGAZINE, the original Tombstone Classic, Doc Holliday Classic, Long Rider Classic, Texas Ranger Classic, Black Widow, Ultimate Bisley, and Arizona Ranger Classic. Also the originator of the ultimate in hunting revolvers, Lucifer's Hammer, The Ultimate 50 and the Ultimate Long Colt.

For more information and full color pictures and brochure, contact:

GARY REEDER CUSTOM GUNS

HIVIZ SIGHT SYSTEMS

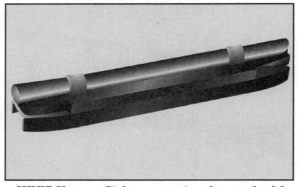

HIVIZ Shotgun Sights are setting the standard for improved performance. The four interchangeable high-glow light pipes and magnetic base have created a revolution. You will shoot better in low and even bright light when hunting or target shooting. Models are available for all guns.

"The HIVIZ Sight System is the most outstanding shooting and training aid I have ever seen. It provides a strong sight reference and clear image of hits and misses resulting in higher scores," –Bob Perigo, former coach, U.S. Olympic Training Center.

HIVIZ Sight Systems are available for shotguns, handguns, muzzle loaders, inline and rifles. HIVIZ— because hitting is everything.

HIVIZ SIGHT SYSTEMS

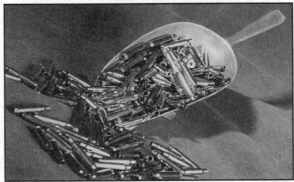

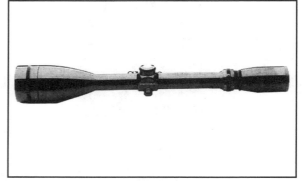

UNDER LEVER DOUBLE RIFLE

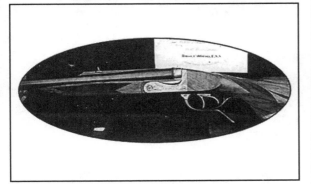

Under Lever Double Rifle

Price: $14,000.00

Send $5.00 for brochure.

B. Searcy & Co.
Established 1975
Rifle Manufacturers

Visa and Mastercard accepted.

B. SEARCY & CO.

STAINLESS STEEL DOUBLE RIFLE

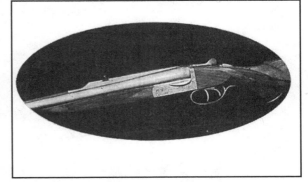

Stainless Steel Double Rifle

The world's first stainless steel double rifle. Stainless steel rifles of same configurations as all blued deluxe rifles.   Price: $13,000.00

Send $5.00 for brochure.

B. Searcy & Co.
Established 1975
Rifle Manufacturers

Visa and Mastercard accepted.

B. SEARCY & CO.

MODEL 70 SAFETY NOW AVAILABLE

The classic Model 70 three position safety is now available to fit Mauser 98, Enfield 1914 & 1917, Springfield 1903 & 1903 A3, Remington right hand M700, and Brno ZKK. The safety and its component parts are fully machined from alloy steel bar stock. The safety lever is color case hardened while the chrome moly sleeve is polished to a #220 finish. They are delivered assembled and ready for final gunsmith installation. Detailed instructions are included.

Other parts are available. Including band ramp front sights, extractors, Kimber, Brownell & Magnum Double Lever Scope rings, two piece scope bases, two position safety kits, gunsmithing fixtures, and custom trigger guard units. Send $2.00 for a 12 page catalog.

PRECISE METALSMITHING ENTERPRISES, INC.

KOWA OPTIMED GETS THE BIG PICTURE

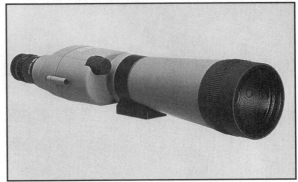

With over 30 years experience in the manufacture of spotting scopes and other precision optical instruments, Kowa has acquired in-depth knowledge about the requirements of field use. The TSN-820 series offers state-of-the-art optics with unmatched quality and fast, easy use under all conditions. Full multi-coating on the 82mm objective lens produces the ultimate in bright, clear, high-definition imagery. The superb sharpness is especially noticeable at extended distances or under low-light conditions. We offer three series of spotting scopes (50mm, 60mm and 82mm diameter objectives) and have binoculars, too. Call, write or send us an e-mail for a free brochure.

KOWA OPTIMED INC.

WINCHESTER

For handloaders who demand ultimate performance of their non-toxic, shotgun ammunition, Bismuth Cartridge Company and Winchester Ammunition are making "the patented bismuth" shot available in all popular shot sizes.

Packaged in 7-pound jugs, bismuth shot is available in sizes: BB, #2, #4, #5, #6.

If you take the time and effort to load your own hunting ammunition, use shot that gives you the knockdown energy, pattern densities and payload you deserve.

Do it right. Load the best non-toxic shot for your shotgun and enjoy the rewards of your hobby. For a local dealer listing and load data information, call 800-759-3333 or www.bismuth-notox.com

THE BISMUTH CARTRIDGE COMPANY

CUSTOM BARRELS

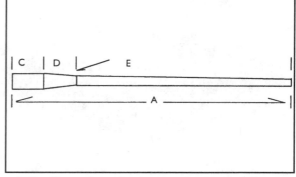

E.R. Shaw barrels are made from AISI-4140 Chrom-Moly resulpherized gun-quality steel with a Rockwell C-scale hardness of 25-28. All barrels are button rifled with right-hand twist and are furnished in-the-white.

BARREL CONTOURS & WEIGHTS*
  Contour No. 1 - Light Sporter
  Contour No. 2 – Medium Sporter.
  Contour No. 3 – Varmint Weight.
  Contour No. 4 – Bull Barrel.
  Contour No. 5 – Heavy Bull.
  *338 cal and larger not available in contours 1 & 2
Many standard and wildcat chamberings available.
Gunsmithing department on premises to assemble and finish your barreled action.

E.R. SHAW INC.

PROTECTIVE METAL CASES

A complete line of 2 pc. and 3 pc. "Flat Style" and "Trunk Style" aluminum transporter/shipping cases are offered by KKAir/ICC. Standard sizes number 40+, with "Special" cases built to customer requirements. These cases are of .063 and.080 aluminum, built for strength with the "Traveling Sportsman" in mind. NEW CONCEALMENT DUFFLES and case jackets are available for all case models, including special cases and cases built by other companies. Write or call KK Air/ICC for more information and pricing.

*You can pay more but
you can't buy better.*

KK AIR / ICC CASE PRODUCTS

GUN LIST

Gun List is the nation's only indexed firearm paper devoted to helping the gun enthusiast find guns, parts, supplies and ammunition for most firearms. Gun List is an essential publication for buyers and sellers because it contains advertisements from the nation's top gun dealers and an extensive list of alphabetized classifieds. Every issue features more than 40,000 firearms for sale.

1 year (26 issues)..........$32.98
2 years (52 issues)........$59.98
3 years (78 issues)........$84.98

Write for foreign rates

KRAUSE PUBLICATIONS, INC.

BOND ARMS INC.
Attn: Lyndol Askew
PO Box 1296
Granbury, TX 76048
Phone: 817-573-4445
Fax: 817-573-5636
Email: bondarms@itexas.net
Web Site:
www2.itexas.net/~bondarms

CASPIAN ARMS LTD.
Attn: Dept SM '99
14 North Main Street
Hardwick, VT 05843
Phone: 802-472-6454
Fax: 802-472-6709

GLASER SAFETY SLUG, INC.
PO Box 8223
Foster City CA 94404
Phone: 800-221-3489
Fax: 510-785-6685
Email: safetyslug@best.com
Web Site: www.safetyslug.com

KK AIR/ICC CASE PRODUCTS
Attn: Brad Knouff
PO Box 9912
Spokane WA 99209
Phone: 800-262-3322
Fax: 509-326-5436
Email:
sales@shellegames.com
Web Site:
www.shellegames.com

LES BAER CUSTOM, INC
Attn: Dept SM'99
29601 34th Ave
Hillsdale, IL 61257
Phone: 309-658-2716
Fax: 309-658-2610

GRUESKIN MARKETING COMMUNICATIONS
204 West 17th Ave Ct
Coal Valley, IL 61240
Phone: 309-799-3859
Fax: 309-799-3853

TRITON CARTRIDGE CORP
PO Box 50
Wappingers Falls, NY 12590
Phone: 800-861-3362
Fax: 914-896-4607
Web Site:
www.triton-ammo.com

STONEY POINT PRODUCTS, INC
Dept. SM'99
PO Box 234
New Ulm MN 56073-0234
Phone: 507-354-3360
Fax: 507-354-7236

MAG-NA PORT
41302 Executive Dr
Harrison Township MI
48045-1306
Phone: 810-469-6727
Fax: 810-469-0425

L.A.R. MFG. INC.
Attn: Advertising
4133 W Farm Rd
West Jordan UT 84088
Phone 801-280-3505
Fax: 801-280-1972
Email: larmfg@sisna.com

SWIFT INSTRUMENTS, INC.
Dept. GD
952 Dorchester Ave
Boston, MA 02125
Phone: 617-436-2960
Fax: 617-436-3232
Web: www.swift-optics.com

COMPETITOR INC.
Appleton Business Center
30 Tricnit Rd Unit 16
PO Box 508
New Ipswich NH 03071
Phone: 603-878-3891

S.W.F.A.
PO Box 69
DeSoto TX 75123
Phone: 972-223-0500
Fax: 972-223-9030

SEARCY ENT.
Attn: Butch Searcy
PO Box
Boron CA 93596-0584
Phone: 760-762-6771
Fax: 760-762-0191

AMERICAN CUSTOM GUNMAKERS GUILD
PO Box 812
Burlington IA 52601
Phone: 319-752-6114
Fax: 319-752-6114

POWER CUSTOM INC.
Dept. SM'99
29739 Hwy J
Gravois Mills, MO 65037
Phone: 573-372-5684
Fax: 573-372-5799
Email: rwpowers@laurie.net

HEAVY EXPRESS INC.
Dept. SM'99
PO Box 60698
Colorado Springs CO
80960-0698
Phone: 800-287-8416

SHOOTING CHRONY INC.
2446 Cawthra Rd
Bldg 1 Unit 10
Mississauga ON L5A 3K6
CANADA

BISMUTH CARTRIDGE COMPANY
3500 Maple Ave - Suite 1470
Dallas TX 75219
Phone: 214-521-5880 or
1-800-759-3333
Fax: 214-521-9035
Web: www.bismuth-notox.com

DOUG TURNBULL RESTORATION INC.
Dept. SM99GD
6680 Rt. 5 & 20 - Box 471
Bloomfield NY 14469
Phone" 716-657-6338
Fax: 716-657-6338
Email:
turnbullrest@mindspring.com
Web: gunshop.com/dougt.htm

CAPE OUTFITTERS, INC.
599 Co Rd 206
Cape Girardeau MO 63701
Phone: 573-335-6260
Fax: 573-335-1555

GARY REEDER CUSTOM GUNS
2710 N Steves Blvd Suite #4
Flagstaff, AZ 86044
Phone: 520-527-4100
Fax: 520-527-0840
Email:
greeder@infomagic.com
Web:
www.reedercustomguns.com

PRECISE METALSMITHING ENTERPRISES, INC.
146 Curtis Hill Rd
Chehalis WA 98532
Phone: 360-748-3743
Fax: 360-748-1802

HIVIZ SIGHT SYSTEMS
North Pass, Ltd.
425 S Bowen St, Suite 6
Longmont CO 80501
Phone: 800-589-4315 or
303-682-4315
Fax: 303-678-5987

ACCURATE ARMS COMPANY INC.
Dept. GDM99
5891 Highway 230 West
McEwen TN 37101
Phone: 800-416-3006
Fax: 931-729-4211

KOWA OPTIMED INC.
Attn: Sporting Optics Division
20001 S Vermont Ave
Torrance CA 90502
Phone: 310-327-1913
Fax: 310-327-4177
Email: dawn@kowa.com
Web: www.kowa-scope.com

SENTRY SOLUTIONS LTD.
Dept. GD
111 Sugar Hill Road,
PO Box 130
Contoocook NH 03229-0130
Phone: 603-746-5687 or
800-546-8049
Fax: 603-746-5847
Email:
info@sentrysolutions.com
Web: www.sentrysolutions.com

MTM CASE-GARD CO.
Dept. SM98
PO Box 14117
Dayton OH 45413
Phone: 937-890-7461
Fax: 937-890-1747
Web: www.mtmcase-gard.com

E.R. SHAW INC.
5312 Thoms Run Road
Bridgeville PA 15017
Phone 412-221-3636
Fax: 412-221-4303

SCHARCH MFG INC.
Dept. Sales
10325 Co Rd 120
Salida CO 81201
Phone: 719-539-7242
Fax: 719-539-3021
Email: scharch@csn.net
Web: www.scharch.com

ASHLEY OUTDOORS INC
2401 Ludelle Street
Fort Worth TX 76105
Phone: 800-734-7939
Fax: 888-744-4880
Email:
sales@ashleyoutdoors.com
Web:
www.ashleyoutdoors.com

HESSE ARMS
1126 70th Street East
Inver Grove Heights, MN
55077-2416
Phone: 612-455-5760
Fax: 612-455-5760
Email: HesseArms@Juno.com
Web: www.HesseArms.com

CUSTOM CONCEALMENT INC.
P.O. Box 455
Zanesville, OH 43702-0455
Phone: 740-453-3702
Fax: 740-455-3865
Email: cci@ghillie.com
Web: www.ghillie.com

BALLARD RIFLE AND CARTRIDGE CO. LLC
Attn. Dept. D
113 W. Yellowstone Ave.
Cody, WY 82414
Phone: 307-587-4914
Fax: 307-527-6097

PACHMAYR, DIV. OF LYMAN PRODUCTS
Attn. Dept. 120
1875 South Mountain Ave.
Monrovia, CA. 91016
Phone: 626-357-7771,
toll free (800) 423-9704
Fax: 626-358-7251
Web: www.pachmayr.com

H&R 1871, INC./NEW ENGLAND FIREARMS
Industrial Rowe
Gardner, MA 01440
Phone: 978-632-9393
Fax: 978-632-2300

RH MACHINE AND CONSULTING, INC.
P.O. Box 394
Pacific, MO 63069-0394
Phone: 314-271-8465
Fax: 314-271-8465

1999
GUN DIGEST
Complete Compact
CATALOG

C

GUNDEX

Includes models suitable for several forms of competition and other sporting purposes.

AA ARMS AP9 MINI PISTOL
Caliber: 9mm Para., 10-shot magazine.
Barrel: 3".
Weight: 3.5 lbs. **Length:** 12" overall.
Stocks: Checkered black synthetic.
Sights: Post front adjustable for elevation, rear adjustable for windage.
Features: Ventilated barrel shroud; blue or electroless nickel finish. Made in U.S. by AA Arms.
Price: 3" barrel, blue **$239.00**
Price: 3" barrel, electroless nickel **$259.00**
Price: Mini/5, 5" barrel, blue.................................. **$259.00**
Price: Mini/5, 5" barrel, electroless nickel **$279.00**

ACCU-TEK BL-9 AUTO PISTOL
Caliber: 9mm Para., 5-shot magazine.
Barrel: 3".
Weight: 22 oz. **Length:** 5.6" overall.
Stocks: Black composition.
Sights: Fixed.
Features: Double action only; black finish. Introduced 1997. Made in U.S. by Accu-Tek.
Price: **$199.00**

Accu-Tek BL-9

Accu-Tek BL-380
Same as the BL-9 except chambered for 380 ACP. Introduced 1997. Made in U.S. by Accu-Tek.
Price: **$199.00**

ACCU-TEK MODEL CP-9SS AUTO PISTOL
Caliber: 9mm Para., 8-shot magazine.
Barrel: 3.2".
Weight: 28 oz. **Length:** 6.25" overall.
Stocks: Black checkered nylon.
Sights: Blade front, rear adjustable for windage; three-dot system.
Features: Stainless steel construction. Double action only. Firing pin block with no external safeties. Lifetime warranty. Introduced 1992. Made in U.S. by Accu-Tek.
Price: Satin stainless **$265.00**

Accu-Tek CP-9SS

Accu-Tek CP-45SS Auto Pistol
Same as the Model CP-9SS except chambered for 45 ACP, 6-shot magazine. Introduced 1995. Made in U.S. by Accu-Tek.
Price: Stainless steel **$265.00**

Accu-Tek CP-40SS Auto Pistol
Same as the Model CP-9SS except chambered for 40 S&W, 7-shot magazine. Introduced 1992.
Price: Stainless **$265.00**

Accu-Tek AT 380SS

ACCU-TEK MODEL AT-380SS AUTO PISTOL
Caliber: 380 ACP, 5-shot magazine.
Barrel: 2.75".
Weight: 20 oz. **Length:** 5.6" overall.
Stocks: Grooved black composition.
Sights: Blade front, rear adjustable for windage.
Features: Stainless steel frame and slide. External hammer; manual thumb safety; firing pin block, trigger disconnect. Lifetime warranty. Introduced 1991. Made in U.S. by Accu-Tek.
Price: Satin stainless **$182.00**
Price: Black finish over steel (AT-380B) **$187.00**

Accu-Tek Model AT-32SS Auto Pistol
Same as the AT-380SS except chambered for 32 ACP. Introduced 1991.
Price: Satin stainless **$176.00**
Price: Black finish over steel (AT-32B) **$181.00**

ACCU-TEK MODEL HC-380SS AUTO PISTOL
Caliber: 380 ACP, 10-shot magazine.
Barrel: 2.75".
Weight: 28 oz. **Length:** 6" overall.
Stocks: Checkered black composition.
Sights: Blade front, rear adjustable for windage.
Features: External hammer; manual thumb safety with firing pin and trigger disconnect; bottom magazine release. Stainless finish. Introduced 1993. Made in U.S. by Accu-Tek.
Price: Satin stainless **$230.00**
Price: Black finish over stainless **$235.00**

Accu-Tek HC-380SS

AMERICAN ARMS MATEBA AUTO/REVOLVER
Caliber: 357 Mag., 6-shot.
Barrel: 4".
Weight: 2.75 lbs. **Length:** 8.77" overall.
Stocks: Smooth walnut.
Sights: Blade on ramp front, adjustable rear.
Features: Double or single action. Cylinder and slide recoil together upon firing. All-steel construction with polished blue finish. Introduced 1957. Imported from Italy by American Arms, Inc.
Price:... **$1,295.00**

AMT AUTOMAG II AUTO PISTOL
Caliber: 22 WMR, 9-shot magazine (7-shot with 3-3/8" barrel).
Barrel: 3-3/8", 4-1/2", 6".
Weight: About 23 oz. **Length:** 9-3/8" overall.
Stocks: Grooved carbon fiber.
Sights: Blade front, adjustable rear.
Features: Made of stainless steel. Gas-assisted action. Exposed hammer. Slide flats have brushed finish, rest is sandblast. Squared trigger guard. Introduced 1986. From AMT.
Price:.. **$399.00**

AMT AUTOMAG III PISTOL
Caliber: 30 Carbine, 8-shot magazine.
Barrel: 6-3/8".
Weight: 43 oz. **Length:** 10-1/2" overall.
Stocks: Carbon fiber.
Sights: Blade front, adjustable rear.
Features: Stainless steel construction. Hammer-drop safety. Slide flats have brushed finish, rest is sandblasted. Introduced 1989. From AMT.
Price:.. **$499.00**

AMT AUTOMAG IV PISTOL
Caliber: 45 Winchester Magnum, 6-shot magazine.
Barrel: 6.5".
Weight: 46 oz. **Length:** 10.5" overall.
Stocks: Carbon fiber.
Sights: Blade front, adjustable rear.
Features: Made of stainless steel with brushed finish. Introduced 1990. Made in U.S. by AMT.
Price:.. **$599.00**

AMT BACK UP II AUTO PISTOL
Caliber: 380 ACP, 5-shot magazine.
Barrel: 2-1/2".
Weight: 18 oz. **Length:** 5" overall.
Stocks: Carbon fiber.
Sights: Fixed, open, recessed.
Features: Concealed hammer, blowback operation; manual and grip safeties. All stainless steel construction. Smallest domestically-produced pistol in 380. From AMT.
Price:.. **$369.00**

AMT 45 ACP HARDBALLER II
Caliber: 45 ACP.
Barrel: 5".
Weight: 39 oz. **Length:** 8-1/2" overall.
Stocks: Wrap-around rubber.
Sights: Adjustable.
Features: Extended combat safety, serrated matte slide rib, loaded chamber indicator, long grip safety, beveled magazine well, adjustable target trigger. All stainless steel. From AMT.
Price:.. **$425.00**
Price: Government model (as above except no rib, fixed sights) ... **$399.00**
Price: 400 Accelerator (400 Cor-Bon, 7" barrel) **$525.00**
Price: Commando (40 S&W, Government Model frame) **$425.00**

AMT 45 ACP HARDBALLER LONG SLIDE
Caliber: 45 ACP.
Barrel: 7". **Length:** 10-1/2" overall.
Stocks: Wrap-around rubber.
Sights: Fully adjustable rear sight.
Features: Slide and barrel are 2" longer than the standard 45, giving less recoil, added velocity, longer sight radius. Has extended combat safety, serrated matte rib, loaded chamber indicator, wide adjustable trigger. From AMT.
Price:.. **$459.00**

AMT 45 ACP Backup

AMT Back Up Double Action Only Pistol
Similar to the standard Back Up except has double-action-only mechanism, enlarged trigger guard, slide is rounded at rear. Has 5-shot magazine. Introduced 1992. From AMT.
Price: 9mm, 40 S&W, 45 ACP.............................. **$319.00**
Price: 38 Super, 357 SIG, 400 Cor-Bon **$369.00**

Arcus-94 Auto

ARCUS-94 AUTO PISTOL
Caliber: 9mm Para., 10-shot magazine.
Barrel: 5.24".
Weight: 32 oz. **Length:** 7.99" overall.
Stocks: Textured rubber.
Sights: Blade front, rear adjustable for windage.
Features: Single-action trigger. Available in blued, brushed chrome and two-tone finishes. Compact and double-action versions also available. Introduced 1998. Imported from Bulgaria by Miltex, Inc.
Price: About **$350.00**

AUTO-ORDNANCE 1911A1 AUTOMATIC PISTOL
Caliber: 9mm Para., 38 Super, 9-shot; 10mm, 45 ACP, 7-shot magazine.
Barrel: 5".
Weight: 39 oz. **Length:** 8-1/2" overall.
Stocks: Checkered plastic with medallion.
Sights: Blade front, rear adjustable for windage.
Features: Same specs as 1911A1 military guns—parts interchangeable. Frame and slide blued; each radius has non-glare finish. Made in U.S. by Auto-Ordnance Corp.
Price: 45 ACP, blue....................................... **$425.00**
Price: 45 ACP, Parkerized................................. **$399.95**
Price: 45 ACP Deluxe (three-dot sights, textured rubber wraparound grips) **$438.95**

Auto-Ordnance 1911A1 Custom High Polish Pistol

Similar to the standard 1911A1 except has a Videcki speed trigger, extended thumb safety, flat mainspring housing, Acurod recoil spring guide system, rosewood grips, custom combat hammer, beavertail grip safety. High-polish blue finish. Introduced 1998. Made in U.S. by Auto-Ordnance Corp.

Price: **$585.00**

Baer Custom Carry

BAER 1911 CONCEPT I AUTO PISTOL

Caliber: 45 ACP, 7-shot magazine.
Barrel: 5".
Weight: 37 oz. **Length:** 8.5" overall.
Stocks: Checkered rosewood.
Sights: Baer dovetail front, Bo-Mar deluxe low-mount rear with hidden leaf.
Features: Baer forged steel frame, slide and barrel with Baer stainless bushing; slide fitted to frame; double serrated slide; Baer beavertail grip safety, checkered slide stop, tuned extractor, extended ejector, deluxe hammer and sear, match disconnector; lowered and flared ejection port; fitted recoil link; polished feed ramp, throated barrel; Baer fitted speed trigger, flat serrated mainspring housing. Blue finish. Made in U.S. by Les Baer Custom, Inc.
Price: **$1,390.00**
Price: Concept II (with Baer adjustable rear sight) **$1,390.00**

Baer 1911 Concept VII Auto Pistol

Same as the Concept I except reduced Commanche size with 4.25" barrel, weighs 27.5 oz., 7.75" overall. Blue finish, checkered front strap. Made in U.S. by Les Baer Custom, Inc.
Price: **$1,495.00**
Price: Concept VIII (stainless frame and slide, Baer adjustable
rear sight) **$1,547.00**

Baer 1911 Concept IX Auto Pistol

Same as the Commanche Concept VII except has Baer lightweight forged aluminum frame, blued steel slide, Baer adjustable rear sight. Chambered for 45 ACP, 7-shot magazine. Made in U.S. by Les Baer Custom, Inc.
Price: **$1,655.00**
Price: Concept X (as above with stainless slide) **$1,675.00**

Baer Premium II

Baer 1911 Prowler III Auto Pistol

Same as the Premier II except also has full-length guide rod, tapered cone stub weight and reverse recoil plug. Made in U.S. by Les Baer Custom, Inc.
Price: Standard size, blued **$1,795.00**

Auto-Ordnance ZG-51 Pit Bull Auto

Same as the 1911A1 except has 3-1/2" barrel, weighs 36 oz. and has an over-all length of 7-1/4". Available in 45 ACP only; 7-shot magazine. Introduced 1989.
Price: **$470.00**

AUTAUGA 32 AUTO PISTOL

Caliber: 32 ACP, 6-shot magazine.
Barrel: 2".
Weight: 11.3 oz. **Length:** 4.3" overall.
Stocks: Black polymer.
Sights: Fixed.
Features: Double-action-only mechansim. Stainless steel construction. Uses Winchester Silver Tip ammunition.
Price: .... **NA**

BAER 1911 CUSTOM CARRY AUTO PISTOL

Caliber: 45 ACP, 7- or 10-shot magazine.
Barrel: 5".
Weight: 37 oz. **Length:** 8.5" overall.
Stocks: Checkered walnut.
Sights: Baer improved ramp-style dovetailed front, Novak low-mount rear.
Features: Baer forged NM frame, slide and barrel with stainless bushing; fitted slide to frame; double serrated slide (full-size only); Baer speed trigger with 4-lb. pull; Baer deluxe hammer and sear, tactical-style extended ambidextrous safety, beveled magazine well; polished feed ramp and throated barrel; tuned extractor; Baer extended ejector, checkered slide stop; lowered and flared ejection port, full-length recoil guide rod; recoil buff. Made in U.S. by Les Baer Custom, Inc.
Price: Standard size, blued **$1,620.00**
Price: Standard size, stainless **$1,690.00**
Price: Commanche size, blued. **$1,640.00**
Price: Commanche size, stainless **$1,690.00**
Price: Commanche size, aluminum frame, blued slide **$1,890.00**
Price: Commanche size, aluminum frame, stainless slide **$1,995.00**

Baer 1911 Concept III Auto Pistol

Same as the Concept I except has forged stainless frame with blued steel slide, Bo-Mar rear sight, 30 lpi checkering on front strap. Made in U.S. by Les Baer Custom, Inc.
Price: **$1,520.00**
Price: Concept IV (with Baer adjustable rear sight) **$1,499.00**
Price: Concept V (all stainless, Bo-Mar sight, checkered front strap)
.... **$1,558.00**
Price: Concept VI (stainless, Baer adjustable sight, checkered
front strap) **$1,558.00**

BAER 1911 PREMIER II AUTO PISTOL

Caliber: 9x23, 38 Super, 400 Cor-Bon, 45 ACP, 7- or 10-shot magazine.
Barrel: 5".
Weight: 37 oz. **Length:** 8.5" overall.
Stocks: Checkered rosewood, double diamond pattern.
Sights: Baer dovetailed front, low-mount Bo-Mar rear with hidden leaf.
Features: Baer NM forged steel frame and barrel with stainless bushing; slide fitted to frame; double serrated slide; lowered, flared ejection port; tuned, polished extractor; Baer extended ejector, checkered slide stop, aluminum speed trigger with 4-lb. pull, deluxe Commander hammer and sear, beavertail grip safety with pad, beveled magazine well, extended ambidextrous safety; flat mainspring housing; polished feed ramp and throated barrel; 30 lpi checkered front strap. Made in U.S. by Les Baer Custom, Inc.
Price: Blued **$1,428.00**
Price: Stainless. **$1,558.00**
Price: 6" model, blued, from **$1,595.00**

BAER 1911 S.R.P. PISTOL

Caliber: 45 ACP.
Barrel: 5".
Weight: 37 oz. **Length:** 8.5" overall.
Stocks: Checkered walnut.
Sights: Trijicon night sights.
Features: Similar to the F.B.I. contract gun except uses Baer forged steel frame. Has Baer match barrel with supported chamber, Wolff springs, complete tactical action job. All parts Mag-na-fluxed; deburred for tactical carry. Has Baer Ultra Coat finish. Tuned for reliability. Contact Baer for complete details. Introduced 1996. Made in U.S. by Les Baer Custom, Inc.
Price: Government or Commanche length **$2,990.00**

BERETTA MODEL 92FS PISTOL

Caliber: 9mm Para., 10-shot magazine.
Barrel: 4.9".
Weight: 34 oz. **Length:** 8.5" overall.
Stocks: Checkered black plastic; wood optional at extra cost.
Sights: Blade front, rear adjustable for windage. Tritium night sights available.
Features: Double action. Extractor acts as chamber loaded indicator, squared trigger guard, grooved front- and backstraps, inertia firing pin. Matte or blued finish. Introduced 1977. Made in U.S. and imported from Italy by Beretta U.S.A.
Price: With plastic grips.....................................$613.00
Price: With wood grips.......................................$635.00
Price: Tritium night sights, add..............................$91.00
Price: Deluxe, gold or silver plated.......................$5,434.00
Price: EL model, blued.......................................$791.00

Beretta Model 92FS

Beretta Models 92FS/96 Centurion Pistols

Identical to the Model 92FS and 96F except uses shorter slide and barrel (4.3"). Tritium or three-dot sight systems. Plastic or wood grips. Available in 9mm or 40 S&W. Also available in D Models (double-action-only). Introduced 1992.
Price: Model 92FS Centurion, three-dot sights, plastic grips......$586.00
Price: Model 92FS Centurion, wood grips......................$635.00
Price: Model 96 Centurion, three-dot sights, plastic grips........$613.00
Price: Model 92D Centurion..............................$586.00
Price: Model 96D Centurion..............................$586.00

Beretta Model 92D Pistol

Same as the Model 92FS except double-action-only and has bobbed hammer, no external safety. Introduced 1992.
Price: With plastic grips, three-dot sights.....................$586.00
Price: As above with tritium sights.........................$676.00

Beretta Model 92F Stainless Pistol

Same as the Model 92FS except has stainless steel barrel and slide, and frame of aluminum-zirconium alloy. Has three-dot sight system. Introduced 1992.
Price: With wood grips.....................................$679.00
Price: With tritium sights, plastic grips.......................$748.00

CONSULT

SHOOTER'S MARKETPLACE

Page 225, This Issue

Beretta Model 92 Compact L Type M Pistol

Similar to the Model 92FS except more compact and lighter: overall length 7.8"; 4.3" barrel; weighs 30.9 oz. Has Bruniton finish, chrome-lined bore, combat trigger guard, ambidextrous safety/decock lever. Single column 8-shot magazine, 9mm only. Introduced 1998. Imported from Italy by Beretta U.S.A.
Price: With three-dot sights.................................$613.00
Price: With tritium sights...................................$704.00
Price: Double action only, three-dot sights....................$586.00
Price: Double action only, tritium sights......................$676.00

Beretta 96D

Beretta Model 96 Pistol

Same as the Model 92F except chambered for 40 S&W. Ambidextrous safety mechanism with passive firing pin catch, slide safety/decocking lever, trigger bar disconnect. Has 10-shot magazine. Available with tritium or three-dot sights. Introduced 1992.
Price: Model 96, plastic grips.............................$676.00
Price: Model 96D, double-action-only, three-dot sights..........$613.00
Price: For tritium sights, add...............................$90.00

Beretta Model 92/96 Combo Kit Pistol

Similar to the 40 S&W Model 96 except comes with an extra 9mm 92FS slide and barrel assembly. Both barrels are 4.66" long and fit flush with the front of the slide. Kit comes in a special plastic case with a 10-round magazine in both calibers. Introduced 1998. From Beretta U.S.A.
Price:...NA

Beretta M9 Special Edition Pistol

Copy of the U.S. M9 military pistol. Similar to the Model 92FS except has special M9 serial number range; one 15-round (pre-ban) magazine; dot-and-post sight system; special M9 military packaging; Army TM 9-1005-317-10 operator's manual; M9 Special Edition patch; certificate of authenticity; Bianchi M12 holster, M1025 magazine pouch, and M1015 web pistol belt. Introduced 1998. From Beretta U.S.A.
Price:..$805.00

BERETTA MODEL 80 CHEETAH SERIES DA PISTOLS

Caliber: 380 ACP, 10-shot magazine (M84); 8-shot (M85); 22 LR, 7-shot (M87).
Barrel: 3.82".
Weight: About 23 oz. (M84/85). 20.8 oz. (M87). **Length:** 6.8" overall.
Stocks: Glossy black plastic (wood optional at extra cost).
Sights: Fixed front, drift-adjustable rear.
Features: Double action, quick takedown, convenient magazine release. Introduced 1977. Imported from Italy by Beretta U.S.A.
Price: Model 84 Cheetah, plastic grips........................$529.00
Price: Model 84 Cheetah, wood grips.........................$557.00
Price: Model 84 Cheetah, wood grips, nickel finish..............$600.00
Price: Model 85 Cheetah, plastic grips, 8-shot..................$500.00
Price: Model 85 Cheetah, wood grips, 8-shot...................$530.00
Price: Model 85 Cheetah, wood grips, nickel, 8-shot.............$559.00
Price: Model 87 Cheetah wood, 22 LR, 7-shot.................$529.00

Beretta Model 86 Cheetah

Similar to the 380-caliber Model 85 except has tip-up barrel for first-round loading. Barrel length is 4.4", overall length of 7.33". Has 8-shot magazine, walnut grips. Introduced 1989.
Price:..$530.00

BERETTA MODEL 950 JETFIRE AUTO PISTOL
Caliber: 25 ACP, 8-shot.
Barrel: 2.4".
Weight: 9.9 oz. **Length:** 4.7" overall.
Stocks: Checkered black plastic or walnut.
Sights: Fixed.
Features: Single action, thumb safety; tip-up barrel for direct loading/unloading, cleaning. From Beretta U.S.A.
Price: Jetfire plastic, blue.................................. $215.00
Price: Jetfire plastic, nickel $293.00
Price: Jetfire wood, EL.................................... $329.00
Price: Jetfire plastic, matte finish........................... $215.00

Beretta Model 21 Bobcat Pistol
Similar to the Model 950 BS. Chambered for 22 LR or 25 ACP. Both double action. Has 2.4" barrel, 4.9" overall length; 7-round magazine on 22 cal.; 8 rounds in 25 ACP, 9.9 oz., available in nickel, matte, engraved or blue finish. Plastic or walnut grips. Introduced in 1985.
Price: Bobcat, 22-cal., blue $266.00
Price: Bobcat, nickel, 22-cal............................... $317.00
Price: Bobcat, 25-cal., blue $266.00
Price: Bobcat, nickel, 25-cal............................... $317.00
Price: Bobcat EL, 22 or 25................................ $307.00
Price: Bobcat plastic matte, 22 or 25....................... $236.00

BERETTA MODEL 3032 TOMCAT PISTOL
Caliber: 32 ACP, 7-shot magazine.
Barrel: 2.45".
Weight: 14.5 oz. **Length:** 5" overall.
Stocks: Checkered black plastic.
Sights: Blade front, drift-adjustable rear.
Features: Double action with exposed hammer; tip-up barrel for direct loading/unloading; thumb safety; polished or matte blue finish. Imported from Italy by Beretta U.S.A. Introduced 1996.
Price: Blue $346.00
Price: Matte $317.00

BERETTA MODEL 8000/8040/8045 COUGAR PISTOL
Caliber: 9mm Para., 10-shot, 40 S&W, 10-shot magazine; 45 ACP, 8-shot.
Barrel: 3.6".
Weight: 33.5 oz. **Length:** 7" overall.
Stocks: Checkered plastic.
Sights: Blade front, rear drift adjustable for windage.
Features: Slide-mounted safety; rotating barrel; exposed hammer. Matte black Bruniton finish. Announced 1994. Imported from Italy by Beretta U.S.A.
Price: $651.00
Price: D models $629.00

Beretta Model 8000/8040 Mini Cougar
Similar to the Model 8000/8040 Cougar except has shorter grip frame and weighs 27.6 oz. Introduced 1998. Imported from Italy by Beretta U.S.A.
Price: 9mm or 40 S&W $651.00
Price: 9mm or 40 S&W, DAO $629.00

BERSA SERIES 95 AUTO PISTOL
Caliber: 380 ACP, 7-shot magazine.
Barrel: 3.5".
Weight: 22 oz. **Length:** 6.6" overall.
Stocks: Wrap-around textured rubber.
Sights: Blade front, rear adjustable for windage; three-dot system.
Features: Double action; firing pin and magazine safeties; combat-style trigger guard. Matte blue or satin nickel. Introduced 1992. Distributed by Eagle Imports, Inc.
Price: Matte blue $241.95
Price: Satin nickel $264.95

BERSA THUNDER 22 AUTO PISTOL
Caliber: 22 LR, 10-shot magazine.
Barrel: 3.5".
Weight: 24.2 oz. **Length:** 6.6" overall.
Stocks: Black polymer.
Sights: Blade front, notch rear adjustable for windage; three-dot system.
Features: Double action; firing pin and magazine safeties. Available in blue or nickel. Introduced 1995. Distributed by Eagle Imports, Inc.
Price: Blue $264.95
Price: Nickel.. $281.95

Beretta 950 Jetfire

Beretta M8000/8040 Cougar

Bersa Series 95

Bersa Thunder 380

BERSA THUNDER 380 AUTO PISTOLS
Caliber: 380 ACP, 7-shot (Thunder 380 Lite), 9-shot magazine (Thunder 380 DLX).
Barrel: 3.5".
Weight: 25.75 oz. **Length:** 6.6" overall.
Stocks: Black polymer.
Sights: Blade front, notch rear adjustable for windage; three-dot system.
Features: Double action; firing pin and magazine safeties. Available in blue or nickel. Introduced 1995. Distributed by Eagle Imports, Inc.
Price: Thunder 380, 7-shot, deep blue finish $264.95
Price: As above, satin nickel $281.95
Price: Thunder 380 DLX, 9-shot, matte blue $274.95

Brolin Legend L45

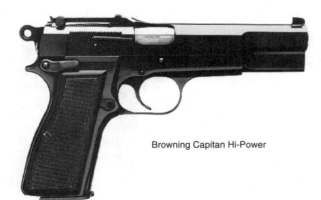

Browning Capitan Hi-Power

BROLIN LEGEND L45 STANDARD PISTOL
Caliber: 45 ACP, 7-shot magazine.
Barrel: 5".
Weight: 35.9 oz. **Length:** 8.5" overall.
Stocks: Checkered walnut.
Sights: Millett High Visibility front, white outline fixed rear.
Features: Throated match barrel; polished feed ramp; lowered and flared ejection port; beveled magazine well; flat top slide; flat mainspring housing; lightened aluminum match trigger; slotted Commander hammer; matte blue finish. Introduced 1996. Made in U.S. by Brolin Arms.
Price: **$499.95**

Brolin Legend L45C Compact Pistol
Similar to the L45 Standard pistol except has 4" barrel with conical lock up; overall length 7.5"; weighs 32 oz. Matte blue finish. Introduced 1996. Made in U.S. by Brolin Arms.
Price: **$519.95**

Brolin L45T Compact Auto Pistol
Same as the L45 Legend except uses compact slide on the standard-size frame. Has 4" barrel, weighs 33.9 oz., and is 7.5" overall. Introduced 1996. Made in U.S. by Brolin Industries.
Price: **$519.95**

BROLIN TAC SERIES SERVICE MODEL DA PISTOL
Caliber: 45 ACP, 8-shot magazine.
Barrel: 5".
Weight: 23 oz. **Length:** 8" overall.
Stocks: Checkered black plastic.
Sights: Blade front, drift adjustable rear.
Features: Skeletonized hammer; low-profile three-dot sight system. Introduced 1998. Imported by Brolin Industries.
Price: Matte blue **$399.95**
Price: Royal blue **$419.95**

Brolin TAC Series Full Size DA Pistol
Similar to the Service Model except available in 9mm Para. 40 S&W (10-shot), and 45 ACP (8-shot). Checkered walnut or plastic grips, checkered full-length slide rib. Introduced 1998. Imported by Brolin Industries.
Price: Matte blue **$399.95**
Price: Royal blue **$419.95**

Brolin L45T Compact

Brolin TAC Series Compact DA Pistol
Similar to the Service Model except has 3-1/2" barrel, 6-1/2" overall length, and weighs 19 oz. Available in 9mm Para. or 40 S&W only. Introduced 1998. Imported by Brolin Industries.
Price: Matte blue **$399.95**
Price: Royal blue **$419.95**

Brolin TAC Series Bantam DA Pistol
Similar to the Compact pistol except has shorter grip frame for 4" overall height. Has 3-1/2" barrel, 6-1/4" overall length, and weighs 17 oz. Chambered for the 9mm Para. and 40 S&W; 6-shot magazine; concealed hammer. Introduced 1998. Imported by Brolin Industries.
Price: Matte blue **$429.95**
Price: Royal blue **$449.95**

BROWNING HI-POWER 9mm AUTOMATIC PISTOL
Caliber: 9mm Para., 40 S&W, 10-shot magazine.
Barrel: 4-21/32".
Weight: 32 oz. **Length:** 7-3/4" overall.
Stocks: Walnut, hand checkered, or black Polyamide.
Sights: 1/8" blade front; rear screw-adjustable for windage and elevation. Also available with fixed rear (drift-adjustable for windage).
Features: External hammer with half-cock and thumb safeties. A blow on the hammer cannot discharge a cartridge; cannot be fired with magazine removed. Fixed rear sight model available. Imported from Belgium by Browning.
Price: Fixed sight model, walnut grips **$584.95**
Price: 9mm with rear sight adj. for w. and e., walnut grips **$635.95**
Price: Mark III, standard matte black finish, fixed sight, moulded grips, ambidextrous safety **$550.75**
Price: Silver chrome, adjustable sight, Pachmayr grips **$650.95**

Browning Capitan Hi-Power Pistol
Similar to the standard Hi-Power except has adjustable tangent rear sight authentic to the early-production model. Also has Commander-style hammer. Checkered walnut grips, polished blue finish. Reintroduced 1993. Imported from Belgium by Browning.
Price: 9mm only **$692.95**

Browning 40 S&W Hi-Power Mark III Pistol
Similar to the standard Hi-Power except chambered for 40 S&W, 10-shot magazine, weighs 35 oz., and has 4-3/4" barrel. Comes with matte blue finish, low profile front sight blade, drift-adjustable rear sight, ambidextrous safety, moulded polyamide grips with thumb rest. Introduced 1993. Imported from Belgium by Browning.
Price: Mark III **$550.95**

Browning Hi-Power HP-Practical Pistol
Similar to the standard Hi-Power except has silver-chromed frame with blued slide, wrap-around Pachmayr rubber grips, round-style serrated hammer and removable front sight, fixed rear (drift-adjustable for windage). Available in 9mm Para. or 40 S&W. Introduced 1991.
Price: **$629.75**
Price: With fully adjustable rear sight **$681.95**

Browning Micro Buck Mark Standard

Browning Buck Mark Varmint

CALICO M-110 AUTO PISTOL
Caliber: 22 LR.
Barrel: 6".
Weight: 3.7 lbs. (loaded). **Length:** 17.9" overall.
Stocks: Moulded composition.
Sights: Adjustable post front, notch rear.
Features: Aluminum alloy frame; flash suppressor; pistol grip compartment; ambidextrous safety. Uses same helical-feed magazine as M-100 Carbine. Introduced 1986. Made in U.S. From Calico.
Price: **$432.00**

CARBON-15 PISTOL
Caliber: 223, 10-shot magazine.
Barrel: 7.25".
Weight: 46 oz. **Length:** 20" overall.
Stock: Checkered composite.
Sights: Ghost ring.
Features: Semi-automatic, gas-operated, rotating bolt action. Carbon fiber upper and lower receiver; chromemoly bolt carrier; fluted stainless match barrel; mil. spec. optics mounting base; uses AR-15-type magazines. Introduced 1992. From Professional Ordnance, Inc.
Price: **$1,607.87**

CENTURY FEG P9R PISTOL
Caliber: 9mm Para., 10-shot magazine.
Barrel: 4.6".
Weight: 35 oz. **Length:** 8" overall.
Stocks: Checkered walnut.
Sights: Blade front, rear drift adjustable for windage.
Features: Double action with hammer-drop safety. Polished blue finish. Comes with spare magazine. Imported from Hungary by Century International Arms.
Price: About **$263.00**

COLT 22 AUTOMATIC PISTOL
Caliber: 22 LR, 10-shot magazine.
Barrel: 4.5".
Weight: 33 oz. **Length:** 8.62" overall.
Stocks: Textured black polymer.
Sights: Blade front, rear drift adjustable for windage.
Features: Stainless steel construction; ventilated barrel rib; single action mechanism; cocked striker indicator; push-button safety. Introduced 1994. Made in U.S. by Colt's Mfg. Co.
Price: **$248.00**

Colt 22 Target Pistol
Similar to the Colt 22 pistol except has 6" bull barrel, full-length sighting rib with lightening cuts and mounting rail for optical sights; fully adjustable rear sight; removable sights; two-point factory adjusted trigger travel. Stainless steel frame. Introduced 1995. Made in U.S. by Colt's Mfg. Co.
Price: **$377.00**

BROWNING BUCK MARK 22 PISTOL
Caliber: 22 LR, 10-shot magazine.
Barrel: 5-1/2".
Weight: 32 oz. **Length:** 9-1/2" overall.
Stocks: Black moulded composite with skip-line checkering.
Sights: Ramp front, Browning Pro Target rear adjustable for windage and elevation.
Features: All steel, matte blue finish or nickel, gold-colored trigger. Buck Mark Plus has laminated wood grips. Made in U.S. Introduced 1985. From Browning.
Price: Buck Mark, blue **$256.95**
Price: Buck Mark, nickel finish with contoured rubber stocks....... **$301.95**
Price: Buck Mark Plus **$313.95**

Browning Micro Buck Mark
Same as the standard Buck Mark and Buck Mark Plus except has 4" barrel. Available in blue or nickel. Has 16-click Pro Target rear sight. Introduced 1992.
Price: Blue **$256.95**
Price: Nickel **$301.95**
Price: Buck Mark Micro Plus **$313.95**
Price: Buck Mark Micro Plus Nickel **$342.95**

Browning Buck Mark Varmint
Same as the Buck Mark except has 9-7/8" heavy barrel with .900" diameter and full-length scope base (no open sights); walnut grips with optional forend, or finger-groove walnut. Overall length is 14", weighs 48 oz. Introduced 1987.
Price: **$390.95**

BRNO ZBP 99 AUTO PISTOL
Caliber: 9mm. Para., 40 S&W, 10-shot magazine.
Barrel: 4".
Weight: 27.5 oz. **Length:** 7.2" overall.
Stocks: Black composition.
Sights: Blade front, rear adjustable for elevation; three-dot system.
Features: Double action mechanism; polymer frame; chamber loaded indicator. Announced 1998. Imported from The Czech Republic by Euro-Imports.
Price: .... **NA**

Calico M-110

Century FEG P9RK Auto Pistol
Similar to the P9R except has 4.12" barrel, 7.5" overall length and weighs 33.6 oz. Checkered walnut grips, fixed sights, 10-shot magazine. Introduced 1994. Imported from Hungary by Century International Arms, Inc.
Price: About **$290.00**

Colt 22 Target

COLT MODEL 1991 A1 AUTO PISTOL

Caliber: 45 ACP, 7-shot magazine.
Barrel: 5".
Weight: 38 oz. **Length:** 8.5" overall.
Stocks: Checkered black composition.
Sights: Ramped blade front, fixed square notch rear, high profile.
Features: Parkerized finish. Continuation of serial number range used on original G.I. 1911 A1 guns. Comes with one magazine and moulded carrying case. Introduced 1991.
Price:. $556.00
Price: Stainless $610.00

Colt Model 1991 A1 Compact Auto Pistol

Similar to the Model 1991 A1 except has 3-1/2" barrel. Overall length is 7", and gun is 3/8" shorter in height. Comes with one 6-shot magazine, moulded case. Introduced 1993.
Price:. $556.00

COLT COMBAT COMMANDER AUTO PISTOL

Caliber: 45 ACP, 8-shot.
Barrel: 4-1/4".
Weight: 36 oz. **Length:** 7-3/4" overall.
Stocks: Textured rubber composite with finger grooves.
Sights: Fixed, glare-proofed blade front, square notch rear; three-dot system.
Features: Long trigger; arched housing; grip and thumb safeties.
Price: 45, stainless $813.00
Price: With stainless slide, blued frame, lightweight trigger, Hogue grips; introduced 1998 . . . . $813.00

COLT MUSTANG 380, GOVERNMENT POCKETLITE

Caliber: 380 ACP, 7-shot magazine.
Barrel: 3-1/4".
Weight: 14-3/4 oz. **Length:** 6" overall.
Stocks: Checkered composition.
Sights: Ramp front, square notch rear, fixed.
Features: Scaled-down version of the 1911 A1 Colt G.M. Has thumb and internal firing pin safeties. Introduced 1983.
Price: Pocketlite 380, stainless $508.00

Colt Mustang 380 Pocketlite

Similar to the standard 380 Government Model except has aluminum alloy frame (12.5 oz.), and is 1/2" shorter than 380 G.M., has 2-3/4" barrel. Introduced 1987.
Price: Mustang Pocketlite STS/N $508.00

COLT PONY AUTOMATIC PISTOL

Caliber: 380 ACP.
Barrel: 2-3/4".
Weight: 19 oz. **Length:** 5-1/2".
Stocks: Black composition.
Sights: Ramp front, fixed rear.
Features: Stainless steel construction. Double-action-only mechanism; recoil-reducing locked breech. Introduced 1997. Made in U.S. by Colt's Mfg. Co.
Price:. $529.00
Price: Pocketlite LW, aluminum frame and stainless steel slide, weighs 13 oz $529.00

> Consult our Directory pages for the location of firms mentioned.

COLT GOVERNMENT MODEL MK IV/SERIES 80

Caliber: 45 ACP, 8-shot magazine.
Barrel: 5".
Weight: 38 oz. **Length:** 8-1/2" overall.
Stocks: Black composite.
Sights: Ramp front, fixed square notch rear; three-dot system.
Features: Grip and thumb safeties and internal firing pin safety, long trigger.
Price: 45 ACP, stainless $813.00

COLT DEFENDER

Caliber: 45 ACP, 7-shot magazine.
Barrel: 3".
Weight: 22-1/2 oz. **Length:** 6-3/4" overall.
Stocks: Pebble-finish rubber wraparound with finger grooves.
Sights: White dot front, snag-free Colt competition rear.
Features: Stainless finish; aluminum frame; combat-style hammer; Hi Ride grip safety, extended manual safety, disconnect safety. Introduced 1998. Made in U.S. by Colt's Mfg. Co.
Price: $750.00

Colt 1991 A1 Compact

Colt Model 1991 A1 Commander Auto Pistol

Similar to the Model 1991 A1 except has 4-1/4" barrel. Parkerized finish. 7-shot magazine. Comes in moulded case. Introduced 1993.
Price: $556.00

Colt Concealed Carry Officer

Similar to the Combat Commander except has stainless slide with aluminum Officers lightweight frame; matte stainless slide, blued frame; weighs 26 oz. Introduced 1998. Made in U.S. by Colt's Mfg. Co. Inc.
Price: $813.00

Colt Mustang 380

Colt Government Model

COLT Z40 DOUBLE-ACTION DAO AUTO PISTOL

Caliber: 40 S&W, 10-shot magazine.
Barrel: 4".
Weight: 34 oz. **Length:** 7-3/4" overall.
Stock: Textured black polymer.
Sights: Dovetailed white dot front, No-Snag™ rear with two white dots.
Features: Double-action-only mechanism; alloy frame, carbon steel slide; matte blue finish. Introduced 1998. Made under license for Colt; imported from The Czech Republic.
Price: $624.00

COONAN 357 MAGNUM, 41 MAGNUM PISTOLS

Caliber: 357 Mag., 41 Magnum, 7-shot magazine.
Barrel: 5".
Weight: 42 oz. **Length:** 8.3" overall.
Stocks: Smooth walnut.
Sights: Interchangeable ramp front, rear adjustable for windage.
Features: Stainless steel construction. Unique barrel hood improves accuracy and reliability. Linkless barrel. Many parts interchange with Colt autos. Has grip, hammer, half-cock safeties, extended slide latch. Made in U.S. by Coonan Arms, Inc.
Price: 5" barrel, from $735.00
Price: 6" barrel, from $768.00
Price: With 6" compensated barrel $1,014.00
Price: Classic model (Teflon black two-tone finish, 8-shot magazine, fully adjustable rear sight, integral compensated barrel) $1,400.00
Price: 41 Magnum Model, from $825.00

Coonan Compact Cadet 357 Magnum Pistol

Similar to the 357 Magnum full-size gun except has 3.9" barrel, shorter frame, 6-shot magazine. Weight is 39 oz., overall length 7.8". Linkless bull barrel, full-length recoil spring guide rod, extended slide latch. Introduced 1993. Made in U.S. by Coonan Arms, Inc.
Price: $855.00

CZ 75 AUTO PISTOL

Caliber: 9mm Para., 40 S&W, 10-shot magazine.
Barrel: 4.7".
Weight: 34.3 oz. **Length:** 8.1" overall.
Stocks: High impact checkered plastic.
Sights: Square post front, rear adjustable for windage; three-dot system.
Features: Single action/double action design; choice of black polymer, matte or high-polish blue finishes. All-steel frame. Imported from the Czech Republic by CZ-USA.
Price: Black polymer $389.00
Price: Glossy blue $409.00
Price: Dual tone or satin nickel $415.00

CZ 85 Auto Pistol

Same gun as the CZ 75 except has ambidextrous slide release and safety-levers; non-glare, ribbed slide top; squared, serrated trigger guard; trigger stop to prevent overtravel. Introduced 1986. Imported from the Czech Republic by CZ-USA.
Price: Black polymer $419.00
Price: Combat, black polymer $475.00
Price: Combat, dual tone $487.00
Price: Combat, glossy blue $499.00

CZ 83 DOUBLE-ACTION PISTOL

Caliber: 380 ACP, 10-shot magazine.
Barrel: 3.8".
Weight: 26.2 oz. **Length:** 6.8" overall.
Stocks: High impact checkered plastic.
Sights: Removable square post front, rear adjustable for windage; three-dot system.
Features: Single action/double action; ambidextrous magazine release and safety. Blue finish; non-glare ribbed slide top. Imported from the Czech Republic by CZ-USA.
Price: Blue $315.00
Price: Nickel $319.95

CZ 100 AUTO PISTOL

Caliber: 9mm Para., 40 S&W, 10-shot magazine.
Barrel: 3.7".
Weight: 24 oz. **Length:** 6.9" overall.
Stocks: Grooved polymer.
Sights: Blade front with dot, white outline rear drift adjustable for windage.
Features: Double action only with firing pin block; polymer frame, steel slide; has laser sight mount. Introduced 1996. Imported from the Czech Republic by CZ-USA.
Price: 9mm Para. $389.00
Price: 40 S&W $399.00

DAVIS P-380 AUTO PISTOL

Caliber: 380 ACP, 5-shot magazine.
Barrel: 2.8".
Weight: 22 oz. **Length:** 5.4" overall.
Stocks: Black composition.
Sights: Fixed.
Features: Choice of chrome or black Teflon finish. Introduced 1991. Made in U.S. by Davis Industries.
Price: $98.00

Coonan 357 Magnum

CZ 75 9MM

CZ 75 Compact Auto Pistol

Similar to the CZ 75 ecept has 10-shot magazine, 3.9" barrel and weighs 32 oz. Has removable fromt sight, non-glare ribbed slide top. Trigger guard is squared and serrated; combat hammer. Introduced 1993. Imported from the Czech Republic by CZ-USA.
Price: Black polymer $429.00
Price: Dual tone or satin nickel $455.00
Price: Compact D, black polymer $449.00

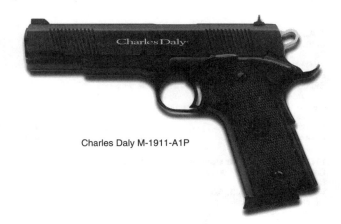

Charles Daly M-1911-A1P

CHARLES DALY M-1911-A1P AUTOLOADING PISTOL

Caliber: 45 ACP, 7- or 10-shot magazine.
Barrel: 5".
Weight: 38 oz. **Length:** 8-3/4" overall.
Stocks: Checkered.
Sights: Blade front, rear drift adjustable for windage; three-dot system.
Features: Skeletonized combat hammer and trigger; beavertail grip safety; extended slide release; oversize thumb safety; Parkerized finish. Introduced 1996. Imported from the Philippines by K.B.I., Inc.
Price: $429.00

DAVIS P-32 AUTO PISTOL
Caliber: 32 ACP, 6-shot magazine.
Barrel: 2.8".
Weight: 22 oz. **Length:** 5.4" overall.
Stocks: Laminated wood.
Sights: Fixed.
Features: Choice of black Teflon or chrome finish. Announced 1986. Made in U.S. by Davis Industries.
Price:. $87.50

Davis P-32

Desert Eagle Magnum

E.A.A. WITNESS DA AUTO PISTOL
Caliber: 9mm Para., 10-shot magazine; 38 Super, 40 S&W, 10-shot magazine; 45 ACP, 10-shot magazine.
Barrel: 4.50".
Weight: 35.33 oz. **Length:** 8.10" overall.
Stocks: Checkered rubber.
Sights: Undercut blade front, open rear adjustable for windage.
Features: Double-action trigger system; round trigger guard; frame-mounted safety. Introduced 1991. Imported from Italy by European American Armory.
Price: 9mm, blue $351.00
Price: 9mm, Wonder finish $366.00
Price: 9mm Compact, blue, 10-shot $351.00
Price: As above, Wonder finish. $366.60
Price: 40 S&W, blue $366.60
Price: As above, Wonder finish. $366.60
Price: 40 S&W Compact, 9-shot, blue. $366.60
Price: As above, Wonder finish. $366.60
Price: 45 ACP, blue $351.00
Price: As above, Wonder finish. $366.60
Price: 45 ACP Compact, 8-shot, blue $351.00
Price: As above, Wonder finish. $366.60

E.A.A. EUROPEAN MODEL AUTO PISTOLS
Caliber: 32 ACP or 380 ACP, 7-shot magazine.
Barrel: 3.88".
Weight: 26 oz. **Length:** 7-3/8" overall.
Stocks: European hardwood.
Sights: Fixed blade front, rear drift-adjustable for windage.
Features: Chrome or blue finish; magazine, thumb and firing pin safeties; external hammer; safety-lever takedown. Imported from Italy by European American Armory.
Price: Blue. $132.60
Price: Wonder finish $163.80

ENTRÉPRISE ELITE P500 AUTO PISTOL
Caliber: 45 ACP, 10-shot magazine.
Barrel: 5".
Weight: 40 oz. **Length:** 8.5" overall.
Stocks: Black ultra-slim, double diamond, checkered synthetic.
Sights: Dovetailed blade front, rear adjustable for windage; three-dot system.
Features: Reinforced dust cover; lowered and flared ejection port; squared trigger guard; adjustable match trigger; bolstered front strap; high grip cut; high ride beavertail grip safety; steel flat mainspring housing; extended thumb lock; skeletonized hammer, match grade sear, disconnector; Wolff springs. Introduced 1998. Made in U.S. by Entréprise Arms.
Price:. $739.00

Entréprise Boxer P500 Auto Pistol
Similar to the Medalist model except has adjustable Competizione "melded" rear sight with dovetailed Patridge front; high mass chiseled slide with sweep cut; machined slide parallel rails; polished breech face and barrel channel. Introduced 1998. Made in U.S. by Entréprise Arms.
Price:. $1,099.00

DESERT EAGLE MAGNUM PISTOL
Caliber: 357 Mag., 9-shot; 44 Mag., 8-shot; 50 Magnum, 7-shot.
Barrel: 6", 10", interchangeable.
Weight: 357 Mag.—62 oz.; 44 Mag.—69 oz.; 50 Mag.—72 oz.
Length: 10-1/4" overall (6" bbl.).
Stocks: Hogue rubber.
Sights: Blade on ramp front, combat-style rear. Adjustable available.
Features: Rotating three-lug bolt; ambidextrous safety; combat-style trigger guard; adjustable trigger optional. Military epoxy finish. Satin, bright nickel, hard chrome, polished and blued finishes available. Made in U.S. From Magnum Research, Inc.
Price: 357, 6" bbl., standard pistol $1,099.00
Price: 44 Mag., 6", standard pistol $1,099.00
Price: 50 Magnum, 6" bbl., standard pistol $1,099.00
Price: 440 Cor-Bon barrel, about $369.00

Entréprise Elite P500

Entréprise Boxer P500

Entréprise Medalist P500 Auto Pistol

Similar to the Elite model except has adjustable Competizione "melded" rear sight with dovetailed Patridge front; machined slide parallel rails with polished breech face and barrel channel; front and rear slide serrations; lowered and flared ejection port; full-length one-piece guide rod with plug; National Match barrel and bushing; stainless firing pin; tuned match extractor; oversize firing pin stop; throated barrel and polished ramp; slide lapped to frame. Introduced 1998. Made in U.S. by Entréprise Arms.
Price: $979.00

ERMA KGP68 AUTO PISTOL

Caliber: 32 ACP, 6-shot, 380 ACP, 5-shot.
Barrel: 4".
Weight: 22-1/2 oz. **Length:** 7-3/8" overall.
Stocks: Checkered plastic.
Sights: Fixed.
Features: Toggle action similar to original "Luger" pistol. Action stays open after last shot. Has magazine and sear disconnect safety systems. Imported from Germany by Mandall Shooting Supplies.
Price: $499.95

FEG MARK II AP PISTOL

Caliber: 380 ACP, 7-shot magazine.
Barrel: 3.9".
Weight: 27 oz. **Length:** 6.9" overall.
Stocks: Checkered black composition.
Sights: Blade front, rear adjustable for windage.
Features: Double action. All-steel construction. Polished blue finish. Comes with two magazines. Introduced 1997. Imported from Hungary by Interarms.
Price: $269.00
Price: Mark II APK, as above with 3.4" barrel, 6.4" overall length, weighs 25 oz. $269.00

FEG MARK II AP22 PISTOL

Caliber: 22 LR, 8-shot magazine.
Barrel: 3.4".
Weight: 23 oz. **Length:** 6.3" overall.
Stocks: Checkered black composition.
Sights: Blade front, rear adjustable for windage.
Features: Double action. All-steel construction. Polished blue finish. Introduced 1997. Imported from Hungary by Interarms.
Price: $269.00

FEG PJK-9HP AUTO PISTOL

Caliber: 9mm Para., 10-shot magazine.
Barrel: 4.75".
Weight: 32 oz. **Length:** 8" overall.
Stocks: Hand-checkered walnut.
Sights: Blade front, rear adjustable for windage; three dot system.
Features: Single action; polished blue or hard chrome finish; rounded combat-style serrated hammer. Comes with two magazines and cleaning rod. Imported from Hungary by K.B.I., Inc.
Price: Blue $349.00
Price: Hard chrome $429.00

FEG SMC-22 DA AUTO PISTOL

Caliber: 22 LR, 8-shot magazine.
Barrel: 3.5".
Weight: 18.5 oz. **Length:** 6.12" overall.
Stocks: Checkered composition with thumbrest.
Sights: Blade front, rear adjustable for windage.
Features: Patterned after the PPK pistol. Alloy frame, steel slide; blue finish. Comes with two magazines, cleaning rod. Introduced 1994. Imported from Hungary by K.B.I., Inc.
Price: $279.00

FEG SMC-380 AUTO PISTOL

Caliber: 380 ACP, 6-shot magazine.
Barrel: 3.5".
Weight: 18.5 oz. **Length:** 6.1" overall.
Stocks: Checkered composition with thumbrest.
Sights: Blade front, rear adjustable for windage.
Features: Patterned after the PPK pistol. Alloy frame, steel slide; double action. Blue finish. Comes with two magazines, cleaning rod. Imported from Hungary by K.B.I., Inc.
Price: $279.00

FEG SMC-918 Auto Pistol

Same as the SMC-380 except chambered for 9x18 Makarov. Alloy frame, steel slide, blue finish. Comes with two magazines, cleaning rod. Introduced 1995. Imported from Hungary by K.B.I., Inc.
Price: $279.00

Entréprise Tactical P500 Auto Pistol

Similar to the Elite model except has Tactical2 Ghost Ring sight or Novak lo-mount sight; ambidextrous thumb safety; front and rear slide serrations; full-length guide rod; throated barrel, polished ramp; tuned match extractor; fitted barrel and bushing; stainless firing pin; slide lapped to frame; dehorned. Introduced 1998. Made in U.S. by Entréprise Arms.
Price: $979.00

FEG Mark II AP

> Consult our Directory pages for the location of firms mentioned.

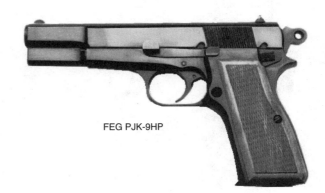

FEG PJK-9HP

FELK MTF 450 AUTO PISTOL

Caliber: 9mm Para. (10-shot); 40 S&W (8-shot); 45 ACP (9-shot magazine).
Barrel: 3.5".
Weight: 19.9 oz. **Length:** 6.4" overall.
Stocks: Checkered.
Sights: Blade front; adjustable rear.
Features: Double-action-only trigger, striker fired; polymer frame; trigger safety, firing pin safety, trigger bar safety; adjustable trigger weight; fully interchangeable slide/barrel to change calibers. Introduced 1998. Imported from Australia by Felk Inc.
Price: $395.00
Price: 45 ACP pistol with 9mm and 40 S&W slide/barrel assemblies $999.00

FORT WORTH HSS

Caliber: 22 LR, 10-shot magazine.
Barrel: 5-1/2" bull.
Weight: 45 oz. **Length:** 10.25" overall.
Stocks: Checkered walnut.
Sights: Ramp front, slide-mounted square notch rear adjustable for windage and elevation.
Features: Stainless steel construction. Military grip. Slide lock; smooth grip straps; push-button takedown; drilled and tapped for barrel weights. Introduced 1995. Made in U.S. by Fort Worth Firearms.
Price: $379.95

FORT WORTH HSSK
Caliber: 22 LR, 10-shot magazine.
Barrel: 4-1/2" or 6-3/4".
Weight: 39 oz. (4-1/2" barrel). **Length:** 9" overall (4-1/2" barrel).
Stocks: Checkered black plastic.
Sights: Blade front, side-mounted rear adjustable for windage.
Features: Stainless steel construction, military grip; standard trigger; push-button barrel takedown. Introduced 1995. Made in U.S. by Fort Worth Firearms.
Price: **$312.95**

GAL COMPACT AUTO PISTOL
Caliber: 45 ACP, 8-shot magazine.
Barrel: 4.25".
Weight: 36 oz. **Length:** 7.75" overall.
Stocks: Rubberized wrap-around.
Sights: Low profile, fixed, three-dot system.
Features: Forged steel frame and slide; competition trigger, hammer, slide stop magazine release, beavertail grip safety; front and rear slide grooves; two-tone finish. Introduced 1996. Imported from Israel by J.O. Arms, Inc.
Price: **$480.00**

Gal Compact

Glock 19

Glock 21

Glock 22 Auto Pistol
Similar to the Glock 17 except chambered for 40 S&W, 10-shot magazine. Overall length is 7.28", weight is 22.3 oz. (without magazine). Fixed or adjustable rear sight. Introduced 1990.
Price: Fixed sight. **$616.00**
Price: Adjustable sight. **$844.00**
Price: Model 22C, ported barrel **$646.00**

GLOCK 26, 27 AUTO PISTOLS
Caliber: 9mm Para. (M26), 10-shot magazine; 40 S&W (M27), 9-shot magazine.
Barrel: 3.47".
Weight: 21.75 oz. **Length:** 6.3" overall.
Stocks: Integral. Stippled polymer.
Sights: Dot on front blade, fixed or fully adjustable white outline rear.
Features: Subcompact size. Polymer frame, steel slide; double-action trigger with "Safe Action" system, three safeties. Matte black Tenifer finish. Hammer-forged barrel. Imported from Austria by Glock, Inc. Introduced 1996.
Price: Fixed sight. **$616.00**
Price: Adjustable sight. **$644.00**

GLOCK 17 AUTO PISTOL
Caliber: 9mm Para., 10-shot magazine.
Barrel: 4.49".
Weight: 21.9 oz. (without magazine). **Length:** 7.28" overall.
Stocks: Black polymer.
Sights: Dot on front blade, white outline rear adjustable for windage.
Features: Polymer frame, steel slide; double-action trigger with "Safe Action" system; mechanical firing pin safety, drop safety; simple takedown without tools; locked breech, recoil operated action. Adopted by Austrian armed forces 1983. NATO approved 1984. Imported from Austria by Glock, Inc.
Price: Fixed sight, with extra magazine, magazine loader, cleaning kit
. . . . **$616.00**
Price: Adjustable sight. **$644.00**
Price: Model 17L (6" barrel). **$800.00**
Price: Model 17C, ported barrel. **$646.00**

Glock 19 Auto Pistol
Similar to the Glock 17 except has a 4" barrel, giving an overall length of 6.85" and weight of 20.99 oz. Magazine capacity is 10 rounds. Fixed or adjustable rear sight. Introduced 1988.
Price: Fixed sight. **$616.00**
Price: Adjustable sight. **$644.00**
Price: Model 19C, ported barrel. **$646.00**

Glock 20 10mm Auto Pistol
Similar to the Glock Model 17 except chambered for 10mm Automatic cartridge. Barrel length is 4.60", overall length is 7.59", and weight is 26.3 oz. (without magazine). Magazine capacity is 10 rounds. Fixed or adjustable rear sight. Comes with an extra magazine, magazine loader, cleaning rod and brush. Introduced 1990. Imported from Austria by Glock, Inc.
Price: Fixed sight. **$668.00**
Price: Adjustable sight. **$697.00**

Glock 21 Auto Pistol
Similar to the Glock 17 except chambered for 45 ACP, 10-shot magazine. Overall length is 7.59", weight is 25.2 oz. (without magazine). Fixed or adjustable rear sight. Introduced 1991.
Price: Fixed sight. **$668.00**
Price: Adjustable sight. **$697.00**

Glock 23 Auto Pistol
Similar to the Glock 19 except chambered for 40 S&W, 10-shot magazine. Overall length is 6.85", weight is 20.6 oz. (without magazine). Fixed or adjustable rear sight. Introduced 1990.
Price: Fixed sight. **$616.00**
Price: Model 23C, ported barrel. **$646.00**
Price: Adjustable sight. **$644.00**

Glock 27 40 S&W

GLOCK 29, 30 AUTO PISTOLS
Caliber: 10mm (M29), 45 ACP (M30), 10-shot magazine.
Barrel: 3.78".
Weight: 24 oz. **Length:** 6.7" overall.
Stocks: Integral. Stippled polymer.
Sights: Dot on front, fixed or fully adjustable white outline rear.
Features: Compact size. Polymer frame steel slide; double-recoil spring re-
duces recoil; Safe Action system with three safeties; Tenifer finish. Two mag-
azines supplied. Introduced 1997. Imported from Austria by Glock, Inc.
Price: Fixed sight **$668.00**
Price: Adjustable sight **$697.00**

GOLAN AUTO PISTOL
Caliber: 9mm Para., 40 S&W, 10-shot magazine.
Barrel: 3.9".
Weight: 34 oz. **Length:** 7" overall.
Stocks: Textured composition.
Sights: Fixed.
Features: Fully ambidextrous double/single action; forged steel slide, alloy frame;
matte blue finish. Introduced 1994. Imported from Israel by J.O. Arms, Inc.
Price: **$649.95**

HECKLER & KOCH USP AUTO PISTOL
Caliber: 9mm Para., 10-shot magazine, 40 S&W, 10-shot magazine.
Barrel: 4.25".
Weight: 28 oz. (USP40). **Length:** 6.9" overall.
Stocks: Non-slip stippled black polymer.
Sights: Blade front, rear adjustable for windage.
Features: New HK design with polymer frame, modified Browning action with
recoil reduction system, single control lever. Special "hostile environment"
finish on all metal parts. Available in SA/DA, DAO, left- and right-hand ver-
sions. Introduced 1993. Imported from Germany by Heckler & Koch, Inc.
Price: Right-hand **$655.00**
Price: Left-hand **$676.00**
Price: Stainless steel, right-hand **$701.00**
Price: Stainless steel, left-hand **$722.00**

Heckler & Koch USP Compact Auto Pistol
Similar to the USP except has 3.58" barrel, measures 6.81" overall, and
weighs 1.60 lbs. (9mm). Available in 9mm Para. or 40 S&W with 10-shot
magazine. Introduced 1996. Imported from Germany by Heckler & Koch,
Inc.
Price: Blue **$685.00**
Price: Blue with control lever on right **$706.00**
Price: Stainless steel **$731.00**
Price: Stainless steel with control lever on right **$752.00**

Heckler & Koch USP45 Auto Pistol
Similar to the 9mm and 40 S&W USP except chambered for 45 ACP, 10-
shot magazine. Has 4.13" barrel, overall length of 7.87" and weighs 30.4 oz.
Has adjustable three-dot sight system. Available in SA/DA, DAO, left- and
right-hand versions. Introduced 1995. Imported from Germany by Heckler &
Koch, Inc.
Price: Right-hand **$717.00**
Price: Left-hand **$737.00**
Price: Stainless steel right-hand **$763.00**
Price: Stainless steel left-hand **$784.00**

Heckler & Koch USP45 Compact
Similar to the USP45 except has stainless slide; 8-shot magazine; modified
and contoured slide and frame; extended slide release; 3.80" barrel, 7.09"
overall length, weighs 1.75 lbs.; adjustable three-dot sights. Introduced
1998. Imported from Germany by Heckler & Koch, Inc.
Price: With control lever on left **$747.00**
Price: With control lever on right **$767.00**

HECKLER & KOCH MARK 23 SPECIAL OPERATIONS PISTOL
Caliber: 45 ACP, 10-shot magazine.
Barrel: 5.87".
Weight: 43 oz. **Length:** 9.65" overall.
Stocks: Integral with frame; black polymer.
Sights: Blade front, rear drift adjustable for windage; three-dot.
Features: Polymer frame; double action; exposed hammer; short recoil, mod-
ified Browning action. Civilian version of the SOCOM pistol. Introduced 1996.
Imported from Germany by Heckler & Koch, Inc.
Price: **$2,055.00**

Heckler & Koch USP 45

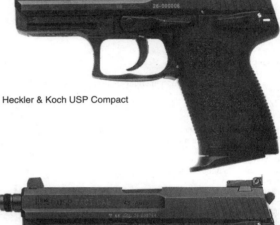

Heckler & Koch USP Compact

Heckler & Koch USP45 Tactical

HECKLER & KOCH USP45 TACTICAL PISTOL
Caliber: 45 ACP, 10-shot magazine.
Barrel: 4.92".
Weight: 2.24 lbs. **Length:** 8.64" overall.
Stocks: Non-slip stippled polymer.
Sights: Blade front, fully adjustable target rear.
Features: Has extended threaded barrel with rubber O-ring; adjustable trigger;
extended magazine floorplate; adjustable trigger stop; polymer frame. Intro-
duced 1998. Imported from Germany by Heckler & Koch, Inc.
Price: **$965.00**

HECKLER & KOCH P7M8 AUTO PISTOL
Caliber: 9mm Para., 8-shot magazine.
Barrel: 4.13".
Weight: 29 oz. **Length:** 6.73" overall.
Stocks: Stippled black plastic.
Sights: Blade front, adjustable rear; three dot system.
Features: Unique "squeeze cocker" in frontstrap cocks the action. Gas-retard-
ed action. Squared combat-type trigger guard. Blue finish. Compact size. Im-
ported from Germany by Heckler & Koch, Inc.
Price: P7M8, blued **$1,222.00**

HERITAGE STEALTH AUTO PISTOL
Caliber: 9mm Para., 40 S&W, 10-shot magazine.
Barrel: 3.9".
Weight: 20.2 oz. **Length:** 6.3" overall.
Stocks: Black polymer; integral.
Sights: Blade front, rear drift adjustable for windage.
Features: Gas retarded blowback action; polymer frame, 17-4 stainless slide; frame mounted ambidextrous trigger safety, magazine safety. Introduced 1996. Made in U.S. by Heritage Mfg., Inc.
Price: **$289.95**
Price: Stainless **$329.95**

HERITAGE H25S AUTO PISTOL
Caliber: 25 ACP, 6-shot magazine.
Barrel: 2.25".
Weight: 13.5 oz. **Length:** 4.5" overall.
Stocks: Smooth hardwood.
Sights: Fixed.
Features: Frame-mounted trigger safety, magazine disconnect safety. Made in U.S. by Heritage Mfg. Inc.
Price: Blue **$149.95**
Price: Nickel **$159.95**

HI-POINT FIREARMS 40 S&W AUTO
Caliber: 40 S&W, 8-shot magazine.
Barrel: 4.5".
Weight: 39 oz. **Length:** 7.72" overall.
Stocks: Checkered acetal resin.
Sights: Fixed; low profile.
Features: Internal drop-safe mechanism; alloy frame. Introduced 1991. From MKS Supply, Inc.
Price: Matte black **$148.95**

HI-POINT FIREARMS 45 CALIBER PISTOL
Caliber: 45 ACP, 7-shot magazine.
Barrel: 4.5".
Weight: 39 oz. **Length:** 7.95" overall.
Stocks: Checkered acetal resin.
Sights: Fixed; low profile.
Features: Internal drop-safe mechanism; alloy frame. Introduced 1991. From MKS Supply, Inc.
Price: Matte black or chrome/black.......................... **$148.95**

HI-POINT FIREARMS 9MM AUTO PISTOL
Caliber: 9mm Para., 9-shot magazine.
Barrel: 4.5".
Weight: 39 oz. **Length:** 7.72" overall.
Stocks: Textured acetal plastic.
Sights: Fixed, low profile.
Features: Single-action design. Scratch-resistant, non-glare blue finish, alloy frame. Introduced 1990. From MKS Supply, Inc.
Price: Matte black **$139.95**

Hi-Point Firearms 9mm Comp Pistol
Similar to the standard 9mm pistol except has 4" barrel, muzzle brake/compensator, 10-shot magazine, adjustable rear sight. Compensator is slotted for laser or flashlight mounting. Introduced 1998. From MKS Supply, Inc.
Price: **$149.95**

HI-POINT FIREARMS MODEL 9MM COMPACT PISTOL
Caliber: 9mm Para., 8-shot magazine.
Barrel: 3.5".
Weight: 29 oz. **Length:** 6.7" overall.
Stocks: Textured acetal plastic.
Sights: Combat-style fixed three-dot system; low profile.
Features: Single-action design; frame-mounted magazine release; polymer or alloy frame. Scratch-resistant matte finish. Introduced 1993. From MKS Supply, Inc.
Price: Black or chrome/black.............................. **$124.95**
Price: With polymer frame (29 oz.), non-slip grips **$124.95**

Hi-Point Firearms Model 380 Polymer Pistol
Similar to the 9mm Compact model except chambered for 380 ACP, 8-shot magazine, adjustable three-dot sights. Weighs 29 oz. Polymer frame. Introduced 1998. Made in U.S. From MKS Supply.
Price: **$99.95**
Price: Chrome slide, black frame **$99.95**

Heritage Stealth

HELWAN "BRIGADIER" AUTO PISTOL
Caliber: 9mm Para., 8-shot magazine.
Barrel: 4.5".
Weight: 32 oz. **Length:** 8" overall.
Stocks: Grooved plastic.
Sights: Blade front, rear adjustable for windage.
Features: Polished blue finish. Single-action design. Cross-bolt safety. Imported by Century International Arms.
Price: **$209.00**

Hi-Point 45 ACP

CONSULT
SHOOTER'S MARKETPLACE
Page 225, This Issue

Hi-Point 9MM Comp

Intratec Cat 9

INTRATEC CAT 45
Caliber: 40 S&W, 45 ACP; 6-shot magazine.
Barrel: 3.25".
Weight: 19 oz. **Length:** 6.35" overall.
Stocks: Moulded composition.
Sights: Fixed, channel.
Features: Black polymer frame. Introduced 1996. Made in U.S. by Intratec.
Price: $255.00

KAHR K9, K40 DA AUTO PISTOLS
Caliber: 9mm Para., 7-shot, 40 S&W, 6-shot magazine.
Barrel: 3.5".
Weight: 25 oz. **Length:** 6" overall.
Stocks: Wrap-around textured soft polymer.
Sights: Blade front, rear drift adjustable for windage; bar-dot combat style.
Features: Trigger-cocking double-action mechanism with passive firing pin block. Made of 4140 ordnance steel with matte black finish. Contact maker for complete price list. Introduced 1994. Made in U.S. by Kahr Arms.
Price: 9mm. $538.00
Price: Matte black, night sights 9mm. $624.00
Price: Matte nickel finish 9mm. $612.00
Price: Matte nickel, night sights 9mm. $699.00
Price: Matte stainless steel, 9mm. $588.00
Price: 40 S&W, matte black. $552.00
Price: 40 S&W, matte black, night sights. $638.00
Price: 40 S&W, matte stainless. $602.00
Price: Lady K9, 9mm, matte black, from $545.00
Price: K9 Elite 98 (high-polish stainless slide flats, Kahr combat trigger), from $631.00
Price: As above, MK9 Elite 98, from $648.00
Price: As above, K40 Elite 98, from. $646.00

Kahr MK9 Micro-Compact Pistol
Similar to the K9 except is 5.5" overall, 4" high, has a 3" barrel. Weighs 22 oz. Has snag-free bar-dot sights, polished feed ramp, dual recoil spring system, DA-only trigger. Comes with 6- and 7-shot magazines. Introduced 1998. Made in U.S. by Kahr Arms.
Price: Matte stainless. $605.00
Price: Matte stainless, tritium night sights $692.00
Price: Duo-Tone (stainless frame, Black-T slide). $749.00
Price: Duo-Tone with tritium night sights $836.00

Kahr KS40 Small Frame Pistol
Same as standard K40 except 1/2" shorter grip. Comes with one 5-shot, one 6-shot magazine. Introduced 1998. Made in U.S. by Kahr Arms.
Price: $594.00
Price: With night sights. $677.00

KAREEN MK II AUTO PISTOL
Caliber: 9mm Para., 10-shot magazine.
Barrel: 4.75".
Weight: 34 oz. **Length:** 7.85" overall.
Stocks: Textured composition.
Sights: Blade front, rear adjustable for windage.
Features: Single-action mechanism; ambidextrous external hammer safety; magazine safety; combat trigger guard. Two-tone finish. Introduced 1985. Imported from Israel by J.O. Arms & Ammunition.
Price: $425.00
Price: Kareen Mk II Compact 9mm (3.75" barrel, 30 oz., 6.75" overall length) $495.00

INTRATEC CAT 9 AUTO PISTOL
Caliber: 380 ACP, 9mm Para., 7-shot magazine.
Barrel: 3".
Weight: 21 oz. **Length:** 5.5" overall.
Stocks: Textured black polymer.
Sights: Fixed channel.
Features: Black polymer frame. Introduced 1993. Made in U.S. by Intratec.
Price: About $235.00

INTRATEC SPORT 22 AUTO PISTOL
Caliber: 22 LR, 10-shot magazine.
Barrel: 4".
Weight: 28 oz. **Length:** 11-3/16" overall.
Stocks: Moulded composition.
Sights: Protected post front, adjustable for windage, rear adjustable elevation.
Features: Ambidextrous cocking knobs and safety. Matte black finish. Accepts any 10/22-type magazine. Introduced 1988. Made in U.S. by Intratec.
Price: $130.00

INTRATEC DOUBLE-ACTION AUTO PISTOLS
Caliber: 22 LR, 10-shot; 25 ACP, 8-shot magazine.
Barrel: 2-1/2".
Weight: 14 oz. **Length:** 5" overall.
Stocks: Wraparound composition in gray, black or driftwood color.
Sights: Fixed.
Features: Double-action only trigger mechanism. Choice of black, satin or TEC-KOTE finish. Announced 1991. Made in U.S. by Intratec.
Price: 22 or 25, black finish $112.00
Price: 22 or 25, satin or TEC-KOTE finish $117.00

Kahr K9 Nickel

Kahr Mk 9

Kareen Mk II Compact

KEL-TEC P-11 AUTO PISTOL
Caliber: 9mm Para., 10-shot magazine.
Barrel: 3.1".
Weight: 14 oz. **Length:** 5.6" overall.
Stocks: Checkered black polymer.
Sights: Blade front, rear adjustable for windage.
Features: Ordnance steel slide, aluminum frame. Double-action-only trigger mechanism. Introduced 1995. Made in U.S. by Kel-Tec CNC Industries, Inc.
Price: Blue. **$309.00**
Price: Stainless **$407.00**
Price: Parkerized. **$350.00**

Jennings J-25

Kel-Tec P-11

JENNINGS J-22, J-25 AUTO PISTOLS
Caliber: 22 LR, 25 ACP, 6-shot magazine.
Barrel: 2-1/2".
Weight: 13 oz. (J-22). **Length:** 4-15/16" overall (J-22).
Stocks: Walnut on chrome or nickel models; grooved black Cycolac or resin-impregnated wood on Teflon model.
Sights: Fixed.
Features: Choice of bright chrome, satin nickel or black Teflon finish. Introduced 1981. From Jennings Firearms.
Price: J-22, about **$79.95**
Price: J-25, about **$79.95**

KIMBER CLASSIC 45 CUSTOM AUTO PISTOL
Caliber: 45 ACP, 7-shot magazine.
Barrel: 5".
Weight: 38 oz. **Length:** 8.5" overall.
Stocks: Black synthetic, walnut (Custom).
Sights: McCormick dovetailed front, low combat rear.
Features: Uses Kimber forged frame and slide, match-grade barrel, extended combat thumb safety, high beavertail grip safety, skeletonized lightweight composite trigger, skeletonized Commander-type hammer, and elongated Commander ejector. Bead-blasted black oxide finish; flat mainspring housing; lowered and flared ejection port; front and rear slide serrations; relief cut under trigger guard; Wolff spring set; beveled magazine well. Introduced 1995. Made in U.S. by Kimber Mfg. Inc.
Price: Custom **$657.00**
Price: Custom Walnut (walnut grips). **$670.00**
Price: Custom Royal (polished blue, rosewood grips) **$787.00**
Price: Custom Stainless **$774.00**

Kimber Classic 45 Custom

Kimber Classic 45 Polymer Frame Auto Pistol
Similar to the Classic 45 Custom except has black polymer frame with stainless steel insert, hooked trigger guard, checkered front strap. Weighs 34.4 oz., overall length 8.75". Introduced 1997. Made in U.S. by Kimber of America.
Price:. **$869.00**
Price: Polymer Stainless. **$948.00**
Price: Polymer Target. **$957.00**
Price: Polymer Stainless Target **$1,036.00**

Kimber Classic Polymer Stainless Target

Kimber Classic 45 Gold Match Auto Pistol
Same as the Custom Royal except also has Kimber low-mount adjustable rear sight, fancy rosewood grips, hand fit slide, barrel, frame and bushing. Comes with one 10-shot and one 8-shot magazine and factory proof target. Introduced 1995. Made in U.S. by Kimber of America, Inc.
Price:. **$1,019.00**

Kimber Compact .45 Auto Pistol
Similar to the Classic Custom except has 4" barrel fitted directly to the slide with no bushing; full-length guide rod; 7-shot magazine; grip is .400" shorter than full-size guns. Weighs 34 oz.; Compact Aluminum weighs 28 oz. Introduced 1998. Made in U.S. by Kimber Mfg. Inc.
Price:. **$677.00**
Price: Compact Stainless **$794.00**
Price: Compact Aluminum. **$677.00**

Kimber Compact Stainless

KORTH SEMI-AUTO PISTOL

Caliber: 9mm Para. (10-shot), 40 S&W (9-shot).
Barrel: 4", 5".
Weight: NA. **Length:** NA.
Stocks: Checkered walnut.
Sights: Ramped front, fully adjustable rear.
Features: Forged steel construction; double action; locked breech; recoil operated. Imported from Germany by Keng's Firearm Specialty, Inc.
Price: High-polish blued finish **$6,999.90**
Price: Plasma-coated silver matte finish **$7,499.90**
Price: Plasma-coated high polish silver finish **$7,999.90**
Price: Interchangeable barrel (9x21 for 9mm Para.) **$2,499.90**
Price: Interchangeable barrel (357 SIG for 40 S&W). **$2,499.90**

L.A.R. GRIZZLY WIN MAG MK I PISTOL

Caliber: 357 Mag., 357/45, 10mm, 44 Mag., 45 Win. Mag., 45 ACP, 7-shot magazine.
Barrel: 5.4", 6.5".
Weight: 51 oz. **Length:** 10-1/2" overall.
Stocks: Checkered rubber, non-slip combat-type.
Sights: Ramped blade front, fully adjustable rear.
Features: Uses basic Browning/Colt 1911A1 design; interchangeable calibers; beveled magazine well; combat-type flat; checkered rubber mainspring housing; lowered and back-chamfered ejection port; polished feed ramp; throated barrel; solid barrel bushings. Available in satin hard chrome, matte blue, Parkerized finishes. Introduced 1983. From L.A.R. Mfg., Inc.
Price: 45 Win. Mag. **$1,000.00**
Price: 357 Mag. **$1,014.00**
Price: Conversion units (357 Mag.) **$248.00**
Price: As above, 45 ACP, 10mm, 45 Win. Mag., 357/45 Win. Mag. . .**$233.00**

PSA-25 Auto

Laseraim Arms Series III Auto Pistol

Similar to the Series II except has 5" barrel only, with dual-port compensator; weighs 43 oz.; overall length is 7-5/8". Choice of fixed or adjustable rear sight. Introduced 1994. Made in U.S. by Laseraim Technologies, Inc.
Price: Fixed sight **$349.00**
Price: Adjustable sight **$349.00**
Price: Fixed sight Dream Team Laseraim laser sight **$349.00**

LLAMA MICROMAX 380 AUTO PISTOL

Caliber: 380 ACP, 7-shot magazine.
Barrel: 3-11/16".
Weight: 23 oz. **Length:** 6-1/2" overall.
Stocks: Checkered high impact polymer.
Sights: 3-dot combat.
Features: Single action design. Mini custom extended slide release; mini custom extended beavertail grip safety; combat-style hammer. Introduced 1997. Imported from Spain by Import Sports, Inc.
Price: Matte blue **$264.95**
Price: Satin chrome **$281.95**

LLAMA MINIMAX SERIES

Caliber: 9mm Para., 8-shot; 40 S&W, 7-shot; 45 ACP, 6-shot magazine.
Barrel: 3-1/2".
Weight: 35 oz. **Length:** 7-1/3" overall.
Stocks: Checkered rubber.
Sights: Three-dot combat.
Features: Single action, skeletonized combat-style hammer, extended slide release, cone-style barrel, flared ejection port. Introduced 1996. Imported from Spain by Import Sports, Inc.
Price: Blue **$281.95**
Price: Duo-Tone finish (45 only) **$298.95**
Price: Satin chrome **$304.95**

L.A.R. Grizzly MK I

L.A.R. Grizzly 50 Mark V Pistol

Similar to the Grizzly Win Mag Mark I except chambered for 50 Action Express with 6-shot magazine. Weight, empty, is 56 oz., overall length 10-5/8". Choice of 5.4" or 6.5" barrel. Has same features as Mark I, IV pistols. Introduced 1993. From L.A.R. Mfg., Inc.
Price: **$1,152.00**
Price: Conversion units for 44 Mag., 45 Win. Mag., 45 ACP, 357/45, 50 A.E **$233.00**

> Consult our Directory pages for the location of firms mentioned.

LASERAIM ARMS SERIES I AUTO PISTOL

Caliber: 10mm Auto, 8-shot, 40 S&W, 400 Cor-Bon, 45 ACP, 7-shot magazine.
Barrel: 6", with compensator.
Weight: 46 oz. **Length:** 9.75" overall.
Stocks: Pebble-grained black composite.
Sights: Blade front, fully adjustable rear.
Features: Single action; barrel compensator; stainless steel construction; ambidextrous safety-levers; extended slide release; matte black Teflon finish; integral mount for laser sight. Introduced 1993. Made in U.S. by Laseraim Technologies, Inc.
Price: Standard, fixed sight **$349.00**
Price: Standard, Compact (4-3/8" barrel), fixed sight. **$349.00**
Price: Adjustable sight **$349.00**
Price: Standard, fixed sight, Auto Illusion red dot sight system **$349.00**
Price: Standard, fixed sight, Laseraim Laser with Hotdot. **$349.00**

Laseraim Arms Series II Auto Pistol

Similar to the Series I except without compensator, has matte stainless finish. Standard Series II has 5" barrel, weighs 43 oz., Compact has 3-3/8" barrel, weighs 37 oz. Blade front sight, rear adjustable for windage or fixed. Introduced 1993. Made in U.S. by Laseraim Technologies, Inc.
Price: Standard or Compact (3-3/8" barrel), fixed sight **$349.00**
Price: Adjustable sight, 5" only **$349.00**
Price: Standard, fixed sight, Auto Illustion red dot sight. **$349.00**
Price: Standard, fixed sight, Laseraim Laser **$349.00**

Llama Minimax

Llama Minimax-II Auto Pistol

Same as the Minimax except in 45 ACP only, with 10-shot staggered magazine. Introduced 1997. Imported from Spain by Import Sports, Inc.
Price: Matte blue **$348.95**
Price: Satin chrome **$368.95**

LLAMA MAX-I AUTO PISTOLS
Caliber: 45 ACP, 7-shot.
Barrel: 5-1/8".
Weight: 36 oz. **Length:** 8-1/2" overall.
Stocks: Black rubber.
Sights: Blade front, rear adjustable for windage; three-dot system.
Features: Single-action trigger; skeletonized combat-style hammer; steel frame; extended manual and grip safeties. Introduced 1995. Imported from Spain by Import Sports, Inc.
Price: 45 ACP, 7-shot, Government model.................... $291.95
Price: As above, satin chrome finish.......................... $314.95

LORCIN L-22 AUTO PISTOL
Caliber: 22 LR, 9-shot magazine.
Barrel: 2.5".
Weight: 16 oz. **Length:** 5.25" overall.
Stocks: Black combat, or pink or pearl.
Sights: Fixed three-dot system.
Features: Available in chrome or black Teflon finish. Introduced 1989. From Lorcin Engineering.
Price: About... $89.00

LORCIN L9MM AUTO PISTOL
Caliber: 9mm Para., 10-shot magazine.
Barrel: 4.5".
Weight: 31 oz. **Length:** 7.5" overall.
Stocks: Grooved black composition.
Sights: Fixed; three-dot system.
Features: Matte black finish; hooked trigger guard; grip safety. Introduced 1994. Made in U.S. by Lorcin Engineering.
Price:... $159.00

LORCIN L-25, LT-25 AUTO PISTOLS
Caliber: 25 ACP, 7-shot magazine.
Barrel: 2.4".
Weight: 14.5 oz. **Length:** 4.8" overall.
Stocks: Smooth composition.
Sights: Fixed.
Features: Available in choice of finishes: chrome, black Teflon or camouflage. Introduced 1989. From Lorcin Engineering.
Price: L-25.. $69.00
Price: LT-25... $79.00

MAKAROV SPECIAL EDITION PISTOL
Caliber: 9x18 Makarov, 8-shot magazine.
Barrel: 3.68".
Weight: 24 oz. **Length:** 6.3" overall.
Stocks: Textured composition.
Sights: Blade front, rear drift-adjustable for windage; three-dot system.
Features: Available in polished blue and brushed chrome finishes. Extended magazine floorplate. Introduced 1998. Imported from Bulgaria by Miltex, Inc.
Price: About.. $250.00

NORTH AMERICAN ARMS GUARDIAN PISTOL
Caliber: 32 ACP, 6-shot magazine.
Barrel: 2.1".
Weight: 13.5 oz. **Length:** 4.36" overall.
Stocks: Black polymer.
Sights: Fixed.
Features: Doube-action-only mechanism. All stainless steel construction; snag-free. Introduced 1998. Made in U.S. by North American Arms.
Price:... $425.00

OLYMPIC ARMS OA-96 AR PISTOL
Caliber: 223.
Barrel: 6", 4140 chromemoly steel.
Weight: 5 lbs. **Length:** 15-3/4" overall.
Stocks: A2 stowaway pistol grip; no buttstock or receiver tube.
Sights: Flat-top upper receiver, cut-down front sight base.
Features: AR-15-type receivers with special bolt carrier; short aluminum hand guard; Vortex flash hider. Introduced 1996. Made in U.S. by Olympic Arms, Inc.
Price:... $940.00

ONE PRO.45 AUTO PISTOL
Caliber: 45 ACP or 400 Corbon, 10-shot magazine.
Barrel: 3.75"
Weight: 31.1 oz. **Length:** 7.04" overall.
Stocks: Tetured composition.
Sights: Blade front, drift-adjustable rear; three-dot system.
Features: All-steel construction; decocking lever and automatic firing pin lock; DA or DAO operation. Introduced 1997. Imported from Switzerland by Magnum Research, Inc.
Price:... $649.00
Price: Conversion kit, 45 ACP/400, 400/45 ACP $249.00

Llama Max-1

Lorcin L9MM

LORCIN L-32, L-380 AUTO PISTOLS
Caliber: 32 ACP, 380 ACP, 7-shot magazine.
Barrel: 3.5".
Weight: 27 oz. **Length:** 6.6" overall.
Stocks: Grooved composition.
Sights: Fixed.
Features: Black Teflon or chrome finish with black grips. Introduced 1992. From Lorcin Engineering.
Price: L-32 32 ACP $89.00
Price: L-380 380 ACP $100.00

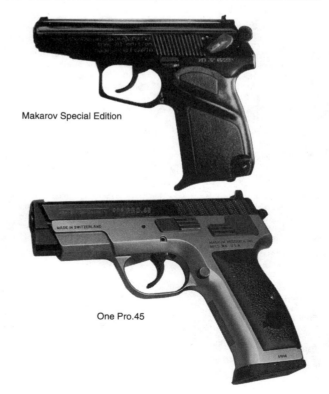

Makarov Special Edition

One Pro.45

Para-Ordnance P16.40

ONE PRO 9 AUTO PISTOL
Caliber: 9mm Para., 10-shot magazine.
Barrel: 3.01".
Weight: 25.1 oz. **Length:** 6.06" overall.
Stocks: Smooth wood.
Sights: Blade front, rear adjustable for windage.
Features: Rotating barrel; short slide; double recoil springs; double-action mechanism; decocking lever. Introduced 1998. Imported from Switzerland by Magnum Research.
Price: . . . . **NA**

PHOENIX ARMS HP22, HP25 AUTO PISTOLS
Caliber: 22 LR, 10-shot (HP22), 25 ACP, 10-shot (HP25).
Barrel: 3".
Weight: 20 oz. **Length:** 5-1/2" overall.
Stocks: Checkered composition.
Sights: Blade front, adjustable rear.
Features: Single action, exposed hammer; manual hold-open; button magazine release. Available in satin nickel, polished blue finish. Introduced 1993. Made in U.S. by Phoenix Arms.
Price: **$99.00**

PHOENIX ARMS MODEL RAVEN AUTO PISTOL
Caliber: 25 ACP, 6-shot magazine.
Barrel: 2-7/16".
Weight: 15 oz. **Length:** 4-3/4" overall.
Stocks: Ivory-colored, black slotted or pink plastic.
Sights: Ramped front, fixed rear.
Features: Available in blue, nickel or chrome finish. Made in U.S. Available from Phoenix Arms.
Price: **$79.00**

PSA-25 AUTO POCKET PISTOL
Caliber: 25 ACP, 6-shot magazine.
Barrel: 2-1/8".
Weight: 9.5 oz. **Length:** 4-1/8" overall.
Stocks: Checkered black polymer, ivory, checkered transparent carbon fiber-filled polymer.
Sights: Fixed.
Features: All steel construction; striker fired; single action only; magazine disconnector; cocking indicator. Introduced 1987. Made in U.S. by Precision Small Arms, Inc.
Price: Traditional (polished black oxide) $269.00
Price: Nouveau - Satin (brushed nickel) $269.00
Price: Nouveau - Mirror (highly polished nickel) $309.00
Price: Featherweight (aluminum frame, nickel slide) $405.00
Price: Diplomat (black oxide with gold highlights, ivory grips) $625.00
Price: Montreaux (gold plated, ivory grips) $692.00
Price: Renaissance (hand engraved nickel, ivory grips) **$1,115.00**
Price: Imperiale (inlaid gold filigree over blue, scrimshawed ivory grips) **$3,600.00**

REPUBLIC PATRIOT PISTOL
Caliber: 45 ACP, 6-shot magazine.
Barrel: 3".
Weight: 20 oz. **Length:** 6" overall.
Stocks: Checkered.
Sights: Blade front, drift-adjustable rear.
Features: Black polymer frame, stainless steel slide; double-action-only trigger system; squared trigger guard. Introduced 1997. Made in U.S. by Republic Arms, Inc.
Price: About **$325.00**

PARA-ORDNANCE P-SERIES AUTO PISTOLS
Caliber: 9mm Para., 40 S&W, 45 ACP, 10-shot magazine.
Barrel: 3", 3-1/2", 4-1/4", 5".
Weight: From 24 oz. (alloy frame). **Length:** 8.5" overall.
Stocks: Textured composition.
Sights: Blade front, rear adjustable for windage. High visibility three-dot system.
Features: Available with alloy, steel or stainless steel frame with black finish (silver or stainless gun). Steel and stainless steel frame guns weighs 40 oz. (P14.45), 36 oz. (P13.45), 34 oz. (P12.45). Grooved match trigger, rounded combat-style hammer. Beveled magazine well. Manual thumb, grip and firing pin lock safeties. Solid barrel bushing. Contact maker for full details. Introduced 1990. Made in Canada by Para-Ordnance.
Price: P14.45ER (steel frame) **$750.00**
Price: P14.45RR (alloy frame) **$740.00**
Price: P12.45RR (3-1/2" bbl., 24 oz., alloy) **$740.00**
Price: P13.45RR (4-1/4" barrel, 28 oz., alloy) **$740.00**
Price: P12.45ER (steel frame) **$750.00**
Price: P16.40ER (steel frame) **$750.00**
Price: P10-9RR (9mm, alloy frame) **$740.00**

Para-Ordnance Limited Pistols
Similar to the P-Series pistols except with full-length recoil guide system; fully adjustable rear sight; tuned trigger with overtravel stop; beavertail grip safety; competition hammer; front and rear slide serrations; ambidextrous safety; lowered ejection port; ramped match-grade barrel; dovetailed front sight. Introduced 1998. Made in Canada by Para-Ordnance.
Price: 9mm, 40 S&W, 45 ACP **$895.00**

Phoenix Arms HP22

PSA-25 Auto

Republic Patriot

ROCKY MOUNTAIN ARMS PATRIOT PISTOL

Caliber: 223, 10-shot magazine.
Barrel: 7", with muzzle brake.
Weight: 5 lbs. **Length:** 20.5" overall.
Stocks: Black composition.
Sights: None furnished.
Features: Milled upper receiver with enhanced Weaver base; milled lower receiver from billet plate; machined aluminum National Match handguard. Finished in DuPont Teflon-S matte black or NATO green. Comes with black nylon case, one magazine. Introduced 1993. From Rocky Mountain Arms, Inc.
Price: With A-2 handle top . . . . $2,500.00 to $2,800.00
Price: Flat top model . . . . $3,000.00 to $3,500.00

RUGER P89 SEMI-AUTO PISTOL

Caliber: 9mm Para., 10-shot magazine.
Barrel: 4.50".
Weight: 32 oz. **Length:** 7.84" overall.
Stocks: Grooved black Xenoy composition.
Sights: Square post front, square notch rear adjustable for windage, both with white dot inserts.
Features: Double action with ambidextrous slide-mounted safety-levers. Slide is 4140 chrome-moly steel or 400-series stainless steel, frame is a lightweight aluminum alloy. Ambidextrous magazine release. Blue or stainless steel. Introduced 1986; stainless introduced 1990.
Price: P89, blue, with extra magazine and magazine loading tool, plastic case with lock $410.00
Price: KP89, stainless, with extra magazine and magazine loading tool, plastic case with lock $452.00

Ruger P89D Decocker Semi-Auto Pistol

Similar to the standard P89 except has ambidextrous decocking levers in place of the regular slide-mounted safety. The decocking levers move the firing pin inside the slide where the hammer can not reach it, while simultaneously blocking the firing pin from forward movement—allows shooter to decock a cocked pistol without manipulating the trigger. Conventional thumb decocking procedures are therefore unnecessary. Blue or stainless steel. Introduced 1990.
Price: P89D, blue with extra magazine and loader, plastic case with lock $410.00
Price: KP89D, stainless, with extra magazine, plastic case with lock $452.00

RUGER P90 SAFETY MODEL SEMI-AUTO PISTOL

Caliber: 45 ACP, 7-shot magazine.
Barrel: 4.50".
Weight: 33.5 oz. **Length:** 7.87" overall.
Stocks: Grooved black Xenoy composition.
Sights: Square post front, square notch rear adjustable for windage, both with white dot inserts.
Features: Double action with ambidextrous slide-mounted safety-levers which move the firing pin inside the slide where the hammer can not reach it, while simultaneously blocking the firing pin from forward movement. Stainless steel only. Introduced 1991.
Price: KP90 with extra magazine, loader, plastic case with lock. . . . $488.65
Price: P90 (blue) $454.00

RUGER P93 COMPACT SEMI-AUTO PISTOL

Caliber: 9mm Para., 10-shot magazine.
Barrel: 3.9".
Weight: 31 oz. **Length:** 7.3" overall.
Stocks: Grooved black Xenoy composition.
Sights: Square post front, square notch rear adjustable for windage.
Features: Front of slide is crowned with a convex curve; slide has seven finger grooves; trigger guard bow is higher for a better grip; 400-series stainless slide, lightweight alloy frame; also in blue. Decocker-only or DAO-only. Introduced 1993. Made in U.S. by Sturm, Ruger & Co.
Price: KP93DAO, double-action-only $520.00
Price: KP93D ambidextrous decocker, stainless $520.00
Price: P93D, ambidextrous decocker, blue $421.50

Ruger KP89D

Ruger P89 Double-Action-Only Semi-Auto Pistol

Same as the KP89 except operates only in the double-action mode. Has a spurless hammer, gripping grooves on each side of the rear of the slide; no external safety or decocking lever. An internal safety prevents forward movement of the firing pin unless the trigger is pulled. Available in 9mm Para., stainless steel only. Introduced 1991.
Price: With lockable case, extra magazine, magazine loading tool . . . $452.00

Ruger KP94 Semi-Auto Pistol

Sized midway between the full-size P-Series and the compact P93. Has 4.25" barrel, 7.5" overall length and weighs about 33 oz. KP94 is manual safety model; KP94DAO is double-action-only (both 9mm Para., 10-shot magazine); KP94D is decocker-only in 40-caliber with 10-shot magazine. Slide gripping grooves roll over top of slide. KP94 has ambidextrous safety-levers; KP94DAO has no external safety, full-cock hammer position or decocking lever; KP94D has ambidextrous decocking levers. Matte finish stainless slide, barrel, alloy frame. Also available in blue. Introduced 1994. Made in U.S. by Sturm, Ruger & Co.
Price: P94, blue $421.50
Price: KP94 (9mm), KP944 (40-caliber) $520.00
Price: KP94DAO (9mm), KP944DAO (40-caliber) $520.00
Price: KP94D (9mm), KP9440 (40-caliber) $520.00

Ruger P90 Decocker Semi-Auto Pistol

Similar to the P90 except has a manual decocking system. The ambidextrous decocking levers move the firing pin inside the slide where the hammer can not reach it, while simultaneously blocking the firing pin from forward movement—allows shooter to decock a cocked pistol without manipulating the trigger. Available only in stainless steel. Overall length 7.87", weighs 34 oz. Introduced 1991.
Price: P90D with lockable case, extra magazine, and magazine loading tool $488.65

Ruger P93DAO

RUGER P95 SEMI-AUTO PISTOL

Caliber: 9mm Para., 10-shot magazine.
Barrel: 3.9".
Weight: 27 oz. **Length:** 7.3" overall.
Stocks: Grooved; integral with frame.
Sights: Blade front, rear drift adjustable for windage; three-dot system.
Features: Moulded polymer grip frame, stainless steel or chrome-moly slide. Suitable for +P+ ammunition. Decocker or DAO. Introduced 1996. Made in U.S. by Sturm, Ruger & Co. Comes with lockable plastic case, spare magazine, loading tool.
Price: P95 DAO double-action-only **$351.00**
Price: P95D decocker only **$351.00**
Price: KP95 stainless steel **$369.00**

RUGER MARK II STANDARD SEMI-AUTO PISTOL

Caliber: 22 LR, 10-shot magazine.
Barrel: 4-3/4" or 6".
Weight: 25 oz. (4-3/4" bbl.). **Length:** 8-5/16" (4-3/4" bbl.).
Stocks: Checkered plastic.
Sights: Fixed, wide blade front, square notch rear adjustable for windage.
Features: Updated design of the original Standard Auto. Has new bolt hold-open latch. 10-shot magazine, magazine catch, safety, trigger and new receiver contours. Introduced 1982.
Price: Blued (MK 4, MK 6) **$252.00**
Price: In stainless steel (KMK 4, KMK 6) **$330.25**

Ruger P4

Ruger MK-4B Compact Pistol

Similar to the Mark II Standard pistol except has 4" bull barrel, Patridge-type front sight, fully adjustable rear, and smooth laminated hardwood thumbrest stocks. Weighs 38 oz., overall length of 8-3/16". Comes with extra magazine, plastic case, lock. Introduced 1996. Made in U.S. by Sturm, Ruger & Co.
Price: **$336.50**

SAFARI ARMS GRIFFON PISTOL

Caliber: 45 ACP, 10-shot magazine.
Barrel: 5", 416 stainless steel.
Weight: 40.5 oz. **Length:** 8.5" overall.
Stocks: Smooth walnut.
Sights: Ramped blade front, LPA adjustable rear.
Features: 10+1 1911 enhanced 45. Beavertail grip safety; long aluminum trigger; full-length recoil spring guide; Commander-style hammer. Throated, polished and tuned. Grip size comparable to standard 1911. Satin stainless steel finish. Introduced 1996. Made in U.S. by Olympic Arms, Inc.
Price: **$920.00**

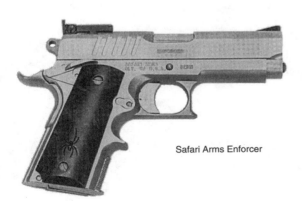

Safari Arms Enforcer

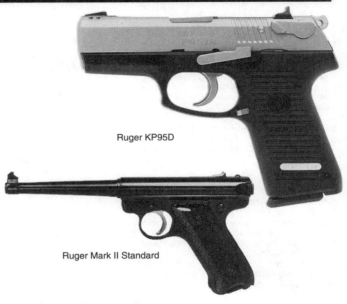

Ruger KP95D

Ruger Mark II Standard

Ruger 22/45 Mark II Pistol

Similar to the other 22 Mark II autos except has grip frame of Zytel that matchs the angle and magazine latch of the Model 1911 45 ACP pistol. Available in 4", 4-3/4" standard and 5-1/2" bull barrel. Introduced 1992.
Price: P4, 4", adjustable sights............................. **$237.50**
Price: KP 4 (4-3/4" barrel) **$280.00**
Price: KP512 (5-1/2" bull barrel)............................ **$330.00**
Price: P512 (5-1/2" bull barrel, all blue) **$237.50**

Ruger Mk-4B

SAFARI ARMS ENFORCER PISTOL

Caliber: 45 ACP, 6-shot magazine.
Barrel: 3.8", stainless.
Weight: 36 oz. **Length:** 7.3" overall.
Stocks: Smooth walnut with etched black widow spider logo.
Sights: Ramped blade front, LPA adjustable rear.
Features: Extended safety, extended slide release; Commander-style hammer; beavertail grip safety; throated, polished, tuned. Parkerized matte black or satin stainless steel finishes. Made in U.S. by Safari Arms.
Price: **$750.00**

Safari Arms Enforcer Carrycomp I Pistol

Similar to the Enforcer except has Wil Schueman-designed hybrid compensator system. Introduced 1993. Made in U.S. by Safari Arms, Inc.
Price: 5" barrel **$1,160.00**

SAFARI ARMS GI SAFARI PISTOL

Caliber: 45 ACP, 7-shot magazine.
Barrel: 5", 416 stainless.
Weight: 39.9 oz. **Length:** 8.5" overall.
Stocks: Checkered walnut.
Sights: G.I.-style blade front, drift-adjustable rear.
Features: Beavertail grip safety; extended thumb safety and slide release; Commander-style hammer. Parkerized finish. Reintroduced 1996.
Price: **$595.00**

SAFARI ARMS RELIABLE PISTOL
Caliber: 45 ACP, 7-shot magazine.
Barrel: 5", 416 stainless steel.
Weight: 39 oz. **Length:** 8.5" overall.
Stocks: Checkered walnut.
Sights: Ramped blade front, LPA adjustable rear.
Features: Beavertail grip safety; long aluminum trigger; full-length recoil spring guide; Commander-style hammer. Throated, polished and tuned. Satin stainless steel finish. Introduced 1996. Made in U.S. by Safari Arms, Inc.
Price:... $825.00

Safari Arms Reliable 4-Star Pistol
Similar to the Reliable except has 4.5" barrel, 7.5" overall length, and weighs 35.7 oz. Introduced 1996. Made in U.S. by Safari Arms, Inc.
Price:... $885.00

SAFARI ARMS COHORT PISTOL
Caliber: 45 ACP, 7-shot magazine.
Barrel: 3.8", 416 stainless.
Weight: 37 oz. **Length:** 8.5" overall.
Stocks: Smooth walnut with laser-etched black widow logo.
Sights: Ramped blade front, LPA adjustable rear.
Features: Combines the Enforcer model, slide and MatchMaster frame. Beavertail grip safety; extended thumb safety and slide release; Commander-style hammer. Throated, polished and tuned. Satin stainless finish. Introduced 1996. Made in U.S. by Safari Arms, Inc.
Price:... $790.00

SIG P210-6 SERVICE PISTOL
Caliber: 9mm Para., 8-shot magazine.
Barrel: 4-3/4".
Weight: 32 oz. **Length:** 8-1/2" overall.
Stocks: Checkered walnut.
Sights: Blade front, notch rear drift adjustable for windage.
Features: Mechanically locked, short-recoil operation; single action only; target trigger with adjustable stop; magazine safety; all-steel construction with matte blue finish. Optional 22 LR conversion kit consists of barrel, slide, recoil spring and magazine. Imported from Switzerland by SIGARMS, Inc.
Price:... $2,100.00
Price: With 22LR conversion kit $2,400.00

SIG SAUER P220 SERVICE AUTO PISTOL
Caliber: 45 ACP, (7- or 8-shot magazine).
Barrel: 4-3/8".
Weight: 27.8 oz. **Length:** 7.8" overall.
Stocks: Checkered black plastic.
Sights: Blade front, drift adjustable rear for windage. Optional Siglite night sights.
Features: Double action. Decocking lever permits lowering hammer onto locked firing pin. Squared combat-type trigger guard. Slide stays open after last shot. Imported from Germany by SIGARMS, Inc.
Price: Blue SA/DA or DAO $750.00
Price: Blue, Siglite night sights $845.00
Price: K-Kote or nickel slide $795.00
Price: K-Kote or nickel slide with Siglite night sights............. $885.00

SIG Sauer P229 DA Auto Pistol
Similar to the P228 except chambered for 9mm Para., 40 S&W, 357 SIG. Has 3.86" barrel, 7.08" overall length and 3.35" height. Weight is 30.5 oz. Introduced 1991. Frame made in Germany, stainless steel slide assembly made in U.S.; pistol assembled in U.S. From SIGARMS, Inc.
Price: Blue, SA/DA or DAO................................. $795.00
Price: With nickel slide $830.00
Price: With nickel frame and slide............................ $898.00
Price: Blue, Siglite night sights $885.00
Price: Nickel slide Siglite night sights $525.00

SIG SAUER P225 COMPACT PISTOL
Caliber: 9mm Para., 8-shot magazine.
Barrel: 3.8".
Weight: 26 oz. **Length:** 7-3/32" overall.
Stocks: Checkered black plastic.
Sights: Blade front, rear adjustable for windage. Optional Siglite night sights.
Features: Double action. Decocking lever permits lowering hammer onto locked firing pin. Square combat-type trigger guard. Imported from Germany by SIGARMS, Inc.
Price: Blue, SA/DA or DAO................................. $725.00
Price: With Siglite night sights............................ $830.00
Price: K-Kote or nickel slide $770.00
Price: K-Kote or nickel slide with Siglite night sights............. $860.00

SAFARI ARMS RENEGADE
Caliber: 45 ACP, 7-shot magazine.
Barrel: 5", 416 stainless steel.
Weight: 39 oz. **Length:** 8.5" overall.
Stocks: Checkered walnut.
Sights: Ramped blade, LPA adjustable rear.
Features: True left-hand pistol. Beavertail grip safety; long aluminum trigger; full-length recoil spring guide; Commander-style hammer. Throated, polished and tuned. Satin stainless finish. Introduced 1996. Made in U.S. by Safari Arms, Inc.
Price:... $1,085.00

SEECAMP LWS 32 STAINLESS DA AUTO
Caliber: 32 ACP Win. Silvertip, 6-shot magazine.
Barrel: 2", integral with frame.
Weight: 10.5 oz. **Length:** 4-1/8" overall.
Stocks: Glass-filled nylon.
Sights: Smooth, no-snag, contoured slide and barrel top.
Features: Aircraft quality 17-4 PH stainless steel. Inertia-operated firing pin. Hammer fired double-action-only. Hammer automatically follows slide down to safety rest position after each shot—no manual safety needed. Magazine safety disconnector. Polished stainless. Introduced 1985. From L.W. Seecamp.
Price:... $425.00

SIG Sauer P220

SIG Sauer P226 Service Pistol
Similar to the P220 pistol except has 4.4" barrel, and weighs 28.3 oz. 357 SIG or 40 S&W. Imported from Germany by SIGARMS, Inc.
Price: Blue SA/DA or DAO $795.00
Price: With Siglite night sights.......................... $885.00
Price: Blue, SA/DA or DAO 357 SIG........................ $795.00
Price: With Siglite night sights.......................... $885.00
Price: K-Kote finish, 40 S&W only or nickel slide $795.00
Price: K-Kote or nickel slide Siglite night sights.............. $885.00
Price: Nickel slide 357 SIG $830.00
Price: Nickel slide, Siglite night sights $925.00

SIG Sauer P225

SIG Sauer P229S

SIG Sauer P239

SMITH & WESSON MODEL 22A SPORT PISTOL

Caliber: 22 LR, 10-shot magazine.
Barrel: 4", 5-1/2", 7".
Weight: 29 oz. **Length:** 8" overall.
Stocks: Two-piece polymer.
Sights: Patridge front, fully adjustable rear.
Features: Comes with a sight bridge with Weaver-style integral optics mount; alloy frame; .312" serrated trigger; stainless steel slide and barrel with matte blue finish. Introduced 1997. Made in U.S. by Smith & Wesson.
Price: 4" **$224.00**
Price: 5-1/2" **$247.00**
Price: 7" **$281.00**

SMITH & WESSON MODEL 457 DA AUTO PISTOL

Caliber: 45 ACP, 7-shot magazine.
Barrel: 3-3/4".
Weight: 29 oz. **Length:** 7-1/4" overall.
Stocks: One-piece Xenoy, wrap-around with straight backstrap.
Sights: Post front, fixed rear, three-dot system.
Features: Aluminum alloy frame, matte blue carbon steel slide; bobbed hammer; smooth trigger. Introduced 1996. Made in U.S. by Smith & Wesson.
Price: **$500.00**

SMITH & WESSON MODEL 908 AUTO PISTOL

Caliber: 9mm Para., 8-shot magazine.
Barrel: 3-1/2".
Weight: 26 oz. **Length:** 6-13/16".
Stocks: One-piece Xenoy, wrap-around with straight backstrap.
Sights: Post front, fixed rear, three-dot system.
Features: Aluminum alloy frame, matte blue carbon steel slide; bobbed hammer; smooth trigger. Introduced 1996. Made in U.S. by Smith & Wesson.
Price: **$453.00**

SMITH & WESSON MODEL 2213, 2214 SPORTSMAN AUTOS

Caliber: 22 LR, 8-shot magazine.
Barrel: 3".
Weight: 18 oz. **Length:** 6-1/8" overall.
Stocks: Checkered black polymer.
Sights: Patridge front, fixed rear; three-dot system.
Features: Internal hammer; serrated trigger; single action. Model 2213 is stainless with alloy frame, Model 2214 is blued carbon steel with alloy frame. Introduced 1990. Made in U.S. by Smith & Wesson.
Price: Model 2213 .... **$330.00**
Price: Model 2214 .... **$284.00**

SIG Sauer P229 S Auto Pistol

Similar to the P229 except available in 357 SIG only; 4.8" heavy barrel; 8.6" overall length; weighs 40.6 oz.; vented compensator; adjustable target sights; rubber grips; extended slide latch and magazine release. Made of stainless steel. Introduced 1998. From SIGARMS, Inc.
Price: **$1,320.00**

SIG SAUER P232 PERSONAL SIZE PISTOL

Caliber: 380 ACP, 7-shot.
Barrel: 3-3/4".
Weight: 16 oz. **Length:** 6-1/2" overall.
Stocks: Checkered black composite.
Sights: Blade front, rear adjustable for windage.
Features: Double action/single action or DAO. Blowback operation, stationary barrel. Introduced 1997. Imported from Germany by SIGARMS, Inc.
Price: Blue SA/DA or DAO **$485.00**
Price: In stainless steel. **$525.00**
Price: With stainless steel slide, blue frame **$505.00**
Price: Stainless steel, Siglite night sights, Hogue grips **$560.00**

SIG SAUER P239 PISTOL

Caliber: 9mm Para., 8-shot, 357 SIG 40 S&W, 7-shot magazine.
Barrel: 3.6"
Weight: 25.2 oz. **Length:** 6.6" overall.
Stocks: Checkered black composite.
Sights: Blade front, rear adjustable for windage. Optional Siglite night sights.
Features: SA/DA or DAO; blackened stainless steel slide, aluminum alloy frame. Introduced 1996. Made in U.S. by SIGARMS, Inc.
Price: SA/DA or DAO **$595.00**
Price: SA/DA or DAO with Siglite night sights **$685.00**

Smith & Wesson Model 22S Sport Pistols

Similar to the Model 22A Sport except with stainless steel frame. Available only with 5-1/2" or 7" barrel. Introduced 1997. Made in U.S. by Smith & Wesson.
Price: 5-1/2" standard barrel. **$303.00**
Price: 5-1/2" bull barrel, wood target stocks with thumbrest. **$368.00**
Price: 7" standard barrel. **$334.00**
Price: 5-1/2" bull barrel, two-piece target stocks with thumbrest **$342.00**

SMITH & WESSON MODEL 410 DA AUTO PISTOL

Caliber: 40 S&W, 10-shot magazine.
Barrel: 4".
Weight: 28.5 oz. **Length:** 7.5 oz.
Stocks: One-piece Xenoy, wrap-around with straight backstrap.
Sights: Post front, fixed rear; three-dot system.
Features: Aluminum alloy frame; blued carbon steel slide; traditional double action with left-side slide-mountd decocking lever. Introduced 1996. Made in U.S. by Smith & Wesson.
Price: **$500.00**

Smith & Wesson Model 457

SMITH & WESSON MODEL 910 DA AUTO PISTOL

Caliber: 9mm Para., 10-shot magazine.
Barrel: 4".
Weight: 28 oz. **Length:** 7-3/8" overall.
Stocks: One-piece Xenoy, wrap-around with straight backstrap.
Sights: Post front with white dot, fixed two-dot rear.
Features: Alloy frame, blue carbon steel slide. Slide-mounted decocking lever. Introduced 1995.
Price: Model 910 .... **$453.00**

SMITH & WESSON MODEL 3913 DOUBLE ACTION
Caliber: 9mm Para., 8-shot magazine.
Barrel: 3-1/2".
Weight: 26 oz. **Length:** 6-13/16" overall.
Stocks: One-piece Delrin wrap-around, textured surface.
Sights: Post front with white dot, Novak LoMount Carry with two dots, adjustable for windage.
Features: Aluminum alloy frame, stainless slide (M3913) or blue steel slide (M3914). Bobbed hammer with no half-cock notch; smooth .304" trigger with rounded edges. Straight backstrap. Extra magazine included. Introduced 1989.
Price: **$643.00**

Smith & Wesson Model 3913 LadySmith Auto
Similar to the standard Model 3913 except has frame that is upswept at the front, rounded trigger guard. Comes in frosted stainless steel with matching gray grips. Grips are ergonomically correct for a woman's hand. Novak Lo-Mount Carry rear sight adjustable for windage, smooth edges for snag resistance. Extra magazine included. Introduced 1990.
Price: **$662.00**

Smith & Wesson Model 3953 DA Pistol
Same as the Model 3913 except double-action-only. Model 3953 has stainless slide with alloy frame. Overall length 7"; weighs 25.5 oz. Extra magazine included. Introduced 1990.
Price: **$643.00**

Smith & Wesson Model 3913TSW/3953TSW Auto Pistols
Similar to the Model 3913 and 3953 except TSW guns have tighter tolerances, ambidextrous manual safety/decocking lever, flush-fit magazine, delayed-unlock firing system. DAO Model 3953 has magazine disconnector. Compact alloy frame, stainless steel slide. Straight backstrap. Introduced 1998. Made in U.S. by Smith & Wesson.
Price: **$674.00**
Price: **$674.00**

SMITH & WESSON MODEL 4006 DA AUTO
Caliber: 40 S&W, 10-shot magazine.
Barrel: 4".
Weight: 38.5 oz. **Length:** 7-7/8" overall.
Stocks: Xenoy wrap-around with checkered panels.
Sights: Replaceable post front with white dot, Novak LoMount Carry fixed rear with two white dots, or micro. click adjustable rear with two white dots.
Features: Stainless steel construction with non-reflective finish. Straight backstrap. Extra magazine included. Introduced 1990.
Price: With adjustable sights **$798.00**
Price: With fixed sight **$768.00**
Price: With fixed night sights **$880.00**

> Consult our Directory pages for the location of firms mentioned.

Smith & Wesson Model 4043, 4046 DA Pistols
Similar to the Model 4006 except is double-action-only. Has a semi-bobbed hammer, smooth trigger, 4" barrel; Novak LoMount Carry rear sight, post front with white dot. Overall length is 7-1/2", weighs 28 oz. Model 4043 has alloy frame. Extra magazine included. Introduced 1991.
Price: Model 4043 . . . . **$750.00**
Price: Model 4046 . . . . **$768.00**
Price: Model 4046 with fixed night sights **$880.00**

SMITH & WESSON MODEL 4500 SERIES AUTOS
Caliber: 45 ACP, 8-shot magazine.
Barrel: 5" (M4506).
Weight: 41 oz. (4506). **Length:** 8-1/2" overall.
Stocks: Xenoy one-piece wrap-around, arched or straight backstrap.
Sights: Post front with white dot, adjustable or fixed Novak LoMount Carry on M4506.
Features: M4506 has serrated hammer spur. Extra magazine included. Contact Smith & Wesson for complete data. Introduced 1989.
Price: Model 4506, fixed sight **$798.00**
Price: Model 4506, adjustable sight **$830.00**
Price: Model 4566 (stainless, 4-1/4", traditional DA, ambidextrous safety, fixed sight) **$798.00**
Price: Model 4586 (stainless, 4-1/4", DA only) **$798.00**

Smith & Wesson 3913 LadySmith

Smith & Wesson 3913 TSW

Smith & Wesson Model 4013 TSW

SMITH & WESSON MODEL 4013, 4053 TSW Autos
Caliber: 40 S&W, 9-shot magazine.
Barrel: 3-1/2".
Weight: 26.4 oz. **Length:** 6-7/8" overall.
Stocks: Checkered black polymer.
Sights: Novak three-dot system.
Features: Traditional double-action system; stainless slide, alloy frame; fixed barrel bushing; ambidextrous decocker; reversible magazine catch. Introduced 1997. Made in U.S. by Smith & Wesson.
Price: Model 4013 . . . . **$799.00**
Price: Model 4053, double-action-only **$824.00**

Smith & Wesson Model 4506

SMITH & WESSON MODEL 4513TSW/4553TSW PISTOLS

Caliber: 45 ACP, 6-shot magazine.
Barrel: 3-3/4".
Weight: 28 oz. (M4513TSW). **Length:** 6-7/8 overall.
Stocks: Checkered Xenoy; straight backstrap.
Sights: White dot front, Novak Lo Mount Carry 2-Dot rear.
Features: Model 4513TSW is traditional double action, Model 4553TSW is double action only. TSW series has tighter tolerances, ambidextrous manual safety/decocking lever, flush-fit magazine, delayed-unlock firing system. DAO has magazine disconnector. Compact alloy frame, stainless steel slide. Introduced 1998. Made in U.S. by Smith & Wesson.
Price: Model 4513TSW $758.00
Price: Model 4553TSW $758.00

SMITH & WESSON MODEL 5900 SERIES AUTO PISTOLS

Caliber: 9mm Para., 10-shot magazine.
Barrel: 4".
Weight: 28-1/2 to 37-1/2 oz. (fixed sight); 38 oz. (adjustable sight).
  Length: 7-1/2" overall.
Stocks: Xenoy wrap-around with curved backstrap.
Sights: Post front with white dot, fixed or fully adjustable with two white dots.
Features: All stainless, stainless and alloy or carbon steel and alloy construction. Smooth .304" trigger, .260" serrated hammer. Extra magazine included. Introduced 1989.
Price: Model 5904 (blue, alloy frame, traditional DA, adjustable sight, ambidextrous safety) $663.00
Price: Model 5906 (stainless, traditional DA, adjustable sight, ambidextrous safety) $765.00
Price: As above, fixed sight $729.00
Price: With fixed night sights $841.00
Price: Model 5946 (as above, stainless frame and slide) $729.00

SMITH & WESSON SIGMA SERIES PISTOLS

Caliber: 9mm Para., 40 S&W, 10-shot magazine.
Barrel: 3-1/4", 4", 4-1/2".
Weight: 26 oz. **Length:** 7.4" overall.
Stocks: Integral.
Sights: White dot front, fixed rear; three-dot system. Tritium night sights available.
Features: Ergonomic polymer frame; low barrel centerline; internal striker firing system; corrosion-resistant slide; Teflon-filled, electroless-nickel coated magazine. Introduced 1994. Made in U.S. by Smith & Wesson.
Price: SW9M, 9mm, 3-1/4" barrel, black polymer, fixed sights $366.00
Price: SW9C, 9mm, 4" barrel, black polymer, fixed night sights $541.00
Price: SW9V, 9mm, 4" barrel, black or gray polymer, stainless finish fixed sights $382.00
Price: SW40C, 40 S&W, 4" barrel, black polymer, fixed sights $541.00
Price: SW40V, 40 S&W, 4" barrel, gray or black polymer, fixed sights $382.00

SMITH & WESSON SIGMA SW380 AUTO

Caliber: 380 ACP, 6-shot magazine.
Barrel: 3".
Weight: 14 oz. **Length:** 5.8" overall.
Stocks: Integral.
Sights: Fixed groove in the slide.
Features: Polymer frame; double-action-only trigger mechanism; grooved/serrated front and rear straps; two passive safeties. Introduced 1995. Made in U.S. by Smith & Wesson.
Price: $319.00

Smith & Wesson 4553 TSW

Smith & Wesson Model 6906 Double-Action Auto

Similar to the Model 5906 except with 3-1/2" barrel, 10-shot magazine, fixed rear sight, .260" bobbed hammer. Extra magazine included. Introduced 1989.
Price: Model 6906, stainless $699.00
Price: Model 6906 with fixed night sights $811.00
Price: Model 6946 (stainless, DA only, fixed sights) $699.00

Smith & Wesson Sigma SW40V

SPRINGFIELD, INC. 1911A1 AUTO PISTOL

Caliber: 9mm Para., 9-shot; 38 Super, 9-shot; 45 ACP, 8-shot.
Barrel: 5".
Weight: 35.6 oz. **Length:** 8-5/8" overall.
Stocks: Checkered plastic or walnut.
Sights: Fixed three-dot system.
Features: Beveled magazine well; lowered and flared ejection port. All forged parts, including frame, barrel, slide. All new production. Introduced 1990. From Springfield, Inc.
Price: Mil-Spec 45 ACP, Parkerized......................... $519.00
Price: Standard, 45 ACP, blued $549.00
Price: Standard, 45 ACP, stainless $589.00
Price: Lightweight (28.6 oz., matte finish) $549.00
Price: Standard, 9mm, 38 Super, blued $549.00
Price: Standard, 9mm, stainless steel $599.00

Springfield, Inc. N.R.A. PPC Pistol

Specifically designed to comply with NRA rules for PPC competition. Has custom slide-to-frame fit; polished feed ramp; throated barrel; total internal honing; tuned extractor; recoil buffer system; fully checkered walnut grips; two fitted magazines; factory test target; custom carrying case. Introduced 1995. From Springfield, Inc.
Price: $1,469.00

Springfield, Inc. TRP Pistols

Similar to the 1911A1 except 45 ACP only; has checkered front strap and mainspring housing; Novak combat rear sight and matching dovetailed front sight; tuned, polished extractor; oversize barrel link; lightweight speed trigger and combat action job; match barrel and bushing; extended thumb safety and fitted beavertail grip safety; Carry bevel on entire pistol; checkered cocobolo wood grips; comes with two Wilson 8-shot magazines. Frame is engraved "Tactical," both sides of frame with "TRP." Introduced 1998. From Springfield, Inc.
Price: Standard with Armory Kote finish...................... $1,098.00
Price: Standard, stainless steel $1,160.00
Price: Champion, Armory Kote............................... $1,098.00

Springfield Standard

Springfield Champion

Springfield, Inc. 1911A1 Defender Pistol

Similar to the 1911A1 Champion except has tapered cone dual-port compensator system, rubberized grips. Has reverse recoil plug, full-length recoil spring guide, serrated frontstrap, extended thumb safety, skeletonized hammer with modified grip safety to match and a Videki speed trigger. Bi-Tone finish. Introduced 1991.

Price: 45 ACP **$993.00**

Springfield, Inc. 1911A1 High Capacity Pistol

Similar to the Standard 1911A1 except available in 45 ACP with 10-shot magazine. Has Commander-style hammer, walnut grips, beveled magazine well, plastic carrying case. Introduced 1993. From Springfield, Inc.

Price: Mil-Spec 45 ACP. **$659.00**
Price: 45 ACP Factory Comp **$1,075.00**
Price: 45 ACP Compact, Ultra. **$689.00**
Price: As above, stainless steel **$759.00**

STOEGER AMERICAN EAGLE LUGER

Caliber: 9mm Para., 7-shot magazine.
Barrel: 4", 6".
Weight: 32 oz. **Length:** 9.6" overall.
Stocks: Checkered walnut.
Sights: Blade front, fixed rear.
Features: Recreation of the American Eagle Luger pistol in stainless steel. Chamber loaded indicator. Introduced 1994. From Stoeger Industries.

Price: 4", or 6" Navy Model **$699.00**
Price: With matte black finish **$789.00**

Sundance Laser 25

SUNDANCE BOA AUTO PISTOL

Caliber: 25 ACP, 7-shot magazine.
Barrel: 2-1/2".
Weight: 16 oz. **Length:** 4-7/8".
Stocks: Grooved ABS or smooth simulated pearl; optional pink.
Sights: Fixed.
Features: Patented grip safety, manual rotary safety; button magazine release; lifetime warranty. Bright chrome or black Teflon finish. Introduced 1991. Made in the U.S. by Sundance Industries, Inc.

Price: **$95.00**

SUNDANCE MODEL A-25 AUTO PISTOL

Caliber: 25 ACP, 7-shot magazine.
Barrel: 2.5".
Weight: 16 oz. **Length:** 4-7/8" overall.
Stocks: Grooved black ABS or simulated smooth pearl; optional pink.
Sights: Fixed.
Features: Manual rotary safety; button magazine release. Bright chrome or black Teflon finish. Introduced 1989. Made in U.S. by Sundance Industries, Inc.

Price: **$79.00**

Springfield, Inc. 1911A1 Custom Carry Gun

Similar to the standard 1911A1 except has Novak low-mount sights, Videki speed trigger, match barrel and bushing; extended thumb safety, beavertail grip safety; beveled, polished magazine well, polished feed ramp and throated barrel; match Commander hammer and sear, tuned extractor; lowered and flared ejection port; recoil buffer system, full-length spring guide rod; walnut grips. Comes with two magazines with slam pads, plastic carrying case. Available in all popular calibers. Introduced 1992. From Springfield, Inc.

Price: **$1,299.00**

Springfield, Inc. 1911A1 Factory Comp

Similar to the standard 1911A1 except comes with bushing-type dual-port compensator, adjustable rear sight, extended thumb safety, Videki speed trigger, and beveled magazine well. Checkered walnut grips standard. Available in 45 ACP, blue only. Introduced 1992.

Price: 45 ACP **$947.00**

> Consult our Directory pages for the location of firms mentioned.

Springfield, Inc. 1911A1 Champion Pistol

Similar to the standard 1911A1 except slide is 4.025". Has low-profile three-dot sight system. Comes with skeletonized hammer and walnut stocks. Available in 45 ACP only; Parkerized or stainless. Introduced 1989.

Price: Parkerized **$549.00**
Price: Stainless **$579.00**
Price: Mil-Spec **$519.00**

Springfield, Inc. V10 Ultra Compact Pistol

Similar to the 1911A1 Compact except has shorter slide, 3.5" barrel, recoil reducing compensator built into the barrel and slide. Beavertail grip safety, beveled magazine well, "hi-viz" combat sights, Videcki speed trigger, flared ejection port, stainless steel frame, blued slide, match grade barrel, walnut grips. Introduced 1996. From Springfield, Inc.

Price: V10 45 ACP. **$675.00**
Price: Ultra Compact (no compensator), 45 ACP **$629.00**

Stoeger American Eagle Luger

SUNDANCE LASER 25 PISTOL

Caliber: 25 ACP, 7-shot magazine.
Barrel: 2-1/2".
Weight: 18 oz. **Length:** 4-7/8" overall.
Stocks: Grooved black ABS.
Sights: Class IIIa laser, 670 NM, 5mW, and fixed open.
Features: Factory installed and sighted laser sight activated by squeezing the grip safety; manual rotary safety; button magazine release. Bright chrome or black finish. Introduced 1995. Made in U.S. by Sundance Industries, Inc.

Price: With laser **$219.95**
Price: Lady Laser (as above except different name, bright chrome only) **$219.95**

TAURUS MODEL PT 22/PT 25 AUTO PISTOLS

Caliber: 22 LR, 9-shot (PT 22); 25 ACP, 8-shot (PT 25).
Barrel: 2.75".
Weight: 12.3 oz. **Length:** 5.25" overall.
Stocks: Smooth rosewood.
Sights: Blade front, fixed rear.
Features: Double action. Tip-up barrel for loading, cleaning. Blue or stainless. Introduced 1992. Made in U.S. by Taurus International.

Price: 22 LR or 25 ACP. **$203.00**
Price: Nickel. **$203.00**
Price: Blue/gold **$220.00**

TAURUS MODEL PT 92AF AUTO PISTOL

Caliber: 9mm Para., 15-shot magazine.
Barrel: 4.92".
Weight: 34 oz. **Length:** 8.54" overall.
Stocks: Black rubber.
Sights: Fixed notch rear. Three-dot sight system.
Features: Double action, exposed hammer, chamber loaded indicator, ambi-dextrous safety, inertia firing pin. Imported by Taurus International.
Price: Blue **$490.00**
Price: Stainless steel **$510.00**

Taurus Model PT 99AF Auto Pistol

Similar to the PT-92 except has fully adjustable rear sight, smooth Brazilian walnut stocks and is available in stainless steel or polished blue. Introduced 1983.
Price: Blue **$530.00**
Price: Stainless steel **$550.00**

TAURUS MODEL PT-111 MILLENNIUM AUTO PISTOL

Caliber: 9mm Para., 10-shot magazine.
Barrel: 3.30".
Weight: 19 oz. **Length:** 6.0" overall.
Stocks: Polymer.
Sights: Fixed. Low profile, three-dot combat.
Features: Double action only. Firing pin lock; polymer frame; striker fired; push-button magazine release. Introduced 1998. Imported by Taurus International.
Price: Blue **$344.00**
Price: Stainless **$360.00**

TAURUS MODEL PT-911 AUTO PISTOL

Caliber: 9mm Para., 10-shot magazine.
Barrel: 3.85".
Weight: 28.2 oz. **Length:** 7.05" overall.
Stocks: Black rubber.
Sights: Fixed. Low profile, three-dot combat.
Features: Double action, exposed hammer; ambidextrous hammer drop; chamber loaded indicator. Introduced 1997. Imported by Taurus International.
Price: Blue **$438.00**
Price: Stainless **$450.00**

TAURUS MODEL PT-945 AUTO PISTOL

Caliber: 45 ACP, 8-shot magazine.
Barrel: 4.25".
Weight: 29.5 oz. **Length:** 7.48" overall.
Stocks: Black rubber.
Sights: Drift-adjustable front and rear; three-dot system.
Features: Double-action mechanism. Has manual ambidextrous hammer drop safety, intercept notch, firing pin block, chamber loaded indicator, last-shot hold-open. Introduced 1995. Imported by Taurus International.
Price: Blue **$470.00**
Price: Stainless **$485.00**
Price: Blue, ported **$510.00**
Price: Stainless, ported **$525.00**

UZI EAGLE AUTO PISTOL

Caliber: 9mm Para., 40 S&W, 45 ACP, 10-shot magazine.
Barrel: 4.4".
Weight: 35 oz. **Length:** 8.1" overall.
Stocks: Textured, high-impact polymer.
Sights: Three-dot tritium night sights.
Features: Double-action mechanism with decocker; polygonal rifling; matte blue/black finish. Introduced 1997. Imported from Israel by Uzi America, Inc.
Price: Full-size, 9mm or 40 S&W **$535.00**
Price: Short Slide, 3.7" barrel, 7.5" overall, 9mm, 40 S&W **$535.00**
Price: Short Slide 45 ACP **$566.00**
Price: Compact, 3.5" barrel, 7.2" overall, DA or DAO 9mm or 40 S&W
. . . . **$535.00**
Price: Polymer Compact, polymer frame, DA or DAO 9mm or 40 S&W
. . . . **$535.00**

WALTHER PP AUTO PISTOL

Caliber: 380 ACP, 7-shot magazine.
Barrel: 3.86".
Weight: 23-1/2 oz. **Length:** 6.7" overall.
Stocks: Checkered plastic.
Sights: Fixed, white markings.
Features: Double action; manual safety blocks firing pin and drops hammer; chamber loaded indicator on 32 and 380; extra finger rest magazine provided. Imported from Germany by Interarms.
Price: 380 . . . . **$999.00**

Taurus PT-92

TAURUS MODEL PT-938 AUTO PISTOL

Caliber: 380 ACP, 10-shot magazine.
Barrel: 3.72".
Weight: 27 oz. **Length:** 6.75" overall.
Stocks: Black rubber.
Sights: Fixed. Low profile, three-dot combat.
Features: Double action only. Chamber loaded indicator; firing pin block; ambidextrous hammer drop. Introduced 1997. Imported by Taurus International.
Price: Blue **$438.00**
Price: Stainless. **$450.00**

TAURUS MODEL PT-940 AUTO PISTOL

Caliber: 40 S&W, 10-shot magazine.
Barrel: 3.35".
Weight: 28.2 oz. **Length:** 7.05" overall.
Stocks: Black rubber.
Sights: Drift-adjustable front and rear; three-dot combat.
Features: Double action, exposed hammer; manual ambidextrous hammer-drop; inertia firing pin; chamber loaded indicator. Introduced 1996. Imported by Taurus International.
Price: Blue **$450.00**
Price: Stainless steel **$470.00**

Taurus PT 945

Walther PP

Walther PPK/S American Auto Pistol
Similar to Walther PP except made entirely in the United States. Has 3.27″ barrel with 6.1″ length overall. Introduced 1980.
Price: 380 ACP only, blue **$540.00**
Price: As above, 32 ACP or 380 ACP, stainless **$540.00**

Walther PPK American Auto Pistol
Similar to Walther PPK/S except weighs 21 oz., has 6-shot capacity. Made in the U.S. Introduced 1986.
Price: Stainless, 32 ACP or 380 ACP **$540.00**
Price: Blue, 380 ACP only **$540.00**

Walther PPK/S American

WALTHER MODEL TPH AUTO PISTOL
Caliber: 22 LR, 25 ACP, 6-shot magazine.
Barrel: 2-1/4″.
Weight: 14 oz. **Length:** 5-3/8″ overall.
Stocks: Checkered black composition.
Sights: Blade front, rear drift-adjustable for windage.
Features: Made of stainless steel. Scaled-down version of the Walther PP/PPK series. Made in U.S. Introduced 1987. From Interarms.
Price: Blue or stainless steel, 22 or 25 . . . . **$440.00**

Walther PPK

Walther TPH

WALTHER P88 COMPACT PISTOL
Caliber: 9mm Para., 10-shot magazine.
Barrel: 3.93″.
Weight: 28 oz. **Length:** NA.
Stocks: Checkered black polymer.
Sights: Blade front, drift adjustable rear.
Features: Double action with ambidextrous decocking lever and magazine release; alloy frame; loaded chamber indicator; matte blue finish. Imported from Germany by Interarms.
Price: **$900.00**

Walther P99

WALTHER P99 AUTO PISTOL
Caliber: 9mm Para., 10-shot magazine.
Barrel: 4″.
Weight: 25 oz. **Length:** 7″ overall.
Stocks: Textured polymer.
Sights: Blade front (comes with three interchangeable blades for elevation adjustment), micrometer rear adjustable for windage.
Features: Double-action mechanism with trigger safety, decock safety, internal striker safety; chamber loaded indicator; ambidextrous magazine release levers; polymer frame with interchangeable backstrap inserts. Comes with two magazines. Introduced 1997. Imported from Germany by Interarms.
Price: **$799.00**

WILKINSON SHERRY AUTO PISTOL
Caliber: 22 LR, 8-shot magazine.
Barrel: 2-1/8″.
Weight: 9-1/4 oz. **Length:** 4-3/8″ overall.
Stocks: Checkered black plastic.
Sights: Fixed, groove.
Features: Cross-bolt safety locks the sear into the hammer. Available in all blue finish or blue slide and trigger with gold frame. Introduced 1985.
Price: **$195.00**

Wilkinson Sherry

WILDEY AUTOMATIC PISTOL
Caliber: 10mm Wildey Mag., 11mm Wildey Mag., 30 Wildey Mag., 357 Peterbuilt, 45 Win. Mag., 475 Wildey Mag., 7-shot magazine.
Barrel: 5″, 6″, 7″, 8″, 10″, 12″, 14″ (45 Win. Mag.); 8″, 10″, 12″, 14″ (all other cals.). Interchangeable.
Weight: 64 oz. (5″ barrel). **Length:** 11″ overall (7″ barrel).
Stocks: Hardwood.
Sights: Ramp front (interchangeable blades optional), fully adjustable rear. Scope base available.
Features: Gas-operated action. Made of stainless steel. Has three-lug rotary bolt. Double or single action. Polished and matte finish. Made in U.S. by Wildey, Inc.
Price: . . . . **$1,175.00 to $1,495.00**

WILKINSON LINDA AUTO PISTOL
Caliber: 9mm Para.
Barrel: 8-5/16″.
Weight: 4 lbs., 13 oz. **Length:** 12-1/4″ overall.
Stocks: Checkered black plastic pistol grip, walnut forend.
Sights: Protected blade front, aperture rear.
Features: Fires from closed bolt. Semi-auto only. Straight blowback action. Cross-bolt safety. Removable barrel. From Wilkinson Arms.
Price: **$533.33**

Includes models suitable for several forms of competition and other sporting purposes.

Baer 1911 Ultimate Master

Baer 1911 Ultimate Master Steel Special Pistol

Similar to the Ultimate Master except chambered for 38 Super with supported chamber (other calibers available), lighter slide, bushing-type compensator; two-piece guide rod. Designed for maximum 150 power factor. Comes without sights—scope and mount only. Hard chrome finish. Made in U.S. by Les Baer Custom, Inc.
Price: $2,980.00

Baer 1911 Bullseye Wadcutter

Benelli MP95E

BERETTA MODEL 89 GOLD STANDARD PISTOL

Caliber: 22 LR, 8-shot magazine.
Barrel: 6″
Weight: 41 oz. **Length:** 9.5″ overall.
Stocks: Target-type walnut with thumbrest.
Sights: Interchangeable blade front, fully adjustable rear.
Features: Single action target pistol. Matte black, Bruniton finish. Imported from Italy by Beretta U.S.A.
Price: $750.00

BAER 1911 ULTIMATE MASTER COMBAT PISTOL

Caliber: 9x23, 38 Super, 400 Cor-Bon 45 ACP (others available), 10-shot magazine.
Barrel: 5″, 6″; Baer NM.
Weight: 37 oz. **Length:** 8.5″ overall.
Stocks: Checkered rosewood.
Sights: Baer dovetail front, low-mount Bo-Mar rear with hidden leaf.
Features: Full-house competition gun. Baer forged NM blued steel frame and double serrated slide; Baer triple port, tapered cone compensator; fitted slide to frame; lowered, flared ejection port; Baer reverse recoil plug; full-length guide rod; recoil buff; beveled magazine well; Baer Commander hammer, sear; Baer extended ambidextrous safety, extended ejector, checkered slide stop; beavertail grip safety with pad, extended magazine release button; Baer speed trigger. Made in U.S. by Les Baer Custom, Inc.
Price: Compensated, open sights $2,560.00
Price: 6″ Model 400 Cor-Bon $2,590.00
Price: Compensated, with Baer optics mount $3,195.00

BAER 1911 NATIONAL MATCH HARDBALL PISTOL

Caliber: 45 ACP, 7-shot magazine.
Barrel: 5″.
Weight: 37 oz. **Length:** 8.5″ overall.
Stocks: Checkered walnut.
Sights: Baer dovetail front with undercut post, low-mount Bo-Mar rear with hidden leaf.
Features: Baer NM forged steel frame, double serrated slide and barrel with stainless bushing; slide fitted to frame; Baer match trigger with 4-lb. pull; polished feed ramp, throated barrel; checkered front strap, arched mainspring housing; Baer beveled magazine well; lowered, flared ejection port; tuned extractor; Baer extended ejector, checkered slide stop; recoil buff. Made in U.S. by Les Baer Custom, Inc.
Price: $1,335.00

Baer 1911 Bullseye Wadcutter Pistol

Similar to the National Match Hardball except designed for wadcutter loads only. Has polished feed ramp and barrel throat; Bo-Mar rib on slide; full-length recoil rod; Baer speed trigger with 3-1/2-lb. pull; Baer deluxe hammer and sear; Baer beavertail grip safety with pad; flat mainspring housing checkered 20 lpi. Blue finish; checkered walnut grips. Made in U.S. by Les Baer Custom, Inc.
Price: From $1,495.00
Price: With 6″ barrel, from $1,690.00

BENELLI MP95E MATCH PISTOL

Caliber: 22 LR, 9-shot magazine, or 32 S&W WC, 5-shot magazine.
Barrel: 4.33″.
Weight: 38.8 oz. **Length:** 11.81″ overall.
Stocks: Checkered walnut match type; anatomically shaped.
Sights: Match type. Blade front, click-adjustable rear for windage and elevation.
Features: Removable, trigger assembly. Special internal weight box on subframe below barrel. Cut for scope rails. Introduced 1993. Imported from Italy by Benelli U.S.A.
Price: Blue, 22 LR $725.00
Price: Chrome, 22 LR....................................... $795.00
Price: Blue, 32 S&W.. $860.00
Price: Chrome, 32 S&W $925.00
Price: Model MP90S (competition version of MP95E), 22 LR $1,165.00
Price: As above, 32 S&W.................................... $1,300.00

Beretta Model 89

BERETTA MODEL 96 COMBAT PISTOL
Caliber: 40 S&W, 10-shot magazine.
Barrel: 4.9″ (5.9″ with weight).
Weight: 34.4 oz. **Length:** 8.5″ overall.
Stocks: Checkered black plastic.
Sights: Blade front, fully adjustable target rear.
Features: Uses heavier Brigadier slide with front and rear serrations; extended frame-mounted safety; extended, reversible magazine release; single-action-only with competition-tuned trigger with extra-short let-off and over-travel adjustment. Comes with tool kit. Introduced 1997. Imported from Italy by Beretta U.S.A.
Price: **$1,593.00**

Beretta Model 96 Stock Pistol
Similar to the Model 96 Combat except is single/double action, with half-cock notch. Has front and rear slide serrations, rubber magazine bumper, replaceable accurizing barrel bushing, ultra-thin fine-checkered grips (aluminum optional), checkered front and back straps, radiused back strap, fitted case. Weighs 35 oz., 8.5″ overall. Introduced 1997. Imported from Italy by Beretta U.S.A.
Price: **$1,371.00**

BF ULTIMATE SINGLE SHOT PISTOL
Caliber: 7mm U.S., 22 LR Match and 100 other chamberings.
Barrel: 10.75" Heavy Match Grade with 11° target crown.
Weight: 3 lbs., 15 oz. **Length:** 16″ overall.
Stocks: Thumbrest target style.
Sights: Bo-Mar/Bond ScopeRib I Combo with hooded post front adjustable for height and width, rear notch available in .032", .062", .080" and .100" widths; 1/2-MOA clicks..
Features: Designed to meet maximum rules for IHMSA Production Gun. Falling block action gives rigid barrel-receiver mating. Hand fitted and headspaced. Etched receiver; gold-colored trigger. Introduced 1988. Made in U.S. by E.A. Brown Mfg.
Price: **$895.00**

Beretta Model 96 Combat

BF Ultimate

BROLIN TAC SERIES MODEL TAC-11 TACTICAL 1911
Caliber: 45 ACP, 8-shot magazine.
Barrel: 5″; conical match design.
Weight: 35.1 oz. **Length:** 8.5″ overall.
Stocks: Black rubber contour.
Sights: Ramp front, Novak Low Profile Combat Sight or Novak tritium.
Features: Throated Conical barrel; polished feed ramp; lowered and flared ejection port; beveled magazine well; flat-top slide; flat mainspring housing; front strap high relief cut; lightened aluminum match trigger; slotted commander hammer; custom beavertail grip safety; Brolin "Iron Claw" extractor. Introduced 1997. Made in the U.S. by Brolin Industries.
Price: Matte blue **$669.95**
Price: Hard chrome **$749.95**

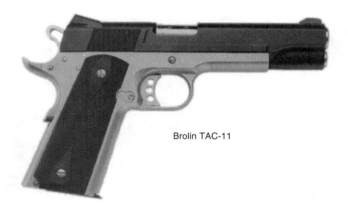

Brolin TAC-11

Browning Buck Mark Target 5.5

BROWNING BUCK MARK SILHOUETTE
Caliber: 22 LR, 10-shot magazine.
Barrel: 9-7/8″.
Weight: 53 oz. **Length:** 14″ overall.
Stocks: Smooth walnut stocks and forend, or finger-groove walnut.
Sights: Post-type hooded front adjustable for blade width and height; Pro Target rear fully adjustable for windage and elevation.
Features: Heavy barrel with .900″ diameter; 12-1/2″ sight radius. Special sighting plane forms scope base. Introduced 1987. Made in U.S. From Browning.
Price: **$434.95**

Browning Buck Mark Unlimited Silhouette
Same as the Buck Mark Silhouette except has 14″ heavy barrel. Conforms to IHMSA 15″ maximum sight radius rule. Introduced 1991.
Price: **$535.95**

Browning Buck Mark Target 5.5
Same as the Buck Mark Silhouette except has a 5-1/2″ barrel with .900″ diameter. Has hooded sights mounted on a scope base that accepts an optical or reflex sight. Rear sight is a Browning fully adjustable Pro Target, front sight is an adjustable post that customizes to different widths, and can be adjusted for height. Contoured walnut grips with thumbrest, or finger-groove walnut. Matte blue finish. Overall length is 9-5/8″, weighs 35-1/2 oz. Has 10-shot magazine. Introduced 1990. From Browning.
Price: **$411.95**
Price: Target 5.5 Gold (as above with gold anodized frame and top rib)
.... **$462.95**
Price: Target 5.5 Nickel (as above with nickel frame and top rib) ... **$462.95**
Browning Buck Mark Field 5.5
Same as the Target 5.5 except has hoodless ramp-style front sight and low profile rear sight. Matte blue finish, contoured or finger-groove walnut stocks. Introduced 1991.
Price: **$411.95**

Browning Buck Mark Bullseye

COLT GOLD CUP TROPHY MK IV/SERIES 80
Caliber: 45 ACP, 8-shot magazine.
Barrel: 5", with new design bushing.
Weight: 39 oz. **Length:** 8-1/2".
Stocks: Checkered rubber composite with silver-plated medallion.
Sights: Patridge-style front, Colt-Elliason rear adjustable for windage and elevation, sight radius 6-3/4".
Features: Arched or flat housing; wide, grooved trigger with adjustable stop; ribbed-top slide, hand fitted, with improved ejection port.
Price: Blue **$1,050.00**
Price: Stainless **$1,116.00**

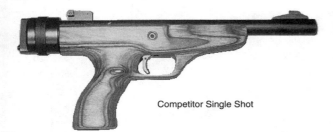

Competitor Single Shot

E.A.A. WITNESS GOLD TEAM AUTO
Caliber: 9mm Para., 9x21, 38 Super, 40 S&W, 45 ACP.
Barrel: 5.1".
Weight: 41.6 oz. **Length:** 9.6" overall.
Stocks: Checkered walnut, competition style.
Sights: Square post front, fully adjustable rear.
Features: Triple-chamber cone compensator; competition SA trigger; extended safety and magazine release; competition hammer; beveled magazine well; beavertail grip. Hand-fitted major components. Hard chrome finish. Match-grade barrel. From E.A.A. Custom Shop. Introduced 1992. From European American Armory.
Price: **$2,150.00**

E.A.A. Witness Silver Team Auto
Similar to the Witness Gold Team except has double-chamber compensator, oval magazine release, black rubber grips, double-dip blue finish. Comes with Super Sight and drilled and tapped for scope mount. Built for the intermediate competition shooter. Introduced 1992. From European American Armory Custom Shop.
Price: 9mm Para., 9x21, 38 Super, 40 S&W, 45 ACP **$968.00**

> Consult our Directory pages for the location of firms mentioned.

FAS 607 MATCH PISTOL
Caliber: 22 LR, 5-shot.
Barrel: 5.6".
Weight: 37 oz. **Length:** 11" overall.
Stocks: Walnut wrap-around; sizes small, medium, large or adjustable.
Sights: Match. Blade front, open notch rear fully adjustable for windage and elevation. Sight radius is 8.66".
Features: Line of sight is only 11/32" above centerline of bore; magazine is inserted from top; adjustable and removable trigger mechanism; single lever takedown. Full 5-year warranty. Imported from Italy by Nygord Precision Products.
Price: **$1,175.00**
Price: Model 603 (32 S&W) **$1,175.00**

Browning Buck Mark Bullseye
Similar to the Buck Mark Silhouette except has 7-1/4" heavy barrel with three flutes per side; trigger is adjustable from 2-1/2 to 5 lbs.; specially designed rosewood target or three-finger-groove stocks with competition-style heel rest, or with contoured rubber grip. Overall length is 11-5/16", weighs 36 oz. Introduced 1996. Made in U.S. From Browning.
Price: With ambidextrous moulded composite stocks **$376.95**
Price: With rosewood stocks, or wrap-around finger groove **$484.95**

Colt Gold Cup Trophy

COMPETITOR SINGLE SHOT PISTOL
Caliber: 22 LR through 50 Action Express, including belted magnums.
Barrel: 14" standard; 10.5" silhouette; 16" optional.
Weight: About 59 oz. (14" bbl.). **Length:** 15.12" overall.
Stocks: Ambidextrous; synthetic (standard) or laminated or natural wood.
Sights: Ramp front, adjustable rear.
Features: Rotary canon-type action cocks on opening; cammed ejector; interchangeable barrels, ejectors. Adjustable single stage trigger, sliding thumb safety and trigger safety. Matte blue finish. Introduced 1988. From Competitor Corp., Inc.
Price: 14", standard calibers, synthetic grip **$414.95**
Price: Extra barrels, from **$159.95**

E.A.A. Witness Gold Team

ENTRÉPRISE TOURNAMENT SHOOTER MODEL I
Caliber: 45 ACP, 10-shot magazine.
Barrel: 5".
Weight: 40 oz. **Length:** 8.5" overall.
Stocks: Black ultra-slim double diamond checkered synthetic.
Sights: Dovetailed Patridge front, adjustable Competizione "melded" rear.
Features: Oversized magazine release button; flared magazine well; fully machined parallel slide rails; polished barrel channel and breech face; front and rear slide serrations; serrated top of slide; stainless ramped bull barrel with fully supported chamber; full-length guide rod with plug; stainless firing pin; match extractor; polished ramp; tuned match extractor; hard chrome finish. Introduced 1998. Made in U.S. by Entréprise Arms.
Price: **$2,300.00**
Price: Model II (6" barrel, black oxide finish) **$2,000.00**
Price: Model III (6", frame-mounted scope base, machined seven-port cone-style compensator, hard chrome finish) **$2,700.00**

FAS 601 Match Pistol
Similar to Model 607 except has different match stocks with adjustable palm shelf, 22 Short only for rapid fire shooting; weighs 40 oz., 5.6" bbl.; has gas ports through top of barrel and slide to reduce recoil; slightly different trigger and sear mechanisms. Imported from Italy by Nygord Precision Products.
Price: **$1,250.00**

FORT WORTH HST TARGET PISTOL
Caliber: 22 LR, 10-shot magazine.
Barrel: 5-1/2" bull or 7-1/4" fluted.
Weight: 44 oz. **Length:** 9.5" overall.
Stocks: Checkered hardwood with thumbrest.
Sights: Undercut ramp front, frame-mounted micro-click rear adjustable for windage and elevation; drilled and tapped for scope mounting.
Features: Gold-plated trigger, slide lock, safety-lever and magazine release; stippled front grip and backstrap; adjustable trigger and sear. Barrel weights optional. Introduced 1995. From Fort Worth Firearms.
Price: 5-1/2" or 71/4" right-hand **$410.95**
Price: 5-1/2" left-hand **$451.95**

Fort Worth HSC Target Pistol
Same as the HST model except has nickel-plated trigger, slide lock, safety lever, magazine release, and has slightly heavier trigger pull. Has stippled front-grip and backstrap, checkered walnut thumbrest grips, adjustable trigger and sear. Matte finish. Drilled and tapped for scope mount and barrel weight. Introduced 1995. From Fort Worth Firearms.
Price: **$388.95**

FORT WORTH HSV TARGET PISTOL
Caliber: 22 LR, 10-shot magazine.
Barrel: 4-1/2" or 5-1/2"; push-button takedown.
Weight: 46 oz. **Length:** 9.5" overall.
Sights: Checkered hardwood with thumbrest.
Stocks: Undercut ramp front, micro-click rear adjustable for windage and elevation. Also available with scope mount, rings, no sights.
Features: Stainless steel construction. Full-length vent rib. Gold-plated trigger, slide lock, safety-lever and magazine release; stippled front grip and backstrap; polished slide; adjustable trigger and sear. Comes with barrel weight. Introduced 1995. From Fort Worth Firearms.
Price: **$472.95**
Price: With Weaver rib **$537.95**
Price: With 8" barrel, Weaver rib, custom grips, sights. **$616.95**
Price: As above, 10" barrel **$629.95**

FORT WORTH MATCHMASTER STANDARD PISTOL
Caliber: 22 LR
Barrel: 3-7/8", 4-1/2", 5-1/2", 7-1/2", 10".
Weight: NA. **Length:** NA.
Stocks: Checkered walnut.
Sights: Ramp front, slide-mounted adjustable rear.
Features: Stainless steel construction. Double extractors; trigger finger magazine release button and standard button; beveled magazine well; grip angle equivalent to M1911; low-profile frame. Introduced 1997. From Fort Worth Firearms.
Price: **$388.95**

Fort Worth Matchmaster Deluxe Pistol
Same as the Matchmaster Standard except comes with Weaver-style rib mount and integral adjustable rear sight system. Introduced 1997. From Fort Worth Firearms.
Price: **$537.95**

FREEDOM ARMS CASULL MODEL 252 SILHOUETTE
Caliber: 22 LR, 5-shot cylinder.
Barrel: 9.95".
Weight: 63 oz. **Length:** NA
Stocks: Black micarta, western style.
Sights: 1/8" Patridge front, Iron Sight Gun Works silhouette rear, click adjustable for windage and elevation.
Features: Stainless steel. Built on the 454 Casull frame. Two-point firing pin, lightened hammer for fast lock time. Trigger pull is 3 to 5 lbs. with pre-set overtravel screw. Introduced 1991. From Freedom Arms.
Price: Silhouette Class **$1,564.00**
Price: Extra fitted 22 WMR cylinder **$343.00**

GAUCHER GP SILHOUETTE PISTOL
Caliber: 22 LR, single shot.
Barrel: 10".
Weight: 42.3 oz. **Length:** 15.5" overall.
Stocks: Stained hardwood.
Sights: Hooded post on ramp front, open rear adjustable for windage and elevation.
Features: Matte chrome barrel, blued bolt and sights. Other barrel lengths available on special order. Introduced 1991. Imported by Mandall Shooting Supplies.
Price: **$425.00**

Fort Worth HST

FORT WORTH HSO AUTO PISTOL
Caliber: 22 Short, 10-shot magazine.
Barrel: 6-3/4" round tapered, with stabilizer and built-in muzzlebrake.
Weight: 40 oz. **Length:** 11-1/4"
Stocks: Checkered walnut with thumbrest.
Sights: Undercut ramp front, frame-mounted click adjustable square notch rear. Drilled and tapped for scope mount.
Features: Integral stabilizer with two removable weights. Trigger adjustable for pull and length of travel; stippled front and backstraps; push-button barrel takedown. Introduced 1995. Made in U.S. by Fort Worth Firearms.
Price: **$599.95**

Fort Worth HSO

Fort Worth Matchmaster Deluxe

Fort Worth Matchmaster Dovetail Pistol
Same as the Matchmaster Standard except has a dovetail-style mount and integral rear sight system. Available with 3-7/8", 4-1/2" or 5-1/2" barrel only. Introduced 1997. From Fort Worth Firearms.
Price: **$472.95**

Freedom Arms 252 Varmint

Freedom Arms Model 252 Varmint
Similar to the Silhouette Class revolver except has 7.5" barrel, weighs 59 oz., has black and green laminated hardwood grips, and comes with brass bead front sight, express shallow V rear sight with windage and elevation adjustments. Introduced 1991. From Freedom Arms.
Price: Varmint Class **$1,497.00**
Price: Extra fitted 22 WMR cylinder **$343.00**

GLOCK 17L COMPETITION AUTO
Caliber: 9mm Para., 10-shot magazine.
Barrel: 6.02″.
Weight: 23.3 oz. **Length:** 8.85″ overall.
Stocks: Black polymer.
Sights: Blade front with white dot, fixed or adjustable rear.
Features: Polymer frame, steel slide; double-action trigger with "Safe Action" system; mechanical firing pin safety, drop safety; simple takedown without tools; locked breech, recoil operated action. Introduced 1989. Imported from Austria by Glock, Inc.
Price: Fixed sight $800.00
Price: Adjustable sight $828.00

GLOCK 24 COMPETITION MODEL PISTOL
Caliber: 40 S&W, 10-shot magazine.
Barrel: 6.02″.
Weight: 29.5 oz. **Length:** 8.85″ overall.
Stocks: Black polymer.
Sights: Blade front with dot, white outline rear adjustable for windage.
Features: Long-slide competition model available as compensated or non-compensated gun. Factory-installed competition trigger; drop-free magazine. Introduced 1994. Imported from Austria by Glock, Inc.
Price: Fixed sight $800.00
Price: Adjustable sight $828.00
Price: Model 24C, ported barrel, fixed sight. $830.00
Price: Model 24C, ported barrel, adjustable sight $855.00

Hammerli SP 20

Heckler & Koch USP45 Match

Kimber Gold Match

Glock 24 Competition

HAMMERLI SP 20 TARGET PISTOL
Caliber: 22 LR, 32 S&W.
Barrel: 4.6″.
Weight: 34.6-41.8 oz. **Length:** 11.8″ overall.
Stocks: Anatomically shaped synthetic Hi-Grip available in five sizes.
Sights: Integral front in three widths, adjustable rear with changeable notch widths.
Features: Extremely low-level sight line; anatomically shaped trigger; adjustable JPS buffer system for different recoil characteristics. Receiver available in red, blue, gold, violet or black. Introduced 1998. Imported from Switzerland by SIGARMS, Inc..
Price: . . . . NA

HARRIS GUNWORKS SIGNATURE JR. LONG RANGE PISTOL
Caliber: Any suitable caliber.
Barrel: To customer specs.
Weight: 5 lbs.
Stock: Gunworks fiberglass.
Sights: None furnished; comes with scope rings.
Features: Right- or left-hand benchrest action of titanium or stainless steel; single shot or repeater. Comes with bipod. Introduced 1992. Made in U.S. by Harris Gunworks, Inc.
Price: $2,700.00

HECKLER & KOCH USP45 MATCH PISTOL
Caliber: 45 ACP, 10-shot magazine.
Barrel: 6.02″.
Weight: 2.38 lbs. **Length:** 9.45″.
Stocks: Textured polymer.
Sights: High profile target front, fully adjustable target rear.
Features: Adjustable trigger stop. Polymer frame, blue or stainless steel slide. Introduced 1997. Imported from Germany by Heckler & Koch, Inc.
Price: Blue $1,369.00
Price: Stainless. $1,441.00

KIMBER CUSTOM TARGET AUTO PISTOL
Caliber: 45 ACP, 7-shot magazine.
Barrel: 5″.
Weight: 38 oz. **Length:** 8.7″ overall.
Stocks: Black synthetic.
Sights: Blade front, Kimber fully adjustable rear; dovetailed.
Features: Match trigger; beveled front and rear slide serrations; lowered, flared ejection port; full-length guide rod; Wolff springs. Introduced 1996. Made in U.S. by Kimber Mfg. Inc.
Price: Custom Target $745.00
Price: Stainless Target $863.00

Kimber Gold Match Target Pistol
Similar to the Custom Target except has highly polished blue finish; hand-fitted stainless steel barrel, bushing, slide and frame; ambidextrous thumb safety; hand-checkered rosewood grips with double diamond pattern; and skeletonized aluminum match-grade trigger. Has 8-shot magazine. Introduced 1998. Made in U.S. by Kimber Mfg. Inc.
Price: Gold Match. $1,019.00
Price: Stainless Target $1,168.00

KORTH MATCH MODEL REVOLVER
Caliber: 22 LR, 32 S&W Long.
Barrel: 5-1/4″, 6″.
Weight: NA. **Length:** NA.
Stocks: Adjustable stippled walnut match type.
Sights: Undercut Patridge front, fully adjustable rear with interchangeable blades.
Features: Forged steel construction; fully adjustable trigger; hammer-forged barrel; interchangeable cylinder. Imported from Germany by Keng's Firearm Specialty, Inc.
Price: High-polish blued finish $6,399.90
Price: Plasma-coated matte silver finish $6,799.90
Price: Plasma-coated high polish silver finish $7,299.90

MORINI MODEL 84E FREE PISTOL
Caliber: 22 LR, single shot.
Barrel: 11.4″.
Weight: 43.7 oz. **Length:** 19.4″ overall.
Stocks: Adjustable match type with stippled surfaces.
Sights: Interchangeable blade front, match-type fully adjustable rear.
Features: Fully adjustable electronic trigger. Introduced 1995. Imported from Switzerland by Nygord Precision Products.
Price: **$1,495.00**

PARDINI MODEL SP, HP TARGET PISTOLS
Caliber: 22 LR, 32 S&W, 5-shot magazine.
Barrel: 4.7″.
Weight: 38.9 oz. **Length:** 11.6″ overall.
Stocks: Adjustable; stippled walnut; match type.
Sights: Interchangeable blade front, interchangeable, fully adjustable rear.
Features: Fully adjustable match trigger. Introduced 1995. Imported from Italy by Nygord Precision Products.
Price: Model SP (22 LR) **$995.00**
Price: Model HP (32 S&W) **$1,095.00**

Ruger Government Target

Ruger Mark II Bull Barrel
Same gun as the Target Model except has 5-1/2″ or 10″ heavy barrel (10″ meets all IHMSA regulations). Weight with 5-1/2″ barrel is 42 oz., with 10″ barrel, 51 oz.
Price: Blued (MK-512) **$310.50**
Price: Blued (MK-10) **$314.50**
Price: Stainless (KMK-10) **$393.00**
Price: Stainless (KMK-512) **$389.00**

SAFARI ARMS BIG DEUCE PISTOL
Caliber: 45 ACP, 7-shot magazine.
Barrel: 6″, 416 stainless steel.
Weight: 40.3 oz. **Length:** 9.5″ overall.
Stocks: Smooth walnut.
Sights: Ramped blade front, LPA adjustable rear.
Features: Beavertail grip safety; extended thumb safety and slide release; Commander-style hammer. Throated, polished and tuned. Parkerized matte black slide with satin stainless steel frame. Introduced 1995. Made in U.S. by Safari Arms, Inc.
Price: **$854.00**

SMITH & WESSON MODEL 41 TARGET
Caliber: 22 LR, 10-shot clip.
Barrel: 5-1/2″, 7″.
Weight: 44 oz. (5-1/2″ barrel). **Length:** 9″ overall (5-1/2″ barrel).
Stocks: Checkered walnut with modified thumbrest, usable with either hand.
Sights: 1/8″ Patridge on ramp base; micro-click rear adjustable for windage and elevation.
Features: 3/8″ wide, grooved trigger; adjustable trigger stop.
Price: S&W Bright Blue, either barrel **$778.00**

SMITH & WESSON MODEL 22A TARGET PISTOL
Caliber: 22 LR, 10-shot magazine.
Barrel: 5-1/2″ bull.
Weight: 38.5 oz. **Length:** 9-1/2″ overall.
Stocks: Dymondwood with ambidextrous thumbrests and flared bottom.
Sights: Patridge front, fully adjustable rear.
Features: Sight bridge with Weaver-style integral optics mount; alloy frame, stainless barrel and slide; matte blue finish. Introduced 1997. Made in U.S. by Smith & Wesson.
Price: **$311.00**

Smith & Wesson Model 22S Target Pistol
Similar to the Model 22A except has stainless steel frame. Introduced 1997. Made in U.S. by Smith & Wesson.
Price: **$368.00**

PARDINI GP RAPID FIRE MATCH PISTOL
Caliber: 22 Short, 5-shot magazine.
Barrel: 4.6″.
Weight: 43.3 oz. **Length:** 11.6″ overall.
Stocks: Wrap-around stippled walnut.
Sights: Interchangeable post front, fully adjustable match rear.
Features: Model GP Schuman has extended rear sight for longer sight radius. Introduced 1995. Imported from Italy by Nygord Precision Products.
Price: Model GP **$995.00**
Price: Model GP Schuman **$1,450.00**

PARDINI K50 FREE PISTOL
Caliber: 22 LR, single shot.
Barrel: 9.8″.
Weight: 34.6 oz. **Length:** 18.7″ overall.
Stocks: Wrap-around walnut; adjustable match type.
Sights: Interchangeable post front, fully adjustable match open rear.
Features: Removable, adjustable match trigger. Barrel weights mount above the barrel. Introduced 1995. Imported from Italy by Nygord Precision Products.
Price: **$1,050.00**

RUGER MARK II TARGET MODEL SEMI-AUTO
Caliber: 22 LR, 10-shot magazine.
Barrel: 6-7/8″.
Weight: 42 oz. **Length:** 11-1/8″ overall.
Stocks: Checkered hard plastic.
Sights: .125″ blade front, micro-click rear, adjustable for windage and elevation. Sight radius 9-3/8″.
Features: Introduced 1982.
Price: Blued (MK-678) **$310.50**
Price: Stainless (KMK-678) **$389.00**

Ruger Mark II Government Target Model
Same gun as the Mark II Target Model except has 6-7/8″ barrel, higher sights and is roll marked "Government Target Model" on the right side of the receiver below the rear sight. Identical in all aspects to the military model used for training U.S. armed forces except for markings. Comes with factory test target. Introduced 1987.
Price: Blued (MK-678G) **$356.50**
Price: Stainless (KMK-678G) **$427.25**

Ruger Stainless Government Competition Model 22 Pistol
Similar to the Mark II Government Target Model stainless pistol except has 6-7/8″ slab-sided barrel; the receiver top is drilled and tapped for a Ruger scope base adaptor of blued, chrome moly steel; comes with Ruger 1″ stainless scope rings with integral scope bases for mounting a variety of optical sights; has checkered laminated grip panels with right-hand thumbrest. Has blued open sights with 9-1/4″ radius. Overall length is 11-1/8″, weight 45 oz. Introduced 1991.
Price: KMK-678GC **$441.00**

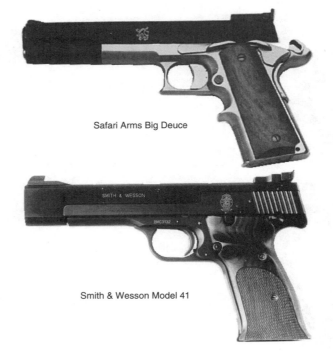

Safari Arms Big Deuce

Smith & Wesson Model 41

Springfield 1911A1 Trophy Match

Springfield, Inc. 1911A1 Trophy Match Pistol
Similar to the 1911A1 except factory accurized, Videki speed trigger, skeletonized hammer; has 4- to 5-1/2-lb. trigger pull, click adjustable rear sight, match-grade barrel and bushing. Comes with checkered walnut grips. Introduced 1994. From Springfield, Inc.
Price: Blue **$989.00**
Price: Stainless steel **$1,029.00**
Price: High Capacity (stainless steel, 10-shot magazine, front slide serrations, checkered slide serrations) **$1,118.00**

Springfield, Inc. Expert Pistol
Similar to the Competition Pistol except has triple-chamber tapered cone compensator on match barrel with dovetailed front sight; lowered and flared ejection port; fully tuned for reliability; fitted slide to frame; extended ambidextrous thumb safety, extended magazine release button; beavertail grip safety; Pachmayr wrap-around grips. Comes with two magazines, plastic carrying case. Introduced 1992. From Springfield, Inc.
Price: 45 ACP, Duotone finish **$1,724.00**
Price: Expert Ltd. (non-compensated) **$1,624.00**

Springfield, Inc. Distinguished Pistol
Has all the features of the 1911A1 Expert except is full-house pistol with deluxe Bo-Mar low-mounted adjustable rear sight; full-length recoil spring guide rod and recoil spring retainer; checkered frontstrap; S&A magazine well; walnut grips. Hard chrome finish. Comes with two magazines with slam pads, plastic carrying case. From Springfield, Inc.
Price: 45 ACP **$2,445.00**
Price: Distinguished Limited (non-compensated) **$2,345.00**

Thompson/Cemter Super 14 Contender

UNIQUE MODEL 96U TARGET PISTOL
Caliber:22 LR, 5- or 6-shot magazine.
Barrel: 5.9″.
Weight: 40.2 oz. **Length:** 11.2″ overall.
Stocks: French walnut. Target style with thumbrest and adjustable shelf.
Sights: Blade front, micrometer rear mounted on frame.
Features: Designed for Sport Pistol and Standard U.I.T. shooting. External hammer; fully adjustable and movable trigger; dry-firing device. Introduced 1997. Imported from France by Nygord Precision Products.
Price: **$1,350.00**

UNIQUE D.E.S. 32U TARGET PISTOL
Caliber: 32 S&W Long wadcutter.
Barrel: 5.9″.
Weight: 40.2 oz.
Stocks: Anatomically shaped, adjustable stippled French walnut.
Sights: Blade front, micrometer click rear.
Features: Trigger adjustable for weight and position; dry firing mechanism; slide stop catch. Optional sleeve weights. Introduced 1990. Imported from France by Nygord Precision Products.
Price: Right-hand, about **$1,350.00**
Price: Left-hand, about **$1,380.00**

SPRINGFIELD, INC. 1911A1 BULLSEYE WADCUTTER PISTOL
Caliber: 38 Super, 45 ACP.
Barrel: 5″.
Weight: 45 oz. **Length:** 8.59″ overall (5″ barrel).
Stocks: Checkered walnut.
Sights: Bo-Mar rib with undercut blade front, fully adjustable rear.
Features: Built for wadcutter loads only. Has full-length recoil spring guide rod, fitted Videki speed trigger with 3.5-lb. pull; match Commander hammer and sear; beavertail grip safety; lowered and flared ejection port; tuned extractor; fitted slide to frame; recoil buffer system; beveled and polished magazine well; checkered front strap and steel mainspring housing (flat housing standard); polished and throated National Match barrel and bushing. Comes with two magazines with slam pads, plastic carrying case, test target. Introduced 1992. From Springfield, Inc.
Price: **$1,499.00**

Springfield, Inc. Basic Competition Pistol
Has low-mounted Bo-Mar adjustable rear sight, undercut blade front; match throated barrel and bushing; polished feed ramp; lowered and flared ejection port; fitted Videki speed trigger with tuned 3.5-lb. pull; fitted slide to frame; recoil buffer system; checkered walnut grips; serrated, arched mainspring housing. Comes with two magazines with slam pads, plastic carrying case. Introduced 1992. From Springfield, Inc.
Price: 45 ACP, blue, 5″ only. **$1,295.00**

Springfield, Inc. 1911A1 N.M. Hardball Pistol
Has Bo-Mar adjustable rear sight with undercut front blade; fitted match Videki trigger with 4-lb. pull; fitted slide to frame; throated National Match barrel and bushing, polished feed ramp; recoil buffer system; tuned extractor; Herrett walnut grips. Comes with two magazines, plastic carrying case, test target. Introduced 1992. From Springfield, Inc.
Price: 45 ACP, blue **$1,336.00**

STI EAGLE 5.1 PISTOL
Caliber: 9mm Para., 38 Super, 40 S&W, 45 ACP, 10-ACP, 10-shot magazine.
Barrel:5″, bull.
Weight: 34 oz. **Length:** 8.62″ overall.
Stocks: Checkered polymer.
Sights: Bo-Mar blade front, Bo-Mar fully adjustable rear.
Features: Modular frame design; adjustable match trigger; skeletonized hammer; extended grip safety with locator pad; match-grade fit of all parts. Many options available. Introduced 1994. Made in U.S. by STI International.
Price: **$1,792.00**

THOMPSON/CENTER SUPER 14 CONTENDER
Caliber: 22 LR, 222 Rem., 223 Rem., 7mm TCU, 7-30 Waters, 30-30 Win., 35 Rem., 357 Rem. Maximum, 44 Mag., 10mm Auto, 445 Super Mag., single shot.
Barrel: 14″.
Weight: 45 oz. **Length:** 17-1/4″ overall.
Stocks: T/C "Competitor Grip" (walnut and rubber).
Sights: Fully adjustable target-type.
Features: Break-open action with auto safety. Interchangeable barrels for both rimfire and centerfire calibers. Introduced 1978.
Price: Blued **$485.00**
Price: Stainless steel **$540.00**
Price: Extra barrels, blued **$228.00**
Price: Extra barrels, stainless steel **$256.00**

Thompson/Center Super 16 Contender
Same as the T/C Super 14 Contender except has 16-1/4″ barrel. Rear sight can be mounted at mid-barrel position (10-3/4″ radius) or moved to the rear (using scope mount position) for 14-3/4″ radius. Overall length is 20-1/4″. Comes with T/C Competitor Grip of walnut and rubber. Available in 22 LR, 22 WMR, 223 Rem., 7-30 Waters, 30-30 Win., 35 Rem., 44 Mag., 45-70 Gov't. Also available with 16″ vent rib barrel with internal choke, caliber 45 Colt/410 shotshell.
Price: Blue **$491.00**
Price: Stainless steel **$545.00**
Price: 45-70 Gov't., blue. **$496.00**
Price: As above, stainless steel **$567.00**
Price: Super 16 Vent Rib, blued. **$522.00**
Price: As above, stainless steel **$578.00**
Price: Extra 16″ barrel, blued **$233.00**
Price: As above, stainless steel **$261.00**
Price: Extra 45-70 barrel, blued **$256.00**
Price: As above, stainless steel **$273.00**
Price: Extra Super 16 vent rib barrel, blue **$265.00**
Price: As above, stainless steel **$294.00**

Unique D.E.S. 69U

UNIQUE D.E.S. 69U TARGET PISTOL
Caliber: 22 LR, 5-shot magazine.
Barrel: 5.91".
Weight: 35.3 oz. **Length:** 10.5" overall.
Stocks: French walnut target-style with thumbrest and adjustable shelf; hand-checkered panels.
Sights: Ramp front, micro. adjustable rear mounted on frame; 8.66" sight radius.
Features: Meets U.I.T. standards. Comes with 260-gram barrel weight; 100, 150, 350-gram weights available. Fully adjustable match trigger; dry-firing safety device. Imported from France by Nygord Precision Products.
Price: Right-hand, about **$1,250.00**
Price: Left-hand, about **$1,290.00**

WICHITA SILHOUETTE PISTOL
Caliber: 308 Win. F.L., 7mm IHMSA, 7mm-308.
Barrel: 14-15/16".
Weight: 4-1/2 lbs. **Length:** 21-3/8" overall.
Stock: American walnut with oil finish. Glass bedded.
Sights: Wichita Multi-Range sight system.
Features: Comes with left-hand action with right-hand grip. Round receiver and barrel. Fluted bolt, flat bolt handle. Wichita adjustable trigger. Introduced 1979. From Wichita Arms.
Price: Center grip stock **$1,800.00**
Price: As above except with Rear Position Stock and target-type
Lightpull trigger **$1,800.00**

WICHITA CLASSIC SILHOUETTE PISTOL
Caliber: All standard calibers with maximum overall length of 2.800".
Barrel: 11-1/4".
Weight: 3 lbs., 15 oz.
Stocks: AAA American walnut with oil finish, checkered grip.
Sights: Hooded post front, open adjustable rear.
Features: Three locking lug bolt, three gas ports; completely adjustable Wichita trigger. Introduced 1981. From Wichita Arms.
Price: **$3,450.00**

> Consult our Directory pages for the location of firms mentioned.

WALTHER GSP MATCH PISTOL
Caliber: 22 LR, 32 S&W Long (GSP-C), 5-shot magazine.
Barrel: 4.22".
Weight: 44.8 oz. (22 LR), 49.4 oz. (32). **Length:** 11.8" overall.
Stocks: Walnut.
Sights: Post front, match rear adjustable for windage and elevation.
Features: Available with either 2.2-lb. (1000 gm) or 3-lb. (1360 gm) trigger. Spare magazine, barrel weight, tools supplied. Imported from Germany by Nygord Precision Products.
Price: GSP, with case **$1,495.00**
Price: GSP-C, with case **$1,595.00**

Includes models suitable for hunting and competitive courses for fire, both police and international.

ARMSCOR M-200DC REVOLVER
Caliber: 38 Spec., 6-shot cylinder.
Barrel: 2-1/2", 4".
Weight: 22 oz. (2-1/2" barrel). **Length:** 7-3/8" overall (2-1/2" barrel).
Stocks: Checkered rubber.
Sights: Blade front, fixed notch rear.
Features: All-steel construction; floating firing pin, transfer bar ignition; shrouded ejector rod; blue finish. Reintroduced 1996. Imported from the Philippines by K.B.I., Inc.
Price: 2-1/2" **$199.99**
Price: 4" **$205.00**

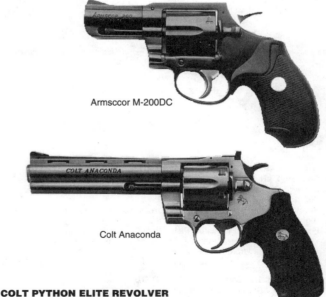

Armsccor M-200DC

Colt Anaconda

COLT ANACONDA REVOLVER
Caliber: 44 Rem. Magnum, 45 Colt, 6-shot.
Barrel: 4", 6", 8".
Weight: 53 oz. (6" barrel). **Length:** 11-5/8" overall.
Stocks: TP combat style with finger grooves.
Sights: Red insert front, adjustable white outline rear.
Features: Stainless steel; full-length ejector rod housing; ventilated barrel rib; offset bolt notches in cylinder; wide spur hammer. Introduced 1990.
Price: **$629.00**
Price: 45 Colt, 6", 8" barrel only **$629.00**

COLT KING COBRA REVOLVER
Caliber: 357 Magnum, 6-shot.
Barrel: 4", 6".
Weight: 42 oz. (4" bbl.). **Length:** 9" overall (4" bbl.).
Stocks: TP combat style.
Sights: Red insert ramp front, adjustable white outline rear.
Features: Full-length contoured ejector rod housing, barrel rib. Introduced 1986.
Price: Stainless **$485.00**

COLT PYTHON ELITE REVOLVER
Caliber: 357 Magnum (handles all 38 Spec.), 6-shot.
Barrel: 6", with ventilated rib.
Weight: 43-1/2 oz. **Length:** 11-1/2" overall.
Stocks: Walnut.
Sights: 1/8" ramp front, adjustable notch rear.
Features: Ventilated rib; grooved, crisp trigger; swing-out cylinder; target hammer.
Price: Stainless steel **$1,018.00**

COLT MAGNUM CARRY REVOLVER

Caliber: 357 Mag., 6-shot.
Barrel: 2".
Weight: 21 oz. **Length:** NA.
Stocks: Combat-style rubber.
Sights: Ramp front, fixed notch rear.
Features: Stainless steel construction. Smooth combat trigger. Introduced 1998. Made in U.S. by Colt's Mfg. Co.
Price: **$460.00**

E.A.A. STANDARD GRADE REVOLVERS

Caliber: 38 Spec., 6-shot; 357 magnum, 6-shot.
Barrel: 2", 4".
Weight: 38 oz. (22 rimfire, 4"). **Length:** 8.8" overall (4" bbl.).
Stocks: Rubber with finger grooves.
Sights: Blade front, fixed or adjustable on rimfires; fixed only on 32, 38.
Features: Swing-out cylinder; hammer block safety; blue finish. Introduced 1991. Imported from Germany by European American Armory.
Price: 38 Special 2" **$180.00**
Price: 38 Special, 4". **$199.00**
Price: 357 Magnum, 2" **$199.00**
Price: 357 Magnum, 4" **$233.00**

HARRINGTON & RICHARDSON 939 PREMIER REVOLVER

Caliber: 22 LR, 9-shot cylinder.
Barrel: 6" heavy.
Weight: 36 oz. **Length:** NA.
Stocks: Walnut-finished hardwood.
Sights: Blade front, fully adjustable rear.
Features: Swing-out cylinder with plunger-type ejection; solid barrel rib; high-polish blue finish; double-action mechanism; Western-style grip. Introduced 1995. Made in U.S. by H&R 1871, Inc.
Price: **$184.95**

HARRINGTON & RICHARDSON 929 SIDEKICK

Caliber: 22 LR, 9-shot cylinder.
Barrel: 4" heavy.
Weight: 30 oz. **Length:** NA.
Stocks: Cinnamon-color laminated wood.
Sights: Blade front, notch rear.
Features: Double action; swing-out cylinder, traditional loading gate; blued frame and barrel. Comes with lockable storage case, Uncle Mike's Sidekick holster. Introduced 1996. Made in U.S. by H&R 1871, Inc.
Price: **$159.95**

Harrington & Richardson 949

HARRINGTON & RICHARDSON SPORTSMAN 999 REVOLVER

Caliber: 22 Short, Long, Long Rifle, 9-shot.
Barrel: 4", 6".
Weight: 30 oz. (4" barrel). **Length:** 8.5" overall.
Stocks: Walnut-finished hardwood.
Sights: Blade front adjustable for elevation, rear adjustable for windage.
Features: Top-break loading; polished blue finish; automatic shell ejection. Reintroduced 1992. From H&R 1871, Inc.
Price: **$279.95**

KORTH COMBAT MODEL REVOLVER

Caliber: 357 Magnum.
Barrel: 3", 4", 5-1/4", 6".
Weight: NA. **Length:** NA.
Stocks: Checkered walnut, round butt.
Sights: Baughman ramp front, fully adjustable rear.
Features: Forged steel construction; trigger adjustable for slack, pull and over-travel; hammer-forged barrel; removable cylinder. Imported from Germany by Keng's Firearm Specialty, Inc.
Price: High-polish blued finish **$5,599.90**
Price: Plasma-coated matte silver finish **$6,199.90**
Price: Plasma-coated high-polish silver finish **$6,699.90**

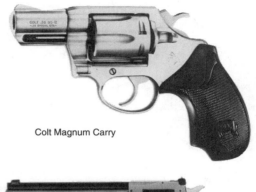

Colt Magnum Carry

Harrington & Richardson 939

HARRINGTON & RICHARDSON 949 WESTERN REVOLVER

Caliber: 22 LR, 9-shot cylinder.
Barrel: 5-1/2", 7-1/2".
Weight: 36 oz. **Length:** NA.
Stocks: Walnut-stained hardwood.
Sights: Blade front, adjustable rear.
Features: Color case-hardened frame and backstrap, traditional loading gate and ejector rod. Introduced 1994. Made in U.S. by H&R 1871, Inc.
Price: About. **$184.95**

Harrington & Richardson Sportsman 999

Korth Sport Model

Korth Sport Model Revolver

Similar to the Combat Model except has square-butt stocks, fully adjustable target rear sight and undercut Patridge front. Imported from Germany by Keng's Firearm Specialty, Inc.
Price: High-polish blued finish **$5,899.90**
Price: Plasma-coated matte silver finish **$6,499.90**
Price: Plasma-coated high polish silver finish **$6,999.00**

MAGNUM RESEARCH LITTLE MAX REVOLVER
Caliber: 22 Hornet, 45 Colt, 454 Casull, 50 A.E.
Barrel: 6-1/2", 7-1/2", 10".
Weight: 45 oz. **Length:** 13" overall (7-1/2" barrel).
Stocks: Rubber.
Sights: Ramp front, adjustable rear.
Features: Single action; stainless steel construction. Announced 1998. Made in U.S. From: Magnum Research.
Price: **$899.00**
Price: Maxline model (7-1/2", 10", 45 Colt, 45-70, 444 Marlin) **$899.00**

NEW ENGLAND FIREARMS LADY ULTRA REVOLVER
Caliber: 32 H&R Mag., 5-shot.
Barrel: 3".
Weight: 31 oz. **Length:** 7.25" overall.
Stocks: Walnut-finished hardwood with NEF medallion.
Sights: Blade front, fully adjustable rear.
Features: Swing-out cylinder; polished blue finish. Comes with lockable storage case. Introduced 1992. From New England Firearms.
Price: **$169.95**

New England Ultra

MANURHIN MR 73 SPORT REVOLVER
Caliber: 357 Magnum, 6-shot cylinder.
Barrel: 6".
Weight: 37 oz. **Length:** 11.1" overall.
Stocks: Checkered walnut.
Sights: Blade front, fully adjustable rear.
Features: Double action with adjustable trigger. High-polish blue finish, straw-colored hammer and trigger. Comes with extra sight. Introduced 1984. Imported from France by Century International Arms.
Price: About **$1,500.00**

REXIO PUCARA M224 REVOLVER
Caliber: 22 LR, 9-shot cylinder.
Barrel: 4".
Weight: 33 oz. **Length:** 9" overall.
Stocks: Checkered hardwood.
Sights:¥ Blade front, square notch rear adjustable for windage.
Features: Alloy frame; hammer block safety; polished blue finish. Introduced 1997. Imported from Argentina by Century International Arms.
Price: **$169.00**
Price: M226, 6" barrel **$169.00**

REXIO PUCARA M384 REVOLVER
Caliber: 38 Spec., 6-shot.
Barrel: 4".
Weight: 30 oz. **Length:** 9" overall.
Stocks: Checkered hardwood.
Sights: Blade front, rear adjustable for windage.
Features: Alloy frame. Polished blue finish. Imported from Argentina by Century International Arms.
Price: **$169.00**
Price: M386, 6" barrel **$169.00**

ROSSI MODEL 68 REVOLVER
Caliber: 38 Spec.
Barrel: 2", 3".
Weight: 22 oz.
Stocks: Checkered wood and rubber.
Sights: Ramp front, low profile adjustable rear.
Features: All-steel frame, thumb latch operated swing-out cylinder. Introduced 1978. Imported from Brazil by Interarms.
Price: 38, blue, 3", wood or rubber grips **$225.00**
Price: M68/2 (2" barrel), wood or rubber grips **$225.00**
Price: 3", nickel **$225.00**

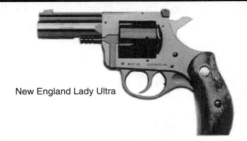

New England Lady Ultra

NEW ENGLAND FIREARMS ULTRA REVOLVER
Caliber: 22 LR, 9-shot; 22 WMR, 6-shot.
Barrel: 4", 6".
Weight: 36 oz. **Length:** 10-5/8" overall (6" barrel).
Stocks: Walnut-finished hardwood with NEF medallion.
Sights: Blade front, fully adjustable rear.
Features: Blue finish. Bull-style barrel with recessed muzzle, high "Lustre" blue/black finish. Introduced 1989. From New England Firearms.
Price: **$169.95**
Price: Ultra Mag 22 WMR **$169.95**

NEW ENGLAND FIREARMS STANDARD REVOLVERS
Caliber: 22 LR, 9-shot; 32 H&R Mag., 5-shot.
Barrel: 3", 4".
Weight: 26 oz. (22 LR, 3"). **Length:** 8-1/2" overall (4" bbl.).
Stocks: Walnut-finished American hardwood with NEF medallion.
Sights: Fixed.
Features: Choice of blue or nickel finish. Introduced 1988. From New England Firearms.
Price: 22 LR, 32 H&R Mag., blue **$134.95**
Price: 22 LR, 3", 4", nickel, 32 H&R Mag. 3" nickel **$144.95**

MEDUSA MODEL 47 REVOLVER
Caliber: Most 9mm, 38 and 357 caliber cartridges; 6-shot cylinder.
Barrel: 2-1/2", 3", 4", 5", 6"; fluted.
Weight: 39 oz. **Length:** 10" overall (4" barrel).
Stocks: Gripper-style rubber.
Sights: Changeable front blades, fully adjustable rear.
Features: Patented extractor allows gun to chamber, fire and extract over 25 different cartridges in the .355- to .357 range, without half-moon clips. Steel frame and cylinder; match quality barrel. Matte blue finish. Introduced 1996. Made in U.S. by Phillips & Rogers, Inc.
Price: **$899.00**

REXIO PUCARA M324 REVOLVER
Caliber: 32 S&W Long, 7-shot cylinder.
Barrel: 4".
Weight: 31 oz. **Length:** 9" overall.
Stocks: Checkered hardwood.
Sights: Blade front, square notch rear adjustable for windage.
Features: Alloy frame; polished blue finish; hammer block safety. Introduced 1997. Imported from Argentina by Century International Arms.
Price: **$169.00**
Price: M326, 6" barrel **$169.00**

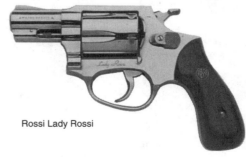

Rossi Lady Rossi

ROSSI LADY ROSSI REVOLVER
Caliber: 38 Spec., 5-shot.
Barrel: 2", 3".
Weight: 21 oz. **Length:** 6.5" overall (2" barrel).
Stocks: Smooth rosewood.
Sights: Fixed.
Features: High-polish stainless steel with "Lady Rossi" engraved on frame. Comes with velvet carry bag. Introduced 1995. Imported from Brazil by Interarms.
Price: **$285.00**

ROSSI CYCLOPS REVOLVER

Caliber: 357 Magnum, 6-shot.
Barrel: 6", 8".
Weight: 44 oz. (6" barrel). **Length:** 11-3/4" overall (6" barrel).
Stocks: Checkered rubber.
Sights: Blade front, fully adjustable rear.
Features: Extra-heavy barrel with four recessed compensator ports on each side of the muzzle. Stainless steel construction. Comes with scope mount and rings. Polished finish. Introduced 1997. Imported from Brazil by Interarms.
Price: **$429.00**

ROSSI MODEL 88 STAINLESS REVOLVER

Caliber: 38 Spec., 5-shot.
Barrel: 2", 3".
Weight: 22 oz. **Length:** 7.5" overall.
Stocks: Checkered wood, service-style, and rubber.
Sights: Ramp front, square notch rear drift adjustable for windage.
Features: All metal parts except springs are of 440 stainless steel; matte finish; small frame for concealability. Introduced 1983. Imported from Brazil by Interarms.
Price: 3" barrel, wood or rubber grips **$255.00**
Price: 2" barrel, wood or rubber grips **$255.00**

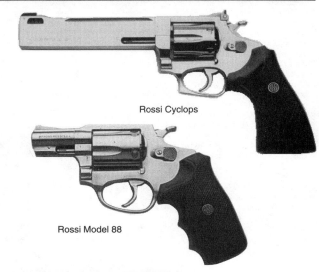

Rossi Cyclops

Rossi Model 88

ROSSI MODEL 515, 518 REVOLVERS

Caliber: 22 LR (Model 518), 22 WMR (Model 515), 6-shot.
Barrel: 4".
Weight: 30 oz. **Length:** 9" overall.
Stocks: Checkered wood and finger-groove wrap-around rubber.
Sights: Blade front with red insert, rear adjustable for windage and elevation.
Features: Small frame; stainless steel construction; solid integral barrel rib. Introduced 1994. Imported from Brazil by Interarms.
Price: Model 518, 22 LR **$255.00**
Price: Model 515, 22 WMR **$270.00**

Rossi Model 518

ROSSI MODEL 720 REVOLVER

Caliber: 44 Spec., 5-shot.
Barrel: 3".
Weight: 27.5 oz. **Length:** 8" overall.
Stocks: Checkered rubber, combat style.
Sights: Red insert front on ramp, fully adjustable rear.
Features: All stainless steel construction; solid barrel rib; full ejector rod shroud. Introduced 1992. Imported from Brazil by Interarms.
Price: **$290.00**
Price: Model 720C, spurless hammer, DA only **$290.00**

ROSSI MODEL 851 REVOLVER

Caliber: 38 Spec., 6-shot.
Barrel: 3" or 4".
Weight: 27.5 oz. (3" bbl.). **Length:** 8" overall (3" bbl.).
Stocks: Checkered Brazilian hardwood.
Sights: Blade front with red insert, rear adjustable for windage.
Features: Medium-size frame; stainless steel construction; ventilated barrel rib. Introduced 1991. Imported from Brazil by Interarms.
Price: **$255.00**

ROSSI MODEL 971 REVOLVER

Caliber: 357 Mag., 6-shot.
Barrel: 2-1/2", 4", 6", heavy.
Weight: 36 oz. **Length:** 9" overall.
Stocks: Checkered Brazilian hardwood. Stainless models have checkered, contoured rubber.
Sights: Blade front, fully adjustable rear.
Features: Full-length ejector rod shroud; matted sight rib; target-type trigger, wide checkered hammer spur. Introduced 1988. Imported from Brazil by Interarms.
Price: 4", stainless **$290.00**
Price: 6", stainless **$290.00**
Price: 4", blue. **$255.00**
Price: 2-1/2", stainless **$290.00**

Rossi Model 971 Comp Gun

Same as the Model 971 stainless except has 3-1/4" barrel with integral compensator. Overall length is 9", weighs 32 oz. Has red insert front sight, fully adjustable rear. Checkered, contoured rubber grips. Introduced 1993. Imported from Brazil by Interarms.
Price: **$290.00**
Price: **$290.00**

Rossi Model 720 Spurless

ROSSI MODEL 877 REVOLVER

Caliber: 357 Mag., 6-shot cylinder.
Barrel: 2".
Weight: 26 oz. **Length:** NA.
Stocks: Stippled synthetic.
Sights: Blade front, fixed groove rear.
Features: Stainless steel construction; fully enclosed ejector rod. Introduced 1996. Imported from Brazil by Interarms.
Price: Model 677 (same as Model 877 except in matte blue steel). . **$260.00**

Rossi Model 971 VRC

Rossi Model 971 VRC Revolver

Similar to the Model 971 except has Rossi's 8-port Vented Rib Compensator; checkered finger-groove rubber grips; stainless steel construction. Available with 2.5", 4", 6" barrel; weighs 30 oz. with 2-5/8" barrel. Introduced 1996. Imported from Brazil by Interarms.
Price: **$340.00**

RUGER GP-100 REVOLVERS
Caliber: 38 Spec., 357 Mag., 6-shot.
Barrel: 3", 3" heavy, 4", 4" heavy, 6", 6" heavy.
Weight: 3" barrel—35 oz., 3" heavy barrel—36 oz., 4" barrel—37 oz., 4" heavy barrel—38 oz.
Sights: Fixed; adjustable on 4" heavy, 6", 6" heavy barrels.
Stocks: Ruger Santoprene Cushioned Grip with Goncalo Alves inserts.
Features: Uses action and frame incorporating improvements and features of both the Security-Six and Redhawk revolvers. Full length and short ejector shroud. Satin blue and stainless steel.
Price: GP-141 (357, 4" heavy, adj. sights, blue) **$440.00**
Price: GP-160 (357, 6", adj. sights, blue) **$440.00**
Price: GP-161 (357, 6" heavy, adj. sights, blue) **$440.00**
Price: GPF-331 (357, 3" heavy), GPF-831 (38 Spec.) **$423.00**
Price: GPF-340 (357, 4"), GPF-840 (38 Spec.) **$423.00**
Price: GPF-341 (357, 4" heavy), GPF-841 (38 Spec.) **$423.00**
Price: KGP-141 (357, 4" heavy, adj. sights, stainless) **$474.00**
Price: KGP-160 (357, 6", adj. sights, stainless) **$474.00**
Price: KGP-161 (357, 6" heavy, adj. sights, stainless) **$474.00**
Price: KGPF-330 (357, 3", stainless), KGPF-830 (38 Spec.) **$457.00**
Price: KGPF-331 (357, 3" heavy, stainless), KGPF-831 (38 Spec.) . . **$457.00**
Price: KGPF-340 (357, 4", stainless), KGPF-840 (38 Spec.) **$457.00**
Price: KGPF-341 (357, 4" heavy, stainless), KGPF-841 (38 Spec.) . **$457.00**

Ruger GP-100

Ruger SP101 DAO

Ruger SP101 Double-Action-Only Revolver
Similar to the standard SP101 except is double-action-only with no single-action sear notch. Has spurless hammer for snag-free handling, floating firing pin and Ruger's patented transfer bar safety system. Available with 2-1/4" barrel in 38 Special +P and 357 Magnum only. Weighs 25-1/2 oz., overall length 7.06". Natural brushed satin or high-polish stainless steel. Introduced 1993.
Price: KSP821L (38 Spec.), KSP321XL (357 Mag.) **$443.00**

Ruger Redhawk

SMITH & WESSON MODEL 10 M&P HB REVOLVER
Caliber: 38 Spec., 6-shot.
Barrel: 4".
Weight: 33.5 oz. **Length:** 9-5/16" overall.
Stocks: Uncle Mike's Combat soft rubber; square butt. Wood optional.
Sights: Fixed; ramp front, square notch rear.
Price: Blue **$408.00**

Smith & Wesson Model 65 Revolver
Similiar to the Model 13 except made of stainless steel. Has Uncle Mike's Combat grips, smooth combat trigger, fixed notch rear sight. Made in U.S. by Smith & Wesson.
Price: 3" or 4" **$445.00**

RUGER SP101 REVOLVERS
Caliber: 22 LR, 32 H&R Mag., 6-shot, 9mm Para., 38 Spec. +P, 357 Mag., 5-shot.
Barrel: 2-1/4", 3-1/16", 4".
Weight: 2-1/4"—25 oz.; 3-1/16"—27 oz.
Sights: Adjustable on 22, 32, fixed on others.
Stocks: Ruger Santoprene Cushioned Grip with Xenoy inserts.
Features: Incorporates improvements and features found in the GP-100 revolvers into a compact, small frame, double-action revolver. Full-length ejector shroud. Stainless steel only. Introduced 1988.
Price: KSP-821 (2-1/2", 38 Spec.) **$443.00**
Price: KSP-831 (3-1/16", 38 Spec.) **$443.00**
Price: KSP-221 (2-1/4", 22 LR) **$443.00**
Price: KSP-240 (4", 22 LR) **$443.00**
Price: KSP-241 (4" heavy bbl., 22 LR) **$443.00**
Price: KSP-3231 (3-1/16", 32 H&R). **$443.00**
Price: KSP-921 (2-1/4", 9mm Para.) **$443.00**
Price: KSP-931 (3-1/16", 9mm Para.) **$443.00**
Price: KSP-321 (2-1/4", 357 Mag.) **$443.00**
Price: KSP-331 (3-1/16", 357 Mag.) **$443.00**
Price: GKSP321X (2-1/4", 357 Mag.), high-gloss stainless. **$443.00**
Price: GKSP331X (3-1/16", 357 Mag.), high-gloss stainless. **$443.00**
Price: GKSP321XL (2-1/4", 357 Mag., spurless hammer, DAO) high-gloss stainless **$443.00**

RUGER REDHAWK
Caliber: 44 Rem. Mag., 45 Colt, 6-shot.
Barrel: 5-1/2", 7-1/2".
Weight: About 54 oz. (7-1/2" bbl.). **Length:** 13" overall (7-1/2" barrel).
Stocks: Square butt Goncalo Alves.
Sights: Interchangeable Patridge-type front, rear adjustable for windage and elevation.
Features: Stainless steel, brushed satin finish, or blued ordnance steel. Has a 9-1/2" sight radius. Introduced 1979.
Price: Blued, 44 Mag., 5-1/2", 71/2" **$490.00**
Price: Blued, 44 Mag., 7-1/2", with scope mount, rings **$527.00**
Price: Stainless, 44 Mag., 5-1/2", 71/2" **$547.00**
Price: Stainless, 44 Mag., 7-1/2", with scope mount, rings **$589.00**
Price: Stainless, 45 Colt, 5-1/2", 7-1/2" **$547.00**
Price: Stainless, 45 Colt, 7-1/2", with scope mount. **$589.00**

Ruger Super Redhawk Revolver
Similar to the standard Redhawk except has a heavy extended frame with the Ruger Integral Scope Mounting System on the wide topstrap. The wide hammer spur has been lowered for better scope clearance. Incorporates the mechanical design features and improvements of the GP-100. Choice of 7-1/2" or 9-1/2" barrel, both with ramp front sight base with Redhawk-style Interchangeable Insert sight blades, adjustable rear sight. Comes with Ruger "Cushioned Grip" panels of Santoprene with Goncalo Alves wood panels. Satin or high-polished stainless steel. Introduced 1987.
Price: KSRH-7 (7-1/2") **$589.00**
Price: KSRH-9 (9-1/2") **$594.00**

SMITH & WESSON MODEL 13 H.B. M&P
Caliber: 357 Mag. and 38 Spec., 6-shot.
Barrel: 4".
Weight: 34 oz. **Length:** 9-5/16" overall (4" bbl.).
Stocks: Uncle Mike's Combat soft rubber; wood optional.
Sights: 1/8" serrated ramp front, fixed square notch rear.
Features: Heavy barrel, K-frame, square butt (4"), round butt (3").
Price: Blue. **$411.00**

Smith & Wesson Model 14

SMITH & WESSON MODEL 17 K-22 MASTERPIECE
Caliber: 22 LR, 10-shot cylinder.
Barrel: 6".
Weight: 42 oz. **Length:** 11-1/8" overall.
Stocks: Hogue rubber.
Sights: Pinned Patridge front, fully adjustable rear.
Features: Polished blue finish; smooth combat trigger; semi-target hammer. The 10-slot version of this model introduced 1996.
Price: **$508.00**

Smith & Wesson Model 19

Smith & Wesson Model 629 Classic DX Revolver
Similar to the Model 629 Classic except offered only with 6-1/2" or 8-3/8" full-lug barrel; comes with five front sights: 50-yard red ramp; 50-yard black Patridge; 100-yard black Patridge with gold bead; 50-yard black ramp; and 50-yard black Patridge with white dot. Comes with Hogue combat-style round butt grip. Introduced 1991.
Price: Model 629 Classic DX, 6-1/2" **$835.00**
Price: As above, 8-3/8" **$862.00**

Smith & Wesson Model 60 .357 Magnum Chiefs Special
Similar to the Model 60 in 38 Special except is 357 Magnum; 2-1/8" or 3" barrel. Weighs 24 oz.; 7-1/2" overall length (3" barrel). Has Uncle Mike's Combat grips.
Price: 2-1/8" barrel **$449.00**
Price: 3" barrel **$476.00**

Smith & Wesson Model 37

Smith & Wesson Model 60 3" Full-Lug Revolver
Similar to the Model 60 Chief's Special except has 3" full-lug barrel, adjustable micrometer click black blade rear sight; rubber Uncle Mike's Custom Grade Boot Grip. Overall length 7-1/2"; weighs 24-1/2 oz. Introduced 1991.
Price: **$476.00**

SMITH & WESSON MODEL 14 FULL LUG REVOLVER
Caliber: 38 Spec., 6-shot.
Barrel: 6", full lug.
Weight: 47 oz. **Length:** 11-1/8" overall.
Stocks: Hogue soft rubber; wood optional.
Sights: Pinned Patridge front, adjustable micrometer click rear.
Features: Has .500" target hammer, .312" smooth combat trigger. Polished blue finish. Reintroduced 1991. Limited production.
Price: **$484.00**

SMITH & WESSON MODEL 15 COMBAT MASTERPIECE
Caliber: 38 Spec., 6-shot.
Barrel: 4".
Weight: 32 oz. **Length:** 9-5/16" (4" bbl.).
Stocks: Uncle Mike's Combat soft rubber; wood optional.
Sights: Front, Baughman Quick Draw on ramp, micro-click rear adjustable for windage and elevation.
Price: Blued **$437.00**

> Consult our Directory pages for the location of firms mentioned.

SMITH & WESSON MODEL 19 COMBAT MAGNUM
Caliber: 357 Mag. and 38 Spec., 6-shot.
Barrel: 2-1/2", 4".
Weight: 36 oz. **Length:** 9-9/16" (4" bbl.).
Stocks: Uncle Mike's Combat soft rubber; wood optional.
Sights: Serrated ramp front 2-1/2" or 4" bbl., red ramp on 4", 6" bbl., micro-click rear adjustable for windage and elevation.
Price: 2-1/2" **$434.00**
Price: 4" **$443.00**

SMITH & WESSON MODEL 29, 629 REVOLVERS
Caliber: 44 Magnum, 6-shot.
Barrel: 6", 8-3/8" (Model 29); 4", 6", 8-3/8" (Model 629).
Weight: 47 oz. (6" bbl.). **Length:** 11-3/8" overall (6" bbl.).
Stocks: Soft rubber; wood optional.
Sights: 1/8" red ramp front, micro-click rear, adjustable for windage and elevation.
Price: S&W Bright Blue, 6" **$574.00**
Price: S&W Bright Blue, 8-3/8" **$586.00**
Price: Model 629 (stainless steel), 4" **$607.00**
Price: Model 629, 6" **$613.00**
Price: Model 629, 8-3/8" barrel **$627.00**

Smith & Wesson Model 629 Classic Revolver
Similar to the standard Model 629 except has full-lug 5", 6-1/2" or 8-3/8" barrel; chamfered front of cylinder; interchangable red ramp front sight with adjustable white outline rear; Hogue grips with S&W monogram; the frame is drilled and tapped for scope mounting. Factory accurizing and endurance packages. Overall length with 5" barrel is 10-1/2"; weighs 51 oz. Introduced 1990.
Price: Model 629 Classic (stainless), 5", 6-1/2" **$650.00**
Price: As above, 8-3/8" **$671.00**

SMITH & WESSON MODEL 36, 37 CHIEFS SPECIAL & AIRWEIGHT
Caliber: 38 Spec.+P, 5-shot.
Barrel: 2".
Weight: 19-1/2 oz. (2" bbl.); 13-1/2 oz. (Airweight). **Length:** 6-1/2" (2" bbl. and round butt).
Stocks: Round butt soft rubber; wood optional.
Sights: Fixed, serrated ramp front, square notch rear.
Price: Blue, standard Model 36 . . . . **$394.00**
Price: Blue, Airweight Model 37, 2" only. **$429.00**

Smith & Wesson Model 60 Chiefs Special Stainless
Similar to the Model 36 except all stainless construction. Has 1-7/8" barrel, 6-5/16" overall length, weighs 21 oz., satin finish.
Price: **$449.00**

Smith & Wesson Model 637 Airweight Revolver
Similar to the Model 37 Airweight except has alloy frame, stainless steel barrel, cylinder and yoke; rated for 38 Spec. +P; Uncle Mike's Boot Grip. Weighs 15 oz. Introduced 1996. Made in U.S. by Smith & Wesson.
Price: **$446.00**

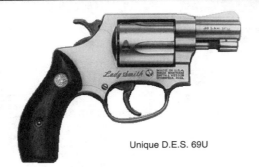

Unique D.E.S. 69U

Smith & Wesson Model 638

Smith & Wesson Model 63

Smith & Wesson Model 317 Kit Gun

SMITH & WESSON MODEL 317 AIRLITE, 317 LADYSMITH REVOLVERS
Caliber: 22 LR, 8-shot.
Barrel: 1-7/8".
Weight: 9.9 oz. **Length:** 6-3/16" overall.
Stocks: Dymondwood Boot or Uncle Mike's Boot.
Sights: Serrated ramp front, fixed notch rear.
Features: Aluminum alloy, carbon and stainless steels, and titanium construction. Short spur hammer, smooth combat trigger. Clear Cote finish. Introduced 1997. Made in U.S. by Smith & Wesson.
Price: With Uncle Mike's Boot grip $451.00
Price: With DymondWood Boot grip $484.00
Price: Model 317 LadySmith (DymondWood only, comes
with display case). $505.00

Smith & Wesson Model 36LS, 60LS LadySmith
Similar to the standard Model 36. Available with 2" barrel, 38 Special. Comes with smooth, contoured rosewood grips with the S&W monogram. Has a speedloader cutout. Comes in a fitted carry/storage case. Introduced 1989.
Price: Model 36LS $425.00
Price: Model 60LS, as above except in stainless, 357 Magnum $479.00

SMITH & WESSON MODEL 38 BODYGUARD
Caliber: 38 Spec., 5-shot.
Barrel: 2".
Weight: 14-1/2 oz. **Length:** 6-5/16" overall.
Stocks: Soft rubber; wood optional.
Sights: Fixed serrated ramp front, square notch rear.
Features: Alloy frame; internal hammer.
Price: Blue $462.00

Smith & Wesson Model 638 Airweight Bodyguard Revolver
Similar to the Model 38 except has alloy frame, stainless steel cylinder and barrel; shrouded hammer. Weighs 14 oz. Has Uncle Mike's Boot Grip. Introduced 1997. Made in U.S. by Smith & Wesson.
Price: $478.00

SMITH & WESSON MODEL 63 KIT GUN
Caliber: 22 LR, 6-shot.
Barrel: 2", 4".
Weight: 24 oz. (4" bbl.). **Length:** 8-3/8" (4" bbl. and round butt).
Stocks: Round butt soft rubber; wood optional.
Sights: Red ramp front, micro-click rear adjustable for windage and elevation.
Features: Stainless steel construction.
Price: 2" $476.00
Price: 4" $481.00

SMITH & WESSON MODEL 64 STAINLESS M&P
Caliber: 38 Spec., 6-shot.
Barrel: 2", 3", 4".
Weight: 34 oz. **Length:** 9-5/16" overall.
Stocks: Soft rubber; wood optional.
Sights: Fixed, 1/8" serrated ramp front, square notch rear.
Features: Satin finished stainless steel, square butt.
Price: 2" $433.00
Price: 3", 4" $441.00

SMITH & WESSON MODEL 65LS LADYSMITH
Caliber: 357 Magnum, 6-shot.
Barrel: 3".
Weight: 31 oz. **Length:** 7.94" overall.
Stocks: Rosewood, round butt.
Sights: Serrated ramp front, fixed notch rear.
Features: Stainless steel with frosted finish. Smooth combat trigger, service hammer, shrouded ejector rod. Comes with soft case. Introduced 1992.
Price: $479.00

SMITH & WESSON MODEL 66 STAINLESS COMBAT MAGNUM
Caliber: 357 Mag. and 38 Spec., 6-shot.
Barrel: 2-1/2", 4", 6".
Weight: 36 oz. (4" barrel). **Length:** 9-9/16" overall.
Stocks: Soft rubber; wood optional.
Sights: Red ramp front, micro-click rear adjustable for windage and elevation.
Features: Satin finish stainless steel.
Price: 2-1/2" $484.00
Price: 4", 6" $490.00

SMITH & WESSON MODEL 67 COMBAT MASTERPIECE
Caliber: 38 Special, 6-shot.
Barrel: 4".
Weight: 32 oz. **Length:** 9-5/16" overall.
Stocks: Soft rubber; wood optional.
Sights: Red ramp front, micro-click rear adjustable for windage and elevation.
Features: Stainless steel with satin finish. Smooth combat trigger, semi-target hammer. Introduced 1994.
Price: $485.00

Smith & Wesson Model 317 Airlite Kit Gun
Similar to the Model 317 Airlite except has 3" barrel, pinned black front sight, micro-click rear adjustable for windage and elevation. Weighs 11 oz. Introduced 1998.
Price: With Uncle Mike's Combat grip $477.00
Price: With DymondWood grip $510.00

SMITH & WESSON MODEL 586, 686 DISTINGUISHED COMBAT MAGNUMS

Caliber: 357 Magnum.
Barrel: 4", 6", full shroud.
Weight: 46 oz. (6"), 41 oz. (4").
Stocks: Soft rubber; wood optional.
Sights: Baughman red ramp front, four-position click-adjustable front, S&W micrometer click rear. Drilled and tapped for scope mount.
Features: Uses L-frame, but takes all K-frame grips. Full-length ejector rod shroud. Smooth combat-type trigger, semi-target type hammer. Trigger stop on 6" models. Also available in stainless as Model 686. Introduced 1981.

Price: Model 586, blue, 4", from............................. **$480.00**
Price: Model 586, blue, 6" **$484.00**
Price: Model 686, 6", ported barrel **$548.00**
Price: Model 686, 8-3/8" **$534.00**
Price: Model 686, 2-1/2" **$499.00**

Smith & Wesson Model 686 Magnum PLUS Revolver

Similar to the Model 686 except has 7-shot cylinder, 2-1/2", 4" or 6" barrel. Weighs 34-1/2 oz., overall length 7-1/2" (2-1/2" barrel). Hogue rubber grips. Introduced 1996. Made in U.S. by Smith & Wesson.

Price: 2-1/2" barrel...................................... **$518.00**
Price: 4" barrel... **$526.00**
Price: 6" barrel... **$534.00**

Smith & Wesson Model 610

SMITH & WESSON MODEL 625 REVOLVER

Caliber: 45 ACP, 6-shot.
Barrel: 5".
Weight: 46 oz. **Length:** 11.375" overall.
Stocks: Soft rubber; wood optional.
Sights: Patridge front on ramp, S&W micrometer click rear adjustable for windage and elevation.
Features: Stainless steel construction with .400" semi-target hammer, .312" smooth combat trigger; full lug barrel. Introduced 1989.

Price: **$618.00**

SMITH & WESSON MODEL 640 CENTENNIAL

Caliber: 357 Mag., 38 Spec., 5-shot.
Barrel: 1-7/8" (38 Spec.), 2-1/8" (357 Magnum).
Weight: 25 oz. **Length:** 6-3/4" overall.
Stocks: Uncle Mike's Boot Grip.
Sights: Serrated ramp front, fixed notch rear.
Features: Stainless steel version of the original Model 40 but without the grip safety. Fully concealed hammer, snag-proof smooth edges. Introduced 1995 in 357 Magnum.

Price: **$488.00**
Price: Model 940 (9mm Para.)............................. **$493.00**

Smith & Wesson Model 442

SMITH & WESSON MODEL 617 FULL LUG REVOLVER

Caliber: 22 LR, 6- or 10-shot.
Barrel: 4", 6", 8-3/8".
Weight: 42 oz. (4" barrel). **Length:** NA.
Stocks: Soft rubber; wood optional.
Sights: Patridge front, adjustable rear. Drilled and tapped for scope mount.
Features: Stainless steel with satin finish; 4" has .312" smooth trigger, .375" semi-target hammer; 6" has either .312" combat or .400" serrated trigger, .375" semi-target or .500" target hammer; 8-3/8" with .400" serrated trigger, .500" target hammer. Introduced 1990.

Price: 4" **$478.00**
Price: 6", target hammer, target trigger **$508.00**
Price: 6", 10-shot...................................... **$549.00**
Price: 8-3/8" **$520.00**

> ## CONSULT
> # SHOOTER'S MARKETPLACE
> *Page 225, This Issue*

SMITH & WESSON MODEL 610 CLASSIC HUNTER REVOLVER

Caliber: 10mm, 6-shot cylinder.
Barrel: 6-1/2" full lug.
Weight: 52 oz. **Length:** 12" overall.
Stocks: Hogue rubber combat.
Sights: Interchangeable blade front, micro-click rear adjustable for windage and elevation.
Features: Stainless steel construction; target hammer, target trigger; unfluted cylinder; drilled and tapped for scope mounting. Introduced 1998.

Price: **$664.00**

Smith & Wesson Model 625

Smith & Wesson Model 442 Centennial Airweight

Similar to the Model 640 Centennial except has alloy frame giving weight of 15.8 oz. Chambered for 38 Special, 2" carbon steel barrel, carbon steel cylinder; concealed hammer; Uncle Mike's Custom Grade Santoprene grips. Fixed square notch rear sight, serrated ramp front. Introduced 1993.

Price: Blue **$445.00**

Smith & Wesson Model 642 Airweight Revolver

Similar to the Model 442 Centennial Airweight except has stainless steel barrel, cylinder and yoke with matte finish; Uncle Mike's Boot Grip; weighs 15.8 oz. Introduced 1996. Made in U.S. by Smith & Wesson.

Price: **$460.00**

Smith & Wesson Model 642LS LadySmith Revolver

Same as the Model 642 except has smooth combat wood grips, and comes with case; aluminum alloy frame, stainless cylinder, barrel and yoke; frosted matte finish. Weighs 15.8 oz. Introduced 1996. Made in U.S. by Smith & Wesson.

Price: **$490.00**

SMITH & WESSON MODEL 649 BODYGUARD REVOLVER

Caliber: 38 Spec., 357 Mag., 5-shot.
Barrel: 1-7/8" (38 Spec.), 2-1/8" (357 Mag.).
Weight: 20 oz. **Length:** 6-5/16" overall.
Stocks: Uncle Mike's Combat.
Sights: Black pinned ramp front, fixed notch rear.
Features: Stainless steel construction; shrouded hammer; smooth combat trigger. Made in U.S. by Smith & Wesson.

Price: **$488.00**

SMITH & WESSON MODEL 651 REVOLVER

Caliber: 22 WMR, 6-shot cylinder.
Barrel: 4".
Weight: 24-1/2 oz. **Length:** 8-11/16" overall.
Stocks: Soft rubber; wood optional.
Sights: Red ramp front, adjustable micrometer click rear.
Features: Stainless steel construction with semi-target hammer, smooth combat trigger. Reintroduced 1991. Limited production.
Price: **$478.00**

SMITH & WESSON MODEL 657 REVOLVER

Caliber: 41 Mag., 6-shot.
Barrel: 6".
Weight: 48 oz. **Length:** 11-3/8" overall.
Stocks: Soft rubber; wood optional.
Sights: Pinned 1/8" red ramp front, micro-click rear adjustable for windage and elevation.
Features: Stainless steel construction.
Price: **$548.00**

Smith & Wesson Model 651

Smith & Wesson Model 696

SMITH & WESSON MODEL 696 REVOLVER

Caliber: 44 Spec., 5-shot.
Barrel: 3".
Weight: 35.5 oz. **Length:** 8-1/4" overall.
Stocks: Uncle Mike's Combat.
Sights: Red ramp front, click adjustable white outline rear.
Features: Stainless steel construction; round butt frame; satin finish. Introduced 1997. Made in U.S. by Smith & Wesson.
Price: **$509.00**

TAURUS MODEL 44 REVOLVER

Caliber: 44 Mag., 6-shot.
Barrel: 4", 6-1/2", 8-3/8".
Weight: 44-3/4 oz. (4" barrel). **Length:** NA.
Stocks: Soft black rubber.
Sights: Serrated ramp front, micro-click rear adjustable for windage and elevation.
Features: Heavy solid rib on 4", vent rib on 6-1/2", 8-3/8". Compensated barrel. Blued model has color case-hardened hammer and trigger. Introduced 1994. Imported by Taurus International.
Price: Blue, 4" **$447.00**
Price: Blue, 6-1/2", 8-3/8" **$465.00**
Price: Stainless, 4" **$508.00**
Price: Stainless, 6-1/2", 8-3/8" **$529.00**

TAURUS MODEL 82 HEAVY BARREL REVOLVER

Caliber: 38 Spec., 6-shot.
Barrel: 4", heavy.
Weight: 34 oz. (4" bbl.). **Length:** 9-1/4" overall (4" bbl.).
Stocks: Soft black rubber.
Sights: Serrated ramp front, square notch rear.
Features: Imported by Taurus International.
Price: Blue **$296.00**
Price: Stainless **$344.00**

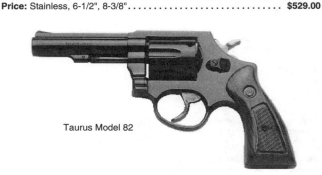
Taurus Model 82

TAURUS MODEL 85 REVOLVER

Caliber: 38 Spec., 5-shot.
Barrel: 2", 3".
Weight: 21 oz.
Stocks: Black rubber, boot grip.
Sights: Ramp front, square notch rear.
Features: Blue finish or stainless steel. Introduced 1980. Imported by Taurus International.
Price: Blue, 2", 3" **$258.00**
Price: Stainless steel **$306.00**
Price: Blue, 2", ported barrel **$276.00**
Price: Stainless, 2", ported barrel **$325.00**
Price: Blue, Ultra-Lite (17 oz.), 2" **$299.00**
Price: Stainless, Ultra-Lite (17 oz.), 2", ported barrel **$330.00**
Price: Blue with gold trim, rosewood boot grip **$315.00**

Taurus Model 85CH

TAURUS MODEL 94 REVOLVER

Caliber: 22 LR, 9-shot cylinder.
Barrel: 2", 4", 5".
Weight: 25 oz.
Stocks: Soft black rubber.
Sights: Serrated ramp front, click-adjustable rear for windage and elevation.
Features: Floating firing pin, color case-hardened hammer and trigger. Introduced 1989. Imported by Taurus International.
Price: Blue **$308.00**
Price: Stainless **$356.00**
Price: Model 94 UL, blue, 2", fixed sight, weighs 14 oz. **$342.00**
Price: As above, stainless **$390.00**

Taurus Model 85CH Revolver

Same as the Model 85 except has 2" barrel only and concealed hammer. Soft rubber boot grip. Introduced 1991. Imported by Taurus International.
Price: Blue **$258.00**
Price: Stainless **$306.00**
Price: Blue, ported barrel **$276.00**
Price: Stainless, ported barrel **$325.00**

TAURUS MODEL 445, 445CH REVOLVERS

Caliber: 44 Special, 5-shot.
Barrel: 2".
Weight: 28.25 oz. **Length:** 6-3/4" overall.
Stocks: Soft black rubber.
Sights: Serrated ramp front, notch rear.
Features: Blue or stainless steel. Standard or concealed hammer. Introduced 1997. Imported by Taurus International.
Price: Blue **$304.00**
Price: Stainless **$351.00**
Price: Blue, concealed hammer **$304.00**
Price: Stainless, concealed hammer **$351.00**

TAURUS MODEL 605 REVOLVER

Caliber: 357 Mag., 5-shot.
Barrel: 2-1/4", 3".
Weight: 24.5 oz. **Length:** NA.
Stocks: Soft black rubber.
Sights: Serrated ramp front, fixed notch rear.
Features: Heavy, solid rib barrel; floating firing pin. Blue or stainless. Introduced 1995. Imported by Taurus International.
Price: Blue **$316.00**
Price: Stainless **$364.00**
Price: Model 605CH (concealed hammer) 2-1/4", blue **$296.00**
Price: Model 605CH, stainless, 21-/4" **$344.00**
Price: Blue, 2-1/4", ported barrel **$333.00**
Price: Stainless, 2-1/4", ported barrel **$381.00**
Price: Blue, 2-1/4", ported barrel, concealed hammer **$315.00**
Price: Stainless, 2-1/4", ported barrel, concealed hammer **$362.00**

TAURUS MODEL 608 REVOLVER

Caliber: 357 Mag., 8-shot.
Barrel: 4", 6-1/2", 8-3/8.
Weight: 44 oz. **Length:** NA.
Stocks: Soft black rubber.
Sights: Serrated ramp front, fully adjustable rear.
Features: Ventilated rib with built-in compensator on 6-1/2" barrel. Available in blue or stainless. Introduced 1995. Imported by Taurus international.
Price: Blue, 4" **$447.00**
Price: Blue, 6-1/2", 8-3/8" **$465.00**
Price: Stainless, 4" **$508.00**
Price: Stainless, 6-1/2", 8-3/8 . . . . **$529.00**

TAURUS MODEL 669 REVOLVER

Caliber: 357 Mag., 6-shot.
Barrel: 4", 6".
Weight: 37 oz., (4" bbl.).
Stocks: Black rubber.
Sights: Serrated ramp front, micro-click rear adjustable for windage and elevation.
Features: Wide target-type hammer, floating firing pin, full-length barrel shroud. Introduced 1988. Imported by Taurus International.
Price: Blue, 4", 6" **$344.00**
Price: Stainless, 4", 6" **$421.00**

Taurus Model 689 Revolver

Same as the Model 669 except has full-length ventilated barrel rib. Available in blue or stainless steel. Introduced 1990. From Taurus International.
Price: Blue, 4" or 6" **$358.00**
Price: Stainless, 4" or 6" **$435.00**

TAURUS MODEL 827 DOUBLE-ACTION REVOLVER

Caliber: 38 Special, 7-shot.
Barrel: 4".
Weight: 36 oz. **Length:** NA.
Stocks: Finger-groove Santoprene.
Sights: Serrated ramp front, notch rear.
Features: Solid rib; shrouded ejector rod. Introduced 1998. Imported by Taurus International.
Price: Blue **$317.00**
Price: Stainless **$364.00**

DAN WESSON FIREARMS MODEL 8 & MODEL 14

Caliber: 38 Special (Model 8); 357 (Model 14), both 6-shot.
Barrel: 2-1/2", 4", 6"; interchangeable.
Weight: 30 oz. (2-1/2"). **Length:** 9-1/4" overall (4" bbl.).
Stocks: Checkered, interchangeable.
Sights: 1/8" serrated front, fixed rear.
Features: Interchangeable barrels and grips; smooth, wide trigger; wide hammer spur with short double-action travel. Available in stainless or Brite blue. Reintroduced 1997. Contact Dan Wesson Firearms for complete price list.
Price: Model 8-2, 2-1/2", blue **$274.00**
Price: As above except in stainless **$319.00**

TAURUS MODEL 454 RAGING BULL REVOLVER

Caliber: 454 Casull, 5-shot.
Barrel: 5", 6-1/2", 8-3/8".
Weight: 53 oz. (6-1/2" barrel). **Length:** 12" overall (6-1/2" barrel).
Stocks: Soft black rubber.
Sights: Patridge front, micrometer click adjustable rear.
Features: Ventilated rib; integral compensating system. Introduced 1997. Imported by Taurus International.
Price: Blue **$795.00**
Price: Stainless **$895.00**

Taurus Model 608

TAURUS MODEL 617, 606CH REVOLVER

Caliber: 357 Magnum, 7-shot.
Barrel: 2".
Weight: 29 oz. **Length:** 6-3/4" overall.
Stocks: Soft black rubber.
Sights: Serrated ramp front, notch rear.
Features: Heavy, solid barrel rib, ejector shroud. Available with porting, concealed hammer. Introduced 1998. Imported by Taurus International.
Price: Blue, regular or concealed hammer **$350.00**
Price: Stainless, regular or concealed hammer **$395.00**
Price: Blue, ported **$367.00**
Price: Stainless, ported **$414.00**

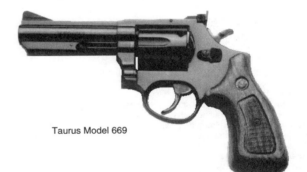

Taurus Model 669

TAURUS MODEL 941 REVOLVER

Caliber: 22 WMR, 8-shot.
Barrel: 2", 4", 5".
Weight: 27.5 oz. (4" barrel). **Length:** NA.
Stocks: Soft black rubber.
Sights: Serrated ramp front, rear adjustable for windage and elevation.
Features: Solid rib heavy barrel with full-length ejector rod shroud. Blue or stainless steel. Introduced 1992. Imported by Taurus International.
Price: Blue **$331.00**
Price: Stainless **$384.00**
Price: Model 941 UL, blue, 2", fixed sight, weighs 14 oz. **$365.00**
Price: As above, stainless **$420.00**

Dan Wesson Firearms Model 9, 15 & 32M Revolvers

Same as Models 8 and 14 except they have adjustable sight. Model 9 chambered for 38 Special, Model 15 for 357 Magnum. Model 32M is chambered for 32 H&R Mag. Same specs and prices as for Model 15 guns. Available in blue or stainless. Reintroduced 1997. Contact Dan Wesson Firearms for complete price list.
Price: Model 9-2 or 15-2, 2-1/2", blue **$346.00**
Price: As above except in stainless **$376.00**

Dan Wesson Firearms Model 15 Gold Series

Similar to the Model 15 except has smoother action to reduce DA pull to 8-10 lbs.; comes with either 6" or 8" vent heavy slotted barrel shroud with bright blue barrel. Shroud is stamped "Gold Series" with the Wesson signature engraved and gold filled. Hammer and trigger are polished bright; rosewood grips. New sights with orange dot Patridge front, white triangle on rear blade. Reintroduced 1997. Made in U.S. by Dan Wesson Firearms.

Price: 6"... **NA**
Price: 8"... **NA**

DAN WESSON FIREARMS MODEL 22 SILHOUETTE REVOLVER

Caliber: 22 LR, 6-shot.
Barrel: 10", regular vent or vent heavy.
Weight: 53 oz.
Stocks: Combat style.
Sights: Partridge-style front, .080" narrow notch rear.
Features: Single action only. Available in blue or stainless. Reintroduced 1997. Made in U.S. by Dan Wesson Firearms.

Price: Blue, regular vent **$474.00**
Price: Blue, vent heavy **$492.00**
Price: Stainless, regular vent **$504.00**
Price: Stainless, vent heavy **$532.00**

DAN WESSON FIREARMS MODEL 322/7322 TARGET REVOLVER

Caliber: 32-20, 6-shot.
Barrel: 2.5", 4", 6", 8", standard vent, vent heavy.
Weight: 43 oz. (6" VH). **Length:** 11.25" overall.
Stocks: Checkered walnut.
Sights: Red ramp interchangeable front, fully adjustable rear.
Features: Bright blue or stainless. Reintroduced 1997. Made in U.S. by Dan Wesson Firearms.

Price: 6", blue **$377.00**
Price: 6", stainless................................... **$419.00**
Price: 8", vent, blue................................. **$429.00**
Price: 8", stainless................................... **$472.00**
Price: 6", vent heavy, blue **$437.00**
Price: 6", vent heavy, stainless **$480.00**
Price: 8", vent heavy, blue **$449.00**
Price: 8", vent heavy, stainless **$501.00**

> Consult our Directory pages for the location of firms mentioned.

DAN WESSON FIREARMS MODEL 40 SILHOUETTE

Caliber: 357 Maximum, 6-shot.
Barrel: 4", 6", 8", 10".
Weight: 64 oz. (8" bbl.). **Length:** 14.3" overall (8" bbl.).
Stocks: Smooth walnut, target-style.
Sights: 1/8" serrated front, fully adjustable rear.
Features: Meets criteria for IHMSA competition with 8" slotted barrel. Blue or stainless steel. Made in U.S. by Dan Wesson Firearms.

Price: Blue, 4"..................................... **$502.00**
Price: Blue, 6"..................................... **$544.00**
Price: Blue, 8"..................................... **$567.00**
Price: Blue, 10"................................... **$597.00**
Price: Stainless, 4".................................. **$567.00**
Price: Stainless, 6".................................. **$610.00**
Price: Stainless, 8" slotted **$645.00**
Price: Stainless, 10" **$671.00**

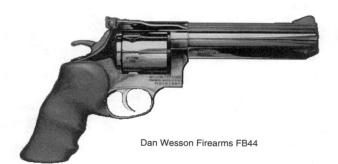

Dan Wesson Firearms FB44

DAN WESSON FIREARMS MODEL 22 REVOLVER

Caliber: 22 LR, 22 WMR, 6-shot.
Barrel: 2-1/2", 4", 6", 8"; interchangeable.
Weight: 36 oz. (2-1/2"), 44 oz. (6"). **Length:** 9-1/4" overall (4" barrel).
Stocks: Checkered; undercover, service or over-size target.
Sights: 1/8" serrated, interchangeable front, white outline rear adjustable for windage and elevation.
Features: Built on the same frame as the Wesson 357; smooth, wide trigger with over-travel adjustment, wide spur hammer, with short double-action travel. Available in Brite blue or stainless steel. Reintroduced 1997. Contact Dan Wesson Firearms for complete price list.

Price: 2-1/2" bbl., blue **$357.00**
Price: As above, stainless **$400.00**
Price: With 4", vent. rib, blue **$392.00**
Price: As above, stainless **$432.00**
Price: Blue Pistol Pac, 22 LR......................... **$653.00**

Dan Wesson Firearms Model 40

Dan Wesson Firearms Model 445 Supermag Revolver

Similar size and weight as the Model 40 revolvers. Chambered for the 445 Supermag cartridge, a longer version of the 44 Magnum. Barrel lengths of 4", 6", 8", 10". Contact maker for complete price list. Reintroduced 1997. Made in the U.S. by Dan Wesson Firearms.

Price: 4", vent heavy, blue.............................. **$542.00**
Price: As above, stainless **$621.00**
Price: 8", vent heavy, blue............................. **$597.00**
Price: As above, stainless **$665.00**
Price: 10", vent heavy, blue............................ **$619.00**
Price: As above, stainless **$687.00**
Price: 8", vent slotted, blue **$577.00**
Price: As above, stainless **$636.00**
Price: 10", vent slotted, blue **$601.00**
Price: As above, stainless **$661.00**

DAN WESSON FIREARMS 45 PIN GUN

Caliber: 45 ACP, 6-shot.
Barrel: 5" with 1:14" twist; Taylor two-stage forcing cone; compensated shroud.
Weight: 54 oz. **Length:** 12.5" overall.
Stocks: Finger-groove Hogue Monogrip.
Sights: Pin front, fully adjustable rear. Has 8.375" sight radius.
Features: Based on 44 Magnum frame. Polished blue or brushed stainless steel. Uses half-moon clips with 45 ACP, or 45 Auto Rim ammunition. Reintroduced 1997. Made in U.S. by Dan Wesson Firearms.

Price: Blue, regular vent **$654.00**
Price: Blue, vent heavy **$663.00**
Price: Stainless, regular vent.......................... **$713.00**
Price: Stainless, vent heavy **$762.00**

DAN WESSON FIREARMS FB44, FB744 REVOLVERS

Caliber: 44 Magnum, 6-shot.
Barrel: 4", 5", 6", 8".
Weight: 50 oz. (4" barrel). **Length:** 9-3/4" overall (4" barrel).
Stocks: Hogue finger-groove rubber.
Sights: Interchangeable blade front, fully adjustable rear.
Features: Fixed, non-vented heavy barrel shrouds, but other features same as other Wesson revolvers. Brushed stainless or polished blue finish. Reintroduced 1997. Made in the U.S. by Dan Wesson Firearms.

Price: FB44-4 (4", blue)................................. **$447.00**
Price: As above, stainless (FB744-4) **$493.00**
Price: FB44-5 (5", blue)................................. **$450.00**
Price: As above, stainless (FB744-5) **$496.00**
Price: FB44-6 (6", blue)................................. **$454.00**
Price: As above, stainless (FB744-6) **$500.00**
Price: FB44-8 (8", blue)................................. **$462.00**
Price: As above, stainless (FB744-8) **$508.00**

DAN WESSON FIREARMS MODEL 738P REVOLVER
Caliber: 38 Special +P, 5-shot.
Barrel: 2".
Weight: 24.6 oz. **Length:** 6.5" overall.
Stocks: Pauferro wood or rubber.
Sights: Blade front, fixed notch rear.
Features: Designed for +P ammunition. Stainless steel construction. Reintroduced 1997. Made in U.S. by Dan Wesson Firearms.
Price: $340.00

DAN WESSON FIREARMS HUNTER SERIES REVOLVERS
Caliber: 357 Supermag, 41 Mag., 44 Mag., 445 Supermag, 6-shot.
Barrel: 6", 7-1/2", depending upon model.
Weight: About 64 oz. **Length:** 14" overall.
Stocks: Hogue finger-groove rubber, wood presentation.
Sights: Blade front, dovetailed Iron Sight Gunworks rear.
Features: Fixed barrel revolvers. Barrels have 1:18.75" twist, Alan Taylor two-stage forcing cone; non-fluted cylinder; bright blue or satin stainless. Reintroduced 1997. Made in U.S. by Dan Wesson Firearms.
Price: Open Hunter (open sights, 7-1/2" barrel), blue $805.00
Price: As above, stainless $849.00
Price: Compensated Open Hunter (6" compensated barrel, 7" shroud),
blue $837.00
Price: As above, stainless $881.00
Price: Scoped Hunter (7-1/2" barrel, no sights, comes with scope rings on shroud),
blue $838.00
Price: As above, stainless $881.00
Price: Compensated Scoped Hunter (6" barrel, 7" shroud, scope rings on shroud), blue $871.00
Price: As above, stainless $914.00

DAN WESSON FIREARMS FB15, FB715 REVOLVERS
Caliber: 357 Magnum, 6-shot.
Barrel: 2-1/2", 4" (Service models), 3", 4", 5", 6" (target models).
Weight: 40 oz. (4" barrel). **Length:** 9-3/4" overall (4" barrel).
Stocks: Service style or Hogue rubber.
Sights: Blade front, adjustable rear (Target); fixed rear on Service.
Features: Fixed barrel, but other features same as other Wesson revolvers. Service models in brushed stainless, satin blue, Traget in brushed stainless or polished blue. Reintroduced 1997. Made in U.S. by Dan Wesson Firearms.
Price: FB14-2 (Service, 2-1/2", blue) $289.00
Price: As above, 4" $296.00
Price: FB714-2 (Service, 2-1/2", stainless) $313.00
Price: As above, 4" $319.00
Price: FB15-3 (Target, 3", blue) $322.00
Price: As above, 5" $331.00
Price: FB715 (Target, 4", stainless) $354.00
Price: As above, 6" $370.00

Dan Wesson Firearms Model 738P

DAN WESSON FIREARMS MODEL 41V, 44V, 45V REVOLVERS
Caliber: 41 Mag., 44 Mag., 45 Colt, 6-shot.
Barrel: 4", 6", 8", 10"; interchangeable.
Weight: 48 oz. (4"). **Length:** 12" overall (6" bbl.)
Stocks: Smooth.
Sights: 1/8" serrated front, white outline rear adjustable for windage and elevation.
Features: Available in blue or stainless steel. Smooth, wide trigger with adjustable over-travel; wide hammer spur. Available in Pistol Pac set also. Reintroduced 1997. Contact Dan Wesson Firearms for complete price list.
Price: 41 Mag., 4", vent $447.00
Price: As above except in stainless $524.00
Price: 44 Mag., 4", blue $447.00
Price: As above except in stainless $524.00
Price: 45 Colt, 4", vent $447.00
Price: As above except in stainless $524.00

Dan Wesson Firearms FB715

Both classic six-shooters and modern adaptations for hunting and sport.

AMERICAN ARMS REGULATOR SINGLE-ACTIONS
Caliber: 357 Mag. 44-40, 45 Colt.
Barrel: 4-3/4", 5-1/2", 7-1/2".
Weight: 32 oz. (4-3/4" barrel). **Length:** 8-1/6" overall (4-3/4" barrel).
Stocks: Smooth walnut.
Sights: Blade front, groove rear.
Features: Blued barrel and cylinder, brass trigger guard and backstrap. Introduced 1992. Imported from Italy by American Arms, Inc.
Price: Regulator, single cylinder $359.00
Price: Regulator, dual cylinder (44-40/44 Spec. or 45 Colt/45 ACP)
.... $399.00
Price: Regulator DLX (all steel) $395.00

American Arms Bisley Single-Action Revolver
Similar to the Regulator except has Bisley-style grip with steel backstrap and trigger guard, Bisley-style hammer. Color case-hardened steel frame. Hammer block safety. Available with 4-3/4", 5-1/2", 7-1/2" barrel, 45, Colt only. Introduced 1997. Imported from Italy by American Arms, Inc.
Price: $475.00

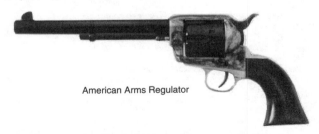

American Arms Regulator

AMERICAN FRONTIER POCKET RICHARDS & MASON NAVY
Caliber: 32, 5-shot cylinder.
Barrel: 4-3/4", 5-1/2".
Weight: NA. **Length:** NA.
Stocks: Varnished walnut.
Sights: Blade front, fixed rear.
Features: Shoots metallic-cartridge ammunition. Non-rebated cylinder; high-polish blue, silver-plated brass backstrap and trigger guard; ejector assembly; color case-hardened hammer and trigger. Introduced 1996. Imported from Italy by American Frontier Firearms Mfg.
Price: From $495.00

American Frontier 1871-1872 Open-Top

American Frontier Remington

AMERICAN FRONTIER 1871-1872 POCKET MODEL REVOLVER
Caliber: 32, 5-shot cylinder.
Barrel: 4-3/4", 5-1/2" round.
Weight: NA. **Length:** NA.
Stocks: Varnished walnut or Tiffany.
Sights: Blade front, fixed rear.
Features: Based on the 1862 Police percussion revolver converted to metallic cartridge. High polish blue finish with silver-plated brass backstrap and trigger guard, color case-hardened hammer. Introduced 1996. Imported from Italy by American Frontier Firearms Mfg.
Price: From $350.00

AMERICAN FRONTIER 1851 NAVY CONVERSION
Caliber: 38, 44.
Barrel: 4-3/4", 5-1/2", 7-1/2", octagon.
Weight: NA. **Length:** NA.
Stocks: Varnished walnut, Navy size.
Sights: Blade front, fixed rear.
Features: Shoots metallic cartridge ammunition. Non-rebated cylinder; blued steel backstrap and trigger guard; color case-hardened hammer, trigger, ramrod, plunger; no ejector rod assembly. Introduced 1996. Imported from Italy by American Frontier Firearms Mfg.
Price: $695.00

American Frontier 1851 Mason

CENTURY GUN DIST. MODEL 100 SINGLE-ACTION
Caliber: 30-30, 375 Win., 444 Marlin, 45-70, 50-70.
Barrel: 6-1/2" (standard), 8", 10".
Weight: 6 lbs. (loaded). **Length:** 15" overall (8" bbl.).
Stocks: Smooth walnut.
Sights: Ramp front, Millett adjustable square notch rear.
Features: Highly polished high tensile strength manganese bronze frame, blue cylinder and barrel; coil spring trigger mechanism. Calibers other than 45-70 start at $2,000.00. Contact maker for full price information. Introduced 1975. Made in U.S. From Century Gun Dist., Inc.
Price: 6-1/2" barrel, 45-70 .... $1,250.00

CIMARRON U.S. CAVALRY MODEL SINGLE-ACTION
Caliber: 45 Colt
Barrel: 7-1/2".
Weight: 42 oz. **Length:** 13-1/2" overall.
Stocks: Walnut.
Sights: Fixed.
Features: Has "A.P. Casey" markings; "U.S." plus patent dates on frame, serial number on backstrap, trigger guard, frame and cylinder, "APC" cartouche on left grip; color case-hardened frame and hammer, rest charcoal blue. Exact copy of the original. Imported by Cimarron Arms.
Price: $499.00

AMERICAN FRONTIER 1871-1872 OPEN-TOP REVOLVERS
Caliber: 38, 44.
Barrel: 4-3/4", 5-1/2", 7-1/2", 8" round.
Weight: NA. **Length:** NA.
Stocks: Varnished walnut.
Sights: Blade front, fixed rear.
Features: Reproduction of the early cartridge conversions from percussion. Made for metallic cartridges. High polish blued steel, silver-plated brass backstrap and trigger guard, color case-hardened hammer; straight non-rebated cylinder with naval engagement engraving; stamped with original patent dates. Does not have conversion breechplate. Introduced 1996. Imported from Italy by American Frontier Firearms Mfg.
Price: $795.00
Price: Tiffany model with Tiffany grips, silver and gold finish with engraving. $995.00

AMERICAN FRONTIER REMINGTON NEW MODEL REVOLVER
Caliber: 38, 44.
Barrel: 5-1/2", 7-1/2"**Weight:** NA. **Length:** NA.
Stocks: Varnished walnut.
Sights: Blade front, fixed rear.
Features: Replica of the factory conversions by Remington between 1863 and 1875. High polish blue or silver finish with color case-hardened hammer; has original loading lever and no gate or ejector assembly. Introduced 1996. Imported from Italy by American Frontier Firearms Mfg.
Price: $695.00

AMERICAN FRONTIER RICHARDS 1860 ARMY
Caliber: 38, 44.
Barrel: 4-3/4", 5-1/2", 7-1/2", round.
Weight: NA. **Length:** NA.
Stocks: Varnished walnut, Army size.
Sights: Blade front, fixed rear.
Features: Shoots metallic cartridge ammunition. Rebated cylinder; available with or without ejector assembly; high-polish blue including backstrap; silver-plated trigger guard; color case-hardened hammer and trigger. Introduced 1996. Imported from Italy by American Frontier Firearms Mfg.
Price: $695.00

AMERICAN FRONTIER REMINGTON NEW ARMY CAVALRY
Caliber: 38, 44, 45.
Barrel: 5-1/2", 7-1/2", 8".
Weight: NA. **Length:** NA.
Stocks: Varnished walnut
Sights: Blade front, fixed rear.
Features: High polish blue finish; color case-hardened hammer. Has ejector assembly, loading gate. Government inspector's cartouche on left grip, sub-inspector's initials on various parts. Introduced 1997. Imported from Italy by American Frontier Firearms Mfg.
Price: Artillery model (5-1/2" barrel only) $795.00
Price: $795.00

American Frontier 1851 Navy Richards & Mason Conversion
Similar to the 1851 Navy Conversion except has Mason ejector assembly. Introduced 1996. Imported from Italy by American Frontier Firearms Mfg.
Price: $695.00

Century Model 100

Cimarron Rough Rider Artillery Model Single-Action
Similar to the U.S. Cavalry model except has 5-1/2" barrel, weighs 39 oz., and is 11-1/2" overall. U.S. markings and cartouche, case-hardened frame and hammer; 45 Colt only.
Price: $499.00

CIMARRON 1873 FRONTIER SIX SHOOTER

Caliber: 38 WCF, 357 Mag., 44 WCF, 44 Spec., 45 Colt.
Barrel: 4-3/4", 5-1/2", 7-1/2".
Weight: 39 oz. **Length:** 10" overall (4" barrel).
Stocks: Walnut.
Sights: Blade front, fixed or adjustable rear.
Features: Uses "old model" blackpowder frame with "Bullseye" ejector or New Model frame. Imported by Cimarron Arms.
Price: 4-3/4" barrel **$469.00**
Price: 5-1/2" barrel **$469.00**
Price: 7-1/2" barrel **$469.00**

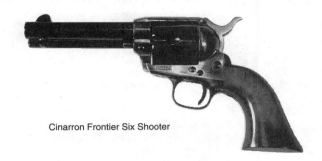

Cimarron Frontier Six Shooter

CIMARRON NEW THUNDERER REVOLVER

Caliber: 357 Mag., 44 WCF, 44 Spec., 45 Colt, 6-shot.
Barrel: 3-1/2", 4-3/4", with ejector.
Weight: 38 oz. (3-1/2" barrel). **Length:** NA.
Stocks: Hand-checkered walnut.
Sights: Blade front, notch rear.
Features: Thunderer grip; color case-hardened frame with balance blued, or nickel finish. Introduced 1993. Imported by Cimarron Arms.
Price: Color case-hardened **$489.00**
Price: Nickeled **$639.00**

COLT SINGLE-ACTION ARMY REVOLVER

Caliber: 44-40, 45 Colt, 6-shot.
Barrel: 4-3/4", 5-1/2", 7-1/2".
Weight: 40 oz. (4-3/4" barrel). **Length:** 10-1/4" overall (4-3/4" barrel).
Stocks: Black Eagle composite.
Sights: Blade front, notch rear.
Features: Available in full nickel finish with nickel grip medallions, or Royal Blue with color case-hardened frame, gold grip medallions. Reintroduced 1992.
Price: **$1,213.00**

E.A.A. BOUNTY HUNTER SA REVOLVERS

Caliber: 22 LR/22 WMR, 357 Mag., 44 Mag., 45 Colt, 6-shot.
Barrel: 4-1/2", 7-1/2".
Weight: 2.5 lbs. **Length:** 11" overall (4-5/8" barrel).
Stocks: Smooth walnut.
Sights: Blade front, grooved topstrap rear.
Features: Transfer bar safety; three position hammer; hammer forged barrel. Introduced 1992. Imported by European American Armory.
Price: Blue or case-hardened **$280.00**
Price: Nickel **$298.00**
Price: 22LR/22WMR, blue **$187.20**
Price: As above, nickel **$204.36**

EMF HARTFORD SINGLE-ACTION REVOLVERS

Caliber: 22 LR, 357 Mag., 32-20, 38-40, 44-40, 44 Spec., 45 Colt.
Barrel: 4-3/4", 5-1/2", 7-1/2".
Weight: 45 oz. **Length:** 13" overall (7-1/2" barrel).
Stocks: Smooth walnut.
Sights: Blade front, fixed rear.
Features: Identical to the original Colts with inspector cartouche on left grip, original patent dates and U.S. markings. All major parts serial numbered using original Colt-style lettering, numbering. Bullseye ejector head and color case-hardening on frame and hammer. Introduced 1990. From E.M.F.
Price: **$600.00**
Price: Cavalry or Artillery **$655.00**
Price: Nickel plated **$725.00**
Price: Engraved, nickel plated **$840.00**

EMF 1894 Bisley Revolver

Similar to the Hartford single-action revolver except has special grip frame and trigger guard, wide spur hammer; available in 45 Colt only, 5-1/2" or 7-1/2" barrel. Introduced 1995. Imported by E.M.F.
Price: Blue **$680.00**
Price: Nickel **$805.00**

EMF Hartford Pinkerton Single-Action Revolver

Same as the regular Hartford except has 4" barrel with ejector tube and birds' head grip. Calibers 32-20, 38-40, 44-40, 44 Special, 45 Colt. Introduced 1997. Imported by E.M.F.
Price: **$475.00**

EMF Hartford Express Single-Action Revolver

Same as the regular Hartford model except uses grip of the Colt Lightning revolver. Barrel lengths of 4", 4-3/4", 5-1/2". Introduced 1997. Imported by E.M.F.
Price: **$475.00**

COLT COWBOY SINGLE-ACTION REVOLVER

Caliber: 45 Colt, 6-shot.
Barrel: 5-1/2".
Weight: 42 oz.
Stocks: Black composition, first generation style.
Sights: Blade front, notch rear.
Features: Dimensional replica of Colt's original Peacemaker with medium-size color case-hardened frame; transfer bar safety system; half-cock loading. Introduced 1998. Made in U.S. by Colt's Mfg. Co.
Price: About **$600.00**

Colt Single Action Army

E.A.A. Bounty Hunter

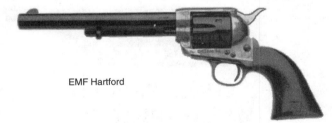

EMF Hartford

EMF 1894 Bisley

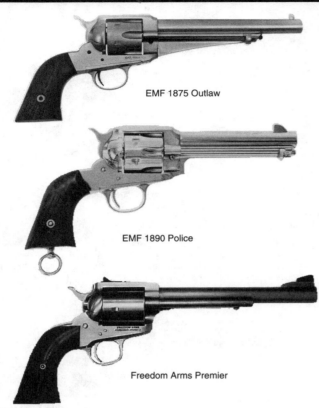

EMF 1875 Outlaw

EMF 1890 Police

Freedom Arms Premier

Freedom Arms Model 654 Revolver

Similar to the 454 except chambered for 41 Magnum with 5-shot cylinder. Introduced 1998. Made in U.S. by Freedom Arms.

Price: Field Grade, adjustable sights $1,310.00
Price: Premier Grade, adjustable sights $1,730.00
Price: Silhouette. $1,417.85

Freedom Arms Model 353 Revolver

Similar to the Premier 454 Casull except chambered for 357 Magnum with 5-shot cylinder; 4-3/4", 6", 7-1/2" or 9" barrel. Weighs 59 oz. with 7-1/2" barrel. Field grade model has adjustable sights, matte finish, Pachmayr grips, 7-1/2" or 10" barrel; Silhouette has 9" barrel, Patridge front sight, Iron Sight Gun Works Silhouette adjustable rear, Pachmayr grips, trigger over-travel adjustment screw. All stainless steel. Introduced 1992.

Price: Field Grade $1,310.00
Price: Premier Grade (brushed finish, impregnated hardwood grips, Premier Grade sights) $1,730.00
Price: Silhouette (9", 357 Mag., 10", 44 Mag.) $1,418.00

CONSULT
SHOOTER'S MARKETPLACE
Page 225, This Issue

HERITAGE ROUGH RIDER REVOLVER

Caliber: 22 LR, 22 LR/22 WMR combo, 6-shot.
Barrel: 2-3/4", 3-1/2", 4-3/4", 6-1/2", 9".
Weight: 31 to 38 oz. Length: NA
Stocks: Exotic hardwood.
Sights: Blade front, fixed rear.
Features: Hammer block safety. High polish blue or nickel finish. Introduced 1993. Made in U.S. by Heritage Mfg., Inc.
Price: . . . . $119.95 to $174.95
Price: 2-3/4", 3-1/2", 4-3/4" birdshead grip . . . . $139.95 to $174.95

EMF 1875 OUTLAW REVOLVER

Caliber: 357 Mag., 44-40, 45 Colt.
Barrel: 7-1/2".
Weight: 46 oz. Length: 13-1/2" overall.
Stocks: Smooth walnut.
Sights: Blade front, fixed groove rear.
Features: Authentic copy of 1875 Remington with firing pin in hammer; color case-hardened frame, blue cylinder, barrel, steel backstrap and brass trigger guard. Also available in nickel, factory engraved. Imported by E.M.F.
Price: All calibers $465.00
Price: Nickel. $550.00
Price: Engraved $600.00
Price: Engraved Nickel $710.00

EMF 1890 Police Revolver

Similar to the 1875 Outlaw except has 5-1/2" barrel, weighs 40 oz., with 12-1/2" overall length. Has lanyard ring in butt. No web under barrel. Calibers 357, 44-40, 45 Colt. Imported by E.M.F.
Price: All calibers $470.00
Price: Nickel. $560.00
Price: Engraved $620.00
Price: Engraved nickel $725.00

FREEDOM ARMS 454 PREMIER SINGLE-ACTION REVOLVER

Caliber: 44 Mag., 454 Casull with 45 Colt, 45 ACP, 45 Win. Mag. optional cylinders, 5-shot.
Barrel: 4-3/4", 6", 7-1/2", 10".
Weight: 50 oz. Length: 14" overall (7-1/2" bbl.).
Stocks: Impregnated hardwood.
Sights: Blade front, notch or adjustable rear.
Features: All stainless steel construction; sliding bar safety system. Lifetime warranty. Made in U.S. by Freedom Arms, Inc.
Price: Field Grade (matte finish, Pachmayr grips), adjustable sights, 4-3/4", 6", 7-1/2", 10" $1,370.00
Price: Field Grade, fixed sights, 4-3/4", 6", 7-1/2", 10" $1,218.00
Price: Field Grade, 44 Rem. Mag., adjustable sights, all lengths . . $1,310.00
Price: Premier Grade 454 (brush finish, impregnated hardwood grips) adjustable sights, 4-3/4", 6", 7-1/2", 10" $1,790.00
Price: Premier Grade, fixed sights, all barrel lengths $1,620.00
Price: Premier Grade, 44 Rem. Mag., adjustable sights, all lengths $1,730.00
Price: Fitted 45 ACP, 45 Colt or 45 Win. Mag cylinder, add $343.00

Freedom Arms Model 555 Revolver

Same as the 454 Casull except chambered for the 50 A.E. (Action Express) cartridge. Offered in Premier and Field Grades with adjustable sights, 4-3/4", 6", 7-1/2" or 10" barrel. Introduced 1994. Made in U.S. by Freedom Arms, Inc.
Price: Premier Grade $1,790.00
Price: Field Grade $1,370.00

FREEDOM ARMS MODEL 97 MID FRAME REVOLVER

Caliber: 357 Mag., 6-shot cylinder.
Barrel: 5-1/2", 7-1/2".
Weight: 40 oz. (5-1/2"barrel). Length: 10-3/4"overall (5-1/2"barrel).
Stocks: Wine wood.
Sights: Blade on ramp front, fixed or fully adjustable rear.
Features: Made of stainless steel; polished cylinder, matte frame. Introduced 1997. Made in U.S. by Freedom Arms.
Price: $1,462.00

Heritage Rough Rider

IAR MODEL 1873 SIX SHOOTER

Caliber: 22 LR/22 WMR combo
Barrel: 5-1/2".
Weight: 36-1/2" oz. Length: 11-3/8" overall.
Stocks: One-piece walnut.
Sights: Blade front, notch rear.
Features: A 3/4-scale reproduction. Color case-hardened frame, blued barrel. All-Steel construction. Made by Uberti. Imported from Italy by IAR, Inc.
Price: $400.00

IAR MODEL 1873 FRONTIER REVOLVER
Caliber: 22 RL, 22 LR/22 WMR.
Barrel: 4-3/4".
Weight: 45 oz. **Length:** 10-1/2"overall.
Stocks: One-piece walnut with inspector's cartouche.
Sights: Blade front, notch rear.
Features: Color case-hardened frame, blued barrel, black nickel-plated brass trigger guard and backstrap. Bright nickel and engraved versions available. Introduced 1997. Imported from Italy by IAR, Inc.
Price: **$400.00**
Price: Nickel-plated **$485.00**
Price: 22 LR/22WMR combo **$425.00**

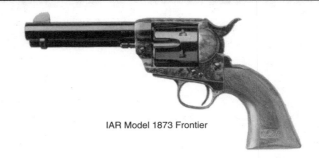

IAR Model 1873 Frontier

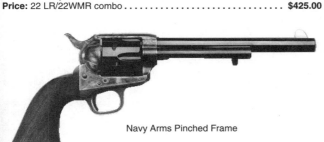

Navy Arms Pinched Frame

Navy Arms Bisley

Navy Arms 1873

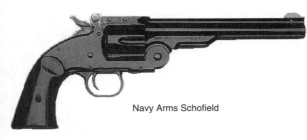

Navy Arms Schofield

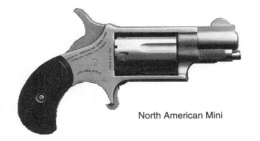

North American Mini

NAVY ARMS FLAT TOP TARGET MODEL REVOLVER
Caliber: 45 Colt, 6-shot cylinder.
Barrel: 7-1/2".
Weight: 40 oz. **Length:** 13-1/4" overall.
Stocks: Smooth walnut.
Sights: Spring-loaded German silver front, rear adjustable for windage.
Features: Replica of Colt's Flat Top Frontier target revolver made from 1888 to 1896. Blue with color case-hardened frame. Introduced 1997. Imported by Navy Arms.
Price: **$430.00**

NAVY ARMS "PINCHED FRAME" SINGLE-ACTION REVOLVER
Caliber: 45 Colt.
Barrel: 7-1/2".
Weight: 37 oz. **Length:** 13" overall.
Stocks: Smooth walnut
Sights: German silver blade, notch rear.
Features: Replica of Colt's original Peacemaker. Color case-hardened frame, hammer, rest charcoal blued. Introduced 1997. Imported by Navy Arms.
Price: **$415.00**

NAVY ARMS BISLEY MODEL SINGLE-ACTION REVOLVER
Caliber: 44-40 or 45 Colt, 6-shot cylinder.
Barrel: 4-3/4", 5-1/2", 7-1/2"
Weight: 40 oz. **Length:** 12-1/2" overall (7-1/2" barrel).
Stocks: Smooth walnut.
Sights: Blade front, notch rear.
Features: Replica of Colt's Bisley Model. Polished blue finish, color case-hardened frame. Introduced 1997. Imported by Navy Arms.
Price: **$445.00**

NAVY ARMS 1873 SINGLE-ACTION REVOLVER
Caliber: 357 Mag., 44-40, 45 Colt, 6-shot cylinder.
Barrel: 3", 4-3/4", 5-1/2", 7-1/2".
Weight: 36 oz. **Length:** 10-3/4" overall (5-1/2" barrel).
Stocks: Smooth walnut.
Sights: Blade front, groove in topstrap rear.
Features: Blue with color case-hardened frame, or nickel. Introduced 1991. Imported by Navy Arms.
Price: Blue **$390.00**
Price: Nickel **$445.00**
Price: 1873 U.S. Cavalry Model (7-1/2", 45 Colt, arsenal markings) **$480.00**
Price: 1895 U.S. Artillery Model (as above, 5-1/2" barrel) **$480.00**

NAVY ARMS 1875 SCHOFIELD REVOLVER
Caliber: 44-40, 45 Colt, 6-shot cylinder.
Barrel: 5", 7".
Weight: 39 oz. **Length:** 10-3/4" overall (5" barrel).
Stocks: Smooth walnut.
Sights: Blade front, notch rear.
Features: Replica of Smith & Wesson Model 3 Schofield. Single-action, top-break with automatic ejection. Polished blue finish. Introduced 1994. Imported by Navy Arms.
Price: Wells Fargo, 5" barrel. **$795.00**
Price: U.S. Cavalry model, 7" barrel, military markings **$795.00**

NORTH AMERICAN MINI-REVOLVERS
Caliber: 22 Short, 22 LR, 22 WMR, 5-shot.
Barrel: 1-1/8", 1-5/8".
Weight: 4 to 6.6 oz. **Length:** 3-5/8" to 6-1/8" overall.
Stocks: Laminated wood.
Sights: Blade front, notch fixed rear.
Features: All stainless steel construction. Polished satin and matte finish. Engraved models available. From North American Arms.
Price: 22 Short, 22 LR **$162.00**
Price: 22 WMR, 1-5/8" bbl. **$184.00**
Price: 22 WMR, 1-1/8" or 1-5/8" bbl. with extra 22 LR cylinder **$218.00**

NORTH AMERICAN MINI-MASTER

Caliber: 22 LR, 22 WMR, 5-shot cylinder.
Barrel: 4".
Weight: 10.7 oz. **Length:** 7.75" overall.
Stocks: Checkered hard black rubber.
Sights: Blade front, white outline rear adjustable for elevation, or fixed.
Features: Heavy vent barrel; full-size grips. Non-fluted cylinder. Introduced 1989.
Price: Adjustable sight, 22 WMR or 22 LR $292.00
Price: As above with extra WMR/LR cylinder $329.00
Price: Fixed sight, 22 WMR or 22 LR $276.00
Price: As above with extra WMR/LR cylinder $314.00

Ruger Bisley Small Frame Revolver

Similar to the Single-Six except frame is styled after the classic Bisley "flat-top." Most mechanical parts are unchanged. Hammer is lower and smoothly curved with a deeply checkered spur. Trigger is strongly curved with a wide smooth surface. Longer grip frame designed with a hand-filling shape, and the trigger guard is a large oval. Adjustable dovetail rear sight; front sight base accepts interchangeable square blades of various heights and styles. Has an unfluted cylinder and roll engraving. Weighs about 41 oz. Chambered for 22 LR, 6-1/2" barrel only. Introduced 1985.
Price: $380.00

Ruger Blackhawk

Ruger Bisley Single-Action Revolver

Similar to standard Blackhawk except the hammer is lower with a smoothly curved, deeply checkered wide spur. The trigger is strongly curved with a wide smooth surface. Longer grip frame has a hand-filling shape. Adjustable rear sight, ramp-style front. Has an unfluted cylinder and roll engraving, adjustable sights. Chambered for 357, 44 Mags. and 45 Colt; 7-1/2" barrel; overall length of 13". Introduced 1985.
Price: $450.00

Ruger New Bearcat

RUGER NEW BEARCAT SINGLE-ACTION

Caliber: 22 LR, 6-shot.
Barrel: 4".
Weight: 23 oz. **Length:** 8-7/8" overall.
Stocks: Smooth rosewood with Ruger medallion.
Sights: Blade front, fixed notch rear.
Features: Reintroduction of the Ruger Super Bearcat with slightly lengthened frame, Ruger patented transfer bar safety system. Available in blue only. Introduced 1993. From Sturm, Ruger & Co.
Price: SBC4, blue $320.00
Price: 9-1/2", blue $318.00

North American Black Widow Revolver

Similar to the Mini-Master except has 2" heavy vent barrel. Built on the 22 WMR frame. Non-fluted cylinder, black rubber grips. Available with either Millett Low Profile fixed sights or Millett sight adjustable for elevation only. Overall length 5-7/8", weighs 8.8 oz. From North American Arms.
Price: Adjustable sight, 22 LR or 22 WMR $259.00
Price: As above with extra WMR/LR cylinder $296.00
Price: Fixed sight, 22 LR or 22 WMR $243.00
Price: As above with extra WMR/LR cylinder $281.00

RUGER SUPER SINGLE-SIX CONVERTIBLE

Caliber: 22 LR, 6-shot; 22 WMR in extra cylinder.
Barrel: 4-5/8", 5-1/2", 6-1/2", (6-groove).
Weight: 34-1/2 oz. (6-1/2" bbl.). **Length:** 11-13/16" overall (6-1/2" bbl.).
Stocks: Smooth American walnut.
Sights: Improved Patridge front on ramp, fully adjustable rear protected by integral frame ribs; or fixed sight.
Features: Ruger transfer bar safety system, gate-controlled loading, hardened chrome-moly steel frame, wide trigger, music wire springs throughout, independent firing pin.
Price: 4-5/8", 5-1/2", 6-1/2", barrel, blue, fixed or adjustable sight (5-1/2", 6-1/2") $313.00
Price: 5-1/2", 6-1/2" bbl. only, high-gloss stainless steel, fixed or adjustable sight $393.00

> Consult our Directory pages for the location of firms mentioned.

RUGER BLACKHAWK REVOLVER

Caliber: 357 Mag./38 Spec., 45 Colt, 6-shot.
Barrel: 4-5/8" or 5-1/2", either caliber; 7-1/2" (45 Colt only).
Weight: 42 oz. (6-1/2" bbl.). **Length:** 12-1/4" overall (5-1/2" bbl.).
Stocks: American walnut.
Sights: 1/8" ramp front, micro-click rear adjustable for windage and elevation.
Features: Ruger transfer bar safety system, independent firing pin, hardened chrome-moly steel frame, music wire springs throughout.
Price: Blue, 357 Mag. (4-5/8", 5-1/2"), BN34, BN36 . . . . $360.00
Price: Blue, 357/9mm Convertible (4-5/8", 5-1/2"), BN34X, BN36X $360.00
Price: Blue, 45 Colt (4-5/8", 5-1/2"), BN42, BN45 . . . . $360.00
Price: Stainless, 357 Mag. (4-5/8", 5-1/2"), KBN34, KBN36 . . . . $443.00
Price: Blue, 45 Colt with extra 45 ACP cylinder, 4-5/8" (BN44X), 5-1/2" (BN455X) $380.00

Ruger Bisley Single-Action

RUGER SUPER BLACKHAWK

Caliber: 44 Mag., 6-shot. Also fires 44 Spec.
Barrel: 4-5/8", 5-1/2", 7-1/2", 10-1/2".
Weight: 48 oz. (7-1/2" bbl.), 51 oz. (10-1/2" bbl.). **Length:** 13-3/8" overall (7-1/2" bbl.).
Stocks: American walnut.
Sights: 1/8" ramp front, micro-click rear adjustable for windage and elevation.
Features: Ruger transfer bar safety system, non-fluted cylinder, steel grip and cylinder frame, square back trigger guard, wide serrated trigger and wide spur hammer.
Price: Blue (S45N, S47N, S411N) $413.00
Price: Stainless (KS45N, KS47N, KS411N) $450.00
Price: Stainless, 10-1/2" bull barrel (KS411N) $455.00
Price: Blue, 10-1/2" bull barrel (S411N) $418.00
Price: Stainless, 4-5/8", hunter grip frame, laminated grips KSH458 . . . . $467.00
Price: Stainless, 7-1/2", hunter grip frame, laminated grips KSH47 . . . . $467.00

Ruger Vaquero

Ruger Bisley-Vaquero Single-Action Revolver

Similar to the Vaquero except has Bisley-style hammer, grip and trigger and is available in 44 Magnum and 45 Colt only, with 5-1/2" barrel. Has smooth rosewood grips with Ruger medallion. Introduced 1997. From Sturm, Ruger & Co.

Price: Color case-hardened frame, blue grip frame, barrel and cylinder, RBNV-475, RBNV-455 ....$450.00
Price: High-gloss stainless steel, KRBNV-475, KRBNV-455 ....$487.00
Price: For simulated ivory grips add $36.00

TRADITIONS 1851 NAVY CONVERSION REVOLVER

Caliber: 38 Spec.
Barrel: 7-1/2".
Weight: 40 oz. **Length:** 14-1/2" overall.
Stocks: Smooth walnut.
Sights: Post front, hammer-notch rear.
Features: Steel frame, brass trigger guard. Introduced 1998. From Traditions.
Price: $365.00

TRADITIONS 1875 SCHOFIELD REVOLVER

Caliber: 44-40, 45 Schofield, 45 Colt, 6-shot cylinder.
Barrel: 5-1/2".
Weight: 40 oz. **Length:** 11-1/4" overall.
Stocks: Walnut.
Sights: Blade front, notch rear.
Features: Blue finish, case-hardened frame, hammer, trigger. Introduced 1998. From Traditions.
Price: $735.00

Uberti Cattleman

Uberti 1873 Buckhorn Single-Action

A slightly larger version of the Cattleman revolver. Available in 44 Magnum or 44 Magnum/44-40 convertible, otherwise has same specs.
Price: Steel backstrap, trigger guard, fixed sights $410.00
Price: Convertible (two cylinders) $475.00

UBERTI 1875 SA ARMY OUTLAW REVOLVER

Caliber: 357 Mag., 44-40, 45 Colt, 45 Colt/45 ACP convertible, 6-shot.
Barrel: 5-1/2", 7-1/2".
Weight: 44 oz. **Length:** 13-3/4" overall.
Stocks: Smooth walnut.
Sights: Blade front, notch rear.
Features: Replica of the 1875 Remington S.A. Army revolver. Brass trigger guard, color case-hardened frame, rest blued. Imported by Uberti U.S.A.
Price: $435.00
Price: 45 Colt/45 ACP convertible $475.00

RUGER VAQUERO SINGLE-ACTION REVOLVER

Caliber: 357 Mag., 44-40, 44 Mag., 45 Colt, 6-shot.
Barrel: 4-5/8", 5-1/2", 7-1/2".
Weight: 41 oz. **Length:** 13-3/8" overall (7-1/2" barrel).
Stocks: Smooth rosewood with Ruger medallion.
Sights: Blade front, fixed notch rear.
Features: Uses Ruger's patented transfer bar safety system and loading gate interlock with classic styling. Blued model has color case-hardened finish on the frame, the rest polished and blued. Stainless model has high-gloss polish. Introduced 1993. From Sturm, Ruger & Co.
Price: 357 Mag. BNV34 (4-5/8"), BNV35 (5-1/2").............. $434.00
Price: 357 Mag. KBNV34 (4-5/8"), KBNV35 (5-1/2") stainless..... $434.00
Price: BNV44 (4-5/8"), BNV445 (5-1/2"), BNV45 (7-1/2"), blue $434.00
Price: KBNV44 (4-5/8"), KBNV455 (5-1/2"), KBNV45 (7-1/2"), stainless
.... $434.00
Price: 44 Mag. BNV475IE (engraved cylinder, simulated ivory grips), blue, 5-1/2".. $583.00
Price: 44 Mag. KBNV475IE (engraved cylinder, simulated ivory grips), stainless, 5-1/2".. $583.00
Price: 45 Colt BNV455IE (engraved cylinder, simulated ivory grips), blue, 5-1/2".. $583.00
Price: 45 Colt KBNV455IE (engraved cylinder, simulated ivory grips), stainless, 5-1/2".. $583.00

TRADITIONS 1873 SINGLE-ACTION REVOLVERS

Caliber: 22 LR, 357 Mag., 44-40, 45 Colt, 6-shot cylinder.
Barrel: 4-3/4", 5-1/2", 7-1/2".
Weight: 44 oz. **Length:** 10-3/4" overall (5-1/2" barrel).
Stocks: Walnut.
Sights: Blade front, groove in topstrap rear.
Features: Blued barrel, cylinder, color case-hardened frame, blue or brass trigger guard. Nickel-plated frame with polished brass trigger guard available in 357 Mag., 44-40, 45 Colt. Introduced 1998. From Traditions.
Price: .... $345.00 to $395.00

Traditions 1894 Bisley Revolver

Similar to the 1873 except has special tight-curl grip frame, modified trigger guard, wide-spur hammer. Available in 45 Colt only with 4-3/4" barrel. Introduced 1998. From Traditions.
Price: $425.00

Traditions Thunderer Revolver

Similar to the 1873 single-action revolver except has special birds-head grip with spur, and smooth or checkered walnut grips. Introduced 1998. From Traditions.
Price: With smooth grips $397.00
Price: With checkered grips $459.00

UBERTI 1873 CATTLEMAN SINGLE-ACTIONS

Caliber: 22 LR/22 WMR, 38 Spec., 357 Mag., 44 Spec., 44-40, 45 Colt/45 ACP, 6-shot.
Barrel: 4-3/4", 5-1/2", 7-1/2"; 44-40, 45 Colt also with 3", 3-1/2", 4".
Weight: 38 oz. (5-1/2" bbl.). **Length:** 10-3/4" overall (5-1/2" bbl.).
Stocks: One-piece smooth walnut.
Sights: Blade front, groove rear; fully adjustable rear available.
Features: Steel or brass backstrap, trigger guard; color case-hardened frame, blued barrel, cylinder. Imported from Italy by Uberti U.S.A.
Price: Steel backstrap, trigger guard, fixed sights $435.00
Price: Brass backstrap, trigger guard, fixed sights.............. $365.00
Price: Bisley model...................................... $435.00

Uberti 1875 Army

UBERTI 1890 ARMY OUTLAW REVOLVER

Caliber: 357 Mag., 44-40, 45 Colt, 45 Colt/45 ACP convertible, 6-shot.
Barrel: 5-1/2", 7-1/2".
Weight: 37 oz. **Length:** 12-1/2" overall.
Stocks: American walnut.
Sights: Blade front, groove rear.
Features: Replica of the 1890 Remington single-action. Brass trigger guard, rest is blued. Imported by Uberti U.S.A.
Price: $435.00
Price: 45 Colt/45 ACP convertible $475.00

U.S. PATENT FIRE-ARMS SINGLE ACTION ARMY REVOLVER
Caliber: 22 LR, 22 WMR, 357 Mag., 44 Russian, 38-40, 44-40, 45 Colt, 6-shot cylinder.
Barrel: 3", 4", 4-3/4", 5-1/2", 7-1/2", 10".
Weight: 37 oz. **Length:** NA.
Stocks: Smooth walnut.
Sights: Blade front, notch rear.
Features: Recreation of original guns; 3" and 4" have no ejector. Available with all-blue, blue with color case-hardening, or full nickel-plate finish. Made in Italy; available from United States Patent Fire-Arms Mfg. Co.
Price: 3" blue $600.00
Price: 4-3/4", blue/cased-colors $732.00
Price: 7-1/2", blue/case-colors $739.00
Price: 10", nickel $847.50

U.S. Patent Fire-Arms Nettleton Cavalry Revolver
Similar to the single Action Army, except in 45 Colt only, with 7-1/2" barrel, color case-hardened/blue finish, and has old-style hand numbering, exact cartouche branding and correct inspector hand-stamp markings. Made in Italy, available from United States Patent Fire-Arms Mfg. Co.
Price: $950.00
Price: Artillery Model, 5-1/2" barrel $950.00

U.S. Patent Fire-Arms Bird Head Model Revolver
Similar to the Single Action Army except has bird's-head grip and comes with 3-1/2", 4" or 4-1/2" barrel. Made in Italy; available from United States Patent Fire-Arms Mfg. Co.
Price: 3-1/2", blue $635.50
Price: 4", blue with color case-hardening $735.00
Price: 4-1/2", nickel-plated $795.50

U.S. Patent Fire-Arms Flattop Target Revolver
Similar to the Single Action Army except 4-3/4", 5-1/2" or 7-1/2" barrel, two-piece hard rubber stocks, flat top frame, adjustable rear sight. Made in Italy; available from United States Patent Fire-Arms Mfg. Co.
Price: 4-3/4", blue, polished hammer $690.00
Price: 4-3/4", blue, case-colored hammer $813.00
Price: 5-1/2", blue, case-colored hammer $816.00
Price: 5-1/2", nickel-plated $765.00
Price: 7-1/2", blue, polished hammer $717.00
Price: 7-1/2", blue, case-colored hammer $822.00

U.S. PATENT FIRE-ARMS BISLEY MODEL REVOLVER
Caliber: 4 Colt, 6-shot cylinder.
Barrel: 4-3/4", 5-1/2", 7-1/2", 10".
Weight: 38 oz. (5-1/2" barrel). **Length:** NA.
Stocks: Smooth walnut.
Sights: Blade front, notch rear.
Features: Available in all-blue, blue with color case-hardening, or full nickel plate finish. Made in Italy; available from United States Patent Fire-Arms Mfg. Co.
Price: 4-3/4", blue $652.00
Price: 5-1/2", blue/case-colors $750.50
Price: 7-1/2", blue/case-colors $756.00
Price: 10", nickel $862.50

HANDGUNS—MISCELLANEOUS

Specially adapted single-shot and multi-barrel arms.

American Derringer Model 1

American Derringer Texas Commemorative
A Model 1 Derringer with solid brass frame, stainless steel barrel and rosewood grips. Available in 38 Spec., 44-40 Win., or 45 Colt. Introduced 1987.
Price: 38 Spec. $295.00
Price: 44-40 or 45 Colt $350.00
Price: Brass frame, 45 Colt $380.00

American Derringer Model 4
Similar to the Model 1 except has 4.1" barrel, overall length of 6", and weighs 16-1/2 oz.; chambered for 357 Mag., 357 Maximum, 45-70, 3" 410-bore shotshells or 45 Colt or 44 Mag. Made of stainless steel. Manual hammer block safety. Introduced 1985.
Price: 3" 410/45 Colt $365.00
Price: 3" 410/45 Colt or 45-70 (Alaskan Survival model) $400.00
Price: 44 Mag. with oversize grips $445.00
Price: Alaskan Survival model (45-70 upper barrel, 410 or 45 Colt lower) $400.00

American Derringer Model 7 Ultra Lightweight
Similar to Model 1 except made of high strength aircraft aluminum. Weighs 7-1/2 oz., 4.82" o.a.l.; rosewood stocks. Available in 22 LR, 22 WMR, 32 H&R Mag., 380 ACP, 38 Spec., 44 Spec. Introduced 1986.
Price: 22 LR, WMR $265.00
Price: 38 Spec. $265.00
Price: 380 ACP $265.00
Price: 32 H&R Mag/32 S&W Long $265.00
Price: 44 Spec. $505.00

AMERICAN DERRINGER MODEL 1
Caliber: 22 LR, 22 WMR, 30 Carbine, 30 Luger, 30-30 Win., 32 H&R Mag., 32-20, 380 ACP, 38 Super, 38 Spec., 38 Spec. shotshell, 38 Spec. +P, 9mm Para., 357 Mag., 357 Mag./45/410, 357 Maximum, 10mm, 40 S&W, 41 Mag., 38-40, 44-40 Win., 44 Spec., 44 Mag., 45 Colt, 45 Win. Mag., 45 ACP, 45 Colt/410, 45-70 single shot.
Barrel: 3".
Weight: 15-1/2 oz. (38 Spec.). **Length:** 4.82" overall.
Stocks: Rosewood, Zebra wood.
Sights: Blade front.
Features: Made of stainless steel with high-polish or satin finish. Two-shot capacity. Manual hammer block safety. Introduced 1980. Available in almost any pistol caliber. Contact the factory for complete list of available calibers and prices. From American Derringer Corp.
Price: 22 LR $260.00
Price: 38 Spec. $260.00
Price: 357 Maximum $285.00
Price: 357 Mag. $275.00
Price: 9mm, 380 .... $260.00
Price: 40 S&W $275.00
Price: 44 Spec., ... $338.00
Price: 44-40 Win., 45 Colt $338.00
Price: 30-30, 41, 44 Mags., 45 Win. Mag. $400.00
Price: 45-70, single shot $327.00
Price: 45 Colt, 410, 2-1/2" $365.00
Price: 45 ACP, 10mm Auto $280.00

American Derringer Model 6
Similar to the Model 1 except has 6" barrel chambered for 3" 410 shotshells or 22 WMR, 357 Mag., 45 ACP, 45 Colt; rosewood stocks; 8.2" o.a.l. and weighs 21 oz. Shoots either round for each barrel. Manual hammer block safety. Introduced 1986.
Price: 22 WMR $365.00
Price: 357 Mag. $365.00
Price: 45 Colt/410 .... $375.00
Price: 45 ACP $365.00

American Derringer Model 10 Lightweight
Similar to the Model 1 except frame is of aluminum, giving weight of 10 oz. Stainless barrels. Available in 38 Spec., 45 Colt or 45 ACP only. Matte gray finish. Introduced 1989.
Price: 45 Colt $325.00
Price: 45 ACP $270.00
Price: 38 Spec. $245.00

American Derringer Lady Derringer

Same as the Model 1 except has tuned action, is fitted with scrimshawed synthetic ivory grips; chambered for 32 H&R Mag. and 38 Spec.; 357 Mag., 45 Colt, 45/410. Deluxe Grade is highly polished; Deluxe Engraved is engraved in a pattern similar to that used on 1880s derringers. All come in a French fitted jewelry box. Introduced 1991.

Price: 32 H&R Mag. $305.00
Price: 357 Mag. $335.00
Price: 38 Spec. $290.00
Price: 45 Colt, 45/410 . . . . $365.00

Consult our Directory pages for the location of firms mentioned.

ANSCHUTZ MODEL 64P SPORT/TARGET PISTOL

Caliber: 22 LR, 22 WMR, 5-shot magazine.
Barrel: 10".
Weight: 3 lbs., 8 oz. **Length:** 18-1/2" overall.
Stock: Choate Rynite.
Sights: None furnished; grooved for scope mounting.
Features: Right-hand bolt; polished blue finish. Introduced 1998. Imported from Germany by AcuSport.
Price: 22 LR $455.95
Price: 22 WMR $479.95

BOND ARMS TEXAS DEFENDER DERRINGER

Caliber: 9mm Para, 38 Spec./357 Mag., 44 Spec./44 Mag., 45 Colt/410 shotshell.
Barrel: 3-1/2".
Weight: 21 oz. **Length:** 5" overall.
Stocks: Laminated black ash or rosewood.
Sights: Blade front, fixed rear.
Features: Interchangeable barrels; retracting firing pins; rebounding firing pins; cross-bolt safety; removable trigger guard; automatic extractor for rimmed calibers. Stainless steel construction with blasted/polished and ground combination finish. Introduced 1997. Made in U.S. by Bond Arms, Inc.
Price: $319.00

DAVIS BIG BORE DERRINGERS

Caliber: 22 WMR, 38 Spec., 9mm Para.
Barrel: 2.75".
Weight: 11.5 oz. **Length:** 4.65" overall.
Stocks: Textured black synthetic.
Sights: Blade front, fixed notch rear.
Features: Alloy frame, steel-lined barrels, steel breech block. Plunger-type safety with integral hammer block. Chrome or black Teflon finish. Introduced 1992. Made in U.S. by Davis Industries.
Price: $98.00
Price: 9mm Para $104.00

Davis D-38 Derringer

DOWNSIZER WSP SINGLE SHOT PISTOL

Caliber: 22 WMR, 32 H&R Mag., 380 ACP, 9mm Para, 357 Magnum, 40 S&W, 45 ACP.
Barrel: 2.10". **Weight:** 11 oz. **Length:** 3.25" overall.
Stocks: Black polymer.
Sights: None.
Features: Single shot, tip-up barrel. Double action only. Stainless steel construction. Measures .900" thick. Introduced 1997. From Downsizer Corp.
Price: $329.00

AMERICAN DERRINGER DA 38 MODEL

Caliber: 22 LR, 9mm Para., 38 Spec., 357 Mag., 40 S&W.
Barrel: 3".
Weight: 14.5 oz. **Length:** 4.8" overall.
Stocks: Rosewood, walnut or other hardwoods.
Sights: Fixed.
Features: Double-action only; two-shots. Manual safety. Made of satin-finished stainless steel and aluminum. Introduced 1989. From American Derringer Corp.
Price: 22 LR, 38 Spec. $325.00
Price: 9mm Para. $335.00
Price: 357 Mag., 40 S&W $365.00

Bond Arms Texas Defender

BROWN CLASSIC SINGLE SHOT PISTOL

Caliber: 17 Ackley Hornet through 45-70 Govt.
Barrel: 15" airgauged match grade.
Weight: About 3 lbs., 7 oz.
Stocks: Walnut; thumbrest target style.
Sights: None furnished; drilled and tapped for scope mounting.
Features: Falling block action gives rigid barrel-receiver mating; hand-fitted and headspaced. Introduced 1998. Made in U.S. by E.A. Brown Mfg.
Price: $499.00

DAVIS LONG-BORE DERRINGERS

Caliber: 22 WMR, 38 Spec., 9mm Para.
Barrel: 3.5".
Weight: 16 oz. **Length:** 5.4" overall.
Stocks: Textured black synthetic.
Sights: Fixed.
Features: Chrome or black teflon finish. Larger than Davis D-Series models. Introduced 1995. Made in U.S. by Davis Industries.
Price: $104.00
Price: 9mm Para. $110.00
Price: Big-Bore models (same calibers, 3/4" shorter barrels) $98.00

DAVIS D-SERIES DERRINGERS

Caliber: 22 LR, 22 WMR, 25 ACP, 32 ACP.
Barrel: 2.4".
Weight: 9.5 oz. **Length:** 4" overall.
Stocks: Laminated wood or pearl.
Sights: Blade front, fixed notch rear.
Features: Choice of black Teflon or chrome finish; spur trigger. Introduced 1986. Made in U.S. by Davis Industries.
Price: $75.00

Downsizer Single Shot

Gaucher GN1 Silhouette

HJS FRONTIER FOUR DERRINGER
Caliber: 22 LR.
Barrel: 2".
Weight: 5-1/2 oz. **Length:** 3-15/16" overall.
Stocks: Brown plastic.
Sights: None.
Features: Four barrels fire with rotating firing pin. Stainless steel construction. Introduced 1993. Made in U.S. by HJS Arms, Inc.
Price: $165.00

HJS Antigua Derringer
   Same as the Frontier Four except blued barrel, brass frame, brass pivot pins. Brown plastic grips. Introduced 1994. Made in U.S. by HJS Arms, Inc.
Price: $180.00

IAR MODEL 1872 DERRINGER
Caliber: 22 Short.
Barrel: 2-3/8".
Weight: 7 oz. **Length:** 5-1/8" overall.
Stocks: Smooth walnut.
Sights: Blade front, notch rear.
Features: Gold or nickel frame with blue barrel. Reintroduced 1996 using original Colt designs and tooling for the Colt model 4 Derringer. Made in U.S. by IAR, Inc.
Price: $85.00
Price: Single cased gun $115.00
Price: Double cased set $189.00

IAR MODEL 1888 DOUBLE DERRINGER
Caliber: 38 Special.
Barrel: 2-3/4".
Weight: 16 oz. **Length:** NA.
Stocks: Smooth walnut.
Sights: Blade front, notch rear.
Features: All steel construction. Blue barrel, color case-hardened frame. Uses original designs and tooling for the Uberti New Maverick Derringer. Introduced 1997. Made in U.S. by IAR, Inc.
Price: $225.00

MAGNUM RESEARCH LONE EAGLE SINGLE SHOT PISTOL
Caliber: 22 Hornet, 223, 22-250, 243, 260 Rem., 7mm BR, 7mm-08, 30-30, 7.62x39, 308, 30-06, 300 Win. Mag., 357 Max., 35 Rem., 358 Win., 44 Mag., 444 Marlin, 440 Cor-Bon.
Barrel: 14", interchangable.
Weight: 4lbs., 3 oz. to 4 lbs., 7 oz. **Length:** 15" overall.
Stocks: Ambidextrous.
Sights: None furnished; drilled and tapped for scope mounting and open sights. Open sights optional.
Features: Cannon-type rotating breech with spring-activated ejector. Ordnance steel with matte blue finish. Cross-bolt safety. External cocking lever on left side of gun. Muzzle break optional. Introduced 1991. Available from Magnum Research, Inc.
Price: Complete pistol, black. $438.00
Price: Barreled action only, black $319.00
Price: Complete pistol, chrome $478.00
Price: Barreled action, chrome $359.00
Price: Scope base. $14.00
Price: Adjustable open sights $35.00

MANDALL/CABANAS PISTOL
Caliber: 177, pellet or round ball; single shot.
Barrel: 9".
Weight: 51 oz. **Length:** 19" overall.
Stock: Smooth wood with thumbrest.
Sights: Blade front on ramp, open adjustable rear.
Features: Fires round ball or pellets with 22 blank cartridge. Automatic safety; muzzlebrake. Imported from Mexico by Mandall Shooting Supplies.
Price: $139.95

GAUCHER GN1 SILHOUETTE PISTOL
Caliber: 22 LR, single shot.
Barrel: 10".
Weight: 2.4 lbs. **Length:** 15.5" overall.
Stocks: European hardwood.
Sights: Blade front, open adjustable rear.
Features: Bolt action, adjustable trigger. Introduced 1990. Imported from France by Mandall Shooting Supplies.
Price: About $525.00
Price: Model GP Silhouette $425.00

HJS Frontier Four

HJS LONE STAR DERRINGER
Caliber: 380 ACP.
Barrel: 2".
Weight: 6 oz. **Length:** 3-15/16" overall.
Stocks: Brown plastic.
Sights: Groove.
Features: Stainless steel construction. Beryllium copper firing pin. Button-rifled barrel. Introduced 1993. Made in U.S. by HJS Arms, Inc.
Price: $185.00

IAR Model 1888 Derringer

CONSULT
SHOOTER'S MARKETPLACE
Page 225, This Issue

Magnum Research Lone Eagle

Maximum Single Shot

REMINGTON MODEL XP-100R LONG RANGE PISTOL
Caliber: 22-250, 223, 260 Rem., 35 Rem., 4-shot magazine (5 in 223).
Barrel: 14-1/2".
Weight: 4-1/2 lbs. **Length:** NA
Stocks: Rear grip fiberglass composite.
Sights: None furnished; drilled and tapped for scope mounting.
Features: Blind magazine; blue finish. Reintroduced 1998. Made in U.S. by Remington.
Price: $665.00

RPM XL SINGLE SHOT PISTOL
Caliber: 22 LR through 45-70.
Barrel: 8", 10-3/4", 12", 14".
Weight: About 60 oz. **Length:** NA.
Stocks: Smooth Goncalo Alves with thumb and heel rests.
Sights: Hooded front with interchangeable post, or Patridge; ISGW rear adjustable for windage and elevation.
Features: Barrel drilled and tapped for scope mount. Visible cocking indicator. Spring-loaded barrel lock, positive hammer-block safety. Trigger adjustable for weight of pull and over-travel. Contact maker for complete price list. Made in U.S. by RPM.
Price: Hunter model (stainless frame, 5/16" underlug, latch lever and positive extractor) $1,295.00
Price: Extra barrel, 8" through 10-3/4".......................... $387.50
Price: Extra barrel with positive extractor, add $100.00
Price: Muzzle brake $100.00

SAVAGE STRIKER BOLT-ACTION HUNTING HANDGUN
Caliber: 22-250, 243, 308, 2-shot magazine.
Barrel: 14".
Weight: About 5 lbs. **Length:** 22-1/2" overall.
Stock: Black composite ambidextrous mid-grip; grooved forend; "Dual Pillar" bedding.
Sights: None furnished; drilled and tapped for scope mounting.
Features: Short left-hand bolt with right-hand ejection; free-floated barrel; uses Savage Model 110 rifle scope rings/bases. Introduced 1998. Made in U.S. by Savage Arms, Inc.
Price: Model 510F (blued barrel and action) $400.00
Price: Model 516FSS (stainless barrel and action) $450.00
Price: Model 516FSAK (stainless, adjustable muzzle brake) $500.00

SUNDANCE POINT BLANK O/U DERRINGER
Caliber: 22 LR, 2-shot.
Barrel: 3".
Weight: 8 oz. **Length:** 4.6" overall.
Stocks: Grooved composition.
Sights: Blade front, fixed notch rear.
Features: Double-action trigger, push-bar safety, automatic chamber selection. Fully enclosed hammer. Matte black finish. Introduced 1994. Made in U.S. by Sundance Industries.
Price: $95.00

MAXIMUM SINGLE SHOT PISTOL
Caliber: 22 LR, 22 Hornet, 22 BR, 22 PPC, 223 Rem., 22-250, 6mm BR, 6mm PPC, 243, 250 Savage, 6.5mm-35M, 270 MAX, 270 Win., 7mm TCU, 7mm BR, 7mm-35, 7mm INT-R, 7mm-08, 7mm Rocket, 7mm Super Mag., 30 Herrett, 30 Carbine, 30-30, 308 Win., 30x39, 32-20, 350 Rem. Mag., 357 Mag., 357 Maximum, 358 Win., 44 Mag., 454 Casull.
Barrel: 8-3/4", 10-1/2", 14".
Weight: 61 oz. (10-1/2" bbl.); 78 oz. (14" bbl.). **Length:** 15", 18-1/2" overall (with 10-1/2" and 14" bbl., respectively).
Stocks: Smooth walnut stocks and forend. Also available with 17" finger groove grip.
Sights: Ramp front, fully adjustable open rear.
Features: Falling block action; drilled and tapped for M.O.A. scope mounts; integral grip frame/receiver; adjustable trigger; Douglas barrel (interchangeable). Introduced 1983. Made in U.S. by M.O.A. Corp.
Price: Stainless receiver, blue barrel $653.00
Price: Stainless receiver, stainless barrel...................... $711.00
Price: Extra blued barrel..................................... $164.00
Price: Extra stainless barrel $222.00
Price: Scope mount $52.00

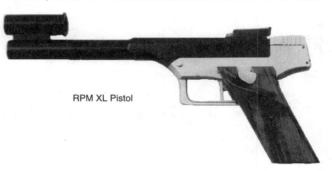

RPM XL Pistol

Savage 510F Striker

Sundance Point Blank

THOMPSON/CENTER ENCORE PISTOL
Caliber: 22-250, 223, 260 Rem., 7mmBR, 7mm-08, 243, 7.62x39, 308, 270, 30-06, 44 Mag., 444 Marlin single shot.
Barrel: 10", 15", tapered round.
Weight: NA. **Length:** 19" overall with 10" barrel.
Stocks: American walnut with finger grooves, walnut forend.
Sights: Blade on ramp front, adjustable rear, or none.
Features: Interchangeable barrels; action opens by squeezing the trigger guard; drilled and tapped for scope mounting; blue finish. Announced 1996. Made in U.S. by Thompson/Center Arms.
Price: $522.00
Price: Extra 10" barrels.................................... $238.00
Price: Extra 15" barrels.................................... $238.50
Price: 45 Colt/410 barrel, 10" $250.28
Price: 45 Colt/410 barrel, 15" $269.50

Thompson/Center Encore

T/C Contender

Thompson/Center Stainless Super 14, Super 16 Contender

Same as the standard Super 14 and Super 16 except they are made of stainless steel with blued sights. Both models have black Rynite forend and finger-groove, ambidextrous grip with a built-in rubber recoil cushion that has a sealed-in air pocket. Receiver has a different cougar etching. Available in 22 LR, 22 LR Match, 22 Hornet, 223 Rem., 30-30 Win., 35 Rem. (Super 14), 45-70 (Super 16 only), 45 Colt/410. Introduced 1993.

Price: 16-1/4" bull barrel **$567.00**
Price: 45 Colt/410, 14" **$573.00**
Price: 45 Colt/410, 16" **$578.00**

Thompson/Center Contender Shooter's Package

Package contains a 14" barrel without iron sights (10" for the 22 LR Match); Weaver-style base and rings; 2.5x-7x Recoil Proof pistol scope; and a soft carrying case. Calibers 22 LR, 223, 7-30 Waters, 30-30. Frame and barrel are blued; grip and forend are black composite. Introduced 1998. Made in U.S. by Thompson/Center Arms.

Price **$730.00**

Consult our Directory pages for the location of firms mentioned.

ULTRA LIGHT ARMS MODEL 20 REB HUNTER'S PISTOL

Caliber: 22-250 thru 308 Win. standard. Most silhouette calibers and others on request. 5-shot magazine.
Barrel: 14", Douglas No. 3.
Weight: 4 lbs.
Stock: Composite Kevlar, graphite reinforced. Du Pont Imron paint in green, brown, black and camo.
Sights: None furnished. Scope mount included.
Features: Timney adjustable trigger; two-position, three-function safety; benchrest quality action; matte or bright stock and metal finish; right- or left-hand action. Shipped in hard case. Introduced 1987. From Ultra Light Arms.
Price: **$1,600.00**

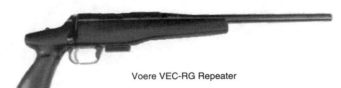

Voere VEC-RG Repeater

Weatherby Mark V CFP

THOMPSON/CENTER CONTENDER

Caliber: 7mm TCU, 30-30 Win., 22 LR, 22 WMR, 22 Hornet, 223 Rem., 270 Ren, 7-30 Waters, 32-20 Win., 357 Mag., 357 Rem. Max., 44 Mag., 10mm Auto, 445 Super Mag., 45/410, single shot.
Barrel: 10", tapered octagon, bull barrel and vent. rib.
Weight: 43 oz. (10" bbl.). **Length:** 13-1/4" (10" bbl.).
Stock: T/C "Competitor Grip." Right or left hand.
Sights: Under-cut blade ramp front, rear adjustable for windage and elevation.
Features: Break-open action with automatic safety. Single-action only. Interchangeable bbls., both caliber (rim & centerfire), and length. Drilled and tapped for scope. Engraved frame. See T/C catalog for exact barrel/caliber availability.
Price: Blued (rimfire cals.) **$475.00**
Price: Blued (centerfire cals.) **$475.00**
Price: Extra bbls. **$219.00**
Price: 45/410, internal choke bbl. **$250.00**

Thompson/Center Stainless Contender

Same as the standard Contender except made of stainless steel with blued sights, black Rynite forend and ambidextrous finger-groove grip with a built-in rubber recoil cushion that has a sealed-in air pocket. Receiver has a different cougar etching. Available with 10" bull barrel in 22 LR, 22 LR Match, 22 Hornet, 223 Rem., 30-30 Win., 357 Mag., 44 Mag., 45 Colt/410. Introduced 1993.

Price: **$529.00**
Price: 45 Colt/410 . . . . **$534.00**
Price: With 22 LR match chamber. **$529.00**

UBERTI ROLLING BLOCK TARGET PISTOL

Caliber: 22 LR, 22 WMR, 22 Hornet, 357 Mag., 45 Colt, single shot.
Barrel: 9-7/8", half-round, half-octagon.
Weight: 44 oz. **Length:** 14" overall.
Stock: Walnut grip and forend.
Sights: Blade front, fully adjustable rear.
Features: Replica of the 1871 rolling block target pistol. Brass trigger guard, color case-hardened frame, blue barrel. Imported by Uberti U.S.A.
Price: **$410.00**

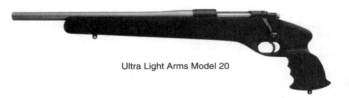

Ultra Light Arms Model 20

VOERE VEC-95CG SINGLE SHOT PISTOL

Caliber: 5.56mm, 6mm UCC caseless, single shot.
Barrel: 12", 14".
Weight: 3 lbs. **Length:** NA.
Stock: Black synthetic; center grip.
Sights: None furnished.
Features: Fires caseless ammunition via electronic ignition; two batteries in the grip last about 500 shots. Bolt action has two forward locking lugs. Tang safety. Drilled and tapped for scope mounting. Introduced 1995. Imported from Austria by JagerSport, Ltd.
Price: **$1,495.00**

Voere VEC-RG Repeater pistol

Similar to the VEC-95CG except has rear grip stock and detachable 5-shot magazine. Available with 12" or 14" barrel. Introduced 1995. Imported from Austria by JagerSport, Ltd.
Price: **$1,495.00**

WEATHERBY MARK V CFP PISTOL

Caliber: 22-250, 243, 7mm-08, 308.
Barrel: 15" fluted stainless.
Weight: NA. **Length:** NA.
Stock: Brown laminate with ambidextrous rear grip.
Sights: None furnished; drilled and tapped for scope mounting.
Features: Uses Mark V lightweight receiver of chrome moly steel, matte blue finish. Introduced 1998. Made in U.S. From Weatherby.
Price: **$1,049.00**

Both classic arms and recent designs in American-style repeaters for sport and field shooting.

AA ARMS AR9 SEMI-AUTOMATIC RIFLE
Caliber: 9mm Para., 10-shot magazine.
Barrel: 16".
Weight: 6 lbs. **Length:** 31" overall.
Stock: Fixed
Sights: Post front adjustable for elevation, open rear for windage.
Features: Blue or electroless nickel finish. Made in U.S. by AA Arms, Inc.
Price: Blue $695.00

ARMALITE MI5A2 CARBINE
Caliber: 223, 7-shot magazine.
Barrel: 16" heavy chrome lined; 1:9" twist.
Weight: 7 lbs. **Length:** 35-11/16" overall.
Stock: Green or black composition.

Thompson 1927 A-1

Auto-Ordnance Thompson M1
Similar to the Model 27 A-1 except is in the M-1 configuration with side cocking knob, horizontal forend, smooth unfinned barrel, sling swivels on butt and forend. Matte black finish. Introduced 1985.
Price: $815.00

ARMALITE AR-10A4 RIFLE.
Caliber: 308 Win., 10-shot magazine.
Barrel: 20" chrome-lined, 1:12" twist.
Weight: 9.6 lbs. **Length:** 41" overall
Stock: Green or black composition.
Sights: Detachable handle, front sight, or scope mount available; comes with international style flattop receiver with Picatinny rail.
Features: Proprietary recoil check. Forged upper receiver with case deflector. Receivers are hard-coat anodized. Introduced 1995. Made in U.S. by ArmaLite, Inc.
Price: $1,378.00

Sights: Standard A2.
Features: Upper and lower receivers have push-type pivot pin; hard coat anodized; A2-style forward assist; M16A2-type raised fence around magazine release button. Made in U.S. by ArmaLite, Inc.
Price: $930.00

AUTO-ORDNANCE 1927 A-1 THOMPSON
Caliber: 45 ACP.
Barrel: 16-1/2".
Weight: 13 lbs. **Length:** About 41" overall (Deluxe).
Stock: Walnut stock and vertical forend.
Sights: Blade front, open rear adjustable for windage.
Features: Recreation of Thompson Model 1927. Semi-auto only. Deluxe model has finned barrel, adjustable rear sight and compensator; Standard model has plain barrel and military sight. From Auto-Ordnance Corp.
Price: Deluxe $825.00
Price: 1927A1C Lightweight model (9-1/2 lbs.) $825.00

Auto-Ordnance 1927A1 Commando
Similar to the 1927A1 except has Parkerized finish, black-finish wood butt, pistol grip, horizontal forend. Comes with black nylon sling. Introduced 1998. Made in U.S. by Auto-Ordnance Corp.
Price: $820.00

Barrett Model 82A-1

BARRETT MODEL 82A-1 SEMI-AUTOMATIC RIFLE
Caliber: 50 BMG, 10-shot detachable box magazine.
Barrel: 29".
Weight: 28.5 lbs. **Length:** 57" overall.
Stock: Composition with Sorbothane recoil pad.
Sights: Scope optional.
Features: Semi-automatic, recoil operated with recoiling barrel. Three-lug locking bolt; muzzlebrake. Self-leveling bipod. Fires same 50-cal. ammunition as the M2HB machinegun. Introduced 1985. From Barrett Firearms.
Price: From $6,800.00

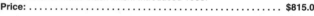

Browning Mark II Safari

BROWNING BAR MARK II SAFARI SEMI-AUTO RIFLE
Caliber: 22-250, 243, 25-06, 270, 30-06, 308.
Barrel: 22" round tapered.
Weight: 7-3/8 lbs. **Length:** 43" overall.
Stock: French walnut pistol grip stock and forend, hand checkered.
Sights: Gold bead on hooded ramp front, click adjustable rear, or no sights.

Browning BAR MARK II Lightweight Semi-Auto
Similar to the Mark II Safari except has lighter alloy receiver and 20" barrel. Available in 243, 308, 270 and 30-06. weighs 7 lbs., 2 oz.; overall length 41". Has dovetailed, gold bead front sight on hooded ramp, open rear click adjustable for windage and elevation. BOSS system not available. Introduced 1997. Imported from Belgium by Browning.
Price: $729.95

Features: Has new bolt release lever; removable trigger assembly with larger trigger guard; redesigned gas and buffer systems. Detachable 4-round box magazine. Scroll-engraved receiver is tapped for scope mounting. BOSS barrel vibration modulator and muzzlebrake system available only on models without sights. Mark II Safari introduced 1993. Imported from Belgium by Browning.
Price: Safari, with sights $729.95
Price: Safari, no sights $713.95
Price: Safari, no sights, 270 Wea. Mag. $765.95
Price: Safari, no sights, BOSS $785.25

Browning BAR Mark II Safari Magnum Rifle
Same as the standard caliber model, except weighs 8-3/8 lbs., 45" overall, 24" bbl., 3-round mag. Cals. 7mm Mag., 300 Win. Mag., 338 Win. Mag. BOSS barrel vibration modulator and muzzlebrake system available only on models without sights. Introduced 1993.
Price: Safari, with sights $781.95
Price: Safari, no sights $765.95
Price: Safari, no sights, BOSS $837.25

Bushmaster M17S

Bushmaster XM15 E2S

Bushmaster XM15 E2S Dissipator Carbine

Similar to the XM15 E2S carbine except has full-length "Dissipator" handguards. Weighs 7.6 lbs.; 34.75" overall; forged aluminum receivers with push-pin style takedown. Made in U.S. by Bushmaster Firearms, Inc.
Price **$925.00**

Colt Match Target Lightweight

CALICO LIBERTY 50, 100 CARBINES

Caliber: 9mm Para.
Barrel: 16.1".
Weight: 7 lbs. **Length:** 34.5" overall.
Stock: Glass-filled, impact resistant polymer.
Sights: Adjustable front post, fixed notch and aperture flip rear.
Features: Helical feed magazine; ambidextrous, rotating sear/striker block safety; static cocking handle; retarded blowback action; aluminum alloy receiver. Introduced 1995. Made in U.S. by Calico.
Price: Liberty 50 .... **$648.00**
Price: Liberty 100 .... **$684.00**

Hi-Point Carbine

Kel-Tec Sub-9

KEL-TEC SUB-9 AUTO RIFLE

Caliber: 9mm Para.

BUSHMASTER M17S BULLPUP RIFLE

Caliber: 223, 10-shot magazine.
Barrel: 21.5", chrome lined;1:9" twist.
Weight: 8.2 lbs. **Length:** 30" overall.
Stock: Fiberglass-filled nylon.
Sights: Designed for optics—carrying handle incorporates scope mount rail for Weaver-type rings; also includes 25-meter open iron sights.
Features: Gas-operated, short-stroke piston system; ambidextrous magazine release. Introduced 1993. Made in U.S. by Bushmaster Firearms, Inc./Quality Parts Co.
Price: **$750.00**

BUSHMASTER SHORTY XM15 E2S CARBINE

Caliber: 223, 30-shot magazine.
Barrel: 16", heavy; 1:9" twist.
Weight: 6.7 lbs. **Length:** 34.75" overall.
Stock: A2 type; fixed black composition.
Sights: Adjustable post front, adjustable aperture rear.
Features: Patterned after Colt M-16A2. Chrome-lined barrel with manganese phosphate finish. "Shorty" handguards. Has forged aluminum receivers with push-pin. Made in U.S. by Bushmaster Firearms Inc.
Price: **$885.00**

COLT MATCH TARGET LIGHTWEIGHT RIFLE

Caliber: 9mm Para., 223 Rem., 5-shot magazine.
Barrel: 16".
Weight: 6.7 lbs. (223); 7.1 lbs. (9mm Para.). **Length:** 34.5" overall.
Stock: Composition stock, grip, forend.
Sights: Post front, rear adjustable for windage and elevation.
Features: 5-round detachable box magazine, flash suppressor, sling swivels. Forward bolt assist included. Introduced 1991.
Price: **$1,010.00**

CONSULT

SHOOTER'S MARKETPLACE

Page 225, This Issue

HI-POINT 9mm CARBINE

Caliber: 9mm Para., 10-shot magazine.
Barrel: 16-1/2".
Weight: NA. **Length:** 31-1/2" overall.
Stock: Black polymer.
Sights: Protected post front, aperture rear. Integral scope mount.
Features: Grip-mounted magazine release. Black or chrome finish. Sling swivels. Introduced 1996. Made in U.S. by MKS Supply, Inc.
Price: **$189.00**

Barrel: 16.1".
Weight: 4.6 lbs. **Length:** 30" overall (extended), 15.9" (closed).
Stock: Metal tube; grooved rubber butt pad.
Sights: Hooded post front, flip-up rear. Interchangeable grip assemblies allow use of most double-column high capacity pistol magazines.
Features: Barrel folds back over the butt for transport and storage. Introduced 1997. Made in U.S. by Kel-Tec CNC Industries, Inc.
Price: **$700.00**

Marlin Model 45

Marlin Model 45 Carbine
Similar to the Model 9 except chambered for 45 ACP, 7-shot magazine. Introduced 1986.
Price: **$438.00**

LR 300 SR LIGHT SPORT RIFLE
Caliber: 223.
Barrel: 16-1/4"; 1:9" twist.
Weight: 7.2 lbs. **Length:** 36" overall (extended stock), 26-1/4" (stock folded).
Stock: Folding, tubular steel, with thumbhold-type grip.

Olympic PCR-5

OLYMPIC ARMS PCR-4 RIFLE
Caliber: 223, 10-shot magazine.
Barrel: 20".
Weight: 8 lbs., 5 oz. **Length:** 38.25" overall.
Stock: A2 stowaway grip, trapdoor buttstock.
Sights: Post front, A1 rear adjustable for windage.
Features: Based on the AR-15 rifle. Barrel is button rifled with 1:9" twist. No bayonet lug. Introduced 1994. Made in U.S. by Olympic Arms, Inc.
Price: **$820.00**

MARLIN MODEL 9 CAMP CARBINE
Caliber: 9mm Para., 10-shot magazine.
Barrel: 16-1/2", Micro-Groove® rifling.
Weight: 6-3/4 lbs. **Length:** 35-1/2" overall.
Stock: Press-checkered walnut-finished Maine birch; rubber buttpad; Mar-Shield™ finish; swivel studs.
Sights: Ramp front with orange post, cutaway Wide-Scan™ hood, adjustable open rear.
Features: Manual bolt hold-open; Garand-type safety, magazine safety; loaded chamber indicator; receiver drilled, tapped for scope mounting. Introduced 1985.
Price: **$438.00**

Sights: Trijicon post front, Trijicon rear.
Features: Uses AR-15 type upper and lower receivers; flat-top receiver with weaver base. Accepts all AR-15/M-16 magazines. Introduced 1996. made in U.S. from Z-M weapons.
Price: **$2,550.00**

OLYMPIC ARMS PCR-5, PCR-6 RIFLES
Caliber: 9mm Para., 40 S&W, 45 ACP, 223, 7.62x39mm (PCR-6), 10-shot magazine.
Barrel: 16".
Weight: 7 lbs. **Length:** 34.75" overall.
Stock: A2 stowaway grip, trapdoor buttstock.
Sights: Post front, A1 rear adjustable for windage.
Features: Based on the CAR-15. No bayonet lug. Button-cut rifling. Introduced 1994. Made in U.S. by Olympic Arms, Inc.
Price: 9mm Para., 40 S&W, 45 ACP **$830.00**
Price: 223 Rem. **$785.00**
Price: 7.62x39mm (PCR-6) **$845.00**

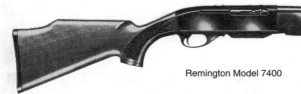

Remington Model 7400

REMINGTON MODEL 7400 AUTO RIFLE
Caliber: 243 Win., 270 Win., 280 Rem., 308 Win., 30-06, 4-shot magazine.
Barrel: 22" round tapered.

Weight: 7-1/2 lbs. **Length:** 42" overall.
Stock: Walnut, deluxe cut checkered pistol grip and forend. Satin or high-gloss finish.
Sights: Gold bead front sight on ramp; step rear sight with windage adjustable.
Features: Redesigned and improved version of the Model 742. Positive cross-bolt safety. Receiver tapped for scope mount. Comes with green Remington hard case. Introduced 1981.
Price: About **$573.00**
Price: Carbine (18-1/2" bbl., 30-06 only) **$573.00**
Price: With black synthetic stock, matte black metal, rifle or carbine **$473.00**

Ruger PC4 Carbine

RUGER PC4, PC9 CARBINES
Caliber: 9mm Para., 40 S&W, 10-shot magazine.
Barrel: 16.25".
Weight: 6 lbs., 4oz. **Length:** 34.75" overall.
Stock: Black DuPont (Zytel) with checkered grip and forend.
Sights: Blade front, open adjustable rear; integral Ruger scope mounts.
Features: Delayed blowback action; manual push-button cross bolt safety and internal firing pin block safety automatic slide lock. Introduced 1997. Made in U.S. by Sturm, Ruger & Co.
Price: PC4, 40 S&W... **$500.00**
Price: PC9, 9mm Para **$550.00**
Price: PC4GR (40 S&W with ghost ring rear sight) **$580.00**
Price: PC9GR (9mm Para. with ghost ring rear sight) **$580.00**

Ruger Mini 14/5

RUGER MINI-14/5 AUTOLOADING RIFLE
Caliber: 223 Rem., 5-shot detachable box magazine.
Barrel: 18-1/2". Rifling twist 1:9".
Weight: 6.4 lbs. **Length:** 37-1/4" overall.
Stock: American hardwood, steel reinforced.
Sights: Ramp front, fully adjustable rear.
Features: Fixed piston gas-operated, positive primary extraction. New buffer system, redesigned ejector system. Ruger S100RH scope rings included. 20-, 30-shot magazine available to police departments and government agencies only.
Price: Mini-14/5R, Ranch Rifle, blued, scope rings **$556.00**
Price: K-Mini-14/5R, Ranch Rifle, stainless, scope rings **$609.00**
Price: Mini-14/5, blued, no scope rings **$516.00**
Price: K-Mini-14/5, stainless, no scope rings **$569.00**

Ruger Mini Thirty Rifle
Similar to the Mini-14 Ranch Rifle except modified to chamber the 7.62x39 Russian service round. Weight is about 7 lbs., 3 oz. Has 6-groove barrel with 1:10″ twist, Ruger Integral Scope Mount bases and folding peep rear sight. Detachable 5-shot staggered box magazine. Blued finish. Introduced 1987.
Price: Blue. **$556.00**
Price: Stainless **$609.00**

Springfield M1A

SPRINGFIELD, INC. M1A RIFLE
Caliber: 7.62mm NATO (308), 5- or 10-shot box magazine.
Barrel: 25-1/16" with flash suppressor, 22" without suppressor.
Weight: 8-3/4 lbs. **Length:** 44-1/4" overall.
Stock: American walnut with walnut-colored heat-resistant fiberglass handguard. Matching walnut handguard available. Also available with fiberglass stock.
Sights: Military, square blade front, full click-adjustable aperture rear.
Features: Commercial equivalent of the U.S. M-14 service rifle with no provision for automatic firing. From Springfield, Inc.
Price: M1A-A1, Scout Rifle, black fiberglass stock **$1,459.00**
Price: Standard M1A rifle, about **$1,381.00**
Price: National Match, about **$1,729.00**
Price: Super Match (heavy premium barrel), about **$2,050.00**
Price: M1A-A1 Bush Rifle, walnut stock, about **$1,359.00**
Price: M1A-A1 Collector, G.I. stock **$1,307.00**

STONER SR-15 M-5 RIFLE
Caliber: 223.
Barrel: 20".
Weight: 7.6 lbs. **Length:** 38" overall.
Stock: Black synthetic.
Sights: Post front, fully adjustable rear.
Features: Modular weapon system. Black finish. Introduced 1998. Made in U.S. by Knight's Mfg.
Price: **$1,295.00**
Price: M-4 Carbine (16" barrel, 6.8 lbs) **$1,295.00**

STONER SR-25 CARBINE
Caliber: 7.62 NATO, 10-shot steel magazine.
Barrel: 16 " free-floating
Weight: 7-3/4 lbs. **Length:** 35.75" overall.
Stock: Black synthetic.
Sights: Integral Weaver-style rail. Scope rings, iron sights optional.
Features: Shortened, non-slip handguard; removable carrying handle. Matte black finish. Introduced 1995. Made in U.S. by Knight's Mfg. Co.
Price: **$2,995.00**

STONER SR-50 LONG RANGE PRECISION RIFLE
Caliber: 50 BMG, 10-shot magazine.
Barrel: 35.5".
Weight: 31.5 lbs. **Length:** 58.37" overall.
Stock: Tubular steel.
Sights: Scope mount.
Features: Gas-operated semi-automatic action; two-stage target-type trigger; M-16-type safety lever; easily removable barrel. Introduced 1996. Made in U.S. by Knight's Mfg. Co.
Price: **$6,995.00**

CENTERFIRE RIFLES—LEVER & SLIDE

Both classic arms and recent designs in American-style repeaters for sport and field shooting.

American Arms/Uberti 1866 Sporting

AMERICAN ARMS/UBERTI 1866 SPORTING RIFLE, CARBINE
Caliber: 22 LR, 22 WMR, 38 Spec., 44-40, 45 Colt.
Barrel: 24-1/4", octagonal.
Weight: 8.1 lbs. **Length:** 43-1/4" overall.
Stock: Walnut.
Sights: Blade front adjustable for windage, rear adjustable for elevation.
Features: Frame, buttplate, forend cap of polished brass, balance charcoal blued. Imported by American Arms, Inc.
Price: $780.00
Price: Yellowboy Carbine (19" round bbl.) **$760.00**

AMERICAN ARMS/UBERTI 1873 SPORTING RIFLE
Caliber: 44-40, 45 Colt.
Barrel: 24-1/4", octagonal.
Weight: 8.1 lbs. **Length:** 43-1/4" overall.
Stock: Walnut.
Sights: Blade front adjustable for windage, open rear adjustable for elevation.
Features: Color case-hardened frame, blued barrel, hammer, lever, buttplate, brass elevator. Imported from Italy by American Arms, Inc.
Price: **$910.00**

AMERICAN ARMS/UBERTI 1860 HENRY RIFLE
Caliber: 44-40, 45 Colt.
Barrel: 24-1/4", half-octagon.
Weight: 9.2 lbs. **Length:** 43-3/4" overall.
Stock: American walnut.
Sights: Blade front, rear adjustable for elevation.
Features: Frame, elevator, magazine follower, buttplate are brass,balance blue (also available in polished steel). Imported by American Arms, Inc.
Price: **$990.00**

Browning BPR

BROWNING BPR PUMP RIFLE
Caliber: 243, 308 (short action); 270, 30-06, 7mm Rem. Mag., 300 Win. Mag., 4-shot magazine (3 for magnums).
Barrel: 22"; 24" for magnum calibers.
Weight: 7 lbs., 3 oz. **Length:** 43" overall (22" barrel).
Stock: Select walnut with full pistol grip, high gloss finish.
Sights: Gold bead on hooded ramp front, open click adjustable rear.
Features: Slide-action mechanism cams forend down away from the barrel. Seven-lug rotary bolt; cross-bolt safety behind trigger; removable magazine; alloy receiver. Introduced 1997. Imported from Belgium by Browning.
Price: Standard calibers **$689.95**
Price: Magnum calibers **$741.95**

Browning Lightning BLR

Browning Lightning BLR Long Action
Similar to the standard Lightning BLR except has long action to accept 30-06, 270, 7mm Rem. Mag. and 300 Win. Mag. Barrel lengths are 22" for 30-06 and 270, 24" for 7mm Rem. Mag. and 300 Win. Mag. Has six-lug rotary bolt; bolt and receiver are full-length fluted. Fold-down hammer at half-cock. Weighs about 7 lbs., overall length 42-7/8" (22" barrel). Introduced 1996.
Price: **$608.95**

BROWNING LIGHTNING BLR LEVER-ACTION RIFLE
Caliber: 223, 22-250, 243, 7mm-08, 308 Win., 4-shot detachable magazine.
Barrel: 20" round tapered.
Weight: 6 lbs., 8 oz. **Length:** 39-1/2" overall.
Stock: Walnut. Checkered grip and forend, high-gloss finish.
Sights: Gold bead on ramp front; low profile square notch adjustable rear.
Features: Wide, grooved trigger; half-cock hammer safety; fold-down hammer. Receiver tapped for scope mount. Recoil pad installed. Introduced 1996. Imported from Japan by Browning.
Price: **$576.95**

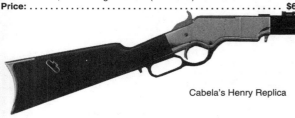

Cabela's Henry Replica

CABELA'S 1858 HENRY REPLICA
Caliber: 44-40, 45 Colt.
Barrel: 24-1/4".
Weight: 9.5 lbs. **Length:** 43" overall.
Stock: European walnut.
Sights: Bead front, open adjustable rear.
Features: Brass receiver and buttplate. Uses original Henry loading system. Faithful to the original rifle. Introduced 1994. Imported by Cabela's.
Price: **$799.99**

CABELA'S 1866 WINCHESTER REPLICA
Caliber: 44-40, 45 Colt.
Barrel: 24-1/4".
Weight: 9 lbs. **Length:** 43" overall.
Stock: European walnut.
Sights: Bead front, open adjustable rear.
Features: Solid brass receiver, buttplate, forend cap. Octagonal barrel. Faithful to the original Winchester `66 rifle. Introduced 1994. Imported by Cabela's.
Price: **$619.99**

Cabela's 1873 Winchester

CABELA'S 1873 WINCHESTER REPLICA
Caliber: 44-40, 45 Colt.
Barrel: 24-1/4", 30".

CIMARRON 1860 HENRY REPLICA
Caliber: 44 WCF, 13-shot magazine.
Barrel: 24-1/4" (rifle), 22" (carbine).
Weight: 9-1/2 lbs. **Length:** 43" overall (rifle).
Stock: European walnut.
Sights: Bead front, open adjustable rear.
Features: Brass receiver and buttplate. Uses original Henry loading system. Faithful to the original rifle. Introduced 1991. Imported by Cimarron Arms.
Price: **$1,029.00**

Weight: 8.5 lbs. **Length:** 43-1/4" overall.
Stock: European walnut.
Sights: Bead front, open adjustable rear; globe front, tang rear.
Features: Color case-hardened steel receiver. Faithful to the original Model 1873 rifle. Introduced 1994. Imported by Cabela's.
Price: With tang sight, globe front **$819.99**
Price: Sporting model, 30" barrel, 44-40, 45 Colt **$769.99**
Price: With half-round/half-octagon barrel, half magazine **$699.99**
Price: Sporting model, 24" or 25" barrel **$729.99**

CIMARRON 1866 WINCHESTER REPLICAS
Caliber: 22 LR, 22 WMR, 38 Spec., 44 WCF.
Barrel: 24-1/4" (rifle), 19" (carbine).
Weight: 9 lbs. **Length:** 43" overall (rifle).
Stock: European walnut.
Sights: Bead front, open adjustable rear.
Features: Solid brass receiver, buttplate, forend cap. Octagonal barrel. Faithful to the original Winchester `66 rifle. Introduced 1991. Imported by Cimarron Arms.
Price: Rifle **$839.00**
Price: Carbine **$829.00**

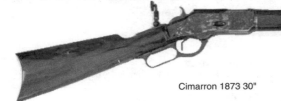

Cimarron 1873 30"

Cimarron 1873 Sporting Rifle

Similar to the 1873 Express except has 24″ barrel with half-magazine.
Price:.. **$949.00**
Price: 1873 Saddle Ring Carbine, 19" barrel **$949.00**

CIMARRON 1873 SHORT RIFLE

Caliber: 22 LR, 22 WMR, 357 Mag., 44-40, 45 Colt.
Barrel: 20" tapered octagon.
Weight: 7.5 lbs. **Length:** 39" overall.
Stock: Walnut.
Sights: Bead front, adjustable semi-buckhorn rear.
Features: Has half "button" magazine. Original-type markings, including caliber, on barrel and elevator and "Kings" patent. From Cimarron Arms.
Price:.. **$799.00**

CIMARRON 1873 30″ EXPRESS RIFLE

Caliber: 22 LR, 22 WMR, 357 Mag., 38-40, 44-40, 45 Colt.
Barrel: 30", octagonal.
Weight: 8-1/2 lbs. **Length:** 48" overall.
Stock: Walnut.
Sights: Blade front, semi-buckhorn ramp rear. Tang sight optional.
Features: Color case-hardened frame; choice of modern blue-black or charcoal blue for other parts. Barrel marked "Kings Improvement." From Cimarron Arms.
Price:.. **$999.00**

> Consult our Directory pages for the location of firms mentioned.

Dixie 1873

E.M.F. 1860 HENRY RIFLE

Caliber: 44-40 or 44 rimfire.
Barrel: 24.25".
Weight: About 9 lbs. **Length:** About 43.75" overall.
Stock: Oil-stained American walnut.
Sights: Blade front, rear adjustable for elevation.
Features: Reproduction of the original Henry rifle with brass frame and buttplate, rest blued. From E.M.F.
Price: Standard **$1,100.00**

E.M.F. MODEL 73 LEVER-ACTION RIFLE

Caliber: 357 Mag., 44-40, 45 Colt.
Barrel: 24".
Weight: 8 lbs. **Length:** 43-1/4" overall.
Stock: European walnut.
Sights: Bead front, rear adjustable for windage and elevation.
Features: Color case-hardened frame (blue on carbine). Imported by E.M.F.
Price: Rifle.. **$1,050.00**
Price: Carbine, 19" barrel **$1,020.00**

DIXIE ENGRAVED 1873 RIFLE

Caliber: 44-40, 11-shot magazine.
Barrel: 20", round.
Weight: 7-3/4 lbs. **Length:** 39" overall.
Stock: Walnut.
Sights: Blade front, adjustable rear.
Features: Engraved and case-hardened frame. Duplicate of Winchester 1873. Made in Italy. From Dixie Gun Works.
Price:.. **$1,295.00**
Price: Plain, blued carbine.............................. **$850.00**

E.M.F. 1866 YELLOWBOY LEVER ACTIONS

Caliber: 38 Spec., 44-40.
Barrel: 19" (carbine), 24" (rifle).
Weight: 9 lbs. **Length:** 43" overall (rifle).
Stock: European walnut.
Sights: Bead front, open adjustable rear.
Features: Solid brass frame, blued barrel, lever, hammer, buttplate. Imported from Italy by E.M.F.
Price: Rifle... **$848.00**
Price: Carbine **$825.00**

E.M.F. HARTFORD MODEL 1892 LEVER-ACTION RIFLE

Caliber: 45 Colt.
Barrel: 24", octagonal.
Weight: 7-1/2 lbs. **Length:** 43" overall.
Stock: European walnut.
Sights: Blade front, open adjustable rear.
Features: Color case-hardened frame, lever, trigger and hammer with blued barrel, or overall blue finish. Introduced 1998. Imported by E.M.F.
Price: Standard **$1,000.00**
Price: Deluxe **$1,085.00**
Price: Premier **$1,250.00**

Marlin Model 1894 Cowboy II

MARLIN MODEL 1894S LEVER-ACTION CARBINE

Caliber: 44 Spec./44 Mag., 10-shot tubular magazine.
Barrel: 20" Micro-Groove®.
Weight: 6 lbs. **Length:** 37-1/2" overall.
Stock: Checkered American black walnut, straight grip and forend. Mar-Shield® finish. Rubber rifle buttpad; swivel studs.
Sights: Wide-Scan" hooded ramp front, semi-buckhorn folding rear adjustable for windage and elevation.
Features: Hammer-block safety. Receiver tapped for scope mount, offset hammer spur, solid top receiver sand blasted to prevent glare.
Price:.. **$477.00**

MARLIN MODEL 1894 COWBOY, COWBOY II

Caliber: 357 Mag., 44 Mag., 44-40, 45 Colt, 10-shot magazine.
Barrel: 24" tapered octagon, deep cut rifling.
Weight: 7-1/2 lbs. **Length:** 41-1/2" overall.
Stock: Straight grip American black walnut with cut checkering, hard rubber buttplate, Mar-Shield® finish.
Sights: Marble carbine front, adjustable Marble semi-buckhorn rear.
Features: Squared finger lever; straight grip stock; blued steel forend tip. Designed for Cowboy Shooting events. Introduced 1996. Made in U.S. by Marlin.
Price: Cowboy I, 45 Colt **$704.00**
Price: Cowboy II, 357 Mag., 44 Mag., 44-40 .... **$704.00**

Marlin Model 1894CS Carbine

Similar to the standard Model 1894S except chambered for 38 Spec./357 Mag. with full-length 9-shot magazine, 18-1/2″ barrel, hammer-block safety, brass bead front sight. Introduced 1983.
Price:.. **$477.00**

Marlin Model 1895G

Marlin Model 1895G Guide Gun Lever Action
Similar to the Model 1895SS except has 18-1/2" ported barrel with deep-cut Ballard-type rifling; straight-grip walnut stock. Overall length is 37", weighs 6-3/4 lbs. Introduced 1998. Made in U.S. by Marlin.
Price: **$562.00**

MARLIN MODEL 1895SS LEVER-ACTION RIFLE
Caliber: 45-70, 4-shot tubular magazine.
Barrel: 22" round.
Weight: 7-1/2 lbs. **Length:** 40-1/2" overall.
Stock: Checkered American black walnut, full pistol grip. Mar-Shield® finish; rubber buttpad; quick detachable swivel studs.
Sights: Bead front with Wide-Scan" hood, semi-buckhorn folding rear adjustable for windage and elevation.
Features: Hammer-block safety. Solid receiver tapped for scope mounts or receiver sights; offset hammer spur.
Price: **$555.00**

Marlin Model 336CS

MARLIN MODEL 444SS LEVER-ACTION SPORTER
Caliber: 444 Marlin, 5-shot tubular magazine.
Barrel: 22" Micro-Groove®.
Weight: 7-1/2 lbs. **Length:** 40-1/2" overall.
Stock: Checkered American black walnut, capped pistol grip with white line spacers, rubber rifle buttpad. Mar-Shield® finish; swivel studs.
Sights: Hooded ramp front, folding semi-buckhorn rear adjustable for windage and elevation.
Features: Hammer-block safety. Receiver tapped for scope mount; offset hammer spur.
Price: **$555.00**

MARLIN MODEL 336CS LEVER-ACTION CARBINE
Caliber: 30-30 or 35 Rem., 6-shot tubular magazine.
Barrel: 20" Micro-Groove®.
Weight: 7 lbs. **Length:** 38-1/2" overall.
Stock: Checkered American black walnut, capped pistol grip with white line spacers. Mar-Shield® finish; rubber buttpad; swivel studs.
Sights: Ramp front with Wide-Scan" hood, semi-buckhorn folding rear adjustable for windage and elevation.
Features: Hammer-block safety. Receiver tapped for scope mount, offset hammer spur; top of receiver sand blasted to prevent glare.
Price: **$459.00**

Marlin Model 30AS Lever-Action Carbine
Same as the Marlin 336CS except has cut-checkered, walnut-finished Maine birch pistol grip stock with swivel studs, 30-30 only, 6-shot. Hammer-block safety. Adjustable rear sight, brass bead front.
Price: **$399.00**
Price: With 4x scope and mount **$443.00**

Marlin Model 30AW

NAVY ARMS MILITARY HENRY RIFLE
Caliber: 44-40 or 45 Colt, 12-shot magazine.
Barrel: 24-1/4".
Weight: 9 lbs., 4 oz.
Stock: European walnut.
Sights: Blade front, adjustable ladder-type rear.
Features: Brass frame, buttplate, rest blued. Recreation of the model used by cavalry units in the Civil War. Has full-length magazine tube, sling swivels; no forend. Imported from Italy by Navy Arms.

Price: $895.00Navy Arms Henry Carbine
Similar to the Military Henry rifle except has 22" barrel, weighs 8 lbs., 12 oz., is 41" overall; no sling swivels. Caliber 44-40. Introduced 1992. Imported from Italy by Navy Arms.
Price: **$875.00**

Marlin Model 30AW Lever-Action Rifle
Similar to the Model 336CS except has walnut-finished, cut-checkered Maine birch stock; blued steel barrel band has integral sling swivel; no front sight hood; comes with padded nylon sling; hard rubber butt plate. Introduced 1998. Made in U.S. by Marlin.
Price: **$402.00**
Price: With 4x scope and mount **$446.00**

Navy Arms Henry Trapper
Similar to the Military Henry Rifle except has 16-1/2" barrel, weighs 7-1/2 lbs. Brass frame and buttplate, rest blued. Introduced 1991. Imported from Italy by Navy Arms.
Price: **$875.00**

Navy Arms Iron Frame Henry
Similar to the Military Henry Rifle except 44-40 only, receiver is blued or color case-hardened steel. Imported by Navy Arms.
Price: **$945.00**

Navy Arms 1866 Yellowboy

NAVY ARMS 1866 YELLOWBOY RIFLE
Caliber: 38 Spec., 44-40, 45 Colt, 12-shot magazine.
Barrel: 24", full octagon.
Weight: 8-1/2 lbs. **Length:** 42-1/2" overall.
Stock: European walnut.
Sights: Blade front, adjustable ladder-type rear.
Features: Brass frame, forend tip, buttplate, blued barrel, lever, hammer. Introduced 1991. Imported from Italy by Navy Arms.
Price: **$685.00**
Price: Carbine, 19" barrel **$675.00**

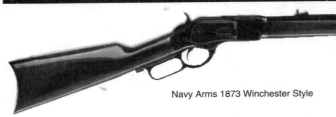

Navy Arms 1873 Winchester Style

NAVY ARMS 1873 WINCHESTER-STYLE RIFLE
Caliber: 357 Mag., 44-40, 45 Colt, 12-shot magazine.
Barrel: 24-1/4".
Weight: 8-1/4 lbs. **Length:** 43" overall.
Stock: European walnut.
Sights: Blade front, buckhorn rear.
Features: Color case-hardened frame, rest blued. Full-octagon barrel. Imported by Navy Arms.
Price: **$820.00**
Price: Carbine, 19" barrel **$800.00**

Navy Arms 1873 Sporting Rifle
Similar to the 1873 Winchester-Style rifle except has checkered pistol grip stock, 30″ octagonal barrel (24″ available). Introduced 1992. Imported by Navy Arms.
Price: 30" barrel **$960.00**
Price: 24" barrel **$930.00**

Navy Arms 1892 Rifle

NAVY ARMS 1892 LEVER-ACTION RIFLE
Caliber: 357 Mag., 44-40, 45 Colt.
Barrel: 24-1/4" octagonal.
Weight: 7 lbs. **Length:** 42" overall.
Stock: American walnut.
Sights: Blade front, semi-buckhorn rear.
Features: Replica of Winchester's early Model 1892 with octagonal barrel, forend cap and crescent buttplate. Blued or color case-hardened receiver; brass-frame model also available, in 44-40 or 45 Colt only. Introduced 1998. Imported by Navy Arms.
Price: **$525.00**

Navy Arms 1892 Carbine
Similar to the 1892 Rifle except has 20" round barrel, weighs 5-3/4 lbs., and is 37-1/2" overall. Introduced 1998. Imported by Navy Arms.
Price: **$465.00**

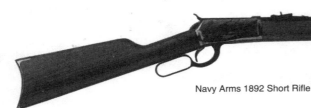

Navy Arms 1892 Short Rifle

Navy Arms 1892 Short Rifle
Similar to the 1892 Rifle except has 20" octagonal barrel, weighs 6-1/4 lbs., and is 37-3/4" overall. Replica of the rare, special order 1892 Winchester nicknamed the "Texas Special." Blued or color case-hardened receiver and furniture. Introduced 1998. Imported by Navy Arms.
Price: $525.00

Remington 7600 Rifle

REMINGTON MODEL 7600 SLIDE ACTION
Caliber: 243, 270, 280, 30-06, 308.
Barrel: 22" round tapered.
Weight: 7-1/2 lbs. **Length:** 42" overall.
Stock: Cut-checkered walnut pistol grip and forend, Monte Carlo with full cheekpiece. Satin or high-gloss finish.
Sights: Gold bead front sight on matted ramp, open step adjustable sporting rear.
Features: Redesigned and improved version of the Model 760. Detachable 4-shot clip. Cross-bolt safety. Receiver tapped for scope mount. Also available in high grade versions. Comes with green Remington hard case. Introduced 1981.
Price: About **$540.00**
Price: Carbine (18-1/2" bbl., 30-06 only) **$540.00**
Price: With black synthetic stock, matte black metal, rifle or carbine. **$440.00**

ROSSI MODEL 92 SADDLE-RING CARBINE
Caliber: 38 Spec./357 Mag., 44 Spec./44-40, 44 Mag., 45 Colt, 10-shot magazine.
Barrel: 20".
Weight: 5-3/4 lbs. **Length:** 37" overall.
Stock: Walnut.
Sights: Blade front, buckhorn rear.
Features: Recreation of the famous lever-action carbine. Handles 38 and 357 interchangeably. Introduced 1978. Imported by Interarms.
Price: **$360.00**
Price: Stainless steel, 38/357, 45 Colt **$415.00**
Price: With 24" half-octagon barrel, 13-shot magazine, brass blade front sight, 45 Colt only, blue only. **$429.00**

Rossi Model 92 Large Logo

Rossi Model 92 Short Carbine
Similar to the standard M92 except has 16″ barrel, overall length of 33-1/2″, weighs 5-1/2 lbs. Introduced 1986.
Price: **$360.00**
Price: Model 92 Large Loop (has oversize cocking lever loop and saddle rings, 44 Mag., 45 Colt only) **$360.00**

Ruger Model 96/44

RUGER MODEL 96/44 LEVER-ACTION RIFLE
Caliber: 44 Mag., 4-shot rotary magazine.
Barrel: 18-1/2".
Weight: 5-7/8 lbs. **Length:** 37-5/16" overall.
Stock: American hardwood.
Sights: Gold bead front, folding leaf rear.
Features: Solid chrome moly steel receiver. Manual cross-bolt safety, visible cocking indicator; short-throw lever action; integral scope mount; blued finish; color case-hardened lever. Introduced 1996. Made In U.S. by Sturm, Ruger & Co.
Price: $419.00

Winchester Model 1886

WINCHESTER MODEL 1886 LEVER-ACTION RIFLE
Caliber: 45-70, 8-shot magazine.
Barrel: 26", full octagon.
Weight: 9-1/4 lbs. **Length:** 45" overall.
Stock: Smooth walnut.
Sights: Bead front, ramp-adjustable buckhorn-style rear.
Features: Recreation of the Model 1886. Polished blue finish; crescent metal butt plate; metal forend cap; pistol grip stock. Reintroduced 1998. From U.S. Repeating Arms.
Price: Grade I.. $996.00
Price: High Grade, select walnut, engraved receiver with gold highlights (1,000 made in 1998 only) $1,588.00

WINCHESTER MODEL 1892 LEVER-ACTION RIFLE
Caliber: 357 Mag., 44-40, 45 Colt, 11-shot magazine.
Barrel: 24", round.
Weight: 6-1/4 lbs. **Length:** 41-1/4" overall.
Stock: Smooth walnut.
Sights: Bead front, ramp-adjustable buckhorn-style rear.
Features: Recreation of the Model 1892. Tang-mounted manual hammer stop; blued crescent butt plate; full magazine tube; straight-grip stock. Reintroduced 1997. From U.S. Repeating Arms Co.
Price: Grade I.. $722.00

Winchester Model 94 Legacy
Similar to the Model 94 Side Eject except has half pistol grip walnut stock, checkered grip and forend. Chambered for 30-30, 357 Mag., 44 Mag., 45 Colt; 20" or 24" barrel. Introduced 1995. Made in U.S. by U.S. Repeating Arms Co., Inc.
Price: With 20" barrel.................................... $393.00
Price: With 24" barrel.................................... $407.00

WINCHESTER MODEL 94 BIG BORE SIDE EJECT
Caliber: 307 Win., 356 Win., 444 Marlin, 6-shot magazine.
Barrel: 20".
Weight: 7 lbs. **Length:** 38-5/8" overall.
Stock: American walnut. Satin finish.
Sights: Hooded ramp front, semi-buckhorn rear adjustable for windage and elevation.
Features: All external metal parts have Winchester's deep blue finish. Rifling twist 1:12". Rubber recoil pad fitted to buttstock. Introduced 1983. From U.S. Repeating Arms Co., Inc.
Price: $404.00

Winchester 94 Slide Eject

Winchester Model 94 Ranger Side Eject Lever-Action Rifle
Same as Model 94 Side Eject except has 6-shot magazine, American hardwood stock and forend, post front sight. Introduced 1985.
Price: $320.00
Price: With 4x32 Bushnell scope, mounts $376.00

Winchester Model 94 Trails End
Similar to the Model 94 Walnut except chambered only for 357 Mag., 44-40, 44 Mag., 45 Colt; 11-shot magazine. Available with standard or large lever loop. Introduced 1997. From U.S. Repeating Arms Co.
Price: With standard lever loop $398.00
Price: With large lever loop $420.00

Winchester Model 94 Trapper Side Eject
Same as the Model 94 except has 16" barrel, 5-shot magazine in 30-30, 9-shot in 357 Mag., 44 Magnum/44 Special, 45 Colt. Has stainless steel claw extractor, saddle ring, hammer spur extension, walnut wood.
Price: $363.00

WINCHESTER MODEL 94 WALNUT SIDE EJECT LEVER-ACTION RIFLE
Caliber: 30-30 Win., 6-shot tubular magazine.
Barrel: 20".
Weight: 6-1/2 lbs. **Length:** 37-3/4" overall.
Stock: Straight grip walnut stock and forend.
Sights: Hooded blade front, semi-buckhorn rear. Drilled and tapped for scope mount. Post front sight on Trapper model.
Features: Solid frame, forged steel receiver; side ejection, exposed rebounding hammer with automatic trigger-activated transfer bar. Introduced 1984.
Price: Checkered walnut $393.00
Price: No checkering, walnut $363.00

Winchester Model 94 Ranger Compact
Similar to the Model 94 Ranger except has 16" barrel and 12-1/2" length of pull, rubber recoil pad, post front sight. Introduced 1998. Made in U.S. by U.S. Repeating Arms.
Price: 357 Mag. or 30-30................................. $320.00

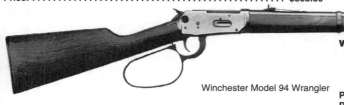

Winchester Model 94 Wrangler

Winchester Model 94 Wrangler Side Eject
Same as the Model 94 except has 16" barrel and large loop lever for large and/or gloved hands. Has 9-shot capacity (5-shot for 30-30), stainless steel claw extractor. Available in 30-30, 44 Magnum/44 Special. Specially inscribed with "1894-1994" on the receiver. Reintroduced 1992.
Price: 30-30 .... $384.00
Price: 44 Magnum/44 Special $404.00

Winchester Model 94 Black Shadow

Winchester Model 1895

Winchester Model 94 Black Shadow Lever-Action Rifle
Similar to the Model 94 Walnut except has black synthetic stock with higher comb for easier scope use, and fuller forend. Non-glare finish; recoil pad. Available in 30-30 with 20" or 24" barrel, 44 Mag. or as Big Bore model in 444 Marlin. Introduced 1998. Made in U.S. by U.S. Repeating Arms.

Price: Black Shadow, 30-30, 44 Mag. $348.00
Price: Black Shadow Big Bore, 444 Marlin $360.00
WINCHESTER MODEL 1895 LEVER-ACTION RIFLE
Caliber: 30-06, 270, 4-shot magazine.
Barrel: 24", round.
Weight: 8 lbs. **Length:** 42" overall.
Stock: American walnut.
Sights: Gold bead front, buckhorn rear adjustable for elevation.
Features: Recreation of the original Model 1895. Polished blue finish with Nimschke-style scroll engraving on receiver. Scalloped receiver, two-piece cocking lever, schnabel forend, straight-grip stock. Introduced 1995. Only 4000 rifles made in 30-06 only. From U.S. Repeating Arms Co., Inc.
Price: Grade I $909.00

Winchester Model 1895 High Grade Rifle
Same as the Grade I except has silvered receiver with extensive engraving: right side shows two scenes portraying large big horn sheep; left side has bull elk and cow elk. Gold borders accent the scenes. Magazine and cocking lever also engraved. Has classic Winchester H-style checkering pattern on fancy grade American walnut. Only 4000 rifles made. Introduced 1995. From U.S. Repeating Arms Co., Inc.
Price: $1,360.00

CENTERFIRE RIFLES—BOLT ACTION

Includes models for a wide variety of sporting and competitive purposes and uses.

ARNOLD ARMS ALASKAN RIFLE
Caliber: 243 to 338 Magnum.
Barrel: 22" to 26".
Weight: NA. **Length:** NA.
Stock: Synthetic; black, woodland or arctic camouflage.
Sights: Optional; drilled and tapped for scope mounting.
Features: Uses the Apollo action with controlled round feed or push feed; chrome-moly steel or stainless; one-piece bolt, handle, knob; cone head bolt and breech; three-position safety; fully adjustable trigger. Introduced 1996. Made in U.S. by Arnold Arms Co.
Price: Chrome-moly steel, matte finish $3,769.00
Price: Stainless steel, matte finish $3,819.00

ARNOLD ARMS SAFARI RIFLE
Caliber: 243 to 458 Win. Mag.
Barrel: 22" to 26".
Weight: NA. **Length:** NA.
Stock: Grade A and AA Fancy English walnut.
Sights: Optional; drilled and tapped for scope mounting.
Features: Uses the Apollo action with controlled or push round feed; one-piece bolt, handle, knob; cone head bolt and breech; three-position safety; fully adjustable trigger; chrome-moly steel in matte blue, polished, or bead blasted stainless. Introduced 1996. Made in U.S. by Arnold Arms Co.
Price: Grade A walnut, chrome-moly $5,528.00
Price: Grade A walnut, stainless steel. $5,578.00
Price: Grade AA walnut, chrome-moly steel $5,588.00
Price: Grade AA walnut, stainless steel $5,638.00

Arnold Arms Serengeti Synthetic Rifle
Similar to the Safari except has Fibergrain synthetic stock in classic or Monte Carlo style; traditional checkering pattern or stipple finish; polished or matte blue or bead-blast stainless finish; chambered for 243 to 300 Magnum. Introduced 1996. Made in U.S. by Arnold Arms Co.
Price: Chrome-moly steel $3,769.00
Price: Stainless steel. $3,819.00

Arnold Arms Grand African Rifle
Similar to the Safari rifle except has Exhibition Grade stock; polished blue chrome-moly steel or bead-blasted or teflon-coated stainless; barrel band; scope mount, express sights; calibers 338 Magnum to 458 Win. Mag.; 24" to 26" barrel. Introduced 1996. Made in U.S. by Arnold Arms Co.
Price: Chrome-moly steel $8,172.00
Price: Stainless steel. $8,022.00

Arnold Arms Alaskan Guide Rifle
Similar to the Alaskan rifle except chambered for 257 to 338 Magnum; choice of A-grade English walnut or synthetic stock; scope mount only. Introduced 1996. Made in U.S. by Arnold Arms Co.
Price: Chrome-moly steel, synthetic stock. $5,528.00
Price: Stainless steel, synthetic stock $5,578.00

Arnold Arms Grand Alaskan Rifle
Similar to the Alaskan rifle except has AAA fancy select or exhibition-grade English walnut; barrel band swivel; comes with iron sights and scope mount; 24" to 26" barrel; 300 Magnum to 458 Win. Mag. Introduced 1996. Made in U.S. by Arnold Arms Co.
Price: Chrome-moly steel, from. $7,570.00
Price: Stainless steel, from $7,620.00

Arnold Arms Alaskan Trophy Rifle
Similar to the Alaskan rifle except chambered for 300 Magnums to 458 Win. Mag.; 24" to 26" barrel; Fibergrain or black synthetic stock, or AA English walnut; comes with barrel band on 375 H&H and larger; scope mount; iron sights. Introduced 1996. Made in U.S. by Arnold Arms Co.
Price: Chrome-moly steel $4,268.00
Price: Stainless steel, polished finish $4,368.00
Price: Stainless steel, matte finish. $4,318.00

Arnold Arms African Trophy Rifle
Similar to the Safari except has AAA Extra Fancy English walnut stock with wrap-around checkering; matte blue chrome-moly or polished or bead blasted stainless steel; scope mount standard or optional Express sights. Introduced 1996. Made in U.S. by Arnold Arms Co.
Price: Blued chrome-moly steel. $6,921.00
Price: Stainless steel $6,971.00

Arnold Arms African Synthetic Rifle
Similar to the Safari except has Fibergrain synthetic stock with or without cheekpiece and traditional checkering pattern, or stipple finish; standard iron sights or Express folding leaf optional; chambered for 338 Magnum to 458 Win. Mag.; 24" to 26" barrel. Introduced 1996. Made in U.S. by Arnold Arms Co.
Price: Chrome-moly steel $4,463.00
Price: Stainless steel $4,513.00

Anschutz 1740 Monte Carlo

Anschutz 1733D Rifle

Similar to the 1740 Monte Carlo except has full-length, walnut, Mannlicher-style stock with skip-line checkering, rosewood schnabel tip, and is chambered for 22 Hornet. Weighs 6.4 lbs., overall length 39", barrel length 19.7". Imported from Germany by AcuSport.

Price: **$1,588.95**

ANSCHUTZ 1743D BOLT-ACTION RIFLE

Caliber: 222 Rem., 3-shot magazine.
Barrel: 19.7".
Weight: 6.4 lbs. **Length:** 39" overall.
Stock: European walnut.
Sights: Hooded blade front, folding leaf rear.
Features: Receiver grooved for scope mounting; single stage trigger; claw extractor; sliging safety; sling swivels. Imported from Germany by AcuSport Corp.

Price: **$1,588.95**

CONSULT
SHOOTER'S MARKETPLACE
Page 225, This Issue

ANSCHUTZ 1740 MONTE CARLO RIFLE

Caliber: 22 Hornet, 5-shot clip; 222 Rem., 3-shot clip.
Barrel: 24".
Weight: 6-1/2 lbs. **Length:** 43.25" overall.
Stock: Select European walnut.
Sights: Hooded ramp front, folding leaf rear; drilled and tapped for scope mounting.
Features: Uses match 54 action. Adjustable single stage trigger. Stock has roll-over Monte Carlo cheekpiece, slim forend with Schnabel tip, Wundhammer palm swell on grip, rosewood grip cap with white diamond insert. Skip-line checkering on grip and forend. Introduced 1997. Imported from Germany by AcuSport.

Price: From. **$1,439.00**
Price: Model 1730 Monte Carlo, as above except in 22 Hornet. . . **$1,439.00**

A-SQUARE CAESAR BOLT-ACTION RIFLE

Caliber: 7mm Rem. Mag., 7mm STW, 30-06, 300 Win. Mag., 300 H&H, 300 Wea. Mag., 8mm Rem. Mag., 338 Win. Mag., 340 Wea. Mag., 338 A-Square, 9.3x62, 9.3x64, 375 Wea. Mag., 375 H&H, 375 JRS, 375 A-Square, 416 Hoffman, 416 Rem. Mag., 416 Taylor, 404 Jeffery, 425 Express, 458 Win. Mag., 458 Lott, 450 Ackley, 460 Short A-Square, 470 Capstick, 495 A-Square.
Barrel: 20" to 26" (no-cost customer option).
Weight: 8-1/2 to 11 lbs.
Stock: Claro walnut with hand-rubbed oil finish; classic style with A-Square Coil-Chek® features for reduced recoil; flush detachable swivels. Customer choice of length of pull.
Sights: Choice of three-leaf express, forward or normal-mount scope, or combination (at extra cost).
Features: Matte non-reflective blue, double cross-bolts, steel and fiberglass reinforcement of wood from tang to forend tip; three-position positive safety; three-way adjustable trigger; expanded magazine capacity. Right- or left-hand. Introduced 1984. Made in U.S. by A-Square Co., Inc.

Price: Walnut stock. **$3,295.00**
Price: Synthetic stock. **$3,745.00**

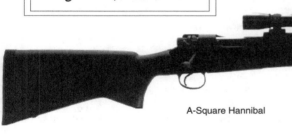

A-Square Hannibal

A-SQUARE HANNIBAL BOLT-ACTION RIFLE

Caliber: 7mm Rem. Mag., 7mm STW, 30-06, 300 Win. Mag., 300 H&H, 300 Wea. Mag., 8mm Rem. Mag., 338 Win. Mag., 340 Wea. Mag., 338 A-Square Mag., 9.3x62, 9.3x64, 375 H&H, 375 Wea. Mag., 375 JRS, 375 A-Square Mag., 378 Wea. Mag., 416 Taylor, 416 Rem. Mag., 416 Hoffman, 416 Rigby, 416 Wea. Mag., 404 Jeffery, 425 Express, 458 Win. Mag., 458 Lott, 450 Ackley, 460 Short A-Square Mag., 460 Wea. Mag., 470 Capstick, 495 A-Square Mag., 500 A-Square Mag.
Barrel: 20" to 26" (no-cost customer option).
Weight: 9 to 11-3/4 lbs.
Stock: Claro walnut with hand-rubbed oil finish; classic style with A-Square Coil-Chek® features for reduced recoil; flush detachable swivels. Customer choice of length of pull. Available with synthetic stock.
Sights: Choice of three-leaf express, forward or normal-mount scope, or combination (at extra cost).
Features: Matte non-reflective blue, double cross-bolts, steel and fiberglass reinforcement of wood from tang to forend tip; Mauser-style claw extractor; expanded magazine capacity; two-position safety; three-way target trigger. Right-hand only. Introduced 1983. Made in U.S. by A-Square Co., Inc.

Price: Walnut stock. **$3,295.00**
Price: Synthetic stock. **$3,745.00**

A-Square Hamilcar Bolt-Action Rifle

Similar to the A-Square Hannibal rifle except chambered for 25-06, 6.5x55, 270 Win., 7x57, 280 Rem., 30-06, 338-06, 9.3x62, 257 Wea. Mag., 264 Win. Mag., 270 Wea. Mag., 7mm Rem. Mag., 7mm Wea. Mag., 7mm STW, 300 Win. Mag., 300 Wea. Mag. Weighs 88-1/2 lbs. Introduced 1994. From A-Square Co., Inc.

Price: **$3,295.00**

Barett Model 95

BARRETT MODEL 95 BOLT-ACTION RIFLE

Caliber: 50 BMG, 5-shot magazine.
Barrel: 29".
Weight: 22 lbs. **Length:** 45" overall.
Stock: Sorbothane recoil pad.
Sights: Scope optional.
Features: Updated version of the Model 90. Bolt-action, bullpup design. Disassembles without tools; extendable bipod legs; match-grade barrel; high efficiency muzzlebrake. Introduced 1995. From Barrett Firearms Mfg., Inc.

Price: From. **$4,700.00**

BERETTA MATO DELUXE BOLT-ACTION RIFLE

Caliber: 270, 280 Rem., 30-06, 7mm Rem. Mag., 300 Win. Mag., 338 Win. Mag., 375 H&H.
Barrel: 23.6".
Weight: 7.9 lbs. **Length:** 44.5" overall.
Stock: XXX claro walnut with ebony forend tip, hand-rubbed oil finish.
Sights: Bead on ramp front, open fully adjustable rear; drilled and tapped for scope mounting.
Features: Mauser-style action with claw extractor; three-position safety; removable box magazine; 375 H&H has muzzle brake. Introduced 1998. From Beretta U.S.A.
Price: **$2,470.00**
Price: 375 H&H **$2,795.00**

Beretta Mato Synthetic Bolt-Action Rifle

Similar to the Mato except has fiberglass/Kevlar/carbon fiber stock in classic American style with shadow line cheekpiece, aluminum bedding block and checkering. Introduced 1998. From Beretta U.S.A.
Price: **$1,660.00**
Price: 375 H&H **$2,015.00**

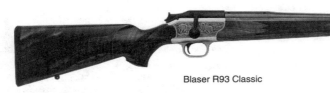

Blaser R93 Classic

BRNO 98 BOLT-ACTION RIFLE

Caliber: 7x64, 243, 270, 308, 30-06, 300 Win. Mag., 9.3x62.
Barrrel: 23.6".
Weight: 7.2 lbs. **Length:** 40.9" overall.
Stock: European walnut.
Sights: Blade on ramp front, open adjustable rear.
Features: Uses Mauser 98-type action; polished blue. Announced 1998. Imported from the Czech Republic by Euro-Imports.
Price: Standard calibers **$507.00**
Price: Magnum calibers. **$547.00**
Price: With set trigger, standard calibers **$615.00**
Price: As above, magnum calibers **$655.00**
Price: With full stock, set trigger, standard calibers **$703.00**
Price: As above, magnum calibers **$743.00**

BLASER R93 BOLT-ACTION RIFLE

Caliber: 22-250, 243, 6.5x55, 270, 7x57, 7mm-08, 308, 30-06, 257 Wea. Mag., 7mm Rem. Mag., 300 Win. Mag., 300 Wea. Mag., 338 Win Mag., 375 H&H, 416 Rem. Mag.
Barrel: 22" (standard calibers), 26" (magnum).
Weight: 7 lbs. **Length:** 40" overall (22" barrel).
Stock: Two-piece European walnut.
Sights: None furnished; drilled and tapped for scope mounting.
Features: Straight pull-back bolt action with thumb-activated safety slide/cocking mechanism; interchangeable barrels and bolt heads. Introduced 1994. Imported from Germany by SIGARMS.
Price: R93 Classic **$3,495.00**
Price: R93 LX **$1,795.00**
Price: R93 Synthetic (black synthetic stock) **$1,495.00**
Price: R93 Safari Synthetic (416 Rem. Mag. only) **$2,120.00**
Price: R93 Safari LX **$2,545.00**
Price: R93 Safari Classic. **$4,245.00**
Price: R93 Safari Attaché **$5,875.00**

Browning A-Bolt II Medallion

BROWNING A-BOLT II RIFLE

Caliber: 25-06, 270, 30-06, 280, 7mm Rem. Mag., 300 Win. Mag., 338 Win. Mag., 375 H&H Mag.
Barrel: 22" medium sporter weight with recessed muzzle; 26" on mag. cals.
Weight: 6-1/2 to 7-1/2 lbs. **Length:** 44-3/4" overall (magnum and standard); 41-3/4" (short action).
Stock: Classic style American walnut; recoil pad standard on magnum calibers.
Features: Short-throw (60") fluted bolt, three locking lugs, plunger-type ejector; adjustable trigger is grooved and gold-plated. Hinged floorplate, detachable box magazine (4 rounds std. cals., 3 for magnums). Slide tang safety. Medallion has glossy stock finish, rosewood grip and forend caps, high polish blue. BOSS barrel vibration modulator and muzzlebrake system not available in 375 H&H. Introduced 1985. Imported from Japan by Browning.
Price: Medallion, no sights. **$636.25**
Price: Hunter, no sights **$545.35**
Price: Hunter, with sights. **$613.75**
Price: Medallion, 375 H&H Mag., with sights. **$737.05**
Price: For BOSS add **$61.70**

Browning A-Bolt II Medallion Left-Hand

Same as the Medallion model A-Bolt except has left-hand action and is available in 25-06, 270, 280, 30-06, 7mm Rem. Mag., 300 Win. Mag., 338 Win. Mag., 375 H&H. Introduced 1987.
Price: **$661.45**
Price: With BOSS **$722.95**
Price: 375 H&H, with sights. **$823.75**

Browning A-Bolt II Gold Medallion

Similar to the standard A-Bolt except has select walnut stock with brass spacers between rubber recoil pad and between the rosewood grip cap and forend tip; gold-filled barrel inscription; palm-swell pistol grip, Monte Carlo comb, 22 lpi checkering with double borders; engraved receiver flats. In 270, 30-06, 7mm Rem. Mag. only. Introduced 1988.
Price: **$854.95**
Price: For BOSS, add **$61.60**

Browning A-Bolt II Stainless Stalker

Similar to the Hunter model A-Bolt except receiver and barrel are made of stainless steel; the rest of the exposed metal surfaces are finished with a durable matte silver-gray. Graphite-fiberglass composite textured stock. No sights are furnished. Available in 223, 22-250, 243, 308, 7mm-08, 270, 30-06, 7mm Rem. Mag., 375 H&H. Introduced 1987.
Price: **$708.25**
Price: With BOSS **$769.75**
Price: Left-hand, no sights. **$730.75**
Price: With BOSS **$792.25**
Price: 375 H&H, with sights **$806.35**
Price: 375 H&H, left-hand with sights **$893.05**

Browning A-Bolt II Varmint Rifle

Same as the A-Bolt II Hunter except has heavy varmint/target barrel, laminated wood stock with special dimensions, flat forend and palm swell grip. Chambered only for 223, 22-250, 308. Comes with BOSS barrel vibration modulator and muzzlebrake system. Introduced 1994.
Price: With BOSS, gloss or matte finish **$819.25**

Browning A-Bolt II Composite Stalker

Similar to the A-Bolt II Hunter except has black graphite-fiberglass stock with textured finish. Matte blue finish on all exposed metal surfaces. Available in 223, 22-250, 243, 7mm-08, 308, 30-06, 270, 280, 25-06, 7mm Rem. Mag., 300 Win. Mag., 338 Win. Mag. BOSS barrel vibration modulator and muzzlebrake system offered in all calibers. Introduced 1994.
Price: No sights **$562.45**
Price: No sights, BOSS **$623.95**

Browning A-Bolt II Short Action

Similar to the standard A-Bolt except has short action for 223, 22-250, 243, 257 Roberts, 7mm-08, 284 Win., 308 chamberings. Available in Hunter or Medallion grades. Weighs 6-1/2 lbs. Other specs essentially the same. BOSS barrel vibration modulator and muzzlebrake system optional. Introduced 1985.
Price: Medallion, no sights **$636.95**
Price: Hunter, no sights. **$545.35**
Price: Hunter, with sights. **$613.75**
Price: Composite, no sights **$562.45**
Price: For BOSS, add **$61.70**

Browning A-Bolt II Custom Trophy

Browning A-Bolt II Custom Trophy Rifle
Similar to the A-Bolt Medallion except has select American walnut stock with recessed swivel studs, octagon barrel, skeleton pistol grip cap, gold highlights, shadowline cheekpiece. Calibers 270, 30-06, 7mm Rem. Mag., 300 Win. Mag. Introduced 1998. Imported from Japan by Browning.
Price: **$1,295.00**

Browning A-Bolt II Micro Medallion
Similar to the standard A-Bolt except is a scaled-down version. Comes with 20" barrel, shortened length of pull (13-5/16"); three-shot magazine capacity; weighs 6 lbs., 1 oz. Available in 22 Hornet, 243, 308, 7mm-08, 257 Roberts, 223, 22-250. BOSS feature not available for this model. Introduced 1988.
Price: No sights $636.25

Browning A-Bolt II Eclipse
Similar to the A-Bolt II except has gray/black laminated, thumbhole stock, BOSS barrel vibration modulator and muzzlebrake. Available in long and short action with standard weight barrel, or short-action Varmint with heavy barrel. Introduced 1996. Imported from Japan by Browning.
Price: Standard barrel **$895.75**
Price: Varmint. **$922.75**

Browning A-Bolt II Eclipse M-1000

Browning A-Bolt II Eclipse M-1000
Similar to the A-Bolt II Eclipse except has long action and heavy target barrel. Chambered only for 300 Win. Mag. Adjustable trigger, bench-style forend, 3-shot magazine; laminated thumbhold stock; BOSS system standard. Introduced 1997. Imported for Japan by Browning.
Price: **$922.75**

CENTURY SWEDISH SPORTER #38
Caliber: 6.5x55 Swede, 5-shot magazine.
Barrel: 24".
Weight: NA. **Length:** 44.1" overall.
Stock: Walnut-finished European hardwood with checkered pistol grip and forend; Monte Carlo comb.
Sights: Blade front, adjustable rear.
Features: Uses M38 Swedish Mauser action; comes with Holden Ironsighter see-through scope mount. Introduced 1987. From Century International Arms.
Price: About $249.00

CENTURY CENTURION 98 SPORTER RIFLE
Caliber: 270 Win., 5-shot magazine.
Barrel: 22" **Weight:** 7 lbs., 13 oz. **Length:** 44" overall.
Stock: Black synthetic.
Sights: None furnished; comes with scope base.
Features: Low-swing safety; polished blue finish. From Century International Arms.
Price: $279.00

Century Centurion 14

CENTURY CENTURION 14 SPORTER
Caliber: 7mm Rem. Mag., 5-shot magazine.
Barrel: 24".
Weight: NA. **Length:** 43.3" overall.
Stock: Walnut-finished European hardwood. Checkered pistol grip and forend. Monte Carlo comb.
Sights: None furnished.
Features: Uses modified Pattern 14 Enfield action. Drilled and tapped; scope base mounted. Blue finish. From Century International Arms.
Price: About $275.00

Cooper Model 22 PV

COOPER ARMS MODEL 22 PRO VARMINT EXTREME
Caliber: 22-250, 220 Swift, 243, 25-06, 6mm PPC, 308, single shot.
Barrel: 26"; stainless steel match grade, straight taper; free-floated.
Weight: NA. **Length:** NA.
Stock: AAA Claro walnut, oil finish, 22 lpi wrap-around borderless ribbon checkering, beaded cheekpiece, steel grip cap, flared varminter forend, Pachmayr pad.
Sights: None furnished; drilled and tapped for scope mounting.
Features: Uses a three front locking lug system. Available with sterling silver inlaid medallion, skeleton grip cap, and French walnut. Introduced 1995. Made in U.S. by Cooper Arms.
Price: **$1,795.00**
Price: Benchrest model with Jewell trigger **$2,195.00**
Price: Black Jack model (McMillan synthetic stock). **$1,795.00**

CZ 550 BOLT-ACTION RIFLE
Caliber: 243, 308 (4-shot detachable magazine), 308, 270, 30-06, 7mm Rem. Mag., 300 Win. Mag. (5-shot internal magazine).
Barrel: 23.6".
Weight: 7.2 lbs. **Length:** 44.7" overall.
Stock: Walnut with high comb; checkered grip and forend.
Sights: None furnished; drilled and tapped for Remington 700-style bases.
Features: Polished blue finish. Introduced 1995. Imported from the Czech Republic by CZ-USA.
Price: From $489.00

COOPER ARMS MODEL 21 VARMINT EXTREME RIFLE
Caliber: 17 Rem., 17 Mach IV, 221 Fireball, 222, 222 Rem. Mag., 223, 22 PPC, single shot.
Barrel: 23.75"; stainless steel, with competition step crown; free-floated.
Weight: NA. **Length:** NA.
Stock: AAA Claro walnut with flared oval forend, ambidextrous palm swell, 22 lpi checkering, oil finish, Pachmayr buttpad.
Sights: None furnished; drilled and tapped for scope mounting.
Features: Action has three mid-bolt locking lugs; adjustable trigger; glass bedded; swivel studs. Introduced 1994. Made in U.S. by Cooper Arms.
Price: **$1,750.00**
Price: Benchrest with Jewell trigger **$2,140.00**
Price: Custom Classic **$1,960.00**

CZ-527

CZ 527 BOLT-ACTION RIFLE
Caliber: 22 Hornet, 222 Rem., 223 Rem., detachable 5-shot magazine.
Barrel: 23-1/2"; standard or heavy barrel.
Weight: 6 lbs., 1 oz. **Length:** 42-1/2" overall.
Stock: European walnut with Monte Carlo.
Sights: Hooded front, open adjustable rear.
Features: Improved mini-Mauser action with non-rotating claw extractor; grooved receiver. Imported from the Czech Republic by CZ-USA.
Price: **$514.00**
Price: Model FS..**$574.00**

Dakota 76 Classic

DAKOTA 76 CLASSIC BOLT-ACTION RIFLE
Caliber: 257 Roberts, 270, 280, 30-06, 7mm Rem. Mag., 338 Win. Mag., 300 Win. Mag., 375 H&H, 458 Win. Mag.
Barrel: 23".
Weight: 7-1/2 lbs. **Length:** 43-1/2" overall.
Stock: Medium fancy grade walnut in classic style. Checkered pistol grip and forend; solid buttpad.
Sights: None furnished; drilled and tapped for scope mounts.
Features: Has many features of the original Model 70 Winchester. One-piece rail trigger guard assembly; steel grip cap. Model 70-style trigger. Many options available. Left-hand rifle available at same price. Introduced 1988. From Dakota Arms, Inc.
Price: **$2,995.00**

Dakota 76 Classic Rifles
A scaled-down version of the standard Model 76. Standard chamberings are 22-250, 243, 6mm Rem., 250-3000, 7mm-08, 308, others on special order. Short Classic Grade has 21" barrel; Alpine Grade is lighter (6-1/2 lbs.), has a blind magazine and slimmer stock. Introduced 1989.
Price: Short Classic **$2,995.00**

DAKOTA 97 VARMINT HUNTER
Caliber: 17 Rem., 222 Rem., 223 Rem., 220 Swift, 22-250, 22 BR, 22 PPC, 6mm BR.
Barrel: 24".
Weight: 8 lbs. **Length:** NA.
Stock: X walnut; 13-5/8" length of pull.
Sights: Optional.
Features: Round short action; solid-bottom single shot; chrome moly #4 barrel; adjustable trigger. Introduced 1998. Made in U.S. by Dakota Arms.
Price: **$1,695.00**

CONSULT
SHOOTER'S MARKETPLACE
Page 225, This Issue

DAKOTA 76 SAFARI BOLT-ACTION RIFLE
Caliber: 270 Win., 7x57, 280, 30-06, 7mm Dakota, 7mm Rem. Mag., 300 Dakota, 300 Win. Mag., 330 Dakota, 338 Win. Mag., 375 Dakota, 458 Win. Mag., 300 H&H, 375 H&H, 416 Rem.
Barrel: 23".
Weight: 8-1/2 lbs. **Length:** 43-1/2" overall.
Stock: XXX fancy walnut with ebony forend tip; point-pattern with wrap-around forend checkering.
Sights: Ramp front, standing leaf rear.
Features: Has many features of the original Model 70 Winchester. Barrel band front swivel, inletted rear. Cheekpiece with shadow line. Steel grip cap. Introduced 1988. From Dakota Arms, Inc.
Price: Wood stock.. **$3,995.00**

Dakota 416 Rigby

Dakota 97 Lightweight Hunter

Dakota 416 Rigby African
Similar to the 76 Safari except chambered for 404 Jeffery, 416 Rigby, 416 Dakota, 450 Dakota, 4-round magazine, select wood, two stock cross-bolts. Has 24" barrel, weight of 9-10 lbs. Ramp front sight, standing leaf rear. Introduced 1989.
Price: **$4,495.00**

DAKOTA LONGBOW TACTICAL E.R. RIFLE
Caliber: 300 Dakota Magnum, 330 Dakota Magnum, 338 Lapua Magnum.
Barrel: 28", .950" at muzzle
Weight: 13.7 lbs. **Length:** 50" to 52" overall.
Stock: Ambidextrous McMillan A-2 fiberglass, black or olive green color; adjustable cheekpiece and buttplate.
Sights: None furnished. comes with Picatinny one-piece optical rail.
Features: Uses the Dakota 76 action with controlled-round feed; three-position firing pin block safety, claw extractor; Model 70-style trigger. comes with bipod, case tool kit. Introduced 1997. Made in U.S. by Dakota Arms, Inc.
Price:.. **$4,250.00**

DAKOTA 97 LIGHTWEIGHT HUNTER
Caliber: 22-250 to 308.
Barrel: 22"-24".
Weight: 6.1-6.5 lbs. **Length:** 43" overall.
Stock: Fiberglass.
Sights: Optional.
Features: Matte blue finish, black stock. Introduced 1998. Made in U.S. by Dakota Arms, Inc.
Price: **$1,695.00**

Dakota Model 97

DAKOTA LONG RANGE HUNTER RIFLE

Caliber: 25-06, 257 Roberts, 270 Win., 280 Rem., 7mm Rem. Mag., 7mm Dakota Mag., 30-06, 300 Win. Mag., 300 Dakota Mag., 338 Win. Mag., 330 Dakota Mag., 375 H&H Mag., 375 Dakota Mag.

Barrel: 24", 26", match-quality; free-floating.
Weight: 7.7 lbs. **Length:** 45" to 47" overall.
Stock: H-S Precision black synthetic, with one-piece bedding block system.
Sights: None furnished. Drilled and tapped for scope mounting.
Features: Cylindrical machined receiver. controlled round feed; Mauser-style extractor; three-position striker blocking safety; fully adjustable match trigger. Introduced 1997. Made in U.S. by Dakota Arms, Inc.
Price: **$1,695.00**

Charles Daly Superior

Charles Daly Empire Grade Rifle

Similar to the Superior except has oil-finished American walnut stock with 18 lpi hand checkering; black hardwood grip cap and forend tip; highly polished barreled action; jewelled bolt; recoil pad; swivel studs. Imported by K.B.I., Inc.
Price: **$439.00**

CHARLES DALY FIELD GRADE MAUSER 98 RIFLE

Caliber: 243, 270, 308, 30-06, 7mm Rem. Mag., 300 Win. Mag., 375 H&H, 458 Win. Mag.
Barrel: 23".
Weight: About 7-1/2 lbs. **Length:** 44-1/2" overall.
Stock: Black fiberglass/graphite composite on Field Grade, hand-checkered European walnut on Superior Grade.
Sights: Hooded front, open fully adjustable rear; drilled and tapped for scope mounts.
Features: Hammer-forged barrel; side safety; steel trigger guard; polished blue finish. Introduced 1998. Imported by K.B.I., Inc.
Price: Field Grade, standard calibers **$349.00**
Price: Field Grade, magnum calibers **$379.00**
Price: Field Grade, 375 H&H, 458 Win. Mag. **$499.00**
Price: Superior Grade, standard calibers. **$399.00**
Price: Superior Grade, magnum calibers. **$429.00**
Price: Superior Grade, 375 H&H, 458 Win. Mag. **$549.00**

Harris Gunworks Signature Titanium Mountain Rifle

Similar to the Classic Sporter except action made of titanium alloy, barrel of chrome-moly steel. Stock is of graphite reinforced fiberglass. Weight is 5-1/2 lbs. Chambered for 270, 280 Rem., 30-06, 7mm Rem. Mag., 300 Win. Mag. Fiberglass stock optional. Introduced 1989.
Price: **$3,200.00**

HARRIS GUNWORKS SIGNATURE CLASSIC SPORTER

Caliber: 22-250, 243, 6mm Rem., 7mm-08, 284, 308 (short action); 25-06, 270, 280 Rem., 30-06, 7mm Rem. Mag., 300 Win. Mag., 300 Wea. (long action); 338 Win. Mag., 340 Wea., 375 H&H (magnum action).
Barrel: 22", 24", 26".
Weight: 7 lbs. (short action).
Stock: Fiberglass in green, beige, brown or black. Recoil pad and 1" swivels installed. Length of pull up to 14-1/4".
Sights: None furnished. Comes with 1" rings and bases.
Features: Uses right- or left-hand action with matte black finish. Trigger pull set at 3 lbs. Four-round magazine for standard calibers; three for magnums. Aluminum floorplate. Wood stock optional. Introduced 1987. From Harris Gunworks, Inc.
Price: **$2,700.00**

CHARLES DALY SUPERIOR BOLT-ACTION RIFLE

Caliber: 22 Hornet, 5-shot magazine.
Barrel: 22.6".
Weight: 6.6 lbs. **Length:** 41.25" overall.
Stock: Walnut-finished hardwood with Monte Carlo comb and cheekpiece.
Sights: Ramped blade front, fully adjustable open rear.
Features: Receiver dovetailed for tip-off scope mount. Introduced 1996. Imported by K.B.I., Inc.
Price: **$339.00**

CHARLES DALY MINI MAUSER 98 RIFLE

Caliber: 22 Hornet, 223 Rem., 22-250, 7.62x39mm.
Barrel: 19-1/4".
Weight: About 6 lbs. **Length:** 40-3/4" overall.
Stock: Black composite fiberglass/graphite on Field Grade, hand-checkered European walnut on Superior Grade.
Sights: Hooded front, fully adjustable open rear; drilled and tapped for scope mounting.
Features: Hammer-forged barrel; side safety; steel trigger guard; polished blue finish. Introduced 1998. Imported by K.B.I., Inc.
Price: Field Grade **$349.00**
Price: Superior Grade. **$399.00**

HARRIS GUNWORKS TALON SAFARI RIFLE

Caliber: 300 Win. Mag., 300 Wea. Mag., 300 Phoenix, 338 Win. Mag., 30/378, 338 Lapua, 300 H&H, 340 Wea., 375 H&H, 404 Jeffery, 416 Rem. Mag., 458 Win. Mag. (Safari Magnum); 378 Wea. Mag., 416 Rigby, 416 Wea. Mag., 460 Wea. Mag. (Safari Super Magnum).
Barrel: 24".
Weight: About 9-10 lbs. **Length:** 43" overall.
Stock: Gunworks fiberglass Safari.
Sights: Barrel band front ramp, multi-leaf express rear.
Features: Uses Harris Gunworks Safari action. Has quick detachable 1" scope mounts, positive locking steel floorplate, barrel band sling swivel. Match-grade barrel. Matte black finish standard. Introduced 1989. From Harris Gunworks, Inc.
Price: Talon Safari Magnum. **$3,900.00**
Price: Talon Safari Super Magnum **$4,200.00**

Consult our Directory pages for the location of firms mentioned.

Harris Gunworks Signature Super Varminter

Similar to the Classic Sporter except has heavy contoured barrel, adjustable trigger, field bipod and special hand-bedded fiberglass stock. Chambered for 223, 22-250, 220 Swift, 243, 6mm Rem., 25-06, 7mm-08, 7mm BR, 308, 350 Rem. Mag. Comes with 1" rings and bases. Introduced 1989.
Price: **$2,700.00**

Harris Gunworks Classic Stainless

Harris Gunworks Classic Stainless Sporter

Similar to the Classic Sporter except barrel and action made of stainless steel. Same calibers, in addition to 416 Rem. Mag. Comes with fiberglass stock, right- or left-hand action in natural stainless, glass bead or black chrome sulfide finishes. Introduced 1990. From Harris Gunworks, Inc.
Price: **$2,700.00**

Harris Gunworks Alaskan

HARRIS GUNWORKS TALON SPORTER RIFLE
Caliber: 22-250, 243, 6mm Rem., 6mm BR, 7mm BR, 7mm-08, 25-06, 270, 280 Rem., 284, 308, 30-06, 350 Rem. Mag. (Long Action); 7mm Rem. Mag., 7mm STW, 300 Win. Mag., 300 Wea. Mag., 300 H&H, 338 Win. Mag., 340 Wea. Mag., 375 H&H, 416 Rem. Mag.
Barrel: 24" (standard).
Weight: About 7-1/2 lbs. **Length:** NA.
Stock: Choice of walnut or fiberglass.
Sights: None furnished; comes with rings and bases. Open sights optional.
Features: Uses pre-'64 Model 70-type action with cone breech, controlled feed, claw extractor and three-position safety. Barrel and action are of stainless steel; chrome-moly optional. Introduced 1991. From Harris Gunworks, Inc.
Price: $2,900.00

Harris Gunworks Signature Alaskan
Similar to the Classic Sporter except has match-grade barrel with single leaf rear sight, barrel band front, 1" detachable rings and mounts, steel floorplate, electroless nickel finish. Has wood Monte Carlo stock with cheekpiece, palm-swell grip, solid buttpad. Chambered for 270, 280 Rem., 30-06, 7mm Rem. Mag., 300 Win. Mag., 300 Wea., 358 Win., 340 Wea., 375 H&H. Introduced 1989.
Price: $3,800.00

HARRIS GUNWORKS SPORTSMAN 97 RIFLE
Caliber: 270, 7mm Rem. Mag., 30-06, 300 Win. Mag., 338 Win. Mag.
Barrel: 24".
Weight: About 7 lbs. **Length:** NA.
Stock: High-grade walnut with hand-rubbed oil finish; choice of American Bastogne or English black walnut.
Sights: None furnished; comes with rings and bases.
Features: Uses Harris Talon action with controlled feed, cone breech, claw extractor, three-position wing safety. Action patterned after pre-64 Model 70. Adjustable trigger. Introduced 1998. Made in U.S. by Harris Gunworks, Inc.
Price: $2,800.00

Howa Lightning

HOWA LIGHTNING BOLT-ACTION RIFLE
Caliber: 223, 22-250, 243, 270, 308, 30-06, 7mm Rem. Mag., 300 Win. Mag., 338 Win. Mag.
Barrel: 22", 24" magnum calibers.
Weight: 7-1/2 lbs. **Length:** 42" overall (22" barrel).
Stock: Black Bell & Carlson Carbelite composite with Monte Carlo comb; checkered grip and forend.
Sights: None furnished. Drilled and tapped for scope mounting.
Features: Sliding thumb safety; hinged floorplate; polished blue/black finish. Introduced 1993. From Interarms.
Price: Standard calibers $425.00
Price: Magnum calibers $445.00

Kimber Model 84C Varmint

Kimber Model 84C Varmint Stainless
Similar to the Model 84C Classic except chambered for 223 Rem-only; 24" medium-heavy, match-grade stainless steel, fluted barrel; with recessed target crown; weighs 7-1/2 lbs.; measures 42-1/2" overall. The Claro walnut stock has 18 lpi hand-checkering. Introduced 1997. Made in U.S. by Kimber of America.
Price: $1,215.00

Kimber Model 84C SuperAmerica
Similar to the Model 84C Classic except has AAA Claro walnut stock with beaded checkpiece, ebony forend tip, wrap-around 22 lpi checkering, and black rubber butt pad. Chambered for 17 Rem., 222 Rem., 223 Rem. Reintroduced 1996. Made in U.S. by Kimber of America, Inc.
Price: $1,595.00

KIMBER MODEL 84C CLASSIC BOLT-ACTION RIFLE
Caliber: 222, 223, 5-shot magazine.
Barrel: 22" match-grade sporter weight.
Weight: 6-3/4 lbs. **Length:** 40-1/2" overall.
Stock: Select A Claro walnut.
Sights: None furnished; drilled and tapped for Warne, Leupold or Millett scope mounts.
Features: Controlled round feed with Mauser-style extractor; pillar-bedded action; free-floating barrel; fully adjustable trigger; steel floorplate and trigger guard. Reintroduced 1996. Made in U.S. by Kimber of America, Inc.
Price: $1,145.00

Kimber Model 84C Single Shot Varmint
Similar to the Model 84C except is a single shot chambered only for 17 Rem. and 223 Rem.; 25" fluted match-grade stainless barrel with target crown; and has varmint-profile stock with wide forend. Introduced 1996. Made in U.S. by Kimber of America, Inc.
Price: 17 Rem. $1,117.00
Price: 223 Rem. $1,032.00

Kongsberg Thumbhole Sporter

KONGSBERG THUMBHOLE SPORTER RIFLE
Caliber: 22-250, 308 Win., 4-shot magazine.
Barrel: 23" heavy barrel (.750" muzzle).
Weight: About 8-1/2 lbs. **Length:** NA.

Stock: Oil-finished American walnut with stippled thumbhole grip, wide stippled forend, cheekpiece fully adjustable for height.
Sights: None furnished. Receiver dovetailed for scope mounting, and is drilled and tapped.
Features: Large bolt knob; rotary magazine; adjustable trigger; three-position safety; 60" bolt throw; claw extractor. Introduced 1993. Imported from Norway by Kongsberg America L.L.C.
Price: Right-hand. $1,580.00
Price: Left-hand $1,718.00

KONGSBERG CLASSIC RIFLE
Caliber: 22-250, 243, 6.5x55, 270 Win., 30-06, 308 Win., 4-shot magazine; 7mm Rem. Mag., 300 Win. Mag., 338 Win. Mag., 3-shot magazine.
Barrel: 23" in standard calibers, 26" for magnums.
Weight: About 7-1/2 lbs. **Length:** 44" overall (23" barrel).
Stock: Oil-finished European walnut with straight fluted comb; 18 lpi checkering; rubber buttpad.
Sights: Hooded blade front, open adjustable rear. Receiver dovetailed for Weaver-type scope mount, and drilled and tapped.
Features: Rotary magazine; adjustable trigger; three-position safety; 60° bolt throw; claw extractor. Introduced 1993. Imported from Norway by Kongsberg America L.L.C.
Price: Right-hand, standard calibers **$995.00**
Price: Right-hand, magnum calibers **$1,109.00**
Price: Left-hand, standard calibers **$1,133.00**
Price: Left-hand, magnum calibers **$1,245.00**

Lakelander 389 Classic Bolt-Action Rifle
Similar to the Premium model except has straight-comb classic-style stock without forend tip and grip cap; solid butt pad. Available in 243, 6.5x55, 308, 270, 30-06, 7mm Rem. Mag. Introduced 1998. Imported from Sweden by Lakelander U.S.A., Inc.
Price: **$1,539.00**

KRICO MODEL 700 BOLT-ACTION RIFLES
Caliber: 17 Rem., 222, 222 Rem. Mag., 223, 5.6x50 Mag., 243, 308, 5.6x57 RWS, 22-250, 6.5x55, 6.5x57, 7x57, 270, 7x64, 30-06, 9.3x62, 6.5x68, 7mm Rem. Mag., 300 Win. Mag., 8x68S, 7.5 Swiss, 9.3x64, 6x62 Freres.
Barrel: 23.6" (std. cals.); 25.5" (mag. cals.).
Weight: 7 lbs. **Length:** 43.3" overall (23.6" bbl.).
Stock: European walnut, Bavarian cheekpiece.
Sights: Blade on ramp front, open adjustable rear.
Features: Removable box magazine; sliding safety. Drilled and tapped for scope mounting. Imported from Germany by Mandall Shooting Supplies.
Price: Model 700 . . . . **$995.00**
Price: Model 700 Deluxe S **$1,495.00**
Price: Model 700 Deluxe **$1,025.00**
Price: Model 700 Stutzen (full stock) **$1,249.00**

LAKELANDER 389 PREMIUM BOLT-ACTION RIFLE
Caliber: 6.5x55, 270, 308, 30-06, 7mm Rem. Mag., 300 Win. Mag.
Barrel: 22".
Weight: 7.6 lbs. **Length:** 43.7" overall.
Stock: European walnut with oil finish, Monte Carlo comb, rosewood forend tip and grip cap.
Sights: None furnished; drilled and tapped for scope mounting.
Features: Special SureSeal protective metal finish; built-in recoil damper; three-position safety; ventilated black recoil pad. Introduced 1998. Imported from Sweden by Lakelander U.S.A., Inc.
Price: **$1,599.00**

L.A.R. Grizzly 50

L.A.R. GRIZZLY 50 BIG BOAR RIFLE
Caliber: 50 BMG, single shot.
Barrel: 36".
Weight: 28.4 lbs. **Length:** 45.5" overall.
Stock: Integral. Ventilated rubber recoil pad.
Sights: None furnished; scope mount.
Features: Bolt-action bullpup design; thumb safety. All-steel construction. Introduced 1994. Made in U.S. by L.A.R. Mfg., Inc.
Price: **$2,570.00**

Marlin Model MR-7

Marlin Model MR-7B
Similar to the MR-7 except available in 270 or 30-06 with Maine birch stock with cut-checkered grip and forend. Introduced 1998. Made in U.S.A. by Marlin.
Price: With sights **$518.00**
Price: Without sights **$478.00**

MARLIN MODEL MR-7 BOLT-ACTION RIFLE
Caliber: 22-250, 243, 25-06, 280, 308, 30-06, 4-shot detachable box magazine.
Barrel: 22"; six-groove rifling.
Weight: 7-1/2 lbs. **Length:** 43" overall.
Stock: American black walnut with cut-checkered grip and forend, rubber buttpad, Mar-Shield® finish.
Sights: Bead on ramp front, adjustable rear, or no sights. (25-06 only available without sights.)
Features: Three-position safety; shrouded striker; red cocking indicator; adjustable 3-6 lb. trigger; quick-detachable swivel studs. Introduced 1996. Made in U.S. by Marlin.
Price: With sights **$638.00**
Price: No sights **$598.00**

Mountain Eagle Varmint

MOUNTAIN EAGLE RIFLE
Caliber: 222 Rem., 223 Rem. (Varmint); 270, 280, 30-06 (long action); 7mm Rem. Mag., 300 Win. Mag., 338 Win. Mag., 300 Wea. Mag., 340 Wea. Mag., 375 H&H, 416 Rem. Mag. (magnum action).

Barrel: 24", 26" (Varmint); match-grade; fluted stainless on Varmint. Free floating.
Weight: 7 lbs., 13 oz. **Length:** 44" overall (24" barrel).
Stock: Kevlar-graphite with aluminum bedding block, high comb, recoil pad, swivel studs; made by H-S Precision.
Sights: None furnished; accepts any Remington 700-type base.
Features: Special Sako action with one-piece forged bolt, hinged steel floorplate, lengthened receiver ring; adjustable trigger. Krieger cut-rifled benchrest barrel. Introduced 1996. From Magnum Research, Inc.
Price: Right-hand **$1,499.00**
Price: Left-hand **$1,549.00**
Price: Varmint Edition **$1,629.00**
Price: 375 H&H, 416 Rem., add **$300.00**

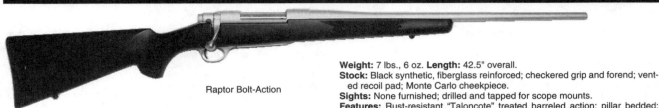

Raptor Bolt-Action

RAPTOR BOLT-ACTION RIFLE
Caliber: 270, 30-06, 243, 25-06, 308; 4-shot magazine.
Barrel: 22".

Weight: 7 lbs., 6 oz. **Length:** 42.5" overall.
Stock: Black synthetic, fiberglass reinforced; checkered grip and forend; vented recoil pad; Monte Carlo cheekpiece.
Sights: None furnished; drilled and tapped for scope mounts.
Features: Rust-resistant "Taloncote" treated barreled action; pillar bedded; stainless bolt with three locking lugs; adjustable trigger. Announced 1997. Made in U.S. by Raptor Arms Co., Inc.
Price: **$249.00**

Remington 700 ADL Synthetic

Remington Model 700 ADL Synthetic
Similar to the 700 ADL except has a fiberglass-reinforced synthetic stock with straight comb, raised cheekpiece, positive checkering, and black rubber buttpad. Metal has matte finish. Available in 223, 243, 270, 308, 30-06 with 22" barrel, 300 Win. Mag., 7mm Rem. Mag. with 24" barrel. Introduced 1996.
Price: From **$425.00**

Remington Model 700 ADL Synthetic Youth
Similar to the Model 700 ADL Synthetic except has 1" shorter stock, 20" barrel. Chambered for 243, 308. Introduced 1998.
Price: **$425.00**

REMINGTON MODEL 700 ADL BOLT-ACTION RIFLE
Caliber: 243, 270, 308, 30-06 and 7mm Rem. Mag.
Barrel: 22" or 24" round tapered.
Weight: 7 lbs. **Length:** 41-1/2" to 43-1/2" overall.
Stock: Walnut. Satin-finished pistol grip stock with fine-line cut checkering, Monte Carlo.
Sights: Gold bead ramp front; removable, step-adjustable rear with windage screw.
Features: Side safety, receiver tapped for scope mounts.
Price: From **$492.00**

Remington Model 700 BDL Bolt-Action Rifle
Same as the 700 ADL except chambered for 222, 223 (short action, 24" barrel), 22-250, 25-06, 6mm Rem. (short action, 22" barrel), 243, 270, 7mm-08, 280, 300 Savage, 30-06, 308; skip-line checkering; black forend tip and grip cap with white line spacers. Matted receiver top, fine-line engraving, quick-release floorplate. Hooded ramp front sight; quick detachable swivels.
Price: From **$585.00**
Also available in 17 Rem., 7mm Rem. Mag., 300 Win. Mag. (long action, 24" barrel), 338 Win. Mag., 35 Whelen (long action, 22" barrel). Overall length 44-1/2", weight about 7-1/2 lbs.
Price: From **$609.00**

Remington 700 VLS

Remington Model 700 Custom KS Mountain Rifle
Similar to the 700 BDL except custom finished with Kevlar reinforced resin synthetic stock. Available in both left- and right-hand versions. Chambered for 270 Win., 280 Rem., 30-06, 7mm Rem. Mag., 7mm STW, 300 Win. Mag., 300 Wea. Mag., 35 Whelen, 338 Win. Mag., 8mm Rem. Mag., 375 H&H, all with 24" barrel only. Weighs 6 lbs., 6 oz. Introduced 1986.
Price: From **$1,136.00**

Remington Model 700 VLS Varmint Laminated Stock
Similar to the 700 BDL except has 26" heavy barrel without sights, brown laminated stock with beavertail forend, grip cap, rubber buttpad. Available in 223 Rem., 22-250, 6mm, 260 Rem., 7mm-08, 243, 308. Polished blue finish. Introduced 1995.
Price: From **$625.00**

Remington Model 700 BDL DM Rifle
Same as the 700 BDL except has detachable box magazine (4-shot, standard calibers, 3-shot for magnums). Has glossy stock finish, fine-line engraving, open sights, recoil pad, sling swivels. Right-hand action calibers: 6mm, 243, 25-06, 270, 280, 7mm-08, 30-06, 308, 7mm Rem. Mag., 300 Win. Mag., 338 Win. Mag.; left-hand calibers: 270, 30-06, 7mm Rem. Mag., 300 Win. Mag. Introduced 1995.
Price: From **$639.00**

Remington Model 700 Safari
Similar to the 700 BDL except custom finished and tuned. In 8mm Rem. Mag., 375 H&H, 416 Rem. Mag. or 458 Win. Mag. calibers only with heavy barrel. Hand checkered, oil-finished stock in classic or Monte Carlo style with recoil pad installed. Delivery time is about 5 months.
Price: From **$1,140.00**
Price: Safari KS (Kevlar stock), right-hand, from **$1,140.00**

Remington Model 700 AWR Alaskan Wilderness Rifle
Similar to the Model 700 BDL except has stainless barreled action with satin blue finish; special 24" Custom Shop barrel profile; matte gray stock of fiberglass and graphite, reinforced with DuPont Kevlar, straight comb with raised cheekpiece, magnum-grade black rubber recoil pad. Chambered for 7mm Rem. Mag., 7mm STW, 300 Win. Mag., 300 Wea. Mag., 338 Win. Mag., 375 H&H. Introduced 1994.
Price: From **$1,376.00**

Remington Model 700 BDL Left Hand
Same as 700 BDL except mirror-image left-hand action, stock. Available in 270, 30-06, 7mm Rem. Mag.
Price: About **$612.00**
Price: 7mm Rem. Mag. **$639.00**

CONSULT

SHOOTER'S MARKETPLACE

Page 225, This Issue

Remington Model 700 BDL SS Rifle
Similar to the 700 BDL rifle except has hinged floorplate, 24" standard weight barrel in all calibers; magnum calibers have magnum-contour barrel. No sights supplied, but comes drilled and tapped. Has corrosion-resistant follower and fire control, stainless BDL-style barreled action with fine matte finish. Synthetic stock has straight comb and cheekpiece, textured finish, positive checkering, plated swivel studs. Calibers—270, 30-06; magnums—7mm Rem. Mag., 300 Win. Mag., 338 Win. Mag., 375 H&H. Weighs 6-3/4 - 7 lbs. Introduced 1993.
Price: From **$641.00**

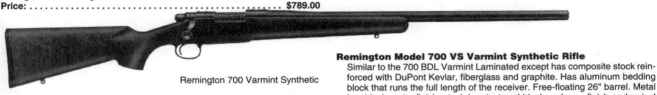

Remington 700 BDL SS DM-B

Remington Model 700 BDL SS DM-B
Same as the 700 BDL SS DM except has muzzlebrake, fine-line engraving. Available only in 7mm Rem. Mag., 7mm STW, 300 Win. Mag., 300 Wea. Mag., 338 Win. Mag. Introduced 1996.
Price: **$789.00**

Remington 700 Varmint Synthetic

Remington Model 700 Sendero Rifle
Similar to the Model 700 Varmint Synthetic except has long action for magnum calibers. Has 26" heavy varmint barrel with spherical concave crown. Chambered for 25-06, 270, 7mm Rem. Mag., 300 Win. Mag. Introduced 1994.
Price: From **$705.00**

Remington 700 Sendero SF

Remington Model 700 BDL SS DM Rifle
Same as the 700 BDL SS except has detachable box magazine. Barrel, receiver and bolt made of #416 stainless steel; black synthetic stock, fine-line engraving. Available in 243, 25-06, 260 Rem., 270, 280, 7mm-08, 308, 30-06, 7mm Rem. Mag., 300 Win. Mag., 300 Wea. Mag., 338 Win. Mag. Introduced 1995.
Price: From **$702.00**

Remington Model 700 VS Varmint Synthetic Rifle
Similar to the 700 BDL Varmint Laminated except has composite stock reinforced with DuPont Kevlar, fiberglass and graphite. Has aluminum bedding block that runs the full length of the receiver. Free-floating 26" barrel. Metal has black matte finish; stock has textured black and gray finish and swivel studs. Available in 220 Swift, 223, 22-250, 243, 308. Also available in left-hand model in 22-250, 223, 308. Introduced 1992.
Price: From **$705.00**

Remington Model 700 Sendero SF Rifle
Similar to the 700 Sendero except has stainless steel action and 26" fluted stainless barrel. Weighs 8-1/2 lbs. Chambered for 25-06, 7mm Rem. Mag., 300 Wea. Mag., 7mm STW, 300 Win. Mag. Introduced 1996.
Price: From **$852.00**

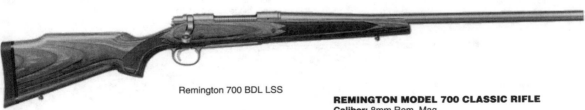

Remington 700 VS SF

Remington Model 700 APR African Plains Rifle
Similar to the Model 700 BDL except has magnum receiver and specially contoured 26" Custom Shop barrel with satin finish, laminated wood stock with raised cheekpiece, satin finish, black buttpad, 20 lpi cut checkering. Chambered for 7mm Rem. Mag., 300 Win. Mag., 300 Wea. Mag., 338 Win. Mag., 375 H&H. Introduced 1994.
Price: **$1,466.00**

Remington Model 700 VS SF Rifle
Similar to the Model 700 Varmint Synthetic except has satin-finish stainless barreled action with 26" fluted barrel, spherical concave muzzle crown, muzzle porting. Chambered for 223, 220 Swift, 22-250, 308. Introduced 1994.
Price: From **$852.00**

Remington Model 700 MTN DM Rifle
Similar to the 700 BDL except weighs 6-3/4 lbs., has a 22" tapered barrel. Redesigned pistol grip, straight comb, contoured cheekpiece, hand-rubbed oil stock finish, deep cut checkering, hinged floorplate and magazine follower, two-position thumb safety. Chambered for 243, 260 Rem., 270 Win., 7mm-08, 25-06, 280 Rem., 30-06, 4-shot detachable box magazine. Overall length is 42-1/2". Introduced 1995.
Price: About **$639.00**

Remington 700 BDL LSS

Remington Model 700 LSS Rifle
Similar to the 700 BDL except has stainless steel barreled action, gray laminated wood stock with Monte Carlo comb and cheekpiece. No sights furnished. Available in 7mm Rem. Mag. and 300 Win. Mag., in right-hand, and 270, 7mm Rem. Mag., 30-06, 300 Win. Mag. in left-hand model. Introduced 1996.
Price: From **$715.00**

REMINGTON MODEL 700 CLASSIC RIFLE
Caliber: 8mm Rem. Mag.
Barrel: 24".
Weight: About 7-3/4 lbs. **Length:** 44-1/2" overall.
Stock: American walnut, 20 lpi checkering on pistol grip and forend. Classic styling. Satin finish.
Sights: None furnished. Receiver drilled and tapped for scope mounting.
Features: A "classic" version of the M700 ADL with straight comb stock. Fitted with rubber recoil pad. Sling swivel studs installed. Hinged floorplate. Limited production in 1998 only.
Price: **$612.00**

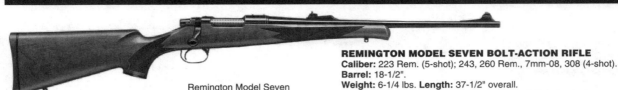

Remington Model Seven

Remington Model Seven Custom MS Rifle

Similar to the Model Seven except has full-length Mannlicher-style stock of laminated wood with straight comb, solid black recoil pad, black steel forend tip, cut checkering, gloss finish. Barrel length 20", weighs 6-3/4 lbs. Available in 222 Rem., 223, 22-250, 243, 6mm Rem., 260 Rem., 7mm-08 Rem., 308, 350 Rem. Mag. Calibers 250 Savage, 257 Roberts, 35 Rem. available on special order. Polished blue finish. Introduced 1993. From Remington Custom Shop.

Price: From **$1,140.00**

Remington Model Seven Youth Rifle

Similar to the Model Seven except has hardwood stock with 12-3/16" length of pull and chambered for 243, 260 Rem., 7mm-08. Introduced 1993.

Price: **$479.00**

Ruger M77 Mark II All-Weather

Ruger M77 Mark II All-Weather Stainless Rifle

Similar to the wood-stock M77 Mark II except all metal parts are of stainless steel, and has an injection-moulded, glass-fiber-reinforced Du Pont Zytel stock. Also offered with laminated wood stock. Chambered for 223, 243, 270, 308, 30-06, 7mm Rem. Mag., 300 Win. Mag., 338 Win. Mag. Has the fixed-blade-type ejector, three-position safety, and new trigger guard with patented floorplate latch. Comes with integral Scope Base Receiver and 1" Ruger scope rings, built-in sling swivel loops. Introduced 1990.

Price: KM77RPMKII **$574.00**
Price: KM77RSPMKII, open sights **$635.00**
Price: KM77RBZMKII, no sights, laminated wood stock, 223, 243, 270, 280 Rem., 7mm Rem. Mag., 30-06, 308, 300 Win. Mag., 338 Win. Mag. **$606.00**
Price: KM77RSBZMKII, open sights, laminated wood stock, 243, 270, 7mm Rem. Mag., 30-06, 300 Win. Mag., 338 Win. Mag. **$667.00**

Ruger M77RSI International Carbine

Same as the standard Model 77 except has 18-1/2" barrel, full-length International-style stock, with steel forend cap, loop-type steel sling swivels. Integral-base receiver, open sights, Ruger 1" steel rings. Improved front sight. Available in 243, 270, 308, 30-06. Weighs 7 lbs. Length overall is 38-3/8".

Price: M77RSIMKII **$642.00**

RUGER M77 MARK II EXPRESS RIFLE

Caliber: 270, 30-06, 7mm Rem. Mag., 300 Win. Mag., 4-shot magazine.
Barrel: 22", with integral steel rib; barrel-mounted front swivel stud; hammer forged.
Weight: 7.5 lbs. **Length:** 42.125" overall.
Stock: Hand-checkered medium quality French walnut with steel grip cap, black rubber butt pad, swivel studs.

REMINGTON MODEL SEVEN BOLT-ACTION RIFLE

Caliber: 223 Rem. (5-shot); 243, 260 Rem., 7mm-08, 308 (4-shot).
Barrel: 18-1/2".
Weight: 6-1/4 lbs. **Length:** 37-1/2" overall.
Stock: Walnut, with modified schnabel forend. Cut checkering.
Sights: Ramp front, adjustable open rear.
Features: Short-action design; silent side safety; free-floated barrel except for single pressure point at forend tip. Introduced 1983.
Price: **$585.00**

Remington Model Seven KS

Similar to the Model Seven except has gray Kevlar reinforced stock with 1" black rubber recoil pad and swivel studs. Metal has black matte finish. No sights on 223, 260 Rem., 7mm-08, 308; 35 Rem. and 350 Rem. have iron sights.

Price: **$1,136.00**

Remington Model Seven SS

Similar to the Model Seven except has stainless steel barreled action and black synthetic stock, 20" barrel. Chambered for 223, 243, 260 Rem., 7mm-08, 308. Introduced 1994.

Price: **$641.00**

RUGER M77 MARK II RIFLE

Caliber: 223, 243, 6mm Rem., 257 Roberts, 25-06, 6.5x55 Swedish, 270, 280 Rem., 308, 30-06, 7mm Rem. Mag., 300 Win. Mag., 338 Win. Mag., 4-shot magazine.
Barrel: 20", 22"; 24" (magnums).
Weight: About 7 lbs. **Length:** 39-3/4" overall.
Stock: Hand-checkered American walnut; swivel studs, rubber butt pad.
Sights: None furnished. Receiver has Ruger integral scope mount base, comes with Ruger 1" rings. Some models have iron sights.
Features: Short action with new trigger and three-position safety. New trigger guard with redesigned floorplate latch. Left-hand model available. Introduced 1989.

Price: M77RMKII (no sights) **$574.00**
Price: M77RSMKII (open sights) **$635.00**
Price: M77LRMKII (left-hand, 270, 30-06, 7mm Rem. Mag., 300 Win. Mag.) **$574.00**

Ruger M77RL Ultra Light

Similar to the M77 except weighs only 6 lbs., chambered for 223, 243, 308, 270, 30-06, 257; barrel tapped for target scope blocks; has 20" Ultra Light barrel. Overall length 40". Ruger's steel 1" scope rings supplied. Introduced 1983.

Price: M77RLMKII **$610.00**

Sights: Ramp front, V-notch two-leaf express rear adjustable for windage mounted on rib.
Features: Mark II action with three-position safety, stainless steel bolt, steel trigger guard, hinged steel floorplate. Introduced 1991.
Price: M77RSEXMKII **$1,550.00**

RUGER 77/22 HORNET BOLT-ACTION RIFLE

Caliber: 22 Hornet, 6-shot rotary magazine.
Barrel: 20".
Weight: About 6 lbs. **Length:** 39-3/4" overall.
Stock: Checkered American walnut, black rubber buttpad.
Sights: Brass bead front, open adjustable rear; also available without sights.
Features: Same basic features as the rimfire model except has slightly lengthened receiver. Uses Ruger rotary magazine. Three-position safety. Comes with 1" Ruger scope rings. Introduced 1994.

Price: 77/22RH (rings only) **$489.00**
Price: 77/22RSH (with sights) **$499.00**
Price: K77/22VHZ Varmint, laminated stock, no sights **$535.00**

Ruger 77/22 Hornet

Ruger M77VT Target

RUGER M77 MARK II MAGNUM RIFLE

Caliber: 375 H&H, 4-shot magazine; 416 Rigby, 3-shot magazine.
Barrel: 26", with integral steel rib; hammer forged.
Weight: 9.25 lbs. (375); 10.25 lbs. (416, 458). **Length:** 40.5" overall.
Stock: Circassian walnut with hand-cut checkering, swivel studs, steel grip cap, rubber butt pad.
Sights: Ramp front, two leaf express on serrated integral steel rib. Rib also serves as base for front scope ring.
Features: Uses an enlarged Mark II action with three-position safety, stainless bolt, steel trigger guard and hinged steel floorplate. Controlled feed. Introduced 1989.
Price: M77RSMMKII $1,550.00

RUGER M77VT TARGET RIFLE

Caliber: 22-250, 220 Swift, 223, 243, 25-06, 308.
Barrel: 26" heavy stainless steel with target gray finish.
Weight: Approx. 9.25 lbs. **Length:** Approx. 44" overall.
Stock: Laminated American hardwood with beavertail forend, steel swivel studs; no checkering or grip cap.
Sights: Integral scope mount bases in receiver.
Features: Ruger diagonal bedding system. Ruger steel 1" scope rings supplied. Fully adjustable trigger. Steel floorplate and trigger guard. New version introduced 1992.
Price: KM77VTMKII $684.00

Ruger 77/44

RUGER 77/44 BOLT-ACTION RIFLE

Caliber: 44 Magnum, 4-shot magazine.
Barrel: 18-1/2".

Weight: 6 lbs. **Length:** 38-1/4" overall.
Stock: American walnut with rubber buttpad and swivel studs.
Sights: Gold bead front, folding leaf rear. Comes with Ruger 1" scope rings.
Features: Uses same action as the Ruger 77/22. Short bolt stroke; rotary magazine; three-position safety. Introduced 1997. Made in U.S. by Sturm, Ruger & Co.
Price: $575.00

Sako 75 Hunter

Sako 75 Stainless Synthetic Rifle

Similar to the 75 Hunter except all metal is of stainless steel, and the synthetic stock has soft composite panels moulded into the forend and pistol grip. Available in 22-250, 243, 308 Win., 25-06, 270, 30-06 with 22" barrel, 7mm Rem. Mag., 300 Win. Mag. with 24" barrel. Introduced 1997. Imported from Finland by Stoeger Industries.
Price: Standard calibers $1,195.00
Price: Magnum calibers $1,225.00

SAKO 75 HUNTER BOLT-ACTION RIFLE

Caliber: 22-250, 243, 7MM-08, 308 Win., 25-06, 270, 280, 30-06; 270 Wea. Mag., 7mm Rem. Mag., 7mm STW, 7mm Wea. Mag., 300 Win. Mag., 300 Wea. Mag., 338 Win. Mag., 340 Wea. Mag., 375 H&H, 416 Rem. Mag.
Barrel: 22", standard calibers; 24", 26" magnum calibers.
Weight: About 6 lbs. **Length:** NA.
Stock: European walnut with matte lacquer finish.
Sights: None furnished; dovetail scope mount rails.
Features: New design with three locking lugs and a mechanical ejector; cold hammer-forged barrel is free-floating; two-position safety; hinged floorplate or detachable magazine that can be loaded from the top; short 70 degree bolt lift. Available in five action lengths. Introduced 1997. Imported form Finland by Stoeger Industries.
Price: Standard calibers $1,099.00
Price: Magnum Calibers $1,129.00

Sako 75 Varmint

Sako 75 Deluxe Rifle

Similar to the 75 Hunter except has select wood rosewood grip cap and forend tip. Available in 25-06, 270, 280, 30-06; 270 Wea. Mag., 7mm Rem. Mag., 7mm STW, 7mm Wea. Mag., 300 Win. Mag., 300 Wea. Mag., 338 Win. Mag., 340 Wea. Mag., 375 H&H, 416 Rem. Mag. Introduced 1997. Imported from Finland by Stoeger Industries.
Price: Standard calibers $1,565.00
Price: Magnum Calibers $1,598.00

Sako 75 Varmint Rifle

Similar to the Model 75 Hunter except chambered only for 17 Rem., 222 Rem., 223 Rem., 22-250 Rem.; 24" heavy barrel with recessed crown; beavertail forend. Introduced 1998. Imported from Finland by Stoeger Industries.
Price: $1,275.00

Sako 75 Super Deluxe Sporter

Similar to Hunter except has select European walnut with high-gloss finish and deep-cut oak leaf carving. Metal has super high polish, deep blue finish. Special order only.
Price: $3,400.00

Sako TRG-S

SAKO TRG-S BOLT-ACTION RIFLE

Caliber: 243, 7mm-08, 270, 6.5x55, 30-06, 7mm Rem. Mag., 300 Win. Mag., 338 Win. Mag., 270 Wea. Mag., 7mm Wea. Mag., 340 Wea. Mag., 375 H&H, 416 Rem. Mag., 5-shot magazine (4-shot for 375 H&H).

Barrel: 22", 24" (magnum calibers).
Weight: 7.75 lbs. **Length:** 45.5" overall.
Stock: Reinforced polyurethane with Monte Carlo comb.
Sights: None furnished.
Features: Resistance-free bolt with 60-degree lift. Recoil pad adjustable for length. Free-floating barrel, detachable magazine, fully adjustable trigger. Matte blue metal. Introduced 1993. Imported from Finland by Stoeger.
Price: 243, 7mm-08, 270, 30-06 . . . . $825.00
Price: Magnum calibers $865.00

SAUER 90 BOLT-ACTION RIFLE

Caliber: 22-250, 243, 6.5x55, 25-06, 270 Win., 308 Win., 30-06, 7mm Rem. Mag., 300 Win. Mag., 300 Wea. Mag., 338 Win. Mag., 375 H&H.
Barrel: 24" (standard calibers); 26" (magnums).
Weight: About 7.5 lbs. **Length:** 42.5" overall (24" barrel).
Stock: Select American Claro walnut with high-gloss epoxy finish, rosewood grip and forend caps; 22 lpi checkering.
Sights: None furnished; drilled and tapped for scope mounting.
Features: Three cam-actuated locking lugs on center of bolt; internal extractor; 65" bolt throw; detachable box magazine; tang safety; loaded chamber indicator; cocking indicator; adjustable trigger. Introduced 1986. Imported from Germany by Sigarms, Inc.
Price: Standard calibers $1,350.00
Price: Magnum calibers. $1,382.00

SAUER 202 BOLT-ACTION RIFLE

Caliber: Standard—243, 6.5x55, 270 Win., 308 Win., 30-06; magnum—7mm Rem. Mag., 300 Win. Mag., 300 Wea. Mag., 375 H&H.
Barrel: 23.6" (standard), 26" (magnum).
Weight: 7.7 lbs. (standard). **Length:** 44.3" overall (23.6" barrel).
Stock: Select American Claro walnut with high-gloss epoxy finish, rosewood grip and forend caps; 22 lpi checkering.
Sights: None furnished; drilled and tapped for scope mounting.
Features: Short 60" bolt throw; detachable box magazine; six-lug bolt; quick-change barrel; tapered bore; adjustable two-stage trigger; firing pin cocking indicator. Introduced 1994. Imported from Germany by Sigarms, Inc.
Price: Standard calibers, right-hand $985.00
Price: Magnum calibers, right-hand. $1,056.00
Price: Standard calibers, left-hand $1,056.00
Price: Magnum calibers, left-hand $1,115.00

Savage Model 10FM

Savage Model 10FM Sierra Ultra Light Rifle

Similar to the Model 110FM Sierra except has a true short action, chambered for 223, 243, 308; weighs 6 lbs. "Dual Pillar" bedding in black synthetic stock with silver medallion in grip cap. Comes with sling and quick-detachable swivels. Introduced 1998. Made in U.S. by Savage Arms, Inc.
Price: $425.00

Savage Model 10FP Tactical Rifle

Similar to the Model 110FP except has true short action, chambered for 223, 308; black synthetic stock with "Dual Pillar" bedding. Introduced 1998. Made in U.S. by Savage Arms, Inc.
Price: $446.00
Price: Model 10FLP (left-hand) $446.00

Savage Model 111FXP3, 111FCXP3 Package Guns

Similar to the Model 110 Series Package Guns except with lightweight, black graphite/fiberglass composite stock with non-glare finish, positive checkering. Same calibers as Model 110 rifles, plus 338 Win. Mag. Model 111FXP3 has fixed top-loading magazine; Model 111FCXP3 has detachable box. Both come with mounted 3-9x32 scope, quick-detachable swivels, sling. Introduced 1994. Made in U.S. by Savage Arms, Inc.
Price: Model 111FXP3, right- or left-hand. $450.00
Price: Model 111FCXP3, right- or left-hand $495.00

SAVAGE MODEL 110 FM SIERRA ULTRA LIGHT WEIGHT RIFLE

Caliber: 243, 270, 308, 30-06.
Barrel: 20"**Weight:** 6-1/4 lbs. **Length:** 41-1/2" overall.
Stock: Graphite/fiberglass-filled composite.
Sights: None furnished; drilled and tapped for scope mounting.
Features: Comes with black nylon sling and quick-detachable swivels. Introduced 1996. Made in U.S. by Savage Arms, Inc.
Price: $410.00

> Consult our Directory pages for the location of firms mentioned.

SAVAGE MODEL 110FP TACTICAL RIFLE

Caliber: 223, 25-06, 308, 30-06, 300 Win. Mag., 7mm Rem. Mag., 4-shot magazine.
Barrel: 24", heavy; recessed target muzzle.
Weight: 8-1/2 lbs. **Length:** 45.5" overall.
Stock: Black graphite/fiberglass composition; positive checkering.
Sights: None furnished. Receiver drilled and tapped for scope mounting.
Features: Pillar-bedded stock. Black matte finish on all metal parts. Double swivel studs on the forend for sling and/or bipod mount. Right or left-hand. Introduced 1990. From Savage Arms, Inc.
Price: Right- or left-hand $429.00

Savage Model 10GY

SAVAGE MODEL 110GXP3, 110GCXP3 PACKAGE GUNS

Caliber: 223, 22-250, 243, 250 Savage, 25-06, 270, 300 Sav., 30-06, 308, 7mm Rem. Mag., 7mm-08, 300 Win. Mag. (Model 110GXP3); 270, 30-06, 7mm Rem. Mag., 300 Win. Mag. (Model 110GCXP3).
Barrel: 22" (standard calibers), 24" (magnum calibers).
Weight: 7.25-7.5 lbs. **Length:** 43.5" overall (22" barrel).
Stock: Monte Carlo-style hardwood with walnut finish, rubber buttpad, swivel studs.
Sights: None furnished.
Features: Model 110GXP3 has fixed, top-loading magazine, Model 110GCXP3 has detachable box magazine. Rifles come with a factory-mounted and bore-sighted 3-9x32 scope, rings and bases, quick-detachable swivels, sling. Left-hand models available in all calibers. Introduced 1991 (GXP3); 1994 (GCXP3). Made in U.S. by Savage Arms, Inc.
Price: Model 110GXP3, right- or left-hand $420.00
Price: Model 110GCXP3, right- or left-hand $485.00

Savage Model 10GY, 110GY Rifle

Similar to the Model 111G except weighs 6.3 lbs., is 42-1/2" overall, and the stock is scaled for ladies, small-framed adults and youths. Chambered for 223, 243, 270, 308. Ramp front sight, open adjustable rear; drilled and tapped for scope mounts. Made in U.S. by Savage Arms, Inc.
Price: Model 110GY $360.00
Price: Model 10GY (short action, calibers 223, 243, 308) $374.00

SAVAGE MODEL 111 CLASSIC HUNTER RIFLES

Caliber: 223, 22-250, 243, 250 Sav., 25-06, 270, 300 Sav., 30-06, 308, 7mm Rem. Mag., 7mm-08, 300 Win. Mag., 338 Win. Mag. (Models 111G, GL, GNS, F, FL, FNS); 270, 30-06, 7mm Rem. Mag., 300 Win. Mag. (Models 111GC, GLC, FAK, FC, FLC).
Barrel: 22", 24" (magnum calibers).
Weight: 6.3 to 7 lbs. **Length:** 43.5" overall (22" barrel).
Stock: Walnut-finished hardwood (M111G, GC); graphite/fiberglass filled composite.
Sights: Ramp front, open fully adjustable rear; drilled and tapped for scope mounting.
Features: Three-position top tang safety, double front locking lugs, free-floated button-rifled barrel. Comes with trigger lock, target, ear puffs. Introduced 1994. Made in U.S. by Savage Arms, Inc.
Price: Model 111FC (detachable magazine, composite stock, right- or left-hand) $420.00
Price: Model 111F (top-loading magazine, composite stock, right- or left-hand) $380.00
Price: Model 111FNS (as above, no sights, right-hand only) $372.00
Price: Model 111G (wood stock, top-loading magazine, right- or left-hand) $360.00
Price: Model 111GC (as above, detachable magazine), right- or left-hand $410.00
Price: Model 111GNS (wood stock, top-loading magzine, no sights, right-hand only). $353.00
Price: Model 111FAK Express (blued, composite stock, top loading magazine, Adjustable Muzzle Brake) $450.00

Savage Model 11G

Savage Model 11 Hunter Rifles

Similar to the Model 111F except has true short action, chambered for 223, 22-250, 243, 308; black synthetic stock with "Dual Pillar" bedding, positive checkering. Introduced 1998. Made in U.S. by Savage Arms, Inc.
Price: Model 11F $395.00
Price: Model 11FL (left-hand) $395.00
Price: Model 11FNS (right-hand, no sights). $387.00
Price: Model 11G (wood stock) $374.00
Price: Model 11GL (as above, left-hand) $374.00
Price: Model 11GNS (wood stock, no sights) $367.00

SAVAGE MODEL 112 LONG RANGE RIFLES
Caliber: 22-250, 223, 5-shot magazine.
Barrel: 26" heavy.
Weight: 8.8 lbs. **Length:** 47.5" overall.
Stock: Black graphite/fiberglass filled composite with positive checkering.
Sights: None furnished; drilled and tapped for scope mounting.
Features: Pillar-bedded stock. Blued barrel with recessed target-style muzzle. Double front swivel studs for attaching bipod. Introduced 1991. Made in U.S. by Savage Arms, Inc.
Price: Model 112FV **$410.00**
Price: Model 112FVSS (cals. 223, 22-250, 25-06, 7mm Rem. Mag., 300 Win. Mag., stainless barrel, bolt handle, trigger guard), right- or left-hand **$515.00**
Price: Model 112FVSS-S (as above, single shot) **$515.00**
Price: Model 112BVSS (heavy-prone laminated stock with high comb, Wundhammer swell, fluted stainless barrel, bolt handle, trigger guard). **$540.00**
Price: Model 112BVSS-S (as above, single shot) **$540.00**

Savage Model 12FV

SAVAGE MODEL 114C CLASSIC RIFLE
Caliber: 270, 30-06, 7mm Rem. Mag., 300 Win. Mag.; 4-shot detachable box magazine in standard calibers, 3-shot for magnums.
Barrel: 22" for standard calibers, 24" for magnums.
Weight: 7-1/8 lbs. **Length:** 45-1/2" overall.
Stock: Oil-finished American walnut; checkered grip and forend.
Sights: None furnished; drilled and tapped for scope mounting.
Features: High polish blue on barrel, receiver and bolt handle; Savage logo laser-etched on bolt body; push-button magazine release. Made in U.S. by Savage Arms, Inc. Introduced 1996.
Price: $525.00

Savage Model 116US Ultra Stainless Rifle
Similar to the Model 116SE except chambered for 270, 30-06, 7mm Rem. Mag., 300 Win. Mag.; stock has high-gloss finish; no open sights. Stainless steel barreled action with satin finish. Introduced 1995. Made in U.S. by Savage Arms, Inc.
Price: $700.00

Savage Model 16FSS Rifle
Similar to the Model 116FSS except has true short action, chambered for 223, 243, 308; 22" free-floated barrel; black graphite/fiberglass stock with "Dual Pillar" bedding. Introduced 1998. Made in U.S. by Savage Arms, Inc.
Price: $515.00
Price: Model 16FLSS (left-hand) $515.00

Savage Model 12 Longe Range Rifles
Similar to the Model 112 Long Range except with true short action, chambered for 223, 22-250, 308. Models 12FV, 12FVSS have black synthetic stocks with "Dual Pillar" bedding, positive checkering, swivel studs; model 12BVSS has brown laminated stock with beavertail forend, fluted stainless barrel. Introduced 1998. Made in U.S. by Savage Arms, Inc.
Price: Model 12FV (223, 22-250 only, blue) **$429.00**
Price: Model 12FVSS (blue action, fluted stainless barrel) **$534.00**
Price: Model 12FLVSS (as above, left-hand) **$534.00**
Price: Model 12FVSS-S (blue action, fluted stainless barrel, single shot) **$534.00**
Price: Model 12BVSS (laminated stock) **$560.00**
Price: Model 12BVSS-S (as above, single shot) **$560.00**

Savage Model 114CE Classic European
Similar to the Model 114C except the oil-finished walnut stock has a schnabel forend tip, cheekpiece and skip-line checkering; bead on blade front sight, fully adjustable open rear; solid red buttpad. Chambered for 270, 30-06, 7mm Rem. Mag., 300 Win. Mag. Introduced 1996. Made in U.S. by Savage Arms, Inc.
Price: $600.00

SAVAGE MODEL 116SE SAFARI EXPRESS RIFLE
Caliber: 300 Win. Mag., 338 Win. Mag., 425 Express, 458 Win. Mag.
Barrel: 24".
Weight: 8.5 lbs. **Length:** 45.5" overall.
Stock: Classic-style select walnut with ebony forend tip, deluxe cut checkering. Two cross bolts; internally vented recoil pad.
Sights: Bead on ramp front, three-leaf express rear.
Features: Controlled-round feed design; adjustable muzzlebrake; one-piece barrel band stud. Satin-finished stainless steel barreled action. Introduced 1994. Made in U.S. by Savage Arms, Inc.
Price: $900.00

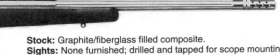

Savage Model 116FCSAK

SAVAGE MODEL 116 WEATHER WARRIORS
Caliber: 223, 243, 270, 30-06, 7mm Rem. Mag., 300 Win. Mag., 338 Win. Mag. (Model 116FSS); 270, 30-06, 7mm Rem. Mag., 300 Win. Mag. (Models 116FCSAK, 116FCS); 270, 30-06, 7mm Rem. Mag., 300 Win. Mag., 338 Win. Mag. (Models 116FSAK, 116FSK).
Barrel: 22", 24" for 7mm Rem. Mag., 300 Win. Mag., 338 Win. Mag. (M116FSS only).
Weight: 6.25 to 6.5 lbs. **Length:** 43.5" overall (22" barrel).

Stock: Graphite/fiberglass filled composite.
Sights: None furnished; drilled and tapped for scope mounting.
Features: Stainless steel with matte finish; free-floated barrel; quick-detachable swivel studs; laser-etched bolt; scope bases and rings. Left-hand models available in all models, calibers at same price. Models 116FCS, 116FSS introduced 1991; Model 116FSK introduced 1993; Model 116FCSAK, 116FSAK introduced 1994. Made in U.S. by Savage Arms, Inc.
Price: Model 116FSS (top-loading magazine) **$495.00**
Price: Model 116FCS (detachable box magazine). **$560.00**
Price: Model 116FCSAK (as above with Savage Adjustable Muzzle Brake system) **$650.00**
Price: Model 116FSAK (top-loading magazine, Savage Adjustable Muzzle Brake system) **$585.00**
Price: Model 116FSK Kodiak (as above with 22" Shock-Suppressor barrel). **$554.00**

Sigarms SHR 970

Weight: 7.2 lbs. **Length:** 41.9" overall.
Stock: Textured black fiberglass.
Sights: None furnished; drilled and tapped for scope mounting.
Features: Quick takedown; interchangeable barrels; removable box magazine; cocking indicator; three-position safety. Introduced 1998. Imported by Sigarms, Inc.
Price: $499.00

SIGARMS SHR 970 SYNTHETIC RIFLE
Caliber: 270, 30-06.
Barrel: 22".

Steyr-Mannlicher SBS

Barrel: 23.6" standard, 26" magnum; 20" full stock standard calibers.
Weight: 7 lbs. **Length:** 40.1" overall.
Stock: Hand-checkered fancy European oiled walnut with schnabel forend.
Sights: Ramp front adjustable for elevation, V-notch rear adjustable for windage.
Features: Single adjustable trigger; 3-position roller safety with "safe-bolt" setting; drilled and tapped for Steyr factory scope mounts. Introduced 1997. Imported from Austria by GSI, Inc.

STEYR MANNLICHER SBS RIFLE
Caliber: 243, 25-06, 308, 6.5x55, 6.5x57, 270, 7x64 Brenneke, 7mm-08, 7.5x55, 30-06, 9.3x62, 6.5x68, 7mm Rem. Mag., 300 Win. Mag., 8x685, 4-shot magazine.

Price: Half-stock, standard calibers $2,795.00
Price: Half-stock, magnum calibers $2,995.00
Price: Full-stock, standard calibers $2,995.00

Steyr SBS Prohunter

STEYR SBS FORESTER RIFLE
Caliber: 243, 25-06, 270, 7mm-08, 308 Win., 30-06, 7mm Rem. Mag., 300 Win. Mag. Detachable 4-shot magazine.
Barrel: 23.6", standard calibers; 25.6", magnum calibers.
Weight: 7.5 lbs. **Length:** 44.5" overall (23.6" barrel).
Stock: Oil-finished American walnut with Monte Carlo cheekpiece. Pachmayr 1" swivels.
Sights: None furnished. Drilled and tapped for Browning A-Bolt mounts.
Features: Steyr Safe Bolt systems, three-position ambidextrous roller tang safety, for Safe, Loading Fire. Matte finish on barrel and receiver; adjustable trigger. Rotary cold-hammer forged barrel. Introduced 1997. Imported by GSI, Inc.

Steyr SBS Prohunter Rifle
Similar to the SBS Forester except has ABS synthetic stock with adjustable butt spacers, straight comb without cheekpiece, palm swell, Pachmayr 1" swivels. Special 10-round magazine conversion kit available. Introduced 1997. Imported by GSI.
Price Standard calibers $799.00
Price Magnum calibers $899.00

Price: Standard caliber $899.00
Price: Magnum calibers $1,045.00

Steyr Scout Rifle

STEYR SSG BOLT-ACTION RIFLES
Caliber: 308 Win., detachable 5-shot rotary magazine.
Barrel: 26"
Weight: 8.5 lbs. **Length:** 44.5" overall.
Stock: Black ABS Cycolac with spacers for length of pull adjustment.
Sights: Hooded ramp front adjustable for elevation, V-notch rear adjustable for windage.
Features: Sliding safety; NATO rail for bipod; 1" swivels; Parkerized finish; single or double-set triggers. Imported from Austria by GSI, Inc.
Price: SSG-PI, iron sights $2,195.00
Price: SSG-PII, heavy barrel, no sights $2,195.00
Price: SSG-PIIK, 20" heavy barrel, no sights $2,195.00
Price: SSG-PIV, 16.75" threaded heavy barrel with flash hider.... $2,660.00

STEYR SCOUT BOLT-ACTION RIFLE
Caliber: 308 Win., 5-shot magazine.
Barrel: 19", fluted.
Weight: NA. **Length:** NA.
Stock: Gray Zytel.
Sights: None furnished; comes with Leupold M8 2.5x28 IER scope on Picatinny optic rail with Steyr mounts.
Features: Comes with luggage case, scout sling, two stock spacers, two magazines. Introduced 1998. From GSI.
Price: From $2,595.00

Tikka Whitetail Hunter

Weight: 7-1/8 lbs. **Length:** 43" overall (std. cals.).
Stock: European walnut with Monte Carlo comb, rubber buttpad, checkered grip and forend.
Sights: None furnished.
Features: Detachable four-shot magazine (standard calibers), three-shot in magnums. Receiver dovetailed for scope mounting. Reintroduced 1996. Imported from Finland by Stoeger Industries.
Price: Standard calibers $598.00
Price: Magnum calibers $624.00

TIKKA WHITETAIL HUNTER BOLT-ACTION RIFLE
Caliber: 22-250, 223, 243, 25-06, 270, 308, 30-06, 7mm Rem. Mag., 300 Win. Mag., 338 Win. Mag.
Barrel: 22-1/2" (std. cals.), 24-1/2" (magnum cals.).

Tikka Whitetail Hunter Synthetic Rifle

Similar to the Whitetail Hunter except has black synthetic stock; calibers 223, 308, 25-06, 270 Win., 30-06, 7mm Rem. Mag., 300 Win. Mag., 338 Win. Mag. Introduced 1996. Imported from Finland by Stoeger.

Price: Standard calibers.....................................$598.00
Price: Magnum calibers....................................$624.00

Tikka Continental Long Range Hunting Rifle

Similar to the Whitetail Hunter except has 26" heavy barrel. Available in 25-06, 270 Win., 7mm Rem. Mag., 300 Win. Mag. Introduced 1996. Imported from Finland by Stoeger.

Price: 25-06, 270 Win......................................$694.00
Price: 7 Rem. Mag., 300 Win. Mag.........................$724.00

Ultra Light Arms Model 28, Model 32, Model 40 Rifles

Ultra Light Arms Model 20

Similar to the Model 20 except in 264, 7mm Rem. Mag., 300 Win. Mag., 338 Win. Mag. (Model 28), 300 Wea. Mag., 416 Rigby (Model 40). Both use 24" Douglas Premium No. 2 contour barrel. Weighs 5-1/2 lbs., 45" overall length. KDF or ULA recoil arrestor built in. Any custom feature available on any ULA product can be incorporated.

Price: Right-hand, Model 28 or 40.........................$2,900.00
Price: Left-hand, Model 28 or 40..........................$3,000.00
Price: Right-hand, Model 32 (7mm STW, 8mm Rem. Mag., 300 Wea. Mag., 340 Wea. Mag., 375 H&H)...................$2,900.00
Price: Left-hand, Model 32, calibers as above.............$3,000.00

Tikka Whitetail Hunter Stainless Synthetic

Similar to the Whitetail Hunter except all metal is of stainless steel, and it has a black synthetic stock. Available in 22-250, 243, 25-06, 308, 30-06, 7mm Rem. Mag., 300 Win. Mag., 338 Win. Mag. Introduced 1997. Imported from Finland by Stoeger.

Price: Standard calibers.....................................$655.00
Price: Magnum calibers....................................$685.00

Tikka Continental Varmint Rifle

Similar to the standard Tikka rifle except has 26" heavy barrel, extra-wide forend. Chambered for 22-250, 223, 308. Reintroduced 1996. Made in Finland by Sako. Imported by Stoeger.

Price: $694.00

ULTRA LIGHT ARMS MODEL 20 RIFLE

Caliber: 17 Rem., 22 Hornet, 222 Rem., 223 Rem. (Model 20S); 22-250, 6mm Rem., 243, 257 Roberts, 7x57, 7x57 Ackley, 7mm-08, 284 Win., 308 Savage. Improved and other calibers on request.
Barrel: 22" Douglas Premium No. 1 contour.
Weight: 4-1/2 lbs. **Length:** 41-1/2" overall.
Stock: Composite Kevlar, graphite reinforced. DuPont imron paint colors— green, black, brown and camo options. Choice of length of pull.
Sights: None furnished. Scope mount included.
Features: Timney adjustable trigger; two-position three-function safety. Benchrest quality action. Matte or bright stock and metal finish. 3" magazine length. Shipped in a hard case. From Ultra Light Arms, Inc.
Price: Right-hand $2,500.00
Price: Model 20 Left Hand (left-hand action and stock) $2,600.00
Price: Model 24 Long Action (25-06, 270, 7mm Express, 30-06, 3-3/8" magazine length) $2,600.00
Price: Model 24 Long Action Left Hand (left-hand action and stock) $2,700.00

Voere VEC-91

Voere VEC-91BR Caseless Rifle

Similar to the VEC-91 except has heavy 20" barrel, synthetic benchrest stock, and is a single shot. Drilled and tapped for scope mounting. Introduced 1995. Imported from Austria by JagerSport, Ltd.

Price: $1,995.00

Voere VEC-91HB Varmint Special Caseless Rifle

Similar to the VEC-91 except has 22" heavy sporter barrel, black synthetic or laminated wood stock. Drilled and tapped for scope mounts. Introduced 1995. Imported from Austria by JagerSport, Ltd.

Price: $1,695.00

VOERE VEC-91 LIGHTNING BOLT-ACTION RIFLE

Caliber: 5.56 UCC (223-cal.), 6mm UCC caseless, 5-shot magazine.
Barrel: 20".
Weight: 6 lbs. **Length:** 39" overall.
Stock: European walnut with cheekpiece, checkered grip and schnabel forend.
Sights: Blade on ramp front, open adjustable rear.
Features: Fires caseless ammunition via electric ignition; two batteries housed in the pistol grip last for about 5000 shots. Trigger is adjustable from 5 oz. to 7 lbs. Bolt action has twin forward locking lugs. Top tang safety. Drilled and tapped for scope mounting. Ammunition available from importer. Introduced 1991. Imported from Austria by JagerSport, Ltd.
Price: About $1,995.00

Voere VEC-91SS Caseless Rifle

Similar to the VEC-91 except has synthetic stock with straight comb, matte-finished metal. Drilled and tapped for scope mounting. No open sights furnished. Introduced 1995. Imported from Austria by JagerSport, Ltd.
Price: 5.56mm UCC or 6mm UCC $1,495.00

Weatherby Mark V

Weatherby Mark V Euromark Rifle

Similar to the Mark V Deluxe except has raised-comb Monte Carlo stock with hand-rubbed oil finish, fine-line hand-cut checkering, ebony grip and forend tips. All metal has low-luster blue. Right-hand only. Uses Mark V action. Introduced 1995. Made in U.S. From Weatherby.

Price: 257, 270, 7mm, 300, 340 Wea. Mags., 26" barrel........$1,499.00
Price: 378 Wea. Mag., 26" barrel..........................$1,586.00
Price: 416 Wea. Mag., 26" barrel..........................$1,758.00
Price: 7mm Rem. Mag., 300 Win. Mag., 338 Win. Mag., 375 H&H, 24"..$1,499.00

WEATHERBY MARK V DELUXE BOLT-ACTION RIFLE

Caliber: All Weatherby calibers.
Barrel: 26" round tapered.
Weight: 8-1/2 lbs. to 10-1/2 lbs. **Length:** 46-5/8" to 46-3/4" overall.
Stock: Walnut, Monte Carlo with cheekpiece; high luster finish; checkered pistol grip and forend; recoil pad.
Sights: None furnished.
Features: Cocking indicator; adjustable trigger; hinged floorplate, thumb safety; quick detachable sling swivels. Made in U.S. From Weatherby.
Price: 257, 270, 7mm. 300, 340 Wea. Mags 26" barrel $1,499.00
Price: 378 Wea. Mag. 26" barrel $1,586.00
Price: 416 Wea. Mag. with Accubrake, 26" barrel $1,758.00
Price: 460 Wea. Mag. with Accubrake, 26" barrel $2,056.00

Weatherby Mark V SLS

Weatherby Mark V SLS Stainless Laminate Sporter

Similar to the Mark V Stainless except all metalwork is 400 series stainless with a corrosion-resistant black oxide bead-blast matte finish. Action is hand-bedded in a laminated stock with a 1" recoil pad. Weighs 8-1/2 lbs. Introduced 1997. Made in U.S. From Weatherby.

Price: 257, 270, 7mm, 300, 340 Wea. Mag., 26" barrel **$1,249.00**
Price: 7mm Rem. Mag., 300 Win. Mag., 338 Win. Mag., 24" barrel. **$1,249.00**

Weatherby Mark V Fluted Stainless

Similar to the Mark V Stainless except has fluted barrel. Weighs 7-1/2 lbs. Introduced 1997. Made in U.S. from Weatherby.

Price: 257, 270, 7mm, 300 Wea. Mag., 26" barrel **$1,149.00**
Price: 7mm Rem. Mag., 300 Win. Mag., 24" barrel. **$1,149.00**

Weatherby Mark V Lazermark Rifle

Same as Mark V Deluxe except stock has extensive oak leaf pattern laser carving on pistol grip and forend. Introduced 1981.

Price: 257, 270, 7mm Wea. Mag., 300, 340, 26" **$1,599.00**
Price: 378 Wea. Mag., 26" **$1,701.00**
Price: 416 Wea. Mag., 26", Accubrake **$1,869.00**
Price: 460 Wea. Mag., 26", Accubrake **$2,196.00**

Weatherby Mark V Fluted Synthetic

Similar to the Mark V Synthetic except has fluted barrel. Weighs 7-1/2 lbs. Introduced 1997. Made in U.S. From Weatherby.

Price: 257, 270, 7mm, 300 Wea. Mag., 26" barrel **$949.00**
Price: 7mm Rem. Mag., 300 Win. Mag., 24" barrel. **$949.00**

Weatherby Accumark Ultra Light

Weatherby Mark V Accumark Ultra Light Weight Rifle

Similar to the Mark V Accumark except weighs 5-3/4 lbs.; free-floated 24" fluted barrel with recessed target crown; hand-laminated stock with CNC-machined aluminum bedding plate and faint gray "spider web" finish. Available in 243, 240 Wea. Mag., 25-06, 270 Win., 280 Rem., 7mm-08, 30-06, 308. Introduced 1998. Made in U.S. from Weatherby.

Price: **$1,199.00**

Weatherby Mark V Stainless Rifle

Similar to the Mark V Deluxe except made of 400-series stainless steel. Also available in 30-378 Wea. Mag. Has lightweight injection-moulded synthetic stock with raised Monte Carlo comb, checkered grip and forend, custom floorplate release. Right-hand only. Introduced 1995. Made in U.S. From Weatherby.

Price: 257, 270, 7mm, 300, 340 Wea. Mags., 26" barrel **$999.00**
Price: 7mm Rem. Mag., 300, 338 Win. Mags., 24" barrel **$999.00**
Price: 375 H&H, 24" barrel **$999.00**
Price: 30-378 Wea. Mag **$1,149.00**

Weatherby Mark V Eurosport Rifle

Similar to the Mark V Deluxe except has raised-comb Monte Carlo stock with hand-rubbed satin oil finish, low-luster blue metal. No grip cap or forend tip. Right-hand only. Introduced 1995. Made in U.S. From Weatherby.

Price: 257, 270, 7mm, 300, 340 Wea. Mags., 26" barrel **$949.00**
Price: 7mm Rem. Mag., 300, 338 Win. Mags., 24" barrel **$949.00**
Price: 375 H&H, 24" barrel **$949.00**

Weatherby Mark V Sporter Rifle

Same as the Mark V Deluxe without the embellishments. Metal has low-luster blue, stock is Claro walnut with high-gloss epoxy finish, Monte Carlo comb, recoil pad. Introduced 1993.

Price: 257 270, 7mm, 300, 340 Wea. Mags., 26" **$949.00**
Price: 375 H&H, 24" **$949.00**
Price: 7mm Rem. Mag., 300 Win. Mag., 338 Win. Mag., 24", ... **$949.00**

Weatherby Mark V Synthetic Rifle

Similar to the Mark V except has synthetic stock with raised Monte Carlo comb, dual-taper checkered forend. Low-luster blued metal. Weighs 8 lbs. Uses Mark V action. Right-hand only. Also available in 30-378 Wea. Mag. Introduced 1995. Made in U.S. From Weatherby.

Price: 257, 270, 7mm, 300, 340 Wea. Mags., 26" barrel **$799.00**
Price: 7mm Rem. Mag., 300, 338 Win. Mags., 24" barrel **$799.00**
Price: 375 H&H, 24" barrel **$799.00**
Price: 30-378 Wea. Mag **$949.00**

WEATHERBY MARK V ACCUMARK RIFLE

Caliber: 257, 270, 7mm, 300, 340 Wea. Mags., 338-378 Wea. Mag., 30-378 Wea. Mag., 7mm STW, 7mm Rem. Mag., 300 Win. Mag.
Barrel: 26".
Weight: 8-1/2 lbs. **Length:** 46-5/8" overall.
Stock: H-S Precision Pro-Series synthetic with aluminum bedding plate.
Sights: None furnished. Drilled and tapped for scope mounting.
Features: Uses Mark V action with heavy-contour stainless barrel with black oxidized flutes, muzzle diameter of .705". Introduced 1996. Made in U.S. From Weatherby.
Price: **$1,299.00**
Price: 30-378 Wea. Mag., 338-378 Wea. Mag., 26", Accubrake . . . **$1,499.00**

Weatherby Mark V Accumark Light Weight Rifle

Similar to the Mark V Accumark except chambered for 22-250, 243, 240 Wea. Mag., 25-06, 270, 280 Rem., 7mm-08, 30-06, 308; fluted 24" heavy-contour stainless barrel; hand-laminated Monte Carlo-style stock with aluminum bedding plate. Weighs 7 lbs.; 44" overall. Introduced 1998. Made in U.S. from Weatherby.

Price: **$1,199.00**

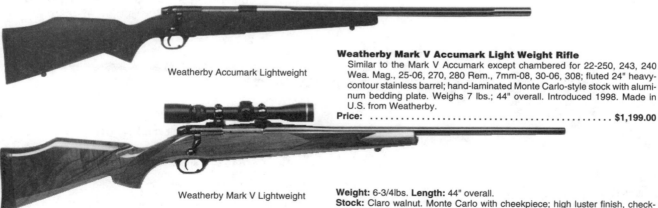

Weatherby Accumark Lightweight

Weatherby Mark V Lightweight

WEATHERBY MARK V LIGHTWEIGHT SPORTER BOLT ACTION RIFLE

Caliber: 22-250, 243, 25-06, 270, 7MM-08, 280, 30-06, 308, 240 Wea. Mag.
Barrel: 24".

Weight: 6-3/4lbs. **Length:** 44" overall.
Stock: Claro walnut. Monte Carlo with cheekpiece; high luster finish, checkered pistol grip and forend, recoil pad.
Sights: None furnished. Drilled and tapped for scope mounting.
Features: Cocking indicator; adjustable trigger; hinged floorplate; thumb safety; six locking lugs; quick detachable swivels. Introduced 1997. Made in U.S. from Weatherby.
Price: **$849.00**

Weatherby Mark V Lightweight Stainless

Similar to the lightweight Sporter except made of 400 series stainless steel; injection moulded synthetic stock with Monte Carlo comb, checkered grip and forend. Weighs 6-1/2 lbs. Introduced 1997. Made in U.S. From Weatherby.

Price: **$899.00**
Price: Lightweight Stainless Carbine (as above with 20" barrel, 243 Win., 7mm-08 Rem., 308 Win.), weighs 6 lbs. **$899.00**

WICHITA VARMINT RIFLE

Caliber: 222 Rem., 222 Rem. Mag., 223 Rem., 22 PPC, 6mm PPC, 22-250, 243, 6mm Rem., 308 Win.; other calibers on special order.
Barrel: 20-1/8".
Weight: 9 lbs. **Length:** 40-1/8" overall.
Stock: AAA Fancy American walnut. Hand-rubbed finish, hand checkered, 20 lpi pattern. Hand-inletted, glass bedded, steel grip cap. Pachmayr rubber recoil pad.
Sights: None. Drilled and tapped for scope mounts.
Features: Right- or left-hand Wichita action with three locking lugs. Available as a single shot only. Checkered bolt handle. Bolt is hand fitted, lapped and jeweled. Side thumb safety. Firing pin fall is 3/16". Non-glare blue finish. From Wichita Arms.
Price: Single shot **$2,695.00**

Wilderness Explorer

Weatherby Mark V Lightweight Carbine

Similar to the Mark V Lightweight Synthetic except has 20" barrel; injection moulded synthetic stock. Available in 243, 7mm-08, 308. Weighs 6 lbs.; overall length 40". Introduced 1997. Made in U.S. From Weatherby.
Price: **$699.00**

Weatherby Mark V Lightweight Synthetic

Similar to the Mark V Lightweight Stainless except made of matte finished blued steel. Injection moulded synthetic stock. Weighs 6-1/2 lbs., 24" barrel. Available in 22-250, 240 Wea. Mag., 243, 25-06, 270, 7mm-08, 280, 30-06, 308. Introduced 1997. Made in U.S. From Weatherby.
Price: **$699.00**

WICHITA CLASSIC RIFLE

Caliber: 17-222, 17-222 Mag., 222 Rem., 222 Rem. Mag., 223 Rem., 6x47; other calibers on special order.
Barrel: 21-1/8".
Weight: 8 lbs. **Length:** 41" overall.
Stock: AAA Fancy American walnut. Hand-rubbed and checkered (20 lpi). Hand-inletted, glass bedded, steel grip cap. Pachmayr rubber recoil pad.
Sights: None. Drilled and tapped for scope mounting.
Features: Available as single shot only. Octagonal barrel and Wichita action, right- or left-hand. Checkered bolt handle. Bolt is hand-fitted, lapped and jeweled. Adjustable trigger is set at 2 lbs. Side thumb safety. Firing pin fall is 3/16". Non-glare blue finish. From Wichita Arms.
Price: Single shot **$3,495.00**

WILDERNESS EXPLORER MULTI-CALIBER CARBINE

Caliber: 22 Hornet, 218 Bee, 44 Magnum, 50 A.E. (interchangeable).
Barrel: 18", match grade.
Weight: 5.5 lbs **Length:** 38-1/2" overall.
Stock: Synthetic or wood.
Sights: None furnished; comes with Weaver-style mount on barrel.
Features: Quick-change barrel and bolt face for caliber switch. Removable box magazine; adjustable trigger with side safety; detachable swivel studs. Introduced 1997. Made in U.S. by Phillips & Rogers, Inc.
Price: **$995.00**

Winchester Model 70 Classic

Winchester Model 70 Synthetic Heavy Varmint Rifle

Similar to the Model 70 Classic Sporter except has fiberglass/graphite stock, 26" heavy stainless steel barrel, blued receiver. Weighs about 10-3/4 lbs. Available in 220 Swift, 222, 22-250, 243, 308. Uses full-length Pillar Plus Accu Block bedding system. Introduced 1993.
Price: **$764.00**
Price: With fluted barrel **$894.00**

Winchester Model 70 Classic Featherweight

Same as the Model 70 Classic except has claw controlled-round feeding system; action is bedded in a standard-grade walnut stock. Available in 22-250, 243, 6.5x55, 308, 7mm-08, 270 Win., 280 Rem., 30-06. Drilled and tapped for scope mounts. Weighs 7.25 lbs. Introduced 1992.
Price: **$620.00**
Price: Classic Featherweight Stainless, as above except made of stainless steel, and available in 22-250, 243, 270, 308, 30-06, 7mm Rem. Mag., 300 Win. Mag. **$716.00**

Winchester Model 70 Classic Featherweight All-Terrain

Similar to the Model 70 Classic Featherweight except has black, fiberglass/graphite stock in same style as the Classic Featherweight, barreled action made of stainless steel. Calibers 270 Win., 30-06, 7mm Rem. Mag., 300 Win. Mag. Introduced 1996.
Price: **$672.00**

WINCHESTER MODEL 70 CLASSIC SPORTER

Caliber: 25-06, 270 Win., 270 Wea., 30-06, 264 Win. Mag., 7mm STW, 7mm Rem. Mag., 300 Win. Mag., 300 Wea. Mag., 338 Win. Mag., 3-shot magazine; 5-shot for 25-06, 270 Win., 30-06.
Barrel: 24", 26" for magnums.
Weight: 7-3/4 lbs. **Length:** 44-3/4" overall.
Stock: American walnut with cut checkering and satin finish. Classic style with straight comb.
Sights: Optional hooded ramp front, adjustable folding leaf rear. Drilled and tapped for scope mounting.
Features: Uses pre-64-type action with controlled round feeding. Three-position safety, stainless steel magazine follower; rubber buttpad; epoxy bedded receiver recoil lug. BOSS barrel vibration modulator and muzzlebrake system optional. From U.S. Repeating Arms Co.
Price: Without sights. **$613.00**
Price: With BOSS (25-06, 264 Win. Mag., 270 Win., 270 Wea. Mag., 30-06, 7mm Rem. Mag., 300 Win. Mag., 300 Wea. Mag., 338 Win. Mag.) **$728.00**
Price: Left-hand, 270, 30-06, 7mm Rem. Mag., 7mm STW, 300 Win. Mag., 338 Win. Mag. **$641.00**
Price: With BOSS, left-hand, 270, 30-06, 7mm Rem. Mag., 7mm STW, 300 Win. Mag. **$756.00**
Price: Classic Sporter Stainless, 270, 30-06, 7mm Rem. Mag., 300 Win. Mag., 338 Win. Mag. **$716.00**
Price: As above, left-hand **$745.00**

Winchester Model 70 Classic Compact

Winchester Model 70 Classic Compact

Similar to the Classic Featherweight except scaled down for smaller shooters. Has 20" barrel, 12-1/2" length of pull. Pre-'64-type action. Available in 243, 308 or 7mm-08. Introduced 1998. Made in U.S. by U. S. Repeating Arms.
Price: **$620.00**

Winchester Model 70
Classic Laminated

WINCHESTER RANGER RIFLE
Caliber: 223, 243, 270, 30-06, 7mm Rem. Mag.
Barrel: 22".
Weight: 7-3/4 lbs. **Length:** 42" overall.
Stock: Stained hardwood.
Sights: Hooded blade front, adjustable open rear.
Features: Three-position safety; push feed bolt with recessed-style bolt face; polished blue finish; drilled and tapped for scope mounting. Introduced 1985. From U.S. Repeating Arms Co.
Price: $482.00
Price: Ranger Ladies/Youth, 223, 243, 7mm-08, 308 only, scaled-down stock $482.00

WINCHESTER MODEL 70 CLASSIC SUPER GRADE
Caliber: 270, 30-06, 5-shot magazine; 7mm Rem. Mag., 300 Win. Mag., 338 Win. Mag., 3-shot magazine.
Barrel: 24", 26" for magnums.
Weight: About 7-3/4 lbs. to 8 lbs. **Length:** 44-1/2" overall (24" bbl.)
Stock: Walnut with straight comb, sculptured cheekpiece, wrap-around cut checkering, tapered forend, solid rubber buttpad.
Sights: None furnished; comes with scope bases and rings.
Features: Controlled round feeding with stainless steel claw extractor, bolt guide rail, three-position safety; all steel bottom metal, hinged floorplate, stainless magazine follower. Introduced 1994. From U.S. Repeating Arms Co.
Price: $840.00

Winchester Model 70 Classic Stainless Rifle
Same as the Model 70 Classic Sporter except has stainless steel barrel and pre-64-style action with controlled round feeding and matte gray finish, black composite stock impregnated with fiberglass and graphite, contoured rubber recoil pad. Available in 22-250, 243, 308, 270 Win., 270 Wea. Mag., 30-06, 7mm Rem. Mag., 300 Win. Mag., 300 Wea. Mag., 338 Win. Mag., 375 H&H Mag. (24" barrel), 3- or 5-shot magazine. Weighs 6.75 lbs. BOSS barrel vibration modulator and muzzlebrake system optional. Introduced 1994.
Price: Without sights $672.00
Price: 375 H&H Mag., with sights $724.00
Price: With BOSS $788.00
Price: Classic Laminated Stainless (gray laminated stock, 270, 30-06, 7mm Rem. Mag., 300 Win. Mag., 338 Win. Mag. $735.00
Price: Classic Camo Stainless (Mossy Oak Treestand camo on composite stock, 270, 30-06, 7mm Rem. Mag., 300 Win. Mag.) $745.00

WINCHESTER MODEL 70 CLASSIC SUPER EXPRESS MAGNUM
Caliber: 375 H&H Mag., 416 Rem. Mag., 458 Win. Mag., 3-shot magazine.
Barrel: 24" (375, 416), 22" (458).
Weight: 8-1/4 to 8-1/2 lbs.
Stock: American walnut with Monte Carlo cheekpiece. Wrap-around checkering and finish.
Sights: Hooded ramp front, open rear.
Features: Controlled round feeding. Two steel cross bolts in stock for added strength. Front sling swivel stud mounted on barrel. Contoured rubber buttpad. From U.S. Repeating Arms Co.
Price: $865.00
Price: Left-hand, 375 H&H only $894.00

Winchester Model 70 Laredo

WINCHESTER MODEL 70 CLASSIC LAREDO
Caliber: 7mm Rem. Mag., 7mm STW, 300 Win. Mag., 3-shot magazine.
Barrel: 26" heavy; 1:10" (300), 1:9.5" (7mm).
Weight: 9-1/2 lbs. **Length:** 46-3/4" overall.

Stock: H-S Precision gray, synthetic with "Pillar Plus Accu-Block" bedding system, wide beavertail forend.
Sights: None furnished; drilled and topped for scope mounting.
Features: Pre-64-style, controlled round action with claw extractor, receiver-mounted blade ejector; matte blue finish. Introduced 1996. Made in U.S. by U.S. Repeating Arms Co.
Price: $764.00
Price: With BOSS $879.00
Price: With fluted barrel $894.00

Classic and modern designs for sporting and competitive use.

ARMSPORT 1866 SHARPS RIFLE, CARBINE
Caliber: 45-70.
Barrel: 28", round or octagonal.
Weight: 8.10 lbs. **Length:** 46" overall.
Stock: Walnut.
Sights: Blade front, folding adjustable rear. Tang sight set optionally available.
Features: Replica of the 1866 Sharps. Color case-hardened frame, rest blued. Imported by Armsport.
Price: $865.00
Price: With octagonal barrel $900.00
Price: Carbine, 22" round barrel $850.00

AMERICAN ARMS/UBERTI 1883 SINGLE SHOT
Caliber: 45-70.
Barrel: 28".
Weight: 8.2 lbs. **Length:** NA.
Stock: European walnut.
Sights: Bead on blade front, open step-adjustable rear.
Features: Recreation of the 1883 Winchester. Color case-hardened receiver and lever, blued barrel. Introduced 1998. Imported from Italy by American Arms, Inc.
Price: $810.00

BROWN MODEL 97D SINGLE SHOT RIFLE
Caliber: 17 Ackley Hornet through 45-70 Govt.
Barrel: Up to 26", air gauged match grade.
Weight: About 5 lbs., 11oz.
Stock: Sporter style with pistol grip, cheekpiece and schnabel forend.
Sights: None furnished; drilled and tapped for scope mounting.
Features: Falling block action gives rigid barrel-receiver mating; polished blue/black finish. Hand-fitted action. Made in U.S. by E. A. Brown Mfg.
Price: $599.00

Brown Model 97D

Browning Model 1885
Traditional Hunter

Browning Model 1885 Traditional Hunter
Similar to the Model 1885 High Wall except chambered for 357 Mag., 44 Mag., 45 Colt, 30-30, 38-55 and 45-70 only; steel crescent buttplate; 1/16" gold bead front sight, adjustable buckhorn rear, and tang-mounted peep sight with barrel-type elevation adjuster and knob-type windage adjustments. Barrel is drilled and tapped for a Browning scope base. Oil-finished select walnut stock with swivel studs. Introduced 1997. Imported for Japan by Browning.
Price: **$1,149.95**

Browning Model 1885 Low Wall

Browning Model 1885 Low Wall Rifle
Similar to the Model 1885 High Wall except has trimmer receiver, thinner 24" octagonal barrel. Forend is mounted to the receiver. Adjustable trigger. Walnut pistol grip stock, trim schnabel forend with high-gloss finish. Available in 22 Hornet, 223 Rem., 243 Win. Overall length 39-1/2", weighs 6 lbs., 4 oz. Rifling twist rates: 1:16" (22 Hornet); 1:12" (223); 1:10" (243). Polished blue finish. Introduced 1995. Imported from Japan by Browning.
Price: **$939.95**

BRNO ZBK 110 SINGLE SHOT RIFLE
Caliber: 222 Rem., 5.6x52R, 22 Hornet, 5.6x50 Mag., 6.5x57R, 7x57R, 8x57JRS.
Barrel: 23.6".
Weight: 5.9 lbs. **Length:** 40.1" overall.
Stock: European walnut.
Sights: None furnished; drilled and tapped for scope mounting.

BROWNING MODEL 1885 HIGH WALL SINGLE SHOT RIFLE
Caliber: 22-250, 30-06, 270, 7mm Rem. Mag., 454 Casull, 45-70.
Barrel: 28".
Weight: About 8-1/2 lbs. **Length:** 43-1/2" overall.
Stock: Walnut with straight grip, schnabel forend.
Sights: None furnished; drilled and tapped for scope mounting.
Features: Replica of J.M. Browning's high-wall falling block rifle. Octagon barrel with recessed muzzle. Imported from Japan by Browning. Introduced 1985.
Price: **$939.95**

Browning Model 1885 BPCR Rifle
Similar to the 1885 High Wall rifle except the ejector system and shell deflector have been removed; chambered only for 40-65 and 45-70; color case-hardened full-tang receiver, lever, buttplate and grip cap; matte blue 30" part octagon, part round barrel. The Vernier tang sight has indexed elevation, is screw adjustable windage, and has three peep diameters. The hooded front sight has a built-in spirit level and comes with sight interchangeable inserts. Adjustable trigger. Overall length 46-1/8", weighs about 11 lbs. Introduced 1996. Imported from Japan by Browning.
Price: **$1,664.95**
Price: BPCR Creedmoor (45-90, 34" barrel with wind gauge sight) . . . **$1,680.00**

Features: Top tang opening lever; cross-bolt safety; polished blue finish. Announced 1998. Imported from The Czech Republic by Euro-Imports.
Price: Standard calibers **$223.00**
Price: 7x57R, 8x57JRS **$245.00**
Price: Lux model, standard calibers **$311.00**
Price: Lux model, 7x57R, 8x57JRS **$333.00**

Cabela's Sharps

CUMBERLAND MOUNTAIN PLATEAU RIFLE
Caliber: 40-65, 45-70.
Barrel: Up to 32"; round.
Weight: About 10-1/2 lbs. (32" barrel). **Length:** 48" overall (32" barrel).
Stock: American walnut.
Sights: Marble's bead front, Marble's open rear.
Features: Falling block action with underlever. Blued barrel and receiver. Stock has lacquer finish, crescent buttplate. Introduced 1995. Made in U.S. by Cumberland Mountain Arms, Inc.
Price: **$1,085.00**

CABELA'S SHARPS SPORTING RIFLE
Caliber: 40-65, 45-70.
Barrel: 32", tapered octagon.
Weight: 9 lbs. **Length:** 47-1/4" overall.
Stock: Checkered walnut.
Sights: Blade front, open adjustable rear.
Features: Color case-hardened receiver and hammer, rest blued. Introduced 1995. Imported by Cabela's.
Price: **$799.99**

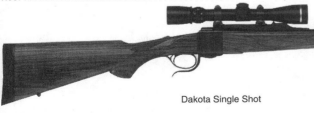

Dakota Single Shot

DAKOTA SINGLE SHOT RIFLE
Caliber: Most rimmed and rimless commercial calibers.
Barrel: 23".
Weight: 6 lbs. **Length:** 39-1/2" overall.
Stock: Medium fancy grade walnut in classic style. Checkered grip and forend.
Sights: None furnished. Drilled and tapped for scope mounting.
Features: Falling block action with under-lever. Top tang safety. Removable trigger plate for conversion to single set trigger. Introduced 1990. Made in U.S. by Dakota Arms.
Price: **$2,995.00**
Price: Barreled action **$2,000.00**
Price: Action only **$1,675.00**

Consult our Directory pages for the location of firms mentioned.

Dixie 1874 Sharps Silhouette

Dixie 1874 Sharps Lightweight Hunter/Target Rifle

Same as the Dixie 1874 Sharps Blackpowder Silhouette model except has a straight-grip buttstock with military-style buttplate. Based on the 1874 military model. Introduced 1995. Imported from Italy by Dixie Gun Works.

Price: **$995.00**

E.M.F. SHARPS RIFLE

Caliber: 45-70.
Barrel: 28", octagon.
Weight: 10-3/4 lbs. **Length:** NA.
Stock: Oiled walnut.
Sights: Blade front, flip-up open rear.

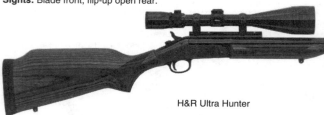

H&R Ultra Hunter

HARRIS GUNWORKS ANTIETAM SHARPS RIFLE

Caliber: 40-65, 45-75.
Barrel: 30", 32", octagon or round, hand-lapped stainless or chrome-moly.
Weight: 11.25 lbs. **Length:** 47" overall.
Stock: Choice of straight grip, pistol grip or Creedmoor with schnabel forend; pewter tip optional. Standard wood is A Fancy; higher grades available.
Sights: Montana Vintage Arms #111 Low Profile Spirit Level front, #108 mid-range tang rear with windage adjustments.
Features: Re-creation of the 1874 Sharps sidehammer. Action is color case-hardened, barrel satin black. Chrome-moly barrel optionally blued. Optional sights include #112 Spirit Level Globe front with windage, #107 Long Range rear with windage. Introduced 1994. Made in U.S. by Harris Gunworks.

Price: **$2,400.00**

MODEL 1885 HIGH WALL RIFLE

Caliber: 30-40 Krag, 32-40, 38-55, 40-65 WCF, 45-70.
Barrel: 26" (30-40), 28" all others. Douglas Premium #3 tapered octagon.
Weight: NA. **Length:** NA.
Stock: Premium American black walnut.
Sights: Marble's standard ivory bead front, #66 long blade top rear with reversible notch and elevator.
Features: Re-creation of early octagon top, thick-wall High Wall with Coil spring action. Tang drilled, tapped for High Wall tang sight. Receiver, lever, hammer and breechblock color case-hardened. Introduced 1991. Available from Montana Armory, Inc.

Price: **$1,095.00**

Navy Arms 1885

NAVY ARMS 1874 SHARPS CAVALRY CARBINE

Caliber: 45-70.
Barrel: 22".
Weight: 7lbs., 12 oz. **Length:** 39" overall.
Stock: Walnut.
Sights: Blade front, military ladder-type rear.
Features: Replica of the 1874 Sharps military carbine. Color case-hardened receiver and furniture. Imported by Navy Arms.

Price: **$935.00**

DIXIE 1874 SHARPS BLACKPOWDER SILHOUETTE RIFLE

Caliber: 45-70.
Barrel: 30"; tapered octagon; blued; 1:18" twist.
Weight: 10 lbs., 3 oz. **Length:** 47-1/2" overall.
Stock: Oiled walnut.
Sights: Blade front, ladder-type hunting rear.
Features: Replica of the Sharps #1 Sporter. Shotgun-style butt with checkered metal buttplate; color case-hardened receiver, hammer, lever and buttplate. Tang is drilled and tapped for tang sight. Double-set triggers. Meets standards for NRA blackpowder cartridge matches. Introduced 1995. Imported from Italy by Dixie Gun Works.

Price: **$995.00**

Features: Replica of the 1874 Sharps Sporting rifle. Color case-hardened lock; double-set trigger; blue finish. Imported by E.M.F.

Price: **$950.00**
Price: With browned finish **$1,000.00**
Price: Carbine (round 22" barrel, barrel band) **$860.00**

HARRINGTON & RICHARDSON ULTRA VARMINT RIFLE

Caliber: 223, 243.
Barrel: 24", heavy.
Weight: About 7.5 lbs. **Length:** NA.
Stock: Hand-checkered laminated birch with Monte Carlo comb.
Sights: None furnished. Drilled and tapped for scope mounting.
Features: Break-open action with side-lever release, positive ejection. Comes with scope mount. Blued receiver and barrel. Swivel studs. Introduced 1993. From H&R 1871, Inc.

Price: **$254.95**

Harrington & Richardson Ultra Hunter Rifle

Similar to the Ultra Varmint rifle except chambered for 25-06 with 26" barrel, or 308 Win., 357 Rem. Max. with 22" barrel. Stock and forend are of cinnamon-colored laminate; hand-checkered grip and forend. Introduced 1995. Made in U.S. by H&R 1871, Inc.

Price: **$249.95**

Harrington & Richardson Ultra Comp Rifle

Similar to the Ultra Varmint except chambered for 270 or 30-06; has compensator to reduce recoil; camo-laminate stock and forend; blued, highly polished frame; scope mount. Made in U.S. by H&R 1871, Inc.

Price: **$289.95**

NAVY ARMS 1885 HIGH WALL RIFLE

Caliber: 45-70; others available on special order.
Barrel: 28" round, 30" octagonal.
Weight: 9.5 lbs. **Length:** 45-1/2" overall (30" barrel).
Stock: Walnut.
Sights: Blade front, buckhorn rear; globe front, Vernier tang-mounted peep rear.
Features: Replica of Winchester's High Wall designed by Browning. Color case-hardened receiver, blued barrel. Introduced 1998. Imported by Navy Arms.

Price: 28", round barrel, buckhorn sights **$745.00**
Price: As above, target sights **$845.00**
Price: 30" octagonal barrel, buckhorn sight **$815.00**
Price: As above, target sights **$915.00**

Navy Arms #2 Creedmoor

Navy Arms #2 Creedmoor Rolling Block Rifle

Similar to the Navy Arms Rolling Block Buffalo Rifle except has 30" tapered octagon barrel, checkered full-pistol grip stock, blade front sight, open adjustable rear sight and Creedmoor tang sight. Imported by Navy Arms.
Price: **$900.00**

Navy Arms Sharps Plains Rifle

Similar to the Sharps Buffalo rifle except 45-70, only has 32" medium-weight barrel, weighs 9 lbs., 8 oz., and is 49" overall. Imported by Navy Arms.
Price: **$1,055.00**

Navy Arms 1874 Sharps Sniper Rifle

Similar to the Navy Arms Sharps Carbine except has 30" barrel, double-set triggers; weighs 8 lbs., 8 oz., overall length 46-3/4". Introduced 1984. Imported by Navy Arms.
Price: **$1,115.00**
Price: 1874 Sharps Infantry Rifle (three-band) **$1,060.00**

NAVY ARMS 1873 SPRINGFIELD CAVALRY CARBINE

Caliber: 45-70.
Barrel: 22".
Weight: 7 lbs. **Length:** 40-1/2" overall.
Stock: Walnut.
Sights: Blade front, military ladder rear.
Features: Blued lockplate and barrel; color case-hardened breechblock; saddle ring with bar. Replica of 7th Cavalry gun. Imported by Navy Arms.
Price: **$870.00**

NAVY ARMS ROLLING BLOCK BUFFALO RIFLE

Caliber: 45-70.
Barrel: 26", 30".
Stock: Walnut.
Sights: Blade front, adjustable rear.
Features: Reproduction of classic rolling block action. Available with full-octagon or half-octagon-half-round barrel. Color case-hardened action. From Navy Arms.
Price: **$745.00**

NAVY ARMS SHARPS BUFFALO RIFLE

Caliber: 45-70, 45-90.
Barrel: 28" heavy octagon.
Weight: 10 lbs., 10 oz. **Length:** 46" overall.
Stock: Walnut; checkered grip and forend.
Sights: Blade front, ladder rear; tang sight optional.
Features: Color case-hardened receiver, blued barrel; double-set triggers. Imported by Navy Arms.
Price: **$1,090.00**

Navy Arms Sharps Sporting Rifle

Same as the Navy Arms Sharps Plains Rifle except has pistol grip stock. Introduced 1997. Imported by Navy Arms.
Price: 45-70 only **$1,090.00**

Navy Arms 1873 Springfield Infantry Rifle

Same action as the 1873 Springfield Cavalry Carbine except in rifle configuration with 32-1/2" barrel, three-band full-length stock. Introduced 1997. Imported by Navy Arms.
Price: **$995.00**

New England Firearms Super Light

New England Firearms Super Light Rifle

Similar to the Handi-Rifle except has new barrel taper, shorter 20" barrel with recessed muzzle and special lightweight synthetic stock and forend. No sights are furnished on the 223 and 243 versions, but have a factory-mounted scope base and offset hammer spur; Monte Carlo stock; 22 Hornet has ramp front, fully adjustable open rear. Overall length is 36", weight is 5.5 lbs. Introduced 1997. Made in U.S. by New England Firearms.
Price: 22 Hornet, 223 Rem. or 243 Win. **$219.95**

NEW ENGLAND FIREARMS HANDI-RIFLE

Caliber: 22 Hornet, 223, 243, 7x57, 7x64 Brenneke, 30-30, 270, 280 Rem., 308, 30-06, 44 Mag., 45-70.
Barrel: 22", 24"; 26" for 280 Rem.
Weight: 7 lbs.
Stock: Walnut-finished hardwood; black rubber recoil pad.
Sights: Ramp front, folding rear (22 Hornet, 30-30, 45-70). Drilled and tapped for scope mount; 223, 243, 270, 280, 30-06 have no open sights, come with scope mounts.
Features: Break-open action with side-lever release. The 223, 243, 270 and 30-06 have recoil pad and Monte Carlo stock for shooting with scope. Swivel studs on all models. Blue finish. Introduced 1989. From New England Firearms.
Price: **$209.95**
Price: 7x57, 7x64 Brenneke, 24" barrel **$211.95**
Price: 280 Rem., 26" barrel **$214.95**
Price: Synthetic Handi-Rifle (black polymer stock and forend, swivels, recoil pad) **$219.95**
Price: Handi-Rifle Youth (223, 243) **$209.95**

New England Firearms Survivor

NEW ENGLAND FIREARMS SURVIVOR RIFLE

Caliber: 223, 357 Mag., single shot.
Barrel: 22".
Weight: 6 lbs. **Length:** 36" overall.
Stock: Black polymer, thumbhole design.
Sights: Blade front, fully adjustable open rear.
Features: Receiver drilled and tapped for scope mounting. Stock and forend have storage compartments for ammo, etc.; comes with integral swivels and black nylon sling. Introduced 1996. Made in U.S. by New England Firearms.
Price: Blue **$219.95**
Price: Electroless nickel **$234.95**

Remington No. 1 Mid-Range

REMINGTON NO.1 ROLLING BLOCK MID-RANGE SPORTER
Caliber: 30-30, 444 Marlin, 45-70.
Barrel: 30" round.
Weight: 8-3/4 lbs. **Length:** 46-1/2" overall.
Stock: American walnut with checkered pistol grip and forend.
Sights: Beaded blade front, adjustable center-notch buckhorn rear.
Features: Recreation of the original. Polished blue metal finish. Many options available. Introduced 1998. Made in U.S. by Remington.
Price: $1,278.00

Ruger No. 18

Ruger No. 1A Light Sporter
Similar to the No. 1B Standard Rifle except has lightweight 22" barrel, Alexander Henry-style forend, adjustable folding leaf rear sight on quarter-rib, dovetailed ramp front with gold bead. Calibers 243, 30-06, 270 and 7x57. Weighs about 7-1/4 lbs.
Price: No. 1A $685.00
Price: Barreled action $465.00

Ruger No. 1V Special Varminter
Similar to the No. 1B Standard Rifle except has 24" heavy barrel. Semi-beavertail forend, barrel tapped for target scope block, with 1" Ruger scope rings. Calibers 22-250, 220 Swift, 223, 25-06. Weight about 9 lbs.
Price: No. 1V $685.00
Price: Barreled action $465.00

RUGER NO. 1B SINGLE SHOT
Caliber: 218 Bee, 22 Hornet, 220 Swift, 22-250, 223, 243, 6mm Rem., 25-06, 257 Roberts, 270, 280, 30-06, 7mm Rem. Mag., 300 Win. Mag., 338 Win. Mag., 270 Wea., 300 Wea.
Barrel: 26" round tapered with quarter-rib; with Ruger 1" rings.
Weight: 8 lbs. **Length:** 43-3/8" overall.
Stock: Walnut, two-piece, checkered pistol grip and semi-beavertail forend.
Sights: None, 1" scope rings supplied for integral mounts.
Features: Under-lever, hammerless falling block design has auto ejector, top tang safety.
Price: $685.00
Price: Barreled action $465.00

Ruger No. 1H Tropical Rifle
Similar to the No. 1B Standard Rifle except has Alexander Henry forend, adjustable folding leaf rear sight on quarter-rib, ramp front with dovetail gold bead, 24" heavy barrel. Calibers 375 H&H, 416 Rem. Mag. (weighs about 8-1/4 lbs.), 416 Rigby, and 458 Win. Mag. (weighs about 9 lbs.).
Price: No. 1H $685.00
Price: Barreled action $465.00

Ruger No. 1 RSI

Ruger No. 1 RSI International
Similar to the No. 1B Standard Rifle except has lightweight 20" barrel, full-length International-style forend with loop sling swivel, adjustable folding leaf rear sight on quarter-rib, ramp front with gold bead. Calibers 243, 30-06, 270 and 7x57. Weight is about 7-1/4 lbs.
Price: No. 1 RSI $699.00
Price: Barreled action $465.00

Ruger No. 1S Medium Sporter
Similar to the No. 1B Standard Rifle except has Alexander Henry-style forend, adjustable folding leaf rear sight on quarter-rib, ramp front sight base and dovetail-type gold bead front sight. Calibers 218 Bee, 7mm Rem. Mag., 338 Win. Mag., 300 Win. Mag. with 26" barrel, 45-70 with 22" barrel. Weighs about 7-1/2 lbs. In 45-70.
Price: No. 1S $685.00
Price: Barreled action $465.00

C. Sharps New Model 1874

C. Sharps Arms 1875 Classic Sharps
Similar to the New Model 1875 Sporting Rifle except has 26", 28" or 30" full octagon barrel, crescent buttplate with toe plate, Hartford-style forend with cast German silver nose cap. Blade front sight, Rocky Mountain buckhorn rear. Weighs 10 lbs. Introduced 1987. From C. Sharps Arms Co. and Montana Armory, Inc.
Price: $1,185.00

C. Sharps Arms New Model 1875 Target & Long Range
Similar to the New Model 1875 except available in all listed calibers except 22 LR; 34" tapered octagon barrel; globe with post front sight, Long Range Vernier tang sight with windage adjustments. Pistol grip stock with cheek rest; checkered steel buttplate. Introduced 1991. From C. Sharps Arms Co. and Montana Armory, Inc.
Price: $1,535.00

C. SHARPS ARMS NEW MODEL 1875 OLD RELIABLEÆ RIFLE
Caliber: 22LR, 32-40 & 38-55 Ballard, 38-56 WCF, 40-65 WCF, 40-90 3-1/4", 40-90 2-5/8", 40-70 2-1/10", 40-70 2-1/4", 40-70 2-1/2", 40-50 1-11/16", 40-50 1-7/8", 45-90, 45-70, 45-100, 45-110, 45-120. Also available on special order only in 50-70, 50-90, 50-140.
Barrel: 24", 26", 30" (standard), 32", 34" optional.
Weight: 8-12 lbs.
Stock: Walnut, straight grip, shotgun butt with checkered steel buttplate.
Sights: Silver blade front, Rocky Mountain buckhorn rear.
Features: Re-creation of the 1875 Sharps rifle. Production guns will have case colored receiver. Available in Custom Sporting and Target versions upon request. Announced 1986. From C. Sharps Arms Co. and Montana Armory, Inc.
Price: 1875 Carbine (24" tapered round bbl.) $810.00
Price: 1875 Saddle Rifle (26" tapered oct. bbl.) $910.00
Price: 1875 Sporting Rifle (30" tapered oct. bbl.) $975.00
Price: 1875 Business Rifle (28" tapered round bbl.) $860.00

C. Sharps New Model 1885

C. SHARPS ARMS NEW MODEL 1874 OLD RELIABLEÆ
Caliber: 40-50, 40-70, 40-90, 45-70, 45-90, 45-100, 45-110, 45-120, 50-70, 50-90, 50-140.
Barrel: 26", 28", 30" tapered octagon.
Weight: About 10 lbs. **Length:** NA.
Stock: American black walnut; shotgun butt with checkered steel buttplate; straight grip, heavy forend with schnabel tip.
Sights: Blade front, buckhorn rear. Drilled and tapped for tang sight.
Features: Re-creation of the Model 1874 Old Reliable Sharps Sporting Rifle. Double set triggers. Reintroduced 1991. Made in U.S. by C. Sharps Arms. Available from Montana Armory, Inc.
Price: $1,175.00

SHILOH SHARPS 1874 LONG RANGE EXPRESS
Caliber: 40-50 BN, 40-70 BN, 40-90 BN, 45-70 ST, 45-90 ST, 45-110 ST, 50-70 ST, 50-90 ST, 50-110 ST, 32-40, 38-55, 40-70 ST, 40-90 ST.
Barrel: 34" tapered octagon.
Weight: 10-1/2 lbs. **Length:** 51" overall.
Stock: Oil-finished semi-fancy walnut with pistol grip, shotgun-style butt, traditional cheek rest, schnabel forend.
Sights: Globe front, sporting tang rear.
Features: Re-creation of the Model 1874 Sharps rifle. Double set triggers. Made in U.S. by Shiloh Rifle Mfg. Co.
Price: $1,434.00
Price: Sporting Rifle No. 1 (similar to above except with 30" bbl., blade front, buckhorn rear sight) $1,408.00
Price: Sporting Rifle No. 3 (similar to No. 1 except straight-grip stock, standard wood) $1,304.00
Price: 1874 Hartford model $1,474.00

SHARPS 1874 RIFLE
Caliber: 45-70.
Barrel: 28", octagonal.
Weight: 9-1/4 lbs. **Length:** 46" overall.
Stock: Checkered walnut.
Sights: Blade front, adjustable rear.

Thompson/Center Encore

THOMPSON/CENTER CONTENDER CARBINE
Caliber: 22 LR, 22 Hornet, 223 Rem., 7mm T.C.U., 7x30 Waters, 30-30 Win., 357 Rem. Maximum, 35 Rem., 44 Mag., 410, single shot.
Barrel: 21".
Weight: 5 lbs., 2 oz. **Length:** 35" overall.
Stock: Checkered American walnut with rubber buttpad. Also with Rynite stock and forend.
Sights: Blade front, open adjustable rear.
Features: Uses the T/C Contender action. Eleven interchangeable barrels available, all with sights, drilled and tapped for scope mounting. Introduced 1985. Offered as a complete Carbine only.
Price: Rifle calibers $540.00
Price: Extra barrels, rifle calibers, each $239.00

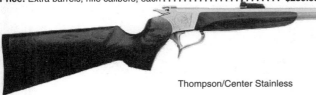

Thompson/Center Stainless

C. SHARPS ARMS NEW MODEL 1885 HIGHWALL RIFLE
Caliber: 22 LR, 22 Hornet, 219 Zipper, 25-35 WCF, 32-40 WCF, 38-55 WCF, 40-65, 30-40-Krag, 40-50 ST or BN, 40-70 ST or BN, 40-90 ST or BN, 45-70 2-1/10" ST, 45-90 2-4/10" ST, 45-100 2-6/10" ST, 45-110 2-7/8" ST, 45-120 3-1/4" ST.
Barrel: 26", 28", 30", tapered full octagon.
Weight: About 9 lbs., 4 oz. **Length:** 47" overall.
Stock: Oil-finished American walnut; schnabel-style forend.
Sights: Blade front, buckhorn rear. Drilled and tapped for optional tang sight.
Features: Single trigger; octagonal receiver top; checkered steel buttplate; color case-hardened receiver and buttplate, blued barrel. Many options available. Made in U.S. by C. Sharps Arms Co. Available from Montana Armory, Inc.
Price: From $1,195.00

Shiloh Sharps 1874 Business Rifle
Similar to No. 3 Rifle except has 28" heavy round barrel, military-style buttstock and steel buttplate. Weight about 9-1/2 lbs. Calibers 40-50 BN, 40-70 BN, 40-90 BN, 45-70 ST, 45-90 ST, 50-70 ST, 50-100 ST, 32-40, 38-55, 40-70 ST, 40-90 ST.
Price: $1,310.00
Price: 1874 Saddle Rifle (similar to Carbine except has 26" octagon barrel, semi-fancy shotgun butt) $1,362.00

Shiloh Sharps 1874 Montana Roughrider
Similar to the No. 1 Sporting Rifle except available with half-octagon or full-octagon barrel in 24", 26", 28", 30", 34" lengths; standard supreme or semi-fancy wood, shotgun, pistol grip or military-style butt. Weight about 8-1/2 lbs. Calibers 30-40, 30-30, 40-50x1-11/16"BN, 40-70x2-1/10" BN, 45-70x2-1/10"ST. Globe front and tang sight optional.
Price: Standard supreme $1,304.00
Price: Semi-fancy $1,414.00

Features: Double set triggers on rifle. Color case-hardened receiver and buttplate, blued barrel. Imported from Italy by E.M.F.
Price: Rifle or carbine $950.00
Price: Military rifle, carbine $860.00
Price: Sporting rifle $860.00

THOMPSON/CENTER ENCORE RIFLE
Caliber: 22-250, 223, 243, 270, 7mm-08, 308, 30-06, 7mm Rem. Mag., 300 Win. Mag.
Barrel: 24", 26".
Weight: 6 lbs., 12 oz. (24" barrel). **Length:** 38-1/2" (24" barrel).
Stock: American walnut. Monte Carlo style; schnabel forend.
Sights: Ramp-style white bead front, fully adjustable leaf-type rear.
Features: Interchangeable barrels; action opens by squeezing trigger guard; drilled and tapped for T/C scope mounts; polished blue finish. Introduced 1996. Made in U.S. by Thompson/Center Arms.
Price: $562.00
Price: Extra barrels. $250.00

Thompson/Center Contender Carbine Youth Model
Same as the standard Contender Carbine except has 16-1/4" barrel, shorter buttstock with 12" length of pull. Comes with fully adjustable open sights. Overall length is 29", weight about 4 lbs., 9 oz. Available in 22 LR, 223 Rem.
Price: $573.00
Price: Extra barrels. $239.00

Thompson/Center Stainless Contender Carbine
Same as the blued Contender Carbine except made of stainless steel with blued sights. Available with walnut or Rynite stock and forend. Chambered for 22 LR, 22 Hornet, 223 Rem., 7-30 Waters, 30-30 Win., 410-bore. Youth model has walnut buttstock with 12" pull length. Introduced 1993.
Price: Rynite stock, forend $556.00

UBERTI ROLLING BLOCK BABY CARBINE

Caliber: 22 LR, 22 WMR, 22 Hornet, 357 Mag., single shot.
Barrel: 22".
Weight: 4.8 lbs. **Length:** 35-1/2" overall.
Stock: Walnut stock and forend.
Sights: Blade front, fully adjustable open rear.
Features: Resembles Remington New Model No. 4 carbine. Brass trigger guard and buttplate; color case-hardened frame, blued barrel. Imported by Uberti USA Inc.
Price: **$490.00**

> ## CONSULT
> # SHOOTER'S MARKETPLACE
> ### Page 225, This Issue

WESSON & HARRINGTON BUFFALO CLASSIC RIFLE

Caliber: 45-70.
Barrel: 32" heavy.
Weight: 9 lbs. **Length:** 52" overall.
Stock: American black walnut.
Sights: None furnished; drilled and tapped for peep sight; barrel dovetailed for front sight.
Features: Color case-hardened Handi-Rifle action with exposed hammer; color case-hardened crescent buttplate; 19th century checkering pattern. Introduced 1995. Made in U.S. by H&R 1871, Inc.
Price: About **$349.95**

Wesson & Harrington 38-55 Target Rifle

Similar to the Buffalo Classic rifle except chambered for 38-55 Win., has 28" barrel. The barrel and steel furniture, including steel trigger guard and forend spacer, are highly polished and blued. Color case-hardened receiver and buttplate. Barrel is dovetailed for a front sight, and drilled and tapped for receiver sight or scope mount. Introduced 1998. Made in U.S. by H&R 1871, Inc.
Price: **$389.95**

DRILLINGS, COMBINATION GUNS, DOUBLE RIFLES

Designs for sporting and utility purposes worldwide.

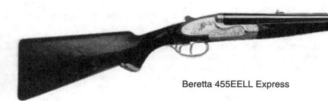

Beretta 455EELL Express

BERETTA EXPRESS SSO O/U DOUBLE RIFLES

Caliber: 375 H&H, 458 Win. Mag., 9.3x74R.
Barrel: 25.5".
Weight: 11 lbs.
Stock: European walnut with hand-checkered grip and forend.
Sights: Blade front on ramp, open V-notch rear.
Features: Sidelock action with color case-hardened receiver (gold inlays on SSO6 Gold). Ejectors; double triggers, recoil pad. Introduced 1990. Imported from Italy by Beretta U.S.A.
Price: SSO6 .... **$21,000.00**
Price: SSO6 Gold **$23,500.00**

BRNO ZH 300 COMBINATION GUN

Caliber: 22 Hornet, 5.6x50R Mag., 5.6x52R, 7x57R, 7x65R, 8x57JRS over 12, 16 (2-3/4" chamber).
Barrel: 23.6".
Weight: 7.9 lbs. **Length:** 40.5" overall.
Stock: European walnut.
Sights: Blade front, open adjustable rear.
Features: Boxlock action; double triggers; automatic safety. Announced 1998. Imported from The Czech Republic by Euro-Imports.
Price: **$724.00**

BERETTA MODEL 455 SxS EXPRESS RIFLE

Caliber: 375 H&H, 458 Win. Mag., 470 NE, 500 NE 3", 416 Rigby.
Barrel: 23-1/2" or 25-1/2".
Weight: 11 lbs.
Stock: European walnut with hand-checkered grip and forend.
Sights: Blade front, folding leaf V-notch rear.
Features: Sidelock action with easily removable sideplates; color case-hardened finish (455), custom big game or floral motif engraving (455EELL). Double triggers, recoil pad. Introduced 1990. Imported from Italy by Beretta U.S.A.
Price: Model 455 .... **$36,000.00**
Price: Model 455EELL.................................. **$47,000.00**

BRNO 500 COMBINATION GUNS

Caliber/Gauge: 12 (2-3/4" chamber) over 5.6x52R, 5.6x50R, 222 Rem., 243, 6.x55, 308, 7x57R, 7x65R, 30-06.
Barrel: 23.6".
Weight: 7.6 lbs. **Length:** 40.5" overall.
Stock: European walnut.
Sights: Bead front, V-notch rear; grooved for scope mounting.
Features: Boxlock action; double set trigger; blue finish with etched engraving. Announced 1998. Imported from The Czech Republic by Euro-Imports.
Price: **$1,023.00**
Price: O/U double rifle, 7x57R, 7x65R, 8x57JRS **$1,125.00**

BRNO ZH Double Rifles

Similar to the ZH 300 combination guns except with double rifle barrels. Available in 7x65R, 7x57R and 8x57JRS. Announced 1998. Imported from The Czech Republic by Euro-Imports.
Price: **$1,125.00**

Charles Daly Superior

Charles Daly Empire Combination Gun

Same as the Superior grade except has deluxe wood with European-style comb and cheekpiece; slim forend. Introduced 1997. Imported from Italy by K.B.I., Inc.
Price: **$1,625.00**

CHARLES DALY SUPERIOR COMBINATION GUN

Caliber/Gauge: 12 ga. over 22 Hornet, 223 Rem., 22-250, 243 Win., 270 Win., 308 Win., 30-06.
Barrel: 23.5", shotgun choked Imp. Cyl.
Weight: About 7.5 lbs.
Stock: Checkered walnut pistol grip buttstock and semi-beavertail forend.
Features: Silvered, engraved receiver; chrome moly steel barrels; double triggers; extractors; sling swivels; gold bead front sight. Introduced 1997. Imported from Italy by K.B.I. Inc.
Price: **$1,159.00**

Hoenig Round Action

GARBI EXPRESS DOUBLE RIFLE
Caliber: 7x65R, 9.3x74R, 375 H&H.
Barrel: 24-3/4".
Weight: 7-3/4 to 8-1/2 lbs. **Length:** 41-1/2" overall.
Stock: Turkish walnut.
Sights: Quarter-rib with express sight.
Features: Side-by-side double; H&H-pattern sidelock ejector with reinforced action, chopper lump barrels of Boehler steel; double triggers; fine scroll and rosette engraving, or full coverage ornamental; coin-finished action. Introduced 1997. Imported from Spain by Wm. Larkin Moore.
Price: **$20,650.00**

HOENIG ROTARY ROUND ACTION DOUBLE RIFLE
Caliber: Most popular calibers from 225 Win. to 9.3x74R.
Barrel: 22"-26".
Weight: NA. **Length:** NA.
Stock: English Walnut; to customer specs.
Sights: Swivel hood front with button release (extra bead stored in trap door grip cap), express-style rear on quarter-rib adjustable for windage and elevation; scope mount.
Features: Round action opens by rotating barrels, pulling forward. Has inertia extractor system; rotary safety blocks the strikers; single lever quick-detachable scope mount. Simple takedown without removing forend. Introduced 1997. Made in U.S. by George Hoenig.
Price: **$19,980.00**

KRIEGHOFF CLASSIC DOUBLE RIFLE
Caliber: 7x65R, 308 Win., 30-06, 30R Blaser, 8x57 JRS, 8x75RS, 9.3x74R.
Barrel: 23.5".
Weight: 7.3 to 8 lbs. **Length:** NA.
Stock: High grade European walnut. Standard has conventional rounded cheekpiece, Bavaria has Bavarian-style cheekpiece.
Sights: Bead front with removable, adjustable wedge (375 H&H and below), standing leaf rear on quarter-rib.
Features: Boxlock action; double triggers; short opening angle for fast loading; quiet extractors; sliding, self-adjusting wedge for secure bolting; Purdey-style barrel extension; horizontal firing pin placement. Many options available. Introduced 1997. Imported from Germany by Krieghoff International.
Price: With small Arabesque engraving. **$7,850.00**
Price: With engraved sideplates **$9,800.00**
Price: For extra barrels **$4,500.00**
Price: Extra 20-ga., 28" shotshell barrels. **$3,200.00**

Krieghoff Classic Double Rifle

Krieghoff Classic Big Five Double Rifle
Similar to the standard Classic excpet available in 375 Flanged Mag. N.E., 500/416 N.E., 470 N.E., 500 N.E. 3". Has hinged front trigger, non-removable muzzle wedge (larger than 375-caliber), Universal Trigger System, Combi Cocking Device, steel trigger guard, specially weighted stock bolt for weight and balance. Many options available. Introduced 1997. Imorted from Germany by Krieghott International.
Price: **$9,450.00**
Price: With engraved sideplates. **$11,400.00**

MERKEL OVER/UNDER COMBINATION GUNS
Caliber/Gauge: 12, 16, 20 (2-3/4" chamber) over 22 Hornet, 5.6x50R, 5.6x52R, 222 Rem., 243 Win., 6.5x55, 6.5x57R, 7x57R, 7x65R, 308 Win., 30-06, 8x57JRS, 9.3x74R.
Barrel: 25.6".
Weight: About 7.6 lbs. **Length:** NA.
Stock: Oil-finished walnut; pistol grip, cheekpiece.
Sights: Bead front, fixed rear.
Features: Kersten double cross-bolt lock; scroll-engraved, color case-hardened receiver; Blitz action; double triggers. Imported from Germany by GSI.
Price: Model 210E **$6,195.00**
Price: Model 211E (silver-grayed receiver, fine hunting scene engraving) **$7,495.00**

MERKEL DRILLINGS
Caliber/Gauge: 12, 20, 3" chambers, 16, 2-3/4" chambers; 22 Hornet, 5.6x50R Mag., 5.6x52R, 222 Rem., 243 Win., 6.5x55, 6.5x57R, 7x57R, 7x65R, 308, 30-06, 8x57JRS, 9.3x74R, 375 H&H.
Barrel: 25.6".
Weight: 7.9 to 8.4 lbs. depending upon caliber. **Length:** NA.
Stock: Oil-finished walnut with pistol grip; cheekpiece on 12- , 16-gauge.
Sights: Blade front, fixed rear.
Features: Double barrel locking lug with Greener cross-bolt; scroll-engraved, case-hardened receiver; automatic trigger safety; Blitz action; double triggers. Imported from Germany by GSI.
Price: Model 95S (selective sear safety), from **$7,995.00**
Price: Model 95K (manually cocked rifle system), from. **$8,595.00**
Price: Model 96K (manually cocked rifle system), from. **$5,895.00**

MERKEL OVER/UNDER DOUBLE RIFLES
Caliber: 22 Hornet, 5.6x50R Mag., 5.6x52R, 222 Rem., 243 Win., 6.5x55, 6.5x57R, 7x57R, 7x65R, 308, 8x57JRS, 9.3x74R.
Barrel: 25.6".
Weight: About 7.7 lbs, depending upon caliber. **Length:** NA.
Stock: Oil-finished walnut with pistol grip, cheekpiece.

Merkel Model 210E

MERKEL MODEL 160 SIDE-BY-SIDE DOUBLE RIFLE
Caliber: 22 Hornet, 5.6x50R Mag., 5.6x52R, 222 Rem., 243 Win., 6.5x55, 6.5x57R, 7x57R, 7x65R, 308, 30-06, 8x57JRS, 9.3x74R, 375 H&H.
Barrel: 25.6".
Weight: About 7.7 lbs, depending upon caliber. **Length:** NA.
Stock: Oil-finished walnut with pistol grip, cheekpiece.
Sights: Blade front on ramp, fixed rear.
Features: Sidelock action. Double barrel locking lug with Greener cross-bolt; fine engraved hunting scenes on sideplates; Holland & Holland ejectors; double triggers. Imported from Germany by GSI.
Price: From. **$13,295.00**

Merkel Boxlock Double Rifles
Similar to the Model 160 double rifle except with Anson & Deely boxlock action with cocking indicators, double triggers, engraved color case-hardened receiver. Introduced 1995. Imported from Germany by GSI.
Price: Model 140-1, from **$5,895.00**
Price: Model 140-1.1 (engraved silver-gray receiver), from **$6,795.00**
Price: Model 150-1 (false sideplates, silver-gray receiver, Arabesque engraving), from **$7,495.00**
Price: Model 150-1.1 (as above with English Arabesque engraving), from **$8,695.00**

Sights: Blade front, fixed rear.
Features: Kersten double cross-bolt lock; scroll-engraved, case-hardened receiver; Blitz action with double triggers. Imported from Germany by GSI.
Price: Model 221 E (silver-grayed receiver finish, hunting scene engraving) **$10,895.00**

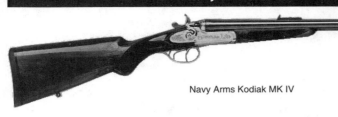

Navy Arms Kodiak MK IV

NAVY ARMS KODIAK MK IV DOUBLE RIFLE
Caliber: 45-70.
Barrel: 24".
Weight: 10 lbs., 3 oz. **Length:** 39-3/4" overall.
Stock: Checkered European walnut.
Sights: Bead front, folding leaf express rear.
Features: Blued, semi-regulated barrels; color case-hardened receiver and hammers; double triggers. Replica of Colt double rifle 1879-1885. Introduced 1996. Imported by Navy Arms.
Price: **$3,125.00**
Price: Engraved satin-finished receiver, browned barrels **$4,000.00**

Rizzini Express

RIZZINI EXPRESS 90L DOUBLE RIFLE
Caliber: 30-06, 7x65R, 9.3x74R.
Barrel: 24".
Weight: NA. **Length:** NA.
Stock: Select European walnut with satin oil finish; English-style cheekpiece.
Sights: Ramp front, quarter-rib with express sight.
Features: Color case-hardened boxlock action; automatic ejectors; single selective trigger; polished blue barrels. Extra 20-gauge shotshell barrels available. Imported for Italy by Wm. Larkin Moore.
Price: With case. **$4,500.00**

Savage 24F Predator

Savage 24F-12/410 Combination Gun
Similar to the 24F-12 except comes with "Four-Tenner" adaptor for shooting 410-bore shotshells. Rifle barrel chambered for 22 Hornet, 223 Rem., 30-30 Win. Introduced 1998. Made in U.S. by Savage Arms, Inc.
Price: **$475.00**

SAVAGE 24F PREDATOR O/U COMBINATION GUN
Caliber/Gauge: 22 Hornet, 223, 30-30 over 12 (24F-12) or 22 LR, 22 Hornet, 223, 30-30 over 20-ga. (24F-20); 3" chambers.
Action: Takedown, low rebounding visible hammer. Single trigger, barrel selector spur on hammer.
Barrel: 24" separated barrels; 12-ga. has Full, Mod., Imp. Cyl. choke tubes, 20-ga. has fixed Mod. choke.
Weight: 8 lbs. **Length:** 40-1/2" overall.
Stock: Black Rynite composition.
Sights: Ramp front, rear open adjustable for elevation. Grooved for tip-off scope mount.
Features: Removable butt cap for storage and accessories. Introduced 1989.
Price: 24F-12 .... **$425.00**
Price: 24F-20 .... **$415.00**

Springfield M6 Scout

SPRINGFIELD, INC. M6 SCOUT RIFLE/SHOTGUN
Caliber/Gauge: 22 LR or 22 Hornet over 410-bore.
Barrel: 18.25".
Weight: 4 lbs. **Length:** 32" overall.
Stock: Folding detachable with storage for 15 22 LR, four 410 shells.
Sights: Blade front, military aperture for 22; V-notch for 410.
Features: All-metal construction. Designed for quick disassembly and minimum maintenance. Folds for compact storage. Introduced 1982; reintroduced 1996. Imported from the Czech Republic by Springfield, Inc.
Price: Parkerized **$167.00**
Price: Stainless steel **$199.00**

Consult our Directory pages for the location of firms mentioned.

TIKKA MODEL 512S DOUBLE RIFLE
Caliber: 300, 30-06, 9.3x74R.
Barrel: 24".
Weight: 8-5/8 lbs.
Stock: American walnut with Monte Carlo style.
Sights: Ramp front, adjustable open rear.
Features: Barrel selector mounted in trigger. Cocking indicators in tang. Recoil pad. Valmet scope mounts available. Introduced 1980. Imported from Italy by Stoeger.
Price: With ejectors **$1,890.00**

TIKKA MODEL 512S COMBINATION GUN
Caliber/Gauge: 12 over 222, 308, 30-06.
Barrel: 24" (Imp. Mod.).
Weight: 7-5/8 lbs.
Stock: American walnut, with recoil pad. Monte Carlo style. Standard measurements 14"x1-3/5"x2"x2-3/5".
Sights: Blade front, flip-up-type open rear.
Features: Barrel selector on trigger. Hand-checkered stock and forend. Barrels are screw-adjustable to change bullet point of impact. Barrels are interchangeable. Introduced 1980. Imported from Italy by Stoeger.
Price: **$1,770.00**
Price: Extra barrels, from **$810.00**

Designs for hunting, utility and sporting purposes, including training for competition.

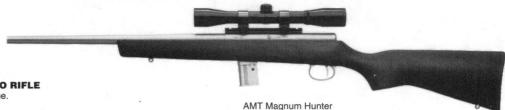

AMT MAGNUM HUNTER AUTO RIFLE
Caliber: 22 WMR, 10-shot magazine.
Barrel: 20".
Weight: 6 lbs. **Length:** 40-1/2" overall.
Stock: Black fiberglass-filled nylon; checkered grip and forend.
Sights: None furnished; drilled and tapped for Weaver mount.
Features: Stainless steel construction. Free-floating target-weight barrel. Introduced 1995. Made in U.S. by AMT.
Price: $459.00

AMT Magnum Hunter

Armscor M-1600

ARMSCOR MODEL AK22 AUTO RIFLE
Caliber: 22 LR, 10-shot magazine.
Barrel: 18.5".
Weight: 7.5 lbs. **Length:** 38" overall.
Stock: Plain mahogany.
Sights: Adjustable post front, leaf rear adjustable for elevation.
Features: Resembles the AK-47. Matte black finish. Introduced 1987. Imported from the Philippines by K.B.I., Inc.
Price: About $199.00

ARMSCOR M-1600 AUTO RIFLE
Caliber: 22 LR, 10-shot magazine.
Barrel: 18.25".
Weight: 6.2 lbs. **Length:** 38.5" overall.
Stock: Black finished mahogany.
Sights: Post front, aperture rear.
Features: Resembles Colt AR-15. Matte black finish. Introduced 1987. Imported from the Philippines by K.B.I., Inc.
Price: About $184.00

Armscor M-20C Auto Carbine

ARMSCOR M-20C AUTO CARBINE
Caliber: 22 LR, 10-shot magazine.
Barrel: 18.25".
Weight: 6.5 lbs. **Length:** 38" overall.
Stock: Walnut-finished mahogany.
Sights: Hooded front, rear adjustable for elevation.
Features: Receiver grooved for scope mounting. Blued finish. Introduced 1990. Imported from the Philippines by K.B.I., Inc.
Price: $139.00

BRNO ZKM 611 AUTO RIFLE
Caliber: 22 WMR, 6- or 10-shot magazine.
Barrel: 20.4".
Weight: 5.9 lbs. **Length:** 38.9" overall.
Stock: European walnut.
Sights: Hooded blade front, open adjustable rear.
Features: Removable box magazine; polished blue finish; cross-bolt safety; grooved receiver for scope mounting; easy takedown for storage. Imported from The Czech Republic by Euro-Imports.
Price: $475.00

Browning Auto-22

Browning Auto-22 Grade VI
Same as the Grade I Auto-22 except available with either grayed or blued receiver with extensive engraving with gold-plated animals: right side pictures a fox and squirrel in a woodland scene; left side shows a beagle chasing a rabbit. On top is a portrait of the beagle. Stock and forend are of high-grade walnut with a double-bordered cut checkering design. Introduced 1987.
Price: Grade VI, blue or gray receiver $819.00

BROWNING AUTO-22 RIFLE
Caliber: 22 LR, 11-shot.
Barrel: 19-1/4".
Weight: 4-3/4 lbs. **Length:** 37" overall.
Stock: Checkered select walnut with pistol grip and semi-beavertail forend.
Sights: Gold bead front, folding leaf rear.
Features: Engraved receiver with polished blue finish; cross-bolt safety; tubular magazine in buttstock; easy takedown for carrying or storage. Imported from Japan by Browning.
Price: Grade I $398.95

CALICO M-100FS CARBINE
Caliber: 22 LR.
Barrel: 16.25".
Weight: 5 lbs. **Length:** 36" overall.
Stock: Glass-filled, impact-resistant polymer.
Sights: Adjustable post front, notch rear.
Features: Has helical-feed magazine; aluminum receiver; ambidextrous safety. Made in U.S. by Calico.
Price: $504.00

Charles Daly Superior Grade

Charles Daly Empire Grade Auto Rifle

Similar to the Field Grade except has select California walnut stock with 24 l.p.i. hand checkering, contrasting forend and grip caps, damascened bolt, high-polish blue. Introduced 1998. Imported by K.B.I.

Price: **$334.00**

Henry U.S. Survival

MAGTECH MT 7022 AUTO RIFLE

Caliber: 22 LR, 10-shot magazine.
Barrel: 18".
Weight: 4.8 lbs. **Length:** 37" overall.
Stock: Brazilian hardwood.
Sights: Hooded blade front, fully adjustable open rear.
Features: Cross-bolt safety; last-shot bolt hold-open; alloy receiver is drilled and tapped for scope mounting. Introduced 1998. Imported from Brazil by Magtech Recreational Products.
Price: . . . . **NA**

Marlin Model 60

Marlin Model 60SS Self-Loading Rifle

Same as the Model 60 except breech bolt, barrel and outer magazine tube are made of stainless steel; most other parts are either nickel-plated or coated to match the stainless finish. Monte Carlo stock is of black/gray Maine birch laminate, and has nickel-plated swivel studs, rubber butt pad. Introduced 1993.

Price: $257.00
Price: Model 60SSK (black fiberglass-filled stock) $223.00
Price: Model 60SSK with 4x scope $236.00
Price: Model 60SB (walnut-finished birch stock) $204.00
Price: Model 60SB with 4x scope $217.00

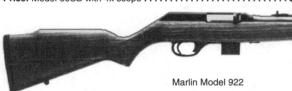

Marlin Model 922

MARLIN 70PSS STAINLESS RIFLE

Caliber: 22 LR, 7-shot magazine.
Barrel: 16-1/4" stainless steel, Micro-Groove® rifling.
Weight: 3-1/4 lbs. **Length:** 35-1/4" overall.
Stock: Black fiberglass-filled synthetic with abbreviated forend, nickel-plated swivel studs, moulded-in checkering.
Sights: Ramp front with orange post, cutaway Wide Scan® hood; adjustable open rear. Receiver grooved for scope mounting.
Features: Takedown barrel; cross-bolt safety; manual bolt hold-open; last shot bolt hold-open; comes with padded carrying case. Introduced 1986. Made in U.S. by Marlin.
Price: $264.00

CHARLES DALY FIELD GRADE AUTO RIFLE

Caliber: 22 LR, 10-shot magazine.
Barrel: 20-3/4".
Weight: 6.5 lbs. **Length:** 40-1/2" overall.
Stock: Walnut-finished hardwood with Monte Carlo.
Sights: Hooded front, adjustable open rear.
Features: Receiver grooved for scope mounting; blue finish; shell deflector. Introduced 1998. Imported by K.B.I.
Price: **$119.00**
Price: Superior Grade (cut checkered stock, fully adjustable sight) **$169.00**

HENRY U.S. SURVIVAL RIFLE .22

Caliber: 22 LR, 8-shot magazine.
Barrel: 16" steel lined.
Weight: 2.5 lbs.
Stock: ABS plastic.
Sights: Blade front on ramp, aperture rear.
Features: Takedown design stores barrel and action in hollow stock. Light enough to float. Silver finish. Comes with two magazines. Introduced 1998. From Henry Repeating Arms Co.
Price: **$165.00**

KRICO MODEL 260 AUTO RIFLE

Caliber: 22 LR, 5-shot magazine.
Barrel: 19.6".
Weight: 6.6 lbs. **Length:** 38.9" overall.
Stock: Beech.
Sights: Blade on ramp front, open adjustable rear.
Features: Receiver grooved for scope mounting. Sliding safety. Imported from Germany by Mandall Shooting Supplies.
Price: **$700.00**

MARLIN MODEL 60 SELF-LOADING RIFLE

Caliber: 22 LR, 14-shot tubular magazine.
Barrel: 22" round tapered.
Weight: About 5-1/2 lbs. **Length:** 40-1/2" overall.
Stock: Press-checkered, walnut-finished Maine birch with Monte Carlo, full pistol grip; Mar-Shield® finish.
Sights: Ramp front, open adjustable rear.
Features: Matted receiver is grooved for scope mount. Manual bolt hold-open; automatic last-shot bolt hold-open.
Price: **$161.00**
Price: With 4x scope **$167.00**

MARLIN MODEL 922 MAGNUM SELF-LOADING RIFLE

Caliber: 22 WMR, 7-shot magazine.
Barrel: 20.5".
Weight: 6.5 lbs. **Length:** 39.75" overall.
Stock: Checkered American black walnut with Monte Carlo comb, swivel studs, rubber buttpad.
Sights: Ramp front with bead and removable Wide-Scan® hood, adjustable folding semi-buckhorn rear.
Features: Action based on the centerfire Model 9 Carbine. Receiver drilled and tapped for scope mounting. Automatic last-shot bolt hold open; magazine safety. Introduced 1993.
Price: **$423.00**

Marlin Model 795

Marlin Model 795 Self-Loading Rifle
Similar to the Model 7000 except has standard-weight 18" barrel with 16-groove Micro-Groove rifling. Comes with ramp front sight with brass bead, screw adjustable open rear. Receiver grooved for scope mount. Introduced 1997. Made in U.S. by Marlin Firearms Co.
Price: **$152.00**
Price: With 4x scope **$159.00**

MARLIN MODEL 995SS SELF-LOADING RIFLE
Caliber: 22 LR, 7-shot clip magazine.
Barrel: 18" Micro-Groove®; stainless steel.
Weight: 5 lbs. **Length:** 37" overall.
Stock: Black fiberglass-filled synthetic with nickel-plated swivel studs, moulded-in checkering.
Sights: Ramp front with orange post and cut-away Wide-Scan® hood; screw-adjustable open rear.
Features: Stainless steel breechbolt and barrel. Receiver grooved for scope mount; bolt hold-open device; cross-bolt safety. Introduced 1979.
Price: **$249.00**

MARLIN MODEL 7000 SELF-LOADING RIFLE
Caliber: 22 LR, 10-shot magazine
Barrel: 18″ heavy target with 12-groove Micro-Groove® rifling, recessed muzzle.
Weight: 5-1/2 lbs. **Length:** 37" overall.
Stock: Black fiberglass-filled synthetic with Monte Carlo combo, swivel studs, moulded-in checkering.
Sights: None furnished; comes with ring mounts.
Features: Automatic last-shot bolt hold-open, manual bolt hold-open; cross bolt safety; steel charging handle; blue finish, nickel-plated magazine. Introduced 1997. Made in U.S. by Marlin Firearms Co.
Price: **$219.00**

REMINGTON MODEL 552 BDL SPEEDMASTER RIFLE
Caliber: 22 S (20), L (17) or LR (15) tubular mag.
Barrel: 21" round tapered.
Weight: About 5-3/4 lbs. **Length:** 40" overall.
Stock: Walnut. Checkered grip and forend.
Sights: Bead front, step open rear adjustable for windage and elevation.
Features: Positive cross-bolt safety, receiver grooved for tip-off mount.
Price: About **$340.00**

Remington 597

Remington 597 LSS Auto Rifle
Similar to the Model 597 except has satin-finish stainless barrel, gray-toned alloy receiver with nickle-plated bolt, and laminated wood stock. Receiver is grooved and drilled and tapped for scope mounting. Introduced 1997. Made in U.S. by Remington.
Price: **$265.00**

REMINGTON 597 AUTO RIFLE
Caliber: 22 LR, 10-shot clip.
Barrel: 20".
Weight: 5-1/2 lbs. **Length:** 40" overall.
Stock: Gray synthetic.
Sights: Bead front, fully adjustable rear.
Features: Matte black finish, nickel-plated bolt. Receiver is grooved and drilled and tapped for scope mounts. Introduced 1997. Made in U.S. by Remington.
Price: **$159.00**
Price: Model 597 Magnum, 22 WMR, 8-shot clip **$305.00**
Price: Model 597 Magnum LS (laminated stock) **$359.00**
Price: Model 597 Sporter (22 LR, wood stock) **$159.00**
Price: Model 597 SS (22 LR, stainless steel, black synthetic stock) **$212.00**

Ruger 10/22 International

Ruger 10/22 International Carbine
Similar to the Ruger 10/22 Carbine except has full-length International stock of American hardwood, checkered grip and forend; comes with rubber butt-pad, sling swivels. Reintroduced 1994.
Price: Blue (10/22RBI) **$262.00**
Price: Stainless (K10/22RBI) **$282.00**

RUGER 10/22 AUTOLOADING CARBINE
Caliber: 22 LR, 10-shot rotary magazine.
Barrel: 18-1/2" round tapered.
Weight: 5 lbs. **Length:** 37-1/4" overall.
Stock: American hardwood with pistol grip and bbl. band.
Sights: Brass bead front, folding leaf rear adjustable for elevation.
Features: Detachable rotary magazine fits flush into stock, cross-bolt safety, receiver tapped and grooved for scope blocks or tip-off mount. Scope base adaptor furnished with each rifle.
Price: Model 10/22 RB (blue) **$213.00**
Price: Model K10/22RB (bright finish stainless barrel) **$255.00**

Ruger 10/22T Target

Ruger 10/22 Deluxe Sporter
Same as 10/22 Carbine except walnut stock with hand checkered pistol grip and forend; straight buttplate, no barrel band, has sling swivels.
Price: Model 10/22 DSP **$274.00**

Ruger 10/22T Target Rifle
Similar to the 10/22 except has 20" heavy, hammer-forged barrel with tight chamber dimensions, improved trigger pull, laminated hardwood stock dimensioned for optical sights. No iron sights supplied. Introduced 1996. Made in U.S. by Sturm, Ruger & Co.
Price: 10/22T **$392.50**
Price: K10/22T, stainless steel **$440.00**

Ruger K10/22RP All-Weather Rifle
Similar to the stainless K10/22/RP except has black composite stock of thermoplastic polyester resin reinforced with fiberglass; checkered grip and forend. Brushed satin, natural metal finish with clear hardcoat finish. Weighs 5 lbs., measures 36-3/4" overall. Introduced 1997. From Sturm, Ruger & Co.
Price: **$255.00**

Savage Model 64FV

Savage Model 64FV Auto Rifle

Similar to the Model 64F except has heavy 21" barrel with recessed crown; no sights provided—comes with Weaver-style bases. Introduced 1998. Imported from Canada by Savage Arms, Inc.

Price: **$149.00**

WINCHESTER MODEL 63 AUTO RIFLE

Caliber: 22 LR, 10-shot magazine.
Barrel: 23".
Weight: 6-1/4 lbs. **Length:** 39" overall.
Stock: Walnut.
Sights: Bead front, open adjustable rear.
Features: Recreation of the original Model 63. Magazine tube loads through a port in the buttstock; forward cocking knob at front of forend; easy takedown for cleaning, storage; engraved receiver. Reintroduced 1997. From U.S. Repeating Arms Co.

Price: Grade I **$678.00**
Price: High grade, select walnut, cut checkering, engraved scenes with gold accents on receiver (made in 1997 only) **$1,083.00**

SAVAGE MODEL 64G AUTO RIFLE

Caliber: 22 LR, 10-shot magazine.
Barrel: 20".
Weight: 5-1/2 lbs. **Length:** 40" overall.
Stock: Walnut-finished hardwood with Monte Carlo-type comb, checkered grip and forend.
Sights: Bead front, open adjustable rear. Receiver grooved for scope mounting.
Features: Thumb-operated rotating safety. Blue finish. Side ejection, bolt hold-open device. Introduced 1990. Made in Canada, from Savage Arms.

Price: **$123.00**
Price: Model 64F, black synthetic stock **$115.00**
Price: Model 64GXP Package Gun includes 4x15 scope and mounts

.... **$129.00**
Price: Model 64FXP (black stock, 4x15 scope) **$120.00**

Classic and modern models for sport and utility, including training.

Browning BL-22

BROWNING BL-22 LEVER-ACTION RIFLE

Caliber: 22 S (22), L (17) or LR (15), tubular magazine.
Barrel: 20" round tapered.

Weight: 5 lbs. **Length:** 36-3/4" overall.
Stock: Walnut, two-piece straight grip Western style.
Sights: Bead post front, folding-leaf rear.
Features: Short throw lever, half-cock safety, receiver grooved for tip-off scope mounts. Imported from Japan by Browning.

Price: Grade I **$345.95**
Price: Grade II (engraved receiver, checkered grip and forend) **$395.95**

Henry Carbine .22

HENRY LEVER-ACTION CARBINE .22

Caliber: 22 Short (21-shot), 22 Long (17-shot), 22 Long Rifle (13-shot).
Barrel: 18-1/4" round.
Weight: 5-1/2 lbs. **Length:** 34" overall.
Stock: Walnut.
Sights: Hooded blade front, open adjustabel rear.
Features: Polished blue finish; full-length tubular magazine; side ejection; receiver grooved for scope mounting. Introduced 1997. Made in U.S. by Henry Repeating Arms Co.

Price: **$239.95**
Price: Youth model (33" overall, 11-rounds 22 LR) **$229.95**

Marlin Model 39AS

MARLIN MODEL 39AS GOLDEN LEVER-ACTION RIFLE

Caliber: 22 S (26), L (21), LR (19), tubular magazine.
Barrel: 24" Micro-Groove®.

Weight: 6-1/2 lbs. **Length:** 40" overall.
Stock: Checkered American black walnut with white line spacers at pistol grip cap and buttplate; Mar-Shield® finish. Swivel studs; rubber buttpad.
Sights: Bead ramp front with detachable Wide-Scan™ hood, folding rear semi-buckhorn adjustable for windage and elevation.
Features: Hammer-block safety; rebounding hammer. Takedown action, receiver tapped for scope mount (supplied), offset hammer spur; gold-plated steel trigger.

Price: **$470.00**

Marlin Annie Oakley

MARLIN MODEL 1897 ANNIE OAKLEY LEVER ACTION
Caliber: 22 Short (19), Long (15), Long Rifle (13).
Barrel: 18-1/2" tapered octagon.

Weight: 5-1/2 lbs. **Length:** 35" overall.
Stock: Semi-fancy American black walnut with straight grip, cut checkering, hard rubber butt plate.
Sights: Marble carbine bead front, Marble semi-buckhorn rear.
Features: Receiver has roll-engraved Annie Oakley likeness with scrolls, gold colored Annie Oakley signature on bolt. Introduced 1998. Made in U.S. by Marlin.
Price: $1,054.00

Remington 572 BDL

REMINGTON 572 BDL FIELDMASTER PUMP RIFLE
Caliber: 22 S (20), L (17) or LR (14), tubular magazine.
Barrel: 21" round tapered.

Weight: 5-1/2 lbs. **Length:** 42" overall.
Stock: Walnut with checkered pistol grip and slide handle.
Sights: Blade ramp front; sliding ramp rear adjustable for windage and elevation.
Features: Cross-bolt safety; removing inner magazine tube converts rifle to single shot; receiver grooved for tip-off scope mount.
Price: About $353.00

Rossi Model 62 SAC

Rossi Model 62 SAC Carbine
Same as standard model except 22 LR, has 16-1/4" barrel. Magazine holds slightly fewer cartridges.
Price: Blue $240.00
Price: Nickel $250.00

ROSSI MODEL 62 SA PUMP RIFLE
Caliber: 22 LR, 22 WMR.
Barrel: 23", round or octagonal.
Weight: 5-3/4 lbs. **Length:** 39-1/4" overall.
Stock: Walnut, straight grip, grooved forend.
Sights: Fixed front, adjustable rear.
Features: Capacity 20 Short, 16 Long or 14 Long Rifle. Quick takedown. Imported from Brazil by Interarms.
Price: Blue $240.00
Price: Nickel $250.00
Price: Blue, with octagonal barrel $250.00
Price: 22 WMR $280.00

Ruger Model 96/22

RUGER MODEL 96/22 LEVER-ACTION RIFLE
Caliber: 22 LR, 10-shot rotary, magazine; 22 WMR, 9-shot rotary magazine.
Barrel: 18-1/2".

Weight: 5-1/4 lbs. **Length:** 37-1/4" overall.
Stock: American hardwood.
Sights: Gold bead front, folding leaf rear.
Features: Cross-bolt safety, visible cocking indicator; short-throw lever action. Screw-on dovetail scope base. Introduced 1996. Made in U.S. by Sturm, Ruger & Co.
Price: 96/22 (22 LR) $327.50
Price: 96/22M (22 WMR) $345.00

Winchester 9422 Large Loop

WINCHESTER MODEL 9422 LEVER-ACTION RIFLE
Caliber: 22 S (21), L (17), LR (15), tubular magazine.
Barrel: 20-1/2".
Weight: 6-1/4 lbs. **Length:** 37-1/8" overall.
Stock: American walnut, two-piece, straight grip (no pistol grip).
Sights: Hooded ramp front, adjustable semi-buckhorn rear.
Features: Side ejection, receiver grooved for scope mounting, takedown action. From U.S. Repeating Arms Co.
Price: Walnut $407.00
Price: With WinTuff laminated stock $407.00
Price: With large lever loop $429.00
Price: Model 9422 Legacy (semi-pistol grip stock) $436.00

Winchester Model 9422 High Grade Series II
Similar to the Model 9422 Walnut except has higher grade of walnut, engraved receiver with a dog and squirrels depicted. Better fit, finish and detailing. Introduced 1998. Made in U.S. by U.S. Repeating Arms.
Price: $504.00

Winchester Model 9422 Magnum Lever-Action Rifle
Same as the 9422 except chambered for 22 WMR cartridge, has 11-round mag. capacity.
Price: Walnut $424.00

Winchester Model 9422 Trapper
Similar to the Model 9422 with walnut stock except has 16-1/2" barrel, overall length of 33-1/8", weighs 5-1/2 lbs. Magazine holds 15 Shorts, 12 Longs, 11 Long Rifles. Introduced 1996.
Price: $407.00
Price: 22 WMR, 8-shot $424.00

Winchester Model 9422 25th Anniversary Edition
Similar to the standard Model 9422 except has better walnut and engraved receiver sides, high-gloss metal finish. Introduced 1997. From U.S. Repeating Arms Co.
Price: Grade I $606.00

RIMFIRE RIFLES—BOLT ACTIONS & SINGLE SHOTS

Includes models for a variety of sports, utility and competitive shooting.

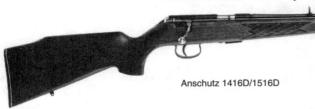

Anschutz 1416D/1516D

Anschutz 1416D/1516D Walnut Luxus Rifles

Similar to the Classic models except have European walnut stocks with Monte Carlo cheekpiece, slim forend with schnabel tip, cut checkering on grip and forend. Introduced 1997. Imported from Germany by AcuSport Corp.

Price: 1416D (22 LR) **$755.95**
Price: 1516D (22 WMR) **$779.95**

ANSCHUTZ 1518D LUXUS BOLT-ACTION RIFLE

Caliber: 22 WMR, 4-shot magazine.
Barrel: 19-3/4".
Weight: 5-1/2 lbs. **Length:** 37-1/2" overall.
Stock: European walnut.
Sights: Blade on ramp front, folding leaf rear.
Features: Receiver grooved for scopt mounting; single stage trigger; skip-line checkering; rosewood forend tip; sling swivels. Imported from Germany by AcuSport Corp.
Price: **$1,186.95**

BRNO ZOM 451 STRAIGHT-PULL RIFLE

Caliber: 22 LR, 7-shot magazine.
Barrel: 22".
Weight: 5.3 lbs. **Length:** 41.7" overall.
Stock: Beech or walnut.
Sights: Blade on ramp front, adjustable open rear.
Features: Straight-pull bolt action; adjustable trigger. Announced 1998. Imported from The Czech Republic by Euro-Imports.
Price: . . . . **NA**

CABANAS MASTER BOLT-ACTION RIFLE

Caliber: 177, round ball or pellet; single shot.
Barrel: 19-1/2".
Weight: 8 lbs. **Length:** 45-1/2" overall.
Stocks: Walnut target-type with Monte Carlo.
Sights: Blade front, fully adjustable rear.
Features: Fires round ball or pellet with 22-cal. blank cartridge. Bolt action. Imported from Mexico by Mandall Shooting Supplies. Introduced 1984.
Price: **$189.95**
Price: Varmint model (has 21-1/2" barrel, 4-1/2 lbs., 41" overall length, varmint-type stock) **$119.95**

ANSCHUTZ 1416D/1516D CLASSIC RIFLES

Caliber: 22 LR (1416D), 5-shot clip; 22 WMR (1516D), 4-shot clip.
Barrel: 22-1/2".
Weight: 6 lbs. **Length:** 41" overall.
Stock: European hardwood with walnut finish; classic style with straight comb, checkered pistol grip and forend.
Sights: Hooded ramp front, folding leaf rear.
Features: Uses Match 64 action. Adjustable single stage trigger. Receiver grooved for scope mounting. Imported from Germany by AcuSport Corp.
Price: 1416D, 22 LR **$755.95**
Price: 1516D, 22 WMR **$779.95**
Price: 1416D Classic left-hand **$679.95**

ANSCHUTZ 1710D CUSTOM RIFLE

Caliber: 22 LR, 5-shot clip.
Barrel: 24-1/4".
Weight: 7-3/8 lbs. **Length:** 42-1/2" overall.
Stock: Select European walnut.
Sights: Hooded ramp front, folding leaf rear; drilled and tapped for scope mounting.
Features: Match 54 action with adjustable single-stage trigger; roll-over Monte Carlo cheekpiece, slim forend with schnabel tip, Wundhammer palm swell on pistol grip, rosewood grip cap with white diamond insert; skip-line checkering on grip and forend. Introduced 1988. Imported from Germany by AcuSport Corp.
Price: **$1,289.95**

CABANAS LASER RIFLE

Caliber: 177.
Barrel: 19".
Weight: 6 lbs., 12 oz. **Length:** 42" overall.
Stock: Target-type thumbhole.
Sights: Blade front, open fully adjustable rear.
Features: Fires round ball or pellets with 22 blank cartridge. Imported from Mexico by Mandall Shooting Supplies.
Price: **$159.95**

Cabanas Leyre Bolt-Action Rifle

Similar to Master model except 44" overall, has sport/target stock.
Price: **$149.95**
Price: Model R83 (17" barrel, hardwood stock, 40" o.a.l.) **$79.95**
Price: Mini 82 Youth (16-1/2" barrel, 33" overall length, 3-1/2 lbs.)
. . . . **$69.95**
Price: Pony Youth (16" barrel, 34" overall length, 3.2 lbs.) **$69.95**

Cabanas Espronceda IV Bolt-Action Rifle

Similar to the Leyre model except has full sporter stock, 18-3/4" barrel, 40" overall length, weighs 5-1/2 lbs.
Price: **$134.95**

Chipmunk Deluxe

COOPER ARMS MODEL 36 CLASSIC SPORTER RIFLE

Caliber: 22 LR, 5-shot magazine.
Barrel: 22-3/4".
Weight: 7 lbs. **Length:** 42-1/2" overall.
Stock: AAA Claro walnut with 22 lpi checkering, oil finish.
Sights: None furnished.
Features: Action has three mid-bolt locking lugs, 45-degree bolt rotation; fully adjustable single stage match trigger; swivel studs. Pachmayr butt pad. Introduced 1991. Made in U.S. by Cooper Arms.
Price: Custom Classic (AAA Claro walnut, Monte Carlo beaded cheekpiece, oil finish) **$1,850.00**
Price: Model 36 Featherweight (black synthetic stock, 6.5 lbs.) . . . **$1,795.00**

CHIPMUNK SINGLE SHOT RIFLE

Caliber: 22, S, L, LR, single shot.
Barrel: 16-1/8".
Weight: About 2-1/2 lbs. **Length:** 30" overall.
Stocks: American walnut.
Sights: Post on ramp front, peep rear adjustable for windage and elevation.
Features: Drilled and tapped for scope mounting using special Chipmunk base ($13.95). Made in U.S. Introduced 1982. From Rogue Rifle Co., Inc.
Price: Standard **$184.95**
Price: Deluxe (better wood, checkering) **$234.95**
Price: With black, brown or camouflage laminate stock **$199.95**
Price: With black polyurethane-coated wood stock **$174.95**
Price: Bull barrel models of above, add **$15.00**

Dakota 22 Sporter

DAKOTA 22 SPORTER BOLT-ACTION RIFLE
Caliber: 22 LR, 5-shot magazine.
Barrel: 22" Premium.
Weight: About 6.5 lbs. **Length:** 42-1/2" overall.
Stock: Claro or English walnut in classic design; 13.6" length of pull. Point panel hand checkering. Swivel studs. Black buttpad.
Sights: None furnished.
Features: Combines features of Winchester 52 and Dakota 76 rifles. Full-sized receiver; rear locking lug and bolt machined from bar stock. Trigger and striker-blocking safety; Model 70-style trigger. Introduced 1992. From Dakota Arms, Inc.
Price: **$1,795.00**

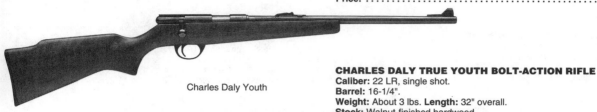

Charles Daly Youth

CHARLES DALY TRUE YOUTH BOLT-ACTION RIFLE
Caliber: 22 LR, single shot.
Barrel: 16-1/4".
Weight: About 3 lbs. **Length:** 32" overall.
Stock: Walnut-finished hardwood.
Sights: Blade front, adjustable rear.
Features: Scaled-down stock for small shooters. Blue finish. Introduced 1998. Imported by K.B.I., Inc.
Price: **$144.00**

Charles Daly Superior Magnum Grade Rifle
Similar to the Superior except chambered for 22 WMR. Has 22.6" barrel, double lug bolt, checkered stock, weighs 6.5 lbs. Introduced 1987.
Price: About **$189.00**

CHARLES DALY SUPERIOR BOLT-ACTION RIFLE
Caliber: 22 LR, 10-shot magazine.
Barrel: 22-5/8".
Weight: 6.7 lbs. **Length:** 41.25" overall.
Stock: Walnut-finished mahogany.
Sights: Bead front, rear adjustable for elevation.
Features: Receiver grooved for scope mounting. Blued finish. Introduced 1998. Imported by K.B.I., Inc.
Price: **$169.00**

Charles Daly Field Grade

Charles Daly Empire Magnum Grade Rifle
Similar to the Superior Magnum except has oil-finished American walnut stock with 18 lpi hand checkering; black hardwood grip cap and forend tip; highly polished barreled action; jewelled bolt; recoil pad; swivel studs. Imported from the Philippines by K.B.I., Inc.
Price: **$359.00**

Charles Daly Field Grade Rifle
Similar to the Superior except has short walnut-finished hardwood stock for small shooters. Introduced 1998. Imported by K.B.I., Inc.
Price: **$119.00**
Price: Field Youth (17.5" barrel). **$119.00**

Charles Daly Empire Grade Rifle
Similar to the Superior except has oil-finished American walnut stock with 18 lpi hand checkering; black hardwood grip cap and forend tip; highly polished barreled action; jewelled bolt; recoil pad; swivel studs. Imported by K.B.I., Inc.
Price: **$334.00**

Kimber Model 82C Classic

KIMBER MODEL 82C CLASSIC BOLT-ACTION RIFLE
Caliber: 22 LR, 4-shot magazine (10-shot available).
Barrel: 22", premium air-gauged, free-floated.
Weight: 6.5 lbs. **Length:** 40.5" overall.
Stock: Classic style of Claro walnut; 13.5" length of pull; hand-checkered; red rubber buttpad; polished steel grip cap.
Sights: None furnished; drilled and tapped for Warne, Leupold or Millett scope mounts.
Features: Action uses aluminum pillar bedding for consistent accuracy; trigger with 2.5-lb. pull is fully adjustable. Reintroduced 1994. Made in U.S. by Kimber of America, Inc.
Price: **$917.00**

Kimber Model 82C Custom Match Bolt-Action Rifle
Same as the Model 82C Classic except has high grade stock of AA French walnut with black ebony forend tip, full coverage 22 lpi borderless checkering, steel Neidner (uncheckered) buttplate, and satin rust blue finish. Reintroduced 1995. Made in U.S. by Kimber of America, Inc.
Price: **$2,158.00**

Kimber Model 82C SuperAmerica Bolt-Action Rifle
Similar to the Model 82C Classic except has AAA fancy grade Claro walnut with beaded cheekpiece, ebony forend tip; hand-checkered 22 lpi patterns with wrap-around coverage; black rubber buttpad. Reintroduced 1994. Made in U.S. by Kimber of America, Inc.
Price: **$1,488.00**

Kimber Model 82C SVT Bolt-Action Rifle
Simliar to the Model 82C except has an offhand high comb target-style stock; 18" fluted, stainless steel, target weight match-grade barrel; single shot action; A Claro walnut; weighs 7-1/2 lbs. Designed for off-hand plinking, varmint shooting and competition. Introduced 1996. Made in U.S. by Kimber of America, Inc.
Price: **$907.00**

Kimber Model 82C HS

Kimber Model 82C Stainless Classic Bolt-Action Rifle

Similar to the Model 82C except has a match-grade stainless steel barrel and matte-finished receiver. Limited edition of 750 guns. Introduced 1996. Made in U.S. by Kimber of America, Inc.

Price: **$899.00**

KRICO MODEL 300 BOLT-ACTION RIFLE

Caliber: 22 LR, 22 WMR, 22 Hornet.
Barrel: 19.6" (22 RF), 23.6" (Hornet).
Weight: 6.3 lbs. **Length:** 38.5" overall (22 RF).
Stock: Walnut-stained beech.
Sights: Blade on ramp front, open adjustable rear.

Marlin Model 880SS

MARLIN MODEL 15YN "LITTLE BUCKAROO"

Caliber: 22 S, L, LR, single shot.
Barrel: 16-1/4" Micro-Groove®.
Weight: 4-1/4 lbs. **Length:** 33-1/4" overall.
Stock: One-piece walnut-finished, press-checkered Maine birch with Monte Carlo; Mar-Shield® finish.
Sights: Ramp front, adjustable open rear.
Features: Beginner's rifle with thumb safety, easy-load feed throat, red cocking indicator. Receiver grooved for scope mounting. Introduced 1989.

Price: **$181.00**
Price: Model 15N (full-sized stock) **$181.00**

Marlin Model 81TS Bolt-Action Rifle

Same as the Marlin 880SS except blued steel, tubular magazine, holds 17 Long Rifle cartridges. Weighs 6 lbs.

Price: **$180.00**
Price: With 4x scope **$187.00**

Kimber Model 82C HS Rifle

Similar to the Model 82C except has 24" medium-heavy barrel fluted on the back half only; high comb stock. Designed for rimfire silhouette competion and small game hunting. Introduced 1997. Made in U.S. by Kimber of America.

Price: **$720.00**

Features: Double triggers, sliding safety. Checkered grip and forend. Imported from Germany by Mandall Shooting Supplies.
Price: Model 300 Standard **$700.00**
Price: Model 300 Deluxe **$795.00**
Price: Model 300 Stutzen (walnut full-length stock) **$825.00**
Price: Model 300 SA (walnut Monte Carlo stock) **$750.00**

MARLIN MODEL 880SS BOLT-ACTION RIFLE

Caliber: 22 LR, 7-shot clip magazine.
Barrel: 22" Micro-Groove®.
Weight: 6 lbs. **Length:** 41" overall.
Stock: Black fiberglass-filled synthetic with nickel-plated swivel studs and moulded-in checkering.
Sights: Ramp front with orange post and cutaway Wide-Scan™ hood, adjustable semi-buckhorn folding rear.
Features: Stainless steel barrel, receiver, front breech bolt and striker; receiver grooved for scope mounting. Introduced 1994. Made in U.S. by Marlin.

Price: **$273.00**

Marlin Model 25MN Bolt-Action Rifle

Similar to the Model 25N except chambered for 22 WMR. Has 7-shot clip magazine, 22" Micro-Groove® barrel, checkered walnut-finished Maine birch stock. Introduced 1989.

Price: **$209.00**
Price: With 4x scope **$216.00**

Marlin Model 25N Bolt-Action Repeater

Similar to Marlin 880, except walnut-finished p.g. stock, adjustable open rear sight, ramp front.

Price: **$183.00**
Price: With 4x scope **$189.00**

Marlin Model 880SQ

Consult our Directory pages for the location of firms mentioned.

Marlin Model 882SS Bolt-Action Rifle

Same as the Marlin Model 882 except has stainless steel front breech bolt, barrel, receiver and bolt knob. All other parts are either stainless steel or nickel-plated. Has black Monte Carlo stock of fiberglass-filled polycarbonate with moulded-in checkering, nickel-plated swivel studs. Introduced 1995. Made in U.S. by Marlin Firearms Co.

Price: **$297.00**

Marlin Model 880SQ Squirrel Rifle

Similar to the Model 880SS except uses the heavy target barrel of Marlin's Model 2000L target rifle. Black synthetic stock with moulded-in checkering; double bedding screws; matte blue finish. Comes without sights, but has plugged dovetail for a rear sight, filled screw holes for front; receiver grooved for scope mount. Weighs 7 lbs. Introduced 1996. Made in U.S. by Marlin.

Price: **$286.00**

Marlin Model 882 Bolt-Action Rifle

Same as the Marlin 880 except 22 WMR cal. only with 7-shot clip magazine; weight about 6 lbs. Comes with swivel studs.

Price: **$280.00**
Price: Model 882L (laminated hardwood stock) **$296.00**

Marlin Model 883 Bolt-Action Rifle

Same as Marlin 882 except tubular magazine holds 12 rounds of 22 WMR ammunition.

Price: **$290.00**

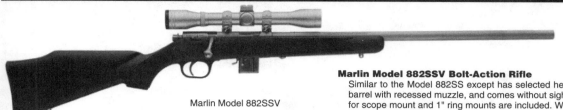

Marlin Model 882SSV

Marlin Model 883SS Bolt-Action Rifle

Same as the Model 883 except front breech bolt, striker knob, trigger stud, cartridge lifter stud and outer magazine tube are of stainless steel; other parts are nickel-plated. Has two-tone brown laminated Monte Carlo stock with swivel studs, rubber butt pad. Introduced 1993.
Price: **$309.00**

Remington 541-T HB Bolt-Action Rifle

Similar to the 541-T except has a heavy target-type barrel without sights. Receiver is drilled and tapped for scope mounting. American walnut stock with straight comb, satin finish, cut checkering, black checkered buttplate, black grip cap and forend tip. Weight is about 6-1/2 lbs. Introduced 1993.
Price: **$492.00**

Marlin Model 882SSV Bolt-Action Rifle

Similar to the Model 882SS except has selected heavy 22" stainless steel barrel with recessed muzzle, and comes without sights; receiver is grooved for scope mount and 1" ring mounts are included. Weighs 7 lbs. Introduced 1997. Made in U.S. by Marlin Firearms Co.
Price: **$293.00**

REMINGTON 541-T

Caliber: 22 S, L, LR, 5-shot clip.
Barrel: 24".
Weight: 5-7/8 lbs. **Length:** 42-1/2" overall.
Stock: Walnut, cut-checkered p.g. and forend. Satin finish.
Sights: None. Drilled and tapped for scope mounts.
Features: Clip repeater. Thumb safety. Reintroduced 1986.
Price: About **$465.00**

Remington 581-S

REMINGTON MODEL 581-S SPORTSMAN

Caliber: 22 LR, 5-shot clip.
Barrel: 24".
Weight: 5-7/8 lbs. **Length:** 42-1/2" overall.
Stock: Stained hardwood.
Sights: Bead on blade front, open adjustable rear.
Features: Polished blue finish. Comes with single-shot adapter. Receiver grooved for scope mounting.
Price: **$239.00**

Ruger K77/22 Varmint

RUGER 77/22 RIMFIRE BOLT-ACTION RIFLE

Caliber: 22 LR, 10-shot rotary magazine; 22 WMR, 9-shot rotary magazine.
Barrel: 20".
Weight: About 5-3/4 lbs. **Length:** 39-3/4" overall.
Stock: Checkered American walnut or injection-moulded fiberglass-reinforced DuPont Zytel with Xenoy inserts in forend and grip, stainless sling swivels.
Sights: Brass bead front, adjustable folding leaf rear or plain barrel with 1" Ruger rings.
Features: Mauser-type action uses Ruger's 10-shot rotary magazine. Three-position safety, simplified bolt stop, patented bolt locking system. Uses the dual-screw barrel attachment system of the 10/22 rifle. Integral scope mounting system with 1" Ruger rings. Blued model introduced in 1983. Stainless steel model and blued model with the synthetic stock introduced in 1989.
Price: 77/22R (no sights, rings, walnut stock) **$473.00**
Price: 77/22RS (open sights, rings, walnut stock) **$481.00**
Price: K77/22RP (stainless, no sights, rings, synthetic stock) **$473.00**
Price: K77/22RSP (stainless, open sights, rings, synthetic stock)
. . . . **$481.00**
Price: 77/22RM (22 WMR, blue, walnut stock) **$473.00**
Price: K77/22RSMP (22 WMR, stainless, open sights, rings, synthetic stock) **$481.00**
Price: K77/22RMP (22 WMR, stainless, synthetic stock) **$473.00**
Price: 77/22RSM (22 WMR, blue, open sights, rings, walnut stock)
. . . . **$481.00**

RUGER K77/22 VARMINT RIFLE

Caliber: 22 LR, 10-shot, 22 WMR, 9-shot detachable rotary magazine.
Barrel: 24", heavy.
Weight: 7.25 lbs. **Length:** 43.25" overall.
Stock: Laminated hardwood with rubber butt pad, quick-detachable swivel studs. No checkering or grip cap.
Sights: None furnished. Comes with Ruger 1" scope rings.
Features: Made of stainless steel with target gray finish. Three-position safety, dual extractors. Stock has wide, flat forend. Introduced 1993.
Price: K77/22VBZ, 22 LR **$499.00**
Price: K77/22VMB, 22 WMR **$499.00**

Sako Finnfire

SAKO FINNFIRE BOLT-ACTION RIFLE

Caliber: 22 LR, 5-shot magazine.
Barrel: 22".
Weight: 5.25 lbs. **Length:** 40" overall.
Stock: European walnut with checkered grip and forend.
Sights: Hooded blade front, open adjustable rear.
Features: Adjustable single-stage trigger; has 50-degree bolt lift. Introduced 1994. Imported from Finland by Stoeger Industries.
Price: **$764.00**
Price: With heavy barrel **$849.00**

SAVAGE MARK I-G BOLT-ACTION RIFLE

Caliber: 22 LR, single shot.
Barrel: 20-3/4".
Weight: 5-1/2 lbs. **Length:** 39-1/2" overall.
Stock: Walnut-finished hardwood with Monte Carlo-type comb, checkered grip and forend.

Savage Mark II-FXP

Savage Mark II-LV Heavy Barrel Rifle

Similar to the Mark II-G except has heavy 21" barrel with recessed target-style crown; gray, laminated hardwood stock with cut checkering. No sights furnished, but has dovetailed receiver for scope mounting. Overall length is 39-3/4", weight is 6-1/2 lbs. Comes with 10-shot clip magazine. Introduced 1997. Imported from Canada by Savage Arms, Inc.
Price: **$200.00**
Price: Mark II-FV, with black graphite/polymer stock **$174.00**

Savage Mark II-FSS Stainless Rifle

Similar to the Mark II-G except has stainless steel barreled action and graphite/polymer filled stock; free-floated barrel. Weighs 5 lbs. Introduced 1997. Imoported from Canada by Savage Arms, Inc.
Price: **$150.00**

Savage Model 93FVSS

Savage Model 93FVSS Magnum Rifle

Similar to the Model 93FSS Magnum except has 21" heavy barrel with recessed target-style crown; satin-finished stainless barreled action; black graphite/fiberglass stock. Drilled and tapped for scope mounting; comes with Weaver-style bases. Introduced 1998. Imported from Canada by Savage Arms, Inc.
Price: **$201.00**

TRISTAR PEE-WEE 22 BOLT-ACTION RIFLE

Caliber: 22 Long Rifle, single shot.
Barrel: 16-1/2".
Weight: 2-3/4 lbs. **Length:** 31" overall.
Stock: Hardwood with hard plastic buttplate; Monte Carlo comb; 12" length of pull.
Sights: Ramp front, fully adjustable rear, both removable; receiver grooved for scope mounting; comes with Simmons 4x15 scope and mount.
Features: Manually cocked action; blued barrel and receiver. Comes with hard gun case. Introduced 1997. Made in U.S. From Tristar Sporting Arms.
Price: **$199.00**

Ultra Light Arms Model 20

WINCHESTER MODEL 52B BOLT-ACTION RIFLE

Caliber: 22 Long Rifle,5-shot magazine.
Barrel: 24".
Weight: 7 lbs. **Length:** 41-3/4" overall.
Stock: Walnut with checkered grip and forend.
Sights: None furnished; grooved receiver and drilled and tapped for scope mounting.
Features: Has Micro Motion trigger adjustable for pull and over-travel; match chamber; detachable magazine. Reintroduced 1997. From U.S. Repeating Arms Co.
Price: **$635.00**

Sights: Bead front, open adjustable rear. Receiver grooved for scope mounting.
Features: Thumb-operated rotating safety. Blue finish. Rifled or smooth bore. Introduced 1990. Made in Canada, from Savage Arms.
Price: Mark I, rifled or smooth bore, right- or left-handed **$119.00**
Price: Mark I-GY (Youth), 19" barrel, 37" overall, 5 lbs. **$119.00**

SAVAGE MARK II-G BOLT-ACTION RIFLE

Caliber: 22 LR, 10-shot magazine.
Barrel: 20-1/2".
Weight: 5-1/2 lbs. **Length:** 39-1/2" overall.
Stock: Walnut-finished hardwood with Monte Carlo-type comb, checkered grip and forend.
Sights: Bead front, open adjustable rear. Receiver grooved for scope mounting.
Features: Thumb-operated rotating safety. Blue finish. Introduced 1990. Made in Canada, from Savage Arms.
Price: **$126.00**
Price: Mark II-GY (youth), 19" barrel, 37" overall, 5 lbs. **$126.00**
Price: Mark II-GL, left-hand **$126.00**
Price: Mark II-GLY (youth) left-hand **$126.00**
Price: Mark II-GXP Package Gun (comes with 4x15 scope), right- or left-handed **$131.00**
Price: Mark II-FXP (as above except with black synthetic stock) **$125.00**
Price: Mark II-F (as above, no scope) **$119.00**

SAVAGE MODEL 93G MAGNUM BOLT-ACTION RIFLE

Caliber: 22 WMR, 5-shot magazine.
Barrel: 20-3/4".
Weight: 5-3/4 lbs. **Length:** 39-1/2" overall.
Stock: Walnut-finished hardwood with Monte Carlo-type comb, checkered grip and forend.
Sights: Bead front, adjustable open rear. Receiver grooved for scope mount.
Features: Thumb-operated rotary safety. Blue finish. Introduced 1994. Made in Canada, from Savage Arms.
Price: About **$145.00**
Price: Model 93F (as above with black graphite/fiberglass stock).... **$139.00**

Savage Model 93FSS Magnum Rifle

Similar to the Model 93G except has stainless steel barreled action and black synthetic stock with positive checkering. Weighs 5-1/2 lbs. Introduced 1997. Imported from Canada by Savage Arms, Inc.
Price: **$175.00**

ULTRA LIGHT ARMS MODEL 20 RF BOLT-ACTION RIFLE

Caliber: 22 LR, single shot or 5-shot repeater.
Barrel: 22" Douglas Premium, #1 contour.
Weight: 5 lbs., 3 oz. **Length:** 41-1/2" overall.
Stock: Composite Kevlar, graphite reinforced. DuPont Imron paint; 13-1/2" length of pull.
Sights: None furnished. Drilled and tapped for scope mounting.
Features: Available as either single shot or repeater with 5-shot removable magazine. Comes with scope mounts. Left-hand model available. Introduced 1993. Made in U.S. by Ultra Light Arms, Inc.
Price: Single shot.. **$800.00**
Price: Repeater **$850.00**

Includes models for classic American and ISU target competition and other sporting and competitive shooting.

ANSCHUTZ 1451R SPORTER TARGET RIFLE
Caliber: 22 LR, 5-shot magazine.
Barrel: 22" heavy match.
Weight: 6.4 lbs. **Length:** 39.75" overall.
Stock: European hardwood with walnut finish.
Sights: None furnished. Grooved receiver for scope mounting or Anschutz micrometer rear sight.
Features: Sliding safety, two-stage trigger. Adjustable buttplate; forend slide rail to accept Anschutz accessories. Imported from Germany by AcuSport Corp.
Price: $549.00

ANSCHUTZ ACHIEVER ST SUPER TARGET RIFLE
Caliber: 22 LR, single shot.
Barrel: 22", .75" diameter.
Weight: About 6.5 lbs. **Length:** 38.75" to 39.75" overall.
Stock: Walnut-finished European hardwood with hand-stippled panels on grip and forend; 13.5" accessory rail on forend.
Sights: Optional. Receiver grooved for scope mounting.
Features: Designed for the advanced junior shooter with adjustable length of pull from 13.25" to 14.25" via removable butt spacers. Two-stage #5066 adjustable trigger factory set at 2.6 lbs. Introduced 1994. Imported from Germany by Gunsmithing, Inc.
Price: $329.95
Price: #6834 Match Sight Set $185.00

ANSCHUTZ 1808D-RT SUPER RUNNING TARGET RIFLE
Caliber: 22 LR, single shot.
Barrel: 32-1/2".
Weight: 9.4 lbs. **Length:** 50.5" overall.
Stock: European walnut. Heavy beavertail forend; adjustable cheekpiece and buttplate. Stippled grip and forend.
Sights: None furnished. Grooved for scope mounting.
Features: Designed for Running Target competition. Nine-way adjustable single-stage trigger, slide safety. Introduced 1991. Imported from Germany by Accuracy International, Gunsmithing, Inc.
Price: Right-hand. . . . .$1,300.10 to $1,410.00

Consult our Directory pages for the location of firms mentioned.

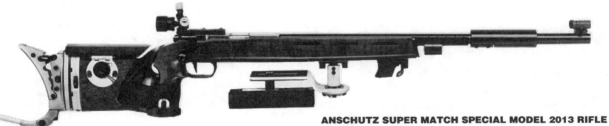

Anschutz 2013

ANSCHUTZ 1903 MATCH RIFLE
Caliber: 22 LR, single shot.
Barrel: 25", .75" diameter.
Weight: 8.6 lbs. **Length:** 43.75" overall.
Stock: Walnut-finished hardwood with adjustable cheekpiece; stippled grip and forend.
Sights: None furnished.
Features: Uses Anschutz Match 64 action and #5098 two-stage trigger. A medium weight rifle for intermediate and advanced Junior Match competition. Introduced 1987. Imported from Germany by Accuracy International, Gunsmithing, Inc.
Price: Right-hand. . . . .$720.40 to $775.00
Price: Left-hand. . . . .$757.90 to $815.00

ANSCHUTZ 64-MSR SILHOUETTE RIFLE
Caliber: 22 LR, 5-shot magazine.
Barrel: 21-1/2", medium heavy; 7/8" diameter.
Weight: 8 lbs. **Length:** 39.5" overall.
Stock: Walnut-finished hardwood, silhouette-type.
Sights: None furnished.
Features: Uses Match 64 action. Designed for metallic silhouette competition. Stock has stippled checkering, contoured thumb groove with Wundhammer swell. Two-stage #5091 trigger. Slide safety locks sear and bolt. Introduced 1980. Imported from Germany by AcuSport Corp., Accuracy International, Gunsmithing, Inc.
Price: 64-MSR . . . .$725.00 to $1,129.95

ANSCHUTZ 2013 BENCHREST RIFLE
Caliber: 22 LR, single shot.
Barrel: 19.75".
Weight: About 11 lbs. **Length:** 37.75" to 42.5" overall.
Stock: Benchrest style of European hardwood. Stock length adjustable via spacers and buttplate.
Sights: None furnished. Receiver grooved for mounts.
Features: Uses the Anschutz 2013 target action, #5018 two-stage adjustable target trigger factory set at 3.9 oz. Introduced 1994. Imported from Germany by Accuracy International, Gunsmithing, Inc.
Price: . . . .$1,725.00 to $2,405.10

ANSCHUTZ 1827B BIATHLON RIFLE
Caliber: 22 LR, 5-shot magazine.
Barrel: 21-1/2".
Weight: 8-1/2 lbs. with sights. **Length:** 42-1/2" overall.
Stock: European walnut with cheekpiece, stippled pistol grip and forend.
Sights: Optional globe front specially designed for Biathlon shooting, micrometer rear with hinged snow cap.
Features: Uses Super Match 54 action and nine-way adjustable trigger; adjustable wooden buttplate, Biathlon butthook, adjustable hand-stop rail. Introduced 1982. Imported from Germany by Accuracy International, Gunsmithing, Inc.
Price: Right-hand, with sights, about . . . . $1,500.50 to $1,555.00

Anschutz 1827BT Fortner Biathlon Rifle
Similar to the Anschutz 1827B Biathlon rifle except uses Anschutz/Fortner system straight-pull bolt action, stainless steel barrel. Introduced 1982. Imported from Germany by Accuracy International, Gunsmithing, Inc.
Price: Right-hand, with sights . . . . $2,155.10 to $2,210.00
Price: Left-hand, with sights . . . . $2,350.00 to $2,395.00
Price: Right-hand, sights, stainless barrel (Gunsmithing, Inc.) $2,295.00

ANSCHUTZ SUPER MATCH SPECIAL MODEL 2013 RIFLE
Caliber: 22 LR, single shot.
Barrel: 19.75" (26" with tube installed).
Weight: 15.5 lbs. **Length:** 43" to 45.5" overall.
Stock: European walnut; target adjustable.
Sights: Optional. Uses #7020/20 sight set.
Features: Improved Super Match 54 action, #5018 trigger give fastest consistent lock time for a production target rifle. Barrel is micro-honed; trigger has nine points of adjustment, two stages. Slide safety. Comes with test target. Introduced 1992. Imported from Germany by Accuracy International, Gunsmithing, Inc.
Price: Right-hand . . . . $2,405.10 to $2,495.00
Price: Left-hand . . . . $2,526.00 to $2,610.00

Anschutz 2007 Match Rifle
Uses same action as the Model 2013, but has a lighter barrel. European walnut stock in right-hand, true left-hand or extra-short models. Sights optional. Available with 19.6" barrel with extension tube, or 26", both in stainless or blue. Introduced 1998. Imported from Germany by Gunsmithing, Inc., Accuracy International.
Price: Right-hand, blue, no sights . . . . $1,697.00 to $1,725.00
Price: Right-hand, blue, no sights, extra-short stock $1,655.70
Price: Left-hand, blue, no sights. . . . . $1,783.40 to $1,795.00

ANSCHUTZ 1808 MSR SILHOUETTE RIFLE
Caliber: 22 LR, 5-shot magazine.
Barrel: 22.4" match; detachable muzzle tube.
Weight: 7.9 lbs. **Length:** 40.9" overall.
Stock: European walnut, thumbhole design.
Sights: None furnished.
Features: Uses Anschutz 54.18 barreled action with two-stage match trigger. Introduced 1997. Imported from Germany by Accuracy International, Acusport Corp.
Price:.. $1,425.00 to $2,219.95

ANSCHUTZ 1911 PRONE MATCH RIFLE
Caliber: 22 LR, single shot.
Barrel: 27-1/4".
Weight: 11 lbs. **Length:** 46" overall.
Stock: Walnut-finished European hardwood; American prone-style with adjustable cheekpiece, textured pistol grip, forend with swivel rail and adjustable rubber buttplate.
Sights: None furnished. Receiver grooved for Anschutz sights (extra).
Features: Two-stage #5018 trigger adjustable from 2.1 to 8.6 oz. Extremely fast lock time. Stainless or blue barrel. Imported from Germany by Accuracy International, Gunsmithing, Inc.
Price: Right-hand, no sights .... $1,656.20 to $2,094.95

ANSCHUTZ 1909 MATCH RIFLE
Caliber: 22 LR, single shot.
Barrel: 26" match.
Weight: 14.3 lbs. **Length:** 44.8" overall.
Stock: European beechwood, thumbhole design with hook buttplate, handstop with swivel.
Sights: None furnished.
Features: Uses Match 54 action. Adjustable comb, buttplate; forend rail accepts Anscuhtz adjustable palm rest. Imported from Germany by Gunsmithing, Inc.
Price: $1,724.50

Anschutz 1913 Super Match Rifle
Same as the Model 1911 except European walnut International-type stock with adjustable cheekpiece, or color laminate, both available with straight or lowered forend, adjustable aluminum hook buttplate, adjustable hand stop, weighs 15.5 lbs., 46" overall. Stainless or blue barrel. Imported from Germany by Accuracy International, Gunsmithing, Inc.
Price: Right-hand, blue, no sights, walnut stock .....$2,139.00 to $2,175.00
Price: Right-hand, blue, no sights, color laminate stock $2,199.40
Price: Right-hand, blue, no sights, walnut, lowered forend $2,181.80
Price: Right-hand, blue, no sights, color laminate, lowered forend . $2,242.20
Price: Left-hand, blue, no sights, walnut stock .....$2,233.10 to $2,275.00

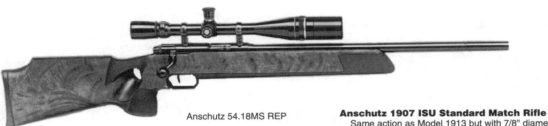

Anschutz 54.18MS REP

Anschutz 54.18MS REP Deluxe Silhouette Rifle
Same basic action and trigger specifications as the Anschutz 1913 Super Match but with removable 5-shot clip magazine, 22" barrel extendable to 30" using optional extension and weight set. Receiver drilled and tapped for scope mounting. Walnut Silhouette stock. Introduced 1990. Imported from Germany by Accuracy International, Gunsmithing, Inc.
Price: .... $1,140.00 to $1,151.70

ARMALITE AR-10 (T) RIFLE
Caliber: 308, 10-shot magazine.
Barrel: 24" target-weight Rock 5R custom.
Weight: 10.4 lbs. **Length:** 43.5" overall.
Stock: Green or black compostion; N.M. fiberglass handguard tube.
Sights: Detachable handle, front sight, or scope mount available. Comes with international-style flattop receiver with Picatinny rail.
Features: National Match two-stage trigger. Forged upper receiver. Receivers hard-coat amodized. Introduced 1995. Made in U.S. by ArmaLite,Inc.
Price: $2,075.00
Price: AR-10 (T) Carbine, lighter 16" barrel, single stage trigger, weighs 8.8 lbs. $1,970.00

BLASER R93 TACTICAL RIFLE
Caliber: 308 Win., 10-shot detachable box magazine.
Barrel: 24".
Weight: 10.4 lbs. **Length:** 44" overall.
Stock: Aluminum with synthetic lining.
Sights: None furnished; accepts detachable scope mount.
Features: Straight-pull bolt action with adjustable trigger; fully adjustable stock; quick takedown; corrosion resistant finish. Introduced 1998. Imported from Germany by Sigarms.
Price:... NA

BUSHMASTER XM15 E2S TARGET MODEL RIFLE
Caliber: 223.
Barrel: 20", 24", 26"; 1:9" twist; heavy.
Weight: 8.3 lbs. **Length:** 38.25" overall (20" barrel).
Stock: Black composition; A2 type.
Sights: Adjustable post front, adjustable aperture rear.

Anschutz 1907 ISU Standard Match Rifle
Same action as Model 1913 but with 7/8" diameter 26" barrel (stainless or blue). Length is 44.5" overall, weighs 10 lbs. Choice of stock configurations. Vented forend. Designed for prone and position shooting ISU requirements; suitable for NRA matches. Also available with walnut flat-forend stock for benchrest shooting. Imported from Germany by Accuracy International, Gunsmithing, Inc.
Price: Right-hand, blue, no sights, hardwood stock ....$1,253.40 to $1,299.00
Price: Right-hand, blue, no sights, colored laminated stock ....$1,316.10 to $1,375.00
Price: Right-hand, blue, no sights, walnut stock .....$1,299.30 to $1,355.00
Price: Left-hand, blue barrel, no sights, hardwood stock ....$1,320.00 to $1,375.00

ARMALITE M15A4 (T) EAGLE EYE RIFLE
Caliber: 223, 7-shot magazine.
Barrel: 24" heavy stainless; 1:8" twist.
Weight: 9.2 lbs. **Length:** 42-3/8" overall.
Stock: Green or black, N.M. fiberglass handguard tube.
Sights: One-piece international-style flat top receiver with Weaver-type rail, including case deflector.
Features: Detachable carry handle, front sight and scope mount (30mm or 1") available. Upper and lower receivers have push-type pivot pin, hard coat anodized. Made in U.S. by ArmaLite, Inc.
Price: $1,378.00

ARMALITE M15A4 ACTION MASTER RIFLE
Caliber: 223, 7-shot magazine.
Barrel: 20" heavy stainless; 1:9" twist.
Weight: 9 lbs. **Length:** 40-1/2" overall.
Stock: Green or black plastic; N.M. fiberglass handguard tube.
Sights: One-piece international-style flattop receiver with Weaver-type rail.
Features: Detachable carry handle, front sight and scope mount available. National Match two-stage trigger group; Picatinny rail; upper and lower receivers have push-type pivot pin; hard coat anodized finish. Made in U.S. by ArmaLite, Inc.
Price: $1,175.00

Features: Patterned after Colt M-16A2. Chrome-lined barrel with manganese phosphate exterior. Forged aluminum receivers with push-pin takedown. Made in U.S. by Bushmaster Firearms Co./Quality Parts Co.
Price: 20" match heavy barrel $895.00
Price: 24" match heavy barrel $915.00
Price: 26" match heavy barrel $935.00

Bushmaster V-Match

BUSHMASTER XM15 E2S V-MATCH RIFLE
Caliber: 223.
Barrel: 20", 24", 26"; 1:9" twist; heavy.

Weight: 8.1 lbs. **Length:** 38.25" overall (20" barrel).
Stock: Black composition. A2 type.
Sights: None furnished; upper receiver has integral scope mount base.
Features: Chrome-lined .950" heavy barrel with counter-bored crown, manganese phosphate finish; free-floating aluminum handguard; forged aluminum receivers with push-pin takedown, hard anodized mil-spec finish. Competition trigger optional. Made in U.S. by Bushmaster Firearms, Inc.
Price: 20" Match heavy barrel **$995.00**
Price: 24" Match heavy barrel **$915.00**
Price: 26" Match heavy barrel **$935.00**
Price: V-Match Commando Carbine (16" barrel) **$950.00**

Bushmaster DCM

Bushmaster DCM Competition Rifle
Similar to the XM15 E2S Target Model except has 20" extra-heavy (1" diameter) barrel with 1.8" twist for heavier competition bullets. Weighs about 12 lbs. with balance weights. Has special competition rear sight with interchangeable apertures, extra-fine 1/2- or 1/4-MOA windage and elevation adjustments; specially ground front sight post in choice of three widths. Full-length handguards over free-floater barrel tube. Introduced 1998. Made in U.S. by Bushmaster Firearms, Inc.
Price: **$1,500.00**

Colt Match Target HBAR

COLT MATCH TARGET MODEL RIFLE
Caliber: 223 Rem., 8-shot magazine.
Barrel: 20".
Weight: 7.5 lbs. **Length:** 39" overall.
Stock: Composition stock, grip, forend.
Sights: Post front, aperture rear adjustable for windage and elevation.
Features: Five-round detachable box magazine, standard-weight barrel, sling swivels. Has forward bolt assist. Military matte black finish. Model introduced 1991.
Price: **$1,040.00**

Colt Match Target Competition HBAR II Rifle
Similar to the Match Target Competition HBAR except has 16.1" barrel, weighs 7.1 lbs., overall length 34.5"; 1:9" twist barrel. Introduced 1995.
Price: **$1,065.00**

Colt Match Target HBAR Rifle
Similar to the Target Model except has heavy barrel, 800-meter rear sight adjustable for windage and elevation. Introduced 1991.
Price: **$1,085.00**

Colt Accurized Rifle
Similar to the Colt Match Target Model except has 24" stainless steel heavy barrel with 1.9" rifling, flattop receiver with scope mount and 1" rings, weighs 9.25 lbs. Introduced 1998. Made in U.S. by Colt's Mfg. Co., Inc.
Price: **$1,295.00**

Colt Match Target Competition HBAR Rifle
Similar to the Sporter Target except has flat-top receiver with integral Weaver-type base for scope mounting. Counter-bored muzzle, 1:9" rifling twist. Introduced 1991.
Price: Model R6700 .... **$1,090.00**

Cooper Model 36 BR-50

COOPER ARMS MODEL 36 BR-50
Caliber: 22 LR, single shot.
Barrel: 22", .860" straight.
Weight: 6.8 lbs. **Length:** 40.5" overall.
Stock: McMillan Benchrest.
Sights: None furnished.
Features: Action has three mid-bolt locking lugs; fully adjustable match grade trigger; stainless barrel. Introduced 1994. Made in U.S. by Cooper Arms.
Price: **$1,950.00**

E.A.A./HW 660 MATCH RIFLE
Caliber: 22 LR.
Barrel: 26".
Weight: 10.7 lbs. **Length:** 45.3" overall.
Stock: Match-type walnut with adjustable cheekpiece and buttplate.
Sights: Globe front, match aperture rear.
Features: Adjustable match trigger; stippled pistol grip and forend; forend accessory rail. Introduced 1991. Imported from Germany by European American Armory.
Price: About **$951.60**
Price: With laminate stock **$998.40**

Harris Gunworks M-86

HARRIS GUNWORKS NATIONAL MATCH RIFLE
Caliber: 7mm-08, 308, 5-shot magazine.
Barrel: 24", stainless steel.
Weight: About 11 lbs. (std. bbl.). **Length:** 43" overall.
Stock: Fiberglass with adjustable buttplate.
Sights: Barrel band and Tompkins front; no rear sight furnished.
Features: Gunworks repeating action with clip slot, Canjar trigger. Match-grade barrel. Available in right-hand only. Fiberglass stock, sight installation, special machining and triggers optional. Introduced 1989. From Harris Gunworks, Inc.
Price: **$3,500.00**

HARRIS GUNWORKS LONG RANGE RIFLE
Caliber: 300 Win. Mag., 7mm Rem. Mag., 300 Phoenix, 338 Lapua, single shot.
Barrel: 26", stainless steel, match-grade.
Weight: 14 lbs. **Length:** 46-1/2" overall.
Stock: Fiberglass with adjustable buttplate and cheekpiece. Adjustable for length of pull, drop, cant and cast-off.
Sights: Barrel band and Tompkins front; no rear sight furnished.
Features: Uses Gunworks solid bottom single shot action and Canjar trigger. Barrel twist 1:12". Introduced 1989. From Harris Gunworks, Inc.
Price: **$3,620.00**

HARRIS GUNWORKS M-86 SNIPER RIFLE
Caliber: 308, 30-06, 4-shot magazine; 300 Win. Mag., 3-shot magazine.
Barrel: 24", Gunworks match-grade in heavy contour.
Weight: 11-1/4 lbs. (308), 11-1/2 lbs. (30-06, 300). **Length:** 43-1/2" overall.
Stock: Specially designed McHale fiberglass stock with textured grip and forend, recoil pad.
Sights: None furnished.
Features: Uses Gunworks repeating action. Comes with bipod. Matte black finish. Sling swivels. Introduced 1989. From Harris Gunworks, Inc.
Price: **$2,700.00**

HECKLER & KOCH PSG-1 MARKSMAN RIFLE
Caliber: 308, 5- and 20-shot magazines.
Barrel: 25.6", heavy.
Weight: 17.8 lbs. **Length:** 47.5" overall.
Stock: Matte black high impact plastic, adjustable for length, pivoting butt cap, vertically-adjustable cheekpiece; target-type pistol grip with adjustable palm shelf.
Sights: Hendsoldt 6x42 scope.
Features: Uses HK-91 action with low-noise bolt closing device, special Marksman trigger group; special forend with T-way rail for sling swivel or tripod. Gun comes in special foam-fitted metal transport case with tripod, two 20-shot and two 5-shot magazines, tripod. Imported from Germany by Heckler & Koch, Inc. Introduced 1986. **Law enforcement sales only.**
Price: **$10,811.00**

KRICO MODEL 360 S2 BIATHLON RIFLE
Caliber: 22 LR, 5-shot magazine.
Barrel: 21.25".
Weight: 9 lbs., 15 oz. **Length:** 40.55" overall.
Stock: Biathlon design of black epoxy-finished walnut with pistol grip.
Sights: Globe front, fully adjustable Diana 82 match peep rear.
Features: Pistol grip-activated action. Comes with five magazines (four stored in stock recess), muzzle/sight snow cap. Introduced 1991. Imported from Germany by Mandall Shooting Supplies.
Price: **$1,595.00**

HARRIS GUNWORKS M-89 SNIPER RIFLE
Caliber: 308 Win., 5-shot magazine.
Barrel: 28" (with suppressor).
Weight: 15 lbs., 4 oz.
Stock: Fiberglass; adjustable for length; recoil pad.
Sights: None furnished. Drilled and tapped for scope mounting.
Features: Uses Gunworks repeating action. Comes with bipod. Introduced 1990. From Harris Gunworks, Inc.
Price: Standard (non-suppressed). **$3,200.00**

Harris Gunworks Long Range Rifle

HARRIS GUNWORKS COMBO M-87 SERIES 50-CALIBER RIFLES
Caliber: 50 BMG, single shot.
Barrel: 29, with muzzlebrake.
Weight: About 21-1/2 lbs. **Length:** 53" overall.
Stock: Gunworks fiberglass.
Sights: None furnished.
Features: Right-handed Gunworks stainless steel receiver, chrome-moly barrel with 1:15" twist. Introduced 1987. From Harris Gunworks, Inc.
Price: **$3,885.00**
Price: M87R 5-shot repeater **$4,000.00**
Price: M-87 (5-shot repeater) "Combo" **$4,000.00**
Price: M-92 Bullpup (shortened M-87 single shot with bullpup stock) **$4,770.00**
Price: M-93 (10-shot repeater with folding stock, detachable magazine) **$4,300.00**

Heckler & Koch PSG-1

KRICO MODEL 400 MATCH RIFLE
Caliber: 22 LR, 22 Hornet, 5-shot magazine.
Barrel: 23.2" (22 LR), 23.6" (22 Hornet).
Weight: 8.8 lbs. **Length:** 42.1" overall (22 RF).
Stock: European walnut, match type.
Sights: None furnished; receiver grooved for scope mounting.
Features: Heavy match barrel. Double-set or match trigger. Imported from Germany by Mandall Shooting Supplies.
Price: **$950.00**

KRICO MODEL 600 SNIPER RIFLE
Caliber: 222, 223, 22-250, 243, 308, 4-shot magazine.
Barrel: 23.6".
Weight: 9.2 lbs. **Length:** 45.2" overall.
Stock: European walnut with adjustable rubber buttplate.
Sights: None supplied; drilled and tapped for scope mounting.
Features: Match barrel with flash hider; large bolt knob; wide trigger shoe. Parkerized finish. Imported from Germany by Mandall Shooting Supplies.
Price: **$2,645.00**

Krico Model 360S Biathlon

KRICO MODEL 600 MATCH RIFLE
Caliber: 222, 223, 22-250, 243, 308, 5.6x50 Mag., 4-shot magazine.
Barrel: 23.6".
Weight: 8.8 lbs. **Length:** 43.3" overall.
Stock: Match stock of European walnut with cheekpiece.
Sights: None furnished; drilled and tapped for scope mounting.
Features: Match stock with vents in forend for cooling, rubber recoil pad, sling swivels. Imported from Germany by Mandall Shooting Supplies.
Price: **$1,250.00**

KRICO MODEL 360S BIATHLON RIFLE
Caliber: 22 LR, 5-shot magazine.
Barrel: 21.25".
Weight: 9.26 lbs. **Length:** 40.55" overall.
Stock: Walnut with high comb, adjustable buttplate.
Sights: Globe front, fully adjustable Diana 82 match peep rear.
Features: Straight-pull action with 17.6-oz. match trigger. Comes with five magazines (four stored in stock recess), muzzle/sight snow cap. Introduced 1991. Imported from Germany by Mandall Shooting Supplies.
Price: **$1,695.00**

LAKELANDER 389 MATCH-MAKER RIFLE
Caliber: 243, 308, 300 Win. Mag.
Barrel: 21.7", heavy.
Weight: 8.4 lbs. **Length:** 43.3" overall.
Stock: American walnut target style with adjustable comb, stippled grip and forend.
Sights: None furnished; drilled and tapped for scope mounting.
Features: Special SureSeal protective metal finish; recoil damper; three-position safety; adjustable trigger. Introduced 1998. Imported from Sweden by Lakelander U.S.A., Inc.
Price: **$2,049.00**

Marlin Model 2000L

OLYMPIC ARMS PCR-SERVICEMATCH RIFLE
Caliber: 223, 10-shot magazine.
Barrel: 20", broach-cut 416 stainless steel.
Weight: About 10 lbs. **Length:** 39.5" overall.
Stock: A2 stowaway grip and trapdoor buttstock.
Sights: Post front, E2-NM fully adjustable operture rear.
Features: Based on the AR-15. Conforms to all DCM standards. Free-floating 1:8.5" or 1:10" barrel; crowned barrel; no bayonet lug. Introduced 1996. Made in U.S. by Olympic Arms, Inc.
Price: **$1,145.00**

MARLIN MODEL 2000L TARGET RIFLE
Caliber: 22 LR, single shot.
Barrel: 22" heavy, Micro-Groove® rifling, match chamber, recessed muzzle.
Weight: 8 lbs. **Length:** 41" overall.
Stock: Laminated black/gray with ambidextrous pistol grip.
Sights: Hooded front with ten aperture inserts, fully adjustable target rear peep.
Features: Buttplate adjustable for length of pull, height and angle. Aluminum forend rail with stop and quick-detachable swivel. Two-stage target trigger; red cocking indicator. Five-shot adaptor kit available. Introduced 1991. From Marlin.
Price: **$639.00**

Olympic PCR-1

Olympic Arms PCR-2, PCR-3 Rifles
Similar to the PCR-1 except has 16" barrel, weighs 8 lbs., 2 oz.; has post front sight, fully adjustable aperture rear. Model PCR-3 has flattop upper receiver, cut-down front sight base. Introduced 1994. Made in U.S. by Olympic Arms, Inc.
Price: **$1,035.00**

REMINGTON 40-XC TARGET RIFLE
Caliber: 223, 7.62 NATO, 5-shot.
Barrel: 24", stainless steel.
Weight: 11 lbs. without sights. **Length:** 43-1/2" overall.
Stock: Kevlar, with palm rail.
Sights: None furnished.
Features: Designed to meet the needs of competitive shooters. Stainless steel barrel and action.
Price: About **$1,548.00**

OLYMPIC ARMS PCR-1 RIFLE
Caliber: 223, 10-shot magazine.
Barrel: 20", 24"; 416 stainless steel.
Weight: 10 lbs., 3 oz. **Length:** 38.25" overall with 20" barrel.
Stock: A2 stowaway grip and trapdoor butt.
Sights: None supplied; flattop upper receiver, cut-down front sight base.
Features: Based on the AR-15 rifle. Broach-cut, free-floating barrel with 1:8.5" or 1:10" twist. No bayonet lug. Crowned barrel; fluting available. Introduced 1994. Made in U.S. by Olympic Arms, Inc.
Price: **$1,100.00**

REMINGTON 40-XBBR KS
Caliber: 22 BR Rem., 222 Rem., 222 Rem. Mag., 223, 6mmx47, 6mm BR Rem., 7.62 NATO (308 Win.).
Barrel: 20" (light varmint class), 24" (heavy varmint class).
Weight: 7-1/4 lbs. (light varmint class); 12 lbs. (heavy varmint class).
Length: 38" (20" bbl.), 42" (24" bbl.).
Stock: Kevlar.
Sights: None. Supplied with scope blocks.
Features: Unblued stainless steel barrel, trigger adjustable from 1-1/2 lbs. to 3-1/2 lbs. Special 2-oz. trigger at extra cost. Scope and mounts extra.
Price: With Kevlar stock **$1,548.00**

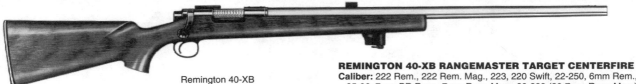

Remington 40-XB

REMINGTON 40-XR KS RIMFIRE POSITION RIFLE
Caliber: 22 LR, single shot.
Barrel: 24", heavy target.
Weight: 10 lbs. **Length:** 43" overall.
Stock: Kevlar. Position-style with front swivel block on forend guide rail.
Sights: Drilled and tapped. Furnished with scope blocks.
Features: Meets all ISU specifications. Deep forend, buttplate vertically adjustable, wide adjustable trigger.
Price: About. $1,441.00

Sako TRG-21

SAKO TRG-21 BOLT-ACTION RIFLE
Caliber: 308 Win., 10-shot magazine.
Barrel: 25.75".

REMINGTON 40-XB RANGEMASTER TARGET CENTERFIRE
Caliber: 222 Rem., 222 Rem. Mag., 223, 220 Swift, 22-250, 6mm Rem., 243, 25-06, 7mm BR Rem., 7mm Rem. Mag., 30-338 (30-7mm Rem. Mag.), 300 Win. Mag., 7.62 NATO (308 Win.), 30-06, single shot.
Barrel: 27-1/4".
Weight: 11-1/4 lbs. **Length:** 47" overall.
Stock: American walnut, laminated thumbhole or Kevlar with high comb and beavertail forend stop. Rubber non-slip buttplate.
Sights: None. Scope blocks installed.
Features: Adjustable trigger. Stainless barrel and action. Receiver drilled and tapped for sights.
Price: Standard single shot, stainless steel barrel, from $1,569.00

Weight: 10.5 lbs. **Length:** 46.5" overall.
Stock: Reinforced polyurethane with fully adjustable cheekpiece and buttplate.
Sights: None furnished. Optional quick-detachable, one-piece scope mount base, 1" or 30mm rings.
Features: Resistance-free bolt, free-floating heavy stainless barrel, 60-degree bolt lift. Two-stage trigger is adjustable for length, pull, horizontal or vertical pitch. Introduced 1993. Imported from Finland by Stoeger.
Price: $3,575.00
Price: Model TRG-41, as above except in 338 Lapua Mag. $4,200.00

Savage Model 112BT

SAVAGE MODEL 900TR TARGET RIFLE
Caliber: 22 LR, 5-shot magazine.
Barrel: 25".
Weight: 8 lbs. **Length:** 43-5/8" overall.
Stock: Target-type, walnut-finished hardwood.
Sights: Target front with inserts, peep rear with 1/4-minute click adjustments.
Features: Comes with shooting rail and hand stop. Introduced 1991. Made in Canada, from Savage Arms.
Price: Right- or left-hand. $415.00

SAVAGE MODEL 112BT COMPETITION GRADE RIFLE
Caliber: 223, 308, 5-shot magazine, 300 Win. Mag., single shot.
Barrel: 26", heavy contour stainless with black finish; 1:9" twist (223), 1:10" (308).
Weight: 10.8 lbs. **Length:** 47.5" overall.
Stock: Laminated wood with straight comb, adjustable cheek rest, Wundhammer palm swell, ventilated forend. Recoil pad is adjustable for length of pull.
Sights: None furnished; drilled and tapped for scope mounting and aperture target-style sights. Recessed target-style muzzle has .812" diameter section for universal target sight base.
Features: Pillar-bedded stock, matte black alloy receiver. Bolt has black titanium nitride coating, large handle ball. Has alloy accessory rail on forend. Comes with safety gun lock, target and ear puffs. Introduced 1994. Made in U.S. by Savage Arms, Inc.
Price: $1,000.00
Price: 300 Win. Mag. (single shot 112BT-S) $1,000.00

Springfield M1A.M-21

STONER SR-15 MATCH RIFLE
Caliber: 223.
Barrel: 20".
Weight: 7.9 lbs. **Length:** 38" overall.
Stock: Black synthetic.
Sights: None furnished; flat-top upper receiver for scope mounting.
Features: Short Picatinny rail; two-stage match trigger. Introduced 1998. Made in U.S. by Knight's Mfg.Co.
Price: $1,595.00

SPRINGFIELD, INC. M1A SUPER MATCH
Caliber: 308 Win.
Barrel: 22", heavy Douglas Premium.
Weight: About 10 lbs. **Length:** 44.31" overall.
Stock: Heavy walnut competition stock with longer pistol grip, contoured area behind the rear sight, thicker butt and forend, glass bedded.
Sights: National Match front and rear.
Features: Has figure-eight-style operating rod guide. Introduced 1987. From Springfield, Inc.
Price: About $2,050.00

Springfield, Inc. M1A/M-21 Tactical Model Rifle
Similar to the M1A Super Match except has special sniper stock with adjustable cheekpiece and rubber recoil pad. Weighs 11.2 lbs. From Springfield, Inc.
Price: $2,204.00

STONER SR-25 MATCH RIFLE
Caliber: 7.62 NATO, 10-shot steel magazine, 5-shot optional.
Barrel: 24" heavy match; 1:11.25" twist.
Weight: 10.75 lbs. **Length:** 44" overall.
Stock: Black synthetic AR-15A2 design. Full floating forend of Mil-spec synthetic attaches to upper receiver at a single point.
Sights: None furnished. Has integral Weaver-style rail. Rings and iron sights optional.

TANNER 50 METER FREE RIFLE
Caliber: 22 LR, single shot.
Barrel: 27.7".
Weight: 13.9 lbs. **Length:** 44.4" overall.
Stock: Seasoned walnut with palm rest, accessory rail, adjustable hook buttplate.
Sights: Globe front with interchangeable inserts, Tanner micrometer-diopter rear with adjustable aperture.
Features: Bolt action with externally adjustable set trigger. Supplied with 50-meter test target. Imported from Switzerland by Mandall Shooting Supplies. Introduced 1984.
Price: About $3,900.00

Stoner SR-25 Match

Features: Improved AR-15 trigger; AR-15-style seven-lug rotating bolt. Gas block rail mounts detachable front sight. Introduced 1993. Made in U.S. by Knight's Mfg. Co.
Price: $2,995.00
Price: SR-25 Lightweight Match (20" medium match target contour barrel, 9.5 lbs., 40" overall) $2,995.00

TANNER STANDARD UIT RIFLE
Caliber: 308, 7.5mm Swiss, 10-shot.
Barrel: 25.9".
Weight: 10.5 lbs. **Length:** 40.6" overall.
Stock: Match style of seasoned nutwood with accessory rail; coarsely stippled pistol grip; high cheekpiece; vented forend.
Sights: Globe front with interchangeable inserts, Tanner micrometer-diopter rear with adjustable aperture.
Features: Two locking lug revolving bolt encloses case head. Trigger adjustable from 1/2 to 6-1/2 lbs.; match trigger optional. Comes with 300-meter test target. Imported from Switzerland by Mandall Shooting Supplies. Introduced 1984.
Price: About $4,700.00

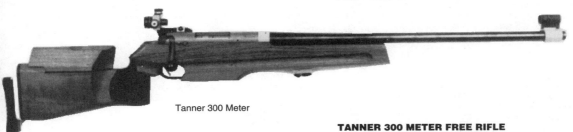

Tanner 300 Meter

TIKKA SPORTER RIFLE
Caliber: 223, 22-250, 308, detachable 5-shot magazine.
Barrel: 23-1/2" heavy.
Weight: 9 lbs. **Length:** 43-5/8" overall.
Stock: European walnut with adjustable comb, adjustable buttplate; stippled grip and forend.
Sights: None furnished; drilled and tapped for scope mounting.
Features: Buttplate is adjustable for distance, angle, height and pitch; adjustable trigger; free-floating barrel. Introduced 1998. Imported from Finland by Stoeger Industries.
Price: $919.00

TANNER 300 METER FREE RIFLE
Caliber: 308 Win., 7.5 Swiss, single shot.
Barrel: 27.58".
Weight: 15 lbs. **Length:** 45.3" overall.
Stock: Seasoned walnut, thumbhole style, with accessory rail, palm rest, adjustable hook butt.
Sights: Globe front with interchangeable inserts, Tanner-design micrometer-diopter rear with adjustable aperture.
Features: Three-lug revolving-lock bolt design; adjustable set trigger; short firing pin travel; supplied with 300-meter test target. Imported from Switzerland by Mandall Shooting Supplies. Introduced 1984.
Price: About $4,900.00

Includes a wide variety of sporting guns and guns suitable for various competitions.

Beretta Pintail

AMERICAN ARMS/FRANCHI 48/AL SHOTGUN
Gauge: 12, 20 or 28, 2-3/4" chamber.
Barrel: 24", 26", 28" (Franchoke Imp. Cyl., Mod., Full choke tubes), 28 ga. has fixed Imp. Cyl. Vent. rib.
Weight: 5.2 lbs. (20-gauge). **Length:** NA
Stock: 14-1/4"x1-5/8"x2-1/2". Walnut with checkered grip and forend.
Features: Recoil-operated action. Chrome-lined bore; cross-bolt safety. Imported from Italy by American Arms, Inc.
Price: 12, 20. . . . . $610.00
Price: 28 ga. $675.00

AMERICAN ARMS/FRANCHI 612VS AUTO SHOTGUN
Gauge: 12, 3" chamber.
Barrel: 24", 26", 28", Franchoke tubes.
Weight: 7 lbs. 2 oz. **Length:** 47-1/2" overall.
Stock: 14-1/4"x1-1/2"x2-1/2". European walnut.
Features: Alloy frame with matte black finish; gas-operated with Variopress System; four-lug rotating bolt; loaded chamber indicator. Introduced 1996. Imported from Italy by American Arms.
Price: $625.00
Price: 612VS Camo (Realtree Extra Brown camo) $649.00
Price: 612VS Synthetic (black synthetic stock, forend) $625.00
Price: 612 Sporting (silvered receiver with black border, target rib, ported 28" barrel) $639.00
Price: 620VS (20-gauge, 26", 28") $625.00

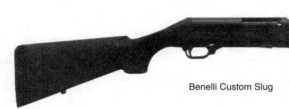

Benelli Sport

Benelli Sport Shotgun

Similar to the Legacy model except has matte blue receiver, two carbon fiber interchangeable ventilated ribs, adjustable buttpad, adjustable buttstock, and functions with ultra-light target loads. Walnut stock with satin finish. Introduced 1997. Imported from Italy by Benelli U.S.A.

Price: **$1,315.00**

Benelli Custom Slug

Benelli Super Black Eagle Custom Slug Gun

Similar to the Benelli Super Black Eagle except has 24" rifled barrel with 3" chamber, and comes with scope mount base. Uses the Montefeltro inertia recoil bolt system. Matte-finish receiver. Weight is 7.5 lbs., overall length 45.5". Wood or polymer stocks available. Introduced 1992. Imported from Italy by Benelli U.S.A.

Price: **$1,255.00**
Price: With polymer stock **$1,245.00**

Benelli Super Black Eagle Camouflage Shotgun

Similar to the Super Black Eagle except covered with Realtree Xtra Brown camouflage pattern. Available with 24", 26", 28" barrel. Introduced 1997. Imported from Italy by Benelli U.S.A.

Price: **$1,300.00**

Benelli Montefeltro 90 Shotgun

Similar to the M1 Super 90 except has checkered walnut stock with high-gloss finish. Uses the Montefeltro rotating bolt system with a simple inertia recoil design. Full, Imp. Mod., Mod., Imp. Cyl. choke tubes. Weighs 7 - 7-1/2 lbs. Finish is matte black. Introduced 1987.

Price: 24", 26", 28" **$925.00**
Price: Left-hand, 26", 28" **$945.00**
Price: 20-ga., Montefeltro, 24", 26", 5-3/4 lbs. **$925.00**

BENELLI M1 FIELD AUTO SHOTGUN

Gauge: 12, 3" chamber.
Barrel: 21", 24", 26", 28" (choke tubes).
Weight: 7 lbs., 4 oz.
Stock: High impact polymer; wood on 26", 28".
Sights: Metal bead front.
Features: Sporting version of the military & police gun. Uses the rotating Montefeltro bolt system. Ventilated rib; blue finish. Comes with set of five choke tubes. Imported from Italy by Benelli U.S.A.

Price: **$905.00**
Price: Wood stock version **$915.00**
Price: 24" rifled barrel, polymer stock **$980.00**

BENELLI LEGACY AUTO SHOTGUN

Gauge: 12, 3" chamber.
Barrel: 26", 28" (Full, Mod., Imp. Cyl., Imp. Mod., Skeet choke tubes). Mid-bead sight.
Weight: 7.1 to 7.6 lbs. **Length:** 49-5/8" overall (26" barrel).
Stock: European walnut with high-gloss finish. Special competition stock comes with drop adjustment kit.
Features: Uses the Montefeltro rotating bolt inertia recoil operating system with a two-piece steel/aluminum etched receiver (bright on lower, blue upper). Drop adjustment kit allows the stock to be custom fitted without modifying the stock. Black lower receiver finish, blued upper. Introduced 1998. Imported from Italy by Heckler & Koch, Inc.

Price: **$1,320.00**

BENELLI SUPER BLACK EAGLE SHOTGUN

Gauge: 12, 3-1/2" chamber.
Barrel: 24", 26", 28" (Imp. Cyl., Mod., Imp. Mod., Full choke tubes).
Weight: 7 lbs., 5 oz. **Length:** 49-5/8" overall (28" barrel).
Stock: European walnut with satin finish, or polymer. Adjustable for drop.
Sights: Bead front.
Features: Uses Montfeltro inertia recoil bolt system. Fires all 12-gauge shells from 2-3/4" to 3-1/2" magnums. Introduced 1991. Imported from Italy by Benelli U.S.A.

Price: With 26" and 28" barrel, wood stock **$1,215.00**
Price: With 24", 26" barrel, polymer stock **$1,200.00**

Benelli Super Black Eagle Limited Edition Shotgun

Similar to the Super Black Eagle except has nickel-plated receiver with finely etched scroll and game scenes highlighted with gold; select-grade walnut stock; 26" vent rib barrel. Limited to 1,000 guns. Introduced 1997. Imported from Italy by Benelli U.S.A.

Price: **$2,095.00**

Benelli Executive Series Shotguns

Similar to the Super Black Eagle except has grayed steel lower receiver, hand-engraved and gold inlaid (Type III), and has highest grade of walnut stock with drop adjustment kit. Barrel lengths of 21", 24", 26", 28"; 3" chamber. **Special order only.** Introduced 1995. Imported from Italy by Benelli U.S.A.

Price: Type I (about two-thirds engraving coverage) **$4,950.00**
Price: Type II (full coverage engraving) **$5,600.00**
Price: Type III (full coverage, gold inlays) **$6,550.00**

Benelli M1 Super 90 Camouflage Field Shotgun

Similar to the M1 Super 90 Field except is covered with Realtree Xtra brown camouflage. Available with 24", 26", 28" barrel, polymer stock. Introduced 1997. Imported from Italy by Benelli U.S.A.

Price: **$990.00**

Benelli Montefeltro 20-Gauge Shotgun

Similar to the 12-gauge Montefeltro Super 90 except chambered for 3" 20-gauge, 24" or 26" barrel (choke tubes), weighs 5 lbs., 12 oz. Has drop-adjustable walnut stock with gloss finish, blued receiver. Overall length 47.5". Introduced 1993. Imported from Italy by Benelli U.S.A.

Price: 24" and 26" barrels **$925.00**
Price: 26", camouflage finish **$1,010.00**

Beretta Pintail

Beretta Pintail Rifled Slug Shotgun

Similar to the Pintail except has 24" fully rifled barrel with 1:28" twist; upper receiver drilled and tapped for scope mounting, and permanently joined for rigidity. Has removable rifle-type sights. Introduced 1998. Imported from Italy by Beretta U.S.A.

Price: **$1,000.00**

BERETTA PINTAIL AUTO SHOTGUN

Gauge: 12, 3" chamber.
Barrel: 24", 26" (choke tubes).
Weight: 7 lbs.
Stock: Checkered walnut.
Features: Montefeltro-type short recoil action. Matte finish on wood and metal. Comes with sling swivels. Introduced 1993. Imported from Italy by Beretta U.S.A.

Price: **$780.00**

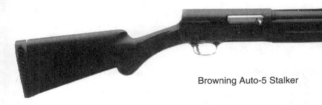

Beretta 390 Silver Mallard

Beretta AL390 Sport Trap/Skeet/Sporting Shotguns

Similar to the AL390 Silver Mallard except has lower-contour, rounded receiver. Available with ported barrel. Trap has 30", 32" barrel (Full, Imp. Mod., Mod. choke tubes); Skeet has 26", 28" barrel (fixed Skeet); Sporting has 28", 30" (Full, Mod., Imp. Cyl., Skeet tubes). Introduced 1995. Imported from Italy by Beretta U.S.A.

Price: AL390 Sport Trap **$900.00**
Price: As above, fixed Full choke. **$890.00**
Price: AL390 Sport Skeet **$890.00**
Price: AL390 Sport Sporting **$900.00**

Beretta A390 Sport Super Skeet Shotgun

Similar to the AL390 Silver Mallard except has adjustable-comb stock that allows height adjustments via interchangeable comb inserts. Rounded recoil pad system allows adjustments for length of pull. Stepped tapered rib. Factory ported barrel in 28" (fixed Skeet). Weighs 8.1 lbs. In 12-gauge only, with 3" chamber. Introduced 1993. Imported from Italy by Beretta U.S.A.

Price: **$1,160.00**

BERETTA AL390 SILVER MALLARD AUTO SHOTGUN

Gauge: 12, 20, 3" chamber.
Barrel: 24", 26", 28", 30", Mobilchoke choke tubes.
Weight: 6.4 to 7.2 lbs.
Stock: Select walnut or matte black synthetic. Adjustable drop and cast.
Features: Gas-operated action with self-compensating valve allows shooting all loads without adjustment. Alloy receiver, reversible safety; chrome-plated bore; floating vent. rib. Matte-finish models for turkey/waterfowl and Deluxe with gold, engraving; camo models have Advantage finish. Youth models in 20-gauge and slug model available. Introduced 1992. Imported from Italy by Beretta U.S.A.

Price: Walnut or synthetic. **$860.00**
Price: Gold Mallard, 12 and 20. . . . . **$1,025.00**
Price: 20-gauge, 20-gauge Youth **$860.00**
Price: Camouflage model **$904.00**

BROLIN BL-12 AUTO SHOTGUN

Gauge: 12, 3" chamber.
Barrel: 18-1/2" (Cyl. or choke tubes), 28" (choke tubes).
Weight: About 7-1/2 lbs.
Stock: Black polymer or hardwood.
Features: Satin blue finish. Introduced 1998. Imported by Brolin Arms.

Price: 18-1/2", fixed choke **$429.95**
Price: 18-1/2", choke tubes **$449.95**
Price: 28", synthetic stock, tubes **$469.95**
Price: 28", wood stock, tubes **$469.95**

Browning Auto-5 Stalker

Browning Auto-5 Stalker

Similar to the Auto-5 Light and Magnum models except has matte blue metal finish and black graphite-fiberglass stock and forend. Stock is scratch and impact resistant and has checkered panels. Light Stalker has 2-3/4" chamber, 26" or 28" vent. rib barrel with Invector choke tubes, weighs 8 lbs., 1 oz. (26"). Magnum Stalker has 3" chamber, 28" or 30" back-bored vent. rib barrel with Invector choke tubes, weighs 8 lbs., 11 oz. (28"). Introduced 1992.

Price: Light Stalker. **$839.95**
Price: Magnum Stalker **$865.95**

Browning Auto-5 Magnum 12

Same as standard Auto-5 except chambered for 3" magnum shells (also handles 2-3/4" magnum and 2-3/4" HV loads). 28" Mod., Full; 30" and 32" (Full) bbls. Back-bored barrel comes with Invector choke tubes. 14"x1-5/8"x2-1/2" stock. Recoil pad. Weighs 8-3/4 lbs.

Price: With back-bored barrel, Invector Plus **$865.95**
Price: Extra Invector Plus barrel **$307.95**

BROWNING AUTO-5 LIGHT 12 AND 20

Gauge: 12, 20, 5-shot; 3-shot plug furnished; 2-3/4" or 3" chamber.
Action: Recoil operated autoloader; takedown.
Barrel: 26", 28", 30" Invector (choke tube) barrel; also available with Light 20-ga. 28" (Mod.) or 26" (Imp. Cyl.) barrel.
Weight: 12-, 16-ga. 7-1/4 lbs.; 20-ga. 6-3/8 lbs.
Stock: French walnut, hand checkered half-pistol grip and forend. 14-1/4"x1-5/8"x2-1/2".
Features: Receiver hand engraved with scroll designs and border. Double extractors, extra bbls. Interchangeable without factory fitting; mag. cut-off; cross-bolt safety. All models except Buck Special and game guns have back-bored barrels with Invector Plus choke tubes. Imported from Japan by Browning.

Price: Light 12, 20, vent. rib., Invector Plus **$839.95**
Price: Extra Invector barrel. **$307.95**
Price: Light 12 Buck Special. **$828.95**
Price: 12, 12 magnum barrel **$307.95**
Price: Buck Special barrel **$296.95**

Browning Gold Sporting Clays Auto

Similar to the Gold Hunter except 12-gauge only with 28" or 30" barrel; front and center beads on tapered ventilated rib; ported and back-bored Invector Plus barrel; 2-3/4" chamber; satin-finished stock with solid, radiused recoil pad with hard heel insert; non-glare black alloy receiver has "Sporting Clays" inscribed in gold. Introduced 1996. Imported from Japan by Browning.

Price: **$759.95**

Browning Gold Deer Hunter

Browning Gold Deer Hunter Auto Shotgun

Similar to the Gold Hunter except 12-gauge only, 22" rifled or smooth Standard Invector barrel with 5" rifled choke tube, cantilever scope mount, extra-thick recoil pad. Weighs 7 lbs., 12 oz., overall length 42-1/2". Sling swivel studs fitted on the magazine cap and butt. Introduced 1997. Imported by Browning.

Price: **$798.95**

BROWNING GOLD HUNTER AUTO SHOTGUN

Gauge: 12, 20, 3" chamber.
Barrel: 12-ga.—26", 28", 30", Invector Plus choke tubes; 20-ga.—26", 30", Invector choke tubes.
Weight: 7 lbs., 9 oz. (12-ga.), 6 lbs., 12 oz. (20-ga.). **Length:** 46-1/4" overall (20-ga., 26" barrel).
Stock: 14"x1-1/2"x2-1/3"; select walnut with gloss finish; palm swell grip.
Features: Self-regulating, self-cleaning gas system shoots all loads; lightweight receiver with special non-glare deep black finish; large reversible safety button; large rounded trigger guard, gold trigger. The 20-gauge has slightly smaller dimensions; 12-gauge have back-bored barrels, Invector Plus tube system. Introduced 1994. Imported by Browning.

Price: 12- or 20-gauge **$734.95**
Price: Extra barrels. **$272.95**

Browning Gold 10 Auto

Browning Gold 10 Stalker Auto Shotgun

Same as the standard Gold 10 except has non-glare metal finish and black graphite-fiberglass composite stock with dull finish and checkering. Introduced 1993. Imported by Browning.

Price: **$1,007.95**
Price: Extra barrel **$261.95**

BROWNING GOLD 10 AUTO SHOTGUN

Gauge: 10, 3-1/2" chamber, 5-shot magazine.
Barrel: 26", 28", 30" (Imp. Cyl., Mod., Full standard Invector).
Weight: 10 lbs. 7 oz. (28" barrel).
Stock: 14-3/8"x1-1/2"x2-3/8". Select walnut with gloss finish, cut checkering, recoil pad.
Features: Short-stroke, gas-operated action, cross-bolt safety. Forged steel receiver with polished blue finish. Introduced 1993. Imported by Browning.

Price: **$1,007.95**
Price: Extra barrel **$261.95**

Fabarm Red Lion

FABARM RED LION AUTO SHOTGUN

Gauge: 12, 3" chamber.
Barrel: 24", 26", 28", choke tubes.
Weight: 7 lbs. **Length:** 45.5" overall.
Stock: European walnut with gloss finish.
Features: Reversible safety; nickel-plated trigger and carrier release button; leather-covered rubber recoil pad. Introduced 1998. Imported from Italy by Heckler & Koch, Inc.

Price: **$804.00**
Price: Gold Lion (as above except gold-plated trigger, carrier release button, olive wood grip cap) **$914.00**

Mossberg Model 9200 Trophy

Mossberg Model 9200 Special Hunter

Similar to the Model 9200 Crown Grade except with 28" vent rib barrel with Accu-II choke set, Parkerized finish, black synthetic stock and forend, and sling and swivels. Introduced 1998. Made in U.S. by Mossberg.

Price: **$456.00**

Mossberg Model 9200 USST Autoloading Shotgun

Same as the Model 9200 Crown Grade except has "United States Shooting Team" custom engraved receiver. Comes with 26" vent. rib barrel with Accu-Choke tubes (including Skeet), cut-checkered walnut stock and forend. Introduced 1993.

Price: **$531.00**

MOSSBERG MODEL 9200 CROWN GRADE AUTO SHOTGUN

Gauge: 12, 3" chamber.
Barrel: 24" (rifled bore), 24", 28" (Accu-Choke tubes); vent. rib.
Weight: About 7.5 lbs. **Length:** 48" overall (28" bbl.).
Stock: Walnut with high-gloss finish, cut checkering.
Features: Shoots all 2-3/4" or 3" loads without adjustment. Alloy receiver, ambidextrous top safety. Introduced 1992.

Price: 28", vent. rib **$534.00**
Price: Trophy, 24" with scope base, rifled bore, Dual-Comb stock . . **$554.00**
Price: 24", Fiber Optic or standard rifle sights, rifled bore **$531.00**

Mossberg Model 9200 Viking

Similar to the Model 9200 Crown Grade except has black matte metal finish, moss-green synthetic stock and forend; 28" Accu-Choke vent. rib barrel with Imp. Cyl., Full and Mod. tubes. Made in U.S. by Mossberg. Introduced 1996.

Price: **$429.00**

Mossberg 9200 Camo

Mossberg Model 9200 Bantam

Same as the Model 9200 Crown Grade except has 1" shorter stock, 22" vent. rib barrel with three Accu-Choke tubes. Made in U.S. by Mossberg. Introduced 1996.

Price: **$531.00**

Remington Model 11-87 Special Purpose Magnum

Similar to the 11-87 Premier except has dull stock finish, Parkerized exposed metal surfaces. Bolt and carrier have dull blackened coloring. Comes with 26" or 28" barrel with Rem Chokes, padded Cordura nylon sling and quick detachable swivels. Introduced 1987.

Price: **$679.00**
Price: With synthetic stock and forend (SPS) **$679.00**
Price: Magnum-Turkey with synthetic stock (SPS-T) **$692.00**

Mossberg Model 9200 Camo Shotgun

Same as the Model 9200 Crown Grade except completely covered with Mossy Oak Tree Stand, Realtree AP gray or OFM camouflage finish. Available with 24" barrel with Accu-Choke tubes. Has synthetic stock and forend. Introduced 1993.

Price: Turkey, 24" vent. rib, Mossy Oak or Realtree finish **$595.00**
Price: 28" vent. rib, Accu-Chokes, Woodlands camo finish. **$516.00**

REMINGTON MODEL 11-87 PREMIER SHOTGUN

Gauge: 12, 3" chamber.
Barrel: 26", 28", 30" Rem Choke tubes. Light Contour barrel.
Weight: About 8-1/4 lbs. **Length:** 46" overall (26" bbl.).
Stock: Walnut with satin or high-gloss finish; cut checkering; solid brown buttpad; no white spacers.
Sights: Bradley-type white-faced front, metal bead middle.
Features: Pressure compensating gas system allows shooting 2-3/4" or 3" loads interchangeably with no adjustments. Stainless magazine tube; redesigned feed latch, barrel support ring on operating bars; pinned forend. Introduced 1987.

Price: **$692.00**
Price: Left-hand **$743.00**
Price: Premier Cantilever Deer Barrel, sling, swivels, Monte Carlo stock **$759.00**

Remington Model 11-87 SPS-T Camo

Remington Model 11-87 Premier Trap

Similar to 11-87 Premier except trap dimension stock with straight or Monte Carlo combs; select walnut with satin finish and Tournament-grade cut checkering; 30" barrel with Rem Chokes (Trap Full, Trap Extra Full, Trap Super Full). Gas system set for 2-3/4" shells only. Introduced 1987.
Price: With Monte Carlo stock **$788.00**

Remington Model 11-87 SPS-T Turkey Camo NWTF Shotgun

Similar to the 11-87 Special Purpose Magnum except with synthetic stock, 21" vent. rib barrel with Super-Full Turkey (.665" diameter with knurled extension) tube. Completely covered with Mossy Oak Break-Up Brown camouflage. Bolt body, trigger guard and recoil pad are non-reflective black. Introduced 1993.
Price: $832.00

Remington Model 11-87 Premier Skeet

Similar to 11-87 Premier except Skeet dimension stock with cut checkering, satin finish, two-piece buttplate; 26" barrel with Skeet or Rem Chokes (Skeet, Imp. Skeet). Gas system set for 2-3/4" shells only. Introduced 1987.
Price: $765.00

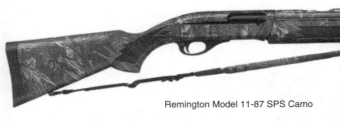

Remington Model 11-87 SPS Camo

Remington Model 11-87 SPS-Deer Shotgun

Similar to the 11-87 Special Purpose Camo except has fully-rifled 21" barrel with rifle sights, black non-reflective, synthetic stock and forend, black carrying sling. Introduced 1993.
Price: $703.00
Price: With wood stock (Model 11-87 SP Deer gun) $659.00

Remington Model 11-87 SPS Cantilever Shotgun

Similar to the 11-87 SPS except has fully rifled barrel; synthetic stock with Monte Carlo comb; cantilever scope mount deer barrel. Comes with sling and swivels. Introduced 1994.
Price: $765.00

Remington Model 11-87 SPS Special Purpose Synthetic Camo

Similar to the 11-87 Special Purpose Magnum except has synthetic stock and all metal (except bolt and trigger guard) and stock covered with Mossy Oak Break-Up camo finish. In 12-gauge only, 26", Rem Choke. Comes with camo sling, swivels. Introduced 1992.
Price: $767.00

CONSULT
SHOOTER'S MARKETPLACE
Page 225, This Issue

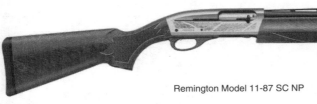

Remington Model 11-87 SC NP

Remington Model 11-87 SC NP Shotgun

Similar to the Model 11-87 Sporting Clays except has low-luster nickel-plated receiver with fine-line engraving, and ported 28" or 30" Rem choke barrel with matte finish. Tournament-grade American walnut stock measures 14-3/16" x 2-1/4" x 1-1/2". Sporting Clays choke tubes have knurled extensions. Introduced 1997. Made in U.S. by Remington.
Price: $827.00

REMINGTON MODEL 11-87 PREMIER SPORTING CLAYS

Gauge: 12, 2-3/4" chamber
Barrel: 26", 28", vent. rib, Rem Choke (Skeet, Imp. Cyl., Mod., Full); Light Contour barrel. Medium height rib.
Weight: 7.5 lbs. **Length:** 46.5" overall (26" barrel).
Stock: 14-3/16"x1-1/2"x2-1/4". Walnut, with cut checkering; sporting clays butt pad.
Features: Top of receiver, barrel and rib have matte finish; shortened magazine tube and forend; lengthened forcing cone; ivory bead front sight; competition trigger. Special no-wrench choke tubes marked on the outside. Comes in two-barrel fitted hard case. Introduced 1992.
Price: $779.00

Remington 1100 Sporting 28

Remington Model 1100 Sporting 28

Similar to the 1100 LT-20 except in 28-gauge with 25" barrel; comes with Skeet, Imp. Cyl., Light Mod., Mod. Rem Choke tubes. Fancy walnut with gloss finish, Sporting rubber buttpad. Made in U.S. by Remington. Introduced 1996.
Price: $781.00

REMINGTON MODEL 1100 LT-20 AUTO

Gauge: 20.
Barrel: 25" (Full, Mod.), 26", 28" with Rem Chokes.
Weight: 7-1/2 lbs.
Stock: 14"x1-1/2"x2-1/2". American walnut, checkered pistol grip and forend.
Features: Quickly interchangeable barrels. Matted receiver top with scroll work on both sides of receiver. Cross-bolt safety.
Price: With Rem Chokes, 20-ga. about $659.00
Price: Youth Gun LT-20 (21" Rem Choke) $659.00
Price: 20-ga., 3" magnum $659.00
Price: Skeet, 26", cut checkering, Rem. Choke $781.00

Remington 1100 Synthetic

Remington Model 1100 LT-20 Synthetic FR RS Shotgun
Similar to the Model 1100 LT-20 except has 21" fully rifled barrel with rifle sights, 2-3/4" chamber, and fiberglass-reinforced synthetic stock. Introduced 1997. Made in U.S. by Remington.
Price: $475.00

Remington Model 1100 Sporting 20 Shotgun
Similar to the Model 1100 LT-20 except has tournament-grade American walnut stock with gloss finish and sporting-style recoil pad, 28" Rem Choke barrel for Skeet, Imp. Cyl., Light Modified and Modified. Introduced 1998.
Price: $781.00

Remington Model 1100 LT-20 Youth Turkey NWTF
Similar to the 1100 LT-20 except has full-coverage Mossy Oak Break-Up camouflage, 13" length of pull, Truglo fiber optic front sight, and 21" barrel with extended Turkey Super Full choke tube. Introduced 1998.
Price: $652.00

Barrel: 26", 28", Rem Chokes.
Remington Model 1100 Synthetic FR CL Shotgun
Similar to the Model 1100 LT-20 except 12-gauge, has 21" fully rifled barrel with cantilever scope mount and fiberglass-reinforced synthetic stock with Monte Carlo comb. Introduced 1997. Made in U.S. by Remington.
Price: $585.00

Remington Model 1100 Synthetic
Simliar to the 1100 LT magnum except in 12- or 20-gauge, and has black synthetic stock; vent. rib 28" barrel on 12-gauge, 26" on 20, both with Mod. Rem Choke tube. Weighs about 7-1/2 lbs. Introduced 1996.
Price: $492.00

Remington Model 1100 Special Field
Similar to Standard Model 1100 except 12- and 20-ga. only, comes with 23" Rem Choke barrel. LT-20 version 6-1/2 lbs.; has straight-grip stock, shorter forend, both with cut checkering. Comes with vent. rib only; matte finish receiver without engraving. Introduced 1983.
Price: 12- and 20-ga., 23" Rem Choke, about $659.00

Remington SP-10 NWTF

Remington Model SP-10 Magnum Camo Auto Shotgun
Similar to the SP-10 Magnum except buttstock, forend, receiver, barrel and magazine cap are covered with Mossy Oak Break-Up camo finish; bolt body and trigger guard have matte black finish. Comes with Extra-Full Turkey Rem Choke tube, 26" vent. rib barrel with mid-rib bead and Bradley-style front sight, swivel studs and quick-detachable swivels, and a non-slip Cordura carrying sling in the same camo pattern. Introduced 1993.
Price: $1,179.00

REMINGTON MODEL SP-10 MAGNUM AUTO SHOTGUN
Gauge: 10, 3-1/2" chamber, 3-shot magazine.
Barrel: 26", 30" (Full and Mod. Rem Chokes).
Weight: 11 to 11-1/4 lbs. **Length:** 47-1/2" overall (26" barrel).
Stock: Walnut with satin finish. Checkered grip and forend.
Sights: Metal bead front.
Features: Stainless steel gas system with moving cylinder; 3/8" ventilated rib. Receiver and barrel have matte finish. Brown recoil pad. Comes with padded Cordura nylon sling. Introduced 1989.
Price: $1,085.00

Remington Model SP-10 Turkey Camo NWTF
Similar to the SP-10 Magnum Camo except has 23" barrel with Turkey Extra Full Rem Choke tube, Truglo fiber optic front sight, and N.W.T.F. 25th Anniversary logo on left side of receiver. Introduced 1998.
Price: $1,225.00

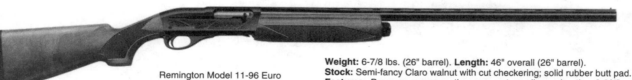

Remington Model 11-96 Euro

REMINGTON MODEL 11-96 EURO LIGHTWEIGHT AUTO SHOTGUN
Gauge: 12, 3" chamber.

Weight: 6-7/8 lbs. (26" barrel). **Length:** 46" overall (26" barrel).
Stock: Semi-fancy Claro walnut with cut checkering; solid rubber butt pad.
Features: Pressure-compensating gas system allows shooting 2-3/4" or 3" loads interchangeably with no adjustments. Lightweight steel receiver with scroll-engraved panels; stainless steel magazine tube; 6mm ventilated rib on light contour barrel. Introduced 1996. Made in U.S. by Remington.
Price: $852.00

SHOTGUNS—SLIDE ACTIONS

Includes a wide variety of sporting guns and guns suitable for competitive shooting.

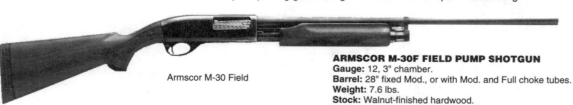

Armscor M-30 Field

ARMSCOR M-30F FIELD PUMP SHOTGUN
Gauge: 12, 3" chamber.
Barrel: 28" fixed Mod., or with Mod. and Full choke tubes.
Weight: 7.6 lbs.
Stock: Walnut-finished hardwood.
Features: Double action slide bars; blued steel receiver; damascened bolt. Introduced 1996. Imported from the Philippines by K.B.I., Inc.
Price: With fixed choke $239.00
Price: With choke tubes. $269.00

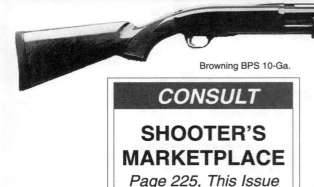

Browning BPS 10-Ga.

CONSULT

SHOOTER'S MARKETPLACE

Page 225, This Issue

Browning BPS Pigeon Grade Pump Shotgun
Same as the standard BPS except has select high grade walnut stock and forend, and gold-trimmed receiver. Available in 12-gauge only with 26" or 28" vent. rib barrels. Introduced 1992.
Price: $602.95

Browning BPS Game Gun Deer Special
Similar to the standard BPS except has newly designed receiver/magazine tube/barrel mounting system to eliminate play, heavy 20.5" barrel with rifle-type sights with adjustable rear, solid receiver scope mount, "rifle" stock dimensions for scope or open sights, sling swivel studs. Gloss or matte finished wood with checkering, polished blue metal. Introduced 1992.
Price: $492.95

Browning BPS Stalker

Browning BPS Pump Shotgun Ladies and Youth Model
Same as BPS Upland Special except 20-ga. only, 22" Invector barrel, stock has pistol grip with recoil pad. Length of pull is 13-1/4". Introduced 1986.
Price: $423.95

Brolin HP9 Combo

Brolin HP9 Combo Pump Shotgun
Same as the HP9 Field except comes with 18-1/2" Cyl.-bored barrel with bead or rifle sights, and 28" vent. rib. barrel with Mod. choke tube. Black synthetic or hardwood stock; pistol grip comes with bead sight on short barrel. Introduced 1997. Imported by Brolin Industries, Inc.
Price: Combo with bead sight $264.95
Price: Combo with rifle sight $299.95

Ithaca Model 37 Turkeyslayer

Ithaca Model 37 Turkeyslayer Pump Shotgun
Similar to the Model 37 Field except has 22" barrel with rifle sights, extended choke tube and full-coverage, Realtree Advantage, Realtree All-Purpose Brown, All-Purpose Grey, or Xtra Brown camouflage finish. Introduced 1996. Made in U.S. by Ithaca Gun Co.
Price: $559.95
Price: Youth Turkeyslayer (20-gauge, 6.5 lbs., shorter stock) $559.95

BROWNING BPS PUMP SHOTGUN
Gauge: 10, 12, 3-1/2" chamber; 12 or 20, 3" chamber (2-3/4" in target guns), 28, 2-3/4" chamber, 5-shot magazine.
Barrel: 10-ga.—24" Buck Special, 28", 30", 32" Invector; 12-, 20- ga.—22", 24", 26", 28", 30", 32" (Imp. Cyl., Mod. or Full). Also available with Invector choke tubes, 12- or 20-ga.; Upland Special has 22" barrel with Invector tubes. BPS 3" and 3-1/2" have back-bored barrel.
Weight: 7 lbs., 8 oz. (28" barrel). **Length:** 48-3/4" overall (28" barrel).
Stock: 14-1/4"x1-1/2"x2-1/2". Select walnut, semi-beavertail forend, full pistol grip stock.
Features: All 12-gauge 3" guns except Buck Special and game guns have back-bored barrels with Invector Plus choke tubes. Bottom feeding and ejection, receiver top safety, high post vent. rib. Double action bars eliminate binding. Vent. rib barrels only. All 12- and 20-gauge guns with 3" chamber available with fully engraved receiver flats at no extra cost. Each gauge has its own unique game scene. Introduced 1977. Imported from Japan by Browning.
Price: 10-ga., Hunting, Invector $508.95
Price: 12-ga., 3-1/2" Mag., Hunting, Invector Plus $508.95
Price: 12-, 20-ga., Hunting, Invector Plus..................... $423.95
Price: 12-ga. Buck Special $408.95
Price: 28-ga., Hunting, Invector $423.95

Browning BPS Game Gun Turkey Special
Similar to the standard BPS except has satin-finished walnut stock and dull-finished barrel and receiver. Receiver is drilled and tapped for scope mounting. Rifle-style stock dimensions and swivel studs. Has Extra-Full Turkey choke tube. Introduced 1992.
Price: $460.95

Browning BPS Stalker Pump Shotgun
Same gun as the standard BPS except all exposed metal parts have a matte blued finish and the stock has a durable black finish with a black recoil pad. Available in 10-ga. (3-1/2") and 12-ga. with 3" or 3-1/2" chamber, 22", 28", 30" barrel with Invector choke system. Introduced 1987.
Price: 12-ga., 3" chamber, Invector Plus $508.95
Price: 10-, 12-ga., 3-1/2" chamber........................... $508.95

BROLIN HP9 FIELD PUMP SHOTGUN
Gauge: 12, 3" chamber.
Barrel: 24", 28" (Mod. choke tube); vent. rib.
Weight: 7.3 lbs. **Length:** 44" overall.
Stock: 14" x 1-1/2" x 2-1/2". Black polymer or oil-finished hardwood.
Sights: Bead front.
Features: Twin action bars; steel receiver; removable sling swivels; cross-bolt safety; matte blue finish. Introduced 1997. Imported by Brolin Industries, Inc.
Price: Synthetic or wood stock, 24" or 28" barrel $239.95
Price: Slug Special (18-1/2", rifle sights, rifled choke) $259.95
Price: Slug Special (22", rifle sights, Imp. Cyl.) $249.95
Price: Slug Special (22", cantilever mount) $289.95
Price: Turkey Special (22", Extra-Full extended turkey choke) $249.95

ITHACA MODEL 37 FIELD PUMP SHOTGUN
Gauge: 12, 20, 3" chamber.
Barrel: 26", 28", 30" (12-gauge), 26", 28" (20-gauge), choke tubes.
Weight: 7 lbs. (12-gauge).
Stock: Walnut with cut-checkered grip and forend.
Features: Steel receiver; bottom ejection; brushed blue finish, vent rib barrels. Reintroduced 1996. Made in U.S. by Ithaca Gun Co.
Price: $539.95
Price: Model 37 New Classic $695.95

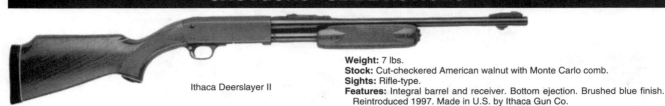

Ithaca Deerslayer II

Weight: 7 lbs.
Stock: Cut-checkered American walnut with Monte Carlo comb.
Sights: Rifle-type.
Features: Integral barrel and receiver. Bottom ejection. Brushed blue finish. Reintroduced 1997. Made in U.S. by Ithaca Gun Co.
Price: $559.95
Price: Smooth Bore Deluxe $509.95
Price: Rifled Deluxe $509.95

ITHACA DEERSLAYER II PUMP SHOTGUN
Gauge: 12, 20, 3" chamber.
Barrel: 20", 25", fully rifled.

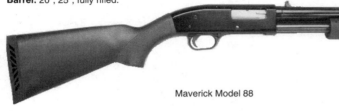

Maverick Model 88

Weight: 7-1/4 lbs. **Length:** 48" overall with 28" bbl.
Stock: Black synthetic with ribbed synthetic forend.
Sights: Bead front.
Features: Alloy receiver with blue finish; dual slide bars; cross-bolt safety in trigger guard; interchangeable barrels. Rubber recoil pad. Mossberg Cable-lock included. Introduced 1989. From Maverick Arms, Inc.
Price: Model 88, synthetic stock, 28" Mod. $221.00
Price: Model 88, synthetic stock, 28" ACCU-TUBE, Mod. $235.00
Price: Model 88, synthetic stock, 24" with rifle sights $235.00

MAVERICK MODEL 88 PUMP SHOTGUN
Gauge: 12, 3" chamber.
Barrel: 18-1/2" (Cyl.), 28" (Mod.).

Mossberg Model 835 Turkey

Mossberg Model 835 Viking
Similar to the Model 835 Crown Grade except has moss-green synthetic stock and forend, matte metal finish, 28" vent. rib Accu-Mag. barrel with Mod. tube. Made in U.S. by Mossberg. Introduced 1996.
Price: $316.00

Mossberg American Field Model 835 Pump Shotgun
Same as the Model 835 Crown Grade except has walnut-stained hardwood stock and comes only with Modified choke tube, 28" barrel. Introduced 1992.
Price: $331.00

Mossberg Model 835 Special Hunter
Similar to the Model 835 Crown Grade except with 24" or 28" ported barrel with Accu-Mag Mod. choke tube, Parkerized finish, black synthetic stock and forend; comes with sling and swivels. Introduced 1998. Made in U.S. by Mossberg.
Price: $335.00

MOSSBERG MODEL 835 CROWN GRADE ULTI-MAG PUMP
Gauge: 12, 3-1/2" chamber.
Barrel: Ported 24" rifled bore, 24", 28", Accu-Mag choke tubes for steel or lead shot.
Weight: 7-3/4 lbs. **Length:** 48-1/2" overall.
Stock: 14"x1-1/2"x2-1/2". Dual Comb. Cut-checkered hardwood or camo synthetic; both have recoil pad.
Sights: White bead front, brass mid-bead; Fiber Optic.
Features: Shoots 2-3/4", 3" or 3-1/2" shells. Backbored and ported barrel to reduce recoil, improve patterns. Ambidextrous thumb safety, twin extractors, dual slide bars. Mossberg Cablelock included. Introduced 1988.
Price: 28" vent. rib, hardwood stock $334.00
Price: 24" Trophy Slugster, rifled bore, scope base, Dual-Comb stock $388.00
Price: Combo, 24" rifled bore, rifle sights, 28" vent. rib, Accu-Mag choke tubes $476.00
Price: Realtree or Mossy Oak Camo Turkey, 24" vent. rib, Accu-Mag Extra-Full tube, synthetic stock $531.00
Price: Realtree Camo, 28" vent. rib, Accu-Mag tubes, synthetic stock $531.00
Price: Realtree Camo Combo, 24" rifled bore, rifle sights, 24" vent. rib, Accu-Mag choke tubes, synthetic stock, hard case $659.00
Price: OFM Camo, 28" vent. rib, Accu-Mag tubes, synthetic stock $531.00
Price: OFM Camo Combo, 24" rifled bore, rifle sights, 28" vent. rib, Accu-Mag tubes, synthetic stock. $476.00

Mossberg Model 500 Sporting

Mossberg Model 500 Viking
Similar to the Model 500 Sporting except in 12-gauge with 24" ported rifled bore, rifle sights or 28" vent. rib with Mod. Accu-Choke tube, or 20-gauge 26" vent. rib with Mod. Accu-Choke tube; moss-green synthetic stock and forend, matte metal finish. Made in U.S. by Mossberg. Introduced 1996.
Price: $287.00
Price: With rifled barrel $327.00
Price: Scope and case combo $394.00

MOSSBERG MODEL 500 SPORTING PUMP
Gauge: 12, 20, 410, 3" chamber.
Barrel: 18-1/2" to 28" with fixed or Accu-Choke, plain or vent. rib.
Weight: 6-1/4 lbs. (410), 7-1/4 lbs. (12). **Length:** 48" overall (28" barrel).
Stock: 14"x1-1/2"x2-1/2". Walnut-stained hardwood. Cut-checkered grip and forend.
Sights: White bead front, brass mid-bead; Fiber Optic.
Features: Ambidextrous thumb safety, twin extractors, disconnecting safety, dual action bars. Quiet Carry forend. Many barrels are ported. Mossberg Ca-blelock included. From Mossberg.
Price: From about $312.00
Price: Sporting Combos (field barrel and Slugster barrel), from $340.00

Mossberg Model 500 Bantam Pump
Same as the Model 500 Sporting Pump except 20-gauge only, 22" vent. rib Accu-Choke barrel with Mod. choke tube; has 1" shorter stock, reduced length from pistol grip to trigger, reduced forend reach. Introduced 1992.
Price: $312.00
Price: With full camouflage finish. $322.00

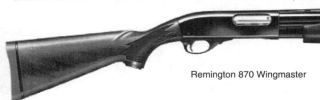

Mossberg Model 500
Trophy Slugster

Mossberg Model 500 Camo Pump
Same as the Model 500 Sporting Pump except 12-gauge only and entire gun is covered with special camouflage finish. Receiver drilled and tapped for scope mounting. Comes with quick detachable swivel studs, swivels, camouflage sling, Mossberg Cablelock.
Price: From about $336.00
Price: Camo Combo (as above with extra Slugster barrel), from about $434.00

MOSSBERG MODEL 500 TROPHY SLUGSTER
Gauge: 12, 20, 3" chamber.
Barrel: 24", ported rifled bore. Integral scope mount.
Weight: 7-1/4 lbs. **Length:** 44" overall.
Stock: 14" pull, 1-3/8" drop at heel. Walnut; Dual Comb design for proper eye positioning with or without scoped barrels. Recoil pad and swivel studs.
Features: Ambidextrous thumb safety, twin extractors, dual slide bars. Comes with scope mount. Mossberg Cablelock included. Introduced 1988.
Price: Rifled bore, with integral scope mount, Dual-Comb stock,
12 or 20 . . . . $369.00
Price: Fiber Optic, rifle sights $371.00
Price: Rifled bore, rifle sights $341.00
Price: 20 ga., Standard or Bantam, from $341.00

Remington 870 Wingmaster

Remington Model 870 Marine Magnum
Similar to the 870 Wingmaster except all metal is plated with electroless nickel and has black synthetic stock and forend. Has 18" plain barrel (Cyl.), bead front sight, 7-shot magazine. Introduced 1992.
Price: $500.00

Remington Model 870 SPS-Deer Shotgun
Has fully-rifled 20" barrel with rifle sights, black non-reflective, synthetic stock and forend, black carrying sling. Introduced 1993.
Price: $436.00

Remington Model 870 SPS-T Turkey Camo NWTF
Similar to the Model 870 SPS-T except has full-coverage Mossy Oak Break-Up camo, Truglo fiber optic front sight, 21" vent rib barrel with extended straight-rifled Turkey Super-Full choke tube. Introduced 1998.
Price: $565.00

Remington Model 870 Express
Similar to the 870 Wingmaster except has a walnut-toned hardwood stock with solid, black recoil pad and pressed checkering on grip and forend. Outside metal surfaces have a black oxide finish. Comes with 26" or 28" vent. rib barrel with a Mod. Rem Choke tube. Introduced 1987.
Price: 12 or 20 . . . . $305.00
Price: Express Combo, 26" vent rib with Mod. Rem Choke and 20" fully rifled barrel with rifle sights $439.00
Price: Express 20-ga., 28" with Mod. Rem Choke tubes $305.00
Price: Express L-H (left-hand), 12-ga., 28" vent rib with Mod. Rem Choke tube $332.00
Price: Express Synthetic $312.00

Remington Model 870 Express Super Magnum
Similar to the 870 Express except has 28" vent. rib barrel with 3-1/2" chamber, vented recoil pad. Introduced 1998.
Price: $332.00
Price: Super Magnum Synthetic $339.00
Price: Super Magnum Turkey Camo (Turkey Extra Full Rem Choke, synthetic stock, full-coverage Realtree Advantage camo) $439.00
Price: Super Magnum Combo (26" with Mod. Rem Choke and 20" fully rifled deer barrel with 3" chamber and rifle sights; wood stock) $465.00

Remington Model 870 Express Youth Gun
Same as the Model 870 Express except comes with 12-1/2" length of pull, 21" barrel with Mod. Rem Choke tube. Hardwood stock with low-luster finish. Introduced 1991.
Price: 20-ga. Express Youth (1" shorter stock), from $305.00

Remington Model 870 Express Rifle-Sighted Deer Gun
Same as the Model 870 Express except comes with 20" barrel with fixed Imp. Cyl. choke, open iron sights, Monte Carlo stock. Introduced 1991.
Price: $300.00
Price: With fully rifled barrel $339.00

REMINGTON MODEL 870 WINGMASTER LC
Gauge: 12, 3" chamber.
Barrel: 26", 28", 30" (Rem Chokes). Light Contour barrel.
Weight: 7-1/4 lbs. **Length:** 46-1/2" overall (26" bbl.).
Stock: 14"x2-1/2"x1". American walnut with satin or high-gloss finish, cut-checkered pistol grip and forend. Rubber buttpad.
Sights: Ivory bead front, metal mid-bead.
Features: Double action bars; cross-bolt safety; blue finish. Available in right- or left-hand style. Introduced 1986.
Price: $519.00
Price: Fully rifled Cantilever, 20" $599.00

Remington Model 870 TC Trap Gun
Similar to the 870 Wingmaster except has tournament-grade, satin-finished American walnut stock with or Monte Carlo comb, over-bored 30" vent. rib barrel with 2-3/4" chamber, over-bore-matched Rem Choke tubes. Made in U.S. by Remington. Reintroduced 1996.
Price: With Monte Carlo stock $680.00

> Consult our Directory pages for the location of firms mentioned.

Remington Model 870 SPS-T Special Purpose Magnum
Similar to the Model 870 except chambered only for 12-ga., 3" shells, 26" or 28" Rem Choke barrel. All exposed metal surfaces are finished in dull, non-reflective black. Black synthetic stock and forend. Comes with padded Cordura 2" wide sling, quick-detachable swivels. Chrome-lined bores. Dark recoil pad. Introduced 1985.
Price: $425.00

Remington Model 870 Special Purpose Synthetic Camo
Similar to the 870 Special Purpose Magnum except has synthetic stock and all metal (except bolt and trigger guard) and stock covered with Mossy Oak Break-Up camo finish, In 12-gauge only, 26" vent. rib, Rem Choke. Comes with camo sling, swivels. Introduced 1992.
Price: $496.00

Remington Model 870 SPS Cantilever Shotgun
Similar to the 870 SPS-Deer except has rifled barrel; synthetic stock with Monte Carlo comb; cantilever scope mount deer barrel. Comes with sling and swivels. Introduced 1994.
Price: With fully rifled barrel $496.00

Remington Model 870 Express Turkey
Same as the Model 870 Express except comes with 3" chamber, 21" vent. rib turkey barrel and Extra-Full Rem Choke Turkey tube; 12-ga. only. Introduced 1991.
Price: $319.00
Price: Express Turkey Camo stock has Realtree Advantage camo, matte black metal $372.00
Price: Express Youth Turkey camo (as above with 1" shorter length of pull) $372.00

Remington 870 Express HD

Remington Model 870 Express Small Gauge

Similar to the 870 Express except is scaled down for 28-gauge and 410-bore. Has 25" vent. rib barrel with fixed Mod. choke; solid black rubber buttpad. Reintroduced 1996.
Price:.. **$332.00**

SARSILMAZ COBRA PUMP SHOTGUN

Gauge: 12, 3" chamber, 7-shot magazine.
Barrel: 16", 28" (Cyl.).
Weight: 6-1/4 lbs. **Length:** 38" overall.
Stock: European hardwood.
Sights: Bead front.
Features: Comes with extra pistol grip. Imported from Turkey by Armsport.
Price:.. **$299.95**

Winchester 1300 Realtree Turkey

Winchester Model 1300 Black Shadow Field Gun

Similar to the Model 1300 Walnut except has black composite stock and forend, matte black finish. Has vent. rib 26" or 28" barrel, 3" chamber, comes with Mod. Winchoke tube. Introduced 1995. From U.S. Repeating Arms Co., Inc.
Price: 12- or 20-gauge **$296.00**

Winchester Model 1300 Black Shadow Turkey Gun

Similar to the Model 1300 Realtree® Turkey except synthetic stock and forend are matte black, and all metal surfaces finished matte black. Drilled and tapped for scope mounting. In 12- or 20-gauge, 3" chamber, 22" vent. rib barrel; comes with one Extra-Full Winchoke tube (20-gauge has Full). Introduced 1994. From U.S. Repeating Arms Co., Inc.
Price:.. **$296.00**

Winchester Model 1300 Black Shadow Deer Gun

Similar to the Model 1300 Black Shadow Turkey Gun except has ramp-type front sight, fully adjustable rear, drilled and tapped for scope mounting. Black composite stock and forend, matte black metal. Smoothbore 22" barrel with one Imp. Cyl. WinChoke tube; 12-gauge only, 3" chamber. Weighs 7-1/4 lbs. Introduced 1994. From U.S. Repeating Arms Co., Inc.
Price:.. **$296.00**
Price: With rifled barrel **$317.00**
Price: Combo, 22" Cyl. barrel with 28" Mod. vent rib barrel **$366.00**

Winchester 1300 Ranger

Winchester Model 1300 Ranger Pump Gun Combo & Deer Gun

Similar to the standard Ranger except comes with two barrels: 22" (Cyl.) deer barrel with rifle-type sights and an interchangeable 28" vent. rib Winchoke barrel with Full, Mod. and Imp. Cyl. choke tubes. Drilled and tapped; comes with rings and bases. Available in 12- and 20-gauge 3" only, with recoil pad. Introduced 1983.
Price: Deer Combo with two barrels **$379.00**
Price: Rifled Deer Combo (22" rifled and 28" vent. rib barrels, 12- or 20-ga.) **$401.00**

Remington Model 870 Express HD

Similar to the 870 Express except in 12-gauge only, 18" (Cyl.) barrel with bead front sight, synthetic stock and forend with non-reflective black finish and positive checkering. Introduced 1995.
Price:.. **$292.00**

Remington Model 870 Express Synthetic

Similar to the 870 Express with 26", 28" barrel except has synthetic stock and forend. Introduced 1994.
Price:.. **$312.00**

TRISTAR MODEL 1887 LEVER-ACTION SHOTGUN

Gauge: 12, 2-3/4" chamber, 5-shot magazine.
Barrel: 30" (Full).
Weight: 8 lbs. **Length:** 48" overall.
Stocks: 12-3/4" pull. Rounded-knob pistol grip; walnut with oil finish; blued, checkered steel buttplate. Dimensions duplicate original WRA Co. specifications.
Sights: Brass, bead front.
Features: Recreation of Browning's original 1885 patents and design as made by Winchester Repeating Arms. External hammer with half- and full-cock positions; has original-type WRA Co. logo on left side of receiver; two-piece walnut forend. Introduced 1997. Imported by Tristar Sporting Arms.
Price:.. **$599.00**

WINCHESTER MODEL 1300 WALNUT PUMP

Gauge: 12, 20, 3" chamber, 5-shot capacity.
Barrel: 26", 28", vent. rib, with Full, Mod., Imp. Cyl. Winchoke tubes.
Weight: 6-3/8 lbs. **Length:** 42-5/8" overall.
Stock: American walnut, with deep cut checkering on pistol grip, traditional ribbed forend; high luster finish.
Sights: Metal bead front.
Features: Twin action slide bars; front-locking rotary bolt; roll-engraved receiver; blued, highly polished metal; cross-bolt safety with red indicator. Introduced 1984. From U.S. Repeating Arms Co., Inc.
Price:.. **$340.00**
Price: Deer Gun (22" rifled barrel, 12-gauge) **$404.00**

Winchester Model 1300 Realtree® Turkey Gun

Similar to the standard Model 1300 except has synthetic Realtree® camo stock and forend, matte finished barrel and receiver, 22" barrel with Extra Full, Full and Mod. Winchoke tubes. Drilled and tapped for scope mounting. Comes with padded, adjustable sling. In 12-gauge only, 3" chamber; weighs about 7 lbs. Introduced 1994. From U.S. Repeating Arms Co., Inc.
Price: Advantage Full Camo **$432.00**
Price: Realtree All-Purpose or Gray Full Camo.................. **$432.00**
Price: Realtree All-Purpose Pattern (matte metal) **$370.00**

Winchester Model 1300 Advantage Camo Deer Gun

Similar to the Model 1300 Black Shadow Deer Gun except has full coverage Advantage camouflage. Has 22" rifled or smoothbore barrel, padded camouflage sling, swivels and swivel posts, rifle sights. Receiver drilled and tapped for scope mounting. Introduced 1995. From U.S. Repeating Arms Co., Inc.
Price: Rifled bore **$432.00**
Price: Smoothbore **$410.00**

WINCHESTER MODEL 1300 RANGER PUMP GUN

Gauge: 12, 20, 3" chamber, 5-shot magazine.
Barrel: 26", 28", vent. rib with Full, Mod., Imp. Cyl. Winchoke tubes.
Weight: 7 to 7-1/4 lbs. **Length:** 48-5/8" to 50-5/8" overall.
Stock: Walnut-finished hardwood with ribbed forend.
Sights: Metal bead front.
Features: Cross-bolt safety, black rubber recoil pad, twin action slide bars, front-locking rotating bolt. From U.S. Repeating Arms Co., Inc.
Price: Vent. rib barrel, Winchoke............................. **$309.00**
Price: Model 1300 Ladies/Youth, 20-ga., 22" vent. rib **$309.00**

Includes a variety of game guns and guns for competitive shooting.

American Arms Silver 1

AMERICAN ARMS SILVER I O/U

Gauge: 12, 20, 28, 410, 3" chamber (28 has 2-3/4").
Barrel: 26" (Imp. Cyl. & Mod., all gauges), 28" (Mod. & Full, 12, 20).
Weight: About 6-3/4 lbs.
Stock: 14-1/8"x1-3/8"x2-3/8". Checkered walnut.
Sights: Metal bead front.
Features: Boxlock action with scroll engraving, silver finish. Single selective trigger, extractors. Chrome-lined barrels. Manual safety. Rubber recoil pad. Introduced 1987. Imported from Italy by American Arms, Inc.
Price: 12- or 20-gauge $635.00
Price: 28 or 410 . . . . $665.00

American Arms Silver II Shotgun

Similar to the Silver I except 26" barrel (Imp. Cyl., Mod., Full choke tubes, 12- and 20-ga.), 28" (Imp. Cyl., Mod., Full choke tubes, 12-ga. only), 26" (Imp. Cyl. & Mod. fixed chokes, 28 and 410), automatic selective ejectors. Weight is about 6 lbs., 15 oz. (12-ga., 26").
Price: $770.00
Price: 28, 410 . . . . $799.00
Price: Two-barrel sets **$1,190.00**

American Arms/Franchi Falconet

AMERICAN ARMS/FRANCHI SPORTING SL IBS O/U

Gauge: 12, 2-3/4" chambers.
Barrel: 28", Franchoke tubes; ported and back-bored.
Weight: 7 lbs., 12 oz. **Length:** 45-3/8" overall.
Stock: 14-1/4"x1-3/8"x2-1/4". Select European walnut.
Features: Wide single selective mechanical trigger, automatic selective ejectors; chrome-lined barrels; ventilated 10mm top rib; detachable sideplates; interchangeable barrels. Imported from Italy by American Arms, Inc.
Price: $1,495.00

American Arms WT/OU 10 Shotgun

Similar to the WS/OU 12 except chambered for 10-gauge 3-1/2" shell, 26" (Full & Full, choke tubes) barrel. Single selective trigger, extractors. Non-reflective finish on wood and metal. Imported by American Arms, Inc.
Price: $1,005.00

BABY BRETTON OVER/UNDER SHOTGUN

Gauge: 12 or 20, 2-3/4" chambers.
Barrel: 27-1/2" (Cyl., Imp. Cyl., Mod., Full choke tubes).
Weight: About 5 lbs.
Stock: Walnut, checkered pistol grip and forend, oil finish.
Features: Receiver slides open on two guide rods, is locked by a large thumb lever on the right side. Extractors only. Light alloy barrels. Imported from France by Mandall Shooting Supplies.
Price: Sprint Standard $895.00
Price: Sprint Deluxe $975.00
Price: Model Fairplay $1,025.00

BAIKAL IJ-27M OVER/UNDER SHOTGUN

Gauge: 12, 2-3/4" chambers.
Barrel: 28.5" (Mod. & Full).
Weight: 7.5 lbs. **Length:** 44.5" overall.
Stock: European hardwood.
Features: Engraved boxlock action with double triggers, extractors; chrome-lined barrels; sling swivels. Imported from Russia by Century International Arms.
Price: About $340.00

AMERICAN ARMS SILVER SPORTING O/U

Gauge: 12, 2-3/4" chambers, 20 3" chambers.
Barrel: 28", 30" (Skeet, Imp. Cyl., Mod., Full choke tubes).
Weight: 7-3/8 lbs. **Length:** 45-1/2" overall.
Stock: 14-3/8"x1-1/2"x2-3/8". Figured walnut, cut checkering; Sporting Clays quick-mount buttpad.
Sights: Target bead front.
Features: Boxlock action with single selective mechanical trigger, automatic selective ejectors; special broadway channeled rib; vented barrel rib; chrome bores. Chrome-nickel finish on frame, with engraving. Introduced 1990. Imported from Italy by American Arms, Inc.
Price: $950.00

AMERICAN ARMS/FRANCHI ALCIONE 97-12 IBS O/U

Gauge: 12, 3" chambers.
Barrel: 26", 28", Franchoke system.
Weight: 7 lbs., 3 oz. **Length:** 43-1/8" overall.
Stock: 14-1/4" x 1-1/2" x 2-1/2". Select European walnut.
Features: Steel alloy receiver; single selective trigger; interchangeable barrels; automatic ejectors; comes with hard case. Introduced 1998. Imported from Italy by American Arms, Inc.
Price: $1,025.00
Price: Alcione SL IBS (detachable side plates) $1,195.00

AMERICAN ARMS/FRANCHI FALCONET 97-12 IBS OVER/UNDER

Gauge: 12, 2-3/4" chambers.
Barrel: 26", Franchoke tubes.
Weight: 6 lbs., 2 oz. **Length:** 43-1/8" overall.
Stock: 14-1/4" x 1-1/2"x2-1/2". European walnut.
Features: Alloy frame with engraving, gold-plated game bird scene engraving; chrome-lined barrels; single selective trigger, automatic selective ejectors; interchangeable barrels. Imported from Italy by American Arms, Inc.
Price: $965.00

AMERICAN ARMS WS/OU 12, TS/OU 12 SHOTGUNS

Gauge: 12, 3-1/2" chambers.
Barrel: WS/OU—28" (Imp. Cyl., Mod., Full choke tubes); TS/OU—24" (Imp. Cyl., Mod., Full choke tubes).
Weight: 6 lbs., 15 oz. **Length:** 46" overall.
Stock: 14-1/8"x1-1/8"x2-3/8". European walnut with cut checkering, black vented recoil pad, matte finish.
Features: Boxlock action with single selective trigger, automatic selective ejectors; chrome bores. Matte metal finish. Imported by American Arms, Inc.
Price: $799.00
Price: With Mossy Oak Break-Up camo $870.00

Consult our Directory pages for the location of firms mentioned.

BAIKAL TOZ-34P OVER/UNDER SHOTGUN

Gauge: 12, 2-3/4" chambers.
Barrel: 28" (Full & Imp. Cyl.).
Weight: 7.5 lbs. **Length:** 44" overall.
Stock: European walnut.
Features: Engraved, blued receiver; cocking indicator; double triggers. Ventilated rib, ventilated rubber buttpad. Imported from Russia by Century International Arms.
Price: About $329.00
Price: With ejectors, about $379.00

Beretta 682 Gold Skeet

BERETTA MODEL 686 SILVER ESSENTIAL O/U

Gauge: 12, 3" chambers.
Barrel: 26", 28", Mobilchoke tubes (Imp. Cyl., Mod., Full).
Weight: 6.7 lbs. **Length:** 45.7" overall (28" barrels).
Stock: 14.5"x2.2"x1.4". American walnut; radiused black buttplate.
Features: Matte chrome finish on receiver, matte and barrels; hard-chrome bores; low-profile receiver with dual conical locking lugs; single selective trigger, ejectors. Introduced 1994. Imported from Italy by Beretta U.S.A.
Price: **$1,070.00**

BERETTA 686 ONYX SPORTING O/U SHOTGUN

Gauge: 12, 3" chambers.
Barrel: 28", 30" (Mobilchoke tubes).
Weight: 7.7 lbs.
Stock: Checkered American walnut.
Features: Intended for the beginning sporting clays shooter. Has wide, vented 12.5mm target rib, radiused recoil pad. Matte black finish on receiver and barrels. Introduced 1993. Imported from Italy by Beretta U.S.A.
Price: **$1,470.00**

BERETTA ULTRALIGHT OVER/UNDER

Gauge: 12, 2-3/4" chambers.
Barrel: 28", Mobilchoke choke tubes.
Weight: About 5 lbs., 13 oz.
Stock: Select American walnut with checkered grip and forend.
Features: Low-profile aluminum alloy receiver with titanium breech face insert. Electroless nickel receiver with game scene engraving. Single selective trigger; automatic safety. Introduced 1992. Imported from Italy by Beretta U.S.A.
Price: **$1,740.00**

Beretta 682 Gold Sporting

Beretta 687EL Gold Pigeon Sporting O/U

Similar to the 687 Silver Pigeon Sporting except has sideplates with gold inlay game scene, vent. side and top ribs, bright orange front sight. Stock and forend are of high grade walnut with fine-line checkering. Available in 12-gauge only with 28" or 30" barrels and Mobilchoke tubes. Weight is 6 lbs., 13 oz. Introduced 1993. Imported from Italy by Beretta U.S.A.
Price: **$4,470.00**

BERETTA OVER/UNDER FIELD SHOTGUNS

Gauge: 12, 20, 28, and 410 bore, 2-3/4", 3" and 3-1/2" chambers.
Barrel: 26" and 28" (Mobilchoke tubes).
Stock: Close-grained walnut.
Features: Highly-figured, American walnut stocks and forends, and a unique, weather-resistant finish on barrels. The 686 Onyx bears a gold P. Beretta signature on each side of the receiver. Silver designates standard 686, 687 models with silver receivers; 686 Silver Pigeon has enhanced engraving pattern, schnabel forend; 686 Silver Essential has matte chrome finish; Gold indicates higher grade 686EL, 687EL models with full sideplates; Diamond is for 687EELL models with highest grade wood, engraving. Case provided with Gold and Diamond grades. Silver Gold, Diamond grades introduced 1994. Imported from Italy by Beretta U.S.A.
Price: 686 Silver Essential **$1,070.00**
Price: 686 Onyx **$1,470.00**
Price: 686 Silver Pigeon two-bbl. set **$2,410.00**
Price: 686 Silver Pigeon **$1,740.00**
Price: 687EL Gold Pigeon (gold inlays, sideplates) **$3,670.00**
Price: 687EL Gold Pigeon, 410, 26", 28-ga., 28" **$3,835.00**
Price: 687EELL Diamond Pigeon (engraved sideplates) **$5,215.00**
Price: 687EELL Diamond Pigeon Combo, 20- and 28-ga., 26" . . . **$5,815.00**

BERETTA SERIES 682 GOLD SKEET, TRAP OVER/UNDERS

Gauge: 12, 2-3/4" chambers.
Barrel: Skeet—28"; trap—30" and 32", Imp. Mod. & Full and Mobilchoke; trap mono shotguns—32" and 34" Mobilchoke; trap top single guns—32" and 34" Full and Mobilchoke; trap combo sets—from 30" O/U, to 32" O/U, 34" top single.
Stock: Close-grained walnut, hand checkered.
Sights: White Bradley bead front sight and center bead.
Features: Receiver has Greystone gunmetal gray finish with gold accents. Trap Monte Carlo stock has deluxe trap recoil pad. Various grades available; contact Beretta U.S.A. for details. Imported from Italy by Beretta U.S.A.
Price: 682 Gold Skeet **$2,850.00**
Price: 682 Gold Trap **$2,910.00**
Price: 682 Gold Trap Top Combo **$3,845.00**
Price: 682 Gold Trap with adjustable stock **$3,725.00**
Price: 686 Silver Pigion Skeet (28"). **$1,760.00**
Price: 687 EELL Diamond Pigeon Trap. **$4,815.00**
Price: 687 EELL Diamond Pigeon Skeet (4-bbl. set). **$8,405.00**
Price: 687 EELL Diamond Pigeon Trap Top Mono . . **$5,055.00** to **$5,105.00**
Price: ASE Gold Skeet **$12,060.00**
Price: ASE Gold Trap **$12,145.00**
Price: ASE Gold Trap Combo **$16,055.00**

BERETTA MODEL SO5, SO6, SO9 SHOTGUNS

Gauge: 12, 2-3/4" chambers.
Barrel: To customer specs.
Stock: To customer specs.
Features: SO5—Trap, Skeet and Sporting Clays models SO5; SO6—SO6 and SO6 EELL are field models. SO6 has a case-hardened or silver receiver with contour hand engraving. SO6 EELL has hand-engraved receiver in a fine floral or "fine English" pattern or game scene, with bas-relief chisel work and gold inlays. SO6 and SO6 EELL are available with sidelocks removable by hand. Imported from Italy by Beretta U.S.A.
Price: SO5 Trap, Skeet, Sporting **$13,000.00**
Price: SO6 Trap, Skeet, Sporting **$17,500.00**
Price: SO6 EELL Field, custom specs. **$28,000.00**
Price: SO9 (12, 20, 28, 410, 26", 28", 30", any choke) **$31,000.00**

BERETTA SPORTING CLAYS SHOTGUNS

Gauge: 12 and 20, 2-3/4" and 3" chambers.
Barrel: 28", 30", 32" Mobilchoke.
Stock: Close-grained walnut.
Features: Equipped with Beretta Mobilchoke flush-mounted screw-in choke tube system. Dual-purpose O/U for hunting and Sporting Clays.12- or 20-gauge, 28", 30" Mobilchoke tubes (four, Skeet, Imp. Cyl., Mod., Full). Wide 12.5mm top rib with 2.5mm center groove; 686 Silver Pigeon has silver receiver with scroll engraving; 687 Silver Pigeon Sporting has silver receiver, highly figured walnut; 687 EL Pigeon Sporting has game scene engraving with gold inlaid animals on full sideplate. Introduced 1994. Imported from Italy by Beretta U.S.A.
Price: 682 Gold Sporting, 28", 30", 31" (with case) **$2,910.00**
Price: 682 Gold Sporting, 28", 30", ported, adj. l.o.p. **$3,035.00**
Price: 686 Silver Pigeon Sporting **$1,795.00**
Price: 686 Silver Pigeon Sporting (20-gauge) **$1,795.00**
Price: 687 Silver Pigeon Sporting **$2,575.00**
Price: 687 Silver Pigeon Sporting (20 gauge) **$2,575.00**
Price: 687 Diamond Pigeon EELL Sporter (hand engraved sideplates, deluxe wood) **$5,310.00**
Price: ASE Gold Sporting Clay **$12,145.00**

BRNO ZH 300 OVER/UNDER SHOTGUN

Gauge: 12, 2-3/4" chambers.
Barrel: 26", 27-1/2", 29" (Skeet, Imp. Cyl., Mod., Full).
Weight: 7 lbs. **Length:** 44.4" overall.
Stock: European walnut.
Features: Double triggers; automatic safety; polished blue finish engraved receiver. Announced 1998. Imported from The Czech Republic by Euro-Imports.
Price: ZH 301, field **$594.00**
Price: ZH 302, Skeet **$608.00**
Price: ZH 303, 12-ga. trap **$608.00**
Price: ZH 321, 16-ga. **$595.00**

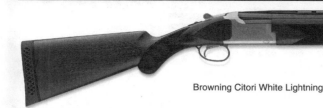

Browning Citori White Lightning

BRNO 501.2 OVER/UNDER SHOTGUN
Gauge: 12, 2-3/4" chambers.
Barrel: 27.5" (Full & Mod.).
Weight: 7 lbs. **Length:** 44" overall.
Stock: European walnut.
Features: Boxlock action with double triggers, ejectors; automatic safety; hand-cut checkering. Announced 1998. Imported from The Czech Republic by Euro-Imports.
Price: $850.00

Browning Citori Sporting Hunter
Similar to the Citori Hunting I except has Sporting Clays stock dimensions, a Superposed-style forend, and Sporting Clays butt pad. Available in 12-gauge with 3" chambers, 26", 28", all with Invector Plus choke tube system. Introduced 1998. Imported from Japan by Browning.
Price: 12-gauge, 3-1/2" **$1,519.00**
Price: 12-, 20-gauge, 3" **$1,435.00**

Browning Superlight Citori Over/Under
Similar to the standard Citori except available in 12, 20 with 24", 26" or 28" Invector barrels, 28 or 410 with 26" barrels choked Imp. Cyl. & Mod. or 28" choked Mod. & Full. Has straight grip stock, schnabel forend tip. Superlight 12 weighs 6 lbs., 9 oz. (26" barrels); Superlight 20, 5 lbs., 12 oz. (26" barrels). Introduced 1982.
Price: Grade I only, 28 or 410, Invector..................... **$1,439.00**
Price: Grade III, Invector, 12 or 20......................... **$2,006.00**
Price: Grade III, 28 or 410, Invector........................ **$2,242.00**
Price: Grade VI, Invector, 12 or 20 .... **$2,919.00**
Price: Grade VI, 28 or 410, Invector **$3,145.00**
Price: Grade I Invector, 12 or 20 .... **$1,386.00**
Price: Grade I Invector, Upland Special (24" bbls.), 12 or 20 ..... **$1,386.00**

Browning Micro Citori Lightning
Similar to the standard Citori 20-ga. Lightning except scaled down for smaller shooter. Comes with 24" Invector Plus back-bored barrels, 13-3/4" length of pull. Weighs about 6 lbs., 3 oz. Introduced 1991.
Price: Grade I.. **$1,428.00**

Browning Citori Ultra Sporter
Similar to the Citori Hunting except has slightly grooved, semi-beavertail forend, satin-finish stock, radiused rubber buttpad. Has three interchangeable trigger shoes, trigger has three length of pull adjustments. Ventilated rib tapers from 13mm to 10mm, 28" or 30" barrels (ported or non-ported) with Invector Plus choke tubes. Ventilated side ribs. Introduced 1989.
Price: With ported barrels, gray or blue receiver **$1,722.00**
Price: Golden Clays.. **$3,203.00**

Browning Citori O/U Special Skeet
Similar to standard Citori except 26", 28" barrels, ventilated side ribs, Invector choke tubes; stock dimensions of 14-3/8"x1-1/2"x2", fitted with Skeet-style recoil pad; conventional target rib and high post target rib.
Price: Grade I Invector, 12-, 20-ga., Invector Plus (high post rib)
.... **$1,586.00**
Price: Grade I, 28 and 410 (high post rib) **$1,549.00**
Price: Grade III, 28, 410 (high post rib) **$2,184.00**
Price: Golden Clays.. **$3,239.00**
Price: Grade III, 12-ga. Invector Plus......................... **$2,179.00**
Price: Adjustable comb stock, add............................... **$210.00**

BROWNING CITORI O/U SHOTGUN
Gauge: 12, 20, 28 and 410.
Barrel: 26", 28" in 28 and 410. Offered with Invector choke tubes. All 12- and 20-gauge models have back-bored barrels and Invector Plus choke system.
Weight: 6 lbs., 8 oz. (26" 410) to 7 lbs., 13 oz. (30" 12-ga.).
Length: 43" overall (26" bbl.).
Stock: Dense walnut, hand checkered, full pistol grip, beavertail forend. Field-type recoil pad on 12-ga. field guns and trap and Skeet models.
Sights: Medium raised beads, German nickel silver.
Features: Barrel selector integral with safety, automatic ejectors, three-piece takedown. Imported from Japan by Browning. Contact Browning for complete list of models and prices.
Price: Grade I, Hunting, Invector, 12 and 20 .... **$1,334.00**
Price: Grade I, Lightning, 28 and 410, Invector **$1,418.00**
Price: Grade III, Lightning, 28 and 410, Invector **$2,242.00**
Price: Grade VI, 28 and 410 Lightning, Invector **$3,145.00**
Price: Grade I, Lightning, Invector Plus, 12, 20 .... **$1,376.00**
Price: Grade I, Hunting, 28", 30" only, 3-1/2", Invector Plus **$1,418.00**
Price: Grade III, Lightning, Invector, 12, 20 .... **$2,006.00**
Price: Grade VI, Lightning, Invector, 12, 20 .... **$2,919.00**
Price: Gran Lightning, 26", 28", Invector, 12 ,20 .... **$1,869.00**
Price: Gran Lightning, 28, 410 .... **$1,969.00**
Price: White Lightning (silver nitride receiver with engraved scroll and rosette, 12-ga., 26", 28") $1,421.00

Browning Citori Special Trap Models
Similar to standard Citori except 12 gauge only; 30", 32" ported or non-ported (Invector Plus); Monte Carlo cheek piece (14-3/8"x1-3/8"x1-3/8"x2"); fitted with trap-style recoil pad; high post target rib, ventilated side ribs.
Price: Grade I, Invector Plus, ported bbls................... **$1,586.00**
Price: Grade III, Invector Plus Ported....................... **$2,179.00**
Price: Golden Clays **$3,239.00**
Price: Adjustable comb stock, add............................ **$210.00**

Browning Special Sporting Clays
Similar to the Citori Ultra Sporter except has full pistol grip stock with palm swell, gloss finish, 28", 30" or 32" barrels with back-bored Invector Plus chokes (ported or non-ported); high post tapered rib. Also available as 28" and 30" two-barrel set. Introduced 1989.
Price: With ported barrels................................... **$1,565.00**
Price: As above, adjustable comb **$1,775.00**
Price: Golden Clays **$3,203.00**
Price: With adjustable comb stock **$3,413.00**

Browning Lightning Sporting Clays
Similar to the Citori Lightning with rounded pistol grip and classic forend. Has high post tapered rib or lower hunting-style rib with 30" back-bored Invector Plus barrels, ported or non-ported, 3" chambers. Gloss stock finish, radiused recoil pad. Has "Lightning Sporting Clays Edition" engraved and gold filled on receiver. Introduced 1989.
Price: Low-rib, ported...................................... **$1,496.00**
Price: High-rib, ported **$1,565.00**
Price: Golden Clays, low rib, ported........................ **$3,092.00**
Price: Golden Clays, high rib, ported....................... **$3,203.00**
Price: Adjustable comb stock, all models, add................ **$210.00**

Browning 802 ES

BROWNING LIGHT SPORTING 802 ES O/U
Gauge: 12, 2-3/4" chambers.
Barrel: 28", back-bored Invector Plus. Comes with flush-mounted Imp. Cyl. and Skeet; 2" extended Imp. Cyl. and Mod.; and 4" extended Imp. Cyl. and Mod. tubes.
Weight: 7 lbs., 5 oz. **Length:** 45" overall.
Stock: 14-3/8" 1/8"x1-9/16"x1-3/4. Select walnut with radiused solid recoil pad, schnabel-type forend.
Features: Trigger adjustable for length of pull; narrow 6.2mm ventilated rib; ventilated barrel side rib; blued receiver. Introduced 1996. Imported from Japan from Browning.
Price: **$1,880.00**

Browning 425 Sporting Clays

Browning 425 WSSF Shotgun

Similar to the 425 Sporting Clays except in 12-gauge only, 28" barrels, has stock dimensions specifically tailored to women shooters (14-1/4"x1-1/2"x1-1/2"); top lever and takedown lever are easier to operate. Stock and forend have teal-colored finish or natural walnut with Women's Shooting Sports Foundation logo. Weighs 7 lbs., 4 oz. Introduced 1995. Imported by Browning.

Price: **$1,775.00**

CHARLES DALY SUPERIOR SKEET

Gauge: 12 and 20, 3" chambers.
Barrel: 26" (Skeet 1 & Skeet 2)
Weight: About 7 lbs.
Stock: Checkered walnut; pistol grip, semi-beavertail forend.
Features: Silvered engraved receiver, chrome moly steel barrels; gold single selective trigger; automatic safety; automatic-ejectors; red bead front sight, metal bead center; recoil pad. Introduced 1997. Imported from Italy by K.B.I., Inc.

Price: **$1,039.00**
Price: Superior Skeet AE-MC (choke tubes). **$1,259.00**

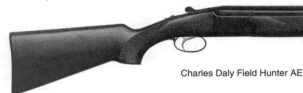

Charles Daly Field Hunter AE

Charles Daly Field Hunter AE Shotgun

Similar to the Field Hunter except 28-gauge and 410-bore only; 26" (Imp. Cyl. & Mod., 28-gauge), 26" (Full & Full, 410); automatic; ejectors. Introduced 1997. Imported from Italy by K.B.I., Inc.

Price: 28 . . . . **$859.00**
Price: 410 . . . . **$899.00**

Charles Daly, Superior Sporting

Charles Daly Field Hunter AE-MC

Similar to the Field Hunter except in 12 or 20 only, 26" or 28" barrels with five multichoke tubes; automatic ejectors. Introduced 1997. Imported from Italy by K.B.I., Inc.

Price: 12 or 20. . . . . **$899.00**

Charles Daly, Empire Trap

CHARLES DALY SUPERIOR TRAP AE

Gauge: 12, 2-3/4" chambers.
Barrel: 30" (Full & Full).
Weight: About 7 lbs.
Stock: Checkered walnut; pistol grip, semi-beavertail forend.
Features: Silver engraved receiver, chrome moly steel barrels; gold single selective trigger; automatic safety, automatic ejectors; red bead front sight, metal bead center; recoil pad. Introduced 1997. Imported from Italy by K.B.I., Inc.

Price: **$1,099.00**
Price: Superior Trap AE-MC model (choke tubes) **$1,219.00**

BROWNING 425 SPORTING CLAYS

Gauge: 12, 20, 2-3/4" chambers.
Barrel: 12-ga.—28", 30", 32" (Invector Plus tubes), back-bored; 20-ga.—28", 30" (Invector Plus tubes).
Weight: 7 lbs., 13 oz. (12-ga., 28").
Stock: 14-13/16" (1/8")x1-7/16"x2-3/16" (12-ga.). Select walnut with gloss finish, cut checkering, schnabel forend.
Features: Grayed receiver with engraving, blued barrels. Barrels are ported on 12-gauge guns. Has low 10mm wide vent rib. Comes with three interchangeable trigger shoes to adjust length of pull. Introduced in U.S. 1993. Imported by Browning.

Price: Grade I, 12-, 20-ga., Invector Plus **$1,775.00**
Price: Golden Clays, 12-, 20-ga., Invector Plus. **$3,308.00**
Price: Adjustable comb stock, add **$210.00**

CENTURY CENTURION OVER/UNDER SHOTGUN

Gauge: 12, 2-3/4" chambers.
Barrel: 28" (Mod. & Full).
Weight: 7.3 lbs. **Length:** 44.5" overall.
Stock: European walnut.
Features: Double triggers; extractors. Polished blue finish. Introduced 1993. Imported by Century International Arms.

Price: About **$380.00**

CHARLES DALY FIELD HUNTER OVER/UNDER SHOTGUN

Gauge: 12, 20, 28 and 410 bore (3" chambers, 28 ga. has 2-3/4").
Barrel: 28" Mod & Full, 26 " Imp. Cyl. & Mod (410 is Full & Full).
Weight: About 7 lbs. **Length:** NA.
Stock: Checkered walnut pistol grip and forend.
Features: Blued engraved receiver, chrome moly steel barrels; gold single selective trigger; automatic safety; extractors; gold bead front sight. Introduced 1997. Imported from Italy by K.B.I., Inc.

Price: 12 or 20 ga. **$699.00**
Price: 28 ga. **$779.00**
Price: 410 bore **$819.00**

Charles Daly Superior Sporting O/U

Similar to the Field Hunter AE-MC except 28" or 30" barrels; silvered, engraved receiver; five choke tubes; ported barrels; red bead front sight. Introduced 1997. Imported from Italy by K.B.I., Inc.

Price: **$1,099.00**

Charles Daly Superior Hunter AE Shotgun

Similar to the Field Hunter AE except has silvered, engraved receiver. Introduced 1997. Imported from Italy by F.B.I., Inc.

Price: 28-ga. **$999.00**
Price: 410-bore **$1,059.00**

CHARLES DALY EMPIRE TRAP AE

Gauge: 12, 2-3/4" chambers.
Barrel: 30" (Full & Full).
Weight: About 7 lbs.
Stock: Checkered walnut; pistol grip, semi-beavertail forend.
Features: Silvered, engraved, reinforced receiver; chrome moly steel barrels; gold single selective trigger; automatic safety, automatic ejector; red bead front sight, metal bead center; recoil pad. Introduced 1997. Imported from Italy by K.B.I., Inc.

Price: **$1,269.00**
Price: Empire Trap AE-MC (choke tubes) **$1,379.00**

Charls Daly Empire DL Hunter

Charles Daly Empire Sporting O/U

Similar to the Empire DL Hunter except 12- or 20-gauge only, 28", 30" barrels with choke tubes; ported barrels; special stock dimensions. Introduced 1997. Imported from Italy by K.B.I., Inc.
Price: **$1,299.00**

CHARLES DALY DIAMOND GTX SKEET AE O/U SHOTGUN
Gauge: 12, 20, 3 " chambers.
Barrel: 26" (SK1 & SK2).
Weight: About 8.5 lbs.
Stock: Checkered deluxed walnut; pistol grip; Skeet dimensions; semi-beavertail forend; hand-rubbed oil finish.
Features: Silvered, hand-engraved receiver; chrome moly steel barrels; GTX detachable single selective trigger system with coil springs, automatic safety; automatic-ejectors; red bead front sight, metal bead center sight; recoil pad. Introduced 1997. Imported from Italy by K.B.I., Inc.
Price: **$5,149.00**
Price: Diamond GTX Skeet AE-MC (choke tubes) **$5,289.00**

CHARLES DALY DIAMOND REGENT GTX DL HUNTER O/U
Gauge: 12, 20, 410, 3" chambers, 28, 2-3/4" chambers.
Barrel: 26", 28", 30" (choke tubes), 26"(Imp. Cyl. & Mod. in 28, 26" (Full & Full) in 410.
Weight: About 7 lbs.
Stock: Extra select fancy European walnut with 24" hand checkering, hand rubbed oil finish.
Features: Boss-type action with internal side lumps. Deep cut hand-engraved scrollwork and game scene set in full sideplates. GTX detachable single selective trigger system with coil springs; chrome moly steel barrels; automatic safety; automatic ejectors, white bead front sight, metal bead center sight. Introduced 1997. Imported from Italy by K.B.I., Inc.
Price: 12 or 20 .... **$22,299.00**
Price: 28 .... **$22,369.00**
Price: 410 .... **$22,419.00**
Price: Diamond Regent GTX EDL Hunter (as above with engraved scroll and birds, 10 gold inlays), 12 or 20 .... **$26,249.00**
Price: As above, 28 .... **$26,499.00**
Price: As above, 410 .... **$26,549.00**

CHARLES DALY EMPIRE DL HUNTER O/U
Gauge: 12, 20, 410, 3" chambers, 28-ga., 2-3/4".
Barrel: 26", 28" (12, 20, choke tubes), 26" (Imp. Cyl. & Mod., 28-ga.), 26" (Full & Full, 410).
Weight: About 7 lbs.
Stocks: Checkered walnut pistol grip buttstock, semi-beavertail forend; recoil pad.
Features: Silvered, engraved receiver; chrome moly barrels; gold single selective trigger; automatic safety; automatic ejectors; red bead front sight, meatal bead middle sight. Introduced 1997. imported from Italy by K.B.I., Inc.
Price: 12 or 20 .... **$1,159.00**
Price: 28 .... **$1,224.00**
Price: 410 .... **$1,269.00**
Price: Empire EDL (dummy sideplates) 12 or 20 .... **$1,319.00**
Price: Empire EDL, 28 .... **$1,384.00**
Price: Empire EDL, 410 .... **$1,424.00**

CHARLES DALY DIAMOND GTX SPORTING O/U SHOTGUN
Gauge: 12, 20, 3" chambers.
Barrel: 28", 30" with choke tubes.
Weight: About 8.5 lbs.
Stock: Checkered deluxe walnut; Sporting clays dimensions. Pistol grip; semi-beavertail forend; hand rubbed oil finish.
Features: Chromed, hand-engraved receiver; chrome moly steel barrels; GTX detachabel single selective trigger system with coil springs, automatic safety; automatic ejectors; red bead front sight; ported barrels. Introduced 1997. Imported from Italy by K.B.I., Inc.
Price: **$5,455.00**

CHARLES DALY DIAMOND GTX TRAP AE O/U SHOTGUN
Gauge: 12, 2-3/4" chambers.
Barrel: 30" (Full & Full).
Weight: About 8.5 lbs.
Stock: Checkered deluxe walnut; pistol grip; trap dimensions; semi-beavertail forend; hand-rubbed oil finish.
Features: Silvered, hand-engraved receiver; chrome moly steel barrels; GTX detachable single selective trigger system with coil springs, automatic safety, automatic-ejectors, red bead front sight, metal bead middle; recoil pad. Introduced 1997. Imported from Italy by K.B.I., Inc.
Price: **$5,289.00**
Price: Diamond GTX Trap AE-MC (choke tubes). **$5,455.00**

FABARM MAX LION OVER/UNDER SHOTGUNS
Gauge: 12, 3" chambers, 20, 3" chambers.
Barrel: 26", 28", 30" (12-ga.); 26", 28" (20-ga.), choke tubes.
Weight: 7.4 lbs. **Length:** 47.5" overall (26" barrel).
Stock: European walnut; leather-covered recoil pad.
Features: Boxlock action with single selective trigger, manual safety, automatic ejectors; chrome-lined barrels; adjustable trigger. Silvered, engraved receiver. Comes with locking, fitted luggage case. Introduced 1998. Imported from Italy by Heckler & Koch, Inc.
Price: 12 or 20 **$1,807.00**

Fabarm Mex Lion

Fabarm Black Lion Competition O/U Shotguns
Similar to the Max Lion except has black receiver finish, deluxe European walnut stock and forend. Introduced 1998. Imported from Italy by Heckler & Koch, Inc.
Price: 12 or 20 .... **$1,529.00**

Fabarm Ultra Mag Lion

FABARM SILVER LION OVER/UNDER SHOTGUNS
Gauge: 12, 3" chambers, 20, 3" chambers.
Barrel: 26", 28", 30" (12-ga.); 26", 28" (20-ga.), choke tubes.
Weight: 7.2 lbs. **Length:** 47.5" overall (26" barrels).
Stock: Walnut; leather-covered recoil pad.
Features: Boxlock action with single selective trigger; silvered receiver with engraving; automatic ejectors. Comes with locking hard plastic case. Introduced 1998. Imported from Italy by Heckler & Koch, Inc.
Price: 12 or 20 .... **$1,331.00**
Price: Super Light Lion (12-ga. only, 24" barrels, weighs 6.5 lbs.) . **$1,053.00**

FABARM ULTRA MAG LION O/U SHOTGUN
Gauge: 12, 3-1/2" chambers.
Barrel: 28" (Cyl., Imp. Cyl., Mod., Imp. Mod., Full, SS-Mod., SS-Full choke tubes).
Weight: 7.9 lbs. **Length:** 50" overall.
Stock: Black-colored walnut.
Features: Matte finished metal surfaces; single selective trigger; non-auto ejectors; leather-covered recoil pad. Comes with locking hard plastic case. Introduced 1998. Imported from Italy by Heckler & Koch, Inc.
Price: **$1,120.00**

CHARLES DALY EMPIRE SKEET AE O/U SHOTGUN

Gauge: 12, 20, 3" chambers.
Barrel: 26" (Skeet 1 & Skeet 2).
Weight: About 7 lbs.
Stock: Checkered walnut; pistol grip; semi-beavertail forend. Skeet dimensions.
Sights:
Features: Silvered, engraved, reinforced receiver; chrome moly steel barrels; gold single selective trigger; automatic safety; automatic-ejectors; red bead front sight, metal bead middle sight; recoil pad. Introduced 1997. Imported from Italy by K.B.I. Inc.
Price:.. **$1,189.00**
Price: Empire Skeet AE-MC (choke tubes)................... **$1,314.00**

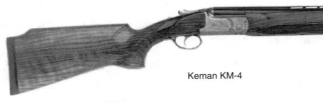

Keman KM-4

KEMEN OVER/UNDER SHOTGUNS

Gauge: 12, 2-3/4" or 3" chambers.
Barrel: 27-5/8" (Hunting, Pigeon, Sporting Clays, Skeet), 30", 32" (Sporting Clays, Trap).
Weight: 7.25 to 8.5 lbs.
Stock: Dimensions to customer specs. High grade walnut.

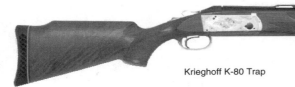

Krieghoff K-80 Trap

KRIEGHOFF K-80 SPORTING CLAYS O/U

Gauge: 12.
Barrel: 28", 30" or 32" with choke tubes.
Weight: About 8 lbs.
Stock: #3 Sporting stock designed for gun-down shooting.
Features: Choice of standard or lightweight receiver with satin nickel finish and classic scroll engraving. Selective mechanical trigger adjustable for position. Choice of tapered flat or 8mm parallel flat barrel rib. Free-floating barrels. Aluminum case. Imported from Germany by Krieghoff International, Inc.
Price: Standard grade with five choke tubes, from **$8,150.00**

KRIEGHOFF K-80 SKEET SHOTGUN

Gauge: 12, 2-3/4" chambers.
Barrel: 28" (Skeet & Skeet, optional Tula or choke tubes).
Weight: About 7-3/4 lbs.
Stock: American Skeet or straight Skeet stocks, with palm-swell grips. Walnut.
Features: Satin gray receiver finish. Selective mechanical trigger adjustable for position. Choice of ventilated 8mm parallel flat rib or ventilated 8-12mm tapered flat rib. Introduced 1980. Imported from Germany by Krieghoff International, Inc.
Price: Standard, Skeet chokes **$6,900.00**
Price: As above, Tula chokes **$7,825.00**
Price: Lightweight model (weighs 7 lbs.), Standard **$6,900.00**
Price: Two-Barrel Set (tube concept), 12-ga., Standard **$11,840.00**
Price: Skeet Special (28", tapered flat rib, Skeet & Skeet choke tubes)
.... **$7,575.00**

LAURONA SILHOUETTE 300 SPORTING CLAYS

Gauge: 12, 2-3/4" or 3" chambers.
Barrel: 28", 29" (Multichoke tubes, flush-type or knurled).
Weight: 7 lbs., 12 oz.
Stock: 14-3/8"x1-3/8"x2-1/2". European walnut with full pistol grip, beavertail forend. Rubber buttpad.
Features: Selective single trigger, automatic selective ejectors. Introduced 1988. Imported from Spain by Galaxy Imports.
Price:.. **$1,250.00**
Price: Silhouette Ultra-Magnum, 3-1/2" chambers **$1,365.00**

CHARLES DALY DIAMOND GTX DL HUNTER O/U

Gauge: 12, 20, 410, 3 " chambers, 28, 2-3/4"chambers.
Barrel: 26", 28", choke tubes in 12 and 20 ga., 26" (Imp. Cyl. & Mod.), 26" (Full & Full) in 410-bore.
Weight: About 8.5 lbs.
Stock: Select fancy European walnut stock, with 24 lpi hand checkering; hand-rubbed oil finish.
Features: Boss-type action with internal side lugs, hand-engraved scrollwork and game scene. GTX detachable single selective trigger system with coil springs; chrome moly steel barrels, automatic safety, automatic ejectors, red bead front sight, recoil pad. Introduced 1997. Imported from Italy by K.B.I., Inc.
Price: 12 or 20 .... **$12,399.00**
Price: 28 .... **$12,489.00**
Price: 410 .... **$12,529.00**
Price: GTX EDL Hunter (with gold inlays), 12, 20 .... **$15,999.00**
Price: As above, 28 .... **$16,179.00**
Price: As above, 410 .... **$16,219.00**

Features: Drop-out trigger assembly; ventilated flat or step top rib, ventilated, solid or no side ribs. Low-profile receiver with black finish on Standard model, antique silver on sideplate models and all engraved, gold inlaid models. Barrels, forend, trigger parts interchangeable with Perazzi. Comes with hard case, accessory tools, spares. Introduced 1989. Imported from Spain by U.S.A. Sporting Clays.
Price: KM-4 Standard **$6,179.00**
Price: KM-4 Luxe-A (engraved scroll), Luxe-B (game scenes) ... **$10,644.00**
Price: KM-4 Super Luxe (engraved game scene) **$12,064.00**
Price: KM-4 Extra Luxe-A (scroll engraved sideplates) **$13,960.00**
Price: KM-4 Extra Luxe-B (game scene sideplates) **$16,030.00**
Price: KM-4 Extra Gold (inlays, game scene) **$19,607.00**

KRIEGHOFF K-80 O/U TRAP SHOTGUN

Gauge: 12, 2-3/4" chambers.
Barrel: 30", 32" (Imp. Mod. & Full or choke tubes).
Weight: About 8-1/2 lbs.
Stock: Four stock dimensions or adjustable stock available; all have palm-swell grips. Checkered European walnut.
Features: Satin nickel receiver. Selective mechanical trigger, adjustable for position. Ventilated step rib. Introduced 1980. Imported from Germany by Krieghoff International, Inc.
Price: K-80 O/U (30", 32", Imp. Mod. & Full), from **$7,375.00**
Price: K-80 Unsingle (32", 34", Full), Standard, from **$7,950.00**
Price: K-80 Combo (two-barrel set), Standard, from **$9,975.00**

Krieghoff K-80 Four-Barrel Skeet Set

Similar to the Standard Skeet except comes with barrels for 12, 20, 28, 410. Comes with fitted aluminum case.
Price: Standard grade **$16,950.00**

Krieghoff K-80 International Skeet

Similar to the Standard Skeet except has 1/2" ventilated Broadway-style rib, special Tula chokes with gas release holes at muzzle. International Skeet stock. Comes in fitted aluminum case.
Price: Standard grade **$7,825.00**

LAURONA SUPER MODEL OVER/UNDERS

Gauge: 12, 20, 2-3/4" or 3" chambers.
Barrel: 26", 28" (Multichoke), 29" (Multichokes and Full).
Weight: About 7 lbs.
Stock: European walnut. Dimensions may vary according to model. Full pistol grip.
Features: Boxlock action, silvered with engraving. Automatic selective ejectors; choke tubes available on most models; single selective or twin single triggers; black chrome barrels. Has 5-year warranty, including metal finish. Imported from Spain by Galaxy Imports.
Price: Model 83 MG, 12- or 20-ga. **$1,215.00**
Price: Model 84S Super Trap (fixed chokes)................ **$1,340.00**
Price: Model 85 Super Game, 12- or 20-ga. **$1,215.00**
Price: Model 85 MS Super Trap (Full/Multichoke)........... **$1,390.00**

Laurona Silhouette 300 Trap

Same gun as the Silhouette 300 Sporting Clays except has 29" barrels, trap stock dimensions of 14-3/8"x1-7/16"x1-5/8", weighs 7 lbs., 15 oz. Available with flush or knurled Multichokes.
Price:.. **$1,310.00**

Ljutic LM-6 Super Deluxe

LJUTIC LM-6 SUPER DELUXE O/U SHOTGUN
Gauge: 12.
Barrel: 28" to 34", choked to customer specs for live birds, trap, International Trap.

Weight: To customer specs.
Stock: To customer specs. Oil finish, hand checkered.
Features: Custom-made gun. Hollow-milled rib, pull or release trigger, push-button opener in front of trigger guard. From Ljutic Industries.
Price: Super Deluxe LM-6 O/U **$17,995.00**
Price: Over/under Combo (interchangeable single barrel, two trigger guards, one for single trigger, one for doubles) **$24,995.00**
Price: Extra over/under barrel sets, 29"-32" **$5,995.00**

Marocchi Lady Sport

Marocchi Lady Sport O/U Shotgun
Ergonomically designed specifically for women shooters. Similar to the Conquista Sporting Clays model except has 28" or 30" barrels with five Contre-choke tubes, stock dimensions of 13-7/8"-14-1/4"x1-11/32"x2-9/32"; weighs about 7-1/2 lbs. Also available as left-hand model—opening lever operates from left to right; stock has left-hand cast. Also available with colored graphics finish on frame and opening lever. Introduced 1995. Imported from Italy by Precision Sales International.
Price: Grade I, right-hand **$2,120.00**
Price: Left-hand, add (all grades) **$101.00**
Price: Lady Sport Spectrum (colored receiver panel) **$2,199.00**
Price: Lady Sport Spectrum, left-hand **$2,300.00**

Marocchi Conquista Trap Over/Under Shotgun
Similar to the Conquista Sporting Clays model except has 30" or 32" barrels choked Full & Full, stock dimensions of 14-1/2"- 14-7/8"x1-11/16"x1-9/32"; weighs about 8-1/4 lbs. Introduced 1994. Imported from Italy by Precision Sales International.
Price: Grade I, right-hand **$1,995.00**
Price: Grade II, right-hand **$2,330.00**
Price: Grade III, right-hand, from **$3,599.00**

Marocchi Conquista Skeet Over/Under Shotgun
Similar to the Conquista Sporting Clays except has 28" (Skeet & Skeet) barrels, stock dimensions of 14-3/8"- 14-3/4"x2-3/16"x1-1/2". Weighs about 7-3/4 lbs. Introduced 1994. Imported from Italy by Precision Sales International.
Price: Grade I, right-hand **$1,995.00**
Price: Grade II, right-hand **$2,330.00**
Price: Grade III, right-hand, from **$3,599.00**

MERKEL MODEL 2001 EL O/U SHOTGUN
Gauge: 12, 20, 3" chambers, 28, 2-3/4" chambers.
Barrel: 12—28"; 20, 28-ga.—26-3/4".
Weight: About 7 lbs. (12-ga.).
Stock: Oil-finished walnut; English or pistol grip.
Features: Self-cocking Blitz boxlock action with cocking indicators; Kersten double cross-bolt lock; silver-grayed receiver with engraved hunting scenes; coil spring ejectors; single selective or doulbe triggers. Imported form Germany by GSI, Inc.
Price: 12, 20 . . . . **$5,895.00**
Price: 28-ga. **$6,495.00**
Price: Model 2000EL (scroll engraving, 12 or 20) **$4,995.00**

PERAZZI MIRAGE SPECIAL SPORTING O/U
Gauge: 12, 2-3/4" chambers.
Barrel: 28-3/8" (Imp. Mod. & Extra Full), 29-1/2" (choke tubes).
Weight: 7 lbs., 12 oz.
Stock: Special specifications.
Features: Has single selective trigger; flat 7/16"x5/16" vent. rib. Many options available. Imported from Italy by Perazzi U.S.A., Inc.
Price: **$9,430.00**

Perazzi Mirage Special Four-Gauge Skeet
Similar to the Mirage Sporting model except has Skeet dimensions, interchangeable, adjustable four-position trigger assembly. Comes with four barrel sets in 12, 20, 28, 410, flat 5/16"x5/16" rib.
Price: From **$20,720.00**

MAROCCHI CLASSIC DOUBLES MODEL 92 SPORTING CLAYS O/U SHOTGUN
Gauge: 12, 3" chambers.
Barrel: 30"; backbored, ported (ContreChoke Plus tubes); 10 mm concave ventilated top rib, ventilated middle rib.
Weight: 8 lbs. 2 oz.
Stock: 14-1/4"- 14-5/8"x 2-1/8"x1-3/8"; American walnut with checkered grip and forend; Sporting Clays buttpad.
Features: Low profile frame; fast lock time; automatic selective ejectors; blued receiver and barrels. Comes with three choke tubes. Ergonomically shaped trgger adjustable for pull length without tools. Barrels are backbored and ported. Introduced 1996. Imported from Italy by Precision Sales International.
Price: **$1,598.00**

MAROCCHI CONQUISTA SPORTING CLAYS O/U SHOTGUNS
Gauge: 12, 2-3/4" chambers.
Barrel: 28", 30", 32" (Contrechoke tubes); 10mm concave vent. rib.
Weight: About 8 lbs.
Stock: 14-1/2"-14-7/8"x2-3/16"x1-7/16"; American walnut with checkered grip and forend; Sporting Clays butt pad.
Sights: 16mm luminescent front.
Features: Has lower monoblock and frame profile. Fast lock time. Ergonomically-shaped trigger is adjustable for pull length. Automatic selective ejectors. Coin-finished receiver, blued barrels. Comes with five choke tubes, hard case. Also available as true left-hand model—opening lever operates from left to right; stock has left-hand cast. Introduced 1994. Imported from Italy by Precision Sales International.
Price: Grade I, right-hand **$1,995.00**
Price: Grade I, left-hand **$2,120.00**
Price: Grade II, right-hand **$2,330.00**
Price: Grade II, left-hand **$2,685.00**
Price: Grade III, right-hand, from **$3,599.00**
Price: Grade III, left-hand, from **$3,995.00**

Merkel Model 303 EL O/U Shotgun
Similar to the Model 2001 EL except has Holland & Holland-style sidelock action with cocking indicators; English-style Arabesque engraving. Available in 12, 20 gauge. Imported from Germany by GSI, Inc.
Price: **$19,995.00**

Merkel Model 2002 EL O/U Shotgun
Similar to the Model 2001 EL except has dummy sideplates, Arabesque engraving with hunting scenes; 12, 20-gauge. Imported from Germany by GSI, Inc.
Price: **$9,995.00**

PERAZZI MX12 HUNTING OVER/UNDER
Gauge: 12, 2-3/4" chambers.
Barrel: 26", 27-5/8", 28-3/8", 29-1/2" (Mod. & Full); choke tubes available in 27-5/8", 29-1/2" only (MX12C).
Weight: 7 lbs., 4 oz.
Stock: To customer specs; Interchangeable.
Features: Single selective trigger; coil springs used in action; schnabel forend tip. Imported from Italy by Perazzi U.S.A., Inc.
Price: From **$8,330.00**
Price: MX12C (with choke tubes), from **$8,935.00**

Perazzi MX20 Hunting Over/Under
Similar to the MX12 except 20-ga. frame size. Available in 20, 28, 410 with 2-3/4" or 3" chambers. 26" standard, and choked Mod. & Full. Weight is 6 lbs., 6 oz.
Price: From **$8,330.00**
Price: MX20C (as above, 20-ga. only, choke tubes), from **$8,935.00**

PERAZZI MX8/MX8 SPECIAL TRAP, SKEET
Gauge: 12, 2-3/4" chambers.
Barrel: Trap—29-1/2" (Imp. Mod. & Extra Full), 31-1/2" (Full & Extra Full). Choke tubes optional. Skeet—27-5/8" (Skeet & Skeet).
Weight: About 8-1/2 lbs. (Trap); 7 lbs., 15 oz. (Skeet).
Stock: Interchangeable and custom made to customer specs.
Features: Has detachable and interchangeable trigger group with flat V springs. Flat 7/16" ventilated rib. Many options available. Imported from Italy by Perazzi U.S.A., Inc.
Price: From $8,330.00
Price: MX8 Special (adj. four-position trigger), from $8,330.00
Price: MX8 Special Combo (o/u and single barrel sets), from . . . $11,620.00

PERAZZI MX28, MX410 GAME O/U SHOTGUNS
Gauge: 28, 2-3/4" chambers, 410, 3" chambers.
Barrel: 26" (Imp. Cyl. & Full).
Weight: NA.
Stock: To customer specifications.
Features: Made on scaled-down frames proportioned to the gauge. Introduced 1993. Imported from Italy by Perazzi U.S.A., Inc.
Price: From $16,650.00

Perazzi Sporting Classic

Piotti Boss

Remington Peerless

Remington 396 Sporting O/U
Similar to the 396 Skeet except the 28", 30" barrels are factory ported, and come with Skeet, Imp. Skeet, Imp. Cyl. and Mod. Rem Choke tubes. Made in U.S. by Remington. Introduced 1996.
Price: $2,126.00

Remington 396 Skeet

RIZZINI S790 EMEL OVER/UNDER SHOTGUN
Gauge: 20, 28, 410.
Barrel: 26", 27.5" (Imp. Cyl. & Imp. Mod.).
Weight: About 6 lbs.
Stock: 14"x1-1/2"x2-1/8". Extra-fancy select walnut.
Features: Boxlock action with profuse engraving; automatic ejectors; single selective trigger; silvered receiver. Comes with Nizzoli leather case. Introduced 1996. Imported from Italy by Wm. Larkin Moore & Co.
Price: From $9,600.00

Perazzi Mirage Special Skeet Over/Under
Similar to the MX8 Skeet except has adjustable four-position trigger, Skeet stock dimensions.
Price: From $8,830.00

Perazzi MX8/20 Over/Under Shotgun
Similar to the MX8 except has smaller frame and has a removable trigger mechanism. Available in trap, Skeet, sporting or game models with fixed chokes or choke tubes. Stock is made to customer specifications. Introduced 1993.
Price: From $8,330.00

PERAZZI MX10 OVER/UNDER SHOTGUN
Gauge: 12, 2-3/4" chambers.
Barrel: 29.5", 31.5" (fixed chokes).
Weight: NA.
Stock: Walnut; cheekpiece adjustable for elevation and cast.
Features: Comes with six pattern adjustment rib inserts. Vent. side rib. Externally selective trigger. Available in single barrel, combo, over/under trap, Skeet, pigeon and sporting models. Introduced 1993. Imported from Italy by Perazzi U.S.A., Inc.
Price: From $10,610.00

Perazzi Sporting Classic O/U
Same as the Mirage Special Sporting except is deluxe version with select wood and engraving, Available with flush mount choke tubes, 29.5" barrels. Introduced 1993.
Price: From $10,510.00

PIOTTI BOSS OVER/UNDER SHOTGUN
Gauge: 12, 20.
Barrel: 26" to 32", chokes as specified.
Weight: 6.5 to 8 lbs.
Stock: Dimensions to customer specs. Best quality figured walnut.
Features: Essentially a custom-made gun with many options. Introduced 1993. Imported from Italy by Wm. Larkin Moore.
Price: From $39,200.00

REMINGTON PEERLESS OVER/UNDER SHOTGUN
Gauge: 12, 3" chambers.
Barrel: 26", 28", 30" (Imp. Cyl., Mod., Full Rem Chokes).
Weight: 7-1/4 lbs. (26" barrels). **Length:** 43" overall (26" barrels).
Stock: 14-3/16"x1-1/2"x2-1/4". American walnut with Imron gloss finish, cut-checkered grip and forend. Black, ventilated recoil pad.
Features: Boxlock action with removable sideplates. Gold-plated, single selective trigger, automatic safety, automatic ejectors. Fast lock time. Mid-rib bead, Bradley-type front. Polished blue finish with light scrollwork on sideplates, Remington logo on bottom of receiver. Introduced 1993.
Price: $1,172.00

REMINGTON 396 SKEET O/U
Gauge: 12, 2-3/4" chambers.
Barrel: 28", 30" (Skeet & Imp. Skeet Rem. Choke tubes).
Weight: 8 lbs.
Stock: 14-3/16"x1-1/2"x2-1/4". Fancy, figured American walnut. Target-style forend, larger-radius comb, grip palm swell.
Features: Boxlock action with removable sideplates. Barrels have lengthened forcing cones; 10mm non-stepped, parallel rib; engraved receiver, sideplates, trigger guard, top lever, forend iron are finished with gray nitride. Made in U.S. by Remington. Introduced 1996.
Price: $1,993.00

Rizzini S792 EMEL Over/Under Shotgun
Similar to the S790 EMEL except has dummy sideplates with extensive engraving coverage. Comes with Nizzoli leather case. Introduced 1996. Imported from Italy by Wm. Larkin Moore & Co.
Price: From $9,400.00

Rizzini Upland EL

Rizzini Artemis Over/Under Shotgun

Same as the Upland EL model except has dummy sideplates with extensive game scene engraving. Fancy European walnut stock. Comes with fitted case. Introduced 1996. Imported from Italy by Wm. Larkin Moore & Co.
Price: From **$2,375.00**

Rizzini S782 EMEL

RIZZINI S790 SPORTING EL OVER/UNDER

Gauge: 12, 2-3/4" chambers.
Barrel: 28", 29.5", Imp. Mod., Mod., Full choke tubes.
Weight: 8.1 lbs.
Stock: 14"x1-1/2"x2". Extra-fancy select walnut.
Features: Boxlock action; automatic ejectors; single selective trigger; 10mm top rib. Comes with case. Introduced 1996. Imported from Italy by Wm. Larkin Moore & Co.
Price: **$6,000.00**

RUGER WOODSIDE OVER/UNDER SHOTGUN

Gauge: 12, 3" chambers.
Barrel: 26", 28" (Full, Mod., Imp. Cyl. and two Skeet tubes), 30" (Mod., Imp. Cyl. and two Skeet tubes).
Weight: 7-1/2 to 8 lbs.
Stock: 14-1/8"x1-1/2"x2-1/2". Select Circassian walnut; pistol grip or straight English grip.
Features: Has a newly patented Ruger cocking mechanism for easier, smoother opening. Buttstock extends forward into action as two side panels. Single selective mechanical trigger, selective automatic ejectors; serrated free-floating rib; back-bored barrels with stainless steel choke tubes. Blued barrels, stainless steel receiver. Engraved action available. Introduced 1995. Made in U.S. by Sturm, Ruger & Co.
Price: **$1,675.00**
Price: Woodside Sporting Clays (30" barrels) **$1,675.00**

RUGER RED LABEL O/U SHOTGUN

Gauge: 12, 20, 3" chambers; 28 2-3/4" chambers.
Barrel: 26", 28" (Skeet, Imp. Cyl., Full, Mod. screw-in choke tubes). Proved for steel shot.
Weight: About 7 lbs. (20-ga.); 7-1/2 lbs. (12-ga.). **Length:** 43" overall (26" barrels).
Stock: 14"x1-1/2"x2-1/2". Straight grain American walnut. Checkered pistol grip and forend, rubber butt pad.
Features: Choice of blue or stainless receiver. Single selective mechanical trigger, selective automatic ejectors; serrated free-floating vent. rib. Comes with two Skeet, one Imp. Cyl., one Mod., one Full choke tube and wrench. Made in U.S. by Sturm, Ruger & Co.
Price: Red Label with pistol grip stock **$1,215.00**
Price: English Field with straight-grip stock **$1,215.00**

SARSILMAZ OVER/UNDER SHOTGUN

Gauge: 12, 3" chambers.
Barrel: 26", 28" (Mod. & Full).
Weight: About 7-1/2 lbs.
Stock: European walnut; checkered grip and forend.

RIZZINI UPLAND EL OVER/UNDER SHOTGUN

Gauge: 12, 16, 20, 28, 410.
Barrel: 26", 27-1/2", Mod. & Full, Imp. Cyl. & Imp. Mod. choke tubes.
Weight: About 6.6 lbs.
Stock: 14"x1-1/2"x2-1/8".
Features: Boxlock action; single selective trigger; ejectors; profuse engraving on silvered receiver. Comes with fitted case. Introduced 1996. Imported from Italy by Wm. Larkin Moore & Co.
Price: From **$3,450.00**

RIZZINI S782 EMEL OVER/UNDER SHOTGUN

Gauge: 12, 2-3/4" chambers.
Barrel: 26", 27.5" (Imp. Cyl. & Imp. Mod.).
Weight: About 6.75 lbs.
Stock: 14"x1-1/2"x2-1/8". Extra fancy select walnut.
Features: Boxlock action with dummy sideplates; extensive engraving with gold inlaid game birds; silvered receiver; automatic ejectors; single selective trigger. Comes with Nizzoli leather case. Introduced 1996. Imported from Italy by Wm. Larkin Moore & Co.
Price: From **$11,250.00**

Ruger Woodside

ROTTWEIL PARAGON OVER/UNDER

Gauge: 12, 2-3/4" chambers.
Barrel: 28", 30", five choke tubes.
Weight: 7 lbs.
Stock: 14-1/2"x1-1/2"x2-1/2"; European walnut.
Features: Boxlock action. Detachable trigger assembly; ejectors can be deactivated; convertible top lever for right- or left-hand use; trigger adjustable for position. Imported from Germany by Dynamit Nobel-RWS, Inc.
Price: **$5,995.00**

Ruger English Field

Ruger Sporting Clays O/U Shotgun

Similar to the Red Label except 30" back-bored barrels, stainless steel choke tubes. Weighs 7.75 lbs., overall length 47". Stock dimensions of 14-1/8"x1-1/2"x2-1/2". Free-floating serrated vent. rib with brass front and mid-rib beads. No barrel side spacers. Comes with two Skeet, one Imp. Cyl., one Mod. choke tubes. Full and Extra-Full available at extra cost. 12 ga. introduced 1992. 20 ga. introduced 1994.
Price: 12 or 20 . . . . **$1,349.00**

Features: Silvered, engraved action, blued barrels. Imported from Turkey by Armsport.
Price: 26" or 28", double triggers **$499.95**
Price: 26" or 28", single selective trigger **$575.00**

Sigarms SA3

SIGARMS SA3 OVER/UNDER SHOTGUN
Gauge: 12, 20, 3" chambers.
Barrel: 26", 27" (Full, Mod, Imp. Cyl. choke tubes).
Weight: 7 lbs.
Stock: Select grade walnut; checkered grip and forend.
Features: Chrome-lined bores; single selective trigger, automatic ejectors; satin nickel receiver finish, rest blued. Introduced 1997. Imported by Sigarms, Inc.
Price: Field, 12-gauge... **$1,335.00**
Price: Sporting Clays.. **$1,675.00**
Price: Field, 20-gauge... **$1,335.00**

SILMA MODEL 70 OVER/UNDER SHOTGUN
Gauge: 12, 3" chambers.
Barrel: 27.5" (Mod. & Imp. Cyl.).
Weight: 6.8 lbs. **Length:** 44.75" overall.
Stock: European walnut.
Features: Engraved, blued boxlock action with single trigger; sling swivels. Introduced 1995. Imported from Italy by Century International Arms.
Price: About.. **$540.00**
Price: With selective trigger................................... **$599.00**
Price: With selective trigger, auto ejectors, tubes................ **$959.00**

SIGARMS SA5 OVER/UNDER SHOTGUN
Gauge: 12, 20, 3" chamber.
Barrel: 26-1/2", 27" (Full, Imp. Mod., Mod., Imp. Cyl., Cyl. choke tubes).
Weight: 6.9 lbs. (12-gauge), 5.9 lbs. (20-gauge).
Stock: 14-1/2" x 1-1/2" x 2-1/2". Select grade walnut; checkered 20 l.p.i. at grip and forend.
Features: Single selective trigger, automatic ejectors; hand-engraved detachable sideplated; matte nickel receiver, rest blued; tapered bolt lock-up. Introduced 1997. Imported by Sigarms, inc.
Price: Field, 12-gauge... **$2,670.00**
Price: Sporting Clays.. **$3,185.00**
Price: Field 20-gauge... **$2,670.00**

CONSULT
SHOOTER'S MARKETPLACE
Page 225, This Issue

SKB Model 585

SKB Model 505 Shotguns
Similar to the Model 585 except blued receiver, standard bore diameter, standard Inter-Choke system on 12, 20, 28, diffrent receiver engraving. Imported from Japan by G.U. Inc.
Price: Field, 12 (26", 28"), 20 (26" only) **$1,049.00**
Price: Sporting Clays, 12 (28", 30")......................... **$1,149.00**

SKB Model 585 Gold Package
Similar to the Model 585 Field except has gold-plated trigger, two gold-plated game inlays, and schnabel forend. Introduced 1998. Imported from Japan by G.U. Inc.
Price: 12-, 20-ga... **$1,489.00**
Price: 28, 410 .... **$1,539.00**

SKB MODEL 585 OVER/UNDER SHOTGUN
Gauge: 12 or 20, 3"; 28, 2-3/4"; 410, 3".
Barrel: 12-ga.—26", 28", 30", 32", 34" (Inter-Choke tube); 20-ga.—26", 28" (Inter-Choke tube); 28—26", 28" (Inter-Choke tube); 410—26", 28" (Imp. Cyl. & Mod., Mod. & Full). Ventilated side ribs.
Weight: 6.6 to 8.5 lbs. **Length:** 43" to 51-3/8" overall.
Stock: 14-1/8"x1-1/2"x2-3/16". Hand checkered walnut with high-gloss finish. Target stocks available in standard and Monte Carlo.
Sights: Metal bead front (field), target style on Skeet, trap, Sporting Clays.
Features: Boxlock action; silver nitride finish with Field or Target pattern engraving; manual safety, automatic ejectors, single selective trigger. All 12-gauge barrels are back-bored, have lengthened forcing cones and longer choke tube system. Sporting Clays models in 12-gauge with 28" or 30" barrels available with optional 3/8" step-up target-style rib, matte finish, nickel center bead, white front bead. Introduced 1992. Imported from Japan by G.U., Inc.
Price: Field.. **$1,329.00**
Price: Two-barrel Field Set, 12 & 20 .... **$2,129.00**
Price: Two-barrel Field Set, 20 & 28 or 28 (& 410)............. **$2,179.00**
Price: Trap, Skeet **$1,429.00**
Price: Two-barrel trap combo **$2,129.00**
Price: Sporting Clays model .... **$1,149.00** to **$1,529.00**
Price: Skeet Set (20, 28, 410) **$3,329.00**

SKB 785 Sporting Clays

SKB MODEL 785 OVER/UNDER SHOTGUN
Gauge: 12, 20, 3"; 28, 2-3/4"; 410, 3".
Barrel: 26", 28", 30", 32" (Inter-Choke tubes).
Weight: 6 lbs., 10 oz. to 8 lbs.
Stock: 14-1/8"x1-1/2"x2-3/16" (Field). Hand-checkered American black walnut with high-gloss finish; semi-beavertail forend. Target stocks available in standard or Monte Carlo styles.
Sights: Metal bead front (Field), target style on Skeet, trap, Sporting Clays models.

Features: Boxlock action with Greener-style cross bolt; single selective chrome-plated trigger, chrome-plated selective ejectors; manual safety. Chrome-plated, over-size, back-bored barrels with lengthened forcing cones. Introduced 1995. Imported from Japan by G.U. Inc.
Price: Field, 12 or 20 .... **$1,949.00**
Price: Field, 28 or 410 .... **$2,029.00**
Price: Field set, 12 and 20 .... **$2,829.00**
Price: Field set, 20 and 28 or 28 and 410 .... **$2,929.00**
Price: Sporting Clays, 12 or 20 .... **$2,099.00**
Price: Sporting Clays, 28 .... **$2,169.00**
Price: Sporting Clays set, 12 and 20 .... **$2,999.00**
Price: Skeet, 12 or 20 .... **$2,029.00**
Price: Skeet, 28 or 410 .... **$2,069.00**
Price: Skeet, three-barrel set, 20, 28, 410...................... **$4,089.00**
Price: Trap, standard or Monte Carlo **$2,029.00**
Price: Trap combo, standard or Monte Carlo **$2,829.00**

Stoeger/IGA Condor Waterfowl

Stoeger/IGA Condor Waterfowl O/U

Similar to the Condor I except has Advantage camouflage on the barrels, stock and forend; all other metal has matte black finish. Comes only with 30" choke tube barrels, 3" chambers, automatic ejectors, single trigger and manual safety. Designed for steel shot. Introduced 1997. Imported from Brazil by Stoeger.

Price: **$729.00**

Stoeger/IGA Deluxe Hunter Clays O/U

Similar to the Condor Supreme except 12-gauge only with 28" choke tube barrels, select semi-fancy American walnut stock with black Pachmayr target-style recoil pad, high luster blued barrels, gold-plated trigger, red bead front and mid-rib sights. Introduced 1997. Imported from Brazil by Stoeger.

Price: **$699.00**

STOEGER/IGA CONDOR I OVER/UNDER SHOTGUN

Gauge: 12, 20, 3" chambers.
Barrel: 26" (Imp. Cyl. & Mod. choke tubes), 28" (Mod. & Full choke tubes).
Weight: 6-3/4 to 7 lbs.
Stock: 14-1/2"x1-1/2"x2-1/2". Oil-finished hardwood with checkered pistol grip and forend.
Features: Manual safety, single trigger, extractors only, ventilated top rib. Introduced 1983. Imported from Brazil by Stoeger Industries.
Price: With choke tubes **$559.00**
Price: Condor Supreme (same as Condor I with single trigger, choke tubes, but with auto. ejectors), 12- or 20-ga., 26", 28" **$629.00**

Stoeger/IGA Turkey Model O/U

Similar to the Condor I model except has Advantage camouflage on the barrels stock and forend. All exposed metal and recoil pad are matte black. Has 26" (Full & Full) barrels, single trigger, manual safety, 3" chambers. Introduced 1997. Imported from Brazil by Stoeger.

Price: **$729.00**

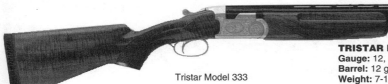

Stoeger/IGA Trap

TIKKA MODEL 512S FIELD GRADE OVER/UNDER

Gauge: 12, 20, 3" chambers.
Barrel: 26", 28", with stainless steel screw-in chokes (Imp. Cyl, Mod., Imp. Mod., Full); 20-ga., 28" only.
Weight: About 7-1/4 lbs.
Stock: American walnut. Standard dimensions—13-9/10"x1-1/2"x2-2/5". Checkered pistol grip and forend.

Stoeger/IGA Trap Model O/U

Similar to the Condor I except 30" barrels with Imp. Mod. & Full choke tubes, single selective trigger, automatic ejectors. Introduced 1998. Imported from Brazil by Stoeger Industries.

Price: **$699.00**

Features: Free interchangeability of barrels, stocks and forends into double rifle model, combination gun, etc. Barrel selector in trigger; auto. top tang safety; barrel cocking indicators. Introduced 1980. Imported from Italy by Stoeger.
Price: Model 512S (ejectors), Field Grade **$1,325.00**
Price: Model 512S Sporting Clays, 12-ga., 28", choke tubes **$1,360.00**

Tristar Model 333

Tristar Model 330 Over/Under

Similar to the Model 333 except has standard grade walnut, etched engraving, fixed chokes, extractors only. Introduced 1996. Imported from Turkey by Tristar Sporting Arms, Ltd.
Price: **$579.00**
Price: Model 330D (as above except with three choke tubes, ejectors) **$709.00**

Tristar Model 333SCL Over/Under

Same as the Model 333SC except has special stock dimensions for female shooters: 13-1/2x1-1/2"x3"x1/4". Introduced 1996. Imported from Turkey by Tristar Sporting Arms, Ltd.
Price: **$899.95**

TRISTAR MODEL 333 OVER/UNDER

Gauge: 12, 20, 3" chambers.
Barrel: 12 ga.—26", 28", 30"; 20 ga.—26", 28"; five choke tubes.
Weight: 7-1/2-7-3/4 lbs. **Length:** 45" overall.
Stock: Hand-checkered fancy grade Turkish walnut; full pistol grip, semi-beavertail forend; black recoil pad.
Features: Boxlock action with slivered, hand-engraved receiver; automatic selective ejectors, mechanical single selective trigger; stainless steel firing pins; auto safety; hard chrome bores. Introduced 1995. Imported from Turkey by Tristar Sporting Arms, Ltd.
Price: **$799.95**

Tristar Model 333SC Over/Under

Same as the Model 333 except has 11mm rib with target sight beads, elongated forcing cones, ported barrels, stainless extended Sporting choke tubes (Skeet, Imp. Cyl., Imp. Cyl., Mod.), Sporting Clays recoil pad. Introduced 1996. Imported from Turkey by Tristar Sporting Arms, Ltd.
Price: **$899.95**

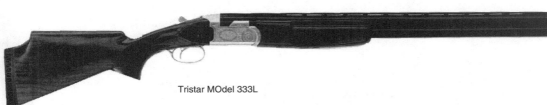

Tristar MOdel 333L

Tristar Model 300 Over/Under

Similar to the Model 333 except has standard grade walnut, extractors, etched frame, double triggers, manual safety, plastic buttplate. Available in 12-ga. only with 26" (Imp. Cyl. & Mod.) or 28" (Mod. & Full) barrels. Introduced 1996. Imported from Turkey by Tristar Sporting Arms, Ltd.
Price: **$429.95**

Tristar Model 333L Over/Under

Same as the Model 333 except has special stock dimensions for female shooters: 13-1/2x1-1/2"x3"x1/4". Available in 12-ga. with 26", 28" or 20 ga. 26", with five choke tubes. Introduced 1996. Imported from Turkey by Tristar Sporting Arms, Ltd.
Price: **$799.95**

Tristar Nova SC

Tristar Nova L "Emillio Rizzinni" Over/Under

Similar to the Nova SC except 12- or 20-ga., 2-3/4" chambers, and has stock dimensions designed for female shooters (1-1/2" x 3" x 13-1/2"). Standard grade walnut. Introduced 1998. Imported from Italy by Tristar Sporting Arms, Ltd.

Price:..$869.00

TRISTAR NOVA SC "EMILLIO RIZZINI" OVER/UNDER

Gauge: 12, 2-3/4" chambers.
Barrel: 28", 30" (Imp. Cyl., Mod., Full choke tubes).
Weight: 7-1/2-8 lbs. **Length:** 46" overall (28" barrel).
Stock: 1-1/2" x 2-3/8" x 14-3/8". Semi-fancy walnut; pistol grip with palm swell; semi-beavertail forend; black Sporting Clays recoil pad.
Features: Silvered boxlock action with Four Locks locking system, auto ejectors, single selective (inertia) trigger, auto safety. Hard chrome bores. Vent. 10mm rib with target-style front and mid-rib beads, vent. spacer rib. Introduced 1998. Imported from Italy by Tristar Sporting Arms, Ltd.

Price:..$869.00

Tristar Nova I

Consult our Directory pages for the location of firms mentioned.

TRISTAR NOVA I, II "EMILLIO RIZZINI" OVER/UNDERS

Gauge: 12, 20, 3" chambers.
Barrel: 12-ga., 26" (Imp. Cyl. & Mod.), 28" (Mod. & Full); 20-ga., 26" (Imp. Cyl. & Mod.), fixed chokes.
Weight: 7-1/2 lbs.
Stock: 1-1/2" x 2-3/8" x 14-3/8". Walnut with palm swell pistol grip, hand checkering, semi-beavertail forend, black recoil pad.
Features: Boxlock action with blued finish, Four Locks locking system, gold single selective (inertia) trigger system, automatic safety, extractors. Introduced 1998. Imported from Italy by Tristar Sporting Arms, Ltd.

Price: Nova I $587.00
Price: Nova II (automatic ejectors, choke tubes)................$779.00

Tristar Nova MAG

Tristar Nova MAG "Emillio Rizzini" Over/Under

Similar to the Nova I except 12-gauge, 3-1/2" chambers; choke tubes; 24" or 28" barrels with three choke tubes; extractors; auto safety. Matte blue finish on all metal, non-reflective wood finish. Introduced 1998. Imported from Italy by Tristar Sporting Arms, Ltd.

Price:..$669.00

Weatherby Athena Grade V Classic

WEATHERBY ATHENA GRADE IV O/U SHOTGUNS

Gauge: 12, 20, 3" chambers.
Action: Boxlock (simulated sidelock) top lever break-open. Selective auto ejectors, single selective trigger (selector inside trigger guard).
Barrel: 26", 28", IMC Multi-Choke tubes.
Weight: 12-ga., 7-3/8 lbs.; 20-ga. 6-7/8 lbs.
Stock: American walnut, checkered pistol grip and forend (14-1/4"x1-1/2"x2-1/2").
Features: Mechanically operated trigger. Top tang safety, Greener cross bolt, fully engraved receiver, recoil pad installed. IMC models furnished with three interchangeable flush-fitting choke tubes. Imported from Japan by Weatherby. Introduced 1982.
Price: 12-ga., IMC, 26", 28"..............................$2,259.00
Price: 20-ga., IMC, 26", 28"..............................$2,259.00

Weatherby Athena Grade V Classic Field O/U

Similar to the Athena Grade IV except has rounded pistol grip, slender forend, oil-finished Claro walnut stock with fine-line checkering, Old English recoil pad. Sideplate receiver has rose and scroll engraving. Available in 12-gauge, 26", 28", 20-gauge, 26", all with 3" chambers. Introduced 1993.

Price:.. $2,599.00

WEATHERBY ORION GRADE III FIELD O/U SHOTGUNS

Gauge: 12, 20, 3" chambers.
Barrel: 26", 28", IMC Mulit-Choke tubes.
Weight: 6-1/2 to 9 lbs.
Stock: 14-1/4"x1-1/2"x2-1/2". American walnut, checkered grip and forend. Rubber recoil pad.
Features: Selective automatic ejectors, single selective inertia trigger. Top tang safety, Greener cross bolt. Has silver-gray receiver with engraving and gold duck/pheasant. Imported from Japan by Weatherby.
Price: Orion III, Field, 12, IMC, 26", 28" $1,699.00
Price: Orion III, Field, 20, IMC, 26", 28" $1,699.00

Weatherby Orion Grade III Classic Field O/U

Similar to the Orion III Field except the stock has a rounded pistol grip, satin oil finish, slender forend, Old English recoil pad. Introduced 1993. Imported from Japan by Weatherby.

Price:.. $1,699.00

Weatherby Orion Grade I Field O/U

Similar to the Orion Grade III Field except has blued receiver with engraving, and the bird is not gold. Available in 12-gauge, 26", 28", 30", 20-gauge, 20", 28", both with 3" chambers and IMC choke tubes. Imported from Japan by Weatherby.

Price:.. $1,329.00

WEATHERBY ORION SSC OVER/UNDER SHOTGUN

Gauge: 12, 3" chambers.
Barrel: 28", 30", 32" (Skeet, SC1, Imp. Cyl., SC2, Mod. IMC choke tubes).
Weight: About 8 lbs.
Stock: 14-3/4"x2-1/4"x1-1/2". Claro walnut with satin oil finish; schnabel forend tip; Sporter-style pistol grip; Pachmayr Decelerator recoil pad.
Features: Designed for Sporting Clays competition. Has lengthened forcing cones and backboring; ported barrels with 12mm grooved rib with mid-bead sight; mechanical trigger is adjustable for length of pull. Introduced 1998. Imported from Japan by Weatherby.

Price:.. $1,749.00

Weatherby Orion II Classic Field

Weatherby Orion Grade II Classic Field O/U
Similar to the Orion III Classic Field except stock has high-gloss finish, and the bird on the receiver is not gold. Available in 12-gauge, 26", 28", 30" barrels, 20-gauge, 26" 28", both with 3" chambers, 28-gauge, 26", 2-3/4" chambers. All have IMC choke tubes. Imported from Japan by Weatherby.
Price: $1,399.00

Weatherby Orion Grade II Sporting Clays
Similar to the Orion II Classic Sporting except has traditional pistol grip with diamond inlay, and standard full-size forend. Available in 12-gauge only, 28", 30" barrels with Skeet, Imp. Cyl., SC2, Mod. Has lengthened forcing cones, backboring, stepped competition rib, radius heel recoil pad, hand-engraved, silver/nitride receiver. Introduced 1992. Imported by Weatherby.
Price: $1,499.00

Weatherby Orion II Classic Sporting

Weatherby Orion Grade II Classic Sporting O/U
Similar to the Orion II Classic Field except in 12 gauge only with (3" chambers), 28", 30" barrels with Skeet, SC1, SC2 Imp. Cyl., Mod. chokes. Weighs 7.5-8 lbs. Competition center vent rib; middle barrel and enlarged front beads. Rounded grip; high gloss stock. Radiused heel recoil pad. Receiver finished in silver nitride with acid-etched, gold-plate clay pigeon monogram. Barrels have lengthened forcing cones. Introduced 1993. Imported by Weatherby.
Price: $1,499.00

Weatherby Orion III English Field O/U
Similar to the Orion III Classic Field except has straight grip English-style stock. Available in 12-gauge (28"), 20-gauge (26", 28") with IMC Multi-Choke tubes. Silver/gray nitride receiver is engraved and has gold-plate overlay. Introduced 1997. Imported from Japan by Weatherby.
Price: $1,699.00

Variety of models for utility and sporting use, including some competitive shooting.

American Arms Brittany

AMERICAN ARMS BRITTANY SHOTGUN
Gauge: 12, 20, 3" chambers.
Barrel: 12-ga.—27"; 20-ga.—25" (Imp. Cyl., Mod., Full choke tubes).
Weight: 6 lbs., 7 oz. (20-ga.).
Stock: 14-1/8"x1-3/8"x2-3/8". Hand-checkered walnut with oil finish, straight English-style with semi-beavertail forend.
Features: Boxlock action with case-color finish, engraving; single selective trigger, automatic selective ejectors; rubber recoil pad. Introduced 1989. Imported from Spain by American Arms, Inc.
Price: $885.00

AMERICAN ARMS TS/SS 12 DOUBLE
Gauge: 12, 3-1/2" chambers.
Barrel: 26", choke tubes; solid raised rib.
Weight: 7 lbs., 6 oz.
Stock: Walnut; cut-checked grip and forend.
Features: Non-reflective metal and wood finishes; boxlock action; single trigger; extractors. Imported by American Arms, Inc.
Price: $799.00

AMERICAN ARMS WT/SS 10 DOUBLE
Gauge: 10, 3-1/2" chambers.
Barrel: 28", choke tubes.
Weight: 10 lbs., 3 oz. **Length:** 45" overall.
Stock: 14-1/4"x1-1/8"x2-3/8".
Features: Boxlock action with extractors; single selective trigger; non-reflective wood and metal finishes. Imported by American Arms, Inc.
Price: $860.00

AMERICAN ARMS GENTRY DOUBLE SHOTGUN
Gauge: 12, 20, 410, 3" chambers; 28 ga. 2-3/4" chambers.
Barrel: 26" (Imp. Cyl. & Mod., all gauges), 28" (Mod., & Full, 12 and 20 gauges).
Weight: 6-1/4 to 6-3/4 lbs.
Stock: 14-1/8"x1-3/8"x2-3/8". Hand-checkered walnut with semi-gloss finish.
Sights: Metal bead front.
Features: Boxlock action with English-style scroll engraving, color case-hardened finish. Double triggers, extractors. Independent floating firing pins. Manual safety. Five-year warranty. Introduced 1987. Imported from Spain by American Arms, Inc.
Price: 12 or 20 . . . . $750.00
Price: 28 or 410 . . . . $795.00

ARRIETA SIDELOCK DOUBLE SHOTGUNS
Gauge: 12, 16, 20, 28, 410.
Barrel: Length and chokes to customer specs.
Weight: To customer specs.
Stock: 14-1/2"x1-1/2"x2-1/2 (standard dimensions), or to customer specs. Straight English with checkered butt (standard), or pistol grip. Select European walnut with oil finish.
Features: Essentially a custom gun with myriad options. Holland & Holland-pattern hand-detachable sidelocks, selective automatic ejectors, double triggers (hinged front) standard. Some have self-opening action. Finish and engraving to customer specs. Imported from Spain by Wingshooting Adventures.
Price: Model 557, auto ejectors, from $2,750.00
Price: Model 570, auto ejectors, from $3,380.00
Price: Model 578, auto ejectors, from $3,740.00
Price: Model 600 Imperial, self-opening, from $4,990.00
Price: Model 601 Imperial Tiro, self-opening, from $5,750.00
Price: Model 801, from $7,950.00
Price: Model 802, from $7,950.00
Price: Model 803, from $5,850.00
Price: Model 871, auto ejectors, from $4,290.00
Price: Model 872, self-opening, from $9,790.00
Price: Model 873, self-opening, from $6,850.00
Price: Model 874, self-opening, from $7,950.00
Price: Model 875, self-opening, from $12,950.00

Beretta Model 470 Silver Hawk

BERETTA MODEL 452 SIDELOCK SHOTGUN
Gauge: 12, 2-3/4" or 3" chambers.
Barrel: 26", 28", 30", choked to customer specs.
Weight: 6 lbs., 13 oz.
Stock: Dimensions to customer specs. Highly figured walnut; Model 452 EELL has walnut briar.
Features: Full sidelock action with English-type double bolting; automatic selective ejectors, manual safety; double triggers, single or single non-selective trigger on request. Essentially custom made to specifications. Model 452 is coin finished without engraving; 452 EELL is fully engraved. Imported from Italy by Beretta U.S.A.
Price: 452 .... **$31,500.00**
Price: 452 EELL **$43,500.00**

BERETTA MODEL 470 SILVER HAWK SHOTGUN
Gauge: 12, 20, 3" chambers.
Barrel: 26" (Imp. Cyl. & Imp. Mod.), 28" (Mod. & Full).
Weight: 5.9 lbs. (20-gauge).
Stock: Select European walnut, straight English grip.
Features: Boxlock action with single selective trigger; selector provides automatic ejection or extraction; silver-chrome action and forend iron with fine engraving; top lever highlighted with gold inlaid hawk's head. Comes with ABS case. Introduced 1997. Imported from Italy by Beretta U.S.A.
Price: **$3,210.00**

Charles Daly Field Hunter

CHARLES DALY FIELD HUNTER DOUBLE SHOTGUN
Gauge: 10, 12, 20, 28, 410 (3" chambers; 28 has 2-3/4").
Barrel: 32" (Mod. & Mod.), 28, 30" (Mod. & Full), 26" (Imp. Cyl. & Mod.) 410 (Full & Full).
Weight: 6 lbs. to 11.4 lbs.
Stock: Checkered walnut pistol grip and forend.
Features: Silvered, engraved receiver; gold single selective trigger in 10-, 12-, and 20-ga.; double triggers in 28 and 410; automatic safety; extractors; gold bead front sight. Introduced 1997. Imported from Spain by K.B.I., Inc.
Price: 10-ga. **$919.00**
Price: 12- or 20-ga. **$749.00**
Price: 28-ga. **$799.00**
Price: 410-bore **$799.00**
Price: Field Hunter AE-MC (choke tubes, 10 ga.) **$1,019.00**
Price: As above, 12 or 20 .... **$879.00**

CHARLES DALY SUPERIOR HUNTER DOUBLE SHOTGUN
Gauge: 12, 20, 3" chambers.
Barrel: 28" (Mod. & Full) 26" (Imp. Cyl. & Mod.).
Weight: About 7 lbs.
Stock: Checkered walnut pistol grip buttstock, splinter forend.
Features: Silvered, engraved receiver; chrome-lined barrels; gold single trigger; automatic safety; extractors; gold bead front sight. Introduced 1997. Imported from Italy by K.B.I., Inc.
Price: **$929.00**

Charles Daly Empire Hunter Double Shotgun
Similar to the Superior Hunter except has deluxe wood, game scene engraving, automatic ejectors. Introduced 1997. Imported from Italy by K.B.I., Inc.
Price: 12 or 20 .... **$1,259.00**

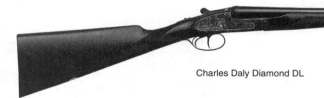

Charles Daly Diamond DL

CHARLES DALY DIAMOND DL DOUBLE SHOTGUN
Gauge: 12, 20, 410, 3" chambers, 28, 2-3/4" chambers.
Barrel: 28" (Mod. & Full), 26" (Imp. Cyl. & Mod.), 26" (Full & Full, 410).
Weight: About 5-7 lbs.
Stock: Select fancy European walnut, English-style butt, beavertail forend; hand-checkered, hand-rubbed oil finish.
Features: Drop-forged action with gas escape valves; demiblock barrels with concave rib; selective automatic-ejectors; hand-detachable double safety sidelocks with hand-engraved rose and scrollwork. Hinged front trigger. Color-case-hardened receiver. Introduced 1997. Imported from Spain by K.B.I., Inc.
Price: 12 or 20 .... **$5,599.00**
Price: 28 .... **$6,079.00**
Price: 410 .... **$6,079.00**

CHARLES DALY DIAMOND REGENT DL DOUBLE SHOTGUN
Gauge: 12, 20, 410, 3" chambers, 28, 2-3/4" chambers.
Barrel: 28" (Mod. & Full), 26" (Imp. Cyl. & Mod.), 26" (Full & Full, 410).
Weight: About 5-7 lbs.
Stock: Special select fancy European walnut, English-style butt, splinter forend; hand-checkered; hand-rubbed oil finish.
Features: Drop-forged action with gas escape valves; demiblock barrels of chrome-nickel steel with concave rib; selective automatic-ejectors; hand-detachable, double-safety H&H sidelocks with demi-relief hand engraving; H&H pattern easy-opening feature; hinged trigger; coin finished action. Introduced 1997. Imported from Spain by K.B.I., Inc.
Price: 12 or 20 .... **$19,999.00**
Price: 28 .... **$20,499.00**
Price: 410 .... **$20,499.00**

Fabarm Classic Lion

FABARM CLASSIC LION DOUBLE SHOTGUN
Gauge: 12, 3" chambers.
Barrel: 26" (Cyl., Imp. Cyl., Mod., Imp. Mod., Full choke tubes).
Weight: 7.2 lbs. **Length:** 47.6" overall.
Stock: Oil-finished European walnut.
Features: Boxlock action with single selective trigger, automatic ejectors, automatic safety. Introduced 1998. Imported from Italy by Heckler & Koch, Inc.
Price: Grade I **$1,488.00**
Price: Grade II (sidelock action) **$2,110.00**

A.H. Fox DE Grade

A.H. FOX SIDE-BY-SIDE SHOTGUNS
Gauge: 16, 20, 28, 410.
Barrel: Length and chokes to customer specifications. Rust-blued Chromox or Krupp steel.
Weight: 5-1/2 to 6-3/4 lbs.
Stock: Dimensions to customer specifications. Hand-checkered Turkish Circassian walnut with hand-rubbed oil finish. Straight, semi- or full pistol grip; splinter, schnabel or beavertail forend; traditional pad, hard rubber buttplate or skeleton butt.

Features: Boxlock action with automatic ejectors; double or Fox single selective trigger. Scalloped, rebated and color case-hardened receiver; hand finished and hand-engraved. Grades differ in engraving, inlays, grade of wood, amount of hand finishing. Add $1,000 for 28 or 410-bore. Introduced 1993. Made in U.S. by Connecticut Shotgun Mfg.
Price: CE Grade **$9,500.00**
Price: XE Grade **$11,000.00**
Price: DE Grade **$13,500.00**
Price: FE Grade **$18,500.00**
Price: Exhibition Grade. **$26,000.000**
Price: 28/410 CE Grade **$8,200.00**
Price: 28/410 XE Grade **$9,700.00**
Price: 28/410 DE Grade **$13,800.00**
Price: 28/410 FE Grade **$14,700.00**
Price: 28/410 Exhibition Grade. **$26,000.00**

Garbi Model 100

Garbi Model 101 Side-by-Side
Similar to the Garbi Model 100 except is hand engraved with scroll engraving, select walnut stock. Better overall quality than the Model 100. Imported from Spain by Wm. Larkin Moore.
Price: From **$5,550.00**

Garbi Model 103A, B Side-by-Side
Similar to the Garbi Model 100 except has Purdey-type fine scroll and rosette engraving. Better overall quality than the Model 101. Model 103B has nickel-chrome steel barrels, H&H-type easy opening mechanism; other mechanical details remain the same. Imported from Spain by Wm. Larkin Moore.
Price: Model 103A, from **$6,850.00**
Price: Model 103B, from **$9,750.00**

GARBI MODEL 100 DOUBLE
Gauge: 12, 16, 20, 28.
Barrel: 26", 28", choked to customer specs.
Weight: 5-1/2 to 7-1/2 lbs.
Stock: 14-1/2"x2-1/4"x1-1/2". European walnut. Straight grip, checkered butt, classic forend.
Features: Sidelock action, automatic ejectors, double triggers standard. Color case-hardened action, coin finish optional. Single trigger; beavertail forend, etc. optional. Five other models are available. Imported from Spain by Wm. Larkin Moore.
Price: From. **$4,300.00**

Garbi Model 200 Side-by-Side
Similar to the Garbi Model 100 except has heavy-duty locks, magnum proofed. Very fine Continental-style floral and scroll engraving, well figured walnut stock. Other mechanical features remain the same. Imported from Spain by Wm. Larkin Moore.
Price: **$9,350.00**

Bill Hanus Birdgun

IAR COWBOY SHOTGUNS
Gauge: 12.
Barrel: 20", 28".
Weight: 7 lbs. (20" barrel). **Length:** 36-7/8" overall (20" barrel).
Stock: Walnut.
Features: Exposed hammers; blued or brown barrels; double triggers. Introduced 1997. Imported from Italy by IAR, Inc.
Price: Gentry model, 20" or 28", engraved, bright-finished locks, blue barrels
. . . . **$1,895.00**
Price: Cowboy model, 20" or 28", no engraving on color case-hardened locks, brown patina barrels **$1,895.00**

BILL HANUS BIRDGUN
Gauge: 16, 20, 28.
Barrel: 27", 20- and 28-ga.; 28", 16-ga. (Skeet 1 & Skeet 2).
Weight: 5 lbs., 4 oz. to 6 lbs., 4 oz.
Stock: 14-3/8"x1-1/2"x2-3/8", with 1/4" cast-off. Select walnut.
Features: Boxlock action with ejectors; splinter forend, straight English grip; checkered butt; English leather-covered handguard included. Made by AYA. Introduced 1998. Imported from Spain by Bill Hanus Birdguns.
Price: **$1,895.00**

> Consult our Directory pages for
> the location of firms mentioned.

Merkel Model 47E

Merkel Model 47SL, 147SL Side-by-Sides
Similar to the Model 122 except with Holland & Holland-style sidelock action with cocking indicators, ejectors. Silver-grayed receiver and sideplates have Arabesque engraving, engraved border and screws (Model 47S), or fine hunting scene engraving (Model 147S). Imported from Germany by GSI.
Price: Model 47SL **$5,295.00**
Price: Model 147SL **$6,695.00**
Price: Model 247SL (English-style engraving, large scrolls) **$6,995.00**
Price: Model 447SL (English-style engraving, small scrolls) **$8,995.00**

MERKEL MODEL, 47E SIDE-BY-SIDE SHOTGUNS
Gauge: 12, 3" chambers, 16, 2-3/4" chambers, 20, 3" chambers.
Barrel: 12-, 16-ga.—28"; 20-ga.—26-3/4" (Imp. Cyl. & Mod., Mod. & Full).
Weight: About 6-3/4 lbs. (12-ga.).
Stock: Oil-finished walnut; straight English or pistol grip.
Features: Anson & Deeley-type boxlock action with single selective or double triggers, automatic safety, cocking indicators. Color case-hardened receiver with standard Arabesque engraving. Imported from Germany by GSI.
Price: Model 47E (H&H ejectors) **$2,695.00**
Price: Model 147 (extractors, silver-grayed receiver with hunting scenes) **$2,995.00**
Price: Model 147E (as above with ejectors) **$3,195.00**
Price: Model 122 (as above with false sideplates, fine engraving)
. . . . **$4,995.00**

Piotti King No. 1

PIOTTI KING NO. 1 SIDE-BY-SIDE
Gauge: 12, 16, 20, 28, 410.
Barrel: 25" to 30" (12-ga.), 25" to 28" (16, 20, 28, 410). To customer specs. Chokes as specified.
Weight: 6-1/2 lbs. to 8 lbs. (12-ga. to customer specs.).
Stock: Dimensions to customer specs. Finely figured walnut; straight grip with checkered butt with classic splinter forend and hand-rubbed oil finish standard. Pistol grip, beavertail forend, satin luster finish optional.
Features: Holland & Holland pattern sidelock action, automatic ejectors. Double trigger with front trigger hinged standard; non-selective single trigger optional. Coin finish standard; color case-hardened optional. Top rib; level, file-cut standard; concave, ventilated optional. Very fine, full coverage scroll engraving with small floral bouquets, gold crown in top lever, name in gold, and gold crest in forend. Imported from Italy by Wm. Larkin Moore.
Price: From $22,500.00

Rizzini Sidelock

PIOTTI PIUMA SIDE-BY-SIDE
Gauge: 12, 16, 20, 28, 410.
Barrel: 25" to 30" (12-ga.), 25" to 28" (16, 20, 28, 410).
Weight: 5-1/2 to 6-1/4 lbs. (20-ga.).
Stock: Dimensions to customer specs. Straight grip stock with walnut checkered butt, classic splinter forend, hand-rubbed oil finish are standard; pistol grip, beavertail forend, satin luster finish optional.
Features: Anson & Deeley boxlock ejector double with chopper lump barrels. Level, file-cut rib, light scroll and rosette engraving, scalloped frame. Double triggers with hinged front standard, single non-selective optional. Coin finish standard, color case-hardened optional. Imported from Italy by Wm. Larkin Moore.
Price: From $12,900.00

SKB Model 385

SKB Model 385 Sporting Clays
Similar to the Field Model 385 except 12-gauge only; 28" barrel with choke tubes; raised ventilated rib with metal middle bead and white front. Stock dimensions 14-1/4"x1-7/16"x1-7/8". Introduced 1998. Imported from Japan by G.U. Inc.
Price: $1,899.00

PARKER REPRODUCTIONS SIDE-BY-SIDE SHOTGUN
Gauge: 12, 16/20 combo, 20, 28, 2-3/4" and 3" chambers.
Barrel: 26" (Skeet 1 & 2, Imp. Cyl. & Mod.), 28" (Mod. & Full, 2-3/4" and 3", 12, 20, 28; Skeet 1 & 2, Imp. Cyl. & Mod., Mod. & Full 16-ga. only).
Weight: 6-3/4 lbs. (12-ga.)
Stock: Checkered (26 lpi) AAA fancy California English or Claro walnut, skeleton steel and checkered butt. Straight or pistol grip, splinter or beavertail forend.
Features: Exact reproduction of the original Parker—parts interchange. Double or single selective trigger, selective ejectors, hard-chromed bores, designed for steel shot. One, two or three (16-20, 20) barrel sets available. Hand-engraved snap caps included. Introduced 1984. Made by Winchester. Imported from Japan by Parker Division, Reagent Chemical.
Price: D Grade, one-barrel set. $3,370.00
Price: Two-barrel set, same gauge $4,200.00
Price: Two-barrel set, 16/20 . . . . $4,870.00
Price: Three-barrel set, 16/20/20. . . . . $5,630.00
Price: A-1 Special two-barrel set. $11,200.00
Price: A-1 Special three-barrel set. $13,200.00

Piotti King Extra Side-by-Side
Similar to the Piotti King No. 1 except highest quality wood and metal work. Choice of either bulino game scene engraving or game scene engraving with gold inlays. Engraved and signed by a master engraver. Exhibition grade wood. Other mechanical specifications remain the same. Imported from Italy by Wm. Larkin Moore.
Price: From $28,200.00

Piotti Lunik Side-by-Side
Similar to the Piotti King No. 1 except better overall quality. Has Renaissance-style large scroll engraving in relief, gold crown in top lever, gold name and gold crest in forend. Best quality Holland & Holland-pattern sidelock ejector double with chopper lump (demi-bloc) barrels. Other mechanical specifications remain the same. Imported from Italy by Wm. Larkin Moore.
Price: From $24,400.00

RIZZINI SIDELOCK SIDE-BY-SIDE
Gauge: 12, 16, 20, 28, 410.
Barrel: 25" to 30" (12-, 16-, 20-ga.), 25" to 28" (28, 410). To customer specs. Chokes as specified.
Weight: 6-1/2 lbs. to 8 lbs. (12-ga. to customer specs).
Stock: Dimensions to customer specs. Finely figured walnut; straight grip with checkered butt with classic splinter forend and hand-rubbed oil finish standard. Pistol grip, beavertail forend, satin luster finish optional.
Features: Holland & Holland pattern sidelock action, auto ejectors. Double triggers with front trigger hinged optional; non-selective single trigger standard. Coin finish standard. Top rib level, file cut standard; concave optional. Imported from Italy by Wm. Larkin Moore.
Price: 12-, 20-ga., from $45,000.00
Price: 28, 410 bore, from. $50,000.00

SKB MODEL 385 SIDE-BY-SIDE
Gauge: 12, 20, 3" chambers; 28, 2-3/4" chambers.
Barrel: 26" (Imp. Cyl., Mod., Skeet choke tubes).
Weight: 6-3/4 lbs. **Length:** 42-1/2" overall.
Stock: 14-1/8"x1-1/2"x2-1/2" American walnut with straight or pistol grip stock, semi-beavertail forend.
Features: Boxlock action. Silver nitrided receiver with engraving; solid barrel rib; single selective trigger, selective automatic ejectors, automatic safety. Introduced 1996. Imported from Japan by G.U. Inc.
Price: $1,769.00
Price: Field Set, 20-, 28-ga., 26", English or pistol grip $2,499.00

SKB Model 485 Side-by-Side
Similar to the Model 385 except has dummy sideplates, extensive upland game scene engraving, semi-fancy American walnut English or pistol grip stock. Imported from Japan by G.U. Inc.
Price: $2,369.00

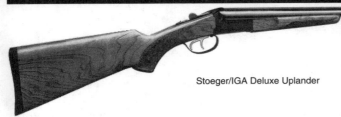

Stoeger/IGA Deluxe Uplander

Stoeger/IGA Deluxe Uplander Shotgun
Similar to the Uplander except with semi-fancy American walnut with thin black Pachmayr rubber recoil pad, matte lacquer finish. Choke tubes and 3" chambers standard 12- and 20-gauge; 28-gauge has 26", 3" chokes, fixed Mod. & Full. Double gold plated triggers; extractors. Introduced 1997. Imported from Brazil by Stoeger.
Price: 12, 20 . . . . **$559.00**
Price: 28, 410 . . . . **$519.00**

Stoeger/IGA English Stock Side-by-Side
Similar to the Uplander except in 410-bore only with 24" barrels (Mod. & Mod.), straight English stock and beavertail forend. Has automatic safety, extractors, double triggers. Intro 1996. Imported from Brazil by Stoeger.
Price: **$424.00**

STOEGER/IGA UPLANDER SIDE-BY-SIDE SHOTGUN
Gauge: 12, 20, 28, 2-3/4" chambers; 410, 3" chambers.
Barrel: 26" (Full & Full, 410 only, Imp. Cyl. & Mod.), 28" (Mod. & Full).
Weight: 6-3/4 to 7 lbs.
Stock: 14-1/2"x1-1/2"x2-1/2". Oil-finished hardwood. Checkered pistol grip and forend.
Features: Automatic safety, extractors only, solid matted barrel rib. Double triggers only. Introduced 1983. Imported from Brazil by Stoeger Industries.
Price: **$424.00**
Price: With choke tubes **$464.00**
Price: Coach Gun, 12, 20, 410, 20" bbls **$409.00**
Price: Coach Gun, nickel finish, black stock **$464.00**
Price: Coach Gun, engraved stock **$479.00**

Stoeger/IGA Ladies Side-by-Side
Similar to the Uplander except in 20-ga. only with 24" barrels (Imp. Cyl. & Mod. choke tubes), 13" length of pull, ventilated rubber recoil pad. Has extractors, double triggers, automatic safety. Introduced 1996. Imported from Brazil by Stoeger.
Price: **$478.00**

Stoeger/IGA Turkey

Stoeger/IGA Youth Side-by-Side
Similar to the Uplander except in 410-bore with 24" barrels (Mod. & Full), 13" length of pull, ventilated recoil pad. Has double triggers, extractors, auto safety. Intro 1996. Imported from Brazil by Stoeger.
Price: **$438.00**

Stoeger/IGA Turkey Side-by-Side
Similar to the Uplander Model except has Advantage camouflage on stock, forend and barrels; 12-gauge only with 3" chambers, and has 24" choke tube barrels. Overall length 40". Introduced 1997. Imported from Brazil by Stoeger.
Price: **$559.00**

Stoeger/IGA Deluxe Coach Gun
Similar to the Uplander except 12- or 20-gauge, 20" barrels, choked Imp. Cyl. & Mod., 3" chambers; select semi-fancy American walnut pistol grip stock with checkering; double triggers; extractors. Introduced 1997. Imported form Brazil by Stoeger.
Price:

Tristar Model 411

TRISTAR MODEL 311 DOUBLE
Gauge: 12, 20, 3" chambers.
Barrel: 26", 28", five choke tubes.
Weight: About 7 lbs.
Stock: 14-3/8"x1-3/8"x2-3/8"x3/8"; hand-checkered Turkish walnut; recoil pad.
Features: Boxlock action; underlug and Greener bolt lockup; extractors, manual safety, double triggers. Black chrome finish. Introduced 1996. Imported from Turkey by Tristar Sporting Arms, Ltd.
Price: **$599.00**
Price: Model 311R (20" Cyl. & Cyl. barrels) **$429.00**

TRISTAR MODEL 411 SIDE-BY-SIDE
Gauge: 12, 20, 410, 3" chambers; 28, 2-3/4".
Barrel: 12-ga., 26", 28"; 20-, 28-ga., 410-bore, 26"; 12- and 20-ga. have three choke tubes, 28 (Imp. Cyl. & Mod.), 410 (Mod. & Full) fixed chokes.
Weight: 6-6-3/4 lbs.
Stock: 14-3/8" l.o.p. Standard walnut with pistol grip, splinter-style forend; hand checkered; black recoil pad.
Features: Engraved, color case-hardened boxlock action; double triggers, extractors; solid barrel rib. Introduced 1998. Imported from Italy by Tristar Sporting Arms, Ltd.
Price: **$749.00**

SHOTGUNS—BOLT ACTIONS & SINGLE SHOTS

Variety of designs for utility and sporting purposes, as well as for competitive shooting.

CONSULT
SHOOTER'S MARKETPLACE
Page 225, This Issue

BRNO ZBK 100 SINGLE BARREL SHOTGUN
Gauge: 12 or 20.
Barrel: 27.5".
Weight: 5.5 lbs. Length: 44" overall.
Stock: Beech.
Features: Polished blue finish; sling swivels. Announced 1998. Imported from The Czech Republic by Euro-Imports.
Price: **$185.00**

Browning A-Bolt Stalker

BROWNING A-BOLT SHOTGUN
Gauge: 12, 3" chamber, 2-shot detachable magazine.
Barrel: 22" (fully rifled), 23" (5" Invector choke tubes).
Weight: 7 lbs., 2 oz. **Length:** 44-3/4" overall.
Stock: 14"x5/8"x1/2". Walnut with satin finish on Hunter; Stalker has black graphite fiberglass composite. Swivel studs.

Sights: Blade front with red insert, open adjustable rear or none. Drilled and tapped for scope mounting.
Features: Uses same bolt system as A-Bolt rifle with 60 bolt throw; front-locking bolt with claw extractor; hinged floorplate. Matte finish on barrel and receiver. Introduced 1995. Imported by Browning.
Price: Hunter, rifled choke tube, open sights $828.95
Price: As above, no sights $804.95
Price: Hunter, rifled barrel, open sights $881.95
Price: As above, no sights $856.95
Price: Stalker, rifled, choke tube, open sights $744.95
Price: As above, no sights $719.95
Price: Stalker, rifled barrel, no sights $772.95

Browning BT-100 Trap

BROWNING BT-100 TRAP SHOTGUN
Gauge: 12, 2-3/4" chamber.
Barrel: 32", 34" (Invector Plus); back-bored; also with fixed Full choke.
Weight: 8 lbs., 9 oz. **Length:** 48-1/2" overall (32" barrel).
Stock: 14-3/8"x1-9/16"x1-7/16x2" (Monte Carlo); 14-3/8"x1-3/4"x1-1/4"x2-1/8" (thumbhole). Walnut with high gloss finish; cut checkering. Wedge-shaped forend with finger groove.

Features: Available in stainless steel or blue. Has drop-out trigger adjustable for weight of pull from 3-1/2 to 5-1/2 lbs., and for three length postions; Ejector-Selector allows ejection or extraction of shells. Available with adjustable comb stock and thumbhole style. Introduced 1995. Imported from Japan by Browning.
Price: Grade I, blue, Monte Carlo, Invector Plus $1,995.00
Price: As above, fixed Full choke $1,948.00
Price: With low-luster wood $1,587.00
Price: Stainless steel, Monte Carlo, Invector Plus $2,415.00
Price: As above, fixed Full choke $2,368.00
Price: Thumbhole stock, blue, Invector Plus $2,270.00
Price: Thumbhole stock, stainless, Invector Plus $2,690.00

H&R Model 928

Harrington & Richardson Model 928 Ultra Slug Hunter Deluxe
Similar to the SB2-980 Ultra Slug except uses 12-gauge action and 12-gauge barrel blank bored to 20-gauge, then fully rifled with 1:35" twist. Has hand-checkered camo laminate Monte Carlo stock and forend. Comes with Weaver-style scope base, offset hammer extension, ventilated recoil pad, sling swivels and camo nylon sling. Introduced 1997. Made in U.S. by H&R 1871 Inc.
Price: $239.95

HARRINGTON & RICHARDSON SB2-980 ULTRA SLUG
Gauge: 12, 20, 3" chamber.
Barrel: 22" (20 ga. Youth) 24", fully rifled.
Weight: 9 lbs. **Length:** NA.
Stock: Walnut-stained hardwood.
Sights: None furnished; comes with scope mount.
Features: Uses the H&R 10-gauge action with heavy-wall barrel. Monte Carlo stock has sling swivels; comes with black nylon sling. Introduced 1995. Made in U.S. by H&R 1871, Inc.
Price: $209.95

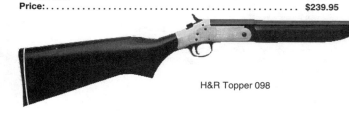

H&R Topper 098

HARRINGTON & RICHARDSON TOPPER MODEL 098
Gauge: 12, 16, 20, 28 (2-3/4"), 410, 3" chamber.
Barrel: 12 ga.—28" (Mod., Full); 16 ga.— 28" (Mod.); 20 ga.—26" (Mod.); 28 ga.—26" (Mod.); 410 bore—26" (Full).
Weight: 5-6 lbs.
Stock: Black-finish hardwood with full pistol grip; semi-beavertail forend.
Sights: Gold bead front.
Features: Break-open action with side-lever release, automatic ejector. Satin nickel frame, blued barrel. Reintroduced 1992. From H&R 1871, Inc.
Price: $114.95
Price: Topper Junior 098 (as above except 22" barrel, 20-ga. (Mod.), 410-bore (Full), 12-1/2" length of pull) $119.95

Harrington & Richardson Topper Deluxe Model 098
Similar to the standard Topper 098 except 12-gauge only with 3-1/2" chamber, 28" barrel with choke tube (comes with Mod. tube, others optional). Satin nickel frame, blued barrel, black-finished wood. Introduced 1992. From H&R 1871, Inc.
Price: $134.95

HARRINGTON & RICHARDSON TAMER SHOTGUN
Gauge: 410, 3" chamber.
Barrel: 19-1/2" (Full).
Weight: 5-6 lbs. **Length:** 33" overall.
Stock: Thumbhole grip of high density black polymer.
Features: Uses H&R Topper action with matte electroless nickel finish. Stock holds four spare shotshells. Introduced 1994. From H&R 1871, Inc.
Price: $124.95

Harrington & Richardson Topper Junior Classic Shotgun
Similar to the Topper Junior 098 except available in 20-gauge (3", Mod.), 410-bore (Full) with 3" chamber; 28-gauge, 2-3/4" chamber (Mod.); all have 22" barrel. Stock is American black walnut with cut-checkered pistol grip and forend. Ventilated rubber recoil pad with white line spacers. Blued barrel, blued frame. Introduced 1992. From H&R 1871, Inc.
Price: $144.95

Harrington & Richardson Topper Deluxe Rifled Slug Gun
Similar to the 12-gauge Topper Model 098 except has fully rifled and ported barrel, ramp front sight and fully adjustable rear. Barrel twist is 1:35". Nickel-plated frame, blued barrel, black-finished stock and forend. Introduced 1995. Made in U.S. by H&R 1871, Inc.
Price: $169.95

Krieghoff KS-5 Trap

KRIEGHOFF K-80 SINGLE BARREL TRAP GUN
Gauge: 12, 2-3/4" chamber.
Barrel: 32" or 34" Unsingle; 34" Top Single. Fixed Full or choke tubes.
Weight: About 8-3/4 lbs.
Stock: Four stock dimensions or adjustable stock available. All hand-checkered European walnut.
Features: Satin nickel finish with K-80 logo. Selective mechanical trigger adjustable for finger position. Tapered step vent. rib. Adjustable point of impact on Unsingle.
Price: Standard grade full Unsingle, from $7,950.00
Price: Standard grade full Top Single combo (special order), from
. . . . $9,975.00
Price: RT (removable trigger) option, add $1,000.00

KRIEGHOFF KS-5 TRAP GUN
Gauge: 12, 2-3/4" chamber.
Barrel: 32", 34"; Full choke or choke tubes.
Weight: About 8-1/2 lbs.
Stock: Choice of high Monte Carlo (1-1/2"), low Monte Carlo (1-3/8") or factory adjustable stock. European walnut.
Features: Ventilated tapered step rib. Adjustable trigger or optional release trigger. Satin gray electroless nickel receiver. Comes with fitted aluminum case. Introduced 1988. Imported from Germany by Krieghoff International, Inc.
Price: Fixed choke, cased $3,695.00
Price: With choke tubes $4,120.00

Krieghoff KS-5 Special
Same as the KS-5 except the barrel has a fully adjustable rib and adjustable stock. Rib allows shooter to adjust point of impact from 50%/50% to nearly 90%/10%. Introduced 1990.
Price: $4,695.00

Ljutic Mono Gun

Ljutic LTX Super Deluxe Mono Gun
Super Deluxe version of the standard Mono Gun with high quality wood, extra-fancy checkering pattern in 24 lpi, double recessed choking. Available in two weights: 8-1/4 lbs. or 8-3/4 lbs. Extra light 33" barrel; medium-height rib. Introduced 1984. From Ljutic Industries.
Price: $6,495.00
Price: With three screw-in choke tubes $6,895.00

LJUTIC MONO GUN SINGLE BARREL
Gauge: 12 only.
Barrel: 34", choked to customer specs; hollow-milled rib, 35-1/2" sight plane.
Weight: Approx. 9 lbs.
Stock: To customer specs. Oil finish, hand checkered.
Features: Totally custom made. Pull or release trigger; removable trigger guard contains trigger and hammer mechanism; Ljutic pushbutton opener on front of trigger guard. From Ljutic Industries.
Price: With standard, medium or Olympic rib, custom 32"-34" bbls., and fixed choke $5,495.00
Price: As above with screw-in choke barrel $5,795.00

Marlin Model 50DL

Marlin Model 50DL Bolt-Action Shotgun
Similar to the Model 55DL except has 28" barrel with Mod. choke. Weighs 7-1/2 lbs., measures 48-3/4" overall. Introduced 1997. Made in U.S. by Marlin Firearms Co.
Price: $326.00

MARLIN MODEL 512 SLUGMASTER SHOTGUN
Gauge: 12, 3" chamber; 2-shot detachable box magazine.
Barrel: 21", rifled (1:28" twist).
Weight: 8 lbs. **Length:** 44-3/4" overall.
Stock: Walnut-finished, press-checkered Maine birch with Mar-Shield® finish, ventilated recoil pad.
Sights: Ramp front with brass bead and removable Wide-Scanô hood, adjustable folding semi-buckhorn rear. Drilled and tapped for scope mounting.
Features: Uses Model 55 action with thumb safety. Designed for shooting saboted slugs. Comes with special Weaver scope mount. Introduced 1994. Made in U.S. by Marlin Firearms Co.
Price: $356.00

MARLIN MODEL 55GDL GOOSE GUN BOLT-ACTION SHOTGUN
Gauge: 12 only, 2-3/4" or 3" chamber.
Action: Bolt action, thumb safety, detachable two-shot clip. Red cocking indicator.
Barrel: 36" (Full) with burnished bore for lead or steel shot.
Weight: 8 lbs. **Length:** 56-3/4" overall.
Stock: Black fiberglass-filled synthetic with moulded-in checkering and swivel studs; ventilated recoil pad.
Sights: Brass bead front, U-groove rear.
Features: Brushed blue finish; thumb safety; red cocking indicator; 2-shot detachable box magazine. Introduced 1997. Made in U.S. by Marlin Firearms Co.
Price: $380.00

Marlin Model 512DL Slugmaster Shotgun
Similar to the Model 512 except has black fiberglass-filled synthetic stock with moulded-in checkering, swivel studs; ventilated recoil pad; padded black nylon sling. Has 21" fully rifled barrel with 1:28" rifling twist. Introduced 1997. Made in U.S. by Marlin Firearms Co.
Price: $372.00

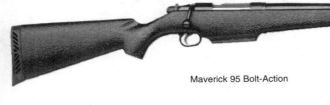

Maverick 95 Bolt-Action

MAVERICK MODEL 95 BOLT-ACTION SHOTGUN
Gauge: 12, 3" chamber, 2-shot magazine.
Barrel: 25" (Mod.).
Weight: 6.5 lbs.
Stock: Textured black synthetic.
Sights: Bead front.
Features: Full-length stock with integral magazine; ambidextrous rotating safety; twin extractors; rubber recoil pad. Blue finish. Introduced 1995. From Maverick Arms.
Price: $184.00

Mossberg Model 695 Shotgun

Mossberg Model 695 Turkey

Same as the Model 695 Slugster except has smoothbore 22" barrel with Extra-Full Turkey Accu-Choke tube, full OFM camouflage finish, fixed U-notch rear sight, bead front. Made in U.S. by Mossberg. Introduced 1996.
Price: **$286.00**

NEW ENGLAND FIREARMS STANDARD PARDNER

Gauge: 12, 20, 410, 3" chamber; 16, 28, 2-3/4" chamber.
Barrel: 12-ga.—28" (Full, Mod.), 32" (Full); 16-ga.—28" (Full), 32" (Full); 20-ga.—26" (Full, Mod.); 28-ga.—26" (Mod.); 410-bore—26" (Full).
Weight: 5-6 lbs. **Length:** 43" overall (28" barrel).
Stock: Walnut-finished hardwood with full pistol grip.
Sights: Bead front.
Features: Transfer bar ignition; break-open action with side-lever release. Introduced 1987. From New England Firearms.
Price: **$99.95**
Price: Youth model (12-, 20-, 28-ga., 410, 22" barrel, recoil pad) .. **$109.95**
Price: 12-ga., 32" (Full) **$104.95**

MOSSBERG MODEL 695 SLUGSTER

Gauge: 12, 3" chamber.
Barrel: 22"; fully rifled, ported.
Weight: 7-1/2 lbs.
Stock: Black synthetic, with swivel studs and rubber recoil pad.
Sights: Blade front, folding rifle-style leaf rear; Fiber Optic. Comes with Weaver-style scope bases.
Features: Matte metal finish; rotating thumb safety; detachable 2-shot magazine. Mossberg Cablelock. Made in U.S. by Mossberg. Introduced 1996.
Price: **$319.00**
Price: With Fiber Optic rifle sights **$351.00**
Price: Scope Combo Model includes Protecto case and Bushnell 1.5-4.5x scope. **$447.00**

NEW ENGLAND FIREARMS TRACKER SLUG GUN

Gauge: 12, 20, 3" chamber.
Barrel: 24" (Cyl.).
Weight: 6 lbs. **Length:** 40" overall.
Stock: Walnut-finished hardwood with full pistol grip, recoil pad.
Sights: Blade front, fully adjustable rifle-type rear.
Features: Break-open action with side-lever release; blued barrel, color case-hardened frame. Introduced 1992. From New England Firearms.
Price: Tracker **$129.95**
Price: Tracker II (as above except fully rifled bore) **$139.95**

New England Turkey and Goose

PERAZZI TMX SPECIAL SINGLE TRAP

Gauge: 12, 2-3/4" chamber.
Barrel: 32" or 34" (Extra Full).
Weight: 8 lbs., 6 oz.
Stock: To customer specs; interchangeable.
Features: Special high rib; adjustable four-position trigger. Also available with choke tubes. Imported from Italy by Perazzi U.S.A., Inc.
Price: From **$6,790.00**

NEW ENGLAND FIREARMS TURKEY AND GOOSE GUN

Gauge: 10, 3-1/2" chamber.
Barrel: 28" (Full), 32" (Mod.).
Weight: 9.5 lbs. **Length:** 44" overall.
Stock: American hardwood with walnut, or matte camo finish; ventilated rubber recoil pad.
Sights: Bead front.
Features: Break-open action with side-lever release; ejector. Matte finish on metal. Introduced 1992. From New England Firearms.
Price: Walnut-finish wood **$149.95**
Price: Camo finish, sling and swivels **$159.95**
Price: Camo finish, 32", sling and swivels **$179.95**
Price: Black matte finish, 24", Turkey Full choke tube, sling and swivels
.... **$184.95**

NEW ENGLAND FIREARMS SURVIVOR

Gauge: 12, 20, 410/45 Colt, 3" chamber.
Barrel: 22" (Mod.); 20" (410/45 Colt, rifled barrel, choke tube).
Weight: 6 lbs. **Length:** 36 overall.
Stock: Black polymer with thumbhole/pistol grip, sling swivels; beavertail forend.
Sights: Bead front.
Features: Buttplate removes to expose storage for extra ammunition; forend also holds extra ammunition. Black or nickel finish. Introduced 1993. From New England Firearms.
Price: Black **$129.95**
Price: Nickel. **$145.95**
Price: 410/45 Colt, black **$145.95**
Price: 410/45 Colt, nickel. **$164.95**

Savage Model 210FT

Savage Model 210FT Master Shot Shotgun

Similar to the Model 210F except has smoothbore barrel threaded for Win-choke-style choke tubes (comes with one Full tube); Advantage camo pattern covers the stock; pillar-bedded synthetic stock; bead front sight, U-notch rear. Introduced 1997. Made in U.S. by Savage Arms, Inc.
Price: **$440.00**

SAVAGE MODEL 210F MASTER SHOT SLUG GUN

Gauge: 12, 3" chamber; 2-shot magazine.
Barrel: 24" 1:35" rifling twist.
Weight: 7-1/2 lbs. **Length:** 43.5 " overall.
Stock: Glass-filled polymer with positive checkering.
Features: Based on the Savage Model 110 action; 60 bolt lift; controlled round feed; comes with scope mount. Introduced 1996. Made in U.S. by Savage Arms.
Price: **$380.00**

SHOTGUNS—BOLT ACTIONS & SINGLE SHOTS

Snake Charmer II

SNAKE CHARMER II SHOTGUN
Gauge: 410, 3" chamber.
Barrel: 18-1/4".
Weight: About 3-1/2 lbs. **Length:** 28-5/8" overall.

Stock: ABS grade impact resistant plastic.
Features: Thumbhole-type stock holds four extra rounds. Stainless steel barrel and frame. Reintroduced 1989. From Sporting Arms Mfg., Inc.
Price: **$149.00**
Price: Snake Charmer II Field Gun (as above except has conventional wood buttstock with 14" length of pull, 24" barrel) .... **NA**
Price: New Generation Snake Charmer (as above except with black carbon steel bbl.) **$139.00**

Tar-Hunt Mountaineer

Tar-Hunt RSG-20 Mountaineer Slug Gun
Similar to the RSG-12 Professional except chambered for 20-gauge (2-3/4") shells; 21" Shaw rifled barrel, with muzzle brake; two-lug bolt; one-shot blind magazine; matte black finish; McMillan fiberglass stock with Pachmayr Decelerator pad; receiver drilled and tapped for Rem.700 bases. Weighs 6-1/2 lbs. Introduced 1997. Made in U.S. by Tar-Hunt Custom Rifles, Inc.
Price: **$1,295.00**

TAR-HUNT RSG-12 PROFESSIONAL RIFLED SLUG GUN
Gauge: 12, 2-3/4" chamber, 1-shot magazine.
Barrel: 21-1/2"; fully rifled, with muzzlebrake.
Weight: 7-3/4 lbs. **Length:** 41-1/2" overall.
Stock: Matte black McMillan fiberglass with Pachmayr Decelerator pad.
Sights: None furnished; comes with Leupold windage bases only.
Features: Uses rifle-style action with two locking lugs; two-position safety; Shaw barrel; single-stage, trigger; muzzlebrake. Many options available. Right- and left-hand models at same prices. Introduced 1991. Made in U.S. by Tar-Hunt Custom Rifles, Inc.
Price: Professional model , right- or left hand **$1,395.00**
Price: Matchless model (400-grit gloss metal finish, McMillan Fibergrain stock), right- or left-hand **$1,783.50**
Price: Peerless model NP-3 nickel/teflon metal finish, McMillan Fibergrain stock), right- or left-hand **$1,973.25**
Price: Block Card model (any barrel length, cartage-type chokes, special McMillan fiberglass stocks, special chamber; fluted barrel, weighted stock, 2-oz. trigger optional), from... **$1,675.00**
Price: RSG-12 Combo (Professional model with extra McMillan Bench Rest heavyweight stock)..................................... **$1,755.00**

Wesson & Harrington Long Tom

WESSON & HARRINGTON LONG TOM CLASSIC SHOTGUN
Gauge: 12, 3" chamber.
Barrel: 32", (Full).

Weight: 7-1/2 lbs. **Length:** 46" overall.
Stock: 14"x1-3/4"x2-5/8". American black walnut with hand-checkered grip and forend.
Features: Color case-hardened receiver and crescent steel buttplate, blued barrel. Receiver engraved with the National Wild Turkey Federation logo. Introduced 1998. Made in U.S. by H&R 1871, Inc.
Price: **$349.95**

SHOTGUNS—MILITARY & POLICE

Designs for utility, suitable for and adaptable to competitions and other sporting purposes.

Armscor M-30SAS Special Purpose

ARMSCOR M-30 SECURITY SHOTGUNS
Gauge: 12, 3" chamber.
Barrel: 18.5", 20" (Cyl.).
Weight: About 7 lbs.
Stock: Walnut-finished hardwood.
Sights: Metal bead front.
Features: Dual action slide bars; damascened bolt; blued steel receiver. Imported from the Philippines by K.B.I., Inc.
Price: M-30R6 (5-shot) **$209.00**
Price: M-30R8 (7-shot) **$224.00**

ARMSCOR M-30 SPECIAL PURPOSE SHOTGUNS
Gauge: 12, 3" chamber.
Barrel: 20" (Cyl.).
Weight: 7.5 lbs.
Stock: Walnut-finished hardwood, or synthetic speedfeed.
Sights: Rifle sights on M-30DG, metal bead front on M-305AS.
Features: M-30DB has 7-shot magazine, polished blue receiver; M-305AS based on Special Air Services gun with 7-shot magazine, ventilated barrel shroud, Parkerized finish. Introduced 1996. Imported from the Philippines by K.B.I., Inc.
Price: M-30DG **$249.00**
Price: M-30SAS **$289.00**

Benelli M1 Tactical

BENELLI M3 PUMP/AUTO SHOTGUN
Gauge: 12, 3" chamber, 7-shot magazine.
Barrel: 19-3/4" (Cyl.).
Weight: 7 lbs., 8 oz. **Length:** 41" overall.
Stock: High-impact polymer with sling loop in side of butt; rubberized pistol grip on stock.
Sights: Post front, buckhorn rear adjustable for windage. Ghost ring system available.
Features: Combination pump/auto action. Alloy receiver with inertia recoil rotating locking lug bolt; matte finish; automatic shell release lever. Introduced 1989. Imported by Benelli USA.
Price: With standard stock **$1,040.00**
Price: With Ghost Ring sight system, standard stock **$1,080.00**

BENELLI M1 TACTICAL SHOTGUN
Gauge: 12, 3", 5-shot magazine.
Barrel: 18.5", choke tubes.
Weight: 6.5 lbs. **Length:** 39.75" overall.
Stock: Black polymer.
Sights: Rifle type with Ghost Ring system, tritium night sights optional.
Features: Semi-auto intertia recoil action. Cross-bolt safety; bolt release button; matte-finish metal. Introduced 1993. Imported from Italy by Benelli USA.
Price: With rifle sights, standard stock **$875.00**
Price: With Ghost Ring rifle sights, standard stock **$905.00**
Price: As above with pistol grip stock **$950.00**

> Consult our Directory pages for the location of firms mentioned.

Beretta Model 1201FP

BROLIN HP9 LAWMAN PUMP SHOTGUN
Gauge: 12, 3" chamber.
Barrel: 18.5" (Cyl.).
Weight: 7 lbs. **Length:** 38.5" overall.
Stock: Black polymer.
Sights: Bead front or rifle type.
Features: Twin action bars; steel receiver; cross-bolt safety. Introduced 1997. Imported by Brolin Industries, Inc.
Price: Matte blue finish. **$217.95**
Price: Satin chrome. **$249.95**
Price: Matte blue finish, rifle sights **$239.95**

BERETTA MODEL 1201FP AUTO SHOTGUN
Gauge: 12, 3" chamber.
Barrel: 18" (Cyl.).
Weight: 6.3 lbs.
Stock: Special strengthened technopolymer, matte black finish.
Stock: Fixed rifle type.
Features: Has 6-shot magazine. Introduced 1988. Imported from Italy by Beretta U.S.A.
Price: **$760.00**
Price: With tritium sights **$840.00**

BROLIN SAS-12 AUTO SHOTGUN
Gauge: 12, 2-3/4" chamber.
Barrel: 24" (choke tubes).
Weight: About 8 lbs.
Stock: Black polymer.
Sights: Bead or rifle-type.
Features: Gas-operated; quick detachable magazine. Introduced 1998. Imported by Brolin Arms.
Price: **$499.95**

Crossfire Shotgun/Rifle

CROSSFIRE SHOTGUN/RIFLE
Gauge/Caliber: 12, 2-3/4" chamber 4-shot/223 Rem. (5-shot).
Barrel: 20" (shotgun), 18" (rifle).
Weight: About 8.6 lbs. **Length:** 40" overall.
Stock: Composite.
Sights: Meprolight night sights. Integral Weaver-style scope rail.
Features: Combination pump-action shotgun, rifle; single selector, single trigger; dual action bars for both upper and lower actions; ambidextrous selector and safety. Introduced 1997. Made in U.S. From Hesco.
Price: About. **$1,895.00**

Fabarm FP6

MAGTECH MT 586P PUMP SHOTGUN
Gauge: 12, 3" chamber, 5-shot magazine (8-shot with 2-3/4" shells).
Barrel: 19" (Cyl.).
Weight: 7.3 lbs. **Length:** 39.5" overall.
Stock: Brazilian hardwood.
Sights: Bead front.
Features: Dual action slide bars, cross-bolt safety. Blue finish. Introduced 1991. Imported from Brazil by Magtech Recreational Products.
Price: About. **$219.00**

FABARM FP6 PUMP SHOTGUN
Gauge: 12, 3" chamber.
Barrel: 20" (Cyl.); accepts choke tubes.
Weight: 6.6 lbs. **Length:** 41.25" overall.
Stock: Black polymer with textured grip, grooved slide handle.
Sights: Blade front.
Features: Twin action bars; anodized finish; free carrier for smooth reloading. Introduced 1998. Imported from Italy by Heckler & Koch, Inc.
Price: **$472.00**

Mossberg Model 500

Mossberg Model HS410 Shotgun

Similar to the Model 500 Security pump except chambered for 20 gauge or 410 with 3" chamber; has pistol grip forend, thick recoil pad, muzzlebrake and has special spreader choke on the 18.5" barrel. Overall length is 37.5", weight is 6.25 lbs. Blue finish; synthetic field stock. Mossberg Cablelock and video included. Introduced 1990.

Price: HS 410. . . . . **$294.00**

Mossberg Model 500, 590 Ghost-Ring Shotguns

Similar to the Model 500 Security except has adjustable blade front, adjustable Ghost-Ring rear sight with protective "ears." Model 500 has 18.5" (Cyl.) barrel, 6-shot capacity; Model 590 has 20" (Cyl.) barrel, 9-shot capacity. Both have synthetic field stock. Mossberg Cablelock included. Introduced 1990. From Mossberg.

Price: Model 500, blue **$333.00**
Price: As above, Parkerized **$386.00**
Price: Model 590, blue. **$341.00**
Price: As above, Parkerized **$393.00**
Price: Parkerized Speedfeed stock **$425.00**

MOSSBERG MODEL 9200A1 JUNGLE GUN

Gauge: 12, 2-3/4" chamber; 5-shot magazine.
Barrel: 18-1/2" (Cyl.).
Weight: About 7 lbs. **Length:** 38-1/2" overall.
Stock: Black synthetic.
Sights: Bead front.
Features: Designed to function only with 2-3/4" 00 Buck loads; Parkerized finish; mil-spec heavy wall barrel; military metal trigger housing; ambidextrous metal tang safety. Introduced 1998. Made in U.S. by Mossberg.
Price: **$654.00**

MOSSBERG MODEL 500 PERSUADER SECURITY SHOTGUNS

Gauge: 12, 20, 410, 3" chamber.
Barrel: 18-1/2", 20" (Cyl.).
Weight: 7 lbs.
Stock: Walnut-finished hardwood or black synthetic.
Sights: Metal bead front.
Features: Available in 6- or 8-shot models. Top-mounted safety, double action slide bars, swivel studs, rubber recoil pad. Blue, Parkerized, Marinecote finishes. Mossberg Cablelock included. From Mossberg.
Price: 12- or 20-ga., 18-1/2", blue, wood or synthetic stock, 6-shot
. . . . **$282.00**
Price: Cruiser, 12- or 20-ga., 18-1/2", blue, pistol grip, heat shield . . . **$274.00**
Price: As above, 410-bore. **$281.00**
Price: 12-ga., 8-shot, blue, wood or synthetic stock. **$282.00**

Mossberg Model 500, 590 Mariner Pump

Similar to the Model 500 or 590 Security except all metal parts finished with Marinecote metal finish to resist rust and corrosion. Synthetic field stock; pistol grip kit included. Mossberg Cablelock included.
Price: 6-shot, 18-1/2" barrel **$412.00**
Price: As above with Ghost-Ring sights **$480.00**
Price: 9-shot, 20" barrel **$425.00**
Price: As above with Ghost-Ring sights **$480.00**

MOSSBERG MODEL 590 SHOTGUN

Gauge: 12, 3" chamber.
Barrel: 20" (Cyl.).
Weight: 7-1/4 lbs.
Stock: Synthetic field or Speedfeed.
Sights: Metal bead front.
Features: Top-mounted safety, double slide action bars. Comes with heat shield, bayonet lug, swivel studs, rubber recoil pad. Blue, Parkerized or Marinecote finish. Mossberg Cablelock included. From Mossberg.
Price: Blue, synthetic stock **$341.00**
Price: Parkerized, synthetic stock **$393.00**
Price: Blue, Speedfeed stock **$374.00**
Price: Parkerized, Speedfeed stock. **$425.00**

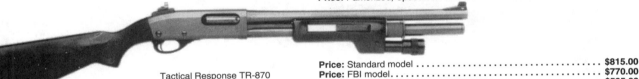

Tactical Response TR-870

TACTICAL RESPONSE TR-870 STANDARD MODEL SHOTGUN

Gauge: 12, 3" chamber, 7-shot magazine.
Barrel: 18" (Cyl.).
Weight: 9 lbs. **Length:** 38" overall.
Stock: Fiberglass-filled polypropolene with non-snag recoil absorbing butt pad. Nylon tactical forend houses flashlight.
Sights: Trak-Lock ghost ring sight system. Front sight has tritium insert.
Features: Highly modified Remington 870P with Parkerized finish. Comes with nylon three-way adjustable sling, high visibility non-binding follower, high performance magazine spring, Jumbo Head safety, and Side Saddle extended 6-shot shell carrier on left side of receiver. Introduced 1991. From Scattergun Technologies, Inc.

Price: Standard model **$815.00**
Price: FBI model. **$770.00**
Price: Patrol model **$595.00**
Price: Border Patrol model **$605.00**
Price: Military model **$690.00**
Price: K-9 model (Rem. 11-87 action) **$860.00**
Price: Urban Sniper, Rem. 11-87 action. **$1,290.00**
Price: Louis Awerbuck model. **$705.00**
Price: Practical Turkey model. **$725.00**
Price: Expert model **$1,350.00**
Price: Professional model. **$815.00**
Price: Entry model **$840.00**
Price: Compact model **$635.00**
Price: SWAT model **$1,050.00**

Winchester Model 1300 Defender

Winchester 8-Shot Pistol Grip Pump Security Shotgun

Same as regular Defender Pump but with pistol grip and forend of high-impact resistant ABS plastic with non-glare black finish. Introduced 1984.
Price: Pistol Grip Defender **$290.00**

Winchester Model 1300 Stainless Marine Pump Gun

Same as the Defender except has bright chrome finish, stainless steel barrel, rifle-type sights only. Phosphate coated receiver for corrosion resistance. Pistol grip optional.
Price: **$460.00**

WINCHESTER MODEL 1300 DEFENDER PUMP GUN

Gauge: 12, 20, 3" chamber, 5- or 8-shot capacity.
Barrel: 18" (Cyl.).
Weight: 6-3/4 lbs. **Length:** 38-5/8" overall.
Stock: Walnut-finished hardwood stock and ribbed forend, or synthetic; or pistol grip.
Sights: Metal bead front.
Features: Cross-bolt safety, front-locking rotary bolt, twin action slide bars. Black rubber buttpad. From U.S. Repeating Arms Co.
Price: 8-shot, wood or synthetic stock **$290.00**
Price: 5-shot, wood stock **$290.00**
Price: Defender Field Combo with pistol grip **$393.00**

Winchester Model 1300 Lady Defender Pump Gun

Similar to the Model 1300 defender except in 20-gauge only, weighs 6-1/4 lbs. Available with synthetic full stock or synthetic pistol grip only. Introduced 1997. From U.S. Repeating Arms Co.
Price: **$290.00**

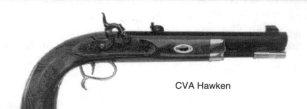

CVA Hawken

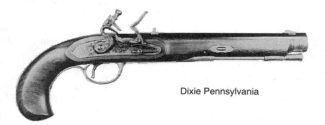

Dixie Pennsylvania

Dixie Harper's Ferry

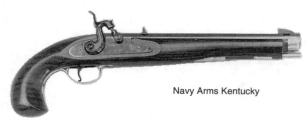

Navy Arms Kentucky

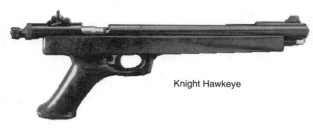

Knight Hawkeye

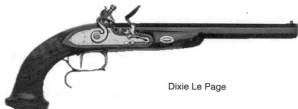

Dixie Le Page

LE PAGE PERCUSSION DUELING PISTOL
Caliber: 44.
Barrel: 10", rifled.
Weight: 40 oz. **Length:** 16" overall.
Stock: Walnut, fluted butt.
Sights: Blade front, notch rear.
Features: Double-set triggers. Blued barrel; trigger guard and buttcap are polished silver. Imported by Dixie Gun Works.
Price: **$259.95**

CVA HAWKEN PISTOL
Caliber: 50.
Barrel: 9-3/4"; 15/16" flats.
Weight: 50 oz. **Length:** 16-1/2" overall.
Stock: Select hardwood.
Sights: Beaded blade front, fully adjustable open rear.
Features: Color case-hardened lock, polished brass wedge plate, nose cap, ramrod thimble, trigger guard, grip cap. Imported by CVA.
Price: **$149.95**
Price: Kit **$109.95**

DIXIE PENNSYLVANIA PISTOL
Caliber: 44 (.430" round ball).
Barrel: 10" (7/8" octagon).
Weight: 2-1/2 lbs.
Stock: Walnut-stained hardwood.
Sights: Blade front, open rear drift-adjustable for windage; brass.
Features: Available in flint only. Brass trigger guard, thimbles, nosecap, wedgeplates; high-luster blue barrel. Imported from Italy by Dixie Gun Works.
Price: Finished **$183.75**
Price: Kit **$174.95**

FRENCH-STYLE DUELING PISTOL
Caliber: 44.
Barrel: 10".
Weight: 35 oz. **Length:** 15-3/4" overall.
Stock: Carved walnut.
Sights: Fixed.
Features: Comes with velvet-lined case and accessories. Imported by Mandall Shooting Supplies.
Price: **$295.00**

HARPER'S FERRY 1806 PISTOL
Caliber: 58 (.570" round ball).
Barrel: 10".
Weight: 40 oz. **Length:** 16" overall.
Stock: Walnut.
Sights: Fixed.
Features: Case-hardened lock, brass-mounted browned barrel. Replica of the first U.S. Gov't.-made flintlock pistol. Imported by Navy Arms, Dixie Gun Works.
Price: . . . . **$275.00 to $405.00**
Price: Kit (Dixie) **$237.00**
Price: Cased set (Navy Arms) **$355.00**

KENTUCKY FLINTLOCK PISTOL
Caliber: 44, 45.
Barrel: 10-1/8".
Weight: 32 oz. **Length:** 15-1/2" overall.
Stock: Walnut.
Sights: Fixed.
Features: Specifications, including caliber, weight and length may vary with importer. Case-hardened lock, blued barrel; available also as brass barrel flint Model 1821. Imported by Navy Arms, The Armoury.
Price: . . . . **$145.00 to $225.00**
Price: In kit form, from . . . . **$90.00 to $112.00**
Price: Single cased set (Navy Arms) **$350.00**
Price: Double cased set (Navy Arms) **$580.00**
Kentucky Percussion Pistol
Similar to flint version but percussion lock. Imported by The Armoury, Navy Arms, CVA (50-cal.).
Price: . . . . **$129.95 to $250.00**
Price: Steel barrel (Armoury) **$179.00**
Price: Single cased set (Navy Arms) **$335.00**
Price: Double cased set (Navy Arms) **$560.00**

KNIGHT HAWKEYE PISTOL
Caliber: 50.
Barrel: 12", 1:20" twist.
Weight: 3-1/4 lbs. **Length:** 20" overall.
Stock: Black composite, autumn brown or shadow black laminate.
Sights: Bead front on ramp, open fully adjustable rear.
Features: In-line ignitiion design; patented double safety system; removable breech plug; fully adjustable trigger; receiver drilled and tapped for scope mounting. Made in U.S. by Modern Muzzle Loading, Inc.
Price: Blued **$359.95**
Price: Stainless. **$429.95**

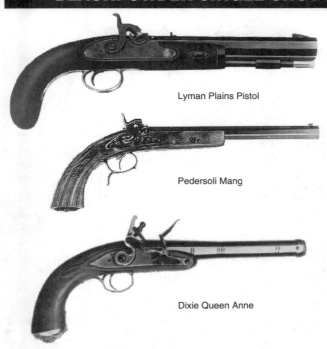

Lyman Plains Pistol

Pedersoli Mang

Dixie Queen Anne

TRADITIONS BUCKHUNTER PRO IN-LINE PISTOL
Caliber: 50, 54.
Barrel: 9-1/2" round.
Weight: 48 oz. **Length:** 14" overall.
Stocks: Smooth walnut or black epoxy coated grip and forend.
Sights: Beaded blade front, folding adjustable rear.
Features: Thumb safety; removable stainless steel breech plug; adjustable trigger, barrel drilled and tapped for scope mounting. From Traditions.
Price: With walnut grip $219.00
Price: Nickel with black grip $234.00
Price: With walnut grip and 12-1/2" barrel.................. $234.00

Traditions Pioneer

TRADITIONS TRAPPER PISTOL
Caliber: 50.
Barrel: 9-3/4", 7/8" flats, 1:20" twist.
Weight: 2-3/4 lbs. **Length:** 16" overall.
Stock: Beech.
Sights: Blade front, adjustable rear.
Features: Double-set triggers; brass buttcap, trigger guard, wedge plate, forend tip, thimble. From Traditions.
Price: Percussion $175.00
Price: Flintlock.................................... $189.00
Price: Kit $131.00

WHITE MUZZLELOADING SYSTEMS JAVELINA PISTOL
Caliber: 41, 45, 50.
Barrel: 14".
Weight: NA. **Length:** NA.
Stock: Black composite with rear grip.
Sights: Blade front, fully adjustable rear. Drilled and tapped for scope mounting.
Features: Stainless steel construction. Action based on the G-Series rifle (Whitetail, Bison) system. Introduced 1996. Made in U.S. by White Muzzleloading Systems.
Price: $499.95

LYMAN PLAINS PISTOL
Caliber: 50 or 54.
Barrel: 8", 1:30" twist, both calibers.
Weight: 50 oz. **Length:** 15" overall.
Stock: Walnut half-stock.
Sights: Blade front, square notch rear adjustable for windage.
Features: Polished brass trigger guard and ramrod tip, color case-hardened coil spring lock, spring-loaded trigger, stainless steel nipple, blackened iron furniture. Hooked patent breech, detachable belt hook. Introduced 1981. From Lyman Products.
Price: Finished... $224.95
Price: Kit $179.95

PEDERSOLI MANG TARGET PISTOL
Caliber: 38.
Barrel: 10.5", octagonal; 1:15" twist,
Weight: 2.5 lbs. **Length:** 17.25" overall.
Stock: Walnut with fluted grip.
Sights: Blade front, open rear adjustable for windage.
Features: Browned barrel, polished breech plug, rest color case-hardened. Imported from Italy by Dixie Gun Works.
Price: $786.00

QUEEN ANNE FLINTLOCK PISTOL
Caliber: 50 (.490" round ball).
Barrel: 7-1/2", smoothbore.
Stock: Walnut.
Sights: None.
Features: Browned steel barrel, fluted brass trigger guard, brass mask on butt. Lockplate left in the white. Made by Pedersoli in Italy. Introduced 1983. Imported by Dixie Gun Works.
Price: $195.00
Price: Kit $170.00

Traditions Buckhunter Pro

TRADITIONS WILLIAM PARKER PISTOL
Caliber: 50.
Barrel: 10-3/8", 15/16" flats; polished steel.
Weight: 37 oz. **Length:** 17-1/2" overall.
Stock: Walnut with checkered grip.
Sights: Brass blade front, fixed rear.
Features: Replica dueling pistol with 1:20" twist, hooked breech. Brass wedge plate, trigger guard, cap guard; separate ramrod. Double-set triggers. Polished steel barrel, lock. Imported by Traditions.
Price: $250.00

TRADITIONS KENTUCKY PISTOL
Caliber: 50.
Barrel: 10"; octagon with 7/8" flats; 1:20" twist.
Weight: 40 oz. **Length:** 15" overall.
Stock: Stained beech.
Sights: Blade front, fixed rear.
Features: Birds-head grip; brass thimbles; color case-hardened lock. Percussion only. Introduced 1995. From Traditions.
Price: Finished... $131.00
Price: Kit $101.00

TRADITIONS PIONEER PISTOL
Caliber: 45.
Barrel: 9-5/8", 13/16" flats, 1:16" twist.
Weight: 31 oz. **Length:** 15" overall.
Stock: Beech.
Sights: Blade front, fixed rear.
Features: V-type mainspring. Single trigger. German silver furniture, blackened hardware. From Traditions.
Price: $139.00
Price: Kit $116.00

ARMY 1860 PERCUSSION REVOLVER
Caliber: 44, 6-shot.
Barrel: 8".
Weight: 40 oz. **Length:** 13-5/8" overall.
Stocks: Walnut.
Sights: Fixed.
Features: Engraved Navy scene on cylinder; brass trigger guard; case-hardened frame, loading lever and hammer. Some importers supply pistol cut for detachable shoulder stock, have accessory stock available. Imported by American Arms, Cabela's (1860 Lawman), E.M.F., Navy Arms, The Armoury, Cimarron, Dixie Gun Works (half-fluted cylinder, not roll engraved), Euroarms of America (brass or steel model), Armsport, Traditions (brass or steel), Uberti U.S.A. Inc., United States Patent Fire-Arms.
Price: About . . . . **$92.95 to $395.00**
Price: Hartford model, steel frame, German silver trim,
cartouches (E.M.F.) **$215.00**
Price: Single cased set (Navy Arms) **$300.00**
Price: Double cased set (Navy Arms) **$490.00**
Price: 1861 Navy: Same as Army except 36-cal., 7-1/2" bbl., weighs 41 oz., cut for shoulder stock; round cylinder (fluted available), from Cabela's, CVA (brass frame, 44-cal.), United States Patent Fire-Arms. . **$99.95 to $385.00**
Price: Steel frame kit (E.M.F., Euroarms) . . . . **$125.00 to $216.25**
Price: Colt Army Police, fluted cyl., 5-1/2", 36-cal. (Cabela's) **$124.95**
Price: With nickeled frame, barrel and backstrap, gold-tone fluted cylinder, trigger and hammer, simulated ivory grips (Traditions) **$199.00**

CABELA'S PATERSON REVOLVER
Caliber: 36, 5-shot cylinder.
Barrel: 7-1/2".
Weight: 24 oz. **Length:** 11-1/2" overall.
Stocks: One-piece walnut.
Sights: Fixed.
Features: Recreation of the 1836 gun. Color case-hardened frame, steel backstrap; roll-engraved cylinder scene. Imported by Cabela's.
Price: **$229.95**

Colt 1847 Walker

COLT 1848 BABY DRAGOON REVOLVER
Caliber: 31, 5-shot.
Barrel: 4".
Weight: About 21 oz.
Stocks: Smooth walnut.
Sights: Brass pin front, hammer notch rear.
Features: Color case-hardened frame; no loading lever; square-back trigger guard; round bolt cuts; octagonal barrel; engraved cylinder scene. Imported by Colt Blackpowder Arms Co.
Price: **$389.95**

Colt 1981 Navy

Uberti 1861 Navy Percussion Revolver
Similar to 1851 Navy except has round 7-1/2" barrel, rounded trigger guard, German silver blade front sight, "creeping" loading lever. Available with fluted or round cylinder. Imported by Uberti USA Inc.
Price: Steel backstrap, trigger guard, cut for stock **$300.00**

American Arms 1860 Army

ARMY 1851 PERCUSSION REVOLVER
Caliber: 44, 6-shot.
Barrel: 7-1/2".
Weight: 45 oz. **Length:** 13" overall.
Stocks: Walnut finish.
Sights: Fixed.
Features: 44-caliber version of the 1851 Navy. Imported by The Armoury, Armsport.
Price: **$129.00**

BABY DRAGOON 1848, 1849 POCKET, WELLS FARGO
Caliber: 31.
Barrel: 3", 4", 5", 6"; seven-groove, RH twist.
Weight: About 21 oz.
Stocks: Varnished walnut.
Sights: Brass pin front, hammer notch rear.
Features: No loading lever on Baby Dragoon or Wells Fargo models. Unfluted cylinder with stagecoach holdup scene; cupped cylinder pin; no grease grooves; one safety pin on cylinder and slot in hammer face; straight (flat) mainspring. From Armsport, Dixie Gun Works, Uberti USA Inc., Cabela's.
Price: 6" barrel, with loading lever (Dixie Gun Works) **$185.00**
Price: 4" (Cabela's, Uberti USA Inc.) **$335.00**

COLT 1847 WALKER PERCUSSION REVOLVER
Caliber: 44.
Barrel: 9", 7 groove, right-hand twist.
Weight: 73 oz.
Stocks: One-piece walnut.
Sights: German silver front sight, hammer notch rear.
Features: Made in U.S. Faithful reproduction of the original gun, including markings. Color case-hardened frame, hammer, loading lever and plunger. Blue steel backstrap, brass square-back trigger guard. Blue barrel, cylinder, trigger and wedge. From Colt Blackpowder Arms Co.
Price: **$419.95**

Colt Walker 150th Anniversary Revolver
Similar to the standard Walker except has original-type "A Company No. 1" markings embellished in gold. Serial numbers begin with 221, a continuation of A Company numbers. Imported by Colt Blackpowder Arms Co.
Price: **$599.95**

COLT 1849 POCKET DRAGOON REVOLVER
Caliber: 31.
Barrel: 4".
Weight: 24 oz. **Length:** 9-1/2" overall.
Stocks: One-piece walnut.
Sights: Fixed. Brass pin front, hammer notch rear.
Features: Color case-hardened frame. No loading lever. Unfluted cylinder with engraved scene. Exact reproduction of original. From Colt Blackpowder Arms Co.
Price: **$389.95**

COLT 1851 NAVY PERCUSSION REVOLVER
Caliber: 36.
Barrel: 7-1/2", octagonal, 7 groove left-hand twist.
Weight: 40-1/2 oz.
Stocks: One-piece oiled American walnut.
Sights: Brass pin front, hammer notch rear.
Features: Faithful reproduction of the original gun. Color case-hardened frame, loading lever, plunger, hammer and latch. Blue cylinder, trigger, barrel, screws, wedge. Silver-plated brass backstrap and square-back trigger guard. From Colt Blackpowder Arms Co.
Price: **$399.95**

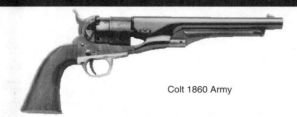

Colt 1860 Army

COLT 1862 POCKET POLICE "TRAPPER MODEL" REVOLVER
Caliber: 36.
Barrel: 3-1/2".
Weight: 20 oz. **Length:** 8-1/2" overall.
Stocks: One-piece walnut.
Sights: Blade front, hammer notch rear.
Features: Has separate 4-5/8" brass ramrod. Color case-hardened frame and hammer; silver-plated backstrap and trigger guard; blued semi-fluted cylinder, blued barrel. From Colt Blackpowder Arms Co.
Price: $389.95

DIXIE WYATT EARP REVOLVER
Caliber: 44.
Barrel: 12" octagon.
Weight: 46 oz. **Length:** 18" overall.
Stocks: Two-piece walnut.
Sights: Fixed.
Features: Highly polished brass frame, backstrap and trigger guard; blued barrel and cylinder; case-hardened hammer, trigger and loading lever. Navy-size shoulder stock ($45) will fit with minor fitting. From Dixie Gun Works.
Price: $130.00

Griswold & Gunnison

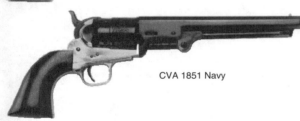

CVA 1851 Navy

Le Mat Revolver

LE MAT REVOLVER
Caliber: 44/65.
Barrel: 6-3/4" (revolver); 4-7/8" (single shot).
Weight: 3 lbs., 7 oz.
Stocks: Hand-checkered walnut.
Sights: Post front, hammer notch rear.
Features: Exact reproduction with all-steel construction; 44-cal. 9-shot cylinder, 65-cal. single barrel; color case-hardened hammer with selector; spur trigger guard; ring at butt; lever-type barrel release. From Navy Arms, Cabela's.
Price: Cavalry model (lanyard ring, spur trigger guard) $595.00
Price: Army model (round trigger guard, pin-type barrel release) . . . $595.00
Price: Naval-style (thumb selector on hammer) $595.00
Price: Engraved 18th Georgia cased set $795.00
Price: Engraved Beauregard cased set $1,000.00

COLT 1860 ARMY PERCUSSION REVOLVER
Caliber: 44.
Barrel: 8", 7 groove, left-hand twist.
Weight: 42 oz.
Stocks: One-piece walnut.
Sights: German silver front sight, hammer notch rear.
Features: Steel backstrap cut for shoulder stock; brass trigger guard. Cylinder has Navy scene. Color case-hardened frame, hammer, loading lever. Reproduction of original gun with all original markings. From Colt Blackpowder Arms Co.
Price: $399.95

Colt 1860 "Cavalry Model" Percussion Revolver
Similar to the 1860 Army except has fluted cylinder. Color case-hardened frame, hammer, loading lever and plunger; blued barrel, backstrap and cylinder, brass trigger guard. Has four-screw frame cut for optional shoulder stock. From Colt Blackpowder Arms Co.
Price: $399.95

COLT 1861 NAVY PERCUSSION REVOLVER
Caliber: 36.
Barrel: 7-1/2".
Weight: 42 oz. **Length:** 13-1/8" overall.
Stocks: One-piece walnut.
Sights: Blade front, hammer notch rear.
Features: Color case-hardened frame, loading lever, plunger; blued barrel, backstrap, trigger guard; roll-engraved cylinder and barrel. From Colt Blackpowder Arms Co.
Price: $399.95

COLT THIRD MODEL DRAGOON
Caliber: 44.
Barrel: 7-1/2".
Weight: 66 oz. **Length:** 13-3/4" overall.
Stocks: One-piece walnut.
Sights: Blade front, hammer notch rear.
Features: Color case-hardened frame, hammer, lever and plunger; round trigger guard; flat mainspring; hammer roller; rectangular bolt cuts. From Colt Blackpowder Arms Co.
Price: Three-screw frame with brass grip straps $419.95
Price: First Dragoon (oval bolt cuts in cylinder, square-back trigger guard) $419.95
Price: Second Dragoon (rectangular bolt cuts in cylinder, square-back trigger guard) $419.95

GRISWOLD & GUNNISON PERCUSSION REVOLVER
Caliber: 36 or 44, 6-shot.
Barrel: 7-1/2".
Weight: 44 oz. (36-cal.). **Length:** 13" overall.
Stocks: Walnut.
Sights: Fixed.
Features: Replica of famous Confederate pistol. Brass frame, backstrap and trigger guard; case-hardened loading lever; rebated cylinder (44-cal. only). Rounded Dragoon-type barrel. Imported by Navy Arms as Reb Model 1860.
Price: $115.00
Price: Kit $90.00
Price: Single cased set $235.00
Price: Double cased set $365.00

NAVY MODEL 1851 PERCUSSION REVOLVER
Caliber: 36, 44, 6-shot.
Barrel: 7-1/2".
Weight: 44 oz. **Length:** 13" overall.
Stocks: Walnut finish.
Sights: Post front, hammer notch rear.
Features: Brass backstrap and trigger guard; some have 1st Model square-back trigger guard, engraved cylinder with navy battle scene; case-hardened frame, hammer, loading lever. Imported by American Arms, The Armoury, Cabela's, Navy Arms, E.M.F., Dixie Gun Works, Euroarms of America, Armsport, CVA (44-cal. only), Traditions (44 only), Uberti USA Inc., United States Patent Fire-Arms.
Price: Brass frame . . . . $99.95 to $385.00
Price: Steel frame . . . . $130.00 to $285.00
Price: Kit form . . . . $110.00 to $123.95
Price: Engraved model (Dixie Gun Works) $139.95
Price: Single cased set, steel frame (Navy Arms) $280.00
Price: Double cased set, steel frame (Navy Arms) $455.00
Price: Confederate Navy (Cabela's) $69.95
Price: Hartford model, steel frame, German silver trim, cartouche (E.M.F.) $190.00

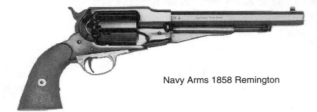

Navy Arms 1858 Remington

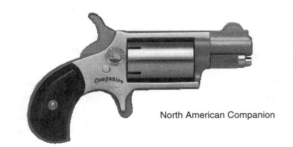

American Arms 1858 Stainless

North American Companion

North American Magnum Companion Percussion Revolver

Similar to the Companion except has larger frame. Weighs 7.2 oz., has 1-5/8" barrel, measures 5-7/16" overall. Comes with bullets, powder measure, bullet seater, leather clip holster, gun rug. Introduced 1996. Made in U.S. by North American Arms.

Price: **$195.00**

POCKET POLICE 1862 PERCUSSION REVOLVER

Caliber: 36, 5-shot.
Barrel: 4-1/2", 5-1/2", 6-1/2", 7-1/2".
Weight: 26 oz. **Length:** 12" overall (6-1/2" bbl.).
Stocks: Walnut.
Sights: Fixed.
Features: Round tapered barrel; half-fluted and rebated cylinder; case-hardened frame, loading lever and hammer; silver or brass trigger guard and backstrap. Imported by CVA (7-1/2" only), Dixie Gun Works, Navy Arms (5-1/2" only), Uberti USA Inc. (5-1/2", 6-1/2" only), United States Patent Fire-Arms.
Price: About . . . . $139.95 to $335.00
Price: Single cased set with accessories (Navy Arms) $365.00
Price: Hartford model, steel frame, German silver trim,
  cartouche (E.M.F.) $215.00

ROGERS & SPENCER PERCUSSION REVOLVER

Caliber: 44.
Barrel: 7-1/2".
Weight: 47 oz. **Length:** 13-3/4" overall.
Stocks: Walnut.
Sights: Cone front, integral groove in frame for rear.
Features: Accurate reproduction of a Civil War design. Solid frame; extra large nipple cut-out on rear of cylinder; loading lever and cylinder easily removed for cleaning. From Dixie Gun Works, Euroarms of America (standard blue, engraved, burnished, target models), Navy Arms.
Price: . . . . $160.00 to $299.95
Price: Nickel-plated $215.00
Price: Engraved (Euroarms) $287.00
Price: Kit version . . . . $245.00 to $252.00
Price: Target version (Euroarms) . . . . $239.00 to $270.00
Price: Burnished London Gray (Euroarms) . . . . $245.00 to $270.00

NAVY ARMS DELUXE 1858 REMINGTON-STYLE REVOLVER

Caliber: 44.
Barrel: 8".
Weight: 2 lbs., 13 oz.
Stocks: Smooth walnut.
Sights: Dovetailed blade front.
Features: First exact reproduction—correct in size and weight to the original, with progressive rifling; highly polished with blue finish. From Navy Arms.
Price: Deluxe model **$415.00**

NEW MODEL 1858 ARMY PERCUSSION REVOLVER

Caliber: 36 or 44, 6-shot.
Barrel: 6-1/2" or 8".
Weight: 38 oz. **Length:** 13-1/2" overall.
Stocks: Walnut.
Sights: Blade front, groove-in-frame rear.
Features: Replica of Remington Model 1858. Also available from some importers as Army Model Belt Revolver in 36-cal., a shortened and lightened version of the 44. Target Model (Uberti USA Inc., Navy Arms) has fully adjustable target rear sight, target front, 36 or 44. Imported by American Arms, Cabela's, CVA (as 1858 Army, brass frame, 44 only), Dixie Gun Works, Navy Arms The Armoury, E.M.F., Euroarms of America (engraved, stainless and plain), Armsport, Traditions (44 only), Uberti USA Inc.
Price: Steel frame, about . . . . **$99.95 to $280.00**
Price: Steel frame kit (Euroarms, Navy Arms) . . . . **$115.95 to $150.00**
Price: Single cased set (Navy Arms) **$290.00**
Price: Double cased set (Navy Arms) **$480.00**
Price: Stainless steel Model 1858 (American Arms, Euroarms, Uberti USA Inc., Cabela's, Navy Arms, Armsport, Traditions) . . . . **$169.95 to $380.00**
Price: Target Model, adjustable rear sight (Cabela's, Euroarms, Uberti USA Inc., Stone Mountain Arms) . . . . **$95.95 to $399.00**
Price: Brass frame (CVA, Cabela's, Traditions, Navy Arms)
  . . . . **$79.95 to $125.00**
Price: As above, kit (Dixie Gun Works, Navy Arms) . . . . **$145.00 to $188.95**
Price: Buffalo model, 44-cal. (Cabela's) **$129.95**
Price: Hartford model, steel frame, German silver trim,
  cartouche (E.M.F.) **$215.00**

CONSULT

SHOOTER'S MARKETPLACE

Page 225, This Issue

NORTH AMERICAN COMPANION PERCUSSION REVOLVER

Caliber: 22.
Barrel: 1-1/8".
Weight: 5.1 oz. **Length:** 4-5/10" overall.
Stocks: Laminated wood.
Sights: Blade front, notch fixed rear.
Features: All stainless steel construction. Uses standard #11 percussion caps. Comes with bullets, powder measure, bullet seater, leather clip holster, gun rag. Long Rifle or Magnum frame size. Introduced 1996. Made in U.S. by North American Arms.
Price: Long Rifle frame **$173.00**

Euroarms Rogers & Spencer

SHERIFF MODEL 1851 PERCUSSION REVOLVER

Caliber: 36, 44, 6-shot.
Barrel: 5".
Weight: 40 oz. **Length:** 10-1/2" overall.
Stocks: Walnut.
Sights: Fixed.
Features: Brass backstrap and trigger guard; engraved navy scene; case-hardened frame, hammer, loading lever. Imported by E.M.F.
Price: Steel frame **$172.00**
Price: Brass frame **$140.00**

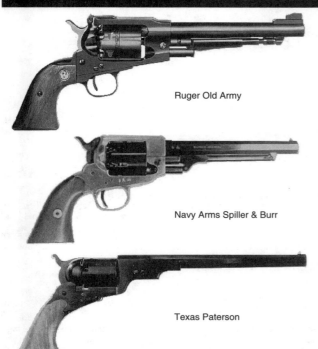

Ruger Old Army

Navy Arms Spiller & Burr

Texas Paterson

UBERTI 1st MODEL DRAGOON
Caliber: 44.
Barrel: 7-1/2", part round, part octagon.
Weight: 64 oz.
Stocks: One-piece walnut.
Sights: German silver blade front, hammer notch rear.
Features: First model has oval bolt cuts in cylinder, square-back flared trigger guard, V-type mainspring, short trigger. Ranger and Indian scene roll-engraved on cylinder. Color case-hardened frame, loading lever, plunger and hammer; blue barrel, cylinder, trigger and wedge. Available with old-time charcoal blue or standard blue-black finish. Polished brass backstrap and trigger guard. From Uberti USA Inc., United States Patent Fire-Arms, Navy Arms.
Price: .... $325.00 to $435.00

Uberti 2nd Model Dragoon Revolver
Similar to the 1st Model except distinguished by rectangular bolt cuts in the cylinder. From Uberti USA, United States Patent Fire-Arms, Navy Arms.
Price: .... $325.00 to $435.00

UBERTI 1862 POCKET NAVY PERCUSSION REVOLVER
Caliber: 36, 5-shot.
Barrel: 5-1/2", 6-1/2", octagonal, 7-groove, LH twist.
Weight: 27 oz. (5-1/2" barrel). **Length:** 10-1/2" overall (5-1/2" bbl.).
Stocks: One-piece varnished walnut.
Sights: Brass pin front, hammer notch rear.
Features: Rebated cylinder, hinged loading lever, brass or silver-plated backstrap and trigger guard, color-cased frame, hammer, loading lever, plunger and latch, rest blued. Has original-type markings. From Uberti USA Inc.
Price: With brass backstrap, trigger guard $310.00

WALKER 1847 PERCUSSION REVOLVER
Caliber: 44, 6-shot.
Barrel: 9".
Weight: 84 oz. **Length:** 15-1/2" overall.
Stocks: Walnut.
Sights: Fixed.
Features: Case-hardened frame, loading lever and hammer; iron backstrap; brass trigger guard; engraved cylinder. Imported by Cabela's, Navy Arms, Dixie Gun Works, Uberti USA Inc., E.M.F., Cimarron, Traditions, United States Patent Fire-Arms.
Price: About. .... $225.00 to $445.00
Price: Single cased set (Navy Arms) $405.00
Price: Deluxe Walker with French fitted case (Navy Arms) $540.00
Price: Hartford model, steel frame, German silver trim, cartouche (E.M.F.) $295.00

RUGER OLD ARMY PERCUSSION REVOLVER
Caliber: 45, 6-shot. Uses .457" dia. lead bullets.
Barrel: 7-1/2" (6-groove, 16" twist).
Weight: 46 oz. **Length:** 13-3/4" overall.
Stocks: Smooth walnut.
Sights: Ramp front, rear adjustable for windage and elevation; or fixed (groove).
Features: Stainless steel; standard size nipples, chrome-moly steel cylinder and frame, same lockwork as in original Super Blackhawk. Also available in stainless steel. Made in USA. From Sturm, Ruger & Co.
Price: Stainless steel (Model KBP-7). $465.00
Price: Blued steel (Model BP-7) $413.00
Price: Blued steel, fixed sight (BP-7F). $413.00
Price: Stainless steel, fixed sight (KBP-7F) $465.00

SPILLER & BURR REVOLVER
Caliber: 36 (.375" round ball).
Barrel: 7", octagon.
Weight: 2-1/2 lbs. **Length:** 12-1/2" overall.
Stocks: Two-piece walnut.
Sights: Fixed.
Features: Reproduction of the C.S.A. revolver. Brass frame and trigger guard. Also available as a kit. From Cabela's, Dixie Gun Works, Navy Arms.
Price: .... $89.95 to $199.00
Price: Kit form (Dixie). $129.95
Price: Single cased set (Navy Arms) $270.00
Price: Double cased set (Navy Arms) $430.00

TEXAS PATERSON 1836 REVOLVER
Caliber: 36 (.375" round ball).
Barrel: 7-1/2".
Weight: 42 oz.
Stocks: One-piece walnut.
Sights: Fixed.
Features: Copy of Sam Colt's first commercially-made revolving pistol. Has no loading lever but comes with loading tool. From Dixie Gun Works, Navy Arms, Uberti USA Inc.
Price: About. .... $310.00 to $395.00
Price: With loading lever (Uberti USA Inc.) $450.00
Price: Engraved (Navy Arms) $485.00

TRADITIONS 1858 STARR REVOLVER
Caliber: 44.
Barrel: 6".
Weight: 42 oz. **Length:** 11-3/4" overall.
Stocks: Smooth.
Sights: Blade front, grooved topstrap rear.
Features: Double-action mechanism; blue finish. Introduced 1998. From Traditions.
Price: $395.00

Uberti 3rd Model Dragoon Revolver
Similar to the 2nd Model except for oval trigger guard, long trigger, modifications to the loading lever and latch. Imported by Uberti USA Inc., United States Patent Fire-Arms.
Price: Military model (frame cut for shoulder stock, steel backstrap) .... $330.00 to $435.00
Price: Civilian (brass backstrap, trigger guard) $325.00

U.S. PATENT FIRE-ARMS 1862 POCKET NAVY
Caliber: 36.
Barrel: 4-1/2", 5-1/2", 6-1/2".
Weight: 27 oz. (5-1/2" barrel). **Length:** 10-1/2" overall (5-1/2" barrel).
Stocks: Smooth walnut.
Sights: Brass pin front, hammer notch rear.
Features: Blued barrel and cylinder, color case-hardened frame, hammer, lever; silver-plated backstrap and trigger guard. Imported from Italy; available from United States Patent Fire-Arms Mfg. Co.
Price: $335.00

Navy Arms Walker

Armoury R140 Hawken

AUSTIN & HALLECK MODEL 420 LR IN-LINE RIFLE
Caliber: 50.
Barrel: 26"; 1" octagon to 3/4" round; 1:28" twist.
Weight: 7-7/8 lbs. **Length:** 47-1/2" overall.
Stock: Lightly figured maple in Classic or Monte Carlo style.
Sights: Ramp front, fully adjustable rear.
Features: Blue or electroless nickel finish; in-line percussion action with removable weather shroud; Timney adjustable target trigger with sear block safety. Introduced 1998. Made in U.S. by Austin & Halleck.
Price: Blue $619.00
Price: Electroless nickel. $689.00
Price: Blue, hand-select highly figured wood $729.00

BOSTONIAN PERCUSSION RIFLE
Caliber: 45.
Barrel: 30", octagonal
Weight: 7-1/4 lbs. **Length:** 46" overall.
Stock: Walnut.
Sights: Blade front, fixed notch rear.
Features: Color case-hardened lock, brass trigger guard, buttplate, patchbox. Imported from Italy by E.M.F.
Price: $285.00

ARMOURY R140 HAWKEN RIFLE
Caliber: 45, 50 or 54.
Barrel: 29".
Weight: 8-3/4 to 9 lbs. **Length:** 45-3/4" overall.
Stock: Walnut, with cheekpiece.
Sights: Dovetail front, fully adjustable rear.
Features: Octagon barrel, removable breech plug; double set triggers; blued barrel, brass stock fittings, color case-hardened percussion lock. From Armsport, The Armoury.
Price: . . . . $225.00 to $245.00

Austin & Halleck Model 320 LR In-Line Rifle
Similar to the Model 420 LR except has black resin synthetic stock with checkered grip and forend. Introduced 1998. Made in U.S. by Austin & Halleck.
Price: Blue $455.00
Price: Electroless nickel $506.00

AUSTIN & HALLECK MOUNTAIN RIFLE
Caliber: 50.
Barrel: 32"; 1:66" twist; 1" flats.
Weight: 7-1/2 lbs. **Length:** 49" overall.
Stock: Curly maple.
Sights: Silver blade front, buckhorn rear.
Features: Available in percussion or flintlock; double throw adjustable set triggers; rust brown finish. Made in U.S. by Austin & Halleck.
Price: Flintlock $499.00
Price: Percussion $499.00
Price: Fancy wood $599.00

Cabela's Blue Ridge

CABELA'S BLUE RIDGE RIFLE
Caliber: 32, 36, 45, 50, 54.
Barrel: 39", octagonal.
Weight: About 7-3/4 lbs. **Length:** 55" overall.
Stock: American black walnut.
Sights: Blade front, rear drift adjustable for windage.
Features: Color case-hardened lockplate and cock/hammer, brass trigger guard and buttplate, double set, double-phased triggers. From Cabela's.
Price: Percussion $349.99
Price: Flintlock $379.95

Cabela's Red River

CABELA'S RED RIVER RIFLE
Caliber: 45, 50, 54, 58.
Barrel: NA.
Weight: About 7 lbs. **Length:** 45" overall.
Stock: Walnut-stained hardwood.
Sights: Blade front, adjustable buckhorn rear.
Features: Brass trigger guard, forend cap, thimbles; color case-hardened lock and hammer; rubber recoil pad. Introduced 1995. Imported by Cabela's.
Price: $129.99

CABELA'S TRADITIONAL HAWKEN
Caliber: 45, 50, 54, 58.
Barrel: 29".
Weight: About 9 lbs.
Stock: Walnut.
Sights: Blade front, open adjustable rear.
Features: Flintlock or percussion. Adjustable double-set triggers. Polished brass furniture, color case-hardened lock. Imported by Cabela's.
Price: Percussion, right-hand. $184.99
Price: Percussion, left-hand. $194.99
Price: Flintlock, right-hand $219.99

> Consult our Directory pages for the location of firms mentioned.

Cabela's Sporterized Hawken Hunter Rifle
Similar to the Traditional Hawken's except has more modern stock style with rubber recoil pad, blued furniture, sling swivels. Percussion only, in 45-, 50-, 54- or 58-caliber.
Price: Carbine or rifle, right-hand $184.99

Cook & Brother

COLT MODEL 1861 MUSKET
Caliber: 58.
Barrel: 40".
Weight: 9 lbs., 3 oz. **Length:** 56" overall.
Stock: Oil-finished walnut.
Sights: Blade front, adjustable folding leaf rear.
Features: Made to original specifications and has authentic Civil War Colt markings. Bright-finished metal, blued nipple and rear sight. Bayonet and accessories available. From Colt Blackpowder Arms Co.
Price: $569.95

CVA Accubolt Pro

CVA AccuBolt Pro In-Line Rifle
Similar to the standard AccuBolt except has 24" Badger barrel, Bell & Carlson composite thumbhole stock, and comes with a hard case. No iron sights. Introduced 1997. From CVA.
Price: $449.95

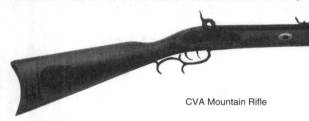

CVA Mountain Rifle

CVA BOBCAT RIFLE
Caliber: 50 and 54.
Barrel: 26"; 1:48" twist.
Weight: 6-1/2 lbs. **Length:** 40" overall.
Stock: Dura-Grip synthetic.
Sights: Blade front, open rear.
Features: Oversize trigger guard; wood ramrod; matte black finish. Introduced 1995. From CVA.
Price: $125.95

CVA ECLIPSE IN-LINE RIFLE
Caliber: 50, 54.
Barrel: 24" round; 1:32" rifling.
Weight: 7 lbs. **Length:** 42" overall.
Stock: Black Advantage camo synthetic.
Sights: Illuminator Fiber Optic Sight System; drilled and tapped for scope mounting.
Features: In-line action uses modern trigger with automatic safety; stainless percussion bolt; swivel studs. From CVA.
Price: 50 or 54, blue, black stock $154.95
Price: 50 or 54, blue, Advantage camo stock $179.95
Price: 50 or 54, Teflon finish, black stock $169.95

CVA Staghorn Rifle
Similar to the Eclipse except has standard open sights, manual safety, black DuraGrip stock and ramrod. From CVA.
Price: 50 or 54 . . . . $134.95

COOK & BROTHER CONFEDERATE CARBINE
Caliber: 58.
Barrel: 24".
Weight: 7-1/2 lbs. **Length:** 40-1/2" overall.
Stock: Select walnut.
Features: Recreation of the 1861 New Orleans-made artillery carbine. Color case-hardened lock, browned barrel. Buttplate, trigger guard, barrel bands, sling swivels and nose cap of polished brass. From Euroarms of America.
Price: $447.00
Price: Cook & Brother rifle (33" barrel) $480.00

CUMBERLAND MOUNTAIN BLACKPOWDER RIFLE
Caliber: 50.
Barrel: 26", round.
Weight: 9-1/2 lbs. **Length:** 43" overall.
Stock: American walnut.
Sights: Bead front, open rear adjustable for windage.
Features: Falling block action fires with shotshell primer. Blued receiver and barrel. Introduced 1993. Made in U.S. by Cumberland Mountain Arms, Inc.
Price: $931.50

CVA ACCUBOLT IN-LINE RIFLE
Caliber: 50.
Barrel: 24" hammer-forged; 1:32" twist.
Weight: 7-1/2 lbs.
Stock: Dura-Grip synthetic, with Monte Carlo comb.
Sights: CVA Illuminator Fiber Optic Sight system. Drilled and tapped for scope mounting.
Features: Uses CVA's AccuSystem copper-coated bullets and special bullet sizer (included). Synthetic ramrod, removable breech plug, swivel studs, rubber recoil pad. Introduced 1997. From CVA.
Price: $339.95

CVA MOUNTAIN RIFLE
Caliber: 50.
Barrel: 32"; 1:66" rifling.
Weight: 8-1/2 lbs. **Length:** NA
Stock: American hard maple.
Sights: Blade front, buckhorn rear.
Features: Browned steel furniture; German silver wedge plates; patchbox. Made in U.S. From CVA.
Price: $499.95

CVA ST. LOUIS HAWKEN RIFLE
Caliber: 50, 54.
Barrel: 28", octagon; 15/16" across flats; 1:48" twist.
Weight: 8 lbs. **Length:** 44" overall.
Stock: Select hardwood.
Sights: Beaded blade front, fully adjustable open rear.
Features: Fully adjustable double-set triggers; synthetic ramrod (kits have wood); brass patch box, wedge plates, nosecap, thimbles, trigger guard and buttplate; blued barrel; color case-hardened, engraved lockplate. V-type mainspring. Button breech. Introduced 1981. From CVA.
Price: St. Louis Hawken, finished (50-, 54-cal.) $199.95
Price: Left-hand, percussion $234.95
Price: Flintlock, 50-cal. only $234.95
Price: Flintlock, left-hand $249.95
Price: Percussion kit (50-cal., blued, wood ramrod) $169.95

DIXIE ENGLISH MATCHLOCK MUSKET
Caliber: 72.
Barrel: 44".
Weight: 8 lbs. **Length:** 57.75" overall.
Stock: Walnut with satin oil finish.
Sights: Blade front, open rear adjustable for windage.
Features: Replica of circa 1600-1680 English matchlock. Getz barrel with 11" octagonal area at rear, rest is round with cannon-type muzzle. All steel finished in the white. Imported by Dixie Gun Works.
Price: $895.00

CVA Firebolt

CVA Monster Buck Rifle

Similar to the Firebolt Rifle except has Realtree X-tra Brown camo finish stock with a rubber coating. Has CVA's Illuminator Fiber Optic Sight System, Bullet Guiding Muzzle. Available in 50- or 54-caliber. From CVA.
Price: $289.95

CVA HunterBolt Rifle

Similar to the Firebolt except has standard open sights, black DuraGrip synthetic stock. From CVA.
Price: 50 or 54 . . . . $189.95

CVA FIREBOLT BOLT-ACTION IN-LINE RIFLES

Caliber: 50, 54.
Barrel: 24".
Weight: 7 lbs. **Length:** NA.
Stock: Dura Grip synthetic; thumbhole, traditional, camo.
Sights: CVA Illuminator Fiber Optic Sight System.
Features: Bolt-action, in-line ignition system. Stainless steel or matte blue barrel; removable breech plug; trigger-block safety. Introduced 1997. From CVA.
Price: Stainless barrel, traditional stock $299.95
Price: Matte blue barrel, Advantage camo stock $279.95
Price: Matte blue barrel, thumbhole stock $279.95
Price: Matte blue barrel, traditional stock $249.95
Price: Left-hand, 50-caliber only, hardwood stock $299.95
Price: With Teflon finish, black stock $279.95
Price: As above, synthetic Sniper stock $299.95
Price: As above, synthetic Advantage camo stock. $299.95

Dixie Inline Carbine

DIXIE INLINE CARBINE

Caliber: 50, 54.
Barrel: 24"; 1:32" twist.
Weight: 6.5 lbs. **Length:** 41" overall.
Stock: Walnut-finished hardwood with Monte Carlo comb.
Sights: Ramp front with red insert, open fully adjustable rear.
Features: Sliding "bolt" fully encloses cap and nipple. Fully adjustable trigger, automatic safety. Aluminum ramrod. Imported from Italy by Dixie Gun Works.
Price: $349.95

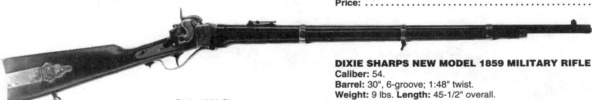

Dixie 1859 Sharps

DIXIE SHARPS NEW MODEL 1859 MILITARY RIFLE

Caliber: 54.
Barrel: 30", 6-groove; 1:48" twist.
Weight: 9 lbs. **Length:** 45-1/2" overall.
Stock: Oiled walnut.
Sights: Blade front, ladder-style rear.
Features: Blued barrel, color case-hardened barrel bands, receiver, hammer, nose cap, lever, patchbox cover and buttplate. Introduced 1995. Imported from Italy by Dixie Gun Works.
Price: $895.00

Dixie Model 1816

DIXIE DELUX CUB RIFLE

Caliber: 40.
Barrel: 28".
Weight: 6-1/2 lbs.
Stock: Walnut.
Sights: Fixed.
Features: Short rifle for small game and beginning shooters. Brass patchbox and furniture. Flint or percussion. From Dixie Gun Works.
Price: Finished $395.00
Price: Kit $350.00
Price: Super Cub (50-caliber) $350.00

DIXIE 1863 SPRINGFIELD MUSKET

Caliber: 58 (.570" patched ball or .575" Minie).
Barrel: 50", rifled.
Stocks: Walnut stained.
Sights: Blade front, adjustable ladder-type rear.
Features: Bright-finish lock, barrel, furniture. Reproduction of the last of the regulation muzzleloaders. Imported from Japan by Dixie Gun Works.
Price: Finished $595.00
Price: Kit $525.00

DIXIE U.S. MODEL 1816 FLINTLOCK MUSKET

Caliber: 69.
Barrel: 42", smoothbore.
Weight: 9.75 lbs. **Length:** 56.5" overall.
Stock: Walnut with oil finish.
Sights: Blade front.
Features: All metal finished "National Armory Bright"; three barrel bands with springs; steel ramrod with button-shaped head. Imported by Dixie Gun Works.
Price: $725.00

DIXIE U.S. MODEL 1861 SPRINGFIELD

Caliber: 58.
Barrel: 40".
Weight: About 8 lbs. **Length:** 55-13/16" overall.
Stock: Oil-finished walnut.
Sights: Blade front, step adjustable rear.
Features: Exact recreation of original rifle. Sling swivels attached to trigger guard bow and middle barrel band. Lockplate marked "1861" with eagle motif and "U.S. Springfield" in front of hammer; "U.S." stamped on top of buttplate. From Dixie Gun Works.
Price: $595.00
Price: From Stone Mountain Arms $599.00
Price: Kit $525.00

DIXIE TENNESSEE MOUNTAIN RIFLE

Caliber: 32 or 50.
Barrel: 41-1/2", 6-groove rifling, brown finish. **Length:** 56" overall.
Stock: Walnut, oil finish; Kentucky-style.
Sights: Silver blade front, open buckhorn rear.
Features: Recreation of the original mountain rifles. Early Schultz lock, interchangeable flint or percussion with vent plug or drum and nipple. Tumbler has fly. Double-set triggers. All metal parts browned. From Dixie Gun Works.
Price: Flint or percussion, finished rifle, 50-cal.. . . . . $575.00
Price: Kit, 50-cal.. . . . . $495.00
Price: Left-hand model, flint or percussion $575.00
Price: Left-hand kit, flint or perc., 50-cal.. . . . . $495.00
Price: Squirrel Rifle (as above except in 32-cal. with 13/16" barrel flats), flint or percussion $575.00
Price: Kit, 32-cal., flint or percussion. $495.00

E.M.F. 1863 SHARPS MILITARY CARBINE

Caliber: 54.
Barrel: 22", round.
Weight: 8 lbs. **Length:** 39" overall.
Stock: Oiled walnut.
Sights: Blade front, military ladder-type rear.
Features: Color case-hardened lock, rest blued. Imported by E.M.F.
Price: $860.00

> Consult our Directory pages for the location of firms mentioned.

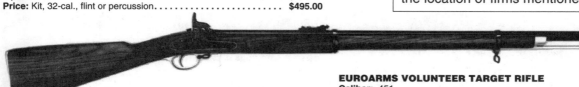

Euroarms Volunteer

EUROARMS BUFFALO CARBINE

Caliber: 58.
Barrel: 26", round.
Weight: 7-3/4 lbs. **Length:** 42" overall.
Stock: Walnut.
Sights: Blade front, open adjustable rear.
Features: Shoots .575" round ball. Color case-hardened lock, blue hammer, barrel, trigger; brass furniture. Brass patchbox. Imported by Euroarms of America.
Price: $440.00

EUROARMS VOLUNTEER TARGET RIFLE

Caliber: .451.
Barrel: 33" (two-band), 36" (three-band).
Weight: 11 lbs. (two-band). **Length:** 48.75" overall (two-band).
Stock: European walnut with checkered wrist and forend.
Sights: Hooded bead front, adjustable rear with interchangeable leaves.
Features: Alexander Henry-type rifling with 1:20" twist. Color case-hardened hammer and lockplate, brass trigger guard and nose cap, rest blued. Imported by Euroarms of America.
Price: Two-band $720.00
Price: Three-band $773.00

Euroarms 1861

EUROARMS 1861 SPRINGFIELD RIFLE

Caliber: 58.
Barrel: 40".
Weight: About 10 lbs. **Length:** 55.5" overall.
Stock: European walnut.
Sights: Blade front, three-leaf military rear.
Features: Reproduction of the original three-band rifle. Lockplate marked "1861" with eagle and "U.S. Springfield." Metal left in the white. Imported by Euroarms of America.
Price: $530.00

Forth Worth Sabine

FORT WORTH FIREARMS RIO GRANDE RIFLE

Caliber: 45, 50.
Barrel: 22"; 1:22" twist.
Weight: 6-1/2 lbs. **Length:** 39" overall.
Stock: Black composite; checkered grip and forend; swivel studs; recoil pad.
Sights: Ramped blade front, open adjustable rear. Drilled and tapped for scope mounting.
Features: Bolt-action design with stainless barrel and receiver. Flash diffuser protects optics from blow-by. Fully adjustable trigger with safety; synthetic Delron ramrod. Introduced 1996. From Fort Worth Firearms.
Price: $457.95

GONIC MODEL 93 M/L RIFLE

Caliber: 50.
Barrel: 26", 1:24" twist.
Weight: 6-1/2 to 7 lbs. **Length:** 43" overall.
Stock: American hardwood with black finish.
Sights: Hooded front, fully adjustable open or aperture rear.
Features: Adjustable trigger with side safety; unbreakable ram rod; comes with scope bases installed. Introduced 1993. Made in U.S. by Gonic Arms, Inc.

FORT WORTH FIREARMS SABINE RIFLE

Caliber: 22.
Barrel: 16-1/4".
Weight: 3-1/2 lbs. **Length:** 32" overall.
Stocks: Walnut-finished hardwood.
Sights: Hooded blade front, open adjustable rear.
Features: In-line design with side cocking lever. Positive click safety; blued finish. Introduced 1997. From Fort Worth Firearms.
Price: $189.95

FORT WORTH FIREARMS PECOS RIFLE

Caliber: 50.
Barrel: 22", stainless; 1:24" twist.
Weight: 6-1/2 lbs. **Length:** 39" overall.
Stock: Black or camo composite with checkered grip and forend.
Sights: Ramped blade front, open adjustable rear. Drilled and tapped for scope mounting.
Features: In-line design with stainless steel barrel and receiver; fully adjustable trigger; synthetic Delron ramrod. Introduced 1997. From Fort Worht Firearms.
Price: $457.95

Price: Blue barrel, Weaver scope bases $438.30
Price: As above with open sights. $500.57
Price: Blue barrel, Weaver scope bases, peep sight. $510.19
Price: Stainless barrel, Weaver scope bases $562.25
Price: As above with open sights. $603.04
Price: Stainless barrel, Weaver scope bases, peep sight $609.76

Gonic Model 93 Deluxe M/L Rifle
Similar to the Model 93 except has gray laminated wood stock. Introduced 1998. Made in U.S. by Gonic Arms, Inc.
Price: Blue barrel, scope bases.............................$619.45
Price: As above with open sights..........................$660.24
Price: Blue barrel, scope bases, peep sight $666.69
Price: Stainless barrel, scope bases $715.65
Price: As above with open sights..........................$756.44
Price: Stainless barrel, scope bases, peep sight.............$763.16

Gonic Model 93 Mountain Classic, Thumbhole M/L Rifles
Similar to the Model 93 except classic model has high-grade walnut or gray laminate stock with extensive hand-checkered panels; integral muzzle brake. Thumbhole model has roll-over Monte Carlo cheekpiece, beavertail forend and palmswell grip. Introduced 1998. Made in U.S. by Gonic Arms, Inc.
Price: Blue or stainless, walnut or gray laminate stock, Classic or Thumbhole model $2,132.00

Gonic Model 93 Safari Classic M/L Rifle
Similar to the Model 93 except has classic-style walnut or laminated stock with cheekpiece and hand-checkered grip and forend; integral muzzle brake. Introduced 1998. Made in U.S. by Gonic Arms, Inc.
Price: Blue or stainless barrel, walnut or gray laminate stock $1,612.00

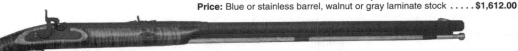

Great American Sporting

HAWKEN RIFLE
Caliber: 45, 50, 54 or 58.
Barrel: 28", blued, 6-groove rifling.
Weight: 8-3/4 lbs. **Length:** 44" overall.
Stock: Walnut with cheekpiece.
Sights: Blade front, fully adjustable rear.
Features: Coil mainspring, double-set triggers, polished brass furniture. From Armsport, Navy Arms, E.M.F.
Price: ....$220.00 to $345.00

KENTUCKIAN RIFLE & CARBINE
Caliber: 44.
Barrel: 35" (Rifle), 27-1/2" (Carbine).
Weight: 7 lbs. (Rifle), 5-1/2 lbs. (Carbine). **Length:** 51" overall (Rifle), 43" (Carbine).
Stock: Walnut stain.
Sights: Brass blade front, steel V-ramp rear.
Features: Octagon barrel, case-hardened and engraved lockplates. Brass furniture. Imported by Dixie Gun Works.
Price: Rifle or carbine, flint, about $269.95
Price: As above, percussion, about........................$259.95

GREAT AMERICAN SPORTING RIFLE
Caliber: 69.
Barrel: 28"; 1-1/4" octagon to 1-1/8" round.
Weight: 10 lbs. **Length:** NA
Stock: Walnut.
Sights: Silver blade front, adjustable semi-buckhorn rear.
Features: Hooked, patent Manton-style breech plug; iron furniture; bedded barrel; brown finish. Made in U.S. by October Country Muzzleloading, Inc.
Price: $1,495.00

HARPER'S FERRY 1803 FLINTLOCK RIFLE
Caliber: 54 or 58.
Barrel: 35".
Weight: 9 lbs. **Length:** 59-1/2" overall.
Stock: Walnut with cheekpiece.
Sights: Brass blade front, fixed steel rear.
Features: Brass trigger guard, sideplate, buttplate; steel patch box. Imported by Euroarms of America, Navy Arms (54-cal. only), Cabela's.
Price: ....$495.95 to $729.00
Price: 54-cal. (Navy Arms) $625.00
Price: 54-caliber (Calela's) $599.99

J.P. HENRY TRADE RIFLE
Caliber: 54.
Barrel: 34", 1" flats.
Weight: 8-1/2 lbs. **Length:** 45" overall.
Stock: Premium curly maple.
Sights: Silver blade front, fixed buckhorn rear.
Features: Brass buttplate, side plate, trigger guard and nose cap; browned barrel and lock; L&R Large English percussion lock; single trigger. Made in U.S. by J.P. Gunstocks, Inc.
Price: $965.50

Navy Arms Kentucky Flintlock

Kentucky Percussion Rifle
Similar to flintlock except percussion lock. Finish and features vary with importer. Imported by Navy Arms, The Armoury, CVA.
Price: About..$259.95
Price: 45- or 50-cal. (Navy Arms) $415.00
Price: Kit, 50-cal. (CVA)...................................$189.95

KNIGHT T-BOLT M/L RIFLE
Caliber: 50.
Barrel: 22", 26", 1:28" twist.
Weight: 6 lbs. **Length:** 41" overall.
Stock: Composite black, Mossy Oak Break-Up or Advantage camo.
Sights: Bead on ramp front, fully adjustable rear; drilled and tapped for scope mounts.
Features: Straight-pull T-Bolt action with double safety system, removable hammer, removable stainless steel breech plug; adjustable trigger. Introduced 1998. Made in U.S. by Knight Rifles.
Price: Blue or stainless ....NA

KENTUCKY FLINTLOCK RIFLE
Caliber: 44, 45, or 50.
Barrel: 35".
Weight: 7 lbs. **Length:** 50" overall.
Stock: Walnut stained, brass fittings.
Sights: Fixed.
Features: Available in carbine model also, 28" bbl. Some variations in detail, finish. Kits also available from some importers. Imported by Navy Arms, The Armoury.
Price: About ....$217.95 to $345.00
Price: Flintlock, 45 or 50-cal. (Navy Arms)....................$425.00

KNIGHT AMERICAN KNIGHT M/L RIFLE
Caliber: 50.
Barrel: 22"; 1:28" twist.
Weight: 6 lbs. **Length:** 41" overall.
Stock: Black composite.
Sights: Bead on ramp front, open fully adjustable rear.
Features: Double safety system; one-piece removable hammer assembly; drilled and tapped for scope mounting. Introduced 1998. Made in U.S. by Knight Rifles.
Price: ....NA

KNIGHT MK-85 RIFLE
Caliber: 50, 54.
Barrel: 24".
Weight: 6-3/4 lbs.
Stock: Walnut, laminated or composition.
Sights: Hooded blade front on ramp, open adjustable rear.
Features: Patented double safety; Sure-Fire in-line percussion ignition; Timney Featherweight adjustable trigger; aluminum ramrod; receiver drilled and tapped for scope bases. Made in U.S. by Knight Rifles.
Price: Hunter, walnut stock $539.95
Price: Stalker, laminated or composition stock $679.95
Price: Predator (stainless steel), laminated or composition stock. . . $759.95
Price: Knight Hawk, blued, composition thumbhole stock. $779.95
Price: As above, stainless steel $869.95

Knight MK-95 Magnum

LONDON ARMORY 2-BAND 1858 ENFIELD
Caliber: .577" Minie, .575" round ball.
Barrel: 33".
Weight: 10 lbs. **Length:** 49" overall.
Stock: Walnut.
Sights: Folding leaf rear adjustable for elevation.
Features: Blued barrel, color case-hardened lock and hammer, polished brass buttplate, trigger guard, nosecap. From Navy Arms, Euroarms of America, Dixie Gun Works.
Price: . . . . $385.00 to $531.00

CONSULT

SHOOTER'S MARKETPLACE

Page 225, This Issue

London Armory 1861

LYMAN COUGAR IN-LINE RIFLE
Caliber: 50 or 54.
Barrel: 22"; 1:24" twist.
Weight: NA. **Length:** NA.
Stock: Smooth walnut; swivel studs.
Sights: Bead on ramp front, folding adjustable rear. Drilled and tapped for Lyman 57WTR receiver sight and Weaver scope bases.
Features: Blued barrel and receiver. Has bolt safety notch and trigger safety. Rubber recoil pad. Delrin ramrod. Introduced 1996. From Lyman.
Price: $299.95
Price: Stainless steel. $382.95

Lyman Great Plains Hunter Rifle
Similar to the Great Plains model except has 1:32" twist shallow-groove barrel and comes drilled and tapped for the Lyman 57GPR peep sight.
Price: $424.95

KNIGHT LK-93 WOLVERINE RIFLE
Caliber: 50.
Barrel: 22", blued.
Weight: 6 lbs.
Stock: Black Fiber-Lite synthetic.
Sights: Blade front on ramp, open adjustable rear.
Features: Patented double safety system; removable breech plug; Sure-Fire in-line percussion ignition system. Made in U.S. by Knight Rifles.
Price: $319.95
Price: LK-93 Stainless $399.95
Price: LK-93 Thumbhole $409.95

KNIGHT BK-92 BLACK KNIGHT RIFLE
Caliber: 50, 54.
Barrel: 24", blued.
Weight: 6-1/2 lbs.
Stock: Black composition.
Sights: Blade front on ramp, open adjustable rear.
Features: Patented double safety system; removable breech plug for cleaning; adjustable Accu-Lite trigger; Green Mountain barrel; receiver drilled and tapped for scope bases. Made in U.S. by Knight Rifles.
Price: With composition stock $399.95

KNIGHT MK-95 MAGNUM ELITE RIFLE
Caliber: 50, 54.
Barrel: 24", stainless.
Weight: 6-3/4 lbs.
Stock: Composition; black or Realtree All-Purpose camouflage.
Sights: Hooded blade front on ramp, open adjustable rear.
Features: Enclosed Posi-Fire ignition system uses large rifle primers; Timney Featherweight adjustable trigger; Green Mountain barrel; receiver drilled and tapped for scope bases. Made in U.S. by Knight Rifles.
Price: Black composition stock $839.95

LONDON ARMORY 3-BAND 1853 ENFIELD
Caliber: 58 (.577" Minie, .575" round ball, .580" maxi ball).
Barrel: 39".
Weight: 9-1/2 lbs. **Length:** 54" overall.
Stock: European walnut.
Sights: Inverted "V" front, traditional Enfield folding ladder rear.
Features: Recreation of the famed London Armory Company Pattern 1853 Enfield Musket. One-piece walnut stock, brass buttplate, trigger guard and nose cap. Lockplate marked "London Armoury Co." and with a British crown. Blued Baddeley barrel bands. From Dixie Gun Works, Euroarms of America, Navy Arms.
Price: About. . . . . $350.00 to $495.00
Price: Assembled kit (Dixie, Euroarms of America). . . . . $425.00 to $431.00

LONDON ARMORY 1861 ENFIELD MUSKETOON
Caliber: 58, Minie ball.
Barrel: 24", round.
Weight: 7 - 7-1/2 lbs. **Length:** 40-1/2" overall.
Stock: Walnut, with sling swivels.
Sights: Blade front, graduated military-leaf rear.
Features: Brass trigger guard, nose cap, buttplate; blued barrel, bands, lockplate, swivels. Imported by Euroarms of America, Navy Arms.
Price: . . . . $300.00 to $427.00
Price: Kit . . . . $365.00 to $373.00

LYMAN TRADE RIFLE
Caliber: 50, 54.
Barrel: 28" octagon, 1:48" twist.
Weight: 8-3/4 lbs. **Length:** 45" overall.
Stock: European walnut.
Sights: Blade front, open rear adjustable for windage or optional fixed sights.
Features: Fast twist rifling for conical bullets. Polished brass furniture with blue steel parts, stainless steel nipple. Hook breech, single trigger, coil spring percussion lock. Steel barrel rib and ramrod ferrules. Introduced 1980. From Lyman.
Price: Percussion. $299.95
Price: Flintlock $324.95

Lyman Great Plains Rifle

LYMAN DEERSTALKER RIFLE

Caliber: 50, 54.
Barrel: 24", octagonal; 1:48" rifling.
Weight: 7-1/2 lbs.
Stock: Walnut with black rubber buttpad.
Sights: Lyman #37MA beaded front, fully adjustable fold-down Lyman #16A rear.
Features: Stock has less drop for quick sighting. All metal parts are blackened, with color case-hardened lock; single trigger. Comes with sling and swivels. Available in flint or percussion. Introduced 1990. From Lyman.

Price: 50- or 54-cal., percussion	**$304.95**
Price: 50- or 54-cal., flintlock	**$329.95**
Price: 50- or 54-cal., percussion, left-hand	**$314.95**
Price: 50-cal., flintlock, left-hand	**$339.95**
Price: Stainless steel	**$382.95**

LYMAN GREAT PLAINS RIFLE

Caliber: 50- or 54-cal.
Barrel: 32", 1:66" twist.
Weight: 9 lbs.
Stock: Walnut.
Sights: Steel blade front, buckhorn rear adjustable for windage and elevation and fixed notch primitive sight included.
Features: Blued steel furniture. Stainless steel nipple. Coil spring lock, Hawken-style trigger guard and double-set triggers. Round thimbles recessed and sweated into rib. Steel wedge plates and toe plate. Introduced 1979. From Lyman.

Price: Percussion	**$424.95**
Price: Flintlock	**$449.95**
Price: Percussion kit	**$344.95**
Price: Flintlock kit	**$369.95**
Price: Left-hand percussion	**$434.95**
Price: Left-hand flintlock	**$459.95**

Lyman Deerstalker Custom Carbine

Similar to the Deerstalker rifle except in 50-caliber only with 21" stepped octagon barrel; 1:24" twist for optimum performance with conical projectiles. Comes with Lyman 37MA front sight, Lyman 16A folding rear. Weighs 6-3/4 lbs., measures 38-1/2" overall. Percussion or flintlock. Comes with Delrin ramrod, modern sling and swivels. Introduced 1991.

Price: Percussion	**$324.95**
Price: Percussion, left-hand	**$329.95**

Markesbery Black Bear

Markesbery Brown Bear and Grizzly Bear M/L Rifles

Similar to the Black Bear except Brown Bear has one-piece thumbhole stock in black composite, crotch walnut, Mossy Oak Treestand, Xtra-B and Xtra-G camouflage. Grizzly Bear has two-piece thumbhole stock. Made in U.S. by Markesbery Muzzle Loaders.

Price: Brown Bear	**$697.69**
Price: Grizzly Bear	**$660.98**

MARKESBERY BLACK BEAR M/L RIFLE

Caliber: 45, 50, 54.
Barrel: 24"; 1:26" twist.
Weight: 6-1/2 lbs. **Length:** 38-1/2" overall.
Stock: Walnut, black laminate or green laminate.
Sights: Bead front, open fully adjustable rear.
Features: Interchangeable barrels; exposed hammer; Magnum Hammer In-Line Ignition System uses small rifle primer or standard No. 11 cap and nipple. Made in U.S. by Markesbery Muzzle Loaders.

Price: Black bear, laminated stock	**$556.27**
Price: Polar bear, one-piece walnut stock	**$556.27**

Marlin Model MLS-50

MARLIN MODELS MLS-50, MLS-54 IN-LINE RIFLES

Caliber: 50, 54.
Barrel: 22", 1:28" twist.
Weight: 6-1/2 lbs. **Length:** 41" overall.
Stock: Black fiberglass-reinforced Rynite with moulded-in checkering, rubber buttpad, swivel studs.
Sights: Ramp front with brass bead, adjustable Marble open rear. Receiver drilled and tapped for scope mounting.
Features: All stainless steel construction. Reversible cocking handle for right- or left- hand shooters; automatic tang safety; one-piece barrel/receiver. Introduced 1997. Made in U.S. by Marlin Firearms Co.

Price:	**$419.00**

Navy Arms J.P. Murray

J.P. MURRAY 1862-1864 CAVALRY CARBINE

Caliber: 58 (.577" Minie).
Barrel: 23".
Weight: 7 lbs., 9 oz. **Length:** 39" overall.
Stock: Walnut.
Sights: Blade front, rear drift adjustable for windage.
Features: Browned barrel, color case-hardened lock, blued swivel and band springs, polished brass buttplate, trigger guard, barrel bands. From Navy Arms, Euroarms of America.

Price:	**$405.00** to **$453.00**

Navy Arms Country Boy

NAVY ARMS HAWKEN HUNTER RIFLE/CARBINE
Caliber: 50, 54, 58.
Barrel: 22-1/2" or 28"; 1:48" twist.
Weight: 6 lbs., 12 oz. **Length:** 39" overall.
Stock: Walnut with cheekpiece.
Sights: Blade front, fully adjustable rear.
Features: Double-set triggers; all metal has matte black finish; rubber recoil pad; detachable sling swivels. Imported by Navy Arms.
Price: Rifle or Carbine **$240.00**

NAVY ARMS COUNTRY BOY IN-LINE RIFLE
Caliber: 50.
Barrel: 24".
Weight: 8 lbs. **Length:** 41" overall.
Stock: Black composition.
Sights: Bead front, fully adjustable open rear.
Features: Chrome-lined barrel; receiver drilled and tapped for scope mount; buttstock has trap containing takedown tool for nipple and breech plug removal. Introduced 1996. From Navy Arms.
Price: **$165.00**
Price: With satin chrome finish **$175.00**

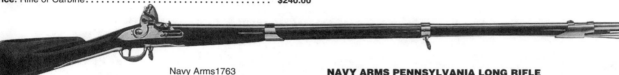

Navy Arms1763

NAVY ARMS 1763 CHARLEVILLE
Caliber: 69.
Barrel: 44-5/8".
Weight: 8 lbs., 12 oz. **Length:** 59-3/8" overall.
Stock: Walnut.
Sights: Brass blade front.
Features: Replica of the French musket used by American troops during the Revolution. Imported by Navy Arms.
Price: **$925.00**

NAVY ARMS PENNSYLVANIA LONG RIFLE
Caliber: 32, 45.
Barrel: 40-1/2".
Weight: 7-1/2 lbs. **Length:** 56-1/2" overall.
Stock: Walnut.
Sights: Blade front, fully adjustable rear.
Features: Browned barrel, brass furniture, polished lock with double-set triggers. Imported by Navy Arms.
Price: Percussion **$475.00**
Price: Flintlock **$485.00**

Navy Arms Whitworth

NAVY ARMS PARKER-HALE VOLUNTEER RIFLE
Caliber: .451".
Barrel: 32".
Weight: 9-1/2 lbs. **Length:** 49" overall.
Stock: Walnut, checkered wrist and forend.
Sights: Globe front, adjustable ladder-type rear.
Features: Recreation of the type of gun issued to volunteer regiments during the 1860s. Rigby-pattern rifling, patent breech, detented lock. Stock is glass bedded for accuracy. Imported by Navy Arms.
Price: **$850.00**

NAVY ARMS 1859 SHARPS CAVALRY CARBINE
Caliber: 54.
Barrel: 22".
Weight: 7-3/4 lbs. **Length:** 39" overall.
Stock: Walnut.
Sights: Blade front, military ladder-type rear.
Features: Color case-hardened action, blued barrel. Has saddle ring. Introduced 1991. Imported from Navy Arms.
Price: **$885.00**

NAVY ARMS PARKER-HALE WHITWORTH MILITARY TARGET RIFLE
Caliber: 45.
Barrel: 36".
Weight: 9-1/4 lbs. **Length:** 52-1/2" overall.
Stock: Walnut. Checkered at wrist and forend.
Sights: Hooded post front, open step-adjustable rear.
Features: Faithful reproduction of the Whitworth rifle, only bored for 45-cal. Trigger has a detented lock, capable of being adjusted very finely without risk of the sear nose catching on the half-cock bent and damaging both parts. Introduced 1978. Imported by Navy Arms.
Price: **$875.00**

NAVY ARMS SMITH CARBINE
Caliber: 50.
Barrel: 21-1/2".
Weight: 7-3/4 lbs. **Length:** 39" overall.
Stock: American walnut.
Sights: Brass blade front, folding ladder-type rear.
Features: Replica of the breech-loading Civil War carbine. Color case-hardened receiver, rest blued. Cavalry model has saddle ring and bar, Artillery model has sling swivels. Imported by Navy Arms.
Price: Cavalry model **$600.00**
Price: Artillery model **$600.00**

Navy Arms Berdan

NAVY ARMS BERDAN 1859 SHARPS RIFLE
Caliber: 54.
Barrel: 30".

Weight: 8 lbs., 8 oz. **Length:** 46-3/4" overall.
Stock: Walnut.
Sights: Blade front, folding military ladder-type rear.
Features: Replica of the Union sniper rifle used by Berdan's 1st and 2nd Sharpshooter regiments. Color case-hardened receiver, patch box, furniture. Double-set triggers. Imported by Navy Arms.
Price: $1,095.00
Price: 1859 Sharps Infantry Rifle (three-band) $1,030.00

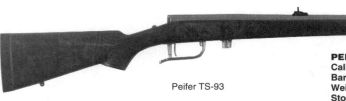

Navy Arms 1863

NAVY ARMS 1863 C.S. RICHMOND RIFLE
Caliber: 58.
Barrel: 40".
Weight: 10 lbs. **Length:** NA.
Stock: Walnut.
Sights: Blade front, adjustable rear.
Features: Copy of the three-band rifle musket made at Richmond Armory for the Confederacy. All steel polished bright. Imported by Navy Arms.
Price:. **$550.00**

NAVY ARMS 1863 SPRINGFIELD
Caliber: 58, uses .575" Minie.
Barrel: 40", rifled.
Weight: 9-1/2 lbs. **Length:** 56" overall.
Stock: Walnut.
Sights: Open rear adjustable for elevation.
Features: Full-size three-band musket. Polished bright metal, including lock. From Navy Arms.
Price: Finished rifle **$550.00**

NAVY ARMS 1861 SPRINGFIELD RIFLE
Caliber: 58.
Barrel: 40"**Weight:** 10 lbs., 4 oz. **Length:** 56" overall.
Stock: Walnut.
Sights: Blade front, military leaf rear.
Features: Steel barrel, lock and all furniture have polished bright finish. Has 1855-style hammer. Imported by Navy Arms.
Price: **$550.00**

PACIFIC RIFLE MODEL 1837 ZEPHYR
Caliber: 62.
Barrel: 30", tapered octagon.
Weight: 7-3/4 lbs. **Length:** NA.
Stocks: Oil-finished fancy walnut.
Sights: German silver blade front, semi-buckhorn rear. Options available.
Features: Improved underhammer action. First production rifle to offer Forsyth rifle, with narrow lands and shallow rifling with 1:144" pitch for high velocity round balls. Metal finish is slow rust brown with nitre blue accents. Optional sights, finishes and integral muzzle brake available. Introduced 1995. Made in U.S. by Pacific Rifle Co.
Price: From **$895.00**

Pacific Model 1837 Zephyr

Pacific Rifle Big Bore, African Rifles
Similar to the 1837 Zephyr except in 72-caliber and 8-bore. The 72-caliber is available in standard form with 28" barrel, or as the African with flat butt-plate, checkered upgraded wood; weight is 9 lbs. The 8-bore African has 24" barrel, weighs 12 lbs., has checkered English walnut, engraving, gold inlays. Introduced 1998. Made in U.S. by Pacific Rifle Co.
Price: 72-caliber, from **$1,150.00**
Price: 8-bore **$2,500.00**

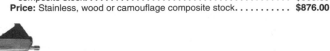

Peifer TS-93

PEIFER MODEL TS-93 RIFLE
Caliber: 45, 50.
Barrel: 24" Douglas premium; 1:20" twist in 45, 1:28" in 50.
Weight: 7 lbs. **Length:** 43-1/4" overall.
Stock: Bell & Carlson solid composite, with recoil pad, swivel studs.
Sights: Williams bead front on ramp, fully adjustable open rear. Drilled and tapped for Weaver scope mounts with dovetail for rear peep.
Features: In-line ignition uses #209 shotshell primer; extremely fast lock time; fully enclosed breech; adjustable trigger; automatic safety; removal primer holder. Blue or stainless. Made in U.S. by Peifer Rifle Co. Introduced 1996.
Price: Blue, black stock **$730.00**
Price: Blue, wood or camouflage composite stock, or stainless with black composite stock **$803.00**
Price: Stainless, wood or camouflage composite stock **$876.00**

Prairie River Bullpup

PRAIRIE RIVER ARMS PRA BULLPUP RIFLE
Caliber: 50, 54.
Barrel: 28"; 1:28" twist.
Weight: 7-1/2 lbs. **Length:** 31-1/2" overall.
Stock: Hardwood or black all-weather.
Sights: Blade front, open adjustable rear.
Features: Bullpup design thumbhole stock. Patented internal percussion ignition system. Left-hand model available. Dovetailed for scope mount. Introduced 1995. Made in U.S. by Prairie River Arms.
Price: 4140 alloy barrel, hardwood stock **$375.00**
Price: As above, black stock **$390.00**
Price: Stainless barrel, hardwood stock **$425.00**
Price: As above, black stock **$440.00**

PRAIRIE RIVER ARMS PRA CLASSIC RIFLE
Caliber: 50, 54.
Barrel: 26"; 1:28" twist.
Weight: 7-1/2 lbs. **Length:** 40-1/2" overall.
Stock: Hardwood or black all-weather.
Sights: Blade front, open adjustable rear.
Features: Patented internal percussion ignition system. Drilled and tapped for scope mount. Introduced 1995. Made in U.S. by Prairie River Arms, Ltd.
Price: 4140 alloy barrel, hardwood stock **$375.00**
Price: As above, stainless barrel. **$425.00**
Price: 4140 alloy barrel, black all-weather stock. **$390.00**
Price: As above, stainless barrel. **$440.00**

Remington Model 700 ML

REMINGTON MODEL 700 ML, MLS RIFLE

Caliber: 50, 54.
Barrel: 24"; 1:28" twist.
Weight: 7-3/4 lbs. **Length:** 44-1/2" overall.
Stock: Black fiberglass-reinforced synthetic with checkered grip and forend; magnum-style buttpad.
Sights: Ramped bead front, open fully adjustable rear. Drilled and tapped for scope mounts.
Features: Uses the Remington 700 bolt action, stock design, safety and trigger mechanisms; removable stainless steel breech plug, No. 11 nipple; solid aluminum ramrod. Comes with cleaning tools and accessories.
Price: ML, blued, 50-caliber only $372.00
Price: MLS, stainless, 50- or 54-caliber $469.00
Price: ML, blued, Mossy Oak Break-Up camo stock $405.00
Price: MLS, stainless, Mossy Oak Break-Up camo stock $503.00
Price: ML Youth (12-3/8" length of pull, 21" barrel) $372.00

C.S. RICHMOND 1863 MUSKET

Caliber: 58.
Barrel: 40".
Weight: 11 lbs. **Length:** 56-1/4" overall.
Stock: European walnut with oil finish.
Sights: Blade front, adjustable folding leaf rear.
Features: Reproduction of the three-band Civil War musket. Sling swivels attached to trigger guard and middle barrel band. Lock plate marked "1863" and "C.S. Richmond." All metal left in the white. Brass buttplate and forend cap. Imported by Euroarms of America, Navy Arms.
Price: $530.00

Ruger 77/50R50 Officers

RUGER 77/50 IN-LINE PERCUSSION RIFLE

Caliber: 50.
Barrel: 22", 1:28" twist.
Weight: 6-1/2 lbs. **Length:** 41-1/2" overall.

Stocks: Birch with rubber buttpad and swivel studs.
Sights: Gold bead front, folding leaf rear. Comes with Ruger scope mounts
Features: Shares design features with the Ruger 77/22 rifle. Stainless steel bolt and nipple/breech plug; uses #11 caps; three-position safety; blued steel ramrod. Introduced 1997. Made in U.S. by Sturm, Ruger & Co.
Price: 77/50RS $429.00
Price: 77/50RSO Officers (straight-grip checkered walnut stock, blued) $550.00
Price: K77/50RSBBZ All-Weather (stainless steel, black laminated stock) $596.00

Navy Arms Brown Bess

SECOND MODEL BROWN BESS MUSKET

Caliber: 75, uses .735" round ball.
Barrel: 42", smoothbore.
Weight: 9-1/2 lbs. **Length:** 59" overall.
Stock: Walnut (Navy); walnut-stained hardwood (Dixie).
Sights: Fixed.
Features: Polished barrel and lock with brass trigger guard and buttplate. Bayonet and scabbard available. From Navy Arms, Dixie Gun Works, Cabela's.
Price: Finished .... $475.00 to $850.00
Price: Kit (Dixie Gun Works, Navy Arms) .... $575.00 to $625.00
Price: Carbine (Navy Arms) $815.00

STONE MOUNTAIN SILVER EAGLE RIFLE

Caliber: 50.
Barrel: 26", octagonal; 15/16" flats; 1:48" twist.
Weight: About 6-1/2 lbs. **Length:** 40" overall.
Stock: Dura-Grip synthetic; checkered grip and forend.
Sights: Blade front, fixed rear.
Features: Weatherguard nickel finish on metal; oversize trigger guard. Introduced 1995. From Stone Mountain Arms.
Price: $139.95

T/C System 1

THOMPSON/CENTER SYSTEM 1 IN-LINE RIFLE

Caliber: 32, 50, 54, 58; 12-gauge.
Barrel: 26" round; 1:38" twist.
Weight: About 7-1/2lbs. **Length:** 44" overall.
Stock: American black walnut or composite.
Sights: Ramp front with white bead, adjustable leaf rear.
Features: In-line ignition. Interchangeable barrels; removable breech plug allows cleaning from the breech; fully adjustable trigger; sliding thumb safety; QLA muzzle system; rubber recoil pad; sling swivel studs. Introduced 1997. Made in U.S. by Thompson/Center Arms.
Price: Blue, walnut stock $388.00
Price: Stainless, composite stock, 50-, 54-caliber $428.00
Price: Stainless, camo composite stock, 50-caliber $465.00
Price: Extra barrels, blue $170.00
Price: Extra barrels, stainless, 50-, 54-caliber $220.00

THOMPSON/CENTER PENNSYLVANIA HUNTER RIFLE

Caliber: 50.
Barrel: 31", half-octagon, half-round.
Weight: About 7-1/2 lbs. **Length:** 48" overall.
Stock: Black walnut.
Sights: Open, adjustable.
Features: Rifled 1:66" for round ball shooting. Available in flintlock or percussion. From Thompson/Center.
Price: Flintlock $405.00

Thompson/Center Pennsylvania Hunter Carbine

Similar to the Pennsylvania Hunter except has 21" barrel, weighs 6.5 lbs., and has an overall length of 38". Designed for shooting patched round balls. Available in flintlock only. Introduced 1992. From Thompson/Center.
Price: Flintlock $394.00

T/C Encore

THOMPSON/CENTER ENCORE 209x50 MAGNUM

Caliber: 50.
Barrel: 26"; interchangeable with centerfire calibers.
Weight: 7 lbs. **Length:** 40-1/2" overall.
Stock: American walnut butt and forend.
Sights: Tru-Glo Fiber Optic front, Tru-Glo Fiber Optic rear.
Features: Uses the stock, frame and forend of the Encore centerfire pistol; break-open design using trigger guard spur; stainless steel universal breech plug; uses #209 shotshell primers. Introduced 1998. Made in U.S. by Thompson/Center Arms.
Price: $562.00

THOMPSON/CENTER NEW ENGLANDER RIFLE

Caliber: 50, 54.
Barrel: 28", round.
Weight: 7 lbs., 15 oz.
Stock: American walnut or Rynite.
Sights: Open, adjustable.
Features: Color case-hardened percussion lock with engraving, rest blued. Also accepts 12-ga. shotgun barrel. Introduced 1987. From Thompson/Center.
Price: Right-hand model $334.00
Price: Accessory 12-ga. barrel, right-hand $184.00

T/C Black Diamond

T/C Hawken

Thompson/Center Hawken Silver Elite Rifle

Similar to the 50-caliber Hawken except all metal is satin-finished stainless steel. Has semi-fancy American walnut stock without patchbox. Percussion only. Introduced 1996. Made in U.S. by Thompson/Center Arms.
Price: $535.00

Traditions Buckhunter Pro In-Line

THOMPSON/CENTER THUNDERHAWK SHADOW

Caliber: 50, 54.
Barrel: 24"; 1:38" twist.
Weight: 7 lbs. **Length:** 41-3/4" overall.
Stock: American walnut or black composite with rubber recoil pad.
Sights: Bead on ramp front, adjustable leaf rear.
Features: Uses modern in-line ignition system, adjustable trigger. Knurled striker handle indicators for Safe and Fire. Black wood ramrod, Drilled and tapped for T/C scope mounts. Introduced 1996. From Thompson/Center Arms.
Price: Blued $289.00
Price: Stainless $340.00
Price: Blued with camo stock $320.00

THOMPSON/CENTER FIRE HAWK RIFLE

Caliber: 50, 54.
Barrel: 24"; 1:38" twist.
Weight: 7 lbs. **Length:** 41-3/4" overall.
Stock: American black walnut or black Rynite; Rynite thumbhole style; all with cheekpiece and swivel studs.
Sights: Ramp front with bead, adjustable leaf-style rear.
Features: In-line ignition with sliding thumb safety; free-floated barrel; exposed nipple; adjustable trigger. Available in blue or stainless. Comes with Weaver-style scope mount bases. Introduced 1995. Made in U.S. by Thompson/Center Arms.
Price: Blue, walnut stock, 50, 54 . . . . $383.00
Price: Stainless, walnut stock, 50, 54 . . . . $433.00
Price: Stainless, Rynite stock, 50, 54 . . . . $423.00
Price: Blue, thumbhole stock, 50, 54 . . . . $404.00
Price: Bantam model with 13-1/4" pull, 21" barrel $383.00
Price: Blue, Advantage camo stock, 50, 54 . . . . $415.00

THOMPSON/CENTER BLACK DIAMOND RIFLE

Caliber: 50.
Barrel: 22-1/2" with QLA; 1:28" twist.
Weight: 6 lbs., 9 oz. **Length:** 41-1/2" overall.
Stock: Black Rynite with moulded-in checkering and grip cap.
Sights: Tru-Glo Fiber Optic ramp-style front, Tru-Glo Fiber Optic open rear.
Features: In-line ignition system with Flame Thrower Musket Nipple; removable universal breech plug; stainless steel construction. Introduced 1998. Made in U.S. by Thompson/Center Arms.
Price: $358.00

THOMPSON/CENTER HAWKEN RIFLE

Caliber: 45, 50 or 54.
Barrel: 28" octagon, hooked breech.
Stock: American walnut.
Sights: Blade front, rear adjustable for windage and elevation.
Features: Solid brass furniture, double-set triggers, button rifled barrel, coil-type mainspring. From Thompson/Center.
Price: Percussion model (45-, 50- or 54-cal.) $448.00
Price: Flintlock model (50-cal.) $459.00
Price: Percussion kit $315.00

TRADITIONS BUCKHUNTER PRO IN-LINE RIFLES

Caliber: 50 (1:32" twist), 54 (1:48" twist).
Barrel: 24" tapered round.
Weight: 7-1/2 lbs. **Length:** 42" overall.
Stock: Beech, composite or laminated; thumbhole available in black, Break-Up or Realtree® Advantage camouflage.
Sights: Beaded blade front, fully adjustable open rear. Drilled and tapped for scope mounting.
Features: In-line percussion ignition system; adjustable trigger; manual thumb safety; removable stainless steel breech plug. Eleven models available. Introduced 1996. From Traditions.
Price: . . . . $169.00 to $270.00

Traditions Buckhunter

TRADITIONS BUCKSKINNER CARBINE
Caliber: 50.
Barrel: 21", 15/16" flats, half octagon, half round; 1:20" or 1:66" twist.
Weight: 6 lbs. **Length:** 37" overall.
Stock: Beech or black laminated.
Sights: Beaded blade front, hunting-style open rear click adjustable for wind-age and elevation.
Features: Uses V-type mainspring, single trigger. Non-glare hardware. From Traditions.
Price: Flintlock **$204.00**
Price: Flintlock, laminated stock **$277.50**
Price: Percussion, 50. . . . . **$189.50**
Price: Percussion, laminated stock, 50 . . . . **$256.00**
Price: Percussion, left-hand. **$212.00**

Traditions Deerhunter

Traditions Deerhunter Composite Rifle
Similar to the Deerhunter except has black composite stock with checkered grip and forend. Blued barrel, C-Nickel or Advantage camouflage finish, 50, 54 percussion, 50-caliber flintlock. Introduced 1996. Imported by Traditions.
Price: Blued, flintlock, 50-cal.. . . . . **$160.00**
Price: Blued, percussion, 50- or 54-cal.. **$152.00**
Price: Blued or Advantage camo, percussion, 50-cal.. . . . . **$175.00**
Price: C-Nickel, percussion, 50-cal.. . . . . **$152.50**
Price: C-Nickel, percussion, 54-cal.. . . . . **$152.50**

TRADITIONS HAWKEN WOODSMAN RIFLE
Caliber: 50 and 54.
Barrel: 28"; 15/16" flats.
Weight: 7 lbs., 11 oz. **Length:** 44-1/2" overall.
Stock: Walnut-stained hardwood.
Sights: Beaded blade front, hunting-style open rear adjustable for windage and elevation.
Features: Percussion only. Brass patchbox and furniture. Double triggers. From Traditions.
Price: 50 or 54 . . . . **$219.00**
Price: 50-cal., left-hand **$233.00**
Price: 50-caliber flintlock **$248.00**

TRADITIONS PANTHER RIFLE
Caliber: 50.
Barrel: 24" octagon (1:48" twist); 15/16" flats.
Weight: 6 lbs. **Length:** 40" overall.
Stock: All-Weather composite.
Sights: Brass blade front, fixed rear.
Features: Percussion only; color case-hardened lock; blackened furniture; sling swivels; PVC ramrod. Introduced 1996. From Traditions.
Price: **$116.00**
Price: With RS Redi-Pak (powder measure, flask, fast loaders, 5-in-1 loader, capper, ball starter, ball puller, cleaning jag, nipple wrench). **$175.00**
Price: With RP Redi-Pak (as above with Pyrodex and percussion caps) **$189.00**

TRADITIONS IN-LINE BUCKHUNTER SERIES RIFLES
Caliber: 50, 54.
Barrel: 24", round; 1:32" (50), 1:48" (54) twist.
Weight: 7 lbs., 6 oz. to 8 lbs. **Length:** 41" overall.
Stock: All-Weather composite.
Sights: Fiber Optic blade front, click adjustable rear. Drilled and tapped for scope mounting.
Features: Removable breech plug; PVC ramrod; sling swivels. Introduced 1995. From Traditions.
Price: **$149.00**
Price: With RS Redi-Pak (powder measure, powder flask, two fast loaders, 5-in-1 loader, capper, ball starter, ball puller, cleaning jag, nipple wrench, bullets) 50- and 54-caliber **$199.00**
Price: With RP Redi-Pak (as above with Pyrodex and percussion caps) 50-caliber only **$233.75**

TRADITIONS DEERHUNTER RIFLE SERIES
Caliber: 32, 50 or 54.
Barrel: 24", octagonal, 15/16" flats; 1:48" or 1:66" twist.
Weight: 6 lbs. **Length:** 40" overall.
Stock: Stained hardwood and All-Weather Composite with rubber buttpad, sling swivels.
Sights: Blade front, fixed rear.
Features: Flint or percussion with color case-hardened lock. Hooked breech, oversized trigger guard, blackened furniture, PVC ramrod. All-Weather has composite stock and C-Nickel barrel. Drilled and tapped for scope mounting. Imported by Traditions, Inc.
Price: Percussion, 50 or 54, 1:48" twist **$152.00**
Price: Flintlock, 50-caliber only, 1:66" twist **$175.00**
Price: Percussion kit, 50 or 54 . . . . **$135.00**
Price: Flintlock, All-Weather, 50-cal. **$160.00**
Price: Percussion, All-Weather, 50 or 54 . . . . **$131.00**

TRADITIONS KENTUCKY RIFLE
Caliber: 50.
Barrel: 33-1/2"; 7/8" flats; 1:66" twist.
Weight: 7 lbs. **Length:** 49" overall.
Stock: Beech; inletted toe plate.
Sights: Blade front, fixed rear.
Features: Full-length, two-piece stock; brass furniture; color case-hardened lock. Introduced 1995. From Traditions.
Price: Finished **$219.00**
Price: Kit **$175.00**

Traditions Lightning

TRADITIONS LIGHTNING BOLT-ACTION MUZZLELOADER
Caliber: 50, 54.
Barrel: 24" round; blued, stainless, C-Nickel or Ultra Coat.
Weight: 7 lbs. **Length:** 43" overall.
Stock: Select hardwood, brown laminated, All-Weather Composite, Advantage, X-tra Brown or Break-Up camouflage.
Sights: Fiber Optic blade front, fully adjustable open rear.
Features: Twenty-one variations available. Field-removable stainless steel bolt; silent thumb safety; adjustable trigger; drilled and tapped for scope mounting. Introduced 1997. Imported by Traditions.
Price: Select hardwood stock. **$219.00**
Price: Laminated stock, stainless steel barrel **$380.00**
Price: All-Weather composite stock, blue finish **$262.00**
Price: All-weather composite, stainless steel **$307.00**
Price: Camouflage composite **$307.00**
Price: All-weather composite, Teflon finish **$307.00**
Price: Camouflage composite, Teflon finish **$351.00**
Price: Composite, with muzzle brake **$249.00**
Price: Composite, with muzzle brake, stainless, fluted barrel **$376.00**

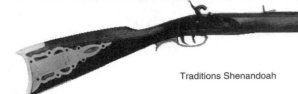

Traditions Shenandoah

TRADITIONS TENNESSEE RIFLE
Caliber: 50.
Barrel: 24", octagon with 15/16" flats; 1:66" twist.
Weight: 6 lbs. **Length:** 40-1/2" overall.
Stock: Stained beech.
Sights: Blade front, fixed rear.
Features: One-piece stock has inletted brass furniture, cheekpiece; double-set trigger; V-type mainspring. Flint or percussion. Introduced 1995. From Traditions.
Price: Percussion **$270.00**
Price: Flintlock. **$285.00**

TRYON TRAILBLAZER RIFLE
Caliber: 50, 54.
Barrel: 28", 30".
Weight: 9 lbs. **Length:** 48" overall.
Stock: European walnut with cheekpiece.
Sights: Blade front, semi-buckhorn rear.
Features: Reproduction of a rifle made by George Tryon about 1820. Double-set triggers, back action lock, hooked breech with long tang. From Armsport.
Price: About. **$825.00**

UFA Grand Teton Rifle
Similar to the Teton model except has 30" tapered octagon barrel in 45- or 50-caliber only. Available in blue or stainless steel with brushed or matte finish, brown or black laminated wood stock and forend. Weighs 9 lbs., overall length 46". Introduced 1994. Made in U.S. by UFA, Inc.
Price: **$995.00**
Price: With premium walnut or maple **$1,145.00**

TRADITIONS SHENANDOAH RIFLE
Caliber: 50.
Barrel: 33-1/2" octagon, 1:66" twist.
Weight: 7 lbs., 3 oz. **Length:** 49-1/2" overall.
Stock: Walnut.
Sights: Blade front, buckhorn rear.
Features: V-type mainspring; double-set trigger; solid brass buttplate, patchbox, nose cap, thimbles, trigger guard. Introduced 1996. From Traditions.
Price: Flintlock **$336.00**
Price: Percussion. **$322.00**

TRADITIONS PENNSYLVANIA RIFLE
Caliber: 50.
Barrel: 40-1/4", 7/8" flats; 1:66" twist, octagon.
Weight: 9 lbs. **Length:** 57-1/2" overall.
Stock: Walnut.
Sights: Blade front, adjustable rear.
Features: Brass patchbox and ornamentation. Double-set triggers. From Traditions.
Price: Flintlock **$463.00**
Price: Percussion. **$454.00**

UFA TETON RIFLE
Caliber: 45, 50, 12-bore (rifled, 72-cal.), 12-gauge.
Barrel: 26".
Weight: 8 lbs. **Length:** 42" overall.
Stock: Black or brown laminated wood; 1" recoil pad.
Sights: Marble's bead front, Marble's fully adjustable rear.
Features: Removable, interchangeable barrel; removable one-piece breech plug/nipple, hammer/trigger assembly; hammer blowback block; glass-bedded stock and forend. Introduced 1994. Made in U.S. by UFA, Inc.
Price: Stainless or blued **$834.00**
Price: With premium walnut or maple **$984.00**
Price: Extra barrels **$165.00**

UFA Teton Blackstone Rifle
Similar to the Teton model except in 50-caliber only, 26" barrel with shallow groove 1:26" rifling. Available only in stainless steel with matte finish. Has hardwood stock with black epoxy coating, 1" recoil pad. Weighs 7-1/2 lbs., overall length 42". Introduced 1994. Made in U.S. by UFA, Inc.
Price: **$534.00**

White Shooting Systems Super 91

WHITE MUZZLELOADING SYSTEMS WHITETAIL RIFLE
Caliber: 41, 45 or 50.
Barrel: 22".
Weight: 6.5 lbs. **Length:** 39.5" overall.
Stock: Black composite; classic style; recoil pad, swivel studs.
Sights: Bead front on ramp, fully adjustable open rear.
Features: Insta-Fire straight-line ignition; action and trigger safeties; adjustable trigger; stainless steel. Introduced 1992. Made in U.S. by White Muzzleloading Systems, Inc.
Price: Blue, wood stock, bull bbl., 50-cal. **$399.00**
Price: Stainless, composite stock **$499.95**
Price: Stainless, laminate stock **$529.95**

> Consult our Directory pages for the location of firms mentioned.

White Muzzleloading Systems Bison Blackpowder Rifle
Similar to the blued Whitetail model except in 54-caliber (1:28" twist) with 22" ball barrel. Uses Insta-Fire in-line percussion system, double safety. Adjustable sight, black-finished hardwood stock, matte blue metal finish, Delron ramrod, swivel studs. Drilled and tapped for scope mounting. Weighs 7-1/4 lbs. Introduced 1993. From White Muzzleloading Systems, Inc.
Price: **$399.95**

WHITE MUZZLELOADING SYSTEMS SUPER 91 BLACKPOWDER RIFLE
Caliber: 41, 45 or 50.
Barrel: 26".
Weight: 7-1/2 lbs. **Length:** 43.5" overall.
Stock: Black laminate or black composite; recoil pad, swivel studs.
Sights: Bead front on ramp, fully adjustable open rear.
Features: Insta-Fire straight-line ignition system; all stainless steel construction; side-swing safety; fully adjustable trigger; full barrel under-rib with two ramrod thimbles. Introduced 1991. Made in U.S. by White Muzzleloading Systems, Inc.
Price: Stainless **$659.95**
Price: Stainless, laminate stock. **$699.95**

White Muzzleloading Systems Super Safari Rifle
Same as the stainless Super 91 except has Mannlicher-style stock of black composite. Introduced 1993. From White Muzzleloading Systems, Inc.
Price: **$799.00**

White Muzzleloading Systems White Lightning Rifle
Similar to the Whitetail stainless rifle except uses smaller action with cocking lever and secondary safety on right side, primary safety on the left. Available only in 50-caliber with 22" barrel. Weighs 6.4 lbs., 40" overall. Has black hardwood stock. Introduced 1995. From White Muzzleloading Systems, Inc.
Price: **$299.95**

Navy Arms 1841 Mississippi

Mississippi 1841 Percussion Rifle
Similar to Zouave rifle but patterned after U.S. Model 1841. Imported by Dixie Gun Works, Euroarms of America, Navy Arms.
Price: About . . . . **$430.00** to **$500.00**

ZOUAVE PERCUSSION RIFLE
Caliber: 58, 59.
Barrel: 32-1/2".
Weight: 9-1/2 lbs. **Length:** 48-1/2" overall.
Stock: Walnut finish, brass patchbox and buttplate.
Sights: Fixed front, rear adjustable for elevation.
Features: Color case-hardened lockplate, blued barrel. From Navy Arms, Dixie Gun Works, Euroarms of America (M1863), E.M.F., Cabela's.
Price: About . . . . **$325.00** to **$465.00**
Price: Kit (Euroarms 58-cal. only). **$335.00**

BLACKPOWDER SHOTGUNS

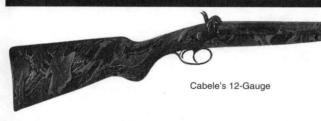

Cabele's 12-Gauge

CABELA'S BLACKPOWDER SHOTGUNS
Gauge: 10, 12, 20.
Barrel: 10-ga., 30"; 12-ga., 28-1/2" (Extra-Full, Mod., Imp. Cyl. choke tubes); 20-ga., 27-1/2" (Imp. Cyl. & Mod. fixed chokes).

CVA TRAPPER PERCUSSION
Gauge: 12.
Barrel: 28".
Weight: 6 lbs. **Length:** 46" overall.
Stock: English-style checkered straight grip of walnut-finished hardwood.
Sights: Brass bead front.
Features: Single blued barrel; color case-hardened lockplate and hammer; screw adjustable sear engagements, V-type mainspring; brass wedge plates; color case-hardened and engraved trigger guard and tang. From CVA.
Price: Finished. **$239.95**

Weight: 6-1/2 to 7 lbs. **Length:** 45" overall (28-1/2" barrel).
Stock: American walnut with checkered grip; 12- and 20-gauge have straight stock, 10-gauge has pistol grip.
Features: Blued barrels, engraved, color case-hardened locks and hammers, brass ramrod tip. From Cabela's.
Price: 10-gauge **$499.99**
Price: 10-gauge, Advantage camo. **$599.99**
Price: 12-gauge **$449.99**
Price: 12-gauge, Advantage camo. **$549.99**
Price: 20-gauge **$429.99**

CVA CLASSIC DOUBLE SHOTGUN
Gauge: 12.
Barrel: 28".
Weight: 9 lbs. **Length:** 45" overall.
Stock: European walnut; classic English style with checkered straight grip, wrap-around forend with bottom screw attachment.
Sights: Bead front.
Features: Hinged double triggers; color case-hardened and engraved lockplates, trigger guard and tang. Polymer-coated fiberglass ramrod. Rubber recoil pad. Not suitable for steel shot. Introduced 1990. Imported by CVA.
Price: **$459.95**

Dixie Magnum

Consult our Directory pages for the location of firms mentioned.

DIXIE MAGNUM PERCUSSION SHOTGUN
Gauge: 10, 12, 20.
Barrel: 30" (Imp. Cyl. & Mod.) in 10-gauge; 28" in 12-gauge.
Weight: 6-1/4 lbs. **Length:** 45" overall.
Stock: Hand-checkered walnut, 14" pull.
Features: Double triggers; light hand engraving; case-hardened locks in 12-gauge, polished steel in 10-gauge; sling swivels. From Dixie Gun Works.
Price: Upland **$449.00**
Price: 12-ga. kit **$375.00**
Price: 20-ga. **$495.00**
Price: 10-ga. **$495.00**
Price: 10-ga. kit **$395.00**

Navy Arms Fowler

NAVY ARMS FOWLER SHOTGUN
Gauge: 10, 12.
Barrel: 28".
Weight: 7 lbs., 12 oz. **Length:** 45" overall.
Stock: Walnut-stained hardwood.
Features: Color case-hardened lockplates and hammers; checkered stock. Imported by Navy Arms.
Price: **$345.00**

BLACKPOWDER SHOTGUNS

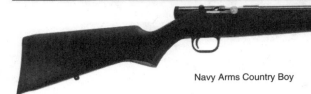

Navy Arms Country Boy

NAVY ARMS STEEL SHOT MAGNUM SHOTGUN
Gauge: 10.
Barrel: 28" (Cyl. & Cyl.).
Weight: 7 lbs., 9 oz. **Length:** 45-1/2" overall.
Stock: Walnut, with cheekpiece.
Features: Designed specifically for steel shot. Engraved, polished locks; sling swivels; blued barrels. Imported by Navy Arms.
Price:.. **$585.00**

NAVY ARMS COUNTRY BOY IN-LINE SHOTGUN
Gauge: 12.
Barrel: 25".
Weight: 7 lbs. **Length:** 42-1/2" overall.
Stock: Checkered black synthetic.
Features: Adjustable rotary choke; chrome-lined bore; sling swivel studs; take-down tool, nipple wrench in butt trap. Introduced 1998. From Navy Arms.
Price:.. **$165.00**

NAVY ARMS T&T SHOTGUN
Gauge: 12.
Barrel: 28" (Full & Full).
Weight: 7-1/2 lbs.
Stock: Walnut.
Sights: Bead front.
Features: Color case-hardened locks, double triggers, blued steel furniture. From Navy Arms.
Price:.. **$560.00**

Traditions Buckhunter Pro

TRADITIONS BUCKHUNTER PRO SHOTGUN
Gauge: 12.
Barrel: 24"; choke tube.
Weight: 6 lbs., 4 oz. **Length:** 43" overall.
Stock: Composite matte black, Break-Up or Advantage camouflage.
Features: In-line action with removable stainless steel breech plug; thumb safety; adjustable trigger; rubber buttpad. Introduced 1996. From Traditions.
Price:.. **$204.00**
Price: With Advantage or Break-Up camouflage stock **$248.00**

White Shooting Systems
White Thunder

White Muzzleloading Systems "Tominator" Shotgun
Similar to the White Thunder except has Imp. Cyl., Mod., Full and Super Full Turkey choke tubes; black laminate stock. Introduced 1995. From White Shooting Systems, Inc.
Price:.. **$499.95**

WHITE MUZZLELOADING SYSTEMS WHITE THUNDER SHOTGUN
Gauge: 12.
Barrel: 26" (Imp. Cyl., Mod., Full choke tubes); ventilated rib.
Weight: About 5-3/4 lbs.
Stock: Black hardwood.
Features: InstaFire in-line ignition; double safeties; match-grade trigger; Delron ramrod. Introduced 1995. From White Muzzleloading Systems, Inc.
Price:.. **$399.95**

AIRGUNS—HANDGUNS

Anics A-101 Magnum

Anics A-101 Magnum Air Pistol
Similar to the A-101 except has 5-1/3" barrel with compensator, gives about 490 fps. Introduced 1996. Imported by Anics Corp.
Price: With case, about.................................. **$75.00**

ANICS A-111 AIR PISTOL
Caliber: 177, 4.5mm, BB; 15-shot magazine.
Barrel: 4" steel smoothbore.
Weight: 35 oz. **Length:** 7" overall.
Power: CO_2
Stocks: Black synthetic, wrap-around style.
Sights: Blade front, fully adjustable rear.
Features: Velocity about 450 fps. Semi-automatic action; double action only; cross-bolt safety; black finish. Comes with two magazines, case. Introduced 1998. Imported by Anics Corp.
Price:.. **$74.00**
Price: Magnum version (5-1/3" barrel, 490 fps)................ **$77.00**

ANICS A-101 SUBCOMPACT AIR PISTOL
Caliber: 177, 4.5mm, BB; 15-shot magazine.
Barrel: 4" steel smoothbore.
Weight: 35 oz. **Length:** 7" overall.
Power: CO_2
Stocks: Ambidextrous black composite.
Sights: Blade front, fixed rear.
Features: Velocity to 450 fps. Semi-automatic action; double action only; cross-bolt safety; black and silver finish. Comes with two 15-shot magazines, case. Introduced 1996. Imported by Anics Corp.
Price: With case, about.................................. **$72.00**

ANICS A-201 AIR REVOLVER
Caliber: 177, 4.5mm, BB; 30-shot cylinder.
Barrel: 4", steel smoothbore.
Weight: 36 oz. **Length:** 9.75" overall.
Power: CO_2
Stocks: Black synthetic.
Sights: Blade front, fully adjustable rear.
Features: Velocity about 410 fps. Fixed barrel; single/double action; black and silver finish. Introduced 1998. Imported by Anics Corp.
Price: $125.00
Price: Magnum version (6" barrel, 460 fps) $130.00

BEEMAN P1 MAGNUM AIR PISTOL
Caliber: 177, 5mm, single shot.
Barrel: 8.4".
Weight: 2.5 lbs. **Length:** 11" overall.
Power: Top lever cocking; spring-piston.
Stocks: Checkered walnut.
Sights: Blade front, square notch rear with click micrometer adjustments for windage and elevation. Grooved for scope mounting.
Features: Dual power for 177 and 20-cal.: low setting gives 350-400 fps; high setting 500-600 fps. Rearward expanding mainspring simulates firearm recoil. All Colt 45 auto grips fit gun. Dry-firing feature for practice. Optional wooden shoulder stock. Introduced 1985. Imported by Beeman.
Price: 177, 5mm $405.00

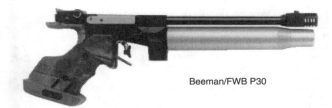

Beeman/FWB P30

BEEMAN/FWB P30 MATCH AIR PISTOL
Caliber: 177, single shot.
Barrel: 10-5/16", with muzzlebrake.
Weight: 2.4 lbs. **Length:** 16.5" overall.
Power: Pre-charged pneumatic.
Stocks: Stippled walnut; adjustable match type.
Sights: Undercut blade front, fully adjustable match rear.
Features: Velocity to 525 fps; up to 200 shots per CO_2 cartridge. Fully adjustable trigger; built-in muzzlebrake. Introduced 1995. Imported from Germany by Beeman.
Price: Right-hand $1,465.00
Price: Left-hand $1,520.00

Beeman/FWB C55

Beeman/Feinwerkbau 103

Beeman P1

Beeman P2 Match Air Pistol
Similar to the Beeman P1 Magnum except shoots only 177 pellets; completely recoilless single-stroke pneumatic action. Weighs 2.2 lbs. Choice of thumbrest match grips or standard style. Introduced 1990.
Price: 177, 5mm, standard grip $445.00
Price: 177, match grip $480.00

BEEMAN/FEINWERKBAU 65 MKII AIR PISTOL
Caliber: 177, single shot.
Barrel: 6.1", removable bbl. wgt. available.
Weight: 42 oz. **Length:** 13.3" overall.
Power: Spring, sidelever cocking.
Stocks: Walnut, stippled thumbrest; adjustable or fixed.
Sights: Front, interchangeable post element system, open rear, click adjustable for windage and elevation and for sighting notch width. Scope mount available.
Features: New shorter barrel for better balance and control. Cocking effort 9 lbs. Two-stage trigger, four adjustments. Quiet firing, 525 fps. Programs instantly for recoil or recoilless operation. Permanently lubricated. Steel piston ring. Imported by Beeman.
Price: Right-hand $1,170.00
Price: Left-hand $1,230.00

BEEMAN/FWB C55 CO₂ RAPID FIRE PISTOL
Caliber: 177, single shot or 5-shot magazine.
Barrel: 7.3".
Weight: 2.5 lbs. **Length:** 15" overall.
Power: Special CO_2 cylinder.
Stocks: Anatomical, adjustable.
Sights: Interchangeable front, fully adjustable open micro-click rear with adjustable notch size.
Features: Velocity 510 fps. Has 11.75" sight radius. Built-in muzzlebrake. Introduced 1993. Imported by Beeman Precision Airguns.
Price: Right-hand $1,705.00
Price: Left-hand $1,755.00

BEEMAN/FEINWERKBAU 103 PISTOL
Caliber: 177, single shot.
Barrel: 10.1", 12-groove rifling.
Weight: 2.5 lbs. **Length:** 16.5" overall.
Power: Single-stroke pneumatic, underlever cocking.
Stocks: Stippled walnut with adjustable palm shelf.
Sights: Blade front, open rear adjustable for windage and elevation. Notch size adjustable for width. Interchangeable front blades.
Features: Velocity 510 fps. Fully adjustable trigger. Cocking effort of 2 lbs. Imported by Beeman.
Price: Right-hand $1,520.00
Price: Left-hand $1,580.00

BEEMAN HW70A AIR PISTOL
Caliber: 177, single shot.
Barrel: 6-1/4", rifled.
Weight: 38 oz. **Length:** 12-3/4" overall.
Power: Spring, barrel cocking.
Stocks: Plastic, with thumbrest.
Sights: Hooded post front, square notch rear adjustable for windage and elevation. Comes with scope base.
Features: Adjustable trigger, 31-lb. cocking effort, 440 fps MV; automatic barrel safety. Imported by Beeman.
Price: $225.00
Price: HW70S, black grip, silver finish $240.00

BEEMAN/WEBLEY TEMPEST AIR PISTOL
Caliber: 177, 22, single shot.
Barrel: 6-7/8".
Weight: 32 oz. **Length:** 8.9" overall.
Power: Spring-piston, break barrel.
Stocks: Checkered black plastic with thumbrest.
Sights: Blade front, adjustable rear.
Features: Velocity to 500 fps (177), 400 fps (22). Aluminum frame; black epoxy finish; manual safety. Imported from England by Beeman.
Price: **$210.00**

Beeman/Webley Hurricane Air Pistol
Similar to the Tempest except has extended frame in the rear for a click-adjustable rear sight; hooded front sight; comes with scope mount. Imported from England by Beeman.
Price: **$240.00**

BEEMAN/WEBLEY NEMESIS AIR PISTOL
Caliber: 177, single shot.
Barrel: 7".
Weight: 2.2 lbs. **Length:** 9.8" overall.
Power: Single-stroke pneumatic.
Stocks: Checkered black composition.
Sights: Blade on ramp front, fully adjustable rear. Integral scope rail.
Features: Velocity to 400 fps. Adjustable two-stage trigger, manual safety. Recoilless action. Introduced 1995. Imported from England by Beeman.
Price: **$200.00**

Benjamin Sheridan CO_2

CONSULT
SHOOTER'S MARKETPLACE
Page 225, This Issue

BRNO TAU-7

COLT GOVERNMENT 1911 A1 AIR PISTOL
Caliber: 177, 8-shot cylinder magazine.
Barrel: 5", rifled.
Weight: 38 oz. **Length:** 8-1/2" overall.
Power: CO_2 cylinder.
Stocks: Checkered black plastic or smooth wood.
Sights: Post front, adjustable rear.
Features: Velocity to 393 fps. Quick-loading cylinder magazine; single and double action; black or silver finish. Introduced 1998. Imported by Colt's Mfg. Co., Inc.
Price: Black finish **$199.00**
Price: Silver finish **$209.00**

Beeman/Webley Tempest

BENJAMIN SHERIDAN CO_2 PELLET PISTOLS
Caliber: 177, 20, 22, single shot.
Barrel: 6-3/8", rifled brass.
Weight: 29 oz. **Length:** 9.8" overall.
Power: 12-gram CO_2 cylinder.
Stocks: Walnut.
Sights: High ramp front, fully adjustable notch rear.
Features: Velocity to 500 fps. Turn-bolt action with cross-bolt safety. Gives about 40 shots per CO_2 cylinder. Black or nickel finish. Made in U.S. by Benjamin Sheridan Co.
Price: Black finish, EB17 (177), EB20 (20), EB22 (22), about...... **$105.00**
Price: Nickel finish, E17 (177), E20 (20), E22 (22), about......... **$120.00**

BENJAMIN SHERIDAN PNEUMATIC PELLET PISTOLS
Caliber: 177, 20, 22, single shot.
Barrel: 9-3/8", rifled brass.
Weight: 38 oz. **Length:** 13-1/8" overall.
Power: Underlever pnuematic, hand pumped.
Stocks: Walnut stocks and pump handle.
Sights: High ramp front, fully adjustable notch rear.
Features: Velocity to 525 fps (variable). Bolt action with cross-bolt safety. Choice of black or nickel finish. Made in U.S. by Benjamin Sheridan Co.
Price: Black finish, HB17 (177), HB20 (20), HB22 (22), about **$115.00**
Price: Nickel finish, H17 (177), H20 (20), H22 (22), about **$120.00**

BRNO TAU-7 CO_2 MATCH PISTOL
Caliber: 177.
Barrel: 10.24".
Weight: 37 oz. **Length:** 15.75" overall.
Power: 12.5-gram CO_2 cartridge.
Stocks: Stippled hardwood with adjustable palm rest.
Sights: Blade front, open fully adjustable rear.
Features: Comes with extra seals and counterweight. Blue finish. Imported by Great Lakes Airguns.
Price: About **$379.50**

BSA 240 MAGNUM AIR PISTOL
Caliber: 177, 22, single shot
Barrel: 6".
Weight: 2 lbs. **Length:** 9" overall.
Power: Spring-air, top-lever cocking.
Stocks: Walnut.
Sights: Blade front, micrometer adjustable rear.
Features: Velocity 510 fps (177), 420 fps (22); crossbolt safety. Combat autoloader styling. Imported from U.K. by Precision Sales International, Inc.
Price: **$293.00**

COPPERHEAD BLACK VENOM PISTOL
Caliber: 177 pellets, BB, 17-shot magazine; darts, single shot.
Barrel: 4.75" smoothbore.
Weight: 16 oz. **Length:** 10.8" overall.
Power: Spring.
Stocks: Checkered.
Sights: Blade front, adjustable rear.
Features: Velocity to 270 fps (BBs), 250 fps (pellets). Spring-fed magazine; cross-bolt safety. Introduced 1996. Made in U.S. by Crosman Corp.
Price: About **$20.00**

COPPERHEAD BLACK FANG PISTOL
Caliber: 177 BB, 17-shot magazine.
Barrel: 4.75" smoothbore.
Weight: 10 oz. **Length:** 10.8" overall.
Power: Spring.
Stocks: Checkered.
Sights: Blade front, fixed notch rear.
Features: Velocity to 250 fps. Spring-fed magazine; cross-bolt safety. Introduced 1996. Made in U.S. by Crosman Corp.
Price: About **$16.00**

Crosman Auto Air II

Crosman Model 1008

Crosman Model 1377

CROSMAN AUTO AIR II PISTOL
Caliber: BB, 17-shot magazine, 177 pellet, single shot.
Barrel: 8-5/8" steel, smoothbore.
Weight: 13 oz. **Length:** 10-3/4" overall.
Power: CO_2 Powerlet.
Stocks: Grooved plastic.
Sights: Blade front, adjustable rear; highlighted system.
Features: Velocity to 480 fps (BBs), 430 fps (pellets). Semi-automatic action with BBs, single shot with pellets. Silvered finish. Introduced 1991. From Crosman.
Price: About **$35.00**

CROSMAN MODEL 357 SERIES AIR PISTOL
Caliber: 177, 6- and 10-shot pellet clips.
Barrel: 4" (Model 3574GT), 6" (Model 3576GT).
Weight: 32 oz. (6"). **Length:** 11-3/8" overall (357-6).
Power: CO_2 Powerlet.
Stocks: Checkered wood-grain plastic.
Sights: Ramp front, fully adjustable rear.
Features: Average 430 fps (Model 3574GT). Break-open barrel for easy loading. Single or double action. Vent. rib barrel. Wide, smooth trigger. Two cylinders come with each gun. Black and gold finish. From Crosman.
Price: 4" or 6", about **$60.00**

CROSMAN MODEL 1008 REPEAT AIR
Caliber: 177, 8-shot pellet clip
Barrel: 4.25", rifled steel.
Weight: 17 oz. **Length:** 8.625" overall.
Power: CO_2 Powerlet.
Stocks: Checkered black plastic.
Sights: Post front, adjustable rear.
Features: Velocity about 430 fps. Break-open barrel for easy loading; single or double semi-automatic action; two 8-shot clips included. Optional carrying case available. Introduced 1992. From Crosman.
Price: About **$60.00**
Price: With case, about **$65.00**
Price: Model 1008SB (silver and black finish), about **$60.00**

CROSMAN MODEL 1322, 1377 AIR PISTOLS
Caliber: 177 (M1377), 22 (M1322), single shot.
Barrel: 8", rifled steel.
Weight: 39 oz. **Length:** 13-5/8".
Power: Hand pumped.
Sights: Blade front, rear adjustable for windage and elevation.
Features: Moulded plastic grip, hand size pump forearm. Cross-bolt safety. Model 1377 also shoots BBs. From Crosman.
Price: About **$60.00**

DAISY/POWER LINE 44 REVOLVER
Caliber: 177 pellets, 6-shot.
Barrel: 6", rifled steel; interchangeable 4" and 8".
Weight: 2.7 lbs.
Power: CO_2.
Stocks: Moulded plastic with checkering.
Sights: Blade on ramp front, fully adjustable notch rear.
Features: Velocity up to 400 fps. Replica of 44 Magnum revolver. Has swing-out cylinder and interchangeable barrels. Introduced 1987. From Daisy Mfg. Co.
Price: **$60.95**

DAISY MODEL 2003 PELLET PISTOL
Caliber: 177 pellet, 35-shot clip.
Barrel: Rifled steel.
Weight: 2.2 lbs. **Length:** 11.7" overall.
Power: CO_2.
Stocks: Checkered plastic.
Sights: Blade front, open rear.
Features: Velocity to 400 fps. Crossbolt trigger-block safety. Made in U.S. by Daisy Mfg. Co.
Price: About **$67.95**

DAISY/POWER LINE 717 PELLET PISTOL
Caliber: 177, single shot.
Barrel: 9.61".
Weight: 2.8 lbs. **Length:** 13-1/2" overall.
Stocks: Moulded wood-grain plastic, with thumbrest.
Sights: Blade and ramp front, micro-adjustable notch rear.
Features: Single pump pneumatic pistol. Rifled steel barrel. Cross-bolt trigger block. Muzzle velocity 385 fps. From Daisy Mfg. Co. Introduced 1979.
Price: About **$69.95**

Daisy/Power Line 747 Pistol
Similar to the 717 pistol except has a 12-groove rifled steel barrel by Lothar Walther, and adjustable trigger pull weight. Velocity of 360 fps. Manual cross-bolt safety.
Price: About **$140.00**

DAISY/POWER LINE 1140 PELLET PISTOL
Caliber: 177, single shot.
Barrel: Rifled steel.
Weight: 1.3 lbs. **Length:** 11.7" overall.
Power: Single-stroke barrel cocking.
Stocks: Checkered resin.
Sights: Hooded post front, open adjustable rear.
Features: Velocity to 325 fps. Made of black lightweight engineering resin. Introduced 1995. From Daisy.
Price: About **$38.95**

Daisy/Power Line 717

DAISY MODEL 454 AIR PISTOL
Caliber: 177 BB, 20-shot clip.
Barrel: Smoothbore steel.
Weight: 1.6 lbs. **Length:** 10.4" overall.
Power: CO_2.
Stocks: Moulded black, ribbed composition.
Sights: Blade front, fixed rear.
Features: Velocity to 420 fps. Semi-automatic action; crossbolt safety; black finish. Introduced 1998. Made in U.S. by Dairy Mfg. Co.
Price: **$61.95**

Daisy/PowerLine 1270

DRULOV DU-10 CONDOR TARGET PISTOL
Caliber: 177, 5-shot magazine.
Barrel: 7.09".
Weight: 2.32 lbs. **Length:** 11.81" overall.
Power: CO_2.
Stocks: Target-type walnut with stippling.
Sights: Blade front, fully adjustable open rear.
Features: Velocity to 472 fps. Developed for Olympic Rapid Fire and 10-meter Sport Pistol events. Introduced 1997. Imported from the Czech Republic by Great Lakes Airguns.
Price: About **$495.50**

"GAT" AIR PISTOL
Caliber: 177, single shot.
Barrel: 7-1/2" cocked, 9-1/2" extended.
Weight: 22 oz.
Power: Spring-piston.
Stocks: Cast checkered metal.
Sights: Fixed.
Features: Shoots pellets, corks or darts. Matte black finish. Imported from England by Stone Enterprises, Inc.
Price: **$24.95**

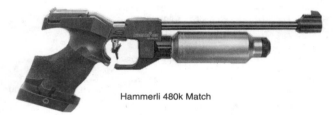

Hammerli 480k Match

MARKSMAN 1010 REPEATER PISTOL
Caliber: 177, 18-shot BB repeater.
Barrel: 2-1/2", smoothbore.
Weight: 24 oz. **Length:** 8-1/4" overall.
Power: Spring.
Features: Velocity to 200 fps. Thumb safety. Black finish. Uses BBs, darts, bolts or pellets. Repeats with BBs only. From Marksman Products.
Price: Matte black finish **$26.00**
Price: Model 2000 (as above except silver-chrome finish) **$27.00**

Consult our Directory pages for the location of firms mentioned.

MARKSMAN 2005 LASERHAWK SPECIAL EDITION AIR PISTOL
Caliber: 177, 24-shot magazine.
Barrel: 3.8", smoothbore.
Weight: 22 oz. **Length:** 10.3" overall.
Power: Spring-air.
Stocks: Checkered.
Sights: Fixed fiber optic front sight.
Features: Velocity to 300 fps with Hyper-Velocity pellets. Square trigger guard with skeletonized trigger; extended barrel for greater velocity and accuracy. Shoots BBs, pellets, darts or bolts. Made in the U.S. From Marksman Products.
Price: **$32.00**

DAISY/POWER LINE 1270 CO_2 AIR PISTOL
Caliber: BB, 60-shot magazine.
Barrel: Smoothbore steel.
Weight: 17 oz. **Length:** 11" overall.
Power: CO_2 pump action.
Stocks: Moulded black polymer.
Sights: Blade on ramp front, adjustable rear.
Features: Velocity to 420 fps. Crossbolt trigger block safety; plated finish. Introduced 1997. Made in U.S. by Daisy Mfg. Co.
Price: About **$40.95**

DAISY/POWER LINE 1700 AIR PISTOL
Caliber: 177 BB, 60-shot magazine.
Barrel: Smoothbore steel.
Weight: 1.4 lbs. **Length:** 11.2" overall.
Power: CO_2.
Stocks: Moulded checkered plastic.
Sights: Blade front, adjustable rear.
Features: Velocity to 420 fps. Cross-bolt trigger block safety; matte finish. Has 3/8" dovetail mount for scope or point sight. Introduced 1994. From Daisy Mfg. Co.
Price: About **$34.95**

Drulov DU-10

HAMMERLI 480 MATCH AIR PISTOL
Caliber: 177, single shot.
Barrel: 9.8".
Weight: 37 oz. **Length:** 16.5" overall.
Power: Air or CO_2.
Stocks: Walnut with 7-degree rake adjustment. Stippled grip area.
Sights: Undercut blade front, fully adjustable open match rear.
Features: Under-barrel cannister charges with air or CO_2 for power supply; gives 320 shots per filling. Trigger adjustable for position. Introduced 1994. Imported from Switzerland by Hammerli Pistols U.S.A.
Price: **$1,325.00**

Marksman 2005 Laserhawk

Hammerli 480k Match Air Pistol
Similar to the 480 except has a short, detachable aluminum air cylinder for use only with compressed air; can be filled while on the gun or off; special adjustable barrel weights. Muzzle velocity of 470 fps, gives about 180 shots. Has stippled black composition grip with adjustable palm shelf and rake angle. Comes with air pressure gauge. Introduced 1996. Imported from Switzerland by SIGARMS, Inc.
Price: **$1,155.00**

MORINI 162E MATCH AIR PISTOL
Caliber: 177, single shot.
Barrel: 9.4".
Weight: 32 oz. **Length:** 16.1" overall.
Power: Pre-charged CO_2.
Stocks: Adjustable match type.
Sights: Interchangeable blade front, fully adjustable match-type rear.
Features: Power mechanism shuts down when pressure drops to a pre-set level. Adjustable electronic trigger. Introduced 1995. Imported from Switzerland by Nygord Precision Products.
Price: **$950.00**

PARDINI K58 MATCH AIR PISTOL
Caliber: 177, single shot.
Barrel: 9.0".
Weight: 37.7 oz. **Length:** 15.5" overall.
Power: Pre-charged compressed air; single-stroke cocking.
Stocks: Adjustable match type; stippled walnut.
Sights: Interchangeable post front, fully adjustable match rear.
Features: Fully adjustable trigger. Introduced 1995. Imported from Italy by Nygord Precision Products.
Price: **$650.00**
Price: K60 model (CO_2) **$650.00**

RECORD JUMBO DELUXE AIR PISTOL
Caliber: 177, single shot.
Barrel: 6", rifled.
Weight: 1.9 lbs. **Length:** 7.25" overall.
Power: Spring-air, lateral cocking lever.
Stocks: Smooth walnut.
Sights: Blade front, fully adjustable open rear.
Features: Velocity to 322 fps. Thumb safety. Grip magazine compartment for extra pellet storage. Introduced 1983. Imported from Germany by Great Lakes Airguns.
Price: **$127.61**

RWS/Diana Model 6M

RWS/Diana Model 6G Air Pistols
Similar to the Model 6M except does not have the movable barrel shroud. Has click micrometer rear sight, two-stage adjustable trigger, interchangeable tunnel front sight. Available in right- or left-hand models.
Price: Right-hand **$450.00**
Price: Left-hand **$490.00**

RWS MODEL C-357 AIR PISTOL
Caliber: 177, 8-shot cylinder.
Barrel: 6", rifled.
Weight: 1.75 lbs. **Length:** 11" overall.
Power: CO_2
Stocks: Checkered black synthetic.
Sights: Blade front, adjustable rear.
Features: Velocity to 380 fps. Manual safety; black finish. Imported from Germany by Dynamit Nobel-RWS Inc.
Price: **$175.00**

Steyr Match LP1C

STEYR LP5C MATCH PISTOL
Caliber: 177, 5-shot magazine.
Barrel: NA.
Weight: 40.2 oz. **Length:** 13.39" overall.
Power: Refillable CO_2 cylinders.
Stocks: Adjustable Morini match with palm shelf; stippled walnut.
Sights: Movable 2.5mm blade front; 2-3mm interchangeable in .2mm increments; fully adjustable open match rear.
Features: Velocity about 500 fps. Fully adjustable trigger; compensator; has dry-fire feature. Barrel and grip weights available. Introduced 1993. Imported from Austria by Nygord Precision Products.
Price: **$1,350.00**

Record Jumbo

RWS/DIANA MODEL 5G AIR PISTOL
Caliber: 177, single shot.
Barrel: 7".
Weight: 2-3/4 lbs. **Length:** 15" overall.
Power: Spring-air, barrel cocking.
Stocks: Plastic, thumbrest design.
Sights: Tunnel front, micro-click open rear.
Features: Velocity of 450 fps. Adjustable two-stage trigger with automatic safety. Imported from Germany by Dynamit Nobel-RWS, Inc.
Price: **$260.00**

RWS/DIANA MODEL 6M MATCH AIR PISTOL
Caliber: 177, single shot.
Barrel: 7".
Weight: 3 lbs. **Length:** 15" overall.
Power: Spring-air, barrel cocking.
Stocks: Walnut-finished hardwood with thumbrest.
Sights: Adjustable front, micro. click open rear.
Features: Velocity of 410 fps. Recoilless double piston system, movable barrel shroud to protect from sight during cocking. Imported from Germany by Dynamit Nobel-RWS, Inc.
Price: Right-hand **$585.00**
Price: Left-hand **$640.00**

RWS C-225 AIR PISTOLS
Caliber: 177, 8-shot rotary magazine.
Barrel: 4", 6".
Weight: NA. **Length:** NA.
Power: CO_2.
Stocks: Checkered black plastic.
Sights: Post front, rear adjustable for windage.
Features: Velocity to 385 fps. Semi-automatic fire; decocking lever. Imported from Germany by Dynamit Nobel-RWS.
Price: 4", blue **$200.00**
Price: 4", nickel **$210.00**
Price: 6", blue **$210.00**
Price: 6", nickel **$235.00**

STEYR CO_2 MATCH LP1C PISTOL
Caliber: 177, single shot.
Barrel: 9".
Weight: 38.7 oz. **Length:** 15.3" overall.
Power: Refillable CO_2 cylinders.
Stocks: Fully adjustable Morini match with palm shelf; stippled walnut.
Sights: Interchangeable blade in 4mm, 4.5mm or 5mm widths, fully adjustable open rear with interchangeable 3.5mm or 4mm leaves.
Features: Velocity about 500 fps. Adjustable trigger, adjustable sight radius from 12.4" to 13.2". With compensator. Imported from Austria by Nygord Precision Products.
Price: **$1,250.00**

STEYR LP 5CP MATCH AIR PISTOL
Caliber: 177, 5-shot magazine.
Barrel: NA.
Weight: 40.7 oz. **Length:** 15.2" overall.
Power: Pre-charged air cylinder.
Stocks: Adjustable match type.
Sights: Interchangeable blade front, fully adjustable match rear.
Features: Adjustable sight radius; fully adjustable trigger. Has barrel compensator. Introduced 1995. Imported from Austria by Nygord Precision Products.
Price: **$1,395.00**

AIRGUNS—HANDGUNS

WALTHER CP88 PELLET PISTOL
Caliber: 177, 8-shot rotary magazine.
Barrel: 4", 6".
Weight: 37 oz. (4" barrel) **Length:** 7" (4" barrel).
Power: CO_2.
Stocks: Checkered plastic.
Sights: Blade front, fully adjustable rear.
Features: Faithfully replicates size, weight and trigger pull of the 9mm Walther P88 compact pistol. Has SA/DA trigger mechanism; ambidextrous safety, levers. Comes with two magazines, 500 pellets, one CO2 cartridge. Introduced 1997. Imported from Germany by Interarms.
Price: Blue... **$179.00**
Price: Nickel **$189.00**

WALTHER CPM-1 CO$_2$ MATCH PISTOL
Caliber: 177, single shot.
Barrel: 8.66".
Weight: NA. **Length:** 15.1" overall.
Power: CO_2.
Stocks: Orthopaedic target type.
Sights: Undercut blade front, open match rear fully adjustable for windage and elevation.
Features: Adjustable velocity; matte finish. Introduced 1995. Imported from Germany by Nygord Precision Products.
Price:.. **$950.00**

Walther CP88

Walther CP88 Competition Pellet Pistol
Similar to the standard CP88 except has 6" match-grade barrel, muzzle weight, wood or plastic stocks. Weighs 41 oz., has overall length of 9". Introduced 1997. Imported from Germany by Interarms.
Price: Blue, plastic stocks **$189.00**
Price: Nickel, plastic stocks **$199.00**
Price: Blue, wood stocks **$220.00**
Price: Nickel, wood stocks................................ **$232.00**

AIRGUNS—LONG GUNS

Air Arms TX 200

AIR ARMS TX 200 AIR RIFLE
Caliber: 177; single shot.
Barrel: 15.7".
Weight: 9.3 lbs. **Length:** 41.5" overall.
Power: Spring-air; underlever cocking.
Stock: Oil-finished hardwood; checkered grip and forend; rubber buttpad.
Sights: None furnished.
Features: Velocity about 900 fps. Automatic safety; adjustable two-stage trigger. Imported from England by Great Lakes Airguns.
Price:.. **$593.27**

AIR ARMS S-300 HI-POWER AIR RIFLE
Caliber: 22.
Barrel: 19-1/2".
Weight: 6.4 lbs. **Length:** 38.5" overall.
Stock: Stained European hardwood; ambidextrous.
Power: Precharged pneumatic.
Sights: None furnished
Features: Velocity about 750 fps. Two-stage trigger. Blue finish. Introduced 1997. Imported from England by Great Lakes Airarms.
Price: **$764.07**

Airrow A-8S1P

AIRROW MODEL A-8SRB STEALTH AIR GUN
Caliber: 177, 22, 25, 38, 9-shot.
Barrel: 19.7"; rifled.
Weight: 6 lbs. **Length:** 34" overall.
Power: CO_2 or compressed air; variable power.
Stock: Telescoping CAR-15-type.
Sights: Variable 3.5-10x scope.
Features: Velocity 1100 fps in all calibers. Pneumatic air trigger. All aircraft aluminum and stainless steel construction. Mil-spec materials and finishes. Introduced 1992. From Swivel Machine Works, Inc.
Price: About... **$2,599.00**

ARS/Magnum 6 Air Rifle
Similar to the King Hunting Master except is 6-shot repeater with 23-3/4" barrel, weighs 8-1/4 lbs. Stock is walnut-stained hardwood with checkered grip and forend; rubber buttpad. Velocity of 1000+ fps with 32-grain pellet. Imported from Korea by Air Rifle Specialists.
Price:.. **$500.00**

AIRROW MODEL A-8S1P STEALTH AIR GUN
Caliber: #2512 16" arrow.
Barrel: 16".
Weight: 4.4 lbs. **Length:** 30.1" overall.
Power: CO_2 or compressed air; variable power.
Stock: Telescoping CAR-15-type.
Sights: Scope rings only.
Features: Velocity to 650 fps with 260-grain arrow. Pneumatic air trigger. All aircraft aluminum and stainless steel construction. Mil-spec materials and finishes. Waterproof case. Introduced 1991. From Swivel Machine Works, Inc.
Price: About... **$1,699.00**

ARS/KING HUNTING MASTER AIR RIFLE
Caliber: 22, 5-shot repeater.
Barrel: 22-3/4".
Weight: 7-3/4 lbs. **Length:** 42" overall.
Power: Pre-compressed air from 3000 psi diving tank.
Stock: Indonesian walnut with checkered grip and forend; rubber buttpad.
Sights: Blade front, fully adjustable open rear. Receiver grooved for scope mounting.
Features: Velocity over 1000 fps with 32-grain pellet. High and low power switch for hunting or target velocities. Side lever cocks action and inserts pellet. Rotary magazine. Imported from Korea by Air Rifle Specialists.
Price:.. **$580.00**
Price: Hunting Master 900 (9mm, limited production) **$1,000.00**

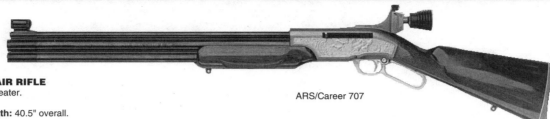

ARS/CAREER 707 AIR RIFLE
Caliber: 22, 6-shot repeater.
Barrel: 23".
Weight: 7.75 lbs. **Length:** 40.5" overall.
Power: Pre-compressed air; variable power.
Stock: Indonesian walnut with checkered grip, gloss finish.
Sights: Hooded post front with interchangeable inserts, fully adjustable diopter rear.
Features: Velocity to 1000 fps. Lever-action with straight feed magazine; pressure gauge in lower front air reservoir; scope mounting rail included. Introduced 1996. Imported from the Philippines by Air Rifle Specialists.
Price: $580.00

ARS/Career 707

ARS/FARCO FP SURVIVAL AIR RIFLE
Caliber: 22, 25, single shot.
Barrel: 22-3/4".
Weight: 5-3/4 lbs. **Length:** 42-3/4" overall.
Power: Multi-pump foot pump.
Stock: Philippine hardwood.
Sights: Blade front, fixed rear.
Features: Velocity to 850 fps (22 or 25). Receiver grooved for scope mounting. Imported from the Philippines by Air Rifle Specialists.
Price: $295.00

ARS HUNTING MASTER AR6 AIR RIFLE
Caliber: 22, 6-shot repeater.
Barrel: 25-1/2".
Weight: 7 lbs. **Length:** 41-1/4" overall.
Power: Pre-compressed air from 3000 psi diving tank.
Stock: Indonesian walnut with checkered grip; rubber buttpad.
Sights: Blade front, adjustable peep rear.
Features: Velocity over 1000 fps with 32-grain pellet. Receiver grooved for scope mounting. Has 6-shot rotary magazine. Imported by Air Rifle Specialists.
Price: $580.00

ARS/FARCO CO_2 AIR SHOTGUN
Caliber: 51 (28-gauge).
Barrel: 30".
Weight: 7 lbs. **Length:** 48-1/2" overall.
Power: 10-oz. refillable CO_2 tank.
Stock: Hardwood.
Sights: Blade front, fixed rear.
Features: Gives over 100 ft. lbs. energy for taking small game. Imported from the Philippines by Air Rifle Specialists.
Price: $460.00

ARS/Farco CO_2 Stainless Steel Air Rifle
Similar to the ARS/Farco CO_2 shotgun except in 22- or 25-caliber with 21-1/2" barrel; weighs 6-3/4 lbs., 42-1/2" overall; Philippine hardwood stock with stippled grip and forend; blade front sight, adjustable rear, grooved for scope mount. Uses 10-oz. refillable CO_2 cylinder. Made of stainless steel. Imported from the Philippines by Air Rifle Specialists.
Price: Including CO_2 cylinder $460.00

ARS/QB77 DELUXE AIR RIFLE
Caliber: 177, 22, single shot.
Barrel: 21-1/2".
Weight: 5-1/2 lbs. **Length:** 40" overall.
Power: Two 12-oz. CO_2 cylinders.
Stock: Walnut-stained hardwood.
Sights: Blade front, adjustable rear.
Features: Velocity to 625 fps (22), 725 fps (177). Receiver grooved for scope mounting. Comes with bulk-fill valve. Imported by Air Rifle Specialists.
Price: $195.00

Anschutz 2002

BEEMAN BEARCUB AIR RIFLE
Caliber: 177, single shot.
Barrel: 13".
Weight: 7.2 lbs. **Length:** 37.8" overall.
Power: Spring-piston, barrel cocking.
Stock: Stained hardwood.
Sights: Hooded post front, open fully adjustable rear.
Features: Velocity to 915 fps. Polished blue finish; receiver dovetailed for scope mounting. Imported from England by Beeman Precision Airguns.
Price: $325.00

BEEMAN CROW MAGNUM AIR RIFLE
Caliber: 20, 22, 25, single shot.
Barrel: 16"; 10-groove rifling.
Weight: 8.5 lbs. **Length:** 46" overall.
Power: Gas-spring; adjustable power to 32 foot pounds muzzle energy. Barrel-cocking.
Stock: Classic-style hardwood; hand checkered.
Sights: For scope use only; built-in base and 1" rings included.
Features: Adjustable two-stage trigger. Automatic safety. Also available in 22-caliber on special order. Introduced 1992. Imported by Beeman.
Price: $1,220.00

ANSCHUTZ 2002 MATCH AIR RIFLE
Caliber: 177, single shot.
Barrel: 26".
Weight: 10-1/2 lbs. **Length:** 44.5" overall.
Stock: European walnut, blonde hardwood or colored laminated hardwood; stippled grip and forend. Also available with flat-forend walnut stock for benchrest shooting.
Sights: Optional sight set #6834.
Features: Muzzle velocity 575 fps. Balance, weight match the 1907 ISU smallbore rifle. Uses #5021 match trigger. Recoil and vibration free. Fully adjustable cheekpiece and buttplate; accessory rail under forend. Introduced 1988. Imported from Germany by Gunsmithing, Inc., Accuracy International.
Price: Right-hand, blonde hardwood stock. . . . . **$1,017.50** to **$1,275.00**
Price: Left-hand, blonde hardwood stock. . . . . **$1,070.60** to **$1,365.00**
Price: Right-hand, walnut stock . . . . **$1,058.40** to **$1,329.00**
Price: Right-hand, color laminated stock . . . . **$1,073.30** to **$1,365.00**
Price: Left-hand, color laminated stock **$1,121.70**
Price: Model 2002D-RT Running Target, right-hand, no sights . . . **$1,185.60**
Price: #6834 Sight Set . . . . **$219.30** to **$225.00**

BEEMAN KODIAK AIR RIFLE
Caliber: 25, single shot.
Barrel: 17.6".
Weight: 9 lbs. **Length:** 45.6" overall.
Power: Spring-piston, barrel cocking.
Stock: Stained hardwood.
Sights: Blade front, open fully adjustable rear.
Features: Velocity to 820 fps. Up to 30 foot pounds muzzle energy. Introduced 1993. Imported by Beeman.
Price: $625.00

Beeman Mako

BEEMAN MAKO AIR RIFLE
Caliber: 177, single shot.
Barrel: 20", with compensator.
Weight: 7.3 lbs. **Length:** 38.5" overall.
Power: Pre-charged pneumatic.
Stock: Stained beech; Monte Carlo cheekpiece; checkered grip.
Sights: None furnished.
Features: Velocity to 930 fps. Gives over 50 shots per charge. Manual safety; brass trigger blade; vented rubber butt pad. Requires scuba tank for air. Introduced 1994. Imported from England by Beeman.
Price: **$1,000.00**
Price: Mako FT (thumbhole stock) **$1,350.00**

Beeman R1 Rifle

BEEMAN R1 AIR RIFLE
Caliber: 177, 20 or 22, single shot.
Barrel: 19.6", 12-groove rifling.
Weight: 8.5 lbs. **Length:** 45.2" overall.
Power: Spring-piston, barrel cocking.
Stock: Walnut-stained beech; cut-checkered pistol grip; Monte Carlo comb and cheekpiece; rubber buttpad.
Sights: Tunnel front with interchangeable inserts, open rear click-adjustable for windage and elevation. Grooved for scope mounting.
Features: Velocity of 940-1000 fps (177), 860 fps (20), 800 fps (22). Non-drying nylon piston and breech seals. Adjustable metal trigger. Milled steel safety. Right- or left-hand stock. Available with adjustable cheekpiece and buttplate at extra cost. Custom and Super Laser versions available. Imported by Beeman.
Price: Right-hand, 177, 20, 22 . . . . **$540.00**
Price: Left-hand, 177, 20, 22. . . . . **$575.00**

BEEMAN R1 CARBINE
Caliber: 177, 20, 22, 25, single shot.
Barrel: 16.1".
Weight: 8.6 lbs. **Length:** 41.7" overall.
Power: Spring-piston, barrel cocking.
Stock: Stained beech; Monte Carlo comb and checkpiece; cut checkered pistol grip; rubber buttpad.
Sights: Tunnel front with interchangeable inserts, open adjustable rear; receiver grooved for scope mounting.
Features: Velocity up to 1000 fps (177). Non-drying nylon piston and breech seals. Adjustable metal trigger. Machined steel receiver end cap and safety. Right- or left-hand stock. Imported by Beeman.
Price: 177, 20, 22, 25, right-hand **$540.00**
Price: As above, left-hand **$575.00**
Price: R1-AW (synthetic stock, nickel plating) **$705.00**

Beeman R1 Laser Mk II

BEEMAN R6 AIR RIFLE
Caliber: 177, single shot.
Barrel: NA.
Weight: 7.1 lbs. **Length:** 41.8" overall.
Power: Spring-piston, barrel cocking.
Stock: Stained hardwood.
Sights: Tunnel post front, open fully adjustable rear.
Features: Velocity to 815 fps. Two-stage Rekord adjustable trigger; receiver dovetailed for scope mounting; automatic safety. Introduced 1996. Imported from Germany by Beeman Precision Airguns.
Price: **$325.00**

BEEMAN R1 LASER MK II AIR RIFLE
Caliber: 177, 20, 22, 25, single shot.
Barrel: 16.1" or 19.6".
Weight: 8.4 lbs. **Length:** 41.7" overall.
Power: Spring-piston, barrel cocking.
Stock: Laminated wood with high cheekpiece, ventilated recoil pad.
Sights: Tunnel front with interchangeable inserts, open adjustable rear; receiver grooved for scope mounting.
Features: Velocity to 1150 fps (177). Special powerplant components. Built from the Beeman R1 rifle by Beeman.
Price: **$995.00**

BEEMAN R7 AIR RIFLE
Caliber: 177, 20, single shot.
Barrel: 17".
Weight: 6.1 lbs. **Length:** 40.2" overall.
Power: Spring piston.
Stock: Stained beech.
Sights: Hooded front, fully adjustable micrometer click open rear.
Features: Velocity to 700 fps (177), 620 fps (20). Receiver grooved for scope mounting; double-jointed cocking lever; fully adjustable trigger; checkered grip. Imported by Beeman.
Price: **$325.00**

> Consult our Directory pages for the location of firms mentioned.

Beeman R9 Deluxe

BEEMAN R9 AIR RIFLE
Caliber: 177, 20, single shot.
Barrel: NA.
Weight: 7.3 lbs. **Length:** 43" overall.
Power: Spring-piston, barrel cocking.
Stock: Stained hardwood.
Sights: Tunnel post front, fully adjustable open rear.
Features: Velocity to 1000 fps (177), 800 fps (20). Adjustable Rekord trigger; automatic safety; receiver dovetailed for scope mounting. Introduced 1996. Imported from Germany by Beeman Precision Airguns.
Price: **$350.00**

Beeman R9 Deluxe Air Rifle
Same as the R9 except has an extended forend stock, checkered pistol grip, grip cap, carved Monte Carlo cheekpiece. Globe front sight with inserts. Introduced 1997. Imported by Beeman.
Price: **$400.00**

Beeman R11

BEEMAN S1 MAGNUM AIR RIFLE

Caliber: 177, single shot.
Barrel: 19".
Weight: 7.1 lbs. **Length:** 45.5" overall.
Power: Spring-piston, barrel cocking.
Stock: Stained beech with Monte Carlo cheekpiece; checkered grip.
Sights: Hooded post front, fully adjustable micrometer click rear.
Features: Velocity to 900 fps. Automatic safety; receiver grooved for scope mounting; two-stage adjustable trigger; curved rubber buttpad. Introduced 1995. Imported by Beeman.
Price: $210.00

BEEMAN SUPER 12 AIR RIFLE

Caliber: 22, 25, 12-shot magazine.
Barrel: 19", 12-groove rifling.
Weight: 7.8 lbs. **Length:** 41.7" overall.
Power: Pre-charged pneumatic; external air reservoir.
Stock: European walnut.
Sights: None furnished; drilled and tapped for scope mounting; scope mount included.
Features: Velocity to 850 fps (25-caliber). Adjustable power setting gives 30-70 shots per 400 cc air bottle. Requires scuba tank for air. Introduced 1995. Imported by Beeman.
Price: $1,675.00

BEEMAN R11 AIR RIFLE

Caliber: 177, single shot.
Barrel: 19.6".
Weight: 8.8 lbs. **Length:** 47" overall.
Power: Spring-piston, barrel cocking.
Stock: Walnut-stained beech; adjustable buttplate and cheekpiece.
Sights: None furnished. Has dovetail for scope mounting.
Features: Velocity 910-940 fps. All-steel barrel sleeve. Imported by Beeman.
Price: $600.00

BEEMAN RX-1 GAS-SPRING MAGNUM AIR RIFLE

Caliber: 177, 20, 22, 25, single shot.
Barrel: 19.6", 12-groove rifling.
Weight: 8.8 lbs.
Power: Gas-spring piston air; single stroke barrel cocking.
Stock: Walnut-finished hardwood, hand checkered, with cheekpiece. Adjustable cheekpiece and buttplate.
Sights: Tunnel front, click-adjustable rear.
Features: Velocity adjustable to about 1200 fps. Uses special sealed chamber of air as a mainspring. Gas-spring cannot take a set. Introduced 1990. Imported by Beeman.
Price: 177, 20, 22 or 25 regular, right-hand $590.00
Price: 177, 20, 22, 25, left-hand $625.00

BEEMAN/HW 97 AIR RIFLE

Caliber: 177, 20, single shot.
Barrel: 17.75".
Weight: 9.2 lbs. **Length:** 44.1" overall.
Power: Spring-piston, underlever cocking.
Stock: Walnut-stained beech; rubber buttpad.
Sights: None. Receiver grooved for scope mounting.
Features: Velocity 830 fps (177). Fixed barrel with fully opening, direct loading breech. Adjustable trigger. Introduced 1994. Imported by Beeman Precision Airguns.
Price: Right-hand only $550.00

Beeman/Feinwerkbau P70

BEEMAN/FEINWERKBAU 300-S SERIES MATCH RIFLE

Caliber: 177, single shot.
Barrel: 19.9", fixed solid with receiver.
Weight: Approx. 10 lbs. with optional bbl. sleeve. **Length:** 42.8" overall.
Power: Spring-piston, single stroke sidelever.
Stock: Match model—walnut, deep forend, adjustable buttplate.
Sights: Globe front with interchangeable inserts. Click micro. adjustable match aperture rear. Front and rear sights move as a single unit.
Features: Recoilless, vibration free. Five-way adjustable match trigger. Grooved for scope mounts. Permanent lubrication, steel piston ring. Cocking effort 9 lbs. Optional 10-oz. barrel sleeve. Available from Beeman.
Price: Right-hand $1,270.00
Price: Left-hand $1,370.00

BEEMAN/FEINWERKBAU 603 AIR RIFLE

Caliber: 177, single shot.
Barrel: 16.6".
Weight: 10.8 lbs. **Length:** 43" overall.
Power: Single stroke pneumatic.
Stock: Special laminated hardwoods and hard rubber for stability. Multi-colored stock also available.
Sights: Tunnel front with interchangeable inserts, click micrometer match aperture rear.
Features: Velocity to 570 fps. Recoilless action; double supported barrel; special, short rifled area frees pellet form barrel faster so shooter's motion has minimum effect on accuracy. Fully adjustable match trigger with separately adjustable trigger and trigger slack weight. Trigger and sights blocked when loading latch is open. Introduced 1997. Imported by Beeman.
Price: $1,755.00

BEEMAN/FEINWERKBAU 300-S MINI-MATCH

Caliber: 177, single shot.
Barrel: 17-1/8".
Weight: 8.8 lbs. **Length:** 40" overall.
Power: Spring-piston, single stroke sidelever cocking.
Stock: Walnut. Stippled grip, adjustable buttplate. Scaled-down for youthful or slightly built shooters.
Sights: Globe front with interchangeable inserts, micro. adjustable rear. Front and rear sights move as a single unit.
Features: Recoilless, vibration free. Grooved for scope mounts. Steel piston ring. Cocking effort about 9-1/2 lbs. Barrel sleeve optional. Left-hand model available. Introduced 1978. Imported by Beeman.
Price: Right-hand $1,270.00
Price: Left-hand $1,370.00

BEEMAN/FEINWERKBAU P70 AIR RIFLE

Caliber: 177, single shot.
Barrel: 16.6".
Weight: 10.6 lbs. **Length:** 42.6" overall.
Power: Precharged pneumatic.
Stock: Laminated hardwoods and hard rubber for stability. Multi-colored stock also available.
Sights: Tunnel front with interchangeable inserts, click micormeter match aperture rear.
Features: Velocity to 570 fps. Recoilless action; double supported barrel; special short rifled area frees pellet from barrel faster so shooter's motion has minimum effect on accuracy. Fully adjustable match trigger with separately adjustable trigger and trigger slack weight. Trigger and sights blocked when loading latch is open. Introduced 1997. Imported by Beeman.
Price: $1,975.00

Benjamin Sheridan Pneumatic

Benjamin Sheridan 397C Pneumatic Carbine

Similar to the standard Model 397 except has 16-3/4" barrel, weighs 4 lbs., 3 oz. Velocity about 650 fps. Introduced 1995. Made in U.S. by Benjamin Sheridan Co.

Price: About. **$125.00**

BENJAMIN SHERIDAN CO_2 AIR RIFLES

Caliber: 177, 20 or 22, single shot.
Barrel: 19-3/8", rifled brass.
Weight: 5 lbs. **Length:** 36-1/2" overall.
Power: 12-gram CO_2 cylinder.
Stock: American walnut with buttplate.

BENJAMIN SHERIDAN PNEUMATIC (PUMP-UP) AIR RIFLES

Caliber: 177 or 22, single shot.
Barrel: 19-3/8", rifled brass.
Weight: 5-1/2 lbs. **Length:** 36-1/4" overall.
Power: Underlever pneumatic, hand pumped.
Stock: American walnut stock and forend.
Sights: High ramp front, fully adjustable notch rear.
Features: Variable velocity to 800 fps. Bolt action with ambidextrous push-pull safety. Black or nickel finish. Introduced 1991. Made in the U.S. by Benjamin Sheridan Co.
Price: Black finish, Model 397 (177), Model 392 (22), about. **$130.00**
Price: Nickel finish, Model S397 (177), Model S392 (22), about. . . . **$140.00**

Sights: High ramp front, fully adjustable notch rear.
Features: Velocity to 680 fps (177). Bolt action with ambidextrous push-pull safety. Gives about 40 shots per cylinder. Black or nickel finish. Introduced 1991. Made in the U.S. by Benjamin Sheridan Co.
Price: Black finish, Model G397 (177), Model G392 (22), about. . . . **$130.00**
Price: Black finish, Model FB9 (20), about **$124.50**

BRNO Tau-200

BRNO TAU-200 AIR RIFLE

Caliber: 177, single shot.
Barrel: 19", rifled.
Weight: 7-1/2 lbs. **Length:** 42" overall.
Power: 6-oz. CO_2 cartridge.
Stock: Wood match style with adjustable comb and buttplate.
Sights: Globe front with interchangeable inserts, fully adjustable open rear.
Features: Adjustable trigger. Comes with extra seals, large CO_2 bottle, counterweight. Introduced 1993. Imported by Century International Arms, Great Lakes Airguns.
Price: About. **$446.50**

Brolin SM1000

BROLIN MAX VELOCITY SM1000 AIR RIFLE

Caliber: 177 or 22, single shot.
Barrel: 19.5".
Weight: 9.2 lbs. **Length:** 46" overall.

BSA MAGNUM SUPERSTAR™ MKII MAGNUM AIR RIFLE, CARBINE

Caliber: 177, 22, 25, single shot.
Barrel: 18".
Weight: 8 lbs., 8 oz. **Length:** 43" overall.
Power: Spring-air, underlever cocking.
Stock: Oil-finished hardwood; Monte Carlo with cheekpiece, checkered at grip; recoil pad.
Sights: Ramp front, micrometer adjustable rear. Maxi-Grip scope rail.
Features: Velocity 1020 fps (177), 800 fps (22), 675 fps (25). Patented rotating breech design. Maxi-Grip scope rail protects optics from recoil; automatic anti-beartrap plus manual safety. Imported from U.K. by Precision Sales International, Inc.
Price:. **$540.00**
Price: MKII Carbine (14" barrel, 39-1/2" overall). **$540.00**

BSA MAGNUM SUPERSPORT™ AIR RIFLE

Caliber: 177, 22, 25, single shot.
Barrel: 18".
Weight: 6 lbs., 8 oz. **Length:** 41" overall.
Power: Spring-air, barrel cocking.
Stock: Oil-finished hardwood; Monte Carlo with cheekpiece, recoil pad.
Sights: Ramp front, micrometer adjustable rear. Maxi-Grip scope rail.

Stock: Walnut-stained hardwood; smooth, checkered or adjustable styles.
Sights: Adjustable blade front, fully adjustable rear. Comes with Weaver-style base mount.
Features: Velocity 1100+ fps (177) 900+ fps (22). Telescoping side cocking lever; double locking safety system. Introduced 1997. Imported by Brolin Industries, Inc.
Price: 177 or 22, smooth stock **$199.95**
Price: 177 or 22, checkered stock **$219.95**
Price: 177 or 22, adjustable stock **$249.95**

BSA MAGNUM AIRSPORTER RB2 MAGNUM AIR RIFLE, CARBINE

Caliber: 177, 22, 25, single shot.
Barrel: 18".
Weight: 8 lbs., 4 oz. **Length:** 44-1/2" overall.
Power: Spring-air, underlever cocking.
Stock: Oil-finished hardwood; Monte Carlo with cheekpiece, checkered at grip; recoil pad.
Sights: Ramp front, micrometer adjustable rear, comes with Maxi-Grip scope rail.
Features: Velocity 1020 fps (177), 800 fps (22), 675 fps (25). Maxi-Grip scope rail protects optics from recoil; automatic anti-beartrap plus manual tang safety. Imported from U.K. by Precision Sales International, Inc.
Price:. **$450.00**
Price: RB2 Carbine (14" barrel, 41" overall, muzzle brake). **$474.50**

Features: Velocity 1020 fps (177), 800 fps (22), 675 fps (25). Patented Maxi-Grip scope rail protects optics from recoil; automatic anti-beartrap plus manual tang safety. Muzzle brake standard. Imported for U.K. by Precision Sales International, Inc.
Price:. **$289.00**
Price: Carbine, 14" barrel, muzzle brake. **$323.00**

BSA Magnum Gold Star

BSA MAGNUM GOLDSTAR MAGNUM AIR RIFLE
Caliber: 177, 22, 10-shot repeater.
Barrel: 18".
Weight: 8 lbs., 8 oz. **Length:** 42.5" overall.
Power: Spring-air, underlever cocking.
Stock: Oil-finished hardwood; Monte Carlo with cheekpiece, checkered at grip; recoil pad.
Sights: Ramp front, micrometer adjustable rear; comes with Maxi-Grip scope rail.
Features: Velocity 1020 fps (177), 800 fps (22). Patented 10-shot indexing magazine; Maxi-Grip scope rail protects optics from recoil; automatic anti-beartrap plus manual safety; muzzlebrake standard. Imported from U.K. by Precision Sales International, Inc.
Price: **$847.00**

BSA MAGNUM SUPERTEN AIR RIFLE
Caliber: 177, 22 10-shot repeater.
Barrel: 17-1/2".
Weight: 7 lbs., 8 oz. **Length:** 37" overall.
Power: Precharged pneumatic via buddy bottle.
Stock: Oil-finished hardwood; Monte Carlo with cheekpiece, cut checkering at grip; adjustable recoil pad.
Sights: No sights; intended for scope use.
Features: Velocity 1300+ fps (177), 1000+ fps (22). Patented 10-shot indexing magazine, bolt-action loading. Left-hand version also available. Imported from U.K. by Precision Sales International, Inc.
Price: **$999.00**
Price: Left-hand **$1,069.00**

COPPERHEAD BLACK FIRE RIFLE
Caliber: 177 BB only.
Barrel: 14" smoothbore steel.
Weight: 2 lbs., 7 oz. **Length:** 31-1/2" overall.
Power: Pneumatic, hand pumped.
Stock: Textured plastic.
Sights: Blade front, open adjustable rear.
Features: Velocity to 437 fps. Introduced 1996. Made in U.S. by Crosman Corp.
Price: About **$25.00**

COPPERHEAD BLACK SERPENT RIFLE
Caliber: 177 pellets, 5-shot, on BB, 195-shot magazine.
Barrel: 19-1/2" smoothbore steel.
Weight: 2 lbs., 14 oz. **Length:** 35-7/8" overall.
Power: Pneumatic, single pump.
Stock: Textured plastic.
Sights: Blade front, open adjustable rear.
Features: Velocity to 405 fps. Introduced 1996. Made in U.S. by Crosman Corp.
Price: About **$40.00**

CROSMAN MODEL 782 BLACK DIAMOND AIR RIFLE
Caliber: 177 pellets (5-shot clip) or BB (195-shot reservoir).
Barrel: 18", rifled steel.
Weight: 3 lbs.
Power: CO$_2$ Powerlet.
Stock: Wood-grained ABS plastic; checkered grip and forend.
Sights: Blade front, open adjustable rear.
Features: Velocity up to 595 fps (pellets), 650 fps (BB). Black finish with white diamonds. Introduced 1990. From Crosman.
Price: About **$60.00**

BSA MAGNUM STUTZEN RB2 AIR RIFLE
Caliber: 177, 22, 25, single shot.
Barrel: 14".
Weight: 8 lbs., 8 oz. **Length:** 37" overall.
Power: Spring-air, underlever cocking.
Stock: Oil-finished hardwood; Monte Carlo with cheekpiece; checkered at grip, recoil pad.
Sights: Ramp front, adjustable leaf rear. Comes with Maxi-Grip scope rail.
Features: Velocity 1020 fps (177), 800 fps (22), 675 fps (25). Maxi-Grip scope rail protects optics from recoil; automatic anti-beartrap plus manual tang safety. Imported from U.K. by Precision Sales International,Inc.
Price: **$698.00**

BSA METEOR MK6 AIR RIFLE
Caliber: 177, 22, single shot.
Barrel: 18".
Weight: 6 lbs. **Length:** 41" overall.
Power: Spring-air, barrel cocking.
Stock: Oil-finished hardwood.
Sights: Ramp front, micrometer adjustable rear.
Features: Velocity 650 fps (177), 500 fps (22). Automatic anti-beartrap; manual tang safety. Receiver grooved for scope mounting. Imported from U.K. by Precision Sales International, Inc.
Price: Rifle or carbine **$224.00**

COPPERHEAD BLACK LIGHTNING RIFLE
Caliber: 177 BB, 15-shot magazine.
Barrel: 14" smoothbore.
Weight: 2 lbs. **Length:** 32" overall.
Power: Single-stroke pneumatic.
Stock: Textured plastic.
Sights: Bead front.
Features: Velocity to 350 fps. Cross-bolt safety. Introduced 1996. Made in U.S. by Crosman Corp.
Price: About **$25.00**

CROSMAN MODEL 66 POWERMASTER
Caliber: 177 (single shot pellet) or BB, 200-shot reservoir.
Barrel: 20", rifled steel.
Weight: 3 lbs. **Length:** 38-1/2" overall.
Power: Pneumatic; hand pumped.
Stock: Wood-grained ABS plastic; checkered pistol grip and forend.
Sights: Ramp front, fully adjustable open rear.
Features: Velocity about 645 fps. Bolt action, cross-bolt safety. Introduced 1983. From Crosman.
Price: About **$55.00**
Price: Model 66RT (as above with Realtree® camo finish), about **$65.00**
Price: Model 664X (as above, with 4x scope) **$70.00**
Price: Model 664SB (as above with silver and black finish), about . . . **$70.00**
Price: Model 664GT (black and gold finish, 4x scope) about **$70.00**

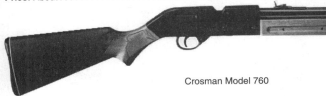

Crosman Model 760

CROSMAN MODEL 760 PUMPMASTER
Caliber: 177 pellets (single shot) or BB (200-shot reservoir).
Barrel: 19-1/2", rifled steel.
Weight: 2 lbs., 12 oz. **Length:** 33.5" overall.
Power: Pneumatic, hand pumped.
Stock: Walnut-finished ABS plastic stock and forend
Features: Velocity to 590 fps (BBs, 10 pumps). Short stroke, power determined by number of strokes. Post front sight and adjustable rear sight. Cross-bolt safety. Introduced 1966. From Crosman.
Price: About **$36.00**
Price: Model 760SB (silver and black finish), about **$50.00**

Crosman Model 1077 Repeatair

CROSMAN MODEL 795 SPRING MASTER RIFLE
Caliber: 177, single shot.
Barrel: Rifled steel.
Weight: 4 lbs., 8 oz. **Length:** 42" overall.
Power: Spring-piston.
Stock: Black synthetic.
Sights: Hooded front, fully adjustable rear.
Features: Velocity about 550 fps. Introduced 1995. From Crosman.
Price: About. $90.00

CROSMAN MODEL 2100 CLASSIC AIR RIFLE
Caliber: 177 pellets (single shot), or BB (200-shot BB reservoir).
Barrel: 21", rifled.
Weight: 4 lbs., 13 oz. **Length:** 39-3/4" overall.
Power: Pump-up, pneumatic.
Stock: Wood-grained checkered ABS plastic.
Features: Three pumps give about 450 fps, 10 pumps about 755 fps (BBs). Cross-bolt safety; concealed reservoir holds over 200 BBs. From Crosman.
Price: About. $70.00
Price: Model 2100SB (silver and black finish), about $80.00
Price: Model 2104GT (black and gold finish, 4x scope), about. $80.00
Price: Model 2100W (walnut stock, pellets only), about $100.00

DAISY MODEL 840
Caliber: 177 pellet single shot; or BB 350-shot.
Barrel: 19", smoothbore, steel.
Weight: 2.7 lbs. **Length:** 36.8" overall.
Power: Pneumatic, single pump.
Stock: Moulded wood-grain stock and forend.
Sights: Ramp front, open, adjustable rear.
Features: Muzzle velocity 335 fps (BB), 300 fps (pellet). Steel buttplate; straight pull bolt action; cross-bolt safety. Forend forms pump lever. Introduced 1978. From Daisy Mfg. Co.
Price: About. $33.95

CROSMAN MODEL 1077 REPEATAIR RIFLE
Caliber: 177 pellets, 12-shot clip
Barrel: 20.3", rifled steel.
Weight: 3 lbs., 11 oz. **Length:** 38.8" overall.
Power: CO_2 Powerlet.
Stock: Textured synthetic or American walnut.
Sights: Blade front, fully adjustable rear.
Features: Velocity 590 fps. Removable 12-shot clip. True semi-automatic action. Introduced 1993. From Crosman.
Price: About. $62.75
Price: 1077SB Silver Series (black stock, silver bbl.) $65.00
Price: 1077W (walnut stock) $100.00

CROSMAN MODEL 1389 BACKPACKER RIFLE
Caliber: 177, single shot.
Barrel: 14", rifled steel.
Weight: 3 lbs. 3 oz. **Length:** 31" overall.
Power: Hand pumped, pneumatic.
Stock: Composition, skeletal type.
Sights: Blade front, rear adjustable for windage and elevation.
Features: Velocity to 560 fps. Detachable stock. Receiver grooved for scope mounting. Metal parts blued. From Crosman.
Price: About. $70.00

CROSMAN MODEL 2200 MAGNUM AIR RIFLE
Caliber: 22, single shot.
Barrel: 19", rifled steel.
Weight: 4 lbs., 12 oz. **Length:** 39" overall.
Stock: Full-size, wood-grained ABS plastic with checkered grip and forend or American walnut.
Sights: Ramp front, open step-adjustable rear.
Features: Variable pump power—three pumps give 395 fps, six pumps 530 fps, 10 pumps 595 fps (average). Full-size adult air rifle. Has white line spacers at pistol grip and buttplate. Introduced 1978. From Crosman.
Price: About. $70.00
Price: 2200W, about $100.00

Daisy 1938 Red Ryder

DAISY/POWER LINE 856 PUMP-UP AIRGUN
Caliber: 177 pellets (single shot) or BB (100-shot reservoir).
Barrel: Rifled steel with shroud.
Weight: 2.7 lbs. **Length:** 37.4" overall.
Power: Pneumatic pump-up.
Stock: Moulded wood-grain with Monte Carlo cheekpiece.
Sights: Ramp and blade front, open rear adjustable for elevation.
Features: Velocity from 315 fps (two pumps) to 650 fps (10 pumps). Shoots BBs or pellets. Heavy die-cast metal receiver. Cross-bolt trigger-block safety. Introduced 1984. From Daisy Mfg. Co.
Price: About. $39.95

DAISY/POWER LINE 853
Caliber: 177 pellets.
Barrel: 20.9"; 12-groove rifling, high-grade solid steel by Lothar Waltherô, precision crowned; bore size for precision match pellets.
Weight: 5.08 lbs. **Length:** 38.9" overall.
Power: Single-pump pneumatic.
Stock: Full-length, select American hardwood, stained and finished; black buttplate with white spacers.
Sights: Globe front with four aperture inserts; precision micrometer adjustable rear peep sight mounted on a standard 3/8" dovetail receiver mount.
Features: Single shot. From Daisy Mfg. Co.
Price: About. $225.00

DAISY 1938 RED RYDER 60th ANNIVERSARY CLASSIC
Caliber: BB, 650-shot repeating action.
Barrel: Smoothbore steel with shroud.
Weight: 2.2 lbs. **Length:** 35.4" overall.
Stock: Walnut stock burned with Red Ryder lariat signature.
Sights: Post front, adjustable V-slot rear.
Features: Walnut forend. Saddle ring with leather thong. Lever cocking. Gravity feed. Controlled velocity. One of Daisy's most popular guns. From Daisy Mfg. Co.
Price: About. $40.95

> Consult our Directory pages for the location of firms mentioned.

DAISY MODEL 990 DUAL-POWER AIR RIFLE
Caliber: 177 pellets (single shot) or BB (100-shot magazine).
Barrel: Rifled steel.
Weight: 4.1 lbs. **Length:** 37.4" overall.
Power: Pneumatic pump-up and 12-gram CO_2.
Stock: Moulded woodgrain.
Sights: Ramp and blade front, adjustable open rear.
Features: Velocity to 650 fps (BB), 630 fps (pellet). Choice of pump or CO_2 power. Shoots BBs or pellets. Heavy die-cast receiver dovetailed for scope mount. Cross-bolt trigger block safety. Introduced 1993. From Daisy Mfg. Co.
Price: About. $62.95

Daisy/Power Line 4880

DAISY/POWER LINE 1170 PELLET RIFLE
Caliber: 177, single shot.
Barrel: Rifled steel.
Weight: 5.5 lbs. **Length:** 42.5" overall.
Power: Spring-air, barrel cocking.
Stock: Hardwood.
Sights: Hooded post front, micrometer adjustable open rear.
Features: Velocity to 800 fps. Monte Carlo comb. Introduced 1995. From Daisy Mfg. Co.
Price: About **$138.95**
Price: Model 131 (velocity to 600 fps) **$120.95**
Price: Model 1150 (black copolymer stock, velocity to 600 fps) **$77.95**

Daisy/Power Line 1000

DAISY/POWER LINE EAGLE 7856 PUMP-UP AIRGUN
Caliber: 177 (pellets), BB, 100-shot BB magazine.
Barrel: Rifled steel with shroud.
Weight: 2-3/4 lbs. **Length:** 37.4" overall.
Power: Pneumatic pump-up.
Stock: Moulded wood-grain plastic.
Sights: Ramp and blade front, open rear adjustable for elevation.
Features: Velocity from 315 fps (two pumps) to 650 fps (10 pumps). Finger grooved forend. Cross-bolt trigger-block safety. Introduced 1985. From Daisy Mfg. Co.
Price: With 4x scope, about **$51.95**

DAISY/YOUTHLINE MODEL 105 AIR RIFLE
Caliber: BB, 400-shot magazine.
Barrel: 13-1/2".
Weight: 1.6 lbs. **Length:** 29.8" overall.
Power: Spring.
Stock: Moulded woodgrain.
Sights: Blade on ramp front, fixed rear.
Features: Velocity to 275 fps. Blue finish. Cross-bolt trigger block safety. Made in U.S. by Daisy Mfg. Co.
Price: **$24.95**

DAISY/POWER LINE 880
Caliber: 177 pellet or BB, 50-shot BB magazine, single shot for pellets.
Barrel: Rifled steel.
Weight: 3.7 lbs. **Length:** 37.6" overall.
Power: Multi-pump pneumatic.
Stock: Moulded wood grain; Monte Carlo comb.
Sights: Hooded front, adjustable rear.
Features: Velocity to 685 fps. (BB). Variable power (velocity and range) increase with pump strokes; resin receiver with dovetail scope mount. Introduced 1997. Made in U.S. by Daisy Mfg. Co.
Price: About **$52.95**
Price: Model 4880 with Glo-Point fiber optic sight **$57.95**

DAISY/POWER LINE 1000 AIR RIFLE
Caliber: 177, single shot.
Barrel: NA.
Weight: 6 lbs. **Length:** 43" overall.
Power: Spring-air, barrel cocking.
Stock: Stained hardwood.
Sights: Hooded blade front on ramp, fully adjustable micrometer rear.
Features: Velocity to 1000 fps. Blued finish; trigger block safety. Introduced 1997. From Daisy Mfg. Co.
Price: About **$214.95**

DAISY/YOUTHLINE MODEL 95 AIR RIFLE
Caliber: BB, 700-shot magazine.
Barrel: 18".
Weight: 2.4 lbs. **Length:** 35.2" overall.
Power: Spring.
Stock: Stained hardwood.
Sights: Blade on ramp front, open adjustable rear.
Features: Velocity to 325 fps. Cross-bolt trigger block safety. Made in U.S. by Daisy Mfg. Co.
Price: **$38.95**

"GAT" AIR RIFLE
Caliber: 177, single shot.
Barrel: 17-1/4" cocked, 23-1/4" extended.
Weight: 3 lbs.
Power: Spring-piston.
Stock: Composition.
Sights: Fixed.
Features: Velocity about 450 fps. Shoots pellets, darts, corks. Imported from England by Stone Enterprises, Inc.
Price: **$38.95**

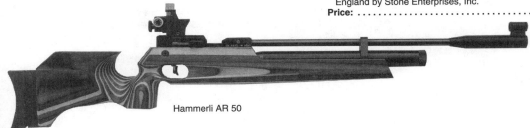

Hammerli AR 50

HAMMERLI MODEL 450 MATCH AIR RIFLE
Caliber: 177, single shot.
Barrel: 19.5".
Weight: 9.8 lbs. **Length:** 43.3" overall.
Power: Pneumatic.
Stock: Match style with stippled grip, rubber buttpad. Beach or walnut.
Sights: Match tunnel front, Hammerli diopter rear.
Features: Velocity about 560 fps. Removable sights; forend sling rail; adjustable trigger; adjustable comb. Introduced 1994. Imported from Switzerland by Sigarms, Inc.
Price: Beech stock **$1,355.00**
Price: Walnut stock **$1,395.00**

HAMMERLI AR 50 AIR RIFLE
Caliber: 177.
Barrel: 19.8".
Weight: 10 lbs. **Length:** 43.2" overall.
Power: Compressed air.
Stock: Anatomically-shaped universal and right-hand; match style; multi-colored laminated wood.
Sights: Interchangeable element tunnel front, fully adjustable Hammerli peep rear.
Features: Vibration-free firing release; fully adjustable match trigger and trigger stop; stainless air tank, built-in pressure gauge. Gives 270 shots per filling. Introduced 1998. Imported from Switzerland by Sigarms, Inc.
Price: . . . . **NA**

Marksman 1710

MARKSMAN 1710 PLAINSMAN AIR RIFLE

Caliber: 177, BB, 20-shot repeater.
Barrel: Smoothbore steel with shroud.
Weight: 2.25 lbs. **Length:** 34" overall.
Power: Spring-air.
Stock: Stained hardwood.
Sights: Blade on ramp front, adjustable V-slot rear.
Features: Velocity about 275 fps. Positive feed; automatic safety. Introduced 1994. Made in U.S. From Marksman Products.
Price: $36.45

MARKSMAN BB BUDDY AIR RIFLE

Caliber: 177, 20-shot magazine.
Barrel: 10.5" smoothbore.
Weight: 1.6 lbs. **Length:** 33" overall.
Power: Spring-air.
Stock: Moulded composition.
Sights: Blade on ramp front, adjustable V-slot rear.
Features: Velocity 275 fps. Positive feed; automatic safety. Youth-sized lightweight design. Introduced 1998. Made in U.S. From Marksman Products.
Price: $27.95

Marksman 1745S

MARKSMAN 1745 BB REPEATER AIR RIFLE

Caliber: 177 BB or pellet, 18-shot BB reservoir.
Barrel: 15-1/2", rifled.
Weight: 4.75 lbs. **Length:** 36" overall.
Power: Spring-air.
Stock: Moulded composition with ambidextrous Monte Carlo cheekpiece and rubber recoil pad.
Sights: Hooded front, adjustable rear.
Features: Velocity about 450 fps. Break-barrel action; automatic safety. Uses BBs, pellets, darts or bolts. Introduced 1997. Made in the U.S. From Marksman Products.
Price: $58.00
Price: Model 1745S (same as above except comes with #1804 4x20 scope) $73.00

MARKSMAN 1750 BB BIATHLON REPEATER RIFLE

Caliber: BB, 18-shot magazine.
Barrel: 15", smoothbore.
Weight: 4.7 lbs.
Power: Spring-piston, barrel cocking.
Stock: Moulded composition.
Sights: Tunnel front, open adjustable rear.
Features: Velocity of 450 fps. Automatic safety. Positive Feed System loads a BB each time gun is cocked. Introduced 1990. From Marksman Products.
Price: $59.75

Marksman 1790

MARKSMAN 1790 BIATHLON TRAINER

Caliber: 177, single shot.
Barrel: 15", rifled.
Weight: 4.7 lbs.
Power: Spring-air, barrel cocking.
Stock: Synthetic.
Sights: Hooded front, match-style diopter rear.
Features: Velocity of 450 fps. Endorsed by the U.S. Shooting Team. Introduced 1989. From Marksman Products.
Price: $70.00

MARKSMAN 1798 COMPETITION TRAINER AIR RIFLE

Caliber: 177, single shot.
Barrel: 15", rifled.
Weight: 4.7 lbs.
Power: Spring-air, barrel cocking.
Stock: Synthetic.
Sights: Laserhawk fiber optic front, match-style diopter rear.
Features: Velocity about 495 fps. Automatic safety. Introduced 1998. Made in U.S. From Marksman Products.
Price: $70.00

MARKSMAN 2015 LASERHAWK™ BB REPEATER AIR RIFLE

Caliber: 177 BB, 20-shot magazine.
Barrel: 10.5" smoothbore.
Weight: 1.6 lbs. **Length:** Adjustable to 33", 34" or 35" overall.
Power: Spring-air.
Stock: Moulded composition.
Sights: Fixed fiber optic front sight, adjustable elevation V-slot rear.
Features: Velocity about 275 fps. Positive feed; automatic safety. Adjustable stock. Introduced 1997. Made in the U.S. From Marksman Products.
Price: $33.00

RWS Model 75S T01

RWS MODEL 75S T01 MATCH
Caliber: 177, single shot.
Barrel: 19".

Weight: 11 lbs. **Length:** 43.7" overall.
Power: Dual spring piston.
Stock: Oil-finished beech with stippled grip; adjustable cheekpiece, buttplate.
Sights: Globe front, fully adjustable match peep rear.
Features: Velocity of 580 fps. Fully adjustable trigger; recoilless action. Introduced 1990. Imported from Germany by Dynamit Nobel-RWS.
Price: **$1,650.00**

RWS Model 24C

RWS/DIANA MODEL 24 AIR RIFLE
Caliber: 177, 22, single shot.
Barrel: 17", rifled.
Weight: 6 lbs. **Length:** 42" overall.
Power: Spring-air, barrel cocking.
Stock: Beech.
Sights: Hooded front, adjustable rear.
Features: Velocity of 700 fps (177). Easy cocking effort; blue finish. Imported from Germany by Dynamit Nobel-RWS, Inc.
Price: **$205.00**
Price: Model 24C **$205.00**

RWS/Diana Model 34 Air Rifle
Similar to the Model 24 except has 19" barrel, weighs 7.5 lbs. Gives velocity of 1000 fps (177), 800 fps (22). Adjustable trigger, synthetic seals. Comes with scope rail.
Price: 177 or 22 . . . . **$285.00**
Price: Model 34N (nickel-plated metal, black epoxy-coated wood stock) **$330.00**
Price: Model 34BC (matte black metal, black stock, 4x32 scope, mounts) **$485.00**

RWS MODEL CA 100 AIR RIFLE
Caliber: 177, single shot.
Barrel: 22".
Weight: 11.4 lbs. **Length:** 44" overall.
Power: Compressed air; interchangeable cylinders.
Stock: Laminated hardwood with adjustable cheekpiece and buttplate.
Sights: Tunnel front, match rear.
Features: Gives 250 shots per full charge. Double-sided power regulator. Introduced 1995. Imported from England by Dynamit Nobel-RWS, Inc.
Price: **$2,200.00**

RWS/DIANA MODEL 45 AIR RIFLE
Caliber: 177, single shot.
Weight: 8 lbs. **Length:** 45" overall.
Power: Spring-air, barrel cocking.
Stock: Walnut-finished hardwood with rubber recoil pad.
Sights: Globe front with interchangeable inserts, micro. click open rear with four-way blade.
Features: Velocity of 820 fps. Dovetail base for either micrometer peep sight or scope mounting. Automatic safety. Imported from Germany by Dynamit Nobel-RWS, Inc.
Price: **$330.00**

RWS/Diana Model 36

RWS/DIANA MODEL 36 AIR RIFLE
Caliber: 177, 22, single shot.
Barrel: 19", rifled.
Weight: 8 lbs. **Length:** 45" overall.

Power: Spring-air, barrel cocking.
Stock: Beech.
Sights: Hooded front (interchangeable inserts available), adjustable rear.
Features: Velocity of 1000 fps (177-cal.). Comes with scope mount; two-stage adjustable trigger. Imported from Germany by Dynamit Nobel-RWS, Inc.
Price: **$415.00**
Price: Model 36 Carbine (same as Model 36 rifle except has 15" barrel) **$415.00**

RWS/Diana Model 52 Deluxe

RWS/DIANA MODEL 52 AIR RIFLE
Caliber: 177, 22, single shot.
Barrel: 17", rifled.
Weight: 8-1/2 lbs. **Length:** 43" overall.
Power: Spring-air, sidelever cocking.
Stock: Beech, with Monte Carlo, cheekpiece, checkered grip and forend.

Sights: Ramp front, adjustable rear.
Features: Velocity of 1100 fps (177). Blue finish. Solid rubber buttpad. Imported from Germany by Dynamit Nobel-RWS, Inc.
Price: **$535.00**
Price: Model 52 Deluxe (select walnut stock, rosewood grip and forend caps, palm swell grip) **$775.00**
Price: Model 48B (as above except matte black metal, black stock) **$535.00**
Price: Model 48 (same as Model 52 except no Monte Carlo, cheekpiece or checkering) **$530.00**

RWS/Diana Model 54 Air King

RWS/DIANA MODEL 54 AIR KING RIFLE
Caliber: 177, 22, single shot.
Barrel: 17".
Weight: 9 lbs. **Length:** 43" overall.
Power: Spring-air, sidelever cocking.
Stock: Walnut with Monte Carlo cheekpiece, checkered grip and forend.
Sights: Ramp front, fully adjustable rear.
Features: Velocity to 1000 fps (177), 900 fps (22). Totally recoilless system; floating action absorbs recoil. Imported from Germany by Dynamit Nobel-RWS, Inc.
Price: **$750.00**

SLAVIA MODEL 631 AIR RIFLE
Caliber: 177, single shot.
Barrel: 21".
Weight: 6.8 lbs. **Length:** 45.5" overall.
Power: Spring-air; barrel cocking.
Stock: Oil-finished European hardwood; checkered forend.
Sights: Hooded post front, fully adjustable open rear.

Slavia Model 631

Features: Velocity to 720 fps. Adjustable two-stage trigger; receiver grooved for scope mounting; automatic safety. Introduced 1996. Imported from the Czech Republic by Great Lakes Airguns.
Price: **$114.40**

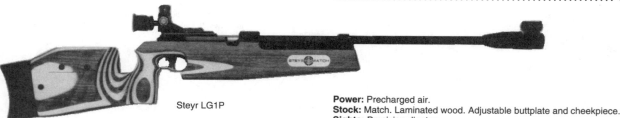

Steyr LG1P

STEYR LG1P AIR RIFLE
Caliber: 177, single shot.
Barrel: 23.75", (13.75" rifled).
Weight: 10.5 lbs. **Length:** 51.7" overall.
Power: Precharged air.
Stock: Match. Laminated wood. Adjustable buttplate and cheekpiece.
Sights: Precision diopter.
Features: Velocity 577 fps. Air cylinders are refillable; about 320 shots per cylinder. Designed for 10-meter shooting. Introduced 1996. Imported from Austria by Nygord Precision Products.
Price: About **$1,295.00**
Price: Left-hand, about **$1,350.00**

WEBLEY PATRIOT AIR RIFLE
Caliber: 22, single shot.
Barrel: 17.5".
Weight: 9 lbs. **Length:** 45.6" overall.
Power: Spring-air; barrel cocking.
Stock: Walnut-stained beech; checkered grip; rubber buttpad.
Sights: Post front, fully adjustable open rear.

Webley Patriot

Features: Velocity to 932 fps. Automatic safety; receiver grooved for scope mounting. Imported from England by Great Lakes Airguns.
Price: **$561.12**

Whiscombe JW70 FB

WHISCOMBE JW SERIES AIR RIFLES
Caliber: 177, 20, 22, 25, single shot.
Barrel: 17", Lothar Walther. Polygonal rifling.
Weight: 9 lbs., 8 oz. **Length:** 39" overall.
Power: Dual spring-piston, multi-stroke; underlever cocking.
Stock: Walnut with adjustable buttplate and cheekpiece.
Sights: None furnished; grooved scope rail.
Features: Velocity 660-1000 (JW80) fps (22-caliber, fixed barrel) depending upon model. Interchangeable barrels; automatic safety; muzzle weight; semi-floating action; twin opposed pistons with counter-wound springs; adjustable trigger. All models include H.O.T. System (Harmonic Optimization Tunable System). Introduced 1995. Imported from England by Pelaire Products.
Price: JW50, MKII fixed barrel only **$1,895.00**
Price: JW60, MKII fixed barrel only **$1,895.00**
Price: JW70, MKII fixed barrel only **$1,950.00**
Price: JW80, MKII **$1,995.00**

A

A-Square Co., Inc., One Industrial Park, Bedford, KY 40006-9667/502-255-7456; FAX: 502-255-7657

A. H&B Service, Inc., 7150 S. Platte Canyon Rd., Littleton, CO 80123/303-979-5447

A.M.T., 6226 Santos Diaz St., Irwindale, CA 91702/818-334-6629; FAX: 818-969-5247

Accu-Tek, 4510 Carter Ct., Chino, CA 91710/909-627-2404; FAX: 909-627-7817

Accuracy Gun Shop, 1240 Hunt Ave., Columbus, GA, 31907/706-561-6386

Accuracy Gun Shop, 5903 Boulder Hwy., E. Las Vegas, NV 89122/702-458-3330

Accuracy International, 9115 Trooper Trail, P.O. Box 2019, Bozeman, MT 59715/406-587-7922; FAX: 406-585-9434

AcuSport Corporation, 1 Hunter Place, Bellefontaine, OH 43311-3001/513-593-7010; FAX: 513-592-5625

Adventure A.G.R., 2991 St. Jude Dr., Waterford, MI 48329/810-673-3090

Ahlman's Inc., 9525 W. 230th St., Morristown, MN 55052/507-685-4243; 507-685-4244; FAX: 507-685-4247

Aimpoint U.S.A., 420 W. Main St., Geneseo, IL 61254/309-944-1702

Aimtech Mount Systems, P.O. Box 223, 101 Inwood Acres, Thomasville, GA 31799/912-226-4313; FAX: 912-227-0222

Air Arms, Hailsham Industrial Park, Diplocks Way, Hailsham, E. Sussex, BN27 3JF ENGLAND/011-0323-845853 (U.S. importers—World Class Airguns)

Air Guns Unlimited, 15866 Main St., LaPuente, CA 91744/818-333-4991

Air Rifle Specialists, P.O. Box 138, 130 Holden Rd., Pine City, NY 14871-0138/607-734-7340; FAX: 607-733-3261

Air Venture Air Guns, 9752 Flower St., Bellflower, CA 90706/310-867-6355

Air Venture, 9752 E. Flower St., Bellflower, CA 90706/310-867-6355

Airguns International, 3451 G Airway Dr., Santa Rosa, CA 95403/707-578-7900

Airrow (See Swivel Machine Works, Inc.)

Alexander, W.R., Gunsmith, 1406 Capital Circle, N.E. #D, Tallahassee, FL 32308/904-656-6176

Allison & Carey Gun Works, Inc., 17311 S.E. Stark, Portland, OR 97233/503-256-5166

Alpine Arms Corp., 6716 Fort Hamilton Pkwy., Brooklyn, NY 11219/718-833-2228

Alpine Range, 5482 Shelby Road, Fort Worth, TX 76140/817-478-6613

American Arms, Inc., 715 Armour Rd., N. Kansas City, MO 64116/816-474-3161; FAX: 816-474-1225

American Derringer Corp., 127 N. Lacy Dr., Waco, TX 76705/800-642-7817, 817-799-9111; FAX: 817-799-7935

Ammo Load, Inc., 1560 E. Edinger, Suite G, Santa Ana, CA 92705/714-558-8858; FAX: 714-569-0319

Amtec 2000, Inc., 84 Industrial Rowe, Gardner, MA 01440/508-632-9608; FAX: 508-632-2300

Anderson Manufacturing Co., Inc., 22602 53rd Ave. SE, Bothell, WA 98021/206-481-1858; FAX: 206-481-7839

Anderson's Gunsmithing, 115 Lincoln Ave. P.O. Box 70, Fall Creek, WI 54732/715-877-2031

Anschutz GmbH, Postfach 1128, D-89001 Ulm, Donau, GERMANY (U.S. importers—Accuracy International; AcuSport Corporation; Champion Shooters' Supply; Champion's Choice; Gunsmithing, Inc.)

Arizaga (See U.S. importer—Mandall Shooting Supplies, Inc.)

Armadillo Air Gun Repair, 5892 Hampshire Rd., Corpus Christi, TX 78408/512-289-5458

ArmaLite, Inc., P.O. Box 299, Geneseo, IL 61254/309-944-6939; FAX: 309-944-6949

Armi Sport (See U.S. importers—Cape Outfitters; Taylor's & Co., Inc.)

Arms United Corp., 1018 Cedar St., Niles, MI 49120/616-683-6837

Armscorp USA, Inc., 4424 John Ave., Baltimore, MD 21227/410-247-6200; FAX: 410-247-6205

Armsport, Inc., 3950 NW 49th St., Miami, FL 33142/305-635-7850; FAX: 305-633-2877

Arrieta, S.L., Morkaiko, 5, 20870 Elgoibar, SPAIN/34-43-743150; FAX: 34-43-743154 (U.S. importers—Griffin & Howe; Jansma, Jack J.; New England Arms Co.; The Orvis Co., Inc.; Quality Arms, Inc.; Wingshooting Adventures)

Article II Gunshop dba Gun World, 421 E. Irving Park Rd., Bensenville, IL 60106/708-595-0310

Aspen Outfitting Co., 520 East Cooper Ave., Aspen, CO 81611

Astra Sport, S.A., Apartado 3, 48300 Guernica, Espagne, SPAIN/34-4-6250100; FAX: 34-4-6255186 (U.S. importer—E.A.A. Corp.; P.S.M.G. Gun Co.)

Atamec-Bretton, 19, rue Victor Grignard, F-42026 St.-Etienne (Cedex 1) FRANCE/77-93-54-69; FAX: 33-77-93-57-98 (U.S. importer—Mandall Shooting Supplies, Inc.)

Atlantic Guns, Inc., 944 Bonifant St., Silver Spring, MD 20910/301-585-4448

Atlas Gun & Repair, 5005 E. St. Bernard Hwy, Violet, LA 70092/504-271-9300

Auto Electric & Parts, Inc., 24 W. Baltimore Ave., Media, PA 19063/610-565-2432

Auto-Ordnance Corp., Williams Lane, West Hurley, NY 12491/914-679-4190

Autumn Sales, Inc. (Blaser), 1320 Lake St., Fort Worth, TX 76102/817-335-1634; FAX: 817-338-0119

AYA (See U.S. importer—New England Custom Gun Service)

B

B&B Gun Refinishing Co., 930 Azalea St., Lake Charles, LA 70605/318-477-8586

B&B Supply Co., 4501 Minnehaha Av., Minneapolis, MN 55406/612-724-5230

B-Square Company, Inc., P.O. Box 11281, 2708 St. Louis Ave., Ft. Worth, TX 76110/817-923-0964, 800-433-2909; FAX: 817-926-7012

Bachelder Master Gunmakers, 1229 Michigan N.E., Grand Rapids, MI 49503/616-459-3636; FAX: 616-459-7442

Badger's Shooters Supply, Inc., 202 N. Hading, Owen, WI 54460-0397/715-229-2101

Baer Custom, Les, Inc., 29601 34th Ave., Hillsdale, IL 61257/309-658-2716; FAX: 309-658-2610

Bain & Davis, Inc., 307 East Valley Blvd., San Gabriel, CA 91776/818-573-4241

Baity's Custom Gunworks, 2623 Boone Trail, N. Wilkesboro, NC 28659/919-667-8785

Barrett Firearms Manufacturer, Inc., P.O. Box 1077, Murfreesboro, TN 37133/615-896-2938; FAX: 615-896-7313

Bartelmay Guns, Geo. M., 911 W. Jefferson St., Morton, IL 61550/309-263-8032

Bartlett, Michael, P.O. Box 26124, Lemarchant Rd., Postal Outlet, St. John's, Newfoundland, CANADA A1C 2H5/709-364-4955

Bausch & Lomb Sports Optics Div. (See Bushnell Sports Optics Worldwide)

Beauchamp & Son, Inc., 160 Rossiter Rd., P.O. Box 181, Richmond, MA 01254/413-698-3822; FAX: 413-698-3866

Bedlans Sporting Goods, 1318 E. St. P.O. Box 244, Fairbury, NE 68352/402-729-6112

Beeman Precision Airguns, 5454 Argosy Dr., Huntington Beach, CA 92649/714-890-4800; FAX: 714-890-4808

Bell's Legendary Country Wear, 22 Circle Dr., Bellmore, NY 11710/516-679-1158

Belleplain Supply, Inc., Box 346 Handsmill Rd., Belleplain, NJ 08270/609-861-2345

Bellrose & Son, L.E., 21 Forge Pond Rd., Granby, MA 01033-0184/413-467-3637

Ben's Gun Shop & Indoor Range, 1151 S. Cedar Ridge Rd., Duncanville, TX 75137/972-780-1807

Benelli Armi, S.p.A., Via della Stazione, 61029 Urbino, ITALY/39-722-307-1; FAX: 39-722-327427 (U.S. importers—Heckler & Koch, Inc.; Whitestone Lumber Co.)

Benjamin/Sheridan Co. (See Crossman)

Benson Gun Shop, 35 Middle Country Rd., Coram, L.I., NY 11727/516-736-0065

Beretta S.p.A., Pietro, Via Beretta, 18-25063 Gardone V.T. (BS) ITALY/XX39/30-8341.1; FAX: XX39/30-8341.421 (U.S. importer—Beretta U.S.A. Corp.)

Beretta U.S.A. Corp., 17601 Beretta Drive, Accokeek, MD 20607/301-283-2191; FAX: 301-283-0435

Bernardelli S.p.A., Vincenzo, 125 Via Matteotti, P.O. Box 74, Gardone V.T., Brescia ITALY, 25063/39-30-8912851-2-3; FAX: 39-30-8910249 (U.S. importer—Armsport, Inc.)

Bertuzzi (See U.S. importer—New England Arms Co.)

Bickford's Gun Repair, 1034 SW 89th Road, Oronogo, MO 64855/417-842-3411; 800-307-6440

Billy Fred's, 2465 I40 Wlfn SC., Amarillo, TX 79109/806-352-2519

Blaser Jagdwaffen GmbH, D-88316 Isny Im Allgau, GERMANY (U.S. importer—Autumn Sales, Inc.)

Blue Ridge Outdoor Sports, 2314 Spartanburg Hwy., E. Flat Rock, NC 28726/704-697-3006

Bob's Crosman Repair, 2510 E. Henry Ave., Cudahy, WI 53110/414-769-8256; FAX: 414-769-9455

Bob's Gun & Tackle Shop, 746 Granby St., Norfolk, VA 23510/804-622-9786

Bohemia Arms Co., 17101 Los Modelos, Fountain Valley, CA 92708/619-442-7005; FAX: 619-442-7005

Bolsa Gunsmithing, 7404 Bolsa Av., Westminister, CA 92683/714-894-9100

Bond Arms, Inc., P.O. Box 1296, Granbury, TX 76048/817-573-5733; FAX: 817-573-5636

Boracci, E. John, Village Sport Center, 38-10 Merrick Rd., Seaford, L.I., NY 11783/516-785-7110

Bosis (See U.S. importer—New England Arms Co.)

Brady's Sportsmans Surplus, Trumpers Shopping Center, P.O. Box 4166, Missoula, MT 59806/406-721-5500; FAX: 406-721-5581

Braverman Corp., R.J., 88 Parade Rd., Meridith, NH 03293/800-736-4867

Brenneke KG, Wilhelm, Ilmenauweg 2, 30851 Langenhagen, GERMANY/ 0511/97262-0; FAX: 0511/97262-62 (U.S. importer—Dynamit Nobel-RWS, Inc.)

Brenner Sport Shop, Charlie, 344 St. George Ave., Rahway, NJ 07065/908-382-4066

Bretton (See Atamec-Bretton)

BRNO (See U.S. importers—Bohemia Arms Co.)

Broadway Arms, 4114 E. Broadway, N. Little Rock, AR 72117/501-945-9348

Brock's Gunsmithing, Inc., North 2104 Division St., Spokane, WA 99207/509-328-9788

Brolin Arms, 2755 Thompson Creek Rd., Pomona, CA 91767/909-392-2350; FAX: 909-392-2354

Brown Co., E. Arthur, 3404 Pawnee Dr., Alexandria, MN 56308/320-762-8847

Browning Arms Co. (see page 447)

Brunswick Gun Shop, 31 Bath Rd., Brunswick, ME 04011/207-729-8322

Bryan & Associates, 201 S. Gosset, Anderson, SC 29623/864-261-6810

BSA Guns Ltd., Armoury Rd. Small Heath, Birmingham, ENGLAND B11 2PX/011-021-772-8543; FAX: 011-021-773-0845 (U.S. importers—Groenewold, John; Precision Sales International, Inc.)

Buffalo Gun Center, Inc., 3385 Harlem Rd., Buffalo, NY 14225/716-833-2581

Bullseye Gun Shop, 7949 E. Frontage Rd., Overland Park, KS 66204/913-648-4867

Burby Gunsmith, Bernard, RR #3, Box 3435, Middlebury, VT 05753/802-388-7365

Burris Co., Inc., P.O. Box 1747, 331 E. 8th St., Greeley, CO 80631/970-356-1670; FAX: 970-356-8702

Bushmaster Firearms (See Quality Parts Co./Bushmaster Firearms)

Bushnell Sports Optics Worldwide, 9200 Cody, Overland Park, KS 66214/913-752-3400, 800-423-3537; FAX: 913-752-3550

C

C-H Tool & Die Corp. (See 4-D Custom Die Co.)

C. Sharps Arms Co. Inc., 100 Centennial, Box 885, Big Timber, MT 59011/406-932-4353

C.R. Specialty, 1701 Baltimore Ave., Kansas City, MO 64108/816-221-3550

Cabanas (See U.S. importer—Mandall Shooting Supplies, Inc.)

Cabela's, 812-13th Ave., Sidney, NE 69160/308-254-6644, 800-237-4444; FAX: 308-254-6745

Cal's Customs, 110 E. Hawthorne, Fallbrook, CA 92026/619-728-5230

Calico Light Weapon Systems, 405 E. 19th St., Bakersfield, CA 93305/805-323-1327; FAX: 805-323-7844

Camdex, Inc., 2330 Alger, Troy, MI 48083/810-528-2300; FAX: 810-528-0989

Cape Outfitters, 599 County Rd. 206, Cape Girardeau, MO 63701/314-335-4103; FAX: 314-335-1555

Capitol Sports & Western Wear, 1092 Helena Ave., Helena, MT 59601/406-443-2978; FAX: 406-442-8136

Carl's Gun Shop, 100 N. Main, Eldorado Springs, MO 64744/417-876-4167

Carpenter's Gun Works, Newton Road RD1 Box 43D, Proctorsville, VT 05153/802-226-7690

Carroll's Gun Shop, Inc., 1612 N. Alabama Rd., Wharton, TX 77488/409-532-3175

Casey's Gun Shop, 59 Des E Rables, P.O. Box 100, Rogersville, New Brunswick, CANADA E0A 2T0/506-775-6822

Catfish Guns, 900 Jeffco-Executive Park, Imperial, MO 63052/314-464-1217

CBC, Avenida Humberto de Campos, 3220, 09400-000 Ribeirao Pires-SP-BRAZIL/55-11-742-7500; FAX: 55-11-459-7385

Central Ohio Police Supply, c/o Wammes Guns, 225 South Main St., Bellefontaine, OH 43311

Century Gun Dist., Inc., 1467 Jason Rd., Greenfield, IN 46140/317-462-4524

Century International Arms, Inc., P.O. Box 714, St. Albans, VT 05478-0714/802-527-1252, 800-527-1252; FAX: 802-527-0470; WEB: http://www.centuryarms.com

Cervera, Albert J., Rt. 1, Box 808, Hanover, VA 23069/804-994-5783

Chalmette Jewelry & Gun, 507 W. St. Bernard Hwy, Chalmette, LA 70043/504-271-2538

Champion Shooters' Supply, P.O. Box 303, New Albany, OH 43054/614-855-1603; FAX: 614-855-1209

Champion's Choice, Inc., 201 International Blvd., LaVergne, TN 37086/615-793-4066; FAX: 615-793-4070

Champlin Firearms, Inc., P.O. Box 3191, Woodring Airport, Enid, OK 73701/405-237-7388; FAX: 405-242-6922

Chapuis Armes, 21 La Gravoux, BP15, 42380 St. Bonnet-le-Chateau, FRANCE/ (33)77.50.06.96 (U.S. importer—Champlin Firearms, Inc.; Chapuis USA)

Chapuis USA, 416 Business Park, Bedford, KY 40006

Charlie's Sporting Goods, Inc., 8908 Menaul Blvd. N.E., Albuquerque, NM 87110/505-884-4545

Charlton Co., Ltd., M.D., Box 153 Brentwood Bay, British Columbia, CANADA V0S 1A0/604-652-5266; FAX: 604-652-4700

Cherry Corners, Inc., 11136 Congress Rd., PO Box 38, Lodi, OH 44254/216-948-1234

Chet Paulson Outfitters, 1901 S. 72nd St., Suite A14, Tacoma, WA 94808/206-475-8831

Chuck's Gun Shop, 235 Paredes Lines Rd., Brownsville, TX 78521/210-504-0243

Chung, Mel, Gunsmith, 39 Ing Place, PO Box 1008, Kaunakakai, HI 96748/808-553-5888

Churchill (See U.S. importer—Ellett Bros.)

Cimarron Arms, P.O. Box 906, Fredericksburg, TX 78624-0906/210-997-9090; FAX: 210-997-0802

Clark's Custom Guns, Inc., 336 Shoot-Out Lane, Princeton, LA 71067/318-949-0072

Colabaugh Gunsmith, Inc., Craig, R.D. #4, Box 4168, Gumm St., Stroudsburg, PA 18360/717-992-4499

Coleman, Ron, Gunsmith, 1600 N. I35, Suite 106, Carrollton, TX 75006/214-245-3030

Colt Blackpowder Arms Co., 110 8th Street, Brooklyn, NY 11215/212-925-2159; FAX: 212-966-4986

Colt's Mfg. Co., Inc., P.O. Box 1868, Hartford, CT 06144-1868/800-962-COLT, 203-236-6311; FAX: 203-244-1449

Comeaux Gun Clinic, 1140 Bernice Lane, Bridge City, TX 77611/409-735-3617

Competitor Corp., Inc., Appleton Business Center, 30 Tricnit Road, Unit 16, New Ipswich, NH 03071-0508/603-878-3891; FAX: 603-878-3950

Connecticut Valley Classics (See CVC)

Contender Vendor, The, Route 1 Box 144, Longdale, OK 73755

Corbin Mfg. & Supply, Inc., 600 Industrial Circle, P.O. Box 2659, White City, OR 97503/541-826-5211; FAX: 541-826-8669

Cosmi Americo & Figlio s.n.c., Via Flaminia 307, Ancona, ITALY I-60020/071-888208; FAX: 39-071-887008 (U.S. importer—New England Arms Co.)

Creekside Gun Shop, Main St., Holcomb, NY 14469/716-657-6131

Crosman Airguns (See page 447)

Crosman Parts & Service Depot, P.O. Box 2421, 427 Pido Rd., Peterborough, Ontario, CANADA K9J 6X7/705-749-0206

Crucelegui, Hermanos (See U.S. importer—Mandall Shooting Supplies, Inc.)

Cumberland Arms, 514 Shafer Road, Manchester, TN 37355/800-797-8414

Cumberland Knife & Gun Works, 5661 Bragg Blvd., Fayetteville, NC 28303/919-867-0009

CVA, 5988 Peachtree Corners East, Norcross, GA 30071/800-251-9412; FAX: 404-242-8546

CVC, 48 Commercial Street, Holyoke, MA 01040/413-552-3184; FAX: 413-552-3276

Cylinder & Slide, 245 E. 4th St., Fremont, NE 68025/402-721-4277

CZ USA, 40356 Oak Park Way, Suite W, Oakhurst, CA 93664

D

D&D Sporting Goods, 108 E. Main, Tishmingo, OK 73460/405-371-3571

D&J Bullet Co., 426 Ferry St., Russel, KY 41169/606-836-2663

D&J Coleman Service, 4811 Guadalupe Ave., Hobbs, NM 88240/505-392-5318

D&L Gunsmithing/Guns & Ammo, 3615 Summer Ave., Memphis, TN 38122/901-327-4384

D&L Shooting Supplies, 2663 W. Shore Rd., Warwick, RI 02886/401-738-1889

Daenzer, Charles E., 142 Jefferson Ave., Otisville, MI 48463/810-631-2415

Daewoo Precision Industries Ltd., 34-3 Yeoeuido-Dong, Yeongdeungoo-GU, 15th, Fl./Seoul, KOREA (U.S. importer—Nationwide Sports Distributors, Inc.)

Daisy Mfg. Co., P.O. Box 220, Rogers, AR 72757/501-636-1200; FAX: 501-636-1601

Dakota (See U.S. importer—EMF Co., Inc.)

Dale's Gun Shop, 3915 18th Ave. S.W., Rochester, MN 55902/507-289-8308

Daly, Charles (See B.C. Miroku/Charles Daly)

Damiano's Field & Stream, 172 N. Highland Ave., Ossining, NY 10562/914-941-6005

Darnall's Gun Works, RR #3, Box 274, Bloomington, IL 61704/309-379-4331

Daryl's Gun Shop, Inc., 1267 A 240th St., State Center, IA 50247/515-483-2656

Dave's Airgun Service, 1525 E. LaVieve Ln., Tempe, AZ 85284/602-491-8304

Davidson's of Canada, 584 Neal Dr., Box 479, Peterborough, Ontario, CANADA K9J 6X7/705-742-5408

Davis Industries, 15150 Sierra Bonita Ln., Chino, CA 91710/909-597-4726; FAX: 909-393-9771

Dayton Traister, 4778 N. Monkey Hill Rd., P.O. Box 593, Oak Harbor, WA 98277/360-679-4657; FAX:360-675-1114

Delisle Thompson Sporting Goods, 1814 A Loren Ave., Saskatoon, Saskatchewan, CANADA S7H 1Y4/306-653-2171

Denny's, 1820 17th St., Cody, WY 82414/307-527-6071

Denver Instrument Co., 6542 Fig St., Arvada, CO 80004/800-321-1135, 303-431-7255; FAX: 303-423-4831

Diana (See U.S. importer—Dynamit Nobel-RWS, Inc.)

Dillon Precision Products, Inc., 8009 East Dillon's Way, Scottsdale, AZ 85260/602-948-8009, 800-762-3845; FAX: 602-998-2786

Dixie Gun & Fish, 1062 E. Tabernacle, St. George, UT 84770/801-674-4008

Dixie Gun Works, Inc., Hwy. 51 South, Union City, TN 38261/901-885-0561, order 800-238-6785; FAX: 901-885-0440

Dollar Drugs, Inc., 15A West 3rd, Lee's Summit, MO 64063/816-524-7600

Don's Sport Shop, Inc., 7803 E. McDowell Rd., Scottsdale, AZ 85257/602-946-5313; 602-945-4051

Dorn's Gun Services, 4388 Mercer University Dr., Macon, GA 31206/912-471-0304

Douglas Sporting Goods, 138 Brick St., Princeton, WV 24740/304-425-8144

Down Under Gunsmiths, 318 Driveway, Fairbanks, AK 99701/907-456-8500

Draper Enterprises, dba Gun Exchange, 5317 W. 65th St., Little Rock, AR 72209/501-562-4668

Dumoulin, Ernest, Rue Florent Boclinville 8-10, 13-4041 Votten, BELGIUM/41 27 78 92 (U.S. importer—New England Arms Co.)

Duncan Gun Shop, 414 2nd St., N. Wilkesboro, NC 28659/919-838-4851

Dynamit Nobel-RWS, Inc., 81 Ruckman Rd., Closter, NJ 07624/201-767-7971; FAX: 201-767-1589

E

E.A.A. Corp., P.O. Box 1299, Sharpes, FL 32959/407-639-4842, 800-536-4442; FAX: 407-639-7006

Eagle Arms (See ArmaLite, Inc.)

EAW (See U.S. importer—New England Custom Gun Service)

Ed's Gun & Tackle Shop, Inc., 2727 Canton Rd., (Hwy. 5), Marietta, GA 30066/770-425-8461

Effebi SNC-Dr. Franco Beretta, via Rossa, 4, 25062 Concesio, Italy/030-2751955; FAX: 030-2180414 (U.S. importer—Nevada Cartridge Co.

Ellett Bros., 267 Columbia Ave., P.O. Box 128, Chapin, SC 29036/803-345-3751, 800-845-3711; FAX: 803-345-1820

Emerging Technologies, Inc. (See Laseraim Technologies, Inc.)

EMF Co., Inc., 1900 E. Warner Ave. Suite 1-D, Santa Ana, CA 92705/714-261-6611; FAX: 714-756-0133

Enstad & Douglas, 211 Hedges, Oregon City, OR 97045/503-655-3751

Epps, Ellwood, R.R. #3, Hwy. 11 North, Orilla, Ontario, CANADA L3V 6H3/705-689-5333

Erma Werke GmbH, Johan Ziegler St., 13/15/FeldiglSt., D-8060 Dachau, GERMANY (U.S. importers—Amtec 2000, Inc.; Mandall Shooting Supplies, Inc.)

Ernie's Gun Shop, Ltd., 1031 Marion St., Winnipeg, Manitoba, CANADA R2J 0L1/204-233-1928

Essex Arms, P.O. Box 345, Island Pond, VT 05846/802-723-4313

Euroarms of America, Inc., P.O. Box 3277, Winchester, VA 22604/540-662-1863; FAX: 540-662-4464

Europtik Ltd., P.O. Box 319, Dunmore, PA 18512/717-347-6049; FAX: 717-969-4330

Eyster, Ken/Heritage Gun, 6441 Bishop Rd., Centerburg, OH 43011/614-625-6131

F

F&D Guns, 5140 Westwood Drive, St. Charles, MO 63304/314-441-5897

Fabarm S.p.A., Via Averolda 31, 25039 Travagliato, Brescia, ITALY/030-6863629; FAX: 030-6863684 (U.S. importer—Ithaca Gun Co., LLC)

Famas (See U.S. importer—Century International Arms, Inc.)

FAS, Via E. Fermi, 8, 20019 Settimo Milanese, Milano, ITALY/02-3285844; FAX: 02-33500196 (U.S. importer—Nygord Precision Products)

Fausti Cav. Stefano & Figlie snc, Via Martiri Dell Indipendenza, 70, Marcheno, ITALY 25060 (U.S. importer—American Arms, Inc.)

FEG, Budapest, Soroksariut 158, H-1095 HUNGARY (U.S. importers—Century International Arms, Inc.; K.B.I., Inc.)

Felton, James, Custom Gunsmith, 1033 Elizabeth St., Eugene, OR 97402/541-689-1687

Fiocchi Munizioni S.p.A. (See U.S. importer—Fiocchi of America, Inc.)

Fiocchi of America, Inc., 5030 Fremont Rd., Ozark, MO 65721/417-725-4118, 800-721-2666; FAX: 417-725-1039

Firearms Co. Ltd./Alpine (See U.S. importer—Mandall Shooting Supplies, Inc.)

Firearms Service Center, Inc., 2140 Old Shepherdsville Rd., Louisville, KY 40218/502-458-1148

Forgett Jr., Valmore J., 689 Bergen Blvd., Ridgefield, NJ 07657/201-945-2500; FAX: 201-945-6859; E-MAIL: ValForgett@msn.com

Forster Products, 82 E. Lanark Ave., Lanark, IL 61046/815-493-6360; FAX: 815-493-2371

4-D Custom Die Co., 711 N. Sandusky St., P.O. Box 889, Mt. Vernon, OH 43050-0889/614-397-7214; FAX: 614-397-6600

Franchi S.p.A., Via del Serpente, 12, 25131 Brescia, ITALY/030-3581833; FAX: 030-3581554 (U.S. importer—American Arms, Inc.)

Francotte & Cie S.A., Auguste, rue du Trois Juin 109, 4400 Herstal-Liege, BELGIUM/32-4-248-13-18; FAX: 32-4-948-11-79

Franklin Sports, Inc., 3941 Atlanta Hwy., Bogart, GA 30622/706-543-7803

Freedom Arms, Inc., P.O. Box 1776, Freedom, WY 83120/307-883-2468, 800-833-4432 (orders only); FAX: 307-883-2005

Freer Gunshop, 8928 Spring Branch Dr., Houston, TX 77080/713-467-3016

Fremont Tool Works, 1214 Prairie, Ford, KS 67842/316-369-2327

Friedman's Army Surplus, 2617 Nolenville Rd., Nashville, TN 37211/615-244-1653

Frontiersman's Soprts, 6925 Wayzata Blvd., St. Louis Park, MN 55426/612-544-3775

FWB, Neckarstrasse 43, 78727 Oberndorf a. N., GERMANY/07423-814-0; FAX: 07423-814-89 (U.S. importer—Beeman Precision Airguns)

G

G.H. Gun Shop, 530 West B St., McCook, NE 69001/308-345-1250

G.I. Loan Shop, Inc., 1004 W. 2nd, Grand Island, NE 68801/308-382-9573

G.U., Inc. (U.S. importer for New SKB Arms Co.; SKB Arms Co.)

G.V.R. Enterprises Ltd., 17552 107 Ave., Edmonton, Alberta, CANADA T5S 1E9/403-453-2681

Galaxy Imports Ltd., Inc., P.O. Box 3361, Victoria, TX 77903/512-573-4867; FAX: 512-576-9622

Gamba S.p.A.-Societa Armi Bresciane Srl., Renato, Via Artigiani, 93, 25063 Gardone Val Trompia (BS), ITALY/30-8911640; FAX: 30-8911648 (U.S. importer—Gamba, USA)

Gamba, USA, P.O. Box 60452, Colorado Springs, CO 80960/719-578-1145; FAX: 719-444-0731

Gamo (See U.S. importers—Arms United Corp.; Daisy Mfg. Co.; Dynamit Nobel-RWS, Inc.; Gamo USA, Inc.)

Gamo USA, Inc., 3911 SW 47th Ave., Suite 914, Ft. Lauderdale, FL 33314/343-640-7248; FAX: 343-654-0900

Gander Mountain, 12400 Fox River Rd., Hwy. W., Wilmot, WI 53192/414-862-5781; FAX: 414-862-3598

Garbi, Armas Urki, 12-14, 20.600 Eibar (Guipuzcoa) SPAIN/43-11 38 73 (U.S. importer—Moore & Co., Wm. Larkin)

Garfield Gunsmithing, 237 Wessington Ave., Garfield, NJ 07026/201-478-0171

Gart Brothers, 1000 Broadway, Denver, CO 80203/303-863-2256

Gary's Gun Shop, Inc., 905 W. 41st St., Souix Falls, SD 57105/605-332-6119

Gatlin Gun Shop, Wallace, 140 Gatlin Rd., Oxford, AL 36203/205-831-6993

Gene's Gunsmithing, Box 34 Group 326 R.R. #3, Selkirk, Manitoba, CANADA R1A 2A8/204-757-2003; FAX: 204-757-4728

Gibbs Rifle Co., Inc., Cannon Hill Industrial Park, Rt. 2, Box 214 Hoffman, Rd./Martinsburg, WV 25401/304-274-0458; FAX: 304-274-0078

Gilbert Equipment Co., Inc., 960 Downtowner Rd., Mobile, AL 36609/205-344-3322

Girard, Florent, Gunsmith, 598 Verreault, Chicoutimi, Quebec, CANADA G7H 2B8/418-696-3329

Glenn's Reel & Rod Repair, 2210 E. 9th St., Des Moines, IA 50316/515-262-2990

Glock GmbH, P.O. Box 50, A-2232 Deutsch Wagram, AUSTRIA (U.S. importer—Glock, Inc.)

Glock, Inc., P.O. Box 369, Smyrna, GA 30081/770-432-1202; FAX: 770-433-8719

Gonic Arms, Inc., 134 Flagg Rd., Gonic, NH 03839/603-332-8456, 603-332-8457

Gordon's Wigwam, 501 South St. Francis, Wichita, KS 67202/316-264-5891

Great Lakes Airguns, 6175 S. Park Ave., Hamburg, NY 14075/716-648-6666; FAX: 716-648-5279

Green Acres Sporting Goods, Inc., 8774 Normandy Blvd., Jacksonville, FL 32221/904-786-5166

Greene's Gun Shop, 4778 N. Monkey Hill Rd., Oak Harbor, WA 98277/360-675-3421

Grice Gun Shop, 307 Healey Ave., P.O. Box 1028, Clearfield, PA 16830/814-765-9273

Griffin & Howe, Inc., 33 Claremont Rd., Bernardsville, NJ 07924/908-766-2287; FAX: 908-766-1068

Griffin & Howe, Inc., 36 W. 44th St., Suite 1011, New York, NY 10036/212-921-0980

Groenwold, John, P.O. Box 830, 1861 Victoria Rd., Mundelein, IL 60060-0830/847-566-2365; FAX: 847-566-4065

Grulla Armes, Apartado 453, Avda Otaloa, 12, Eiber, SPAIN (U.S. importer—American Arms, Inc.)

Grundman's, Inc., 75 Wildwood Av., Rio Dell, CA 85562/707-764-5744

GSI, Inc., 108 Morrow Ave., P.O. Box 129, Trussville, AL 35173/205-655-8299; FAX: 205-655-7078

Gun & Tackle Store, The, 6041 Forrest Lane, Dallas, TX 75230/214-239-8181

Gun Center, The, 5831 Buckeystown Pike, Frederick, MD 21701/301-694-6887

Gun City USA, Inc., 573 Murfreesboro Rd., Nashville, TN 37210/615-256-6127

Gun Hospital, The, 45 Vinyard Ave., E. Providence, RI 02914/401-438-3495

Gun Rack, Inc. The, 213 Richland Ave., Aiken, SC 29801/803-648-7100

Gun Shop, The, 716-A South Rogers Road, Olathe, KS 66062

Gun Shop, The, 5550 S. 900 East, Salt Lake City, UT 84117/801-263-3633

Gun Shop, The, 62778 Spring Creek Rd., Montrose, CO 81401

Gun World, 392 5th St., Elko, NV 89801/702-738-2666

Guncrafters, 2767 Commercial St. N.E., Salem, OR 97303/503-362-6197; FAX: 503-362-6237

Gunshop, The, 44622 N. Sierra Hwy., Lancaster, CA 93534/805-942-8377

Gunsmith Company, The, 3435 S. State St., Salt Lake City, UT 84115/801-467-8244; FAX: 801-467-8256

Gunsmithing Specialties Co., 110 N. Washington St., Buffalo, NY 14225/402-339-1222

Gunsmithing Specialty, 110 No. Washington St., Papillion, NE 68046/402-339-1222

Gunsmithing, Inc., 208 West Buchanan St., Colorado Springs, CO 80907/719-632-3795; FAX: 719-632-3493

Gunsmithing, Ltd., 57 Unquowa Rd., Fairfield, CT 06430/203-254-0436

H

H&R 1871, Inc., 60 Industrial Rowe, Gardner, MA 01440/508-632-9393; FAX: 508-632-2300

H-S Precision, Inc., 1301 Turbine Dr., Rapid City, SD 57701/605-341-3006; FAX: 605-342-8964

Hagstrom, E.G., 2008 Janis Dr., Memphis, TN 38116/901-398-5333

Hammerli Ltd., Seonerstrasse 37, CH-5600 Lenzburg, SWITZERLAND/064-50 11 44; FAX: 064-51 38 27 (U.S. importer—Hammerli USA; Mandall Shooting Supplies, Inc.; Sigarms, Inc.)

Hammerli USA, 19296 Oak Grove Circle, Groveland, CA 95321/209-962-5311; FAX: 209-962-5931

Hampel's Key & Gun Shop, 710 Randolph St., Traverse City, MI 49684/616-946-5485

Hanus Birdguns, Bill, P.O. Box 533, Newport, OR 97365/541-265-7433; FAX: 541-265-7400

Harris Gunworks, 3840 N. 28th Ave., Phoenix, AZ 85017-4733/602-230-1414; FAX: 602-230-1422

Harry's Army & Navy, 691 Route 130, Robbinsville, NJ 08691/609-585-5450

Hart & Son, Robert W., 401 Montgomery St., Nescopeck, PA 18635/717-752-3655

Hartford (See U.S. importer— EMF Co., Inc.)

Hawken Shop, The (See Dayton Traister)

Heckler & Koch GmbH, P.O. Box 1329, 78722 Oberndorf, Neckar, GERMANY/49-7423179-0; FAX: 49-7423179-2406 (U.S. importer—Heckler & Koch, Inc.)

Heckler & Koch, Inc., 21480 Pacific Blvd., Sterling, VA 20166-8903/703-450-1900; FAX: 703-450-8160

Heckman Arms Company, 1736 Skyline Drive, Richmond Heights, OH 44143/216-289-9182

Helwan (See U.S. importer—Interarms)

Henry's Airguns, 1204 W. Locust, Belvidere, IL 61008/815-547-5091

Herold's Gun Shoppe, 1498 East Main, Waynesboro, PA 17268/717-762-4010

Hi-Point Firearms, 5990 Philadelphia Dr., Dayton, OH 45415/513-275-4991; FAX: 513-522-8330

High Standard Mfg. Co., Inc., 4601 S. Pinemont, Suite 144, Houston, TX 77041/713-462-4200; FAX: 713-462-6437

Hill Top Hunting & Fishing Supply, Route 3, Box 85, Canton, NY 13617/315-385-4875

Hill's Hardware & Sporting Goods, 1234 S. Second St., Union City, TN 38281/901-885-1510

Hill's Inc., 1720 Capital Blvd., Raleigh, NC 27604/919-833-4884

HJS Arms, Inc., P.O. Box 3711, Brownsville, TX 78523-3711/800-453-2767, 210-542-2767

Hollywood Engineering, 10642 Arminta St., Sun Valley, CA 91352/818-842-8376

Horchler's Gun Shop, 100 Ratlum Rd., RFD, Collinsville, CT 06022/203-379-1977

Hornady Mfg. Co., P.O. Box 1848, Grand Island, NE 68802/800-338-3220, 308-382-1390; FAX: 308-382-5761

Howa Machinery, Ltd., Sukaguchi, Shinkawa-cho, Nishikasugai-gun, Aichi 452, JAPAN (U.S. importer—Interarms)

Huntington Die Specialties, 601 Oro Dam Blvd., Oroville, CA 95965/916-534-1210; FAX: 916-534-1212

Huntington Sportsmen's Store, 601 Oro Dam Blvd., Oroville, CA 95965/916-534-8000; FAX: 916-534-1212

Hutch's, 50 E. Main St., Lehi, UT 84043/7801-768-3461

Hutchinson's Gun Repair, 507 Clifton St., Pineville, LA 71360/318-640-4315

I

IAR, Inc., 33171 Camino Capistrano, San Juan Capistrano, CA 92675/714-443-3642; FAX: 714-443-3647

IGA (See U.S. importer—Stoeger Industries)

Imbert & Smithers, 1144 El Camino Real, San Carlos, CA 94070/415-593-4207

Import Sports Inc., 1750 Brielle Ave., Unit B1, Wanamassa, NJ 07712/908-493-0302; FAX: 908-493-0301

Interarms, 10 Prince St., Alexandria, VA 22314/703-548-1400; FAX: 703-549-7826

Intermountain Arms & Tackle, Inc., 1375 E. Fairview, Meridian, ID 83642/208-888-4911; FAX: 208-888-4381

Intratec, 12405 SW 130th St., Miami, FL 33186-6224/305-232-1821; FAX: 305-253-7207

Island Pond Gun Shop, Main St., Island Pond, VT 05846/802-723-4546

Israel Arms International, Inc., 5709 Hartsdale, Houston, TX 77036/713-789-0745; FAX: 713-789-7513

J

J&M Gun Shop, Inc., 2106 Russellville Rd., Bowling Green, KY 42101/502-782-1962

J&T Services, 12 1/2 Woodlawn Ave., Bradford, PA 16701/814-368-3634

Jack First, Inc., 1201 Turbine Dr., Rapid City, SD 57701/605-343-9544; 605-343-8481

Jack's Lock & Gun Shop, 32 4th St., Fond Du Lac, WI 54935/414-922-4420; FAX: 414-922-0619

Jackalope Gun Shop, 1048 S. 5th St., Douglas, WY 82633/307-358-3441

Jacobson's Gun Center, 612 Broad St., Story City, LA 50248/515-733-2995; FAX: 515-733-4838

Jaeger, Inc./Dunn's, Paul, P.O. Box 449, 1 Madison Ave., Grand Junction, TN 38039/901-764-6909; FAX: 901-764-6503

JägerSport, Ltd., One Wholesale Way, Cranston, RI 02920/800-962-4867, 401-944-9682; FAX: 401-946-2587

Jay's Sports, Inc., N88 W15263 Main St., Menomonee Falls, WI 53051/414-251-0550

Jay-Cee's Warranty Service, 547 Vaughan Ave., Selkirk, Manitoba, CANADA R1A 0T2/204-482-7477

Jensen's Custom Ammunition Supply, 5146 E. Pima, Tuscon, AZ 85712/520-325-3346

Jim's Trading Post, 10 SW Plaza, Box 1345, Pine Bluff, AR 71603/501-534-8591

Joe's Gun Shop, 4430 14th St., Dorr, MI 49323/616-877-4615

Joe's Gun Shop, 5215 W. Edgemont Ave., Phoenix, AZ 85035/602-233-0694

Johnson Service, Inc., W., 3654 N. Adrian Hwy., Adrian, ME 49221/517-265-2545

Jordan, Charles Don, 218 N. Magnolia Dr., Tifton, GA 31794/912-382-4251

K

K&M Services, 5430 Salmon Run Rd., Dover, PA 17315/717-292-3175

K.B.I., Inc., P.O. Box 6625, Harrisburg, PA 17112/717-540-8518; FAX: 717-540-8567

Kahles, A Swarovski Company, 1 Wholesale Way, Cranston, RI 02920-5540/800-426-3089; FAX: 401-946-2587

Kahr Arms, P.O. Box 220, 630 Route 303, Blauvelt, NY 10913/914-353-5996; FAX: 914-353-7833

Keidel's Gunsmithing Service, 927 Jefferson Ave., Washington, PA 15301/412-222-6379

Kel-Tec CNC Industries, Inc., P.O. Box 3427, Cocoa, FL 32924/407-631-0068; FAX: 407-631-1169

Keng's Firearms Specialty, Inc., 875 Wharton Dr., P.O. Box 44405, Atlanta, GA 30336-1405/404-691-7611: FAX: 404-505-8445

Kesselring Gun Shop, 400 Hwy. 99 North, Burlington, WA 98233/206-724-3113; FAX: 206-724-7003

Kesselring Gun Shop, 400 Pacific Hwy 99 No., Burlington, WA 98233/360-724-3113

Kielon, Gunsmith, Dave, 57 Kittleberger Park, Webster, NY 14580/716-872-2256

Kimber of America, Inc., 1 Lawton St., Yonkers, NY 10705/800-880-2418

King's Gun Shop, Inc., 32301 Walters Hwy., Franklin, VA 23851/804-562-4725

Kirkpatrick, Gunsmith, Larry, 707 79th, Lubbock, TX 79404/806-745-5308

Knight's Mfg. Co., 7750 9th St. SW, Vero Beach, FL 32968/561-562-5697; FAX: 561-569-2955

Korth, Robert-Bosch-Str. 4, P.O. Box 1320, 23909 Ratzeburg, GERMANY/451-4991497; FAX: 451-4993230 (U.S. importer—Interarms; Mandall Shooting Supplies, Inc.)

Kowa Optimed, Inc., 20001 S. Vermont Ave., Torrance, CA 90502/310-327-1913; FAX: 310-327-4177

Krico Jagd-und Sportwaffen GmbH, Nurnbergerstrasse 6, D-90602 Pyrbaum GERMANY/09180-2780; FAX: 09180-2661 (U.S. importer—Mandall Shooting Supplies, Inc.)

Krieghoff Gun Co., H., Boschstrasse 22, D-89079 Ulm, GERMANY/731-401820; FAX: 731-4018270 (U.S. importer—Krieghoff International, Inc.)

Krieghoff International, Inc., 7528 Easton Rd., Ottsville, PA 18942/610-847-5173; FAX: 610-847-8691

KSN Industries, Ltd. (See U.S. importer—Israel Arms International, Inc.)

L

L&S Technologies, Inc. (See Aimtech Mount Systems)

L'Armurier A. Richard Lusignant, 15820 St. Michel, St. Hyacinthe, Quebec, CANADA J2T 3R7/514-773-7007

L'Armurier Alain Bouchard, 420 Route 143, Ulverton/MLB, Quebec, CANADA J0B 2B0/819-826-6611

L'Armurier C.A.F. Gunshop, 10 Rue Perron, St-Mathias Sur Richelie, Quebec, CANADA J0L 2G0/514-658-8512

L'Armurier De L'Outaouais Ent., 28 Rue Bourque, Hull, Quebec, CANADA J8Y 1X1/819-777-9824

L.A.R. Mfg., Inc., 4133 W. Farm Rd., West Jordan, UT 84088/801-280-3505; FAX: 801-280-1972

Labs Air Gun Shop, 2307 N. 62nd St., Omaha, NE 68104/402-553-0990

Ladwig Gunsmithing, Inc., Jack, 2339 S. 43rd St., West Wilwaukee, WI 53219/414-383-0885

Lafayette Shooters, 3520 AMB Caffrey Pky., LaFayette, LA 70503/318-988-1191

Lakefield Arms Ltd. (See Savage Arms, Inc.)

Lapua Ltd., P.O. Box 5, Lapua, FINLAND SF-62101/6-310111; FAX: 6-4388991 (U.S. importer—Keng's Firearms Specialty, Inc.)

Laser Devices, Inc., 2 Harris Ct. A-4, Monterey, CA 93940/408-373-0701; FAX: 408-373-0903

Laseraim Technologies, Inc., P.O. Box 3548, Little Rock, AR 72203/501-375-2227; FAX: 501-372-1445

Laurona Armas Eibar, S.A.L., Avenida de Otaola 25, P.O. Box 260, 20600 Eibar, SPAIN/34-43-700600; FAX: 34-43-700616 (U.S. importer—Galaxy Imports Ltd., Inc.)

Lawson Custom Firearms, Inc., Art, 313 S. Magnolia Ave., Ocala, FL 34471/352-629-7793

Lebeau-Courally, Rue St. Gilles, 386, 4000 Liege, BELGIUM/042-52-48-43; FAX: 32-042-52-20-08 (U.S. importer—New England Arms Co.)

Lee Precision, Inc., 4275 Hwy. U, Hartford, WI 53027/414-673-3075; FAX: 414-673-9273

Leica USA, Inc., 156 Ludlow Ave., Northvale, NJ 07647/201-767-7500; FAX: 201-767-8666

Leo's Custom Stocks, 1767 Washington Ave., Library, PA 15129/412-835-4126

Leupold & Stevens, Inc., P.O. Box 688, Beaverton, OR 97075/503-646-9171; FAX: 503-526-1455

Levan Sporting Goods Store, Martin, 433 North 9th St., Lebanon, PA 17042/717-273-3148

Lewis Arms, 1575 Hooksett Rd., Hooksett, NH 03106/603-485-7334

Lion Country Supply, P.O. Box 480, Port Matilda, PA 16870

Llama Gabilondo Y Cia, Apartado 290, E-01080, Victoria, SPAIN (U.S. importer—Import Sports, Inc.)

Log Cabin Sport Shop, 8010 Lafayette Rd., Rt. 1, Lodi, OH 44254/216-948-1082

Log Cabin Sport Shop, 8010 Lafayette Rd., Lodi, OH 44254/216-948-1082

Lone Star Guns, 1170 Park Blvd., Plano, TX 75074/972-424-4501

Long Beach Uniform Co., Inc., 2789 Long Beach Blvd., Long Beach, CA 90806/310-424-0220

Long, Gunsmith, Ltd., W.R., P.O. Box 876, 2007 Brook Road N., Cobourg, Ontario, CANADA K9A 4H1/416-372-5955

Longacre's, Inc., 358 Chestnut, Abilene, TX 79602/915-672-9521

Lorcin Engineering Co., Inc., 10427 San Sevaine Way, Ste. A, Mira Loma, CA 91752

Lounsbury Sporting Goods, Bob, 104 North St., Middletown, NY 10940/914-343-1808

Lutter, Robert E., 3547 Auer Dr., Fort Wayne, IN 46835/219-485-8319

Lyman Products Corp., 475 Smith Street, Middletown, CT 06457-1541/860-632-2020, 800-22-LYMAN; FAX: 860-632-1699

M

M.O.A. Corp., 2451 Old Camden Pike, Eaton, OH 45320/513-456-3669

MAC1, 13974 VanNess, Gardena, CA 90249/310-327-3582

Mac-1 Distributors, 13974 Van Ness Ave., Gardena, CA 90249/310-327-3582

Magasin Latulippe, 637 Rue St. Vallier, PO Box 395, Quebec City, Quebec, CANADA G1K 6W8/418-529-0024

Magma Engineering Co., P.O. Box 161, 20955 E. Ocotillo Rd., Queen Creek, AZ 85242/602-987-9008; FAX: 602-987-0148

Magnum Research, Inc., 7110 University Ave. NE, Minneapolis, MN 55432/800-772-6168, 612-574-1868; FAX: 612-574-0109; WEB:http://www.magnumresearch.com

Mandall Shooting Supplies, Inc., 3616 N. Scottsdale Rd., Scottsdale, AZ 85252/602-945-2553; FAX: 602-949-0734

Marksman Products, 5482 Argosy Dr., Huntington Beach, CA 92649/714-898-7535, 800-822-8005; FAX: 714-891-0782

Marlin Firearms Co., 100 Kenna Dr., North Haven, CT 06473/203-239-5621; FAX: 203-234-7991

Marocchi F.lli S.p.A, Via Galileo Galilei 8, I-25068 Zanano di Sarezzo, ITALY/ (U.S. importers—Precision Sales International, Inc.)

Martins Gun Shop, Henry, 1100 Kay Lane, Shreveport, LA 71115/318-797-1119

Mason Guns & Ammo, Tom, 68 Lake Ave., Danbury, CT 06810/203-778-6421

Master Gunsmiths, 12621 Ticonderoga, Houston, TX 77044/713-459-1631

Matt's 10X Gunsmithing, Inc., 5906 Castle Rd., Duluth, MN 55803/218-721-3961

Mauser Werke Oberndorf Waffensysteme GmbH, Postfach 1349, 78722 Oberndorf/N. GERMANY/ (U.S. importer—GSI, Inc.)

Maverick Arms, Inc., 7 Grasso Ave., P.O. Box 497, North Haven, CT 06473/203-230-5300; FAX: 203-230-5420

May & Company, Inc., P.O. Box 1111, 838 W. Capitol St., Jackson, MS 39203/601-354-5781; FAX: 601-355-4804

McBride's, Inc., 2915 San Gabriel, Austin, TX 78705/512-472-3532

McBros Rifle Co., P.O. Box 86549, Phoenix, AZ 85080/602-582-3713; FAX: 602-581-3825

McClelland Gun Shop, 1533 Centerville Rd., Dallas, TX 75228/214-321-0231

McDaniel Co., Inc., B., 8880 Pontiac Trail, S. Lyon, MI 48178/810-437-8989

McGuns, W.H., 124 North 22nd Av., Humboldt, TN 38343/901-784-5746; FAX: 901-784-7661

MCS, Inc., 34 Delmar Dr., Brookfield, CT 06804/203-775-1013; FAX: 203-775-9462

MEC-Gar S.r.l., Via Madonnina 64, Gardone V.T., Brescia, ITALY 25063/39-30-8912687; FAX: 39-30-8910065 (U.S. importer—MEC-Gar U.S.A., Inc.)

MEC-Gar U.S.A., Inc., Box 112, 500B Monroe Turnpike, Monroe, CT 06468/203-635-8662; FAX: 203-635-8662

Merkel Freres, Strasse 7 October, 10, Suhl, GERMANY/ (U.S. importer—GSI, Inc.)

Metro Rod & Reel, 236 S.E. Grand Ave., Portland, OR 97214/503-232-3193

Meydag, Peter, 12114 East 16th, Tulsa, OK 74128/918-437-1928

Miclean, Bill, 499 Theta Ct., San Jose, CA 95123/408-224-1445

Midwestern Shooters Supply, Inc., 150 Main St., Lomira, WI 53048/414-269-4995

Mike's Crosman Service, 5995 Renwood Dr., Winston-Salem, NC 27106/910-922-1031

Miller's Sport Shop, 2 Summit View Dr., Mountaintop, PA 18707/717-474-6931

Millers Gun Shop, 915 23rd St., Gulfport, MS 39501/601-684-1765

Millers Rod & Gun, P.O. Box 178, McCain St., Florenceville, New Brunswick, CANADA E0J 1K0/506-392-6105

Mirador Optical Corp., P.O. Box 11614, Marina Del Rey, CA 90295-7614/310-821-5587; FAX: 310-305-0386

Miroku, B.C./Daly, Charles (See U.S. importer—Bell's Legendary Country Wear; K.B.I., Inc.; U.S. distributor—Outdoor Sports Headquarters, Inc.)

MKS Supply, Inc. (See Hi-Point Firearms)

Moates Sport Shop, Bob, 10418 Hull St. Rd., Midlothian, VA 23112/804-276-2293

Modern Guncraft, 148 N. Branford Rd., Wallingford, CT 06492/203-265-1015

Modern MuzzleLoading, Inc., 234 Airport Rd., P.O. Box 130, Centerville, IA 52544/515-856-2626; FAX: 515-856-2628

Montana Armory, Inc. (See C. Sharps Arms Co. Inc.)

Moore & Co., Wm. Larkin, 8727 E. Via de Commencio, Suite A, Scottsdale, AZ 85258/602-951-8913; FAX: 602-951-8913

Moreau, Gunsmith, Pete, 1807 S. Erie, Bay City, MI 48706/517-893-7106

Morini (See U.S. importers—Mandall Shooting Supplies, Inc.; Nygord Precision Products)

Mossberg & Sons, Inc., O.F, 7 Grasso Ave., North Haven, CT 06473/203-230-5300; FAX: 203-230-5420

Mountain Gun Works, 3017 10th Ave. S., Great Falls, MT 59405/406-761-4346

Murray, John, 27 Clearview St., Moncton, New Brunswick, CANADA E1A 4H1/506-382-5271

N

N.A. Guns, 10220 Florida Blvd., Baton Rouge, LA 70815/504-272-3620

Nagel's Gun Shop, 6201 San Pedro Ave., San Antonio, TX 78216/210-342-5420

Nationwide Sports Distributors, Inc., 70 James Way, Southampton, PA 18966/215-322-2050, 800-355-3006; FAX: 702-358-2093

Navy Arms Co., 689 Bergen Blvd., Ridgefield, NJ 07657/201-945-2500; FAX: 201-945-6859

Nelson's Engine Shop, 620 State St., Cedar Falls, IA 50613/319-266-4497

Nevada Air Guns, 3297 "J" Las Vegas Blvd. N, Las Vegas, NV 89115/702-643-8532

Nevada Cartridge Co., 44 Montgomery St., Suite 500, San Francisco, CA 94104/415-925-9394; FAX: 415-925-9396

New England Arms Co., Box 278, Lawrence Lane, Kittery Point, ME 03905/207-439-0593; FAX: 207-439-6726

New England Custom Gun Service, 438 Willow Brook Rd., RR2, Box 122W, W. Lebanon, NH 03784/603-469-3450; FAX: 603-469-3471

New SKB Arms Co., C.P.O. Box 1401, Tokyo, JAPAN/81-3-3943-9550; FAX: 81-3-3943-0695

Newby, Stewart, Gunsmith, Main & Cross Streets, Newburgh, Ontario, CANADA K0K 2S0/613-378-6613

Nikon, Inc., 1300 Walt Whitman Rd., Melville, NY 11747/516-547-8623; FAX: 516-547-0309

Norinco, 7A, Yun Tan N Beijing, CHINA/ (U.S. importers—Century International Arms, Inc.; Interarms)

Norma Precision AB (See U.S. importers—Dynamit Nobel-RWS Inc.; Paul Co. Inc., The)

North American Arms, Inc., 2150 South 950 East, Provo, UT 84606-6285/800-821-5783, 801-374-9990; FAX: 801-374-9998

Northern Precision Airguns, 1161 Grove St., Tawas City, MI 48763/517-362-6949

Northern Virginia Gun Works, Inc., 7518-K Fullerton Rd., Springfield, VA 22153/703-644-6504

Northland Sport Center, Inc., Route 2, Box 185, Bagley, MN 56621/218-694-2464

Northridge Pistol & Rifle Range, 19015 Parthenia St., Northridge, CA 91324/818-886-4867

Northwest Arms Service, No. So. 2nd, Alwood, KS 67730/913-626-3078

Nu-Line Guns, Inc., 1053 Caulks Hill Rd., Harvester, MO 63303/314-441-4500; FAX: 314-447-5018

Nusbaum Enterprises, Inc., 136 Ridgewood Dr., Mobile, AL 36608/334-344-1079

Nygord Precision Products, P.O. Box 12578, Prescott, AZ 86304/520-717-2315; FAX: 520-717-2198

O

Oakland Custom Arms, Inc., 4690 West Walton, Waterford, MI 48329/810-674-8261

Old Western Scrounger, Inc., 12924 Hwy. A-l2, Montague, CA 96064/916-459-5445; FAX: 916-459-3944

On Target Gun Shop, Inc., 6984 W. Main St., Kalamazoo, MI 49009/616-375-4570

Orvis Co., The, Rt. 7, Manchester, VT 05254/802-362-3622 ext. 283; FAX: 802-362-3525

Oshman's Sporting Goods, Inc., 975 Gessner, Houston, TX 77024/713-467-1098

Ott's Gun Service, Route 2, Box 169-A, Atmore, AL 36502/334-862-2588

Outdoor Sports Headquarters, Inc., 967 Watertower Ln., West Carrollton, OH 45449/513-865-5855; FAX: 513-865-5962

Outdoorsman Sporting Goods Co., The, 1707 Radner Ct., Geneva, IL 60134/630-232-9518

Outdoorsman, The, Village West Shopping Center, 4101 13th Ave. South, Fargo, ND 58103/701-282-0131; FAX: 701-282-0133

Outpost, The, 2451 E. Maple Rapids Rd., Eureka, MI 48833/517-224-9562

P

P&D Rod, Reel & Airguns, 7540 Hwy. 62, White City, OR 97503/541-826-3893

P.S.M.G. Gun Co., 10 Park Ave., Arlington, MA 02174/617-646-8845; FAX: 617-646-2133

Pachmayr, Ltd., 1875 S. Mountain Ave., Monrovia, CA 91016/818-357-7771, 800-423-9704; FAX: 818-358-7251

Pacific International Service Co., P.O. Box 3, Mountain Way, Janesville, CA 96114/916-253-2218

Paducah Shooters Supply, Inc., 3919 Cairo Rd., Paducah, KY 42001/502-442-3242

Para-Ordnance Mfg., Inc., 980 Tapscott Rd., Scarborough, Ont. M1X 1E7, CANADA/416-297-7855; FAX: 416-297-1289 (U.S. importer—Para-Ordnance, Inc.)

Para-Ordnance, Inc., 1919 NE 45th St., Ft. Lauderdale, FL 33308

Pardini Armi Srl, Via Italica 154, 55043 Lido Di Camaiore Lu, ITALY/584-90121; FAX: 584-90122 (U.S. importers—Nygord Precision Products;MCS, Inc.)

Pasadena Gun Center, Box 6125, 206 E. Shaw, Pasadena, TX 77506/713-472-0417

Paul Co., The, 27385 Pressonville Rd., Wellsville, KS 66092/913-883-4444; FAX: 913-883-2525

Pedersen & Son, C.R., 2717 S. Pere Marquette Hwy., Ludington, MI 49431/616-843-2061

Pedersoli and Co., Davide, Via Artigiani 57, Gardone V.T., Brescia, ITALY 25063/030-8912402; FAX: 030-8911019 (U.S. importers—Beauchamp & Son, Inc.; Cabela's; Cape Outfitters; Cimarron Arms; Dixie Gun Works; EMF Co., Inc.; Navy Arms Co.; Track of the Wolf, Inc.)

Pekin Gun & Sporting Goods, 1304 Derby St., Pekin, IL 61554/309-347-6060

Pentax Corp., 35 Inverness Dr. E., Englewood, CO 80112/800-709-2020; FAX: 303-643-0393

Perazzi m.a.p. S.p.A. (See ARMI Perazzi S.p.A.)

Perazzi USA, Inc., 1207 S. Shamrock Ave., Monrovia, CA 91016/818-303-0068; FAX: 818-303-2081

Phoenix Arms, 1420 S. Archibald Ave., Ontario, CA 91761/909-947-4843; FAX: 909-947-6798

Phoxx Mfg., 200 E. Hickory, Linton, ND 58552/800-280-8668; 701-254-4597

Phoxx Shooters Supply, 5807 Watt Ave., N. Highlands, CA 95660/916-348-9827

Pietta (See U.S. importers—Navy Arms Co.; Taylor's & Co., Inc.)

Pintos Gun Shop, 827 N. Central #102, Kent, WA 98032/206-859-6333

Pioneer Arms Co., 355 Lawrence Rd., Broomall, PA 19008/215-356-5203

Piotti (See U.S. importer—Moore & Co., Wm. Larkin)

Plaza Gunworks, Inc., 983 Gadsden Hwy., Birmingham, AL 35235/205-836-6206

Ponsness/Warren, P.O. Box 8, Rathdrum, ID 83858/208-687-2231; FAX: 208-687-2233

Potter Gunsmithing, 13960 Boxhorn Dr., Muskego, WI 53150/414-425-4830

Powell & Son (Gunmakers) Ltd., William, 35-37 Carrs Lane, Birmingham B4 7SX ENGLAND/121-643-0689; FAX: 121-631-3504 (U.S. importer—The William Powell Agency)

Powell Agency, William, The, 22 Circle Dr., Bellmore, NY 11710/516-679-1158

Precision Airgun Sales, 5139 Warrensville Center Rd., Maple Heights, OH 44137/216-587-5005

Precision Airgun Sales, Inc., 5139 Warrensville Center Rd., Maple Hts., OH 44137-1906/216-587-5005

Precision Arms & Gunsmithing, Ltd., Hwy. 27 & King Rd., Box 809, Nobleton, Ontario, CANADA L0G 1N0/416-859-0965

Precision Gun Works, 4717 St. Rd. 44, Oshkosh, WI 54904/414-233-2274

Precision Gunsmithing, 2723 W. 6th, Amarillo, TX 79106/806-376-7223

Precision Pellet, 1016 Erwin Dr., Joppa, MD 21085/410-679-8179

Precision Reloading, Inc., P.O. Box 122, Stafford Springs, CT 06076/860-684-7979; FAX: 860-684-6788

Precision Sales International, Inc., P.O. Box 1776, Westfield, MA 01086/413-562-5055; FAX: 413-562-5056

Precision Small Arms, 9777 Wilshire Blvd., Suite 1005, Beverly Hills, CA 90212/310-859-4867; FAX: 310-859-2868

Precision Sport Optics, 15571 Producer Lane, Unit G, Huntington Beach, CA 92649/714-891-1309; FAX: 714-892-6920

Preuss Gun Shop, 39046 Woodlawn, Box 650, Shaver Lake, CA 93664/209-841-3405

PrimeTime Sports dba A&M Sales, 412 Ogden Ave., Downers Grove, IL 60515/630-241-2055

Professional Armaments Co., 3695 S. Redwood Rd., West Valley City, UT 84119/801-975-7422; FAX: 801-975-9333

Q

Quad City Gun Repair, 220 N. 2nd St., Eldridge, IA 52748/319-285-4153

Quality Arms, Inc., Box 19477, Dept. GD, Houston, TX 77224/713-870-8377; FAX: 713-870-8524

Quality Firearms, 114 13th Avenue So., Nampa, ID 83651/208-466-1631

Quality Parts Co./Bushmaster Firearms, 999 Roosevelt Trail, Bldg. 3, Windham, ME 04062/800-998-7928, 207-892-2005; FAX: 207-892-8068

R

R&R Shooters Supply, W 6553 North Rd., Mauston, WI 53948/608-847-4562

Rajo Corporation, 2106 W. Franklin St., Evansville, IN 47712/812-422-6945

Ralph's Gun Shop, 200 Fourth St. South, Niverville, Manitoba, CANADA R0A 1E0/204-388-4581

Ram-Line Blount, Inc., P.O. Box 39, Onalaska, WI 54650-0039

Randy's Gun Repair & Sales, P.O. Box 106, Tabustinac, New Brunswick, CANADA E0C 2A0/506-779-4768

Ranging, Inc., Routes 5 & 20, East Bloomfield, NY 14443/716-657-6161; FAX: 716-657-5405

Ransberger, David W., 110 E. Hawthorne, Fallbrook, CA 92028/619-728-5230

Rapids Gun Shop, 7811 Buffalo Ave., Niagara Falls, NY 14304/716-283-7873

Ray's Gunsmith Shop, 3199 Elm Ave., Grand Junction, CO 81504/970-434-6162

Ray's Hardware & Sporting Goods, 730 Singleton Blvd., Dallas, TX 75212/214-747-7916; FAX: 214/744-3415

Ray's Liquor & Sporting Goods, 1956 Solano St., Box 677, Corning, CA 96021/916-824-5625

Ray's Sport Shop, Inc., 559 Hwy. 22, No. Plainfield, NJ 07060/908-561-4400

RCBS, Div. of Blount, Inc., Sporting Equipment Div., 605 Oro Dam Blvd., Oroville, CA 95965/800-533-5000, 916-533-5191; FAX: 916-533-1647

Redding Reloading Equipment, 1089 Starr Rd., Cortland, NY 13045/607-753-3331; FAX: 607-756-8445

Redfield, Inc., 5800 E. Jewell Ave., Denver, CO 80224/303-757-6411; FAX: 303-756-2338

Reliable Gun & Tackle, Inc., 3227 Fraser St., Vancouver, British Columbia, CANADA V5V 4B8/604-874-4710

Reloading Center, 515 W. Main, Burley, ID 83318/208-678-5053

Remington Arms Co. (See page 447)

Rigby & Co., John, 66 Great Suffolk St., London SE1 OBU, ENGLAND/0171-620-0690; FAX: 0171-928-9205

River Bend Sport Shop, 230 Grand Seasons Dr., Waupaca, WI 54981/715-258-3583

Rizzini F.lli (See U.S. importers—Moore & Co., Wm. Larkin; New England Arms Co.)

Rizzini, Battista, Via 2 Giugno, 7/7Bis-25060 Marcheno (Brescia), ITALY/ (U.S. importers—Wm. Larkin Moore & Co.; New England Arms Co.)

Robinson's Sporting Goods, Ltd., 1307 Broad St., Victoria, British Columbia, CANADA V8W 2A8/604-385-3429

Rocking "S" Gun Shop, P.O. Box 1469, Ennis, MT 59729-1469/406-682-5229

Rocky Mountain Arms, Inc., 600 S. Sunset, Unit C, Longmont, CO 80501/303-768-8522; FAX: 303-678-8766

Ron's Gun Repair, 1212 E. Benson Rd., Souix Falls, SD 57104/605-338-7398

Rossi S.A., Amadeo, Rua: Amadeo Rossi, 143, Sao Leopoldo, RS, BRAZIL 93030-220/051-592-5566 (U.S. importer—Interarms)

Rusk Gun Shop, Inc., 6904 Watts Rd., Madison, WI 53719/608-274-8740; FAX: 608-274-8791

Russell's Sporting Goods, 8228 Macleod Trail S.E., Calgary, Alberta, CANADA T2M 2B8/403-276-9222

RWS (See U.S. importer—Dynamit Nobel-RWS, Inc.)

S

S.E.M. Gun Works, 6002 Augusta Rd., Greenville, SC 29605/864-277-5428

Sabatti S.r.l., via Alessandro Volta 90, 25063 Gardone V.T., Brescia, ITALY/030-8912207-831312; FAX: 030-8912059 (U.S. importer—E.A.A. Corp.)

Sako Ltd. (See U.S. importer—Stoeger Industries)

Sams Gunsmithing, David, 225 Front St., Lititz, PA 17543/717-626-0021

San Marco (See U.S. importers—Cape Outfitters; EMF Co., Inc.)

Sanders Gun Shop, 3001 5th St., Meridian, MS 39301/601-485-5301

Saskatoon Gunsmith Shoppe, Ltd., 2310 Avenue "C" N., Saskatoon, Saskatchewan, CANADA S7L 5X5/306-244-2023

Sauer (See U.S. importers—Paul Co., The; Sigarms, Inc.)

Savage Arms (Canada), Inc., 248 Water St., P.O. Box 1240, Lakefield, Ont. K0L 2H0, CANADA/705-652-8000; FAX: 705-652-8431

Savage Arms, Inc., 100 Springdale Rd., Westfield, MA 01085/413-568-7001; FAX: 413-562-7764

Scalzo's Sporting Goods, 1520 Farm to Market Rd., Endwell, NY 13760/607-748-7586

Scharch Mfg., Inc., 10325 CR 120, Salida, CO 81201/719-539-7242, 800-836-4683; FAX: 719-539-3021

Schmidt & Bender, Inc., Brook Rd., P.O. Box 134, Meriden, NH 03770/603-469-3565, 800-468-3450; FAX: 603-469-3471

Schultheis Sporting Goods, Inc., 8 Main, Box 463, Arkport, NY 14807/607-295-7485

Seecamp Co., Inc., L.W., P.O. Box 255, New Haven, CT 06502/203-877-3429

Selin Gunsmith Ltd., Del, 2803 28th St., Vernon, British Columbia, CANADA V1T 4Z5/604-545-6413

Shepherd Scope Ltd., Box 189, Waterloo, NE 68069/402-779-2424; FAX: 402-779-4010

Shiloh Rifle Mfg., 201 Centennial Dr., Big Timber, MT 59011/406-932-4454; FAX: 406-932-5627

Shooter's Choice, Inc., RD #4 Box 168A, Dover, DE 19901/302-736-5166

Shooters Service Center, 8242 N. Lombard, Portland, OR 97203/503-289-1280

Shooters Supply, 1120 Tieton Dr., Yakima, WA 98902/509-482-1181; FAX: 509-575-0315

Shooting Gallery, The, 249 Seneca, Weirton, WV 26062/304-723-3298

Siegles Guns, 508 W. McArthur Blvd., Oakland, CA 94609/510-655-8789

Sievert's Guns, 4107 W. Northern, Pueblo, CO 81005/719-564-0035

SIG, CH-8212 Neuhausen, SWITZERLAND/ (U.S. importer—Mandall Shooting Supplies, Inc.)

SIG-Sauer (See U.S. importer—Sigarms, Inc.)

Sigarms, Inc., Corporate Park, Exeter, NH 03833/603-772-2302; FAX: 603-772-9082

Sile Distributors, Inc., 7 Centre Market Pl., New York, NY 10013/212-925-4111; FAX: 212-925-3149

Sillman, Hal, Associated Services, P.O. Box 4706, 20625 NE 16th Ave., Hollywood, FL 33083/954-894-6717; FAX: 954-894-6717

Simmons Enterprises, Ernie, 709 East Elizabethtown Rd., Manheim, PA 17545/717-664-4040

Simmons Gun Repair, Inc., 700 S. Rogers Rd., Olathe, KS 66062/913-782-3131

Simmons Gun Shop, Al, 122 Locke St. S., Hamilton, Ontario, CANADA L8P 4A8/905-522-1131

Simmons Outdoor Corp., 201 Plantation Oak Parkway, Thomasville, GA 31792/912-227-9053; FAX: 912-227-9054

SKB Arms Co. (See New SKB Arms Co.)

Skip's Gun Shop, 3 Pleasant St., Bristol, NH 03222/603-744-3100

Smith & Smith Gun Shop, 2589 Oscar Johnson Dr., No. Charleston, SC 29405/803-744-2024

Smith & Wesson (See page 447)

Smith's Lawn & Marine Service, 9100 Main St., Clarence, NY 14031/716-633-7868

Societa Armi Bresciane Srl. (See U.S. importer—Cape Outfitters; Gamba, USA)

Sodak Sport & Bait, 850 So. Hwy 281, Aberdeen, SD 57401/605-225-2737

Solvay Police Supply, 102 First St., Solvay, NY 13209/315-468-6287; FAX: 315-468-6751

Southland Gun Works, 1228 Harry Byrd Hwy., Darlington, SC 29532/803-393-6291

Southwest Airguns, 3311 Ryan St., Lake Charles, LA 70601/318-474-6038

Southwest Shooters Supply, 1940 Linwood Blvd., Oklahoma City, OK 73106/405-235-4476

Sporting Arms Mfg., Inc., 801 Hall Ave., Littlefield, TX 79339/806-385-5665; FAX: 806-385-3394

Sportman's Haven, 14695 E. Pike Road, Cambridge, OH 43725/614-432-7243; FAX: 614-432-3204

Sports Mart, The, 828 Ford St., Ogdensburg, NY 13669/315-3983-2865

Sports World, Inc., 5800 S. Lewis Ave., Suite 154, Tulsa, OK 74105/918-742-4027

Sports World, Route 52, Liberty, NY 12754/914-292-3077

Sportsman's Exchange, Inc., 560 C St., Oxnard, CA 93030/805-483-1917

Sportsman's Haven, Inc., 14695 East Pike Rd., Cambridge, OH 43725/614-432-7243

Sportsman's Shop, The, 101 W. Main St., New Holland, PA 17557/717-354-4311

Sportsmans Depot, 2222 N. U.S. Hwy 68, Urban, OH 43078/513-653-4429

Sportsmen's Repair Center., Inc., 106 S. High St., Box 134, Columbus Groves, OH 45830/419-659-5818

Spradlin's, 113 Arthur, Pueblo, CO 81004/719-543-9462

Springfield, Inc., 420 W. Main St., Geneseo, IL 61254/309-944-5631; FAX: 309-944-3676

Stalwart Corporation, 76 Imperial, Unit A, Evanston, WY 82930/307-789-7687; FAX: 307-789-7688

Stan's Gun Repair, R.R. #2, Westbrook, MN 56183/507-274-5649

Star Bonifacio Echeverria S.A., Torrekva 3, Eibar, SPAIN 20600/43-107340; FAX: 43-101524 (U.S. importer—E.A.A. Corp.; Interarms; P.S.M.G. Gun Co.)

Star Machine Works, 418 10th Ave., San Diego, CA 92101/619-232-3216

Starnes, Gunmaker, Ken, 32900 S.W. Laurel View Rd., Hillsboro, OR 97123/503-628-0705

Steyr Mannlicher AG & CO KG, Mannlicherstrasse 1, A-4400 Steyr, AUSTRIA/0043-7252-78621; FAX: 0043-7252-68621 (U.S. importer—GSI, Inc.; Nygord Precision Products)

Stock & Barrel, 6 Chapel Court, Charlottetown, P.E.I., CANADA C1A 8L4/902-368-3154

Stocker's Shop, 5199 Mahoning Ave., Warren, OH 44483/216-847-9579

Stoeger Industries, 5 Mansard Ct., Wayne, NJ 07470/201-872-9500, 800-631-0722; FAX: 201-872-2230

Stonewall Range, 10 Ken-Mar Dr., Broadview Hts., OH 44147/216-526-0029

Sturm, Ruger & Co., Inc., 200 Ruger Rd., Prescott, AZ 86301/520-541-8820; FAX: 520-541-8850

Sundance Industries, Inc., 25163 W. Avenue Stanford, Valencia, CA 91355/805-257-4807

Surplus Center, 515 S.E. Spruce, Roseburg, OR 97470/541-672-4312

Survival Arms, Inc., P.O. Box 965, Orange, CT 06477/203-924-6533; FAX: 203-924-2581

Swarovski Optik North America Ltd., One Wholesale Way, Cranston, RI 02920/401-946-2220, 800-426-3089; FAX: 401-946-2587

Swift Instruments, Inc., 952 Dorchester Ave., Boston, MA 02125/617-436-2960; FAX: 617-436-3232

Swivel Machine Works, Inc., 11 Monitor Hill Rd., Newtown, CT 06470/203-270-6343

T

T.J.'s Firing Line Gunsmith, 692-A Peoria St., Aurora, CO 80011/303-363-1911

Tanfoglio Fratelli S.r.l., via Valtrompia 39, 41, 25068 Gardone V.T., Brescia, ITALY/30-8910361; FAX: 30-8910183 (U.S. importer—E.A.A. Corp.)

Tanner (See U.S. importer—Mandall Shooting Supplies, Inc.)

Tar-Hunt Custom Rifles, Inc., RR3, P.O. Box 572, Bloomsburg, PA 17815-9351/717-784-6368; FAX: 717-784-6368

Tasco Sales, Inc., 7600 NW 26th St., Miami, FL 33122-1494/305-591-3670; FAX: 305-592-5895

Taurus Firearms, Inc., 16175 NW 49th Ave., Miami, FL 33014/305-624-1115; FAX: 305-623-7506

Taurus International Firearms (See U.S. importer—Taurus Firearms, Inc.)

Taylor & Vadney, Inc., 303 Central Ave., ALbany, NY 12206/518-472-9183

Taylor's & Co., Inc., 304 Lenoir Dr., Winchester, VA 22603/540-722-2017; FAX: 540-722-2018

Taylor's Sportsman Supply, Gene, 445 W. Gunnison, Grand Junction, CO 81505/970-242-8165

Ten Ring Service, 2227 W. Lou Dr., Jacksonville, FL 32216/904-724-7419

Texas Armory (See Bond Arms, Inc.)

Texas Longhorn Arms, Inc., 5959 W. Loop South, Suite 424, Bellaire, TX 77401/713-660-6323; FAX: 713-660-0493

Thompson's Gunshop, Inc., 10254 84th St., Alto, MI 49302/616-891-0440

Thompson/Center Arms (See page 447)

300 Gunsmith Service, 12500 East Bellview Ave., Englewood, CO 80111/303-690-3300

Thunder Mountain Arms, P.O. Box 593, Oak Harbor, WA 98277/206-679-4657; FAX: 206-675-1114

Tikka (See U.S. importer—Stoeger Industries)

TOZ (See U.S. importer—Nygord Precision Products)

Track of the Wolf, Inc., P.O. Box 6, Osseo, MN 55369-0006/612-424-2500; FAX: 612-424-9860

Traders, The, 885 E. 14th St., San Leandro, CA 94577/510-569-0555

Trading Post, The, 412 Erie St. S., Massillon, OH 44646/216-833-7761

Traditions, Inc., P.O. Box 776, 1375 Boston Post Rd., Old Saybrook, CT 06475/860-388-4656; FAX: 860-388-4657

Trester, Inc., Verne, 3604 W. 16th St., Indianapolis, IN 46222/317-638-6921

Trijicon, Inc., 49385 Shafer Ave., P.O. Box 930059, Wixom, MI 48393-0059/810-960-7700; FAX: 810-960-7725

U

Uberti USA, Inc., P.O. Box 469, Lakeville, CT 06039/860-435-8068; FAX: 860-435-8146

Uberti, Aldo, Casella Postale 43, I-25063 Gardone V.T., ITALY/ (U.S. importers—American Arms, Inc.; Cabela's; Cimarron Arms; Dixie Gun Works; EMF Co., Inc.; Forgett Jr., Valmore J.; IAR, Inc.; Navy Arms Co; Taylor's & Co., Inc.; Uberti USA, Inc.)

Ugartechea S.A., Ignacio, Chonta 26, Eibar, SPAIN 20600/43-121257; FAX: 43-121669 (U.S. importer—Aspen Outfitting Co.; The Gun Shop; Bill Hanus Birdguns; Lion Country Supply)

Ultra Light Arms, Inc., P.O. Box 1270, 214 Price St., Granville, WV 26505/304-599-5687; FAX: 304-599-5687

Ultralux (See U.S. importer—Keng's Firearms Specialty, Inc.)

Unertl Optical Co., Inc., John, 308 Clay Ave., P.O. Box 818, Mars, PA 16046-0818/412-625-3810

Unique Sporting Goods, 1538 Columbia St., Lorreto, PA 15940/814-674-8889

Unique/M.A.P.F., 10, Les Allees, 64700 Hendaye, FRANCE 64700/33-59 20 71 93 (U.S. importer—Nygord Precision Products)

Upper Missouri Trading Co., 304 N. Harold St., Crofton, NE 68730/402-388-4844

V

Valley Gun Shop, 7719 Harford Rd., Baltimore, MD 21234/410-668-2171; FAX: 410-668-6693

Valley Gunsmithing, 619 Second St., Webster City, IA 50595/515-832-5102

VanBurne's Gun Shop, 5337 Cowan Ave., Toledo, OH 43613/419-475-3150

Voere-KGH m.b.H., P.O. Box 416, A-6333 Kufstein, Tirol, AUSTRIA/0043-5372-62547; FAX: 0043-5372-65752 (U.S. importers—JäagerSport, Ltd.)

W

Wailea Supply Outdoor Sports, 22 Alahele Pl., Kihei, HI 96753/808-874-9457; FAX: 808-874-8686

Walker Arms Co., 499 County Road 820, Hwy. 80 West, Selma, AL 36701/334-872-6231; FAX: 334-872-6262

Walther GmbH, Carl, B.P. 4325, D-89033 Ulm, GERMANY/ (U.S. importer—Champion's Choice; Interarms; P.S.M.G. Gun Co.)

Wanamaker Guns, 7915 Southeastern Ave., Indianapolis, IN 46239/317-862-4867; FAX: 317-862-2666

Wardle's Appliance Service, 1420 Youville Dr., #13, Orleans, Ontario, CANADA K1C 7B3/613-830-4768

Way It Was Sporting, The, 620 Chestnut St., Moorestown, NJ 08057/609-231-0111

Weatherby (See page 447)

Weaver Scope Repair Service, 1121 Larry Mahan Dr., Suite B, El Paso, TX 79925/915-593-1005

Webley and Scott Ltd., Frankley Industrial Park, Tay Rd., Rubery, Rednal, Birmingham B45 0PA, ENGLAND/011-021-453-1864; FAX: 021-457-7846 (U.S. importer—Beeman Precision Airguns; Groenewold, John)

Weihrauch KG, Hermann, Industriestrasse 11, 8744 Mellrichstadt, GERMANY/ 09776-497-498 (U.S. importers—Beeman Precision Airguns; E.A.A. Corp.)

Wessell Gun Service, 4000 E. 9 Mile Road, Warren, MI 48091/313-756-2660

West Gate Gunsports, Inc., 10116 175th St., Edmonton, Alberta, CANADA T5S 1A1/403-489-0633

West Luther Gun Repair, R.R. #1, Conn, Ontario, CANADA N0G 1N0/519-848-6260

Westley Richards & Co., 40 Grange Rd., Birmingham, ENGLAND B29 6AR/010-214722953 (U.S. importer—Westley Richards Agency USA)

Westley Richards Agency USA (U.S. importer for Westley Richards & Co.)

White Dog Gunsmithing, 62 Central Ave., Ilion, NY 13357/315-894-6211

White Muzzleloading Systems, 25 E. Hwy. 40, Suite 330-12, Roosevelt, UT 84066/801-722-5996; FAX: 801-722-5909

White Shooting Systems (See White Muzzleloading Systems)

Whitestone Lumber Corp., 148-02 14th Ave., Whitestone, NY 11357/718-746-4400; FAX: 718-767-1748

Wholesale Sports, 12505 97 St., Edmonton, Alberta, CANADA T5G 1Z8/403-477-3737

Wichita Arms, Inc., 923 E. Gilbert, P.O. Box 11371, Wichita, KS 67211/316-265-0661; FAX: 316-265-0760

Wichita Guncraft, Inc., 4607 Barnett, Wichita Falls, TX 76310/817-692-5622

Wild West Guns, Inc., 7521 Old Seward Hwy. #A, Anchorage, AK 99518/907-344-4500

Wildey, Inc., P.O. Box 475, Brookfield, CT 06804/203-355-9000; FAX: 203-354-7759

Wilkinson Arms, 26884 Pearl Rd., Parma, ID 83660/208-722-6771; FAX: 208-722-5197

Will's Gun Shop, 5603 N. Hubbard Lake Rd., Spruce, MI 48762/517-727-2500

William's Gun Shop, Ben, 1151 S. Cedar Ridge, Duncanville, TX 75137/214-780-1807

Williams Gun Shop, Inc., Dick, 4985 Cole Rd., Saginaw, MI 48601/517-777-1240

Williams Gun Sight Co., 7389 Lapeer Rd., Box 329, Davison, MI 48423/810-653-2131, 800-530-9028; FAX: 810-658-2140

Williams Gun Sight, 7389 Lapeer Road, Box 329, Davison, MI 48423/810-653-2131, ext. 139

Williamson Precision Gunsmithing, 117 W. Pipeline, Hurst, TX 76053/817-285-0064

Winchester (See page 447)

Wingshooting Adventures, 0-1845 W. Leonard, Grand Rapids, MI 49544/616-677-1980; FAX: 616-677-1986

Wise Choice Sporting Goods & Gunsmithing, RR #2, Hwy. 11 N., Kilworthy, Ontario, CANADA P0E 1G0/705-689-9473

Wisner's Gun Shop, Inc., 146 Curtis Hill Rd., Chehalis, WA 98532/360-748-8942

Wolf Custom Gunsmithing, Gregory, c/o Albrights Gun Shop, 36 E. Dover St., Easton, MD 21601/410-820-8811

Wolfer Brothers, Inc., 1701 Durham Dr., Houston, TX 77007/713-869-7640

Woodman's Sporting Goods, 223 Main St., Norway, ME 04268/207-743-6602

World Class Airguns, 2736 Morningstar Dr., Indianapolis, IN 46229/317-897-5548

Wortner Gun Works, Ltd., 433 Queen St., Box 411, Chatham, Ontario, CANADA N7M 5K5/519-352-0924

Y, Z

Ye Olde Black Powder Shop, 994 W. Midland Road, Auburn, MI 48611/517-662-2271; FAX: 517-662-2666

Zabala Hermanos S.A., P.O. Box 97, Eibar, SPAIN 20600/43-768085, 43-768076; FAX: 34-43-768201 (U.S. importer—American Arms, Inc.)

Zanes Gun Rack, 4167 N. High St., Columbus, OH 43214/614-263-0369

Zanoletti, Pietro, Via Monte Gugielpo, 4, I-25063 Gardone V.T., ITALY/ (U.S. importer—Mandall Shooting Supplies, Inc.)

Zeiss Optical, Carl, 1015 Commerce St., Petersburg, VA 23803/804-861-0033, 800-388-2984; FAX: 804-733-4024

Warranty Service Centers

SERVICE CENTER	CITY	BR	CR	RE	SW	TC	WN	WE
ALABAMA								
Gatlin Gun, Wallace	Oxford			✓				
Nusbaum Enterprises, Inc.	Mobile			✓				
Ott's Gun Service	Atmore	✓		✓				
Plaza Gunworks, Inc.	Birmingham			✓	✓			
Walker Arms Co., Inc.	Selma	✓		✓	✓	✓	✓	✓
ALASKA								
Down Under Gunsmiths	Fairbanks	✓		✓			✓	
Wild West Guns, Inc.	Anchorage	✓		✓			✓	
ARIZONA								
Dave's Airgun Service	Tempe		✓					
Don's Sport Shop, Inc.	Scottsdale		✓	✓			✓	
Jensens's Custom Ammunition	Tucson		✓	✓	✓	✓	✓	
Joe's Gun Shop	Phoenix		✓					
ARKANSAS								
Broadway Arms	North Little Rock			✓				
Draper Enterprises dba Gun Exchange, Inc.	Little Rock				✓			
Jim's Trading Post	Pine Bluff	✓						
CALIFORNIA								
Air Guns Unlimited	La Puente		✓					
Air Venture Air Guns	Bellflower		✓					
Airguns International	Santa Rosa		✓					
Bain & Davis	San Gabriel			✓				
Bolsa Gunsmithing	Westminster	✓		✓				
Cal's Customs	Fallbrook		✓	✓				
Grundman's	Rio Dell			✓				
Gunshop, Inc., The	Lancaster			✓				
Huntington Sportsman's Store	Oroville	✓		✓				✓
Imbert & Smiters, Inc.	San Carlos	✓		✓				
Long Beach Uniform., Inc.	Long Beach	✓		✓	✓			
Mac1	Gardena		✓					
Miclean, Bill	San Jose		✓					
Northridge Pistol & Rifle Range	Northridge			✓	✓			
Pacific International Service Co.	Janesville	✓	✓	✓	✓			
Phoxx Shooters Supply	N. Highlands		✓					
Preuss Gun Shop	Shaver Lake			✓				
Ransberger, David W.	Fallbrook			✓				
Ray's Liquor and Sporting Goods	Corning		✓					
Siegle's Gunshop, Inc.	Oakland		✓					
Sportsman's Exchange, Inc.	Oxnard			✓				
Traders, The	San Leandro		✓					

SERVICE CENTER	CITY	BR	CR	RE	SW	TC	WN	WE
COLORADO								
A. H&B Service, Inc.	Littleton	✓		✓				
Gart Brothers Sporting Goods	Denver	✓	✓				✓	
Ray's Gunsmith Shop	Grand Junction	✓	✓					
Sievert's Guns	Pueblo				✓	✓		
Spradin's	Pueblo			✓	✓			
Taylor's Sportman's Supply, Gene	Grand Junction			✓	✓			
300 Gunsmith Service (Wichita Guncraft)	Englewood			✓	✓		✓	
T.J.'s Firing Line Gunsmith	Aurora			✓	✓		✓	
CONNECTICUT								
Gunsmithing Limited	Fairfield	✓		✓			✓	
Horchler's Gun Shop	Collinsville		✓	✓				
Mason, Gun & Ammo Co., Tom	Danbury			✓	✓			
Modern Guncraft	Wallingford		✓					
DELAWARE								
Shooter's Choice, Inc.	Dover				✓			
FLORIDA								
Alexander, Gunsmith. W.R.	Tallahassee	✓	✓	✓				
Green Acres Sporting Goods, Inc.	Jacksonville	✓	✓	✓				
Lawsons Custom Firearms, Inc., Art	Ocala	✓	✓					
Sillman, Hal, Associated Services	Miami		✓					
Ten Ring Service	Jacksonville					✓		
GEORGIA								
Accuracy Gun Shop	Columbus	✓		✓	✓			
Dorn's Outdoor Center	Macon	✓	✓				✓	
Ed's Gun & Tackle Shop, Inc.	Marietta	✓	✓	✓				
Franklin Sports, Inc.	Bogart	✓		✓	✓			
Jordan, Charles Don	Tifton	✓		✓		✓		
HAWAII								
Chung, Gunsmith, Mel	Kaunakakai	✓		✓	✓		✓	
Wailea Supply Outdoor Sports	Kihie	✓	✓					
IDAHO								
Intermountain Arms & Tackle, Inc.	Meridian	✓		✓		✓	✓	
Quality Firearms	Nampa	✓		✓		✓		
Reloading Center	Burley			✓				
ILLINOIS								
Article II Gunshop dba Gun World	Bensenville				✓			
Betelmay Guns, Geo. M.	Morton	✓						
Damall's Gun Works	Bloomington			✓			✓	
Groenwold, John	Mundelein		✓					
Henry's Airguns	Belvidere		✓					

Warranty Service Centers

BR=Browning CR=Crosman/Benjamin RE=Remington SW=Smith & Wesson TC=Thompson/Center WN=Winchester WE=Weatherby

SERVICE CENTER	CITY	BR	CR	RE	SW	TC	WN	WE
Outdoorsman Sporting Goods Co.	Geneva		✓					
Pekin Gun & Sporting Goods	Pekin		✓				✓	
Prime Time Sports dba A&M Sales	Downers Grove		✓				✓	
INDIANA								
Lutter, Robert E.	Ft. Wayne	✓	✓					
Rajo Corporation	Evansville		✓					
Trester, Inc., Verne	Indianapolis			✓				
Wanamaker Guns	Indianapolis		✓					
IOWA								
Daryl's Gun Shop, Inc.	State Center			✓				
Glenn's Reel & Rod Repair	Des Moines		✓					
Jacobson's Gun Center	Story City							✓
Nelson's Engine Shop	Cedar Falls		✓					
Quad City Gun Repair	Eldridge			✓				
Valley Gunsmithing	Webster City			✓				
KANSAS								
Bullseye Gun Shop	Overland Park			✓				
Gordan's Wigwam	Wichita	✓						
Northwest Arms Service	Alwood			✓				
Simmons Gun Repair	Olathe			✓	✓		✓	
KENTUCKY								
D&J Bullet Co.	Russel				✓			
Firearms Service Center	Louisville			✓				
J&M Gun Shop, Inc.	Bowling Green				✓			
Paducah Shooters Supply, Inc.	Paducah			✓				
LOUISIANA								
Atlas Gun Repair	Violet	✓						
B&B Gun Refinishing	Lake Charles			✓				
Chalmette Jewelry & Guns	Chalmette	✓						
Clark's Custom Guns, Inc.	Princeton				✓			
Hutchinson's Gun Repair	Pineville	✓		✓				
Martin Gun Shop, Henry	Shreveport			✓				
N.A. Guns, Inc.	Baton Rouge	✓		✓				
Southwest Airguns	Lake Charles		✓					
MAINE								
Brunswick Gun Shop	Brunswick			✓	✓			
Johnson Service, Inc., W.	Adrian			✓	✓			
Woodman's Sporting Goods	Norway			✓				✓
MARYLAND								
Atlantic Guns, Inc.	Silver Spring	✓		✓	✓			
Gun Center, The	Frederick		✓					

SERVICE CENTER	CITY	BR	CR	RE	SW	TC	WN	WE
Precision Pellet	Joppa		✓					
Valley Gun Shop	Baltimore	✓	✓	✓			✓	
Wolf Custom Gunsmithing, Gregory, c/o Albright's Gun Shop	Easton	✓		✓				
MASSACHUSETTS								
Bellrose & Son, L.E.	Granby		✓					
MICHIGAN								
Adventure A.G.R.	Waterford		✓	✓				✓
Bachelder Master Gunmakers	Grand Rapids		✓	✓	✓		✓	✓
Daenzer, Charles E.	Otisville		✓	✓				
Hampel's Key & Gun Shop	Traverse City		✓	✓				
Joe's Gun Shop	Dorr		✓					
McDaniel Co., Inc., B.	South Lyon		✓	✓				
Moreau, Gunsmith, Pete	Bay City		✓					
Northern Precision Airguns	Tawas City		✓					
Oakland Custom Arms, Inc.	Waterford			✓				
On Target Gun Shop, Inc.	Kalamazoo			✓				
Outpost, The	Eureka		✓					
Pederson Co., C.R.	Ludington			✓				
Thompson's Gunshop, Inc.	Alto							
Wessel Gun Service	Warren	✓						
Williams Gun Sight & Outfitters	Davison	✓					✓	
Williams Gun Shop, Inc., Dick	Saginaw		✓	✓				
Will's Gun Shop	Spruce							✓
Ye Olde Blk Powder Shop	Auburn					✓		
MINNESOTA								
Ahlman's	Morristown	✓		✓	✓		✓	✓
B&B Supply Co.	Minneapolis		✓					
Dale's Gunshop	Rochester			✓				
Frontiersman's Sports	St. Louis Park	✓						
Matt's 10X Gunsmithing, Inc.	Duluth			✓				
Northland Sport Center	Bagley			✓				
Stan's Gun Repair	Westbrook			✓				
MISSISSIPPI								
May & Company, Inc.	Jackson		✓					
Millers Gun Shop	Gulfport			✓		✓		
Sanders Gun Shop	Meridian			✓				
MISSOURI								
Bickford's Gun Repair	Orongo			✓			✓	✓
CR Specialty	Kansas City	✓						
Carl's Gun Shop	Eldorado Springs			✓			✓	
Catfish Guns	Imperial			✓	✓		✓	

Warranty Service Centers

BR=Browning CR=Crosman/Benjamin RE=Remington SW=Smith & Wesson TC=Thompson/Center WN=Winchester WE=Weatherby

SERVICE CENTER	CITY	BR	CR	RE	SW	TC	WN	WE
Dollar Drugs, Inc.	Lee's Summit		✓					
F&D Guns	St. Charles							
Nu-Line Guns, Inc.	Harvester	✓		✓	✓		✓	✓
MONTANA								
Brady's Sportsmans Surplus	Missoula		✓			✓		
Capitol Sports & Western Wear	Helena			✓	✓		✓	✓
Montana Gun Works	Great Falls				✓			
Rocking S Gunshop	Ennis			✓				
NEBRASKA								
Bedlan's Sporting Good, Inc.	Fairbury	✓						
Cylinder & Slide, Inc.	Fremont				✓			
G.H. Gun Shop	McCook			✓				✓
G.I. Loan Shop	Grand Island			✓				
Gunsmithing Specialties, Co.	Papillion	✓						
Labs Air Gun Shop	Omaha		✓					
Upper Missouri Trading Co., Inc.	Crofton			✓		✓		
NEVADA								
Accuracy Gun Shop, Inc.	Las Vegas			✓				
Gun World	Elko			✓				
Nevada Air Guns	Las Vegas		✓					
NEW HAMPSHIRE								
Lewis Arms	Hooksett	✓					✓	✓
Skip's Gunshop	Bristol			✓			✓	✓
NEW JERSEY								
Belleplain Supply, Inc.	Belleplain		✓					
Brenner Sport Shop, Charlie	Rahway		✓					
Garfield Gunsmithing	Garfield	✓		✓				✓
Harry's Army & Navy Store	Robbinsville	✓	✓		✓			
Ray's Sport Shop, Inc.	North Plainfield	✓		✓	✓			
The Way It Was Sporting	Moorestown	✓						
NEW MEXICO								
Charlie's Sporting Goods, Inc.	Albuquerque		✓		✓			
D&J Coleman Service	Hobbs		✓					
NEW YORK								
Alpine Arms Corp.	Brooklyn				✓			
Benson Gun Shop	Coram L.I.		✓					
Boracci, E. John. Village Sport Ctr.	Seaford L.I.		✓					
Buffalo Gun Center, Inc.	Buffalo			✓				
Creekside Gun Shop	Holcomb	✓						
Damiano's Field & Stream	Ossining		✓					
Gunsmithing Specialties Co.	Buffalo			✓				

SERVICE CENTER	CITY	BR	CR	RE	SW	TC	WN	WE
Hill Top Hunting & Fishing Supply	Webster			✓				
Kielon, Gunsmith, Dave	Middleton		✓					
Lounsbury Sporting Goods, Bob	Niagara Falls		✓					
Rapids Gun Shop	Endwell		✓					
Scalzo's Sporting Goods	Arkport		✓	✓				
Schultheis Sporting Goods	Clarence			✓				
Smith's Lawn & Marine Svc.	Solvay			✓				
Solvay Police Supply	Ogdensburg		✓					
Sports Mar, The	Liberty		✓					
Sports World	Albany		✓					
Taylor & Vadney, Inc.	Ilion			✓				
White Dog Gunsmithing					✓			
NORTH CAROLINA								
Baity's Custom Gunworks	North Wilksboro	✓						
Blue Ridge Outdoor Sports, Inc.	E. Flat Rock				✓			
Duncan Gun Shop, Inc.	North Wilksboro					✓		
Hill's, Inc.	Raleigh	✓						
Mike's Crosman Service	Winston-Salem		✓					
NORTH DAKOTA								
Outdoorsman, The	Fargo	✓		✓				
Phoxx Mfg.	Linton		✓	✓				
OHIO								
Central Ohio Police Supply, c/o Wammes Guns	Bellefontaine	✓		✓				
Cherry Corners, Inc.	Lodi			✓		✓		
Eyster Hertige Gunsmiths, Ken	Centerburg	✓						
Heckman Arms Company	Richmond Heights						✓	
Log Cabin Sport Shop	Lodi					✓		
Precision Airgun Sales	Maple Heights		✓					
Sportman's Depot	Urban		✓					
Sportman's Haven	Cambridge	✓		✓	✓	✓		✓
Sportmen's Repair Ctr., Inc.	Columbus Groves		✓					
Stocker's Shop	Warren		✓					
Stonewall Range	Broadview Heights				✓			
Trading Post, The	Massillon		✓					
VanBurne's Gun Shop	Toledo		✓					
Zanes Gun Rack	Columbus		✓					
OKLAHOMA								
Contender Vender, The	Longdale					✓		
Meydag, Peter	Tulsa		✓					
Southwest Shooters Supply, Inc.	Oklahoma City	✓					✓	✓
Sports World, Inc.	Tulsa	✓		✓	✓	✓	✓	✓

Warranty Service Centers

BR=Browning CR=Crosman/Benjamin RE=Remington SW=Smith & Wesson TC=Thompson/Center WN=Winchester WE=Weatherby

SERVICE CENTER	CITY	BR	CR	RE	SW	TC	WN	WE
OREGON								
Allison & Carey Gun Works	Portland	✓					✓	
Enstad & Douglas	Oregon City					✓		
Felton, James, Custom Gunsmith	Eugene			✓				
Guncrafters	Salem							✓
P&D Rod, Reel & Airguns	White City		✓					
Shooters Service Center	Portland				✓			
Stames, Gunmaker, Ken	Hillsboro			✓				
Surplus Center	Roseburg			✓				
PENNSYLVANIA								
Auto Electric & Parts, Inc.	Media		✓					
Colabaugh Gunsmith, Inc., Craig	Stroudsburg			✓				
Grice Gun Shop, Inc.	Clearfield			✓			✓	
Hart & Son, Robert W.	Nescopeck			✓	✓			
Herold's Gun Shoppe	Waynesboro			✓				
J&T Services	Bradford		✓					
Keidel's Gunsmithing Service	Washington			✓				
Leo's Custom Stocks	Library	✓		✓				
Levan's Sporting Goods	Lebanon		✓	✓				
Miller's Sport Shop	Mountaintop		✓				✓	
Sams Gunsmithing, David	Lititz			✓				
Sportman's Shop	New Holland	✓			✓			
Unique Sporting Goods	Lorreto		✓					
RHODE ISLAND								
K&L Shooting Supplies	Warwick			✓				
Gun Hospital, The	E. Providence		✓					
SOUTH CAROLINA								
Bryan & Associates	Anderson		✓					
Gun Rack, Inc., The	Aiken			✓				
S.E.M. Gun Works	Greenville		✓					
Smith & Smith Gun Shop, Inc.	North Charleston	✓		✓				
Southland Gun Works, Inc.	Darlington	✓		✓				
SOUTH DAKOTA								
Gary's Gun Shop	Sioux Falls	✓		✓	✓			
Jack First	Rapid City	✓		✓	✓		✓	✓
Ron's Gun Repair	Sioux Falls	✓		✓	✓		✓	
Sodak Sport & Bait	Aberdeen	✓					✓	
TENNESSEE								
D&L Gunsmithing/Guns & Ammo	Memphis	✓		✓			✓	
Friedman's Army Surplus	Nashville		✓					
Gun City USA, Inc.	Nashville	✓			✓	✓		

SERVICE CENTER	CITY	BR	CR	RE	SW	TC	WN	WE
Hagstrom, E.G.	Memphis		✓					
Hill's Hardware & Sporting Goods	Union City			✓				
McGuns, W.H.	Humboldt	✓		✓			✓	✓
TEXAS								
Alpine Range	Fort Worth	✓						✓
Armadillo Air Gun Repair	Corpus Christi		✓	✓				
Ben's Gun Shop & Indoor Range	Duncanville		✓	✓				
Billy Fred's	Amarillo	✓						
Carroll's Gun Shop, Inc.	Wharton	✓		✓				
Chuck's Gun Shop	Brownsville		✓					
Coleman, Inc., Ron	Carrollton	✓		✓				
Comeaux Gun Clinic	Bridge City	✓	✓	✓			✓	
Freer's Gun Shop	Houston			✓			✓	
Gun & Tackle Store, The	Dallas			✓				
Kirkpatrick, Gunsmith, Larry	Lubbock			✓				
Lone Star Guns, Inc.	Plano	✓		✓	✓			
Longacre's, Inc.	Abilene			✓				
Master Gunsmiths, Inc.	Houston	✓		✓	✓		✓	
McBride's Guns, Inc.	Austin	✓	✓	✓	✓		✓	
McClelland Gun Shop	Dallas	✓		✓			✓	
Nagal Gun Shop, Inc.	San Antonio	✓		✓				
Oshman's Sporting Goods, Inc.	Houston	✓	✓	✓				
Pasadena Gun Center	Pasadena			✓		✓		
Precision Gunsmithing	Amarillo	✓		✓				
Ray's Sporting Goods	Dallas	✓						
Wichita Guncraft, Inc.	Wichita Falls			✓		✓		
Williamson Precision	Hurst							✓
Wolfer Brothers, Inc.	Houston		✓					
UTAH								
Dixie Gun & Fish	St. George	✓		✓				
Gunsmith Co., The	Salt Lake City	✓		✓		✓		
Hutch's	Lehi		✓					
Professional Armaments, Inc.	West Valley City	✓	✓	✓	✓			
VERMONT								
Burby, Inc. Guns & Gunsmithing	Middlebury			✓				
Carpenter's Gun Works	Proctorsville			✓		✓		
Island Gun Shop	Island Pond	✓						
VIRGINIA								
Bob's Gun & Tackle Shop, (Blaustein & Reich, Inc.)	Norfolk	✓		✓	✓		✓	
Cervera, Albert J.	Hanover		✓					
King's Gun Shop, Inc.	Franklin	✓		✓				

Warranty Service Centers

BR=Browning CR=Crosman/Benjamin RE=Remington SW=Smith & Wesson TC=Thompson/Center WN=Winchester WE=Weatherby

SERVICE CENTER	CITY	BR	CR	RE	SW	TC	WN	WE
Moates Sport Shop, Bob	Midlothian	✓						
Northern Virginia Gun Works, Inc.	Springfield			✓				
WASHINGTON								
Brock's Gunsmithing, Inc.	Spokane			✓				
Chet Paulson Outfitters	Tacoma	✓						
Greene's Gun Shop	Oak Harbor			✓				
Kesselring Gun Shop	Burlington	✓						
Pintos Gun Shop	Kent		✓					
Shooters Supply	Yakima					✓		
Wisner's Gun Shop, Inc.	Chehalis			✓				
WEST VIRGINIA								
Douglas Sporting Goods	Princeton				✓			
Shooting Gallery, The	Weirton		✓					
WISCONSIN								
Anderson's Gunsmithing	Fall Creek	✓						
Badger's Shooters Supply, Inc.	Owen			✓				
Bob's Crosman Repair	Cudahy		✓					
Gander Mountain, Inc.	Wilmot	✓		✓	✓		✓	
Jack's Lock & Gun Shop	Fond Du Lac	✓	✓	✓				
Jay's Sports, Inc.	Menomonee Falls						✓	
Ladwig Gunsmithing, Inc., Jack	West Milwaukee			✓				
Midwestern Shooters Supply, Inc.	Lomira	✓		✓				
Potter Gunsmithing	Muskego			✓				
Precision Gun Works	Oshkosh			✓				
River Bend Sport Shop	Waupaca		✓					
R&R Shooters Supply	Mauston		✓	✓				
Rusk Gun Shop, Inc.	Madison	✓		✓			✓	✓
WYOMING								
Denny's	Cody				✓			
Jackalope Gun Shop	Douglas			✓				
CANADA								
Bartlett, Michael	St. John's, NF		✓					
Casey's Gun Shop	Rogersville, NB	✓		✓			✓	
Charlton Co., Ltd., M.D.	Brentwood Bay, BC				✓			
Crosman Parts & Service Center	Peterborough, ON		✓					
Davidson's of Canada	Peterborough, ON			✓				
Delisle Thompson Sporting Goods	Saskatoon, SK			✓				
Epps, Ellwood	Orillia, ON			✓				
Ernie's Gun Shop, Ltd.	Winnipeg, MB			✓		✓		
G.V.R. Enterprises, Ltd.	Edmonton, AB		✓					
Gene's Gunsmithing	Selkirk, MB			✓		✓		✓

SERVICE CENTER	CITY	BR	CR	RE	SW	TC	WN	WE
Girard, Florent, Gunsmith	Chicoutimi, PQ			✓				
Jay-Cee's Warranty Service	Selkirk, MB		✓					
L'Armurier, A. Richard, Lusignant	St. Hyacinthe, PQ			✓		✓	✓	
L'Armurier Alain Bouchard, Inc.	Ulverton, PQ	✓				✓		
L'Armurier C.A.F. Gunshop	St. Mathias Sur Richelie, PQ		✓					
L'Armurier De L'Outaouais	Hull, PQ			✓			✓	
Long Gunsmithing Ltd., W.R.	Cobourg, ON	✓					✓	
Magasin Latulippe, Inc.	Quebec City, PQ	✓	✓	✓				✓
Millers Rod & Gun	Florenceville, NB		✓	✓				
Murray, John	Moncton, NB		✓					
Newby, Stewart, Gunsmith	Newburgh, ON			✓				
Precision Arms & Gunsmithing Ltd.	Nobleton, ON		✓				✓	
Ralph's Gun Shop	Niverville, MB			✓			✓	
Randy's Gun Repair & Sales	Tabustinac, NB							
Reliable Gun & Tackle, Ltd.	Vancouver, BC	✓	✓				✓	
Robinson's Sporting Goods, Ltd.	Victoria, BC		✓				✓	
Russell's Sporting Goods	Calgary, AB						✓	
Saskatoon Gunsmith Shoppe, Ltd.	Saskatoon, SK			✓			✓	
Selin Gunsmith, Ltd., Del	Vernon, BC		✓					
Simmons Gun Shoop, Al	Hamilton, ON		✓	✓				
Stock & Barrel	Charlottetown, PEI		✓					
Wardie's Appliance Service	Orleans, ON		✓					
West Gate Gunsports, Inc.	Edmonton, AB			✓			✓	
West Luther Gun Repair	Conn, ON			✓			✓	
Wholesale Sports	Edmonton, AB	✓						✓
Wise Choice Sporting Goods & Gunsmithing	Kilworth, ON			✓			✓	
Wortner Gun Works, Ltd.	Chatham, ON		✓	✓	✓		✓	✓

Sporting Leaf and Open Sights

ERA EXPRESS SIGHTS A wide variety of open sights and bases for custom installation. Partial listing shown. From New England Custom Gun Service.
Price: One-leaf express $66.00
Price: Two-leaf express $71.50
Price: Three-leaf express $77.00
Price: Bases for above $27.50
Price: Standing rear sight, straight $13.25
Price: Base for above $16.50

ERA PROFESSIONAL EXPRESS SIGHTS Standing or folding leaf sights are securely locked to the base with the ERA Magnum Clamp, but can be loosened for sighting in. Base can be attached with two socket-head cap screws or soldered. Finished and blued. Barrel diameters from .600″ to .930″.
Price: Standing leaf $54.00
Price: One-leaf express $96.00
Price: Two-leaf express $101.00
Price: Three-leaf express $109.00

ERA MASTERPIECE REAR SIGHT Adjustable for windage and elevation, and adjusted and locked with a small screwdriver. Comes with 8-36 socket-head cap screw and wrench. Barrel diameters from .600″ to .930″.
Price: $75.00

G.G. & G. SAME PLANE APERTURE M-16/AR-15 A2-style dual aperture rear sight with both large and small apertures centered on the same plane.
Price: $45.00

LYMAN No.16 Middle sight for barrel dovetail slot mounting. Folds flat when scope or peep sight is used. Sight notch plate adjustable for elevation. White triangle for quick aiming. 3 heights: A-.400" to.500", B-.345" to .445", C-.500" to .600".
Price: $12.25

MARBLE FALSE BASE #76, #77, #78 New screw-on base for most rifles replaces factory base. 3/8″ dovetail slot permits installation of any folding rear sight. Can be had in sweat-on models also.
Price: $7.95

MARBLE FOLDING LEAF Flat-top or semi-buckhorn style. Folds down when scope or peep sights are used. Reversible plate gives choice of "U" or "V" notch. Adjustable for elevation.
Price: $14.95
Price: Also available with both windage and elevation adjustment $16.95

MARBLE SPORTING REAR With white enamel diamond, gives choice of two "U" and two "V" notches or different sizes. Adjustment in height by means of double step elevator and sliding notch piece. For all rifles; screw or dovetail installation.
Price: .... $14.95-$16.95

MARBLE #20 UNIVERSAL New screw or sweat-on base. Both have .100″ elevation adjustment. In five base sizes. Three styles of U-notch, square notch, peep. Adjustable for windage and elevation.
Price: Screw-on $23.00
Price: Sweat-on $21.00

MILLETT SPORTING & BLACKPOWDER RIFLE Open click adjustable rear fits 3/8″ dovetail cut in barrel. Choice of white outline, target black or open express V rear blades. Also available is a replacement screw-on sight with express V, .562″ hole centers. Dovetail fronts in white or blaze orange in seven heights (.157″-.540″).
Price: Dovetail or screw-on rear $55.60
Price: Front sight $12.34

MILLETT SCOPE-SITE Open, adjustable or fixed rear sights dovetail into a base integral with the top scope-mounting ring. Blaze orange front ramp sight is integral with the front ring half. Rear sights have white outline aperture. Provides fast, short-radius, Patridge-type open sights on the top of the scope. Can be used with all Millett rings, Weaver-style bases, Ruger 77 (also fits Redhawk), Ruger Ranch Rifle, No. 1, No. 3, Rem. 870, 1100; Burris, Leupold and Redfield bases.
Price: Scope-Site top only, windage only $31.15
Price: As above, fully adjustable $66.10
Price: Scope-Site Hi-Turret, fully adjustable, low, medium, high $66.10

WICHITA MULTI RANGE SIGHT SYSTEM Designed for silhouette shooting. System allows you to adjust the rear sight to four repeatable range settings, once it is pre-set. Sight clicks to any of the settings by turning a serrated wheel. Front sight is adjustable for weather and light conditions with one adjustment. Specify gun when ordering.
Price: Rear sight $120.00
Price: Front sight $90.00

WILLIAMS DOVETAIL OPEN SIGHT (WDOS) Open rear sight with windage and elevation adjustment. Furnished with "U" notch or choice of blades. Slips into dovetail and locks with gib lock. Heights from .281″ to .531″.
Price: With blade $15.86
Price: Less Blade $9.92

WILLIAMS GUIDE OPEN SIGHT (WGOS) Open rear sight with windage and elevation adjustment. Bases to fit most military and commercial barrels. Choice of square "U" or "V" notch blade, 3/16″, 1/4″, 5/16″, or 3/8″ high.
Price: Less blade $16.34
Price: Extra blades, each $6.37

WILLIAMS WGOS OCTAGON Open rear sight for 1″ octagon barrels. Installs with two 6-48 screws and uses same hole spacing as most T/C muzzleloading rifles. Four heights, choice of square, U, V, B blade.
Price: $21.80

WILLIAMS WSKS, WAK47 Replaces original military-type rear sight. Adjustable for windage and elevation. No drilling or tapping. Peep aperture or open. For SKS carbines, AK-47.
Price: Aperture $24.67
Price: Open $22.61

WILLIAMS WM-96 Fits Mauser 96-type military rifles, replaces original rear sight with open blade or aperture. Fully adjustable for windage and elevation. No drilling; tapping.
Price: Aperture $24.67
Price: Open $22.61

WILLIAMS FRONT FIRE SIGHTS Fiber optic light gathering rifle beads in red or yellow; glow with natural light.
Price: $13.95
Price: Sight set for newer style Remington rifles $24.95

Micrometer Receiver Sights

BEEMAN/FEINWERKBAU 5454 MATCH APERTURE SIGHT Small size, new-design sight uses constant-pressure flat springs to eliminate point of impact shifts.
Price: $350.00

BEEMAN SPORT APERTURE SIGHT Positive click micrometer adjustments. Standard units with flush surface screwdriver adjustments. Deluxe version has target knobs. For air rifles with grooved receivers.
Price: Standard $40.00
Price: Deluxe $50.00

EAW RECEIVER SIGHT A fully adjustable aperture sight that locks securely into the EAW quick-detachable scope mount rear base. Made by New England Custom Gun Service.
Price: $95.00

G.G.&G. MAD IRIS Multiple Aperture Device is a four sight, rotatins aperture disk with small and large apertures on the same plane . Mounts on M-16/AR-15 flat top receiver. Fully adjustable.
Price: $129.00
Price: A2 IRIS, two apertures, full windage adjustments $120.00

LYMAN NO. 2 TANG SIGHT Designed for the Winchester Model 94. Has high index marks on aperture post; comes with both .093″ quick sighting aperture, .040″ large disk aperture, and replacement mounting screws.
Price: $68.00
Price: For Marlin lever actions $70.00

LYMAN No. 57 1/4-minute clicks. Stayset knobs. Quick release slide, adjustable zero scales. Made for almost all modern rifles.
Price: $61.50
Price: No. 57SME, 57SMET (for White Systems Model 91 and Whitetail rifles) $61.50

LYMAN No. 66 Fits close to the rear of flat-sided receivers, furnished with Stayset knobs. Quick release slide, 1/4-min. adjustments. For most lever or slide action or flat-sided automatic rifles.
Price: $61.50
Price: No. 66MK (for all current versions of the Knight MK-85 in-line rifle with flat-sided receiver) $61.50
Price: No. 66 SKS fits Russian and Chinese SKS rifles; large and small apertures $61.50

LYMAN No. 66U Light weight, designed for most modern shotguns with a flat-sided, round-top receiver. 1/4-minute clicks. Requires drilling, tapping. Not for Browning A-5, Rem. M11.
Price: $61.50

LYMAN 90MJT RECEIVER SIGHT Mounts on standard Lyman and Williams FP bases. Has 1/4-minute audible micrometer click adjustments, target knobs with direction indicators. Adjustable zero scales, quick release slide. Large 7/8″ diameter aperture disk.
Price: $68.75

LYMAN 90MJT RECEIVER SIGHT Mounts on standard Lyman and Williams FP bases. Has 1/4-minute audible micrometer click adjustments, target knobs with direction indicators. Adjustable zero scales, quick release slide. Large 7/8″ diameter aperture disk.
Price: $68.75

MARBLE PEEP TANG SIGHT All-steel construction. Micrometer-like click adjustments for windage and elevation. For most popular old and new lever-action rifles.
Price: $99.00

MILLETT PEEP RIFLE SIGHTS Fully adjustable, heat-treated nickel steel peep aperture receiver sight for the Mini-14. Has fine windage and elevation adjustments; replaces original.
Price: Rear sight, Mini-14 .... $49.00
Price: Front sight, Mini-14 .... $18.75
Price: Front and rear combo with hood $64.00

WILLIAMS FP Internal click adjustments. Positive locks. For virtually all rifles, T/C Contender, Heckler & Koch HK-91, Ruger Mini-14, plus Win., Rem. and Ithaca shotguns.
Price: From $59.95
Price: With Target Knobs $71.20
Price: With Square Notched Blade $63.03
Price: With Target Knobs & Square Notched Blade $74.45
Price: FP-GR (for dovetail-grooved receivers, 22s and air guns) $59.95
Price: FP-94BBSE (for Win. 94 Big Bore A.E.; uses top rear scope mount holes) $59.95

WILLIAMS TARGET FP Similar to the FP series but developed for most bolt-action rimfire rifles. Target FP High adjustable from 1.250″ to 1.750″ above centerline of bore; Target FP Low adjustable from .750″ to 1.250″. Attaching bases for Rem. 540X, 541-S, 580, 581, 582 (#540); Rem. 510, 511, 512, 513-T, 521-T (#510); Win. 75 (#75); Savage/Anschutz 64 and Mark 12 (#64). Some rifles require drilling, tapping.
Price: High or Low $77.15

Price: Base only $12.98
Price: FP-T/C Scout rifle, from. $59.95
Price: FP-94BBSE (for Win. 94 Big Bore A.E.; uses top rear scope mount holes). $59.95

WILLIAMS 5-D SIGHT Low cost sight for shotguns, 22s and the more popular big game rifles. Adjustment for windage and elevation. Fits most guns without drilling and tapping. Also for British SMLE, Winchester M94 Side Eject.
Price: From. $31.47
Price: With Shotgun Aperture $31.47

WILLIAMS GUIDE (WGRS) Receiver sight for 30 M1 Carbine, M1903A3 Springfield, Savage 24s, Savage-Anschutz and Weatherby XXII. Utilizes military dovetail; no drilling. Double-dovetail windage adjustment, sliding dovetail adjustment for elevation.
Price: $30.85
Price: WGRS-CVA (for rifles with octagon barrels, receivers) $30.85

Front Sights

ERA FRONT SIGHTS European-type front sights inserted from the front. Various heights available. From New England Custom Gun Service.
Price: 1/16″ silver bead $11.50
Price: 3/32″ silver bead $16.00
Price: Sourdough bead $14.50
Price: Tritium night sight $44.00
Price: Folding night sight with ivory bead $39.50

LYMAN HUNTING SIGHTS Made with gold or white beads 1/16″ to 3/32″ wide and in varying heights for most military and commercial rifles. Dovetail bases.
Price: $8.75

MARBLE STANDARD Ivory, red, or gold bead. For all American-made rifles, 1/16″ wide bead with semi-flat face which does not reflect light. Specify type of rifle when ordering.
Price: $8.95

MARBLE CONTOURED Has 3/8″ dovetail base, .090″ deep, is 5/8″ long. Uses standard 1/16″ or 3/32″ bead, ivory, red, or gold. Specify rifle type.
Price: $10.50

WILLIAMS RISER BLOCKS For adding .250″ height to front sights when using a receiver sight. Two widths available: .250″ for Williams Streamlined Ramp or .340″ on all standard ramps having this base width. Uses standard 3/8″ dovetail.
Price: $5.46

Globe Target Front Sights

LYMAN 20 MJT TARGET FRONT Has 7/8″ diameter, one-piece steel globe with 3/8″ dovetail base. Height is .700″ from bottom of dovetail to center of aperture; height on 20 LJT is .750″. Comes with seven Anschutz-size steel inserts—two posts and five apertures .126″ through .177″.
Price: 20 MJT or 20 LJT $30.00

LYMAN No. 17A TARGET Includes seven interchangeable inserts: four apertures, one transparent amber and two posts .50″ and .100″ in width.
Price: $26.00
Price: Insert set $9.00

LYMAN No. 93 MATCH Has 7/8″ diameter, fits any rifle with a standard dovetail mounting block. Comes with seven target inserts and accepts most Anschutz accessories. Hooked locking bolt and nut allows quick removal, installation. Base available in .860″ (European) and .562″ (American) hole spacing.
Price: $41.25

WILLIAMS TARGET GLOBE FRONT Adapts to many rifles. Mounts to the base with a knurled locking screw. Height is .545″ from center, not including base. Comes with inserts.
Price: $30.85
Price: Dovetail base (low) .220″ $17.00
Price: Dovetail base (high) .465″. $17.00
Price: Screw-on base, .300″ height, .300″ radius. $15.45
Price: Screw-on base, .450″ height, .350″ radius. $15.45
Price: Screw-on base, .215″ height, .400″ radius. $15.45

Ramp Sights

ERA MASTERPIECE Banded ramps; 21 sizes; hand-detachable beads and hood; beads inserted from the front. Various heights available. From New England Custom Gun Service.
Price: Banded ramp. $54.00
Price: Hood $10.50
Price: 1/16″ silver bead $11.50
Price: 3/32″ silver bead $16.00
Price: Sourdough bead $14.50
Price: Tritium night sight $47.00
Price: Folding night sight with ivory bead $39.50

LYMAN NO. 18 SCREW-ON RAMP Used with 8-40 screws but may also be brazed on. Heights from .10″ to .350″. Ramp without sight.
Price: $13.75

MARBLE FRONT RAMPS Available in polished or dull matte finish or serrated style. Standard 3/8x.090″ dovetail slot. Made for MR-width (.340″) front sights. Can be used as screw-on or sweat-on. Heights: .100″, .150″, .300″.
Price: Polished or matte. $14.00
Price: Serrated. $10.00

WILLIAMS SHORTY RAMP Companion to "Streamlined" ramp, about 1/2″ shorter. Screw-on or sweat-on. It is furnished in 1/8″, 3/16″, 9/32″, and 3/8″ heights without hood only. Also for shotguns.
Price: $15.90
Price: With dovetail lock. $18.55

WILLIAMS STREAMLINED RAMP Available in screw-on or sweat-on models. Furnshined in 9/16″, 7/16″, 3/8″, 5/16″, 3/16″ heights.
Price: $17.35
Price: Sight hood $3.95

WILLIAMS STREAMLINED FRONT SIGHTS Narrow (.250″ width) for Williams Streamlined ramps and others with 1/4″ top width; medium (.340″ width) for all standard factory ramps. Available with white, gold or flourescent beads, 1/16″ or 3/32″.
Price:. . . . . $8.93 to $9.25

Handgun Sights

BO-MAR DELUXE BMCS Gives 3/8″ windage and elevation adjustment at 50 yards on Colt Gov't 45; sight radius under 7″. For GM and Commander models only. Uses existing dovetail slot. Has shield-type rear blade.
Price:. $68.95
Price: BMCS-2 (for GM and 9mm) $68.95
Price: Flat bottom. $68.95
Price: BMGC (for Colt Gold Cup), angled serrated blade, rear $68.95
Price: BMGC front sight. $12.95
Price: BMCZ-75 (for CZ-75,TZ-75, P-9 and most clones). Works with factory front $68.95

BO-MAR FRONT SIGHTS Dovetail style for S&W 4506, 4516, 1076; undercut style (.250″, .280″, 5/16″ high); Fast Draw style (.210″, .250″, .230″ high).
Price $12.95

BO-MAR BMU XP-100/T/C CONTENDER No gunsmithing required; has .080″ notch.
Price:. $77.00

BO-MAR BMML For muzzleloaders; has .062″ notch, flat bottom.
Price:. $65.95
Price: With 3/8″ dovetail. $65.95

BO-MAR RUGER "P" ADJUSTABLE SIGHT Replaces factory front and rear sights.
Price: Rear sight. $65.95
Price: Front sight $12.00

BO-MAR BMR Fully adjustable rear sight for Ruger MKI, MKII Bull barrel autos.
Price: Rear $65.95
Price: Undercut front sight $12.00

BO-MAR GLOCK Fully adjustable, all-steel replacement sights. Sight fits factory dovetail. Longer sight radius. Uses Novak Glock .275″ high, .135″ wide front, or similar.
Price: Rear sight. $68.95
Price: Front sight $20.95

BO-MAR LOW PROFILE RIB & ACCURACY TUNER Streamlined rib with front and rear sights; 71/8″ sight radius. Brings sight line closer to the bore than standard or extended sight and ramp. Weight 5 oz. Made for Colt Gov't 45, Super 38, and Gold Cup 45 and 38.
Price:. $123.00

BO-MAR COMBAT RIB For S&W Model 19 revolver with 4″ barrel. Sight radius 53/4″, weight 51/2 oz.
Price:. $110.00

BO-MAR WINGED RIB For S&W 4″ and 6″ length barrels—K-38, M10, HB 14 and 19. Weight for the 6″ model is about 71/4 oz.
Price:. $123.00

BO-MAR COVER-UP RIB Adjustable rear sight, winged front guards. Fits right over revolver's original front sight. For S&W 4″ M-10HB, M-13, M-58, M-64 & 65, Ruger 4″ models SDA-34, SDA-84, SS-34, SS-84, GF-34, GF-84.
Price:. $117.00

C-MORE SIGHTS Replacement front sight blades offered in two types and five styles. Made of Du Pont Acetal, they come in a set of five high-contrast colors: blue, green, pink, red and yellow. Easy to install. Patridge style for Colt Python (all barrels), Ruger Super Blackhawk (71/2″), Ruger Blackhawk (45/8″); ramp style for Python (all barrels), Blackhawk (45/8″), Super Blackhawk (71/2″ and 101/2″). From C-More Systems.
Price: Per set $19.95

G.G. & G. GHOST RINGS Replaces the factory rear sight without gunsmithing. Black phosphate finish. Available for Colt M1911 and Commander, Beretta M92F, Glock, S&W, SIG Sauer.
Price:. $65.00

JP GHOST RING Replacement bead front, ghost ring rear for Glock and M1911 pistols. From JP Enterprises.
Price:. $79.95
Price: Bo-Mar replacement leaf with JP dovetail front bead. $99.95

MMC TACTICAL ADJUSTABLE SIGHTS Low-profile, snag free design. Twenty-two click positions for elevation, drift adjustable for windage. Machined from 4140 steel and heat treated to 40 RC. Tritium and non-tritium. Ten different configurations and colors. Three different finishes. For 1911s, all Glock, HK USP, S&W, Browning Hi-Power.
Price: Sight set, tritium. $144.92
Price: Sight set, white ouline or white dot $99.90
Price: Sight set, black. $93.90

MEPROLIGHT TRITIUM NIGHT SIGHTS Replacement sight assemblies for use in low-light conditions. Available for rifles, shotguns, handguns and bows. **TRU-DOT** models carry a 12-year warranty on the useable illumination, while non-TRU-DOT have a 5-year warranty. Contact Hesco, Inc. for complete list of available models.
Price: Kahr K9, K40, fixed, TRU-DOT. $100.00
Price: Ruger P85, P89, P94, adjustable, TRU-DOT. $156.00
Price: Ruger Mini-14R sights. $140.00
Price: SIG Sauer P220, P225, P226, P228, adjustable, TRU-DOT. $156.00
Price: Smith&Wesson autos, fixed or adjustable, TRU-DOT $100.00
Price: Taurus PT92, PT100, adjustable, TRU-DOT $156.00
Price: Walther P-99, fixed, TRU-DOT $100.00
Price: Shotgun bead $32.00
Price: Beretta M92, Cougar, Brigadier, fixed, TRU-DOT $100.00
Price: Browning Hi-Power, adjustable, TRU-DOT $156.00
Price: Colt M1911 Govt., adjustable, TRU-DOT $156.00

MILLETT SERIES 100 REAR SIGHTS All-steel highly visible, click adjustable. Blades in white outline, target black, silhouette, 3-dot, and tritium bars. Fit most popular revolvers and autos.
Price: .... **$49.30** to **$80.00**

MILLETT ULTRA SIGHT Fully adjustable rear works with factory front. Steel and carbon fiber. Easy to install. For most automatics. White outline, target black or 3-dot.
Price: **$49.95**

MILLETT BAR-DOT-BAR TRITIUM NIGHT SIGHTS Replacement front and rear combos fit most automatics. Horizontal tritium bars on rear, dot front sight.
Price: **$145.00**

MILLETT 3-DOT SYSTEM SIGHTS The 3-Dot System sights use a single white dot on the front blade and two dots flanking the rear notch. Fronts available in Dual-Crimp and Wide Stake-On styles, as well as special applications. Adjustable rear sight available for most popular auto pistols and revolvers.
Price: Front, from **$16.00**
Price: Adjustable rear .... **$55.60** to **$56.80**

MILLETT REVOLVER FRONT SIGHTS All-steel replacement front sights with either white or orange bar. Easy to install. For Ruger GP-100, Redhawk, Security-Six, Police-Six, Speed-Six, Colt Trooper, Diamondback, King Cobra, Peacemaker, Python, Dan Wesson 22 and 15-2.
Price: .... **$13.60** to **$16.00**

MILLETT DUAL-CRIMP FRONT SIGHT Replacement front sight for automatic pistols. Dual-Crimp uses an all-steel two-point hollow rivet system. Available in eight heights and four styles. Has a skirted base that covers the front sight pad. Easily installed with the Millett Installation Tool Set. Available in Blaze Orange Bar, White Bar, Serrated Ramp, Plain Post.
Price: **$16.00**

MILLETT STAKE-ON FRONT SIGHT Replacement front sight for automatic pistols. Stake-On sights have skirted base that covers the front sight pad. Easily installed with the Millet Installation Tool Set. Available in seven heights and four styles—Blaze Orange Bar, White Bar, Serrated Ramp, Plain Post.
Price: **$16.00**

OMEGA OUTLINE SIGHT BLADES Replacement rear sight blades for Colt and Ruger single action guns and the Interarms Virginian Dragoon. Standard Outline available in gold or white notch outline on blue metal. From Omega Sales, Inc.
Price: **$8.95**

OMEGA MAVERICK SIGHT BLADES Replacement "peep-sight" blades for Colt, Ruger SAs, Virginian Dragoon. Three models available—No. 1, Plain; No. 2, Single Bar; No. 3, Double Bar Rangefinder. From Omega Sales, Inc.
Price: Each.......... **$6.95**

PACHMAYR ACCU-SET Low-profile, fully adjustable rear sight to be used with existing front sight. Available with target, white outline or 3-dot blade. Blue finish. Uses factory dovetail and locking screw. For Browning, Colt, Glock, SIG Sauer, S&W and Ruger autos. From Pachmayr.
Price: .... **NA**

P-T TRITIUM NIGHT SIGHTS Self-luminous tritium sights for most popular handguns, Colt AR-15, H&K rifles and shotguns. Replacement handgun sight sets available in 3-Dot style (green/green, green/yellow, green/orange) with bold outlines around inserts; Bar-Dot available in green/green with or without white outline rear sight. Functional life exceeds 15 years. From Innovative Weaponry, Inc.
Price: Handgun sight sets **$99.95**
Price: Rifle sight sets.......... **$99.95**
Price: Rifle, front only.......... **$49.95**
Price: Shotgun, front only **$49.95**

TRIJICON NIGHT SIGHTS Three-dot night sight system uses tritium lamps in the front and rear sights. Tritium "lamps" are mounted in silicone rubber inside a metal cylinder. A polished crystal sapphire provides protection and clarity. Inlaid white outlines provide 3-dot aiming in daylight also. Available for most popular handguns. From Trijicon, Inc.
Price: .... **$50.00 to $175.00**

WICHITA SERIES 70/80 SIGHT Provides click windage and elevation adjustments with precise repeatability of settings. Sight blade is grooved and angled back at the top to reduce glare. Available in Low Mount Combat or Low Mount Target styles for Colt 45s and their copies, S&W 645, Hi-Power, CZ 75 and others.
Price: Rear sight, target or combat **$75.00**
Price: Front sight, Patridge or ramp **$15.00**

WICHITA GRAND MASTER DELUXE RIBS Ventilated rib has wings machined into it for better sight acquisition and is relieved for Mag-Na-Porting. Milled to accept Weaver see-thru-style rings. Made of stainless or blued steel; front and rear sights blued. Has Wichita Multi-Range rear sight system, adjustable front sight. Made for revolvers with 6″ barrel.
Price: Model 301S, 301B (adj. sight K frames with custom bbl. of 1″ to 1.032″ dia. L and N frame with 1.062″ to 1.100″ dia. bbl.) **$180.00**
Price: Model 303S, 303B (adj. sight K, L, N frames with factory barrel) . **$180.00**

WILLIAMS FIRE SIGHTS Fiber optic light gathering sights in red or yellow, glow with natural light. Front and rear sight sets. For Glock, Ruger P-Series (except P-85), S&W 910/915, Colt Gov't Series 80.
Price: **$39.95**

Shotgun Sights

ACCURA-SITE For shooting shotgun slugs. Three models to fit most shotguns—"A" for vent. rib barrels, "B" for solid ribs, "C" for plain barrels. Rear sight has windage and elevation provisions. Easily removed and replaced. Includes front and rear sights. From All's, The Jim Tembeils Co.
Price: .... **$27.95** to **$34.95**

FIRE FLY EM-109 SL SHOTGUN SIGHT Made of aircraft-grade aluminum, this 1/4-oz. "channel" sight has a thick, sturdy hollowed post between the side rails to give a Patridge sight picture. All shooting is done with both eyes open, allowing the shooter to concentrate on the target, not the sights. The hole in the sight post gives reduced-light shooting capability and allows for fast, precise aiming. For sport or combat shooting. Model EM-109 fits all vent. rib and double barrel shotguns and muzzleloaders with octagon barrel. Model MOC-110 fits all plain barrel shotguns without screw-in chokes. From JAS, Inc.
Price: **$35.00**

LYMAN Three sights of over-sized ivory beads. No. 10 Front (press fit) for double barrel or ribbed single barrel guns...**$4.50**; No. 10D Front (screw fit) for non-ribbed single barrel guns (comes with wrench)...**$5.50**; No. 11 Middle (press fit) for double and ribbed single barrel guns...**$4.75**.

MMC M&P COMBAT SHOTGUN SIGHT SET A durable, protected ghost ring aperture, combat sight made of steel. Fully adjustable for windage and elevation.
Price: M&P Sight Set (front and rear) **$73.45**
Price: As above, installed **$83.95**

MMC TACTICAL GHOST RING SIGHT Click adjustable for elevation with 30 MOA total adjustment in 3 MOA increments. Click windage adjustment. Machined from 4140 steel, heat treated to 40 RC. Front sight available in banded tactical or serrated ramp. Front and rear sights avialable with or without tritium. Available in three different finishes.
Price: Rear Ghost Ring with tritium **$119.95**
Price: Rear Ghost Ring without tritium **$99.95**
Price: Front Banded Tactical with tritium.......... **$59.95**
Price: Front Banded Tactical without tritium **$39.95**
Price: Front serrated ramp.......... **$24.95**

MARBLE SHOTGUN BEAD SIGHTS No. 214—Ivory front bead, 11/64″, tapered shank...**$4.40**; No. 223—Ivory rear bead, .080″, tapered shank...**$4.40**; No. 217—Ivory front bead, 11/64″, threaded shank...**$4.75**; No. 223-T—Ivory rear bead, .080″, threaded shank...**$5.95**. Reamers, taps and wrenches available from Marble Arms.

MILLETT SHURSHOT SHOTGUN SIGHT A sight system for shotguns with ventilated rib. Rear sight attaches to the rib, front sight replaces the front bead. Front has an orange face, rear has two orange bars. For 870, 1100 or other models.
Price: Rear.......... **$13.15**
Price: Adjustable front and rear set.......... **$31.00**
Price: Front.......... **$12.95**

POLY-CHOKE Replacement front shotgun sights in four styles—Xpert, Poly Bead, Xpert Mid Rib sights, and Bev-L-Block. Xpert Front available in 3x56, 6x48 thread, 3/32″ or 5/32″ shank length, gold, ivory...**$4.70**; or Sun Spot orange bead...**$5.95**; Poly Bead is standard replacement 1/8″ bead, 6x48...**$2.95**; Xpert Mid Rib in tapered carrier (ivory only) **$5.95**, or 3x56 threaded shank (gold only)...**$2.95**; Hi and Lo Blok sights with 6x48 thread, gold or ivory...**$5.25**. From Marble Arms.

SLUG SIGHTS Made of non-marring black nylon, front and rear sights stretch over and lock onto the barrel. Sights are low profile with blaze orange front blade. Adjustable for windage and elevation. For plain-barrel (non-ribbed) guns in 12-, 16- and 20-gauge, and for shotguns with 5/16″ and 3/8″ ventilated ribs. From Innovision Ent.
Price: **$11.95**

WILLIAMS GUIDE BEAD SIGHT Fits all shotguns, 1/8″ ivory, red or gold bead. Screws into existing sight hole. Various thread sizes and shank lengths.
Price: **$4.77**

WILLIAMS SLUGGER SIGHTS Removable aluminum sights attach to the shotgun rib. High profile front, fully adjustable rear. Fits 1/4″, 5/16″ or 3/8″ (special) ribs.
Price: **$34.95**

WILLIAMS FIRE SIGHTS Fiber optic light gathering front sights in red or yellow, glow with natural light. Fit 1/4″, 5/16″ or 3/8″ vent. ribs, most popular shotguns.
Price: **$13.95**

Sight Attachments

MERIT IRIS SHUTTER DISC Eleven clicks give 12 different apertures. No. 3 Disc and Master, primarily target types, 0.22″ to .125″; No. 4, 1/2″ dia. hunting type, .025″ to .155″. Available for all popular sights. The Master, with flexible rubber light shield, is particularly adapted to extension, scope height, and tang sights. All models have internal click springs; are hand fitted to minimum tolerance.
Price: Master Target **$66.00**
Price: No. 3 Disc (Plain Face) **$55.00**
Price: No. 4 Hunting Disc.......... **$45.00**

MERIT LENS DISC Similar to Merit Iris Shutter (Model 3 or Master) but incorporates provision for mounting prescription lens integrally. Lens may be obtained locally from your optician. Sight disc is 7/16″ wide (Model 3), or 3/4″ wide (Master).
Price: Model 3 Target.......... **$68.00**
Price: Master **$78.00**

MERIT OPTICAL ATTACHMENT For revolver and pistol shooters, instantly attached by rubber suction cup to regular or shooting glasses. Swings aside. Any aperture .020″ to .156″.
Price: **$63.00**

WILLIAMS APERTURES Standard thread, fits most sights. Regular series 3/8″ to 1/2″ O.D., .050″ to .125″ hole. "Twilight" series has white reflector ring.
Price: Regular series **$4.97**
Price: Twilight series **$6.79**
Price: Wide open 5/16″ aperture for shotguns fits 5-D or Foolproof sights (specify model).......... **$8.77**

Briley Screw-In Chokes

Installation of these choke tubes requires that all traces of the original choking be removed, the barrel threaded internally with square threads and then the tubes are custom fitted to the specific barrel diameter. The tubes are thin and, therefore, made of stainless steel. Cost of installation for single-barrel guns (pumps, autos), lead shot, 12-gauge **$129.00**, 20-gauge **$139.00**; steel shot **$159.00** and **$169.00**, all with three chokes; un-single target guns run **$190.00**; over/unders and side-by-sides, lead shot, 12-gauge, **$349.00**, 20-gauge **$369.00**; steel shot **$449.00** and **$469.00**, all with five chokes. For 10-gauge auto or pump with two steel shot chokes, **$149.00**; over/unders, side-by-sides with three steel shot chokes, **$329.00**. For 16-gauge auto or pump, three lead shot chokes, **$239.00**; over/unders, side-by-sides with five lead shot chokes, **$429.00**. The 28 and 410-bore run **$159.00** for autos and pumps with three lead shot chokes, **$429.00** for over/unders and side-by-sides with five lead shot chokes.

Cutts Compensator

The Cutts Compensator is one of the oldest variable choke devices available. Manufactured by Lyman Gunsight Corporation, it is available with a steel body. A series of vents allows gas to escape upward and downward. For the 12-ga. Comp body, six fixed-choke tubes are available: the Spreader—popular with Skeet shooters; Improved Cylinder; Modified; Full; Superfull, and Magnum Full. Full, Modified and Spreader tubes are available for 12 or 20, and an Adjustable Tube, giving Full through Improved Cylinder chokes, is offered in 12 and 20 gauges. Cutts Compensator, complete with wrench, adaptor and any single tube **$87.50**; with adjustable tube **$112.50**. All single choke tubes **$25.00** each; adjustable tube **$50.00**. No factory installation available.

Dayson Automatic Brake System

This system fits most single barrel shotguns threaded for choke tubes, and cuts away 30 grooves on the exterior of a standard one-piece wad as it exits the muzzle. This slows the wad, allowing shot and wad to separate faster, reducing shot distortion and tightening patterns. The A.B.S. Choke Tube is claimed to reduce recoil by about 25 percent, and with the Muzzle Brake up to 60 percent. Ventilated Choke Tubes available from .685″ to .725″, in .005″ increments. Model I Ventilated Choke Tube for use with A.B.S. Muzzle Brake, **$49.95**; for use without Muzzle Brake, **$52.95**; A.B.S. Muzzle Brake, from **$69.95**. Contact Dayson Arms for more data.

Gentry Quiet Muzzle Brake

Developed by gunmaker David Gentry, the "Quiet Muzzle Brake" is said to reduce recoil by up to 85 percent with no loss of accuracy or velocity. There is no increase in noise level because the noise and gases are directed away from the shooter. The barrel is threaded for installation and the unit is blued to match the barrel finish. Price, installed, is **$150.00**. Add **$15.00** for stainless steel, **$45.00** for knurled cap to protect threads. Shipping extra.

JP Muzzle Brake

Designed for single shot handguns, AR-15, Ruger Mini-14, Ruger Mini Thirty and other sporting rifles, the JP Muzzle Brake redirects high pressure gases against a large frontal surface which applies forward thrust to the gun. All gases are directed up, rearward and to the sides. Priced at **$79.95** (AR-15 or sporting rifles), **$89.95** (bull barrel and SKS, AK models), **$89.95** (Ruger Minis), Dual Chamber model **$79.95**. From JP Enterprises, Inc.

KDF Slim Line Muzzle Brake

This threaded muzzlebrake has 30 pressure ports that direct combustion gases in all directions to reduce felt recoil up to a claimed 80 percent without affecting accuracy or ballistics. It is said to reduce felt recoil of a 30-06 to that of a 243. Price, installed, is **$179.00**. From KDF, Inc.

Mag-Na-Port

Electrical Discharge Machining works on any firearm except those having non-conductive shrouded barrels. EDM is a metal erosion technique using carbon electrodes that control the area to be processed. The Mag-Na-Port venting process utilizes small trapezoidal openings to direct powder gases upward and outward to reduce recoil. No effect is had on bluing or nickeling outside the Mag-Na-Port area so no refinishing is needed. Rifle-style porting on single shot or large caliber handguns with barrels 71/2″ or longer is **$110.00**; Dual Trapezoidal porting on most handguns with minimum barrel length of 3″, **$100.00**; standard revolver porting, **$78.50**; porting through the slide and barrel for semi-autos, **$115.00**; traditional rifle porting, **$125.00**. Prices do not include shipping, handling and insurance. From Mag-Na-Port International.

Mag-Na-Brake

A screw-on brake under 2″ long with progressive integrated exhaust chambers to neutralize expanding gases. Gases dissipate with an opposite twist to prevent the brake from unscrewing, and with a 5-degree forward angle to minimize sound pressure level. Available in blue, satin blue, bright or satin stainless. Standard and Light Contour installation cost **$179.00** for bolt-action rifles, many single action and single shot handguns. A knurled thread protector supplied at extra cost. Also available in Varmint style with exhaust chambers covering 220 degrees for prone-position shooters. From Mag-Na-Port International.

Poly-Choke

Marble Arms Corp., manufacturer of the Poly-Choke adjustable shotgun choke, now offers two models in 12-, 16-, 20-, and 28-gauge—the Ventilated and Standard style chokes. Each provides nine choke settings including Xtra-Full and Slug. The Ventilated model reduces 20 percent of a shotgun's recoil, the company claims, and is priced at **$105.00**. The Standard Model is **$95.00**. Postage not included. Contact Marble Arms for more data.

Pro-port

A compound ellipsoid muzzle venting process similar to Mag-Na-Porting, only exclusively applied to shotguns. Like Mag-Na-Porting, this system reduces felt recoil, muzzle jump, and shooter fatigue. Very helpful for trap doubles shooters. Pro-Port is a patented process and installation is available in both the U.S. and Canada. Cost for the Pro-Port process is **$129.50** for over/unders (both barrels); **$99.50** for only the top or bottom barrel; and **$78.50** for single-barrel shotguns. Optional pigeon porting costs **$25.00** extra per barrel. Prices do not include shipping and handling. From Pro-port Ltd.

SSK Arrestor Brake

This is a true muzzlebrake with an expansion chamber. It takes up about 1" of barrel and reduces velocity accordingly. Some Arrestors are added to a barrel, increasing its length. Said to reduce the felt recoil of a 458 to that approaching a 30-06. Can be set up to give zero muzzle rise in any caliber, and can be added to most guns. For handgun or rifle. Prices start at **$95.00**. Contact SSK Industries for full data.

Weigand Hybra-Port

This series of ports through the top or top sides of the revolver barrel is said to reduce muzzle flip up to 70 percent. The system directs gases up instead of away from the muzzle, with no perceived increase in muzzle flash. Velocity loss averages 3 to 5 percent. Price, **$99.95**. From Weigand Combat Handguns, Inc.

Maker and Model	Magn.	Field at 100 Yds. (feet)	Eye Relief (in.)	Length (in.)	Tube Dia. (in.)	W & E Adjustments	Weight (ozs.)	Price	Other Data
ADCO									[1]Multi-Color Dot system changes from red to green. [2]For airguns, paintball, rimfires. Uses common lithium water battery. [3]Comes with standard dovetail mount. [4].75" dovetail mount; poly body; adj. intensity diode. [5]10 MOA dot; black or nickel. [6]Square format; with mount battery. [7]Adjustable dot size; black or nickel finish.
Magnum 45 mm[5]	0	—	—	4.1	45 mm	Int.	6.8	$289.00	
MIRAGE Ranger 1"	0	—	—	5.2	1	Int.	3.9	159.00	
MIRAGE Ranger 30mm	0	—	—	5.5	30mm	Int.	5	179.00	
MIRAGE Sportsman[1]	0	—	—	5.2	1	Int.	4.5	249.00	
MIRAGE Trident[7]	0	—	—	6	30mm	Int.	6.5	369.00	
MIRAGE Competitor	0	—	—	5.5	30mm	Int.	5.5	269.00	
IMP Sight[2]	0	—	—	4.5	—	Int.	1.3	17.95	
Square Shooter[3]	0	—	—	5	—	Int.	5	125.00	
MIRAGE Eclipse[1]	0	—	—	5.5	30mm	Int.	5.5	249.00	
MIRAGE Champ Red Dot	0	—	—	4.5	—	Int.	2	33.95	
Vantage 1"	0	—	—	3.9	1	Int.	3.9	129.00	
Vantage 30mm	0	—	—	4.2	30mm	Int.	4.9	132.00	
Vision 2000[6]	0	60	—	4.7	—	Int.	6.2	89.00	
T-10 Target/Sniper Scope	10	11.6	NA	13.8	30mm	Int.	21.6	NA	
AIMPOINT									Illuminates red dot in field of view. No parallax (dot does not need to be centered). Unlimited field of view and eye relief. On/off, adj. intensity. Dot covers 3" @100 yds. [1]Comes with 30mm rings, battery, lense cloth. [2]Requires 1" rings. Black or stainless finish. 3x scope attachment (for rifles only). $129.95. [3]Black finish (AP 5000-B) or stainless (AP-5000-S); avail. with regular 3-min. or 10-min. Mag Dot as B2 or S2. From Aimpoint U.S.A. [4]Band pass reflection coating for compatibility with night vision equipment; U.S. Army contract model; with anti-reflex coated lenses (Comp ML), $349.00.
Comp	0	—	—	4.6	30mm	Int.	4.3	308.00	
Comp M[4]	0	—	—	5	36mm	Int.	6.1	379.00	
Series 5000[3]	0	—	—	5.75	30mm	Int.	5.8	277.00	
Series 3000 Universal[2]	0	—	—	5.5	1	Int.	5.5	232.00	
Series 5000/2x[1]	2	—	—	7	30mm	Int.	9	367.00	
ARMSON O.E.G.									Shown red dot aiming point. No batteries needed. Standard mounts 1" fits (not incl.). Other O.E.G. models for shotguns and rifles can be special ordered. [1]Daylight Only Sight with .375" dovetail mount for 22s. Does not contain tritium. From Trijicon, Inc.
Standard	0	—	—	5.125	1	Int.	4.3	202.00	
22 DOS[1]	0	—	—	3.75	—	Int.	3	127.00	
22 Day/Night	0	—	—	3.75	—	Int.	3	169.00	
M16/AR-15	0	—	—	5.125	—	Int.	5.5	226.00	
BAUSCH & LOMB									[1]Adj. objective, sunshade. [2]Also in matte finish. [3]Also in matte finish. [4]Also in matte and silver finish. [5]Also in matte finish. [6]50mm objective; also in matte finish. [7]Also in silver finish. **Partial listings shown. Contact Bushnell Sports Optics for details.**
Elite 4000									
40-6244A[1]	6-24	18-4.5	3	16.9	1	Int.	20.2	640.95	
40-2104G[2]	2.5-10	41.5-10.8	3	13.5	1	Int.	16	560.95	
40-1636G[3]	1.5-6	61.8-16.1	3	12.8	1	Int.	15.4	528.95	
40-1040	10	10.5	3.6	13.8	1	Int.	22.1	1,858.00	
Elite 3000									
30-5155M	5-15	21-7	3	15.9	1	Int.	24	471.95	
30-4124A[1]	4-12	26.9-9	3	13.2	1	Int.	15	417.95	
30-3940G[4]	3-9	33.8-11.5	3	12.6	1	Int.	13	319.95	
30-2732G[5]	2-7	44.6-12.7	3	11.6	1	Int.	12	303.95	
30-3950G[6]	3-9	31.5-10.5	3	15.7	1	Int.	19	382.95	
30-1545M	1.5-4.5	63-20	3.3	12.5	1	Int.	13	433.95	
30-3955E	3-9	31.5-10.5	3	15.6	30mm	Int.	22	592.95	
Elite 3000 Handgun									
30-2632G[7]	2-6	10-4	20	9	1	Int.	10	417.95	
30-2632G[7]	2-6	10-4	20	9	1	Int.	10	417.95	
BEEMAN									All scopes have 5 point reticle, all glass fully coated lenses. [1]Parallel adjustable. [2]Reticle lighted by ambient light. Imported by Beeman. [3]Available with lighted Electro-Dot reticle.
Rifle Scopes									
5045[1]	4-12	26.9-9	3	13.2	1	Int.	15	NA	
5046[1]	6-24	18-4.5	3	16.9	1	Int.	20.2	NA	
5050[1]	4	26	3.5	11.7	1	Int.	11	NA	
5055[1]	3-9	38-13	3.5	10.75	1	Int.	11.2	NA	
5060[1]	4-12	30-10	3	12.5	1	Int.	16.2	NA	
5065[1]	6-18	17-6	3	14.7	1	Int.	17.3	NA	
5066RL[2]	2-7	58-15	3	11.4	1	Int.	17	380.00	
5047L[2]	4	25	3.5	7	1	Int.	13.7	NA	
Pistol Scopes									
5025	2	19	10-24	9.1	1	Int.	7.4	NA	
5020	1.5	14	11-16	8.3	.75	Int.	3.6	NA	
BURRIS									All scopes avail. with Plex reticle. Steel-on-steel click adjustments. [1]Dot reticle on some models. [2]Post crosshair reticle extra. [3]Matte satin finish. [4]Available with parallax adjustment (standard on 10x, 12x, 4-12x, 6-12x, 6-18x, 6x HBR and 3-12x Signature). [5]Silver matte finish extra. [6]Target knobs extra, standard on silhouette models. LER and XER with P.A., 6x HBR. [7]Sunshade avail. [8]Avail. with Fine Plex reticle. [9]Available with Heavy Plex reticle. [10]Available with Posi-Lock. [11]Available with Peep Plex reticle. [12]Also avail. for rimfires, airguns. Selected models available with camo finish. **Partial listing shown.** Contact Burris for complete details.
Black Diamond									
3-12x50[3,4,6]	3.2-11.9	34-12	3.5-4	13.8	30mm	Int.	25	854.00	
Fullfield									
1.50x9[9]	1.6	62	3.5-3.75	10.25	1	Int.	9	293.00	
2.50x9[9]	2.5	55	3.5-3.75	10.25	1	Int.	9	302.00	
4x[1,2,3]	3.75	36	3.5-3.75	11.25	1	Int.	11.5	307.00	
6x[1,3]	5.8	23	3.5-3.75	13	1	Int.	12	336.00	
12x[1,4,6,7,8]	11.8	10.5	3.5-3.75	15	1	Int.	15	454.00	
1.75-5x[1,2,9,10]	1.7-4.6	66-25	3.5-3.75	10.875	1	Int.	13	366.00	
2-7x[1,2,3]	2.5-6.8	47-18	3.5-3.75	12	1	Int.	14	391.00	
3-9x[1,2,3,10]	3.3-8.7	38-15	3.5-3.75	12.625	1	Int.	15	356.00	
3.5-10x50mm[3,5,10]	3.7-9.7	29.5-11	3.5-3.75	14	1	Int.	19	486.00	
4-12x[1,4,8,11]	4.4-11.8	27-10	3.5-3.75	15	1	Int.	18	493.00	
6-18x[1,3,4,6,7,8]	6.5-17.6	16.7	3.5-3.75	15.8	1	Int.	18.5	517.00	
Compact Scopes									
1x XER[3]	1	51	4.5-20	8.8	1	Int.	7.9	290.00	
4x[4,5]	3.6	24	3.75-5	8.25	1	Int.	7.8	257.00	
6x[1,4]	5.5	17	3.75-5	9	1	Int.	8.2	273.00	
6x HBR[1,5,8]	6	13	4.5	11.25	1	Int.	13	429.00	
1-4x XER[3]	1-3.8	53-15	4.25-30	8.8	1	Int.	10.3	360.00	
3-9x[4,5]	3.6-8.8	25-11	3.75-5	12.625	1	Int.	11.5	361.00	
4-12x[1,4,6]	4.5-11.6	19-8	3.75-4	15	1	Int.	15	475.00	

CAUTION: PRICES SHOWN ARE SUPPLIED BY THE MANUFACTURER OR IMPORTER. CHECK YOUR LOCAL GUNSHOP.

Maker and Model	Magn.	Field at 100 Yds. (feet)	Eye Relief (in.)	Length (in.)	Tube Dia. (in.)	W & E Adjustments	Weight (ozs.)	Price	Other Data
Signature Series									LER=Long Eye Relief; IER=Intermediate Eye Relief; XER=Extra Eye Relief. Partial listing shown, contact maker for complete data. From Burris.
1.5-6x[2,3,5,9,10]	1.7-5.8	70-20	3.5-4	10.8	1	Int.	13	465.00	
4x[3]	4	30	3.5-4	12.125	1	Int.	14	359.00	
6x[3]	6	20	3.5-4	12.125	1	Int.	14	397.00	
2-8x[3,5,11]	2.1-7.7	53-17	3.5-4	11.75	1	Int.	14	536.00	
3-9x[3,5,10,13]	3.3-8.8	36-14	3.5-4	12.875	1	Int.	15.5	549.00	
2.50-10x[3,5,10]	2.7-9.5	37-10.5	3.5-4	14	1	Int.	19	669.00	
3-12x[3,10]	3.3-11.7	34-9	3.5-4	14.25	1	Int.	21	677.00	
4-16x[1,3,5,6,8,10]	4.3-15.7	33-9	3.5-4	15.4	1	Int.	23.7	695.00	
6-24x[1,3,5,6,8,10,13]	6.6-23.8	17-6	3.5-4	16	1	Int.	22.7	713.00	
8-32x[8,10,12]	8.6-31.4	13-3.8	3.5-4	17	1	Int.	24	767.00	
Handgun									
1.50-4x LER[1,5,10]	1.6-3.	16-11	11-25	10.25	1	Int.	11	352.00	
2-7x LER[3,4,5,10]	2-6.5	21-7	7-27	9.5	1	Int.	12.6	390.00	
3-9x LER[4,5,10]	3.4-8.4	12-5	22-14	11	1	Int.	14	440.00	
2x LER[4,5,6]	1.7	21	10-24	8.75	1	Int.	6.8	257.00	
4x LER[1,4,5,6,10]	3.7	11	10-22	9.625	1	Int.	9	288.00	
10x LER[1,4,6]	9.5	4	8-12	13.5	1	Int.	14	447.00	
Scout Scope									
1.50 XER[3,9]	1.5	22	7-18	9	1	Int.	7.3	290.00	
2.75x XER[3,9]	2.7	15	7-14	9.375	1	Int.	7.5	295.00	
BUSHNELL									
Trophy									[1]Wide Angle. [2]Also silver finish. [3]Also silver finish. [4]56mm objective. [5]Selective red L.E.D. dot for low light hunting. [6]Also silver finish. [7]Adj. obj. [8]Variable intensity; interchangeable extra reticles (Dual Rings, Open Cross Hairs) **$111.95**; fits Weaver-style base. Comp model 430 with diamond reticle and 1911 No-hole or 5-hole pattern mount, or STI mount, **$631.00.** (2x magnification adapter **$248.95**). [9]Blackpowder scope; extended eye relief, Circle-X reticle. [10]50mm objective.
73-1420	1.75-4	73-30	3.5	10.8	1	Int.	10.9	237.95	
73-1500[1]	1.75-5	68-23	3.5	10.8	1	Int.	12.3	243.95	
73-4124[1]	4-12	32-11	3	12.5	1	Int.	16.1	285.95	
73-3940	3-9	42-14	3	11.7	1	Int.	13.2	159.95	
73-6184	6-18	17.3-6	3	14.8	1	Int.	17.9	360.95	
Turkey & Brush									
73-1420	1.75-4	73-30	3.5	10.8	32mm	Int.	10.9	237.95	
HOLOsight Model 400[8]	1	—	—	6	—	Int.	8.7	562.95	
Trophy Handgun									
73-0232[2]	2	20	9-26	8.7	1	Int.	7.7	262.95	
73-2632[3]	2-6	21-7	9-26	9.1	1	Int.	9.6	268.95	
Banner									
71-1545	1.5-4.5	67-23	3.5	10.5	1	Int.	10.5	116.95	
71-3944[9]	3-9	36-13	4	11.5	1	Int.	12.5	120.95	
71-3950[10]	3-9	31-10	3	16	1	Int.	19	186.95	
71-4124[7]	4-12	29-11	3	12	1	Int.	15	157.95	
71-6185[10]	6-18	17-6	3	16	1	Int.	18	209.95	
Sportview									
79-0428	4	25	3	7.6	1	Int.	8.5	75.95	
79-0004	4	31	4	11.7	1	Int.	11.2	97.95	
79-0039	3-9	38-13	3.5	10.75	1	Int.	11.2	116.95	
79-0412[7]	4-12	27-9	3.2	13.1	1	Int.	14.6	141.95	
79-1393[6]	3-9	35-12	3.5	11.75	1	Int.	10	68.95	
79-1545	1.5-4.5	69-24	3	10.7	1	Int.	8.6	86.95	
79-3145	3.5-10	36-13	3	12.75	1	Int.	13.9	154.95	
79-1403	4	29	4	11.75	1	Int.	9.2	56.95	
79-6184	6-18	19.1-6.8	3	14.5	1	Int.	15.9	170.95	
79-3940M	3-9	42-14	3	12.7	1	Int.	12.5	95.95	
COLT OPTICS									
Classic AR[1]	4	225	3	7.2	35mm	Int.	14.6	249.00	[1]Duplex reticle; with range finding reticle, **$299.00**; with illuminated range finding reticle, **$399.99**. [2]Bullet drop compensator for 308 match, parallax adj. on turret; also in 10x, **$529.00** and 16x, **$549.00**. [3]Oversize knobs, 1/4-MOA clicks, Mil Dot reticle; 10x, **$499.00**, 16x, **$529.00**. [4]Ring and dot reticle; illuminated reticle **$479.00**. [5]10x **$469.00**, 16x **$499.00**. [6]Also 2.5x20, **$159.00**.
SSE[2]	6	159	3.3	12.8	30mm	Int.	22.8	499.00	
Tactical Elite[3]	6	159	3.38	13	30mm	Int.	22.6	469.00	
Compact 1-5x20[4]	1-5	301-62	3.45	9.5	30mm	Int.	14.2	359.00	
Tactical[5]	6	157	3.35	12.2	30mm	Int.	13.8	449.00	
Handgun 1.5x20[6]	1.5	183	11-22	5.4	1	Int.	6.8	159.00	
Handgun 4x32	4	91	11-22	8.6	1	Int.	7.6	165.00	
Handgun 1.5-4.5x20	1.5-4.5	190-88	11-22	7.7	1	Int.	7.6	215.00	
Handgun 2.5-7x28	2.5-7	135-52	11-22	9.3	1	Int.	8.6	245.00	
Red Dots									
Railway	1	—	—	4.8	—	Int.	5	299.00	
Scout	1	—	—	11	—	Int.	7.5	368.00	
Serendipity	1	—	—	5.3	—	Int.	3.75	299.00	
Slide Ride	1	—	—	4.8	—	Int.	3	NA	
Tactical	1	—	—	8	—	Int.	12	444.00	
DOCTER OPTIC									
Fixed Power									Matte black and matte silver finish available. All lenses multi-coated. Illuminated reticle avail., choice of reticles. [1]Rail mount, aspherical lenses avail. Aspherical lens model, **$1,375.00.** Imported from Germany by Docter Optic Technologies, Inc.
4x32	4	31	3	10.7	26mm	Int.	10	898.00	
6x42	6	20	3	12.8	26mm	Int.	12.7	1,004.00	
8x56[1]	8	15	3	14.7	26mm	Int.	15.6	1,240.00	
Variables									
1-4x24	1-4	79.7-31.3	3	10.8	30mm	Int.	13	1,300.00	
1.2-5x32	1.2-5	65-25	3	11.6	30mm	Int.	15.4	1,345.00	
1.5-6x42	1.5-6	41.3-20.6	3	12.7	30mm	Int.	16.8	1,378.00	
2.5-10x48	2.5-10	36.6-12.4	3	13.7	30mm	Int.	18.6	1,378.00	
2-12x56	3-12	44.2-13.8	3	14.8	30mm	Int.	20.3	1,425.00	
3-10x40	3-10	34.4-11.7	3	13	1	Int.	18	795.00	
EUROPTIK SUPREME									[1]Military scope with adjustable parallax. Fixed powers have 26mm tubes, variables have 30mm tubes. Some models avail. with steel tubes. All lenses multi-coated. Dust and water tight. From Europtik.
4x36K	4	39	3.5	11.6	26mm	Int.	14	795.00	
6x42K	6	21	3.5	13	26mm	Int.	15	875.00	
8x56K	8	18	3.5	14.4	26mm	Int.	20	925.00	
1.5-6x42K	1.5-6	61.7-23	3.5	12.6	30mm	Int.	17	1,095.00	
2-8x42K	2-8	52-17	3.5	13.3	30mm	Int.	17	1,150.00	
2.5-10x56K	2.5-10	40-13.6	3.5	15	30mm	Int.	21	1295.00	
3-12x56 Super	3-12	10.8-34.7	3.5-2.5	15.2	30mm	Int.	24	1,495.00	

CAUTION: PRICES SHOWN ARE SUPPLIED BY THE MANUFACTURER OR IMPORTER. CHECK YOUR LOCAL GUNSHOP.

53rd EDITION, 1999 **457**

Maker and Model	Magn.	Field at 100 Yds. (feet)	Eye Relief (in.)	Length (in.)	Tube Dia. (in.)	W & E Adjustments	Weight (ozs.)	Price	Other Data
4-16x56 Super	4-16	9.8-3.9	3.1	18	30mm	Int.	26	1,575.00	
3-9x40 Micro	3-9	3.2-12.1	2.7	13	1	Int.	14	1,450.00	
2.5-10x46 Micro	2.5-10	13.7-33.4	2.7	14	30mm	Int.	20	1,395.00	
4-16x56 EDP[1]	4-16	22.3-7.5	3.1	18	30mm	Int.	29	1,995.00	
7-12x50 Target	7-12	8.8-5.5	3.5	15	30mm	Int.	21	1,495.00	
KAHLES									[1]Steel tube. [2]Ballistic cam system with military range finder. Waterproof, fogproof, nitrogen filled. Choice of reticles. Imported from Austria by Swarovski Optic NA.
K1.5-6x42-L	1.5-6	61-21	—	12.5	30mm	Int.	15.8	770.00	
K2.2-9x42-L	2.2-9	39.5-15	—	13.3	30mm	Int.	15.5	943.00	
K3-12x56-L	3-12	30-11	—	15.2	30mm	Int.	18	999.00	
KZF84-6[1,2]	6	23	—	12.5	1	Int.	17.6	1,165.00	
KZF84-10[1,2]	10	13	—	13.25	1	Int.	18	1,199.00	
KILHAM									Unlimited eye relief; internal click adjustments; crosshair reticle. Fits Thompson/Center rail mounts, for S&W K, N, Ruger Blackhawk, Super, Super Single-Six, Contender.
Hutson Handgunner II	1.7	8	—	5.5	.875	Int.	5.1	119.95	
Hutson Handgunner	3	8	10-12	6	.875	Int.	5.3	119.95	
LEICA									Aluminum tube with hard anodized matte black finish with titanium accents; finger-adjustable windage and elevation with 1/4-MOA clicks. Made in U.S. From Leica.
Ultravid 1.75-6x32	1.75-6	47-18	4.8-3.7	11.25	30mm	Int.	14	749.00	
Ultravid 3.5-10x42	3.5-10	29.5-10.7	4.6-3.6	12.62	30mm	Int.	16	849.00	
Ultravid 4.5-14x42	4.5-14	20.5-7.4	5-3.7	12.28	30mm	Int.	18	949.00	
LEUPOLD									Constantly centered reticles, choice of Duplex, tapered CPC, Leupold Dot, Crosshair and Dot. CPC and Dot reticles extra. [1]2x and 4x scopes have from 12"-24" of eye relief and are suitable for handguns, top ejection arms and muzzleloaders. [2]3x9 Compact, 6x Compact, 12x, 3x9, and 6.5x20 come with adjustable objective. Sunshade available for all adjustable objective scopes, $23.20-41.10. [3]Silver finish about $15.00 extra. [4]Long Range scopes have side focus parallax adjustment, additional windage and elevation travel. Partial listing shown. Contact Leupold for complete details.
Vari-X III 3.5x10 Tactical	3.5-10	29.5-10.7	3.6-4.6	12.5	1	Int.	13.5	764.30	
M8-2X EER[1]	1.7	21.2	12-24	7.9	1	Int.	6	292.20	
M8-2X EER Silver[1]	1.7	21.2	12-24	7.9	1	Int.	6	314.30	
M8-2.5x28 IER Scout	2.3	22	9.3	10.1	1	Int.	7.5	380.40	
M8-4X EER[1]	3.7	9	12-24	8.4	1	Int.	7	394.60	
M8-4X EER Silver[1]	3.7	9	12-24	8.4	1	Int.	7	394.60	
Vari-X 2.5-8 EER	2.5-8	13-4.3	11.7-12	9.7	1	Int.	10.9	574.40	
M8-4X Compact	3.6	25.5	4.5	9.2	1	Int.	7.5	362.50	
Vari-X 2-7x Compact	2.5-6.6	41.7-16.5	5-3.7	9.9	1	Int.	8.5	453.60	
Vari-X 3-9x Compact	3.2-8.6	34-13.5	4-3	11-11.3	1	Int.	11	491.10	
M8-4X	4	24	4	10.7	1	Int.	9.3	362.50	
M8-6X36mm	5.9	17.7	4.3	11.4	1	Int.	10	385.70	
M8-6x 42mm	6	17	4.5	12	1	Int.	11.3	478.60	
M8-6x42 A.O. Tactical	6	17	4.2	12.1	1	Int.	11.3	616.10	
M8-12x A.O. Varmint	11.6	9.1	4.2	13	1	Int.	13.5	535.90	
Vari-X 3-9x Compact EFR A.O.	3.8-8.6	34-13.5	4-3	11	1	Int.	11	525.00	
Vari-X-II 1x4	1.6-4.2	70.5-28.5	4.3-3.8	9.2	1	Int.	9	375.00	
Vari-X-II 2x7	2.5-6.6	42.5-17.8	4.9-3.8	11	1	Int.	10.5	407.10	
Vari-X-II 3x9[1,3]	3.3-8.6	32.3-14	4.1-3.7	12.3	1	Int.	13.5	410.70	
Vari-X-II 3-9x50mm	3.3-8.6	32.3-14	4.1-3.7	12	1	Int.	13.6	489.30	
Vari-X II 3-9x40 Tactical	3-9	32.3-14	4.7-3.7	12.2	1	Int.	13	510.70	
Vari-X-II 4-12 A.O. Matte	4.4-11.6	22.8-11	5-3.3	12.3	1	Int.	13.5	564.30	
Vari-X-III 1.5-5x20	1.5-4.5	66-23	5.3-3.7	9.4	1	Int.	9.5	592.90	
Vari-X-III 1.75-6x32	1.9-5.6	47-18	4.8-3.7	9.8	1	Int.	11	641.10	
Vari-X-III 2.5x8	2.6-7.8	37-13.5	4.7-3.7	11.3	1	Int.	11.5	639.30	
Vari-X-III 3.5-10x40 Long Range M3[4]	3.9-9.7	29.8-11	4-3.5	13.5	30mm	Int.	19.5	1,098.20	
Vari-X-III 3.5-10x50	3.3-9.7	29.5-10.7	4.6-3.6	12.4	1	Int.	13	762.50	
Vari-X-III 4.5-14 A.O.	4.7-13.7	20.8-7.4	5-3.7	12.4	1	Int.	14.5	742.90	
Vari-X-III 4.5-14x50 A.O.	4.7-13.7	20.8-7.4	5-3.7	12.4	1	Int.	14.5	783.90	
Vari-X III 4.5-14x 50 Long Range Tactical[4]	4.9-14.3	19-6	5-3.7	12.1	30mm	Int.	17.5	1,026.80	
Vari-X-III 6.5-20 A.O. Varmint	6.5-19.2	14.2-5.5	5.3-3.6	14.2	1	Int.	17.5	876.80	
Vari-X-III 6.5x20xTarget EFR A.O.	6.5-19.2	—	5.3-3.6	14.2	1	Int.	16.5	894.60	
Vari-X III 6.5-20x 50 Long Range Target[4]	6.8-19.2	14.7-5.4	4.9-3.7	14.3	30mm	Int.	19	1,107.10	
Vari-X III 8.5-25x40 A.O. Target	8.5-25	10.86-4.2	5.3	14.3	1	Int.	17.5	883.90	
Vari-X III 8.5-25x 50 Long Range Target[4]	8.3-24.2	11.4-4.3	4.4-3.6	14.3	30mm	Int.	19	1,196.40	
Mark 4 M1-10x	10	11.1	3.6	13.125	30mm	Int.	21	1,735.70	
Mark 4 M1-16x	16	6.6	4.1	12.875	30mm	Int.	22	1,735.70	
Mark 4 M3-10x	10	11.1	3.6	13.125	30mm	Int.	21	1,735.70	
Vari-X III 6.5x20[2] A.O.	6.5-19.2	14.2-5.5	5.3-3.6	14.2	1	Int.	16	796.40	
BR-D 24x40 A.O. Target	24	4.7	3.2	13.6	1	Int.	15.3	964.30	
BR-D 36x-40 A.O. Target	36	3.2	3.4	14.1	1	Int.	15.6	1,008.90	
LPS 1.5-6x42	1.5-6	58.7-15.7	4	11.2	30mm	Int.	16	1,476.80	
LPS 3.5-14x52 A.O.	3.5-14	28-7.2	4	13.1	30mm	Int.	22	1,569.60	
Rimfire									
Vari-X II 2-7x RF Special	3.6	25.5	4.5	9.2	1	Int.	7.5	453.60	
Shotgun									
M8 4x	3.7	9	12-24	8.4	1	Int.	6	383.90	
Vari-X II 1x4	1.6-4.2	70.5-28.5	4.3-3.8	9.2	1	Int.	9	396.40	
Vari-X-II 2x7	2.5-6.6	42.5-17.8	4.9-3.8	11	1	Int.	9	428.60	
LYMAN									Made under license from Lyman to Lyman's orig. specs. Blue steel. Three-point suspension rear mount with .25-min. click adj. Data listed are for 20x model. [1]Price approximate. Made in U.S. by Parsons Optical Mfg. Co.
Super TargetSpot[1]	10, 12, 15, 20, 25, 30	5.5	2	24.3	.75	Int.	27.5	685.00	
McMILLAN									42mm obj. lens; .25-MOA clicks; nitrogen filled, fogproof, waterproof; etched duplex-type reticle. [1]Tactical Scope with external adj. knobs, military reticle; 60+ min. adj.
Vision Master 2.5-10x	2.5-10	14.2-4.4	4.3-3.3	13.3	30mm	Int.	17	1,250.00	
Vision Master Model 1[1]	2.5-10	14.2-4.4	4.3-3.3	13.3	30mm	Int.	17	1,250.00	

CAUTION: PRICES SHOWN ARE SUPPLIED BY THE MANUFACTURER OR IMPORTER. CHECK YOUR LOCAL GUNSHOP.

Maker and Model	Magn.	Field at 100 Yds. (feet)	Eye Relief (in.)	Length (in.)	Tube Dia. (in.)	W & E Adjustments	Weight (ozs.)	Price	Other Data
MILLETT									[3]3-MOA dot. [2]5-MOA dot. [3]3-, 5-, 8-, 10-MOA dots. [4]10-MOA dot. All have click adjustments; waterproof, shockproof; 11 dot intensity settings. All avail. in matte/black or silver finish. From Millett Sights.
Buck 3-9x44	3-9	38-14	3.25-4	13	1	Int.	16.2	549.00	
SP-1 Compact[1]	1	36.65	—	4.1	1	Int.	3.2	149.95	
SP-2 Compact[2]	1	58	—	4.5	30mm	Int.	4.3	149.95	
MultiDot SP[3]	1	50	—	4.8	30mm	Int.	5.3	289.95	
30mm Wide View[4]	1	60	—	5.5	30mm	Int.	5	289.95	
MIRADOR									[1]Wide angle scope. Multi-coated objective lens. Nitrogen filled; waterproof; shockproof. From Mirador Optical Corp.
RXW 4x40[1]	4	37	3.8	12.4	1	Int.	12	179.95	
RXW 1.5-5x20[1]	1.5-5	46-17.4	4.3	11.1	1	Int.	10	188.95	
RXW 3-9x40	3-9	43-14.5	3.1	12.9	1	Int.	13.4	251.95	
NIGHTFORCE									Lighted reticles with eleven intensity levels. Most scopes have choice of reticles. From Lightforce U.S.A.
FIXED POWER									
36x56	36	2.6	3	17	30mm	Int.	35	846.25	
Variable Power									
1.75-6x42	1.75-6	47.2-15.7	4.1	12.5	30mm	Int.	22	730.75	
2.5-10x50	2.5-10	31.4-9.4	3.3	13.9	30mm	Int.	28	738.25	
3.5-15x56	3.5-15	24.5-6.9	3	15.8	30mm	Int.	32	825.25	
5.5-22x56	5.5-22	15.7-4.4	3	19.4	30mm	Int.	38.5	877.75	
8-32x56	8-32	9.4-3.1	3	16.6	30mm	Int.	36	909.25	
12-42x56	12-42	6.7-2.3	3	17	30mm	Int.	36	940.75	
NIKON									Super multi-coated lenses and blackening of all internal metal parts for maximum light gathering capability; positive .25-MOA; fogproof; waterproof; shockproof; luster and matte finish. [1]Also available in matte silver finish. [2]Available in silver matte finish. From Nikon, Inc.
4x40[2]	4	26.7	3.5	11.7	1	Int.	11.7	284.00	
1.5-4.5x20	1.5-4.5	67.8-22.5	3.7-3.2	10.1	1	Int.	9.5	358.00	
1.5-4.5x24 EER	1.5-4.4	13.7-5.8	24-18	8.9	1	Int.	9.3	352.00	
2-7x32	2-7	46.7-13.7	3.9-3.3	11.3	1	Int.	11.3	367.00	
3-9x40[1]	3-9	33.8-11.3	3.6-3.2	12.5	1	Int.	12.5	371.00	
3.5-10x50	3.5-10	25.5-8.9	3.9-3.8	13.7	1	Int.	15.5	489.00	
4-12x40 A.O.	4-12	25.7-8.6	3.6-3.5	14	1	Int.	16.6	476.00	
4-12x50 A.O.	4-12	25.4-8.5	3.6-3.5	14	1	Int.	18.3	578.00	
6.5-20x44	6.5-19.4	16.2-5.4	3.5-3.1	14.8	1	Int.	19.6	591.00	
2x20 EER	2	22	26.4	8.1	1	Int.	6.3	213.00	
NORINCO									Partial listing shown. Some with Ruby Lens coating, blue/black and matte finish. Imported by Nic Max, Inc.
N2520	2.5	44.1	4	—	1	Int.	—	52.28	
N420	4	29.3	3.7	—	1	Int.	—	52.70	
N640	6	20	3.1	—	1	Int.	—	67.88	
N154520	1.5-4.5	63.9-23.6	4.1-3.2	—	1	Int.	—	80.14	
N251042	2.5-10	27-11	3.5-2.8	—	1	Int.	—	206.60	
N3956	3-9	35.1-6.3	3.7-2.6	—	1	Int.	—	231.88	
N31256	3-12	26-10	3.5-2.8	—	1	Int.	—	290.92	
NC2836M	2-8	50.8-14.8	3.6-2.7	—	1	Int.	—	255.60	
PARSONS									Adjustable for parallax, focus. Micrometer rear mount with .25-min. click adjustments. Price is approximate. Made in U.S. by Parsons Optical Mfg. Co.
Parsons Long Scope	6	10	2	28-34+	.75	Ext.	13	475.00-525.00	
PENTAX									[1]Glossy finish; matte finish, $594.00. [2]Glossy finish; matte finish, $628.00; electroless nickel, $638.00. [3]Glossy finish; matte finish. $652.00. [4]Glossy-XL finish. [5]Glossy finish, matte finish, $816.00. [6]Glossy finish, Fine Plex; matte finish, Fine Plex, $856.00; dot reticle, add $10.00. [7]Glossy finish; matte finish. $504.00; electroless nickel, $524.00. [8]Glossy finish; matte finish, $420.00; electroless nickel $440.00. [9]Lightseeker II $636.00 glossy, $660.00 matte. [10]Lightseeker II $844.00 matte. [11]Glossy finish; matte finish, $372.00; also with Mossy Oak, Advantage, Mossy Oak Break-Up Camo, $364.00. [12]Matte finish, $440.00. [13]Glossy finish; matte finish, $310.00; Mossy Oak, $330.00. [14]Lightseeker II; $878.00 matte. Imported by Pentax Corp.
Lightseeker 2-8x[1]	2-8	53-17	3-3.5	11.7	1	Int.	14	560.00	
Lightseeker 3-9x[2,9]	3-9	36-14	3-3.5	12.7	1	Int.	15	594.00	
Lightseeker 1.75-6x[7]	1.75-6	71-20	3.5-4	10.75	1	Int.	13	526.00	
Lightseeker 3.5-10x[3]	3.5-10	29.5-11	3.-3.25	14	1	Int.	19.5	630.00	
Lightseeker 3-11x[4]	3-11	38.5-13	3-3.25	13.3	1	Int.	19	720.00	
Lightseeker 4-16x A.O.[5,10]	4-16	3-3.5	33-9	15.4	1	Int.	23.7	796.00	
Lightseeker 6-24 A.O.[6,17]	6-24	18-5.5	3-3.25	16	1	Int.	22.7	836.00	
Lightseeker 8.5-32x	8.5-32	13-3.8	3.5-4	17.2	1	Int.	24	880.00	
Shotgun									
Lightseeker Zero-X SG Plus[11]	0	51	4.5-15	8.9	1	Int.	7.9	340.00	
Lightseeker Zero-X/V SG Plus[12]	0-4	53.8-15	3.5-7	8.9	1	Int.	10.3	454.00	
Lightseeker Turkey Still-Target Comp.	0-4	54.15	3.5-7	8.9	1	Int.	10.3	476.00	
Lightseeker 2.5x SG Plus[13]	2.5	55	3-3.5	10	1	Int.	9	350.00	
RWS									Air gun scopes. All have Dyna-Plex reticle. Model 800 is for air pistols. M450, 3-9x40mm $200.00. Imported from Japan by Dynamit Nobel-RWS.
300	4	36	3.5	11.75	1	Int.	13.2	170.00	
400[1]	2-7	55-16	3.5	11.75	1	Int.	13.2	190.00	
450	3-9	43-14	3.5	12	1	Int.	14.3	215.00	
500	4	36	3.5	12.25	1	Int.	13.9	225.00	
550	2-7	55-16	3.5	12.75	1	Int.	14.3	235.00	
600	3-9	43-14	3.5	13	1	Int.	16.5	260.00	
REDFIELD									[1]Accutrac feature avail. on these scopes at extra cost. Traditionals have round lenses. 4-Plex reticle is standard. Selected models shown. **Contact Redfield for full data.**
Ultimate Illuminator 3-12x	2.9-11.7	27-10.5	3-3.5	15.4	30mm	Int.	23	826.95	
Widefield Illuminator 2-7x	2-6.8	56-17	3-3.5	11.7	1	Int.	13.5	549.95	
Widefield Illuminator 3-9x[1]	2.9-8.7	38-13	3.5	12.75	1	Int.	17	623.95	
Widefield Illuminator 3-10x	3-10.1	29-10.5	3.5	14.75	1	Int.	18	703.95	
Target 8-32x	8-32	13.3-3.4	2.9	16.4	1	Int.	16.1	712.95	
TX-27									
4x40	4	28.9	3-3.5	14.5	27mm	Int.	9	473.95	
2.5-10x44	2.5-10.1	35.5-10.7	3-3.5	12.7	27mm	Int.	11.7	566.95	
3.5-14x40	3.5-14	33.3-7.3	3-3.5	13.2	27mm	Int.	15.5	600.95	
5-20x44	5.1-19.9	22.5-4.7	3-3.5	13.7	27mm	Int.	17.1	686.95	
Target Benchrest									
40x40	40	2.7	3.5	19.5	1	Int.	15.5	878.95	
Tracker SE									
4x	4.1	28.9	3.5	11.7	1	Int.	9.9	200.95	
6x	6.2	18	3.5	12.4	1	Int.	11.1	200.95	
2-7x	2.3-7	36.6-12.2	3-3.5	11.4	1	Int.	11.7	241.95	

CAUTION: PRICES SHOWN ARE SUPPLIED BY THE MANUFACTURER OR IMPORTER. CHECK YOUR LOCAL GUNSHOP.

53rd EDITION, 1999 **459**

Maker and Model	Magn.	Field at 100 Yds. (feet)	Eye Relief (in.)	Length (in.)	Tube Dia. (in.)	W & E Adjustments	Weight (ozs.)	Price	Other Data
3-9x	3-9	34.4-11.3	3-3.5	12.3	1	Int.	12.6	270.95	
4-12x	3.9-11.4	27-9	3-3.75	13.8	1	Int.	16.8	292.95	
6-18x	6.1-18.1	18-5.8	3-3.75	14.4	1	Int.	19	344.95	
Scout Scope	2	24	9.5-20	7.8	1	Int.	6	241.95	
Golden Five Star 3-9x40[6]	3-9.1	34-11	3-3.75	12.5	1	Int.	13	363.95	
Golden Five Star 4-12x A.O. *	3.9-11.4	279	3-3.75	13.8	1	Int.	216	508.95	
Golden Five Star 6-18x A.O. *	6.1-18.1	18.6	3-3.75	14.3	1	Int.	18	500.95	
6-24x Varmint	5.9-23.8	15-5.5	3-3.5	15.75	1	Int.	26	659.95	
Handgun Scopes									
Handgun 2x	2	24	9.5-20	7.88	1	Int.	6	234.95	
Handgun 4x	4	75	13-19	8.63	1	Int.	6.1	234.95	
Handgun 2.50-7x	2.50-7	11-3.75	11-26	9.4	1	Int.	9.3	316.95	
ESD	1	14.9	—	5.25	30mm	Int.	6.1	366.95	
Low Profile Scopes									
Widefield 2.75xLP	2.75	55.5	3.50	10.5	1	Int.	8	292.95	
Widefield 4xLP	3.6	37.5	3.5	11.5	1	Int.	10	319.95	
Widefield 6xLP	5.5	23	3.5	12.75	1	Int.	11	345.95	
Widefield 1.75-5xLP	1.75-5	70-27	3.5	10.75	1	Int.	11.5	397.95	
Widefield 2x-7xLP*	2-7	49-19	3.5	11.75	1	Int.	13	408.95	
Widefield 3x-9xLP*	3-9	39-15	3.5	12.5	1	Int.	14	455.95	
SCHMIDT & BENDER									
Fixed									
4x36	4	30	3.25	11	1	Int.	14	725.00	
6x42	6	21	3.25	13	1	Int.	17	795.00	
8x56	8	16.5	3.25	14	1	Int.	22	915.00	
10x42	10	10.5	3.25	13	1	Int.	18	910.00	
Variables									
1.25-4x20[1]	1.25-4	96-16	3.25	10	30mm	Int.	15.5	945.00	
1.25-4x20 Safari[5]	1.25-4	96-16	3.75	10	30mm	Int.	15.5	990.00	
1.5-6x42[1,5]	1.5-6	60-19.5	3.25	12	30mm	Int.	19.7	1,073.00	
2.5-10x56[1,5]	2.5-10	37.5-12	3.25	14	30mm	Int.	24.6	1,298.00	
3-12x42[2]	3-12	34.5-11.5	3.25	13.5	30mm	Int.	19	1,222.00	
3-12x50[1,5]	3-12	33.3-12.6	3.25	13.5	30mm	Int.	22.9	1,262.00	
4-16x50 Varmint[4,6]	4-16	22.5-7.5	3.25	14	30mm	Int.	26	1,495.00	
Police/Marksman Fixed									
6x42[1]	6	21	3.25	13	30mm	Int.	17	900.00	
10x42[3]	10	10.5	3.25	13	30mm	Int.	18	950.00	
Variables									
1.5-6x42[3]	1.5-6	60-19.5	3.25	12	30mm	Int.	NA	1,200.00	
3-12x42[3]	3-12	34.5-11.5	3.25	13.5	30mm	Int.	NA	1,360.00	
3-12x50[3]	3-12	33.3-12.6	3.25	13.5	30mm	Int.	NA	1,400.00	
SHEPHERD									
3940-E	3-9	43.5-15	3.3	13	1	Int.	17	1,039.40	
310-2[1,2]	3-10	35.3-11.6	3-3.75	12.8	1	Int.	18	524.25	
SIGHTRON									
Electronic Red Dot									
S33-3[2,4]	1	58	—	5.15	33mm	Int.	5.43	248.99	
S33-3D[3,4]	1	58	—	5.74	30mm	Int.	6.27	369.99	
Riflescopes Variables									
SII 1.56x42	1.5-6	50-15	3.8-4	11.69	1	Int.	15.35	377.99	
SII 2.5-7x32SG[8]	2.5-7	26-7	4.3	10.9	1	Int.	8.46	374.99	
SII2.58x42	2.5-8	36-12	3.6-4.2	11.89	1	Int.	12.82	339.99	
SII 39x42[4,6,7]	3-9	34-12	3.6-4.2	12.00	1	Int.	13.22	358.99	
SII312x42[6]	3-12	32-9	3.6-4.2	11.89	1	Int.	12.99	379.99	
SII3.510x42	3.5-10	32-11	3.6	11.89	1	Int.	13.16	379.99	
SII4.514x42[1]	4.5-14	22-7.9	3.6	13.88	1	Int.	16.07	426.99	
Fixed									
SII 4x42	4	31	4	12.48	1	Int.	12.34	249.99	
SII 6x42[4]	6	20	4	12.48	1	Int.	12.34	249.99	
SII 8x42[4]	8	16	4	12.28	1	Int.	12.34	249.99	
Target									
SII 24x44	24	4.1	4.33	13.30	1	Int.	15.87	406.99	
SII 416x42[1,4,5,6,7]	4-16	26-7	3.6	13.62	1	Int.	16	466.99	
SII 624-42[1,4,5,7]	6-24	16-5	3.6	14.6	1	Int.	18.7	489.99	
Compact									
SII 4x32	4	25	4.5	9.69	1	Int.	9.34	179.99	
SII2.5-10x32	2.5-10	41-10.5	3.75-3.5	10.9	1	Int.	10.39	339.99	
Shotgun									
SII 2.5x20SG	2.5	41	4.3	10.28	1	Int.	8.46	193.99	
Pistol									
SII 1x28P[4]	1	30	9-24	9.49	1	Int.	8.46	197.99	
SII 2x28P[4]	2	16-10	9-24	9.49	1	Int.	8.28	197.99	
Rimfire									
SII4x32RF	4	25	4.5	9.69	1	Int.	9.34	179.99	

All scopes have 30-yr. warranty, click adjustments, centered reticles. rotation indicators. [1]Glass reticle; aluminum. Available in aluminum with mounting rail. [2]Aluminum only. [3]Aluminum tube. Choice of two bullet drop compensators, choice of two sunshades, two range finding reticles. From Schmidt & Bender, Inc. [4]Parallax adjustment in thrid turret; extremely fine crosshairs. [5]Available with illuminated reticle that glows red; third turret houses on/off switch, dimmer and battery. Also with Long Eye Relief. From Schmidt & Bender, Inc.

[1]Also avail. as 310-P, 310-PE, $524.25. [2]Also avail. as 310-P1, 310-P2, 310-P3, 310-Pla, 310-PE1. 310-P22, 310-P22 Mag., 310-PE, $524.95. All have patented Dual Reticle system with range finder bullet drop compensation; multi-coated lenses, waterproof, shockproof, nitrogen filled, matte finish. From Shepherd Scope, Ltd.

[1]Adjustable objective. [2]3MOA dot; also with 5 or 10 MOA dot. [3]Variable 3,5,10 MOA dot; black finish; also stainless. [4]Satin black; also stainless. Electronic Red Dot scopes come with ring mount, front and rear extension tubes, polarizing filter, battery, haze filter caps, wrench. Rifle, pistol, shotgun scopes have aluminum tubes, Exac Trak adjustments. Lifetime warranty. From Sightron, Inc. [5]3" sun shade. [6]Mil Dot or Plex reticle. [7]Dot or Plex reticle. [8]Double Diamond reticle.

CAUTION: PRICES SHOWN ARE SUPPLIED BY THE MANUFACTURER OR IMPORTER. CHECK YOUR LOCAL GUNSHOP.

Maker and Model	Magn.	Field at 100 Yds. (feet)	Eye Relief (in.)	Length (in.)	Tube Dia. (in.)	W & E Adjustments	Weight (ozs.)	Price	Other Data
SIMMONS									
AETEC									
2100[8]	2.8-10	44-14	5	11.9	1	Int.	15.5	356.95	
2104[16]	3.8-12	33-11	4	13.5	1	Int.	20	389.95	
2107[14,20]	6-24	20-6.4	3.2	17.3	1	Int.	22.1	412.95	
V-TAC									
3006[15]	3-9	39-14.5	4.1-3	12.5	1	Int.	17	807.95	
3007	4.5-14	22-9.4	4.1-2.8	15.2	1	Int.	20.6	877.95	
44Mag									
M-1044[11]	3-10	34-10.5	3	12.75	1	Int.	15.5	253.95	
M-1045	4-12	29.5-9.5	3	13.2	1	Int.	18.25	310.95	
M-1047	6.5-20	14-.5	2.6-3.4	12.8	1	Int.	19.5	322.95	
M-1050M[19]	3.8-12	30-9.5	3	13.2	1	Int.	18.25	356.95	
Prohunter									
7700[1]	2-7	53-16.25	3	11.5	1	Int.	12.5	137.95	
7710[2]	3-9	36-13	3	12.6	1	Int.	13.5	148.95	
7716	4-12	26-9	3	12.6	1	Int.	14	176.95	
7720	6-18	18.5-6	3	13.75	1	Int.	12	195.95	
7740[3]	6	21.75	3	12.5	1	Int.	12	130.95	
Prohunter Handgun									
7732[18]	2	22	9-17	8.75	1	Int.	7	148.95	
7738[18]	4	15	10.5-26.4	8.5	1	Int.	8	160.95	
Whitetail Classic									
WTC11	1.5-5	75-23	3.4-3.2	9.3	1	Int.	9.7	199.95	
WTC12	2.5-8	45-14	3.2-3	11.3	1	Int.	13	218.95	
WTC13	3.5-10	30-10.5	3.2-3	12.4	1	Int.	13.5	229.95	
WTC 15	3.5-10	29.5-11.5	3.2	12.75	1	Int.	13.5	310.95	
WTC16	4	36.8	4	9.9	1	Int.	12	158.95	
WTC 45	4.5-14	22.5-8.6	3.2	13.2	1	Int.	14	287.95	
Pro50									
8800[10]	4-12	27-9	3.5	13.2	1	Int.	18.25	238.95	
8810[10]	6-18	17-5.8	3.6	13.2	1	Int.	18.25	259.95	
Deerfield									
21006	4	29.5	3.3	11.5	1	Int.	10	45.95	
21029	3-9	37-13	3.4-3	12.1	1	Int.	12.25	82.95	
21031	4-12	27-9	3-2.8	13.25	1	Int.	14.6	83.95	
Gold Medal Silhoutte									
23002	6-20	18-5.4	2.6-3.4	14.75	1	Int.	19.75	646.95	
Gold Medal Handgun									
22002[6]	2.5-7	11-4	15.7-19.7	9.25	1	Int.	9	299.95	
22004[6]	2	21.5	10.5-26.4	7.8	1	Int.	5.75	229.95	
22008	1.5-4	14-6.3	10-26	8.7	1	Int.	7.25	287.95	
Shotgun									
21004	4	16	5.5	8.8	1	Int.	9.1	90.95	
21005	2.5	24	6	7.4	1	Int.	7	67.95	
7789D	2	31	5.5	8.8	1	Int.	8.75	114.95	
7790D	4	17	5.5	8.5	1	Int.	8.75	125.95	
7791D	1.5-5	76-23.5	3.4	9.5	1	Int.	10.75	148.95	
Rimfire									
1022[7]	4	29.5	3	11.75	1	Int.	11	77.95	
1022T	3-9	42-14	3.5	11.5	1	Int.	12	183.95	
Blackpowder									
BP0420M[17]	4	19.5	4	7.5	1	Int.	8.3	125.95	
BP2732M[12]	2-7	57.7-16.6	3	11.6	1	Int.	12.4	144.95	
Pro Air Gun									
21608 A.O.	4	28.5	3	11.32	1	Int.	11.5	123.95	
21613 A.O.	4-12	27.5-10.25	3.1-2.9	13.2	1	Int.	13.2	213.95	
21619 A.O.	6-18	17-6	2.9-2.7	14.2	1	Int.	14.2	230.90	
SPRINGFIELD ARMORY									
6x40 Government Model 7.62mm[1]	6	—	3.5	13	1	Int.	14.7	339.00	
4-14x70 Tactical Government Model[2]	4-14	—	3.5	14.25	1	Int.	15.8	339.00	
4-14x56 1st Gen. Government Model[3]	4-14	—	3.5	14.75	30mm	Int.	23	466.00	
10x56 Mil Dot Government Model[4]	10	—	3.5	14.75	30mm	Int.	28	659.00	
6-20x56 Mil Dot Government Model	6-20	—	3.5	18.25	30mm	Int.	33	769.00	
STEINER									
Hunting Z									
1.5-5x20[1]	1.5-5	32-12	4.3	9.6	30mm	Int.	11.7	1,399.00	
2.5-8x36[1]	2.5-8	40-15	4	11.6	30mm	Int.	13.4	1,599.00	
3.5-10x50[1]	3.5-10	77-25	4	12.4	30mm	Int.	16.9	1,799.00	
SWAROVSKI HABICHT									
PH Series									
1.25-4x24[1]	1.25-4	86-27	4.5	10.6	30mm	Int.	15.9	998.89	
1.5-6x42[2]	1.5-6	65.4-21	3.75	13	30mm	Int.	20.5	1,132.22	
2.5-10x42[3]	2.5-10	39.6-12.3	3.75	13.2	30mm	Int.	19.4	1,298.89	
2.5-10x56[4]	2.5-10	39.6-12.3	3.75	14.7	30mm	Int.	24.3	1,398.89	
3-12x50[5]	3-12	33-10.5	3.75	14.3	30mm	Int.	22.0	1,376.6	
6-24x50	6-24	18.6-5.4	3.1	15.4	30mm	Int.	22.6	1,665.56	
6x42	6	23	3.25	12.6	1	Int.	17.9	921.11	
8x50	8	17	3.25	14.4	30mm	Int.	19.9	954.44	
8x56	8	17	3.25	14.4	30mm	Int.	23	998.89	
AL Series									
4x32A	4	30	3.2	11.5	1	Int.	10.8	554.44	

[1]Matte; also polished finish. [2]Silver; also black matte or polished. [3]Black matte finish. [4]Granite finish; black polish **$216.95**; silver **$218.95**; also with 50mm obj., black granite **$336.95**. [5]Camouflage. [6]Black polish. [7]With ring mounts. [8]Black polished; also black or silver matte. [9]Lighted reticle, Black Granite finish. [10]50mm obj.; black matte. [11]Black or silver matte. [12]75-yd. parallax; black or silver matte. [13]TV view. [14]Adj. obj. [15]V-TAC reticle in 1st focal plane; 4" sunshade; black matte. [16]Adj. objective; 4" sunshade; black matte. [17]Octagon body; rings included; black matte or silver finish. [18]Black matte finish; also available in silver. **Only selected models shown.** Contact Simmons Outdoor Corp. for complete details. [19]Smart reticle. [20]44mm A.O.; also available with 50mm A.O., **$435.95.**

[1]Range finding reticle with automatic bullet drop compensator for 308 match ammo to 700 yds. [2]Range finding reticle with automatic bullet drop compensator for 223 match ammo to 700 yds. [3]Also avail. as 2nd Gen. with target knobs and adj. obj., **$549.00**; as 3rd Gen. with illuminated reticle, **$698.00**; as Mil Dot model with illuminated Target Tracking reticle, target knobs, adj. obj., **$698.00**. [4]Unlimited range finding, target knobs, adj. obj., illuminated Target Tracking green reticle. All scopes have matte black finish, internal bubble level, 1/4-MOA clicks. From Springfield, Inc.

Waterproof, fogproof, nitrogn filled, accordion-type eye cup. [1]Heavy-Duplex, Duplex or European #4 reticle. Aluminum tubes; matte black finish. From Pioneer Research.

All models offered in either steel or lightweight alloy tubes. Weights shown are for lightweight versions. Choice of nine constantly centered reticles. Eyepiece recoil mechanism and rubber ring shield to protect face. American-style plex reticle available in 2.2-9x42 and 3-12x56 traditional European scopes. [1]Alloy weighs 12.3 oz. [2]Alloy weighs 15.9 oz. [3]Alloy weighs 14.8 oz. [4]Alloy weighs 18.3 oz. [5]Alloy weighs 16.6 oz. Imported by Swarovski Optik North America Ltd.

Maker and Model	Magn.	Field at 100 Yds. (feet)	Eye Relief (in.)	Length (in.)	Tube Dia. (in.)	W & E Adjustments	Weight (ozs.)	Price	Other Data
6x36A	6	21	3.2	11.9	1	Int.	11.5	610.00	
1.5-4.5x20A	1.5-4.5	75-25.8	3.5	9.53	1	Int.	10.6	665.56	
3-9x36	3-9	39-13.5	3.3	11.9	1	Int.	13	588.88	
3-10x42	3-10	33-11.7	3.3	12.5	1	Int.	13.7	776.67	
AV Series									
3-10x42A	3.3-10	33-11.7	3.35	12.36	1	Int.	12.5	776.67	
4-12x50A	4-12	29.1-9.9	3.35	13.46	1	Int.	13.3	799.00	
SWIFT									All Swift scopes, with the exception of the 4x15, have Quadraplex reticles and are fogproof and waterproof. The 4x15 has crosshair reticle and is non-waterproof. [1]Available in black or silver finish—same price. [2]Comes with ring mounts, wrench, lens caps, extension tubes, filter, battery. From Swift Instruments.
600 4x15	4	16.2	2.4	11	.75	Int.	4.7	24.00	
601 3-7x20	3-7	25-12	3-2.9	11	1	Int.	5.6	53.00	
649 4-12x50	4-12	30-10	3-2.8	13.2	1	Int.	14.6	216.00	
650 4x32	4	29	3.5	12	1	Int.	9	80.00	
653 4x40WA[1]	4	35.5	3.75	12.25	1	Int.	12	98.00	
654 3-9x32	3-9	35.75-12.75	3	12.75	1	Int.	13.75	95.00	
656 3-9x40WA[1]	3-9	42.5-13.5	2.75	12.75	1	Int.	14	103.00	
657 6x40	6	18	3.75	13	1	Int.	10	99.50	
660 4x20	4	25	4	11.8	1	Int.	9	80.00	
664 4-12x40[1]	4-12	27-9	3-2.8	13.3	1	Int.	14.8	143.00	
665 1.5-4.5x21	1.5-4.5	69-24.5	3.5-3	10.9	1	Int.	9.6	98.00	
666 Shotgun 1x20	1	113	3.2	7.5	1	Int.	9.6	102.00	
667 Fire-Fly[2]	1	—	—	5.3	30mm	Int.	5	215.00	
668M 4x32	4	25	4	10	1	Int.	8.9	95.00	
Pistol Scopes									
661 4x32	4	90	10-22	9.2	1	Int.	9.5	115.00	
662 2.5x32	2.5	14.3	9-22	8.9	1	Int.	9.3	110.00	
663 2x20[1]	2	18.3	9-21	7.2	1	Int.	8.4	115.00	
TASCO									
Titan									[1]Water, fog & shockproof; fully coated optics; .25-min. click stops; haze filter caps; 30-day/limited lifetime warranty. [2]30/30 range finding reticle. [3]World Class Wide Angle; Supercon mulit-coated optics; Opti-Centered® 30/30 range finding reticle; lifetime warranty. [4]1/3 greater zoom range. [5]Trajectory compensating scopes, Opti-Centered® stadia reticle. [6]Anodized finish. [7]True one-power scope. [8]Coated optics; crosshair reticle; ring mounts included to fit most 22, 10mm receivers. [9]Fits Remington 870, 1100, 11-87. [10]Electronic dot reticle with rheostat; coated optics; adj. for windage and elevation; waterproof, shockproof, fogproof; Lithium battery; 3x power booster avail.; matte black or matte aluminum finish; dot or T-3 reticle. [11]TV view. [12]Also matte aluminum finish. [13]11-position rheostat, 10-MOA dot; built-in sovetail-style mount. Also with crosshair reticle. [14]Also 30/30 reticle. [15]Also in stainless finish. [16]Black matte or stainless finish. [17]Also with stainless finish. [18]Also in matte black. [19]Available with 5-min. or 10-min. dot. [20]Red dot device; can be used on rifles, shotguns, handguns; 3.5 or 7 MOA dot. Available with 10, 15, 20-min. dot. [21]20mm; also 32mm. [22]20mm; black matte; also stainless steel; also 32mm. [23]Pro-Shot reticle. [24]Has 4, 8, 12, 16MOA dots (switchable). [25]Available with BDC. **Contact Tasco for details on complete line.**
T1.254.5x26NG	1.25-4.5	59-20	3.5	12	30mm	Int.	16.4	594.00	
T1.56x42N	1.5-6	59-20	3.5	12	30mm	Int.	16.4	680.00	
T39x42N	3-9	37-13	3.5	12.5	30mm	Int.	16.8	645.00	
T312x52N	3-12	27-10	4.5	14	30mm	Int.	20.7	764.00	
Big Horn									
BH2.510x50	2.5-10	44-11	4	13.5	1	Int.	18.7	611.00	
BH4.510x50	4.5-10	30-7.3	4	13.5	1	Int.	18.9	679.00	
World Class									
WA13.5x20[1,3,10]	1-3.5	115-31	3.5	9.75	1	Int.	10.2	161.00	
WA1.75-5x20[1,3]	1.75-5	72-24	3	10.625	1	Int.	10	152.00	
WA2.58x40[18]	2.5-8	44-14	3	11.75	1	Int.	14.25	178.00	
WA27x32[1,3,9]	2-7	56-17	3.25	11.5	1	Int.	12	161.00	
WA39x40[1,3,6,11,17,18]	3-9	43.5-15	3	12.75	1	Int.	13	199.00	
World Class Airgun									
AG4x40WA	4	36	3	13	1	Int.	14	374.00	
AG39x50WA	3-9	41-14	3	15	1	Int.	17.5	509.00	
World Class Electronic									
ERD39x40WA	3-9	41-14	3	12.75	1	Int.	16	323.00	
World Class TS									
TS24x44[18]	24	4.5	3	14	1	Int.	17.9	407.00	
TS36x44[18]	36	3	3	14	1	Int.	17.9	441.00	
TS832x44[18]	8-24	11-3.5	3	14	1	Int.	19.5	492.00	
TS624x44[18]	6-24	15-4.5	3	14	1	Int.	18.5	475.00	
TS832x44[18]	8-32	11-3.5	4.5	17	1	Int.	19.5	1,127.00	
World Class Pistol									
PWC2x22[12]	2	25	11-20	8.75	1	Int.	7.3	288.00	
PWC4x28[12]	4	8	12-19	9.45	1	Int.	7.9	340.00	
P1.254x28[12]	1.25-4	23-9	15-23	9.25	1	Int.	8.2	339.00	
Mag IV									
W312x40[1,2,4]	3-12	35-9	3	12.25	1	Int.	12	152.00	
W416x40[1,2,4,15,16]	4-16	26-7	3	14.25	1	Int.	15.6	203.00	
W416x50	4-16	31-8	4	13.5	1	Int.	16	350.00	
W520x50[25]	5-20	24-6	4	13.5	1	Int.	16	NA	
W624x40	6-24	17-4	3	15.25	1	Int.	16.8	255.00	
Golden Antler									
GA4x32TV	4	32	3	13	1	Int.	12.7	79.00	
GA39x32TV[1]	3-9	39-13	3	—	1	Int.	12.2	102.00	
GA39x40TV	3-9	39-13	3	12.5	1	Int.	13	135.00	
GA39x40WA	3-9	41-15	3	12.75	1	Int.	13	152.00	
Silver Antler									
SA2.5x32	2.5	42	3.25	11	1	Int.	10	99.00	
SA2.5x32A	2.5	32	6	8.5	1	Int.	8.5	87.00	
SA4x40	4	32	3	12	1	Int.	12.5	85.00	
SA39x32	3-9	39-13	3	13.25	1	Int.	12.2	101.00	
SA39x40WA[12]	3-9	41-15	3	12.75	1	Int.	13	152.00	
SA4x32[12]	4	32	3	13	1	Int.	12.7	79.00	
Pronghorn									
PH4x32	4	32	3	12	1	Int.	12.5	61.00	
PH39x32	3-9	39-13	3	12	1	Int.	11	83.00	
PH39x40	3-9	39-13	3	13	1	Int.	12.1	110.00	
High Country									
HC416x40	4-16	26-7	3.25	14.25	1	Int.	15.6	254.00	
HC624x10	6-24	17.4	3	15.25	1	Int.	16.8	280.00	
HC39x40	3-9	41-15	3	12.75	1	Int.	13	195.00	
HC3.510x40	3.5-10	30-10.5	3	11.75	1	Int.	14.25	220.00	
Rubber Armored									
RC39x40A	3-9	35-12	3.25	12.5	1	Int.	14.3	255.00	

Maker and Model	Magn.	Field at 100 Yds. (feet)	Eye Relief (in.)	Length (in.)	Tube Dia. (in.)	W & E Adjustments	Weight (ozs.)	Price	Other Data
World Class TR Scopes									
TR416x40	4-16	26-7	3	14.25	1	Int.	16.8	373.00	
TR624x40	6-24	17.4	3	15.5	1	Int.	17.5	407.00	
Bantam									
S1.5-45x20A[21,23]	1.5-4.5	69.5-23	4	10.25	1	Int.	10	102.00	
S1.54x32A[23]	1.5-4.5	69.5-23	4	11.25	1	Int.	12	110.00	
S2.5x20A[22,23]	2.5	22	6	7.5	1	Int.	7.5	80.00	
SA2.5x32A	2.5	32	6	8.5	1	Int.	8.5	87.00	
Airgun									
AG4x20	4	20	2.5	10.75	.75	Int.	5	40.00	
AG4x40WA	4	36	3	13	1	Int.	14	373.00	
AG4x32N	4	30	3	—	1	Int.	12.25	144.00	
AG27x32	2-7	48-17	3	12.25	1	Int.	14	178.00	
AG37x20	3-7	24-11	3	11.5	1	Int.	6.5	73.00	
AG39x50WA	3-9	41-14	3	15	1	Int.	17.5	475.00	
Rimfire									
RF4x15[8]	4	22.5	2.5	11	.75	Int.	4	17.00	
RF4x20WA	4	23	2.5	10.5	.75	Int.	3.8	24.00	
RF4x32[18]	4	31	3	12.25	1	Int.	12.6	86.00	
RF37x20	3-7	24-11	2.5	11.5	.75	Int.	5.7	45.00	
P1.5x15	1.5	22.5	9.5-20.75	8.75	.75	Int.	3.25	37.00	
Propoint									
PDP2[10,12,19]	1	40	Unltd.	5	30mm	Int.	5	254.00	
PDP3[10,12,19]	1	52	Unltd.	5	30mm	Int.	5	367.00	
PDP3CMP	1	68	4.75	33mm		Int.	—	390.00	
PDP5CMP[24]	1	82	Unltd.	4	47mm	Int.	8	407.00	
PDPGCMP[13]	1	—	Unltd.	3	—	Int.	5.8	390.00	
Optima 2000[20]	—	—	Unltd.	1.5	—	Int.	.5	596.00	
World Class Plus									
WCP4x44	4	32	3.25	12.75	1	Int.	13.5	271.00	
WCP3.510x50[18]	3.5-10	30-10.5	3.75	13	1	Int.	17.1	407.00	
WCP6x44	6	21	3.25	12.75	1	Int.	13.6	288.00	
WCP39x44[1,16]	3-9	39-14	3.5	12.75	1	Int.	15.8	305.00	
DWC832x50 Target	8-32	13-4	3	14.5	1	Int.	25.1	560.00	
DWCP1040x50 Target	10-40	11-2.5	3	14.5	1	Int.	25.3	611.00	
THOMPSON/CENTER RECOIL PROOF SERIES									[1]Black finish; silver, **$256.00**. [2]Black finish; silver, **$339.00**. [3]Black; silver, **$290.00**. [4]Lighted reticle, black. [5]Red dot scope. [6]Adj. obj. [7]Matte black; silver finish **$157.00**. From Thompson/Center. [8]Silver finish; black **$157.00**.
Pistol Scopes									
8356[1]	2	22.1	10.5-26.4	7.8	1	Int.	6.4	250.00	
8315[2]	2.5-7	15-5	8-21, 8-11	9.25	1	Int.	9.2	308.00	
8352[3]	4	22.1	10.5-26.4	7.8	1	Int.	6.4	285.00	
8322	2.5	15	9-21	7.4	1	Int.	7.2	298.00	
8326[4]	2.5-7	15-5	8-21, 8-11	9.25	1	Int.	10.5	370.00	
8650[5]	1	40	—	5.25	30mm	Int.	4.8	252.00	
8626[4]	3-9	33-11	3	10.75	1	Int.	10.1	390.00	
8668[8]	3-9	36.5-13.5	3	12.625	1	Int.	13.5	161.00	
8654	3-9	34.5-13.5	3	13.12	1	Int.	13.5	251.00	
Muzzleloader Scopes									
8658	1	60	3.8	9.125	1	Int.	10.2	122.00	
8656[7]	1.5-5	53-16	3	11.5	1	Int.	12.5	152.00	
8662	4	16	3	8.8	1	Int.	9.1	123.00	
8664[6]	6-18	18.8-6.2	3	14.33	1	Int.	13.5	200.00	
TRIJICON									[1]Advanced Combat Optical Gunsight for AR-15, M-16, with Intergral mount. Other mounts available. From Trijicon, Inc.
Reflex 1x24	1	—	—	4.25	1	Int.	4.6	299.00	
TA44 1.5x16[1]	1.5	43.8	2.4	4.1	—	Int.	3.5	595.00	
TA45 1.5x24[1]	1.5	28.9	3.6	5.6	—	Int.	3.9	595.00	
TA47 2x20[1]	2	33.1	2.1	4.5	—	Int.	3.8	595.00	
TA50 3x24[1]	3	28.9	1.4	4.8	—	Int.	3.9	619.00	
TA11 3.5x35[1]	3.5	28.9	2.4	8	—	Int.	14	1,295.00	
TAO1 4x32[1]	4	36.8	1.5	5.8	—	Int.	9.9	895.00	
Variable AccuPoint 3-9x40	3-9	—	3.2-3.6	12.2	1	Int.	12.8	649.00	
ULTRA DOT									[1]Brightness-adjustable fiber optic red dot reticle. Waterproof, nitrogen-filled one-piece tube. Tinted see-through lens covers and battery included. [2]Parallax adjustable. [3]Ultra Dot sights include rings, battery, polarized filter, and 5-year warranty. All models available in black or satin finish. [4]Illuminated red dot has eleven brightness settings. Shock-proof aluminum tube. From Ultra Dot Distribution.
Micro-Dot Scopes[1]									
1.5-4.5x20 Rifle	1.5-4.5	80-26	3	9.8	1	Int.	10.5	297.00	
2-7x32	2-7	54-18	3	11	1	Int.	12.1	308.00	
3-9x40	3-9	40-14	3	12.2	1	Int.	13.3	327.00	
4x-12x56[2]	4-12	30-10	3	14.3	1	Int.	18.3	417.00	
Ultra-Dot Sights[3]									
Ultra-Dot 25[4]	1	—	—	5.1	1	Int.	3.9	159.00	
Ultra-Dot 30[4]	1	—	—	5.1	30mm	Int.	4	179.00	
UNERTL									[1]Dural .25-MOA click mounts. Hard coated lenses. Non-rotating objective lens focusing. [2].25-MOA click mounts. [3]With target mounts. [4]With calibrated head. [5]Same as 1" Target but without objective lens focusing. [6]With new Posa mounts. [7]Range focus unit near rear of tube. Price is with Posa or standard mounts. Magnum clamp. From Unertl.
1" Target	6, 8, 10	16-10	2	21.5	.75	Ext.	21	358.00	
1.25: Target[1]	8, 10, 12, 14	12-16	2	25	.75	Ext.	21	466.00	
1.5" Target	10, 12, 14, 16, 18, 20	11.5-3.2	2.25	25.5	.75	Ext.	31	487.00	
2" Target[2]	10, 12, 14, 16, 18, 24, 30, 32, 36,	8	2.25	26.25	1	Ext.	44	642.00	
Varmint, 1.25"[3]	6, 8, 10, 12, 8, 10, 12,	1-7	2.50	19.50	.875	Ext.	26	466.00	
Ultra Varmint, 2"[4]	15	12.6-7	2.25	24	1	Ext.	34	630.00	
Small Game[5]	3, 4, 6	25-17	2.25	18	.75	Ext.	16	284.00	
Programmer 200[7]	10, 12, 14, 16, 18, 20, 24, 30, 36	11.3-4	—	26.5	1	Ext.	45	805.00	
BV-20[8]	2	8	4.4	17.875	1	Ext.	21.25	595.00	
Tube Sight	—	—	—	17	—	Ext.	—	262.50	

CAUTION: PRICES SHOWN ARE SUPPLIED BY THE MANUFACTURER OR IMPORTER. CHECK YOUR LOCAL GUNSHOP.

Maker and Model	Magn.	Field at 100 Yds. (feet)	Eye Relief (in.)	Length (in.)	Tube Dia. (in.)	W & E Adjustments	Weight (ozs.)	Price	Other Data
U.S. OPTICS									Prices are shown are estimates; scopes built as ordered, to order; choice of reticles; choice of front or rear focal plane; extra-heavy MIL-SPEC construction; extra-long turrets; individual w&e rebound springs; up to 88mm dia. objectives; up to 50mm tubes; all lenses multi-coated. Made in U.S. by U.S. Optics.
SN-1/TAR Fixed Power System									
16.2x	15	8.6	4.3	16.5	30mm	Int.	27	1,700.00	
22.4x	20	5.8	3.8	18	30mm	Int.	29	1,800.00	
26x	24	5	3.4	18	30mm	Int.	31	1,900.00	
31x	30	4.6	3.5	18	30mm	Int.	32	2,100.00	
37x	36	4	3.6	18	30mm	Int.	32	2,300.00	
48x	50	3	3.8	18	30mm	Int.	32	2,500.00	
Variables									
SN-2	4-22	26.8-5.8	5.4-3.8	18	30mm	Int.	24	1,762.00	
SN-3	1.6-8	—	4.4-4.8	18.4	30mm	Int.	36	1,435.00	
SN-4	1-4	116-31.2	4.6-4.9	18	30mm	Int.	35	1,065.00	
Fixed Power									
SN-6	4, 6, 8, 10	—	4.2-4.8	9.2	30mm	Int.	18	1,195.00	
SN-8	4, 10, 20, 40	32	3.3	7.5	30mm	Int.	11.1	890.00-4,000.00	
WEAVER									[1]Gloss black, [2]Matte black, [3]Silver, [4]Satin, [5]Silver and black (slightly higher in price). [6]Field of view measured at 18" eye relief..25 MOA click adjustments, except T-Series which vary from .125 to .25 clicks. One-piece tubes with multi-coated lenses. All scopes are shock-proof, waterproof, and fogproof. Dual-X reticle available in all except V24 which has a fine X-hair and ot; T-Series in which certain models are available in fine X-hair and dots; Qwik-Point red dot scopes which are available in fixed 4 or 12 MOA, or variable 4-8-12 MOA. V16 also available with fine X-hair, dot or Dual-X reticle. T-Series scopes have Micro-Trac® adjustments.
Riflescopes									
K2.5[1]	2.5	35	3.7	9.5	1	Int.	7.3	166.95	
K4[1,2]	3.7	26.5	3.3	11.3	1	Int.	10	175.95	
K6[1]	5.7	18.5	3.3	11.4	1	Int.	10	186.95	
KT15[1]	14.6	7.5	3.2	12.9	1	Int.	14.7	353.95	
V3[1,2]	1.1-2.8	88-32	3.9-3.7	9.2	1	Int.	8.5	210.95	
V9[1,2]	2.8-8.7	33-11	3.5-3.4	12.1	1	Int.	11.1	221.95	
V9x50[1,2]	3-9	29.4-9.9	3.6-3	13.1	1	Int.	14.5	295.95	
V10[1,2,3]	2.2-9.6	38.5-9.5	3.4-3.3	12.2	1	Int.	11.2	245.95	
V10-50[1,2,3]	2.3-9.7	40.2-9.2	2.9-2.8	13.75	1	Int.	15.2	337.95	
V16 MDX[2,3]	3.8-15.5	26.8-6.8	3.1	13.9	1	Int.	16.5	412.95	
V16 MFC[2,3]	3.8-15.5	26.8-6.8	3.1	13.9	1	Int.	16.5	412.95	
V16 MDT[2,3]	3.8-15.5	26.8-6.8	3.1	13.9	1	Int.	16.5	412.95	
V24 Varmint[2]	6-24	15.3-4	3.15	14.3	1	Int.	17.5	480.95	
Handgun									
H2[1,3]	2	21	4-29	8.5	1	Int.	6.7	202.95	
H4[1,3]	4	18	11.5-18	8.5	1	Int.	6.7	220.95	
VH4[1,3]	1.5-4	13.6-5.8	11-17	8.6	1	Int.	8.1	270.95	
VH8[1,2,3]	2.5-8	8.5-3.7	12.16	9.3	1	Int.	8.3	282.95	
Rimfire									
R4[2,3]	3.9	29	3.9	9.7	1	Int.	8.8	144.95	
RV7[2,3]	2.5-7	37-13	3.7-3.3	10.75	1	Int.	10.7	166.95	
T-Series									
T-6[4]	614	14	3.58	12.75	1	Int.	14.9	412.95	
T-10[4]	10	9.3	3	15.1	1	Int.	16.7	752.95	
T16[4]	16	6.5	3	15.1	1	Int.	16.7	758.95	
T-24[4]	24	4.4	3	15.1	1	Int.	16.7	764.95	
T-36[3,4]	36	3	3	15.1	1	Int.	16.7	770.95	
ZEISS									All scopes have .25-minute click-stop adjustments. Choice of Z-Plex or fine crosshair reticles. Rubber armored objective bell, rubber eyepiece ring. Lenses have T-Star coating for highest light transmission. Z-Series scopes offered in non-rail, tubes with duplex reticles only; 1" and 30mm. [1]Black matte finish. [2]Also in stainless matte finish. [3]Also with illuminated reticle, $1,810.00. [4]Matte finish. Also with illuminated reticle, $1,740.00. Bullet Drop Compensator avail. for all Z-Series scopes. Imported from Germany by Carl Zeiss Optical, Inc.
Diatal Z 6x42	6	22.9	3.2	12.7	1	Int.	13.4	955.00	
Diatal Z 8x56	8	18	3.2	13.8	1	Int.	17.6	1,135.00	
Diavari 1.25-4x24	1.25-4	105-33	3.2	11.46	30mm	Int.	17.3	1,085.00	
Diavari Z 2.5x10x48[1,2,5]	2.5-10	33-11.7	3.2	14.5	30mm	Int.	24	1,465.00	
Diavari C 3-9x36MC[4]	3-9	36-13	3.5	11.9	1	Int.	15	615.00	
Diavari Z 1.5-6x42[1,2]	1.5-6	65.5-22.9	3.2	12.4	1.18 (30mm)	Int.	18.5	1,240.00	
Diavari Z 3-12x56[1,2,3]	3-12	27.6-9.9	3.2	15.3	1.18 (30mm)	Int.	25.8	1,575.00	

Hunting scopes in general are furnished with a choice of reticle—crosshairs, post with crosshairs, tapered or blunt post, or dot crosshairs, etc. The great majority of target and varmint scopes have medium or fine crosshairs but post or dot reticles may be ordered. W—Windage E—Elevation MOA—Minute of Angle or 1" (approx.) at 100 yards, etc.

CAUTION: PRICES SHOWN ARE SUPPLIED BY THE MANUFACTURER OR IMPORTER. CHECK YOUR LOCAL GUNSHOP.

Maker and Model	Wavelength (nm)	Beam Color	Lens	Operating Temp. (degrees F.)	Weight (ozs.)	Price	Other Data
ALPEC							
Power Shot[1]	635	Red	Glass	NA	2.5	$199.95	[1]Range 1000 yards. [2]Range 300 yards. Mini Shot II range 500 yards, output 650mm, **$129.95.** [3]Range 300 yards; Laser Shot II 500 yards; Super Laser Shot 1000 yards. Black or stainless finish aluminum; removable pressure or push-button switch. Mounts for most handguns, many rifles and shotguns. From Alpec Team, Inc.
Mini Shot[2]	670	Red	Glass	NA	2.5	109.95	
Laser Shot[3]	670	Red	Glass	NA	3.0	89.95	
LASERAIM							
LA3X Dualdot[1]	—	—	—	—	12	199.00	[1]Red dot/laser combo; 300-yd. range: LA3xHD Hotdot has 500-yd. range **$249.00;** 4 MOA dot size, laser gives 2" dot size at 100 yrds. [2]30mm obj. lens: 4 MOA dot at 100 yds: fits Weaver base. [3]300-yd range; 2" dot at 100 yds.; rechargeable Nicad battery [4]1.5-mile range; 1" dot at 100 yds.;20+ hrs. batt. life. [5]1.5-mile range; 1" dot at 100 yds; rechargeable Nicad battery (comes with in-field charger); [6]Black or satin finish. With mount, **$169.00** [7]Laser projects 2" dot at 100 yds.: with rotary switch; with Hotdot **$237.00;** with Hotdot touch switch **$357.00.** [8]For Glock 17-27; G1 Hotdot **$299.00;** price installed. [10]Fits std. Weaver base, no rings required; 6-MOA dot; seven brightness settings. All have w&e adj.; black or satin silver finish. From Laseraim Technologies, Inc.
LA5[3]	—	—	—	—	1.2	150.00	
LA10 Hotdot[4]	—	—	—	—	NA	199.00	
LA11 Hotdot[5]	—	—	—	—	NA	199.00	
LA16 Hotdot Mighty Sight[6]	—	—	—	—	1.5	149.00	
Red Dot Sights							
LA93 Illusion III[2]	—	—	—	—	5.0	99.00	
LA9750 Grand Illusion[10]	—	—	—	—	7.0	199.00	
Lasers							
MA3 Mini Aimer[7]	—	—	—	—	1.0	99.00	
G1 Laser[8]	—	—	—	—	2.0	229.00	
LASER DEVICES							
He Ne FA-6	—	—	—	—	11	229.50	Projects high intensity beam of laser light onto target as an aiming point. Adj. for w.&e. [1]Diode laser system. From Laser Devices, Inc.
He Ne FA-9	—	—	—	—	16	299.00	
He Ne FA-9P	—	—	—	—	14	299.00	
FA-4[1]	—	—	—	—	3.5	299.00	
LASERGRIPS							
LG-201[1]	633	Red-Orange	Glass	NA	—	349.00	Replaces existing grips with built-in laser high in the right grip panel. Integrated pressure sensitive pad in grip activates the laser. Also has master on/off switch. [1]For Beretta 92, 96, Colt 1911/Commander, Ruger MkII, S&W J-frames, SIG Sauer P228, P229. [2]For all Glock models. Option on/off switch. Requires factory installation. From Crimson Trace Corp.
GLS-630[2]	633	Red-Orange	Glass	NA	—	595.00	
LASERLYTE							
LLX-0006-140/090[1]	635/645	Red	—	—	1.4	159.95	[1]Dot/circle or dot/crosshair projection; black or stainless. [2]Also 635/645mm model. From TacStar Laserlyte.
WPL-0004-140/090[2]	670	Red	—	—	1.2	109.95	
TPL-0004-140/090[2]	670	Red	—	—	1.2	109.95	
T7S-0004-140[2]	670	Red	—	—	0.8	109.95	
LASERMAX							
Guide Rod	650/635	Red-Orange	Glass	40-120	.25	From 494.95	Replaces the recoil spring guide rod; includes a customized takedown lever that serves as the laser's instant on/off switch. For Glock, Smith & Wesson, Sigarms and Beretta. From LaserMax.
NIGHT STALKER							
S0 Smart	635	Red	NA	NA	2.46	515.00	Waterproof; LCD panel displays power remaining; programmable blink rate; constant or memory on. From Wilcox Industries Corp.

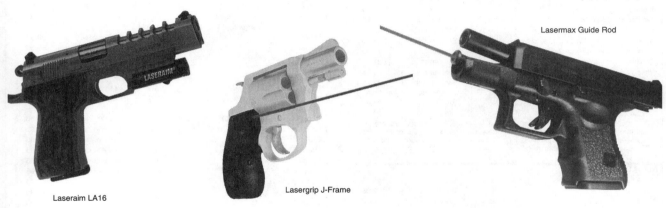

Laseraim LA16

Lasergrip J-Frame

Lasermax Guide Rod

CAUTION: PRICES SHOWN ARE SUPPLIED BY THE MANUFACTURER OR IMPORTER. CHECK YOUR LOCAL GUNSHOP.

53rd EDITION, 1999 **465**

Maker, Model, Type	Adjust.	Scopes	Price
AIMTECH			
Handguns			
AMT Auto Mag II 22 Mag.	No	Weaver rail	$56.99
AMT Auto Mag III 30 Carb.	No	Weaver rail	64.95
Auto Mag IV 45WM	No	Weaver rail	64.95
Astra 44 Mag Revolver	No	Weaver rail	63.25
Beretta/Taurus 92/99	No	Weaver rail	63.25
Browning Buckmark/Challenger II	No	Weaver rail	56.99
Browning Hi-Power	No	Weaver rail	63.25
CZ75	No	Weaver rail	63.25
EA9/P9 Tanfoglio frame	No	Weaver rail	63.25
Glock 17, 17L, 19, 22, 23	No	Weaver rail	63.25
Glock 20, 21	No	Weaver rail	63.25
Govt. 45 Autos/38 Super	No	Weaver rail	63.25
Hi-Standard 22 all makes	No	Weaver rail	63.25
Rossi 85/851/951 Revolvers	No	Weaver rail	63.25
Ruger Mk I, Mk II	No	Weaver rail	49.95
Ruger P89	No	Weaver rail	63.25
S&W K, L, N frames	No	Weaver rail	63.25
S&W K, L, N with tapped top strap[1]	No	Weaver rail	69.95
S&W Model 41 Target 22	No	Weaver rail	63.25
S&W Model 52 Target 38	No	Weaver rail	63.25
S&W 2nd Gen. 59/459/659	No	Weaver rail	56.99
S&W 3rd Gen. 59 Series	No	Weaver rail	69.95
S&W 422/622/2206/2206TGT	No	Weaver rail	56.99
S&W 645/745	No	Weaver rail	56.99
S&W Sigma	No	Weaver rail	64.95
Taurus PT908	No	Weaver rail	63.25
Taurus 44 6.5" bbl.	No	Weaver rail	69.95
Shotguns			
Benelli M-1 Super 90	No	Weaver rail	40.95
Benelli Montefeltro 12-ga.	No	Weaver rail	40.95
Benelli Super Black Eagle	No	Weaver rail	49.95
Browning Auto-5 12-ga.	No	Weaver rail	40.95
Browning BPS	No	Weaver rail	40.95
Ithaca 37/87 12-ga.	No	Weaver rail	40.95
Mossberg 500/Maverick 12-ga.[2]	No	Weaver rail	40.95
Mossberg 500/Maverick 20-ga.[2]	No	Weaver rail	40.95
Mossberg 835 Ulti-Mag[2]	No	Weaver rail	40.95
Mossberg 5500/9200[2]	No	Weaver rail	40.95
Remington 1100/1187 12-ga.[2]	No	Weaver rail	40.95
Remington 1100/1187 12-ga. LH	No	Weaver rail	40.95
Remington 1100/1187 20-ga.	No	Weaver rail	40.95
Remington 1100/1187 20-ga. LH	No	Weaver rail	40.95
Remington 870 12-ga.[2]	No	Weaver rail	40.95
Remington 870 12-ga. LH	No	Weaver rail	40.95
Remington 870 20-ga.	No	Weaver rail	40.95
Remington 870 20-ga. LH	No	Weaver rail	40.95
Winchester 1300[2]	No	Weaver rail	40.95
Winchester 1400[2]	No	Weaver rail	40.95
Rifles			
AR-15/M16	No	Weaver rail	21.95
Browning A-Bolt	No	Weaver rail	21.95
Browning BAR	No	Weaver rail	21.95
Browning BLR	No	Weaver rail	21.95
CVA Apollo	No	Weaver rail	21.95
Marlin 336	No	Weaver rail	21.95
Mauser Mark X	No	Weaver rail	21.95
Modern Muzzleloading MK85	No	Weaver rail	21.95
Remington 700 Short	No	Weaver rail	21.95
Remington 700 Long	No	Weaver rail	21.95
Remington 7400/7600	No	Weaver rail	21.95
Ruger 10/22	No	Weaver rail	21.95
Savage 110, 111, 113, 114, 115, 116	No	Weaver rail	21.95
Thompson/Center Thunderhawk	No	Weaver rail	21.95
Traditions Buckhunter	No	Weaver rail	21.95
White W Series	No	Weaver rail	21.95
White G Series	No	Weaver rail	21.95
White WG Series	No	Weaver rail	21.95
Winchester Model 70	No	Weaver rail	21.95
Winchester 94 AE	No	Weaver rail	21.95

All mounts no-gunsmithing, see-through/iron sight usable. Rifle mounts are solid see-through bases. All mounts accommodate standard split rings of all makes. From Aimtech, L&S Technologies, Inc. [3] blade sight and mount combination. [2]These models also available in RSP camouflage.

Maker, Model, Type	Adjust.	Scopes	Price
A.R.M.S.			
M16A1,A2,AR-15	No	Weaver rail	59.95
Multibase	No	Weaver rail	59.95
#19 acog Throw Lever Mt.	No	Weaver rail	150.00
#19 Weaver/STANAG Throw Lever Rail	No	Weaver rail	140.00

Maker, Model, Type	Adjust.	Scopes	Price
STANAG Rings	No	30mm	75.00
Throw Lever Rings	No	Weaver rail	95.00
Ring Inserts	No	1", 30mm	29.00
#38 Std. Swan Sleeve[1]	No	—	150.00
#39 A2 Plus Mod. Mt.	No	#39T rail	125.00
#39T Bi-level Rail	No	—	39.95
[1]Avail. in three lengths. From A.R.M.S., Inc.			
ARMSON			
AR-15[1]	No	1"	45.00
Mini-14[2]	No	1"	66.00
H&K[3]	No	1"	82.00
[1]Fastens with one nut. [2]Models 181, 182, 183, 184, etc. [3]Claw mount. From Trijicon, Inc.			
ARMSPORT			
100 Series[1]	No	1" rings, Low, med., high	10.75
104 22-cal.	No	1"	10.75
201 See-Thru	No	1"	13.00
1-Piece Base[2]	No	—	5.50
2-Piece Base[2]	No	—	2.75
[1]Weaver-type ring. [2]Weaver-type base; most popular rifles. Made in U.S. From Armsport.			
B-SQUARE			
Pistols (centerfire)			
Beretta 92/Taurus 99	No	Weaver rail	64.95
Colt M1911	E only	Weaver rail	64.95
Desert Eagle	No	Weaver rail	64.95
Glock	No	Weaver rail	64.95
H&K USP, 9mm and 40 S&W	No	Weaver rail	64.95
Ruger P85/89	E only	Weaver rail	64.95
SIG Sauer P226	E only	Weaver rail	64.95
Pistols (rimfire)			
Browning Buck Mark	No	Weaver rail	49.95
Colt 22	No	Weaver rail	49.95
Ruger Mk I/II, bull or taper	No	Weaver rail	49.95
Smith & Wesson 41, 2206	No	Weaver rail	49.95
Revolvers			
Colt Anaconda/Python	No	Weaver rail	64.95
Ruger Single-Six	No	Weaver rail	64.95
Ruger GP-100	No	Weaver rail	64.95
Ruger Blackhawk, Super	No	Weaver rail	64.95
Ruger Redhawk, Super	No	Weaver rail	64.95
Smith & Wesson K, L. N	No	Weaver rail	64.95
Taurus 66, 669, 689	No	Weaver rail	64.95
Rifles (sporting)			
Browning BAR, A-Bolt	No	Weaver rail	39.95
Marlin MR7	No	Weaver rail	39.95
Mauser 98 Large Ring	No	Weaver rail	39.95
Mauser 91/93/95/96 Small Ring	No	Weaver rail	39.95
Remington 700, 740, 742, 760	No	Weaver rail	39.95
Remington 7400, 7600	No	Weaver rail	39.95
Remington Seven	No	Weaver rail	39.95
Rossi 22 Pump	No	Weaver rail	39.95
Ruger Mini-14	W&E	Weaver rail	64.95
Ruger 96/22	No	Weaver rail	54.95
Ruger M77 (short and long)	No	Weaver rail	69.96
Ruger 10/22 (reg. and See-Thru)	No	Weaver rail	39.95
Savage 110-116, 10-16	No	Weaver rail	39.95
Modern Military (rings incl.)			
AK-47/MAC 90	No	Weaver rail	64.95
Colt AR-15 (See-Thru & Flat Top)	No	Weaver rail	74.95
FN/FAL/LAR (See-Thru rings)	No	Weaver rail	99.95
Classic Military (rings incl.)			
FN 49	No	Weaver rail	69.95
Hakim	No	Weaver rail	69.95
Mauser 38, 94, 96, 98	E only	Weaver rail	64.95
Mosin-Nagant 91	E only	Weaver rail	64.95
Air Rifles			
RWS, Diana, BSA, Gamo	W&E	11mm rail	59.95
Weihrauch, Anschutz, Beeman	W&E	11mm rail	59.95
Shotguns/Slug Guns			
Benelli Super 90 (See-Thru)	No	Weaver rail	49.95
Browning BPS, A-5 9 (See-Thru)	No	Weaver rail	49.95
Browning Gold 10/12/20-ga. (See-Thru)	No	Weaver rail	49.95
Ithaca 37, 87	No	Weaver rail	49.95
Mossberg 500/Mav. 88	No	Weaver rail	49.95
Mossberg 835/Mav. 91	No	Weaver rail	49.95
Remington 870/1100/11-87	No	Weaver rail	49.95
Remington SP10	No	Weaver rail	49.95
Winchester 1200-1500	No	Weaver rail	49.95
Prices shown for anodized black finish; add $10 for stainless finish. Partial listing of mounts shown here. Contact B-Square for complete listing and details.			

Maker, Model, Type	Adjust.	Scopes	Price
BEEMAN			
Two-Piece, Med.	No	1"	31.50
Deluxe Two-Piece, High	No	1"	33.00
Deluxe Two-Piece	No	30mm	41.00
Deluxe One-Piece	No	1"	50.00
Dampamount	No	1"	120.00

All grooved receivers and scope bases on all known air rifles and 22-cal. rimfire rifles (1/2" to 5/8"—6mm to 15mm).

Maker, Model, Type	Adjust.	Scopes	Price
BOCK			
Swing ALK[1]	W&E	1", 26mm, 30mm	349.00
Safari KEMEL[2]	W&E	1", 26mm, 30mm	149.00
Claw KEMKA[3]	W&E	1", 26mm, 30mm	224.00
ProHunter Fixed[4]	No	1", 26mm, 30mm	95.00

[1]Q.D.: pivots right for removal. For Steyr-Mannlicher, Win. 70, Rem. 700, Mauser 98, Dakota, Sako, Sauer 80, 90. Magnum has extra-wide rings, same price. [2]Heavy-duty claw-type reversible for front or rear removal. For Steyr-Mannlicher rifles. [3]True claw mount for bolt-action rifles. Also in extended model. For Steyr-Mannlicher, Win. 70, Rem. 700. Also avail. as Gunsmith Bases—bases not drilled or contoured—same price. [4]Extra-wode rings. Imported from Germany by GSI, Inc.

Maker, Model, Type	Adjust.	Scopes	Price
BURRIS			
Supreme (SU) One Piced (T)[1]	W only	1" split rings, 3 heights	1 piece base - 23.00-27.00
Trumount (TU) Two Piece (T)	W only	1" split rings, 3 heights	2 piece base - 21.00-30.00
Trumount (TU) Two Piece Ext.	W only	1" split rings	26.00
Browning 22-cal. Auto Mount[2]	No	1" split rings	20.00
1" 22-cal. Ring Mounts[3]	No	1" split rings	1"rings - 24.00-47.00
L.E.R. (LU) Mount Bases[4]	W only	1" split rings	24.00-51.00
L.E.R. No Drill-No Tap Bases[4,7,8]	W only	1" split rings	47.00-51.00
Extension Rings[5]	No	1" scopes	25.00-44.00
Ruger Ring Mount[6,9]	W only	1" split rings	44.00-61.00
Std. 1" Rings[9]	—	Low, medium, high heights	38.00-44.00
Zee Rings[9]	—	Fit Weaver bases; medium and high heights	29.00-44.00
Signature Rings	No	30mm split rings	64.00
Rimfire/Airgun Rings	W only	1" split rings, med. & high	24.00-47.00
Double Dovetail (DD) Bases	No	30mm Signature	23.00-26.00

[1]Most popular rifles. Universal rings, mounts fit Burris, Universal, Redfield, Leupold and Browning bases. Comparable prices. [2]Browning Standard 22 Auto rifle. [3]Grooved receivers. [4]Universal dovetail; accepts Burris, Universal, Redfield, Leupold rings. For Dan Wesson, S&W, Virginian, Ruger Blackhawk, Win. 94. [5]Medium standard front, extension rear, per pair. Low standard front, extension rear per pair. [6]Compact scopes, scopes with 2" bell for M77R. [7]Selected rings and bases available with matte Safari or silver finish. [8]For S&W K, L, N frames, Colt Python, Dan Wesson with 6" or longer barrels. [9]Also in 30mm.

Maker, Model, Type	Adjust.	Scopes	Price
CATCO			
Enfield Drop-In	No	1"	39.95

Uses Weaver-style rings (not incl.). No gunsmithing required. See-Thru design. From CATCO.

Maker, Model, Type	Adjust.	Scopes	Price
CLEAR VIEW			
Universal Rings, Mod. 101[1]	No	1" split rings	21.95
Standard Model[2]	No	1" split rings	21.95
Broad View[3]	No	1"	21.95
22 Model[4]	No	3/4" 7/8" 1"	13.95
SM-94 Winchester[5]	No	1" split rings	23.95
94 EJ[6]	No	1" split rings	21.95

[1]Most rifles by using Weaver-type base; allows use of iron sights. [2]Most popular rifles; allows use of iron sights. [3]Most popular rifles; low profile, wide field of view. [4]22 rifles with grooved receiver. [5]Side mount. [6]For Win. A.E. From Clear View Mfg.

Maker, Model, Type	Adjust.	Scopes	Price
CONETROL			
Huntur[1]	W only	1", split rings, 3 heights	76.92
Gunnur[2]	W only	1", split rings, 3 heights	99.96
Custom[3]	W only	1", split rings, 3 heights	119.88
One Piece Side Mount Base[4]	W only	1", 26mm, 26.5mm solid or split rings, 3 heights	—
Dap Tar Basses[5]	W only	1", 26mm, 26.5mm solid or split rings, 3 heights	—
Pistol Bases, 2 or 3-ring[6]	W only	1" scopes	—
Fluted Bases[7]	W only	Standard Conetrol rings	99.96
30mm Rings[8]	W only	26mm, 26.5mm, 30mm	79.92-97.96

[1]All popular rifles, including metric-drilled foreign guns. Price shown for base, two rings. Matte finish. [2]Gunnur grade has mirror-finished rings, satin-finish base. Price shown for base, two rings. [3]Custom grade has mirror-finished rings and mirror-finished, streamlined base. Price shown for base, two rings. [4]Win. 94, Krag, older split-bridge Mannlicher-Schoenauer, Mini-14, etc. Prices same as above. [5]For all popular guns with integral mounting provision, including Sako. BSA Ithacagun, Ruger, Tikka, H&K, BRNO—$39.96-$59.94—and many others. Also for grooved-receiver rimfires and air rifles. Prices same as above. [6]For XP-100, T/C Contender, Colt SAA, Ruger Blackhawk, S&W. [7]Sculptured two-piece bases as found on fine custom rifles. Price shown is for base alone. Also available unfinished—$79.92, or finished but unblued—$89.94. [8]30mm rings made in projectionless style, medium height only. Three-ring mount for T/C Contender and other pistols in Conetrol's three grades. Any Conetrol mount available in stainless or Teflon for double regular cost of grade.

Maker, Model, Type	Adjust.	Scopes	Price
CUSTOM QUALITY			
Custom See-Thru	No	Up to 44mm	29.95
Dovetail 101-1 See-Thru	No	1"	29.95
Removable Rings	No	1"	29.95
Solid Dovetail	No	1", 30mm vertically split	29.95
Dovetail 22 See-Thru	No	1"	29.95

Mounts for many popular rifles. From Custom Quality Products, Inc.

Maker, Model, Type	Adjust.	Scopes	Price
EAW			
Quick-Loc Mount	W&E	1", 26mm	253.00
	W&E	30mm	291.00
Magnum Fixed Mount	W&E	1", 26mm	198.00
	W&E	30mm	215.00

Fit most popular rifles. Avail. in 4 heights, 4 extensions. Reliable return to zero. Stress-free mounting. Imported by New England Custom Gun Svc.

Maker, Model, Type	Adjust.	Scopes	Price
GENTRY			
Feather-Light Bases	No	—	39.00-59.00
Feather-Light Rings	No	1", 30mm	48.00-65.00

Bases for Rem. Seven, 700, Mauser 98, Browning A-Bolt, Weatherby Mk. V, Win. 70, HVA, Dakota. Two-piece base for Rem. Seven, chrome moly or stainless. Rings in matte or regular blue, or stainless gray; four heights. From David Gentry.

Maker, Model, Type	Adjust.	Scopes	Price
GRIFFIN & HOWE			
Topmount[1]	No	1", 30mm	625.00
Sidemount[2]	No	1", 30mm	255.00
Garand Mount[3]	No	1"	255.00

[1]Quick-detachable, double-lever mount with 1" rings, installed; with 30mm rings $875.00. [2]Quick-detachable, double-lever mount with 1" rings; with 30mm rings $375.00; installed, 1" rings. $405.00; installed, 30mm rings $525.00. [3]Price installed, with 1" rings $405.00. From Griffin & Howe.

Maker, Model, Type	Adjust.	Scopes	Price
G. G. & G.			
Remington 700 Rail	No	Weaver base	115.00
Sniper Grade Rings	No	1", 30mm	145.00
M16/AR15 F.I.R.E. Std.	No	Weaver rail	65.00
M16/AR15 F.I.R.E. Scout	No	Weaver rail	75.00
Aimpoint Single Ring[2]	No	—	155.00
Galil Side Mount	No	Weaver rail	NA
H&K MP-5 Low Boy Mount[3]	No	Weaver rail	NA

[1]For M16/A3, AR15 flat top receivers; also in extended length. [2]For Aimpoint 5000 and Comp; quick detachable; spare barrety compartment. [3]Low profile; quick release. From G, G&G.

Maker, Model, Type	Adjust.	Scopes	Price
IRONSIGHTER			
Wide Ironsighter™	No	1" split rings	35.98
Ironsighter Center Fire[1]	No	1" split rings	32.95
Ironsighter S-94	No	1" split rings	39.95
Ironsighter AR-15/M-16[8]	No	1", 30mm	$103.95
Ironsighter 22-Cal.Rimfire			
Model #570[9]	No	1" split rings	32.95
Model #573[9]	No	30mm split rings	32.95
Model #722	No	1" split rings	17.75
Model #727	No	.875" split rings	17.75
Model #700[5]	No	1" split rings	32.95
Ruger Base Mounts[6]	No	1" split rings	83.95
Ironsighter Handguns[4]	No	1" split rings	83.95
Blackpowder Mount[7]	No	1"	32.95-76.95

[1]Most popular rifles, including Ruger Mini-14, H&R M700, and muzzleloaders. Rings have oval holes to permit use of iron sights. [2]For 1" dia. scopes. [3]For .875 dia. scopes. [4]For 1" dia. extended eye relief scopes. [5]702—Browning A-Bolt; 709—Marlin 39A. [6]732—Ruger 77/22 R&RS, No. 1, Ranch Rifle; 778 fits Ruger 77R, RS. Both 733, 778 fit Ruger Integral bases. Fits most popular blackpowder rifles, one model for Holden Ironsighter mounts, one for Weaver rings. [8]Model 716 with 1" #540 rings; Model 717 with 30mm #530 rings. [9]Fits mount rail on Rem. 522 Viper. Adj. rear sight is integral. Some models in stainless finish. From Ironsighter Co.

Maker, Model, Type	Adjust.	Scopes	Price
K MOUNT By KENPATABLE			
Shotgun Mount	No	1", laser or red dot device	49.95
SKS[1]	No	1"	39.95

Wrap-around design; no gunsmithing required. Models for Browning BPS, A-5 12-ga. Sweet 16, 20, Rem. 870/1100 (LTW, and L.H.), S&W 916, Mossberg 500, Ithaca 37 & 51 12-ga., S&W 1000/3000, Win. 1400. [1]Requires simple modification to gun. From KenPatable Ent.

Maker, Model, Type	Adjust.	Scopes	Price
KRIS MOUNTS			
Side-Saddle[1]	No	1",26mm split rings	12.98

Maker, Model, Type	Adjust.	Scopes	Price
Two-Piece (T)[2]	No	1", 26mm split rings	8.98
One Piece (T)[3]	No	1", 26mm split rings	12.98

[1]One-piece mount for Win. 94. [2]Most popular rifles and Ruger. [3]Blackhawk revolver. Mounts have oval hole to permit use of iron sights.

KWIK-SITE

Maker, Model, Type	Adjust.	Scopes	Price
KS-See-Thru[1]	No	1"	31.95
KS-22 See-Thru[2]	No	1"	23.95
KS-W94[3]	No	1"	39.95
Kwik-Site (cont.)			
Bench Rest	No	1'	31.95
KS-WEV	No	1'	31.95
KS-WEV-HIGH	No	1'	37.95
KS-T22 1"[4]	No	1'	23.95
KS-FL Flashlite[5]	No	Mini or C cell flashlight	49.95
KS-T88[6]	No	1"	11.95
KS-T89	No	30mm	14.95
KSN 22 See-Thru	No	1", 7/8"	20.95
KSN-T22	No	1", 7/8	20.95
KSN-M-16 See-Thru	No	1"	99.95
KS-202[1]	No	1"	31.95
KS-203	No	30mm	43.95
KSBP[7]	No	Intergral	76.95
KSSM8	No	1"	31.95
KSB Base Set	—	—	5.95
Combo Bases & Rings	No	1"	31.95

Bases interchangeable with Weaver bases. [1]Most rifles. Allows use of iron sights. [2]22-cal. rifles with grooved receivers. Allows use of iron sights. [3]Model 94, 94 Big Bore. No drilling or tapping. Also in adjustable model **$49.95.** [4]Non-See-Thru model for grooved receivers. [5]Allows Mag Lite or C or D, Mini Mag Lites to be mounted atop See-Thru mounts. [6]Fits any Redfield, Tasco, Weaver or Universal-style Kwik-Site dovetail base. [7]Blackpowder mount with integral base and sights. [8]Shotgun side mount. Bright blue, black matte or satin finish. Standard, high heights.

LASER AIM

Maker, Model, Type	Adjust.	Scopes	Price
	No	Laser Aim	19.99-69.00

Mounts Laser Aim above or below barrel. Avail. for most popular handguns, rifles, shotguns, including militaries. From Laser Aim Technologies, Inc.

LEUPOLD

Maker, Model, Type	Adjust.	Scopes	Price
STD Bases[1]	W only	One- or two-piece bases	23.80
STD Rings[1]	—	1" super low, low, medium, high	31.40
DD RBH Handgun mounts[3]	No	—	57.60
Dual Dovetail Bases[1,4]	No	—	23.80
Dual Dovetail Rings[9]	—	1", super low, low, low	31.40
Ring Mounts[5,6,7]	No	7/8", 1"	78.60
22 Rimfire[9]	No	7/8", 1"	58.20
Gunmaker Base[8]	W only	—	16.50
Quick Release Rings	—	1", low, med., high	31.90-68.90
Quick Release Bases[10]	No	1", one- or two-piece	69.30

[1]Rev. front and rear combinations; matte finish **$22.90.** [2]Avail. polished, matte or silver (low, med. only) finish. [3]Base and two rings; Casull, Ruger, S&W, T/C; add $5.00 for silver finish. [4] Rem. 700, Win. 70-type actions. [5]For Ruger No. 1, 77, 77/22; interchangeable with Ruger units. [6]For dovetailed rimfire rifles. [7]Sako; high, medium, low. [8]Must be drilled, tapped for each action. [9]13mm dovetail receiver. [10]BSA Monarch, Rem. 40x, 700, 721, 725, Ruger M77, S&W 1500, Weatherby Mark V, Vanguard, Win. M70.

MARLIN

Maker, Model, Type	Adjust.	Scopes	Price
One Piece QD (T)	No	1" split rings	10.10
Most Marlin lever actions			

MILLETT

Maker, Model, Type	Adjust.	Scopes	Price
Black Onyx Smooth	—	1", low, medium, high	31.15
Chaparral Engraved	—	engraved	46.15
One-piece Bases[6]	Yes	1"	23.95
Universal Two-Piece Bases			
700 Series	W only	Two-piece bases	25.15
FN Series	W only	Two-piece bases	25.15
70 Series[1]	W only	1", two-piece bases	25.15
Angle-Loc Rings[2]	W only	1", low, medium, high	32.20-47.20
Ruger 77 Rings[3]	—	1"	47.20
Shotgun Rings[4]	—	1"	28.29
Handgun Bases, Rings[5]	—	1"	34.60-69.15
30mm rings[7]	—	30mm	37.75-42.95
Extension Rings[8]	—	1"	35.65
See-Thru Mounts[9]	No	1"	27.95-32.95
Shotgun Mounts[10]	No	1"	49.95
Timber Mount	No	1"	78.00

BRNO, Rem. 40x, 700, 722, 725, 7400 Ruger 77 (round top), Marlin, Weatherby, FN Mauser, FN Brownings, Colt 57, Interarms Mark X, Parker-Hale, Savage 110, Sako (round receiver), many others. [1]Fits Win. M70 70XTR, 670, Browning BBR, BAR, BLR, A-Bolt, Rem. 7400/7600, Four, Six, Marlin 336, Win. 94 A. E., Sav. 110. [2]To fit Weaver-type bases. [3]Engraved. Smooth **$34.60.** [4]For Rem. 870, 1100; smooth. [5]Two and three-ring sets for Colt Python, Trooper, Diamondback, Peacekeeper, Dan Wesson, Ruger Redhawk, Super Redhawk. [6]Turn-in bases and Weaver-style for most popular rifles and T/C Contender, XP-100 pistols. [7]Both Weaver and turn-in styles; three heights. [8]Med. or high; ext. front—std. rear, ext. rear—std. front, ext. front—ext. rear; **$40.90** for double extension. [9]Many popular rifles, Knight MK-85, T/C Hawken, Renegade, Mossberg 500 Slugster, 835 slug. [10]For Rem. 879/1100, Win. 1200, 1300/1400, 1500, Mossberg 500. Some models available in nickel at extra cost. From Millett Sights. [11]For T/C Hawken and Renegade; See-Thru with adj. open sight inside.

MMC

Maker, Model, Type	Adjust.	Scopes	Price
AK[1]	No	—	39.95
FN FAL/LAR[2]	No	—	59.95

[1]Fits all AK derivative receivers; Weaver-style base; low-profile scope position. [2]Fits all FAL versions; Weaver-style base. From MMC.

PEM'S

Maker, Model, Type	Adjust.	Scopes	Price
22T Mount[1]	No	1"	17.95
The Mount[2]	Yes	1"	29.50

[1]Fit all 3/8" dovetail on rimfire rifles. [2]Base and ring set; for over 100 popular rifles; low, medium base. From Pem's.

RAM-LINE

Maker, Model, Type	Adjust.	Scopes	Price
Mini-14 Mount	Yes	1"	24.97

No drilling or tapping. Use std. dovetail rings. Has built-in shell deflector. Made of solid black polymer. From Ram-Line, Inc.

REDFIELD

Maker, Model, Type	Adjust.	Scopes	Price
NGS	No	Weaver rail	30.95-78.95
American Rings[6]	No	1", low, med., high	27.95-37.95
All American Aluminum Rings	No	1"	8.95-12.95
American Bases[6]	No	—	4.95-10.95
American Widefield See-Thru[7]	No	1"	15.95
JR-SR (T)[1]. One/two-piece bases.	W only	3/4", 1", 26mm, 30mm	JR-23.95-52.95 SR-18.95-22.95
Ring (T)[2]	No	3/4" and 1"	27.95-29.95
Three-Ring Pistol System SMP[3]	No	1", split rings (three)	49.95-52.95
Widefield See-Thru Mounts	No	1"	15.95
Ruger Rings[4]	No	1", med., high	34.95-36.95
Ruger 30mm[5]	No	1"	42.95
Midline Ext. Rings	No	1"	24.95

[1]Low, med. & high, split rings, Reversible extension front rings for 1". 2-piece bases for Sako. Colt Sauer bases **$39.95.** Med. Top Access JR rings nickel-plated, **$28.95.** SR two-piece ABN mount nickel-plated, **$22.95.** [2]Split rings for grooved 22s; 30mm, black matte **$42.95.** [3]Used with MP scopes for; S&W K, L or N frame, XP-100, M-14, M-1, Ger. K-43, T/C Contender, Ruger receivers. [4]For Ruger Model 77 rifles, medium and high; medium only for M77/22. [5]For Model 77. Also in matte finish **$45.95.** [6]Aluminun 22 groove mount **$14.95;** base and medium rings **$18.95.** [7]Fits American or Weaver-style base, Non-Gunsmithing mount system. For many popular shotguns, rifles, handguns and blackpowder rifles. Uses existing screw holes.

S&K

Maker, Model, Type	Adjust.	Scopes	Price
Insta-Mount (T) bases amd rings[1]	W only	Use S&K rings only	47.00-117.00
Conventional rings and bases[2]	W only	1" split rings	From 65.00
Skulptured Bases, Rings[2]	W only	1", 26mm, 30mm	From 65.00
Smooth Kontoured Rings[3]	Yes	1", 26mm, 30mm	90.00-120.00

[1]1903, A3, M1 Carbine, Lee Enfield #1. Mk.III, #4, #5, M1917, M98 Mauser, AR-15, AR-180, M-14, M-1, Ger. K-43, Mini-14, M1-A, Krag, AKM, Win. 94, SKS Type 56, Daewoo, H&K. [2]Most popular rifles already drilled and tapped. [3]No projections; weigh 1/2-oz. each; matte or gloss finish. Horizontally and vertically split rings, matte or high gloss.

SSK INDUSTRIES

Maker, Model, Type	Adjust.	Scopes	Price
T'SOB	No	1"	65.00-145.00
Quick Detachable	No	1"	From 160.00

Custom installation using from two to four rings (included). For T/C Contender, most 22 auto pistols, Ruger and other S.A. revolvers, Ruger, Dan Wesson, S&W, Colt DA revolvers. Black or white finish. Uses Kimber rings in two- or three-ring sets. In blue or SSK Khrome. For T/C Contender or most popular revolvers. Standard, non-detachable model also available, from $65.00.

SAKO

Maker, Model, Type	Adjust.	Scopes	Price
QD Dovetail	W only	1"	70.00-155.00

Sako, or any rifle using Sako action, 3 heights available, Stoeger, importer.

SPRINGFIELD, INC

Maker, Model, Type	Adjust.	Scopes	Price
M1A Third Generation	No	1" or 30mm	123.00
M1A Standard	NO	1" or 30mm	77.00
SAR-4800 Mount	No	—	96.00
M6 Scout Mount	No	—	29.00
Weaver-style bases. From Springfield, Inc.			

TALBOT

Maker, Model, Type	Adjust.	Scopes	Price
QD Bases	No	—	180.00-190.00
Rings	No	1", 30mm	40.00-60.00

Blue or stainless steel; standard or extended bases; rings in three heights. For most popular rifles. From Talbot QD Mounts.

Maker, Model, Type	Adjust.	Scopes	Price
TASCO			
World Class			
Aluminum Ringsets	Yes	1", 30mm	12.00-17.00
See-Thru	No	1"	19.00
Shotgun Bases	Yes	—	34.00
From Tasco.			
THOMPSON/CENTER			
Duo-Ring Mount[1]	No	1"	60.00
Weaver-Style Bases[2]	No	—	14.00
Weaver-Style Rings[3]	No	1"	28.00-39.00
Weaver-Style See-Thru Rings[4]	No	1"	26.00

[1]Attaches directly to T/C Contender bbl., no drilling/tapping; also for T/C M/L rifles, needs base adapter; blue or stainless; for M/L guns, **$59.80**. [2]For T/C ThunderHawk, FireHawk rifles; blue; silver, **$37.00**. [3]Medium and high; blue or silver finish. [4]For T.C FireHawk, ThunderHawk; blue; silver, **$29.00**. From Thompson/Center.

Maker, Model, Type	Adjust.	Scopes	Price
UNERTL			
1/4 Click[1]	Yes	3/4", 1" target scopes	Per set 186.00

[1]Unertl target or varmint scopes. Posa or standard mounts, less bases. From Unertl.

Maker, Model, Type	Adjust.	Scopes	Price
WARNE			
Premier Series (all steel)			
T.P.A. (Permanently Attacker)	No	1", 4 heights	78.00
		30mm, 2 heights	87.60
Sako	No	1", 4 heights	78.00
		30mm, 3 heights	87.60
Premier Series Rings fit Premier Series Bases			
Premier Series (all-steel Q.D. rings)			
Premier Series (all steel).	No	1", 4 heights	111.00
Quick detachable lever.		26mm, 2 heights	115.50
		30mm, 3 heights	121.50
Brno 19mm	No	1", 3 heights	111.50
		30mm, 2 heights	121.50
Brno 16mm		1" 2 heights	111.50
Ruger	No	1", 4 heights	111.50
		30mm, 3 heights	121.50
Ruger M77	No	1", 3 heights	111.50
		30mm, 2 heights	121.50
Sako Medium & Long Action	No	1", 4 heights	111.50
		30mm, 3 heights	121.50
Sako Short Action	No	1", 3 heights	111.50
All-steel One-Piece Base, ea.			35.00
All-Steel Two-Piece Base, ea.			12.50
Maxima Series (fits all Weaver-style bases)			
Permanently Attached[1]	No	1", 3 heights	31.40
		30mm, 3 heights	45.50
Adjustable Double Lever[2]	No	1", 3 heights	66.00
		30mm, 3 heights	73.40
Thumb Knob	No	1", 3 heights	54.50
		39mm, 3 heights	62.00
All-Steel Two-Piece Base, ea.			12.50

Vertically split rings with dovetail clamp, precise return to zero. Fit most popular rifles, handguns. Regular blue, matte blue, silver finish. [1]All-Steel, non-q.d. rings. [2]All-steel, q.d. rings. From Warne Mfg. Co.

Maker, Model, Type	Adjust.	Scopes	Price
WEAVER			
Detachable Mounts			
Top Mount	No	7/8", 1",30mm, 33mm	24.95-34.95
Side Mount	No	1", 1" long	13.95-34.95
Tip-Off Rings	No	7/8", 1"	21.95-32.95
Pivot Mounts	No	1"	38.95
Complete Mount Systems			
Pistol	No	1"	75.00-105.00
Rifle	No	1"	20.00
SKS Mount System	No	1"	49.75
Pro-View (no base required)	No	1"	15.00-17.00
Converta-Mount, 12-ga. (Rem. 870), Moss. 500)	No	1", 30mm	75.00
See-Thru Mounts			
Detachable	No	1"	27.00-32.00
System (no base required)	No	1"	15.00-35.00
Tip-Off	No	1"	15.00

Nearly all modern rifles, pistols, and shotguns. Detachable rings in standard, See-Thru, and extension styles, in Low, Medium, High or X-High heights; gloss (blued), silver and matte finishes to match scopes. Extension rings are only available in 1" High style and See-Thru X-tensions only in gloss finsih. Tip-Off rings only for 3/8" grooved receivers or 3/8"grooved adaptor bases; no base required. See-Thru & Pro-View mounts for most modern big bore rifles, some in silver. No Drill & Tap Pistol systems in gloss or silver for: Colt Python, Trooper, 357, Officer's Model; Ruger Single-Six, Security-Six (gloss finish only), Blackhawk, Super Blackhawk, Blackhawk SRM 357, Redhawk, Mini-14 Series (not Ranch), Ruger 22 Auto Pistols, Mark II; Smith & Wesson I- and current K-frames with adj. rear sights. Converta-Mount Systems in Standard and See-Under for: Mossberg 500 (12- and 20-ga.); Remington 870, 11-87 (12- and 20-ga. lightweight); Winchester 1200, 1300, 1400, 1500. Converta Brackets, Bases Rings also avail. for Beretta A303 and A390; Browning A-5, BPS Pump; Ithaca 37, 87. From Weaver.

Maker, Model, Type	Adjust.	Scopes	Price
WEIGAND			
Browning Buck Mark[1]	No	—	29.95
Colt 22 Aiutomatic[1]	No	—	19.95
Integramounts[2]	No	—	39.95-69.00
S&W Revolver[3]	No	—	29.95
Ruger 10/22[4]	No	—	14.95-39.95
Ruger Revolver[5]	No	—	29.95
Taurus Revolver[4]	No	—	29.95-65.00
T/C Encore Monster Mount	No	—	69.00
T/C Contender Monster Mount	No	—	69.00
Lightweight Rings	No	1", 30mm	29.95-39.95
1911, P-9 Scopemounts			
SM3[6]	No	Weaver rail	99.95
SRS 1911[7]	No	30mm	99.95
APCMNT[8]	No	—	69.95

[1]No gunsmithing. [2]S&W K, L, N frames; Taurus vent rib models; Colt Anaconda/Python; Ruger Redhawk; Ruger 10/22. [3]K, L, N frames. [4]Three models. [5]Redhawk, Blackhawk, GP-100. [6]3rd Gen.; drill and tap; without slots, **$59.95**. [7]Ringless design, silver only; SRS 1911-2, **$79.95**; for P-9, **$59.95**. [8]For Aimpoint Comp Red Dot scope, silver only. From Weigand Combat Handguns, Inc.

Maker, Model, Type	Adjust.	Scopes	Price
WIDEVIEW			
Premium 94 Angle Eject	No	1"	24.00
Premium See-Thru	No	1"	22.00
22 Premium See-Thru	No	3/4", 1"	16.00
Universal Ring Angle Cut	No	1'	24.00
Universal Ring Straight Cut	No	1"	22.00
Solid Mounts			
Lo Ring Solid[1]	No	1"	16.00
Hi Ring Solid[1]	No	1"	16.00
SR Rings	—	1", 30mm	18.64
22 Grooved Receiver	No	1"	16.00
94 Side Mount	No	1"	26.00
Blackpowder Mounts[2]	No	1"	22.00-44.00

[1]For Weaver-type base. Models for many, popular rifles. Low ring, high ring and grooved receiver types. [2]No drilling, tapping; for T/C Renegade, Hawken, CVA, Knight Traditions guns. From Wideview Scope Mount Corp.

Maker, Model, Type	Adjust.	Scopes	Price
WILLIAMS			
Sidemount with HCO Rings[1]	No	1", split or extension rings.	74.21
Sidemount, offset rings[2]	No	Same	61.08
Sight-Thru Mounts[3]	No	1", 7/8" sleeves	18.95
Streamline Mounts	No	1" (bases form rings).	25.70
Guideline Handgun[4]	No	1" split rings	61.75

[1]Most rifles, Br. S.M.L.E. (roune rec.) **$14.41** extra. [2]Mmost rifles including Win. 94 Big Bore. [3]Many modern rifles, including CVA Apollo, others with 1" octagon barrels. [4]No drilling, tapping required; heat treated alloy. For Ruger MkII Bull Barrel (**$61.75**); Streamline Top Mount for T.C Contender (**$14.15**), Scout Rifle, (**$24.00**), High Top Mount with sub-base (**$51.45**). From Williams Gunsight Co.

Maker, Model, Type	Adjust.	Scopes	Price
YORK			
M-1 Garand	Yes	1"	39.95

Centers scope over the action. No drilling, tapping or gunsmithing. Uses standard dovetail rings. From York M-1 Conversions.

NOTES

(S)—Side Mount (T)—Top Mount; 22mm=.866"; 25.4mm=1.024"; 26.5mm=1.045"; 30mm=1.81".

SPOTTING SCOPES

BAUSCH & LOMB PREMIER HDR 60mm objective, 15-45x zoom. Straight or 45 eyepiece. Field at 1000 yds. 125 ft. (15x), 68 ft. (45x). Length 13.0″; weight 38 oz. Interchangeable bayonet-style eyepieces.
Price: Straight or angled, 15-45x ... **$590.95**
Price: Angled, 15-45x ... **$638.95**
Price: 22x wide angle eyepiece ... **$86.95**
Price: 30x long eye relief eyepiece ... **$136.95**

BAUSCH & LOMB DISCOVERER 15x to 60x zoom, 60mm objective. Constant focus throughout range. Field at 1000 yds. 38 ft (60x), 150 ft. (15x). Comes with lens caps. Length 171/2″; weight 48.5 oz.
Price: ... **$391.95**

BAUSCH & LOMB ELITE 15x to 45x zoom, 60mm objective. Field at 1000 yds., 119-62 ft. Length is 12.2″; weight, 26.5 oz. Waterproof, armored. Tripod mount. Comes with black case.
Price: ... **$766.95**

BAUSCH & LOMB 77MM ELITE 20x, 30x or 20-60x zoom, 77mm objective. Field of view at 1000 yds. 175 ft. (20x), 78 ft. (30x), 108-62 ft. (zoom). Weight 51 oz. (20x, 30x), 54 oz. (zoom); length 16.8″. Interchangeable bayonet-style eyepieces. Built-in peep sight.
Price: With EDPrime Glass ... **$1,251.95**
Price: 20-60x zoom eyepiece ... **$335.95**
Price: 20x wide angle eyepiece ... **$221.95**
Price: 30x eyepiece ... **$221.95**

BURRIS 18-45x SPOTTER 60mm objective, 18-45x, constant focus, Field at 1000 yds. 112-63 ft.; weighs 29oz.; length 12.6". Camera adapters available.
Price: ... **$795.00**

BURRIS 20x SPOTTER 20x, 50mm objective. Straight type. Field at 100 yds. 15 ft. Length 10″; weight 21 oz. Rubber armor coating, multi-coated lenses, 22mm eye relief. Recessed focus adjustment. Nitrogen filled. Retractable sunshade.
Price: 24x 60mm ... **$598.00**
Price: 30x 60mm ... **$625.00**

BUSHNELL COMPACT TROPHY 50mm objective, 20-50x zoom. Field at 1000 yds. 84 ft. (20x), 48 ft. (50x). Length 11″; weight 16.5 oz. Black rubber armored, waterproof.
Price: ... **$325.95**

BUSHNELL BANNER SENTRY 18-36x zoom, 50mm objective. Field at 1000 yds. 115-78 ft. Length 14.5″, weight 27 oz. Black rubber armored. Built-in peep sight. Comes with tripod and hardcase.
Price: ... **$180.95**
Price: With 45 field eyepiece, includes tripod ... **$202.95**

BUSHNELL SENTRY WATERPROOF 18-36X zoom, 50mm objective. Field at 1000 yds. 115 ft. (18x), 38 ft. (36x). Overall length 14.7″, weighs 31 oz. Black rubber armored. Built-in peep sight.
Price: With tripod ... **$248.95**

BUSHNELL SPACEMASTER 20x-45x zoom. Long eye relief. Rubber armored, prismatic. 60mm objective. Field at 1000 yds. 125-65 ft. Minimum focus 20 ft. Length with caps 11.6″; weight 38.4 oz.
Price: With tripod, carrying case and 20-45x LER eyepiece. ... **$533.95**
Price: Interchangeable eyepieces 20x, 25x, 60x, each ... **$63.95**
Price: 22x Wide Angle ... **$86.95**
Price: 15-45x zoom eyepiece ... **$182.95**

BUSHNELL SPORTVIEW 12-36x 200m, 50mm objective. Field at 100 yds. 160 ft. (12x), 90 ft. (36x). Length 14.6″; weight 25 oz.
Price: With tripod and carrying case ... **$159.95**

KOWA TSN SERIES Offset 45 or straight body. 77mm objective, 20x WA, 25x, 25x LER, 30x WA, 40x, 60x, 77x and 20-60x zoom. Field at 1000 yds. 179 ft. (20xWA), 52 ft. (60x). Available with flourite lens.
Price: TSN-1 (without eyepiece) 45 offset scope ... **$696.00**
Price: TSN-2 (without eyepiece) Straight scope ... **$660.00**
Price: 20x W.A. (wide angle) eyepiece ... **$230.00**
Price: 25x eyepiece ... **$143.00**
Price: 25x LER (long eye relief) eyepiece ... **$214.00**
Price: 30x W.A. (wide angle) eyepiece ... **$266.00**
Price: 40x eyepiece ... **$159.00**
Price: 60x W.A. (wide angle) eyepiece ... **$230.00**
Price: 77x eyepiece ... **$235.00**
Price: 20-60x zoom eyepiece ... **$302.00**

KOWA TS-610 SERIES Offset 45 or straight body. 60mm objective, 20x WA, 25x, 25x LER, 27x WA, 40x and 20-60x zoom. Field at 1000 yds. 162 ft. (20x WA), 51 ft. (60x). Available with ED lens.
Price: TS-611 (without eyepiece) 45 offset scope ... **$510.00**
Price: TS-612 (without eyepiece) Straight scope ... **$462.00**
Price: 20x W.A. (wide angle) eyepiece ... **$111.00**
Price: 25x eyepiece ... **$95.00**
Price: 25x LER (long eye relief) eyepiece ... **$214.00**
Price: 27x W.A. (wide angle) eyepiece ... **$166.00**
Price: 40x eyepiece ... **$98.00**
Price: 20-60x zoom eyepiece ... **$207.00**

KOWA TS-9 SERIES Offset 45 , straight or rubber armored (straight only). 50mm objective, 15x, 20x and 11-33x zoom. Field at 1000 yds. 188 ft. (15x), 99 ft. (33x).
Price: TS-9B (without eyepiece) 45 offset scope ... **$223.00**
Price: TS-9C (without eyepiece) straight scope ... **$176.00**
Price: TS-9R (without eyepiece) straight rubber armored scope/black ... **$197.00**
Price: 15x eyepiece ... **$38.00**
Price: 20x eyepiece ... **$36.00**
Price: 11-33x zoom eyepiece ... **$122.00**

LEUPOLD 12-40x60 VARIABLE 60mm objective, 12-40x. Field at 100 yds. 17.5-5.3 ft.; eye relief 1.2″ (20x). Overall length 11.5″, weight 32 oz. Rubber armored.
Price: ... **$1,132.10**

LEUPOLD 25x50 COMPACT 50mm objective, 25x. Field at 100 yds. 8.3 ft.; eye relief 1″; length overall 9.4″; weight 20.5 oz.
Price: Armored model ... **$789.30**
Price: Packer Tripod ... **$92.90**

MIRADOR TTB SERIES Draw tube armored spotting scopes. Available with 75mm or 80mm objective. Zoom model (28x-62x, 80mm) is 117/8″ (closed), weighs 50 oz. Field at 1000 yds. 70-42 ft. Comes with lens covers.
Price: 28-62x80mm ... **$1,133.95**
Price: 32x80mm ... **$971.95**
Price: 26-58x75mm ... **$989.95**
Price: 30x75mm ... **$827.95**

MIRADOR SSD SPOTTING SCOPES 60mm objective, 15x, 20x, 22x, 25x, 40x, 60x, 20-60x; field at 1000 yds. 37 ft.; length 101/4″; weight 33 oz.
Price: 25x ... **$575.95**
Price: 22x Wide Angle ... **$593.95**
Price: 20-60x Zoom ... **$746.95**
Price: As above, with tripod, case ... **$944.95**

MIRADOR SIA SPOTTING SCOPES Similar to the SSD scopes except with 45 eyepiece. Length 121/4″; weight 39 oz.
Price: 25x ... **$809.95**
Price: 22x Wide Angle ... **$827.95**
Price: 20-60x Zoom ... **$980.95**

MIRADOR SSR SPOTTING SCOPES 50mm or 60mm objective. Similar to SSD except rubber armored in black or camouflage. Length 111/8″; weight 31 oz.
Price: Black, 20x ... **$521.95**
Price: Black, 18x Wide Angle ... **$539.95**
Price: Black, 16-48x Zoom ... **$692.95**
Price: Black, 20x, 60mm, EER ... **$692.95**
Price: Black, 22x Wide Angle, 60mm ... **$701.95**
Price: Black, 20-60x Zoom ... **$854.95**

MIRADOR SSF FIELD SCOPES Fixed or variable power, choice of 50mm, 60mm, 75mm objective lens. Length 93/4″; weight 20 oz. (15-32x50).
Price: 20x50mm ... **$359.95**
Price: 25x60mm ... **$440.95**
Price: 30x75mm ... **$584.95**
Price: 15-32x50mm Zoom ... **$548.95**
Price: 18-40x60mm Zoom ... **$629.95**
Price: 22-47x75mm Zoom ... **$773.95**

MIRADOR SRA MULTI ANGLE SCOPES Similar to SSF Series except eyepiece head rotates for viewing from any angle.
Price: 20x50mm ... **$503.95**
Price: 25x60mm ... **$647.95**
Price: 30x75mm ... **$764.95**
Price: 15-32x50mm Zoom ... **$692.95**
Price: 18-40x60mm Zoom ... **$836.95**
Price: 22-47x75mm Zoom ... **$953.95**

MIRADOR SIB FIELD SCOPES Short-tube, 45 scopes with porro prism design. 50mm and 60mm objective. Length 101/4″; weight 18.5 oz. (15-32x50mm); field at 1000 yds. 129-81 ft.
Price: 20x50mm ... **$386.95**
Price: 25x60mm ... **$449.95**
Price: 15-32x50mm Zoom ... **$575.95**
Price: 18-40x60mm Zoom ... **$638.95**

NIKON FIELDSCOPES 60mm and 78mm lens. Field at 1000 yds. 105 ft. (60mm, 20x), 126 ft. (78mm, 25x). Length 12.8″ (straight 60mm), 12.6″ (straight 78mm); weight 34.5-47.5 oz. Eyepieces available separately.
Price: 60mm straight body ... **$610.00**
Price: 60mm angled body ... **$740.00**
Price: 60mm straight ED body ... **$1,090.00**
Price: 60mm angled ED body ... **$1,190.00**
Price: 78mm straight ED body ... **$1,860.00**
Price: 78mm angled ED body ... **$1,980.00**
Price: Eyepieces (15x to 60x) ... **$134.00** to **$290.00**
Price: 15-45x eyepiece (25-56x for 78mm) ... **$281.00**

NIKON SPOTTING SCOPE 60mm objective, 20x fixed power or 15-45x zoom. Field at 1000 yds. 145 ft. (20x). Gray rubber armored. Straight or angled eyepiece. Weighs 44.2 oz., length 12.1″ (20x).
Price: 20x60 fixed ... **$426.00**
Price: 15-45x zoom ... **$658.00**

PENTAX 30x60 HG 60mm objective lens, 30x. Field of view 86 ft. at 1000 yds. Length 12.1″; weight 35 oz. Waterproof, rubber armor, multi-coated lenses. Comes with lens cap, case, neck strap.
Price: ... **$450.00**

REDFIELD AURORA PACK SPOTTER 60mm objective, 30x catadioptric lens system. Field at 100 yds, 9.5ft. Length 7.5"; weight 11.5oz.
Price: Scope only ... **$349.00**
Price: Kit (with 10" folding tripod, carrying case) ... **$419.00**

REDFIELD AURORA 20-60X 66mm objective, 20-60x zoom; straight or 45 eyepiece. Has integral pull-out sunshade, rubber-like finish. Field at 100 yds. 95-50 ft.; length 12.5″, weight 46 oz.
Price: ... **$942.95**
Price: Kit, includes softside carrying case, tripod, vinyl case ... **$1,045.95**

REDFIELD AURORA 27-80X 80mm objective, 27-80x zoom. Straight or 45 eyepiece. Has pull-out sunshade, armor coating. Field at 100 yds. 72-38 ft.; length 14.2″, weight 60 oz.
Price: **$1,148.95**
Price: Kit, includes soft side carrying case, tripod vinyl case **$1,251.95**
REDFIELD WIDEFIELD 20-45x SPOTTER 60mm objective, 20-45x. Field at 1000 yds. 45-63 ft. Length 12.5″; weight 23 oz. Black rubber armor coat. With vinyl carrying case.
Price: **$515.95**
Price: As above, with adjustable tripod, aluminum carrying case with shoulder strap........................... **$668.95**
SIMMONS 1280 50mm objective, 15-45x zoom. Black matte finish. Ocular focus. Peep finder sight. Waterproof.
Price: With tripod.. **$289.95**
SIMMONS 1281 60mm objective, 20-60x zoom. Black matte finish. Ocular focus. Peep finder sight. Waterproof.
Price: With tripod.. **$319.95**
SIMMONS 2482, 2483 PRESIDENTIAL 50mm objective, 20x fixed power. Waterproof. Nitrogen filled. Field at 1000 yds. 142 ft. Black rubber armored. Comes with case and tripod.
Price: 2482 .... **$451.95**
Price: 2483, 16-46x60mm **$659.95**
SIMMONS 77206 PROHUNTER 50mm objectives, 25x fixed power. Field at 1000yds. 110 ft.; length 10.25″; weighs 32oz. Black rubber armored.
Price: With tripod case....................................... **$173.95**
SIMMONS 41200 EUROSTYLE 50mm objective, 15-45x zoom. Field at 1000 yds. 104-41 ft.; length 16.75″; weighs 32.75 oz.
Price: With hard case and tripod **$103.95**
Price: 20-60x, Model 412001 .... **$142.95**
SWAROVSKI CT EXTENDIBLE SCOPES 75mm or 85mm objective, 20-60x zoom, or fixed 15x, 22x, 30x, 32x eyepieces. Field at 1000 yds. 135 ft. (15x), 99 ft. (32x); 99 ft. (20x), 5.2 ft. (60x) for zoom. Length 12.4″ (closed), 17.2″ (open) for the CT75; 9.7″/17.2″ for CT85. Weight 40.6 oz. (CT75), 49.4 oz. (CT85). Green rubber armored.
Price: CT75 body **$765.56**
Price: CT85 body **$1,094.44**
Price: 20-60x eyepiece....................................... **$343.33**
Price: 15x, 22x eyepiece..................................... **$232.22**
Price: 30x eyepiece.. **$265.55**
SWAROVSKI AT-80/ST-80 SPOTTING SCOPES 80mm objective, 20-60x zoom, or fixed 15x, 22x, 30x, 32x eyepieces. Field at 1000 yds. 135 ft. (15x), 99 ft. (32x); 99 ft. (20x), 52.5 ft. (60x) for zoom. Length 16″ (AT-80), 15.6″ (ST-80); weight 51.8 oz. Available with HD (high density) glass.
Price: AT-80 (angled) body **$1,094.44**
Price: ST-80 (straight) body **$1,094.44**
Price: With HD glass **$1,555.00**
Price: 20-60x eyepiece....................................... **$343.33**
Price: 15x, 22x eyepiece..................................... **$232.22**
Price: 30x eyepiece.. **$265.55**
SWIFT NIGHTHAWK M849U 80mm objective, 28-75x zoom, or fixed 25x, 31x, 50x, 75x eyepieces. Has rubber armored body, 1.8x optical finder, retractable lens hood, 45 eyepiece. Field at 1000 yds. 60 ft. (28x), 41 ft. (75x). Length 13.4 oz.; weight 39 oz.
Price: Body only **$850.00**
Price: 28-75x eyepiece **$285.00**
Price: Fixed eyepieces .... **$90.00 to $200.00**
Price: Model 849 (straight) body............................. **$780.00**
SWIFT NIGHTHAWK M850U 65mm objective, 22-60x zoom, or fixed 20x, 25x, 40x, 60x eyepieces. Rubber armored with a 1.8x optical finder, retractable lens hood. Field at 1000 yds. 83 ft. (22x), 52 ft. (60x). Length 12.3″; weight 30 oz. Has 45 eyepiece.
Price: Body only **$630.00**
Price: 22-60x eyepiece....................................... **$285.00**
Price: Fixed eyepieces .... **$90.00 to $200.00**
Price: Model 850 (straight) body............................. **$560.00**
SWIFT LEOPARD M837 50mm objective, 25x. Length 911/16″ to 101/2″. Weight with tripod 28 oz. Rubber armored. Comes with tripod.

Price: **$150.00**
SWIFT TELEMASTER M841 60mm objective. 15x to 60x variable power. Field at 1000 yds. 160 feet (15x) to 40 feet (60x). Weight 3.25 lbs.; length 18″ overall.
Price: **$399.50**
SWIFT M700R 10x-40x, 40mm objective. Field of 210 feet at 10x, 70 feet at 40x. Length 16.3″, weight 21.4 oz. Has 45 eyepiece.
Price: **$198.00**
SWIFT SEARCHER M839 60mm objective, 20x, 40x. Field at 1000 yds. 118 ft. (30x), 59 ft. (40x). Length 12.6″; weight 3 lbs. Rotating eyepiece head for straight or 45 viewing.
Price: **$460.00**
Price: 30x, 50x eyepieces, each.............................. **$65.00**
TASCO 29TZBWP WATERPROOF SPOTTER 60mm objective lens, 20-60x zoom. Field at 100 yds. 7 ft., 4 in. to 3 ft., 8 in. Black rubber armored. Comes with tripod, hard case.
Price: **$356.50**
TASCO WC28TZ WORLD CLASS SPOTTING SCOPE 50mm objective, 12-36x zoom. Field at 100 yds. World Class. 13-3.8 ft. Comes with tripod and case.
Price: **$220.00**
TASCO CW5001 COMPACT ZOOM 50mm objective, 12-36x zoom. Field at 100 yds. 16 ft., 9 in. Includes photo adapter tube, tripod with panhead lever, case.
Price: **$280.00**
TASCO 3700WP WATERPROOF SPOTTER 50mm objective, 18-36x zoom. Field at 100 yds. 12ft., 6 in. to 7 ft., 9 in. Black rubber armored. Comes with tripod, hard case.
Price: **$288.60**
TASCO 3700, 3701 SPOTTING SCOPE 50mm objective. 18-36x zoom. Field at 100 yds. 12 ft., 6 in. to 7 ft., 9 in. Black rubber armored.
Price: Model 3700 (black, with tripod, case)................. **$237.00**
Price: Model 3701 (as above, brown camo).................... **$237.00**
TASCO 21EB ZOOM 50mm objective lens, 15-45x zoom. Field at 100 yds. 11 ft. (15x). Weight 22 oz.; length 18.3″ overall. Comes with panhead lever tripod.
Price: **$119.00**
TASCO 22EB ZOOM 60mm objective lens, 20-60x zoom. Field at 100 yds. 7 ft., 2 in. (20x). Weight 28 oz.; length 21.5″ overall. Comes with micro-adjustable tripod.
Price: **$183.00**
UNERTL "FORTY-FIVE" 54mm objective. 20x (single fixed power). Field at 100 yds. 10',10″; eye relief 1″; focusing range infinity to 33 ft. Weight about 32 oz.; overall length 153/4″. With lens covers.
Price: With multi-layer lens coating.......................... **$662.00**
Price: With mono-layer magnesium coating.................... **$572.00**
UNERTL STRAIGHT PRISMATIC 63.5mm objective, 24x. Field at 100 yds., 7 ft. Relative brightness, 6.96. Eye relief 1/2″. Weight 40 oz.; length closed 19″. Push-pull and screw-focus eyepiece. 16x and 32x eyepieces **$125.00** each.
Price: **$515.00**
UNERTL 20x STRAIGHT PRISMATIC 54mm objective, 20x. Field at 100 yds. 8.5 ft. Relative brightness 6.1. Eye relief 1/2″. Weight 36 oz.; length closed 131/2″. Complete with lens covers.
Price: **$477.00**
UNERTL TEAM SCOPE 100mm objective. 15x, 24x, 32x eyepieces. Field at 100 yds. 13 to 7.5 ft. Relative brightness, 39.06 to 9.79. Eye relief 2″ to 11/2″. Weight 13 lbs.; length 297/8″ overall. Metal tripod, yoke and wood carrying case furnished (total weight 80 lbs.).
Price: **$2,810.00**
WEAVER 20x50 50mm objective. Field of view 12.4 ft at 100 yds. Eye relief .85″; weighs 21 oz.; overall length 10″. Waterproof, armored.
Price: **$352.95**
WEAVER 15-40x60 ZOOM 60mm objective. 15-40x zoom. Field at 100 yds. 119 ft. (15x), 66 ft. (60x). Overall length 12.5″, weighs 26 oz. Waterproof, armored.
Price: **$528.95**

AAFTA News (M)
5911 Cherokee Ave., Tampa, FL 33604. Official newsletter of the American Airgun Field Target Assn.

Action Pursuit Games Magazine (M)
CFW Enterprises, Inc., 4201 W. Vanowen Pl., Burbank, CA 91505 818-845-2656. $3.95 single copy U.S., $4.50 Canada. Editor: Jessica Sparks, 818-845-2656. World's leading magazine of paintball sports.

Air Gunner Magazine
4 The Courtyard, Denmark St., Wokingham, Berkshire RG11 2AZ, England/011-44-734-771677. $U.S. $44 for 1 yr. Leading monthly airgun magazine in U.K.

Airgun Ads
Box 33, Hamilton, MT 59840/406-363-3805; Fax: 406-363-4117. $35 1 yr. (for first mailing; $20 for second mailing; $35 for Canada and foreign orders.) Monthly tabloid with extensive For Sale and Wanted airgun listings.

The Airgun Letter
Gapp, Inc., 4614 Woodland Rd., Ellicott City, MD 21042-6329/410-730-5496; Fax: 410-730-9544; e-mail: staff@airgnltr.net; http://www.airgunletter.com. $21 U.S., $24 Canada, $27 Mexico and $33 other foreign orders, 1 yr. Monthly newsletter for airgun users and collectors.

Airgun World
4 The Courtyard, Denmark St., Wokingham, Berkshire RG40 2AZ, England/011-44-734-771677. Call for subscription rates. Oldest monthly airgun magazine in the U.K., now a sister publication to *Air Gunner.*

Alaska Magazine
4220 B St., Suite 210, Achorage, AK 99503. $24.00 yr. Hunting, Fishing and Life on the Last Frontier articles of Alaska and western Canada. Outdoors Editor, Ken Marsh.

American Firearms Industry
Nat'l. Assn. of Federally Licensed Firearms Dealers, 2455 E. Sunrise Blvd., Suite 916, Ft. Lauderdale, FL 33304. $35.00 yr. For firearms retailers, distributors and manufacturers.

American Guardian
NRA, 11250 Waples Mill Rd., Fairfax, VA 22030. Publications division. $15.00 1 yr. Magazine features personal protection; home-self-defense; family recreation shooting; women's issues; etc.

American Gunsmith
Belvoir Publications, Inc., 75 Holly Hill Lane, Greenwich, CT 06836-2626/203-661-6111. $49.00 (12 issues). Technical journal of firearms repair and maintenance.

American Handgunner
591 Camino de la Reina, Suite 200, San Diego, CA 92108. $16.95 yr. Articles for handgun enthusiasts, competitors, police and hunters.

American Hunter (M)
National Rifle Assn., 11250 Waples Mill Rd., Fairfax, VA 22030 (Same address for both.) Publications Div. $35.00 yr. Wide scope of hunting articles.

American Rifleman (M)
National Rifle Assn., 11250 Waples Mill Rd., Fairfax, VA 22030 (Same address for both.) Publications Div. $35.00 yr. Firearms articles of all kinds.

American Single Shot Rifle News* (M)
Membership Secy. Tim Mather, 1180 Easthill SE, N. Canton, Ohio. Annual dues $20 for 6 issues. Official journal of the American Single Shot Rifle Assn.

American Survival Guide
McMullen Angus Publishing, Inc., 774 S. Placentia Ave., Placentia, CA 92670-6846. 12 issues $19.95/714-572-2255; FAX: 714-572-1864.

Arms Collecting (Q)
Museum Restoration Service, P.O. Box 70, Alexandria Bay, NY 13607-0070. $22.00 yr.; $62.00 3 yrs.; $112.00 5 yrs.

Australian Shooters Journal
Sporting Shooters' Assn. of Australia, Inc., P.O. Box 2066, Kent Town SA 5071, Australia. $45.00 yr. locally; $55.00 yr. overseas surface mail only. Hunting and shooting articles.

The Backwoodsman Magazine
P.O. Box 627, Westcliffe, CO 81252. $16.00 for 6 issues per yr.; $30.00 for 2 yrs.; sample copy $2.75. Subjects include muzzle-loading, woodslore, primitive survival, trapping, homesteading, blackpowder cartridge guns, 19th century how-to.

Black Powder Cartridge News (Q)
SPG, Inc., P.O. Box 761, Livingston, MT 59047/Phone/Fax: 406-222-8416. $17 yr. (4 issues) ($6 extra 1st class mailing). For the blackpowder cartridge enthusiast.

Blackpowder Hunting (M)
Intl. Blackpowder Hunting Assn., P.O. Box 1180Z, Glenrock, WY 82637/307-436-9817. $20.00 1 yr.; $36.00 2 yrs. How-to and where-to features by experts on hunting; shooting; ballistics; traditional and modern blackpowder rifles, shotguns, pistols and cartridges.

Black Powder Times
P.O. Box 234, Lake Stevens, WA 98258. $20.00 yr.; add $5 per year for Canada, $10 per year other foreign. Tabloid newspaper for blackpowder activities; test reports.

Blade Magazine*
700 East State St., Iola, WI 54990-0001. $19.95 for 12 issues. Foreign price (including Canada-Mexico) $50.00. A magazine for all enthusiasts of handmade, factory and antique knives.

Caliber
GFI-Verlag, Theodor-Heuss Ring 62, 50668 K"ln, Germany. For hunters, target shooters and reloaders.

The Caller (Q) (M)
National Wild Turkey Federation, P.O. Box 530, Edgefield, SC 29824. Tabloid newspaper for members; 4 issues per yr. (membership fee $25.00)

Cartridge Journal (M)
Robert Mellichamp, 907 Shirkmere, Houston, TX 77008/713-869-0558. Dues $12 for U.S. and Canadian members (includes the newsletter); 6 issues.

The Cast Bullet*(M)
Official journal of The Cast Bullet Assn. Director of Membership, 203 E. 2nd St., Muscatine, IA 52761. Annual membership dues $14, includes 6 issues.

COLTELLI, che Passione (Q)
Casella postale N.519, 20101 Milano, Italy/Fax:02-48402857. $15 1 yr., $27 2 yrs. Covers all types of knives—collecting, combat, historical. Italian text.

Combat Handguns*
Harris Publications, Inc., 1115 Broadway, New York, NY 10010. Single copy $3.25 U.S.A.; $3.75 Canada.

Deer & Deer Hunting Magazine
700 E. State St., Iola, WI 54990-0001. $18.95 yr. (8 issues)

The Derringer Peanut (M)
The National Association of Derringer Collectors, P.O. Box 20572, San Jose, CA 95160. A newsletter dedicated to developing the best derringer information. Write for details.

Deutsches Waffen Journal
Journal-Verlag Schwend GmbH, Postfach 100340, D-74503 Schwäbisch Hall, Germany/0791-404-500; FAX:0791-404-505 and 404-424. DM102 p. yr. (interior); DM125.30 (abroad), postage included. Antique and modern arms and equipment. German text.

Double Gun Journal
P.O. Box 550, East Jordan, MI 49727/800-447-1658. $35 for 4 issues.

Ducks Unlimited, Inc. (M)
1 Waterfowl Way, Memphis, TN 38120

The Engraver (M) (Q)
P.O. Box 4365, Estes Park, CO 80517/970-586-2388; Fax: 970-586-0394. Mike Dubber, editor. The journal of firearms engraving.

The Field
King's Reach Tower, Stamford St., London SE1 9LS England. £36.40 U.K. 1 yr.; 49.90 (overseas, surface mail) yr.; £82.00 (overseas, air mail) yr. Hunting and shooting articles, and all country sports.

Field & Stream
Times Mirror Magazines, Two Park Ave., New York, NY 10016. $11.94 yr. Monthly shooting column. Articles on hunting and fishing.

Field Tests
Belvoir Publications, Inc., 75 Holly Hill Lane; P.O. Box 2626, Greenwich, CT 06836-2626/203-661-6111; 800-829-3361 (subscription line). U.S. & Canada $29 1 yr.; $58 2 yrs.; all other countries $45 1 yr., $90 2 yrs. (air).

Fur-Fish-Game
A.R. Harding Pub. Co., 2878 E. Main St., Columbus, OH 43209. $15.95 yr. "Gun Rack" column by Don Zutz.

The Gottlieb-Tartaro Report
Second Amendment Foundation, James Madison Bldg., 12500 NE 10th Pl., Bellevue, WA 98005/206-454-7012;Fax:206-451-3959. $30 for 12 issues. An insiders guide for gun owners.

Gray's Sporting Journal
Gray's Sporting Journal, P.O. Box 1207, Augusta, GA 30903. $36.95 per yr. for 6 issues. Hunting and fishing journals. Expeditions and Guides Book (Annual Travel Guide).

Gun List†
700 E. State St., Iola, WI 54990. $32.98 yr. (26 issues); $59.98 2 yrs. (52 issues). Indexed market publication for firearms collectors and active shooters; guns, supplies and services.

Gun News Digest (Q)
Second Amendment Fdn., P.O. Box 488, Station C, Buffalo, NY 14209/716-885-6408;Fax:716-884-4471. $10 U.S.; $20 foreign.

The Gun Report
World Wide Gun Report, Inc., Box 38, Aledo, IL 61231-0038. $33.00 yr. For the antique and collectable gun dealer and collector.

Gunmaker (M) (Q)
ACGG, P.O. Box 812, Burlington, IA 52601-0812. The journal of custom gunmaking.

The Gunrunner
Div. of Kexco Publ. Co. Ltd., Box 565G, Lethbridge, Alb., Canada T1J 3Z4. $23.00 yr., sample $2.00. Monthly newspaper, listing everything from antiques to artillery.

Gun Show Calendar (Q)
700 E. State St., Iola, WI 54990. $14.95 yr. (4 issues). Gun shows listed; chronologically and by state.

Gun Tests
11 Commerce Blvd., Palm Coast, FL 32142. The consumer resource for the serious shooter. Write for information.

Gun Trade News
Bruce Publishing Ltd., P.O. Box 82, Wantage, Ozon OX12 7A8, England/44-1-235-771770; Fax: 44-1-235-771848. Britain's only "trade only" magazine exclusive to the gun trade.

Gun Week†
Second Amendment Foundation, P.O. Box 488, Station C, Buffalo, NY 14209. $35.00 yr. U.S. and possessions; $40.00 yr. other countries. Tabloid paper on guns, hunting, shooting and collecting (36 issues).

Gun World
Y-Visionary Publishing, LP 265 South Anita Drive, Ste. 120, Orange, CA 92868. $21.97 yr.; $34.97 2 yrs. For the hunting, reloading and shooting enthusiast.

Guns & Ammo
Petersen Publishing Co., 6420 Wilshire Blvd., Los Angeles, CA 90048. $21.94 yr. Guns, shooting, and technical articles.

Guns
Guns Magazine, P.O. Box 85201, San Diego, CA 92138. $19.95 yr.; $34.95 2 yrs.; $46.95 3 yrs. In-depth articles on a wide range of guns, shooting equipment and related accessories for gun collectors, hunters and shooters.

Guns Review
Ravenhill Publishing Co. Ltd., Box 35, Standard House, Bonhill St., London EC 2A 4DA, England. £20.00 sterling (approx. U.S. $38 USA & Canada) yr. For collectors and shooters.

H.A.C.S. Newsletter (M)
Harry Moon, Pres., P.O. Box 50117, South Slope RPO, Burnaby BC, V5J 5G3, Canada/604-438-0950;Fax:604-277-3646. $25 p. yr. U.S. and Canada. Official newsletter of The Historical Arms Collectors of B.C. (Canada).

Handgunner*
Richard A.J. Munday, Seychelles house, Brightlingsen, Essex CO7 ONN, England/012063-305201. £ 18.00 (sterling).

Handloader*
Wolfe Publishing Co., 6471 Airpark Dr., Prescott, AZ 86301/520-445-7810;Fax:520-778-5124. $22.00 yr. The journal of ammunition reloading.

INSIGHTS*
NRA, 11250 Waples Mill Rd., Fairfax, VA 22030. Editor, John E. Robbins. $15.00 yr., which includes NRA junior membership; $10.00 for adult subscriptions (12 issues). Plenty of details for the young hunter and target shooter; emphasizes gun safety, marksmanship training, hunting skills.

International Arms & Militaria Collector (Q)
Arms & Militaria Press, P.O. Box 80, Labrador, Qld. 4215, Australia. A$39.50 yr. (U.S. & Canada), 2 yrs. A$77.50; A$37.50 (others), 1 yr., 2 yrs. $73.50 all air express mail; surface mail is less. Editor: Ian D. Skennerton.

International Shooting Sport*/UIT Journal
International Shooting Union (UIT), Bavariaring 21, D-80336 Munich, Germany. Europe: (Deutsche Mark) DM44.00 yr., 2 yrs. DM83.00; outside Europe: DM50.00 yr., 2 yrs. DM95.00 (air mail postage included.) For international sport shooting.

Internationales Waffen-Magazin
Habegger-Verlag Zürich, Postfach 9230, CH-8036 Zürich, Switzerland. SF 105.00 (approx. U.S. $73.00) surface mail for 10 issues. Modern and antique arms, self-defense. German text; English summary of contents.

The Journal of the Arms & Armour Society (M)
A. Dove, P.O. Box 10232, London, SW19 2ZD England. £15.00 surface mail; £20.00 airmail sterling only yr. Articles for the historian and collector.

Journal of the Historical Breechloading Smallarms Assn.
Published annually. P.O. Box 12778, London, SE1 6XB, England. $21.00 yr. Articles for the collector plus mailings of short articles on specific arms, reprints, newsletters, etc.

Knife World
Knife World Publications, P.O. Box 3395, Knoxville, TN 37927. $15.00 yr.; $25.00 2 yrs. Published monthly for knife enthusiasts and collectors. Articles on custom and factory knives; other knife-related interests, monthly column on knife identification, military knives.

Man At Arms*
P.O. Box 460, Lincoln, RI 02865. $27.00 yr., $52.00 2 yrs. plus $8.00 for foreign subscribers. The N.R.A. magazine of arms collecting-investing, with excellent articles for the collector of antique arms and militaria.

The Mannlicher Collector (Q)(M)
Mannlicher Collectors Assn., Inc., P.O. Box 1455, Kalispell, MT 59903. $20 yr. subscription included i. membership.

MAN/MAGNUM
S.A. Man (Pty) Ltd., P.O. Box 35204, Northway, Durban 4065, Republic of South Africa. SA Rand 200.00 for 12 issues. Africa's only publication on hunting, shooting, firearms, bushcraft, knives, etc.

The Marlin Collector (M)
R.W. Paterson, 407 Lincoln Bldg., 44 Main St., Champaign, IL 61820.

Muzzle Blasts (M)
National Muzzle Loading Rifle Assn., P.O. Box 67, Friendship, IN 47021. $30.00 yr. annual membership. For the blackpowder shooter.

Muzzleloader Magazine*
Scurlock Publishing Co., Inc., Dept. Gun, Route 5, Box 347-M, Texarkana, TX 75501. $18.00 U.S.; $22.50 U.S. for foreign subscribers a yr. The publication for blackpowder shooters.

National Defense (M)*
American Defense Preparedness Assn., Two Colonial Place, Suite 400, 2101 Wilson Blvd., Arlington, VA 22201-3061/703-522-1820; FAX: 703-522-1885. $35.00 yr. Articles on both military and civil defense field, including weapons, materials technology, management.

National Knife Magazine (M)
Natl. Knife Coll. Assn., 7201 Shallowford Rd., P.O. Box 21070, Chattanooga, TN 37424-0070. Membership $35 yr.; $65.00 International yr.

National Rifle Assn. Journal (British) (Q)
Natl. Rifle Assn. (BR.), Bisley Camp, Brookwood, Woking, Surrey, England. GU24, OPB. £24.00 Sterling including postage.

National Wildlife*
Natl. Wildlife Fed., 1400 16th St. NW, Washington, DC 20036, $16.00 yr. (6 issues); *International Wildlife*, 6 issues, $16.00 yr. Both, $22.00 yr., includes all membership benefits. Write attn.: Membership Services Dept., for more information.

New Zealand GUNS*
Waitekauri Publishing, P.O. 45, Waikino 3060, New Zealand. $NZ90.00 (6 issues) yr. Covers the hunting and firearms scene in New Zealand.

New Zealand Wildlife (Q)
New Zealand Deerstalkers Assoc., Inc., P.O. Box 6514, Wellington, N.Z. $30.00 (N.Z.). Hunting, shooting and firearms/game research articles.

North American Hunter* (M)
P.O. Box 3401, Minnetonka, MN 55343/612-936-9333; e-mail: huntingclub@pclink.com. $18.00 yr. (7 issues). Articles on all types of North American hunting.

Outdoor Life
Times Mirror Magazines, Two Park Ave., New York, NY 10016. Special 1-yr. subscription, $11.97. Extensive coverage of hunting and shooting. Shooting column by Jim Carmichel.

La Passion des Courteaux (Q)
Phenix Editions, 25 rue Mademoiselle, 75015 Paris, France. French text.

Paintball Games International Magazine
Aceville Publications, Castle House, 97 High St., Colchester, Essex, England CO1 1TH/011-44-206-564840. Write for subscription rates. Leading magazine in the U.K. covering competitive paintball activities.

Paintball News
PBN Publishing, P.O. Box 1608, 24 Henniker St., Hillsboro, NH 03244/603-464-6080. $35 U.S. 1 yr. Bi-weekly. Newspaper covering the sport of paintball, new product reviews and industry features.

Paintball Sports (Q)
Paintball Publications, Inc., 540 Main St., Mount Kisco, NY 10549/941-241-7400. $24.75 U.S. 1 yr., $32.75 foreign. Covering the competitive paintball scene.

Performance Shooter
Belvoir Publications, Inc., 75 Holly Hill Lane, Greenwich, CT 06836-2626/203-661-6111. $45.00 yr. (12 issues). Techniques and technology for improved rifle and pistol accuracy.

Petersen's HUNTING Magazine
Petersen Publishing Co., 6420 Wilshire Blvd., Los Angeles, CA 90048. $19.94 yr.; Canada $29.34 yr.; foreign countries $29.94 yr. Hunting articles for all game; test reports.

P.I. Magazine
America's Private Investigation Journal, 755 Bronx Dr., Toledo, OH 43609. Chuck Klein, firearms editor with column about handguns.

Pirsch
BLV Verlagsgesellschaft mbH, Postfach 400320, 80703 Munich, Germany/089-12704-0;Fax:089-12705-354. German text.

Point Blank
Citizens Committee for the Right to Keep and Bear Arms (sent to contributors), Liberty Park, 12500 NE 10th Pl., Bellevue, WA 98005

POINTBLANK (M)
Natl. Firearms Assn., Box 4384 Stn. C, Calgary, AB T2T 5N2, Canada. Official publication of the NFA.

The Police Marksman*
6000 E. Shirley Lane, Montgomery, AL 36117. $17.95 yr. For law enforcement personnel.

Police Times (M)
3801 Biscayne Blvd., Miami, FL 33137/305-573-0070.

Popular Mechanics
Hearst Corp., 224 W. 57th St., New York, NY 10019. $15.94 yr. Firearms, camping, outdoor oriented articles.

Precision Shooting
Precision Shooting, Inc., 222 McKee St., Manchester, CT 06040. $32.00 yr. U.S. Journal of the International Benchrest Shooters, and target shooting in general. Also considerable coverage of varmint shooting, as well as big bore, small bore, schuetzen, lead bullet, wildcats and precision reloading.

Rifle*
Wolfe Publishing Co., 6471 Airpark Dr., Prescott, AZ 86301/520-445-7810; Fax: 520-778-5124. $19.00 yr. The sporting firearms journal.

Rifle's Hunting Annual
Wolfe Publishing Co., 6471 Airpark Dr., Prescott, AZ 86301/520-445-7810; Fax: 520-778-5124. $4.99 Annual. Dedicated to the finest pursuit of the hunt.

Rod & Rifle Magazine
Lithographic Serv. Ltd., P.O. Box 38-138, Wellington, New Zealand. $50.00 yr. (6 issues). Hunting, shooting and fishing articles.

Safari* (M)
Safari Magazine, 4800 W. Gates Pass Rd., Tucson, AZ 85745/602-620-1220. $55.00 (6 times). The journal of big game hunting, published by Safari Club International. Also publish *Safari Times*, a monthly newspaper, included in price of $55.00 national membership.

Second Amendment Reporter
Second Amendment Foundation, James Madison Bldg., 12500 NE 10th Pl., Bellevue, WA 98005. $15.00 yr. (non-contributors).

Shooter's News
23146 Lorain Rd., Box 349, North Olmsted, OH 44070/216-979-5258;Fax:216-979-5259. $29 U.S. 1 yr., $54 2 yrs.; $52 foreign surface. A journal dedicated to precision riflery.

Shooting Industry
Publisher's Dev. Corp., 591 Camino de la Reina, Suite 200, San Diego, CA 92108. $50.00 yr. To the trade $25.00.

Shooting Sports USA
National Rifle Assn. of America, 11250 Waples Mill Road, Fairfax, VA 22030. Annual subscriptions for NRA members are $5 for classified shooters and $10 for non-classified shooters. Non-NRA member subscriptions are $15. Covering events, techniques and personalities in competitive shooting.

Shooting Sportsman*
P.O. Box 11282, Des Moines, IA 50340/800-666-4955 (for subscriptions). Editorial: P.O. Box 1357, Camden, ME 04843. $19.95 for six issues. The magazine of wingshooting and fine guns.

The Shooting Times & Country Magazine (England)†
IPC Magazines Ltd., King's Reach Tower, Stamford St, 1 London SE1 9LS, England/0171-261-6180;Fax:0171-261-7179. £65 (approx. $98.00) yr.; £79 yr. overseas (52 issues). Game shooting, wild fowling, hunting, game fishing and firearms articles. Britain's best selling field sports magazine.

Shooting Times
Primedia, News Plaza, P.O. Box 1790, Peoria, IL 61656/309-682-6626. $23.98 yr. Guns, shooting, reloading; articles on every gun activity.

The Shotgun News‡
Primedia, News Plaza, P.O. Box 1790, Peoria, IL 61656/800-495-8362. $29.00 yr.; foreign subscription call for rates. Sample copy $4.00. Gun ads of all kinds.

SHOT Business
Flintlock Ridge Office Center, 11 Mile Hill Rd., Newtown, CT 06470-2359/203-426-1320; FAX: 203-426-1087. For the shooting, hunting and outdoor trade retailer.

Shotgun Sports
P.O. Box 6810, Auburn, CA 95604/916-889-2220; FAX:916-889-9106. $28.00 yr. Trapshooting how-to's, shotshell reloading, shotgun patterning, shotgun tests and evaluations, Sporting Clays action, waterfowl/upland hunting. Call 1-800-676-8920 for a free sample copy.

The Sixgunner (M)
Handgun Hunters International, P.O. Box 357, MAG, Bloomingdale, OH 43910

The Skeet Shooting Review
National Skeet Shooting Assn., 5931 Roft Rd., San Antonio, TX 78253. $20.00 yr. (Assn. membership of $30.00 includes mag.) Competition results, personality profiles of top Skeet shooters, how-to articles, technical, reloading information.

Soldier of Fortune
Subscription Dept., P.O. Box 348, Mt. Morris, IL 61054. $29.95 yr.; $39.95 Canada; $50.95 foreign.

Sporting Clays Magazine
5211 South Washington Ave., Titusville, FL 32780/407-268-5010; FAX: 407-267-7216. $29.95 yr. (12 issues).

Sporting Goods Business
Miller Freeman, Inc., One Penn Plaza, 10th Fl., New York, NY 10119-0004. Trade journal.

Sporting Goods Dealer
Two Park Ave., New York, NY 10016. $100.00 yr. Sporting goods trade journal.

Sporting Gun
Bretton Court, Bretton, Peterborough PE3 8DZ, England. £27.00 (approx. U.S. $36.00), airmail £35.50 yr. For the game and clay enthusiasts.

Sports Afield
The Hearst Corp., 250 W. 55th St., New York, NY 10019. $13.97 yr. Tom Gresham on firearms, ammunition; Grits Gresham on shooting and Thomas McIntyre on hunting.

The Squirrel Hunter
P.O. Box 368, Chireno, TX 75937. $14.00 yr. Articles about squirrel hunting.

Stott's Creek Calendar
Stott's Creek Printers, 2526 S 475 W, Morgantown, IN 46160/317-878-5489. 1 yr (3 issues) $11.50; 2 yrs. (6 issues) $20.00. Lists all gun shows everywhere in convenient calendar form; call for information.

Super Outdoors
2695 Aiken Road, Shelbyville, KY 40065/502-722-9463; 800-404-6064; Fax: 502-722-8093. Mark Edwards, publisher. Contact for details.

TACARMI
Via E. De Amicis, 25; 20123 Milano, Italy. $100.00 yr. approx. Antique and modern guns. (Italian text.)

Territorial Dispatch—1800s Historical Publication (M)
National Assn. of Buckskinners, 4701 Marion St., Suite 324, Livestock Exchange Bldg., Denver, CO 80216. Michael A. Nester & Barbara Wyckoff, editors. 303-297-9671.

Trap & Field
1000 Waterway Blvd., Indianapolis, IN 46202. $25.00 yr. Official publ. Amateur Trapshooting Assn. Scores, averages, trapshooting articles.

Turkey Call* (M)
Natl. Wild Turkey Federation, Inc., P.O. Box 530, Edgefield, SC 29824. $25.00 with membership (6 issues per yr.)

Turkey & Turkey Hunting*
Krause Publications, 700 E. State St., Iola, WI 54990-0001. $13.95 (6 issue p. yr.). Magazine with leading-edge articles on all aspects of wild turkey behavior, biology and the successful ways to hunt better with that info. Learn the proper techniques to calling, the right equipment, and more.

The U.S. Handgunner* (M)
U.S. Revolver Assn., 40 Larchmont Ave., Taunton, MA 02780. $10.00 yr. General handgun and competition articles. Bi-monthly sent to members.

U.S. Airgun Magazine
P.O. Box 2021, Benton, AR 72018/800-247-4867; Fax: 501-316-8549. 10 issues a yr. Cover the sport from hunting, 10-meter, field target and collecting. Write for details.

The Varmint Hunter Magazine (Q)
The Varmint Hunters Assn., Box 759, Pierre, SD 57501/800-528-4868. $24.00 yr.

Waffenmarkt-Intern
GFI-Verlag, Theodor-Heuss Ring 62, 50668 K"ln, Germany. Only for gunsmiths, licensed firearms dealers and their suppliers in Germany, Austria and Switzerland.

Wild Sheep (M) (Q)
Foundation for North American Wild Sheep, 720 Allen Ave., Cody, WY 82414. Website: http://iigi.com/os/non/fnaws/fnaws.htm; e-mail: fnaws@wyoming.com. Official journal of the foundation.

Wisconsin Outdoor Journal
Krause Publications, 700 E. State St., Iola, WI 54990-0001. $16.95 yr. (8 issues). For Wisconsin's avid hunters and fishermen, with features from all over that state with regional reports, legislative updates, etc.

Women & Guns
P.O. Box 488, Sta. C, Buffalo, NY 14209. $24.00 yr. U.S.; $72.00 foreign (12 issues). Only magazine edited by and for women gun owners.

World War II*
Cowles History Group, 741 Miller Dr. SE, Suite D-2, Leesburg, VA 20175-8920. Annual subscriptions $19.95 U.S.; $25.95 Canada; 43.95 foreign. The title says it—WWII; good articles, ads, etc.

---

*Published bi-monthly
† Published weekly
‡Published three times per month. All others are published monthly.

M=Membership requirements; write for details. Q=Published Quarterly.

THE ARMS LIBRARY

FOR COLLECTOR ◆ HUNTER ◆ SHOOTER ◆ OUTDOORSMAN

IMPORTANT NOTICE TO BOOK BUYERS

Books listed here may be bought from Ray Riling Arms Books Co., 6844 Gorsten St., P.O. Box 18925, Philadelphia, PA 19119, phone 215/438-2456; FAX: 215-438-5395. Joe Riling is the researcher and compiler of "The Arms Library" and a seller of gun books for over 30 years.

The Riling stock includes books classic and modern, many hard-to-find items, and many not obtainable elsewhere. These pages list a portion of the current stock. They offer prompt, complete service, with delayed shipments occurring only on out-of-print or out-of-stock books.

NOTICE FOR ALL CUSTOMERS: Remittance in U.S. funds must accompany all orders. For U.S. add $2.00 per book for postage and insurance. Minimum order $10.00. For UPS add 50% to mailing costs.

All foreign countries add $5.00 per book. All foreign orders are shipped at the buyer's risk unless an additional $5 for insurance is included.

Payments in excess of order or for "Backorders" are credited or fully refunded at request. Books "As-Ordered" are not returnable except by permission and a handling charge on these of $2.00 per book is deducted from refund or credit. Only Pennsylvania customers must include current sales tax.

A full variety of arms books also available from Rutgers Book Center, 127 Raritan Ave., Highland Park, NJ 08904/908-545-4344; FAX: 908-545-6686 or I.D.S.A. Books, 1324 Stratford Drive, Piqua, OH 45356/937-773-4203; FAX: 937-778-1922.

***New Book**

BALLISTICS and HANDLOADING

***ABC's of Reloading, 6th Edition,** by C. Rodney James and the editors of *Handloader's Digest*, DBI Books, a division of Krause Publications, Iola, WI, 1997. 288 pp., illus. Paper covers. $21.95.

The definitive guide to every facet of cartridge and shotshell reloading.

Ammunition Making, by George E. Frost, National Rifle Association of America, Washington, D.C., 1990. 160 pp., illus. Paper covers. $17.95.

Reflects the perspective of "an insider" with half a century's experience in successful management of ammunition manufacturing operations.

Barnes Reloading Manual #1, Barnes Bullets, American Fork, UT, 1995. 350 pp., illus. $24.95.

Data for more than 65 cartridges from 243 to 50 BMG.

Basic Handloading, by George C. Nonte, Jr., Outdoor Life Books, New York, NY, 1982. 192 pp., illus. Paper covers. $6.95.

How to produce high-quality ammunition using the safest, most efficient methods.

Big Bore Rifles And Cartridges, Wolfe Publishing Co., Prescott, AZ, 1991. Paper covers. $26.00.

This book covers cartridges from 8mm to .600 Nitro with loading tables.

Black Powder Guide, 2nd Edition, by George C. Nonte, Jr., Stoeger Publishing Co., So. Hackensack, NJ, 1991. 288 pp., illus. Paper covers. $14.95.

How-to instructions for selection, repair and maintenance of muzzleloaders, making your own bullets, restoring and refinishing, shooting techniques.

Blackpowder Loading Manual, 3rd Edition, by Sam Fadala, DBI Books, a division of Krause Publications, Inc., Iola, WI, 1995. 368 pp., illus. Paper covers. $19.95.

Revised and expanded edition of this landmark blackpowder loading book. Covers hundreds of loads for most of the popular blackpowder rifles, handguns and shotguns.

The Bullet Swage Manual. by Ted Smith, Corbin Manufacturing and Supply Co., White City, OR, 1988. 45 pp., illus. Paper covers. $10.00.

A book that fills the need for information on bullet swaging.

***Cartridges of the World, 8th Edition,** by Frank Barnes, edited by M. L. McPherson, DBI Books, a division of Krause Publications, Inc., Iola, WI, 1997. 480 pp., illus. Paper covers. $24.95.

Completely revised edition of the general purpose reference work for which collectors, police, scientists and laymen reach first for answers to cartridge identification questions.

Cast Bullets for the Black Powder Rifle, by Paul A. Matthews, Wolfe Publishing Co., Prescott, AZ, 1996. 133 pp., illus. Paper covers. $22.50.

The tools and techniques used to make your cast bullet shooting a success.

***Complete Blackpowder Handbook, 3rd Edition,** by Sam Fadala, DBI Books, a division of Krause Publications, Inc., Iola, WI, 1997. 400 pp., illus. Paper covers. $21.95.

Expanded and completely rewritten edition of the definitive book on the subject of blackpowder.

The Complete Handloader for Rifles, Handguns and Shotguns, by John Wootters, Stackpole Books, Harrisburg, PA, 1988. 214 pp., $29.95.

Loading-bench know-how.

Complete Reloading Guide, by robert & John Traister, Stoeger Publishing Co., Wayne, NJ, 1997. 608 pp., illus. Paper covers. $34.95

Perhaps the finest, most comprehensive work ever published on the subject of reloading.

Designing and Forming Custom Cartridges, by Ken Howell, Ken Howell, Stevensville, MT, 1995. 596 pp., illus. $59.95.

Covers cartridge dimensions and includes complete introductory material on cartridge manufacture and appendices on finding loading data and equipment.

Game Loads and Practical Ballistics for the American Hunter, by Bob Hagel, Wolfe Publishing Co., Prescott, AZ, 1992. 310 pp., illus. $27.90.

Hagel's knowledge gained as a hunter, guide and gun enthusiast is gathered in this informative text.

Handbook of Bullet Swaging No. 7, by David R. Corbin, Corbin Manufacturing and Supply Co., White City, OR, 1986. 199 pp., illus. Paper covers. $10.00.

This handbook explains the most precise method of making quality bullets.

Handbook for Shooters and Reloaders, by P.O. Ackley, Salt Lake City, UT, 1970, (Vol. I), 567 pp., illus. (Vol. II), a new printing with specific new material. 495 pp., illus. $18.95 each.

Handbook of Metallic Cartridge Reloading, by Edward Matunas, Winchester Press, Piscataway, NJ, 1981. 272 pp., illus. $19.95.

Up-to-date, comprehensive loading tables prepared by four major powder manufacturers.

Handgun Reloading, The Gun Digest Book of, by Dean A. Grennell and Wiley M. Clapp, DBI Books, a division of Krause Publications, Inc., Iola, WI, 1987. 256 pp., illus. Paper covers. $16.95.

Detailed discussions of all aspects of reloading for handguns, from basic to complex. New loading data.

Handloader's Digest, 18th Edition, edited by Bob Bell, DBI Books, a division of Krause Publications, Inc., Iola, WI, 1998. 480 pp., illus. Paper covers. $27.95.

Top Writers in the field contribute helpful information on techniques and components. Greatly expanded and fully indexed catalog of all currently available tools, accessories and components for metallic, blackpowder cartridge, shotshell reloading and swaging.

Handloader's Guide, by Stanley W. Trzoniec, Stoeger Publishing Co., So. Hackensack, NJ, 1985. 256 pp., illus. Paper covers. $14.95.

The complete step-by-step fully illustrated guide to handloading ammunition.

Handloader's Manual of Cartridge Conversions, by John J. Donnelly, Stoeger Publishing Co., So. Hackensack, NJ, 1986. Unpaginated. $49.95.

From 14 Jones to 70-150 Winchester in English and American cartridges, and from 4.85 U.K. to 15.2x28R Gevelot in metric cartridges. Over 900 cartridges described in detail.

Handloading, by Bill Davis, Jr., NRA Books, Wash., D.C., 1980. 400 pp., illus. Paper covers. $15.95.

A complete update and expansion of the NRA Handloader's Guide.

Handloading for Hunters, by Don Zutz, Winchester Press, Piscataway, NJ, 1977. 288 pp., illus. $30.00.

Precise mixes and loads for different types of game and for various hunting situations with rifle and shotgun.

Hatcher's Notebook, by S. Julian Hatcher, Stackpole Books, Harrisburg, PA, 1992. 488 pp., illus. $39.95.

A reference work for shooters, gunsmiths, ballisticians, historians, hunters and collectors.

Hodgdon Data Manual No. 26, Hodgdon Powder Co., Shawnee Mission, KS, 1993. 797 pp. $22.95.

Includes Hercules, Winchester and Dupont powders; data on cartridge cases; loads; silhouette; shotshell; pyrodex and blackpowder; conversion factors; weight equivalents, etc.

The Home Guide to Cartridge Conversions, by Maj. George C. Nonte Jr., The Gun Room Press, Highland Park, NJ, 1976. 404 pp., illus. $24.95.

Revised and updated version of Nonte's definitive work on the alteration of cartridge cases for use in guns for which they were not intended.

Hornady Handbook of Cartridge Reloading, 4th Edition, Vol. I and II, Hornady Mfg. Co., Grand Island, NE, 1991. 1200 pp., illus. $28.50.

New edition of this famous reloading handbook. Latest loads, ballistic information, etc.

Hornady Handbook of Cartridge Reloading, Abridged Edition, Hornady Mfg. Co., Grand Island, NE, 1991. $19.95.

Ballistic data for 25 of the most popular cartridges.

Hornady Load Notes, Hornady Mfg. Co., Grand Island, NE, 1991. $4.95.

Complete load data and ballistics for a single caliber. Eight pistol 9mm-45ACP; 16 rifle, 222-45-70.

How-To's for the Black Powder Cartridge Rifle Shooter, by Paul A. Matthews, Wolfe Publishing Co., Prescott, AZ, 1995. 45 pp. Paper covers. $22.50.

Covers lube recipes, good bore cleaners and over-powder wads. Tips include compressing powder charges, combating wind resistance, improving ignition and much more.

The Illustrated Reference of Cartridge Dimensions, edited by Dave Scovill, Wolfe Publishing Co., Prescott, AZ, 1994. 343 pp., illus. Paper covers. $19.00

A comprehensive volume with over 300 cartridges. Standard and metric dimensions have been taken from SAAMI drawings and/or fired cartridges.

Loading the Black Powder Rifle Cartridge, by Paul A Matthews, Wolfe Publishing Co., Prescott, AZ, 1993. 121 pp., illus. Paper covers. $22.50.

Author Matthews brings the blackpowder cartridge shooter valuable information on the basics, including cartridge care, lubes and moulds, powder charges and developing and testing loads in his usual authoritative style.

***Loading the Peacemaker—Colt's Model P,** by Dave Scovill, Wolfe Publishing Co., Prescott, AZ, 1996. 227 pp., illus. $24.95.

A comprehensive work about the history, maintenance and repair of the most famous revolver ever made, including the most extensive load data ever published.

Lyman Cast Bullet Handbook, 3rd Edition, edited by C. Kenneth Ramage, Lyman Publications, Middlefield, CT, 1980. 416 pp., illus. Paper covers. $19.95.

Information on more than 5000 tested cast bullet loads and 19 pages of trajectory and wind drift tables for cast bullets.

Lyman Black Powder Handbook, edited by C. Kenneth Ramage, Lyman Products for Shooters, Middlefield, CT, 1975. 239 pp., illus. Paper covers. $14.95.

Comprehensive load information for the modern blackpowder shooter.

Lyman Pistol & Revolver Handbook, 2nd Edition, edited by Thomas J. Griffin, Lyman Products Co., Middlefield, CT, 1996. 287 pp., illus. Paper covers. $18.95.

The most up-to-date loading data available including the hottest new calibers, like 40 S&W, 9x21, 9mm Makarov, 9x25 Dillon and 454 Casull.

Lyman Reloading Handbook No. 47, edited by Edward A. Matunas, Lyman Publications, Middlefield, CT, 1992. 480 pp., illus. Paper covers. $23.00.

A comprehensive reloading manual complete with "How to Reload" information. Expanded data section with all the newest rifle and pistol calibers.

Lyman Shotshell Handbook, 4th Edition, edited by Edward A. Matunas, Lyman Products Co., Middlefield, CT, 1996. 330 pp., illus. Paper covers. $24.95.

Has 9000 loads, including slugs and buckshot, plus feature articles and a full color I.D. section.

Lyman's Guide to Big Game Cartridges & Rifles, by Edward Matunas, Lyman Publishing Corporation, Middlefield, CT, 1994. 287 pp., illus. Paper covers. $17.95.

A selection guide to cartridges and rifles for big game—antelope to elephant.

Making Loading Dies and Bullet Molds, by Harold Hoffman, H&P Publishing, San Angelo, TX, 1993. 230 pp., illus. Paper covers. $24.95.

A good book for learning tool and die making.

Metallic Cartridge Reloading, 3rd Edition, by M.L. McPherson, DBI Books, a division of Krause Publications, Inc., Iola, WI., 1996. 352 pp., illus. Paper covers. $21.95.

A true reloading manual with over 10,000 loads fro all popular metallic cartridges and a wealth of invaluable technical data provided by a recognized expert.

Modern Handloading, by Maj. Geo. C. Nonte, Winchester Press, Piscataway, NJ, 1972. 416 pp., illus. $15.00.

Covers all aspects of metallic and shotshell ammunition loading, plus more loads than any book in print.

***Modern Reloading,** by Richard Lee, Inland Press, 1996. 510 pp., illus. $24.98.
The how-tos of rifle, pistol amd shotgun reloading plus load data for rifle and pistol calibers.

Modern Practical Ballistics, by Art Pejsa, Pejsa Ballistics, Minneapolis, MN, 1990. 150 pp., illus. $24.95.
Covers all aspects of ballistics and new, simplified methods. Clear examples illustrate new, easy but very accurate formulas.

Mr. Single Shot's Cartridge Handbook, by Frank de Haas, Mark de Haas, Orange City, IA, 1996. 116 pp., illus. Paper covers. $21.50.
This book covers most of the cartridges, both commercial and wildcat, that the author has known and used.

Nick Harvey's Practical Reloading Manual, by Nick Harvey, Australian Print Group, Maryborough, Victoria, Australia, 1995. 235 pp., illus. Paper covers. $24.95.
Contains data for rifle and handgun including many popular wildcat and improved cartridges. Tools, powders, components and techniques for assembling optimum reloads with particular application to North America.

Nosler Reloading Manual No. 3, edited by Gail Root, Nosler Bullets, Inc., Bend, OR, 1989. 516 pp., illus. $21.95.
All-new book. New format including featured articles and cartridge introductions by well-known shooters, gun writers and editors.

The Paper Jacket, by Paul Matthews, Wolfe Publishing Co., Prescott, AZ, 1991. Paper covers. $13.50.
Up-to-date and accurate information about paper-patched bullets.

Precision Handloading, by John Withers, Stoeger Publishing Co., So. Hackensack, NJ, 1985. 224 pp., illus. Paper covers. $14.95.
An entirely new approach to handloading ammunition.

Propellant Profiles New and Expanded, 3rd Edition, Wolfe Publishing Co., Prescott, AZ, 1991. Paper covers. $16.95.

Reloader's Guide, 3rd Edition, by R.A. Steindler, Stoeger Publishing Co., So. Hackensack, NJ, 1984. 224 pp., illus. Paper covers. $11.95.
Complete, fully illustrated step-by-step guide to handloading ammunition.

***Reloading for Shotgunners, 4th Edition,** by Kurt D. Fackler and M.L. McPherson, DBI Books, a division of Krause Publications, Inc., Iola, WI, 1997. 320 pp., illus. Paper covers. $19.95.
Expanded reloading tables with over 11,000 loads. Bushing charts for every major press and component maker. All new presentation on all aspects of shotshell reloading by two of the top experts in the field.

Sierra Handgun Manual, 3rd Edition, edited by Kenneth Ramage, Sierra Bullets, Santa Fe Springs, CA, 1990. 704 pp., illus. 3-ring binder. $19.95.
New listings for XP-100 and Contender pistols and TCU cartridges...part of a new single shot section. Covers the latest loads for 10mm Auto, 455 Super Mag, and Accurate powders.

Sierra Rifle Manual, 3rd Edition, edited by Kenneth Ramage, Sierra Bullets, Santa Fe Springs, CA, 1990. 856 pp., illus. 3-ring binder. $24.95.
Updated load information with new powder listings and a wealth of inside tips.

Sixgun Cartridges and Loads, by Elmer Keith, The Gun Room Press, Highland Park, NJ, 1986. 151 pp., illus. $24.95.
A manual covering the selection, uses and loading of the most suitable and popular revolver cartridges. Originally published in 1936. Reprint.

Speer Reloading Manual Number 12, edited by members of the Speer research staff, Omark Industries, Lewiston, ID, 1987. 621 pp., illus. $18.95.
Reloading manual for rifles and pistols.

Understanding Ballistics, by Robert A. Rinker, Mulberry House Publishing Co., Corydon, IN, 1997. 373 pp., illus Paper covers. $19.95.
Explains basic to advanced firearm ballistics in understandable terms.

Why Not Load Your Own?, by Col. T. Whelen, A. S. Barnes, New York, 1957, 4th ed., rev. 237 pp., illus. $20.00.
A basic reference on handloading, describing each step, materials and equipment. Includes loads for popular cartridges.

Wildcat Cartridges Volumes 1 & 2 Combination, by the editors of Handloaders magazine, Wolfe Publishing Co., Prescott, AZ, 1997. 350 pp., illus. Paper covers. $39.95.
A profile of the most popular information on wildcat cartridges that appeared in the Handloader magazine.

Yours Truly, Harvey Donaldson, by Harvey Donaldson, Wolfe Publ. Co., Inc., Prescott, AZ, 1980. 288 pp., illus. $19.50.
Reprint of the famous columns by Harvey Donaldson which appeared in "Handloader" from May 1966 through December 1972.

COLLECTORS

Air Guns, by Eldon G. Wolff, Duckett's Publishing Co., Tempe, AZ, 1997. 204 pp., illus Paper covers. $35.00
Historical reference covering many makers, European and American guns, canes and more.

The American B.B. Gun, by Arni Dunathan, R&R Books, Livonia, N.Y. 1997. 154 pp., illus. $30.00.
A collector's guide.

The American Cartridge, by Charles R. Suydam, Borden Publishing Co., Alhambra, CA, 1986. 184 pp., illus. $24.95.
An illustrated study of the rimfire cartridge in the United States.

Antique Guns, the Collector's Guide, 2nd Edition, edited by John Traister, Stoeger Publishing Co., S. Hackensack, NJ, 1994. 320 pp., illus. Paper covers. $19.95.
Covers a vast spectrum of pre-1900 firearms: those manufactured by U.S. gunmakers as well as Canadian, French, German, Belgian, Spanish and other foreign firms.

Arms & Accoutrements of the Mounted Police 1873-1973, by Roger F. Phillips and Donald J. Klancher, Museum Restoration Service, Ont., Canada, 1982. 224 pp., illus. $49.95.
A definitive history of the revolvers, rifles, machine guns, cannons, ammunition, swords, etc. used by the NWMP, the RNWMP and the RCMP during the first 100 years of the Force.

Arms and Armor in the Art Institute of Chicago, by Walter J. Karcheski, Jr., Books Sales, Edison, NJ, 1998. 128 pp., illus. $22.95
This book highlights one of the greatest collections of arms and armour in North America. Describes the use, craftsmanship and significance of suits nad weapons throughout the ages.

Arms Makers of Maryland, by Daniel D. Hartzler, George Shumway, York, PA, 1975. 200 pp., illus. $50.00.
A thorough study of the gunsmiths of Maryland who worked during the late 18th and early 19th centuries.

Artistry in Arms: The Guns of Smith & Wesson, by Roy G. Jinks, Smith & Wesson, Springfield, MA, 1991. 85 pp., illus. Paper covers. $19.95.
Catalog of the Smith & Wesson International Museum Tour 1991-1995 organized by the Connecticut Valley Historical Museum and Springfield Library and Museum Association.

Assault Weapons, 4th Edition, The Gun Digest Book of, edited by Jack Lewis, DBI Books, a division of Krause Publications, Iola, WI, 1996. 256 pp., illus. Paper covers. $19.95.
An in-depth look at the history and uses of these arms.

Astra Automatic Pistols, by Leonardo M. Antaris, FIRAC Publishing Co., Sterling, CO, 1989. 248 pp., illus. $45.00.
Charts, tables, serial ranges, etc. The definitive work on Astra pistols.

Basic Documents on U.S. Marital Arms, commentary by Col. B. R. Lewis, reissue by Ray Riling, Phila., PA, 1956 and 1960. *Rifle Musket Model 1855*. The first issue rifle of musket caliber, a muzzle loader equipped with the Maynard Primer, 32 pp. *Rifle Musket Model 1863*. The typical Union muzzle-loader of the Civil War, 26 pp. *Breech-Loading Rifle Musket Model 1866*. The first of our 50-caliber breechloading rifles, 12 pp. *Remington Navy Rifle Model 1870*. A commercial type breech-loader made at Springfield, 16 pp. *Lee Straight Pull Navy Rifle Model 1895*. A magazine cartridge arm of 6mm caliber. 23 pp. *Breech-Loading Arms* (five models) 27 pp. *Ward-Burton Rifle Musket 1871*-16 pp. Each $10.00.

Battle Weapons of the American Revolution, by George C. Neuman, Scurlock Publishing Co., Texarkana, TX, 1998. 400 pp. Illus. $65.00.
The most extensive photographic collection of Revolutionary War weapons ever in one volume. More that 1,600 photos of over 500 muskets, rifles, swords, bayonets, knives and other arms used by both sides in America's War for Independence.

Behold, the Longrifle Again, by James B. Whisker, Old Bedford Village Press, Bedford, PA, 1997. 176 pp., illus. $45.00
Excellent reference work for the ocllector profusely illustrated with photographs of some of the finest Kentucky rifles showing front and back profiles and overall view.

Beretta Automatic Pistols, by J.B. Wood, Stackpole Books, Harrisburg, PA, 1985. 192 pp., illus. $24.95.
Only English-language book devoted to the Beretta line. Includes all important models.

***Birmingham Gunmakers,** by Douglas Tate, Safari Press, Inc., Huntington Beach, CA, 1997. 300 pp., illus. $50.00.
An invaluable work for anybody interested in the fine sporting arms crafted in this famous British gunmakers' city.

Blacksmith Guide to Ruger Flat-Top & Super Blackhawks, by H.W. Ross, Jr., Blacksmith Corp., Chino Valley, AZ, 1990. 96 pp., illus. Paper covers. $9.95.
A key source on the extensively collected Ruger Blackhawk revolvers.

Blue Book of Gun Values, 19th Edition, edited by S.P. Fjestad, Blue Book Publications, Inc., Minneapolis, MN, 1998. 1301 pp., illus. Paper covers. $27.95
Covers all new 1998 firearm prices. Gives technical data on both new and discontinued domestic and foreign commercial and military guns.

The Blunderbuss 1500-1900, by James D. Forman, Museum Restoration Service, Bloomfield, Ont., Canada, 1995. 40 pp., illus. Paper covers. $4.95.
The guns that had no peer as an anti-personal weapon throughout the flintlock era.

Boarders Away, Volume II: Firearms of the Age of Fighting Sail, by William Gilkerson, Andrew Mowbray, Inc. Publishers, Lincoln, RI, 1993. 331 pp., illus. $65.00.
Covers the pistols, muskets, combustibles and small cannon used aboard American and European fighting ships, 1626-1826.

The Book of Colt Engraving, by R.L. Wilson, Random House, New York, NY, 1998. 560 pp., illus. $89.95.
A fresh look at the subject matter, not a reprinting expanded from the earlier edition.

The Book of the Springfield, by Edward C. Crossman and Roy F. Dunlap, Wolfe Publishing Co., Prescott, AZ, 1990. 567 pp., illus. $36.00.
A textbook covering the military, sporting and target rifles chambered for the caliber 30 Model 1906 cartridge; their metallic and telescopic sights and ammunition used in them.

Boothroyd's Revised Directory of British Gunmakers, by Geoffrey and Susan Boothroyd, Sand Lake Press, Amity, OR, 1997. 412 pp., illus. $34.95.
A new revised and enlarged edition. Lists all makers in alphabetically order.

Breech-Loading Carbines of the United States Civil War Period, by Brig. Gen. John Pitman, Armory Publications, Tacoma, WA, 1987. 94 pp., illus. $29.95.
The first in a series of previously unpublished manuscripts originated by the late Brigadier General John Putnam. Exploded drawings showing parts actual size follow each sectioned illustration.

The Breech-Loading Single-Shot Rifle, by Major Ned H. Roberts and Kenneth L. Waters, Wolfe Publishing Co., Prescott, AZ, 1995. 333 pp., illus. $28.50.
A comprehensive and complete history of the evolution of the Schutzen and single-shot rifle.

The British Enfield Rifles, Volume 1, The SMLE Mk I nad Mk III Rifles, by Charles R. Stratton, North Cape Publications, Tustin, CA, 1997. 150 pp., illus. Paper covers. $19.95.
A systematic and thorough examination on a part-by-part basis of the famous British battle rifle that endured for nearly 70 years as the British Army's number one battle rifle.

The British Falling Block Breechloading Rifle from 1865, by Jonathan Kirton, tom rowe Books, Maynardsville, TN, 2nd edition, 1997. 380 pp., illus. $70.00.
Expanded 2nd edition of a comprehensive work on the British falling block rifle.

British Military Firearms 1650-1850, by Howard L. Blackmore, Stackpole Books, Mechanicsburg, PA, 1994. 224 pp., illus. $50.00.
The definitive work on British military firearms.

British Service Rifles and Carbines 1888-1900, by Alan M. Petrillo, Excaliber Publications, Latham, NY, 1994. 72 pp., illus, Paper covers. $11.95.
A complete review of the Lee-Metford and Lee-Enfield rifles and carbines.

British Single Shot Rifles, Volume 1, Alexander Henry, by Wal Einfer, Tom Rowe, Manardville, TN, 1998, 200 pp., illus. $50.00.
Detailed Study of the single shot rifles made by Henry. Illustrated with hundreds of photographs and drawings.

British Single Shot Rifles Volume 2, George Gibbs, by Wal Winfer, Tom Rowe, Maynardville, TN, 1998. 177 pp., illus. $50.00
Detailed study of the Farquharson as made by Gibbs. Hundreds of photos.

British Small Arms Ammunition, 1864-1938, by Peter Labett, Armory Publications, Oceanside, CA, 1994. 352 pp., illus. $75.00.
The military side of the story illustrating the rifles, carbines, machine guns, revolvers and automatic pistols and their ammunition, experimental and adopted, from 577 Snider to modern times.

The British Soldier's Firearms from Smoothbore to Rifled Arms, 1850-1864, by Dr. C.H. Roads, R&R Books, Livonia, NY, 1994. 332 pp., illus. $49.00.
A reprint of the classic text covering the development of British military hand and shoulder firearms in the crucial years between 1850 and 1864.

***British Sporting Guns & Rifles,** compiled by George Hoyem, Armory Publications, Coeur d'Alene, ID, 1997. 1024 pp., illus. In two volumes. $240.00.
Eighteen old sporting firearms trade catalogs and a rare book reproduced with their color covers in a limited, signed and numbered edition.

British Sporting Rifle Cartridges, by Bill Fleming, Armory Publications, Oceanside, CA, 1994. 302 pp., illus. $75.00.

An expanded study of volume three of *The History & Development of Small Arms Ammunition.* Includes pertinent trade catalog pages, etc.

Browning Dates of Manufacture, compiled by George Madis, Art and Reference House, Brownsboro, TX, 1989. 48 pp. $5.00.

Gives the date codes and product codes for all models from 1824 to the present.

Browning Sporting Arms of Distinction 1903-1992, by Matt Eastman, Matt Eastman Publications, Fitzgerald, GA, 1995. 450 pp., illus. $49.95.

The most recognized publication on Browning sporting arms; covers all models.

Bullard Arms, by G. Scott Jamieson, The Boston Mills Press, Ontario, Canada, 1989. 244 pp., illus. $35.00.

The story of a mechanical genius whose rifles and cartridges were the equal to any made in America in the 1880s.

Burning Powder, compiled by Major D.B. Wesson, Wolfe Publishing Company, Prescott, AZ, 1992. 110 pp. Soft cover. $10.95.

A rare booklet from 1932 for Smith & Wesson collectors.

The Burnside Breech Loading Carbines, by Edward A. Hull, Andrew Mowbray, Inc., Lincoln, RI, 1986. 95 pp., illus. $16.00.

No. 1 in the "Man at Arms Monograph Series." A model-by-model historical/technical examination of one of the most widely used cavalry weapons of the American Civil War based upon important and previously unpublished research.

California Gunsmiths 1846-1900, by Lawrence P. Sheldon, Far Far West Publ., Fair Oaks, CA, 1977. 289 pp., illus. $30.00.

A study of early California gunsmiths and the firearms they made.

Canadian Military Handguns 1855-1985, by Clive M. Law, Museum Restoration Service, Bloomfield, Ont. Canada, 1994. 130pp., illus. $40.00.

A long-awaited and important history for arms historians and pistol collectors.

Cap Guns, by James Dundas, Schiffer Publishing, Atglen, PA, 1996. 160 pp., illus. Paper covers. $29.95.

Over 600 full-color photos of cap guns and gun accessories with a current value guide.

Carbines of the Civil War, by John D. McAulay, Pioneer Press, Union City, TN, 1981. 123 pp., illus. Paper covers. $7.95.

A guide for the student and collector of the colorful arms used by the Federal cavalry.

*__Carbines of the U.S. Cavalry 1861-1905,__ by John D. McAulay, Andrew Mowbray Publishers, Lincoln, RI, 1996. #35.00.

Covers the crucial use of carbines from the beginning of the Civil War to the end of the cavalry carbine era in 1905.

*__Cartridge Catalogues,__ compiled by George Hoyem, Armory Publications, Coeur d'Alene, ID., 1997. 504 pp., illus. $125.00.

Fourteen old ammunition makers' and designers' catalogs reproduced with their color covers in a limited, signed and numbered edition.

Cartridges for Breechloading Rifles, by A. Mattenheimer, Armory Publications, Oceanside, CA, 1989. 90 pp. with two 15"x19" color lithos containing 163 drawings of cartridges and firearms mechanisms. $29.95.

Reprinting of this German work on cartridges. Text in German and English.

*__Cartridges of the World, 8th Edition,__ by Frank Barnes, edited by M. L. McPherson, DBI Books, a division of Krause Publications, Inc., Iola, WI, 1997. 480 pp., illus. Paper covers. $24.95.

Completely revised edition of the general purpose reference work for which collectors, police, scientists and laymen reach first for answers to cartridge identification questions. Available October, 1996.

Civil War Breech Loading Rifles, by John D. McAulay, Andrew Mowbray, Inc., Lincoln, RI, 1991. 144 pp., illus. Paper covers. $15.00.

All the major breech-loading rifles of the Civil War and most, if not all, of the obscure types are detailed, illustrated and set in their historical context.

Civil War Carbines Volume 2: The Early Years, by John D. McAulay, Andrew Mowbray, Inc., Lincoln, RI, 1991. 144 pp., illus. Paper covers. $15.00.

Covers the carbines made during the exciting years leading up to the outbreak of war and used by the North and South in the conflict.

*__Civil War Firearms,__ by Joseph G. Bilby, Combined Books, Conshohocken, PA, 1996. 252 pp., illus. $34.95.

A unique work combining background data on each firearm including its battlefield use, and a guide to collecting and firing surviving relics and modern reproductions.

Civil War Guns, by William B. Edwards, Thomas Publications, Gerrysburg, PA, 1997. 444 pp., illus. $40.00.

The complete story of Federal and Confederate small arms; design, manufacture, identifications, procurement issue, employment, effectiveness, and postwar disposal by the recognized expert.

Civil War Pistols, by John D. McAulay, Andrew Mowbray Inc., Lincoln, RI, 1992. 166 pp., illus. $38.50.

A survey of the handguns used during the American Civil War.

*__Civil War Sharps Carbines and Rifles,__ by Earl J. Coates and John D. McAulay, Thomas Publications, Gettysburg, PA, 1996. 108 pp., illus. Paper covers. $12.95.

Traces the history and development of the firearms including short histories of specific serial numbers and the soldiers who received them.

Col. Burton's Spiller & Burr Revolver, by Matthew W. Norman, Mercer University Press, Macon, GA, 1997. 152 pp., illus. $22.95.

A remarkable archival research project on the arm together with a comprehensive story of the establishment and running of the factory.

*__Collecting Western Toy Guns Identification and Value Guide,__ by Jim Schleyer, Books Americana, a division of Krause Publications, Iola, WI, 1997. 480 pp., illus. Paper covers, $29.95.

Well-illustrated and loaded with information, descriptions and current values of toy pistols, rifles, holsters, spurs, etc.

A Collector's Guide to United States Combat Shotguns, by Bruce N. Canfield, Andrew Mowbray Inc., Lincoln, RI, 1992. 184 pp., illus. Paper covers. $24.00

This book provides full coverage of combat shotguns, from the earliest examples right up to the Gulf War and beyond.

A Collector's Guide to Winchester in the Service, by Bruce N. Canfield, Andrew Mowbray, Inc., Lincoln, RI, 1991. 192 pp., illus. Paper covers. $22.00.

The firearms produced by Winchester for the national defense. From Hotchkiss to the M14, each firearm is examined and illustrated.

A Collector's Guide to the M1 Garand and the M1 Carbine, by Bruce N. Canfield, Andrew Mowbray, Inc., Publisher, Lincoln, RI, 1988. 144 pp., illus., paper covers. $22.00.

A comprehensive guide to the most important and ubiquitous American arms of WWII and Korea.

A Collector's Guide to the '03 Springfield, by Bruce N. Canfield, Andrew Mowbray Inc, Lincoln, RI, 1989. 160 pp., illus. Paper covers. $22.00.

A comprehensive guide follows the '03 through its unparalleled tenure of service. Covers all of the interesting variations, modifications and accessories of this highly collectible military rifle.

Collector's Illustrated Encyclopedia of the American Revolution, by George C. Neumann and Frank J. Kravic, Rebel Publishing Co., Inc., Texarkana, TX, 1989. 286 pp., illus. $29.95.

A showcase of more than 2,300 artifacts made, worn, and used by those who fought in the War for Independence.

Colonial Frontier Guns, by T.M. Hamilton, Pioneer Press, Union City, TN, 1988. 176 pp., illus. Paper covers. $13.95.

A complete study of early flint muskets of this country.

The Colt Armory, by Ellsworth Grant, Man-at-Arms Bookshelf, Lincoln, RI, 1996. 232 pp., illus. $35.00.

A history of Colt's Manufacturing Company.

Colt Heritage, by R.L. Wilson, Simon & Schuster, 1979. 358 pp., illus. $75.00.

The official history of Colt firearms 1836 to the present.

Colt Memorabilia Price Guide, by John Ogle, Krause Publications, Inc., Iola, WI, 1998. 256 pp., illus. Paper covers. $29.95

The first book ever compiled about the vast array of non-gun merchandise produced by Sam Colt's companies, and other companies using the Colt name.

The Colt Model 1905 Automatic Pistol, by John Potocki, Mowbray Publishers, Lincoln, RI, 1997. 192 pp., illus. $28.00

Covers all aspects of the Colt Model 1905 Automatic pistol, from its invention by the legendary John Browning to its numerous production variations.

Colt Peacemaker British Model, by Keith Cochran, Cochran Publishing Co., Rapid City, SD, 1989. 160 pp., illus. $35.00.

Covers those revolvers Colt squeezed in while completing a large order of revolvers for the U.S. Cavalry in early 1874, to those magnificent cased target revolvers used in the pistol competitions at Bisley Commons in the 1890s.

Colt Peacemaker Encyclopedia, by Keith Cochran, Keith Cochran, Rapid City, SD, 1986. 434 pp., illus. $65.00.

A must book for the Peacemaker collector.

Colt Peacemaker Encyclopedia, Volume 2, by Keith Cochran, Cochran Publishing Co., SD, 1992. 416 pp., illus. $60.00.

Included in this volume are extensive notes on engraved, inscribed, historical and noted revolvers, as well as those revolvers used by outlaws, lawmen, movie and television stars.

Colt Percussion Accoutrements 1834-1873, by Robin Rapley, Robin Rapley, Newport Beach, CA, 1994. 432 pp., illus. Paper covers. $39.95.

The complete collector's guide to the identification of Colt percussion accoutrements; including Colt conversions and their values.

Colt Pocket Pistols, by Dr. John W. Brunner, Phillips Publications, Williamstown, NJ, 1996. 200 pp., illus. $50.00.

The definitive reference guide on the 25, 32 and 380 Colt automatic pistols.

Colt Revolvers and the Tower of London, by Joseph G. Rosa, Royal Armouries of the Tower of London, London, England, 1988. 72 pp., illus. Soft covers. $15.00.

Details the story of Colt in London through the early cartridge period.

Colt Rifles and Muskets from 1847-1870, by Herbert Houze, Krause Publications, Iola, WI, 1996. 192 pp., illus. $34.95.

Discover previously unknown Colt models along with an extensive list of production figures for all models.

Colt's SAA Post War Models, by George Garton, The Gun Room Press, Highland Park, NJ, 1995. 166 pp., illus. $39.95.

Complete facts on the post-war Single Action Army revolvers. Information on calibers, production numbers and variations taken from factory records.

Colt Single Action Army Revolvers and the London Agency, by C. Kenneth Moore, Andrew Mowbray Publishers, Lincoln, RI, 1990. 144 pp., illus. $35.00.

Drawing on vast documentary sources, this work chronicles the relationship between the London Agency and the Hartford home office.

The Colt U.S. General Officers' Pistols, by Horace Greeley IV, Andrew Mowbray Inc., Lincoln, RI, 1990. 199 pp., illus. $38.00.

These unique weapons, issued as a badge of rank to General Officers in the U.S. Army from WWII onward, remain highly personal artifacts of the military leaders who carried them. Includes serial numbers and dates of issue.

*__Colts from the William M. Locke Collection,__ by Frank Sellers, Andrew Mowbray Publishers, Lincoln, RI, 1996. 192 pp., illus. $55.00.

This important book illustrates all of the famous Locke Colts, with captions by arms authority Frank Sellers.

Colt's Dates of Manufacture 1837-1978, by R.L. Wilson, published by Maurie Albert, Coburg, Australia; N.A. distributor I.D.S.A. Books, Hamilton, OH, 1983. 61 pp. $10.00.

An invaluable pocket guide to the dates of manufacture of Colt firearms up to 1978.

Colt's 100th Anniversary Firearms Manual 1836-1936: A Century of Achievement, Wolfe Publishing Co., Prescott, AZ, 1992. 100 pp., illus. Paper covers. $12.95.

Originally published by the Colt Patent Firearms Co., this booklet covers the history, manufacturing procedures and the guns of the first 100 years of the genius of Samuel Colt.

The Complete Guide to U.S. Infantry Weapons of World War Two, by Bruce Canfield, Andrew Mowbray, Publisher, Lincoln, RI, 1995. 303 pp., illus. $35.00.

A definitive work on the weapons used by the United States Armed Forces in WWII.

Compliments of Col. Ruger: A Study of Factory Engraved Single Action Revolvers, by John C. Dougan, Taylor Publishing Co., El Paso, TX, 1992. 238 pp., illus. $46.50.

Clearly detailed black and white photographs and a precise text present an accurate istory of the Sturm, Ruger & Co. single-action revolver engraving project.

Confederate Revolvers, by William A. Gary, Taylor Publishing Co., Dallas, TX, 1987. 174 pp., illus. $49.95.

Comprehensive work on the rarest of Confederate weapons.

Cowboy Collectibles and Western Memorabilia, by Bob Bell and Edward Vebell, Schiffer Publishing, Atglen, PA, 1992. 160 pp., illus. Paper covers. $29.95.

The exciting era of the cowboy and the wild west collectibles including rifles, pistols, gun rigs, etc.

Cowboy and Gunfighter Collectible, by Bill Mackin, Mountain Press Publishing Co., Missoula, MT, 1995. 178 pp., illus. Paper covers. $25.00.

A photographic encyclopedia with price guide and makers' index.

Cowboy Hero Cap Pistols, by Rudy D'Angelo, Antique Trader Books, Dubuque, IA, 1998. 196 pp., illus. Paper covers. $34.95.

Aimed at collectors of cap pistols created and named for famous film and television cowboy heros, this in-depth guide hits all the marks. Current values are given.

The Deringer in America, Volume 1, The Percussion Period, by R.L. Wilson and L.D. Eberhart, Andrew Mowbray Inc., Lincoln, RI, 1985. 271 pp., illus. $48.00.

A long awaited book on the American percussion deringer.

The Deringer in America, Volume 2, The Cartridge Period, by L.D. Eberhart and R.L. Wilson, Andrew Mowbray Inc., Publishers, Lincoln, RI, 1993. 284 pp., illus. $65.00.

Comprehensive coverage of cartridge deringers organized alphabetically by maker. Includes all types of deringers known by the authors to have been offered to the American market.

The Devil's Paintbrush: Sir Hiram Maxim's Gun, by Dolf Goldsmith, 2nd Edition, expanded and revised, Collector Grade Publications, Toronto, Canada, 1993. 384 pp., illus. $69.95

The classic work on the world's first true automatic machine gun.

Drums A'beating Trumpets Sounding, by William H. Guthman, The Connecticut Historical Society, Westport, CT, 1993. 232 pp., illus. $75.00.

Artistically carved powder horns in the provincial manner, 1746-1781.

The Dutch Luger (Parabellum) A Complete History, by Bas J. Martens and Guus de Vries, Ironside International Publishers, Inc., Alexandria, VA, 1995. 268 pp., illus. $49.95.

The history of the Luger in the Netherlands. An extensive description of the Dutch pistol and trials and the different models of the Luger in the Dutch service.

The Eagle on U.S. Firearms, by John W. Jordan, Pioneer Press, Union City, TN, 1992. 140 pp., illus. Paper covers. $14.95.
Stylized eagles have been stamped on government owned or manufactured firearms in the U.S. since the beginning of our country. This book lists and illustrates these various eagles in an informative and refreshing manner.

Early Indian Trade Guns: 1625-1775, by T.M. Hamilton, Museum of the Great Plains, Lawton, OK, 1968. 34 pp., illus. Paper covers. $12.95.
Detailed descriptions of subject arms, compiled from early records and from the study of remnants found in Indian country.

Encyclopedia of Ruger Rimfire Semi-Automatic Pistols: 1949-1992, by Chad Hiddleson, Krause Publications, Iola, WI, 1993. 250 pp., illus. $29.95.
Covers all physical aspects of Ruger 22-caliber pistols including important features such as boxes, grips, muzzlebrakes, instruction manuals, serial numbers, etc.

Encyclopedia of Ruger Semi-Automatic Rimfire Pistols 1949-1992, by Chad Hiddleson, Krause Publications, Iola, WI, 1994. 304 pp., illus. $29.95.
This book is a compilation of years of research, outstanding photographs and technical data on Ruger.

European Firearms in Swedish Castles, by Kaa Wennberg, Bohuslaningens Boktryckeri AB, Uddevalla, Sweden, 1986. 156 pp., illus. $50.00.
The famous collection of Count Keller, the Ettersburg Castle collection, and others. English text.

European Gun Makers, by Hans Pfingsten & Robert Jones, Armory Publications, Inc., Coeur d'Alene, ID. 300 pp., illus. $63.00
A study of the double-barrel shotguns and rifles, three-barrel guns (drilling) and four-barrel guns (vierling) made by German and Austrian gun makers.

European Sporting Cartridges, Part 1, by W.B. Dixon, Armory Publications, inc., Coeur d'Alene, ID, 1997. 250 pp., illus. $63.00
Photographs and drawings of over 550 centerfire cartridge case types in 1,300 illustrations produced in German and Austria from 1875 to 1995.

Fifteen Years in the Hawken Lode, by John D. Baird, The Gun Room Press, Highland Park, NJ, 1976. 120 pp., illus. $24.95.
A collection of thoughts and observations gained from many years of intensive study of the guns from the shop of the Hawken brothers.

'51 Colt Navies, by Nathan L. Swayze, The Gun Room Press, Highland Park, NJ, 1993. 243 pp., illus. $59.95.
The Model 1851 Colt Navy, its variations and markings.

Firearms and Tackle Memorabilia, by John Delph, Schiffer Publishing, Ltd., West Chester, PA, 1991. 124 pp., illus. $39.95.
A collector's guide to signs and posters, calendars, trade cards, boxes, envelopes, and other highly sought after memorabilia. With a value guide.

Firearms of the American West 1866-1894, by Louis A. garavaglia and Charles g. Worman, University of Colorado Press, Niwot, CO, 1998. 416 pp., illus. $59.95.
A monumental work that offers both technical information on lall of the important firearms used in the West during this period and a highly entertaining history of how they were used, who used them, and why.

Flayderman's Guide to Antique American Firearms and Their Values, 7th Edition, edited by Norm Flayderman, DBI books, a division of Krause Publications, Inc., Iola, WI, 1998. 656 pp., illus. Paper covers. $32.95.
A completely updated and new edition with more than 3,600 models and variants extensively described with all marks and specifications necessary for quick identification.

*__The .45-70 Springfield,__ by Joe Poyer and Craig Riesch, North Cape Publications, Tustin, CA, 1996. 150 pp., illus. Paper covers. $15.95.
A revised and expanded second edition of a best-selling reference work organized by serial number and date of production to aid the collector in identifying popular "Trapdoor" rifles and carbines.

Frank and George Freund and the Sharps Rifle, by Gerald O. Kelver, Gerald O. Kelver, Brighton, CO, 1986. 60 pp., illus. Paper covers. $12.00.
Pioneer gunmakers of Wyoming Territory and Colorado.

The French 1935 Pistols, by Eugene Medlin and Colin Doane, Eugene Medlin, El Paso, TX, 1995. 172 pp., illus. Paper covers. $25.95.
The development and identification of successive models, fakes and variants, holsters and accessories, and serial numbers by dates of production.

From the Kingdom of Lilliput: The Miniature Firearms of David Kucer, by K. Corey Keeble and **The Making of Miniatures,** by David Kucer, Museum Restoration Service, Ontario, Canada, 1994. 51 pp., illus, $25.00.
An overview of the subject of miniatures in general combined with an outline by the artist himself on the way he makes a miniature firearm.

Frontier Pistols and Revolvers, by Dominique Venner, Book Sales, Edison, NJ, 1998. 144 pp., illus. $19.95.
Colt, Smith & Wesson, Remington and other early-brand revolvers which tamed the American frontier are shown amid vintage photographs, etchings and paintings to evoke the wild West, the civil War and our early history.

The Fusil de Tulole in New France, 1691-1741, by Russel Bouchard, Museum Restorations Service, Bloomfield, Ontario, Canada, 1997. 36 pp., illus. Paper covers. $6.95
The development of the company and the identification of their arms.

Game Guns & Rifles: Percussion to Hammerless Ejector in Britain, by Richard Akehurst, Trafalgar Square, N. Pomfret, VT, 1993. 192 pp., illus. $39.95.
Long considered a classic this important reprint covers the period of British gunmaking between 1830-1900.

George Schreyer, Sr. and Jr., Gunmakers of Hanover, Pennsylvania, by George Shumway, George Shumway Publishers, York, PA, 1990. 160pp., illus. $50.00.
This monograph is a detailed photographic study of almost all known surviving long rifles and smoothbore guns made by highly regarded gunsmiths George Schreyer, Sr. and Jr.

The German Assault Rifle 1935-1945, by Peter R. Senich, Paladin Press, Boulder, CO, 1987. 328 pp., illus. $49.95.
A complete review of machine carbines, machine pistols and assault rifles employed by Hitler's Wehrmacht during WWII.

The German K98k Rifle, 1934-1945: The Backbone of the Wehrmacht, by Richard D. Law, Collector Grade Publications, Inc., Toronto, Canada, 1993. 336 pp., illus. $69.95.
The most comprehensive study ever published on the 14,000,000 bolt-action K98k rifles produced in Germany between 1934 and 1945.

German Machineguns, by Daniel D. Musgrave, Revised edition, Ironside International Publishers, Inc. Alexandria, VA, 1992. 586 pp., 650 illus. $49.95.
The most definitive book ever written on German machineguns. Covers the introduction and development of machineguns in Germany from 1899 to the rearmament period after WWII.

German Military Rifles and Machine Pistols, 1871-1945, by Hans Dieter Gotz, Schiffer Publishing Co., West Chester, PA, 1990. 245 pp., illus. $35.00.
This book portrays in words and pictures the development of the modern German weapons and their ammunition including the scarcely known experimental types.

German 7.9mm Military Ammunition, by Daniel W. Kent, Daniel W. Kent, Ann Arbor, MI, 1991. 244 pp., illus. $35.00.
The long-awaited revised edition of a classic among books devoted to ammunition.

German Pistols and Holsters, 1934-1945, Volume 4, by Lt. Col. Robert D. Whittington, 3rd, U.S.A.R., Brownlee Books, Hooks, TX, 1991. 208 pp. $30.00.
Pistols and holsters issued in 412 selected armed forces, army and Waffen-SS units including information on personnel, other weapons and transportation.

The Golden Age of Remington, by Robert W.D. Ball, Krause publications, Iola, WI, 1995. 194 pp., illus. $29.95.
For Remington collectors or firearms historians, this book provides a pictorial history of Remington through World War I. Includes value guide.

A Guide to Ballard Breechloaders, by George j. Layman, Pioneer Press, Union City, TN, 1997. 261 pp., illus. Paper covers. $19.95
Documents the saga of this fine rifle from the first models made by Ball & Williams of Worchester, to its production by the Marlin Firearms Co, to the cessation of 19th century manufacture in 1891, and finally to the modern reproductions made in the 1990's.

A Guide to the Maynard Breechloader, by George J. Layman, George J. Layman, Ayer, MA, 1993. 125 pp., illus. Paper covers. $17.95.
The first book dedicated entirely to the Maynard family of breech-loading firearms. Coverage of the arms is given from the 1850s through the 1880s.

Guide to Ruger Single Action Revolvers Production Dates, 1953-73, by John C. Dougan, Blacksmith Corp., Chino Valley, AZ, 1991. 22 pp., illus. Paper covers. $9.95.
A unique pocket-sized handbook providing production information for the popular Ruger single-action revolvers manufactured during the first 20 years.

Gun Collecting, by Geoffrey Boothroyd, Sportsman's Press, London, 1989. 208 pp., illus. $29.95.
The most comprehensive list of 19th century British gunmakers and gunsmiths ever published.

Gun Collector's Digest, 5th Edition, edited by Joseph J. Schroeder, DBI Books, a division of Krause Publications, Inc., Iola, WI, 1989. 224 pp., illus. Paper covers. $17.95.
The latest edition of this sought-after series.

Gunmakers of Illinois, 1683-1900, Vol. 1, by Curtis L. Johnson, George Shumway Publisher, York, PA, 1997. 200 pp., illus. $50.00
This first volume covering the alphabet from A to F of a projected three-volume series, records the available names, dates, biographical details, and illustrates the work undertaken, by almost 1600 Illinois gunsmiths and gunmakers.

Gunmakers of London 1350-1850, by Howard L. Blackmore, George Shumway Publisher, York, PA, 1986. 222 pp., illus. $35.00.
A listing of all the known workmen of gun making in the first 500 years, plus a history of the guilds, cutlers, armourers, founders, blacksmiths, etc. 260 gunmarks are illustrated.

Gunsmiths of Illinois, by Curtis L. Johnson, George Shumway Publishers, York, PA, 1995. 160 pp., illus. $50.00.
Genealogical information is provided for nearly one thousand gunsmiths. Contains hundreds of illustrations of handmade origin, from Illinois.

The Gunsmiths of Manhattan, 1625-1900: A Checklist of Tradesmen, by Michael H. Lewis, Museum Restoration Service, Bloomfield, Ont., Canada, 1991. 40 pp., illus. Paper covers. $4.95.
This listing of more than 700 men in the arms trade in New York City prior to about the end of the 19th century will provide a guide for identification and further research.

The Guns of Dagenham: Lanchester, Patchett, Sterling, by Peter Laidler and David Howroyd, Collector Grade Publications, Inc., Cobourg, Ont., Canada, 1995. 310 pp., illus. $39.95.
An in-depth history of the small arms made by the Sterling Company of Dagenham, Essex, England, from 1940 until Sterling was purchased by British Aerospace in 1989 and closed.

Guns of the Western Indian War, by R. Stephen Dorsey, Collector's Library, Eugene, OR, 1997. 220 pp., illus. Paper covers. $30.00.
The full story of the guns and ammunition that made western history in the turbulent period of 1865-1890.

Gun Tools, Their History and Identification by James B. Shaffer, Lee A. Rutledge and R. Stephen Dorsey, Collector's Library, Eugene, OR, 1992. 375 pp., illus. $32.00.
Written history of foreign and domestic gun tools from the flintlock period to WWII.

Gun Tools, their History and Identifications, Volume 2, by Stephen Dorsey and James B. Shaffer, Collectors' Library, Eugene, OR, 1997. 396 pp., illus. Paper covers. $30.00.
Gun tools from the Royal Armouries Museum in england, Pattern Room, Royal Ordnance Reference Collection in Nottingham and from major private collections.

*__Hall's Military Breechloaders,__ by Peter A. Schmidt, Andrew Mowbray Publishers, Lincoln, RI, 1996. 232 pp., illus. $55.00.
The whole story behind these bold and innovative firearms.

Handbook of Military Rifle Marks 1870-1950, by Richard A. Hoffman and Noel P. Schott, Mapleleaf Militaria Publishing, St. Louis, MO, 1995. 42 pp., illus. Spiral bound. $15.00.
An illustrated guide to identifying military rifle and marks.

The Handgun, by Geoffrey Boothroyd, David and Charles, North Pomfret, VT, 1989. 566 pp., illus. $60.00.
Every chapter deals with an important period in handgun history from the 14th century to the present.

The Hawken Rifle: Its Place in History, by Charles E. Hanson, Jr., The Fur Press, Chadron, NE, 1979. 104 pp., illus. Paper covers. $15.00.
A definitive work on this famous rifle.

Hawken Rifles, The Mountain Man's Choice, by John D. Baird, The Gun Room Press, Highland Park, NJ, 1976. 95 pp., illus. $29.95.
Covers the rifles developed for the Western fur trade. Numerous specimens are described and shown in photographs.

High Standard: A Collector's Guide to the Hamden & Hartford Target Pistols, by Tom Dance, Andrew Mowbray, Inc., Lincoln, RI, 1991. 192 pp., illus. Paper covers. $24.00.
From Citation to Supermatic, all of the production models and specials made from 1951 to 1984 are covered according to model number or series.

Historic Pistols: The American Martial Flintlock 1760-1845, by Samuel E. Smith and Edwin W. Bitter, The Gun Room Press, Highland Park, NJ, 1986. 353 pp., illus. $45.00.
Covers over 70 makers and 163 models of American martial arms.

Historical Hartford Hardware, by William W. Dalrymple, Colt Collector Press, Rapid City, SD, 1976. 42 pp., illus. Paper covers. $10.00.
Historically associated Colt revolvers.

The History and Development of Small Arms Ammunition, Volume 1, by George A. Hoyem, Armory Publications, Oceanside, CA, 1991. 230 pp., illus. $65.00.
Military musket, rifle, carbine and primitive machine gun cartridges of the 18th and 19th centuries, together with the firearms that chambered them.

The History and Development of Small Arms Ammunition, Volume 2, by George A. Hoyem, Armory Publications, Oceanside, CA, 1991. 303 pp., illus. $65.00.
Covers the blackpowder military centerfire rifle, carbine, machine gun and volley gun ammunition used in 28 nations and dominions, together with the firearms that chambered them.

The History of Smith and Wesson, by Roy G. Jinks, Willowbrook Enterprises, Springfield, MA, 1988. 290 pp., illus. $27.95.
Revised 10th Anniversary edition of the definite book on S&W firearms.

The History of Winchester Firearms 1866-1992, sixth edition, updated, expanded, and revised by Thomas Henshaw, New Win Publishing, Clinton, NJ, 1993. 280 pp., illus. $24.95.
This classic is the standard reference for all collectors and others seeking the facts about any Winchester firearm, old or new.

History of Winchester Repeating Arms Company, by Herbert G. Houze, Krause Publications, Iola, WI, 1994. 800 pp., illus. $50.00.
The complete Winchester history from 1856-1981.

Honour Bound: The Chauchat Machine Rifle, by Gerard Demaison and Yves Buffetaut, Collector Grade Publications, Inc., Cobourg, Ont., Canada, 1995. $39.95.
The story of the CSRG (Chauchat) machine rifle, the most manufactured automatic weapon of World War One.

How to Buy and Sell Used Guns, by John Traister, Stoeger Publishing Co., So. Hackensack, NJ, 1984. 192 pp., illus. Paper covers. $10.95.
A new guide to buying and selling guns.

Identification Manual on the .303 British Service Cartridge, No. 1-Ball Ammunition, by B.A. Temple, I.D.S.A. Books, Piqua, OH, 1986. 84 pp., 57 illus. $12.50

Identification Manual on the .303 British Service Cartridge, No. 2-Blank Ammunition, by B.A. Temple, I.D.S.A. Books, Piqua, OH, 1986. 95 pp., 59 illus. $12.50

Identification Manual on the .303 British Service Cartridge, No. 3-Special Purpose Ammunition, by B.A. Temple, I.D.S.A. Books, Piqua, OH, 1987. 82 pp., 49 illus. $12.50

Identification Manual on the .303 British Service Cartridge, No. 4-Dummy Cartridges Henry 1869-c.1900, by B.A. Temple, I.D.S.A. Books, Piqua, OH, 1988. 84 pp., 70 illus. $12.50

Identification Manual on the .303 British Service Cartridge, No. 5-Dummy Cartridges (2), by B.A. Temple, I.D.S.A. Books, Piqua, OH, 1994. 78 pp. $12.50

The Illustrated Encyclopedia of Civil War Collectibles, by Chuck Lawliss, Henry Holt and Co., New York, NY, 1997. 316 pp., illus. Paper covers. $22.95.
A comprehensive guide to Union and Confederate arms, equipment, uniforms, and other memorabilia.

Illustrations of United States Military Arms 1776-1903 and Their Inspector's Marks, compiled by Turner Kirkland, Pioneer Press, Union City, TN, 1988. 37 pp., illus. Paper covers. $4.95.
Reprinted from the 1949 Bannerman catalog. Valuable information for both the advanced and beginning collector.

Indian War Cartridge Pouches, Boxes and Carbine Boots, by R. Stephen Dorsey, Collector's Library, Eugene, OR, 1993. 156 pp., illus. Paper Covers. $25.00.
The key reference work to the cartridge pouches, boxes, carbine sockets and boots of the Indian War period 1865-1890.

An Introduction to the Civil War Small Arms, by Earl J. Coates and Dean S. Thomas, Thomas Publishing Co., Gettysburg, PA, 1990. 96 pp., illus. Paper covers. $10.00.
The small arms carried by the individual soldier during the Civil War.

Iver Johnson's Arms & Cycle Works Handguns, 1871-1964, by W.E. "Bill" Goforth, Blacksmith Corp., Chino Valley, AZ, 1991. 160 pp., illus. Paper covers. $14.95.
Covers all of the famous Iver Johnson handguns from the early solid-frame pistols and revolvers to optional accessories, special orders and patents.

Jaeger Rifles, by George Shumway, George Shumway Publisher, York, PA, 1994. 108 pp., illus. Paper covers. $30.00.
Thirty-six articles previously published in *Muzzle Blasts* are reproduced here. They deal with late-17th, and 18th century rifles from Vienna, Carlsbad, Bavaria, Saxony, Brandenburg, Suhl, North-Central Germany, and the Rhine Valley.

Japanese Rifles of World War Two, by Duncan O. McCollum, Excalibur Publications, Latham, NY, 1996. 64 pp., illus. Paper covers. $18.95.
A sweeping view of the rifles and carbines that made up Japan's arsenal during the conflict.

The Kentucky Pistol, by Roy Chandler and James Whisker, Old Bedford Village Press, Bedford, PA, 1997. 225 pp., illus. $45.00
A photographic study of Kentucky pistols from famous collections.

The Kentucky Rifle, by Captain John G.W. Dillin, George Shumway Publisher, York, PA, 1993. 221 pp., illus. $50.00.
This well-known book was the first attempt to tell the story of the American longrifle. This edition retains the original text and illustrations with supplemental footnotes provided by Dr. George Shumway.

The Kentucky Rifle, a True American Heritage in Picture, by the Kentucky rifle Associations, Washington, D.C., 1997. Published by the Forte Group, Alexandria, VA. 109 pp., illus. $35.00.
This photographic essay reveals both the beauty and the decorative nature of the Kentucky by providing detailed photos of some of the most significant examples of American rifles, pistols and accoutrements.

Know Your Broomhandle Mausers, by R.J. Berger, Blacksmith Corp., Southport, CT, 1985. 96 pp., illus. Paper covers. $9.95.
An interesting story on the big Mauser pistol and its variations.

Krag Rifles, by William S. Brophy, The Gun Room Press, Highland Park, NJ, 1980. 200 pp., illus. $35.00.
The first comprehensive work detailing the evolution and various models, both military and civilian.

The Krieghoff Parabellum, by Randall Gibson, Midland, TX, 1988. 279 pp., illus. $40.00.
A comprehensive text pertaining to the Lugers manufactured by H. Krieghoff Waffenfabrik.

The Lee-Enfield Story, by Ian Skennerton, Ian Skennerton, Ashmore City, Australia, 1993. 503 pp., illus. $59.95.
The Lee-Metford, Lee-Enfield, S.M.L.E. and No. 4 series rifles and carbines from 1880 to the present.

***LeMat, the Man, the Gun,** by Valmore J. Forgett and Alain F. and Marie-Antoinette Serpette, Navy Arms Co., Ridgefield, NJ, 1996. 218 pp., illus. $49.95.
The first definitive study of the Confederate revolvers invention, development and delivery by Francois Alexandre LeMat.

Les Pistolets Automatiques Francaise 1890-1990, by Jean Huon, Combined Books, Inc., Conshohocken, PA, 1997. 160 pp., illus. French text. $34.95
French automatic pistols from the earliest experiments through the World Wars and Indo-China to modern security forces.

***Levine's Guide to Knives And Their Values, 4th Edition,** by Bernard Levine, DBI Books, a division of Krause Publications, Iola, WI, 1997. 512 pp., illus. Paper covers. $27.95
All the basic tools for identifying, valuing and collecting folding and fixed blade knives.

The London Gunmakers and the English Duelling Pistol, 1770-1830, by Keith R. Dill, Museum Restoration Service, Bloomfield, Ontario, Canada, 1997. 36 pp., illus. Paper covers. $6.95
Ten gunmakers made London one of the major gunmaking centers of the world. This book examines how the design nad construction of their pistols contributed to that reputation and how these characteristics may be used to date flintlock arms.

Longrifles of North Carolina, by John Bivens, George Shumway Publisher, York, PA, 1988. 256 pp., illus. $50.00.
Covers art and evolution of the rifle, immigration and trade movements. Committee of Safety gunsmiths, characteristics of the North Carolina rifle.

Longrifles of Pennsylvania, Volume 1, Jefferson, Clarion & Elk Counties, by Russel H. Harringer, George Shumway Publisher, York, PA, 1984. 200 pp., illus. $50.00.
First in series that will treat in great detail the longrifles and gunsmiths of Pennsylvania.

***The Luger Handbook,** by Aarron Davis, Krause Publications, Iola, WI, 1997. 112 pp., illus. Paper covers. $9.95.
Quick reference to classify Luger models and variations with complete details including proofmarks.

Lugers at Random, by Charles Kenyon, Jr., Handgun Press, Glenview, IL, 1990. 420 pp., illus. $49.95.
A new printing of this classic, comprehensive reference for all Luger collectors.

The Luger Story, by John Walter, Stackpole Books, Mechanicsburg, PA, 1995. 256 pp., illus. $39.95.
The standard history of the world's most famous handgun.

The M1 Garand Serial Numbers and Data Sheets, by Scott A. Duff, Export, PA, 1995. 101 pp., illus. Paper covers. $9.95.
Provides the reader with serial numbers related to dates of manufacutre and a large sampling of data sheets to aid in identification or restoration.

The M1 Garand: Owner's Guide, by Scott A. Duff, Scott A. Duff, Wxport, PA, 1997. 126 pp., illus. Paper covers. $16.95.
This Book answers the questions M1 owners most often ask concerning maintenance activities not encounted by military users.

Machine Guns of World War 1, by Robert Bruce, Combined Publishing, Conshohocken, PA, 1998. 128 pp., illus. $39.95.
Live firing classic military weapons in color photographs.

Maine Made Guns and Their Makers, by Dwight B. Demeritt, Friends of the Maine State Museum, Augusta, ME, 1997. 438 pp., illus. $55.00.
An enlarged and updated edition of the definitive work on Maine made guns and their makers.

Marlin Firearms: A History of the Guns and the Company That Made Them, by Lt. Col. William S. Brophy, USAR, Ret., Stackpole Books, Harrisburg, PA, 1989. 672 pp., illus. $75.00.
The definitive book on the Marlin Firearms Co. and their products.

***Martini-Henry .450 Rifles & Carbines,** by Dennis Lewis, Excalibur Publications, Latham, NY, 1996. 72 pp., illus. Paper covers. $11.95.
The stories of the rifles and carbines that were the mainstay of the British soldier through the Victorian wars.

Massachusetts Military Shoulder Arms 1784-1877, by George D. Moller, Andrew Mowbray Publisher, Lincoln, RI, 1989. 250 pp., illus. $24.00.
A scholarly and heavily researched study of the military shoulder arms used by Massachusetts during the 90-year period following the Revolutionary War.

Matt Eastman's Guide to Browning Belgium Firearms 1903-1994, by Matt Eastman, Matt Eastman Publications, Fitzgerald, GA, 1995. 150 pp. Paper covers. $14.95.
Covers all Belgium models through 1994. Manufacturing production figures on the Auto-5 and Safari rifles.

Mauser Bolt Rifles, by Ludwig Olson, F. Brownell & Son, Inc., Montezuma, IA, 1976. 364 pp., illus. $51.95.
The most complete, detailed, authoritative and comprehensive work ever done on Mauser bolt rifles.

Mauser Military Rifles of the World, by Robert W.D. Ball, Krause Publications, Iola, WI, 1996. 272 pp., illus. $39.95.
The rifles produced by the Mauser Co. for their international market with complete production quantities, rarity and technical specifications.

Military Handguns of France 1858-1958, by Eugene Medlin and Jean Huon, Excalibur Publications, Latham, NY, 1994. 124 pp., illus. Paper covers. $24.95.
The first book written in English that provides students of arms with a thorough history of French military handguns.

Military Pistols of Japan, by Fred L. Honeycutt, Jr., Julin Books, Palm Beach Gardens, FL, 1991. 168 pp., illus. $42.00.
Covers every aspect of military pistol production in Japan through WWII.

***The Military Remington Rolling Block Rifle,** by George Layman, George Layman, Ayer, MA, 1996. 146 pp., illus. Paper covers. $24.95.
A standard reference for those with an interest in the Remington rolling block family of firearms.

Military Rifles of Japan, 4th Edition, by F.L. Honeycutt, Julin Books, Lake Park, FL, 1989. 208 pp., illus. $42.00.
A new revised and updated edition. Includes the early Murata-period markings, etc.

Military Small Arms of the 20th Century, 6th Edition, by Ian V. Hogg, DBI Books, a division of Krause Publications, Inc., Iola, WI, 1991. 352 pp., illus. Paper covers. $20.95.
Fully revised and updated edition of the standard reference in its field.

M1 Carbine, by Larry Ruth, Gunroom Press, Highland Park, NJ, 1987. 291 pp., illus. Paper $19.95.
The origin, development, manufacture and use of this famous carbine of World War II.

***The M1 Garand 1936 to 1957,** by Joe Poyer and Craig Riesch, North Cape Publications, Tustin, CA, 1996. 216 pp., illus. Paper covers. $19.95.
Describes the entire range of M1 Garand production in text and quick-scan charts.

The M1 Garand: Post World War, by Scott A. Duff, Scott A. Duff, Export, PA, 1990. 139 pp., illus. Soft covers. $19.95.
A detailed account of the activities at Springfield Armory through this period. International Harvester, H&R, Korean War production and quantities delivered. Serial numbers.

The M1 Garand: World War 2, by Scott A. Duff, Scott A. Duff, Export, PA, 1993. 210 pp., illus. Paper covers. $39.95.
The most comprehensive study available to the collector and historian on the M1 Garand of World War II.

Modern Beretta Firearms, by Gene Gangarosa, Jr., Stoeger Publishing Co., S. Hackensack, NJ, 1994. 288 pp., illus. Paper covers. $16.95.
Traces all models of modern Beretta pistols, rifles, machine guns and combat shotguns.

Modern Gun Values, The Gun Digest Book of, 10th Edition, by the Editors of Gun Digest, DBI Books, a division of Krause Publications, Inc., Iola, WI., 1996. 560 pp. illus. Paper covers. $21.95.
Greatly updated and expanded edition describing and valuing over 7,000 firearms manufactured from 1900 to 1996. The standard for valuing modern firearms.

***Modern Guns Identification & Value Guide, Eleventh Edition,** by Russell and Steve Quartermous, Collector Books, Paducah, KY, 1996. 504 pp., illus. Paper covers. $12.95.
A popular guidebook featuring 2500 models of rifle, handgun and shotgun from 1900 to the present with detailed descriptions and prices.

More Single Shot Rifles, by James C. Grant, The Gun Room Press, Highland Park, NJ, 1976. 324 pp., illus. $29.95.
Details the guns made by Frank Wesson, Milt Farrow, Holden, Borchardt, Stevens, Remington, Winchester, Ballard and Peabody-Martini.

Mortimer, the Gunmakers, 1753-1923, by H. Lee Munson, Andrew Mowbray Inc., Lincoln, RI, 1992. 320 pp., illus. $65.00.
Seen through a single, dominant, English gunmaking dynasty this fascinating study provides a window into the classical era of firearms artistry.

Mossberg: More Gun for the Money, by V. and C. Havlin, Investment Rarities, Inc., Minneapolis, MN, 1995. 304 pp., illus. Paper covers. $24.95.
The history of O. F. Mossberg and Sons, Inc.

The Muzzle-Loading Cap Lock Rifle, by Ned H. Roberts, reprinted by Wolfe Publishing Co., Prescott, AZ, 1991. 432 pp., illus. $30.00.
Originally published in 1940, this fascinating study of the muzzle-loading cap lock rifle covers rifles on the frontier to hunting rifles, including the famous Hawken.

The Navy Luger, by Joachim Gortz and John Walter, Handgun Press, Glenview, IL, 1988. 128 pp., illus. $24.95.
The 9mm Pistole 1904 and the Imperial German Navy. A concise illustrated history.

The Number 5 Jungle Carbine, by Alan M. Petrillo, Excalibur Publications, Latham, NY, 1994. 32 pp., illus. Paper covers. $7.95.
A comprehensive treatment of the rifle that collectors have come to call the "Jungle Carbine"—the Lee-Enfield Number 5, Mark 1.

The '03 Era: When Smokeless Revolutionized U.S. Riflery, by Clark S. Campbell, Collector Grade Publications, Inc., Ontario, Canada, 1994. 334 pp., illus. $44.50.
A much-expanded version of Campbell's *The '03 Springfields*, representing forty years of in-depth research into "all things '03."

Observations on Colt's Second Contract, November 2, 1847, by G. Maxwell Longfield and David T. Basnett, Museum Restoration Service, Bloomfield, Ontario, Canada, 1997. 36 pp., illus. Paper covers. $6.95.
This study traces the history and the construction of the Second Model Colt Dragoon supplied in 1848 to the U.S. Cavalry.

Official Guide to Gunmarks, 3rd edition, by Robert H. Balderson, House of collectibles, New York, NY, 1996. 367 pp., illus. Paper covers. $15.00.
Identifies manufacturers' marks that appear on American and foreign pistols, rifles and shotguns.

Official Price Guide to Antique and Modern Firearms, by Robert H. Balderson, House of Collectibles, New York, NY, 1996. 300 pp., illus. Paper covers. $17.00.
More than 30,000 updated prices for firearms manufactured from the 1600's to the present.

Official Price Guide to Civil War Collectibles, by Richard Friz, House of Collectibles, New York, NY, 1995. 375 pp., illus. Paper covers. $17.00.
Price listings and current market values for thousands of Civil War items.

Official Price Guide to Gun Collecting, by R.L. Wilson, Ballantine/House of Collectibles, New York, NY, 1998. 450 pp., illus. Paper covers. $21.50.
covers more than 30,000 prices from Colt revolvers to Winchester rifles and shotguns to German Lugers and British sporting rifles and game guns.

The P-08 Parabellum Luger Automatic Pistol, edited by J. David McFarland, Desert Publications, Cornville, AZ, 1982. 20 pp., illus. Paper covers. $10.00.
Covers every facet of the Luger, plus a listing of all known Luger models.

Packing Iron, by Richard C. Rattenbury, Zon International Publishing, Millwood, NY, 1993. 216 pp., illus. $45.00.
The best book yet produced on pistol holsters and rifle scabbards. Over 300 variations of holster and scabbards are illustrated in large, clear plates.

Patents for Inventions, Class 119 (Small Arms), 1855-1930. British Patent Office, Armory Publications, Oceanside, CA, 1993. 7 volume set. $350.00.
Contains 7980 abridged patent descriptions and their sectioned line drawings, plus a 37-page alphabetical index of the patentees.

Pattern Dates for British Ordnance Small Arms, 1718-1783, by Dr. DeWitt Bailey, Thomas Publications, Gettysburg, PA, 1997. 128 pp., illus. Paper covers. $20.00.
A heavy illustrated guide to pistols, carbines, rifles and muskets produced during the period.

Pistols of the World, 3rd Edition, by Ian Hogg and John Weeks, DBI Books, a division of Krause Publications, Inc., Iola, WI, 1992. 320 pp., illus. Paper covers. $20.95.
A totally revised edition of one of the leading studies of small arms.

The Pitman Notes on U.S. Martial Small Arms and Ammunition, 1776-1933, Volume 2, Revolvers and Automatic Pistols, by Brig. Gen. John Pitman, Thomas Publications, Gettysburg, PA, 1990. 192 pp., illus. $29.95.
A most important primary source of information on United States military small arms and ammunition.

The Plains Rifle, by Charles Hanson, Gun Room Press, Highland Park, NJ, 1989. 169 pp., illus. $35.00.
All rifles that were made with the plainsman in mind, including pistols.

Powder and Ball Small Arms, by Martin Pegler, Windrow & Green, London, 1998. 128 pp., illus. $39.95.
Part of the new "Live Firing classic Weapons" series featuring full color photos of experienced shooters dressed in authentic costumes handling, loading and firing historic weapons.

The Powder Flask Book, by Ray Riling, R&R Books, Livonia, NY, 1993. 514 pp., illus. $70.00.
The complete book on flasks of the 19th century. Exactly scaled pictures of 1,600 flasks are illustrated.

Proud Promise: French Autoloading Rifles, 1898-1979,by Jean Huon, Collector Grade Publications, Inc., Cobourg, Ont., Canada, 1995. 216 pp., illus. $39.95.
The author has finally set the record straight about the importance of French contributions to modern arms design.

E. C. Prudhomme's Gun Engraving Review, by E. C. Prudhomme, R&R Books, Livonia, NY, 1994. 164 pp., illus. $60.00.
As a source for engravers and collectors, this book is an indispensable guide to styles and techniques of the world's foremost engravers.

The Rare and Valuable Antique Arms, by James E. Serven, Pioneer Press, Union City, TN, 1976. 106 pp., illus. Paper covers. $4.95.
A guide to the collector in deciding which direction his collecting should go, investment value, historic interest, mechanical ingenuity, high art or personal preference.

Reloading Tools, Sights and Telescopes for Single Shot Rifles, by Gerald O. Kelver, Brighton, CO, 1982. 163 pp., illus. Paper covers. $15.00.
A listing of most of the famous makers of reloading tools, sights and telescopes with a brief description of the products they manufactured.

The Remington-Lee Rifle, by Eugene F. Myszkowski, Excalibur Publications, Latham, NY, 1995. 100 pp., illus. Paper covers. $22.50.
Features detailed descriptions, including serial number ranges, of each model from the first Lee Magazine Rifle produced for the U.S. Navy to the last Remington-Lee Small Bores shipped to the Cuban Rural Guard.

Revolvers of the British Services 1854-1954, by W.H.J. Chamberlain and A.W.F. Taylerson, Museum Restoration Service, Ottawa, Canada, 1989. 80 pp., illus. $27.50.
Covers the types issued among many of the United Kingdom's naval, land or air services.

Rhode Island Arms Makers & Gunsmiths, by William O. Archibald, Andrew Mowbray, Inc., Lincoln, RI, 1990. 108 pp., illus. $16.50.
A serious and informative study of an important area of American arms making.

Rifles of the World, by Jean-Noel Mouret, Book Sales, Edison, NJ, 1998. 144 pp., illus. $17.99.
This highly illustrated book recounts the fascinating story of the rifle and its development. Military, sporting and hunting.

***Rifles of the World, 2nd Edition,** by John Walter, DBI Books, a division of Krause Publications, Inc., Iola, WI. 512 pp., illus. Paper covers. $24.95.

The Rock Island '03, by C.S. Ferris, C.S. Ferris, Arvada, CO, 1993. 58 pp., illus. Paper covers. $12.50.
A monograph of interenst to the collector or historian concentrating on the U.S. M1903 rifle made by the less publicized of our two producing facilities.

Round Ball to Rimfire, Vol. 1, by Dean Thomas, Thomas Publications, Gerrysburg, PA, 1997. 144 pp., illus. $40.00.
The first of a two-volume set of the most complete history and guide for all small arms ammunition used in the Civil War. The information includes data from research and development to the arsenals that created it.

Ruger, edited by Joseph Roberts, Jr., the National Rifle Association of America, Washington, D.C., 1991. 109 pp. illus. Paper covers. $14.95.
The story of Bill Ruger's indelible imprint in the history of sporting firearms.

***Ruger and his Guns,** by R.L. Wilson, Simon & Schuster, New Tork, NY, 1996. 358 pp., illus. $65.00.
A history of the man, the company and their firearms.

The SAFN-49 and The FAL, by Joe Poyer and Dr. Richard Feirman, North Cape Publications, Tustin, CA, 1998. 160 pp., illus. Paper covers. $14.95.
The first complete overview of the SAFN-49 battle rifle, from its pre-World War 2 beginnings to its military service in countries as diverse as the Belgian Congo and Argentina. The FAL was "light" version of the SAFN-49 nad it became the Free World's most adopted battle rifle.

Sam Colt's Own Record 1847, by John Parsons, Wolfe Publishing Co., Prescott, AZ, 1992. 167 pp., illus. $24.50.
Chronologically presented, the correspondence published here completes the account of the manufacture, in 1847, of the Walker Model Colt revolver.

J.P. Sauer & Sohn, Suhl, by Jim Cate & Nico Van Gun, CBC Book Co., Chattanoga, TN, 1998. 406 pp., illus. $65.00.
A historical study of Sauer automatic pistols. Over 500 photos showing the different variations of pistols, grips, magazines and holsters.

Scottish Firearms, by Claude Blair and Robert Woosnam-Savage, Museum Restoration Service, Bloomfield, Ont., Canada, 1995. 52 pp., illus. Paper covers. $4.95.
This revision of the first book devoted entirely to Scottish firearms is supplemented by a register of surviving Scottish long guns.

The Scottish Pistol, by Martin Kelvin. Fairleigh Dickinson University Press, Dist. By Associated University Presses, Cranbury, NJ, 1997. 256 pp., illus. $49.50.
The Scottish pistol, its history, manufacture and design.

Scouts, Peacemakers and New Frontiers in .22 Caliber, by Don Wilkerson, Cherokee Publications, Kansas City, MO, 1995. 224 pp., illus. $40.00.
Covers the 48 variations and numerous subvariants of the later rimfire Single Actions.

Sharps Firearms, by Frank Seller, Frank M. Seller, Denver, CO, 1982. 358 pp., illus. $50.00.
Traces the development of Sharps firearms with full range of guns made including all martial variations.

Simeon North: First Official Pistol Maker of the United States, by S. North and R. North, The Gun Room Press, Highland Park, NJ, 1972. 207 pp., illus. $15.95.
Reprint of the rare first edition.

***The SKS Carbine,** by Steve Kehaya and Joe Poyer, North Cape Publications, Tustin, CA, 1997. 150 pp., illus. Paper covers. $16.95.
The first comprehensive examination of a major historical firearm used through the Vietnam conflict to the diamond fields of Angola.

The SKS Type 45 Carbines, by Duncan Long, Desert Publications, El Dorado, AZ, 1992. 110 pp., illus. Paper covers.
Covers the history and practical aspects of operating, maintaining and modifying this abundantly available rifle.

Small Arms of the East India Company 1600-1856, by D. F. Harding, Volume 1 & 2, Foresight Books, London, England, $185.00.
Over 100 patterns of East India Company muskets, fusils, rifles, carbines, pistols, blunderbusses, wallpieces and bayonets identified for the first time in print.

Smith & Wesson 1857-1945, by Robert J. Neal and Roy G. Jinks, R&R Books, Livonia, NY, 1996. 434 pp., illus. $50.00.
The bible for all existing and aspiring Smith & Wesson collectors.

Sniper Variations of the German K98k Rifle, by Richard D. Law, Collector Grade Publications, Ontario, Canada, 1997. 240 pp., illus. $47.50.
Volume 2 of "Backbone of the Wehrmacht" the author's in-depth study of the German K98k rifle. This volume concentrates on the telescopic-sighted rifle of choice for most German snipers during World War 2.

Southern Derringers of the Mississippi Valley, by Turner Kirkland, Pioneer Press, Tenn., 1971. 80 pp., illus., paper covers. $10.00.
A guide for the collector, and a much-needed study.

Soviet Russian Postwar Military Pistols and Cartridges, by Fred A. Datig, Handgun Press, Glenview, IL, 1988. 152 pp., illus. $29.95.
Thoroughly researched, this definitive sourcebook covers the development and adoption of the Makarov, Stechkin and the new PSM pistols. Also included in this source book is coverage on Russian clandestine weapons and pistol cartridges.

Soviet Russian Tokarev "TT" Pistols and Cartridges 1929-1953, by Fred Datig, Graphic Publishers, Santa Ana, CA, 1993. 168 pp., illus. $39.95.
Details of rare arms and their accessories are shown in hundreds of photos. It also contains a complete bibliography and index.

Soviet Small-Arms and ammunition, by David Bolotin, Handgun Press, Glenview, IL, 1996. 264 pp., illus. $49.95.
An authoritative and complete book on Soviet small arms.

Spencer Firearms, by Roy Marcot, R&R Books, Livonia, NY, 1995. 237 pp., illus. $60.00.
The definitive work on one of the most famous Civil War firearms.

Sporting Collectibles, by Jim and Vivian Karsnitz, Schiffer Publishing Ltd., West Chester, PA, 1992. 160 pp., illus. Paper covers. $29.95.
The fascinating world of hunting related collectibles presented in an informative text.

The Springfield 1903 Rifles, by Lt. Col. William S. Brophy, USAR, Ret., Stackpole Books Inc., Harrisburg, PA, 1985. 608 pp., illus. $75.00.
The illustrated, documented story of the design, development, and production of all the models, appendages, and accessories.

Springfield Armory Shoulder Weapons 1795-1968, by Robert W.D. Ball, Antique Trader Books, Dubuque, IA, 1998. 264 pp., illus. $34.95.
This book documents the 255 basic models of rifles, including test and trial rifles, produced by the Springfield Armory. It features the entire history of rifles and carbines manufactured at the Armory, the development of each weapon with specific operating characteristics and procedures.

***Springfield Model 1903 Service Rifle Production and Lateration, 1905-1910,** by C.S. Ferris and John Beard, Arvada, CO, 1995. 66 pp., illus. Paper covers. $12.50.
A highly recommended work for any serious student of the Springfield Model 1903 rifle.

Springfield Shoulder Arms 1795-1865, by Claud E. Fuller, S. & S. Firearms, Glendale, NY, 1986. 76 pp., illus. Paper covers. $17.95.
Exact reprint of the scarce 1930 edition of one of the most definitive works on Springfield flintlock and percussion muskets ever published.

Standard Catalog of Firearms, 8th Edition, edited by Ned Schwing, Krause Publications, Iola, WI, 1998. 1,200 pp., illus. Paper covers. $29.95.
The world's number one guide for firearms collectors with over more than 4,000 photos.

Standard Catalog of Smith and Wesson, by Jim Supica and Richard Nahas, Krause Publications, Iola, WI, 1996. 240 pp., illus. $29.95.

Clearly details hundreds of products by the legendary manufacturer. How to identify, evaluate the condition and assess the value of 752 Smith & Wesson models and variations.

Steel Canvas: The Art of American Arms, by R.L. Wilson, Random House, NY, 1995, 384 pp., illus. $65.00.

Presented here for the first time is the breathtaking panorama of America's extraordinary engravers and embellishers of arms, from the 1700s to modern times.

Stevens Pistols & Pocket Rifles, by K.L. Cope, Museum Restoration Service, Alexandria Bay, NY, 1992. 114 pp., illus. $24.50.

This is the story of the guns and the man who designed them and the company which he founded to make them.

*__A Study of Colt Conversions and Other Percussion Revolvers,__ by R. Bruce McDowell, Krause Publications, Iola, WI, 1997. 464 pp., illus. $39.95.

The ultimate reference detailing Colt revolvers that have been converted from percussion to cartridge.

The Sumptuous Flaske, by Herbert G. Houze, Andrew Mowbray, Inc., Lincoln, RI, 1989. 158 pp., illus. Soft covers. $35.00.

Catalog of a recent show at the Buffalo Bill Historical Center bringing together some of the finest European and American powder flasks of the 16th to 19th centuries.

Textbook of Automatic Pistols, by R.K. Wilson, Wolfe Publishing Co., Prescott, AZ, 1990. 349 pp., illus. $54.00.

Reprint of the 1943 classic being a treatise on the history, development and functioning of modern military self-loading pistols.

Thompson: The American Legend,by Tracie L. Hill, Collector Grade Publications, Ontario, Canada, 1996. 584 pp., illus. $85.00.

The story of the first American submachine gun. All models are featured and discussed.

Trade Guns of the Hudson's Bay Company, 1670-1870, by S. James gooding, Museum Restoration Service, Bloomfield, Ontario, Canada, 1998. 35 pp., illus. Paper covers. $6.95.

The various styles and patterns of muzzle loading guns brought by the Hudson Bay Co. to North America to trade with the Indians.

The Trapdoor Springfield, by M.D. Waite and B.D. Ernst, The Gun Room Press, Highland Park, NJ, 1983. 250 pp., illus. $39.95.

The first comprehensive book on the famous standard military rifle of the 1873-92 period.

U.S. Breech-Loading Rifles and Carbines, Cal. 45, by Gen. John Pitman, Thomas Publications, Gettysburg, PA, 1992. 192 pp., illus. $29.95.

The third volume in the Pitman Notes on U.S. Martial Small Arms and Ammunition, 1776-1933. This book centers on the "Trapdoor Springfield" models.

United States Martial Flintlocks, by Robert M. Reilly, Mowbray Publishing Co., Lincoln, RI, 1997. 264 pp., illus. $40.00.

A comprehensive history of American flintlock longarms and handguns (mostly military) c. 1775 to c. 1840.

U.S. Martial Single Shot Pistols, by Daniel D. Hartzler and James B. Whisker, Old Bedford Village Pess, Bedford, PA, 1998. 128 pp., illus. $45.00.

A photographic chronicle of military and semi-martial pistols supplied to the U.S. Government and the several States.

U.S. Military Arms Dates of Manufacture from 1795, by George Madis, David Madis, Dallas, TX, 1989. 64 pp. Soft covers. $5.00.

Lists all U.S. military arms of collector interest alphabetically, covering about 250 models.

U.S. Military Small Arms 1816-1865, by Robert M. Reilly, The Gun Room Press, Highland Park, NJ, 1983. 270 pp., illus. $39.95.

Covers every known type of primary and secondary martial firearms used by Federal forces.

U.S. Military Small Arms Production Dates, 1770's to 1970's, by D. R. & M.T. Morse, Firing Pin Enterprises, Phoenix, AZ, 1997. 96 pp., Spiral bound. $22.95.

Production quantities, serial numbers, manufacturing dates, disposition information, and much more.

U.S. M1 Carbines: Wartime Production, by Craig Riesch, North Cape Publications, Tustin, CA, 1994. 72 pp., illus. Paper covers. $15.95.

Presents only verifiable and accurate information. Each part of the M1 Carbine is discussed fully in its own section; including markings and finishes.

U.S. Naval Handguns, 1808-1911, by Fredrick R. Winter, Andrew Mowbray Publishers, Lincoln, RI, 1990. 128 pp., illus. $26.00.

The story of U.S. Naval Handguns spans an entire century—included are sections on each of the important naval handguns within the period.

Walther Models PP and PPK, 1929-1945, by James L. Rankin, assisted by Gary Green, James L. Rankin, Coral Gables, FL, 1974. 142 pp., illus. $35.00.

Complete coverage on the subject as to finish, proofmarks and Nazi Party inscriptions.

Walther P-38 Pistol, by Maj. George Nonte, Desert Publications, Cornville, AZ, 1982. 100 pp., illus. Paper covers. $11.95.

Complete volume on one of the most famous handguns to come out of WWII. All models covered.

Walther Volume II, Engraved, Presentation and Standard Models, by James L. Rankin, J.L. Rankin, Coral Gables, FL, 1977. 112 pp., illus. $35.00.

The new Walther book on embellished versions and standard models. Has 88 photographs, including many color plates.

Walther, Volume III, 1908-1980, by James L. Rankin, Coral Gables, FL, 1981. 226 pp., illus. $35.00.

Covers all models of Walther handguns from 1908 to date, includes holsters, grips and magazines.

The Webley Story, by William C. Dowell, commonwealth Heritage Society, Bellingham, WA, 1998. 337 pp., illus. Each book serial numberd. $69.95.

The Definitive work on Webley firearms and a must for the collectors of them.

Weimar and Early Lugers, by Jan C. Still, Jan C. Still, Douglas, AK, 1994. 312 pp., illus.

Volume 5 of the series *The Pistol of Germany and Here Allies in Two World Wars.*

The Whitney Firearms, by Claud Fuller, Standard Publications, Huntington, WV, 1946, 334 pp., many plates and drawings, $50.00.

An authoritative history of all Whitney arms and their maker. Highly recommended. An exclusive with Ray Riling Arms Books Co.

Winchester: An American Legend, by R.L. Wilson, Random House, New York, NY, 1991. 403 pp., illus. $65.00.

The official history of Winchester firearms from 1849 to the present.

The Winchester Book, by George Madis, David Madis Gun Book Distributor, Dallas, TX, 1986. 650 pp., illus. $49.50.

A new, revised 25th anniversary edition of this classic book on Winchester firearms. Complete serial ranges have been added.

Winchester Dates of Manufacture 1849-1984, by George Madis, Art & Reference House, Brownsboro, TX, 1984. 59 pp. $5.95.

A most useful work, compiled from records of the Winchester factory.

Winchester Engraving, by R.L. Wilson, Beinfeld Books, Springs, CA, 1989. 500 pp., illus. $125.00.

A classic reference work, of value to all arms collectors.

The Winchester Handbook, by George Madis, Art & Reference House, Lancaster, TX, 1982. 287 pp., illus. $19.95.

The complete line of Winchester guns, with dates of manufacture, serial numbers, etc.

Winchester Lever Action Repeating Firearms, Vol. 1, The Models of 1866, 1873 and 1876, by Arthur Pirkie, North Cape Publications, Tustin, CA, 1995. 112 pp., illus. Paper covers. $19.95.

Complete, part-by-part description, including dimensions, finishes, markings and variations throughout the production run of these fine, collectible guns.

*__Winchester Lever Action Repeating Rifles, Vol. 2, The Models of 1886 and 1892,__ by Arthur Pirkle, North Cape Publications, Tustin, CA, 1996. 150 pp., illus. Paper covers. $19.95.

Describes each model on a part-by-part basis by serial number range complete with finishes, markings and changes.

Winchester Lever Action Repeating Rifles, Volume 3, The Model of 1894, by Arthur Pirkle, North Cape Publications, Tustin, CA, 1998. 150 pp., illus. Paper covers. $16.95.

The first book ever provide a detailed description of the Model 1894 rifle and carbine.

The Winchester Model 94: The First 100 Years, by Robert C. Renneberg, Krause Publications, Iola, WI, 1991. 208 pp., illus. $34.95.

Covers the design and evolution from the early years up to the many different editions that exist today.

Winchester Shotguns and Shotshells, by Ronald W. Stadt, Krause Publications, Iola, WI, 1995. 256 pp., illus. $34.95.

The definitive book on collectible Winchester shotguns and shotshells manufactured through 1961.

The Winchester Single-Shot, by John Cambell, Andrew Mowbray, Inc., Lincoln RI, 1995. 272 pp., illus. $55.00.

Covers every important aspect of this highly-collectible firearm.

Winchester Slide-Action Rifles, Volume 1: Model 1890 & 1906, by Ned Schwing, Krause Publications, Iola, WI, 1992. 352 pp., illus. $39.95.

First book length treatment of models 1890 & 1906 with over 50 charts and tables showing significant new information about caliber style and rarity.

Winchester Slide-Action Rifles, Volume 2: Model 61 & Model 62, by Ned Schwing, Krause Publications, Iola, WI, 1993. 256 pp., illus. $34.95.

A complete historic look into the Model 61 and the Model 62. These favorite slide-action guns receive a thorough presentation which takes you to the factory to explore receivers, barrels, markings, stocks, stampings and engraving in complete detail.

Winchester's 30-30, Model 94, by Sam Fadala, Stackpole Books, Inc., Harrisburg, PA, 1986. 223 pp., illus. $24.95.

The story of the rifle America loves.

EDGED WEAPONS

The American Blade Collectors Association Price Guide to Antique Knives, by J. Bruce Voyles, Krause Publications, Iola, WI, 1995. 480 pp., illus. Paper covers. $16.95.

In this complete guide to pocketknives there are 40,000 current values in six grades of condition for knives produced from 1800-1970.

*__The American Eagle Pommel Sword: The Early Years 1794-1830,__ by Andrew Mowbray, Manrat Arms Publications, Lincoln, RI, 1997. 244 pp., illus. $65.00.

The standard guide to the most popular style of American sword.

American Indian Tomahawks, by Harold L. Peterson, The Gun Room Press, Highland Park, NJ, 1993. 142 pp., illus. $49.95.

The tomahawk of the American Indian, in all its forms, as a weapon and as a tool.

American Knives; The First History and Collector's Guide, by Harold L. Peterson, The Gun Room Press, Highland Park, NJ, 1980. 178 pp., illus. $24.95.

A reprint of this 1958 classic. Covers all types of American knives.

American Military Bayonets of the 20th Century, by Gary M. Cunningham, Scott A. Duff Publications, Export, PA, 1997. 116 pp., illus. Paper covers. $19.95.

A guide for collectors, including notes on makers, markings, finishes, variations, scabbards, and production data.

*__American Premium Guide to Pocket Knives and Razors, Identification and Value Guide, 4th Edition,__ by Jim Sargent, Books Americana, a division of Krause Publications, Iola, WI, 1996. Paper covers. $22.95.

Hundreds of rare photos have been added to the huge sections on Case, Remington, Pal and Browning knives and sheaths.

American Primitive Knives 1770-1870, by G.B. Minnes, Museum Restoration Service, Ottawa, Canada, 1983. 112 pp., illus. $24.95.

Origins of the knives, outstanding specimens, structural details, etc.

American Socket Bayonets and Scabbards, by Robert M. Reilly, Andrew Mowbray, Inc., Lincoln, RI, 1990. 209 pp., illus. $45.00.

A comprehensive illustrated history of socket bayonets, scabbards and frogs in America from the Colonial period through the Civil War period.

The American Sword, 1775-1945, by Harold L. Peterson, Ray Riling Arms Books, Co., Phila., PA, 1980. 286 pp. plus 60 pp. of illus. $45.00.

1977 reprint of a survey of swords worn by U.S. uniformed forces, plus the rare "American Silver Mounted Swords, (1700-1815)."

American Swords and Sword Makers, by Richard H. Bezdek, Paladin Press, Boulder, CO, 1994. 648 pp., illus. $79.95.

The long-awaited definitive reference volume to American swords, sword makers and sword dealers from Colonial times to the present.

The Ames Sword Company, 1829-1935, by John D. Hamilton, Andrew Mowbray Publisher, Linclon, RI, 1995. 255 pp., illus. $45.00.

An exhaustively researched and comprehensive history of America's foremost sword manufacturer and arms supplier during the Civil War.

Battle Blades: A Professional's Guide to Combat/Fighting Knives, by Greg Walker; Foreword by Al Mar, Paladin Press, Boulder, CO, 1993. 168 pp., illus. $30.00.

The author evaluates daggers, Bowies, switchblades and utility blades according to their design, performance, reliability and cost.

Bayonets from Janzen's Notebook, by Jerry L. Janzen, Cedar Ridge Publications, Broken Arrow, OK, 1994. 512 pp., illus. $34.50.

A very popular reference book covering bayonets of the World.

The Bayonet in New France, 1665-1760, by Erik Goldstein, Museum Restroation Service, Bloomfield, Ontario, Canada, 1997. 36 pp., illus. Paper covers. $6.95.

Traces bayonets from the recently developed plug bayonet, through the regulation socket bayonets which saw service in North America.

Bayonets of the Remington Cartridge Period, by Jerry L. Janzen, Cedar Ridge Publications, Broken Arrow, OK, 1994. 200 pp., illus. $39.95.

The story of the bayonets which accompanied the Remington Rolling Block and its many successors. Included are the rifles, the countries who used them, pictures of the bayonets in use and detailed descriptions of each bayonet.

The Book of the Sword, by Richard F. Burton, Dover Publications, New York, NY, 1987. 199 pp., illus. Paper covers. $12.95.

Traces the swords origin from its birth as a charged and sharpened stick through diverse stages of development.

Borders Away, Volume 1: With Steel, by William Gilkerson, Andrew Mowbray, Inc., Lincoln, RI, 1991. 184 pp., illus. $48.00.

A comprehensive study of naval armament under fighting sail. This first voume covers axes, pikes and fighting blades in use between 1626-1826.

The Bowie Knife, by Raymond Thorp, Phillips Publications, Wiliamstown, NJ, 1992. 167 pp., illus. $9.95.

After forty-five years, the classic work on the Bowie knife is once again available.

British & Commonwealth Bayonets, by Ian D. Skennerton and Robert Richardson, I.D.S.A. Books, Piqua, OH, 1986. 404 pp., 1300 illus. $40.00.

Collecting the Edged Weapons of Imperial Germany, by Thomas M. Johnson and Thomas T. Wittmann, Johnson Reference Books, Fredricksburg, VA, 1989. 363 pp., illus. $39.50.

An in-depth study of the many ornate military, civilian, and government daggers and swords of the Imperial era.

***Collecting North American Indian Knives,** by Lara Hothem, Books Americana, a division of Krause Publications, Iola, WI, 1996. 152 pp., illus. Paper covers. $41.95.

A complete guide to the identification and value of sharp-edged weapons and ceremonial knives of the Native Americans from every region.

Collector's Guide to Ames U.S. Contract Military Edged Weapons: 1832-1906, by Ron G. Hickox, Pioneer Press, Union City, IN, 1993. 70 pp., illus. Paper covers. $14.95.

While this book deals primarily with edged weapons made by the Ames Manufacturing Company, this guide refers to other manufactureres of United States swords.

Collector's Handbook of World War 2 German Daggers, by LtC. Thomas M. Johnson, Johnson Reference Books, Fredericksburg, VA, 2nd edition, 1991. 252 pp., illus. Paper covers. $25.00.

Concise pocket reference guide to Third Reich daggers and accoutrements in a convenient format. With value guide.

***Collins Machetes and Bowies 1845-1965,** by Danial E. Henry, Krause Publications, Iola, WI, 1996. 232 pp., illus. Paper covers. $19.95.

A comprehensive history of Collins machetes and bowies including more than 1200 blade instruments and accessories.

The Complete Bladesmith: Forging Your Way to Perfection, by Jim Hrisoulas, Paladin Press, Boulder, CO, 1987. 192 pp., illus. $25.00.

Novice as well as experienced bladesmith will benefit from this definitive guide to smithing world-class blades.

The Complete Book of Pocketknife Repair, by Ben Kelly, Jr., Krause Publications, Iola, WI, 1995. 130 pp., illus. Paper covers. $10.95.

Everything you need to know about repairing knives can be found in this step-by-step guide to knife repair.

Confederate Edged Weapons, by W.A. Albaugh, R&R Books, Lavonia, NY, 1994. 198 pp., illus. $30.00.

The master reference to edged weapons of the Confederate forces. Features precise line drawings and an extensive text.

The Craft of the Japanese Sword, by Leon and Hiroko Kapp, Yoshindo Yoshihara, Kodanska Internantional, Tokyo, Japan, 1990. 167 pp., illus. $39.00.

The first book in English devoted to contemporary sword manufacturing in Japan.

Eickhorn Edged Weapons Exports, Vol. 1: Latin America, by A.M. de Quesada, Jr. And Ron G. Hicock, Pioneer Press, Union City, TN, 1996. 120 pp., illus. Paper covers. $15.00.

This research studies the various Eickhorn edged weapons and accessories manufactured for various countries outside of Germany.

Exploring the Dress Daggers of the German Army, by Thomas T. Wittmann, Johnson Reference Books, Fredericksburg, VA, 1995. 350 pp., illus. $59.95.

The first in-depth analysis of the dress daggers worn by the German Army.

German Clamshells and Other Bayonets, by G. Walker and R.J. Weinard, Johnson Reference Books, Fredericksburg, VA, 1994. 157 pp., illus. $22.95.

Includes unusual bayonets, many of which are shown for the first time. Current market values are listed.

German Military Fighting Knives 1914-1945, by Gordon A. Hughes, Johnson Reference Books, Fredericksburg, VA, 1994. 64 pp., illus. Paper covers. $24.50.

Documents the different types of German military fighting knives used during WWI and WWII. Makers' proofmarks are shown as well as details of blade inscriptions, etc.

The Halberd and other European Polearms 1300-1650, by George Snook, Museum Restoration Service, Bloomfield, Ontario, Canada, 1998. 40 pp., illus. Paper covers. $6.95

A comprehensive introduction to the history, use, and identification of the staff weapons of Europe.

The Handbook of British Bayonets, by Ian D. Skennerton, I.D.S.A. Books, Piqua, OH. 64 pp. $4.95

The Hand Forged Knife, Krause Publications, Inc., Iola, WI. 136 pp., illus., #|$12.95.

Explains the techniques for forging, hardening and tempering knives and other stailess steel tools.

How to Make Folding Knives, by Ron Lake, Frank Centofante and Wayne Clay, Krause Publications, Iola, WI, 1995. 193 pp., illus. Paper covers. $13.95.

With step-by-step instructions, learn how to make your own folding knife from three top custom makers.

How to Make Knives, by Richard W. Barney and Robert W. Loveless, Krause Publications, Iola, WI, 1995. 182 pp., illus. Paper covers. $13.95.

Complete instructions from two premier knife makers on making high-quality, handmade knives.

***How to Make Multi-Blade Folding Knives,** by Eugene Shdley & Terry Davis, Krause Publications, Iola, WI, 1997. 192 pp., illus. Paper covers. $19.95.

This step-by-step instructional guide teaches knifemakers how to craft these complex folding knives.

IBCA Price Guide to Commemorative Knives 1960-1990 by Bruce Voyles, Krause Publications, Ioloa, WI. 256 pp., illus., $16.95.

IBCA Price Guide to Antique Knives edited by Bruce Voyles, Krause Publications, Ioloa, WI. 480 pp., illus., $17.95.

Japanese Military and Civil Swords and Dirks, by Richard Fuller and Ron Gregory, Howell Press, Charlottesville, VA, 1997. 288 pp., illus. $49.95.

This essential reference covers both military and civil Japanese swords and dirks form 1868 to 1945. More than 110 sword and dirk patterns are described and illustrated.

Kentucky Knife Traders Manual No. 6, by R.B. Ritchie, Hindman, KY, 1980. 217 pp., illus. Paper covers. $10.00.

Guide for dealers, collectors and traders listing pocket knives and razor values.

Knife and Tomahawk Throwing: The Art of the Experts, by Harry K. McEvoy, Charles E. Tuttle, Rutland, VT, 1989. 150 pp., illus. Soft covers. $8.95.

The first book to employ side-by-side the fascinating art and science of knives and tomahawks.

Knifemaking, The Gun Digest Book of, by Jack Lewis and Roger Combs, DBI Books, a division of Krause Publications, Inc., Iola, WI, 1989. 256 pp., illus. Paper covers. $16.95.

All the ins and outs from the world of knifemaking in a brand new book.

Knife Talk: The Art & Sculence of Knifemaking, by Ed Fowler, Krause Publications, Iola, WI, 160 pp., illus. Paper covers. $14.95

How to make knives, why we make knives nad the use of knives. A compilation of the author's most memorable articles from Blade magazine.

***Knives, 5th Edition, The Gun Digest Book of,** edited by Jack Lewis and Roger Combs, DBI Books, a division of Krause Publications, Iola, WI, 1997. 256 pp., illus. Paper covers. $19.95.

Covers practically every aspect of the knife world.

Knives '99, 19th Edition, edited by Ken Warner, DBI Books, a division of Krause Publications, Iola, WI, 1998. 304 pp., illus. Paper covers. $21.95.

Visual presentation of current factory and custom designs in both folding and straight patterns, in swords, miniatures and commerical cutlery. Available September 1998.

***Levine's Guide to Knives And Their Values, 4th Edition,** by Bernard Levine, DBI Books, a division of Krause Publications, Iola, WI, 1997. 512 pp., illus. Paper covers. $27.95.

All the basic tools for identifying, valuing and collecting folding and fixed blade knives.

The Master Bladesmith: Advanced Studies in Steel, by Jim Hrisoulas, Paladin Press, Boulder, CO, 1990. 296 pp., illus. $45.00.

The author reveals the forging secrets that for centuries have been protected by guilds.

Military Swords of Japan 1868-1945, by Richard Fuller and Ron Gregory, Arms and Armour Press, London, England, 1986. 127 pp., illus. Paper covers. $18.95.

A wide-ranging survey of the swords and dirks worn by the armed forces of Japan until the end of World War II.

Modern Combat Blades, by Duncan Long, Paladin Press, Boulder, CO, 1993. 128 pp., illus. $25.00.

Long discusses the pros and cons of bowies, bayonets, commando daggers, kukris, switchblades, butterfly knives, belt-buckle blades and many more.

Official Price Guide to Collector Knives, 11th Edition, by C. Houston Price, Krause Publications, Inc., Iola, WI. 531 pp., illus. $17.00

Invaluable information on grading, buying, selling, age determination, and how to spot fakes. More than 13,000 price lists.

On Damascus Steel, by Dr. Leo S. Figiel,Atlantis Arts Press, Atlantis, FL, 1991. 145 pp., illus. $65.00.

The historic, technical and artistic aspects of Oriental and mechanical Damascus. Persian and Indian sword blades, from 1600-1800, which have never been published, are illustrated.

The Pattern-Welded Blade: Artistry in Iron, by Jim Hrisoulas, Paladin Press, Boulder, CO, 1994. 120 pp., illus. $35.00.

Reveals the secrets of this craft—from the welding of the starting billet to the final assembly of the complete blade.

Randall Made Knives, Krause Publications, Inc., Iola, WI. 292 pp., illus. $50.00.

Plots the designs of all 24 of Randall's unique knives.

Randall Made Knives: The History of the Man and the Blades, by Robert L. Gaddis, Paladin Press, Boulder, CO, 1993. 304 pp., illus. $50.00.

The authorized history of Bo Randall and his blades, told in his own words and those of the people who knew him best.

Renaissance Swordsmanship, by John Clements, Paladin Press, Boulder, CO, 1997. 152 pp., illus. Paper covers. $25.00.

The illustrated use of rapiers and cut-and-thrust swords.

Rice's Trowel Bayonet, reprinted by Ray Riling Arms Books, Co., Phila., PA, 1968. 8 pp., illus. Paper covers. $3.00.

A facsimile reprint of a rare circular originally published by the U.S. government in 1875 for the information of U.S. troops.

The Samurai Sword, by John M. Yumoto, Charles E. Tuttle Co., Rutland, VT, 1958. 191 pp., illus. $23.95.

A must for anyone interested in Japanese blades, and the first book on this subject written in English.

The Scottish Dirk, by James D. Forman, Museum Restoration Service, Bloomfield, Ont., Canada, 1991. 60 pp., illus. Paper covers. $5.95.

More than 100 dirks are illustrated with a text that sets the dirk and Sgian Dubh in their socio-historic content following design changes through more than 300 years of evolution.

Scottish Swords from the Battlefield at Culloden, by Lord Archibald Campbell, The Mowbray Co., Providence, RI, 1973. 63 pp., illus. $15.00.

A modern reprint of an exceedingly rare 1894 privately printed edition.

The Sheffield Knife Book, by Geoffrey Tweedale, Krause Publications, Inc., Iola, WI. 320 pp., illus., $50.00.

Small Arms Identification Series, No. 6-British Service Sword & Lance Patterns, by Ian Skennerton, I.D.S.A. Books, Piqua, OH, 1994. 48 pp. $9.50.

Small Arms Series, No. 2. The British Spike Bayonet, by Ian Skennerton, I.D.S.A. Books, Piqua, OH, 1982. 32 pp., 30 illus. $9.00.

Sure Defence, The Bowie Knife Book, by Kenneth J. Burton, I.D.S.A. Books, Piqua, OH, 1988. 100 pp., 115 illus. $37.50.

***The Standard Knife Collector's Guide, 3rd Edition,** by Roy Ritchie and Ron Stewart, Collector Books, Paducah, KY, 1996. 688 pp., illus. Paper covers. $12.95.

Includes virtually all knife manufacturers both old and new, plus custom made and commemorative knives.

Swords and Sword Makers of the War of 1812, by Richard Bezdek, Paladin Press, Boulder, CO, 1997. 104 pp., illus. $40.00.

The complete history of the men and companies that made swords during and before the war. Includes examples of cavalry and artillery sabers.

Swords of Imperial Japan 1868-1845, by Jim Dawson, Krause Publications, Inc. 160 pp., illus. $29.95.

Details the military, civilian, diplomatic and civil, police and colonial swords of post-Samurai era.

Sword of the Samurai, by George R. Parulski, Jr., Paladin Press, Boulder, CO, 1985. 144 pp., illus. $34.95.

The classical art of Japanese swordsmanship.

Swords from Public Collections in the Commonwealth of Pennsylvania, edited by Bruce S. Bazelon, Andrew Mowbray Inc., Lincoln, RI, 1987. 127 pp., illus. Paper covers. $12.00.

Contains new information regarding swordmakers of the Philadelphia area.

Swords and Blades of the American Revolution, by George C. Neumann, Rebel Publishing Co., Inc., Texarkana, TX, 1991. 288 pp., illus. $35.95.

The encyclopedia of bladed weapons—swords, bayonets, spontoons, halberds, pikes, knives, daggers, axes—used by both sides, on land and sea, in America's struggle for independence.

Tomahawks Illustrated, by Robert Kuck, Robert Kuck, New Knoxville, OH, 1977. 112 pp., illus. Paper covers. $15.00.

A pictorial record to provide a reference in selecting and evaluating tomahawks.

The Working Folding Knife, by Steven Dick, Stoeger Publishing Co., Wayne, NJ, 1998. 280 pp., illus. Paper covers. $21.95

From the classic American Barlow to exotic folders like the spanish Navaja this book has it all.

GENERAL

Advanced Muzzleloader's Guide, by Toby Bridges, Stoeger Publishing Co., So. Hackensack, NJ, 1985. 256 pp., illus. Paper covers. $14.95.

The complete guide to muzzle-loading rifles, pistols and shotguns—flintlock and percussion.

*__Aids to Musketry for Officers & NCOs__, by Capt. B.J. Friend, Excalibur Publications, Latham, NY, 1996. 40 pp., illus. Paper covers. $7.95.
A facsimile edition of a pre-WWI British manual filled with useful information for training the common soldier.

Air Gun Digest, 3rd Edition, by J.I. Galan, DBI Books, a division of Krause Publications, Inc., Iola, WI, 1995. 258 pp., illus. Paper covers. $18.95
Everything from A to Z on air gun history, trends and technology.

American Gunsmiths, by Frank M. Sellers, The Gun Room Press, Highland Park, NJ, 1983. 349 pp. $39.95.
A comprehensive listing of the American gun maker, patentee, gunsmith and entrepreneur.

American and Imported Arms, Ammunition and Shooting Accessories, Catalog No. 18 of the Shooter's Bible, Stoeger, Inc., reprinted by Fayette Arsenal, Fayetteville, NC, 1988. 142 pp., illus. Paper covers. $10.95.
A facsimile reprint of the 1932 Stoeger's Shooter's Bible.

America's Great Gunmakers, by Wayne van Zwoll, Stoeger Publishing Co., So. Hackensack, NJ, 1992. 288 pp., illus. Paper covers. $16.95.
This book traces in great detail the evolution of guns and ammunition in America and the men who formed the companies that produced them.

Armed and Female, by Paxton Quigley, E.P. Dutton, New York, NY, 1989. 237 pp., illus. $16.95.
The first complete book on one of the hottest subjects in the media today, the arming of the American woman.

Arms and Armour in Antiquity and the Middle Ages, by Charles Boutell, Stackpole Books, Mechanicsburg, PA, 1996. 352 pp., illus. $22.95.
Detailed descriptions of arms and armor, the development of tactics and the outcome of specific battles.

Arms & Armor in the Art Institute of Chicago, by Walter J. Karcheski, Jr., Bulfinch Press, Boston, MA, 1995. 128 pp., illus. $35.00.
Now, for the first time, the Art Institute of Chicago's arms and armor collection is presented in the visual delight of 103 color illustrations.

Arms for the Nation: Springfield Longarms, edited by David C. Clark, Scott A. Duff, Export, PA, 1994. 73 pp., illus. Paper covers. $9.95.
A brief history of the Springfield Armory and the arms made there.

Arsenal of Freedom, The Springfield Armory, 1890-1948: A Year-by-Year Account Drawn from Official Records, compiled and edited by Lt. Col, William S. Brophy, USAR Ret., Andrew Mowbray, Inc., Lincoln, RI, 1991. 400 pp., illus. Soft covers. $29.95.
A "must buy" for all students of American military weapolns, equipment and accoutrements.

Assault Weapons, 4th Edition, The Gun Digest Book of, edited by Jack Lewis, DBI Books, a division of Krause Publications, Inc., Iola, WI. 256 pp. illus. Paper covers. $19.95.
An in-depth look at the history and uses of these arms.

The Big Guns: Civil War Siege, Seacoast, and Naval Cannon, by Edwin Olmstead, Wayne E. Stark and Spencer C. Tucker, Museum Restoration Service, Bloomfield, Ontario, Canada, 1997. 360 pp., illus. $80.00.
This book is designed to identify and record the heavy guns available to both sides during the Civil War.

Blackpowder Loading Manual, 3rd Edition, by Sam Fadala, DBI Books, a division of Krause Publications, Inc., Iola, WI, 1995. 368 pp., illus. Paper covers. $19.95.
Revised and expanded edition of this landmark blackpowder loading book. Covers hundreds of loads for most of the popular blackpowder rifles, handguns and shotguns.

The Blackpowder Notebook, by Sam Fadala, Wolfe Publishing Co., Prescott, AZ, 1994. 212 pp., illus. $22.50.
For anyone interested in shooting muzzleloaders, this book will help improve scores and obtain accuracy and reliability.

Bolt Action Rifles, 3rd Edition, by Frank de Haas, DBI Books, a division of Krause Publications, Inc., Iola, WI, 1995. 528 pp., illus. Paper covers. $24.95.
A revised edition of the most definitive work on all major bolt-action rifle designs.

The Book of the Crossbow, by Sir Ralph Payne-Gallwey, Dover Publications, Mineola, NY, 1996. 416 pp., illus. Paper covers. $14.95.
Unabridged republication of the scarce 1907 London edition of the book on one of the most devastating hand weapons of the Middle Ages.

Bows and Arrows of the Native Americans, by Jim Hamm, Lyons & Burford Publishers, New York, NY, 1991. 156 pp., illus. $19.95.
A complete step-by-step guide to wooden bows, sinew-backed bows, composite bows, strings, arrows and quivers.

Bowhunter's Digest, 3rd Edition, by Chuck Adams, DBI Books, a division of Krause Publications, Inc., Iola, WI, 1990. 288 pp., illus. Soft covers. $17.95.
All-new edition covers all the necessary equipment and how to use it, plus the fine points on how to improve your skill.

British Small Arms of World War 2, by Ian D. Skennerton, I.D.S.A. Books, Piqua, OH, 1988. 110 pp., 37 illus. $25.00.

British Sniper, by Ian Skennerton, I.D.S.A. Books, Piqua, OH, 1983. 26 pp., over 375 illus. $40.00.

*__Cartridges of the World, 8th Edition__, by Frank Barnes, edited by M. L. McPherson, DBI Books, a division of Krause Publications, Inc., Iola, WI, 1997. 480 pp., illus. Paper covers. $24.95.
Completely revised edition of the general purpose reference work for which collectors, police, scientists and laymen reach first for answers to cartridge identification questions.

*__Combat Handgunnery, 4th Edition, The Gun Digest Book of,__ by Chuck Taylor, DBI Books, a division of Krause Publications, Inc., Iola, WI, 1997. 256 pp., illus. Paper covers. $18.95.
This edition looks at real world combat handgunnery from three different perspectives—military, police and civilian.

*__The Complete Blackpowder Handbook, 3rd Edition,__ by Sam Fadala, DBI Books, a division of Krause Publications, Inc., Iola, WI, 1997. 400 pp., illus. Paper covers. $21.95.
Expanded and completely rewritten edition of the definitive book on the subject of blackpowder.

The Complete Guide to Game Care and Cookery, 3rd Edition, by Sam Fadala, DBI Books, a division of Krause Publications, Inc., Iola, WI, 1994. 320 pp., illus. Paper covers. $18.95.
Over 500 photos illustrating the care of wild game in the field and at home with a separate recipe section providing over 400 tested recipes.

Complete Guide to Guns & Shooting, by John Malloy, DBI Books, a division of Krause Publications, Inc., Iola, WI, 1995. 256 pp., illus. Paper covers. $18.95.
What every shooter and gun owner should know about firearms, ammunition, shooting techniques, safety, collecting and much more.

Cowboy Action Shooting, by Charly Gullett, Wolfe Publishing Co., Prescott, AZ, 1995. 400 pp., illus. Paper covers. $24.50.
The fast growing of the shooting sports is comprehensively covered in this text—the guns, loads, tactics and the fun and flavor of this Old West era competition.

Crossbows, edited by Roger Combs, DBI Books, a division of Krause Publications, Inc., Iola, WI, 1986. 192 pp., illus. Paper covers. $15.95.
Complete, up-to-date coverage of the hottest bow going—and the most controversial.

Death from Above: The German FG42 Paratrooper Rifle, by Thomas B. Dugelby and R. Blake Stevens, Collector Grade Publications, Toronto, Canada, 1990. 147 pp., illus. $39.95.
The first comprehensive study of all seven models of the FG42.

Encyclopedia of Modern Firearms, Vol. 1, compiled and publ. by Bob Brownell, Montezuma, IA, 1959. 1057 pp. plus index, illus. $60.00. Dist. By Bob Brownell, Montezuma, IA 50171.
Massive accumulation of basic information of nearly all modern arms pertaining to "parts and assembly." Replete with arms photographs, exploded drawings, manufacturers' lists of parts, etc.

Exploded Handgun Drawings, The Gun Digest Book of, edited by Harold A. Murtz, DBI Books, a division of Krause Publications, Inc., Iola, WI, 1992. 512 pp., illus. Paper covers. $20.95.
Exploded or isometric drawings for 494 of the most popular handguns.

Exploded Long Gun Drawings, The Gun Digest Book of, edited by Harold A. Murtz, DBI Books, a division of Krause Publications, Inc., Iola, WI, 512 pp., illus. Paper covers. $20.95.
Containing almost 500 rifle and shotgun exploded drawings.

Firearms Engraving as Decorative Art, by Dr. Fredric A. Harris, Barbara R. Harris, Seattle, WA, 1989. 172 pp., illus. $115.00.
The origin of American firearms engraving motifs in the decorative art of the Middle East. Illustrated with magnificent color photographs.

Firing Back, by Clayton E. Cramer, Krause Publications, Iola, WI, 1995. 208 pp., Paper covers. $9.95.
Proposes answers and arguments to counter the popular anti-gun sentiments.

Frank Pachmayr: The Story of America's Master Gunsmith and his Guns, by John Lachuk, Safari Press, Huntington Beach, CA, 1996. 254 pp., illus. First edition, limited, signed and slipcased. $85.00; Second printing trade edition. $50.00.
The colorful and historically significant biography of Frank A Pachmayr, America's own gunsmith emeritus.

The Frontier Rifleman, by H.B. LaCrosse Jr., Pioneer Press, Union City, TN, 1989. 183 pp., illus. Soft covers. $14.95.
The Frontier rifleman's clothing and equipment during the era of the American Revolution, 1760-1800.

Gatling: A Photographic Remembrance, by E. Frank Stephenson, Jr., Meherrin River Press, Murfreesboro, NC, 1994. 140 pp., illus. Paper covers. $25.00.
A new book on Richard Gatling and his famous gun; featuring 145 photographs, many rare and never before published.

The Gatling Gun: 19th Century Machine Gun to 21st Century Vulcan, by Joseph Berk, Paladin Press, Boulder, CO, 1991. 136 pp., illus. $29.95.
Here is the fascinating on-going story of a truly timeless weapon, from its beginnings during the Civil War to its current role as a state-of-the-art modern combat system.

*__German Artillery of World War Two,__ by Ian V. Hogg, Stackpole Books, Mechanicsburg, PA, 1997. 304 pp., illus. $44.95.
Complete details of German artillery use in WWII.

Good Guns Again, by Stephen Bodio, Wilderness Adventures Press, Bozeman, MT, 1994. 183 pp., illus. $29.00.
A celebration of fine sporting arms.

Grand Old Lady of No Man's Land: The Vickers Machine Gun, by Dolf L. Goldsmith, Collector Grade Publications, Cobourg, Canada, 1994. 600 pp., illus. $79.95.
Goldsmith brings his years of experience as a U.S. Army armourer, machine gun collector and shooter to bear on the Vickers, in a book sure to become a classic in its field.

Great Shooters of the World, by Sam Fadala, Stoeger Publishing Co., So. Hackensack, NJ, 1991. 288 pp., illus. Paper covers. $18.95.
This book offers gun enthusiasts an overview of the men and women who have forged the history of firearms over the past 150 years.

Gun Digest 1999, 53rd Edition, edited by Ken Warner, DBI Books, a division of Krause Publications, Inc., Iola, WI, 1998. 544 pp., illus. Paper covers. $24.95
An all-new edition of the most read and respected gun book in the world for the last half century.

Gun Digest Treasury, 7th Edition, edited by Harold A. Murtz, DBI Books, a division of Krause Publications, Inc., Iola, WI, 1994. 320 pp., illus. Paper covers. $17.95.
A collection of some of the most interesting articles which have appeared in Gun Digest over its first 45 years.

Gunfitting: The Quest for Perfection, by Michael Yardley, Safari Press, Huntington Beach, CA, 1995. 128 pp., illus. $24.95.
The author, a very experienced shooting instructor, examines gun stocks and gunfitting in depth.

Gun Notes, by Elmer Keith, Safari Press, Huntington Beach, CA, 1995. 280 pp., illus. $35.00.
A collection of Elmer Keith's most interesting columns and feature stories that appeared in *Guns and Ammo* magazine from 1961 to the late 1970s.

Gun Notes, Volume 2, by Elmer Keith, Safari Press, Huntington Beach, CA, 1997. 292 pp., illus. Limited 1st edition, numbered and signed by Keith's son. Slipcased. $75.00. Second edition. $35.00.
covers Articles from Keith's monthly column in "Guns & Ammo" magazine during the period from 1971 through Keith's passing in 1982.

Gunshot Injuries: How They Are Inflicted, Their Complications and Treatment, by Col. Louis A. La Garde, 2nd revised edition, Lancer Militaria, Mt. Ida, AR, 1991. 480 pp., illus. $34.95.
A classic work which was the standard textbook on the subject at the time of WWI.

Guns of the Wild West, by George Markham, Sterling Publishing Co., New York, NY, 1993. 160 pp., illus. Paper covers. $19.95.
Firearms of the American Frontier, 1849-1917.

Gun Talk, edited by Dave Moreton, Winchester Press, Piscataway, NJ, 1973. 256 pp., illus. $9.95.
A treasury of original writing by the top gun writers and editors in America. Practical advice about every aspect of the shooting sports.

The Gun That Made the Twenties Roar, by Wm. J. Helmer, rev. and enlarged by George C. Nonte, Jr., The Gun Room Press, Highland Park, NJ, 1977. Over 300 pp., illus. $24.95.
Historical account of John T. Thompson and his invention, the infamous "Tommy Gun."

Gun Trader's Guide, 21st Edition, published by the Stoeger Publishing Co., Wayne, NJ, 1998. 592 pp., illus. Paper covers. $23.95.
Complete specifications and curretn prices for used guns. Prices of over 5,000 handguns, rifles and shotguns both domestic and foreign.

The Gunfighter, Man or Myth? by Joseph G. Rosa, Oklahoma Press, Norman, OK, 1969. 229 pp., illus. (including weapons). Paper covers. $14.95.
A well-documented work on gunfights and gunfighters of the West and elsewhere. Great treat for all gunfighter buffs.

*__Gun Notes Volume 2,__ by Elmer Keith, Safari Press, Inc., Huntington Beach, CA, 1996. 288 pp., illus. $35.00.
This second volume contains excerpts from Keith's *Guns & Ammo* magazine columns from the years 1971 through 1980.

Guns & Shooting: A Selected Bibliography, by Ray Riling, Ray Riling Arms Books Co., Phila., PA, 1982. 434 pp., illus. Limited, numbered edition. $75.

A limited edition of this superb bibliographical work, the only modern listing of books devoted to guns and shooting.

*Guns, Bullets, and Gunfighters, by Jim Cirillo, Paladin Press, Boulder, CO, 1996. 119 pp., illus. Paper covers. $15.00.

Lessons and tales from a modern-day gunfighter.

*Guns Illustrated 1999, 31st Edition, edited by Harold A. Murtz, DBI Books, a division of Krause Publications, Inc., Iola, WI, 1998. 352 pp., illus. Paper covers. $22.95

The journal for gun buffs. Timely, top-of-the-line writing packed with highly informative, technical articles on a wide range of shooting topics covered by some the top writers in the industry.

Guns, Loads, and Hunting Tips, by Bob Hagel, Wolfe Publishing Co., Prescott, AZ, 1986. 509 pp., illus. $19.95.

A large hardcover book packed with shooting, hunting and handloading wisdom.

Gun Writers of Yesteryear, compiled by James Foral, Wolfe Publishing Co., Prescott, AZ, 1993. 449 pp. $35.00.

Here, from the pre-American rifleman days of 1898-1920, are collected some 80 articles by 34 writers from eight magazines.

Handgun Digest, 3rd Edition, edited by Chris Christian, DBI Books, a division of Krause Publications, Inc., Iola, WI, 1995. 256 pp., illus. Paper covers. $18.95.

Full coverage of all aspects of handguns and handgunning from a highly readable and knowledgeable author.

HK Assault Rifle Systems, by Duncan Long, Paladin Press, Boulder, CO, 1995. 110 pp., illus. Paper covers. $27.95.

The little known history behind this fascinating family of weapons tracing its beginnings from the ashes of World War Two to the present time.

I Remember Skeeter, compiled by Sally Jim Skelton, Wolfe Publishing Co., Prescott, AZ, 1998. 401 pp., illus. Paper covers. $19.95.

A collection of some of the beloved storyteller's famous works interspersed with anecdotes and tales from the people who knew best.

Jim Dougherty's Guide to Bowhunting Deer, by Jim Dougherty, DBI Books, a division of Krause Publications, Inc., Iola, WI, 1992. 256 pp., illus. Paper covers. $17.95.

Dougherty sets down some important guidelines for bowhunting and bowhunting equipment.

Kill or Get Killed, by Col. Rex Applegate, Paladin Press, Boulder, CO, 1996. 400 pp., illus. $29.95.

The best and longest-selling book on close combat in history.

The Long-Range War: Sniping in Vietnam, by Peter R. Senich, Paladin Press, Boulder, CO, 1994. 280 pp., illus. $39.95.

The most complete report on Vietnam-era sniping ever documented.

Manual for H&R Reising Submachine Gun and Semi-Auto Rifle, edited by George P. Dillman, Desert Publications, El Dorado, AZ, 1994. 81 pp., illus. Paper covers. $12.95.

A reprint of the Harrington & Richardson 1943 factory manual and the rare military manual on the H&R submachine gun and semi-auto rifle.

The Manufacture of Gunflints, by Sydney B.J. Skertchly, facsimile reprint with new introduction by Seymour de Lotbiniere, Museum Restoration Service, Ontario, Canada, 1984. 90 pp., illus. $24.50.

Limited edition reprinting of the very scarce London edition of 1879.

Master Tips, by J. Winokur, Potshot Press, Pacific Palisades, CA, 1985. 96 pp., illus. Paper covers. $11.95.

Basics of practical shooting.

Military Rifle & Machine Gun Cartridges, by Jean Huon, Paladin Press, Boulder, CO, 1990. 392 pp., illus. $34.95.

Describes the primary types of military cartridges and their principal loadings, as well as their characteristics, origin and use.

Military Small Arms of the 20th Century, 6th Edition, by Ian V. Hogg, DBI Books, a division of Krause Publications, Inc., Iola, WI, 1991. 352 pp., illus. Paper covers. $21.95.

Fully revised and updated edition of the standard reference in its field.

Modern Custom Guns, Walnut, Steel, and Uncommon Artistry, by Tom Turpin, Krause Publications, Iola, WI, 1997. 206 pp., illus. $49.95.

From exquisite engraving to breathtaking exotic woods, the mystique of today's custom guns is expertly detailed in word and awe-inspiring color photos of rifles, shotguns and handguns.

Modern Gun Values, 10th Edition, The Gun Digest Book of by the editors of Gun Digest, DBI Books, a division of Krause Publications, Inc., Iola, WI, 1996. 560 pp., illus. paper covers. $21.95.

Greatly updated and expanded edition describing and valuing over 7,000 firearms manufactured between 1900 and 1995. The standard reference for valuing modern firearms.

Modern Law Enforcement Weapons & Tactics, 2nd Edition, by Tom Ferguson, DBI Books, a division of Krause Publications, Inc., Iola, WI, 1991. 256 pp., illus. Paper covers. $18.95.

An in-depth look at the weapons and equipment used by law enforcement agencies of today.

Modern Sporting Guns, by Christopher Austyn, Safari Press, Huntington Beach, CA, 1994. 128 pp., illus. $40.00.

A discussion of the "best" English guns; round action, over-and-under, boxlocks, hammer guns, bolt action and double rifles as well as accessories.

The More Complete Cannoneer, by M.C. Switlik, Museum & Collectors Specialties Co., Monroe, MI, 1990. 199 pp., illus. $19.95.

Compiled agreeably to the regulations for the U.S. War Department, 1861, and containing current observations on the use of antique cannon.

The MP-40 Machine Gun, Desert Publications, El Dorado, AZ, 1995. 32 pp., illus. Paper covers. $11.95.

A reprint of the hard-to-find operating and maintenance manual for one of the most famous machine guns of World War II.

Naval Percussion Locks and Primers, by Lt. J. A. Dahlgren, Museum Restoration Service, Bloomfield, Canada, 1996. 140 pp., illus. $35.00

First published as an Ordnance Memoranda in 1853, this is the finest existing study of percussion locks and primers origin and development.

L.D. Nimschke Firearms Engraver, by R.L. Wilson, R&R Books, Livonia, NY, 1992. 108 pp., illus. $100.00.

The personal work record of one of the 19th century America's foremost engravers. Augmented by a comprehensive text, photographs of deluxe-engraved firearms, and detailed indexes.

The One-Round War: U.S.M.C. Scout-Snipers in Vietnam, by Peter Senich, Paladin Press, Boulder, CO, 1996. 384 pp., illus. $59.95.

Sniping in Vietnam focusing specifically on the Marine Corps program.

OSS Weapons, by Dr. John W. Brunner, Phillips Publications, Williamstown, NJ, 1996. 224 pp., illus. $44.95.

The most definitive book ever written on the weapons and equipment used by the supersecret warriors of the Office of Strategic Services.

Pin Shooting: A Complete Guide, by Mitchell A. Ota, Wolfe Publishing Co., Prescott, AZ, 1992. 145 pp., illus. Paper covers. $14.95.

Traces the sport from its humble origins to today's thoroughly enjoyable social event, including the mammoth eight-day Second Chance Pin Shoot in Michigan.

E.C. Prudhomme, Master Gun Engraver, A Retrospective Exhibition: 1946-1973, intro. by John T. Amber, The R. W. Norton Art Gallery, Shreveport, LA, 1973. 32 pp., illus. Paper covers. $9.95.

Examples of master gun engravings by Jack Prudhomme.

A Rifleman Went to War, by H. W. McBride, Lancer Militaria, Mt. Ida, AR, 1987. 398 pp., illus. $24.95.

The classic account of practical marksmanship on the battlefields of World War I.

Second to None, edited by John Culler and Chuck Wechsler, Live Oak Press, Inc., Camden, SC, 1988. 227 pp., illus. $39.95.

The most popular articles from *Sporting Classics* magazine on great sporting firearms.

Sharpshooting for Sport and War, by W.W. Greener, Wolfe Publishing Co., Prescott, AZ, 1995. 192 pp., illus. $30.00.

This classic reprint explores the *first* expanding bullet; service rifles; shooting positions; trajectories; recoil; external ballistics; and other valuable information.

The Shooter's Bible 1999, No. 90, edited by William S. Jarrett, Stoeger Publishing co. Wayne, NJ, 1998. 576 pp., illus. Paper covers. $23.95.

Over 3,000 firearms currently offered by major American and foreign gunmakers. Represented are handguns, rifles, shotguns and black powder arms with complete specifications and retail prices.

Shooting, by J.H. FitzGerald, Wolfe Publishing Co., Prescott, AZ, 1993. 421 pp., illus. $29.00.

A classic book and reference for anyone interested in pistol and revolver shooting.

Sniper: The World of Combat Sniping, by Adrian Gilbert, St Martin's Press, NY, 1995. 290 pp., illus. $24.95.

The skills, the weapons and the experiences.

Sniper Training, FM 23-10, Reprint of the U.S. Army field manual of August, 1994, Paladin Press, Boulder, CO, 1995. 352pp., illus. Paper covers. $25.00

The most up-to-date U.S. military sniping information and doctrine.

Sniping in France, by Major H. Hesketh-Prichard, Lancer Militaria, Mt. Ida, AR, 1993. 224 pp., illus. $24.95.

The author was a well-known British adventurer and big game hunter. He was called upon in the early days of "The Great War" to develop a program to offset an initial German advantage in sniping. How the British forces came to overcome this advantage.

*Special Warfare: Special Weapons, by Kevin Dockery, Emperor's Press, Chicago, IL, 1997. 192 pp., illus. $29.95.

The arms and equipment of the UDT and SEALS from 1943 to the present.

The SPIW: Deadliest Weapon that Never Was, by R. Blake Stevens, and Edward C. Ezell, Collector Grade Publications, Inc., Toronto, Canada, 1985. 138 pp., illus. $29.95.

The complete saga of the fantastic flechette-firing Special Purpose Individual Weapon.

Sporting Collectibles, by Dr. Stephen R. Irwin, Stoeger Publishing Co., Wayne, NJ, 1997. 256 pp., illus. Paper covers. $19.95.

A must book for serious collectors nad admirers of sporting collectibles.

The Sporting Craftsmen: A Complete Guide to Contemporary Makers of Custom-Built Sporting Equipment, by Art Carter, Countrysport Press, Traverse City, MI, 1994. 240 pp., illus. $49.50.

Profiles leading makers of centerfire rifles; muzzleloading rifles; bamboo fly rods; fly reels; flies; waterfowl calls; decoys; handmade knives; and traditional longbows and recurves.

*Sporting Rifle Takedown & Reassembly Guide, 2nd Edition, by J.B. Wood, DBI Books, a division of Krause Publications, Iola, WI, 1997. 480 pp., illus. $19.95.

An updated edition of the reference guide for anyone who wants to properly care for their sporting rifle. (Available September 1997)

The Street Smart Gun Book, by John Farnam, Police Bookshelf, Concord, NH, 1986. 45 pp., illus. Paper covers. $11.95.

Weapon selection, defensive shooting techniques, and gunfight-winning tactics from one of the world's leading authorities.

Stress Fire, Vol. 1: Stress Fighting for Police, by Massad Ayoob, Police Bookshelf, Concord, NH, 1984. 149 pp., illus. Paper covers. $9.95.

Gunfighting for police, advanced tactics and techniques.

Survival Guns, by Mel Tappan, Desert Publications, El Dorado, AZ, 1993. 456 pp., illus. Paper covers. $21.95.

Discusses in a frank and forthright manner which handguns, rifles and shotguns to buy for personal defense and securing food, and the ones to avoid.

Tactical Marksman, by Dave M. Lauch, Paladin Press, Boulder, CO, 1996. 165 pp., illus. Paper covers. $35.00.

A complete training manual for police and practical shooters.

Thompson Guns 1921-1945, Anubis Press, Houston, TX, 1980. 215 pp., illus. Paper covers. $11.95.

Facsimile reprinting of five complete manuals on the Thompson submachine gun.

The Ultimate Sniper, by Major John L. Plaster, Paladin Press, Boulder, CO, 1994. 464 pp., illus. Paper covers. $39.95.

An advanced training manual for military and police snipers.

U.S. Marine Corp Rifle and Pistol Marksmanship, 1935, reprinting of a government publication, Lancer Militaria, Mt. Ida, AR, 1991. 99 pp., illus. Paper covers. $11.95.

The old corps method of precision shooting.

U.S. Marine Corps Scout/Sniper Training Manual, Lancer Militaria, Mt. Ida, AR, 1989. Soft covers. $14.95.

Reprint of the original sniper training manual used by the Marksmanship Training Unit of the Marine Corps Development and Education Command in Quantico, Virginia.

U.S. Marine Corps Scout-Sniper, World War II and Korea, by Peter R. Senich, Paladin Press, Boulder, CO, 1994. 236 pp., illus. $39.95.

The most thorough and accurate account ever printed on the training, equipment and combat experiences of the U.S. Marine Corps Scout-Snipers.

U.S. Marine Corps Sniping, Lancer Militaria, Mt. Ida, AR, 1989. Irregular pagination. Soft covers. $14.95.

A reprint of the official Marine Corps FMFM1-3B.

Unrepentant Sinner, by Charles Askins, Tejano Publications, San Antonio, TX, 1985. 322 pp., illus. Soft covers. $19.95.

The autobiography of Colonel Charles Askins.

Weapons of the Waffen-SS, by Bruce Quarrie, Sterling Publishing Co., Inc., 1991. 168 pp., illus. $24.95.

An in-depth look at the weapons that made Hitler's Waffen-SS the fearsome fighting machine it was.

Weatherby: The Man, The Gun, The Legend, by Grits and Tom Gresham, Cane River Publishing Co., Natchitoches, LA, 1992. 290 pp., illus. $24.95.

A fascinating look at the life of the man who changed the course of firearms development in America.

The Winchester Era, by David Madis, Art & Reference House, Brownsville, TX, 1984. 100 pp., illus. $14.95.

Story of the Winchester company, management, employees, etc.

Winchester Repeating Arms Company by Herbert Houze, Krause Publications, Inc., Iola, WI. 512 pp., illus. $50.00.

With British Snipers to the Reich, by Capt. C. Shore, Lander Militaria, Mt. Ida, AR, 1988. 420 pp., illus. $24.95.

One of the greatest books ever written on the art of combat sniping.

You Can't Miss, by John Shaw and Michael Bane, John Shaw, Memphis, TN, 1983. 152 pp., illus. Paper covers. $12.95.
The secrets of a successful combat shooter; how to better defensive shooting skills.

GUNSMITHING

Advanced Rebarreling of the Sporting Rifle, by Willis H. Fowler, Jr., Willis H. Fowler, Jr., Anchorage, AK, 1994. 127 pp., illus. Paper covers. $32.50.
A manual outlining a superior method of fitting barrels and doing chamber work on the sporting rifle.

The Art of Engraving, by James B. Meek, F. Brownell & Son, Montezuma, IA, 1973. 196 pp., illus. $33.95.
A complete, authoritative, imaginative and detailed study in training for gun engraving. The first book of its kind—and a great one.

Artistry in Arms, The R. W. Norton Gallery, Shreveport, LA, 1970. 42 pp., illus. Paper covers. $9.95.
The art of gunsmithing and engraving.

Barrels & Actions, by Harold Hoffman, H&P Publishers, San Angelo, TX, 1990. 309 pp., illus. Sprial bound. $27.95.
A manual on barrel making.

Black Powder Hobby Gunsmithing, by Sam Fadala and Dale Storey, DBI Books, a division of Krause Publications, Inc., Iola, WI., 1994. 256 pp., illus. Paper covers. $18.95.
A how-to guide for gunsmithing blackpowder pistols, rifles and shotguns from two men at the top of their respective fields.

Checkering and Carving of Gun Stocks, by Monte Kennedy, Stackpole Books, Harrisburg, PA, 1962. 175 pp., illus. $39.95.
Revised, enlarged cloth-bound edition of a much sought-after, dependable work.

The Complete Metal Finishing Book, by Harold Hoffman, H&P Publishers, San Angelo, TX, 1992. 364 pp., illus. Paper covers. $29.95.
Instructions for the different metal finishing operations that the normal craftsman or shop will use. Primarily firearm related.

Custom Gunstock Carving, by Philip Eck, Stackpole Books, Mechanicsburg, PA, 1995. 232 pp., illus. $34.95.
Featuring a gallery of more than 100 full-size patterns for buttstocks, grips, accents and borders that carvers can use for their own projects.

Exploded Handgun Drawings, The Gun Digest Book of, edited by Harold A. Murtz, DBI Books, a division of Krause Publications, Inc., Iola, WI. 1992. 512 pp., illus. Paper covers. $20.95.
Exploded or isometric drawings for 494 of the most popular handguns.

Exploded Long Gun Drawings, The Gun Digest Book of, edited by Harold A. Murtz, DBI Books, a division of Krause Publications, Inc., Iola, WI. 512 pp., illus. Paper covers. $20.95.
Containing almost 500 rifle and shotgun exploded drawings. An invaluable aid to both professionals and hobbyists.

The Finishing of Gun Stocks, by Harold Hoffman, H&P Publishers, San Angelo, TX, 1994. 98 pp., illus. Paper covers. $17.95.
Covers different types of finishing methods and finishes.

Firearms Assembly/Disassembly, Part I: Automatic Pistols, Revised Edition, The Gun Digest Book of, by J.B. Wood, DBI Books, a division of Krause Publications, Inc., Iola, WI, 1990. 480 pp., illus. Paper covers. $19.95.
Covers 58 popular autoloading pistols plus nearly 200 variants of those models integrated into the text and completely cross-referenced in the index.

Firearms Assembly/Disassembly Part II: Revolvers, Revised Edition, The Gun Digest Book of, by J.B. Wood, DBI Books, a division of Krause Publications, Inc., Iola, WI, 1990. 480 pp., illus. Paper covers. $19.95.
Covers 49 popular revolvers plus 130 variants. The most comprehensive and professional presentation available to either hobbyist or gunsmith.

Firearms Assembly/Disassembly Part III: Rimfire Rifles, Revised Edition, The Gun Digest Book of, by J. B. Wood, DBI Books, a division of Krause Publications, Inc., Iola, WI., 1994. 480 pp., illus. Paper covers. $19.95.
Greatly expanded edition covering 65 popular rimfire rifles plus over 100 variants all completely cross-referenced in the index.

Firearms Assembly/Disassembly Part IV: Centerfire Rifles, Revised Edition, The Gun Digest Book of, by J.B. Wood, DBI Books, a division of Krause Publications, Inc., Iola, WI, 1991. 480 pp., illus. Paper covers. $19.95.
Covers 54 popular centerfire rifles plus 300 variants. The most comprehensive and professional presentation available to either hobbyist or gunsmith.

Firearms Assembly/Disassembly, Part V: Shotguns, Revised Edition, The Gun Digest Book of, by J.B. Wood, DBI Books, a division of Krause Publications, Inc., Iola, WI, 1992. 480 pp., illus. Paper covers. $19.95.
Covers 46 popular shotguns plus over 250 variants with step-by-step instructions on how to dismantle and reassemble each. The most comprehensive and professional presentation available to either hobbyist or gunsmith.

Firearms Assembly/Disassembly Part VI: Law Enforcement Weapons, The Gun Digest Book of, by J.B. Wood, DBI Books, a division of Krause Publications, Inc., Iola, WI, 1981. 288 pp., illus. Paper covers. $16.95.
Step-by-step instructions on how to completely dismantle and reassemble the most commonly used firearms found in law enforcement arsenals.

Firearms Assembly 3: The NRA Guide to Rifle and Shotguns, NRA Books, Wash., DC, 1980. 264 pp., illus. Paper covers. $13.95.
Text and illustrations explaining the takedown of 125 rifles and shotguns, domestic and foreign.

Firearms Assembly 4: The NRA Guide to Pistols and Revolvers, NRA Books, Wash., DC, 1980. 253 pp., illus. Paper covers. $13.95.
Text and illustrations explaining the takedown of 124 pistol and revolver models, domestic and foreign.

Firearms Bluing and Browning, By R.H. Angier, Stackpole Books, Harrisburg, PA. 151 pp., illus. $18.95.
A world master gunsmith reveals his secrets of building, repairing and renewing a gun, quite literally, lock, stock and barrel. A useful, concise text on chemical coloring methods for the gunsmith and mechanic.

Firearms Disassembly—With Exploded Views, by John A. Karns & John E. Traister, Stoeger Publishing Co., S. Hackensack, NJ, 1995. 320 pp., illus. Paper covers. $19.95.
Provides the do's and don'ts of firearms disassembly. Enables owners and gunsmiths to disassemble firearms in a professional manner.

Guns and Gunmaking Tools of Southern Appalachia, by John Rice Irwin, Schiffer Publishing Ltd., 1983. 118 pp., illus. Paper covers. $9.95.
The story of the Kentucky rifle.

Gunsmithing Tips and Projects, a collection of the best articles from the *Handloader* and *Rifle* magazines, by various authors, Wolfe Publishing Co., Prescott, AZ, 1992. 443 pp., illus. Paper covers. $25.00.
Includes such subjects as shop, stocks, actions, tuning, triggers, barrels, customizing, etc.

Gunsmith Kinks, by F.R. (Bob) Brownell, F. Brownell & Son, Montezuma, IA, 1st ed., 1969. 496 pp., well illus. $18.95.
A widely useful accumulation of shop kinks, short cuts, techniques and pertinent comments by practicing gunsmiths from all over the world.

Gunsmith Kinks 2, by Bob Brownell, F. Brownell & Son, Publishers, Montezuma, IA, 1983. 496 pp., illus. $18.95.
A collection of gunsmithing knowledge, shop kinks, new and old techniques, shortcuts and general know-how straight from those who do them best—the gunsmiths.

Gunsmith Kinks 3, edited by Frank Brownell, Brownells Inc., Montezuma, IA, 1993. 504 pp., illus. $19.95.
Tricks, knacks and "kinks" by professional gunsmiths and gun tinkerers. Hundreds of valuable ideas are given in this volume.

Gunsmithing, by Roy F. Dunlap, Stackpole Books, Harrisburg, PA, 1990. 742 pp., illus. $34.95.
A manual of firearm design, construction, alteration and remodeling. For amateur and professional gunsmiths and users of modern firearms.

Gunsmithing at Home: Lock, Stock and Barrel, by John Traister, Stoeger Publishing Co., Wayne, NJ, 1997. 320 pp., illus. Paper covers. $19.95.
A Complete step-by-step fully illustrated guide to the art of gunsmithing.

Gunsmithing: Pistols & Revolvers, by Patrick Sweeney, DBI Books, a division of Krause Publications, Inc., Iola, WI, 1998. 352 pp., illus. Paper covers. $24.95.
Do-it-Yourself projects, diagnosis and repair for pistols and revolvers.

The Gunsmith's Manual, by J.P. Stelle and Wm. B. Harrison, The Gun Room Press, Highland Park, NJ, 1982. 376 pp., illus. $19.95.
For the gunsmith in all branches of the trade.

Handbook of Hard-to Find Guns Parts Drawings, by LeeRoy Wisner, Brownells, Inc., Montezuma, IA, 1997. Unpaginated. Deluxe edition. $54.95.
Over 2901 dimensioned drawings covering 147 guns from 36 manufacturers. The most valuable tool you'll ever buy for your shop.

Home Gunsmithing the Colt Single Action Revolvers, by Loren W. Smith, Ray Riling Arms Books, Co., Phila., PA, 1995. 119 pp., illus. $24.95.
Affords the Colt Single Action owner detailed, pertinent information on the operating and servicing of this famous and historic handgun.

How to Convert Military Rifles, Williams Gun Sight Co., Davision, MI, new and enlarged seventh edition, 1997. 76 pp., illus. Paper covers. $13.95.
This latest edition updated the cahnges that have occured over the past thirty years. Tips, instructions and illustratons on how to convert popular military rifles as the Enfield, Mauser 96 nad SKS just to name a few are presented.

Mr. Single Shot's Gunsmithing-Idea-Book, by Frank de Haas, Mark de Haas, Orange City, IA, 1996. 168 pp., illus. Paper covers. $21.50.
Offers easy to follow, step-by-step instructions for a wide variety of gunsmithing procedures all reinforced by plenty of photos.

The NRA Gunsmithing Guide—Updated, by Ken Raynor and Brad Fenton, National Rifle Association, Wash., DC, 1984. 336 pp., illus. Paper covers. $19.95.
Material includes chapters and articles on all facets of the gunsmithing art.

Pistolsmithing, The Gun Digest Book of, by Jack Mitchell, DBI Books, a division of Krause Publications, Inc., Iola, WI, 1980. 256 pp., illus. Paper covers. $16.95.
An expert's guide to the operation of each of the handgun actions with all the major functions of pistolsmithing explained.

Pistolsmithing, by George C. Nonte, Jr., Stackpole Books, Harrisburg, PA, 1974. 560 pp., illus. $29.95.
A single source reference to handgun maintenance, repair, and modification at home, unequaled in value.

Practical Gunsmithing, by the editors of American Gunsmith, DBI Books, a division of Krause Publications, Inc., Iola, WI, 1996. 256 pp., illus. Paper covers. $19.95.
A book intended primarily for home gunsmithing, but one that will be extremely helpful to professionals as well.

Professional Stockmaking, by D. Wesbrook, Wolfe Publishing Co., Prescott AZ, 1995. 308 pp., illus. $54.00.
A step-by-step how-to with complete photographic support for every detail of the art of working wood into riflestocks.

Riflesmithing, The Gun Digest Book of, by Jack Mitchell, DBI Books, a division of Krause Publications, Inc., Iola, WI, 1982. 256 pp., illus. Paper covers. $16.95.
The art and science of rifle gunsmithing. Covers tools, techniques, designs, finishing wood and metal, custom alterations.

Shotgun Gunsmithing, The Gun Digest Book of, by Ralph Walker, DBI Books, a division of Krause Publications, Inc., Iola, WI, 1983. 256 pp., illus. Paper covers. $16.95.
The principles and practices of repairing, individualizing and accurizing modern shotguns by one of the world's premier shotgun gunsmiths.

Sporting Rifle Take Down & reassembly Guide, 2nd Edition, by J.B. Wood, Krause Publications, Iola, WI, 1997. 480 pp., illus. Paper covers. $19.95.
Hunters and shooting enthusiasts must have this reference featuring 52 of the most popular and widely used sporting centerfire and rimfire rifles.

The Story of Pope's Barrels, by Ray M. Smith, R&R Books, Livonia, NY, 1993. 203 pp., illus. $39.00.
A reissue of a 1960 book whose author knew Pope personally. It will be of special interest to Schuetzen rifle fans, since Pope's greatest days were at the height of the Schuetzen-era before WWI.

Survival Gunsmithing, by J.B. Wood, Desert Publications, Cornville, AZ, 1986. 92 pp., illus. Paper covers. $9.95.
A guide to repair and maintenance of the most popular rifles, shotguns and handguns.

The Trade Rifle Sketchbook, by Charles E. Hanson, The Fur Press, Chadron, NE, 1979. 48 pp., illus. Paper covers. $9.95.
Includes full-scale plans for 10 rifles made for Indian and mountain men; from 1790 to 1860, plus plans for building three pistols.

HANDGUNS

Advanced Master Handgunning, by Charles Stephens, Paladin Press, Boulder, CO., 1994. 72 pp., illus. Paper covers. $10.00.
Secrets and surefire techniques for winning handgun competitions.

The Ayoob Files: The Book,by Massad Ayoob, Police Bookshelf, Concord, NH, 1995. 223 pp., illus. Paper covers. $14.95.
The best of Massad Ayoob's acclaimed series in American Handgunner magazine.

Big Bore Sixguns, by John Taffin, Krause Publications, Iola, WI, 1997. 336 pp., illus. $39.95.
The author takes aim on the entire range of big bores from .357 Magnums to .500 Maximums, single actions and cap-and-ball sixguns to custom touches for big bores.

Black Powder Hobby Gunsmithing, by Sam Fadala and Dale Storey, DBI Books, a division of Krause Publications, Inc., Iola, WI., 1994. 256 pp., illus. Paper covers. $18.95.
A how-to guide for gunsmithing blackpowder pistols, rifles and shotguns from two men at the top of their respective fields.

Browning Hi-Power Pistols, Desert Publications, Cornville, AZ, 1982. 20 pp., illus. Paper covers. $9.95.

Covers all facets of the various military and civilian models of the Browning Hi-Power pistol.

Colt Automatic Pistols, by Donald B. Bady, Borden Publ. Co., Alhambra, CA, 1974, 368 pp., illus. $45.00.
The rev. and enlarged ed. of a key work on a fascinating subject. Complete information on every automatic marked with Colt's name.

The Colt .45 Auto Pistol, compiled from U.S. War Dept. Technical Manuals, and reprinted by Desert Publications, Cornville, AZ, 1978. 80 pp., illus. Paper covers. $9.95.
Covers every facet of this famous pistol from mechanical training, manual of arms, disassembly, repair and replacement of parts.

***Combat Handgunnery, 4th Edition,** by Chuck Taylor, DBI Books, a division of Krause Publications, Inc., Iola, WI, 1997. 256 pp., illus. Paper covers. $18.95.
This all-new edition looks at real world combat handgunnery from three different perspectives—military, police and civilian. Available, October, 1996.

Combat Raceguns, by J.M. Ramos, Paladin Press, Boulder, CO, 1994. 168 pp., illus. Paper covers. $25.00.
Learn how to put together precision combat raceguns with the best compensators, frames, controls, sights and custom accessories.

Competitive Pistol Shooting,by Dr. Laslo Antal, A&C Black, London, England, 2nd edition, 1995. 176 pp., illus. Paper covers. $24.95.
Covers the basic principles followed in each case by a well illustrated and detailed discussion of the rules, technique, and training as well as the choice and maintenance of weapons.

The Complete Book of Combat Handgunning, by Chuck Taylor, Desert Publications, Cornville, AZ, 1982. 168 pp., illus. Paper covers. $16.95.
Covers virtually every aspect of combat handgunning.

Complete Guide to Compact Handguns, by Gene Gangarosa, Jr., Stoeger Publishing Co., Wayne, NJ, 1997. 228 pp., illus. Paper covers. $22.95.
Includes hundreds of compact firearms, along with text results conducted by the author.

Complete Guide to Service Handguns, by Gene Gangarosa, Jr., Stoeger Publishing Co., Wayne, NJ, 1998. 320 pp., illus. Paper covers. $22.95.
The author explores the revolvers and pistols that are used around the globe by military, law enforcement and civilians.

The Custom Government Model Pistol, by Layne Simpson, Wolfe Publishing Co., Prescott, AZ, 1994. 639 pp., illus. Paper covers. $24.50.
The book about one of the world's greatest firearms and the things pistolsmiths do to make it even greater.

The CZ-75 Family: The Ultimate Combat Handgun, by J.M. Ramos, Paladin Press, Boulder, CO, 1990. 100 pp., illus. Soft covers. $16.00.
An in-depth discussion of the early-and-late model CZ-75s, as well as the many newest additions to the Czech pistol family.

Encyclopedia of Pistols & Revolvers, by A.E. Hartnik, Knickerbocker Press, New York, NY, 1997. 272 pp., illus. $19.95.
A comprehensive encyclopedia specially written for collectors and owners of pistols and revolvers.

Experiments of a Handgunner, by Walter Roper, Wolfe Publishing Co., Prescott, AZ, 1989. 202 pp., illus. $37.00.
A limited edition reprint. A listing of experiments with functioning parts of handguns, with targets, stocks, rests, handloading, etc.

Exploded Handgun Drawings, The Gun Digest Book of, edited by Harold A. Murtz, DBI Books, a division of Krause Publications, Inc., Iola, WI. 1992. 512 pp., illus. Paper covers. $20.95.
Exploded or isometric drawings for 494 of the most popular handguns.

The Farnam Method of Defensive Handgunning, by John S. Farnam, DTI, Inc., Seattle, WA, 1994. 191 pp., illus. Paper covers. $13.95.
A book intended to not only educate the new shooter, but also to serve as a guide and textbook for his and his instructor's training courses.

Fast and Fancy Revolver Shooting, by Ed. McGivern, Anniversary Edition, Winchester Press, Piscataway, NJ, 1984. 484 pp., illus. $18.95.
A fascinating volume, packed with handgun lore and solid information by the acknowledged dean of revolver shooters.

Firearms Assembly/Disassembly, Part I: Automatic Pistols, Revised Edition, The Gun Digest Book of, by J.B. Wood, DBI Books, a division of Krause Publications, Inc., Iola, WI, 1990. 480 pp., illus. Soft covers. $19.95.
Covers 58 popular autoloading pistols plus nearly 200 variants of those models integrated into the text and completely cross-referenced in the index.

Firearms Assembly/Disassembly Part II: Revolvers, Revised Edition, The Gun Digest Book of, by J.B. Wood, DBI Books, a division of Krause Publications, Inc., Iola, WI, 1990. 480 pp., illus. Soft covers. $19.95.
Covers 49 popular revolvers plus 130 variants. The most comprehensive and professional presentation available to either hobbyist or gunsmith.

.45 ACP Super Guns, by J.M. Ramos, Paladin Press, Boulder, CO, 1991. 144 pp., illus. Paper covers. $24.00.
Modified .45 automatic pistols for competition, hunting and personal defense.

The .45, The Gun Digest Book of, by Dean A. Grennell, DBI Books, a division of Krause Publications, Inc., Iola, WI, 1989. 256 pp., illus. Paper covers. $17.95.
Definitive work on one of America's favorite calibers.

Glock: The New Wave in Combat Handguns, by Peter Alan Kasler, Paladin Press, Boulder, CO, 1993. 304 pp., illus. $25.00.
Kasler debunks the myths that surround what is the most innovative handgun to be introduced in some time.

***Glock's Handguns,** by Duncan Long, Desert Publications, El Dorado, AR, 1996. 180 pp., illus. Paper covers. $18.95.
An outstanding volume on one of the world's newest and most successful firearms of the century.

Hand Cannons: The World's Most Powerful Handguns, by Duncan Long, Paladin Press, Boulder, CO, 1995. 208 pp., illus. Paper covers. $20.00.
Long describes and evaluates each powerful gun according to their features.

Handgun Digest, 3rd Edition, edited by Chris Christian, DBI Books, a division of Krause Publications, Inc., Iola, WI, 1995. 256 pp., illus. Paper covers. $18.95.
Full coverage of all aspects of handguns and handgunning from a highly readable and knowledgeable author.

Handgun Reloading, The Gun Digest Book of, by Dean A. Grennell and Wiley M. Clapp, DBI Books, a division of Krause Publications, Inc., Iola, WI, 1987. 256 pp., illus. Paper covers. $16.95.
Detailed discussions of all aspects of reloading for handguns, from basic to complex. New loading data.

***Handguns '99, 11th Edition,** edited by Ray Ordorica, DBI Books, a division of Krause Publications, Inc., Iola, WI, 1998. 352 pp., illus. Paper covers. $22.95.
Top writers in the handgun industry give you a complete report on new handgun developments, testfire reports on the newest introductions and previews of what's ahead.

***Heckler & Koch's Handguns,** by Duncan Long, Desert Publications, El Dorado, AR, 1996. 142 pp., illus. Paper covers. $18.95.
Traces the history and the evolution of H&K's pistols from the company's beginning at the end of WWII to the present.

Hidden in Plain Sight,by Trey Bloodworth & Mike Raley, Professional Press, Chapel Hill, NC, 1995. Paper covers. $13.00.
A practical guide to concealed handgun carry.

High Standard Automatic Pistols 1932-1950, by Charles E. Petty, The Gunroom Press, Highland Park, NJ, 1989. 124 pp., illus. $19.95.
A definitive source of information for the collector of High Standard arms.

The Hi-Standard Pistol Guide, by Burr Leyson, Duckett's Sporting Books, Tempe AZ, 1995. 128 pp., illus. Paper covers. $22.00.
Complete information on selection, care and repair, ammunition, parts, and accessories.

How to Become a Master Handgunner: The Mechanics of X-Count Shooting, by Charles Stephens, Paladin Press, Boulder, CO, 1993. 64 pp., illus. Paper covers. $10.00.
Offers a simple formula for success to the handgunner who strives to master the technique of shooting accurately.

Hunting for Handgunners, by Larry Kelly and J.D. Jones, DBI Books, a division of Krause Publications, Inc., Iola, WI, 1990. 256 pp., illus. Paper covers. $16.95.
Covers the entire spectrum of hunting with handguns in an amusing, easy-flowing manner that combines entertainment with solid information.

Illustrated Encyclopedia of Handguns, by A.B. Zhuk, Stackpole Books, Mechanicsburg, PA, 1994. 256 pp., illus. Cloth cover, $49.95; paper cover, $29.95.
Identifies more than 2,000 military and commercial pistols and revolvers with details of more than 100 popular handgun cartridges.

Instinct Combat Shooting, by Chuck Klein, Chuck Klein, The Goose Creek, IN, 1989. 49 pp., illus. Paper covers. $12.00.
Defensive handgunning for police.

Know Your Czechoslovakian Pistols, by R.J. Berger, Blacksmith Corp., Chino Valley, AZ, 1989. 96 pp., illus. Soft covers. $9.95.
A comprehensive reference which presents the fascinating story of Czech pistols.

Know Your 45 Auto Pistols—Models 1911 & A1, by E.J. Hoffschmidt, Blacksmith Corp., Southport, CT, 1974. 58 pp., illus. Paper covers. $9.95.
A concise history of the gun with a wide variety of types and copies.

Know Your Walther P38 Pistols, by E.J. Hoffschmidt, Blacksmith Corp., Southport, CT, 1974. 77 pp., illus. Paper covers. $9.95.
Covers the Walther models Armee, M.P., H.P., P.38—history and variations.

Know Your Walther PP & PPK Pistols, by E.J. Hoffschmidt, Blacksmith Corp., Southport, CT, 1975. 87 pp., illus. Paper covers. $9.95.
A concise history of the guns with a guide to the variety and types.

The Mauser Self-Loading Pistol, by Belford & Dunlap, Borden Publ. Co., Alhambra, CA. Over 200 pp., 300 illus., large format. $24.95.
The long-awaited book on the "Broom Handles," covering their inception in 1894 to the end of production. Complete and in detail: pocket pistols, Chinese and Spanish copies, etc.

Modern American Pistols and Revolvers, by A.C. Gould, Wolfe Publishing Co., Prescott, AZ, 1988. 222 pp., illus. $37.00.
A limited edition reprint. An account of the development of those arms as well as the manner of shooting them.

The Modern Technique of the Pistol, by Gregory Boyce Morrison, Gunsite Press, Paulden, AZ, 1991. 153 pp., illus. $45.00.
The theory of effective defensive use of modern handguns.

9mm Handguns, 2nd Edition, The Gun Digest Book of, edited by Steve Comus, DBI Books, a division of Krause Publications, Inc., Iola, WI, 1993. 256 pp., illus. Paper covers. $18.95.
Covers the 9mmP cartridge and the guns that have been made for it in greater depth than any other work available.

9mm Parabellum; The History & Developement of the World's 9mm Pistols & Ammunition, by Klaus-Peter Konig and Martin Hugo, Schiffer Publishing Ltd., Atglen, PA, 1993. 304 pp., illus. $39.95.
Detailed history of 9mm weapons from Belguim, Italy, Germany, Israel, France, USA, Czechoslovakia, Hungary, Poland, Brazil, Finland and Spain.

The Official 9mm Markarov Pistol Manual,translated into English by Major James Gebhardt, U.S. Army (Ret.), Desert Publications, El Dorado, AR, 1996. 84 pp., illus. Paper covers. $12.95.
The information found in this book will be of enormous benefit and interest to the owner or a prospective owner of one of these pistols.

The 100 Greatest Combat Pistols, by Timothy J. Mullin, Paladin Press, Boulder, CO, 1994. 409 pp., illus. Paper covers. $40.00.
Hands-on tests and evaluations of handguns from around the world.

P-38 Automatic Pistol, by Gene Gangarosa, Jr., Stoeger Publishing Co., S. Hackensack, NJ, 1993. 272 pp., illus. Paper covers. $16.95
This book traces the origins and development of the P-38, including the momentous political forces of the World War II era that caused its near demise and, later, its rebirth.

Pistol & Revolver Guide, 3rd Ed., by George C. Nonte, Stoeger Publ. Co., So. Hackensack, NJ, 1975. 224 pp., illus. Paper covers. $11.95.
The standard reference work on military and sporting handguns.

Pistol Guide, by George C. Nonte, Jr., Stoeger Publishing Co., So. Hackensack, NJ, 1991. 280 pp., illus. Paper covers. $13.95.
Covers handling and marksmanship, care and maintenance, pistol ammunition, how to buy a used gun, military pistols, air pistols and repairs.

Pistols of the World, 3rd Edition, by Ian Hogg and John Weeks, DBI Books, a division of Krause Publications, Inc., Iola, WI, 1992. 352 pp., illus. Paper covers. $20.95.
A totally revised edtion of one of the leading studies of small arms.

Pistolsmithing, The Gun Digest Book of, by Jack Mitchell, DBI Books, a division of Krause Publications, Inc., Iola, WI, 1980, 288 pp., illus. Paper covers. $16.95.
An expert's guide to the operation of each of the handgun actions with all the major functions of pistolsmithing explained.

Powerhouse Pistols—The Colt 1911 and Browning Hi-Power Source Book, by Duncan Long, Paladin Press, Boulder, CO, 1989. 152 pp., illus. Soft covers. $19.95.
The author discusses internal mechanisms, outward design, test-firing results, maintenance and accessories.

Practical Shooting: Beyond Fundamentals,by Brian Enos, Zediker Publishing, Clifton, CO, 1997. 201 pp., illus. $27.95.
This prize-winning master covers technique of combat shooting in all its aspects.

Report of Board on Tests of Revolvers and Automatic Pistols, From the Annual Report of the Chief of Ordnance, 1907. Reprinted by J.C. Tillinghast, Marlow, NH, 1969. 34 pp., 7 plates, paper covers. $9.95.
A comparison of handguns, including Luger, Savage, Colt, Webley-Fosbery and other makes.

Revolver Guide, by George C. Nonte, Jr., Stoeger Publishing Co., So. Hackensack, NJ, 1991. 288 pp., illus. Paper covers. $10.95.
A detailed and practical encyclopedia of the revolver, the most common handgun to be found.

Ruger Automatic Pistols and Single Action Revolvers, by Hugo A. Lueders, edited by Don Findley, Blacksmith Corp., Chino Valley, AZ, 1993. 79 pp., illus. Paper covers. $14.95.
The definitive work on Ruger automatic pistols and single action revolvers.

The Ruger "P" Family of Handguns, by Duncan Long, Desert Publications, El Dorado, AZ, 1993. 128 pp., illus. Paper covers. $14.95.
A full-fledged documentary on a remarkable series of Sturm Ruger handguns.

The Ruger .22 Automatic Pistol, Standard/Mark I/Mark II Series, by Duncan Long, Paladin Press, Boulder, CO, 1989. 168 pp., illus. Paper covers. $12.00.
The definitive book about the pistol that has served more than 1 million owners so well.

The Semiautomatic Pistols in Police Service and Self Defense, by Massad Ayoob, Police Bookshelf, Concord, NH, 1990. 25 pp., illus. Soft covers. $9.95.
First quantitative, documented look at actual police experience with 9mm and 45 police service automatics.

The Sharpshooter—How to Stand and Shoot Handgun Metallic Silhouettes, by Charles Stephens, Yucca Tree Press, Las Cruces, NM, 1993. 86 pp., illus. Paper covers. $10.00.
A narration of some of the author's early experiences in silhouette shooting, plus how-to information.

Shoot to Win, by John Shaw, Blacksmith Corp., Southport, CT, 1985. 160 pp., illus. Paper covers. $15.50.
The lessons taught here are of interest and value to all handgun shooters.

Shooting, by J.H. FitzGerald, Wolfe Publishing Co., Prescott, AZ, 1993. 421 pp., illus. $29.00
Exhaustive coverage of handguns and their use for target shooting, defense, trick shooting, and in police work by an noted firearms expert.

*__Shooting Colt Single Actions,__ by Mike Venturino, Livingston, MT, 1995.
A definitive work on the famous Colt SAA and the ammunition it shoots.

Sig/Sauer Handguns, by Duncan Long, Desert Publications, El Dorado, AZ, 1995. 150 pp., illus. Paper covers. $16.95.
The history of Sig/Sauer handguns, including Sig, Sig-Hammerli and Sig/Sauer variants.

Sixgun Cartridges and Loads, by Elmer Keith, reprint edition by The Gun Room Press, Highland Park, NJ, 1984. 151 pp., illus. $24.95.
A manual covering the selection, use and loading of the most suitable and popular revolver cartridges.

Sixguns, by Elmer Keith, Wolfe Publishing Company, Prescott, AZ, 1992. 336 pp. Paper covers. $29.95.
The history, selection, repair, care, loading, and use of this historic frontiersman's friend—the one-hand firearm.

Smith & Wesson's Automatics, by Larry Combs, Desert Publications, El Dorado, AZ, 1994. 143 pp., illus. Paper covers. $27.95.
A must for every S&W auto owner or prospective owner.

Standard Catalog of Smith and Wesson by Jim Supica and Richard Nahas, Kruase Publications, Inc. Iola, WI, 1996. 240 pp., illus. $29.95.
Clearly details hundreds of products by the legendary manufacturer. How to identify, evaluate the conitions and asses the value of 752 Smith & Wesson models and variations.

*__Street Stoppers: The Latest Handgun Stopping Power Street Results,__ by Evan P. Marshall & Edwin J. Sandow, Paladin Press, Boulder, CO, 1997. 392 pp., illus. Paper covers. $39.95.
Compilation of the results of real-life shooting incidents involving every major handgun caliber.

The Tactical Pistol, by Gabriel Suarez with a foreword by Jeff Cooper, Paladin Press, Boulder, CO, 1996. 216 pp., illus. Paper covers. $25.00.
Advanced gunfighting concepts and techniques.

The Thompson/Center Contender Pistol, by Charles Tephens, Paladin Press, Boulder, CO, 1997. 58 pp., illus. Paper covers. $12.00.
How to tune and time, load and shoot accurately with the Contender pistol.

The .380 Enfield No. 2 Revolver, by Mark Stamps and Ian Skennerton, I.D.S.A. Books, Piqua, OH, 1993. 124 pp., 80 illus. Paper covers. $19.95.

The Truth About Handguns, by Duane Thomas, Paladin Press, Boulder, CO, 1997. 136 pp., illus. Paper covers. $14.00.
Exploding the myths, hype, and misinformation about handguns.

U.S. Handguns of World War 2, The Secondary Pistols and Revolvers, by charles W. Pate, Mowbray Publishers, Lincoln, RI, 1997. 368 pp., illus. $39.00.
This indispensable new book covers all of the American military handguns of W.W.2 except for the M1911A1.

World's Deadliest Rimfire Battleguns, by J.M. Ramos, Paladin Press, Boulder, CO, 1990. 184 pp., illus. Paper covers. $14.00.
This heavily illustrated book shows international rimfire assault weapon innovations from World War II to the present.

HUNTING

NORTH AMERICA

Advanced Black Powder Hunting, by Toby Bridges, Stoeger Publishing Co., Wayne, NJ, 1998. 288 pp., illus. Paper covers. $21.95.
The first modern day publication to be filled from cover to cover with guns, loads, projectiles, accessories and the techniques to get the most from today's front loading guns.

Advanced Wild Turkey Hunting & World Records, by Dave Harbour, Winchester Press, Piscataway, NJ, 1983. 264 pp., illus. $19.95.
The definitive book, written by an authority who has studied turkeys and turkey calling for over 40 years.

After the Hunt With Lovett Williams,by Lovett Williams, Krause Publications, Iola, WI, 1996. 256 pp., illus. Paper covers. $15.95.
The author carefully instructs you on how to prepare your trophy turkey for a trip to the taxidermist. Plus help on planning a grand slam hunt.

Aggressive Whitetail Hunting, by Greg Miller, Krause Publications, Iola, WI, 1995. 208 pp., illus. Paper covers. $14.95.
Learn how to hunt trophy bucks in public forests, private farmlands and exclusive hunting grounds from one of America's foremost hunters.

*__Alaskan Adventures, Volume 2,__ by Russell Annabel, Safari Press, Inc., Huntington Beach, CA, 1997. 351 pp., illus. $50.00.
More of this famous writer's previously unpublished magazine articles in book form.

All About Bears, by Duncan Gilchrist, Stoneydale Press Publishing Co., Stevensville, MT, 1989. 176 pp., illus. $19.95.
Covers all kinds of bears—black, grizzly, Alaskan brown, polar and leans on a lifetime of hunting and guiding experiences to explore proper hunting techniques.

All-American Deer Hunter's Guide, edited by Jim Zumbo and Robert Elman, Winchester Press, Piscataway, NJ, 1983. 320 pp., illus. $29.95.
The most comprehensive, thorough book yet published on American deer hunting.

American Duck Shooting, by George Bird Grinnell, Stackpole Books, Harrisburg, PA, 1991. 640 pp., illus. Paper covers. $19.95.
First published in 1901 at the height of the author's career. Describes 50 species of waterfowl, and discusses hunting methods common at the turn of the century.

*__American Hunting and Fishing Books, 1800-1970, Volume 1,__ by Morris Heller, Nimrod and Piscator Press, Mesilla, NM, 1997. 220 pp., illus. A limited, numbered edition. $125.00.
An up-to-date, profusely illustrated, annotated bibliography on American hunting and fishing books and booklets.

American Man-Killers, by Don Zaidle, Safari Press, Long Beach, CA, 1997. 240 pp., illus. $24.95.
Gripping tales about our continents most fearsome kollers from grizzles to cougars, to alligators and a whole host of lesser known potentially dangerous species.

*__The Art of Super-Accurate Hunting with Scoped Rifles,__ by Don Judd, Wolfe Publishing Co., Prescott, AZ, 1996. 99 pp., illus. Paper covers. $14.95.
The philosophy of super-accurate hunting and the rewards of making your shot a trophy.

Autumn Passages, Compiled by the editors of Ducks Unlimited Magazine, Willow Creek Press, Minocqua, WI, 1997. 320 pp. $27.50.
An exceptional collection of duck hunting stories.

Awesome Antlers of North America, by Odie Sudbeck, HTW Publications, Seneca, KS, 1993. 150 pp., illus. $35.00.
500 world-class bucks in color and black and white. This book starts up where the Boone & Crockett recordbook leaves off.

Bare November Days, by George Bird Evans et al, Countrysport Press, Traverse City, MI, 1992. 136 pp., illus. $39.50.
A new, original anthology, a tribute to ruffed grouse, king of upland birds.

Bear Attacks, by K. Etling, Safari Press, Long Beach, CA, 1998. 574 pp., illus. In 2 volumes. $80.00.
Classic tales of dangerous North American bears.

The Bear Hunter's Century, by Paul Schullery, Stackpole Books, Harrisburg, PA, 1989. 240 pp., illus. $19.95.
Thrilling tales of the bygone days of wilderness hunting.

The Best of Babcock, by Havilah Babcock, selected and with an introduction by Hugh Grey, The Gunnerman Press, Auburn Hills, MI, 1985. 262 pp., illus. $19.95.
A treasury of memorable pieces, 21of which have never before appeared in book form.

The Best of Field & Stream, edited by J.I. Merritt, with Margaret G. Nichols and the editor of *Field & Stream,* Lyons & Burford, New York, NY, 1995. 352 pp., illus. $25.00.
100 years of great writing from America's premier sporting magazine.

The Best of Nash Buckingham, by Nash Buckingham, selected, edited and annotated by George Bird Evans, Winchester Press, Piscataway, NJ, 1973. 320 pp., illus. $35.00.
Thirty pieces that represent the very cream of Nash's output on his whole range of outdoor interests—upland shooting, duck hunting, even fishing.

The Best of Sheep Hunting, by John Batten, Amwell Press, Clinton, NJ, 1992. 616 pp., illus. $47.50.
This "Memorial Edition" is a collection of 40 articles and appendices covering sheep hunting in the North American area of Canada, Alaska, the West and Midwest as well as Africa and Europe.

*__Better on a Rising Tide,__ by Tom Kelly, Lyons & Burford Publishers, New York, NY, 1995. 184 pp. $22.95.
Tales of wild turkeys, turkey hunting and Southern folk.

Big December Canvasbacks, by Worth Mathewson, Sand Lake Press, Amity, OR, 1997. 171 pp., illus. By David Hagenbaumer. Limited, signed and numbered edition. $29.95.
Duck hunting stories.

Big Woods, by William Faulkner, wilderness adventures, Gallatin Gateway, MT, 1998. 208 pp., illus. Slipcased. $60.00.
A colleiton of Faulkner's best hunting stories that belongs in the library of every sportsman.

Birdhunter, by Richard s. Grozik, Safari Press, Huntington Beach, CA, 1998. 180 pp., illus. Limited, numbered and signed edition. Slipcased. $60.00.
An entertaining salute to the closeness between man and his dog, man and his gun, and man and the great outdoors.

Birds on the Horizon, by Stuart Williams, Countrysport Press, Traverse City, MI, 1993. 288 pp., illus. $49.50.
Wingshooting adventures around the world.

Blacktail Trophy Tactics, by Boyd Iverson, Stoneydale Press, Stevensville, MI, 1992. 166 pp., illus. Paper covers. $14.95.
A comprehensive analysis of blacktail deer habits, describing a deer's and man's use of scents, still hunting, tree techniques, etc.

Bowhunter's Digest, 3rd Edition, by Chuck Adams, DBI Books, a division of Krause Publications, Inc., Iola, WI, 1990. 288 pp., illus. Soft covers. $17.95.
All-new edition covers all the necessary equipment and how to use it, plus the fine points on how to improve your skill.

*__Bowhunter's Handbook, Expert Strategies and Techniques,__ by M.R. James with Fred Asbell, Dave Holt, Dwight Schuh & Dave Samuel, DBI Books, a division of Krause Publications, Iola, WI, 1997. 256 pp., illus. Paper covers. $19.95.
Tips from the top on taking your bowhunting skills to the next level.

The Buffalo Harvest,by Frank Mayer as told to Charles Roth, Pioneer Press, Union City, TN, 1995. 96 pp., illus. Paper covers. $7.50.
The story of a hide hunter during his buffalo hunting days on the plains.

Bugling for Elk, by Dwight Schuh, Stoneydale Press Publishing Co., Stevensville, MT, 1983. 162 pp., illus. $18.95.
A complete guide to early season elk hunting.

Call of the Quail: A Tribute to the Gentleman Game Bird, by Michael McIntosh, et al., Countrysport Press, Traverse City, MI, 1990. 175 pp., illus. $39.50.
A new anthology on quail hunting.

Calling All Elk, by Jim Zumbo, Jim Zumbo, Cody, WY, 1989. 169 pp., illus. Paper covers. $14.95.
The only book on the subject of elk hunting that covers every aspect of elk vocalization.

Campfires and Game Trails: Hunting North American Big Game, by Craig Boddington, Winchester Press, Piscataway, NJ, 1985. 295 pp., illus. $23.95.
How to hunt North America's big game species.

Come October, by Gene Hill et al, Countrysport Press, Inc., Traverse City, MI, 1991. 176 pp., illus. $39.50.
A new and all-original anthology on the woodcock and woodcock hunting.

The Complete Guide to Bird Dog Training, by John R. Falk, Lyons & Burford, New York, NY, 1994. 288 pp., illus. $22.95.
The latest on live-game field training techniques using released quail and recall pens. A new chapter on the services available for entering field trials and other bird dog competitions.

The Complete Guide to Bowhunting Deer, by Chuck Adams, DBI Books, a division of Krause Publications, Inc., Iola, WI, 1984. 256 pp., illus. Paper covers. $16.95.
Plenty on equipment, bows, sights, quivers, arrows, clothes, lures and scents, stands and blinds, etc.

The Complete Guide to Game Care & Cookery, 3rd Edition, by Sam Fadala, DBI Books, a division of Krause Publications, Inc., Iola, WI, 1994. 320 pp., illus. Paper covers. $18.95.
Over 500 photos illustrating the care of wild game in the field and at home with a separate recipe section providing over 400 tested recipes.

The Complete Smoothbore Hunter, by Brook Elliot, Winchester Press, Piscataway, NJ, 1986. 240 pp., illus. $16.95.
Advice and information on guns and gunning for all varieties of game.

***The Complete Venison Cookbook from Field to Table,** by Jim & Ann Casada, Krause Publications, Iola, WI, 1996. 208 pp., Comb-bound. $12.95.
More than 200 kitchen tested recipes make this book the answer to a table full of hungry hunters or guests.

Covey Rises and Other Pleasures, by David H. Henderson, Amwell Press, Clinton, NJ, 1983. 155 pp., illus. $17.50.
A collection of essays and stories concerned with field sports.

Coveys and Singles: The Handbook of Quail Hunting, by Robert Gooch, A.S. Barnes, San Diego, CA, 1981. 196 pp., illus. $11.95.
The story of the quail in North America.

Coyote Hunting, by Phil Simonski, Stoneydale Press, Stevensville, MT, 1994. 126 pp., illus. Paper covers. $12.95.
Probably the most thorough "How-to-do-it" book on coyote hunting ever written.

Dabblers & Divers: A Duck Hunter's Book, compiled by the editors of Ducks Unlimited Magazine, Willow Creek Press, Minocqua, WI, 1997. 160 pp., illus. $39.95.
A word-and-photographic portrayal of waterfowl hunter's singular intimacy with, and passion for, watery haunts and wildfowl.

Dancers in the Sunset Sky, by Robert F. Jones, The Lyons Press, New York, NY, 1997. 192 pp., illus. $22.95.
The musings of a bird hunter.

Deer & Deer Hunting, by Al Hofacker, Krause Publications, Iola, WI, 1993. 208 pp., illus. $34.95.
Coffee-table volume packed full of how-to-information that will guide hunts for years to come.

Deer and Deer Hunting: The Serious Hunter's Guide, by Dr. Robert Wegner, Stackpole Books, Harrisburg, PA, 1984. 384 pp., illus. Paper covers. $18.95.
In-depth information from the editor of "Deer & Deer Hunting" magazine. Major bibliography of English language books on deer and deer hunting from 1838-1984.

Deer and Deer Hunting Book 2, by Dr. Robert Wegner, Stackpole Books, Harrisburg, PA, 1987. 400 pp., illus. Paper covers. $18.95.
Strategies and tactics for the advanced hunter.

Deer and Deer Hunting, Book 3, by Dr. Robert Wegner, Stackpole Books, Harrisburg, PA, 1990. 368 pp., ilus. $29.95.
This comprehensive volume covers natural history, deer hunting lore, profiles of deer hunters, and discussion of important issues facing deer hunters today.

Deer Hunter's Guide to Guns, Ammunition, and Equipment, by Edward A. Matunas, an Outdoor Life Book, distributed by Stackpole Books, Harrisburg, PA, 1983. 352 pp., illus. $24.95.
Where to hunt for North American deer. An authoritative guide that will help every deer hunter get maximum enjoyment and satisfaction from his sport.

The Deer Hunters: The Tactics, Lore, Legacy and Allure of American Deer Hunting, Edited by Patrick Durkin, Krause Publications, Iola, WI, 1997. 208 pp., illus. $29.95.
More than twenty years of research form America's top whitetail hunters, researchers, and photographers have gone in to the making of this book.

Deer Hunting, by R. Smith, Stackpole Books, Harrisburg, PA, 1978. 224 pp., illus. Paper covers. $14.95.
A professional guide leads the hunt for North America's most popular big game animal.

Deer Hunting Coast to Coast, by C. Boddington and R. Robb, Safari Press, Long Beach, CA, 1989. 248 pp., illus. $24.95.
Join the authors as they hunt whitetail deer in eastern woodlot, southern swamps, midwestern prairies, and western river bottom; mule deer in badland, deserts, and high alpine basins; blacktails in oak grasslands and coastal jungles.

Doves and Dove Shooting, by Byron W. Dalrymple, New Win Publishing, Inc., Hampton, NJ, 1992. 256 pp., illus. $17.95.
The author reveals in this classic book his penchant for observing, hunting, and photographing this elegantly fashioned bird.

Dove Hunting, by Charley Dickey, Galahad Books, NY, 1976. 112 pp., illus. $10.00.
This indispensable guide for hunters deals with equipment, techniques, types of dove shooting, hunting dogs, etc.

Dreaming the Lion, by Thomas McIntyre, Countrysport Press, Traverse City, MI, 1994. 309 pp., illus. $35.00.
Reflections on hunting, fishing and a search for the wild. Twenty-three stories by *Sports Afield* editor, Tom McIntyre.

Drummer in the Woods, by Burton L. Spiller, Stackpole Books, Harrisburg, PA, 1990. 240 pp., illus. Soft covers. $16.95.
Twenty-one wonderful stories on grouse shooting by "the Poet Laureate of Grouse."

Duck Decoys and How to Rig Them, by Ralf Coykendall, revised by Ralf Coykendall, Jr., Nick Lyons Books, New York, NY, 1990. 137 pp., illus. Paper covers. $14.95.
Sage and practical advice on the art of decoying ducks and geese.

The Duck Hunter's Handbook, by Bob Hinman, revised, expanded, updated edition, Winchester Press, Piscataway, NJ, 1985. 288 pp., illus. $15.95.
The duck hunting book that has it all.

Eastern Upland Shooting, by Dr. Charles C. Norris, Countrysport Press, Traverse City, MI, 1990. 424 pp., illus. $29.50.
A new printing of this 1946 classic with a new, original Foreword by the author's friend and hunting companion, renowned author George Bird Evans.

Elk and Elk Hunting, by Hart Wixom, Stackpole Books, Harrisburg, PA, 1986. 288 pp., illus. $34.95.
Your practical guide to fundamentals and fine points of elk hunting.

Elk Hunting in the Northern Rockies, by Ed. Wolff, Stoneydale Press, Stevensville, MT, 1984. 162 pp., illus. $18.95.
Helpful information about hunting the premier elk country of the northern Rocky Mountain states—Wyoming, Montana and Idaho.

Elk Hunting with the Experts, by Bob Robb, Stoneydale Press, Stevensville, MT, 1992. 176 pp., illus. Paper covers. $15.95.
A complete guide to elk hunting in North America by America's top elk hunting expert.

Elk Rifles, Cartridges and Hunting Tactics, by Wayne van Zwoll, Larsen's Outdoor Publishing, Lakeland, FL, 1992. 414 pp., illus. $24.95.
The definitive work on which rifles and cartridges are proper for hunting elk plus the tactics for hunting them.

Encyclopedia of Deer, by G. Kenneth Whitehead, Safari Press, Huntington, CA, 1993. 704 pp., illus. $130.00.
This massive tome will be the reference work on deer for well into the next century.

Fair Chase, by Jim Rikhoff, Amwell Press, Clinton, NJ, 1984. 323 pp., illus. $25.00.
A collection of hunting experiences from the Arctic to Africa, Mongolia to Montana, taken from over 25 years of writing.

A Fall of Woodcock, by Tom Huggler, Countrysport Press, Selman, AL, 1997. 256 pp., illus. $39.00.
A book devoted to the woodcock and to those who await his return to their favorite converts each autumn.

Firelight, by Burton L. Spiller, Gunnerman Press, Auburn Hills, MI, 1990. 196 pp., illus. $19.95.
Enjoyable tales of the outdoors and stalwart companions.

The Formidable Game, by John H. Batten, Amwell Press, Clinton, NJ. 1983. 264 pp., illus. $40.00.
Big game hunting in India, Africa and North America by a world famous hunter.

Fresh Looks at Deer Hunting, by Byron W. Dalrymple, New Win Publishing, Inc., Hampton, NJ, 1993. 288 pp., illus. $24.95.
Tips and techniques abound throughout the pages of this latest work by Mr. Dalrymple whose name is synonymous with hunting proficiency.

From the Peace to the Fraser, by Prentis N. Gray, Boone and Crockett Club, Missoula, MT, 1995. 400 pp., illus. $49.95.
Newly discovered North American hunting and exploration journals from 1900 to 1930.

Fur Trapping In North America, by Steven Geary, Winchester Press, Piscataway, NJ, 1985. 160 pp., illus. Paper covers. $19.95.
A comprehensive guide to techniques and equipment, together with fascinating facts about fur bearers.

A Gallery of Waterfowl and Upland Birds, by Gene Hill, with illustrations by David Maass, Petersen Prints, Los Angeles, CA, 1978. 132 pp., illus. $44.95.
Gene Hill at his best. Liberally illustrated with 51 full-color reproductions of David Maass' finest paintings.

Game in the Desert Revisited, by Jack O'Connor, Amwell Press, Clinton, NJ, 1984. 306 pp., illus. $27.50.
Reprint of a Derrydale Press classic on hunting in the Southwest

Getting the Most Out of Modern Waterfowling, by John O. Cartier, St. Martin's Press, NY, 1974. 396 pp., illus. $22.50.
The most comprehensive, up-to-date book on waterfowling imaginable.

Getting a Stand, by Miles Gilbert, Pioneer Press, Union City, TN, 1993. 204 pp., illus. Paper covers. $10.95.
An anthology of 18 short personal experiences by buffalo hunters of the late 1800s, specifically from 1870-1882.

Gordon MacQuarrie Trilogy: Stories of the Old Duck Hunters, by Gordon MacQuarrie, Willow Creek Press, Minocqua, WI, 1994. $49.00.
A slip-cased three volume set of masterpieces by one of America's finest outdoor writers.

The Grand Passage: A Chronicle of North American Waterfowling, by Gene Hill, et al., Countrysport Press, Traverse City, MI, 1990. 175 pp., illus. $39.50.
A new original anthology by renowned sporting authors on our world of waterfowling.

Grouse and Woodcock, A Gunner's Guide, by Don Johnson, Krause Publications, Iola, WI, 1995. 256 pp., illus. Paper covers. $14.95.
Find out what you need in guns, ammo, equipment, dogs and terrain.

Grouse of North America, by Tom Huggler, NorthWord Press, Inc., Minocqua, WI, 1990. 160 pp., illus. $29.95.
A cross-continental hunting guide.

Grouse Hunter's Guide, by Dennis Walrod, Stackpole Books, Harrisburg, PA, 1985. 192 pp., illus. $18.95.
Solid facts, observations, and insights on how to hunt the ruffed grouse.

Gunning for Sea Ducks, by George Howard Gillelan, Tidewater Publishers, Centreville, MD, 1988. 144 pp., illus. $14.95.
A book that introduces you to a practically untouched arena of waterfowling.

Heartland Trophy Whitetails, by Odie Sudbeck, HTW Publications, Seneca, KS, 1992. 130 pp., illus. $35.00.
A completely revised and expanded edition which includes over 500 photos of Boone & Crockett class whitetail, major mulies and unusual racks.

***The Heck with Moose Hunting,** by Jim Zumbo, Wapiti Valley Publishing Co., Cody, WY, 1996. 199 pp., illus. $17.95.
Jim's hunts around the continent including encounters with moose, caribou, sheep, antelope and mountain goats.

***High Pressure Elk Hunting,** by Mike Lapinski, Stoneydale Press Publishing Co., Stevensville, MT, 1996. 192 pp., illus. $19.95.
The secrets of hunting educated elk revealed.

***Hill Country,** by Gene Hill, Countrysport Press, Traverse City, MI, 1996. 180 pp., illus. $25.00.
Stories about hunting, fishing, dogs and guns.

Home from the Hill, by Fred Webb, Safari Press, Huntington Beach, CA, 1997. 283 pp., illus. Limited edition, signed and numbered. In a slipcase. $50.00.
The story of a big-game guide in the Canadian wilderness.

Horns in the High Country, by Andy Russell, Alfred A. Knopf, NY, 1973. 259 pp., illus. Paper covers. $12.95.
A many-sided view of wild sheep and their natural world.

How to Hunt, by Dave Bowring, Winchester Press, Piscataway, NJ, 1982. 208 pp., illus. Paper covers. $10.95; cloth, $15.00.
A basic guide to hunting big game, small game, upland birds, and waterfowl.

Hunt Alaska Now: Self-Guiding for Trophy Moose & Caribou, by Dennis W. Confer, Wily Ventures, Anchorage, AK, 1997. 309 pp., illus. Paper covers. $26.95.
How to plan affordable, successful, safe hunts you can do yourself.

The Hunters and the Hunted, by George Laycock, Outdoor Life Books, New York, NY, 1990. 280 pp., illus. $34.95.
The pursuit of game in America from Indian times to the present.

A Hunter's Fireside Book, by Gene Hill, Winchester Press, Piscataway, NJ, 1972. 192 pp., illus. $16.95.
An outdoor book that will appeal to every person who spends time in the field—or who wishes he could.

A Hunter's Road, by Jim Fergus, Henry Holt & Co., NY, 1992. 290 pp. $22.50
A journey with gun and dog across the American uplands.

Hunt High for Rocky Mountain Goats, Bighorn Sheep, Chamois & Tahr, by Duncan Gilchrist, Stoneydale Press, Stevensville, MT, 1992. 192 pp., illus. Paper covers. $19.95.
The source book for hunting mountain goats.

The Hunter's Shooting Guide, by Jack O'Connor, Outdoor Life Books, New York, NY, 1982. 176 pp., illus. Paper covers. $5.95.
A classic covering rifles, cartridges, shooting techniques for shotguns/rifles/handguns.

The Hunter's World, by Charles F. Waterman, Winchester Press, Piscataway, NJ, 1983. 250 pp., illus. $29.95.
A classic. One of the most beautiful hunting books that has ever been produced.

Hunting Adventure of Me and Joe, by Walt Prothero, Safari Press, Huntington Beach, CA, 1995. 220 pp., illus. $22.50.
A collection of the author's best and favorite stories.

Hunting America's Game Animals and Birds, by Robert Elman and George Peper, Winchester Press, Piscataway, NJ, 1975. 368 pp., illus. $16.95.
A how-to, where-to, when-to guide—by 40 top experts—covering the continent's big, small, upland game and waterfowl.

Hunting Ducks and Geese, by Steven Smith, Stackpole Books, Harrisburg, PA, 1984. 160 pp., illus. $19.95.
Hard facts, good bets, and serious advice from a duck hunter you can trust.

Hunting for Handgunners, by Larry Kelly and J.D. Jones, DBI Books, a division of Krause Publications, Inc., Iola, WI, 1990. 256 pp., illus. Soft covers. $16.95.
A definitive work on an increasingly popular sport.

Hunting in Many Lands, edited by Theodore Roosevelt and George Bird Grinnell, et al., Boone & Crockett Club, Dumphries, VA, 1990. 447 pp., illus. $40.00.
A limited edition reprinting of the original Boone & Crockett Club 1895 printing.

Hunting Mature Bucks, by Larry L. Weishuhn, Krause Publications, Iola, WI, 1995. 256 pp., illus. Paper covers. $14.95.
One of North America's top white-tailed deer authorities shares his expertise on hunting those big, smart and elusive bucks.
Hunting Open-Country Mule Deer, by Dwight Schuh, Sage Press, Nampa, ID, 1989. 180 pp., illus. $18.95.
A guide taking Western bucks with rifle and bow.
Hunting Predators for Hides and Profits, by Wilf E. Pyle, Stoeger Publishing Co., So. Hackensack, NJ, 1985. 224 pp., illus. Paper covers. $11.95.
The author takes the hunter through every step of the hunting/marketing process.
Hunting the American Wild Turkey, by Dave Harbour, Stackpole Books, Harrisburg, PA, 1975. 256 pp., illus. $24.95.
The techniques and tactics of hunting North America's largest, and most popular, woodland game bird.
***Hunting the Rockies, Home of the Giants,** by Kirk Darner, Marceline, MO, 1996. 291 pp., illus. $25.00.
Understand how and where to hunt Western game in the Rockies.
Hunting the Sun, by Ted Nelson Lundrigan, Countrysport Press, Selma, AL, 1997. 240 pp., illus. $30.00.
One of the best books on grouse and woodcock ever published.
Hunting Trips in North America, by F.C. Selous, Wolfe Publishing Co., Prescott, AZ, 1988. 395 pp., illus. $52.00.
A limited edition reprint. Coverage of caribou, moose and other big game hunting in virgin wilds.
Hunting Trophy Deer, by John Wootters, The Lyons Press, New York, NY, 1997. 272 pp., illus. $24.95.
A revised edition of the definitve manual for identifying, scouting, and successfully hunting a deer of a lifetime.
Hunting Trophy Whitetails, by David Morris, Stoneydale Press, Stevensville, MT, 1993. 483 pp., illus. $29.95.
This is one of the best whitetail books published in the last two decades. The author is the former editor of *North American Whitetail* magazine.
Hunting Upland Birds, by Charles F. Waterman, Countrysport Press, Selma, AL, 1997. 220 pp., illus. $30.00.
Originally published a quarter of a century ago, this classic has been newly updated with the latest information for today's wingshooter.
Hunting Western Deer, by Jim and Wes Brown, Stoneydale Press, Stevensville, MT, 1994. 174 pp., illus. Paper covers. $14.95.
A pair of expert Oregon hunters provide insight into hunting mule deer and blacktail deer in the western states.
Hunting Wild Turkeys in the West, by John Higley, Stoneydale Press, Stevensville, MT, 1992. 154 pp., illus. Paper covers. $12.95.
Covers the basics of calling, locating and hunting turkeys in the western states.
Hunting with the Twenty-two, by Charles Singer Landis, R&R Books, Livonia, NY, 1994. 429 pp., illus. $45.00.
A miscellany of articles touching on the hunting and shooting of small game.
I Don't Want to Shoot an Elephant, by Havilah Babcock, The Gunnerman Press, Auburn Hills, MI, 1985. 184 pp., illus. $19.95.
Eighteen delightful stories that will enthrall the upland gunner for many pleasurable hours.
***In Search of the Buffalo,** by Charles G. Anderson, Pioneer Press, Union City, TN, 1996. 144 pp., illus. Paper civers. $13.95.
The primary study of the life of J. Wright Mooar one of the few hunters fortunate enough to kill a white buffalo.
In Search of the Wild Turkey, by Bob Gooch, Greatlakes Living Press, Ltd., Waukegan, IL, 1978. 182 pp., illus. $9.95.
A state-by-state guide to wild turkey hot spots, with tips on gear and methods for bagging your bird.
Indian Hunts and Indian Hunters of the Old West, by Dr. Frank C. Hibben, Safari Press, Long Beach, CA, 1989. 228 pp., illus. $24.95.
Tales of some of the most famous American Indian hunters of the Old West as told to the author by an old Navajo hunter.
Jack O'Connor's Gun Book, by Jack O'Connor, Wolfe Publishing Company, Prescott, AZ, 1992. 208 pp. Hardcover. $26.00.
Jack O'Connor imparts a cross-section of his knowledge on guns and hunting. Brings back some of his writings that have here-to-fore been lost.
Jaybirds Go to Hell on Friday, by Havilah Babcock, The Gunnerman Press, Auburn Hills, MI, 1985. 149 pp., illus. $19.95.
Sixteen jewels that reestablish the lost art of good old-fashioned yarn telling.
Jim Dougherty's Guide to Bowhunting Deer, by Jim Dougherty, DBI Books, a division of Krause Publications, Inc., Iola, WI, 1992. 256 pp., illus. Paper covers. $17.95.
Dougherty sets down some important guidelines for bowhunting and bowhunting equipment.
Last Casts and Stolen Hunts, edited by Jim Casada and Chuck Wechsler, Countrysport Press, Traverse City, MI, 1994. 270 pp., illus. $29.95.
The world's best hunting and fishing stories by writers such as Zane Grey, Jim Corbett, Jack O'Connor, Archibald Rutledge and others.
A Listening Walk...and Other Stories, by Gene Hill, Winchester Press, Piscataway, NJ, 1985. 208 pp., illus. $15.95.
Vintage Hill. Over 60 stories.
Longbows in the Far North, by E. Donnall Thomas, Jr. Stackpole Books, Mechanicsburg, PA, 1994. 200 pp., illus. $18.95.
An archer's adventures in Alaska and Siberia.
The Longwalkers: 25 Years of Tracking the Northern Cougar, by Jerry A. Lewis, Wolfe Publishing Co., Prescott, AZ, 1996. 140 pp., illus. Paper covers. $24.95.
Trek the snow-covered mountain forests of Idaho, Montana, British Columbia, and Alberta with the author as he follows cougars/mountain lions on foot, guided by his keen hounds.
Mammoth Monarchs of North America, by Odie Sudbeck, HTW Publications, Seneca, KA, 1995. 288 pp., illus. $35.00.
This book reveals eye-opening big buck secrets.
Matching the Gun to the Game, by Clair Rees, Winchester Press, Piscataway, NJ, 1982. 272 pp., illus. $17.95.
Covers selection and use of handguns, blackpowder firearms for hunting, matching rifle type to the hunter, calibers for multiple use, tailoring factory loads to the game.
Measuring and Scoring North American Big Game Trophies, by Wm. H. Nesbitt and Philip L. Wright, The Boone and Crockett Club, Alexandria, VA, 1986. 176 pp., illus. $15.00.
The Boone and Crockett Club official scoring system, with tips for trophy evaluation.
Meditation on Hunting, by Jose Ortego y Gasset, Wilderness Adventures Press, Bozeman, MT, 1996. 140 pp., illus. In a slipcase. $60.00.
The classic work on the philosophy of hunting.
Mixed Bag, by Jim Rikhoff, National Rifle Association of America, Wash., DC, 1981. 284 pp., illus. Paper covers. $9.95.
Reminiscences of a master raconteur.
Modern Pheasant Hunting, by Steve Grooms, Stackpole Books, Harrisburg, PA, 1982. 224 pp., illus. Paper covers. $10.95.
New look at pheasants and hunters from an experienced hunter who respects this splendid gamebird.
Modern Waterfowl Guns and Gunning, by Don Zutz, Stoeger Publishing Co., So. Hackensack, NJ, 1985. 224 pp., illus. Paper covers. $11.95.
Up-to-date information on the fast-changing world of waterfowl guns and loads.
Montana—Land of Giant Rams, by Duncan Gilchrist, Stoneydale Press Publishing Co., Stevensville, MT, 1990. 208 pp., illus. $19.95.
Latest information on Montana bighorn sheep and why so many Montana bighorn rams are growing to trophy size.
Montana—Land of Giant Rams, Volume 2, by Duncan Gilchrist, Outdoor Expeditions and Books, Corvallis, MT, 1992. 208 pp., illus. $34.95.
The reader will find stories of how many of the top-scoring trophies were taken.
More and Better Pheasant Hunting, by Steve Smith, Winchester Press, Piscataway, NJ, 1986. 192 pp., illus. $15.95.
Complete, fully illustrated, expert coverage of the bird itself, the dogs, the hunt, the guns, and the best places to hunt.
More Grouse Feathers, by Burton L. Spiller, Crown Publ., NY, 1972. 238 pp., illus. $25.00.
Facsimile of the original Derrydale Press issue of 1938. Guns and dogs, the habits and shooting of grouse, woodcock, ducks, etc. Illus. by Lynn Bogue Hunt.
More Tracks: 78 Years of Mountains, People & Happinesss, by Howard Copenhaver, Stoney dale Press, Stevensville, MT, 1992. 150 pp., illus. $18.95.
A collection of stories by one of the back country's best storytellers about the people who shared with Howard his great adventure in the high places and wild Montana country.
Mostly Huntin', by Bill Jordan, Everett Publishing Co., Bossier City, LA, 1987. 254 pp., illus. $21.95.
Jordan's hunting adventures in North America, Africa, Australia, South America and Mexico.
Mostly Tailfeathers, by Gene Hill, Winchester Press, Piscataway, NJ, 1975. 192 pp., illus. $15.95.
An interesting, general book about bird hunting.
"Mr. Buck": The Autobiography of Nash Buckingham, by Nash Buckingham, Countrysport Press, Traverse City, MI, 1990. 288 pp., illus. $39.50.
A lifetime of shooting, hunting, dogs, guns, and Nash's reflections on the sporting life, along with previously unknown pictures and stories written especially for this book.
Murry Burnham's Hunting Secrets, by Murry Burnham with Russell Tinsley, Winchester Press, Piscataway, NJ, 1984. 244 pp., illus. $17.95.
One of the great hunters of our time gives the reasons for his success in the field.
My Health is Better in November, by Havilah Babcock, University of S. Carolina Press, Columbia, SC, 1985. 284 pp., illus. $19.95.
Adventures in the field set in the plantation country and backwater streams of SC.
North American Big Game Animals, by Byron W. Dalrymple and Erwin Bauer, Outdoor Life Books/Stackpole Books, Harrisburg, PA, 1985. 258 pp., illus. $29.95.
Complete illustrated natural histories. Habitat, movements, breeding, birth and development, signs, and hunting.
North American Elk: Ecology and Management, edited by Jack Ward Thomas and Dale E. Toweill, Stackpole Books, Harrisburg, PA, 1982. 576 pp., illus. $39.95.
The definitive, exhaustive, classic work on the North American elk.
The North American Waterfowler, by Paul S. Bernsen, Superior Publ. Co., Seattle, WA, 1972. 206 pp. Paper covers. $9.95.
The complete inside and outside story of duck and goose shooting. Big and colorful, illustrations by Les Kouba.
Of Bears and Man, by Mike Cramond, University of Oklahoma Press, Norman, OK, 1986. 433 pp., illus. $29.95.
The author's lifetime association with bears of North America. Interviews with survivors of bear attacks.
The Old Man and the Boy, by Robert Ruark, Henry Holt & Co., New York, NY, 303 pp., illus. $24.95.
A timeless classic, telling the story of a remarkable friendship between a young boy and his grandfather as the hunt and fish together.
The Old Man's Boy Grows Older, by Robert Ruark, Henry Holt & Co., Inc., New York, NY, 1993. 300 pp., illus. $24.95.
The heartwarming sequel to the best-selling *The Old Man and the Boy*.
***Old Wildfowling Tales, Volume 2,** edited by Worth Mathewson, Sand Lake Press, Amity, OR, 1996. 240 pp. $21.95.
A collection of duck and geese hunting stories based around accounts from the past.
Once Upon a Time, by Nash Buckingham, Beaver Dam Press, Brentwood, TN, 1995. 170 pp., illus. $29.50.
161 Waterfowling Secrets, edited by Matt Young, Willow Creek Press, Minocqua, WI, 1997. 78 pp., Paper covers. $10.95.
Time-honored, field-tested waterfowling tips and advice.
The Only Good Bear is a Dead Bear, by Jeanette Hortick Prodgers, Falcon Press, Helena, MT, 1986. 204 pp. Paper covers. $12.50.
A collection of the West's best bear stories.
Outdoor Pastimes of an American Hunter, by Theodore Roosevelt, Stackpole Books, Mechanicsburg, PA, 1994. 480 pp., illus. Paper covers. $18.95.
Stories of hunting big game in the West and notes about animal pursued and observed.
Outdoor Yarns & Outright Lies, by Gene Hill and Steve Smith, Stackpole Books, Harrisburg, PA, 1984. 168 pp., illus. $18.95.
Fifty or so stories by two good sports.
The Outlaw Gunner, by Harry M. Walsh, Tidewater Publishers, Cambridge, MD, 1973. 178 pp., illus. $22.95.
A colorful story of market gunning in both its legal and illegal phases.
***Passing a Good Time,** by Gene Hill, Countrysport Press, Traverse City, MI, 1996. 200 pp., illus. $25.00.
Filled with insights and observations of guns, dogs and fly rods that make Gene Hill a master essayist.
Pear Flat Philosophies, by Larry Weishuhn, Safari Press, Huntington Beach, CA, 1995. 234 pp., illus. $24.95.
The author describes his more lighthearted adventures and funny anecdotes while out hunting.
Pheasant Days, by Chris Dorsey, Voyageur Press, Stillwater, MN, 1992. 233 pp., illus. $24.95.
The definitive resource on ringnecks. Includes everything from basic hunting techniques to the life cycle of the bird.
Pheasant Hunter's Harvest, by Steve Grooms, Lyons & Burford Publishers, New York, NY, 1990. 180 pp. $22.95.
A celebration of pheasant, pheasant dogs and pheasant hunting. Practical advice from a passionate hunter.
***Pheasant Tales,** by Gene Hill et al, Countrysport Press, Traverse City, MI, 1996. 202 pp., illus. $39.00.
Charley Waterman, Michael McIntosh and Phil Bourjaily join the author to tell some of the stories that illustrate why the pheasant is America's favorite game bird.
Pheasants of the Mind, by Datus Proper, Wilderness Adventures Press, Bozeman, MT, 1994. 154 pp., illus. $25.00.

No single title sums up the life of the solitary pheasant hunter like this masterful work.

Pinnell and Talifson: Last of the Great Brown Bear Men, by Marvin H. Clark, Jr., Great Northwest Publishing and Distributing Co., Spokane, WA, 19880. 224 pp., Illus. $39.95
The story of these famous Alaskan guides and some of the record bears taken by both of them.

***Predator Calling with Gerry Blair,** by Gerry Blair, Krause Publications, Iola, WI, 1996. 208 pp., illus. Paper covers. $14.95.
Time-tested secrets lure predators closer to your camera or gun.

Proven Whitetail Tactics, by Greg Miller, Krause Publications, Iola, WI, 1997. 224 pp., illus. Paper covers. $19.95.
Proven tactics for scouting, calling and still-hunting whitetail.

Quail Hunting in America, by Tom Huggler, Stackpole Books, Harrisburg, PA, 1987. 288 pp., illus. $19.95.
Tactics for finding and taking bobwhite, valleys, Gambel's Mountain, scaled-blue, and Mearn's quail by season and habitat.

Quest for Dall Rams, by Duncan Gilchrist, Duncan Gilchrist Outdoor Expeditions and Books, Corvallis, MT, 1997. 224 pp., illus. Limited numbered edition. $34.95.
The most complete book o Dall sheep ever written. Covers information on Alaska and provinces with Dall sheep and explains hunting techniques, equipment, etc.

Quest for Giant Bighorns, by Duncan Gilchrist, Outdoor Expeditions and Books, Corvallis, MT, 1994. 224 pp., illus. Paper covers. $19.95.
How some of the most successful sheep hunters hunt and how some of the best bighorns were taken.

Radical Elk Hunting Strategies, by Mike Lapinski, Stoneydale Press Publishing Co., Stevensville, MT, 1988. 161 pp., illus. $18.95.
Secrets of calling elk in close.

Records of North American Big Game 1932, by Prentis N. Grey, Boone and Crockett Club, Dumfries, VA, 1988. 178 pp., illus. $79.95.
A reprint of the book that started the Club's record keeping for native North American big game.

Records of North American Caribou and Moose, Craig Boddington et al, The Boone & Crockett Club, Missoula, MT, 1997. 250 pp., illus. $24.95.
More than 1,800 caribou listings and more than 1,500 moose listings, organized by the state or Canadian province where they were taken.

***Records of North American Elk and Mule Deer, 2nd Edition,** edited by Jack and Susan Reneau, Boone & Crockette Club, Missoula, MT, 1996. 360 pp., illus. Paper cover, $18.95; hardcover, $24.95.
Updated and expanded edition featuring more than 150 trophy, field and historical photos of the finest elk and mule deer trophies ever recorded.

***Records of North American Sheep, Rocky Mountain Goats and Pronghorn** edited by Jack and Susan Reneau, Boone & Crockette Club, Missoula, MT, 1996. 400 pp., illus. Paper cover, $18.95; hardcover, $24.95.
The first B&C Club records book featuring all 3941 accepted wil sheep, Rocky Mountain goats and pronghorn trophies.

The Rifles, the Cartridges, and the Game, by Clay Harvey, Stackpole Books, Harrisburg, PA, 1991. 254 pp., illus. $32.95.
Engaging reading combines with exciting photos to present the hunt with an intense level of awareness and respect.

Ringneck! Pheasants & Pheasant Hunting, by Ted Janes, Crown Publ., NY, 1975. 120 pp., illus. $15.95.
A thorough study of one of our more popular game birds.

Ruffed Grouse, edited by Sally Atwater and Judith Schnell, Stackpole Books, Harrisburg, PA, 1989. 370 pp., illus. $59.95.
Everything you ever wanted to know about the ruffed grouse. More than 25 wildlife professionals provided in-depth information on every aspect of this popular game bird's life. Lavishly illustrated with over 300 full-color photos.

The Russell Annabel Adventure Series, by Russell Anabel, Safari Press, Huntington Beach, CA: **Vol. 1, Alaskan Adventure, The Early Years.**.$35.00, **Vol. 2, Adventure is My Business, 1951-1955.**.$50.00, **Vol. 3, Adventure is in My Blood, 1957-1964.**.$55.00, **Vol. 4, High Road to Adventure, 1964-1970.**.$55.00, **Vol. 5, The Way We Were, 1970-1979.**.$55.00.
A complete collection of previously unpublished magazine articles in book form by this gifted outdoor writer.

***The Season,** by Tom Kelly, Lyons & Burford, New York, NY, 1997. 160 pp., illus. $22.95.
The delight and challenges of a turkey hunter's Spring season.

Secret Strategies from North America's Top Whitetail Hunters, compiled by Nick Sisley, Krause Publications, Iola, WI, 1995. 256 pp., illus. Paper covers. $14.95.
Bow and gun hunters share their success stories.

Sheep Hunting in Alaska—The Dall Sheep Hunter's Guide, by Tony Russ, Outdoor Expeditions and Books, Corvallis, MT, 1994. 160 pp., illus. Paper covers. $19.95.
A how-to guide for the Dall sheep hunter.

Shorebirds: The Birds, The Hunters, The Decoys, by John M. Levinson & Somers G. Headley, Tidewater Publishers, Centreville, MD, 1991. 160 pp., illus. $49.95.
A thorough study of shorebirds and the decoys used to hunt them. Photographs of more than 200 of the decoys created by prominent carvers are shown.

Shots at Big Game, by Craig Boddington, Stackpole Books, Harrisburg, PA, 1989. 198 pp., illus. $24.95.
How to shoot a rifle accurately under hunting conditions.

Some Bears Kill!: True-Life Tales of Terror, by Larry Kanuit, Safari Press, Huntington Beach, CA, 1997. 313 pp., illus. $24.95.
A collection of 38 stories as told by the victims, and in the case of fatality, recounted by the author from institutional records, Episodes involve all three species of North American bears.

Southern Deer & Deer Hunting, by Larry Weishuhn and Bill Bynum, Krause Publications, Iola, WI, 1995. 256 pp., illus. Paper covers. $14.95.
Mount a trophy southern whitetail on your wall with this firsthand account of stalking big bucks below the Mason-Dixon line.

Spring Gobbler Fever, by Michael Hanback, Krause Publications, Iola, WI, 1996. 256 pp., illus. Paper covers. $15.95.
Your complete guide to spring turkey hunting.

Spirit of the Wilderness, Compiled by Theodore J. Holsten, Jr., Susan c. Reneau and Jack Reneau, the Boone & Crockett Club, Missoula, MT, 19971 300 pp., illus. $29.95.
Stalking wild sheep, tracking a trophy cougar, hiking the back country of British Columbia, fishing for striped bass and coming face to face with a grizzly bear are some of the adventures found in this book.

Stand Hunting for Whitetails, by Richard P. Smith, Krause Publications, Iola, WI, 1996. 256 pp., illus. Paper covers. $14.95.
The author explains the tricks and strategies for successful stand hunting.

Successful Goose Hunting, by Charles L. Cadieux, Stone Wall Press, Inc., Washington, DC, 1986. 223 pp., illus. $24.95.
Here is a complete book on modern goose hunting by a lifetime waterfowler and professional wildlifer.

The Sultan of Spring: A Hunter's Odyssey Through the World of the Wild Turkey, by Bob Saile, The Lyons Press, New York, NY, 1998. 176 pp., illus. $22.95.
A literary salute to the magic and mysticism of spring turkey hunting.

Taking Big Bucks, by Ed Wolff, Stoneydale Press, Stevensville, MT, 1987. 169 pp., illus. $18.95.
Solving the whitetail riddle.

Taking Chances in the High Country, compiled and with an introduction by Jim Rikhoff, The Amwell Press, Clinton, NJ, 1995. 411 pp., illus. In a slipcase. $85.00.
An anthology by some thirty stories by different authors on hunting sheep in the high country.

Taking More Birds, by Dan Carlisle and Dolph Adams, Lyons & Burford Publishers, New York, NY, 1993. 160 pp., illus. Paper covers. $15.95.
A practical handbook for success at Sporting Clays and wing shooting.

Tales of Alaska's Big Bears, by Jim Rearden, Wolfe Publishing Co., Prescott, AZ, 1989. 125 pp., illus. Soft covers. $12.95.
A collection of bear yarns covering nearly three-quarters of a century.

Tales of Quails 'n Such, by Havilah Babcock, University of S. Carolina Press, Columbia, SC, 1985. 237 pp. $19.95.
A group of hunting stories, told in informal style, on field experiences in the South in quest of small game.

***Tears and Laughter,** by Gene Hill, Countrysport Press, Traverse City, MI, 1996. 176 pp., illus. $25.00.
In twenty-six stories, Gene Hill explores the ancient and honored bond between man and dog.

Tenth Legion, by Tom Kelly, the Lyons Press, New York, NY, 1998. 128 pp., illus. $21.95.
The classid work on that frustrating yet wonderful sport of turkey hunting.

They Left Their Tracks, by Howard Coperhaver, Stoneydale Press Publishing Co., Stevensville, MT, 1990. 190 pp., illus. $18.95.
Recollections of 60 years as an outfitter in the Bob Marshall Wilderness.

Timberdoodle, by Frank Woolner, Nick Lyons Books, N. Y., NY, 1987. 168 pp., illus. $18.95.
The classic guide to woodcock and woodcock hunting.

***Timberdoodle Tales,** by T. Waters, Safari Press, Inc., Huntington Beach, CA, 1997. 220 pp., illus. $30.00.
A fresh appreciation of this captivating bird and the ethics of its hunt.

Timberdoodle Tales: Adventures of a Minnesota Woodcock Hunter, Safari Press, Huntington Beach, CA, 1997. 220 pp., illus. $35.00.
The life history and hunt of the American woodcock by the author.

Trail and Campfire, edited by George Bird Grinnel and Theodore Roosevelt, The Boone and Crockett Club, Dumfries, VA, 1989. 357 pp., illus. $39.50.
Reprint of the Boone and Crockett Club's 3rd book published in 1897.

Trail of the Eagle, by Bud Conkle, as told to Jim Rearden, Great Northwest Publishing & Distributing Co., Anchorage, AK, 1991. 280 pp., illus. $35.00.
Hunting Alaska with master guide Bud Conkle.

Trailing a Bear, by Robert S. Munger, The Munger Foundation, Albion, MI, 1997. 352 pp., illus. Paper covers. $19.95.
An exciting and humorous account of hunting with legendary archer Fred Bear.

The Trickiest Thing in Feathers, by Corey Ford; compiled and edited by Laurie Morrow and illustrated by Christopher Smith , Wilderness Adventures, Gallatin Gateway, MT, 1998. 208 pp., illus. $29.95.
Here is a collection of Corey Ford's best wing-shooting stories, many of them previously unpublished.

Trophy Mule Deer: Finding & Evaluating Your Trophy, by Lance Stapleton, Outdoor Experiences Unlimited, Salem, OR, 1993. 290 pp., illus. Paper covers. $24.95.
The most comprehensive reference book on mule deer.

The Turkey Hunter's Book, by John M. McDaniel, Amwell Press, Clinton, NJ, 1980. 147 pp., illus. Paper covers. $11.95.
One of the most original turkey hunting books to be published in many years.

Turkey Hunter's Digest, Revised Edition, by Dwain Bland, DBI Books, a division of Krause Publications, Inc., Iola, WI, 1994. 256 pp., illus. Paper covers. $17.95.
A no-nonsense approach to hunting all five sub-species of the North American wild turkey that make up the Royal Grand Slam.

Turkey Hunting with Gerry Blair, by Gerry Blair, Krause Publications, Iola, WI, 1993. 280 pp., illus. $19.95.
Novice and veteran turkey hunters alike will enjoy this complete examination of the varied wild turkey subspecies, their environments, equipment needed to pursue them and the tactics to outwit them.

The Upland Equation: A Modern Bird-Hunter's Code, by Charles Fergus, Lyons & Burford Publishers, New York, NY, 1996. 86 pp. $18.00
A book that deserves space in every sportsman's library. Observations based on firsthand experience.

The Upland Gunner's Book, edited by George Bird Evans, The Amwell Press, Clinton, NJ, 1985. 263 pp., illus. In slipcase. $27.50.
An anthology of the finest stories ever written on the sport of upland game hunting.

Upland Tales, by Worth Mathewson (Ed.), Sand Lake Press, Amity, OR, 1996. 271 pp., illus. $21.95.
A collection of articles on grouse, snipe and quail.

Varmint and Small Game Rifles and Cartridges, by various authors, Wolfe Publishing Co., Prescott, AZ, 1993. 228 pp., illus. Paper covers. $26.00.
This is a collection of reprints of articles originally appearing in Wolfe's *Rifle* and *Handloader* magazines from 1966 through 1990.

Waterfowling Horizons: Shooting Ducks and Geese in the 21st Century, by Chris and Jason Smith, Wilderness Adventures, Gallatin Gateway, MT, 1998. 320 pp., illus. $49.95.
A compendium of the very latest in everything for the duck and goose hunter today.

Wegner's Bibliography on Dear and Deer Hunting, by Robert Wegner, St. Hubert's Press, Deforest, WI, 1993. 333 pp., 16 full-page illustrations. $45.00.
A comprehensive annotated compilation of books in English pertaining to deer and their hunting 1413-1991.

Western Hunting Guide, by Mike Lapinski, Stoneydale Press Publishing Co., Stevensville, MT, 1989. 168 pp., illus. $18.95.
A complete where-to-go and how-to-do-it guide to Western hunting.

Whispering Wings of Autumn, by Gene Hill and Steve Smith, Wilderness Adventures Press, Bozeman, MT, 1994. 150 pp., illus. $29.00.
Hill and Smith, masters of hunting literature, treat the reader to the best stories of grouse and woodcock hunting.

***Whitetail: Behavior Through the Seasons,** by Charles J. Alsheimer, Krause Publications, Iola, WI, 1996. 208 pp., illus. $34.95.
In-depth coverage of whitetail behavior presented through striking portraits of the whitetail in every season.

Whitetail: The Ultimate Challenge, by Charles J. Alsheimer, Krause Publications, Iola, WI, 1995. 228 pp., illus. Paper covers. $14.95.
Learn deer hunting's most intriguing secrets—fooling deer using decoys, scents and calls—from America's premier authority.

Wildfowlers Season, by Chris Dorsey, Lyons & Burford Publishers, New York, NY, 1998. 224 pp., illus. $37.95.
Modern methods for a classic sport.

The Wild Turkey Book, edited and with special commentary by J. Wayne Fears, Amwell Press, Clinton, NJ, 1982. 303 pp., illus. $22.50.
An anthology of the finest stories on wild turkey ever assembled under one cover.

The Wilderness Hunter, by Theodore Roosevelt, Wolfe Publishing Co., Prescott, AZ, 1994. 200 pp., illus. $25.00.
Reprint of a classic by one of America's most famous big game hunters.

Wings for the Heart, by Jerry A. Lewis, West River Press, Corvallis, MT, 1991. 324 pp., illus. Paper covers. $14.95.
A delightful book on hunting Montana's upland birds and waterfowl.

Wisconsin Hunting, by Brian Lovett, Krause Publications, Iola, WI, 1997. 208 pp., illus. Paper covers. $16.95.
A comprehensive guide to Wisconsin's public hunting lands.

The Woodchuck Hunter, by Paul C. Estey, R&R Books, Livonia, NY, 1994. 135 pp., illus. $25.00.
This book contains information on woodchuck equipment, the rifle, telescopic sights and includes interesting stories.

Woodcock Shooting, by Steve Smith, Stackpole Books, Inc., Harrisburg, PA, 1988. 142 pp., illus. $16.95.
A definitive book on woodcock hunting and the characteristics of a good woodcock dog.

World Record Whitetail: The Hanson Buck Story, by Milo Hanson with Ian McMurchy, Krause Publications, Iola, WI, 1995. 144 pp., illus. Paper covers. $9.95.
How do you top a deer hunting record that stood for 80 years? Milo Hanson shares in his firsthand account of bagging the largest whitetail ever scored in the history of B&C measurements.

AFRICA/ASIA/ELSEWHERE

African Adventures, by J.F. Burger, Safari Press, Huntington Beach, CA, 1993. 222 pp., illus. $35.00.
The reader shares adventures on the trail of the lion, the elephant and buffalo.

The African Adventures: A Return to the Silent Places, by Peter Hathaway Capstick, St. Martin's Press, New York, NY, 1992. 220 pp., illus. $22.95.
This book brings to life four turn-of-the-century adventurers and the savage frontier they braved. Frederick Selous, Constatine "Iodine" Ionides, Johnny Boyes and Jim Sutherland.

African Camp-fire Nights, by J.E. Burger, Safari Press, Huntington Beach, CA, 1993. 192 pp., illus. $32.50.
In this book the author writes of the men who made hunting their life's profession.

African Hunter, by James Mellon, Safari Press, Huntington Beach, CA, 1996. 522 pp., illus. Clothbound, $125.00; paper covers, $75.00.
Regarded as the most comprehensive title ever published on African hunting.

African Hunting and Adventure, by William Charles Baldwin, Books of Zimbabwe, Bulawayo, 1981. 451 pp., illus. $75.00.
Facsimile reprint of the scarce 1863 London edition. African hunting and adventure from Natal to the Zambezi.

African Jungle Memories, by J.F. Burger, Safari Press, Huntington Beach, CA, 1993. 192 pp., illus. $32.50.
A book of reminiscences in which the reader is taken on many exciting adventures on the trail of the buffalo, lion, elephant and leopard.

African Rifles & Cartridges, by John Taylor, The Gun Room Press, Highland Park, NJ, 1977. 431 pp., illus. $35.00.
Experiences and opinions of a professional ivory hunter in Africa describing his knowledge of numerous arms and cartridges for big game. A reprint.

African Safaris, by Major G.H. Anderson, Safari Press, Long Beach, CA, 1997. 173 pp., illus. $35.00.
A reprinting of one of the rarest books on African hunting, with a foreword by Tony Sanchez.

African Twilight, by Robert F. Jones, Wilderness Adventure Press, Bozeman, MT, 1994. 208 pp., illus. $36.00.
Details the hunt, danger and changing face of Africa over a span of three decades.

After Big Game in Central Africa, by Edouard Foa, St. Martin's Press, New York, NY, 1989. 400 pp., illus. $16.95.
Reprint of the scarce 1899 edition. This sportsman covered 7200 miles, mostly on foot—from Zambezi delta on the east coast to the mouth of the Congo on the west.

A Man Called Lion: The Life and Times of John Howar "Pondoro" Taylor, by P.H. Capstick, Safari Press, Huntington Beach, CA, 1994. 240 pp., illus. $24.95.
With the help of Brian Marsh, an old Taylor acquaintance, Peter Capstick has cumulated over ten years of research into the life of this mysterious man.

Argali: High-Mountain Hunting, by Ricardo Medem, Safari Press, Huntington Beach, CA, 1995. 304 pp., illus. Limited, signed edition. $150.00.
Medem describes hunting seven different countries in the pursuit of sheep and other mountain game.

*__Baron in Africa,__ by W. Alvensleben, Safari Press, Inc., Huntington Beach, CA, 1997. 100 pp., illus. $60.00.
A must-read adventure story on one of the most interesting characters to have come out of Africa after WWII.

*__The Best of Big Game,__ by Terry Wieland, John Culler and Sons, Camden, SC, 1996. 200 pp., illus. $49.95.
Twenty detailed accounts of the best hunters from around the world.

*__The Big Five,__ by Tony Dyer, Trophy Room Books, Angoura, CA, 1996. 224 pp., illus. Limited, numbered edition signed by both the artist and author. $100.00.
A new edition of this classic study of the big five by two of the men who know them best.

Big Game and Big Game Rifles, by John Taylor, Safari Press, Huntington Beach, CA, 1993. 215 pp., illus. $24.95.
A classic by the man who probably knew more about ammunition and rifles for African game than any other hunter.

Big Game Hunting and Collecting in East Africa 1903-1926, by Kalman Kittenberger, St. Martin's Press, New York, NY, 1989. 496 pp., illus. $16.95.
One of the most heart stopping, charming and funny accounts of adventure in the Kenya Colony ever penned.

Big Game Hunting Around the World, by Bert Klineburger and Vernon W. Hurst, Exposition Press, Jericho, NY, 1969. 376 pp., illus. $30.00.
The first book that takes you on a safari all over the world.

Big Game Hunting in Asia, Africa, and Elsewhere, by Jacques Vettier, Trophy Room Books, Agoura, CA, 1993. 400 pp., illus. Limited, numbered edition. $150.00.
The first English language edition of the book that set a new standard in big game hunting book literature.

Big Game Hunting in North-Eastern Rhodesia, by Owen Letcher, St. Martin's Press, New York, NY, 1986. 272 pp., illus. $15.95.
A classic reprint and one of the very few books to concentrate on this fascinating area, a region that today is still very much safari country.

Big Game Shooting in Cooch Behar, the Duars and Assam, by The Maharajah of Cooch Behar, Wolfe Publishing Co., Prescott, AZ, 1993. 461 pp., illus. $49.50.
A reprinting of the book that has become legendary. This is the Maharajah's personal diary of killing 365 tigers.

The Book of the Lion, by Sir Alfred E. Pease, St. Martin's Press, New York, NY, 1986. 305 pp., illus. $15.95.
Reprint of the finest book ever published on the subject. The author describes all aspects of lion history and lion hunting, drawing heavily on his own experiences in British East Africa.

*__Bwana Cotton,__ by Cotton Gordon, Trophy Room Books, Agoura, CA, 1996. 300 pp., illus. Limited, numbered and signed edition. $85.00.
Rambling, witty, wonderful reminiscences of an African hunter.

Chui! A Guide to Hunting the African Leopard, by Lou Hallamore and Bruce Woods, Trophy Room Books, Agoura, CA, 1994. 239 pp., illus. $75.00.
Tales of exciting leopard encounters by one of today's most respected pros.

Death in a Lonely Land, by Peter Capstick, St. Martin's Press, New York, NY, 1990. 284 pp., illus. $22.95.
Twenty-three stories of hunting as only the master can tell them.

Death in the Dark Continent, by Peter Capstick, St. Martin's Press, New York, NY, 1983. 238 pp., illus. $22.95.
A book that brings to life the suspense, fear and exhilaration of stalking ferocious killers under primitive, savage conditions, with the ever present threat of death.

Death in the Long Grass, by Peter Hathaway Capstick, St. Martin's Press, New York, NY, 1977. 297 pp., illus. $22.95.
A big game hunter's adventures in the African bush.

Death in the Silent Places, by Peter Capstick, St. Martin's Press, New York, NY, 1981. 243 pp., illus. $22.95.
The author recalls the extraordinary careers of legendary hunters such as Corbett, Karamojo Bell, Stigand and others.

Duck Hunting in Australia, by Dick Eussen, Australia Outdoor Publishers Pty Ltd., Victoria, Australia, 1994. 106 pp., illus. Paper covers. $17.95.
Covers the many aspects of duck hunting from hides to hunting methods.

East Africa and its Big Game, by Captain Sir John C. Willowghby, Wolfe Publishing Co., Prescott, AZ, 1990. 312 pp., illus. $52.00.
A deluxe limited edition reprint of the very scarce 1889 edition of a narrative of a sporting trip from Zanzibar to the borders of the Masai.

East of the Sun and West of the Moon, by Theodore and Kermit Roosevelt, Wolfe Publishing Co., Prescott, AZ, 1988. 284 pp., illus. $25.00.
A limited edition reprint. A classic on Marco Polo sheep hunting. A life experience unique to hunters of big game.

Elephant, by Commander David Enderby Blunt, The Holland Press, London, England, 1985. 260 pp., illus. $45.00.
A study of this phenomenal beast by a world-leading authority.

Elephant Hunting in East Equatorial Africa, by A. Neumann, St. Martin's Press, New York, NY, 1994. 455 pp., illus. $26.95.
This is a reprint of one of the rarest elephant hunting titles ever.

Elephants of Africa, by Dr. Anthony Hall-Martin, New Holland Publishers, London, England, 1987. 120 pp., illus. $75.00.
A superbly illustrated overview of the African elephant with reproductions of paintings by the internationally acclaimed wildlife artist Paul Bosman.

Encounters with Lions, by Jan Hemsing, Trophy Room books, Agoura, CA, 1995. 302 pp., illus. $75.00.
Some stories fierce, fatal, frightening and even humorous of when man and lion meet.

First Wheel, by Bunny Allen, Amwell Press, Clinton, NJ, 1984. Limited, signed and numbered edition in the NSFL "African Hunting Heritage Series." 292 pp., illus. $100.00.
A white hunter's diary, 1927-47.

The Formidable Game, by John Batten, The Amwell Press, Clinton, NJ, 1994. 336 pp., illus. $40.00.
Batten and his wife cover the globe in search of the world's dangerous game. Includes a section on the development of the big bore rifle for formidable game.

*__"For the Honour of a Hunter....",__ by A.M.D. (Tony) Seth-Smith, Trophy Room Books, Agoura, CA, 1996. 320 pp., illus. Limited, numbered and signed edition. $85.00.
Autobiography of one of the breed of "hard safari men" whose lives are full of changes and charges.

Fourteen Years in the African Bush, by Tony Marsh, Safari Press, Huntington Beach, CA, 1998. 300 pp., illus. Limited numbered and signed edition. Slipcased. $70.00
An account of a Kenya game warden.

From Sailor to Professional Hunter: The Autobigraphy of John Northcote, Trophy Room Books, Agoura, CA, 1997. 400 pp., illus. Limited edition, signed and numbered. $125.00.
Only a handfull of men can boast of having a fifty-year professional hunting career throughout Africa as John Northcote has had.

*__Glory Days of Baja,__ by Larry Stanton, John Culler and Sons, Camden, SC, 1996. 184 pp., illus. $21.95.
This book represents twenty-five years of hunting in Mexico's Baja.

The Great Arc of the Wild Sheep, by J.L. Clark, Safari Press, Huntington Beach, CA, 1994. 247 pp., illus. $24.95.
Perhaps the most complete work done on all the species and subspecies of the wild sheep of the world.

Great Hunters Their Trophy Rooms and Collections, Various contributors, Safari Press, Hunington Beach, CA, 1997. 176 pp., illus. $60.00.
The greatest hunters from around the world had their rooms professionally photographed for this book. Each has its own descriptive text, written by the hunter, with details on the animals and the hunter.

Horned Death, by John F. Burger, Safari Press, Huntington Beach, CA, 1992. 343 pp., illus. $35.00.
The classic work on hunting the African buffalo.

Horn of the Hunter, by Robert Ruark, Safari Press, Long Beach, CA, 1987. 315 pp., illus. $35.00.
Ruark's most sought-after title on African hunting, here in reprint.

Hunters of Man, by Capt. J. Brandt, Safari Press, Huntington Beach, CA, 1997. 242 pp., illus. Paper covers. $18.95.
True stories of man-eaters, man killers and rogues in Southeast Asia.

Hunting Adventures Worldwide, by Jack Atcheson, Jack Stcheson & Sons, Butte, MT, 1995. 256 pp., illus. $29.95.
The author chronicles the richest adventures of a lifetime spent in quest of big game across the world – including Africa, North America and Asia.

Hunting in Ethiopia, An Anthology, by Tony Sanchez-Arino, Safari Press, Huntington Beach, CA, 1996. 350 pp., illus. Limited, signed and numbered edition. $135.00.
The finest selection of hunting stories ever compiled on hunting in this great game country.

Hunting in Many Lands, by Theodore Roosevelt and George Bird Grinnel, The Boone and Crockett Club, Dumfries, VA, 1987. 447 pp., illus. $40.00.
Limited edition reprint of this 1895 classic work on hunting in Africa, India, Mongolia, etc.

Hunting in the Sudan, An Anthology, compiled by Tony Sanchez-Arino, Safari Press, Huntington Beach, CA, 1992. 350 pp., illus. Limited, signed and numbered edition in a slipcase. $125.00.
The finest selection of hunting stories ever compiled on hunting in this great game country.

Hunting, Settling and Remembering, by Philip H. Percival, Trophy Room Books, Agoura, CA, 1997. 230 pp., illus. Limited, numbered and signed edition. $85.00

If Philip Percival is to come alive again, it will be through this, the first edition of his easy, intricate and magical book illustrated with some of the best historical big game hunting photos ever taken.

Hunting the Elephant in Africa, by Captain C.H. Stigand, St. Martin's Press, New York, NY, 1986. 379 pp., illus. $14.95.
A reprint of the scarce 1913 edition; vintage Africana at its best.

Jaguar Hunting in the Mato Grosso and Bolivia, by T. Almedia, Safari Press, Long Beach, CA, 1989. 256 pp., illus. $35.00.
Not since Sacha Siemel has there been a book on jaguar hunting like this one.

Jim Corbett's India, stories selected by R.E. Hawkins, Oxford University Press, New York, NY, 1993. 250 pp. $24.95.
Stories and extracts from Jim Corbett's writings on tiger hunting by his publisher and editor.

Jim Corbett, Master of the Jungle, by Tim Werling, Safari Press, Huntington Beach, CA, 1998. 215 pp., illus. $30.00
A biography of India's most famous hunter of man-eating tigers and leopards.

King of the Wa-Kikuyu, by John Boyes, St. Martin Press, New York, NY, 1993. 240 pp., illus. $19.95.
In the 19th and 20th centuries, Africa drew to it a large number of great hunters, explorers, adventurers and rogues. Many have become legendary, but John Boyes (1874-1951) was the most legendary of them all.

Lake Ngami, by Charles Anderson, New Holland Press, London, England, 1987. 576 pp., illus. $35.00.
Originally published in 1856. Describes two expeditions into what is now Botswana, depicting every detail of landscape and wildlife.

Last Horizons: Hunting, Fishing and Shooting on Five Continents, by Peter Capstick, St. Martin's Press, New York, NY, 1989. 288 pp., illus. $19.95.
The first in a two volume collection of hunting, fishing and shooting tales from the selected pages of The American Hunter, Guns & Ammo and Outdoor Life.

Last of the Few: Forty-Two Years of African Hunting, by Tony Sanchez-Arino, Safari Press, Huntington Beach, CA, 1996. 250 pp., illus. $85.00.
The story of the author's career with all the highlights that come from pursuing the unusual and dangerous animals that are native to Africa.

Last of the Ivory Hunters, by John Taylor, Safari Press, Long Beach, CA, 1990. 354 pp., illus. $29.95.
Reprint of the classic book "Pondoro" by one of the most famous elephant hunters of all time.

Legends of the Field: More Early Hunters in Africa, by W.R. Foran, Trophy Room Press, Agoura, CA, 1997. 319 pp., illus. Limited edition. $100.00.
This book contains the biographies of some very famous hunters: William Cotton Oswell, F.C. Selous, sir Samuel Baker, Arthur Neumann, Jim Sutherland, W.D.M. Bell and others.

The Lost Classics, by Robert Ruark, Safari Press, Huntington Beach, CA, 1996. 260 pp., illus. $35.00.
The magazine stories that Ruark wrote in the 1950s and 1960s finally in print in book form.

The Man-Eaters of Tsavo, by Lt. Colonel J.H. Patterson, Peter Capstick, series editor, St. Martin's Press, New York, NY, 1986, 5th printing. 346 pp., illus. $22.95.
The classic man-eating story of the lions that halted construction of a railway line and reportedly killed one hundred people, told by the man who risked his life to successfully shoot them.

Memoirs of an African Hunter, by Terry Irwin, Safari Press, Huntington Beach, CA, 1998. 350 pp., illus. Limited signed and numbered edition. Slipcased. $85.00.
A narrative of a professional hunter's experiences in Africa.

***Men for all Seasons: The Hunters and Pioneers,** by Tony Dyers, Trophy Room Books, Agoura, CA, 1996. 440 pp., illus. Limited, numbered and signed edition. $125.00.
The men, women and warriors who created the great Safari Industry of East Africa.

Months of the Sun; Forty Years of Elephant Hunting in the Zambezi Valley, by Ian Nyschens, Safari Press, Huntington Beach, CA, 1998. 420 pp., illus. Limited signed and numbered edition. Slipcased. $85.00.
The author has shot equally as many elephants as Walter Bell, and under much more difficult circumstances. His book will rank, or surpass, the best elephant-ivory hunting books published this century.

Mundjamba: The Life Story of an African Hunter, by Hugo Seia, Trophy Room Books, Agoura, CA, 1996. 400 pp., illus. Limited, numbered and signed by the author. $125.00.
An autobiography of one of the most respected and appreciated professional African hunters.

My Last Kambaku, by Leo Kroger, Safari Press, Huntington Beach, CA, 1997. 272 pp., illus. Limited edition signed and numbered and slipcased. $60.00.
One fo the most engaging hunting memoirs ever published.

The Nature of the Game, by Ben Hoskyns, Quiller Press, Ltd., London, England, 1994. 160 pp., illus. $37.50.
The first complete guide to British, European and North American game.

***Nine Man-Eaters and One Rogue,** by Kenneth Anderson, John Culler and Sons, Camden, SC, 1996. 256 pp., illus. $29.95.
Exciting true stories of hunting man-eating tigers in India's jungle.

One Happy Hunter, by George Barrington, Safari Press, Huntington Beach, CA, 1994. 240 pp., illus. $40.00.
A candid, straightforward look at safari hunting.

The Path of a Hunter, by Gilles Tre-Hardy, Trophy Room Books, Agoura, CA, 1997. 318 pp., illus. Limited Edition, signed and numbered. $85.00.
A most unusual hunting autobiography with much about elephant hunting in Africa.

Peter Capstick's Africa: A Return to the Long Grass, by Peter Hathaway Capstick, St. Martin's Press, N. Y., NY, 1987. 213 pp., illus. $29.95.
A first-person adventure in which the author returns to the long grass for his own dangerous and very personal excursion.

The Recollections of an Elephant Hunter 1864-1875, by William Finaughty, Books of Zimbabwe, Bulawayo, Zimbabwe, 1980. 244 pp., illus. $85.00.
Reprint of the scarce 1916 privately published edition. The early game hunting exploits of William Finaughty in Matabeleland and Nashonaland.

Safari: A Chronicle of Adventure, by Bartle Bull, Viking/Penguin, London, England, 1989. 383 pp., illus. $40.00.
The thrilling history of the African safari, highlighting some of Africa's best-known personalities.

Safari Rifles: Double, Magazine Rifles and Cartridges for African Hunting, by Craig Boddington, Safari Press, Huntington Beach, CA, 1990. 416 pp., illus. $37.50.
A wealth of knowledge on the safari rifle. Historical and present double-rifle makers, ballistics for the large bores, and much, much more.

Safari: The Last Adventure, by Peter Capstick, St. Martin's Press, New York, NY, 1984. 291 pp., illus. $19.95.
A modern comprehensive guide to the African Safari.

Sands of Silence, by Peter H. Capstick, Saint Martin's Press, New York, NY, 1991. 224 pp., illus. $35.00.
Join the author on safari in Nambia for his latest big-game hunting adventures.

Shoot Straight and Stay Alive: A Lifetime of Hunting Experiences, by Fred Bartlett, Trophy Room Books, Argoura, CA, 1994. 262 pp., illus. $85.00.
A book written by a man who has left his mark on the maps of Africa's great game-lands.

Skyline Pursuits, by John Batten, The Amwell Press, Clinton, NJ, 1994. 372 pp., illus. $40.00.
A chronicle of Batten's own hunting adventures in the high country on four continents since 1928, traces a sheep hunting career that has accounted for both North American and International Grand Slams.

Solo Safari, by T. Cacek, Safari Press, Huntington Beach, CA, 1995. 270 pp., illus. $30.00.
Here is the story of Terry Cacek who hunted elephant, buffalo, leopard and plains game in Zimbabwe and Botswana on his own.

South Pacific Trophy Hunter, by Murray Thomas, Safari Press, Long Beach, CA, 1988. 181 pp., illus. $37.50.
A record of a hunter's search for a trophy of each of the 15 major game species in the South Pacific region.

Spiral-Horn Dreams, by Terry Wieland, Trophy Room Books, Agoura, CA, 1996. 362 pp., illus. Limited, numbered and signed by the author. $85.00.
Everyone who goes to hunt in Africa is looking for something; this is for those who go to hunt the spiral-horned antelope—the bongo, myala, mountain nyala, greater and lesser kudu, etc.

Sport on the Pamirs and Turkestan Steppes, by Major C.S. Cumberland, Moncrieff & Smith, Victoria, Autralia, 1992. 278 pp., illus. $45.00.
The first in a series of facsimile reprints of great trophy hunting books by Moncrieff & Smith.

Theodore Roosevelt Outdoorsman, by R.L. Wilson, Trophy Room Books, Agoura, CA, 1994. 326 pp., illus. $85.00.
This book presents Theodore Roosevelt as a rancher, Rough Rider, Governor, President, naturalist and international big game hunter.

Those Were the Days, by Rudolf Sand, Safari Press, Huntington Beach, CA, 1993. 300 pp., illus. $100.00.
Travel with Rudolf Sand to the pinnacles of the world in his pursuit of wild sheep and goats.

Through the Brazilian Wilderness, by Theodore Roosevelt, Stackpole Books, Mechanicsburg, PA, 1994. 448 pp., illus. Paper covers. $16.95.
Adventure and drama in the South American jungle.

***The Tiger Walks,** by Kenneth Anderson, John Culler and Sons, Camden, SC, 1996. 400 pp., illus. $29.95.
The best of Anderson's eight books bound in one big volume.

To Heck with Moose Hunting, by Jim Zumbo, Wapiti Publishing Co., cody, WY, 1996. 199 pp., illus. $17.95.
Jim's hunts around the continent and even an African adventure.

Trophy Hunter in Africa, by Elgin Gates, Safari Press, Huntington Beach, CA, 1994. 315 pp., illus. $29.95.
This is the story of one man's adventure in Africa's wildlife paradise.

Uganda Safaris, by Brian Herne, Winchester Press, Piscataway, NJ, 1979. 236 pp., illus. $12.95.
The chronicle of a professional hunter's adventures in Africa.

Under the Shadow of Man Eaters, by Jerry Jaleel, The Jim Corbett Foundation, Edmonton, Alberta, Canada, 1997. 152 pp., illus. A limited, numbered and signed edition. Paper covers. $35.00.
The life and legend of Jim Corbett of Kumaon.

Use Enough Gun, by Robert Ruark, Safari Press, Huntington Beach, CA, 1997. 333 pp., illus. $35.00.
Robert Ruark on big game hunting.

Warrior: The Legend of Col. Richard Meinertzhagen, by Peter H. Capstick, St. Martins Press, New York, NY, 1998. 320 pp., illus. $23.95.
A stirring and vivid biography of the famous British colonial officer Richard Meinertzhagen, whose exploits earned him fame and notoriety as one of the most daring and ruthless men to serve during the glory days of the British Empire.

Where Lions Roar: Ten More Years of African Hunting, by Craig Boddington, Safari Press, Huntington Beach,CA, 1997. 250 pp., illus. Limited edition, signed and numbered. In a slipcase. $60.00.
The story of Boddington's hunts in the Dark Continent during the last ten years.

A White Hunters Life, by Angus MacLagan, an African Heritage Book, published by Amwell Press, Clinton, NJ, 1983. 283 pp., illus. Limited, signed, and numbered deluxe edition, in slipcase. $100.00.
True to life, a sometimes harsh yet intriguing story.

Wild Sports of Southern Africa, by William Cornwallis Harris, New Holland Press, London, England, 1987. 376 pp., illus. $35.00.
Originally published in 1863, describes the author's travels in Southern Africa.

With a Gun in Good Country, by Ian Manning, Trophy Room Books, Agoura, CA, 1996. Limited, numbered and signed by the author. $85.00.
A book written about that splendid period before the poaching onslaught which almost closed Zambia and continues to the granting of her independence. It then goes on to recount Manning's experiences in Botswana, Congo, and briefly in South Africa.

RIFLES

The Accurate Varmint Rifle, by Boyd Mace, Precision Shooting, Inc., Whitehall, NY, 1991. 184 pp., illus. $24.95.
A long overdue and long needed work on what factors go into the selection of components for and the subsequent assembly of...the accurate varmint rifle.

The AK-47 Assault Rifle, Desert Publications, Cornville, AZ, 1981. 150 pp., illus. Paper covers. $10.00.
Complete and practical technical information on the only weapon in history to be produced in an estimated 30,000,000 units.

American Hunting Rifles: Their Application in the Field for Practical Shooting, by Craig Boddington, Safari Press, Huntington Beach, CA, 1996. 446 pp., illus. First edition, limited, signed and slipcased. $85.00. Second printing trade edition. $35.00.
Covers all the hunting rifles and calibers that are needed for North America's diverse game,

The AR-15/M16, A Practical Guide, by Duncan Long. Paladin Press, Boulder, CO, 1985. 168 pp., illus. Paper covers. $16.95.
The definitive book on the rifle that has been the inspiration for so many modern assault rifles.

***The Art of Shooting With the Rifle,** by Col. Sir H. St. John Halford, Excalibur Publications, Latham, NY, 1996. 96 pp., illus. Paper covers. $12.95.
A facsimile edition of the 1888 book by a respected rifleman providing a welath of detailed information.

The Art of the Rifle, by Jeff Cooper, Paladin Press, Boulder, CO, 1997. 104 pp., illus. $29.95.
Everthing you need to know about the rifle whether you use it for security, meat or target shooting.

Assault Weapons, 4th Edition, by Jack Lewis, DBI Books, a division of Krause Publications, Inc., Iola, WI, 1996. 256 pp., illus. Paper covers. $19.95.
An in-depth look at the history and uses of these arms.

Australian Military Rifles & Bayonets, 200 Years of, by Ian Skennerton, I.D.S.A. Books, Piqua, OH, 1988. 124 pp., 198 illus. Paper covers. $19.50.

Australian Service Machineguns, 100 Years of, by Ian Skennerton, I.D.S.A. Books, Piqua, OH, 1989. 122 pp., 150 illus. Paper covers. $19.50.

The Big-Bore Rifle, by Michael McIntosh, Countrysport Press, Traverse City, MI, 1990. 224 pp., illus. $39.95.
The book of fine magazine and double rifles 375 to 700 calibers.

The Big Game Rifle, by Jack O'Connor, Safari Press, Huntington Beach, CA, 1994. 370 pp., illus. $37.50.
An outstanding description of every detail of construction, purpose and use of the big game rifle.

Big Game Rifles and Cartridges, by Elmer Keith, reprint edition by The Gun Room Press, Highland Park, NJ, 1984. 161 pp., illus. $29.95.
Reprint of Elmer Keith's first book, a most original and accurate work on big game rifles and cartridges.

The Black Rifle, M16 Retrospective, R. Blake Stevens and Edward C. Ezell, Collector Grade Publications, Toronto, Canada, 1987. 400 pp., illus. $59.95
The complete story of the M16 rifle and its development.

Bolt Action Rifles, 3rd Edition, by Frank de Haas, DBI Books, a division of Krause Publications, Inc., Iola, WI, 1995. 528 pp., illus. Paper covers. $24.95.
A revised edition of the most definitive work on all major bolt-action rifle designs.

The Book of the Garand, by Maj. Gen. J.S. Hatcher, The Gun Room Press, Highland Park, NJ, 1977. 292 pp., illus. $26.95.
A new printing of the standard reference work on the U.S. Army M1 rifle.

The Book of the Twenty-Two: The All American Caliber, by Sam Fadala, Stoeger Publishing Co., So. Hackensack, NJ, 1989. 288 pp., illus. Soft covers. $16.95.
The All American Caliber from BB caps up to the powerful 226 Barnes. It's about ammo history, plinking, target shooting, and the quest for the one-hole group.

British Military Martini, Treatise on the, Vol. 1, by B.A. Temple and Ian Skennerton, I.D.S.A. Books, Piqua, OH, 1983. 256 pp., 114 illus. $40.00.

British Military Martini, Treatise on the, Vol. 2, by B.A. Temple and Ian Skennerton, I.D.S.A. Books, Piqua, OH, 1989. 213 pp., 135 illus. $40.00.

British .22RF Training Rifles, by Dennis Lewis and Robert Washburn, Excaliber Publications, Latham, NY, 1993. 64 pp., illus. Paper covers. $10.95.
The story of Britain's training rifles from the early Aiming Tube models to the post-WWII trainers.

Classic Sporting Rifles, by Christopher Austyn, Safari Press, Huntington Beach, CA, 1997. 128 pp., illus. $50.00.
As the head of the gun department at Christie's Auction House the author examines the "best" rifles built over the last 150 years.

Combat Rifles of the 21st Century, by Duncan Long, Paladin Press, Boulder, CO, 1991. 115 pp., illus. Paper covers. $16.50.
An inside look at the U.S. Army's program to develop a super advanced combat rifle to replace the M16.

The Complete AR15/M16 Sourcebook, by Duncan Long, Paladin Press, Boulder, CO, 1993. 232 pp., illus. Paper covers. $35.00.
The latest development of the AR15/M16 and the many spin-offs now available, selective-fire conversion systems for the 1990s, the vast selection of new accessories.

Exploded Long Gun Drawings, The Gun Digest Book of, edited by Harold A. Murtz, DBI Books, a division of Krause Publications, Inc., Iola, WI, 512 pp., illus. Paper covers. $20.95.
Containing almost 500 rifle and shotgun exploded drawings. An invaluable aid to both professionals and hobbyists.

The FAL Rifle, by R. Blake Stevens and Jean van Rutten, Collector Grade Publications, Cobourg, Canada, 1993. 848 pp., illus. $129.95.
Originally published in three volumes, this classic edition covers North American, UK and Commonwealth and the metric FAL's.

The Fighting Rifle, by Chuck Taylor, Paladin Press, Boulder, CO, 1983. 184 pp., illus. Paper covers. $20.00.
The difference between assault and battle rifles and auto and light machine guns.

Firearms Assembly/Disassembly Part III: Rimfire Rifles, Revised Edition, The Gun Digest Book of, by J.B. Wood, DBI Books, a division of Krause Publications, Inc., Iola, WI., 1994. 480 pp., illus. Paper covers. $19.95.
Covers 65 popular rimfires plus over 100 variants, all cross-referenced in the index.

Firearms Assembly/Disassembly Part IV: Centerfire Rifles, Revised Edition, The Gun Digest Book of, by J.B. Wood, DBI Books, a division of Krause Publications, Inc., Iola, WI, 1991. 480 pp., illus. Paper covers. $19.95.
Covers 54 popular centerfire rifles plus 300 variants. The most comprehensive and professional presentation available to either hobbyist or gunsmith.

Forty Years with the .45-70, second edition, revised and expanded, by Paul A. Matthews, Wolfe Publishing Co., Prescott, AZ, 1997. 184 pp., illus. Paper covers. $14.95.
This book is pure gun lore-lore of the .45-70. It not only contains a history of the cartridge but also years of the author's personal experiences.

F.N.-F.A.L. Auto Rifles, Desert Publications, Cornville, AZ, 1981. 130 pp., illus. Paper covers. $13.95.
A definitive study of one of the free world's finest combat rifles.

The Hammerless Double Rifle, by Alexander Gray, Wolfe Publishing Co., Prescott, AZ, 1994. 154 pp., illus. $39.50.
The history, design, construction and maintenance are explored for a better understanding of these firearms.

Hints and Advice on Rifle-Shooting, by Private R. McVittie with new introductory material by W.S. Curtis, W.S. Curtis Publishers, Ltd., Clwyd, England, 1993. 32 pp. Paper covers. $10.00.
A reprint of the original 1886 London edition.

*How-To's for the Black Powder Cartridge Rifle Shooter, by Paul A. Matthews, Wolfe Publishing Co., Prescott, AZ, 1996. 136 pp., illus. Paper covers. $22.00.
Practices and procedures used in the reloading and shooting of blackpowder cartridges.

Hunting with the .22, by C.S. Landis, R&R Books, Livonia, NY, 1995. 429 pp., illus. $45.00.
A reprinting of the classical work on .22 rifles.

Illustrated Handbook of Rifle Shooting, by A.L. Russell, Museum Restoration Service, Alexandria Bay, NY, 1992. 194 pp., illus. $24.50.
A new printing of the 1869 edition by one of the leading military marksman of the day.

Know Your M1 Garand, by E. J. Hoffschmidt, Blacksmith Corp., Southport, CT, 1975, 84 pp., illus. Paper covers. $9.95.
Facts about America's most famous infantry weapon. Covers test and experimental models, Japanese and Italian copies, National Match models.

Know Your Ruger 10/22 Carbine, by William E. Workman, Blacksmith Corp., Chino Valley, AZ, 1991. 96 pp., illus. Paper covers. $9.95.
The story and facts about the most popular 22 autoloader ever made.

The Lee Enfield No. 1 Rifles, by Alan M. Petrillo, Excaliber Publications, Latham, NY, 1992. 64 pp., illus. Paper covers. $10.95.
Highlights the SMLE rifles from the Mark 1-VI.

The Lee Enfield Number 4 Rifles, by Alan M. Petrillo, Excalibur Publications, Latham, NY, 1992. 64 pp., illus. Paper covers. $10.95.
A pocket-sized, bare-bones reference devoted entirely to the .303 World War II and Korean War vintage service rifle.

The Lee Enfield Story, by Ian Skennerton, I.D.S.A. Books, Piqua, OH, 1993. 504 pp., nearly 1,000 illus. $59.95.

The Lee Enfield Story, Deluxe Presentation Edition by Ian Skennerton, I.D.S.A. Books, Piqua, OH, 1993. 504 pp., nearly 1,000 illus. Leather cover. $150.00.

Legendary Sporting Rifles, by Sam Fadala, Stoeger Publishing Co., So. Hackensack, NJ, 1992. 288 pp., illus. Paper covers. $16.95.
Covers a vast span of time and technology beginning with the Kentucky Long-rifle.

The Li'l M1 .30 Cal. Carbine, by Duncan Long, Desert Publications, El Dorado, AZ, 1995. 203 pp., illus. Paper covers. $14.95.
Traces the history of this little giant from its original creation.

M14/M14A1 Rifles and Rifle Markmanship, Desert Publications, El Dorado, AZ, 1995. 236 pp., illus. Paper covers. $16.95.
Contains a detailed description of the M14 and M14A1 rifles and their general characteristics, procedures for disassembly and assembly, operating and functioning of the rifles, etc.

*The M14 Owner's Guide and Match Conditioning Instructions, by Scott A. Duff and John M. Miller, Scott A. Duff Publications, Export, PA, 1996. 180 pp., illus. Paper covers. $19.95.
Traces the history and development from the T44 through the adoption and production of the M14 rifle.

The M-14 Rifle, facsimile reprint of FM 23-8, Desert Publications, Cornville, AZ, 50 pp., illus. Paper $7.95.
Well illustrated and informative reprint covering the M-14 and M-14E2.

The M14-Type Rifle: A Shooter's and Collector's Guide, by Joe Poyer, North Cape Publications, Tustin, CA, 1997. 82 pp., illus. Paper covers. $14.95.
covers the history and development, commercial copies, cleaning and maintenance instructions, and targeting and shooting.

Military Bolt Action Rifles, 1841-1918, by Donald B. Webster, Museum Restoration Service, Alexander Bay, NY, 1993. 150 pp., illus. $34.50.
A photographic survey of the principal rifles and carbines of the European and Asiatic powers of the last half of the 19th century and the first years of the 20th century.

Military and Sporting Rifle Shooting, by Captain E.C. Crossman, Wolfe Publishing Co., Prescott, AZ, 1988. 449 pp., illus. $45.00.
A limited edition reprint. A complete and practical treatise covering the use of rifles.

The Mini-14, by Duncan Long, Paladin Press, Boulder, CO, 1987. 120 pp., illus. Paper covers. $12.00.
History of the Mini-14, the factory-produced models, specifications, accessories, suppliers, and much more.

Mr. Single Shot's Book of Rifle Plans, by Frank de Haas, Mark de Haas, Orange City, IA, 1996. 85 pp., illus. Paper covers. $22.50.
Contains complete and detailed drawings, plans and instructions on how to build four different and unique breech-loading single shot rifles of the author's own proven design.

M1 Carbine Owner's Manual, M1, M2 & M3 .30 Caliber Carbines, Firepower Publications, Cornville, AZ, 1984. 102 pp., illus. Paper covers. $10.95.
The complete book for the owner of an M1 Carbine.

The M1 Garand Serial Numbers & Data Sheets, by Scott A. Duff, Scott A. Duff, Export, PA, 1995. 101 pp. Paper covers. $9.95.
This pocket reference book includes serial number tables and data sheets on the Springfield Armory, Gas Trap Rifles, Gas Port Rifles, Winchester Repeating Arms, International Harvester and H&R Arms Co. and more.

More Single Shot Rifles and Actions, by Frank de Haas, Mark de Haas, Orange City, IA, 1996. 146 pp., illus. Paper covers. $22.50.
Covers 45 different single shot rifles. Includes the history plus photos, drawings and personal comments.

The Muzzle-Loading Rifle...Then and Now, by Walter M. Cline, National Muzzle Loading Rifle Association, Friendship, IN, 1991. 161 pp., illus. $32.00.
This extensive compilation of the muzzleloading rifle exhibits accumulative preserved data concerning the development of the "hallowed old arms of the Southern highlands."

The No. 4 (T) Sniper Rifle: An Armourer's Perspective, by Peter Laidler with Ian Skennerton, I.D.S.A. Books, Piqua, OH, 1993. 125 pp., 75 illus. Paper covers. $19.95.

Notes on Rifle-Shooting, by Henry William Heaton, reprinted with a new introduction by W.S. Curtis, W.S. Curtis Publishers, Ltd., Clwyd, England, 1993. 89 pp. $19.95.
A reprint of the 1864 London edition. Captain Heaton was one of the great rifle shots from the earliest days of the Volunteer Movement.

*The Official SKS Manual, Translation by Major James F. Gebhardt (Ret.), Paladin Press, Boulder, CO, 1997. 96 pp., illus. Paper covers. $15.00.
This Soviet military manual covering the widely distributed SKS is now available in English.

The Pennsylvania Rifle, by Samuel E. Dyke, Sutter House, Lititz, PA, 1975. 61 pp., illus. Paper covers. $5.00.
History and development, from the hunting rifle of the Germans who settled the area. Contains a full listing of all known Lancaster, PA, gunsmiths from 1729 through 1815.

Police Rifles, by Richard Fairburn, Paladin Press, Boulder, CO, 1994. 248 pp., illus. Paper covers. $30.00.
Selecting the right rifle for street patrol and special tactical situations.

The Poor Man's Sniper Rifle, by D. Boone, Paladin Press, Boulder, CO, 1995. 152 pp., illus. Paper covers. $14.95.
Here is a complete plan for converting readily available surplus military rifles to high-performance sniper weapons.

A Potpourri of Single Shot Rifles and Actions, by Frank de Haas, Mark de Haas, Ridgeway, MO, 1993. 153 pp., illus. Paper covers. $22.50.
The author's 6th book on non-bolt-action single shots. Covers more than 40 single-shot rifles in historical and technical detail.

The Remington 700, by John F. Lacy, Taylor Publishing Co., Dallas, TX, 1990. 208 pp., illus. $44.95.
Covers the different models, limited editions, chamberings, proofmarks, serial numbers, military models, and much more.

The Revolving Rifles, by Edsall James, Pioneer Press, Union City, TN, 1975. 23 pp., illus. Paper covers. $2.50.
Valuable information on revolving cylinder rifles, from the earliest matchlock forms to the latest models of Colt and Remington.

Rifle Guide, by Sam Fadala, Stoeger Publishing Co., S. Hackensack, NJ, 1993. 288 pp., illus. Paper covers. $16.95.
This comprehensive, fact-filled book beckons to both the seasoned rifleman as well as the novice shooter.

The Rifle: Its Development for Big-Game Hunting, by S.R. Truesdell, Safari Press, Huntington Beach, CA, 1992. 274 pp., illus. $35.00.
The full story of the development of the big-game rifle from 1834-1946.

Rifleman's Handbook: A Shooter's Guide to Rifles, Reloading & Results, by Rick Jamison, NRA Publications, Washington, DC, 1990. 303 pp., illus. $21.95.
Helpful tips on precision reloading, how to squeeze incredible accuracy out of an "everyday" rifle, etc.

Riflesmithing, The Gun Digest Book of, by Jack Mitchell, DBI Books, a division of Krause Publications, Inc., Iola, WI, 1982. 256 pp., illus. Paper covers. $16.95.
Covers tools, techniques, designs, finishing wood and metal, custom alterations.

Rifles of the World, 2nd Edition, edited by John Walter, DBI Books, a division of Krause Publications, Inc., Iola, WI, 1998. 384 pp., illus. $24.95
the definitive guide to the world's centerfire and rimfire rifles.

Ned H. Roberts and the Schuetzen Rifle, edited by Gerald O. Kelver, Brighton, CO, 1982. 99 pp., illus. $15.00.
A compilation of the writings of Major Ned H. Roberts which appeared in various gun magazines.

The Ruger 10/22, by William E. Workman, Krause Publications, Iola, WI, 1994. 320 pp., illus. Paper covers. $19.95.
Learn all about the most popular, best-selling and perhaps best-built 22 caliber semi-automatic rifles of all time.

Schuetzen Rifles, History and Loading, by Gerald O. Kelver, Gerald O. Kelver, Publisher, Brighton, CO, 1972. Illus. $15.00.
Reference work on these rifles, their bullets, loading, telescopic sights, accuracy, etc. A limited, numbered ed.

Semi-Auto Rifles: Data and Comment, edited by Robert W. Hunnicutt, The National Rifle Association, Washington, DC, 1988. 156 pp., illus. Paper covers. $15.95.
A book for those who find military-style self-loading rifles interesting for their history, intriguing for the engineering that goes into their design, and a pleasure to shoot.

Shooting the Blackpowder Cartridge Rifle, by Paul A. Matthews, Wolfe Publishing Co., Prescott, AZ, 1994. 129 pp., illus. Paper covers. $22.50.
A general discourse on shooting the blackpowder cartridge rifle and the procedure required to make a particular rifle perform.

Single-Shot Actions, Their Design and Construction, by Frank and Mark Delisse, de Haas Books, Orange City, IA 1991. 247 pp., illus. $45.00.
Covers the best single shot rifles of the past plus a potpourri of modern single shot rifle actions.

Single-Shot Rifle Finale, by James Grant, Wolfe Publishing Co., Prescott, AZ, 1992. 556 pp., illus. $36.00.
The master's 5th book on the subject and his best.

Single Shot Rifles and Actions, by Frank de Haas, Orange City, IA, 1990. 352 pp., illus. Soft covers. $27.00.
The definitive book on over 60 single shot rifles and actions.

Sixty Years of Rifles, by Paul A. Matthews, Wolfe Publishing Co., Prescott, AZ, 1991. 224 pp., illus. $19.50.
About rifles and the author's experience and love affair with shooting and hunting.

S.L.R.—Australia's F.N. F.A.L. by Ian Skennerton and David Balmer, I.D.S.A. Books, Piqua, OH, 1989. 124 pp., 100 illus. Paper covers. $19.50.

Small Arms Identification Series, No. 2—.303 Rifle, No. 4 Marks I, & I*, Marks 1/2, 1/3 & 2, by Ian Skennerton, I.D.S.A. Books, Piqua, OH, 1994. 48 pp. $9.50.

Small Arms Identification Series, No. 3—9mm Austen Mk I & 9mm Owen Mk I Sub-Machine Guns, by Ian Skennerton, I.D.S.A. Books, Piqua, OH, 1994. 48 pp. $9.50.

Small Arms Identification Series, No. 4—.303 Rifle, No. 5 Mk I, by Ian Skennerton, I.D.S.A. Books, Piqua, OH, 1994. 48 pp. $9.50.

Small Arms Identification Series, No. 5—.303-in. Bren Light Machine Gun, by Ian Skennerton, I.D.S.A. Books, Piqua, OH, 1994. 48 pp. $9.50.

Small Arms Series, No. 1 DeLisle's Commando Carbine, by Ian Skennerton, I.D.S.A. Books, Piqua, OH, 1981. 32 pp., 24 illus. $9.00.

Small Arms Identification Series, No. 1—.303 Rifle, No. 1 S.M.L.E. Marks III and III*, by Ian Skennerton, I.D.S.A. Books, Piqua, OH, 1981. 48 pp. $9.50.

***Sporting Rifle Takedown & Reassembly Guide, 2nd Edition,** by J.B. Wood, DBI Books, a division of Krause Publications, Iola, WI, 1997. 480 pp., illus. $19.95.
An updated edition of the reference guide for anyone who wants to properly care for their sporting rifle. (Available September 1997)

The Springfield Rifle M1903, M1903A1, M1903A3, M1903A4, Desert Publications, Cornville, AZ, 1982. 100 pp., illus. Paper covers. $12.00.
Covers every aspect of disassembly and assembly, inspection, repair and maintenance.

Still More Single Shot Rifles, by James J. Grant, Pioneer Press, Union City, TN, 1995. 211 pp., illus. $27.50.
This is Volume Four in a series of Single-Shot Rifles by America's foremost authority. It gives more in-depth information on those single-shot rifles which were presented in the first three books.

The Sturm, Ruger 10/22 Rifle and .44 Magnum Carbine, by Duncan Long, Paladin Press, Boulder, CO, 1988. 108 pp., illus. Paper covers. $12.00.
An in-depth look at both weapons detailing the elegant simplicity of the Ruger design. Offers specifications, troubleshooting procedures and ammunition recommendations.

Target Rifle in Australia, by J.E. Corcoran, R&R, Livonia, NY, 1996. 160 pp., illus. $40.00.
A most interesting study of the evolution of these rifles from 1860 - 1900. British rifles from the percussion period through the early smokeless era are discussed.

To the Dreams of Youth: The .22 Caliber Single Shot Winchester Rifle, by Herbert Houze, Krause Publications, Iola, WI, 1993. 192 pp., illus. $34.95.
A thoroughly researched history of the 22-caliber Winchester single shot rifle, including interesting photographs.

U.S. Marine Corps AR15/M16 A2 Manual, reprinted by Desert Publications, El Dorado, AZ, 1993. 262 pp., illus. Paper covers. $16.95.
A reprint of TM05538C-23&P/2, August, 1987. The A-2 manual for the Colt AR15/M16.

U.S. Rifle M14—From John Garand to the M21, by R. Blake Stevens, Collector Grade Publications, Inc., Toronto, Canada, revised second edition, 1991. 350 pp., illus. $49.50.
A classic, in-depth examination of the development, manufacture and fielding of the last wood-and-metal ("lock, stock, and barrel") battle rifle to be issued to U.S. troops.

War Baby!: The U.S. Caliber 30 Carbine, Volume I, by Larry Ruth, Collector Grade Publications, Toronto, Canada, 1992. 512 pp., illus. $69.95.
Volume 1 of the in-depth story of the phenomenally popular U.S. caliber 30 carbine. Concentrates on design and production of the military 30 carbine during World War II.

War Baby Comes Home: The U.S. Caliber 30 Carbine, Volume 2, by Larry Ruth, Collector Grade Pulications, Toronto, Canada, 1993. 386 pp., illus. $49.95.
The triumphant competion of Larry Ruth's two-volume in-depth series on the most popular U.S. military small arm in history.

The Winchester Model 52, Perfection in Design, by Herbert G. Houze, Krause Publicaitons, Iola, WI, 1997. 192 pp., illus. $34.95.
This book covers the complete story of this technically superior gun.

The Winchester Model 94: The First 100 Years, by Robert C. Renneberg, Krause Publications, Iola, WI, 1991. 208 pp., illus. $34.95.
Covers the design and evolution from the early years up to today.

Winchester Slide-Action Rifles, Volume I: Model 1890 and Model 1906 by Ned Schwing, Krause Publications, Inc., Iola, WI. 352 pp., illus. $39.95
Traces the history through word and picture in this chronolgy of the Model 1890 and 1906.

Winchester Slide-Action Rifles, Volume II: Model 61 & Model 62 by Ned Schwing, Krause Publications, Inc., Iola, WI. 256 pp., illus. $34.95
Historical look complete with markings, stampings and engraving.

SHOTGUNS

Advanced Combat Shotgun: The Stress Fire Concept, by Massad Ayoob, Police Bookshelf, Concord, NH, 1993. 197 pp., illus. Paper covers. $9.95.
Advanced combat shotgun fighting for police.

The American Shotgun, by Charles Askins, Wolfe Publishing Co., Prescott, AZ, 1988. 321 pp., illus. $39.00.
A limited edition reprint. Askins covers shotguns and patterning extremely well.

The American Shotgun, by David F. Butler, edited by C. Kenneth Ramage, Lyman Publications, Middlefield, CT, 1973. 243 pp., illus. Paper covers. $14.95.
A comprehensive history of the American smoothbore's evolution from Colonial times to the present day.

American Shotgun Design and Performance, by L.R. Wallack, Winchester Press, Piscataway, NJ, 1977. 184 pp., illus. $16.95.
An expert lucidly recounts the history and development of American shotguns.

Best Guns, by Michael McIntosh, Countrysport, Inc., Traverse City, MI, 1989. 288 pp., illus. $39.50.
Devoted to the best shotguns ever made in the United States and the best presently being made in the world.

The Better Shot, by Ken Davies, Quiller Press, London, England, 1992. 136 pp., illus. $39.95.
Step-by-step shotgun technique with Holland and Holland.

Black Powder Hobby Gunsmithing, by Sam Fadala and Dale Storey, DBI Books, a division of Krause Publications, Inc., Iola, WI, 1994. 256 pp., illus. Paper covers. $18.95
A how-to-guide for gunsmithing blackpowder pistols, rifles and shotguns from two men at the top of their respective fields.

The British Shotgun, Volume 1, 1850-1870, by I.M. Crudington and D.J. Baker, Barrie & Jenkins, London, England, 1979. 256 pp., illus. $59.95.
An attempt to trace, as accurately as is now possible, the evolution of the shotgun during its formative years in Great Britain.

***Boothroyd on British Shotguns,** by Geoffrey Boothroyd, Sand Lake Press, Amity, OR, 1996. 221 pp., illus. plus a 32 page reproduction of the 1914 Webley & Scott catalog. A limited, numbered edition. $34.95.
Based on articles by the author that appeared in the British Publication *Shooting Times & Country Magazine*.

***The British Over-and-Under Shotgun,** by Geoffrey and Susan Boothroyd, Sand Lake Press, Amity, OR, 1996. 137 pp., illus. $34.95.
Historical outline of the development of the O/U shotgun with individual chapters devoted to the twenty-two British makers.

Boss & Co. Builders of Best Guns Only, by Donald Dallas, Safari Press, Huntington Beach, CA, 1996. 336 pp., illus. $75.00

The Browning Superposed: John M. Browning's Last Legacy, by Ned Schwing, Krause Publications, Iola, WI, 1996. 496 pp., illus. $49.95.
An exclusive story of the man, the company and the best-selling over-and-under shotgun in North America.

Clay Pigeon Shooting for Beginners and Enthusiasts, by John King, The Sportsman's Press, London, England, 1991. 94 pp., illus. $24.95.
John King has devised this splendid guide to clay pigeon shooting in the same direct style in which he teaches at his popular Barbury Shooting School near Swindon.

Clay Shooting, by Peter Croft, Ward Lock, London, England, 1990. 160 pp., illus, $29.95.
A complete guide to Skeet, trap and sporting shooting.

Clay Target Handbook, by Jerry Meyer, Lyons & Buford, Publisher, New York, NY, 1993. 182 pp., illus. $22.95.
Contains in-depth, how-to-do-it information on trap, skeet, sporting clays, international trap, international skeet and clay target games played around the country.

Clay Target Shooting, by Paul Bentley, A&C Black, London, England, 1987. 144 pp., illus. $25.00.
Practical book on clay target shooting written by a very successful international competitor, providing valuable professional advice and instruction for shooters of all disciplines.

A Collector's Guide to United States Combat Shotguns, by Bruce N. Canfield, Andrew Mowbray Inc., Publishers, Lincoln, RI, 1993. 184 pp., illus. Paper covers. $24.00.
Full coverage of the combat shotgun, from the earliest examples to the Gulf War and beyond.

The Complete Clay Shot, by Mike Barnes, Trafalgar Square, N. Pomfret, VT, 1993. 192 pp., illus. $39.95.
The latest compendium on the clay sports by Mike Barnes, a well-known figure in shotgunning in the U.S. and England.

Cradock on Shotguns, by Chris Cradock, Banford Press, London, England, 1989. 200 pp., illus. $45.00.
A definitive work on the shotgun by a British expert on shotguns.

The Defensive Shotgun, by Louis Awerbuck, S.W.A.T. Publications, Cornville, AZ, 1989. 77 pp., illus. Soft covers. $12.95.
Cuts through the myths concerning the shotgun and its attendant ballistic effects.

The Double Shotgun, by Don Zutz, Winchester Press, Piscataway, NJ, 1985. 304 pp., illus. $20.95.
Revised, updated, expanded edition of the history and development of the world's classic sporting firearms.

Ed Scherer on Sporting Clays, by Ed Scherer, Ed Scherer, Elk Grove, WI, 1993. 200 pp., illus. Paper covers. $29.95.
Covers footwork, gun fit, master eye checks, recoil reduction, noise abatement, eye and ear protection, league shooting, shot sizes and chokes.

Exploded Long Gun Drawings, The Gun Digest Book of, edited by Harold A. Murtz, DBI Books, a division of Krause Publications, Inc., Iola, WI. 512 pp., illus. Paper covers. $20.95.
Containing almost 500 rifle and shotgun exploded drawings. An invaluable aid to both professionals and hobbyists.

Field, Cover and Trap Shooting, by Adam H. Bogardus, Wolfe Publishing Co., Prescott, AZ, 1988. 446 pp., illus. $45.00.
A limited edition reprint. Hints for skilled marksmen as well as young sportsmen. Includes haunts and habits of game birds and waterfowl.

Finding the Extra Target, by Coach John R. Linn & Stephen A. Blumenthal, Shotgun Sports, Inc., Auburn, CA, 1989. 126 pp., illus. Paper covers. $14.95.
The ultimate training guide for all the clay target sports.

Firearms Assembly/Disassembly, Part V: Shotguns, Revised Edition, The Gun Digest Book of, by J.B. Wood, DBI Books, a division of Krause Publications, Inc., Iola, WI, 1992. 480 pp., illus. Paper covers. $19.95.
Covers 46 popular shotguns plus over 250 variants. The most comprehensive and professional presentation available to either hobbyist or gunsmith.

A.H. Fox "The Finest Gun in the World", revised and enlarged edition, by Michael McIntosh, Countrysport, Inc., New Albany, OH, 1995. 408 pp., illus. $49.00.
The first detailed history of one of America's finest shotguns.

Game Gun, by Richard Grozik, country Sport Press, Traverse City, MI, 1997. 203 pp., illus. $39.00.
A revision of a classic on the craftsmanship and function of double guns.

Game Shooting, by Robert Churchill, Countrysport Press, Selma, AL, 1998. 258 pp., illus. $34.95.
The basis for every shotgun instructional technique devised and the foundation for all wingshooting and the game of sporting clays.

The Golden Age of Shotgunning, by Bob Hinman, Wolfe Publishing Co., Inc., Prescott, AZ, 1982. $22.50.
A valuable history of the late 1800s detailing that fabulous period of development in shotguns, shotshells and shotgunning.

Grand Old Shotguns, by Don Zutz, Shotgun Sports Magazine, Auburn, CA, 1995. 136 pp., illus. Paper covers. $19.95
A study of the great smoothbores, their history and how and why they were discontinued. Find out the most sought-after and which were the best shooters.

Hartman on Skeet, By Barney Hartman, Stackpole Books, Harrisburg, PA, 1973. 143 pp., illus. $19.95.
A definitive book on Skeet shooting by a pro.

The Italian Gun, by Steve Smith & Laurie Morrow, wilderness Adventures, Gallatin Gateway, MT, 1997. 325 pp., illus. $49.95.
The first book ever written entirely in English for American enthusiasts who own, aspire to own, or simply admire Italian guns.

The Ithaca Featherlight Repeater; the Best Gun Going, by Walter C. Snyder, Southern Pines, NC, 1998. 300 pp., illus. $89.95.
Describes the complete history of each model of the legendary Ithaca Model 37 and Model 87 Repeaters from their conception in 1930 throught 1997.

L.C. Smith Shotguns, by Lt. Col. William S. Brophy, The Gun Room Press, Highland Park, NJ, 1979. 244 pp., illus. $35.00.
The first work on this very important American gun and manufacturing company.

The Little Trapshooting Book, by Frank Little, Shotgun Sports Magazine, Auburn, CA, 1994. 168 pp., illus. Paper covers. $19.95
Packed with know-how from one of the greatest trapshooters of all time.

Lock, Stock, and Barrel, by C. Adams & R. Braden, Safari Press, Huntington Beach, CA, 1996. 254 pp., illus. $24.95.
The process of making a best grade English gun from a lump of steel and a walnut tree trunk to the ultimate product plus practical advise on consistent field shooting with a double gun.

A Manual of Clayshooting, by Chris Cradock, Hippocrene Books, Inc., New York, NY, 1983. 192 pp., illus. $39.95.
Covers everything from building a range to buying a shotgun, with lots of illus. & dia.

*****Mental Training for the Shotgun Sports,** by Michael J. Keyes, Shotgun Sports, Auburn, CA, 1996. 160 pp., illus. Paper covers. $24.95.
The most comprehensive book ever published on what it takes to shoot winning scores at trap, Skeet and Sporting Clays.

The Model 12, 1912-1964,by Dave Riffle, Dave Riffle, Ft. Meyers, FL, 1995. 274 pp., illus. $49.95.
The story of the greatest hammerless repeating shotgun ever built.

The Mysteries of Shotgun Patterns, by George G. Oberfell and Charles E. Thompson, Oklahoma State University Press, Stillwater, OK, 1982. 164 pp., illus. Paper covers. $25.00.
Shotgun ballistics for the hunter in non-technical language.

The Orvis Wing-Shooting Handbook, by Bruce Bowlen, Nick Lyons Books, New York, NY, 1985. 83 pp., illus. Paper covers. $10.95.
Proven techniques for better shotgunning.

*****Parker Guns "The Old Reliable",** by Ed Muderiak, Safari Press, Inc., Huntington Beach, CA, 1997. 325 pp., illus. $40.00.
A look at the small beginnings, the golden years, and the ultimate decline of the most famous of all American shotgun manufacturers.

Positive Shooting, by Michael Yardley, Safari Press, Huntington Beach, CA, 1995. 160 pp., illus. $30.00.
This book will provide the shooter with a sound foundation from which to develop an effective, personal technique that can dramatically improve shooting performance.

Purdey's, the Guns and the Family, by Richard Beaumont, David and Charles, Pomfret, VT, 1984. 248 pp., illus. $39.95.
Records the history of the Purdey family from 1814 to today, how the guns were and are built and daily functioning of the factory.

*****Reloading for Shotgunners, 4th Edition,** by Kurt D. Fackler and M.L. McPherson, DBI Books, a division of Krause Publications, Inc., Iola, WI, 1997. 320 pp., illus. Paper covers. $19.95.
Expanded reloading tables with over 11,000 loads. Bushing charts for every major press and component maker. All new presentation on all aspects of shotshell reloading by two of the top experts in the field. (Available October 1997.)

Remington Double Shotguns, by Charles G. Semer, Denver, CO, 1997. 617 pp., illus. $60.00.
This book deals with the entire production and all grades of double shotguns made by Remington during the period of their production 1873-1910.

75 Years with the Shotgun, by C.T. (Buck) Buckman, Valley, Publ., Fresno, CA, 1974. 141 pp., illus. $10.00.
An expert hunter and trapshooter shares experiences of a lifetime.

The Shooting Field with Holland & Holland, by Peter King, Quiller Press, London, England, new & enlarged edition, 1990. 184 pp., illus. $49.95.
The story of a company which has produced excellence in all aspects of gunmaking.

The Shotgun in Combat, by Tony Lesce, Desert Publications, Cornville, AZ, 1979. 148 pp., illus. Paper covers. $10.00.
A history of the shotgun and its use in combat.

Shotgun Digest, 4th Edition, edited by Jack Lewis, DBI Books, a division of Krause Publications, Inc., Iola, WI, 1993. 256 pp., illus. Paper covers. $17.95.
A look at what's happening with shotguns and shotgunning today.

Shotgun Gunsmithing, The Gun Digest Book of, by Ralph Walker, DBI Books, a division of Krause Publications, Inc., Iola, WI, 1983. 256 pp., illus. Paper covers. $16.95.
The principles and practices of repairing, individualizing and accurizing modern shotguns by one of the world's premier shotgun gunsmiths.

The Shotgun: History and Development, by Geoffrey Boothroyd, Safari Press, Huntington Beach, CA, 1995. 240 pp., illus. $35.00.
The first volume in a series that traces the development of the British shotgun from the 17th century onward.

Shotgun Stuff, by Don Zutz, Shotgun Sports, Inc., Auburn, CA, 1991. 172 pp., illus. Paper covers. $19.95.
This book gives shotgunners all the "stuff" they need to achieve better performance and get more enjoyment from their favorite smoothbore.

Shotgunner's Notebook: The Advice and Reflections of a Wingshooter, by Gene Hill, Countrysport Press, Traverse City, MI, 1990. 192 pp., illus. $24.50.
Covers the shooting, the guns and the miscellany of the sport.

Shotgunning: The Art and the Science, by Bob Brister, Winchester Press, Piscataway, NJ, 1976. 321 pp., illus. $18.95.
Hundreds of specific tips and truly novel techniques to improve the field and target shooting of every shotgunner.

Shotgunning Trends in Transition, by Don Zutz, Wolfe Publishing Co., Prescott, AZ, 1990. 314 pp., illus. $29.50.
This book updates American shotgunning from post WWII to present.

Shotguns and Cartridges for Game and Clays, by Gough Thomas, edited by Nigel Brown, A & C Black, Ltd., Cambs, England, 1989. 256 pp., illus. Soft covers. $24.95.
Gough Thomas' well-known and respected book for game and clay pigeon shooters in a thoroughly up-dated edition.

Shotguns and Gunsmiths: The Vintage Years, by Geoffrey Boothroyd, Safari Press, Huntington Beach, CA, 1995. 240 pp., illus. $35.00.
A fascinating insight into the lives and skilled work of gunsmiths who helped develop the British shotgun during the Victorian and Edwardian eras.

Shotguns and Shooting, by Michael McIntosh, Countrysport Press, New Albany, OH, 1995. 258 pp., illus. $30.00.
The art of guns and gunmaking, this book is a celebration no lover of fine doubles should miss.

Side by Sides of the World, by Charles E. Carder, Avil Onze Publications, Delphos, OH, 1997. 181 pp., illus. Paper covers. $24.95.
Double barrel shotguns from the early 1800's to the present. 1,295 different names found on side by sides.

Sidelocks & Boxlocks, by Geoffrey Boothroyd, Sand Lake Press, Amity, OR, 1991. 271 pp., illus. $35.00.
The story of the classic British shotgun.

Spanish Best: The Fine Shotguns of Spain, by Terry Wieland, Countrysport, Inc., Traverse City, MI, 1994. 264 pp., illus. $49.50.
A practical source of information for owners of Spanish shotguns and a guide for those considering buying a used shotgun.

The Sporting Clay Handbook, by Jerry Meyer, Lyons and Burford Publishers, New York, NY, 1990. 140 pp., illus. Soft covers. $17.95.
Introduction to the fastest growing, and most exciting, gun game in America.

Sporting Clays, The Gun Digest Book of, by Jack Lewis and Steve Comus, DBI Books, a division of Krause Publications, Inc., Iola, WI, 1991. 256 pp., illus. Paper covers. $18.95.
A superb introduction to the fastest growing gun game in America.

Sporting Clays, by Michael Pearce, Stackpole Books, Harrisburg, PA, 1991. 192 pp., illus. $18.95.
Expert techniques for every kind of clays course.

Successful Clay Pigeon Shooting, compiled by T. Hoare, Trafalgar Square, N. Pomfret, VT, 1993. 176 pp., illus. $39.95.
This comprehensive guide has been written by ten leading personalities for all aspiring clay pigeon shooters.

*****The Tactical Shotgun,** by Gabriel Suzrez, Paladin Press, Boulde, CO, 1996. 232 pp., illus. Paper covers. $25.00.
The best techniques and tactics for employing the shotgun in personal combat.

Taking More Birds, by Dan Carlisle & Dolph Adams, Lyons & Burford, New York, NY, 1993. 120 pp., illus. $19.95.
A practical guide to greater success at sporting clays and wing shooting.

Trap & Skeet Shooting, 3rd Edition, by Chris Christian, DBI Books, a division of Krause Publications, Inc., Iola, WI, 1994. 288 pp., illus. Paper covers. $17.95.
A detailed look at the contemporary world of trap, Skeet and Sporting Clays.

*****Trapshooting is a Game of Opposites,** by Dick Bennett, Shotgun Sports, Inc., Auburn, CA, 1996. 129 pp., illus. Paper covers. $19.95.
Discover everything you need to know about shooting trap like the pros.

Turkey Hunter's Digest, Revised Edition, by Dwain Bland, DBI Books, a division of Krause Publications, Inc., Iola, WI, 1994. 256 pp., illus. Paper covers. $17.95.
Presents no-nonsense approach to hunting all five sub-species of the North American wild turkey.

U.S. Shotguns, All Types, reprint of TM9-285, Desert Publications, Cornville, AZ, 1987. 257 pp., illus. Paper covers. $9.95.
Covers operation, assembly and disassembly of nine shotguns used by the U.S. armed forces.

U.S. Winchester Trench and Riot Guns and Other U.S. Military Combat Shotguns, by Joe Poyer, North Cape Publications, Tustin, CA, 1992. 124 pp., illus. Paper covers. $15.95.
A detailed history of the use of military shotguns, and the acquisition procedures used by the U.S. Army's Ordnance Department in both World Wars.

The Winchester Model Twelve, by George Madis, David Madis, Dallas, TX, 1984. 176 pp., illus. $19.95.
A definitive work on this famous American shotgun.

The Winchester Model 42, by Ned Schwing, Krause Pub., Iola, WI, 1990. 160 pp., illus. $34.95.
Behind-the-scenes story of the model 42's invention and its early development. Production totals and manufacturing dates; reference work.

Winchester Shotguns and Shotshells, by Ron Stadt, Krause Pub., Iola, WI. 288 pp., illus. $34.95.
Must-have for Winchester collectors of shotguns manufactured through 1961.

Winchester's Finest, the Model 21, by Ned Schwing, Krause Publicatons, Inc., Iola, WI, 1990. 360 pp., illus. $49.95.
The classic beauty and the interesting history of the Model 21 Winchester shotgun.

The World's Fighting Shotguns, by Thomas F. Swearengen, T.B.N. Enterprises, Alexandria, VA, 1979. 500 pp., illus. $34.95.
The complete military and police reference work from the shotgun's inception to date, with up-to-date developments.

UNITED STATES

ALABAMA

Alabama Gun Collectors Assn.
Secretary, P.O. Box 70965, Tuscaloosa, AL 35407

ALASKA

Alaska Gun Collectors Assn., Inc.
C.W. Floyd, Pres., 5240 Little Tree, Anchorage, AK 99507

ARIZONA

Arizona Arms Assn.
Don DeBusk, President, 4837 Bryce Ave., Glendale, AZ 85301

CALIFORNIA

California Cartridge Collectors Assn.
Rick Montgomery, 1729 Christina, Stockton, CA 95204/209-463-7216 evs.

California Waterfowl Assn.
4630 Northgate Blvd., #150, Sacramento, CA 95834

Greater Calif. Arms & Collectors Assn.
Donald L. Bullock, 8291 Carburton St., Long Beach, CA 90808-3302

Los Angeles Gun Ctg. Collectors Assn.
F.H. Ruffra, 20810 Amie Ave., Apt. #9, Torrance, CA 90503

Stock Gun Players Assn.
6038 Appian Way, Long Beach, CA, 90803

COLORADO

Colorado Gun Collectors Assn.
L.E.(Bud) Greenwald, 2553 S. Quitman St., Denver, CO 80219/303-935-3850

Rocky Mountain Cartridge Collectors Assn.
John Roth, P.O. Box 757, Conifer, CO 80433

CONNECTICUT

Ye Connecticut Gun Guild, Inc.
Dick Fraser; P.O. Box 425, Windsor, CT 06095

FLORIDA

Unified Sportsmen of Florida
P.O. Box 6565, Tallahassee, FL 32314

GEORGIA

Georgia Arms Collectors Assn., Inc.
Michael Kindberg, President, P.O. Box 277, Alpharetta, GA 30239-0277

ILLINOIS

Illinois State Rifle Assn.
P.O. Box 637, Chatsworth, IL 60921

Mississippi Valley Gun & Cartridge Coll. Assn.
Bob Filbert, P.O. Box 61, Port Byron, IL 61275/309-523-2593

Sauk Trail Gun Collectors
Gordell M. Matson, P.O. Box 1113, Milan, IL 61264

Wabash Valley Gun Collectors Assn., Inc.
Roger L. Dorsett, 2601 Willow Rd., Urbana, IL 61801/217-384-7302

INDIANA

Indiana State Rifle & Pistol Assn.
Thos. Glancy, P.O. Box 552, Chesterton, IN 46304

Southern Indiana Gun Collectors Assn., Inc.
Sheila McClary, 309 W. Monroe St., Boonville, IN 47601/812-897-3742

IOWA

Beaver Creek Plainsmen Inc.
Steve Murphy, Secy., P.O. Box 298, Bondurant, IA 50035

Central States Gun Collectors Assn.
Dennis Greischar, Box 841, Mason City, IA 50402-0841

KANSAS

Kansas Cartridge Collectors Assn.
Bob Linder, Box 84, Plainville, KS 67663

KENTUCKY

Kentuckiana Arms Collectors Assn.
Charles Billips, President, Box 1776, Louisville, KY 40201

Kentucky Gun Collectors Assn., Inc.
Ruth Johnson, Box 64, Owensboro, KY 42302/502-729-4197

LOUISIANA

Washitaw River Renegades
Sandra Rushing, P.O. Box 256, Main St., Grayson, LA 71435

MARYLAND

Baltimore Antique Arms Assn.
Mr. Cillo, 1034 Main St., Darlington, MD 21304

MASSACHUSETTS

Bay Colony Weapons Collectors, Inc.
John Brandt, Box 111, Hingham, MA 02043

Massachusetts Arms Collectors
Bruce E. Skinner, P.O. Box 31, No. Carver, MA 02355/508-866-5259

MICHIGAN

Association for the Study and Research of .22 Caliber Rimfire Cartridges
George Kass, 4512 Nakoma Dr., Okemos, MI 48864

MINNESOTA

Sioux Empire Cartridge Collectors Assn.
Bob Cameron, 14597 Glendale Ave. SE, Prior Lake, MN 55372

MISSISSIPPI

Mississippi Gun Collectors Assn.
Jack E. Swinney, P.O. Box 16323, Hattiesburg, MS 39402

MISSOURI

Greater St. Louis Cartridge Collectors Assn.
Don MacChesney, 634 Scottsdale Rd., Kirkwood, MO 63122-1109

Mineral Belt Gun Collectors Assn.
D.F. Saunders, 1110 Cleveland Ave., Monett, MO 65708

Missouri Valley Arms Collectors Assn., Inc.
L.P Brammer II, Membership Secy., P.O. Box 33033, Kansas City, MO 64114

MONTANA

Montana Arms Collectors Assn.
Dean E. Yearout, Sr., Exec. Secy., 1516 21st Ave. S., Great Falls, MT 59405

Weapons Collectors Society of Montana
R.G. Schipf, Ex. Secy., 3100 Bancroft St., Missoula, MT 59801/406-728-2995

NEBRASKA

Nebraska Cartridge Collectors Club
Gary Muckel, P.O. Box 84442, Lincoln, NE 68501

NEW HAMPSHIRE

New Hampshire Arms Collectors, Inc.
James Stamatelos, Secy., P.O. Box 5, Cambridge, MA 02139

NEW JERSEY

Englishtown Benchrest Shooters Assn.
Michael Toth, 64 Cooke Ave., Carteret, NJ 07008

Jersey Shore Antique Arms Collectors
Joe Sisia, P.O. Box 100, Bayville, NJ 08721-0100

New Jersey Arms Collectors Club, Inc.
Angus Laidlaw, Vice President, 230 Valley Rd., Montclair, NJ 07042/201-746-0939; e-mail: acclaidlaw@juno.com

NEW YORK

Iroquois Arms Collectors Assn.
Bonnie Robinson, Show Secy., P.O. Box 142, Ransomville, NY 14131/716-791-4096

Mid-State Arms Coll. & Shooters Club
Jack Ackerman, 24 S. Mountain Terr., Binghamton, NY 13903

NORTH CAROLINA

North Carolina Gun Collectors Assn.
Jerry Ledford, 3231-7th St. Dr. NE, Hickory, NC 28601

OHIO

Ohio Gun Collectors Assn.
P.O. Box 9007, Maumee, OH 43537-9007/419-897-0861; Fax:419-897-0860

Shotshell Historical and Collectors Society
Madeline Bruemmer, 3886 Dawley Rd., Ravenna, OH 44266

The Stark Gun Collectors, Inc.
William I. Gann, 5666 Waynesburg Dr., Waynesburg, OH 44688

OREGON

Oregon Arms Collectors Assn., Inc.
Phil Bailey, P.O. Box 13000-A, Portland, OR 97213-0017/503-281-6864; off.:503-281-0918

Oregon Cartridge Collectors Assn.
Boyd Northrup, P.O. Box 285, Rhododendron, OR 97049

PENNSYLVANIA

Presque Isle Gun Collectors Assn.
James Welch, 156 E. 37 St., Erie, PA 16504

SOUTH CAROLINA

Belton Gun Club, Inc.
J.K. Phillips, 195 Phillips Dr., Belton, SC 29627

Gun Owners of South Carolina
Membership Div.: William Strozier, Secretary, P.O. Box 70, Johns Island, SC 29457-0070/803-762-3240; Fax:803-795-0711; e-mail:76053.222@compuserve.com

SOUTH DAKOTA

Dakota Territory Gun Coll. Assn., Inc.
Curt Carter, Castlewood, SD 57223

TENNESSEE

Smoky Mountain Gun Coll. Assn., Inc.
Hugh W. Yabro, President, P.O. Box 23225, Knoxville, TN 37933

Tennessee Gun Collectors Assn., Inc.
M.H. Parks, 3556 Pleasant Valley Rd., Nashville, TN 37204-3419

TEXAS

Houston Gun Collectors Assn., Inc.
P.O. Box 741429, Houston, TX 77274-1429

Texas Cartridge Collectors Assn., Inc.
Robert Mellichamp, Memb. Contact, 907 Shirkmere, Houston, TX 77008/713-869-0558

Texas Gun Collectors Assn.
Bob Eder, Pres., P.O. Box 12067, El Paso, TX 79913/915-584-8183

Texas State Rifle Assn.
1131 Rockingham Dr., Suite 101, Richardson, TX 75080-4326

VIRGINIA

Virginia Gun Collectors Assn., Inc.
Addison Hurst, Secy., 38802 Charlestown
Height, Waterford, VA 20197/540-882-3543

WASHINGTON

**Association of Cartridge Collectors on the
Pacific Northwest**
Robert Jardin, 14214 Meadowlark Drive KPN,
Gig Harbor, WA 98329

Washington Arms Collectors, Inc.
Joyce Boss, P.O. Box 389, Renton, WA,
98057-0389/206-255-8410

WISCONSIN

Great Lakes Arms Collectors Assn., Inc.
Edward C. Warnke, 2913 Woodridge Lane,
Waukesha, WI 53188

Wisconsin Gun Collectors Assn., Inc.
Lulita Zellmer, P.O. Box 181, Sussex, WI 53089

WYOMING

Wyoming Weapons Collectors
P.O. Box 284, Laramie, WY
82070/307-745-4652 or 745-9530

NATIONAL ORGANIZATIONS

Amateur Trapshooting Assn.
David D. Bopp, Exec. Director, 601 W. National
Rd., Vandalia, OH 45377/937-898-4638;
Fax:937-898-5472

American Airgun Field Target Assn.
5911 Cherokee Ave., Tampa, FL 33604

American Coon Hunters Assn.
Opal Johnston, P.O. Cadet, Route 1, Box 492,
Old Mines, MO 63630

American Custom Gunmakers Guild
Jan Billeb, Exec. Director, P.O. Box 812,
Burlington, IA 52601-0812/319-752-6114 (Phone
or Fax)

American Defense Preparedness Assn.
Two Colonial Place, 2101 Wilson Blvd., Suite
400, Arlington, VA 22201-3061

American Paintball League
P.O. Box 3561, Johnson City, TN
37602/800-541-9169

American Pistolsmiths Guild
Alex B. Hamilton, Pres., 1449 Blue Crest Lane,
San Antonio, TX 78232/210-494-3063

American Police Pistol & Rifle Assn.
3801 Biscayne Blvd., Miami, FL 33137

American Single Shot Rifle Assn.
Gary Staup, Secy., 709 Carolyn Dr., Delphos,
OH 45833/419-692-3866

American Society of Arms Collectors
George E. Weatherly, P.O. Box 2567,
Waxahachie, TX 75165

American Tactical Shooting Assn.(A.T.S.A.)
c/o Skip Gochenour, 2600 N. Third St.,
Harrisburg, PA 17110/717-233-0402;
Fax:717-233-5340

**Association of Firearm and Tool Mark
Examiners**
Lannie G. Emanuel, Secy., Southwest Institute
of Forensic Sciences, P.O. Box 35728, Dallas, TX
75235/214-920-5979; Fax:214-920-5928;
Membership Secy., Ann D. Jones, VA Div. of
Forensic Science, P.O. Box 999, Richmond, VA
23208/804-786-4706; Fax:804-371-8328

Boone & Crockett Club
250 Station Dr., Missoula, MT 59801-2753

Browning Collectors Assn.
Secretary:Scherrie L. Brennac, 2749 Keith Dr.,
Villa Ridge, MO 63089/314-742-0571

The Cast Bullet Assn., Inc.
Ralland J. Fortier, Editor, 4103 Foxcraft Dr.,
Traverse City, MI 49684

**Citizens Committee for the Right to Keep and
Bear Arms**
Natl. Hq., Liberty Park, 12500 NE Tenth Pl.,
Bellevue, WA 98005

Colt Collectors Assn.
25000 Highland Way, Los Gatos, CA 95030

Ducks Unlimited, Inc.
Natl. Headquarters, One Waterfowl Way,
Memphis, TN 38120

Fifty Caliber Shooters Assn.
11469 Olive St. Rd., Suite 50, St. Louis, MO
63141/601-475-7545;Fax:601-475-0452

Firearms Coalition/Neal Knox Associates
Box 6537, Silver Spring, MD
20906/301-871-3006

Firearms Engravers Guild of America
Rex C. Pedersen, Secy., 511 N. Rath Ave.,
Lundington, MI 49431/616-845-7695(Phone and
Fax)

Foundation for North American Wild Sheep
720 Allen Ave., Cody, WY 82414-3402/web site:
http://iigi.com/os/non/fnaws/fnaws.htm; e-mail:
fnaws@wyoming.com

Freedom Arms Collectors Assn.
P.O. Box 160302, Miami, FL 33116-0302

Garand Collectors Assn.
P.O. Box 181, Richmond, KY 40475

Golden Eagle Collectors Assn. (G.E.C.A.)
Chris Showler, 11144 Slate Creek Rd., Grass
Valley, CA 95945

Gun Owners of America
8001 Forbes Place, Suite 102, Springfield, VA
22151/703-321-8585

Handgun Hunters International
J.D. Jones, Director, P.O. Box 357 MAG,
Bloomingdale, OH 43910

Harrington & Richardson Gun Coll. Assn.
George L. Cardet, 330 S.W. 27th Ave., Suite 603,
Miami, FL 33135

High Standard Collectors' Assn.
John J. Stimson, Jr., Pres., 540 W. 92nd St.,
Indianapolis, IN 46260

**Hopkins & Allen Arms & Memorabilia Society
(HAAMS)**
P.O. Box 187, Delphos, OH 45833

International Ammunition Association, Inc.
C.R. Punnett, Secy., 8 Hillock Lane, Chadds
Ford, PA
19317/610-358-1285;Fax:610-358-1560

International Benchrest Shooters
Joan Borden, RR1, Box 250BB, Springville, PA
18844/717-965-2366

International Blackpowder Hunting Assn.
P.O. Box 1180, Glenrock, WY
82637/307-436-9817

IHMSA (Intl. Handgun Metallic Silhouette Assn.)
Frank Scotto, P.O. Box 5038, Meriden, CT 06451

**International Society of Mauser Arms
Collectors**
Michael Kindberg, Pres., P.O. Box 277,
Alpharetta, GA 30239-0277

**Jews for the Preservation of Firearms
Ownership (JPFO) 501(c)(3)**
2872 S. Wentworth Ave., Milwaukee, WI
53207/414-769-0760; Fax:414-483-8435

The Mannlicher Collectors Assn.
Thomas Seefeldt, Membership Secy., P.O. Box
1455, Kalispell, MT 59903

Marlin Firearms Collectors Assn., Ltd.
Dick Paterson, Secy., 407 Lincoln Bldg., 44 Main
St., Champaign, IL 61820

Miniature Arms Collectors/Makers Society, Ltd.
Ralph Koebbeman, Pres., 4910 Kilburn Ave.,
Rockford, IL 61101/815-964-2569

M1 Carbine Collectors Assn. (M1-CCA)
623 Apaloosa Ln., Gardnerville, NV 89410-7840

National Association of Buckskinners (NAB)
Territorial Dispatch—1800s Historical
Publication, 4701 Marion St., Suite 324,
Livestock Exchange Bldg., Denver, CO
80216/303-297-9671

**The National Association of Derringer
Collectors**
P.O. Box 20572, San Jose, CA 95160

**National Assn. of Federally Licensed Firearms
Dealers**
Andrew Molchan, 2455 E. Sunrise, Ft.
Lauderdale, FL 33304

National Association to Keep and Bear Arms
P.O. Box 78336, Seattle, WA 98178

National Automatic Pistol Collectors Assn.
Tom Knox, P.O. Box 15738, Tower Grove
Station, St. Louis, MO 63163

National Bench Rest Shooters Assn., Inc.
Pat Ferrell, 2835 Guilford Lane, Oklahoma City,
OK 73120-4404/405-842-9585; Fax:
405-842-9575

National Muzzle Loading Rifle Assn.
Box 67, Friendship, IN 47021

National Professional Paintball League (NPPL)
540 Main St., Mount Kisco, NY
10549/914-241-7400

National Reloading Manufacturers Assn.
One Centerpointe Dr., Suite 300, Lake Oswego,
OR 97035

National Rifle Assn. of America
11250 Waples Mill Rd., Fairfax, VA 22030

National Shooting Sports Foundation, Inc.
Robert T. Delfay, President, Flintlock Ridge
Office Center, 11 Mile Hill Rd., Newtown, CT
06470-2359/203-426-1320; FAX: 203-426-1087

National Skeet Shooting Assn.
Mike Hampton, Exec. Director, 5931 Roft Road,
San Antonio, TX 78253-9261

National Sporting Clays Association
5931 Roft Road, San Antonio, TX
78253-9261/800-877-5338

National Wild Turkey Federation, Inc.
P.O. Box 530, 770 Augusta Rd., Edgefield, SC
29824

North American Hunting Club
P.O. Box 3401, Minnetonka, MN
55343/612-936-9333; Fax: 612-936-9755

**North American Paintball Referees Association
(NAPRA)**
584 Cestaric Dr., Milpitas, CA 95035

North-South Skirmish Assn., Inc.
Stevan F. Meserve, Exec. Secretary, 507 N.
Brighton Court, Sterling, VA 20164-3919

Remington Society of America
Leon W. Wier Jr., President, 8268 Lone Feather
Ln., Las Vegas, NV 89123

Rocky Mountain Elk Foundation
P.O. Box 8249, Missoula, MT
59807-8249/406-523-4500;Fax:406-523-4581

Ruger Collector's Assn., Inc.
P.O. Box 240, Greens Farms, CT 06436

Safari Club International
Philip DeLone, Executive Dir., 4800 W. Gates
Pass Rd., Tucson, AZ 85745/602-620-1220

Sako Collectors Assn., Inc.
Jim Lutes, 202 N. Locust, Whitewater, KS 67154

Second Amendment Foundation
James Madison Building, 12500 NE 10th Pl.,
Bellevue, WA 98005

Single Action Shooting Society
1938 North Batavia St., Suite M, Orange, CA 92865/714-998-1899; Fax:714-998-1992

Smith & Wesson Collectors Assn.
George Linne, 2711 Miami St., St. Louis, MO 63118

The Society of American Bayonet Collectors
P.O. Box 234, East Islip, NY 11730-0234

Southern California Schuetzen Society
Dean Lillard, 34657 Ave. E., Yucaipa, CA 92399

Sporting Arms and Ammunition Manufacturers' Institute (SAAMI)
Flintlock Ridge Office Center, 11 Mile Hill Rd., Newtown, CT 06470-2359/203-426-4358; FAX: 203-426-1087

Sporting Clays of America (SCA)
Ron L. Blosser, Pres., 9257 Buckeye Rd., Sugar Grove, OH 43155-9632/614-746-8334; Fax: 614-746-8605

The Thompson/Center Assn.
Joe Wright, President, Box 792, Northboro, MA 01532/508-845-6960

U.S. Practical Shooting Assn./IPSC
Dave Thomas, P.O. Box 811, Sedro Woolley, WA 98284/360-855-2245

U.S. Revolver Assn.
Brian J. Barer, 40 Larchmont Ave., Taunton, MA 02780/508-824-4836

U.S. Shooting Team
U.S. Olympic Shooting Center, One Olympic Plaza, Colorado Springs, CO 80909/719-578-4670

The Varmint Hunters Assn., Inc.
Box 759, Pierre, SD 57501/Member Services 800-528-4868

Weatherby Collectors Assn., Inc.
P.O. Box 888, Ozark, MO 65721

The Wildcatters
P.O. Box 170, Greenville, WI 54942

Winchester Arms Collectors Assn.
Richard Berg, Executive Secy., P.O. Box 6754, Great Falls, MT 59406

The Women's Shooting Sports Foundation (WSSF)
1505 Highway 6 South, Suite 101, Houston, TX 77077

ARGENTINA

Asociacion Argentina de Coleccionistas de Armes y Municiones
Castilla de Correos No. 28, Succursal I B, 1401 Buenos Aires, Republica Argentina

AUSTRALIA

Antique & Historical Arms Collectors of Australia
P.O. Box 5654, GCMC Queensland 9726, Australia

The Arms Collector's Guild of Queensland Inc.
Ian Skennerton, P.O. Box 433, Ashmore City 4214, Queensland, Australia

Australian Cartridge Collectors Assn., Inc.
Bob Bennett, 126 Landscape Dr., E. Doncaster 3109, Victoria, Ausrtalia

Sporting Shooters Assn. of Australia, Inc.
P.O. Box 2066, Kent Town, SA 5071, Australia

CANADA

ALBERTA

Canadian Historical Arms Society
P.O. Box 901, Edmonton, Alb., Canada T5J 2L8

National Firearms Assn.
Natl. Hq: P.O. Box 1779, Edmonton, Alb., Canada T5J 2P1

BRITISH COLUMBIA

The Historical Arms Collectors of B.C. (Canada)
Harry Moon, Pres., P.O. Box 50117, South Slope RPO, Burnaby, BC V5J 5G3, Canada/604-438-0950; Fax:604-277-3646

ONTARIO

Association of Canadian Cartridge Collectors
Monica Wright, RR 1, Millgrove, ON, LOR IVO, Canada

Tri-County Antique Arms Fair
P.O. Box 122, RR #1, North Lancaster, Ont., Canada K0C 1Z0

EUROPE

BELGIUM

European Catridge Research Assn.
Graham Irving, 21 Rue Schaltin, 4900 Spa, Belgium/32.87.77.43.40; Fax:32.87.77.27.51

CZECHOSLOVAKIA

Spolecnost Pro Studium Naboju (Czech Cartridge Research Assn.)
JUDr. Jaroslav Bubak, Pod Homolko 1439, 26601 Beroun 2, Czech Republic

DENMARK

Aquila Dansk Jagtpatron Historic Forening (Danish Historical Cartridge Collectors Club)
Steen Elgaard Møller, Ulriksdalsvej 7, 4840 Nr. Alslev, Denmark 10045-53846218;Fax:004553846209

ENGLAND

Arms and Armour Society
Hon. Secretary A. Dove, P.O. Box 10232, London, 5W19 2ZD, England

Dutch Paintball Federation
Aceville Publ., Castle House 97 High Street, Colchester, Essex C01 1TH, England/011-44-206-564840

European Paintball Sports Foundation
c/o Aceville Publ., Castle House 97 High St., Colchester, Essex, C01 1TH, England

Historical Breechloading Smallarms Assn.
D.J. Penn M.A., Secy., P.O. Box 12778, London SE1 6BX, England.
Journal and newsletter are $23 a yr., including airmail.

National Rifle Assn.
(Great Britain) Bisley Camp, Brookwood, Woking Surrey GU24 OPB, England/01483.797777; Fax: 014730686275

United Kingdom Cartridge Club
Ian Southgate, 20 Millfield, Elmley Castle, Nr. Pershore, Worcestershire, WR10 3HR, England

FRANCE

STAC-Western Co.
3 Ave. Paul Doumer (N.311); 78360 Montesson, France/01.30.53-43-65; Fax: 01.30.53.19.10

GERMANY

Bund Deutscher Sportschützen e.v. (BDS)
Borsigallee 10, 53125 Bonn 1, Germany

Deutscher Schützenbund
Lahnstrasse 120, 65195 Wiesbaden, Germany

SPAIN

Asociacion Espanola de Colleccionistas de Cartuchos (A.E.C.C.)
Secretary: Apdo. Correos No. 1086, 2880-Alcala de Henares (Madrid), Spain. President: Apdo. Correos No. 682, 50080 Zaragoza, Spain

SWEDEN

Scandinavian Ammunition Research Assn.
Box 107, 77622 Hedemora, Sweden

NEW ZEALAND

New Zealand Cartridge Collectors Club
Terry Castle, 70 Tiraumea Dr., Pakuranga, Auckland, New Zealand

New Zealand Deerstalkers Assn.
P.O. Box 6514 TE ARO, Wellington, New Zealand

SOUTH AFRICA

Historical Firearms Soc. of South Africa
P.O. Box 145, 7725 Newlands, Republic of South Africa

Republic of South Africa Cartridge Collectors Assn.
Arno Klee, 20 Eugene St., Malanshof Randburg, Gauteng 2194, Republic of South Africa

S.A.A.C.A. (Southern Africa Arms and Ammunition Assn.)
Gauteng Office: P.O. Box 7597, Weltevreden Park, 1715, Republic of South Africa/011-679-1151; Fax: 011-679-1131; e-mail: saaaca@iafrica.com. Kwa-Zulu Natal office: P.O. Box 4065, Northway, Kwazulu-Natal 4065, Republic of South Africa

SAGA (S.A. Gunowners' Assn.)
P.O. Box 35203, Northway, Kwazulu-Natal 4065, Republic of South Africa

1999
GUN DIGEST
DIRECTORY OF THE
ARMS TRADE

The **Product Directory** contains 53 product categories. Note that in the Product Directory, a black bullet preceeding a manufacturer's name indicates the availability of a Warranty Service Center address, which can be found on page 437.

The **Manufacturers' Directory** alphabetically lists the manufacturers with their addresses, phone numbers, FAX numbers and Internet addresses, if available.

DIRECTORY OF THE ARMS TRADE INDEX

AMMUNITION, COMMERCIAL

ACTIV Industries, Inc.
American Ammunition
Arizona Ammunition, Inc.
Arms Corporation of the Philippines
A-Square Co., Inc.
Atlantic Rose, Inc.
Bergman & Williams
Big Bear Arms & Sporting Goods, Inc.
Black Hills Ammunition, Inc.
Blammo Ammo
Blount, Inc., Sporting Equipment Div.
Brenneke KG, Wilhelm
Brown Dog Ent.
Buffalo Bullet Co., Inc.
BulletMakers Workshop, The
Bull-X, Inc.
California Magnum
Casull Arms Corp.
CBC
Clean Shot Technologies Inc.
Colorado Sutlers Arsenal
Cor-Bon Bullet & Ammo Co.
Cubic Shot Shell Co. Inc.
Cumberland States Arsenal
Dead Eye's Sport Center
Delta Frangible Ammunition, LLC
Denver Bullets, Inc.
Diana
Dynamit Nobel-RWS, Inc.
Effebi SNC, Dr. Franco Beretta
Eldorado Cartridge Corp.
Eley Ltd.
Elite Ammunition
Estate Cartridge, Inc.
Executive Protection Institue
Federal Cartridge Co.
Fiocchi of America, Inc.
4W Ammunition
Hunters Supply
Garrett Cartridges, Inc.
Garthwaite Pistolsmith, Jim
Gibbs Rifle Co., Inc.
Glaser Safety slug Inc.
Goldcoast Reloaders, Inc.
Groenewold, John
Gun City Inc
Hansen & Co.
Hansen Cartridge Co.
Hart & Son, Inc., Robert W.
Hirtenberger Aktiengesellschaft
Hornady Mfg. Co.
ICI-America

IMI
Ion Industries Inc.
Israel Military Industries Ltd.
Jones, J.D.
Keng's Firearms Specialty, Inc.
Kent Cartridge Mfg. Co. Ltd.
Lapua Ltd.
Lightfield Ammunition Corp.
Lock's Philadelphia Gun Exchange
M&D Munitions Ltd.
MagSafe Ammo Co.
Maionchi-L.M.I.
Markell, Inc.
Mathews & Son, Inc., George E.
McBros Rifle Co.
Men—Metallwerk Elisenhuette, GmbH
Mullins Ammunition
NECO
New England Ammunition Co.
Oklahoma Ammunition Co.
Parker & Sons Gunsmithing
Omark Industries
Outdoor Sports Hdqtr
Pacific Cartridge, Inc.
Paragon Sales & Serv
PMC/Eldorado Cartridge Corp.
Polywad, Inc.
Pony Express Reloaders
Precision Delta Corp.
Pro Load Ammunition, Inc.
R.E.I.
Remington Arms Co., Inc.
Rucker Dist. Inc.
RWS
Slug Group, Inc.
Spence, George W.
Talon Mfg. Co., Inc.
TCCI
Thompson Bullet Lube Co.
3-D Ammunition & Bullets
3-Ten Corp.
USAC
Valor Corp.
Victory USA
Vihtavuori Oy/Kaltron-Pettibone
Voere-KGH m.b.H.
Vom Hoffe
Weatherby, Inc.
Westley Richards & Co.
Widener's Reloading & Shooting
  Supply, Inc.
Winchester Div., Olin Corp.
Zero Ammunition Co., Inc.

AMMUNITION, CUSTOM

Accuracy Unlimited (Littleton, CO)
AFSCO Ammunition
Allred Bullet Co.
American Derringer Corp.
Arizona Ammunition, Inc.
Arms Corporation of the Philippines
A-Square Co., Inc.
Atlantic Rose, Inc.
Belding Custom Gun Shop
Berger Bullets, Ltd.
Black Hills Ammunition, Inc.
Blue Mountain Bullets
Bruno Shooters Supply
Brynin, Milton
Buckskin Bullet Co.
BulletMakers Workshop, The
Calhoon Varmint Bullets, James
Carroll Bullets
CBC
Country Armourer, The
Cubic Shot Shell Co., Inc.
Custom Tackle and Ammo
Dakota Arms, Inc.
Dead Eye's Sport Center
Delta Frangible Ammunition, LLC
DKT, Inc.
Elite Ammunition
Estate Cartridge, Inc.
4W Ammunition
Freedom Arms, Inc.
GDL Enterprises
GOEX, Inc.
Gonzalez Guns, Ramon B
"Gramps" Antique Cartridges
Granite Custom Bullets

Grayback Wildcats
Gun Accessories
Heidenstrom Bullets
Hirtenberger Aktiengesellschaft
Hoelscher, Virgil
Horizons Unlimited
Hornady Mfg. Co.
Hunters Supply
IMI
Israel Military Industries Ltd.
Jensen Bullets
Jensen's Custom Ammunition
Jensen's Firearms Academy
Kaswer Custom, Inc.
Keeler, R.H.
Kent Cartridge Mfg. Co. Ltd.
KJM Fabritek, Inc.
L A R Mfg. Inc.
Lindsley Arms Cartridge Co.
Linebaugh Custom Sixguns
MagSafe Ammo Co.
MAST Technology
McBros Rifle Co.
McKillen & Heyer, Inc.
McMurdo, Lynn
Men-Metallwerk Elisenhuette, GmbH
Milstor Corp.
Mountain Rifles Inc.
Mullins Ammunition
Naval Ordnance Works
NECO
Northern Precision Custom Swaged
  Bullets
Nygord Precision Products
Old Western Scrounger, Inc.

Oklahoma Ammunition Company
Precision Delta Corp.
Precision Munitions, Inc.
Precision Reloading, Inc.
Professional Hunter Supplies
R.E.I.
Sanders Custom Gun Service
Sandia Die & Cartridge Co.
SOS Products Co.
Specialty Gunsmithing
Spence, George W.
Spencer's Custom Guns
Star Custom Bullets

State Arms Gun Co.
Stewart's Gunsmithing
Talon Mfg. Co., Inc.
3-D Ammunition & Bullets
3-Ten Corp.
Unmussig Bullets, D.L.
Vitt/Boos
Vom Hoffe
Vulpes Ventures, Inc.
Warren Muzzleloading Co., Inc.
Weaver Arms Corp. Gun Shop
Worthy Products, Inc.
Yukon Arms Classic Ammunition

AMMUNITION, FOREIGN

AFSCO Ammunition
Armscorp USA, Inc.
A-Square Co., Inc.
Atlantic Rose, Inc.
Beeman Precision Airguns
BulletMakers Workshop, The
B-West Imports, Inc.
CBC
Cheddite France, S.A.
Cubic Shot Shell Co., Inc.
Dead Eye's Sport Center
Diana
DKT, Inc.
Dynamit Nobel-RWS, Inc.
E Arthur Brown Co
Fiocchi of America, Inc.
First, Inc., Jack
Fisher Enterprises, Inc.
Fisher, R. Kermit
FN Herstal
Forgett Jr., Valmore J.
Gibbs Rifle Co., Inc.
GOEX, Inc.
Groenewold, John
Hansen & Co.
Hansen Cartridge Co.
Heidenstrom Bullets
Hirtenberger Aktiengesellschaft
Hornady Mfg. Co.
IMI
IMI Services USA, Inc.

Israel Military Industries Ltd.
JägerSport, Ltd.
K.B.I., Inc.
Keng's Firearms Specialty, Inc.
Magnum Research, Inc.
MagSafe Ammo Co.
MagTech Recreational Products, Inc.
Maionchi-L.M.I.
MAST Technology
Merkuria Ltd.
Mullins Ammunition
Naval Ordnance Works
Oklahoma Ammunition Co.
Old Western Scrounger, Inc.
Paragon Sales & Serv
Paul Company Inc.
Petro-Explo, Inc.
Precision Delta Corp.
R.E.T. Enterprises
RWS
Sentinel Arms
Southern Ammunition Co., Inc.
Spence, George W.
Stratco, Inc.
SwaroSports, Inc.
T.F.C. S.p.A.
USA Sporting Inc.
Vom Hoffe
Vihtavuori Oy/Kaltron-Pettibone
Yukon Arms Classic Ammunition

AMMUNITION COMPONENTS—BULLETS, POWDER, PRIMERS, CASES

Acadian Ballistic Specialties
Accuracy Unlimited (Littleton, CO)
Accurate Arms Co., Inc.
Accurate Bullet Co.
Action Bullets, Inc.
ACTIV Industries, Inc.
Alaska Bullet Works, Inc.
Alliant Techsystems
Allred Bullet Co.
Alpha LaFranck Enterprises
American Products Inc.
Arco Powder
Armfield Custom Bullets
A-Square Co., Inc.
Atlantic Rose, Inc.
Baer's Hollows
Ballard Built
Ballistic Products, Inc.
Barnes Bullets, Inc.
Beartooth Bullets
Beeline Custom Bullets Limited
Bell Reloading, Inc.
Belt MTN Arms
Berger Bullets, Ltd.
Bergman & Williams
Berry's Mfg., Inc.
Bertram Bullet Co.
Big Bore Bullets of Alaska
Big Bore Express
Bitterroot Bullet Co.
Black Belt Bullets
Black Hills Shooters Supply
Black Powder Products
Blount, Inc., Sporting Equipment Div.
Brenneke KG, Wilhelm
Briese Bullet Co., Inc.
Brown Co., E. Arthur
Brown Dog Ent.
BRP, Inc.
Bruno Shooters Supply
Buck Stix—SOS Products Co.

Buckeye Custom Bullets
Buckskin Bullet Co.
Buffalo Arms Co.
Buffalo Rock Shooters Supply
Bullet, Inc.
Bullseye Bullets
Bull-X, Inc.
Butler Enterprises
Buzztail Brass
Calhoon Varmint Bullets, James
Canyon Cartridge Corp.
Carnahan Bullets
Cascade Bullet Co., Inc.
Casull Arms Corp.
Cast Performance Bullet Company
CCI
Champion's Choice, Inc.
Cheddite France, S.A.
CheVron Bullets
C.J. Ballistics, Inc.
Colorado Sutlers Arsenal
Competitor Corp., Inc.
Cook Engineering Service
Cor-Bon Bullet & Ammo Co.
Cumberland States Arsenal
Cummings Bullets
Curtis Cast Bullets
Curtis Gun Shop
Custom Bullets by Hoffman
D&J Bullet Co. & Custom Gun Shop,
  Inc.
Dakota Arms, Inc.
Dixie Gun Works, Inc.
DKT, Inc.
Dohring Bullets
Double A Ltd.
Eichelberger Bullets, Wm.
Eldorado Cartridge Corp.
Elkhorn Bullets
Epps, Ellwood
Federal Cartridge Co.

Fiocchi of America, Inc.
Forkin, Ben
4W Ammunition
Fowler, Bob
Fowler Bullets
Foy Custom Bullets
Freedom Arms, Inc.
Fusilier Bullets
G&C Bullet Co., Inc.
Gander Mountain, Inc.
Gehmann, Walter
GOEX, Inc.
Golden Bear Bullets
Gonic Bullet Works
Gotz Bullets
"Gramps" Antique Cartridges
Granite Custom Bullets
Grayback Wildcats
Green Mountain Rifle Barrel Co., Inc.
Grier's Hard Cast Bullets
Group Tight Bullets
Gun City
Hammets VLD Bullets
Hardin Specialty Dist.
Harris Enterprises
Harrison Bullets
Hart & Son, Inc., Robert W.
Hawk, Inc.
Hawk Laboratories, Inc.
Haydon Shooters' Supply, Russ
Heidenstrom Bullets
Hercules, Inc.
Hi-Performance Ammunition Company
Hirtenberger Aktiengesellschaft
Hobson Precision Mfg. Co.
Hodgdon Powder Co.
Hornady Mfg. Co.
HT Bullets
Huntington Die Specialties
Hunters Supply
IMI Services USA, Inc.
Imperial Magnum Corp.
IMR Powder Co.
J-4, Inc.
J&D Components
J&L Superior Bullets
Jensen Bullets
Jensen's Firearms Academy
Jericho Tool & Die Co. Inc.
Jester Bullets
JLK Bullets
JRP Custom Bullets
Ka Pu Kapili
Kasmarsik Bullets
Kaswer Custom, Inc.
Keith's Bullets
Ken's Kustom Kartridge
Keng's Firearms Specialty, Inc.
Kent Cartridge Mfg. Co. Ltd.
KJM Fabritek, Inc.
KLA Enterprises
Knight Rifles
Lage Uniwad
Lapua Ltd.
Lawrence Brand Shot
Legend Products Corp.
Liberty Shooting Supplies
Lightfield Ammunition Corp.
Slug Group, Inc.
Lightning Performance Innovations, Inc.
Lindsley Arms Cartridge Co.
Littleton, J.F.
Loweth, Richard H.R.
Lomont Precision Bullets
M&D Munitions Ltd.
Magnus Bullets
Maine Custom Bullets
Maionchi-L.M.I.
Marchmon Bullets
Markesbery Muzzle Loaders, Inc.
MarMik, Inc.
Marple & Associates, Dick
MAST Technology
Mathews & Son, Inc., George E.
McMurdo, Lynn
Meister Bullets
Men—Metallwerk Elisenhuette, GmbH
Merkuria Ltd.
Michael's Antiques
Mitchell Bullets, R.F.
MI-TE Bullets
Modern Muzzleloading, Inc.
MoLoc Bullets

Montana Armory, Inc.
Montana Precision Swaging
Mountain State Muzzleloading Supplies, Inc.
Mt. Baldy Bullet Co.
Mulhern, Rick
Murmur Corp.
Mushroom Express Bullet Co.
Nagel's Bullets
National Bullet Co.
Naval Ordnance Works
Navy Arms Co.
Necromancer Industries, Inc.
Norma
North American Shooting Systems
North Devon Firearms Services
Northern Precision Custom Swaged Bullets
Nosler, Inc.
Oklahoma Ammunition Co.
Old Wagon Bullets
Old Western Scrounger, Inc.
Ordnance Works, The
Oregon Trail Bullet Company
Pacific Cartridge, Inc.
Pacific Rifle Co.
Page Custom Bullets
Patrick Bullets
Pease Accuracy, Bob
Petro-Explo, Inc.
Phillippi Custom Bullets, Justin
Pinetree Bullets
PMC/Eldorado Cartridge Corp.
Polywad, Inc.
Pomeroy, Robert
Precision Components
Precision Components and Guns
Precision Delta Corp.
Precision Munitions, Inc.
Prescott Projectile Co.
Price Bullets, Patrick W.
PRL Bullets
Professional Hunter Supplies
Rainier Ballistics Corp.
Ranger Products
Red Cedar Precision Mfg.
Redwood Bullet Works
Reloading Specialties, Inc.
Remington Arms Co., Inc.
Rhino
Rifle Works & Armory
R.I.S. Co., Inc.
R.M. Precision, Inc.
Robinson H.V. Bullets
Rolston, Inc., Fred W.
Rubright Bullets
SAECO
Scharch Mfg., Inc.
Schmidtman Custom Ammunition
Schneider Bullets
Schroeder Bullets
Scot Powder
Seebeck Assoc., R.E.
Shappy Bullets
Shilen, Inc.
Sharps Arms Co. Inc., C.
Sierra Bullets
SOS Products Co.
Specialty Gunsmithing
Speer Products
Spencer's Custom Guns
Stanley Bullets
Star Ammunition, Inc.
Star Custom Bullets
Stark's Bullet Mfg.
Starke Bullet Company
Stewart's Gunsmithing
Swift Bullet Co.
Talon Mfg. Co., Inc.
Taracorp Industries
TCCI
TCSR
T.F.C. S.p.A.
Thompson Precision
3-D Ammunition & Bullets
TMI Products
Traditions, Inc.
Trico Plastics
Trophy Bonded Bullets, Inc.
True Flight Bullet Co.
Tucson Mold, Inc.
Unmussig Bullets, D.L.
USAC
Vann Custom Bullets
Vihtavuori Oy/Kaltron-Pettibone

Vincent's Shop
Viper Bullet and Brass Works
Vom Hoffe
Warren Muzzleloading Co., Inc.
Watson Trophy Match Bullets
Weatherby, Inc.
Western Nevada West Coast Bullets
Widener's Reloading & Shooting Supply
Williams Bullet Co., J.R.
Winchester Div., Olin Corp.

ANTIQUE ARMS DEALERS

Ackerman & Co.
Ad Hominem
Antique American Firearms
Antique Arms Co.
Aplan Antiques & Art, James O.
Armoury, Inc., The
Bear Mountain Gun & Tool
Bob's Tactical Indoor Shooting Range & Gun Shop
British Antiques
Buckskin Machine Works
Buffalo Arms Co.
Bustani, Leo R.
Cape Outfitters
Carlson, Douglas R.
Chadick's Ltd.
Chambers Flintlocks Ltd., Jim
Champlin Firearms, Inc.
Chuck's Gun Shop
Classic Guns, Inc.
Clements' Custom Leathercraft, Chas
Cole's Gun Works
Colonial Arms, Inc.
D&D Gunsmiths, Ltd.
Dixie Gun Works, Inc.
Dixon Muzzleloading Shop, Inc.
Duffy, Charles E.
Dyson & Son Ltd., Peter
Ed's Gun House
Enguix Import-Export
Fagan & Co., William
Fanzoj GmbH
Fish Mfg. Gunsmith Sptg. Co., Marshall F.
Flayderman & Co., N.
Forgett Jr., Valmore J.
Frielich Police Equipment
Fulmer's Antique Firearms, Chet
Getz Barrel Co.
Glass, Herb
Goergen's Gun Shop Inc.
Golden Age Arms Co.
Gun Hunter Trading

Gun Room, The
Gun Room Press, The
Guncraft Sports, Inc.
Gun Works, The
Guns Antique & Modern DBA/Charles E. Duffy
Hallowell & Co.
Hamilton, Jim
Handgun Press
HandiCrafts Unltd.
Hansen & Co.
Hunkeler, A.
Johns Master Engraver, Bill
Kelley's
Knight's Manufacturing
Ledbetter Airguns, Riley
LeFever Arms Co., Inc.
Lever Arms Service Ltd.
Log Cabin Shop Inc.
Mandall Shooting Supplies, Inc.
Martin's Gun Shop
Montana Outfitters
Museum of Historical Arms, Inc.
Muzzleloaders Etcetera, Inc.
New England Arms Co.
Pony Express Sport Shop, Inc.
Powder Horn Antiques
Retting, Inc., Martin B.
R.G.-G., Inc.
Samco Global Arms
Scott Fine Guns, Inc., Thad
Shootin' Shack, The
Steves House of Guns
Stott's Creek Armory, Inc.
Strawbridge, Victor W.
Vic's Gun Refinishing
Vintage Arms, Inc.
Wallace, Terry
Westley Richards & Co.
Wiest, M.C.
Winchester Sutler, Inc., The
• Wood, Frank
Yearout, Lewis E.

Windjammer Tournament Wads, Inc.
Winkle Bullets
Woodleigh
Worthy Products, Inc.
Wosenitz VHP, Inc.
Wyant Bullets
Wyoming Bonded Bullets
Wyoming Custom Bullets
Yukon Arms Classic Ammunition
Zero Ammunition Co., Inc.

APPRAISERS—GUNS, ETC.

Antique Arms Co.
Armoury, Inc., The
Arundel Arms & Ammunition, Inc., A.
Barsotti, Bruce
Beitzinger, George
Blue Book Publications, Inc.
Bob's Tactical Indoor Shooting Range & Gun Shop
British Antiques
Bustani, Leo
Butterfield & Butterfield
Camilli, Lou
Cannon's, Andy Cannons
Cape Outfitters
Chadick's Ltd.
Champlin Firearms, Inc.
Christie's East
Clark Firearms Engraving
Classic Guns, Inc.
Cleland's Outdoor World
Clements' Custom Leathercraft, Chas
Cole's Gun Works
Colonial Arms, Inc.
Colonial Repair
Corry, John
Custom Tackle and Ammo
D&D Gunsmiths, Ltd.
Dilliott Gunsmithing, Inc.
DGR Custom Rifles
Dixon Muzzleloading Shop, Inc.
Duane's Gun Repair
Ed's Gun House
Epps, Ellwood
Eversull Co., Inc., K.
Fagan & Co., William

Ferris Firearms
Fish Mfg. Gunsmith Sptg. Co, Marshall F.
Flayderman & Co., Inc., N.
Forgett, Valmore J., Jr.
Forty Five Ranch Enterprises
Francotte & Cie S.A., Auguste
Frontier Arms Co., Inc.
Gene's Custom Guns
Getz Barrel Co.
Gillmann, Edwin
Golden Age Arms Co.
Gonzalez Guns, Ramon B.
Griffin & Howe, Inc.
Goergen's Gun Shop Inc.
Gun City
Gun Hunter Trading Co.
Gun Room Press, The
Gun Shop, The
Guncraft Sports, Inc.
Guns
Hallberg Gunsmith, Fritz
Hallowell & Co.
Hammans, Charles E.
Handgun Press
HandiCrafts Unltd.
Hank's Gun Shop
Hansen & Co.
Hughes, Steven Dodd
Irwin, Campbell H.
Island Pond Gun Shop
Jackalope Gun Shop
Jaeger, Inc., Paul/Dunn's
Jensen's Custom Ammunition
Kelley's

LaRocca Gun Works, Inc.
Ledbetter Airguns, Riley
LeFever Arms Co., Inc.
L.L. Bean, Inc.
Log Cabin Shop Inc.
Mac's .45 Shop
Madis, George
Mandall Shooting Supplies, Inc.
Martin's Gun Shop
McCann Industries
McCann's Muzzle-Gun Works
Montana Outfitters
Museum of Historical Arms, Inc.
Muzzleloaders Etcetera, Inc.
Navy Arms Co.
New England Arms Co.
Nitex, Inc.
Orvis Co., The
Pasadena Gun Center
Pentheny de Pentheny
Perazzi USA, Inc.
Peterson Gun Shop, Inc., A.W.
Pettinger Books, Gerald
Pony Express Sport Shop, Inc.
Powder Horn Antiques

R.E.T. Enterprises
Retting, Inc., Martin B.
Richards, John
River Road Sporting Clays
Rogers Gunsmithing, Bob
Safari Outfitters Ltd.
Scott Fine Guns, Inc., Thad
Shootin' Shack, Inc.
Steger, James R.
Stott's Creek Armory, Inc.
Stratco, Inc.
Strawbridge, Victor W.
Swampfire Shop, The
Thurston Sports, Inc.
Vic's Gun Refinishing
Walker Arms Co. Inc.
Wayne Firearms for Collectors and
  Investors, James
Wells Custom Gunsmith, R.A.
Whildin & Sons Ltd., E.H.
Wiest, M.C.
Williams Shootin' Iron Service
Winchester Sutler, Inc., The
Wood, Frank
Yearout, Lewis E.
Yee, Mike

AUCTIONEERS—GUNS, ETC.

Buck Stix—SOS Products Co.
Butterfield & Butterfield
Christie's East
Fagan & Co, William

Kelley's
"Little John's" Antique Arms
Sotheby's

BOOKS (Publishers and Dealers)

Accurate Arms Co. Inc.
American Handgunner Magazine
Armory Publications, Inc.
Arms & Armour Press
Ballistic Products, Inc.
Barnes Bullets, Inc.
Beeman Precision Airguns
Blackhawk West
Blacksmith Corp.
Blacktail Mountain Books
Blue Book Publications, Inc.
Blue Ridge Machinery & Tools, Inc.
Boone's Custom Ivory Grips
Brown Co., E. Arthur
Brownell Checkering Tools, W.E.
Brownell's, Inc.
Bullet'n Press
Calibre Press, Inc.
Cape Outfitters
Clearview Products
Colonial Repair
Colorado Sutlers Arsenal
Corbin Mfg. & Supply, Inc.
Cumberland States Arsenal
DBI Books
Dixon Muzzleloading Shop Inc.
Flores Publications, Inc., J.
Forgett Jr., Valmore J.
Golden Age Arms Co.
Groenewold, John
Gun City
Gun Hunter Books
Gun Hunter Trading Co.
Gun List
Gun Parts Corp., The
Gun Room Press, The
Gun Works, The
Guncraft Books
Guncraft Sports, Inc.
Gunnerman Books
GUNS Magazine
H&P Publishing
Handgun Press
Harris Publications
Hawk Laboratories, Inc.
Hawk, Inc.
Heritage/VSP Gun Books
High North Products Inc.
Hodgdon Powder Co., Inc.
Home Shop Machinist, The
Hornady Mfg. Co.
Hungry Horse Books
I.D.S.A. Books
Info-Arm
Ironside International Publishers, Inc.
Koval Knives
Krause Publications, Inc.
Lapua Ltd.

Lethal Force Institute
Lyman Products Corp.
Madis Books
Magma Enginerring Co.
Marmik Inc.
Martin Bookseller, J.
McKee Publications
Montana Armory, Inc.
Mountain South
Mulberry House Publishing
New Win Publishing, Inc.
NgraveR Co., The
OK Weber, Inc.
Outdoor Sports Hdqtr
Outdoorsman's Bookstore, The
Paintball Games International
  Magazine (Aceville Publications)
Petersen Publishing Co.
Pettinger Books, Gerald
Police Bookshelf
Precision Shooting, Inc.
PWL Gunleather
Remington Double Shotguns
R.G.-G., Inc.
Riling Arms Books Co., Ray
Rocky Mountain Wildlife Products
Rutgers Book Center
S&S Firearms
Safari Press, Inc.
Saunders Gun & Machine Shop
Semmer, Charles
Sharps Arms Co. Inc., C.
Shootin' Accessories, Ltd.
Sierra Bullets
SPG, Inc.
Stackpole Books
Stewart Game Calls, Inc., Johnny
Stoeger Industries
Stoeger Publishing Co.
"Su-Press-On" Inc.
Thomas, Charles C.
Track of the Wolf, Inc.
Trafalgar Square
Trotman, Ken
Tru-Balance Knife Co.
Vintage Industries, Inc.
VSP Publishers
WAMCO—New Mexico
Wells Creek Knife & Gun Work
Wilderness Sound Products Ltd.
Williams Gun Sight Co.
Winchester Press
Wolfe Publishing Co.
Wolf's Western Traders

BULLET AND CASE LUBRICANTS

Blackhawk West
Bonanza
Brown Co., E. Arthur
Camp-Cap Products Division
Chem-Pak, Inc.
C-H Tool & Die Corp.
Cooper-Woodward
CVA
Elkhorn Bullets
E-Z-Way Systems
Forster Products
4-D Custom Die Co.
Guardsman Products
HEBB Resources
Hollywood Engineering
Hornady Mfg. Co.
Imperial
Knoell, Doug
Le Clear Industries

Lee Precision, Inc.
Lestrom Laboratories, Inc.
Lithi Bee Bullet Lube
M&N Bullet Lube
Michaels of Oregon Co.
MI-TE Bullets
NECO
Paco's
RCBS
Reardon Products
Rooster Laboratories
Shay's Gunsmithing
Small Custom Mould & Bullet Co.
Tamarack Products, Inc.
Uncle Mike's
Warren Muzzleloading Co., Inc.
Widener's Reloading & Shooting
  Supply, Inc.
Young Country Arms

BULLET SWAGE DIES AND TOOLS

Brynin, Milton
Bullet Swaging Supply, Inc.
Camdex, Inc.
Corbin Mfg. & Supply, Inc.
Cumberland Arms
Eagan, Donald V.
Heidenstrom Bullets

Holland's
Hollywood Engineering
Necromancer Industries, Inc.
Niemi Engineering, W.B.
North Devon Firearms Services
Rorschach Precision Products
Sport Flite Manufacturing Co.

CARTRIDGES FOR COLLECTORS

Ad Hominem
Cameron's
Campbell, Dick
Cartridge Transfer Group
Cole's Gun Works
Colonial Repair
Country Armourer, The
de Coux, Pete
DGR Custom Rifles
Duane's Gun Repair
Enguix Import-Export
Epps, Ellwood
First, Inc., Jack
Fitz Pistol Grip Co.
Forty Five Ranch Enterprises
Goergen's Gun Shop, Inc.

"Gramps" Antique Cartridges
Grayback Wildcats
Gun City
Gun Parts Corp., The
Gun Room Press, The
Mandall Shooting Supplies, Inc.
MAST Technology
Michael's Antiques
Montana Outfitters
Pasadena Gun Center
San Francisco Gun Exchange
SOS Products Co.
Stone Enterprises, Ltd.
Ward & Van Valkenburg
Yearout, Lewis E.

CASES, CABINETS, RACKS AND SAFES—GUN

Alco Carrying Cases
All Rite Products, Inc.
Allen Co., Bob
Allen Co., Inc.
Allen Sportswear, Bob
Alumna Sport by Dee Zee
American Display Co.
American Security Products Co.
Americase
Ansen Enterprises
Arkfeld Mfg. & Dist. Co., Inc.
Art Jewel Enterprises Ltd.
Ashby Turkey Calls
Bagmaster Mfg., Inc.
Barramundi Corp.
BEC, Inc.
Berry's Mfg., Inc.
Big Sky Racks, Inc.
Big Spring Enterprises "Bore Stores"
Bill's Custom Cases
Bison Studios
Black Sheep Brand
Boyt
Brauer Bros. Mfg. Co.
Brown, H.R.
Browning Arms Co.
Bucheimer, J.M.
Bushmaster Hunting & Fishing
Cannon Safe, Inc.
Chipmunk
Cobalt Mfg. Inc.
CONKKO
Connecticut Shotgun Mfg. Co.
D&L Industries
Dara-Nes, Inc.
Dayson Arms, Ltd.
Deepeeka Exports Pvt. Ltd.
D.J. Marketing
Doskocil Mfg. Co., Inc.
DTM International, Inc.
Elk River, Inc.
English, Inc., A.G.
Enhanced Presentations, Inc.

Eutaw Co., Inc.,, The
Eversull Co., Inc. K.
Fort Knox Security Products
Frontier Safe Co.
Galati Internationl
GALCO International Ltd.
Granite Custom Bullets
Gun Locker
Gun-Ho Sports Cases
Hafner Creations, Inc.
Hall Plastics, Inc., John
Hastings Barrels
Homak
Hoppe's Div.
Huey Gun Cases
Hugger Hooks Co.
Hunter Co., Inc.
Impact Case Co.
Johanssons Vapentillbehor, Bert
Johnston Bros.
Jumbo Sports Products
Kalispel Case Line
Kane Products, Inc.
KK Air International
Knock on Wood Antiques
Kolpin Mfg., Inc.
Lakewood Products, LLC
Liberty Safe
Marsh, Mike
Maximum Security Corp.
McWelco Products
Morton Booth Co.
MPC
MTM Molded Products Co., Inc.
Nalpak
National Security Safe Co., Inc.
Necessary Concepts, Inc.
Nesci Enterprises, Inc.
Oregon Arms, Inc.
Outa-Site Gun Carriers
Outdoor Connection, Inc., The
Palmer Security Products
Penguin Industries, Inc.

Perazzi USA, Inc.
Pflumm Mfg. Co.
Poburka, Philip
Powell & Son (Gunmakers) Ltd.,
    William
Protecto Plastics
Prototech Industries, Inc.
Quality Arms, Inc.
Schulz Industries
Silhouette Leathers
Southern Security

Sportsman's Communicators
Sun Welding Safe Co.
Surecase Co., The
Sweet Home, Inc.
Tinks & Ben Lee Hunting Products
Waller & Son, Inc., W.
WAMCO, Inc.
Wilson Case, Inc.
Woodstream
Zanotti Armor, Inc.
Ziegel Engineering

CHOKE DEVICES, RECOIL ABSORBERS AND RECOIL PADS

Accuright
Action Products, Inc.
Allen Co., Bob
Allen Sportswear, Bob
Answer Products Co.
Arms Ingenuity Co.
Baer Custom, Inc., Les
Baker, Stan
Bansner's Gunsmithing Specialties
Bartlett Engineering
Briley Mfg., Inc.
Brooks Tactical Systems
Brownells Inc.
B-Square Co., Inc.
Buffer Technologies
Bull Mountain Rifle Co.
C&H Research
Cape Outfitters
Cation
Chuck's Gun Shop
Clearview Products
Colonial Arms, Inc.
Connecticut Shotgun Mfg. Co.
CRR, Inc./Marble's Inc.
Danuser Machine Co.
Dayson Arms Ltd.
Dever Co., Jack
Dina Arms Corporation
Elsen, Inc., Pete
Galazan
Gentry Custom Gunmaker, David
Graybill's Gun Shop
Guns
ings Barrels
Holland's
I.N.C., Inc.

Jackalope Gun Shop
Jaeger, Inc., Paul/Dunn's
J.P. Enterprises, Inc.
Kick Eez
Lawson Co., Harry
London Guns Ltd.
Lyman Products Corp.
Mag-Na-Port International, Inc.
Marble Arms
Mathews & Son, Inc., George E.
Meadow Industries
Menck, Gunsmith Inc., T.W.
Michaels of Oregon Co.
Middlebrooks Custom Shop
Morrow, Bud
Nelson/Weather-rite, Inc.
Nu-Line Guns Inc.
One Of A Kind
Original Box, Inc.
Palsa Outdoor Products
PAST Sporting Goods, Inc.
Pro-Port Ltd.
Protektor Model
Que Industries
R.M. Precision, Inc.
Shell Shack
Shotguns Unlimited
Simmons Gun Repair, Inc.
Spencer's Custom Guns
Stone Enterprises Ltd.
3-Ten Corp.
Trulock Tool
Uncle Mike's
Vortek Products Inc.
Wise Guns, Dale

CHRONOGRAPHS AND PRESSURE TOOLS

Brown Co., E. Arthur
Canons Delcour
Clearview Products
Competition Electronics, Inc.
Custom Chronograph, Inc.
D&H Precision Tooling
Hege Jagd-u. Sporthandels, GmbH
Hornady Mfg. Co.
Hutton Rifle Ranch

Kent Cartridge Mfg. Co. Ltd.
Oehler Research, Inc.
P.A.C.T., Inc.
Shooting Chrony, Inc.
SKAN A.R.
Stratco, Inc.
Tepeco
Williamson Precision Gunsmith

CLEANING AND REFINISHING SUPPLIES

AC Dyna-tite Corp.
Acculube II, Inc.
Accupro Gun Care
American Gas & Chemical Co., Ltd.
Answer Products Co.
Armite Laboratories
Armsport, Inc.
Atlantic Mills, Inc.
Atsko/Sno-Seal, Inc.
Barnes Bullets, Inc.
Beeman Precision Airguns
Bill's Gun Repair
Birchwood Casey
Blackhawk East
Blount, Inc., Sporting Equipment Div.
Blue and Gray Products, Inc.
Break-Free, Inc.
Bridgers Best
Brown Co., E. Arthur
Brownells Inc.
Camp-Cap Products Division
Cape Outfitters
Chem-Pak, Inc.
CONKKO
Connecticut Shotgun Mfg. Co
Crane & Crane Ltd.
Creedmoor Sports, Inc.
CRR, Inc./Marble's Inc.
Custom Products
D&H Prods. Co., Inc.

Dara-Nes, Inc.
Decker Shooting Products
Deepeeka Exports Pvt. Ltd.
Desert Mountain Mfg.
Dewey Mfg. Co., Inc., J.
Du-Lite Corp.
Dutchman's Firearms, Inc., The
Dykstra, Doug
E&L Mfg., Inc.
Eezox, Inc.
Ekol Leather Care
Faith Associates, Inc.
Flashette Co.
Flitz International Ltd.
Fluoramics, Inc.
Frontier Products Co.
G96 Products Co., Inc.
Goddard, Allen
Golden Age Arms Co.
Gozon Corp., U.S.A.
Great Lakes Airguns
Groenewold, John
Guardsman Products
Gunsmithing Inc
Heatbath Corp.
Hoppe's Div.
Hornady Mfg. Co.
Hydrosorbent Products
  Iosso Products
Jedediah Starr Trading Co.

Johnston Bros.
K&M Service
Kellogg's Professional Products
Kent Cartridge Mfg. Co. Ltd.
Kesselring Gun Shop
Kleen-Bore, Inc.
Laurel Mountain Forge
Lee Supplies, Mark
LEM Gun Specialties, Inc.
Lewis Lead Remover, The
List Precision Engineering
Lone Star Rifle Co., Inc.
LPS Laboratories, Inc.
Marble Arms
Markesberry Bros.
Micro Sight Co.
Minute Man High Tech Industries
Mountain View Sports, Inc.
MTM Molded Products Co., Inc.
Muscle Products Corp.
Nesci Enterprises, Inc.
Northern Precision Custom Swaged
  Bullets
Now Products, Inc.
October Country
Old World Oil Products
Omark Industries
Original Mink Oil, Inc.
Outers Laboratories, Div. of Blount
Ox-Yoke Originals, Inc.
P&M Sales and Service
PanaVise Products, Inc.
Parker & Sons Gunsmithing
Parker Gun Finishes
Paul Company Inc.
Pendleton Royal
Penguin Industries, Inc.
Precision Reloading, Inc.

ProlixÆ Lubricants
Pro-Shot Products, Inc.
R&S Industries Corp.
Radiator Specialty Co.
Rickard, Inc., Pete
RIG Products Co.
Rooster Laboratories
Rusteprufe Laboratories
Rusty Duck Premium Gun Care
  Products
Saunders Gun & Machine Shop
Shiloh Creek
Shooter's Choice
Shootin' Accessories, Ltd.
Silencio/Safety Direct
Sinclair International
Sno-Seal, Inc.
Southern Bloomer Mfg Co.
Spencer's Custom Guns
Stoney Point Products, Inc.
Svon Corp.
Tag Distributors
TDP Industries, Inc.
Tetra Gun Lubricants
Texas Platers Supply Co.
T.F.C. S.p.A.
Thompson Bullet Lube Co.
Thompson/Center Arms
Track of the Wolf, Inc.
United States Products Co.
Venco Industries, Inc.
Warren Muzzleloading Co., Inc.
WD-40 Co.
Wick, David E.
Willow Bend
Wolf's Western Traders
Young Country Arms
Z-Coat Industrial Coatings, Inc.

COMPUTER SOFTWARE—BALLISTICS

Action Target, Inc.
AmBr Software Group Ltd.
Arms, Programming Solutions
Arms Software
Ballistic Engineering & Software, Inc.
Ballistic Program Co., Inc., The
Barnes Bullets, Inc.
Beartooth Bullets
Blackwell, W.
Canons Delcour
Corbin Mfg. & Supply, Inc.
Country Armourer, The
Data Tech Software Systems
Exe, Inc.
FlashTek, Inc.
Gun Hunter Trading

Hodgdon Powder Co., Inc.
Jensen Bullets
J.I.T. Ltd.
Kent Cartridge Mfg. Co. Ltd.
Load From A Disk
Maionchi-L.M.I.
Oehler Research, Inc.
Outdoor Sports Hdqtr
P.A.C.T., Inc.
PC Bullet
Pejsa Ballistics
Powley Computer
Sierra Bullets
Tioga Engineering Co., Inc.
Vancini, Carl
W. Square Enterprises

CUSTOM GUNSMITHS

A&W Repair
A.A. Arms, Inc.
Acadian Ballistic Specialties
Ackerman & Co.
Ace Custom 45's, Inc.
Ad Hominem
Accuracy Unlimited (Glendale, AZ)
Acra-Bond Laminates
Actions by "T"
Adair Custom Shop, Bill
Ahlman Guns
Aldis Gunsmithing & Shooting Supply
Alpha Gunsmith Division
Alpine's Precision Gunsmithing &
  Indoor Shooting Range
Amrine's Gun Shop
Answer Products Co.
Antique Arms Co.
Armament Gunsmithing Co., Inc.
Arms Craft Gunsmithing
Arms Ingenuity Co.
Armscorp USA Inc.
Arnold Arms Co., Inc.
Art's Gun & Sport Shop, Inc.
Arundel Arms & Ammunition, Inc., A.
Baelder, Harry
Baer Custom, Inc., Les
Bain & Davis, Inc.
Baity's Custom Gunworks
Ballard Rifle & Cartridge Co. LLC
Bansner's Gunsmithing Specialties
Barnes Bullets, Inc.
Barsotti, Bruce
Barta's Gunsmithing
Bear Arms

Bear Mountain Gun & Tool
Beaver Lodge
Behlert Precision, Inc.
Beitzinger, George
Belding's Custom Gun Shop
Bellm Contenders
Belt MTN Arms
Benchmark Guns
Bengtson Arms Co., L.
Biesen, Al
Biesen, Roger
Billeb, Stephen L.
Billings Gunsmiths, Inc.
BlackStar AccuMax Barrels
BlackStar Barrel Accurizing
Boltin, John
Bond Custom Firearms
Borden's Accuracy
Borovnik KG, Ludwig
Bowen Classic Arms
Brace, Larry D.
Brgoch, Frank
Briese Bullet Co., Inc.
Briley Mfg. Inc.
Briganti, A.J.
Briley Mfg., Inc.
Broad Creek Rifle Works
Brockman's Custom Gunsmithing
Broken Gun Ranch
Broughton Rifle Barrels
Brown Precision, Inc.
Buckhorn Gun Works
Buckskin Machine Works
Budin, Dave
Bull Mountain Rifle Co.

Bullberry Barrel Works, Ltd.
Burkhart Gunsmithing, Don
C&J Enterprises, Inc.
Cache La Poudre Rifleworks
CAM Enterprises
Camilli, Lou
Cannon's, Andy Cannon
Carolina Precision Rifles
Carter's Gun Shop
Caywood, Shane J.
Chambers Flintlocks Ltd., Jim
Champlin Firearms, Inc.
Chicasaw Gun Works
Christman Jr., Gunmaker, David
Chuck's Gun Shop
Clark Custom Guns, Inc.
Clark Firearms Engraving
Classic Arms Corp.
Classic Guns, Inc.
Clearview Products
Cleland's Outdoor World
Cloward's Gun Shop
Cochran, Oliver
Cogar's Gunsmithing
Cole's Gun Works
Coleman's Custom Repair
Colonial Repair
Colorado Gunsmithing Academy
Colorado School of Trades
Colt's Mfg. Co., Inc.
Competitive Pistol Shop, The
Conrad, C.A.
Corkys Gun Clinic
Cox, C. Ed
Craig Custom Ltd.
Creekside Gun Shop, Inc.
Cullity Restoration, Daniel
Cumberland Knife & Gun Works
Curtis Custom Shop
Custom Checkering Service
Custom Gun Products
Custom Gun Stocks
Custom Gunsmiths
Custom Shop, The
Cylinder & Slide, Inc.
D&D Gunsmiths, Ltd.
D&J Bullet Co. & Custom Gun Shop,
    Inc.
Dangler, Homer L.
Darlington Gun Works, Inc.
Dave's Gun Shop
Davis, Don
Davis Service Center, Bill
Delorge, Ed
Del-Sports Inc.
Dever Co., Jack
DGS, Inc.
DGR Custom Rifles
Dietz Gun Shop & Range, Inc.
Dilliott Gunsmithing, Inc.
Donnelly, C.P.
Dowtin Gunworks
Duane's Gun Repair
Duffy, Charles E.
Duncan's Gun Works, Inc.
Dyson & Son Ltd., Peter
E Arthur Brown Co
Echols & Co., D'Arcy
Eckelman Gunsmithing
Eggleston, Jere D.
EGW Evolution Gun Works
Erhardt, Dennis
Eskridge Rifles, Steven Eskridge
Eversull Co., Inc., K.
Eyster Heritage Gunsmiths, Inc., Ken
Fanzoj GmbH
Ferris Firearms
Fish Mfg. Gunsmith Spt. Co., Fulton
    Armory
Marshall F.
Fisher, Jerry A.
Flaig's
Fleming Firearms
Flynn's Custom Guns
Forkin, Ben
Forster, Kathy
Forster, Larry L.
Forthofer's Gunsmithing &
    Knifemaking
Francesca, Inc.
Francotte & Cie S.A., Auguste
Frank Custom Classic Arms, Ron
Frontier Arms Co., Inc.
Fullmer, Geo. M.
G.G. & G.

Gator Guns & Repair
Genecco Gun Works, K.
Gentry Custom Gunmaker, David
Gilkes, Anthony W.
Gillmann, Edwin
Gilman-Mayfield, Inc.
Giron, Robert E.
Goens, Dale W.
Gonzalez Guns, Ramon B.
Goodling's Gunsmithing
Goodwin, Fred
Gordie's Gun Shop
Grace, Charles E.
Graybill's Gun Shop
Green, Roger M.
Greg Gunsmithing Repair
GrÇ-Tan Rifles
Griffin & Howe, Inc.
Gun Shop, The
Gun Works, The
Guncraft Sports, Inc.
Guns
Guns Antique & Modern DBA/Charles
    E. Duffy
Gunsite Custom Shop
Gunsite Gunsmithy
Gunsite Training Center
Gunsmithing Ltd.
Hagn Rifles & Actions, Martin
Hallberg Gunsmith, Fritz
Halstead, Rick
Hamilton, Alex B.
Hamilton, Jim
Hammans, Charles E.
Hammond Custom Guns Ltd.
Hank's Gun Shop
Hanus, Bill Birdguns
Hanson's Gun Center, Dick
Harold's Custom Gun Shop, Inc.
Harris Gunworks
Hart & Son, Inc., Robert W.
Hart Rifle Barrels, Inc.
Hartmann & Weiss GmbH
Harwood, Jack O.
Hawken Shop, The
Hecht, Hubert J.
Heilmann, Stephen
Heinie Specialty Products
Hensler, Jerry
Hensley, Gunmaker, Darwin
Heppler, Keith M.
Heppler's Machining
Heydenberk, Warren R.
High Bridge Arms, Inc.
High Performance International
Highline Machine Co.
Hill, Loring F.
Hiptmayer, Armurier
Hiptmayer, Klaus
Hoag, James W.
Hobbie Gunsmithing, Duane A.
Hodgson, Richard
Hoehn Sales, Inc.
Hoelscher, Virgil
Hoenig & Rodman
Hofer Jagdwaffen, P.
Holland, Dick
Holland's
Hollis Gun Shop
Horst, Alan K.
Huebner, Corey O.
Hughes, Steven Dodd
Hunkeler, Al
Hyper-Single, Inc.
Ide, Kenneth G.
Imperial Magnum Corp.
Irwin, Campbell N.
Island Pond Gun Shop
Ivanoff, Thomas G.
J&S Heat Treat
Jackalope Gun Shop
Jaeger, Inc., Paul/Dunn's
Jamison's Forge Works
Jarrett Rifles, Inc.
Jarvis, Inc.
Jensen's Custom Ammunition
Jim's Gun Shop
Jim's Precision
Johnston, James
Jones, J.D.
Juenke, Vern
Jurras, L.E.
K-D, Inc.
KDF, Inc.

Keith's Custom Gunstocks
Ken's Gun Specialties
Ketchum, Jim
Kilham & Co.
Kimball, Gary
King's Gun Works
KLA Enterprises
Klein Custom Guns, Don
Kleinendorst, K.W.
Kneiper Custom Guns, Jim
Knippel, Richard
KOGOT
Kopp, Terry K.
Korzinek Riflesmith, J.
LaFrance Specialties
Lair, Sam
Lampert, Ron
LaRocca Gun Works, Inc.
Lathrop's, Inc.
Laughridge, William R.
Lawson Co., Harry
Lazzeroni Arms Co.
Lee's Red Ramps
LeFever Arms Co., Inc.
Liberty Antique Gunworks
Lind Custom Guns, Al
Linebaugh Custom Sixguns
List Precision Engineering
Lock's Philadelphia Gun Exchange
Long, George F.
Lyons Gunworks, Larry
Mac's .45 Shop
Mag-Na-Port International, Inc.
Mahony, Philip Bruce
Makinson, Nicholas
Mandall Shooting Supplies, Inc.
Martin's Gun Shop
Martz, John V.
Masker, Seely
Mathews & Son, Inc., George E.
Mazur Restoration, Pete
McCament, Jay
McCann Industries
McCann's Muzzle-Gun Works
McCluskey Precision Rifles
McFarland, Stan
McGowen Rifle Barrels
McKinney, R.P.
McMillan Rifle Barrels
MCS, Inc.
Mercer Custom Stocks, R.M.
Michael's Antiques
Mid-America Recreation, Inc.
Middlebrooks Custom Shop
Miller Co., David
Miller Arms, Inc.
Miller Custom
Mills Jr., Hugh B.
Mo's Competitor Supplies
Moeller, Steve
Monell Custom Guns
Morrison Custom Rifles, J.W.
Morrow, Bud
Mowrey's Guns & Gunsmithing
Mullis Guncraft
Nastoff's 45 Shop, Inc., Steve
Nelson, Stephen
Nettestad Gun Works
New England Arms Co.
New England Custom Gun Service
Newman Gunshop
NCP Products, Inc.
Nicholson Custom
Nickels, Paul R.
Nicklas, Ted
Nitex, Inc.
Norman Custom Gunstocks, Jim
Norrell Arms, John
North American Shooting Systems
North Fork Custom Gunsmithing
Nu-Line Guns, Inc.
Oakland Custom Arms, Inc.
Old World Gunsmithing
Olson, Vic
Orvis Co., The
Ottmar, Maurice
Ozark Gun Works
P&S Gun Service
Pagel Gun Works, Inc.
Parker Gun Finishes
Pasadena Gun Center
Paterson Gunsmithing
PEM's Mfg. Co.
Pence Precision Barrels

Penrod Precision
Pentheny de Pentheny
Perazone, Brian
Performance Specialists
Peterson Gun Shop, Inc., A.W.
Powell & Son (Gunmakers) Ltd.,
    William
Power Custom, Inc.
Professional Hunter Supplies
P.S.M.G. Gun Co.
Quality Firearms of Idaho, Inc.
R&J Gun Shop
Ray's Gunsmith Shop
Renfrew Guns & Supplies
Ridgetop Sporting Goods
Ries, Chuck
Rifles Inc.
Rigby & Co., John
River Road Sporting Clays
RMS Custom Gunsmithing
Robar Co.'s, Inc., The
Robinson, Don
Rocky Mountain Arms, Inc.
Rocky Mountain Rifle Works Ltd.
Rogers Gunsmithing, Bob
Romain's Custom Guns, Inc.
RPM
Rudnicky, Susan
Rupert's Gun Shop
Ryan, Chad L.
Sanders Custom Gun Service
Schiffman, Mike
Schumakers Gun Shop
Schwartz Custom Guns, Wayne E.
Score High Gunsmithing
Scott, Dwight
Scott, McDougall & Associates
Sharp Shooter Supply
Shaw, Inc., E.R.
Shay's Gunsmithing
Shell Shack
Shockley, Harold H.
Shooten' Haus, The
Shooters Supply
Shootin' Shack, Inc.
Shooting Specialties
Shotguns Unlimited
Sile Distributors Inc.
Silver Ridge Gun Shop
Simmons Gun Repair, Inc.
Singletary, Kent
Sipes Gun Shop
Siskiyou Gun Works
Skeoch, Brian R.
Slezak, Jerome F.
Small Arms Mfg. Co.
Smith, Art
Smith, Sharmon
Snapp's Gunshop
Speiser, Fred D.
Spencer's Custom Guns
Spencer Reblue Service
Sportsmen's Exchange & Western
    Gun Traders, Inc.
Springfield Inc.
SSK Industries
Star Custom Bullets
Starnes Gunmaker, Ken
Steelman's Gun Shop
Steffens, Ron
Steger, James R.
Stiles Custom Guns
Storey, Dale A.
Stott's Creek Armory, Inc.
Strawbridge, Victor W.
Sturgeon Valley Sporters
Sullivan, David S.
Swampfire Shop, The
Swann, D.J.
Swenson's 45 Shop, A.D.
Swift River Gunworks
Szweda, Robert
Taconic Firearms Ltd.
Talmage, William G.
Tank's Rifle Shop
Tarnhelm Supply Co., Inc.
Taylor & Robbins
Ten-Ring Precision, Inc.
Thompson, Randall
Tom's Gunshop
300 Gunsmith Service, Inc.
Thurston Sports, Inc.
Time Precision, Inc.
Titus, Daniel
Tom's Gun Repair

Tooley Custom Rifles
Trevallion Gunstocks
Trulock Tool
Tucker, James C.
Unmussig Bullets, D.L.
Upper Missouri Trading Co.
USA Sporting Inc.
Van Horn, Gil
Van Patten, J.W.
Van's Gunsmith Service
Vest, John
Vic's Gun Refinishing
Vintage Arms, Inc.
Volquartsen Custom Ltd.
Von Minden Gunsmithing Services
Walker Arms Co., Inc.
Wallace, Terry
Wasmundt, Jim
Weaver Arms Corp. Gun Shop
Weber & Markin Custom Gunsmiths
Weems, Cecil
Weigand Combat Handguns, Inc.
Wiest, M. C
Wells, Fred F.
Wells Custom Gunsmith, R.A.

Welsh, Bud
Wenig Custom Gunstocks, Inc.
Werth, T.W.
Wessinger Custom Guns & Engraving
Western Design
Westley Richards & Co.
Westwind Rifles, Inc.
White Muzzleloading Systems
White Shooting Systems, Inc.
Wichita Arms, Inc.
Wiebe, Duane
Wild West Guns
Williams Gun Sight Co.
Williams Shootin' Iron Service
Williamson Precision Gunsmithing
Wilson Gun Shop
Winter, Robert M.
Wise Guns, Dale
Wiseman and Co., Bill
Wood, Frank
Wright's Hardwood Gunstock Blanks
Yankee Gunsmith
Yee, Mike
Zeeryp, Russ

CUSTOM METALSMITHS

A&W Repair
Ahlman Guns
Aldis Gunsmithing & Shooting Supply
Amrine's Gun Shop
Answer Products Co.
Arnold Arms Co., Inc.
Arundel Arms & Ammunition, Inc., A.
Baer Custom, Inc., Les
Bansner's Gunsmithing Specialties
Baron Technology
Barsotti, Bruce
Bear Mountain Gun & Tool
Behlert Precision, Inc.
Beitzinger, George
Bell, Sid
Benchmark Guns
Bengtson Arms Co., L.
Biesen, Al
Billings Gunsmiths, Inc.
Billingsley & Brownell
Brace, Larry D.
Briganti, A.J.
Broad Creek Rifle Works
Brown Precision, Inc.
Buckhorn Gun Works
Bull Mountain Rifle Co.
Bullberry Barrel Works, Ltd.
Burkhart Gunsmithing, Don
Bustani, Leo R.
C&J Enterprises Inc.
Campbell, Dick
Carter's Gun Shop
Champlin Firearms, Inc.
Checkmate Refinishing
Chicasaw Gun Works
Christman Jr., Gunmaker, David
Classic Guns, Inc.
Cochran, Oliver
Colonial Repair
Colorado Gunsmithing Academy
Craftguard
Crandall Tool & Machine Co.
Cullity Restoration, Daniel
Custom Gun Products
Custom Gunsmiths
Custom Shop, The
D&D Gunsmiths, Ltd.
D&H Precision Tooling
Dave's Gun Shop
Delorge, Ed
DGR Custom Rifles
DGS, Inc.
Duane's Gun Repair
Duncan's Gunworks, Inc.
Eversull Co., Inc., K.
Eyster Heritage Gunsmiths, Inc., Ken
Ferris Firearms
Forster, Larry L.
Forthofer's Gunsmithing &
    Knifemaking
Francesca, Inc.
Frank Custom Classic Arms, Ron
Fullmer, Geo. M.
Gene's Custom Guns
Gentry Custom Gunmaker, David
Gilkes, Anthony W.
Gordie's Gun Shop

Grace, Charles E.
Graybill's Gun Shop
Green, Roger M.
Griffin & Howe, Inc.
Gun Shop, The
Guns
Hagn Rifles & Actions, Martin
Hallberg Gunsmith, Fritz
Hamilton, Alex B.
Hamilton, John
Hart & Son, Inc., Robert W.
Hartmann & Weiss GmbH
Harwood, Jack O.
Hecht, Hubert J.
Heilmann, Stephen
Heppler's Machining
Heritage Wildlife Carvings
Highline Machine Co.
Hiptmayer, Armurier
Hiptmayer, Klaus
Hoag, James W.
Hoelscher, Virgil
Holland's
Hollis Gun Shop
Horst, Alan
Hyper-Single, Inc.
Island Pond Gun Shop
Ivanoff, Thomas G.
J&S Heat Treat
Jaeger, Inc., Paul/Dunn's
Jamison's Forge Works
Jeffredo Gunsight
Johnston, James
KDF, Inc.
Ken's Gun Specialties
Kilham & Co.
Klein Custom Guns, Don
Kleinendorst, K.W.
Kopp, Terry K.
Lampert, Ron
Lawson Co., Harry
List Precision Engineering
Mac's .45 Shop
Makinson, Nicholas
Mazur Restoration, Pete
McCament, Jay
McCann Industries
McCann's Machine & Gun Shop
McFarland, Stan
Miller Arms Inc.
Morrison Custom Rifles, J.W.
Morrow, Bud
Mullis Guncraft
Nelson, Stephen
Nettestad Gun Works
New England Custom Gun Service
Nicholson Custom
Nitex, Inc.
Noreen, Peter H.
North Fork Custom Gunsmithing
Nu-Line Guns, Inc.
Olson, Vic
Ozark Gun Works
P&S Gun Service
Pagel Gun Works, Inc.
Parker Gun Finishes
Pasadena Gun Center

Penrod Precision
Precision Metal Finishing
Precise Metalsmithing Enterprises
Precision Metal Finishing, John
    Westrom
Precision Specialties
Rice, Keith
Rifles Inc.
River Road Sporting Clays
Robar Co.'s, Inc., The
Rocky Mountain Arms, Inc.
Rogers Gunsmithing, Bob
Score High Gunsmithing
Simmons Gun Repair, Inc.
Sipes Gun Shop
Skeoch, Brian R.
Smith, Art
Snapp's Gunshop
Spencer's Custom Guns
Sportsmen's Exchange & Western
    Gun Traders, Inc.
Starnes Gunmaker, Ken
Steffens, Ron
Steger, James R.
Stiles Custom Guns
Storey, Dale A.
Strawbridge, Victor W.

DECOYS

A&M Waterfowl, Inc.
Baekgaard Ltd.
Boyds' Gunstock Industries, Inc.
Carry-Lite, Inc.
Deer Me Products Co.
Fair Game International
Farm Form Decoys, Inc.
Feather Flex Decoys
Flambeau Products Corp.
G&H Decoys, Inc.
Herter's Manufacturing, Inc.
Hiti-Schuch, Atelier Wilma

Klingler Woodcarving
L.L. Bean, Inc.
Molin Industries
North Wind Decoy Co.
Penn's Woods Products, Inc.
Russ Trading Post
Quack Decoy & Sporting Clays
Sports Innovations, Inc.
Tanglefree Industries
Waterfield Sports, Inc.
Woods Wise Products

Taylor & Robbins
Ten-Ring Precision, Inc.
Thompson, Randall
Tom's Gun Repair
Tooley Custom Rifles
Van Horn, Gil
Van Patten, J.W.
Von Minden Gunsmithing Services
Waldron, Herman
Wallace, Terry
Weber & Markin Custom Gunsmiths
Wells, Fred F.
Wells Custom Gunsmith, R.A.
Werth, T.W.
Wessinger Custom Guns & Engraving
Westrom, John
White Rock Tool & Die
Wiebe, Duane
Wild West Guns Inc.
Williams Gun Sight Co.
Williams Shootin' Iron Service
Williamson Precision Gunsmithing
Winter, Robert M.
Wise Guns, Dale
Wood, Frank
Zufall, Joseph F.

ENGRAVERS, ENGRAVING TOOLS

Ackerman & Co.
Adair Custom Shop, Bill
Adams, John J. & Son Engravers
Adams Jr., John J.
Ahlman Guns
Alfano, Sam
Allard, Gary
Allen Firearm Engraving
Altamont Co.
American Pioneer Video
Anthony and George Ltd.
Baron Technology
Barraclough, John K.
Bates Engraving, Billy
Bell, Sid
Blair Engraving, J.R.
Bleile, C. Roger
Boessler, Erich
Bone Engraving, Ralph
Bratcher, Dan
Brgoch, Frank
Brooker, Dennis
Brownell Checkering Tools, W.E.
Burgess, Byron
CAM Enterprises
Churchill, Winston
Clark Firearms Engraving
Collings, Ronald
Creek Side Metal & Woodcrafters
Cullity Restoration, Daniel
Cupp, Custom Engraver, Alana
Custom Gun Engraving
Davidson, Jere
Dayton Traister
Delorge, Ed
Desquesnes, Gerald
Dolbare, Elizabeth
Drain, Mark
Dubber, Michael W.
Engraving Artistry
Evans Engraving, Robert
Eversull Co., Inc., K.
Eyster Heritage Gunsmiths, Inc., Ken
Firearms Engraver's Guild of America
Flannery Engraving Co., Jeff W.
Forty Five Ranch Enterprises
Fountain Products
Francote & Cie S.A., Auguste
Frank E. Hendricks Master En
Frank Knives

French, Artistic Engraving, J.R.
Gene's Custom Guns
George, Tim
Glimm, Jerome C.
Golden Age Arms Co.
Gournet, Geoffroy
Grant, Howard V.
Griffin & Howe, Inc.
Gun Room, The
Guns
Gurney, F.R.
Gwinnell, Bryson J.
Hale/Engraver, Peter
Hamilton, Jim
Hands Engraving, Barry Lee
Harris Gunworks
Harris Hand Engraving, Paul A.
Harwood, Jack O.
Hawken Shop, The
Hendricks, Frank E.
Heritage Wildlife Carvings
Hiptmayer, Armurier
Hiptmayer, Heidemarie
Horst, Alan K.
Ingle, Engraver, Ralph W.
Jaeger, Inc., Paul/Dunn's
Jantz Supply
Johns Master Engraver, Bill
Kamyk Engraving Co., Steve
Kane, Edward
Kehr, Roger
Kelly, Lance
Klingler Woodcarving
Koevenig's Engraving Service
Kudlas, John M.
LeFever Arms Co., Inc.
Leibowitz, Leonard
Lindsay, Steve
Little Trees Ramble
Lutz Engraving, Ron
Lyons Gunworks, Larry
Master Engravers, Inc.
McCombs, Leo
McDonald, Dennis
McKenzie, Lynton
Mele, Frank
Metals Hand Engraver
Mittermeier, Inc., Frank
Montgomery Community College
Mountain States Engraving

Nelson, Gary K.
New England Custom Gun Service
New Orleans Jewelers Supply Co.
NgraveR Co., The
Oker's Engraving
P&S Gun Service
Pedersen, C.R.
Pedersen, Rex C.
Pilgrim Pewter, Inc.
Pilkington, Scott
Piquette, Paul R.
Potts, Wayne E.
Rabeno, Martin
Reed, Dave
Reno, Wayne
Riggs, Jim
Roberts, J.J.
Rohner, Hans
Rohner, John
Rosser, Bob
Rundell's Gun Shop
Runge, Robert P.
Sampson, Roger
Scott Pilkington Little Tree
Schiffman, Mike

Sherwood, George
Singletary, Kent
Smith, Mark A.
Smith, Ron
Smokey Valley Rifles
Theis, Terry
Thiewes, George W.
Thirion Gun Engraving, Denise
Thompson/Center Arms
Valade Engraving, Robert
Vest, John
Viramontez, Ray
Vorhes, David
Wagoner, Vernon G.
Wallace, Terry
Warenski, Julie
Warren, Kenneth W.
Weber & Markin Custom Gunsmiths
Welch, Sam
Wells, Rachel
Wessinger Custom Guns & Engraving
Wood, Mel
Yee, Mike
Ziegel Engineering

GAME CALLS

Adventure Game Calls
Arkansas Mallard Duck Calls
Ashby Turkey Calls
Bostick Wildlife Calls, Inc.
Cedar Hill Game Calls, Inc.
Creative Concepts USA Inc.
Crit'R Call
Custom Calls
D&H Prods. Co., Inc.
D-Boone Ent., Inc.
Deepeeka Exports Pvt. Ltd.
Dr. O's Products Ltd.
Duck Call Specialists
Faulhaber Wildlocker
Faulk's Game Call Co., Inc.
Flow-Rite of Tennessee, Inc.
Gander Mountain, Inc.
Green Head Game Call Co.
Hally Caller
Haydel's Game Calls, Inc.
Herter's Manufacturing, Inc.
Hunter's Specialties, Inc.
Keowee Game Calls
Kingyon, Paul L.
Knight & Hale Game Calls
Lohman Mfg. Co., Inc.
Mallardtone Game Calls

Marsh, Johnny
Moss Double Tone, Inc.
Mountain Hollow Game Calls
Oakman Turkey Calls
Olt Co., Philip S.
Outdoor Sports Hdqtr
Penn's Woods Products, Inc.
Primos, Inc.
Quaker Boy, Inc.
Rickard, Inc., Pete
Rocky Mountain Wildlife Products
Russ Trading Post
Salter Calls, Inc., Eddie
Sceery Game Calls
Scobey Duck & Goose Calls, Glynn
Scruggs' Game Calls, Stanley
Simmons Outdoor Corp.
Sports Innovations, Inc.
Stewart Game Calls, Inc., Johnny
Sure-Shot Game Calls, Inc.
Tanglefree Industries
Tink's & Ben Lee Hunting Products
Tink's Safariland Hunting Corp.
Wellington Outdoors
Wilderness Sound Products Ltd.
Woods Wise Products
Wyant's Outdoor Products, Inc.

GUN PARTS, U.S. AND FOREIGN

A.A. Arms, Inc.
Actions by "T"
Ahlman Guns
Amherst Arms
Armscorp USA, Inc.
Auto-Ordnance Corp.
Badger Shooters Supply, Inc.
Bear Mountain Gun & Tool
Billings Gunsmiths, Inc.
Bill's Gun Repair
Bob's Gun Shop
Briese Bullet Co., Inc.
British Antiques
Brown Products, Inc., Ed
Buffer Technologies
Bushmaster Firearms
Bustani, Leo
Cape Outfitters
Caspian Arms Ltd.
Chicasaw Gun Works
Cochran, Oliver
Cole's Gun Works
Colonial Repair
Cryo-Accurizing
Cylinder & Slide, Inc.
Delta Arms Ltd.
DGR Custom Rifles
Dibble, Derek A.
Duane's Gun Repair
Duffy, Charles E.
Dyson & Son Ltd., Peter
E&L Mfg., Inc.
E.A.A. Corp.
EGW Evolution Gun Works
Elliott Inc., G.W.
EMF Co., Inc.
Enguix Import-Export

European American Armory Corp.
Federal Arms Corp. of America
Fleming Firearms
Forrest, Inc., TomGalati International
Glimm, Jerome C.
Goodwin, Fred
Greider Precision
Groenewold, John
Gun Parts Corp., The
Gun Shop, The
Gun Works, The
Guns Antique & Modern DBA/Charles
    E. Duffy
Gunsmithing, Inc.
Gun-Tec
Hastings Barrels
Hawken Shop, The
High Performance International
Irwin, Campbell H.
I.S.S.
Jaeger, Inc., Paul/Dunn's
Jamison's Forge Works
Johnson's Gunsmithing, Inc., Neal G
J.R. Distributing (Wolf competiition
    guns)
K&T Co.
Kimber of America, Inc.
K.K. Arms Co.
Knight's Manufacturing
Krico Jagd-und Sportwaffen GmbH
Laughridge, William R.
List Precision Engineering
Ljutic Industries, Inc.
Lodewick, Walter H.
Long, George F.
Mac's .45 Shop
Mandall Shooting Supplies, Inc.

Markell, Inc.
Martin's Gun Shop
Martz, John V.
McCormick Corp., Chip
MCS, Inc.
Merkuria Ltd.
Mid-America Recreation, Inc.
Mo's Competitor Supplies
Morrow, Bud
NCP Products, Inc.
North Star West
Nu-Line Guns, Inc.
Nygord Precision Products
Olympic Arms
Parts & Surplus
Pennsylvania Gun Parts
Perazone, Brian
Perazzi USA, Inc.
Performance Specialists
Peterson Gun Shop, Inc., A.W.
Pre-Winchester 92-90-62 Parts Co.
P.S.M.G. Gun Co.
Quality Firearms of Idaho, Inc.
Quality Parts Co.
Ranch Products
Randco UK
Raptor Arms Co. Inc.
Ravell Ltd.
Retting, Inc., Martin B.
R.G.-G., Inc.
Ruger
S&S Firearms
Sabatti S.R.L.
Samco Global Arms
Sarco, Inc.

Scherer
Shockley, Harold H.
Shootin' Shack, Inc.
Silver Ridge Gun Shop
Simmons Gun Repair, Inc.
Sipes Gun Shop
Smires, C.L.
Smith & Wesson
Southern Ammunition Co., Inc.
Southern Armory, The
Sportsmen's Exchange & Western
    Gun Traders, Inc.
Springfield, Inc.
Springfield Sporters, Inc.
Steyr Mannlicher AG & CO KG
STI International
Sturm, Ruger & Co., Inc.
"Su-Press-On" Inc.
Swampfire Shop, The
Tank's Rifle Shop
Tarnhelm Supply Co., Inc.
Triple-K Mfg. Co., Inc.
Twin Pine Armory
USA Sporting Inc.
Vintage Arms, Inc.
Volquartsen Custom Ltd.
Walker Arms Co., Inc.
Waller & Son, Inc. W.
Weaver Arms Corp. Gun Shop
Wescombe, Bill
Whitestone Lumber Corp.
Williams Mfg. of Oregon
Winchester Sutler, Inc., The
Wise Guns, Dale
Wolff Co., W.C.

GUNS, AIR

●Air Arms
●Air Venture
●Airrow
Allred Bullet Co.
●Anschutz GmbH
    Arms Corporation of the Philippines
    Baikal
●Beeman Precision Airguns
●Benjamin/Sheridan Co.
    Brass Eagle, Inc.
    Brocock Ltd.
    Brolin Industries Inc.
●BSA Guns Ltd.
    Catoctin Cutlery
    Compasseco, Ltd.
    Component Concepts, Inc.
    Creedmoor Sports, Inc.
●Crosman Airguns
    Crosman Products of Canada Ltd.
●Daisy Mfg. Co.
    Daystate Ltd.
●Diana
●Dynamit Nobel-RWS, Inc.
●FAS
    Frankonia Jagd
●FWB
Gamo USA, Inc.
    Gaucher Armes, S.A.
Great Lakes Airguns
    Hebard Guns, Gil
    Hofmann & Co.
●Interarms
Israel Arms International
    Labanu, Inc.

List Precision Engineering
Loch Leven Industries/Convert-A-Pell
Mac-1 Distributors
Marksman Products
Maryland Paintball Supply
Merkuria Ltd.
Nygord Precision Products
●Pardini Armi Srl
    Park Rifle Co., Inc.
    Penguin Industries, Inc.
●Precision Airgun Sales, Inc.
●Precision Sales Int'l., Inc.
    Ripley Rifles
    Robinson, Don
●RWS
    S.G.S. Sporting Guns Srl
    Scott Pilkington Little Tree
    SKAN A.R.
    Smart Parts
●Steyr Mannlicher AG & CO KG
    Stone Enterprises Ltd.
●Swivel Machine Works, Inc.
    Theoben Engineering
    Tippman Pneumatics, Inc.
    Tristar Sporting Arms, Ltd.
    Trooper Walsh
    UltraSport Arms, Inc.
    Valor Corp.
    Vortek Products Inc
●Walther GmbH, Carl
●Webley and Scott Ltd.
●Weihrauch KG, Hermann
    Whiscombe
●World Class Airguns

GUNS, FOREIGN—IMPORTERS (Manufacturers)

●Accuracy International (Anschutz
    GmbH target rifles)
●AcuSport Corporation (Anschutz
    GmbH)
●Air Rifle Specialists (airguns)
●American Arms, Inc. (Fausti Cav.
    Stefano & Figlie snc; Franchi S.p.A.;
    Grulla Armes; Uberti, Aldo; Zabala
    Hermanos S.A.; blackpowder arms)
American Frontier Firearms Mfg. Inc.
    (single-action revolvers)
●Amtec 2000, Inc. (Erma Werke
    GmbH)
●Armsport, Inc. (Bernardelli S.p.A.,
    Vincenzo)
●Auto-Ordnance Corp. (Techno Arms)
●●Beauchamp & Son, Inc. (Pedersoli
    and Co., Davide)
●Bell's Legendary Country Wear
    (Miroku, B.C./Daly, Charles)

Benelli USA Corp.
●Beretta U.S.A. Corp. (Beretta S.p.A.,
    Pietro)
Big Bear Arms & Sporting Goods, Inc.
    (Russian/Big Bear Arms)
●Bohemia Arms Co. (BRNO)
British Sporting Arms
●Browning Arms Co. (Browning Arms
    Co.)
B-West Imports, Inc.
●Cabela's (Pedersoli and Co., Davide;
    Uberti, Aldo; blackpowder arms)
●Cape Outfitters (Armi Sport; Pedersoli
    and Co., Davide; San Marco; Societa
    Armi Bresciane Srl.; blackpowder
    arms)
●Century International Arms, Inc.
    (FEG)
●Champion Shooters' Supply
    (Anschutz GmbH)

• **See page 437 for Warranty Service Center Addresses**

- Champion's Choice (Anschutz GmbH; Walther GmbH, Carl; target rifles)
- Chapuis USA (Chapuis Armes)
- Champlin Firearms, Inc. (Chapuis Armes; M.Thys)
- Christopher Firearms Co., Inc., E.
- Cimarron Arms (Uberti, Aldo; Armi San Marco; Pedersoli)
- CVA (blackpowder arms)
- CZ USA
- Dixie Gun Works, Inc. (Pedersoli and Co., Davide; Uberti, Aldo; blackpowder arms)
- Dynamit Nobel-RWS, Inc. (Brenneke KG, Wilhelm; Diana; Gamo; Norma Precision AB; RWS)
- E.A.A. Corp. (Astra-Sport, S.A.; Sabatti S.r.l.; Tanfoglio Fratelli S.r.l.; Weihrauch KG, Hermann; Star Bonifacio Echeverria S.A.)
- Eagle Imports, Inc. (Bersa S.A.)
- Ellett Bros. (Churchill)
- EMF Co., Inc. (Dakota; Hartford; Pedersoli and Co., Davide; San Marco; Uberti, Aldo; blackpowder arms)
- Euroarms of America, Inc. (blackpowder arms)
- Eversull Co., Inc., K.
- Fiocchi of America, Inc. (Fiocchi Munizioni S.p.A.)
- Forgett Jr., Valmore J. (Navy Arms Co.; Uberti, Aldo)
- Franzen International, Inc. (Peters Stahl GmbH)
- Galaxy Imports Ltd., Inc. (Hanus Birdguns, Bill; Ignacio Ugartechea S.A.; Laurona Armas Eibar, S.A.D.)
- Gamba, USA (Societa Armi Bresciane Srl.)
- Gamo USA, Inc. (Gamo airguns)
- Giacomo Sporting, Inc.
- Glock, Inc. (Glock GmbH)
- Great Lakes Airguns (air pistols & rifles)
- Griffin & Howe, Inc. (Arrieta, S.L.)
- GSI, Inc. (Mauser Werke Oberndorf; Merkel Freres; Steyr- Mannlicher AG)
- G.U., Inc. (New SKB Arms Co.; SKB Arms Co.)
- Gun Shop, The (Ugartechea S.A., Ignacio)
- Gunsite Custom Shop (Accuracy International Precision Rifles)
- Gunsite Training Center (Accuracy International Precision Rifles)
- Gunsmithing, Inc. (Anschutz GmbH)
- Hammerli USA (Hammerli Ltd.)
- Hanus Birdguns, Bill (Ugartechea S.A., Ignacio)
- Heckler & Koch, Inc. (Benelli Armi S.p.A.; Heckler & Koch, GmbH)
- IAR, Inc. (Uberti, Kimar, Armi San Marco, S.I.A.C.E.)
- Imperial Magnum Corp. (Imperial Magnum Corp.)
- Import Sports Inc. (Llama Gabilondo Y Cia)
- Interarms (Helwan; Howa Machinery Ltd.; Interarms; Korth; Norinco; Rossi S.A., Amadeo; Star Bonifacio Echeverria S.A.; Walther GmbH, Carl)
- Israel Arms International, Inc. (KSN Industries, Ltd.)
- Ithaca Gun Co., LLC (Fabarm S.p.A.)
- I.S.S.
- JägerSport, Ltd. (Voere-KGH m.b.H.)
- J.R. Distributing (Wolf competition guns)
- K.B.I., Inc. (FEG; Miroku, B.C./ Daly, Charles)
- Kemen American (Armas Kemen S.A.)
- Keng's Firearms Specialty, Inc. (Lapua Ltd.; Ultralux)
- Kongsberg America L.L.C. (Kongsberg)
- Krieghoff International, Inc (Krieghoff Gun Co., H.)
- K-Sports Imports, Inc.
- Labanu, Inc. (Rutten; air rifles)
- Lion Country Supply (Ugartechea S.A., Ignacio)

London Guns Ltd. (London Guns Ltd.)
- Magnum Research, Inc.
MagTech Recreational Products, Inc. (MagTech)
- Mandall Shooting Supplies, Inc. (Arizaga; Atamec-Bretton; Cabanas; Crucelegui, Hermanos; Erma Werke GmbH; Firearms Co. Ltd./Alpine; Hammerli Ltd.; Korth; Krico Jagd-und Sportwaffen GmbH; Morini; SIG; Tanner; Zanoletti, Pietro; blackpowder arms)
Marx, Harry (FERLIB)
MCS, Inc. (Pardini)
- MEC-Gar U.S.A., Inc. (MEC-Gar S.R.L.)
- Moore & Co., Wm. Larkin (Garbi; Piotti; Rizzini, Battista; Rizzini F.lli)
- Nationwide Sports Distributors, Inc. (Daewoo Precision Industries Ltd.)
- Navy Arms Co. (Navy Arms Co. Pedersoli and Co., Davide; Pietta; Uberti, Aldo; blackpowder and cartridge arms)
- New England Arms Co. (Arrieta, S.L.; Bertuzzi; Bosis; Cosmi Americo & Figlio s.n.c.; Dumoulin, Ernest; Lebeau-Courally; Rizzini, Battista; Rizzini F.lli)
- New England Custom Gun Service (AYA; EAW)
- Nygord Precision Products (FAS; Morini; Pardini Armi Srl; Steyr-Mannlicher AG; TOZ; Unique/M.A.P.F.)
OK Weber, Inc. (target rifles)
- Orvis Co., Inc., The (Arrieta, S.L.)
- Para-Ordnance, Inc. (Para- Ordnance Mfg., Inc.)
- Paul Co., The (Norma Precision AB; Sauer)
Pelaire Products (Whiscombe air rifle)
- Perazzi USA, Inc. (Armi Perazzi S.p.A.)
- Powell Agency, William, The (William Powell & Son [Gunmakers] Ltd.)
- Precision Sales International, Inc. (BSA Guns Ltd.; Marocchi o/u shotguns)
P.S.M.G. Gun Co. (Astra Sport, S.A.; Interarms; Star Bonifacio Echeverria S.A.; Walther GmbH, Carl)
- Quality Arms, Inc. (Arrieta, S.L.)
Sarco, Inc.
- Savage Arms, Inc. (Lakefield Arms Ltd.; Savage Arms [Canada], Inc.)
Schuetzen Pistol Works (Peters Stahl GmbH)
Scott Fine Guns Inc., Thad
- Sigarms, Inc. (Hammerli Ltd.; Sauer rifles; SIG-Sauer)
- SKB Shotguns (SKB Arms Co.)
Specialty Shooters Supply, Inc. (JSL Ltd.)
Sphinx USA Inc. (Sphinx Engineering SA)
- Springfield, Inc. (Springfield, Inc.)
- Stoeger Industries (IGA; Sako Ltd.; Tikka; target pistols)
Stone Enterprises Ltd. (airguns)
- Swarovski Optik North America Ltd.
- Taurus Firearms, Inc. (Taurus International Firearms)
- Taylor's & Co., Inc. (Armi San Marco; Armi Sport; I.A.B.; Pedersoli and Co., Davide; Pietta; Uberti, Aldo)
- Track of the Wolf, Inc. (Pedersoli and Co., Davide)
Tradewinds, Inc. (blackpowder arms)
Tristar Sporting Arms, Ltd. (Turkish, German, Italian and Spanish made firearms)
Trooper Walsh
Turkish Firearms Corp. (Turkish Firearms Corp.)
- Uberti USA, Inc. (Uberti, Aldo; blackpowder arms)
USA Sporting Inc. (Armas Kemen S.A.)
Vintage Arms, Inc.
- Weatherby, Inc. (Weatherby, Inc.)
- Westley Richards Agency USA (Westley Richards)
- Whitestone Lumber Corp. (Heckler & Koch; Bennelli Armi S.p.A.)
- Wingshooting Adventures (Arrieta, S.L.)
- World Class Airguns (Air Arms)

GUNS, FOREIGN—MANUFACTURERS (Importers)

- Accuracy International Precision Rifles (Gunsite Custom Shop; Gunsite Training Center)
- Air Arms (World Class Airguns)
- Armas Kemen S.A. (Kemen America; USA Sporting Inc.)
- Armi Perazzi S.p.A. (Perazzi USA, Inc.)
Armi San Marco (Taylor's & Co., Inc.; Cimarron Arms; IAR, Inc.)
- Armi Sport (Cape Outfitters; Taylor's & Co., Inc.)
Arms Corporation of the Philippines Armscorp USA Inc.
- Arrieta, S.L. (Griffin & Howe, Inc. New England Arms Co.; The Orvis Co., Inc.; Quality Arms, Inc.; Wingshooting Adventures)
- Astra Sport, S.A. (E.A.A. Corp.; P.S.M.G. Gun Co.)
- Atamec-Bretton (Mandall Shooting Supplies, Inc.)
- AYA (New England Custom Gun Service)
BEC Scopes (BEC, Inc.)
- Benelli Armi S.p.A. (Heckler & Koch, Inc.; Whitestone Lumber Co.)
- Beretta S.p.A., Pietro (Beretta U.S.A. Corp.)
- Bernardelli S.p.A., Vincenzo (Armsport, Inc.)
Bersa S.A. (Eagle Imports, Inc.)
- Bertuzzi (New England Arms Co.)
- Blaser Jagdwaffen GmbH (Bondini Paolo (blackpowder arms)
Borovnik KG, Ludwig
- Bosis (New England Arms Co.)
- Brenneke KG, Wilhelm (Dynamit Nobel-RWS, Inc.)
- BRNO (Bohemia Arms Co.)
Brocock Ltd.
Brolin Industries Inc. (Mauser)
- Browning Arms Co. (Browning Arms Co.)
- BSA Guns Ltd. (Groenewold, John; Precision Sales International, Inc.)
- Cabanas (Mandall Shooting Supplies, Inc.)
- CBC
- Chapuis Armes (Champlin Firearms, Inc.; Chapuis USA)
- Churchill (Ellett Bros.)
- Cosmi Americo & Figlio s.n.c. (New England Arms Co.)
- Crucelegui, Hermanos (Mandall Shooting Supplies, Inc.)
Cryo-Accurizing
- Daewoo Precision Industries Ltd. (Nationwide Sports Distributors, Inc.)
- Dakota (EMF Co., Inc.)
- Diana (Dynamit Nobel-RWS, Inc.)
- Dumoulin, Ernest (New England Arms Co.)
- EAW (New England Custom Gun Service)
- Effebi SNC-Dr. Franco Beretta (Erma Werke GmbH (Amtec 2000, Inc.; Mandall Shooting Supplies, Inc.)
- Fabarm S.p.A. (Ithaca Gun Co., LLC)
Ed's Gun House
Euro-Imports
F.A.I.R. Techni-Mec s.n.c.
Fanzoj GmbH
- FAS (Nygord Precision Products)
- Fausti Cav. Stefano & Figlie snc (American Arms, Inc.)
- FEG (Century International Arms, Inc.; K.B.I., Inc.)
Felk Inc.
FERLIB (Marx, Harry)
- Fiocchi Munizioni S.p.A. (Fiocchi of America, Inc.)
- Firearms Co. Ltd./Alpine (Mandall Shooting Supplies, Inc.)
Firearems International
FN Herstal
- Franchi S.p.A (American Arms, Inc.)
- FWB (Beeman Precision Airguns)
Galaxy Imports LTD Inc.
- Gamba S.p.A.-Societa Armi Bresciane Srl., Renato (Gamba, USA)

- Gamo (Daisy Mfg. Co.; Dynamit Nobel-RWS, Inc.; Gamo USA, Inc.)
- Garbi, Armas Urki (Moore & Co., Wm. Larkin)
Gaucher Armes S.A.
- Glock GmbH (Glock, Inc.)
Goergen's gun Shop Inc.
- Grulla Armes (American Arms, Inc.)
Gunsmithing Inc
- Hammerli Ltd. (Hammerli USA; Mandall Shooting Supplies, Inc.; Sigarms, Inc.)
- Hartford (EMF Co., Inc.)
Hartmann & Weiss GmbH
- Heckler & Koch, GmbH (Heckler & Koch, Inc.)
Hege Jagd-u. Sporthandels, GmbH
- Helwan (Interarms)
Holland & Holland Ltd.
- Howa Machinery Ltd. (Interarms)
I.A.B. (Taylor's & Co., Inc.)
- IGA (Stoeger Industries)
IMI
- Imperial Magnum Corp. (Imperial Magnum Corp.)
Inter Ordnance of America
- Interarms (Interarms; P.S.M.G. Gun Co.)
JSL Ltd. (Specialty Shooters Supply, Inc.)
- Kimar (IAR, Inc.)
- Kongsberg (Kongsberg America L.L.C.)
- Korth (Interarms; Mandall Shooting Supplies, Inc.)
- Krico Jagd-und Sportwaffen GmbH (Mandall Shooting Supplies, Inc.)
- Krieghoff Gun Co., H. (Krieghoff International, Inc.)
- KSN Industries, Ltd. (Israel Arms International, Inc.)
- Lakefield Arms Ltd. (Savage Arms, Inc.)
Lakelander U.S.A. Inc.
Lanber Armas, S.A.
- Lapua Ltd. (Keng's Firearms Specialty, Inc.)
- Laurona Armas Eibar S.A.D. (Galaxy Imports Ltd., Inc.)
- Lebeau-Courally (New England Arms Co.)
- Llama Gabilondo Y Cia (Import Sports Inc.)
London Guns Ltd. (London Guns Ltd.)
Madis, George
Mandell Shooting Supply
MagTech (MagTech Recreational Products, Inc.)
- Marocchi F.lli S.p.A. (Precision Sales International, Inc.)
- Mauser Werke Oberndorf (GSI, Inc.)
- MEC-Gar S.R.L. (MEC-Gar U.S.A., Inc.)
- Merkel Freres (GSI, Inc.)
- Miroku, B.C./Daly, Charles (Bell's Legendary Country Wear; K.B.I., Inc.)
Miltex Inc.
- Morini (Mandall Shooting Supplies; Nygord Precision Products)
M.Thys (Champlin Firearms, Inc.)
- Navy Arms Co. (Forgett Jr., Valmore J.; Navy Arms Co.)
- New SKB Arms Co. (G.U., Inc.)
Norica, Avnda Otaola
- Norinco (Century International Arms, Inc.; Interarms)
- Norma Precision AB (Dynamit Nobel-RWS Inc.; The Paul Co., Inc.)
- Para-Ordnance Mfg., Inc. (Para-Ordnance, Inc.)
- Pardini Armi Srl. (Nygord Precision Products; MCS, Inc.)
- Pedersoli and Co., Davide (Beauchamp & Son, Inc.; Cabela's; Cape Outfitters; Cimarron Arms; Dixie Gun Works, Inc.; EMF Co., Inc.; Navy Arms Co.; Track of the Wolf, Inc.)
Pease International
Perugini-Visini & Co. s.r.l.
Peters Stahl GmbH (Franzen International, Inc.)

- Pietta (Navy Arms Co.; Taylor's & Co., Inc.)
- Piotti (Moore & Co., Wm. Larkin)
- Powell & Son Ltd., William (Powell Agency, The, William)
- Rigby & Co., John
- Rizzini, Battista (Moore & Co., Wm. Larkin; New England Arms Co.)
- Rizzini F.lli (Moore & Co., Wm. Larkin; New England Arms Co.)
- Rossi S.A., Amadeo (Interarms) Rutten (Labanu, Inc.)
- RWS (Dynamit Nobel-RWS, Inc.)
- Sabatti S.R.L. (E.A.A. Corp.)
- Sako Ltd. (Stoeger Industries)
- San Marco (Cape Outfitters; EMF Co., Inc.)
- S.A.R.L. G. Granger
- Sauer (Paul Co., The; Sigarms, Inc.)
- Savage Arms (Canada), Inc. (Savage Arms, Inc.)
- S.I.A.C.E. (IAR, Inc.)
- SIG (Mandall Shooting Supplies, Inc.)
- SIG-Sauer (Sigarms, Inc.) Scott Pilkington Little Tree
- Societa Armi Bresciane Srl. (Cape Outfitters; Gamba, USA)
- Sphinx Engineering SA (Sphinx USA Inc.)
- Springfield, Inc. (Springfield, Inc.)
- Star Bonifacio Echeverria S.A. (E.A.A. Corp.; Interarms; P.S.M.G. Gun Co.)
- Steyr-Mannlicher AG (GSI, Inc.; Nygord Precision Products)
- Tanfoglio Fratelli S.r.l. (E.A.A. Corp.)
- Tanner (Mandall Shooting Supplies, Inc.)
- Taurus International Firearms (Taurus Firearms, Inc.)

Taurus S.A., Forjas
Techno Arms (Auto-Ordnance Corp.)
T.F.C. S.p.A.
- Tikka (Stoeger Industries)
- TOZ (Nygord Precision Products) Turkish Firearms Corp. (Turkish Firearms Corp.)
- Uberti, Aldo (American Arms, Inc.; Cabela's; Cimarron Arms; Dixie Gun Works, Inc.; EMF Co., Inc.; Forgett Jr., Valmore J.; IAR, Inc.; Navy Arms Co.; Taylor's & Co., Inc.; Uberti USA, Inc.)
- Ugartechea S.A., Ignacio (Aspen Out fitting Co.; Gun Shop, The; Hanus Birdguns, Bill; Lion Country Supply)
- Ultralux (Keng's Firearms Specialty, Inc.)
- Unique/M.A.P.F. (Nygord Precision Products) Valtro USA Inc.
- Voere-KGH m.b.H. (JägerSport, Ltd.)
- Walther GmbH, Carl (Champion's Choice; Interarms; P.S.M.G. Gun Co.)
- Weatherby, Inc. (Weatherby, Inc.)
- Webley & Scott Ltd. (Beeman Precision Airguns; Groenewold, John)
- Weihrauch KG, Hermann (Beeman Precision Airguns; E.A.A. Corp.)
- Westley Richards & Co. (Westley Richards Agency USA) Whiscombe (Pelaire Products)
- Wolf (J.R. Distributing)
- Zabala, Hermanos S.A. (American Arms, Inc.)
- Zanoletti, Pietro (Mandall Shooting Supplies, Inc.) Zoli, Antonio

LaFrance Specialties
- Lakefield Arms Ltd.
* L A R Mfg., Inc.
- Laseraim, Inc. Lever Arms Service Ltd. Ljutic Industries, Inc. Lock's Philadelphia Gun Exchange
- Lorcin Engineering Co., Inc. Madis, George Mag-Na-Port International, Inc.
- Magnum Research, Inc. Mandell Shooting Supply
- Marlin Firearms Co.
- Maverick Arms, Inc.
- McBros Rifle Co. Miller Arms, Inc.
- MKS Supply, Inc. M.O.A. Corp.
- Montana Armory, Inc.
- Mossberg & Sons, Inc., O.F. Mountain Rifles Inc. MPI Stocks New England Firearms NCP Products, Inc.
- North American Arms, Inc. North Star West Nowlin Mfg. Co. Nowling Gun Shop October Country Olympic Arms, Inc. Oregon Arms, Inc. Parker & Sons Gunsmithing Phillips & Rogers, Inc.
- Phoenix Arms Professional Ordnance, Inc. Proware Inc.
- Quality Parts Co. Raptor Arms Co., Inc.
- Remington Arms Co., Inc. Republic Arms, Inc.

Rifle Works & Armory
- Rocky Mountain Arms, Inc.
- Rogue Rifle Co., Inc. Rogue River Rifleworks RPM Ruger
- Savage Arms (Canada), Inc. Scattergun Technologies, Inc.
- Seecamp Co., Inc., L.W. Sharps Arms Co., Inc., C. Shepherd & Turpin Dist. Company
- Shiloh Rifle Mfg. Small Arms Specialties
- Smith & Wesson
- Sporting Arms Mfg., Inc.
- Springfield, Inc. STI International
- Stoeger Industries
- Sturm, Ruger & Co., Inc.
- Sundance Industries, Inc.
- Sunny Hill Enterprizes, Inc.
- Swivel Machine Works, Inc.
- Tar-Hunt Custom Rifles, Inc.
- Texas Armory
- Taurus Firearms, Inc.
- Thompson/Center Arms Time Precision, Inc. Tristar Sporting Arms, Ltd.
- Ultra Light Arms, Inc. UFA, Inc. U.S. Repeating Arms Co. Wallace, Terry
- Weatherby, Inc. Wescombe, Bill Wesson Firearms Co., Inc. Wesson Firearms, Dan Whildin & Sons Ltd., E.H.
- Wildey, Inc.
- Wilkinson Arms Z-M Weapons

GUNS, U.S.-MADE

A.A. Arms, Inc.
- Accu-Tek Acra-Bond Laminates
- Airrow Allred Bullet Co.
- American Arms, Inc.
- American Derringer Corp. American Frontier Firearms Co. A.M.T. Angel Arms Inc.
- ArmaLite, Inc. Armscorp USA Inc. A-Square Co., Inc. Austin & Halleck
- Auto-Ordnance Corp.
- Baer Custom, Inc., Les
- Barrett Firearms Mfg., Inc. Bar-Sto Precision Machine
- Beretta S.p.A., Pietro
- Beretta U.S.A. Corp. Big Bear Arms & Sporting Goods, Inc.
- Bond Arms, Inc.
- Braverman Corp., R.J. Brockman's Custom Gunsmithin
- Brolin Industries Inc.
- Brown Co., E. Arthur Brown Products, Inc., Ed
- Browning Arms Co. (Parts & Service)
- Bushmaster Firearms Calhoon Varmint Bullets, James
- Calico Light Weapon Systems
- Cape Outfitters Casull Arms Corp.
- Century Gun Dist., Inc.
- Champlin Firearms, Inc.
- Colt's Mfg. Co., Inc.
- Competitor Corp., Inc. Conetrol Scope Mounts
- Connecticut Shotgun Mfg. Co.
- Connecticut Valley Classics Coonan Arms Cooper Arms Crossfire LLC Cryo-Accurizing
- Cumberland Arms Cumberland Mountain Arms
- CVA
- CVC Daisy manufacturing
- Dakota Arms, Inc. Dangler, Homer L.

- Davis Industries
- Dayton Traister
- Dixie Gun Works, Inc. Downsizer Corp.
- Eagle Arms, Inc.
- Emerging Technologies, Inc.
- Essex Arms E Arthur Brown Co Ed's Gun House
- Enterprise Arms Inc. FN Herstal
- Forgett Jr., Valmore J. Fort Worth Firearms Frank Custom Classic Arms, Ron
- Freedom Arms, Inc. Fulton Armory Galazan Genecco Gun Works, K. Gentry Custom Gunmaker, David
- Gibbs Rifle Co., Inc.
- Gilbert Equipment Co., Inc.
- Gonic Arms, Inc. Gunsite Custom Shop Gunsite Gunsmithy
- H&R 1871, Inc.
- Harris Gunworks Harrington & Richardson
- Hawken Shop, The Heritage Firearms Heritage Manufacturing, Inc. Hesco-Meprolight Hi-Point Firearms
- HJS Arms, Inc. Hoenig, George Holston Ent. Inc. H-S Precision, Inc. Hutton Rifle Ranch IAR Inc. Imperial Russian Armory
- Intratec Ithaca Gun Co., LLC Jones, J.D. J.P. Enterprises, Inc. J.P. Gunstocks Inc. JS Worldwide DBA
- Kahr Arms Kelbly, Inc.
- Kel-Tec CNC Industries, Inc.
- Kimber of America, Inc. K.K. Arms Co.
- Knight's Mfg. Co.

GUNS AND GUN PARTS, REPLICA AND ANTIQUE

Ahlman Guns
Armi San Paolo
Auto-Ordnance Corp.
Bear Mountain Gun & Tool
Beauchamp & Son, Inc.
Billings Gunsmiths, Inc.
Bob's Gun Shop
British Antiques
Buckskin Machine Works
Buffalo Arms Co.
Cache La Poudre Rifleworks
Cape Outfitters
Chambers Flintlocks Ltd., Jim
Chicasaw Gun Works
Cochran, Oliver
Cogar's Gunsmithing
Cole's Gun Works
Colonial Arms, Inc.
Colonial Repair
Custom Riflestocks, Inc.
Dale's Gun Shop
Dangler, Homer L.
Day & Sons, Inc., Leonard
Delhi Gun House
Delta Arms Ltd.
Dilliott Gunsmithing, Inc.
Dyson & Son., Ltd. Peter
Ed's Gun House
Euroarms of Armerica Inc.
Flintlocks, Etc.
Forgett, Valmore J., Jr.
Galaxy Imports Ltd Inc.
Getz Barrel Co.
Golden Age Arms Co.
Goodwin, Fred
Groenewold, John
Gun Parts Corp., The
Gun Works, The
Guns
Gun-Tec
Hastings Barrels
Hunkeler, A.
IAR, Inc.
Jedediah Starr Trading Co.
Kokolus, Michael
Liberty Antique Gunworks
List Precision Engineering
Lock's Philadelphia Gun Exchange
L&R Lock Co.
Lucas, Edw. E.

Mandall Shooting Supplies, Inc.
Martin's Gun Shop
McKee Publications
McKinney, R.P.
Mountain State Muzzleloading Supplies, Inc.
Muzzleloaders Etcetera Inc
Mowrey Gun Works
Munsch Gunsmithing, Tommy
Museum of Historical Arms, Inc.
Navy Arms Co.
Neumann GmbH
North Star West
Nu-Line Guns Inc.
Pasadena Gun Center
Pecatonica River Longrifle
PEM's Mfg. Co.
Pony Express Sport Shop, Inc.
Precise Metalsmithing Enterprises
Quality Firearms of Idaho, Inc.
Randco UK
Ravell Ltd.
Retting, Inc., Martin B.
R.G.-G., Inc.
S&S Firearms
Samco Global Arms
Sarco, Inc.
Shootin' Shack, Inc.
Silver Ridge Gun Shop
Simmons Gun Repair, Inc.
Southern Ammunition Co., Inc.
Starnes Gunmaker, Ken
Stott's Creek Armory, Inc.
Taylor's & Co., Inc.
Tennessee Valley Mfg.
Tiger-Hunt
Triple-K Mfg. Co., Inc.
Uberti USA, Inc.
Vintage Industries, Inc.
Vortek Products, Inc.
Walker Arms Co., Inc.
Weisz Parts
Wells Custom Guns, R.A.
Wescombe, Bill
Winchester Sutler, Inc., The

• See page 437 for Warranty Service Center Addresses

GUNS, SURPLUS—PARTS AND AMMUNITION

Ad Hominem
Ahlman Guns
Alpha 1 Drop Zone
Armscorp USA, Inc.
Arundel Arms & Ammunition, Inc., A.
Bolin Industries Inc.
Bondini Paolo
Century International Arms, Inc.
Chuck's Gun Shop
Cole's Gun Works
Combat Military Ordnance Ltd.
Delta Arms Ltd.
Ed's Gun House
First, Inc., Jack
Flaig's
Fleming Firearms
Forgett, Valmore J., Jr.
Forrest, Inc., Tom
Frankonia Jagd
Garcia National Gun Traders, Inc.
Goodwin, Fred
Gun City
Gun Parts Corp., The
Hallberg Gunsmith, Fritz
Hart & Son, Inc., Robert W.
Hank's Gun Shop
Hege Jagd-u. Sporthandels, GmbH
Hofmann & Co.
Interarms
Jackalope Gun Shop
LaRocca Gun Works, Inc.
Lever Arms Service Ltd.

Log Cabin Shop Inc.
Lomont Precision Bullets
Mandall Shooting Supplies, Inc.
Navy Arms Co.
Nevada Pistol Academy Inc.
Oil Rod and Gun Shop
Paragon Sales & Services, Inc.
Parts & Surplus
Pasadena Gun Center
Perazone, Brian
Quality Firearms of Idaho, Inc.
Ravell Ltd.
Retting, Inc., Martin B.
Samco Global Arms, Inc.
San Francisco Gun Exchange
Sarco, Inc.
Shootin' Shack, Inc.
Silver Ridge Gun Shop
Simmons Gun Repair, Inc.
Sportsmen's Exchange & Western
    Gun Traders, Inc.
Springfield Sporters, Inc.
Starnes Gunmaker, Ken
Tarnhelm Supply Co., Inc.
T.F.C. S.p.A.
Thurston Sports, Inc.
Williams Shootin' Iron Service
Whitestone Lumber Corp.
GUNSMITHS, CUSTOM
    (see Custom Gunsmiths)
GUNSMITHS, HANDGUN
    (see Pistolsmiths)

GUNSMITH SCHOOLS

American Gunsmithing Institute
Bull Mountain Rifle Co.
Colorado Gunsmithing Academy
Colorado School of Trades
Cylinder & Slide, Inc.
Lassen Community College, GRS
    Corp, Glendo
    Gunsmithing Dept.
Laughridge, William R.
Log Cabin Shop Inc.
Modern Gun Repair School
Montgomery Community College
Murray State College
North American Correspondence
    Schools

Nowlin Mfg. Co.
Nowling Gun Shop
NRI Gunsmith School
Pennsylvania Gunsmith School
Piedmont Community College
Pine Technical College
Professional Gunsmiths of America
Southeastern Community College
Smith & Wesson
Spencer's Custom Guns
Trinidad State Junior College
    Gunsmithing Dept.
Wright's Hardwood Gunstock Blanks
Yavapai College

GUNSMITH SUPPLIES, TOOLS, SERVICES

Ace Custom 45's, Inc.
Actions by "T"
Aldis Gunsmithing & Shooting Supply
Alley Supply Co.
Allred Bullet Co.
American Frontier Firearms Co.
Baer Custom, Inc., Les
Bar-Sto Precision Machine
Bear Mountain Gun & Tool
Belt MTN Arms
Bengtson Arms Co., L.
Biesen, Al
Biesen, Roger
Bill's Gun Repair
Blue Ridge Machinery & Tools, Inc.
Break-Free, Inc.
Briley Mfg., Inc.
Brockman's Custom Gunsmithin
Brown Products Inc., Ed
Brownells, Inc.
B-Square Co., Inc.
Bull Mountain Rifle Co.
Burkhart Gunsmithing, Don
C&J Enterprises Inc.
Carbide Checkering Tools
Caywood, Shane J.
Chapman Manufacturing Co.
Chem-Pak, Inc.
Choate Machine & Tool Co., Inc.
Chopie Mfg., Inc.
Chuck's Gun Shop
Clark Custom Guns, Inc.
Colonial Arms, Inc.
Colorado School of Trades
Conetrol Scope Mounts
Craig Custom Ltd.
CRR, Inc./Marble's Inc.
Cumberland Arms
Cumberland Mountain Arms
Custom Checkering Service

Custom Gun Products
D&J Bullet Co. & Custom Gun Shop,
    Inc.
Decker Shooting Products
Dem-Bart Checkering Tools, Inc.
Dever Co., Jack
Dewey Mfg. Co., Inc., J.
Dremel Mfg. Co.
Du-Lite Corp.
Dutchman's Firearms, Inc., The
Dyson & Son, Ltd., Peter
Echols & Co., D'Arcy
EGW Evolution Gun Works
Erhardt, Dennis A
Faith Associates, Inc.
FERLIB
Fisher, Jerry A.
Forgreens Tool Mfg., Inc.
Forkin, Ben
Forster, Kathy
Gilkes, Anthony W.
Grace Metal Products, Inc.
Greider Precision
GRS Corp, Glendo
GrÇ-Tan Rifles
Gun Hunter Trading
Gunline Tools
Gun-Tec
Half Moon Rifle Shop
Halstead, Rick
Hammon Custom Guns Ltd.
Hastings Barrels
Henriksen Tool Co., Inc.
High Performance International
Hines Co., S.C.
Hoelscher, Virgil
Holland's
Huey Gun Cases
Ivanoff, Thomas G.
J&R Engineering

J&S Heat Treat
Jacobson, Teddy
Jantz Supply
  Jedediah Starr Trading Co.
JGS Precision Tool Mfg.
Kasenit Co., Inc.
Kimball, Gary
Kleinendorst, K.W.
Kmount
Kopp Professional Gunsmithing, Terry
  K.
Korzinek Riflesmith, J.
Kwik Mount Corp.
LaBounty Precision Reboring
Lea Mfg. Co.
Lee's Red Ramps
Lee Supplies, Mark
List Precision Engineering
London Guns Ltd.
Mahovsky's Metalife
Marble Arms
Marsh, Mike
McKillen & Heyer, Inc.
Menck, Thomas W.
Metalife Industries
Metaloy Inc.
Michael's Antiques
MMC
Morrow, Bud
Mo's Competitor Supplies
Mowrey's Guns & Gunsmithing
N&J Sales
New England Custom Gun Service
Now Products Inc
Nowlin Custom Mfg.
Nowling Gun Shop
Nu-Line Guns, Inc.
Ole Frontier Gunsmith Shop
Parker Gun Finishes
PEM's Mfg. Co.
Perazone, Brian
P.M. Enterprises, Inc.
Power Custom, Inc.
Practical Tools, Inc.
Precision Metal Finishing
Precision Specialties
Professional Gunsmiths of America
Prolix/Æ Lubricants

Ransom International Corp.
Reardon Products
Rice, Keith
Robar Co.'s, Inc., The
Rocky Mountain Arms Inc.
Romain's Custom Guns, Inc.
Roto Carve
Royal Arms Gunstocks
Rusteprufe Laboratories
Scott, McDougall & Associates
Shooter's Choice
Simmons Gun Repair, Inc.
Smith Abrasives, Inc.
Southern Bloomer Mfg Co.
Spradlin's
Starrett Co., L.S.
Stiles Custom Guns
Sullivan, David S.
Texas Platers Supply
Time Precision, Inc.
Tom's Gun Repair
Track of the Wolf, Inc.
Trinidad State Junior College
    Gunsmithing Dept.
United States Products Co.
Trulock Tool
Turnbull Restoration, Doug
Van Gorden & Son, Inc., C.S.
Venco Industries, Inc.
Volquartsen Custom Ltd.
Warne Manufacturing Co.
Washita Mountain Whetstone Co.
Weaver Arms Corp. Gun Shop
Weigand Combat Handguns, Inc.
Wells, Fred F.
Welsh, Bud
Westrom, John
Westwind Rifles, Inc.
White Rock Tool & Die
Wilcox All-Pro Tools & Supply
Will-Burt Co.
Williams Gun Sight Co.
Williams Shootin' Iron Service
Willow Bend
Wise Guns, Dale
Wright's Hardwood Gunstock Blanks
Wolff Co., W.C.
Yavapai College

HANDGUN ACCESSORIES

A.A. Arms, Inc.
Ace Custom 45's, Inc.
Action Direct, Inc.
ADCO Sales, Inc.
Adventurer's Outpost
African Import Co.
Aimpoint U.S.A.
Aimtech Mount Systems
Ajax Custom Grips, Inc.
Alpha Gunsmith Division
American Derringer Corp.
American Frontier Firearms Co.
Arms Corporation of the Philippines
Aro-Tek, Ltd.
Astra Sport, S.A.
Baer Custom, Inc., Les
Bagmaster Mfg. Inc.
Bar-Sto Precision Machine
BEC, Inc.
Behlert Precision, Inc.
Berry's Mfg. Inc.
Blue and Gray Products, Inc.
Bohemia Arms Co.
Bolin Industries Inc.
Bond Custom Firearms
Broken Gun Ranch
Brooks Tactical Systems
Brown Products, Inc., Ed
Bucheimer, J.M.
Bushmaster Firearms
Bushmaster Hunting & Fishing
Butler Creek Corp.
C3 Systems
Cannon Safe Co. Inc.
CATCO
Centaur Systems, Inc.
Central Specialties Ltd.
Ciener Inc., Jonathan Arthur
Conetrol Scope Mounts
Craig Custom Ltd.
CRR, Inc./Marble's Inc.
D&L Industries
Dade Screw Machine Products
Dayson Arms Ltd.

Delhi Gun House
D.J. Marketing
Doskocil Mfg. Co., Inc
E Arthur Brown Co
E&L Mfg., Inc.
E.A.A. Corp.
Eagle International Sporting Goods,
    Inc.
Euroarms of America Inc.
European American Armory Corp.
Faith Associates, Inc.
Federal Arms Corp. of America
Feminine Protection, Inc.
Fisher Custom Firearms
Fleming Firearms
Flores Publications, Inc., J.
Frielich Police Equipment
FWB
Galati International
GALCO International Ltd.
Garthwaite Pistolsmith, Jim
G.G. & G.
Glock, Inc.
Gould & Goodrich
Greider Precision
Gremmel Enterprises
Gun Parts Corp., The
Gun-Alert
Gun-Ho Sports Cases
Haselbauer Products, Jerry
Hebard Guns, Gil
Heinie Specialty Products
Henigson & Associates
Hill Speed Leather, Ernie
H.K.S. Products
Hoppe's Div.
H-S Precision Inc.
Hunter Co., Inc.
Impact Case Co.
Israel Arms International
Jarvis, Inc.
JB Custom
Jeffredo Gunsight
Jones, J.D.

J.P. Enterprises, Inc.
Jumbo Sports Products
Kalispel Case Line
KeeCo Impressions
KK Air International
Keller Co., The
King's Gun Works
K.K. Arms Co.
L&S Technologies, Inc.
Lasermax Inc.
Lee's Red Ramps
Loch Leven Industries
Lohman Mfg. Co., Inc.
Mac's .45 Shop
Mag-Na-Port International, Inc.
Magnolia Sports, Inc.
Marble Arms
Markell, Inc.
Maxi-Mount
MCA Sports
McCormick Corp., Chip
MEC-Gar S.R.L.
Menck Gunsmith Inc., T. W.
Merkuria Ltd.
Michaels of Oregon Co.
Mid-America Guns and Ammo
Middlebrooks Custom Shop
Millett Sights
MTM Molded Products Co., Inc.
MCA Sports
Noble Co., Jim
No-Sho Mfg. Co.
Nowling Gun Shop
Omega Sales
Outdoor Sports Hdqtr
Ox-Yoke Originals, Inc.
Pachmayr LTD

PAST Sporting Goods, Inc.
Pearce Grip, Inc.
Penguin Industries, Inc.
Phoenix Arms
Practical Tools, Inc.
Protector Mfg. Co., Inc., The
Quality Parts Co.
Ram-Line Blount, Inc.
Ranch Products
Ransom International Corp.
Redfield, Inc.
Ringler Custom Leather Co.
Round Edge, Inc.
RPM
Simmons Gun Repair, Inc.
Slings 'N Things, Inc.
Southern Bloomer Mfg. Co.
Southwind Sanctions
Springfield Inc.
"Su-Press-On" Inc.
TacStar Industries, Inc.
TacTell, Inc.
Tanfoglio Fratelli S.r.l.
T.F.C. S.p.A.
Thompson/Center Arms
Trigger Lock Division
Trijicon, Inc.
Triple-K Mfg. Co., Inc.
Tyler Manufacturing & Distributing
Valor Corp.
Volquartsen Custom Ltd.
Waller & Son, Inc., W.
Weigand Combat Handguns, Inc.
Western Design
Wichita Arms, Inc.
Wilson Gun Shop
Wolff Co., W.C.

HANDGUN GRIPS

A.A. Arms, Inc.
Ahrends, Kim
Ajax Custom Grips, Inc.
Altamont Co.
American Derringer Corp.
American Frontier Firearms Co.
American Gripcraft
Arms Corporation of the Philippines
Aro-Tek Ltd.
Art Jewel Enterprises Ltd.
Baelder, Harry
Baer Custom, Inc., Les
Barami Corp.
Bear Hug Grips, Inc.
Big Bear Arms & Sporting Goods, Inc.
Bohemia Arms Co.
Boone's Custom Ivory Grips, Inc.
Boone Trading Co. Inc.
Boyds' Gunstock Industries, Inc.
Brooks Tactical Systems
Brown Products, Inc., Ed
CAM Enterprises
Cole-Grip
Colonial Repair
Crimson Trace
Custom Firearms
E.A.A. Corp.
EMF Co., Inc.
Essex Arms
European American Armory Corp.
Eyears Insurance
Fisher Custom Firearms
Fitz Pistol Grip Co.
Forrest, Inc., Tom
FWB

Garthwaite Pistolsmith, Jim
Herrett's Stocks, Inc.
Hogue Grips
H-S Precision Inc.
Huebner, Corey O.
KeeCo Impressions
Korth
Lee's Red Ramps
Lett Custom Grips
Linebaugh Custom Sixgun
Mac's .45 Shop
Masen Co., Inc., John
Michaels of Oregon Co.
Mid-America Guns and Ammo
Millett Sights
N.C. Ordnance Co.
Newell, Robert H.
Norman Custom Gunstocks, Jim
Northern Precision Custom SW
Pachmayr LTD
Pardini Armi Srl
Pilgrim Pewter, Inc.
Radical Concepts
Rosenberg & Sons, Jack A.
Roy's Custom Grips
Sile Distributors, Inc.
Smith & Wesson
Spegel, Craig
Stoeger Industries
Taurus Firearms, Inc.
Tyler Manufacturing & Distributing
Uncle Mike's
Vintage Industries, Inc.
Volquartsen Custom Ltd.
Western Gunstock Mfg. Co.

HEARING PROTECTORS

Aero Peltor
Ajax Custom Grips, Inc.
Autauga Arms, Inc.
Brown Co., E. Arthur
Brown Products, Inc., Ed
Browning Arms Co.
Clark Co., Inc., David
E-A-R, Inc.
Electronic Shooters Protection, Inc.
Faith Associates, Inc.
Flents Products Co., Inc.

Gentex Corp.
Hoppe's Div.
Kesselring Gun Shop
North Specialty Products
Paterson Gunsmithing
Peltor, Inc.
Penguin Industries, Inc.
R.E.T. Enterprises
Rucker Dist. Inc.
Silencio/Safety Direct
Willson Safety Prods. Div.

HOLSTERS AND LEATHER GOODS

AA Arms, Inc.
A&B Industries, Inc.
Action Direct, Inc.

Action Products, Inc.
Aker Leather Products
Alessi Holsters, Inc.

American Sales & Mfg. Co.
Arratoonian, Andy
Bagmaster, Inc.
Baker's Leather Goods, Roy
Bandcor Industries
Bang-Bang Boutique
Barami Corp.
Bear Hug Grips, Inc.
Beretta S.p.A., Pietro
Bianchi International, Inc.
Bill's Custom Cases
Blocker Holsters, Inc., Ted
Brauer Bros. Mfg. Co.
Brooks Tactical Systems
Brown, H.R.
Browning Arms Co.
Bucheimer, J.M.
Bull-X, Inc.
Bushwacker Backpack & Supply Co.
Cathey Enterprises, Inc.
Chace Leather Products
Churchill Glove Co., James
Cimarron Arms
Clements' Custom Leathercraft, Chas
Cobra Sport
Colonial Repair
Counter Assault
Creedmoor Sports, Inc.
Davis Leather Co., G. Wm.
Delhi Gun House
DeSantis Holster & Leather Goods,
  Inc.
Dixie Gun Works, Inc.
Ekol Leather Care
El Dorado Leather (c/o Dill)
El Paso Saddlery Co.
EMF Co., Inc.
Eutaw Co., Inc., The
F&A Inc.
Faust, Inc., T.G.
Feminine Protection, Inc.
Flores Publications, Inc., J.
Fobus International Ltd.
Forgett Jr., Valmore J.
Frankonia Jagd
Gage Manufacturing
GALCO International Ltd.
GML Products, Inc.
Gould & Goodrich
Gun Leather Limited
Gunfitters, The
Gun Works, The
Gusty Winds Corp.
Hafner Creations, Inc.
HandiCrafts Unltd.
Hank's Gun Shop
Hebard Guns, Gil
Heinie Specialty Products
Hellweg Ltd.
Henigson & Associates, Steve
Hill Speed Leather, Ernie
High North Products Inc.
Hofmann & Co.
Holster Shop, The
Horseshoe Leather Products
Hoyt Holster Co., Inc.
Hume, Don

Hunter Co., Inc.
Israel Arms International
John's Custom Leather
Jumbo Sports Products
Kane Products, Inc.
Keller Co., The
Kirkpatrick Leather Co.
KL Null Holsters Ltd.
Kolpin Mfg., Inc.
Korth
Kramer Handgun Leather, Inc.
L A R Mfg., Inc.
Law Concealment Systems, Inc.
Lawrence Leather Co.
Leather Arsenal
Lock's Philadelphia Gun Exchange
Lone Star Gunleather
Magnolia Sports, Inc.
Markell, Inc.
Michaels of Oregon Co.
Minute Man High Tech Industries
Noble Co., Jim
No-Sho Mfg. Co.
Null Holsters Ltd., K.L.
October Country
Ojala Holsters, Arvo
Oklahoma Leather Products, Inc.
Old West Reproductions, Inc.
Paser Pal
Pathfinder Sports Leather
PWL Gunleather
Renegade
Ringler Custom Leather Co.
Rumanya Inc.
Rybka Custom Leather Equipment,
  Thad
Safariland Ltd., Inc.
Safety Speed Holster, Inc.
Schulz Industries
Second Chance Body Armor
Shoemaker & Sons, Inc., Tex
ShurKatch Corporation
Sile Distributors Inc.
Silhouette Leathers
Smith Saddlery, Jesse W.
Southwind Sanctions
Sparks, Milt
Stalker, Inc.
Starr Trading Co., Jedediah
Strong Holster Co.
Stuart, V. Pat
Tabler Marketing
Top-Line USA Inc.
Torel, Inc.
Triple-K Mfg. Co., Inc.
Tristar Sporting Arms, Ltd.
Tyler
Tyler Manufacturing & Distributing
Uncle Mike's
Valor Corp.
Venus Industries
Viking Leathercraft, Inc.
Walt's Custom Leather
Westley Richards & Co.
Whinnery, Walt
Wild Bill's Originals
Wilson Gun Shop

HUNTING AND CAMP GEAR, CLOTHING, ETC.

A&M Waterfowl, Inc.
Ace Sportswear, Inc.
Action Direct, Inc.
Action Products, Inc.
Adventure Game Calls
Adventure 16, Inc.
Allen Co., Bob
Allen Sportswear, Bob
Armor
Atlanta Cutlery Corp.
Atsko/Sno-Seal, Inc.
Baekgaard Ltd.
Bagmaster Mfg., Inc.
Barbour, Inc.
Bauer, Eddie
Bear Archery
Beaver Park Products, Inc
Beretta S.p.A., Pietro
Better Concepts Co.
Big Beam Emergency Systems, Inc.
Boss Manufacturing Co.
Brown, H.R.
Brown Manufacturing
Browning Arms Co.
Buck Stop Lure Co., Inc.

Bushmaster Hunting & Fishing
Camofare Co.
Camp-Cap Products Division
Carhartt, Inc.
Catoctin Cutlery
Chippewa Shoe Co.
Churchill Glove Co., James
Clarkfield Enterprises, Inc.
Coghlan's Ltd.
Cold Steel, Inc.
Coleman Co., Inc.
Coulston Products, Inc.
Creative Concepts USA Inc.
Creedmoor Sports, Inc.
D&H Prods. Co., Inc.
Dakota Corp.
Danner Shoe Mfg. Co.
DeckSlider of Florida
Deer Me Products
Dr. O's Products Ltd.
Dunham Co.
Duofold, Inc.
Dynalite Products, Inc.
E-A-R, Inc.
Ekol Leather Care

Erickson's Mfg., Inc., C.W.
Eutaw Co., Inc., The
F&A Inc.
Flores Publications, Inc., J.
Flow-Rite of Tennessee, Inc.
Forrest Tool Co.
Fortune Products Inc.
Fox River Mills, Inc.
G&H Decoys, Inc.
Gander Mountain, Inc.
Gerber Legendary Blades
Glacier Glove
Gozon Corp
Co.
Hafner Creations, Inc.
Heritage Wildlife Carvings
Hinman Outfitters, Bob
Hodgman, Inc.
Houtz & Barwick
Hunter's Specialties, Inc.
Just Brass, Inc.
K&M Industries, Inc.
Kamik Outdoor Footwear
Kolpin Mfg., Inc.
LaCrosse Footwear, Inc.
Langenberg Hat Co.
Lectro Science, Inc.
Liberty Trouser Co.
L.L. Bean, Inc.
MAG Instrument, Inc.
Mag-Na-Port International, Inc.
Marathon Rubber Prods. Co., Inc.
McCann's Machine & Gun Shop
Melton Shirt Co., Inc.
Molin Industries
Mountain Hollow Game Calls
Nelson/Weather-Rite, Inc.
North Specialty Products
Northlake Outdoor Footwear
Original Mink Oil, Inc.
Orvis Co., The
Outdoor Connection, Inc., The
Palsa Outdoor Products
Partridge Sales Ltd., John

Pointing Dog Journal
Powell & Son (Gunmakers) Ltd.,
William
Pro-Mark
Pyramid, Inc.
Randolph Engineering, Inc.
Ranger Mfg. Co., Inc.
Ranging, Inc.
Rattlers Brand
Red Ball
Re-Heater, Inc.
Rocky, Shoes & Boots
Ringler Custom Leather Co.
Scansport, Inc.
Sceery Game Calls
Servus Footwear Co.
ShurKatch Corporation
Simmons Outdoor Corp.
Slings 'N Things, Inc.
Sno-Seal
Streamlight, Inc.
Swanndri New Zealand
10-X Products Group
Thompson, Norm
T.H.U. Enterprises, Inc.
Tink's Safariland Hunting Corp.
Thompson/Center Arms
Torel, Inc.
TrailTimer Co.
Triple-K Mfg. Co., Inc.
United Cutlery Corp.
Venus Industries
Wakina by Pic
Walker Co., B.B.
Walls Industries
Wideview Scope Mount Corp.
Wilderness Sound Products Ltd.
Willson Safety Prods. Div.
Winchester Sutler, Inc., The
Wolverine Boots & Outdoor Footwear
Division
Woolrich Woolen Mills
Wyoming Knife Corp.
Yellowstone Wilderness Supply

KNIVES AND KNIFEMAKER'S SUPPLIES FACTORY AND MAIL ORDER

Action Direct, Inc.
Adventure 16, Inc.
Aitor-Cuchilleria Del Norte, S.A.
All Rite Products, Inc.
American Target Knives
Aristocrat Knives
Art Jewel Enterprises Ltd.
Atlanta Cutlery Corp.
B&D Trading Co., Inc.
Barteaux Machetes, Inc.
Benchmark Knives
Beretta S.p.A., Pietro
Beretta U.S.A. Corp.
Big Bear Arms & Sporting Goods, Inc.
Bill's Custom Cases
Blackjack Knives, Ltd.
Boker USA, Inc.
Boone's Custom Ivory Grips I
Boone Trading Co.
Bowen Knife Co. Inc.
Brooks Tactical Systems
Brown, H.R.
Browning Arms Co.
Buck Knives, Inc.
Buster's Custom Knives
CAM Enterprises
Camillus Cutlery Co.
Campbell, Dick
Case & Sons Cutlery Co., W.R.
Catoctin Cutlery
Chicago Cutlery Co.
Christopher Firearms Co., Inc., E.
Clements' Custom Leathercraft, Chas
Cold Steel, Inc.
Coleman Co., Inc.
Colonial Knife Co., Inc.
Compass Industries, Inc.
Creative Craftsman, Inc., The
Crosman Blades
CRR, Inc./Marble's Inc.
Cutco Cutlery
Cutlery Shoppe
DAMASCUS-U.S.A.
Dan's Whetstone Co., Inc.
Degen Inc.
Delhi Gun House

DeSantis Holster & Leather Goods,
Inc.
Diamond Machining Technology, Inc.
EdgeCraft Corp./P.B. Tuminello
EK Knife Co.
Empire Cutlery Corp.
Eze-Lap Diamond Prods.
Flitz International Ltd.
Flores Publications, Inc., J.
Forrest Tool Co.
Forthofer's Gunsmithing &
Knifemaking
Fortune Products, Inc.
Frank Knives
Frost Cutlery Co.
Gerber Legendary Blades
Gibbs Rifle Co., Inc.
Glock, Inc.
Golden Age Arms Co.
Gun Room, The
H&B Forge Co.
HandiCrafts Unltd.
Harrington Cutlery, Inc., Russell
Harris Publications
Henckels Zwillingswerk, Inc., J.A.
Hoppe's Div.
Hubertus Schneidwarenfabrik
Hunter Co., Inc.
Hunting Classics
Ibberson (Sheffield) Ltd., George
Imperial Schrade Corp.
J.A. Blades, Inc.
Jackalope Gun Shop
Jantz Supply
Jenco Sales, Inc.
Johnson Wood Products
KA-BAR Knives
Kasenit Co., Inc.
Kershaw Knives
Knife Importers, Inc.
Koval Knives
Lamson & Goodnow Mfg. Co.
Leapers Inc.
Leatherman Tool Group, Inc.
Linder Solingen Knives
Marble Arms
Mar Knives, Inc., Al

Matthews Cutlery
McCann Industries
McCann's Machine & Gun Shop
Molin Industries
Mountain State Muzzleloading
Supplies, Inc.
Murphy Co., Inc., R.
Normark Corp.
October Country
Outdoor Edge Cutlery Corp.
Penguin Industries, Inc.
Pilgrim Pewter, Inc.
Plaza Cutlery, Inc.
Precise International
Queen Cutlery Co.
R&C Knives & Such
Randall-Made Knives
Rodgers & Sons Ltd., Joseph
Russell Knives, Inc., A.G.
Scansport, Inc.
Schiffman, Mike

Schrimsher's Custom Knifemaker's
Supply, Bob
Sheffield Knifemakers Supply, Inc.
Shell Shack
Smith Saddlery, Jesse W.
Soque River Knives
Spyderco, Inc.
Swiss Army Knives, Inc.
T.F.C. S.p.A.
Traditions, Inc.
Tru-Balance Knife Co.
United Cutlery Corp.
Utica Cutlery Co.
Venus Industries
Washita Mountain Whetstone Co.
Weber Jr., Rudolf
Wells Creek Knife & Gun Works
Western Cutlery Co.
Whinnery, Walt
Wideview Scope Mount Corp.
Wostenholm
Wyoming Knife Corp.

LABELS, BOXES, CARTRIDGE HOLDERS

Ballistic Products, Inc.
Berry's Mfg., Inc.
Blackhawk East
Brown Co., E. Arthur
Cabinet Mountain Outfitters Scents &
Lures
Cape Outfitters
Crane & Crane Ltd.
Del Rey Products
DeSantis Holster & Leather Goods,
Inc.

Fitz Pistol Grip Co.
Flambeau Products Corp.
J&J Products Co.
Kolpin Mfg., Inc.
Liberty Shooting Supplies
Midway Arms, Inc.
MTM Molded Products Co., Inc.
Pendleton Royal
Ziegel Engineering

LOAD TESTING AND PRODUCT TESTING
(Chronographing, Ballistic Studies)

Accurate Arms Co. Inc.
Ballistic Research
Briese Bullet Co., Inc.
Clerke Co., J.A.
D&H Precision Tooling
Dale's Gun Shop
Defense Training International, Inc.
DGR Custom Rifles
Duane's Gun Repair
Henigson & Associates, Steve
Hensler, Jerry
Hoelscher, Virgil
Hutton Rifle Ranch
Jackalope Gun Shop
Jensen Bullets
KJM Fabritek Inc.
Liberty Shooting SPP

Linebaugh Custom Sixguns
Lomont Precision Bullets
Maionchi-L.M.I.
MAST Technology
McMurdo, Lynn
Middlebrooks Custom Shop
Multiplex International
Oil Rod and Gun Shop
Rupert's Gun Shop
SOS Products Co.
Spencer's Custom Guns
Vancini, Carl
Vulpes Ventures, Inc.
Wells Custom Gunsmith, R.A.
White Laboratory, Inc., H.P.
X-Spand Target Systems

MISCELLANEOUS

Actions, Rifle
Hall Manufacturing
Accurizing, Rifle
Richards, John
Stoney Baroque Shooters Supply
Adapters, Cartridge
Alex, Inc.
Adapters, Shotshell
PC Co.
Airgun Accessories
BSA Guns Ltd.
Airgun Repair
Airgun Repair Centre
Nationwide Airgun Repairs
Assault Rifle Accessories
Ram-Line Blount, Inc.
Barrel Stress Relieving
300° Below Services
Bi-Pods
B.M.F. Activator, Inc.
Body Armor
A&B Industries, Inc.
Faust, Inc., T.G.
Second Chance Body Armor
Top-Line USA Inc.
Bore Illuminator
Flashette Co.
Bore Lights
MDS, Inc.
Brass Catcher
Gage Manufacturing
M.A.M. Products, Inc.
Bullets, Rubber
CIDCO

Bullets, Moly Coat
NECO
Starke Bullet Company
Calendar, Gun Shows
Stott's Creek Printers
Cannons, Miniature Replicas
Furr Arms
Dehumidifiers
Buenger Enterprises
Hydrosorbent Products
Dryers
Peet Shoe Dryer, Inc.
E-Z Loader
Del Rey Products
Field Carts
Firearm Refinishers
Armoloy Co. of Ft. Worth
Firearm Restoration
Adair Custom Shop, Bill
Johns Master Engraver, Bill
Mazur Restoration, Pete
Moeller, Steve
Nicholson Custom
FFL Record Keeping
Basics Information Systems, Inc.
PFRB Co.
R.E.T. Enterprises
Hunting Trips
J/B Adventures & Safaris, Inc.
Professional Hunter Specialties
Safaris Plus
Wild West Guns
Hypodermic Rifles/Pistols

Multipropulseurs
Industrial Dessicants
WAMCO—New Mexico
Insert Barrels
MCA Sports
Lettering Restoration System
Pranger, Ed G.
Locks, Gun
Brown Manufacturing
Central Specialties Ltd.
L&R Lock Co.
Trigger Lock Division
Voere-KGH m.b.H.
Master Lock Co.
Magazines
Mag-Pack Corp.
Mech-Tech Systems Inc.
Mats
Brigade Quartermasters
Military Equipment/Accessories
Amherst Arms
Ruvel & Co., Inc.
Photographers, Gun
Bilal, Mustafa
Hanusin, John
Macbean, Stan
Payne Photography, Robert
Radack Photography, Lauren
Smith, Michael
Weyer International
White Pine Photographic Services
Pistol Barrel Maker
Bar-Sto Precision Machine
Power Tools, Rotary Flexible Shaft
Foredom Electric Co.
RF Barrel Vibration Reducer
Hoehn Sales, Inc.
RF Device
B.M.F. Activator Inc.
Saddle Rings, Studs
Silver Ridge Gun Shop
Safety Devices
P&M Sales and Service
Safeties
P.M. Enterprises, Inc.
Scents and Lures
Buck Stop Lure Co., Inc.
Cabinet Mountain Outfitters Scents & Lures
Dr. O's Products Ltd.
Flow-Rite of Tennessee, Inc.
Mountain Hollow Game Calls
Russ Trading Post
Tink's Safariland Hunting Corp.
Tinks & Ben Lee Hunting Products
Wellington Outdoors
Wildlife Research Center, Inc.
Wyant's Outdoor Products, Inc.
Scrimshaw
Dolbare, Elizabeth
Hoover, Harvey

Lovestrand, Erik
Reno, Wayne
Shooting Range Equipment
Caswell International Corp.
Shotgun Barrel Maker
Baker, Stan
Eyster Heritage Gunsmiths, Inc., Ken
Shotgun Conversion Tubes
Dina Arms Corporation
Silencers
AWC Systems Technology
DLO Mfg.
Fleming Firearms
S&H Arms Mfg. Co.
S.C.R.C.
Sound Technology
Ward Machine
Silver Sportsmen's Art
Bell, Sid
Heritage Wildlife Carvings
Slings and Swivels
DTM International, Inc.
Pathfinder Sports Leather
Schulz Industries
Torel, Inc.
Stock Finish
Richards, John
Treestands and Steps
A&J Products
Dr. O's Products Ltd.
Russ Trading Post
Silent Hunter
Summit Specialties, Inc.
Trax America, Inc.
Treemaster
Warren & Sweat Mfg. Co.
Trophies
Blackinton & Co., Inc., V.H.
Ventilated Rib
Simmons Gun Repair, Inc.
Ventilation
ScanCo Environmental Systems
Video Tapes
American Pioneer Video
Calibre Press, Inc.
Cedar Hill Game Calls, Inc.
Clements' Custom Leathercraft, Chas
Eastman Products, R.T.
Foothills Video Productions, Inc.
HandiCraft Unltd.
Lethal Force Institute
Police Bookkshelf
Primos, Inc.
Trail Visions
Wilderness Sound Products Ltd.
Wind Flags
Time Precision, Inc.
Xythos-Miniature Revolver
Andres & Dworsky

Flintlocks, Etc.
●Forgett Jr., Valmore J.
Fort Hill Gunstocks
Fowler, Bob
Frankonia Jagd
Frontier
Getz Barrel Co.
Golden Age Arms Co.
●Gonic Arms, Inc.
Green Mountain Rifle Barrel Co., Inc.
Gun Works, The
Hastings Barrels
●Hawken Shop, The
Hege Jagd-u. Sporthandels, GmbH
Hofmann & Co.
Hodgdon Powder Co., Inc.
Hoppe's Div.
●Hornady Mfg. Co.
House of Muskets, Inc., The
Hunkeler, A.
Impact Case Co.
J.P. Gunstocks Inc.
Jamison's Forge Works
Jedediah Starr Trading Co.
Jones Co., Dale
Kalispel Case Line
K&M Industries, Inc.
Kennedy Firearms
Knight Rifles
L&R Lock Co.
●L&S Technologies, Inc.
Legend Products Corp.
Lestrom Laboratories, Inc.
Lothar Walther Precision Tool, Inc.
Lutz Engraving, Ron
●Lyman
●Marlin Firearms Co.
Mathews & Son, Inc., George E.
McCann's Muzzle-Gun Works
Michaels of Oregon Co.
MMP
●Modern MuzzleLoading, Inc.
Montana Precision Swaging
Mountain State Muzzleloading Supplies, Inc.
Mowrey Gun Works
MSC Industrial Supply Co.
Mt. Alto Outdoor Products
Mushroom Express Bullet Co.
Naval Ordnance Works
Newman Gunshop
North Star West
October Country
Oklahoma Leather Products, Inc.

Olson, Myron
Orion Rifle Barrel Co.
Ox-Yoke Originals, Inc.
Pacific Rifle Co.
Parker & Sons Gunsmithing
Parker Gun Finishes
Pecatonica River Longrifle
●Pedersoli and Co., Davide
Penguin Industries, Inc.
●Pioneer Arms Co.
Prairie River Arms
Prolix Lubricants
R.E. Davis
Rusty Duck Premium Gun Care Products
R.V.I.
S&B Industries
S&S Firearms
Selsi Co., Inc.
Shiloh Creek
●Shooter's Choice
Simmons Gun Repair, Inc.
Sklany's Machine Shop
Slings 'N Things, Inc.
Smokey Valley Rifles
South Bend Replicas, Inc.
Southern Bloomer Mfg. Co.
Starr Trading Co., Jedediah
Stone Mountain Arms
●Taylor's & Co., Inc.
Tennessee Valley Mfg.
Thompson Bullet Lube Co.
●Thompson/Center Arms
●Thunder Mountain Arms
Tiger-Hunt
●Track of the Wolf, Inc.
●Traditions, Inc.
Treso, Inc.
UFA, Inc.
Uberti, Aldo
Uncle Mike's
●Upper Missouri Trading Co.
Venco Industries, Inc.
●Voere-KGH m.b.H.
Walters, John
Warne Manufacturing
Warren Muzzleloading Co., Inc.
Wescombe, Bill
White Owl Enterprises
White Muzzleloading Systems
●White Shooting Systems, Inc.
●Williams Gun Sight Co.
Woodworker's Supply
Wright's Hardwood Gunstock Blanks
Young Country Arms

MUZZLE-LOADING GUNS, BARRELS AND EQUIPMENT

Accuracy Unlimited (Littleton, CO)
Adkins, Luther
Allen Manufacturing
Armi San Paolo
Armoury, Inc., The
Austing & Halleck
Bauska Barrels
●Beauchamp & Son, Inc.
Beaver Lodge
Bentley, John
Big Bore Bullets
Birdsong & Associates, W.E.
Black Powder Specialties
Blackhawk East
Blackhawk West
Black Powder Products
Blue and Gray Products, Inc.
Bridgers Best
Buckskin Bullet Co.
Buckskin Machine Works
Butler Creek Corp.
Cache La Poudre Rifleworks
California Sights
Cash Manufacturing Co., Inc.
CenterMark
Chambers Flintlocks, Ltd., Jim

Chopie Mfg., Inc.
●Cimarron Arms
Cogar's Gunsmithing
Colonial Repair
●Colt Blackpowder Arms Co.
Conetrol Scope Mounts
Cousin Bob's Mountain Products
●Cumberland Arms
Cumberland Mountain Arms
●Cumberland Knife & Gun Works
Curly Maple Stock Blanks
●CVA
Dangler, Homer L.
Day & Sons, Inc., Leonard
●Dayton Traister
deHaas Barrels
Delhi Gun House
●Dixie Gun Works, Inc.
DGS Inc.
Dixon Muzzleloading Shop Inc.
Dyson & Son Ltd., Peter
●EMF Co., Inc.
●Euroarms of America, Inc.
Eutaw Co., Inc., The
Feken, Dennis
Fellowes, Ted

PISTOLSMITHS

Acadian Ballistic Specialties
Acuracy Unlimited (Glendale, AZ)
Actions by "T"
Adair Custom Shop, Bill
Ahlman Guns
Ahrends, Kim
Aldis Gunsmithing & Shooting Supply
Alpha Precision, Inc.
Alpine's Precision Gunsmithing & Indoor Shooting Range
Armament Gunsmithing Co., Inc.
Arundel Arms & Ammunition, Inc., A.
Baer Custom, Inc., Les
Bain & Davis, Inc.
Baity's Custom Gunworks
Banks, Ed
Behlert Precision, Inc.
Bellm Contenders
Belt MTN Arms
Bengtson Arms Co., L.
Bowen Classic Arms Corp.
Broken Gun Ranch
Burkhart Gunsmithing, Don
Cannon's, Andy Cannon
Caraville Manufacturing
Carter's Gun Shop
Chicasaw Gun Works
Clark Custom Guns, Inc.
Cleland's Outdoor World
Cochran, Oliver
Colonial Repair
Colorado School of Trades
Coonan Arms
Corkys Gun Clinic
Craig Custom Ltd.
Curtis Custom Shop

Custom Firearms
Custom Gunsmiths
D&D Gunsmiths, Ltd.
D&L Sports
Dale's Gun Shop
Davis Service Center, Bill
Dayton Traister
EGW Evolution Gun Works
Ellicott Arms, Inc./Woods Pistolsmithing
Ferris Firearms
Fisher Custom Firearms
Forkin, Ben
Francesca, Inc.
Frielich Police Equipment
Garthwaite, Pistolsmith, Inc., Jim
G.G. & G.
Greider Precision
Gun Room Press, The
Guncraft Sports, Inc.
Gunsite Custom Shop
Gunsite Gunsmithy
Gunsite Training Center
Hallberg Gunsmith, Fritz
Hamilton, Alex B.
Hamilton, Keith
Hammond Custom Guns Ltd.
Hank's Gun Shop
Hanson's Gun Center, Dick
Harwood, Jack O.
Harris Gunworks
Hawken Shop, The
Hebard Guns, Gil
Heinie Specialty Products
High Bridge Arms, Inc.
Hoag, James W.

Irwin, Campbell H.
Island Pond Gun Shop
Ivanoff, Thomas G.
J&S Heat Treat
Jacobson, Teddy
Jarvis, Inc.
Jensen's Custom Ammunition
Johnston, James
Jones, J.D.
Jungkind, Reeves C.
K-D, Inc.
Kaswer Custom, Inc.
Ken's Gun Specialties
Kilham & Co.
Kimball, Gary
Kopp, Terry K.
La Clinique du .45
LaFrance Specialties
LaRocca Gun Works, Inc.
Lathrop's, Inc.
Lawson, John G.
Lee's Red Ramps
Leckie Professional Gunsmithing
Liberty Antique Gunworks
Linebaugh Custom Sixguns
List Precision Engineering
Long, George F.
Mac's .45 Shop
Mag-Na-Port International, Inc.
Mahony, Philip Bruce
Mandall Shooting Supplies, Inc.
Marent, Rudolf
Marvel, Alan
Maxi-Mount
McCann Industries
McCann's Machine & Gun Shop
MCS, Inc.
Middlebrooks Custom Shop
Miller Custom
Mitchell's Accuracy Shop
MJK Gunsmithing, Inc.
Mo's Competitor Supplies
Mowrey's Guns & Gunsmithing
Mullis Guncraft
Nastoff's 45 Shop, Inc., Steve
NCP Products, Inc.
North Fork Custom Gunsmithing
Novak's Inc.
Nowlin Custom Mfg.
Nowling Gun Shop

Nygord Precision Products
Oglesby & Oglesby Gunmakers, Inc.
Paris, Frank J.
Pace Marketing, Inc.
Pasadena Gun Center
Peacemaker Specialists
PEM's Mfg. Co.
Performance Specialists
Pierce Pistols
Plaxco, J. Michael
Power Custom Inc.
Precision Specialties
Randco UK
Ries, Chuck
Rim Pac Sports, Inc.
Robar Co.'s, Inc., The
RPM
Score High Gunsmithing
Scott, McDougall & Associates
Seecamp Co., Inc., L.W.
Shooters Supply
Shootin' Shack, Inc.
Sight Shop, The
Singletary, Kent
Sipes Gun Shop
Spokhandguns, Inc.
Springfield, Inc.
SSK Industries
Starnes Gunmaker, Ken
Steger, James R.
Swenson's 45 Shop, A.D.
Swift River Gunworks
Ten-Ring Precision, Inc.
Thompson, Randall
300 Gunsmith Service, Inc.
Thurston Sports, Inc.
Tom's Gun Repair
Vic's Gun Refinishing
Volquartsen Custom Ltd.
Walters Industries
Walters, Thomas David
Wardell Precision Handguns Ltd.
Weigand Combat Handguns, Inc.
Wessinger Custom Guns & Engraving
Wild West Guns Inc.
Williams Gun Sight Co.
Williamson Precision Gunsmithing
Wilson Gun Shop
Wichita Arms, Inc.

REBORING AND RERIFLING

Ahlman Guns
A.M.T.
Arundel Arms & Ammunition, Inc., A.
Bauska Barrels
BlackStar AccuMax Barrels
BlackStar Barrel Accurizing
Chicasaw Gun Works
Cochran, Oliver
Ed's Gun House
Flaig's
Gun Works, The
IAI
H&S Liner Service
Ivanoff, Thomas G.
Jackalope Gun Shop
K-D, Inc.
Kopp, Terry K.
LaBounty Precision Reboring

Matco, Inc.
NCP Products, Inc.
Pence Precision Barrels
Pro-Port Ltd.
Redman's Rifling & Reboring
Rice, Keith
Ridgetop Sporting Goods
Shaw, Inc., E.R.
Siegrist Gun Shop
Simmons Gun Repair, Inc.
Stratco, Inc.
300 Gunsmith Service, Inc.
Time Precision, Inc.
Tom's Gun Repair
Van Patten, J.W.
White Rock Tool & Die
Zufall, Joseph F.

RELOADING TOOLS AND ACCESSORIES

Accurate Arms Co. Inc.
Action Bullets, Inc.
Advance Car Mover Co., Rowell Div.
Alaska Bullet Works, Inc.
American Products Inc.
Ames Metal Products
Armfield Custom Bullets
Armite Laboratories
Arms Corporation of the Philippines
Atlantic Rose, Inc.
Atsko/Sno-Seal, Inc.
Bald Eagle Precision Machine Co.
Ballistic Products, Inc.
Belltown, Ltd.
Ben's Machines
Berger Bullets, Ltd.
Berry's Mfg., Inc.
Birchwood Casey
Black Powder Specialties
Blackhawk East
Blount, Inc., Sporting Equipment Div.

Blue Mountain Bullets
Blue Ridge Machinery & Tools, Inc.
Bonanza
Break-Free, Inc.
●Brown Co., E. Arthur
BRP Inc.
Bruno Shooters Supply
Brynin, Milton
B-Square Co., Inc.
Buck Stix—SOS Products Co.
Bull Mountain Rifle Co.
Bullet Swaging Supply, Inc.
Bullseye Bullets
C&D Special Products
●Camdex, Inc.
Camp-Cap Products Division
Canyon Cartridge Corp.
Carbide Die & Mfg. Co., Inc.
Case Sorting System
CFVentures
C-H Tool & Die Corp.

Chem-Pak, Inc.
CheVron Case Master
Claybuster Wads & Harvester Bullets
Cleanzoil Corp.
Clymer Manufacturing Co., Inc.
Colorado Shooter's Supply
CONKKO
Cook Engineering Service
Cooper-Woodward
Crouse's Country Cover
●Cumberland Arms
Curtis Cast
Custom Products, Neil A. Jones
●CVA
Davis, Don
Davis Products, Mike
D.C.C. Enterprises
Denver Bullets, Inc.
●Denver Instrument Co.
Dever Co., Jack
Dewey Mfg. Co., Inc., J.
●Dillon Precision Products, Inc.
Dropkick
Dutchman's Firearms, Inc., The
E&L Mfg., Inc.
Eagan, Donald V.
Eezox, Inc.
Efficient Machinery Co.
Eichelberger Bullets, Wm.
Elkhorn Bullets
Engineered Accessories
Enguix Import-Export
Estate Cartridge, Inc.
Euroarms of America Inc.
E-Z-Way Systems
F&A Inc.
Federal Cartridge Co.
Federated-Fry
Feken, Dennis
Ferguson, Bill
First, Inc., Jack
Fisher Custom Firearms
Fitz Pistol Grip Co.
Flambeau Products Corp.
Flitz International Ltd.
●Forgett Jr., Valmore J.
●Forster Products
●4-D Custom Die Co.
4W Ammunition
Fremont Tool Works
Fry Metals
Fusilier Bullets
G&C Bullet Co., Inc.
GAR
Gehmann, Walter
Goddard, Allen
Gozon Corp., U.S.A.
Graf & Sons
"Gramps" Antique Cartridges
Graphics Direct
Graves Co.
Green, Arthur S.
Greenwood Precision
Groupt Tight Bullets
Gun city Inc
Gun Works, The
Hanned Line, The
Hanned Precision
Harrell's Precision
Harris Enterprises
Harrison Bullets
Haselbauer Products, Jerry
Haydon's Shooters' Supply, Russ
Heidenstrom Bullets
Hensley & Gibbs
Hirtenberger Aktiengesellschaft
Hobson Precision Mfg. Co.
Hoch Custom Bullet Moulds
Hodgdon Powder Co., Inc.
Hoehn Sales, Inc.
Hoelscher, Virgil
Holland's Gunsmithing
Hollywood Engineering
Hondo Industries
Hornady Mfg. Co.
Howell Machine
Hunters Supply
●Huntington Die Specialties
Hutton Rifle Ranch
Image Ind. Inc.
IMI Services USA, Inc.
Imperial
Imperial Magnum Corp.

INTEC International, Inc.
Iosso Products
Javelina Lube Products
Jedediah Starr Trading Co.
JGS Precision Tool Mfg.
J&L Superior Bullets
JLK Bullets
Jonad Corp.
Jones Custom Products, Neil A.
Jones Moulds, Paul
●K&M Services
Kapro Mfg. Co., Inc.
King & Co.
Kleen-Bore, Inc.
Knoell, Doug
Korzinek Riflesmith, J.
●Lapua Ltd.
L A R Mfg. Inc.
LBT
Le Clear Industries
●Lee Precision, Inc.
Legend Products Corp.
Liberty Metals
Liberty Shooting Supplies
Lightning Performance Innovations, Inc.
Lithi Bee Bullet Lube
Littleton, J.F.
Lortone, Inc.
Loweth Firearms, Richard H.R.
Luch Metal Merchants, Barbara
Lyman Instant Targets, Inc.
●Lyman Products Corp.
M&D Munitions Ltd.
MA Systems
●Magma Engineering Co.
MarMik, Inc.
Marquart Precision Co.
MAST Technology
Match Prep—Doyle Gracey
Mayville Engineering Co.
McKillen & Heyer, Inc.
MCRW Associates Shooting Supplies
●MCS, Inc.
MEC, Inc.
Midway Arms, Inc.
Miller Engineering
MI-TE Bullets
MMP
Mo's Competitor Supplies
Montana Armory, Inc.
Mountain South
Mountain State Muzzleloading Supplies, Inc.
Mt. Baldy Bullet Co.
MTM Molded Products Co., Inc.
Multi-Scale Charge Ltd.
MWG Company
Necromancer Industries, Inc.
Newman Gunshop
NEI Handtools, Inc.
Niemi Engineering, W.B.
North Devon Firearms Services
Northern Precision Custom
Now Products Inc
SSK Industries
October Country
Old West Bullet Moulds
Omark Industries
Original Box, Inc.
Outdoor Sports Hdqtr
Paco's
Paragon Sales & Serv
Pease Accuracy, Bob
●Pedersoli and Co., Davide
Peerless Alloy, Inc.
Pinetree Bullets
Plum City Ballistic Range
Pomeroy, Robert
●Ponsness/Warren
Prairie River Arms
Precision Castings & Equipment, Inc.
●Precision Reloading, Inc.
Prime Reloading
Professional Hunter Supplies
ProlixÆ Lubricants
Proofmark Corp.
Pro-Shot Products, Inc.
Protector Mfg. Co., Inc., The
Quinetics Corp.
R&D Engineering & Manufacturing
Rapine Bullet Mould Mfg. Co.
Raytech

RCBS
R.D.P. Tool Co., Inc.
Redding Reloading Equipment
R.E.I.
Reloading Specialties, Inc.
Rice, Keith
Riebe Co., W.J.
RIG Products
R.I.S. Co., Inc.
Roberts Products
Rochester Lead Works, Inc.
Rolston, Inc., Fred. W.
Rooster Laboratories
Rorschach Precision Products
Rosenthal, Brad and Sallie
Royal Arms Gunstocks
SAECO
Sandia Die & Cartridge Co.
Saunders Gun & Machine Shop
Saville Iron Co.
●Scharch Mfg., Inc.
Scot Powder Co. of Ohio, Inc.
Scott, Dwight
Seebeck Assoc., R.E.
Sharp Shooter Supply
Sharps Arms Co. Inc., C.
Shiloh Creek
●Shiloh Rifle Mfg.
●Shooter's Choice
ShurKatch Corporation
Sierra Specialty Prod. Co.
Silver Eagle Machining
Simmons, Jerry
Sinclair International, Inc.
Skip's Machine
S.L.A.P. Industries
Small Custom Mould & Bullet Co.
Sno-Seal
SOS Products Co.
Spence, George W.
Spencer's Custom Guns
SPG, Inc.
Sport Flite Manufacturing Co.
Sportsman Supply Co.
Stalwart Corp.
Star Custom Bullets
●Star Machine Works

Starr Trading Co., Jedediah
Stillwell, Robert
Stoney Point Products, Inc.
Stratco, Inc.
Tamarack Products Inc.
Taracorp Industries
TCCI
TCSR
TDP Industries, Inc.
Tetra Gun Lubricants
Thompson Bullet Lube Co.
●Thompson/Center Arms
Timber Heirloom Products
Time Precision, Inc.
TMI Products
TR Metals Corp.
Trammco, Inc.
Tru-Square Metal Prods., Inc.
TTM
United States Products Inc.
Varner's Service
Vega Tool Co.
Venco Industries, Inc.
VibraShine, Inc.
Vibra-Tek Co.
Vihtavuori Oy/Kaltron-Pettibone
Vitt/Boos
Von Minden Gunsmithing Services
Walters, John
Webster Scale Mfg. Co.
WD-40 Co.
Welsh, Bud
Wells Custom Gunsmith, R.A.
Werner, Carl
White Rock Tool & Die
Whitetail Design & Engineering Ltd.
Widener's Reloading & Shooting
  Supply
William's Gun Shop, Ben
Wilson, Inc., L.E.
Wise Guns, Dale
Wolf's Western Traders
Woodleigh
WTA Manufacturing, Bill Wood
Yesteryear Armory & Supply
Young Country Arms

RESTS—BENCH, PORTABLE—AND ACCESSORIES

Accuright
Adventure 16, Inc.
Armor Metal Products
Bald Eagle Precision Machine Co.
Bartlett Engineering
Borden's Accuracy
Browning Arms Co.
B-Square Co., Inc.
Bull Mountain Rifle Co.
Canons Delcour
Chem-Pak, Inc.
Clift Mfg., L.R.
Clift Welding Supply
Cravener's Gun Shop
Decker Shooting Products
Desert Mountain Mfg.
Erickson's Mfg., Inc., C.W.
F&A Inc.
Greenwood Precision
Harris Engineering, Inc.
Hidalgo, Tony
Hoehn Sales, Inc.

Hoelscher, Virgil
Hoppe's Div.
Kolpin Mfg., Inc.
Kramer Designs
Midway Arms, Inc.
Millett Sights
MJM Manufacturing
Outdoor Connection, Inc., The
PAST Sporting Goods, Inc.
Penguin Industries, Inc.
Protektor Model
Ransom International Corp
Saville Iron Co.
ShurKatch Corporation
Sinclair International
Stoney Point Products, Inc.
Thompson Target Technology
T.H.U. Enterprises, Inc.
Tonoloway Tack Drivers
Varner's Service
Wichita Arms, Inc.
Zanotti Armor, Inc.

RIFLE BARREL MAKERS (See also Muzzle-Loading Guns, Barrels and Equipment)

Airrow
American Safe Arms Inc.
Arundel Arms & Ammunition, Inc., A.
A.M.T.
Bauska Barrels
BlackStar AccuMax Barrels
BlackStar Barrel Accurizing
Border Barrels Ltd.
Broad Creek Rifle Works
Broughton Rifle Barrels
Brown Co., E. Arthur
Bullberry Barrel Works, Ltd.
C&J Enterprises Inc.
Canons Delcour
Carter's Gun Shop
Chicasaw Gun Works
Christensen Arms
Cincinnati Swaging

Clerke Co., J.A.
Competition Limited
Cryo-Accurizing
D&J Bullet Co. & Custom Gun Shop,
  Inc.
deHaas Barrels
DKT, Inc.
Donnelly, C.P.
Douglas Barrels, Inc.
Fanzoj GmbH
Gaillard Barrels
Getz Barrel Co.
Green Mountain Rifle Barrel Co., Inc.
Gun Works, The
Half Moon Rifle Shop
Harold's Custom Gun Shop, Inc.
Harris Gunworks
Hart Rifle Barrels, Inc.

Hastings Barrels
Hoelscher, Virgil
H-S Precision, Inc.
IAI
Jackalope Gun Shop
K-D, Inc.
KOGOT
Kopp, Terry K.
Krieger Barrels, Inc.
LaBounty Precision Reboring
Lilja Precision Rifle Barrels
Lothar Walther Precision Tool, Inc.
Mac's .45 Shop
Matco, Inc.
McGowen Rifle Barrels
McMillan Rifle Barrels
Mid-America Recreation, Inc.
Nowlin Custom Mfg.
Obermeyer Rifled Barrels
Orion Rifle Barrel Co.
Olympic Arms, Inc.
Pac-Nor Barreling

Pell, John T.
Pence Precision Barrels
Perazone, Brian
Raptor Arms Co., Inc.
Rocky Mountain Rifle Works Ltd.
Rosenthal, Brad and Sallie
Sabatti S.R.L.
Sanders Custom Gun Service
Schneider Rifle Barrels, Inc., Gary
Shaw, Inc., E.R.
Shilen, Inc.
Siskiyou Gun Works
Small Arms Mfg. Co.
Specialty Shooters Supply, Inc.
Strutz Rifle Barrels, Inc., W.C.
Swift River Gunworks
Swivel Machine Works, Inc.
Unmussig Bullets, D.L.
Verney-Carron
Wells, Fred F.
Wilson Arms Co., The
Wiseman and Co., Bill

SCOPES, MOUNTS, ACCESSORIES, OPTICAL EQUIPMENT

Accuracy Innovations, Inc.
Ackerman, Bill
ADCO Sales, Inc.
Adventurer's Outpost
●Aimpoint U.S.A.
●Aimtech Mount Systems
●Air Venture
Alley Supply Co.
Apel GmbH, Ernst
Armalite Inc.
A.R.M.S., Inc.
●Armscorp USA, Inc.
Autauga Arms, Inc.
●Baer Custom, Inc., Les
●Barrett Firearms Mfg., Inc.
●Bausch & Lomb Sports Optics Div.
Beaver Park Products, Inc.
BEC, Inc.
Beeman Precision Airguns
Blount, Inc., Sporting Equipment Div.
●Boonie Packer Products
Borden's Accuracy
Brockman's Custom Gunsmithin
●Brown Co., E Arthur
Brownells, Inc.
Brunton U.S.A.
BSA Optics
B-Square Co., Inc.
Bull Mountain Rifle Co.
Burris
●Bushnell Sports Optics Worldwide
Butler Creek Corp.
California Grip
CATCO
Celestron International
Center Lock Scope Rings
Champion's Choice
Clearview Mfg. Co., Inc.
Combat Military Ordnance Ltd.
Compass Industries, Inc.
Concept Development Corp.
Conetrol Scope Mounts
Creedmoor Sports, Inc.
Crimson Trace
Custom Quality Products, Inc.
D&H Prods. Co., Inc.
D.C.C. Enterprises
Dale's Gun Shop
Del-Sports, Inc.
DHB Products
E Arthur Brown Co
Eagle International Sporting Goods,
  Inc.
Edmund Scientific Co.
Ednar, Inc.
Eggleston, Jere D.
EGW Evolution Gun Works
Eclectic Technologies, Inc.
Emerging Technologies, Inc.
Europtik Ltd.
Excalibur Enterprises
Farr Studio, Inc.
Federal Arms Corp. of America
Forgett Jr., Valmore J.
Fotar Optics
Frankonia Jagd
Fujinon, Inc.
G.G. & G.
Gentry Custom Gunmaker, David

Great Lakes Airguns
Groenewold, John
GSI, Inc.
Guns
Accessories
Gun South, Inc.
Guns, (Div. of D.C. Engineering, Inc.)
Gunsmithing, Inc.
Hakko Co. Ltd.
●Hammerli USA
●Harris Gunworks
Harvey, Frank
Hertel & Reuss
Hines Co., S.C.
Hiptmayer, Armurier
Hiptmayer, Klaus
Hitek International
Hofmann & Co.
Holland's
Ironsighter Co.
Jaeger, Inc., Paul/Dunn's
●JägerSport, Ltd.
Jeffredo Gunsight
Jewell Triggers, Inc.
●Kahles, A Swarovski Company
Kalispel Case Line
KDF, Inc.
KenPatable Ent., Inc.
●Kesselring Gun Shop
●Kimber of America, Inc.
Kmount
●Kowa Optimed, Inc.
Kris Mounts
KVH Industries, Inc.
Kwik Mount Corp.
Kwik-Site Co.
●L&S Technologies, Inc.
L.A.R. Mfg., Inc.
●Laser Devices, Inc.
Laseraim
Laserlyte
LaserMax, Inc.
Leapers, Inc.
Lectro Science, Inc.
Lee Co., T.K.
Leica USA, Inc.
●Leupold & Stevens, Inc.
Lightforce U.S.A. Inc.
List Precision Engineering
Lohman Mfg. Co., Inc.
London Guns Ltd.
Lyte Optronics
Mac-1 Distributors
Mac's .45 Shop
Mag-Na-Port International, Inc.
Masen Co., Inc., John
Maxi-Mount
●McBros Rifle Co.
McCann Industries
McCann's Machine & Gun Shop
McMillan Optical Gunsight Co.
●MCS, Inc.
MDS
Merit Corp.
Michaels of Oregon Co.
Military Armament Corp.
Millett Sights
●Mirador Optical Corp.
Mitchell Optics Inc.

Mo's Competitor Supplies
Mountain Rifles Inc.
MWG Co.
●New England Custom Gun Service
Nic Max, Inc.
Nightforce
Nikon, Inc.
Norincoptics
Nygord Precision Products
Oakshore Electronic Sights, Inc.
Olympic Optical Co.
Optical Services Co.
Orchard Park Enterprise
Oregon Arms, Inc.
Outdoor Connection, Inc., The
Parsons Optical Mfg. Co.
PECAR Herbert Schwarz, GmbH
PEM's Mfg. Co.
●Pentax Corp.
Perazone, Brian
P.M. Enterprises, Inc.
Precise Metalsmithing Enterprises
●Precision Sport Optics
Premier Reticles
Quarton USA, Ltd. Co.
●Ram-Line Blount, Inc.
Ranch Products
Randolph Engineering, Inc.
●Ranging, Inc.
●Redfield, Inc.
Rice, Keith
Rocky Mountain High Sports Glasses
Rogue Rifle Co., Inc.
S&K Mfg. Co.
Sanders Custom Gun Service
Saunders Gun & Machine Shop
●Schmidt & Bender, Inc.
Scope Control Inc.
ScopLevel
Score High Gunsmithing
Segway Industries
Selsi Co., Inc.
Sharp Shooter Supply
Shepherd Scope Ltd.
Sightron, Inc.
●Simmons Enterprises, Ernie
●Simmons Outdoor Corp.

Sinclair International
Six Enterprises
SKAN A.R.
SKB Shotguns
Slug Group, Inc.
Southern Bloomer Mfg. Co.
Sportsmatch U.K. Ltd.
●Springfield, Inc.
SSK Industriies
Stiles Custom Guns
●Stoeger Industries
SwaroSports, Inc.
●Swarovski Optik North America Ltd.
●Swift Instruments, Inc.
TacStar Industires, Inc.
Talley, Dave
●Tasco Sales, Inc.
Tele-Optics
●Thompson/Center Arms
●Trijicon, Inc.
Ultra Dot Distribution
Uncle Mike's
●Unertl Optical Co., Inc., John
United Binocular Co.
United States Optics Tech., Inc.
Valor Corp.
●Voere-KGH m.b.H.
Warne Manufacturing Co.
Warren Muzzleloading Co., Inc.
WASP Shooting Systems
●Weatherby, Inc.
Weaver Products
●Weaver Scope Repair Service
Weigand Combat Handguns, Inc.
Wells Custom Guns, R.A.
●Westley Richards & Co.
White Muzzleloading Systems
●White Shooting Systems, Inc.
White Rock Tool & Die
Wilcox Industries Corp.
Wild West Guns Inc.
Wideview Scope Mount Corp.
●Williams Gun Sight Co.
York M-1 Conversions
Zanotti Armor, Inc.
●Zeiss Optical, Carl

SHOOTING/TRAINING SCHOOLS

Alpine Precision Gunsmithing & Indoor
   Shooting Range
American Gunsmithing Institute
American Small Arms Academy
Auto Arms
Barsotti, Bruce
Bob's Tactical Indoor Shooting Range
   & Gun Shop
Cannon's, Andy Cannon
Chapman Academy of Practical
   Shooting
Chelsea Gun Club of New York City,
   Inc.
CQB Training
Defense Training International, Inc.
Dowtin Gunworks
Executive Protection Institute
Feminine Protection, Inc.
Ferris Firearms
Firearm Training Center, The
G.H. Enterprises Ltd.
Front Sight Firearms Training Institute
Gene's Custom Guns
Gunsite Training Center
Guncraft Sports, Inc.
Henigson & Associates, Steve
International Shootists, Inc.
Israel Arms International

Jensen's Custom Ammunition
Jensen's Firearms Acadamy
Ljutic Industries, Inc.
L.L. Bean, Inc.
McMurdo, Lynn
Mendez, John A.
Montgomery Community College
NCP Products, Inc.
Nevada Pistol Academy Inc.
North American Shooting Systems
North Mountain Pine Training Center
Performance Specialists
Quigley's Personal Protection
   Strategies, Paxton
River Road Sporting Clays
SAFE
Shooter's World
Shooting Gallery, The
Smith & Wesson
Specialty Gunsmithing
Starlight Training Center, Inc.
Steger, James R.
Tactical Defense Institute
Thunder Ranch
300 Gunsmith Service, Inc.
Western Missouri Shooters Alliance
Yankee Gunsmith
Yavapai Firearms Academy Ltd.

SIGHTS, METALLIC

Accura-Site
Alley Supply Co.
All's, The Jim J. Tembelis Co., Inc.
Alpec Team, Inc.
Andela Tool & Machine, Inc.
Anschutz GmbH
Armsport, Inc.
Baer Custom, Inc., Les
BEC, Inc.
Black Powder Specialties
Bo-Mar Tool & Mfg. Co.
Bond Custom Firearms
Bowen Classic Arms Corp.

Bradley Gunsight Co.
Brockman's Custom Gunsmithin
Brown Co., E. Arthur
Brown Products, Inc., Ed
Brownell Inc.
California Sights
Cape Outfitters
Center Lock Scope Rings
Champion's Choice
C-More Systems
Colonial Repair
CRR, Inc./Marble's Inc.
Dale's Gun Shop

DHB Products
E Arthur Brown Co
Eagle International Sporting Goods,
   Inc.
Engineered Accessories
Evans, Andrew
Evans Gunsmithing
Farr Studio, Inc.
Forgett Jr., Valmore J.
G.G. & G.
Garthwaite Pistolsmith, Jim
Gun Doctor, The
Gun Works, The
Hank's Gun Shop
Heinie Specialty Products
Hesco-Meprolight
Hiptmayer, Armurier
Hiptmayer, Klaus
Innovative Weaponry, Inc.
Innovision Enterprises
Jaeger, Inc., Paul/Dunn's
J.P. Enterprises, Inc.
Kris Mounts
Leapers
Lee's Red Ramps
List Precision Engineering
London Guns Ltd.
L.P.A. Snc
Lyman Instant Targets, Inc.
Lyman Products Corp.
Mac's .45 Shop
Madis, George
Marble Arms
MCS, Inc.
MEC-Gar S.R.L.
Meier Works

Meprolight
Merit Corp.
Mid-America Recreation, Inc.
Middlebrooks Custom Shop
Millett Sights
MMC
Mo's Competitor Supplies
Montana Armory, Inc.
Montana Vintage Arms
New England Custom Gun Service
Newman Gunshop
North Pass
Novak's Inc.
Oakshore Electronic Sights, Inc.
OK Weber, Inc.
PEM's Mfg. Co.
P.M. Enterprises, Inc.
Quarton USA, Ltd. Co.
Redfield, Inc.
RPM
Sharps Arms Co. Inc., C.
Slug Site
STI International
Talley, Dave
T.F.C. S.p.A.
Thompson/Center Arms
Trijicon, Inc.
United States Optics Technologies,
   Inc.
Warne Manufacturing
WASP Shooting Systems
Wichita Arms, Inc.
Wild West Guns Inc.
Williams Gun Sight Co.
Wilson Gun Shop

STOCKS (Commercial and Custom)

Accuracy Unlimited (Glendale, AZ)
Ackerman & Co.
Acra-Bond Laminates
Ahlman Guns
Amrine's Gun Shop
Arms Ingenuity Co.
Arundel Arms & Ammunition, Inc., A.
Baelder, Harry
Bain & Davis, Inc.
Balickie, Joe
Bansner's Gunsmithing Specialties
Barnes Bullets, Inc.
Beitzinger, George
Belding's Custom Gun Shop
Bell & Carlson, Inc.
Benchmark Guns
Biesen, Al
Biesen, Roger
Billeb, Stephen L.
Billings Gunsmiths, Inc.
Black Powder Specialties
Bohemia Arms Co.
Blount, Inc., Sporting Equipment Div.
Boltin, John M.
Borden's Accuracy
Bowerly, Kent
Boyds' Gunstock Industries, Inc.
Brace, Larry D.
Brgoch, Frank
Briganti, A.J.
Broad Creek Rifle Works
Brockman's Custom Gunsmithin
Brown Co., E. Arthur
Brown Precision, Inc.
Buckhorn Gun Works
Bull Mountain Rifle Co.
Bullberry Barrel Works, Ltd.
Burkhart Gunsmithing, Don
Butler Creek Corp.
Calico Hardwoods, Inc.
Cape Outfitters
Camilli, Lou
Campbell, Dick
Carter's Gun Shop
Caywood, Shane J.
Chambers Flintlocks Ltd., Jim
Chicasaw Gun Works
Christman Jr., Gunmaker, David
Churchill, Winston
Claro Walnut Gunstock Co.
Clifton Arms, Inc.
Cloward's Gun Shop
Cochran, Oliver
Coffin, Charles H.
Coffin, Jim
Colonial Repair

Colorado Gunsmithing Academy
Colorado School of Trades
Conrad, C.A.
Creedmoor Sports, Inc.
Curly Maple Stock Blanks
Custom Checkering Service
Custom Gun Products
Custom Gun Stocks
Custom Riflestocks, Inc.
D&D Gunsmiths, Inc.
D&G Presicion Duplicators
D&J Bullet Co. & Custom Gun Shop,
   Inc.
Dakota Arms Inc.
Dangler, Homer L.
D.D. Custom Stocks
de Treville & Co., Stan
Dever Co., Jack
Devereaux, R.H. "Dick"
DGR Custom Rifles
DGS, Inc.
Dillon, Ed
Dowtin Gunworks
Dressel Jr., Paul G.
Duane Custom Stocks, Randy
Duane's Gun Repair
Duncan's Gunworks, Inc.
Echols & Co., D'Arcy
Eggleston, Jere D.
Erhardt, Dennis
Eversull Co., Inc., K.
Fajen, Inc., Reinhart
Farmer-Dressel, Sharon
Fibron Products, Inc.
Fisher, Jerry A.
Flaig's
Folks, Donald E.
Forster, Kathy
Forster, Larry L.
Forthofer's Gunsmithing &
   Knifemaking
Francotte & Cie S.A., Auguste
Frank Custom Classic Arms, Ron
Game Haven Gunstocks
Gene's Custom Guns
Gervais, Mike
Gillmann, Edwin
Giron, Robert E.
Glaser Safety Slug Inc.
Goens, Dale W.
Golden Age Arms Co.
Gordie's Gun Shop
Goudy Classic Stocks, Gary
Grace, Charles E.
Great American Gun Co.
Green, Roger M.

Greene, M.L.
Greene Precision Duplicators
Greenwood Precision
Griffin & Howe, Inc.
Gun Shop, The
Guns
Gunsmithing Ltd.
Hallberg Gunsmith, Fritz
Halstead, Rick
Hamilton, Jim
Hanson's Gun Center, Dick
Harper's Custom Stocks
Harris Gunworks
Hart & Son, Inc., Robert W.
Harwood, Jack O.
Hastings Barrels
Hecht, Hubert J.
Heilmann, Stephen
Hensley Gunmaker, Darwin
Heppler, Keith M.
Heydenberk, Warren R.
High Tech Specialties, Inc.
Hillmer Custom Gunstocks, Paul D.
Hines Co., S.C.
Hiptmayer, Armurier
Hiptmayer, Klaus
Hoelscher, Virgil
Hoenig & Rodman
H-S Precision, Inc.
Huebner, Corey O.
Hughes, Steven Dodd
Ide, Kenneth G.
Island Pond Gun Shop
Ivanoff, Thomas G.
Jackalope Gun Shop
Jaeger, Inc., Paul/Dunn's
Jamison's Forge Works
Jarrett Rifles, Inc.
Johnson Wood Products
J.P. Gunstocks, Inc.
KDF, Inc.
Keith's Custom Gunstocks
Kelbly, Inc.
Ken's Rifle Blanks
Kilham & Co.
Kimber
Klein Custom Guns, Don
Klingler Woodcarving
Knippel, Richard
Kokolus, Michael M.
Lawson Co., Harry
Lind Custom Guns, Al
Lynn's Custom Gunstocks
Lyons Gunworks, Larry
Mac's .45 Shop
Marple & Associates, Dick
Masen Co., Inc., John
Mazur Restoration, Pete
McBros Rifle Co.
McCann's Muzzle-Gun Works
McCament, Jay
McCullough, Ken
McDonald, Dennis
McFarland, Stan
McGowen Rifle Barrels
McGuire, Bill
McKinney, R.P.
McMillan Fiberglass Stocks, Inc.
Mercer Custom Stocks, R.M.
Michaels of Oregon Co.
Mid-America Recreation, Inc.
Miller Arms, Inc.
Morrison Custom Rifles, J.W.
MPI Fiberglass Stocks
MWG Co.
NCP Products, Inc.
Nelson, Stephen
Nettestad Gun Works
New England Arms Co.
New England Custom Gun Service
Newman Gunshop
Nickels, Paul R.
Norman Custom Gunstocks, Jim
Oakland Custom Arms, Inc.
Oil Rod and Gun Shop
OK Weber, Inc.
Old World Gunsmithing
One Of A Kind

Or-ön
Orvis Co., The
Ottmar, Maurice
P&S Gun Service
Pacific Research Laboratories, Inc.
Pagel Gun Works, Inc.
Paragon Sales & Serv
Paulsen Gunstocks
Pecatonica River Longrifle
PEM's Mfg. Co.
Perazone, Brian
Perazzi USA, Inc.
Pohl, Henry A.
Powell & Son (Gunmakers) Ltd.,
  William
R&J Gun Shop
Ram-Line Blount, Inc.
Rampart International
Reagent Chemical and Research, Inc.
Reiswig, Wallace E.
Richards Micro-Fit Stocks
Rimrock Rifle Stocks
RMS Custom Gunsmithing
Robinson, Don
Robinson Firearms Mfg. Ltd.
Rogers Gunsmithing, Bob
Roto Carve
Royal Arms Gunstocks
Ryan, Chad L.
Sanders Custom Gun Service
Saville Iron Co.
Schiffman, Curt
Schiffman, Mike
Schiffman, Norman
Schumakers Gun Shop
Schwartz Custom Guns, David W.
Schwartz Custom Guns, Wayne E.
Score High Gunsmithing
Shell Shack
Sile Distributors, Inc.
Simmons Gun Repair, Inc.
Six Enterprises
Skeoch, Brian R.
Smith, Sharmon
Speiser, Fred D.
Stiles Custom Guns
Storey, Dale A.
Stott's Creek Armory, Inc.
Strawbridge, Victor W.
Sturgeon Valley Sporters
Swan, D.J.
Swift River Gunworks
Szweda, Robert
Talmage, William G.
Taylor & Robbins
Tecnolegno S.p.A.
T.F.C. S.p.A.
Thompson/Center Arms
Tiger-Hunt
Tirelli
Tom's Gun Repair
Track of the Wolf, Inc.
Trevallion Gunstocks
Tucker, James C.
Turkish Firearms Corp.
Tuttle, Dale
Vest, John
Vic's Gun Refinishing
Vintage Industries, Inc.
Volquartsen Custom Ltd.
Von Minden Gunsmithing Services
Walker Arms Co., Inc.
Walnut Factory, The
Weber & Markin Custom Gunsmiths
Weems, Cecil
Wells Custom Gunsmith, R.A.
Wells, Fred F.
Wenig Custom Gunstocks, Inc.
Werth, T.W.
Wessinger Custom Guns & Engraving
Western Gunstock Mfg. Co.
Williams Gun Sight Co.
Williamson Precision Gunsmithing
Windish, Jim
Winter, Robert M.
Working Guns
Wright's Hardwood Gunstock Blanks
Yee, Mike
Zeeryp, Russ

TARGETS, BULLET AND CLAYBIRD TRAPS

Action Target, Inc.
American Target
American Whitetail Target Systems

A-Tech Corp.
Autauga Arms, Inc.
Beomat of America Inc.

Birchwood Casey
Blount, Inc., Sporting Equipment Div.
Blue and Gray Products, Inc.
Brown Manufacturing
Bull-X, Inc.
Caswell International Corp.
Champion Target Co.
Dapkus Co., Inc., J.G.
Datumtech Corp.
Dayson Arms Ltd.
D.C.C. Enterprises
Detroit-Armor Corp.
Diamond Mfg. Co.
Estate Cartridge, Inc.
Federal Champion Target Co.
Freeman Animal Targets
G.H. Enterprises Ltd.
Gozan Corp.
Hiti-Schuch, Atelier Wilma
H-S Precision, Inc.
Hunterjohn
Innovision Enterprises
Kennebec Journal
Kleen-Bore, Inc.
Lakefield Arms Ltd.
Littler Sales Co.
Lyman Instant Targets, Inc.
Lyman Products Corp.
M&D Munitions Ltd.

Mendez, John A.
MSR Targets
National Target Co.
N.B.B., Inc.
North American Shooting Systems
Nu-Teck
Outers Laboratories, Div. of Blount
Ox-Yoke Originals, Inc.
Passive Bullet Traps, Inc.
PlumFire Press, Inc.
Quack Decoy & Sporting Clays
Redfield, Inc.
Remington Arms Co., Inc.
Rockwood Corp., Speedwell Div.
Rocky Mountain Target Co.
Savage Arms (Canada), Inc.
Savage Range Systems, Inc.
Schaefer Shooting Sports
Seligman Shooting Products
Shooters Supply
Shoot-N-C Targets
Thompson Target Technology
Trius Products, Inc.
White Flyer Targets
World of Targets
X-Spand Target Systems
Z's Metal Targets & Frames
Zriny's Metal Targets

TAXIDERMY

African Import Co.
Jonas Appraisers—Taxidermy
  Animals, Jack

Kulis Freeze Dry Taxidermy
Montgomery Community College
World Trek, Inc.

TRAP AND SKEET SHOOTER'S EQUIPMENT

Allen Co., Bob
Allen Sportswear, Bob
Bagmaster Mfg., Inc.
Baker, Stan
Beomat of America Inc.
Beretta S.p.A., Pietro
Cape Outfitters
Clymer Manufacturing Co., Inc.
Crane & Crane Ltd.
Dayson Arms Ltd.
Estate Cartridge, Inc.
F&A Inc.
Fiocchi of America, Inc.
Game Winner Inc,
G.H. Enterprises Ltd.
Hastings Barrels
Hillmer Custom Gunstocks, Paul D.
Hoppe's Div.
Hunter Co., Inc.
Jenkins Recoil Pads Inc
K&T Co.
Kalispel Case Line
Lakewood Products, LLC
Lynn's Custom Gunstocks

Mag-Na-Port International, Inc.
Maionchi-L.M.I.
Meadow Industries
MEC Inc.
Moneymaker Guncraft Corp.
MTM Molded Products Co., Inc.
NCP Products, Inc.
Noble Co., Jim
Pachmayr LTD
PAST Sporting Goods, Inc.
Penguin Industries, Inc.
Perazzi USA, Inc.
Pro-Port Ltd.
Protektor Model
Quack Decoy & Sporting Clays
Remington Arms Co., Inc.
Rhodeside, Inc.
Shootin' Accessories, Ltd.
Shooting Specialties
ShurKatch Corporation
Titus, Daniel
Trius Products, Inc.
Warne Manufacturing
X-Spand Target Systems

TRIGGERS, RELATED EQUIPMENT

Actions By T
A.M.T.
B&D Trading Co., Inc.
Baer Custom, Inc., Les
Behlert Precision, Inc.
Bond Custom Firearms
Boyds' Gunstock Industries, Inc.
Bull Mountain Rifle Co.
Canjar Co., M.H.
Cycle Dynamics, Inc.
Dayton Traister
Electronic Trigger Systems, Inc.
Eversull Co., Inc., K.
FWB
Galati International
Guns
ings Barrels
Hawken Shop, The
Hoelscher, Virgil
Hoehn Sales Inc.
Holland's
IAI
Impact Case Co.
Jacobson, Teddy
Jaeger, Inc., Paul/Dunn's
Jewell Triggers, Inc.
J.P. Enterprises, Inc.
KK Air International
L&R Lock Co.

List Precision Engineering
London Guns Ltd.
Mahony, Philip Bruce
Masen Co., Inc., John
Master Lock Co.
Miller Single Trigger Mfg. Co.
NCP Products, Inc.
OK Weber, Inc.
PEM's Mfg. Co.
Penrod Precision
Perazone, Brian
Perazzi USA, Inc.
S&B Industries
Sharp Shooter Supply
Shilen, Inc.
Simmons Gun Repair, Inc.
Slug Group, Inc

A

A&B Industries, Inc. (See Top-Line USA, Inc.)

A&J Products, Inc., 5791 Hall Rd., Muskegon, MI 49442-1964

A&M Waterfowl, Inc., P.O. Box 102, Ripley, TN 38063/901-635-4003; FAX: 901-635-2320

A&W Repair, 2930 Schneider Dr., Arnold, MO 63010/314-287-3725

A.A. Arms, Inc., 4811 Persimmont Ct., Monroe, NC 28110/704-289-5356, 800-935-1119; FAX: 704-289-5859

A.B.S. III, 9238 St. Morritz Dr., Fern Creek, KY 40291

AC Dyna-tite Corp., 155 Kelly St., P.O. Box 0984, Elk Grove Village, IL 60007/847-593-5566; FAX: 847-593-1304

Acadian Ballistic Specialties, P.O. Box 61, Covington, LA 70434

Acculube II, Inc., 4366 Shackleford Rd., Norcross, GA 30093-2912

Accupro Gun Care, 15512-109 Ave., Surrey, BC U3R 7E8, CANADA/604-583-7807

Accuracy Den, The, 25 Bitterbrush Rd., Reno, NV 89523/702-345-0225

Accuracy Innovations, Inc., P.O. Box 376, New Paris, PA 15554/814-839-4517; FAX: 814-839-2601

Accuracy International, 9115 Trooper Trail, P.O. Box 2019, Bozeman, MT 59715/406-587-7922; FAX: 406-585-9434

Accuracy International Precision Rifles (See U.S. importer—Gunsite Custom Shop; Gunsite Training Center)

Accuracy Unlimited, 7479 S. DePew St., Littleton, CO 80123

Accuracy Unlimited, 16036 N. 49 Ave., Glendale, AZ 85306/602-978-9089; FAX: 602-978-9089

Accura-Site (See All's, The Jim Tembelis Co., Inc.)

Accurate Arms Co., Inc., 5891 Hwy. 230 West, McEwen, TN 37101/931-729-4207, 800-416-3006; FAX 931-729-4211

Accurate Bullet Co., 159 Creek Road, Glen Mills, PA 19342/610-399-6584

Accuright, RR 2 Box 397, Sebeka, MN 56477/218-472-3383

Accu-Tek, 4510 Carter Ct., Chino, CA 91710/909-627-2404; FAX: 909-627-7817

Ace Custom 45's, Inc., 18801/2 Upper Turtle Creek Rd., Kerrville, TX 78028/210-257-4290; FAX: 210-257-5724

Ace Sportswear, Inc., 700 Quality Rd., Fayetteville, NC 28306/919-323-1223; FAX: 919-323-5392

Ackerman & Co., 16 Cortez St., Westfield, MA 01085/413-568-8008

Ackerman, Bill (See Optical Services Co.)

Acra-Bond Laminates, 134 Zimmerman Rd, Kalispell, MT 59901/406-257-9003; FAX 406-257-9003

Action Bullets, Inc., RR 1, P.O. Box 189, Quinter, KS 67752/913-754-3609; FAX: 913-754-3629

Action Direct, Inc., P.O. Box 830760, Miami, FL 33283/305-559-4652; FAX: 305-559-4652

Action Products, Inc., 22 N. Mulberry St., Hagerstown, MD 21740/301-797-1414; FAX: 301-733-2073

Action Target, Inc., P.O. Box 636, Provo, UT 84603/801-377-8033; FAX: 801-377-8096

Actions by "T," Teddy Jacobson, 16315 Redwood Forest Ct., Sugar Land, TX 77478/281-277-4008; WEB www.actionsbyt.com

ACTIV Industries, Inc., 1000 Zigor Rd., P.O. Box 339, Kearneysville, WV 25430/304-725-0451; FAX: 304-725-2080

AcuSport Corporation, 1 Hunter Place, Bellefontaine, OH 43311-3001/513-593-7010; FAX: 513-592-5625

Ad Hominem, 3130 Gun Club Lane, RR Orillia, Ont. L3V 6H3, CANADA/705-689-5303; FAX: 705-689-5303

Adair Custom Shop, Bill, 2886 Westridge, Carrollton, TX 75006

Adams & Son Engravers, John J., 87 Acorn Rd., Dennis, MA 02638/508-385-7971

Adams Jr., John J., 87 Acorn Rd., Dennis, MA 02638/508-385-7971

ADCO Sales Inc., 10 Cedar St., Unit 17, Woburn, MA 01801/617-935-1799; FAX: 617-935-1011

Adkins, Luther, 1292 E. McKay Rd., Shelbyville, IN 46176-9353/317-392-3795

Advance Car Mover Co., Rowell Div., P.O. Box 1, 240 N. Depot St., Juneau, WI 53039/414-386-4464; FAX: 414-386-4416

Adventure 16, Inc., 4620 Alvarado Canyon Rd., San Diego, CA 92120/619-283-6314

Adventure Game Calls, R.D. 1, Leonard Rd., Spencer, NY 14883/607-589-4611

Adventurer's Outpost, P.O. Box 70, Cottonwood, AZ 86326/800-762-7471; FAX: 602-634-8781

Aero Peltor, 90 Mechanic St., Southbridge, MA 01550/508-764-5500; FAX: 508-764-0188

African Import Co., 20 Braunecker Rd., Plymouth, MA 02360/508-746-8552

AFSCO Ammunition, 731 W. Third St., P.O. Box L, Owen, WI 54460/715-229-2516

Ahlman Guns, 9525 W. 230th St., Morristown, MN 55052/507-685-4243; FAX: 507-685-4280

Ahrends, Kim, Custom Firearms, Inc., Box 203, Clarion, IA 50525/515-532-3449; FAX: 515-532-3926

Aimpoint U.S.A., 420 W. Main St., Geneseo, IL 61254/309-944-1702

Aimtech Mount Systems, P.O. Box 223, 101 Inwood Acres, Thomasville, GA 31799/912-226-4313; FAX: 912-227-0222

Air Arms, Hailsham Industrial Park, Diplocks Way, Hailsham, E. Sussex, BN27 3JF ENGLAND/011-0323-845853 (U.S. importers—World Class Airguns)

Air Rifle Specialists, P.O. Box 138, 130 Holden Rd., Pine City, NY 14871-0138/607-734-7340; FAX: 607-733-3261

Air Venture Airguns, 9752 E. Flower St., Bellflower, CA 90706/562-867-6355

Airgun Repair Centre, 3227 Garden Meadows, Lawrenceburg, IN 47025/812-637-1463; FAX: 812-637-1463

Airrow (See Swivel Machine Works, Inc.)

Aitor-Cuchilleria Del Norte, S.A., Izelaieta, 17, 48260 Ermua (Vizcaya), SPAIN/43-17-08-50; FAX: 43-17-00-01

Ajax Custom Grips, Inc., 9130 Viscount Row, Dallas, TX 75247/214-630-8893; FAX: 214-630-4942; WEB: http://www.ajaxgrips.com

A.K.'s Gun Shop, 3221 2nd Ave. N., Great Falls, MT 59401/406-454-1831

Aker International, Inc., 2248 Main St., Suite 6, Chula Vista, CA 91911/619-423-5182; FAX: 619-423-1363

Alaska Bullet Works, Inc., 9978 Crazy Horse Drive, Juneau, AK 99801/907-789-3834; FAX: 907-789-3433

Alcas Cutlery Corp. (See Cutco Cutlery)

Alco Carrying Cases, 601 W. 26th St., New York, NY 10001/212-675-5820; FAX: 212-691-5935

Aldis Gunsmithing & Shooting Supply, 502 S. Montezuma St., Prescott, AZ 86303/602-445-6723; FAX: 602-445-6763

Alessi Holsters, Inc., 2465 Niagara Falls Blvd., Amherst, NY 14228-3527/716-691-5615

Alex, Inc., Box 3034, Bozeman, MT 59772/406-282-7396; FAX: 406-282-7396

Alfano, Sam, 36180 Henry Gaines Rd., Pearl River, LA 70452/504-863-3364; FAX: 504-863-7715

All American Lead Shot Corp., P.O. Box 224566, Dallas, TX 75062

All Rite Products, Inc., 5752 N. Silverstone Circle, Mountain Green, UT 84050/801-876-3330; 801-876-2216

All's, The Jim J. Tembelis Co., Inc., P.O. Box 108, Winnebago, WI 54985-0108/414-725-5251; FAX: 414-725-5251

Allard, Gary, Creek Side Metal & Woodcrafters, Fishers Hill, VA 22626/703-465-3903

Allen Co., Bob, 214 SW Jackson, P.O. Box 477, Des Moines, IA 50315/515-283-2191; 800-685-7020; FAX: 515-283-0779

Allen Co., Inc., 525 Burbank St., Broomfield, CO 80020/303-469-1857, 800-876-8600; FAX: 303-466-7437

Allen Firearm Engraving, 339 Grove Ave., Prescott, AZ 86301/520-778-1237

Allen Mfg., 6449 Hodgson Rd., Circle Pines, MN 55014/612-429-8231

Allen Sportswear, Bob (See Allen Co., Bob)

Alley Supply Co., P.O. Box 848, Gardnerville, NV 89410/702-782-3800

Alliant Techsystems, Smokeless Powder Group, 200 Valley Rd., Suite 305, Mt. Arlington, NJ 07856/800-276-9337; FAX: 201-770-2528

Allred Bullet Co., 932 Evergreen Drive, Logan, UT 84321/801-752-6983; FAX: 801-752-6983

Alpec Team, Inc., 201 Ricken Backer Cir., Livermore, CA 94550/510-606-8245; FAX: 510-606-4279

Alpha 1 Drop Zone, 2121 N. Tyler, Wichita, KS 67212/316-729-0800

Alpha Gunsmith Division, 1629 Via Monserate, Fallbrook, CA 92028/619-723-9279, 619-728-2663

Alpha LaFranck Enterprises, P.O. Box 81072, Lincoln, NE 68501/402-466-3193

Alpha Precision, Inc., 2765-B Preston Rd. NE, Good Hope, GA 30641/770-267-6163

Alpine's Precision Gunsmithing & Indoor Shooting Range, 2401 Government Way, Coeur d'Alene, ID 83814/208-765-3559; FAX: 208-765-3559

Altamont Co., 901 N. Church St., P.O. Box 309, Thomasboro, IL 61878/217-643-3125, 800-626-5774; FAX: 217-643-7973

Alumna Sport by Dee Zee, 1572 NE 58th Ave., P.O. Box 3090, Des Moines, IA 50316/800-798-9899

AmBr Software Group Ltd., P.O. Box 301, Reistertown, MD 21136-0301/800-888-1917; FAX: 410-526-7212

American Ammunition, 3545 NW 71st St., Miami, FL 33147/305-835-7400; FAX: 305-694-0037

American Arms, Inc., 715 Armour Rd., N. Kansas City, MO 64116/816-474-3161; FAX: 816-474-1225

American Derringer Corp., 127 N. Lacy Dr., Waco, TX 76705/800-642-7817, 817-799-9111; FAX: 817-799-7935

American Display Co., 55 Cromwell St., Providence, RI 02907/401-331-2464; FAX: 401-421-1264

American Frontier Firearms Mfg. Inc., P.O. 744, Aguanga, CA 92536/909-763-0014; FAX: 909-763-0014

American Gas & Chemical Co., Ltd., 220 Pegasus Ave., Northvale, NJ 07647/201-767-7300

American Gripcraft, 3230 S. Dodge 2, Tucson, AZ 85713/602-790-1222

American Gunsmithing Institute, 1325 Imola Ave., #504, Napa, CA 94559/707-253-0462; FAX: 707-253-7149

American Handgunner Magazine, 591 Camino de la Reina, Suite 200, San Diego, CA 92108/619-297-5350; FAX: 619-297-5353

American Pioneer Video, P.O. Box 50049, Bowling Green, KY 42102-2649/800-743-4675

American Products Inc., 14729 Spring Valley Road, Morrison, IL 61270/815-772-3336; FAX: 815-772-8046

American Safe Arms, Inc., 1240 Riverview Dr., Garland, UT 84312/801-257-7472; FAX: 801-785-8156

American Sales & Mfg Co., P.O. Box 677, Laredo, TX 78042/210-723-6893; FAX: 210-725-0672

American Security Products Co., 11925 Pacific Ave., Fontana, CA 92337/909-685-9680, 800-421-6142; FAX: 909-685-9685

American Small Arms Academy, P.O. Box 12111, Prescott, AZ 86304/602-778-5623

American Target, 1328 S. Jason St., Denver, CO 80223/303-733-0433; FAX: 303-777-0311

American Target Knives, 1030 Brownwood NW, Grand Rapids, MI 49504/616-453-1998

American Whitetail Target Systems, P.O. Box 41, 106 S. Church St., Tennyson, IN 47637/812-567-4527

Americase, P.O. Box 271, 1610 E. Main, Waxahachie, TX 75165/800-880-3629; FAX: 214-937-8373

Ames Metal Products, 4323 S. Western Blvd., Chicago, IL 60609/773-523-3230; FAX: 773-523-3854

Amherst Arms, P.O. Box 1457, Englewood, FL 34295/941-475-2020; FAX: 941-473-1212

Amrine's Gun Shop, 937 La Luna, Ojai, CA 93023/805-646-2376

Amsec, 11925 Pacific Ave., Fontana, CA 92337

A.M.T., 6226 Santos Diaz St., Irwindale, CA 91702/818-334-6629; FAX: 818-969-5247

Amtec 2000, Inc., 84 Industrial Rowe, Gardner, MA 01440/508-632-9608; FAX: 508-632-2300

Analog Devices, Box 9106, Norwood, MA 02062

Andela Tool & Machine, Inc., RD3, Box 246, Richfield Springs, NY 13439

Andres & Dworsky, Bergstrasse 18, A-3822 Karlstein, Thaya, Austria, EUROPE, 0 28 44-285

Angel Arms, Inc., 1825 Addison Way, Haywood, CA 94545/510-783-7122

Angelo & Little Custom Gun Stock Blanks, P.O. Box 240046, Dell, MT 59724-0046

Anschutz GmbH, Postfach 1128, D-89001 Ulm, Donau, GERMANY (U.S. importers—Accuracy International; AcuSport Corporation; Champion Shooters' Supply; Champion's Choice; Gunsmithing, Inc.)

Ansen Enterprises, Inc., 1506 W. 228th St., Torrance, CA 90501-5105/310-534-1837; FAX: 310-534-3162

Answer Products Co., 1519 Westbury Drive, Davison, MI 48423/810-653-2911

Anthony and George Ltd., Rt. 1, P.O. Box 45, Evington, VA 24550/804-821-8117

Antique American Firearms (See Carlson, Douglas R.)

Antique Arms Co., 1110 Cleveland Ave., Monett, MO 65708/417-235-6501

AO Safety Products, Div. of American Optical Corp. (See E-A-R, Inc., Div. of Cabot Safety Corp.

Apel GmbH, Ernst, Am Kirschberg 3, D-97218 Gerbrunn, GERMANY/0 (931) 707192

Aplan Antiques & Art, James O., HC 80, Box 793-25, Piedmont, SD 57769/605-347-5016

Arcadia Machine & Tool, Inc. (See AMT)

Arco Powder, HC-Rt. 1, P.O. Box 102, County Rd. 357, Mayo, FL 32066/904-294-3882; FAX: 904-294-1498

Aristocrat Knives, 1701 W. Wernsing Ave., Effingham, IL 62401/800-953-3436; FAX: 217-347-3083

Arizaga (See U.S. importer—Mandall Shooting Supplies, Inc.)

Arizona Ammunition, Inc., 21421 No. 14th Ave., Suite E, Phoenix, AZ 85727/602-516-9004; FAX: 602-516-9012

Arkansas Mallard Duck Calls, Rt. Box 182, England, AR 72046/501-842-3597

Arkfeld Mfg. & Dist. Co., Inc., 1230 Monroe Ave., Norfolk, NE 68702-0054/402-371-9430; 800-533-0676

ArmaLite, Inc., P.O. Box 299, Geneseo, IL 61254/309-944-6939; FAX: 309-944-6949

Armament Gunsmithing Co., Inc., 525 Rt. 22, Hillside, NJ 07205/908-686-0960

Armas Kemen S.A. (See U.S. importers—Kemen America; USA Sporting)

Armfield Custom Bullets, 4775 Caroline Drive, San Diego, CA 92115/619-582-7188; FAX: 619-287-3238

Armi Perazzi S.p.A., Via Fontanelle 1/3, 1-25080 Botticino Mattina, ITALY/030-2692591; FAX: 030 2692594 (U.S. importer—Perazzi USA, Inc.)

Armi San Marco (See U.S. importers—Taylor's & Co., Inc.; Cimarron Arms; IAR, Inc.)

Armi San Paolo, via Europa 172-A, I-25062 Concesio, 030-2751725 (BS) ITALY

Armi Sport (See U.S. importers—Cape Outfitters; Taylor's & Co., Inc.)

Armite Laboratories, 1845 Randolph St., Los Angeles, CA 90001/213-587-7768; FAX: 213-587-5075

Armoloy Co. of Ft. Worth, 204 E. Daggett St., Fort Worth, TX 76104/817-332-5604; FAX: 817-335-6517

Armor (See Buck Stop Lure Co., Inc.)

Armor Metal Products, P.O. Box 4609, Helena, MT 59604/406-442-5560; FAX: 406-442-5650

Armory Publications, Inc., 2615 N. 4th St., No. 620, Coeur d'Alene, ID 83814-3781/208-664-5061; FAX: 208-664-9906

Armoury, Inc., The, Rt. 202, Box 2340, New Preston, CT 06777/860-868-0001; FAX: 860-868-2919

A.R.M.S., Inc., 230 W. Center St., West Bridgewater, MA 02379-1620/508-584-7816; FAX: 508-588-8045

Arms & Armour Press, Wellington House, 125 Strand, London WC2R 0BB ENGLAND/0171-420-5555; FAX: 0171-240-7265

Arms Corporation of the Philippines, Bo. Parang Marikina, Metro Manila, PHILIPPINES/632-941-6243, 632-941-6244; FAX: 632-942-0682

Arms Craft Gunsmithing, 1106 Linda Dr., Arroyo Grande, CA 93420/805-481-2830

Arms Ingenuity Co., P.O. Box 1, 51 Canal St., Weatogue, CT 06089/203-658-5624

Arms, Programming Solutions (See Arms Software)

Arms Software, 4851 SW Madrona St., Lake Oswego, OR 97035/800-366-5559; FAX: 503-697-3337

Armscorp USA, Inc., 4424 John Ave., Baltimore, MD 21227/410-247-6200; FAX: 410-247-6205

Armsport, Inc., 3950 NW 49th St., Miami, FL 33142/305-635-7850; FAX: 305-633-2877

Arnold Arms Co., Inc., P.O. Box 1011, Arlington, WA 98223/800-371-1011, 360-435-1011; FAX: 360-435-7304

Aro-Tek, Ltd., 206 Frontage Rd. North, Suite C, Pacific, WA 98047/206-351-2984; FAX: 206-833-4483

Arratoonian, Andy (See Horseshoe Leather Products)

Arrieta, S.L., Morkaiko, 5, 20870 Elgoibar, SPAIN/34-43-743150; FAX: 34-43-743154 (U.S. importers—Griffin & Howe; Jansma, Jack J.; New England Arms Co.; The Orvis Co., Inc.; Quality Arms, Inc.; Wingshooting Adventures)

Art Jewel Enterprises Ltd., Eagle Business Ctr., 460 Randy Rd., Carol Stream, IL 60188/708-260-0400

Art's Gun & Sport Shop, Inc., 6008 Hwy. Y, Hillsboro, MO 63050

Artistry in Leather (See Stuart, V. Pat)

Arundel Arms & Ammunition, Inc., A., 24A Defense St., Annapolis, MD 21401/410-224-8683

Ashby Turkey Calls, P.O. Box 1466, Ava, MO 65608-1466/417-967-3787

A-Square Co., Inc., One Industrial Park, Bedford, KY 40006-9667/502-255-7456; FAX: 502-255-7657

Astra Sport, S.A., Apartado 3, 48300 Guernica, Espagne, SPAIN/34-4-6250100; FAX: 34-4-6255186 (U.S. importer—E.A.A. Corp.; P.S.M.G. Gun Co.)

Atamec-Bretton, 19, rue Victor Grignard, F-42006 St.-Etienne (Cedex 1) FRANCE/77-93-54-69; FAX: 33-77-93-57-98 (U.S. importer—Mandall Shooting Supplies, Inc.)

A-Tech Corp., P.O. Box 1281, Cottage Grove, OR 97424

Atlanta Cutlery Corp., 2143 Gees Mill Rd., Box 839 CIS, Conyers, GA 30207/800-883-0300; FAX: 404-388-0246

Atlantic Mills, Inc., 1295 Towbin Ave., Lakewood, NJ 08701-5934/800-242-7374

Atlantic Research Marketing Systems (See A.R.M.S., Inc.)

Atlantic Rose, Inc., P.O. Box 1305, Union, NJ 07083

Atsko/Sno-Seal, Inc., 2530 Russell SE, Orangeburg, SC 29115/803-531-1820; FAX: 803-531-2139

Audette, Creighton, 19 Highland Circle, Springfield, VT 05156/802-885-2331

Austin & Halleck, 1099 Welt, Weston, MO 64098/816-386-2176; FAX: 816-386-2177

Austin's Calls, Bill, Box 284, Kaycee, WY 82639/307-738-2552

Autauga Arms, Inc., Pratt Plaza Mall No. 13, Prattville, AL 36067/800-262-9563; FAX: 334-361-2961

Auto Arms, 738 Clearview, San Antonio, TX 78228/512-434-5450

Automatic Equipment Sales, 627 E. Railroad Ave., Salesburg, MD 21801

Auto-Ordnance Corp., Williams Lane, West Hurley, NY 12491/914-679-4190

Autumn Sales, Inc. (Blaser), 1320 Lake St., Fort Worth, TX 76102/817-335-1634; FAX: 817-338-0119

AWC Systems Technology, P.O. Box 41938, Phoenix, AZ 85080-1938/602-780-1050

AYA (See U.S. importer—New England Custom Gun Service)

A Zone Bullets, 2039 Walter Rd., Billings, MT 59105/800-252-3111; 406-248-1961

Aztec International Ltd., P.O. Box 2616, Clarkesville, GA 30523/706-754-8282; FAX: 706-754-6889

B

B&D Trading Co., Inc., 3935 Fair Hill Rd., Fair Oaks, CA 95628/800-334-3790, 916-967-9366; FAX: 916-967-4873

B&G Bullets (See Northside Gun Shop)

Badger Shooters Supply, Inc., P.O. Box 397, Owen, WI 54460/800-424-9069; FAX: 715-229-2332

Baekgaard Ltd., 1855 Janke Dr., Northbrook, IL 60062/708-498-3040; FAX: 708-493-3106

Baelder, Harry, Alte Goennebeker Strasse 5, 24635 Rickling, GERMANY/04328-722732; FAX: 04328-722733

Baer Custom, Les, Inc., 29601 34th Ave., Hillsdale, IL 61257/309-658-2716; FAX: 309-658-2610

Baer's Hollows, P.O. Box 284, Eads, CO 81036/719-438-5718

Bagmaster Mfg., Inc., 2731 Sutton Ave., St. Louis, MO 63143/314-781-8002; FAX: 314-781-3363; WEB: http://www.bagmaster.com

Bain & Davis, Inc., 307 E. Valley Blvd., San Gabriel, CA 91776-3522/818-573-4241, 213-283-7449

Baker, Stan, 10,000 Lake City Way, Seattle, WA 98125/206-522-4575

Baker's Leather Goods, Roy, P.O. Box 893, Magnolia, AR 71753/501-234-0344

Balaance Co., 340-39 Ave. S.E. Box 505, Calgary, AB, T2G 1X6 CANADA

Bald Eagle Precision Machine Co., 101-A Allison St., Lock Haven, PA 17745/717-748-6772; FAX: 717-748-4443

Balickie, Joe, 408 Trelawney Lane, Apex, NC 27502/919-362-5185

Balland Rifle & Cartridge Co. LLC, 113 W Yellowstone Ave., Cody WY 82414/307-587-4914; FAX: 307-527-6097

Ballard Built, P.O. Box 1443, Kingsville, TX 78364/512-592-0853

Ballard Industries, 10271 Lockwood Dr., Suite B, Cupertino, CA 95014/408-996-0957; FAX: 408-257-6828

Ballistic Engineering & Software, Inc., 185 N. Park Blvd., Suite 330, Lake Orion, MI 48362/313-391-1074

Ballistic Products, Inc., 20015 75th Ave. North, Corcoran, MN 55340-9456/612-494-9237; FAX: 612-494-9236

Ballistic Program Co., Inc., The, 2417 N. Patterson St., Thomasville, GA 31792/912-228-5739, 800-368-0835

Ballistic Research, 1108 W. May Ave., McHenry, IL 60050/815-385-0037

Bandcor Industries, Div. of Man-Sew Corp., 6108 Sherwin Dr., Port Richey, FL 34668/813-848-0432

Bang-Bang Boutique (See Holster Shop, The)

Banks, Ed, 2762 Hwy. 41 N., Ft. Valley, GA 31030/912-987-4665

Bansner's Gunsmithing Specialties, 261 East Main St. Box VH, Adamstown, PA 19501/800-368-2379; FAX: 717-484-0523

Barami Corp., 6689 Orchard Lake Rd. No. 148, West Bloomfield, MI 48322/248-738-0462; FAX: 248-738-2542

Barbour, Inc., 55 Meadowbrook Dr., Milford, NH 03055/603-673-1313; FAX: 603-673-6510

Barnes Bullets, Inc., P.O. Box 215, American Fork, UT 84003/801-756-4222, 800-574-9200; FAX: 801-756-2465; WEB: http://www.itsnet.com/home/bbullets

Baron Technology, 62 Spring Hill Rd., Trumbull, CT 06611/203-452-0515; FAX: 203-452-0663

Barraclough, John K., 55 Merit Park Dr., Gardena, CA 90247/310-324-2574

Barramundi Corp., P.O. Drawer 4259, Homosassa Springs, FL 32687/904-628-0200

Barrett Firearms Manufacturer, Inc., P.O. Box 1077, Murfreesboro, TN 37133/615-896-2938; FAX: 615-896-7313

Barsotti, Bruce (See River Road Sporting Clays)

Bar-Sto Precision Machine, 73377 Sullivan Rd., P.O. Box 1838, Twentynine Palms, CA 92277/619-367-2747; FAX: 619-367-2407

Barta's Gunsmithing, 10231 US Hwy. 10, Cato, WI 54206/414-732-4472

Barteaux Machete, 1916 SE 50th Ave., Portland, OR 97215-3238/503-233-5880

Bartlett Engineering, 40 South 200 East, Smithfield, UT 84335-1645/801-563-5910

Basics Information Systems, Inc., 1141 Georgia Ave., Suite 515, Wheaton, MD 20902/301-949-1070; FAX: 301-949-5326

Bates Engraving, Billy, 2302 Winthrop Dr., Decatur, AL 35603/256-355-3690

Bauer, Eddie, 15010 NE 36th St., Redmond, WA 98052

Baumgartner Bullets, 3011 S. Alane St., W. Valley City, UT 84120

Bausch & Lomb Sports Optics Div. (See Bushnell Sports Optics Worldwide)

Bauska Barrels, 105 9th Ave. W., Kalispell, MT 59901/406-752-7706

Bear Archery, RR 4, 4600 Southwest 41st Blvd., Gainesville, FL 32601/904-376-2327

Bear Arms, 121 Rhodes St., Jackson, SC 29831/803-471-9859

Bear Hug Grips, Inc., P.O. Box 16649, Colorado Springs, CO 80935-6649/800-232-7710

Bear Mountain Gun & Tool, 120 N. Plymouth, New Plymouth, ID 83655/208-278-5221; FAX: 208-278-5221

Beartooth Bullets, P.O. Box 491, Dept. HLD, Dover, ID 83825-0491/208-448-1865

Beauchamp & Son, Inc., 160 Rossiter Rd., P.O. Box 181, Richmond, MA 01254/413-698-3822; FAX: 413-698-3866

Beaver Lodge (See Fellowes, Ted)

Beaver Park Products, Inc., 840 J St., Penrose, CO 81240/719-372-6744

BEC, Inc., 1227 W. Valley Blvd., Suite 204, Alhambra, CA 91803/818-281-5751; FAX:818-293-7073

Beeline Custom Bullets Limited, P.O. Box 85, Yarmouth, Nova Scotia CANADA B5A 4B1/902-648-3494; FAX: 902-648-0253

Beeman Precision Airguns, 5454 Argosy Dr., Huntington Beach, CA 92649/714-890-4800; FAX: 714-890-4808

Behlert Precision, Inc., P.O. Box 288, 7067 Easton Rd., Pipersville, PA 18947/215-766-8681, 215-766-7301; FAX: 215-766-8681

Beitzinger, George, 116-20 Atlantic Ave., Richmond Hill, NY 11419/718-847-7661

Belding's Custom Gun Shop, 10691 Sayers Rd., Munith, MI 49259/517-596-2388

Bell & Carlson, Inc., Dodge City Industrial Park/101 Allen Rd., Dodge City, KS 67801/800-634-8586, 316-225-6688; FAX: 316-225-9095

Bell Alaskan Silversmith, Sid (See Heritage Wildlife Carvings)

Bell Reloading, Inc., 1725 Harlin Lane Rd., Villa Rica, GA 30180

Bell's Gun & Sport Shop, 3309-19 Mannheim Rd, Franklin Park, IL 60131

Bell's Legendary Country Wear, 22 Circle Dr., Bellmore, NY 11710/516-679-1158

Bellm Contenders, P.O. Box 459, Cleveland, UT 84518/801-653-2530

Belltown, Ltd., 11 Camps Rd., Kent, CT 06757/860-354-5750

Belt MTN Arms, 107 10th Ave. SW, White Sulphur Springs, MT 59645/406-586-4495

Ben's Machines, 1151 S. Cedar Ridge, Duncanville, TX 75137/214-780-1807; FAX: 214-780-0316

Benchmark Guns, 12593 S. Ave. 5 East, Yuma, AZ 85365

Benchmark Knives (See Gerber Legendary Blades)

Benelli Armi, S.p.A., Via della Stazione, 61029 Urbino, ITALY/39-722-307-1; FAX: 39-722-327427 (U.S. importers—Heckler & Koch, Inc.; Whitestone Lumber Co.)

Benelli USA Corp., 17603 Indian Head Hwy., Ascokeek, MD 20607/301-283-6981; FAX: 301-283-6988

Bengtson Arms Co., L., 6345-B E. Akron St., Mesa, AZ 85205/602-981-6375

Benjamin/Sheridan Co., Crossman, Rts. 5 and 20, E. Bloomfield, NY 14443/716-657-6161; FAX: 716-657-5405

Bentley, John, 128-D Watson Dr., Turtle Creek, PA 15145

Beomat of America Inc., 300 Railway Ave., Campbell, CA 95008/408-379-4829

Beretta S.p.A., Pietro, Via Beretta, 18-25063 Gardone V.T. (BS) ITALY/XX39/30-8341.1; FAX: XX39/30-8341.421 (U.S. importer—Beretta U.S.A. Corp.)

Beretta U.S.A. Corp., 17601 Beretta Drive, Accokeek, MD 20607/301-283-2191; FAX: 301-283-0435

Berger Bullets, Ltd., 5342 W. Camelback Rd., Suite 200, Glendale, AZ 85301/602-842-4001; FAX: 602-934-9083

Bergman & Williams, 2450 Losee Rd., Suite F, Las Vegas, NV 89030/702-642-1901; FAX: 702-642-1540

Bernardelli S.p.A., Vincenzo, 125 Via Matteotti, P.O. Box 74, Gardone V.T., Brescia ITALY, 25063/39-30-8912851-2-3; FAX: 39-30-8910249 (U.S. importer—Armsport, Inc.)

Berry's Bullets (See Berry's Mfg., Inc.)

Berry's Mfg., Inc., 401 North 3050 East St., St. George, UT 84770/801-634-1682; FAX: 801-634-1683

Bersa S.A., Gonzales Castillo 312, 1704 Ramos Mejia, ARGENTINA/541-656-2377; FAX: 541-656-2093 (U.S. importer—Eagle Imports, Inc.)

Bertram Bullet Co., P.O. Box 313, Seymour, Victoria 3660, AUSTRALIA/61-57-922912; FAX: 61-57-991650

Bertuzzi (See U.S. importer—New England Arms Co.)

Better Concepts Co., 663 New Castle Rd., Butler, PA 16001/412-285-9000

Beverly, Mary, 3201 Horseshoe Trail, Tallahassee, FL 32312

Bianchi International, Inc., 100 Calle Cortez, Temecula, CA 92590/909-676-5621; FAX: 909-676-6777

Biesen, Al, 5021 Rosewood, Spokane, WA 99208/509-328-9340

Biesen, Roger, 5021 W. Rosewood, Spokane, WA 99208/509-328-9340

Big Beam Emergency Systems, Inc., 290 E. Prairie St., Crystal Lake, IL 60039

Big Bear Arms & Sporting Goods, Inc., 1112 Milam Way, Carrollton, TX 75006/972-416-8051, 800-400-BEAR; FAX: 972-416-0771

Big Bore Bullets of Alaska, P.O. Box 872785, Wasilla, AK 99687/907-373-2673; FAX: 907-373-2673

Big Bore Express, 7154 W. State St., Boise, ID 83703/800-376-4010; FAX:208-376-4020

Big Sky Racks, Inc., P.O. Box 729, Bozeman, MT 59771-0729/406-586-9393; FAX: 406-585-7378

Big Spring Enterprises "Bore Stores", P.O. Box 1115, Big Spring, Rd./Yellville, AR 72687/870-449-5297; FAX: 870-449-4446; E-MAIL: BIGSPRNG@mtnhome.com

Bilal, Mustafa, 908 NW 50th St., Seattle, WA 98107-3634/206-782-4164

Bill's Custom Cases, P.O. Box 2, Dunsmuir, CA 96025/916-235-0177; FAX: 916-235-4959

Bill's Gun Repair, 1007 Burlington St., Mendota, IL 61342/815-539-5786

Billeb, Stephen L., 1101 N. 7th St., Burlington, IA 52601/319-753-2110

Billings Gunsmiths, Inc., 1841 Grand Ave., Billings, MT 59102/406-256-8390

Billingsley & Brownell, P.O. Box 25, Dayton, WY 82836/307-655-9344

Birchwood Casey, 7900 Fuller Rd., Eden Prairie, MN 55344/800-328-6156, 612-937-7933; FAX: 612-937-7979

Birdsong & Assoc., W.E., 1435 Monterey Rd., Florence, MS 39073-9748/601-366-8270

Bismuth Cartridge Co., 3500 Maple Ave., Suite 1650, Dallas, TX 75219/800-759-3333, 214-521-5880; FAX: 214-521-9035

Bison Studios, 1409 South Commerce St., Las Vegas, NV 89102/702-388-2891; FAX: 702-383-9967

Bitterroot Bullet Co., Box 412, Lewiston, ID 83501-0412/208-743-5635

Black Belt Bullets (See Big Bore Express)

Black Hills Ammunition, Inc., P.O. Box 3090, Rapid City, SD 57709-3090/605-348-5150; FAX: 605-348-9827

Black Hills Shooters Supply, P.O. Box 4220, Rapid City, SD 57709/800-289-2506

Black Powder Products, 67 Township Rd. 1411, Chesapeake, OH 45619/614-867-8047

Black Sheep Brand, 3220 W. Gentry Parkway, Tyler, TX 75702/903-592-3853; FAX: 903-592-0527

Blackhawk East, Box 2274, Loves Park, IL 61131

Blackhawk West, Box 285, Hiawatha, KS 66434

Blackinton & Co., V.H., 221 John L. Dietsch, Attleboro Falls, MA 02763-0300/508-699-4436; FAX: 508-695-5349

Blackjack Knives, Ltd., 1307 W. Wabash, Effingham, IL 62401/217-347-7700; FAX: 217-347-7737

Blacksmith Corp., 830 N. Road No. 1 E., P.O. Box 1752, Chino Valley, AZ 86323/520-636-4456; FAX: 520-636-4457

BlackStar AccuMax Barrels, 11501 Brittmoore Park Drive, Houston, TX 77041/281-721-6040; FAX: 281-721-6041

BlackStar Barrel Accurizing (See BlackStar AccuMax Barrels)

Blacktail Mountain Books, 42 First Ave. W., Kalispell, MT 59901/406-257-5573

Blair Engraving, J.R., P.O. Box 64, Glenrock, WY 82637/307-436-8115

Blammo Ammo, P.O. Box 1677, Seneca, SC 29679/803-882-1768

Blaser Jagdwaffen GmbH, D-88316 Isny Im Allgau, GERMANY (U.S. importer—Autumn Sales, Inc.)

Bleile, C. Roger, 5040 Ralph Ave., Cincinnati, OH 45238/513-251-0249

Blocker Holsters, Inc., Ted., Clackamas Business Park Bld. A, 14787 S.E. 82nd, Dr./Clackamas, OR 97015/503-557-7757; FAX: 503-557-3771

Blount, Inc., Sporting Equipment Div., 2299 Snake River Ave., P.O. Box 856, Lewiston, ID 83501/800-627-3640, 208-746-2351; FAX: 208-799-3904

Blue and Gray Products, Inc. (See Ox-Yoke Originals, Inc.)

Blue Book Publications, Inc., One Appletree Square, 8009 34th Ave. S., Suite, 175/Minneapolis, MN 55425/800-877-4867, 612-854-5229; FAX: 612-853-1486

Blue Mountain Bullets, HCR 77, P.O. Box 231, John Day, OR 97845/541-820-4594

Blue Ridge Machinery & Tools, Inc., P.O. Box 536-GD, Hurricane, WV 25526/800-872-6500; FAX: 304-562-5311

BMC Supply, Inc., 26051 - 179th Ave. S.E., Kent, WA 98042

B.M.F. Activator, Inc., 803 Mill Creek Run, Plantersville, TX 77363/409-894-2005, 800-527-2881

Bob's Gun Shop, P.O. Box 200, Royal, AR 71968/501-767-1970; FAX 501-767-1970

Bob's Tactical Indoor Shooting Range & Gun Shop, 122 Lafayette Rd., Salisbury, MA 01952/508-465-5561

Boessler, Erich, Am Vogeltal 3, 97702 Munnerstadt, GERMANY/9733-9443

Bohemia Arms Co., 17101 Los Modelos St., Fountain Valley, CA 92708/619-442-7005; FAX: 619-442-7005

Boker USA, Inc., 1550 Balsam Street, Lakewood, CO 80215/303-462-0662; FAX: 303-462-0668

Boltin, John M., P.O. Box 644, Estill, SC 29918/803-625-2185

Bo-Mar Tool & Mfg. Co., Rt. 8, Box 405, Longview, TX 75604/903-759-4784; FAX: 903-759-9141

Bonanza (See Forster Products)

Bond Arms, Inc., P.O. Box 1296, Granbury, TX 76048/817-573-5733; FAX: 817-573-5636

Bond Custom Firearms, 8954 N. Lewis Ln., Bloomington, IN 47408/812-332-4519

Bondini Paolo, Via Sorrento, 345, San Carlo di Cesena, ITALY I-47020/0547 663 240; FAX: 0547 663 780 (U.S. importer—blackpowder arms)

Bone Engraving, Ralph, 718 N. Atlanta, Owasso, OK 74055/918-272-9745

Boone Trading Co., Inc., P.O. Box BB, Brinnan, WA 98320

Boone's Custom Ivory Grips, Inc., 562 Coyote Rd., Brinnon, WA 98320/206-796-4330

Boonie Packer Products, P.O. Box 12204, Salem, OR 97309/800-477-3244, 503-581-3244; FAX: 503-581-3191

Borden's Accuracy, RD 1, Box 250BC, Springville, PA 18844/717-965-2505; FAX: 717-965-2328

Border Barrels Ltd., Riccarton Farm, Newcastleton SCOTLAND U.K. TD9 0SN

Borovnik KG, Ludwig, 9170 Ferlach, Bahnhofstrasse 7, AUSTRIA/042 27 24 42; FAX: 042 26 43 49

Bosis (See U.S. importer—New England Arms Co.)

Boss Manufacturing Co., 221 W. First St., Kewanee, IL 61443/309-852-2131, 800-447-4581; FAX: 309-852-0848

Bostick Wildlife Calls, Inc., P.O. Box 728, Estill, SC 29918/803-625-2210, 803-625-4512

Bowen Classic Arms Corp., P.O. Box 67, Louisville, TN 37777/423-984-3583

Bowen Knife Co., Inc., P.O. Box 590, Blackshear, GA 31516/912-449-4794

Bowerly, Kent, 26247 Metolius Meadows Dr., Camp Sherman, OR 97730/541-595-6028

Boyds' Gunstock Industries, Inc., 3rd & Main, P.O. Box 305, Geddes, SD 57342/605-337-2125; FAX: 605-337-3363

Boyt, 509 Hamilton, P.O. Drawer 668, Iowa Falls, IA 50126/515-648-4626; FAX: 515-648-2385

Brace, Larry D., 771 Blackfoot Ave., Eugene, OR 97404/541-688-1278; FAX 541-607-5833

Bradley Gunsight Co., P.O. Box 340, Plymouth, VT 05056/860-589-0531; FAX: 860-582-6294

Brass and Bullet Alloys, P.O. Box 1238, Sierra Vista, AZ 85636/602-458-5321; FAX: 602-458-9125

Brass Eagle, Inc., 7050A Bramalea Rd., Unit 19, Mississauga, Ont. L4Z 1C7, CANADA/416-848-4844

Bratcher, Dan, 311 Belle Air Pl., Carthage, MO 64836/417-358-1518

Brauer Bros. Mfg. Co., 2020 Delman Blvd., St. Louis, MO 63103/314-231-2864; FAX: 314-249-4952

Braverman Corp., R.J., 88 Parade Rd., Meridith, NH 03293/800-736-4867

Break-Free, Inc., P.O. Box 25020, Santa Ana, CA 92799/714-953-1900; FAX: 714-953-0402

Brenneke KG, Wilhelm, Ilmenauweg 2, 30851 Langenhagen, GERMANY/0511/97262-0; FAX: 0511/97262-62 (U.S. importer—Dynamit Nobel-RWS, Inc.)

Bretton (See Atamec-Bretton)

Bridgers Best, P.O. Box 1410, Berthoud, CO 80513

Briese Bullet Co., Inc., RR1, Box 108, Tappen, ND 58487/701-327-4578; FAX: 701-327-4579

Brigade Quartermasters, 1025 Cobb International Blvd., Dept. VH, Kennesaw, GA 30144-4300/404-428-1248, 800-241-3125; FAX: 404-426-7726

Briganti, A.J., 512 Rt. 32, Highland Mills, NY 10930/914-928-9573

Briley Mfg., Inc., 1230 Lumpkin, Houston, TX 77043/800-331-5718; Web: www.briley.com

British Antiques, P.O. Box 7, Latham, NY 12110/518-783-0773

British Sporting Arms, RR1, Box 130, Millbrook, NY 12545/914-677-8303

BRNO (See U.S. importers—Bohemia Arms Co.)

Broad Creek Rifle Works, 120 Horsey Ave., Laurel, DE 19956/302-875-5446; FAX 302-875-1448

Brockman's Custom Gunsmithing, P.O. Box 357, Gooding, ID 83330/208-934-5050

Brocock Ltd., 43 River Street, Digbeth, Birmingham, B5 5SA ENGLAND/011-021-773-1200

Broken Gun Ranch, 10739 126 Rd., Spearville, KS 67876/316-385-2587; FAX: 316-385-2597

Brolin Industries Inc., 2755 Thompson Creek Rd., Pomona, CA 91767/909-392-7822; FAX: 909-392-7824

Brooker, Dennis, Rt. 1, Box 12A, Derby, IA 50068/515-533-2103

Brooks Tactical Systems, 279-C Shorewood Ct., Fox Island, WA 98333-9725/253-549-2866; FAX 253-549-2703

Brown Co., E. Arthur, 3404 Pawnee Dr., Alexandria, MN 56308/320-762-8847

Brown, H.R. (See Silhouette Leathers)

Brown Dog Ent., 2200 Calle Camelia, 1000 Oaks, CA 91360/805-497-2318; FAX: 805-497-1618

Brown Manufacturing, P.O. Box 9219, Akron, OH 44305/800-837-GUNS

Brown Precision, Inc., 7786 Molinos Ave., Los Molinos, CA 96055/916-384-2506; FAX: 916-384-1638

Brown Products, Inc., Ed, 43825 Muldrow Trail, Perry, MO 63462/573-565-3261; FAX: 573-565-2791

Brownell Checkering, W.E., 9390 Twin Mountain Circle, San Diego, CA 92126/619-695-2479; FAX: 619-695-2479

Brownells, Inc., 200 S. Front St., Montezuma, IA 50171/515-623-5401; FAX: 515-623-3896

Browning Arms Co., One Browning Place, Morgan, UT 84050/801-876-2711; FAX: 801-876-3331

Browning Arms Co. (Parts & Service), 3005 Arnold Tenbrook Rd., Arnold, MO 63010-9406/314-287-6800; FAX: 314-287-9751

BRP, Inc., High Performance Cast Bullets, 1210 Alexander Rd., Colorado Springs, CO 80909-3932/719-633-0658

Bruno Shooters Supply, 111 N. Wyoming St., Hazleton, PA 18201/717-455-2281; FAX: 717-455-2211

Brunton U.S.A., 620 E. Monroe Ave., Riverton, WY 82501/307-856-6559; FAX: 307-856-1840

Brynin, Milton, P.O. Box 383, Yonkers, NY 10710/914-779-4333

BSA Guns Ltd., Armoury Rd. Small Heath, Birmingham, ENGLAND B11 2PX/011-021-772-8543; FAX: 011-021-773-0845 (U.S. importers—Groenewold, John; Precision Sales International, Inc.)

BSA Optics, 3911 SW 47th Ave., #914, Ft. Lauderdale, FL 33314/954-581-2144; FAX: 954-581-3165

B-Square Company, Inc., P.O. Box 11281, 2708 St. Louis Ave., Ft. Worth, TX 76110/817-923-0964, 800-433-2909; FAX: 817-926-7012

Bucheimer, J.M., Jumbo Sports Products, 721 N. 20th St., St. Louis, MO 63103/314-241-1020

Buck Knives, Inc., 1900 Weld Blvd., P.O. Box 1267, El Cajon, CA 92020/619-449-1100, 800-326-2825; FAX: 619-562-5774, 800-729-2825

Buck Stix—SOS Products Co., Box 3, Neenah, WI 54956

Buck Stop Lure Co., Inc., 3600 Grow Rd. NW, P.O. Box 636, Stanton, MI 48888/517-762-5091; FAX: 517-762-5124

Buckeye Custom Bullets, 6490 Stewart Rd., Elida, OH 45807/419-641-4463

Buckhorn Gun Works, 8109 Woodland Dr., Black Hawk, SD 57718/605-787-6472

Buckskin Bullet Co., P.O. Box 1893, Cedar City, UT 84721/801-586-3286

Buckskin Machine Works, A. Hunkeler, 3235 S. 358th St., Auburn, WA 98001/206-927-5412

Budin, Dave, Main St., Margaretville, NY 12455/914-568-4103; FAX: 914-586-4105

Buenger Enterprises/Goldenrod Dehumidifier, 3600 S. Harbor Blvd., Oxnard, CA 93035/800-451-6797; FAX: 805-985-1534

Buffalo Arms Co., 3355 Upper Gold Creek Rd., Samuels, ID 83864/208-263-6953; FAX: 208-265-2096

Buffalo Bullet Co., Inc., 12637 Los Nietos Rd., Unit A, Santa Fe Springs, CA 90670/310-944-0322; FAX: 310-944-5054

Buffalo Rock Shooters Supply, R.R. 1, Ottawa, IL 61350/815-433-2471

Buffer Technologies, P.O. Box 104930, Jefferson City, MO 65110/573-634-8529; FAX: 573-634-8522

Bull Mountain Rifle Co., 6327 Golden West Terrace, Billings, MT 59106/406-656-0778

Bullberry Barrel Works, Ltd., 2430 W. Bullberry Ln. 67-5, Hurricane, UT 84737/801-635-9866; FAX: 801-635-0348

Bullet, Inc., 3745 Hiram Alworth Rd., Dallas, GA 30132

Bullet'n Press, 19 Key St., Eastport, Maine 04631/207-853-4116

Bullet Swaging Supply, Inc., P.O. Box 1056, 303 McMillan Rd, West Monroe, LA 71291/318-387-3266; FAX: 318-387-7779

BulletMakers Workshop, The, RFD 1 Box 1755, Brooks, ME 04921

Bullseye Bullets, 1610 State Road 60, No. 12, Valrico, FL 33594/813-654-6563

Bull-X, Inc., 520 N. Main, Farmer City, IL 61842/309-928-2574; FAX: 309-928-2130

Burgess, Byron, P.O. Box 6853, Los Osos, CA 93412/805-528-1005

Burkhart Gunsmithing, Don, P.O. Box 852, Rawlins, WY 82301/307-324-6007

Burnham Bros., P.O. Box 1148, Menard, TX 78659/915-396-4572; FAX: 915-396-4574

Burris Co., Inc., P.O. Box 1747, 331 E. 8th St., Greeley, CO 80631/970-356-1670; FAX: 970-356-8702

Bushmann Hunters & Safaris, P.O. Box 293088, Lewisville, TX 75029/214-317-0768

Bushmaster Firearms (See Quality Parts Co./Bushmaster Firearms)

Bushmaster Hunting & Fishing, 451 Alliance Ave., Toronto, Ont. M6N 2J1 CANADA/416-763-4040; FAX: 416-763-0623

Bushnell Sports Optics Worldwide, 9200 Cody, Overland Park, KS 66214/913-752-3400, 800-423-3537; FAX: 913-752-3550

Bushwacker Backpack & Supply Co. (See Counter Assault)

Bustani, Leo, 8195 No. Mil Tr., Suite A Box 13, W. Palm Beach, FL 33410/305-622-2710

Buster's Custom Knives, P.O. Box 214, Richfield, UT 84701/801-896-5319

Butler Creek Corp., 290 Arden Dr., Belgrade, MT 59714/800-423-8327, 406-388-1356; FAX: 406-388-7204

Butler Enterprises, 834 Oberting Rd., Lawrenceburg, IN 47025/812-537-3584

Butterfield & Butterfield, 220 San Bruno Ave., San Francisco, CA 94103/415-861-7500

Buzztail Brass (See Grayback Wildcats)

B-West Imports, Inc., 2425 N. Huachuca Dr., Tucson, AZ 85745-1201/602-628-1990; FAX: 602-628-3602

C

C3 Systems, 678 Killingly St., Johnston, RI 02919

C&D Special Products (See Claybuster Wads & Harvester Bullets)

C&H Research, 115 Sunnyside Dr., Box 351, Lewis, KS 67552/316-324-5445

C&J Enterprises, Inc., 7101 Jurupa Ave., No. 12, Riverside, CA 92504/909-689-7758; FAX 909-689-7791

C&T Corp. TA Johnson Brothers, 1023 Wappoo Road, Charleston, SC 29407-5960

Cabanas (See U.S. importer—Mandall Shooting Supplies, Inc.)

Cabela's, 812-13th Ave., Sidney, NE 69160/308-254-6644, 800-237-4444; FAX: 308-254-6745

Cabinet Mtn. Outfitters Scents & Lures, P.O. Box 766, Plains, MT 59859/406-826-3970

Cache La Poudre Rifleworks, 140 N. College, Ft. Collins, CO 80524/303-482-6913

Cadre Supply (See Parts & Surplus)

Calhoon Varmint Bullets, James, Shambo Rt., 304, Havre, MT 59501/406-395-4079

Calibre Press, Inc., 666 Dundee Rd., Suite 1607, Northbrook, IL 60062-2760/800-323-0037; FAX: 708-498-6869

Cali'co Hardwoods, Inc., 3580 Westwind Blvd., Santa Rosa, CA 95403/707-546-4045; FAX: 707-546-4027

Calico Light Weapon Systems, 405 E. 19th St., Bakersfield, CA 93305/805-835-9605; FAX: 805-835-9605

California Magnum, 20746 Dearborn St., Chatsworth, CA 91313/818-341-7302; FAX: 818-341-7304

California Sights (See Fautheree, Andy)

Camdex, Inc., 2330 Alger, Troy, MI 48083/810-528-2300; FAX: 810-528-0989

Cameron's, 16690 W. 11th Ave., Golden, CO 80401/303-279-7365; FAX: 303-628-5413

Camilli, Lou, 600 Sandtree Dr., Suite 212, Lake Park, FL 33403-1538

Camillus Cutlery Co., 54 Main St., Camillus, NY 13031/315-672-8111; FAX: 315-672-8832

Campbell, Dick, 20,000 Silver Ranch Rd., Conifer, CO 80433/303-697-0150; FAX 303-697-0150

Camp-Cap Products, P.O. Box 173, Chesterfield, MO 63006/314-532-4340; FAX: 314-532-4340

Canjar Co., M.H., 500 E. 45th Ave., Denver, CO 80216/303-295-2638; FAX: 303-295-2638

Cannon's, Andy Cannon, Box 1026, 320 Main St., Polson, MT 59860/406-887-2048

Cannon Safe, Inc., 9358 Stephens St., Pico Rivera, CA 90660/310-692-0636, 800-242-1055; FAX: 310-692-7252

Canons Delcour, Rue J.B. Cools, B-4040 Herstal, BELGIUM 32.(0)42.40.61.40; FAX: 32(0)42.40.22.88

Canyon Cartridge Corp., P.O. Box 152, Albertson, NY 11507/FAX: 516-294-8946

Cape Outfitters, 599 County Rd. 206, Cape Girardeau, MO 63701/314-335-4103; FAX: 314-335-1555

Caraville Manufacturing, P.O. Box 4545, Thousand Oaks, CA 91359/805-499-1234

Carbide Checkering Tools (See J&R Engineering)

Carbide Die & Mfg. Co., Inc., 15615 E. Arrow Hwy., Irwindale, CA 91706/818-337-2518

Carhartt, Inc., P.O. Box 600, 3 Parklane Blvd., Dearborn, MI 48121/800-358-3825, 313-271-8460; FAX: 313-271-3455

Custom Gun Engraving, D-97422 Schweinfurt, Siedlerweg 17, GERMANY/01149-9721-41446; FAX: 01149-9721-44413

Carlson, Douglas R., Antique American Firearms, P.O. Box 71035, Dept. GD, Des Moines, IA 50325/515-224-6552

Carnahan Bullets, 17645 110th Ave. SE, Renton, WA 98055

Carolina Precision Rifles, 1200 Old Jackson Hwy., Jackson, SC 29831/803-827-2069

Carrell's Precision Firearms, 643 Clark Ave., Billings, MT 59101-1614/406-962-3593

Carroll Bullets (See Precision Reloading, Inc.)

Carry-Lite, Inc., 5203 W. Clinton Ave., Milwaukee, WI 53223/414-355-3520; FAX: 414-355-4775

Carter's Gun Shop, 225 G St., Penrose, CO 81240/719-372-6240

Cartridge Transfer Group, Pete de Coux, 235 Oak St., Butler, PA 16001/412-282-3426

Cascade Bullet Co., Inc., 2355 South 6th St., Klamath Falls, OR 97601/503-884-9316

Cascade Shooters, 2155 N.W. 12th St., Redwood, OR 97756

Case & Sons Cutlery Co., W.R., Owens Way, Bradford, PA 16701/814-368-4123, 800-523-6350; FAX: 814-768-5369

Case Sorting System, 12695 Cobblestone Creek Rd., Poway, CA 92064/619-486-9340

Cash Mfg. Co., Inc., P.O. Box 130, 201 S. Klein Dr., Waunakee, WI 53597-0130/608-849-5664; FAX: 608-849-5664

Caspian Arms Ltd., 14 North Main St., Hardwick, VT 05843/802-472-6454; FAX: 802-472-6709

Cast Performance Bullet Company, 12441 U.S. Hwy. 26, Riverton, WY 82501/307-856-4347

Casull Arms Corp., P.O. Box 1629, Afton, WY 83110/307-886-0200

Caswell International Corp., 1221 Marshall St. NE, Minneapolis, MN 55413-1055/612-379-2000; FAX: 612-379-2367

CATCO, 316 California Ave., #341N, Reno, NV 89509/707-253-8338; FAX: 707-253-7149

Catco-Ambush, Inc., P.O.Box 300, Corte Madera, CA 94926

Cathey Enterprises, Inc., P.O. Box 2202, Brownwood, TX 76804/915-643-2553; FAX: 915-643-3653

Cation, 2341 Alger St., Troy, MI 48083/810-689-0658; FAX: 810-689-7558

Catoctin Cutlery, P.O. Box 188, 17 S. Main St., Smithsburg, MD 21783/301-824-7416; FAX: 301-824-6138

Caywood, Shane J., P.O. Box 321, Minocqua, WI 54548/715-277-3866 evenings

CBC, Avenida Humberto de Campos, 3220, 09400-000 Ribeirao Pires-SP-BRAZIL/55-11-742-7500; FAX: 55-11-459-7385

CCG Enterprises, 5217 E. Belknap St., Halton City, TX 76117/800-819-7464

CCI, Div. of Blount, Inc., Sporting Equipment Div., 2299 Snake River Ave.,,, P.O. Box 856/Lewiston, ID 83501

800-627-3640, 208-746-2351; FAX: 208-746-2915

Cedar Hill Game Calls, L.L.C., Rt. 2 Box 236, Downsville, LA 71234/318-982-5632; FAX: 318-368-2245

Celestron International, P.O. Box 3578, 2835 Columbia St., Torrance, CA 90503/310-328-9560; FAX: 310-212-5835

Centaur Systems, Inc., 1602 Foothill Rd., Kalispell, MT 59901/406-755-8609; FAX: 406-755-8609

Center Lock Scope Rings, 9901 France Ct., Lakeville, MN 55044/612-461-2114

CenterMark, P.O. Box 4066, Parnassus Station, New Kensington, PA 15068/412-335-1319

Central Specialties Ltd. (See Trigger Lock Division/Central Specialties Ltd.)

Century Gun Dist., Inc., 1467 Jason Rd., Greenfield, IN 46140/317-462-4524

Century International Arms, Inc., P.O. Box 714, St. Albans, VT 05478-0714/802-527-1252, 800-527-1252; FAX: 802-527-0470; WEB: www.centuryarms.com

CFVentures, 509 Harvey Dr., Bloomington, IN 47403-1715

C-H Tool & Die Corp. (See 4-D Custom Die Co.)

Chace Leather Products, 507 Alden St., Fall River, MA 02722/508-678-7556; FAX: 508-675-9666

Chadick's Ltd., P.O. Box 100, Terrell, TX 75160/214-563-7577

Chambers Flintlocks Ltd., Jim, Rt. 1, Box 513-A, Candler, NC 28715/704-667-8361

Champion Shooters' Supply, P.O. Box 303, New Albany, OH 43054/614-855-1603; FAX: 614-855-1209

Champion Target Co., 232 Industrial Parkway, Richmond, IN 47374/800-441-4971

Champion's Choice, Inc., 201 International Blvd., LaVergne, TN 37086/615-793-4066; FAX: 615-793-4070

Champlin Firearms, Inc., P.O. Box 3191, Woodring Airport, Enid, OK 73701/580-237-7388; FAX: 580-242-6922

Chapman Academy of Practical Shooting, 4350 Academy Rd., Hallsville, MO 65255/573-696-5544, 573-696-2266

Chapman Manufacturing Co., 471 New Haven Rd., P.O. Box 250, Durham, CT 06422/203-349-9228; FAX: 203-349-0084

Chapuis Armes, 21 La Gravoux, BP15, 42380 St. Bonnet-le-Chateau, FRANCE/(33)77.50.06.96 (U.S. importer—Champlin Firearms, Inc.; Chapuis USA)

Chapuis USA, 416 Business Park, Bedford, KY 40006

Checkmate Refinishing, 370 Champion Dr., Brooksville, FL 34601/904-799-5774

Cheddite France, S.A., 99, Route de Lyon, F-26501 Bourg-les-Valence, FRANCE/33-75-56-4545; FAX: 33-75-56-3587

Chelsea Gun Club of New York City, Inc., 237 Ovington Ave., Apt. D53, Brooklyn, NY 11209/718-836-9422, 718-833-2704

Chem-Pak, Inc., 11 Oates Ave., P.O. Box 1685, Winchester, VA 22604/800-336-9828, 703-667-1341; FAX: 703-722-3993

Cherry's Fine Guns, P.O. Box 5307, Greensboro, NC 27435-0307/919-854-4182

Chesapeake Importing & Distributing Co. (See CIDCO)

CheVron Bullets, RR1, Ottawa, IL 61350/815-433-2471

CheVron Case Master (See CheVron Bullets)

Chicago Cutlery Co., 1536 Beech St., Terre Haute, IN 47804/800-457-2665

Chicasaw Gun Works, 4 Mi. Mkr., Pluto Rd., Box 868, Shady Spring, WV 25918-0868/304-763-2848; FAX: 304-763-2848

Chipmunk (See Oregon Arms, Inc.)

Chippewa Shoe Co., P.O. Box 2521, Ft. Worth, TX 76113/817-332-4385

Choate Machine & Tool Co., Inc., P.O. Box 218, 116 Lovers Ln., Bald Knob, AR 72010/501-724-6193, 800-972-6390; FAX: 501-724-5873

Chopie Mfg., Inc., 700 Copeland Ave., LaCrosse, WI 54603/608-784-0926

Christensen Arms, 385 North 3050 East, St. George, UT 84790/435-624-9535; FAX: 435-674-9293

Christie's East, 219 E. 67th St., New York, NY 10021/212-606-0400

Christman Jr., David, Gunmaker, 937 Lee Hedrick Rd., Colville, WA 99114/509-684-1438

Christopher Firearms Co., Inc., E., Route 128 & Ferry St., Miamitown, OH 45041/513-353-1321

Chu Tani Ind., Inc., P.O. Box 2064, Cody, WY 82414-2064

Chuck's Gun Shop, P.O. Box 597, Waldo, FL 32694/904-468-2264

Churchill (See U.S. importer—Ellett Bros.)

Churchill, Winston, Twenty Mile Stream Rd., RFD P.O. Box 29B, Proctorsville, VT 05153/802-226-7772

Churchill Glove Co., James, P.O. Box 298, Centralia, WA 98531

CIDCO, 21480 Pacific Blvd., Sterling, VA 22170/703-444-5353

Ciener, Inc., Jonathan Arthur, 8700 Commerce St., Cape Canaveral, FL 32920/407-868-2200; FAX: 407-868-2201

Cimarron Arms, P.O. Box 906, Fredericksburg, TX 78624-0906/210-997-9090; FAX: 210-997-0802

Cincinnati Swaging, 2605 Marlington Ave., Cincinnati, OH 45208

Citadel Mfg., Inc., 5220 Gabbert Rd., Moorpark, CA 93021/805-529-7294; FAX: 805-529-7297

C.J. Ballistics, Inc., P.O. Box 132, Acme, WA 98220/206-595-5001

Clark Co., Inc., David, P.O. Box 15054, Worcester, MA 01615-0054/508-756-6216; FAX: 508-753-5827

Clark Custom Guns, Inc., 336 Shootout Lane, Princeton, LA 71067/318-949-9884; FAX: 318-949-9829

Clark Firearms Engraving, P.O. Box 80746, San Marino, CA 91118/818-287-1652

Clarkfield Enterprises, Inc., 1032 10th Ave., Clarkfield, MN 56223/612-669-7140

Claro Walnut Gunstock Co., 1235 Stanley Ave., Chico, CA 95928/530-342-5188; FAX 530-342-5199

Classic Arms Corp., P.O. Box 106, Dunsmuir, CA 96025-0106/916-235-2000

Classic Guns, Inc., Frank S. Wood, 3230 Medlock Bridge Rd., Suite 110, Norcross, GA 30092/404-242-7944

Claybuster Wads & Harvester Bullets, 309 Sequoya Dr., Hopkinsville, KY 42240/800-922-6287, 800-284-1746, 502-885-8088; FAX: 502-885-1951

Clean Shot Technologies, Inc., 21218 St. Andrews Blvd., #504, Boca Raton, FL 33433/888-866-2532; FAX: 561-479-7039

Clearview Mfg. Co., Inc., 413 S. Oakley St., Fordyce, AR 71742/501-352-8557; FAX: 501-352-7120

Clearview Products, 3021 N. Portland, Oklahoma City, OK 73107

Cleland's Outdoor World, Inc., 10306 Airport Hwy., Swanton, OH 43558/419-865-4713; FAX 419-865-5865

Clements' Custom Leathercraft, Chas, 1741 Dallas St., Aurora, CO 80010-2018/ 303-364-0403; FAX:303-739-9824

Clenzoil Corp., P.O. Box 80226, Sta. C, Canton, OH 44708-0226/330-833-9758; FAX: 330-833-4724

Clerke Co., J.A., P.O. Box 627, Pearblossom, CA 93553-0627/805-945-0713

Clift Mfg., L.R., 3821 Hammonton Rd., Marysville, CA 95901/916-755-3390; FAX: 916-755-3393

Clift Welding Supply & Cases, 1332-A Colusa Hwy., Yuba City, CA 95993/916-755-3390; FAX: 916-755-3393

Cloward's Gun Shop, 4023 Aurora Ave. N, Seattle, WA 98103/206-632-2072

Clymer Manufacturing Co., Inc., 1645 W. Hamlin Rd., Rochester Hills, MI 48309-1530/810-853-5555, 810-853-5627; FAX: 810-853-1530

C-More Systems, P.O. Box 1750, 7553 Gary Rd., Manassas, VA 22110/703-361-2663; FAX: 703-361-5881

Cobalt Mfg., Inc., 1020 Shady Oak Dr., Denton, TX 76205/800-690-9923; FAX: 940-383-4281

Cobra Sport S.r.l., Via Caduti Nei Lager No. 1, 56020 San Romano, Montopoli v/Arno (Pi), ITALY/0039-571-450490; FAX: 0039-571-450492

Coffin, Charles H., 3719 Scarlet Ave., Odessa, TX 79762/915-366-4729

Coffin, Jim (See Working Guns)

Cogar's Gunsmithing, P.O. Box 755, Houghton Lake, MI 48629/517-422-4591

Coghlan's Ltd., 121 Irene St., Winnipeg, Man., CANADA R3T 4C7/204-284-9550; FAX: 204-475-4127

Cold Steel, Inc., 2128-D Knoll Dr., Ventura, CA 93003/800-255-4716, 800-624-2363 (in CA); FAX: 805-642-9727

Cole's Gun Works, Old Bank Building, Rt. 4, Box 250, Moyock, NC 27958/919-435-2345

Cole-Grip, 16135 Cohasset St., Van Nuys, CA 91406/818-782-4424

Coleman Co., Inc., 250 N. St. Francis, Wichita, KS 67201

Coleman's Custom Repair, 4035 N. 20th Rd., Arlington, VA 22207/703-528-4486

Collings, Ronald, 1006 Cielta Linda, Vista, CA 92083

Colonial Arms, Inc., P.O. Box 636, Selma, AL 36702-0636/334-872-9455; FAX: 334-872-9540

Colonial Knife Co., Inc., P.O. Box 3327, Providence, RI 02909/401-421-1600; FAX: 401-421-2047

Colonial Repair, P.O. Box 372, Hyde Park, MA 02136-9998/617-469-4951

Colorado Gunsmithing Academy, 27533 Highway 287 South, Lamar, CO 81052/719-336-4099, 800-754-2046; FAX: 719-336-9642

Colorado School of Trades, 1575 Hoyt St., Lakewood, CO 80215/800-234-4594; FAX: 303-233-4723

Colorado Shooter's Supply, 1163 W. Paradise Way, Fruita, CO 81521/303-858-9191

Colorado Sutlers Arsenal (See Cumberland States Arsenal)

Colt Blackpowder Arms Co., 110 8th Street, Brooklyn, NY 11215/212-925-2159; FAX: 212-966-4986

Colt's Mfg. Co., Inc., P.O. Box 1868, Hartford, CT 06144-1868/800-962-COLT, 860-236-6311; FAX: 860-244-1449

Combat Military Ordnance Ltd., 3900 Hopkins St., Savannah, GA 31405/912-238-1900; FAX: 912-236-7570

Companhia Brasileira de Cartuchos (See CBC)

Compass Industries, Inc., 104 East 25th St., New York, NY 10010/212-473-2614, 800-221-9904; FAX: 212-353-0826

Compasseco, Ltd., 151 Atkinson Hill Ave., Bardtown, KY 40004/502-349-0910

Competition Electronics, Inc., 3469 Precision Dr., Rockford, IL 61109/815-874-8001; FAX: 815-874-8181

Competitive Pistol Shop, The, 5233 Palmer Dr., Ft. Worth, TX 76117-2433/817-834-8479

Competitor Corp., Inc., Appleton Business Center, 30 Tricnit Road, Unit 16, New Ipswich, NH 03071-0508/603-878-3891; FAX: 603-878-3950

Component Concepts, Inc., 10240 SW Nimbus Ave., Suite L-8, Portland, OR 97223/503-684-9262; FAX: 503-620-4285

Concept Development Corp., 14715 N. 78th Way, Suite 300, Scottsdale, AZ 85260/800-472-4405; FAX: 602-948-7560

Condon, Inc., David, 109 E. Washington St., Middleburg, VA 22117/703-687-5642

Conetrol Scope Mounts, 10225 Hwy. 123 S., Seguin, TX 78155/210-379-3030, 800-CONETROL; FAX: 210-379-3030

CONKKO, P.O. Box 40, Broomall, PA 19008/215-356-0711

Connecticut Shotgun Mfg. Co., P.O. Box 1692, 35 Woodland St., New Britain, CT 06051-1692/860-225-6581; FAX: 860-832-8707

Connecticut Valley Classics (See CVC)

Conrad, C.A., 3964 Ebert St., Winston-Salem, NC 27127/919-788-5469

Continental Kite & Key (See CONKKO)

Cook Engineering Service, 891 Highbury Rd., Vermont VICT 3133 AUSTRALIA

Coonan Arms (JS Worldwide DBA), 1745 Hwy. 36 E., Maplewood, MN 55109/612-777-3156; FAX: 612-777-3683

Cooper Arms, P.O. Box 114, Stevensville, MT 59870/406-777-5534; FAX: 406-777-5228

Cooper-Woodward, 3800 Pelican Rd., Helena, MT 59602/406-458-3800

Corbin Mfg. & Supply, Inc., 600 Industrial Circle, P.O. Box 2659, White City, OR 97503/541-826-5211; FAX: 541-826-8669

Cor-Bon Bullet & Ammo Co., 1311 Industry Rd., Sturgis, SD 57785/800-626-7266; FAX: 800-923-2666

Corkys Gun Clinic, 4401 Hot Springs Dr., Greeley, CO 80634-9226/970-330-0516

Corry, John, 861 Princeton Ct., Neshanic Station, NJ 08853/908-369-8019

Cosmi Americo & Figlio s.n.c., Via Flaminia 307, Ancona, ITALY I-60020/071-888208; FAX: 39-071-887008 (U.S. importer—New England Arms Co.)

Costa, David (See Island Pond Gun Shop)

Coulston Products, Inc., P.O. Box 30, 201 Ferry St., Suite 212, Easton, PA 18044-0030/215-253-0167, 800-445-9927; FAX: 215-252-1511

Counter Assault, Box 4721, Missoula, MT 59806/406-728-6241; FAX: 406-728-8800

Country Armourer, The, P.O. Box .308, Ashby, MA 01431-0308/508-827-6797; FAX: 508-827-4845

Cousin Bob's Mountain Products, 7119 Ohio River Blvd., Ben Avon, PA 15202/412-766-5114; FAX: 412-766-5114

Cox, Ed C., RD 2, Box 192, Prosperity, PA 15329/412-228-4984

CQB Training, P.O. Box 1739, Manchester, MO 63011

Craftguard, 3624 Logan Ave., Waterloo, IA 50703/319-232-2959; FAX: 319-234-0804

Craig Custom Ltd., Research & Development, 629 E. 10th, Hutchinson, KS 67501/316-669-0601

Crandall Tool & Machine Co., 19163 21 Mile Rd., Tustin, MI 49688/616-829-4430

Crane & Crane Ltd., 105 N. Edison Way 6, Reno, NV 89502-2355/702-856-1516; FAX: 702-856-1616

Creative Concepts USA, Inc., P.O. Box 1705, Dickson, TN 37056/615-446-8346, 800-874-6965; FAX: 615-446-0646

Creative Craftsman, Inc., The, 95 Highway 29 North, P.O. Box 331, Lawrenceville, GA 30246/404-963-2112; FAX: 404-513-9488

Creedmoor Sports, Inc., P.O. Box 1040, Oceanside, CA 92051/619-757-5529

Creek Side Metal & Woodcrafters (See Allard, Gary)

Creekside Gun Shop, Inc., Main St., Holcomb, NY 14469/716-657-6338; FAX: 716-657-7900

Crimson Trace, 1433 N.W. Quimby, Portland, OR 97209/503-295-2406; 503-295-2225

Crit'R Call (See Rocky Mountain Wildlife Products)

Crosman Airguns, Rts. 5 and 20, E. Bloomfield, NY 14443/716-657-6161; FAX: 716-657-5405

Crosman Blades (See Coleman Co., Inc.)

Crosman Products of Canada Ltd., 1173 N. Service Rd. West, Oakville, Ontario, L6M 2V9 CANADA/905-827-1822

Crossfire LLC, 2169 Greenville Rd., La Grange, GA 30241/706-882-8070; FAX: 706-882-9050

Crouse's Country Cover, P.O. Box 160, Storrs, CT 06268/860-423-8736

CRR, Inc./Marble's Inc., 420 Industrial Park, P.O. Box 111, Gladstone, MI 49837/906-428-3710; FAX: 906-428-3711

Crucelegui, Hermanos (See U.S. importer—Mandall Shooting Supplies, Inc.)

Cryo-Accurizing, 2101 East Olive, Decatur, IL 62526/217-423-3070; FAX: 217-423-3075

Cubic Shot Shell Co., Inc., 98 Fatima Dr., Campbell, OH 44405/330-755-0349

Cullity Restoration, Daniel, 209 Old County Rd., East Sandwich, MA 02537/508-888-1147

Cumberland Arms, 514 Shafer Road, Manchester, TN 37355/800-797-8414

Cumberland Knife & Gun Works, 5661 Bragg Blvd., Fayetteville, NC 28303/919-867-0009

Cumberland Mountain Arms, P.O. Box 710, Winchester, TN 37398/615-967-8414; FAX: 615-967-9199

Cumberland States Arsenal, 1124 Palmyra Road, Clarksville, TN 37040

Cummings Bullets, 1417 Esperanza Way, Escondido, CA 92027

Cupp, Alana, Custom Engraver, P.O. Box 207, Annabella, UT 84711/801-896-4834

Curly Maple Stock Blanks (See Tiger-Hunt)

Curtis Custom Shop, RR1, Box 193A, Wallingford, KY 41093/703-659-4265

Curtis Cast Bullets, 527 W Babcock St., Bozeman, MT 59715/406-587-8117; FAX: 406-587-8117

Curtis Gun Shop (See Curtis Cast Bullets)

Custom Barreling & Stocks, 937 Lee Hedrick Rd., Colville, WA 99114/509-684-5686 (days), 509-684-3314 (evenings)

Custom Bullets by Hoffman, 2604 Peconic Ave., Seaford, NY 11783

Custom Calls, 607 N. 5th St., Burlington, IA 52601/319-752-4465

Custom Checkering Service, Kathy Forster, 2124 SE Yamhill St., Portland, OR 97214/503-236-5874

Custom Chronograph, Inc., 5305 Reese Hill Rd., Sumas, WA 98295/360-988-7801

Custom Firearms (See Ahrends, Kim)

Custom Gun Products, 5021 W. Rosewood, Spokane, WA 99208/509-328-9340

Custom Gun Stocks, Rt. 6, P.O. Box 177, McMinnville, TN 37110/615-668-3912

Custom Gunsmiths, 4303 Friar Lane, Colorado Springs, CO 80907/719-599-3366

Custom Hunting Ammo & Arms (See CHAA, Ltd.)

Custom Products (See Jones Custom Products, Neil A.)

Custom Quality Products, Inc., 345 W. Girard Ave., P.O. Box 71129, Madison Heights, MI 48071/810-585-1616; FAX: 810-585-0644

Custom Riflestocks, Inc., Michael M. Kokolus, 7005 Herber Rd., New Tripoli, PA 18066/610-298-3013

Custom Shop, The, 890 Cochrane Crescent, Peterborough, Ont. K9H 5N3 CANADA/705-742-6693

Custom Tackle and Ammo, P.O. Box 1886, Farmington, NM 87499/505-632-3539

Cutco Cutlery, P.O. Box 810, Olean, NY 14760/716-372-3111

Cutlery Shoppe, 5461 Kendall St., Boise, ID 83706-1248/800-231-1272

CVA, 5988 Peachtree Corners East, Norcross, GA 30071/800-251-9412; FAX: 404-242-8546

CVC, 48 Commercial Street, Holyoke, MA 01040/413-552-3184; FAX: 413-552-3276

Cylinder & Slide, Inc., William R. Laughridge, 245 E. 4th St., Fremont, NE 68025/402-721-4277; FAX: 402-721-0263

CZ USA, 40356 Oak Park Way, Suite W, Oakhurst, CA 93664

D

D&D Gunsmiths, Ltd., 363 E. Elmwood, Troy, MI 48083/810-583-1512; FAX: 810-583-1524

D&G Precision Duplicators (See Greene Precision Duplicators)

D&H Precision Tooling, 7522 Barnard Mill Rd., Ringwood, IL 60072/815-653-4011

D&H Prods. Co., Inc., 465 Denny Rd., Valencia, PA 16059/412-898-2840, 800-776-0281; FAX: 412-898-2013

D&J Bullet Co. & Custom Gun Shop, Inc., 426 Ferry St., Russell, KY 41169/606-836-2663; FAX: 606-836-2663

D&L Industries (See D.J. Marketing)

D&L Sports, P.O. Box 651, Gillette, WY 82717/307-686-4008

D&R Distributing, 308 S.E. Valley St., Myrtle Creek, OR 97457/503-863-6850

Dade Screw Machine Products, 2319 NW 7th Ave., Miami, FL 33127/305-573-5050

Daewoo Precision Industries Ltd., 34-3 Yeoeuido-Dong, Yeongdeungoo-GU, 15th, Fl./Seoul, KOREA (U.S. importer—Nationwide Sports Distributors, Inc.)

Daisy Mfg. Co., P.O. Box 220, Rogers, AR 72757/501-621-4210; FAX: 501-636-0573

Dakota (See U.S. importer—EMF Co., Inc.)

Dakota Arms, Inc., HC 55, Box 326, Sturgis, SD 57785/605-347-4686; FAX: 605-347-4459

Dakota Corp., 77 Wales St., P.O. Box 543, Rutland, VT 05701/802-775-6062, 800-451-4167; FAX: 802-773-3919

Daly, Charles (See B.C. Miroku/Charles Daly)

DAMASCUS-U.S.A., 149 Deans Farm Rd., Tyner, NC 27980/252-221-2010; FAX: 252-221-2009

Dan's Whetstone Co., Inc., 130 Timbs Place, Hot Springs, AR 71913/501-767-1616; FAX: 501-767-9598

Dangler, Homer L., Box 254, Addison, MI 49220/517-547-6745

Danner Shoe Mfg. Co., 12722 NE Airport Way, Portland, OR 97230/503-251-1100, 800-345-0430; FAX: 503-251-1119

Danuser Machine Co., 550 E. Third St., P.O. Box 368, Fulton, MO 65251/573-642-2246; FAX: 573-642-2240

Dapkus Co., Inc., J.G., Commerce Circle, P.O. Box 293, Durham, CT 06422

Dara-Nes, Inc. (See Nesci Enterprises, Inc.)

Darlington Gun Works, Inc., P.O. Box 698, 516 S. 52 Bypass, Darlington, SC 29532/803-393-3931

Data Tech Software Systems, 19312 East Eldorado Drive, Aurora, CO 80013

Datumtech Corp., 2275 Wehrle Dr., Buffalo, NY 14221

Dave's Gun Shop, 555 Wood Street, Powell, Wyoming 82435/307-754-9724

Davidson, Jere, Rt. 1, Box 132, Rustburg, VA 24588/804-821-3637

Davis, Don, 1619 Heights, Katy, TX 77493/713-391-3090

Davis Co., R.E., 3450 Pleasantville NE, Pleasantville, OH 43148/614-654-9990

Davis Industries, 15150 Sierra Bonita Ln., Chino, CA 91710/909-597-4726; FAX: 909-393-9771

Davis Leather Co., Gordon Wm., P.O. Box 2270, Walnut, CA 91788/909-598-5620

Davis Products, Mike, 643 Loop Dr., Moses Lake, WA 98837/509-765-6178, 509-766-7281 orders only

Davis Service Center, Bill, 7221 Florin Mall Dr., Sacramento, CA 95823/916-393-4867

Day & Sons, Inc., Leonard, P.O. Box 122, Flagg Hill Rd., Heath, MA 01346/413-337-8369

Dayson Arms Ltd., P.O. Box 532, Vincennes, IN 47591/812-882-8680; FAX: 812-882-8680

Daystate Ltd., Birch House Lanee, Cotes Heath, Staffs, ST15.022 ENGLAND/ 01782-791755; FAX: 01782-791617

Dayton Traister, 4778 N. Monkey Hill Rd., P.O. Box 593, Oak Harbor, WA 98277/360-679-4657; FAX:360-675-1114

DBASE Consultants (See Arms, Peripheral Data Systems)

DBI Books, Division of Krause Publications, (Editorial office) 700 E. State St., Iola, WI 54990/715-445-2214: FAX: 715-445-4087; Orders: 800-258-0929

D-Boone Ent., Inc., 5900 Colwyn Dr., Harrisburg, PA 17109

D.C.C. Enterprises, 259 Wynburn Ave., Athens, GA 30601

D.D. Custom Stocks, R.H. "Dick" Devereaux, 5240 Mule Deer Dr., Colorado Springs, CO 80919/719-548-8468

de Coux, Pete (See Cartridge Transfer Group)

de Treville & Co., Stan, 4129 Normal St., San Diego, CA 92103/619-298-3393

Dead Eye's Sport Center, RD 1, Box 147B, Shickshinny, PA 18655/717-256-7432

Decker Shooting Products, 1729 Laguna Ave., Schofield, WI 54476/715-359-5873

DeckSlider of Florida, 27641-2 Reahard Ct., Bonita Springs, FL 33923/800-782-1474

Deepeeka Exports Pvt. Ltd., D-78, Saket, Meerut-250-006, INDIA/011-91-121-512889, 011-91-121-545363; FAX: 011-91-121-542988, 011-91-121-511599

Deer Me Products Co., Box 34, 1208 Park St., Anoka, MN 55303/612-421-8971; FAX: 612-422-0526

Defense Training International, Inc., 749 S. Lemay, Ste. A3-337, Ft. Collins, CO 80524/303-482-2520; FAX: 303-482-0548

Degen Inc. (See Aristocrat Knives)

deHaas Barrels, RR 3, Box 77, Ridgeway, MO 64481/816-872-6308

Del Rey Products, P.O. Box 91561, Los Angeles, CA 90009/213-823-0494

Delhi Gun House, 1374 Kashmere Gate, Delhi, INDIA 110 006/(011)2940974 2940814; FAX: 91-11-2917344

Delorge, Ed, 2231 Hwy. 308, Thibodaux, LA 70301/504-447-1633

Del-Sports, Inc., Box 685, Main St., Margaretville, NY 12455/914-586-4103; FAX: 914-586-4105

Delta Arms Ltd., P.O. Box 1000, Delta, VT 84624-1000

Delta Enterprises, 284 Hagemann Drive, Livermore, CA 94550

Delta Frangible Ammunition, LLC, P.O. Box 2350, Stafford, VA 22555-2350/540-720-5778, 800-339-1933; FAX: 540-720-5667

Dem-Bart Checkering Tools, Inc., 6807 Bickford Ave., Old Hwy. 2, Snohomish, WA 98290/360-568-7356; FAX: 360-568-1798

Denver Bullets, Inc., 1811 W. 13th Ave., Denver, CO 80204/303-893-3146; FAX: 303-893-9161

Denver Instrument Co., 6542 Fig St., Arvada, CO 80004/800-321-1135, 303-431-7255; FAX: 303-423-4831

DeSantis Holster & Leather Goods, Inc., P.O. Box 2039, 149 Denton Ave., New Hyde Park, NY 11040-0701/516-354-8000; FAX: 516-354-7501

Desert Mountain Mfg., P.O. Box 130184, Coram, MT 59913/800-477-0762, 406-387-5361; FAX 406-387-5361

Detroit-Armor Corp., 720 Industrial Dr. No. 112, Cary, IL 60013/708-639-7666; FAX: 708-639-7694

Dever Co., Jack, 8590 NW 90, Oklahoma City, OK 73132/405-721-6393

Devereaux, R.H. "Dick" (See D.D. Custom Stocks)

Dewey Mfg. Co., Inc., J., P.O. Box 2014, Southbury, CT 06488/203-264-3064; FAX: 203-262-6907

DGR Custom Rifles, RR1, Box 8A, Tappen, ND 58487/701-327-8135

DGS, Inc., Dale A. Storey, 1117 E. 12th, Casper, WY 82601/307-237-2414; FAX 307-237-2414

DHB Products, P.O. Box 3092, Alexandria, VA 22302/703-836-2648

Diamond Machining Techonology (See DMT—Diamond Machining Technology)

Diamond Mfg. Co., P.O. Box 174, Wyoming, PA 18644/800-233-9601

Diana (See U.S. importer—Dynamit Nobel-RWS, Inc.)

Dibble, Derek A., 555 John Downey Dr., New Britain, CT 06051/203-224-2630

Dietz Gun Shop & Range, Inc., 421 Range Rd., New Braunfels, TX 78132/210-885-4662

Dilliott Gunsmithing, Inc., 657 Scarlett Rd., Dandridge, TN 37725/423-397-9204

Dillon, Ed, 1035 War Eagle Dr. N., Colorado Springs, CO 80919/719-598-4929; FAX: 719-598-4929

Dillon Precision Products, Inc., 8009 East Dillon's Way, Scottsdale, AZ 85260/602-948-8009, 800-762-3845; FAX: 602-998-2786

Dina Arms Corporation, P.O. Box 46, Royersford, PA 19468/610-287-0266; FAX: 610-287-0266

Division Lead Co., 7742 W. 61st Pl., Summit, IL 60502

Dixie Gun Works, Inc., Hwy. 51 South, Union City, TN 38261/901-885-0561, order 800-238-6785; FAX: 901-885-0440

Dixon Muzzleloading Shop, Inc., 9952 Kunkels Mill Rd., Kempton, PA 19529/610-756-6271

D.J. Marketing, 10602 Horton Ave., Downey, CA 90241/310-806-0891; FAX: 310-806-6231

DKT, Inc., 14623 Vera Drive, Union, MI 49130-9744/616-641-7120, 800-741-7083 orders only; FAX: 616-641-2015

DLO Mfg., 10807 SE Foster Ave., Arcadia, FL 33821-7304

DMT—Diamond Machining Technology, Inc., 85 Hayes Memorial Dr., Marlborough, MA 01752/508-481-5944; FAX: 508-485-3924

Dogtown Varmint Supplies, 1048 Irvine Ave. No. 333, Newport Beach, CA 92660/714-642-3997

Dohring Bullets, 100 W. 8 Mile Rd., Ferndale, MI 48220

Dolbare, Elizabeth, P.O. Box 222, Sunburst, MT 59482-0222

Donnelly, C.P., 405 Kubli Rd., Grants Pass, OR 97527/541-846-6604

Doskocil Mfg. Co., Inc., P.O. Box 1246, 4209 Barnett, Arlington, TX 76017/817-467-5116; FAX: 817-472-9810

Double A Ltd., P.O. Box 11306, Minneapolis, MN 55411/612-522-0306

Douglas Barrels, Inc., 5504 Big Tyler Rd., Charleston, WV 25313-1398/304-776-1341; FAX: 304-776-8560

Downsizer Corp., P.O. Box 710316, Santee, CA 92072-0316/619/448-5510; FAX: 619-448-5780

Dowtin Gunworks, Rt. 4, Box 930A, Flagstaff, AZ 86001/602-779-1898

Dr. O's Products Ltd., P.O. Box 111, Niverville, NY 12130/518-784-3333; FAX: 518-784-2800

Drain, Mark, SE 3211 Kamilche Point Rd., Shelton, WA 98584/206-426-5452

Dremel Mfg. Co., 4915-21st St., Racine, WI 53406

Dressel Jr., Paul G., 209 N. 92nd Ave., Yakima, WA 98908/509-966-9233; FAX: 509-966-3365

Dri-Slide, Inc., 411 N. Darling, Fremont, MI 49412/616-924-3950

Dropkick, 1460 Washington Blvd., Williamsport, PA 17701/717-326-6561; FAX: 717-326-4950

DTM International, Inc., 40 Joslyn Rd., P.O. Box 5, Lake Orion, MI 48362/313-693-6670

Duane Custom Stocks, Randy, 110 W. North Ave., Winchester, VA 22601/703-667-9461; FAX: 703-722-3993

Duane's Gun Repair (See DGR Custom Rifles)

Dubber, Michael W., P.O. Box 312, Evansville, IN 47702/812-424-9000; FAX: 812-424-6551

Duck Call Specialists, P.O. Box 124, Jerseyville, IL 62052/618-498-9855

Duffy (See Guns Antique & Modern DBA/Charles E. Duffy)

Du-Lite Corp., Charles E., 171 River Rd., Middletown, CT 06457/203-347-2505; FAX: 203-347-9404

Dumoulin, Ernest, Rue Florent Boclinville 8-10, 13-4041 Votten, BELGIUM/41 27 78 92 (U.S. importer—New England Arms Co.)

Duncan's Gun Works, Inc., 1619 Grand Ave., San Marcos, CA 92069/619-727-0515

Dunham Co., P.O. Box 813, Brattleboro, VT 05301/802-254-2316

Dunphy, Ted, W. 5100 Winch Rd., Rathdrum, ID 83858/208-687-1399; FAX: 208-687-1399

Duofold, Inc., RD 3 Rt. 309, Valley Square Mall, Tamaqua, PA 18252/717-386-2666; FAX: 717-386-3652

DuPont (See IMR Powder Co.)

Dutchman's Firearms, Inc., The, 4143 Taylor Blvd., Louisville, KY 40215/502-366-0555

Dybala Gun Shop, P.O. Box 1024, FM 3156, Bay City, TX 77414/409-245-0866

Dykstra, Doug, 411 N. Darling, Fremont, MI 49412/616-924-3950

Dynalite Products, Inc., 215 S. Washington St., Greenfield, OH 45123/513-981-2124

Dynamit Nobel-RWS, Inc., 81 Ruckman Rd., Closter, NJ 07624/201-767-7971; FAX: 201-767-1589

Dyson & Son Ltd., Peter, 3 Cuckoo Lane, Honley, Huddersfield, Yorkshire HD7 2BR, ENGLAND/44-1484-661062; FAX: 44-1484-663709

E

E&L Mfg., Inc., 4177 Riddle by Pass Rd., Riddle, OR 97469/541-874-2137; FAX: 541-874-3107

E.A.A. Corp., P.O. Box 1299, Sharpes, FL 32959/407-639-4842, 800-536-4442; FAX: 407-639-7006

Eagan, Donald V., P.O. Box 196, Benton, PA 17814/717-925-6134

Eagle Arms (See ArmaLite, Inc.)

Eagle Grips, Eagle Business Center, 460 Randy Rd., Carol Stream, IL 60188/800-323-6144, 708-260-0400; FAX: 708-260-0486

Eagle Imports, Inc., 1750 Brielle Ave., Unit B1, Wanamassa, NJ 07712/908-493-0333; FAX: 908-493-0301

Eagle International Sporting Goods, Inc., P.O. Box 67, Zap, ND 58580/888-932-4536; FAX: 701-948-2282

E-A-R, Inc., Div. of Cabot Safety Corp., 5457 W. 79th St., Indianapolis, IN 46268/800-327-3431; FAX: 800-488-8007

Eastman Products, R.T., P.O. Box 1531, Jackson, WY 83001/307-733-3217, 800-624-4311

EAW (See U.S. importer—New England Custom Gun Service)

Echols & Co., D'Arcy, 164 W. 580 S., Providence, UT 84332/801-753-2367

Eclectic Technologies, Inc., 45 Grandview Dr., Suite A, Farmington, CT 06034

Eckelman Gunsmithing, 3125 133rd St. SW, Fort Ripley, MN 56449/218-829-3176

Ed's Gun House, P.O. Box 62, Minnesota City, MN 55959/507-689-2925

Edenpine, Inc. c/o Six Enterprises, Inc., 320 D Turtle Creek Ct., San Jose, CA 95125/408-999-0201; FAX: 408-999-0216

EdgeCraft Corp./Sam Weiner, 825 Southwood Road, Avondale, PA 19311-9765/610-268-0500, 800-342-3255; FAX: 610-268-3545

Edmisten Co., P.O. Box 1293, Boone, NC 28607

Edmund Scientific Co., 101 E. Gloucester Pike, Barrington, NJ 08033/609-543-6250

Ednar, Inc., 2-4-8 Kayabacho, Nihonbashi, Chuo-ku, Tokyo, JAPAN 103/81(Japan)-3-3667-1651; FAX: 81-3-3661-8113

Eezox, Inc., P.O. Box 772, Waterford, CT 06385-0772/860-447-8282, 800-462-3331; FAX: 860-447-3484

Effebi SNC-Dr. Franco Beretta, via Rossa, 4, 25062 Concesio, Italy/030-2751955; FAX: 030-2180414 (U.S. importer—Nevada Cartridge Co.)

Efficient Machinery Co., 12878 N.E. 15th Pl., Bellevue, WA 98005

Eggleston, Jere D., 400 Saluda Ave., Columbia, SC 29205/803-799-3402

EGW Evolution Gun Works, 4050 B-8 Skyron Dr., Doylestown, PA 18901/215-348-9892; FAX: 215-348-1056

Eichelberger Bullets, Wm., 158 Crossfield Rd., King of Prussia, PA 19406

EK Knife Co., c/o Blackjack Knives, Ltd., 1307 Wabash Ave., Effingham, IL 62401

Ekol Leather Care, P.O. Box 2652, West Lafayette, IN 47906/317-463-2250; FAX: 317-463-7004

El Dorado Leather (c/o Dill), P.O. Box 566, Benson, AZ 85602/520-586-4791; FAX: 520-586-4791

El Paso Saddlery Co., P.O. Box 27194, El Paso, TX 79926/915-544-2233; FAX: 915-544-2535

Eldorado Cartridge Corp. (See PMC/Eldorado Cartridge Corp.)

Electro Prismatic Collimators, Inc., 1441 Manatt St., Lincoln, NE 68521

Electronic Shooters Protection, Inc., 11997 West 85th Place, Arvada, CO 80005/303-456-8964; 800-797-7791; FAX: 303-456-7179

Electronic Trigger Systems, Inc., P.O. Box 13, 230 Main St. S., Hector, MN 55342/320-848-2760; FAX: 320-848-2760

Eley Ltd., P.O. Box 705, Witton, Birmingham, B6 7UT, ENGLAND/021-356-8899; FAX: 021-331-4173

Elite Ammunition, P.O. Box 3251, Oakbrook, IL 60522/708-366-9006

Elk River, Inc., 1225 Paonia St., Colorado Springs, CO 80915/719-574-4407

Elkhorn Bullets, P.O. Box 5293, Central Point, OR 97502/541-826-7440

Ellett Bros., 267 Columbia Ave., P.O. Box 128, Chapin, SC 29036/803-345-3751, 800-845-3711; FAX: 803-345-1820

Ellicott Arms, Inc./Woods Pistolsmithing, 3840 Dahlgren Ct., Ellicott City, MD 21042/410-465-7979

Elliott Inc., G.W., 514 Burnside Ave., East Hartford, CT 06108/203-289-5741; FAX: 203-289-3137

Elsen, Inc., Pete, 1529 S. 113th St., West Allis, WI 53214

Emerging Technologies, Inc. (See Laseraim Technologies, Inc.)

EMF Co., Inc., 1900 E. Warner Ave. Suite 1-D, Santa Ana, CA 92705/714-261-6611; FAX: 714-756-0133

Empire Cutlery Corp., 12 Kruger Ct., Clifton, NJ 07013/201-472-5155; FAX: 201-779-0759

Engineered Accessories, 1307 W. Wabash Ave., Effingham, IL 62401/217-347-7700; FAX: 217-347-7737

English, Inc., A.G., 708 S. 12th St., Broken Arrow, OK 74012/918-251-3399

Englishtown Sporting Goods Co., Inc., David J. Maxham, 38 Main St., Englishtown, NJ 07726/201-446-7717

Engraving Artistry, 36 Alto Rd., RFD 2, Burlington, CT 06013/203-673-6837

Enguix Import-Export, Alpujarras 58, Alzira, Valencia, SPAIN 46600/(96) 241 43 95; FAX: (96) (241 43 95) 240 21 53

Enhanced Presentations, Inc., 5929 Market St., Wilmington, NC 28405/910-799-1622; FAX: 910-799-5004

Enlow, Charles, 895 Box, Beaver, OK 73932/405-625-4487

Ensign-Bickford Co., The, 660 Hopmeadow St., Simsbury, CT 06070

Entre`prise Arms Inc., 15861 Business Center Dr., Irwindale, CA 91706

EPC, 1441 Manatt St., Lincoln, NE 68521/402-476-3946

Epps, Ellwood (See "Gramps" Antique Cartridges)

Erhardt, Dennis, 3280 Green Meadow Dr., Helena, MT 59601/406-442-4533

Erickson's Mfg., Inc., C.W., 530 Garrison Ave. N.E., P.O. Box 522, Buffalo, MN 55313/612-682-3665; FAX: 612-682-4328

Erma Werke GmbH, Johan Ziegler St., 13/15/FeldiglSt., D-8060 Dachau, GERMANY (U.S. importers—Amtec 2000, Inc.; Mandall Shooting Supplies, Inc.)

Eskridge Rifles, Steven Eskridge, 218 N. Emerson, Mart, TX 76664/817-876-3544

Essex Arms, P.O. Box 345, Island Pond, VT 05846/802-723-4313

Essex Metals, 1000 Brighton St., Union, NJ 07083/800-282-8369

Estate Cartridge, Inc., 12161 FM 830, Willis, TX 77378/409-856-7277; FAX: 409-856-5486

Euber Bullets, No. Orwell Rd., Orwell, VT 05760/802-948-2621

Euro-Imports, 614 Millar Ave., El Cajon, CA 92020/619-442-7005; FAX: 619-442-7005

Euroarms of America, Inc., P.O. Box 3277, Winchester, VA 22604/540-662-1863; FAX: 540-662-4464

European American Armory Corp. (See E.A.A. Corp.)

Europtik Ltd., PO Box 319, Dunmore PA 18512/717-347-6049;717-969-4330

Eutaw Co., Inc., The, P.O. Box 608, U.S. Hwy. 176 West, Holly Hill, SC 29059/803-496-3341

Evans, Andrew, 2325 NW Squire St., Albany, OR 97321/541-928-3190; FAX: 541-928-4128

Evans Engraving, Robert, 332 Vine St., Oregon City, OR 97045/503-656-5693

Evans Gunsmithing (See Evans, Andrew)

Eversull Co., Inc., K., 1 Tracemont, Boyce, LA 71409/318-793-8728; FAX: 318-793-5483

Excalibur Enterprises, P.O. Box 400, Fogelsville, PA 18051-0400/610-391-9105; FAX: 610-391-9220

Exe, Inc., 18830 Partridge Circle, Eden Prairie, MN 55346/612-944-7662

Executive Protection Institute, Rt. 2, Box 3645, Berryville, VA 22611/540-955-1128

C. Eyears, Roland, 576 Binns Blvd., Columbus, OH 43204-2441

Eyster Heritage Gunsmiths, Inc., Ken, 6441 Bishop Rd., Centerburg, OH 43011/614-625-6131

Eze-Lap Diamond Prods., P.O. Box 2229, 15164 Weststate St., Westminster, CA 92683/714-847-1555; FAX: 714-897-0280

E-Z-Way Systems, P.O. Box 4310, Newark, OH 43058-4310/614-345-6645, 800-848-2072; FAX: 614-345-6600

F

F&A Inc. (See ShurKatch Corporation)

Fabarm S.p.A., Via Averolda 31, 25039 Travagliato, Brescia, ITALY/030-6863629; FAX: 030-6863684 (U.S. importer—Ithaca Gun Co., LLC)

Fagan & Co., William, 22952 15 Mile Rd., Clinton Township, MI 48035/810-465-4637; FAX: 810-792-6996

Fair Game International, P.O. Box 77234-34053, Houston, TX 77234/713-941-6269

F.A.I.R. Techni-Mec s.n.c. di Isidoro Rizzini & C., Via Gitti, 41 Zona I, dustriale/25060 Marcheno (Brescia), ITALY 030/861162-8610344; FAX: 030/8610179

Faith Associates, Inc., 1139 S. Greenville Hwy., Hendersonville, NC 28792/828-692-1916; FAX: 828-697-6827

Famas (See U.S. importer—Century International Arms, Inc.)

Fanzoj GmbH, Griesgasse 1, 9170 Ferlach, AUSTRIA 9170/(43) 04227-2283; FAX: (43) 04227-2867; email: jfanzoj@netway.at

Far North Outfitters, Box 1252, Bethel, AK 99559

Farm Form Decoys, Inc., 1602 Biovu, P.O. Box 748, Galveston, TX 77553/409-744-0762, 409-765-6361; FAX: 409-765-8513

Farmer-Dressel, Sharon, 209 N. 92nd Ave., Yakima, WA 98908/509-966-9233; FAX: 509-966-3365

Farr Studio, Inc., 1231 Robinhood Rd., Greeneville, TN 37743/615-638-8825

Farrar Tool Co., Inc., 12150 Bloomfield Ave., Suite E, Santa Fe Springs, CA 90670/310-863-4367; FAX: 310-863-5123

FAS, Via E. Fermi, 8, 20019 Settimo Milanese, Milano, ITALY/02-3285844; FAX: 02-33500196 (U.S. importer—Nygord Precision Products)

Faulhaber Wildlocker, Dipl.-Ing. Norbert Wittasek, Seilergasse 2, A-1010 Wien, AUSTRIA/OM-43-1-5137001; FAX: OM-43-1-5137001

Faulk's Game Call Co., Inc., 616 18th St., Lake Charles, LA 70601/318-436-9726

Faust, Inc., T.G., 544 Minor St., Reading, PA 19602/610-375-8549; FAX: 610-375-4488

Fausti Cav. Stefano & Figlie snc, Via Martiri Dell Indipendenza, 70, Marcheno, ITALY 25060 (U.S. importer—American Arms, Inc.)

Fautheree, Andy, Black Powder Specialties, P.O. Box 4607, Pagosa Springs, CO 81157/970-731-5003; FAX 970-731-5009

Feather, Flex Decoys, 1655 Swan Lake Rd., Bossier City, LA 71111/318-746-8596; FAX: 318-742-4815

Federal Arms Corp. of America, 7928 University Ave., Fridley, MN 55432/612-780-8780; FAX: 612-780-8780

Federal Cartridge Co., 900 Ehlen Dr., Anoka, MN 55303/612-323-2300; FAX: 612-323-2506

Federal Champion Target Co., 232 Industrial Parkway, Richmond, IN 47374/800-441-4971; FAX: 317-966-7747

Federated-Fry (See Fry Metals)

FEG, Budapest, Soroksariut 158, H-1095 HUNGARY (U.S. importers—Century International Arms, Inc.; K.B.I., Inc.)

Feinwerkbau Westinger & Altenburger GmbH (See FWB)

Feken, Dennis, Rt. 2 Box 124, Perry, OK 73077/405-336-5611

Felk Inc., 2121 Castlebridge Rd., Midlothian, VA 23113/804-794-3744

Fellowes, Ted, Beaver Lodge, 9245 16th Ave. SW, Seattle, WA 98106/206-763-1698

Feminine Protection, Inc., 10514 Shady Trail, Dallas, TX 75220/214-351-4500; FAX: 214-352-4686

Ferguson, Bill, P.O. Box 1238, Sierra Vista, AZ 85636/520-458-5321; FAX: 520-458-9125

FERLIB, Via Costa 46, 25063 Gardone V.T. (Brescia) ITALY/30-89-12-586; FAX: 30-89-12-586 (U.S. importer—Harry Marx)

Ferris Firearms, 7110 F.M. 1863, Bulverde, TX 78163/210-980-4424

Fibron Products, Inc., P.O. Box 430, Buffalo, NY 14209-0430/716-886-2378; FAX: 716-886-2394

Fiocchi Munizioni S.p.A. (See U.S. importer—Fiocchi of America, Inc.)

Fiocchi of America, Inc., 5030 Fremont Rd., Ozark, MO 65721/417-725-4118, 800-721-2666; FAX: 417-725-1039

Firearm Training Center, The, 9555 Blandville Rd., West Paducah, KY 42086/502-554-5886

Firearms Co. Ltd./Alpine (See U.S. importer—Mandall Shooting Supplies, Inc.)

Firearms Engraver's Guild of America, 332 Vine St., Oregon City, OR 97045/503-656-5693

Firearms International, 5709 Hartsdale, Houston, TX 77036/713-460-2447

First, Inc., Jack, 1201 Turbine Dr., Rapid City, SD 57701/605-343-9544; FAX: 605-343-9420

Fish Mfg. Gunsmith Sptg. Co., Marshall F., Rd. Box 2439, Rt. 22 North, Westport, NY 12993/518-962-4897

Fisher, Jerry A., 553 Crane Mt. Rd., Big Fork, MT 59911/406-837-2722

Fisher Custom Firearms, 2199 S. Kittredge Way, Aurora, CO 80013/303-755-3710

Fisher Enterprises, Inc., 1071 4th Ave. S., Suite 303, Edmonds, WA 98020-4143/206-771-5382

Fisher, R. Kermit (See Fisher Enterprises, Inc.)

Fitz Pistol Grip Co., P.O. Box 610, Douglas City, CA 96024/916-778-0240

Flaig's, 2200 Evergreen Rd., Millvale, PA 15209/412-821-1717

Flambeau Products Corp., 15981 Valplast Rd., Middlefield, OH 44062/216-632-1631; FAX: 216-632-1581

Flannery Engraving Co., Jeff W., 11034 Riddles Run Rd., Union, KY 41091/606-384-3127

Flashette Co., 15620 Oak Park Ave., Oak Forest, IL 60452/708-532-9193; FAX: 708-532-9624

Flayderman & Co., Inc., N., P.O. Box 2446, Ft. Lauderdale, FL 33303/305-761-8855

Fleming Firearms, 7720 E 126th St. N, Collinsville, OK 74021-7016/918-665-3624

Flents Products Co., Inc., P.O. Box 2109, Norwalk, CT 06852/203-866-2581; FAX: 203-854-9322

Flintlocks, Etc. (See Beauchamp & Son, Inc.)

Flitz International Ltd., 821 Mohr Ave., Waterford, WI 53185/414-534-5898; FAX: 414-534-2991

Flores Publications, Inc., J. (See Action Direct, Inc.)

Flow-Rite of Tennessee, Inc., 107 Allen St., P.O. Box 196, Bruceton, TN 38317/901-586-2271; FAX: 901-586-2300

Fluoramics, Inc., 18 Industrial Ave., Mahwah, NJ 07430/800-922-0075, 201-825-7035

Flynn's Custom Guns, P.O. Box 7461, Alexandria, LA 71306/318-455-7130

FN Herstal, Voie de Liege 33, Herstal 4040, BELGIUM/(32)41.40.82.83; FAX: (32)41.40.86.79

Fobus International Ltd., P.O. Box 64, Kfar Hess, ISRAEL/40692 972-9-7964170; FAX: 972-9-7964169

Folks, Donald E., 205 W. Lincoln St., Pontiac, IL 61764/815-844-7901

Foothills Video Productions, Inc., P.O. Box 651, Spartanburg, SC 29304/803-573-7023, 800-782-5358

Foredom Electric Co., Rt. 6, 16 Stony Hill Rd., Bethel, CT 06801/203-792-8622

Forgett Jr., Valmore J., 689 Bergen Blvd., Ridgefield, NJ 07657/201-945-2500; FAX: 201-945-6859; E-MAIL: ValForgett@msn.com

Forgreens Tool Mfg., Inc., P.O. Box 990, 723 Austin St., Robert Lee, TX 76945/915-453-2800; FAX: 915-453-2460

Forkin, Ben (See Belt MTN Arms)

Forrest, Inc., Tom, P.O. Box 326, Lakeside, CA 92040/619-561-5800; FAX: 619-561-0227

Forrest Tool Co., P.O. Box 768, 44380 Gordon Lane, Mendocino, CA 95460/707-937-2141; FAX: 717-937-1817

Forster, Kathy (See Custom Checkering Service)

Forster, Larry L., P.O. Box 212, 220 First St. NE, Gwinner, ND 58040-0212/701-678-2475

Forster Products, 82 E. Lanark Ave., Lanark, IL 61046/815-493-6360; FAX: 815-493-2371

Fort Hill Gunstocks, 12807 Fort Hill Rd., Hillsboro, OH 45133/513-466-2763

Fort Knox Security Products, 1051 N. Industrial Park Rd., Orem, UT 84057/801-224-7233, 800-821-5216; FAX: 801-226-5493

Fort Worth Firearms, 2006-B Martin Luther King Fwy., Ft. Worth, TX 76104-6303/817-536-0718; FAX: 817-535-0290

Forthofer's Gunsmithing & Knifemaking, 5535 U.S. Hwy 93S, Whitefish, MT 59937-8411/406-862-2674

Fortune Products, Inc., HC04, Box 303, Marble Falls, TX 78654/830-693-6111; FAX: 830-693-6394

Forty Five Ranch Enterprises, Box 1080, Miami, OK 74355-1080/918-542-5875

Fotar Optics, 1756 E. Colorado Blvd., Pasadena, CA 91106/818-579-3919; FAX: 818-579-7209

Fouling Shot, The, 6465 Parfet St., Arvada, CO 80004

Fountain Products, 492 Prospect Ave., West Springfield, MA 01089/413-781-4651; FAX: 413-733-8217

4-D Custom Die Co., 711 N. Sandusky St., P.O. Box 889, Mt. Vernon, OH 43050-0889/614-397-7214; FAX: 614-397-6600

Fowler, Bob (see Black Powder Products)

4W Ammunition (See Hunters Supply)

Fowler Bullets, 806 Dogwood Dr., Gastonia, NC 28054/704-867-3259

Fox River Mills, Inc., P.O. Box 298, 227 Poplar St., Osage, IA 50461/515-732-3798; FAX: 515-732-5128

Foy Custom Bullets, 104 Wells Ave., Daleville, AL 36322

Francesca, Inc., 3115 Old Ranch Rd., San Antonio, TX 78217/512-826-2584; FAX: 512-826-8211

Franchi S.p.A., Via del Serpente, 12, 25131 Brescia, ITALY/030-3581833; FAX: 030-3581554 (U.S. importer—American Arms, Inc.)

Francotte & Cie S.A., Auguste, rue du Trois Juin 109, 4400 Herstal-Liege, BELGIUM/32-4-248-13-18; FAX: 32-4-948-11-79

Frank Custom Classic Arms, Ron, 7131 Richland Rd., Ft. Worth, TX 76118/817-284-9300; FAX: 817-284-9300

Frank Knives, 13868 NW Keleka Pl., Seal Rock, OR 97376/541-563-3041; FAX: 541-563-3041

Frankonia Jagd, Hofmann & Co., D-97064 Wurzburg, GERMANY/09302-200; FAX: 09302-20200

Franzen International, Inc. (U.S. importer for Peters Stahl GmbH)

Freedom Arms, Inc., P.O. Box 1776, Freedom, WY 83120/307-883-2468, 800-833-4432 (orders only); FAX: 307-883-2005

Freeman Animal Targets, 5519 East County Road, 100 South, Plainsfield, IN 46168/317-272-2663; FAX: 317-272-2674; E-MAIL: Signs@indy.net; WEB: http://www.freemansighs.com

Fremont Tool Works, 1214 Prairie, Ford, KS 67842/316-369-2327

French, J.R., Artistic Engraving, 1712 Creek Ridge Ct., Irving, TX 75060/214-254-2654

Frielich Police Equipment, 211 East 21st St., New York, NY 10010/212-254-3045

Europtik Ltd., P.O. Box 319,, Dunmore, PA 18512/717-347-6049; FAX: 717-969-4330

Front Sight Firearms Training Institute, P.O. Box 2619, Aptos, CA 95001/800-987-7719; FAX: 408-684-2137

Frontier, 2910 San Bernardo, Laredo, TX 78040/956-723-5409; FAX: 956-723-1774

Frontier Arms Co., Inc., 401 W. Rio Santa Cruz, Green Valley, AZ 85614-3932

Frontier Products Co., 164 E. Longview Ave., Columbus, OH 43202/614-262-9357

Frontier Safe Co., 3201 S. Clinton St., Fort Wayne, IN 46806/219-744-7233; FAX: 219-744-6678

Frost Cutlery Co., P.O. Box 22636, Chattanooga, TN 37422/615-894-6079; FAX: 615-894-9576

Fry Metals, 4100 6th Ave., Altoona, PA 16602/814-946-1611

FTI, Inc., 72 Eagle Rock Ave., Box 366, East Hanover, NJ 07936-3104

Fujinon, Inc., 10 High Point Dr., Wayne, NJ 07470/201-633-5600; FAX: 201-633-5216

Fullmer, Geo. M., 2499 Mavis St., Oakland, CA 94601/510-533-4193

Fulmer's Antique Firearms, Chet, P.O. Box 792, Rt. 2 Buffalo Lake, Detroit Lakes, MN 56501/218-847-7712

Fulton Armory, 8725 Bollman Place No. 1, Savage, MD 20763/301-490-9485; FAX: 301-490-9547

Furr Arms, 91 N. 970 W., Orem, UT 84057/801-226-3877; FAX: 801-226-3877

Fusilier Bullets, 10010 N. 6000 W., Highland, UT 84003/801-756-6813

FWB, Neckarstrasse 43, 78727 Oberndorf a. N., GERMANY/07423-814-0; FAX: 07423-814-89 (U.S. importer—Beeman Precision Airguns)

G

G96 Products Co., Inc., River St. Station, P.O. Box 1684, Paterson, NJ 07544/201-684-4050; FAX: 201-684-3848

G&C Bullet Co., Inc., 8835 Thornton Rd., Stockton, CA 95209/209-477-6479; FAX: 209-477-2813

G&H Decoys, Inc., P.O. Box 1208, Hwy. 75 North, Henryetta, OK 74437/918-652-3314; FAX: 918-652-3400

Gage Manufacturing, 663 W. 7th St., A, San Pedro, CA 90731/310-832-3546

Gaillard Barrels, P.O. Box 21, Pathlow, Sask., S0K 3B0 CANADA/306-752-3769; FAX: 306-752-5969

Galati International, P.O. Box 326, Catawissa, MO 63015/314-257-4837; FAX: 314-257-2268

Galaxy Imports Ltd., Inc., P.O. Box 3361, Victoria, TX 77903/512-573-4867; FAX: 512-576-9622

GALCO International Ltd., 2019 W. Quail Ave., Phoenix, AZ 85027/602-258-8295, 800-874-2526; FAX: 602-582-6854

Gamba S.p.A.-Societa Armi Bresciane Srl., Renato, Via Artigiani, 93, 25063 Gardone Val Trompia (BS), ITALY/30-8911640; FAX: 30-8911648 (U.S. importer—Gamba, USA)

Gamba, USA, P.O. Box 60452, Colorado Springs, CO 80960/719-578-1145; FAX: 719-444-0731

Gamco, 1316 67th Street, Emeryville, CA 94608/510-527-5578

Game Haven Gunstocks, 13750 Shire Rd., Wolverine, MI 49799/616-525-8257

Game Winner, Inc., 2625 Cumberland Parkway, Suite 220, Atlanta, GA 30339/770-434-9210; FAX: 770-434-9215

Gamo (See U.S. importers—Arms United Corp.; Daisy Mfg. Co.; Dynamit Nobel-RWS, Inc.; Gamo USA, Inc.)

Gamo USA, Inc., 3911 SW 47th Ave., Ft. Lauderdale, FL 33314/954-581-5822; FAX: 954-581-3165

Gander Mountain, Inc., P.O. Box 128, Hwy. W,, Wilmot, WI 53192/414-862-2331,Ext. 6425

GAR, 590 McBride Avenue, West Paterson, NJ 07424/201-754-1114; FAX: 201-754-1114

Garbi, Armas Urki, 12-14, 20.600 Eibar (Guipuzcoa) SPAIN/43-11 38 73 (U.S. importer—Moore & Co., Wm. Larkin)

Garcia National Gun Traders, Inc., 225 SW 22nd Ave., Miami, FL 33135/305-642-2355

Garrett Cartridges, Inc., P.O. Box 178, Chehalis, WA 98532/360-736-0702

Garthwaite, Pistolsmith, Inc., Jim, Rt. 2, Box 310, Watsontown, PA 17777/717-538-1566; FAX: 717-538-2965
Gator Guns & Repair, 6255 Spur Hwy., Kenai, AK 99611/907-283-7947
Gaucher Armes, S.A., 46, rue Desjoyaux, 42000 Saint-Etienne, FRANCE/04-77-33-38-92; FAX: 04-77-61-95-72
G.C.C.T., 4455 Torrance Blvd., Ste. 453, Torrance, CA 90509-2806
GDL Enterprises, 409 Le Gardeur, Slidell, LA 70460/504-649-0693
Gehmann, Walter (See Huntington Die Specialties)
Genco, P.O. Box 5704, Asheville, NC 28803
Genecco Gun Works, K., 10512 Lower Sacramento Rd., Stockton, CA 95210/209-951-0706
General Lead, Inc., 1022 Grand Ave., Phoenix, AZ 85007
Gene's Custom Guns, P.O. Box 10534, White Bear Lake, MN 55110/612-429-5105
Gentex Corp., 5 Tinkham Ave., Derry, NH 03038/603-434-0311; FAX: 603-434-3002
Gentner Bullets, 109 Woodlawn Ave., Upper Darby, PA 19082/610-352-9396
Gentry Custom Gunmaker, David, 314 N. Hoffman, Belgrade, MT 59714/406-388-GUNS
George & Roy's, 2950 NW 29th, Portland, OR 97210/503-228-5424, 800-553-3022; FAX: 503-225-9409
George, Tim, Rt. 1, P.O. Box 45, Evington, VA 24550/804-821-8117
Gerber Legendary Blades, 14200 SW 72nd Ave., Portland, OR 97223/503-639-6161, 800-950-6161; FAX: 503-684-7008
Gervais, Mike, 3804 S. Cruise Dr., Salt Lake City, UT 84109/801-277-7729
Getz Barrel Co., P.O. Box 88, Beavertown, PA 17813/717-658-7263
G.G. & G., 3602 E. 42nd Stravenue, Tucson, AZ 85713/520-748-7167; FAX: 520-748-7583
G.H. Enterprises Ltd., Bag 10, Okotoks, Alberta T0L 1T0 CANADA/403-938-6070
Giacomo Sporting USA, 6234 Stokes Lee Center Rd., Lee Center, NY 13363
Gibbs Rifle Co., Inc., Cannon Hill Industrial Park, Rt. 2, Box 214 Hoffman, Rd./Martinsburg, WV 25401
304-274-0458; FAX: 304-274-0078
Gilbert Equipment Co., Inc., 960 Downtowner Rd., Mobile, AL 36609/205-344-3322
Gilkes, Anthony W., 5950 Sheridan Blvd., Arvada, CO 80003/303-657-1873; FAX: 303-657-1885
Gillmann, Edwin, 33 Valley View Dr., Hanover, PA 17331/717-632-1662
Gilman-Mayfield, Inc., 3279 E. Shields, Fresno, CA 93703/209-221-9415; FAX: 209-221-9419
Gilmore Sports Concepts, 5949 S. Garnett, Tulsa, OK 74146/918-250-4867; FAX: 918-250-3845
Giron, Robert E., 1328 Pocono St., Pittsburgh, PA 15218/412-731-6041
Glacier Glove, 4890 Aircenter Circle, Suite 210, Reno, NV 89502/702-825-8225; FAX: 702-825-6544
Glaser Safety Slug, Inc., P.O. Box 8223, Foster City, CA 94404/800-221-3489; FAX: 510-785-6685
Glass, Herb, P.O. Box 25, Bullville, NY 10915/914-361-3021
Glimm's Custom Gun Engraving, 19 S. Maryland, Conrad, MT 59425/406-278-3574
Glock GmbH, P.O. Box 50, A-2232 Deutsch Wagram, AUSTRIA (U.S. importer—Glock, Inc.)
Glock, Inc., P.O. Box 369, Smyrna, GA 30081/770-432-1202; FAX: 770-433-8719
GML Products, Inc., 394 Laredo Dr., Birmingham, AL 35226/205-979-4867
Gner's Hard Cast Bullets, 1107 11th St., LaGrande, OR 97850/503-963-8796
Goddard, Allen, 716 Medford Ave., Hayward, CA 94541/510-276-6830
Goens, Dale W., P.O. Box 224, Cedar Crest, NM 87008/505-281-5419
Goergen's Gun Shop, Inc., Rt. 2, Box 182BB, Austin, MN 55912/507-433-9280
Goldcoast Reloaders, Inc., 4260 NE 12th Terrace, Pompano Beach, FL 33064/954-783-4849; FAX: 954-942-3452
Golden Age Arms Co., 115 E. High St., Ashley, OH 43003/614-747-2488
Golden Bear Bullets, 3065 Fairfax Ave., San Jose, CA 95148/408-238-9515
Gonic Arms, Inc., 134 Flagg Rd., Gonic, NH 03839/603-332-8456, 603-332-8457
Gonic Bullet Works, P.O. Box 7365, Gonic, NH 03839
Gonzalez Guns, Ramon B., P.O. Box 370, 93 St. Joseph's Hill Road, Monticello, NY 12701/914-794-4515
Goodling's Gunsmithing, R.D. 1, Box 1097, Spring Grove, PA 17362/717-225-3350
Goodwin, Fred, Silver Ridge Gun Shop, Sherman Mills, ME 04776/207-365-4451
Gordie's Gun Shop, 1401 Fulton St., Streator, IL 61364/815-672-7202
Gotz Bullets, 7313 Rogers St., Rockford, IL 61111
Goudy Classic Stocks, Gary, 263 Hedge Rd., Menlo Park, CA 94025-1711/415-322-1338
Gould & Goodrich, 709 E. McNeil St., Lillington, NC 27546/910-893-2071; FAX: 910-893-4742
Gournet, Geoffroy, 820 Paxinosa Ave., Easton, PA 18042/610-559-0710
Gozon Corp., U.S.A., P.O. Box 6278, Folson, CA 95763/916-983-2026; FAX: 916-983-9500
Grace, Charles E., 1305 Arizona Ave., Trinidad, CO 81082/719-846-9435
Grace Metal Products, Inc., P.O. Box 67, Elk Rapids, MI 49629/616-264-8133
Graf & Sons, Route 3 Highway 54 So., Mexico, MO 65265/573-581-2266; FAX: 573-581-2875
"Gramps" Antique Cartridges, Box 341, Washago, Ont. L0K 2B0 CANADA/705-689-5348
Granite Custom Bullets, Box 190, Philipsburg, MT 59858/406-859-3245
Grant, Howard V., Hiawatha 15, Woodruff, WI 54568/715-356-7146
Graphics Direct, P.O. Box 372421, Reseda, CA 91337-2421/818-344-9002
Graves Co., 1800 Andrews Ave., Pompano Beach, FL 33069/800-327-9103; FAX: 305-960-0301
Grayback Wildcats, 5306 Bryant Ave., Klamath Falls, OR 97603/541-884-1072

Graybill's Gun Shop, 1035 Ironville Pike, Columbia, PA 17512/717-684-2739
Great American Gunstock Co., 3420 Industrial Drive, Yuba City, CA 95993/916-671-4570; FAX: 916-671-3906
Great Lakes Airguns, 6175 S. Park Ave., Hamburg, NY 14075/716-648-6666; FAX: 716-648-5279
Green, Arthur S., 485 S. Robertson Blvd., Beverly Hills, CA 90211/310-274-1283
Green Genie, Box 114, Cusseta, GA 31805
Green Head Game Call Co., RR 1, Box 33, Lacon, IL 61540/309-246-2155
Green Mountain Rifle Barrel Co., Inc., P.O. Box 2670, 153 West Main St., Conway, NH 03818/603-447-1095; FAX: 603-447-1099
Green, Roger M., P.O. Box 984, 435 E. Birch, Glenrock, WY 82637/307-436-9804
Greene Precision Duplicators, M.L. Greene Engineering Services, P.O. Box, 1150, Golden, CO 80402-1150/303-279-2383
Greenwood Precision, P.O. Box 468, Nixa, MO 65714-0468/417-725-2330
Greg Gunsmithing Repair, 3732 26th Ave. North, Robbinsdale, MN 55422/612-529-8103
Greg's Superior Products, P.O. Box 46219, Seattle, WA 98146
Greider Precision, 431 Santa Marina Ct., Escondido, CA 92029/619-480-8892; FAX: 619-480-9800; E-MAIL: Greider@msn.com
Gremmel Enterprises, 2111 Carriage Drive, Eugene, OR 97408-7537/541-302-3000
GrÈ-Tan Rifles, 29742 W.C.R. 50, Kersey, CO 80644/970-353-6176; FAX: 970-356-9133
Grier's Hard Cast Bullets, 1107 11th St., LaGrande, OR 97850/503-963-8796
Griffin & Howe, Inc., 33 Claremont Rd., Bernardsville, NJ 07924/908-766-2287; FAX: 908-766-1068
Griffin & Howe, Inc., 36 W. 44th St., Suite 1011, New York, NY 10036/212-921-0980
Grifon, Inc., 58 Guinam St., Waltham, MS 02154
Groenewold, John, P.O. Box 830, Mundelein, IL 60060/847-566-2365
Group Tight Bullets, 482 Comerwood Court, San Francisco, CA 94080/650-583-1550
GRS Corp., Glendo, P.O. Box 1153, 900 Overlander St., Emporia, KS 66801/316-343-1084, 800-835-3519
Grulla Armes, Apartado 453, Avda Otaloa, 12, Eiber, SPAIN (U.S. importer—American Arms, Inc.)
GSI, Inc., 108 Morrow Ave., P.O. Box 129, Trussville, AL 35173/205-655-8299; FAX: 205-655-7078
G.U., Inc. (U.S. importer for New SKB Arms Co.; SKB Arms Co.)
Guardsman Products, 411 N. Darling, Fremont, MI 49412/616-924-3950
Gun Accessories (See Glaser Safety Slug, Inc.)
Gun-Alert, 1010 N. Maclay Ave., San Fernando, CA 91340/818-365-0864; FAX: 818-365-1308
Gun City, 212 W. Main Ave., Bismarck, ND 58501/701-223-2304
Gun Doctor, The, 435 East Maple, Roselle, IL 60172/708-894-0668
Gun Doctor, The, P.O. Box 39242, Downey, CA 90242/310-862-3158
Gun-Ho Sports Cases, 110 E. 10th St., St. Paul, MN 55101/612-224-9491
Gun Hunter Books (See Gun Hunter Trading Co.)
Gun Hunter Trading Co., 5075 Heisig St., Beaumont, TX 77705/409-835-3006
Gun Leather Limited, 116 Lipscomb, Ft. Worth, TX 76104/817-334-0225; 800-247-0609
Gun List (See Krause Publications, Inc.)
Gun Locker, Div. of Airmold, W.R. Grace & Co.-Conn., Becker Farms Ind. Park,, P.O. Box 610/Roanoke Rapids, NC 27870
800-344-5716; FAX: 919-536-2201
Gun Parts Corp., The, 226 Williams Lane, West Hurley, NY 12491/914-679-2417; FAX: 914-679-5849
Gun Room, The, 1121 Burlington, Muncie, IN 47302/317-282-9073; FAX: 317-282-5270
Gun Room Press, The, 127 Raritan Ave., Highland Park, NJ 08904/908-545-4344; FAX: 908-545-6686
Gun Shop, The, 5550 S. 900 East, Salt Lake City, UT 84117/801-263-3633
Gun Shop, The, 62778 Spring Creek Rd., Montrose, CO 81401
Gun Shop, The, 716-A South Rogers Road, Olathe, KS 66062
Gun South, Inc. (See GSI, Inc.)
Gun-Tec, P.O. Box 8125, W. Palm Beach, FL 33407
Gun Works, The, 247 S. 2nd, Springfield, OR 97477/541-741-4118; FAX: 541-988-1097
Guncraft Books (See Guncraft Sports, Inc.)
Guncraft Sports, Inc., 10737 Dutchtown Rd., Knoxville, TN 37932/423-966-4545; FAX: 423-966-4500
Gunfitters, The, P.O. 426, Cambridge, WI 53523-0426/608-764-8128
Gunline Tools, 2950 Saturn St., "O", Brea, CA 92821/714-993-5100; FAX: 714-572-4128
Gunnerman Books, P.O. Box 217, Owosso, MI 48867/517-729-7018; FAX: 517-725-9391
Guns, 81 E. Streetsboro St., Hudson, OH 44236/330-650-4563
Guns Antique & Modern DBA/Charles E. Duffy, Williams Lane, West Hurley, NY 12491/914-679-2997
Guns, Div. of D.C. Engineering, Inc., 8633 Southfield Fwy., Detroit, MI 48228/313-271-7111, 800-886-7623 (orders only); FAX: 313-271-7112
GUNS Magazine, 591 Camino de la Reina, Suite 200, San Diego, CA 92108/619-297-5350; FAX: 619-297-5353
Gunsight, The, 1712 North Placentia Ave., Fullerton, CA 92631
Gunsite Custom Shop, P.O. Box 451, Paulden, AZ 86334/520-636-4104; FAX: 520-636-1236
Gunsite Gunsmithy (See Gunsite Custom Shop)
Gunsite Training Center, P.O. Box 700, Paulden, AZ 86334/520-636-4565; FAX: 520-636-1236
Gunsmith in Elk River, The, 14021 Victoria Lane, Elk River, MN 55330/612-441-7761

Gunsmithing, Inc., 208 West Buchanan St., Colorado Springs, CO 80907/719-632-3795; FAX: 719-632-3493

Gunsmithing Ltd., 57 Unquowa Rd., Fairfield, CT 06430/203-254-0436; FAX: 203-254-1535

Gurney, F.R., Box 13, Sooke, BC V0S 1N0 CANADA/604-642-5282: FAX: 604-642-7859

Gusdorf Corp., 11440 Lackland Rd., St. Louis, MO 63146/314-567-5249

Gusty Winds Corp., 2950 Bear St., Suite 120, Costa Mesa, CA 92626/714-536-3587

Gwinnell, Bryson J., P.O. Box 248C, Maple Hill Rd., Rochester, VT 05767/802-767-3664

H

H&B Forge Co., Rt. 2 Geisinger Rd., Shiloh, OH 44878/419-895-1856

H&P Publishing, 7174 Hoffman Rd., San Angelo, TX 76905/915-655-5953

H&R 1871, Inc., 60 Industrial Rowe, Gardner, MA 01440/508-632-9393; FAX: 508-632-2300

H&S Liner Service, 515 E. 8th, Odessa, TX 79761/915-332-1021

Hafner Creations, Inc., P.O. Box 1987, Lake City, FL 32055/904-755-6481; FAX: 904-755-6595

Hagn Rifles & Actions, Martin, P.O. Box 444, Cranbrook, B.C. VIC 4H9, CANADA/604-489-4861

Hakko Co. Ltd., Daini-Tsunemi Bldg., 1-13-12, Narimasu, Itabashiku Tokyo 175, JAPAN/03-5997-7870/2; FAX: 81-3-5997-7840

Hale, Engraver, Peter, 800 E. Canyon Rd., Spanish Fork, UT 84660/801-798-8215

Half Moon Rifle Shop, 490 Halfmoon Rd., Columbia Falls, MT 59912/406-892-4409

Hall Manufacturing, 142 CR 406, Clanton, AL 35045/205-755-4094

Hall Plastics, Inc., John, P.O. Box 1526, Alvin, TX 77512/713-489-8709

Hallberg Gunsmith, Fritz, 532 E. Idaho Ave., Ontario, OR 97914/541-889-3135; FAX: 541-889-2633

Hallowell & Co., 340 W. Putnam Ave., Greenwich, CT 06830/203-869-2190; FAX: 203-869-0692

Hally Caller, 443 Wells Rd., Doylestown, PA 18901/215-345-6354

Halstead, Rick, RR4, Box 272, Miami, OK 74354/918-540-0933

Hamilton, Alex B. (See Ten-Ring Precision, Inc.)

Hamilton, Jim, Rte. 5, Box 278, Guthrie, OK 73044/405-282-3634

Hamilton, Keith, P.O. Box 871, Gridley, CA 95948/916-846-2316

Hammans, Charles E., P.O. Box 788, 2022 McCracken, Stuttgart, AR 72106/501-673-1388

Hammerli USA, 19296 Oak Grove Circle, Groveland, CA 95321/209-962-5311; FAX: 209-962-5931

Hammerli Ltd., Seonerstrasse 37, CH-5600 Lenzburg, SWITZERLAND/064-50 11 44; FAX: 064-51 38 27 (U.S. importer—Hammerli USA; Mandall Shooting Supplies, Inc.; Sigarms, Inc.)

Hammets VLD Bullets, P.O. Box 479, Rayville, LA 71269/318-728-2019

Hammond Custom Guns Ltd., 619 S. Pandora, Gilbert, AZ 85234/602-892-3437

Hammonds Rifles, RD 4, Box 504, Red Lion, PA 17356/717-244-7879

Handgun Press, P.O. Box 406, Glenview, IL 60025/847-657-6500; FAX: 847-724-8831

HandiCrafts Unltd. (See Clements' Custom Leathercraft, Chas)

Hands Engraving, Barry Lee, 26192 E. Shore Route, Bigfork, MT 59911/406-837-0035

Hank's Gun Shop, Box 370, 50 West 100 South, Monroe, UT 84754/801-527-4456

Hanned Line, The, P.O. Box 2387, Cupertino, CA 95015-2387

Hanned Precision (See Hanned Line, The)

Hansen & Co. (See Hansen Cartridge Co.)

Hansen Cartridge Co., 244-246 Old Post Rd., Southport, CT 06490/203-259-6222, 203-259-7337; FAX: 203-254-3832

Hanson's Gun Center, Dick, 233 Everett Dr., Colorado Springs, CO 80911

Hanus Birdguns, Bill, P.O. Box 533, Newport, OR 97365/541-265-7433; FAX: 541-265-7400

Hanusin, John, 3306 Commercial, Northbrook, IL 60062/708-564-2706

Hardin Specialty Dist., P.O. Box 338, Radcliff, KY 40159-0338/502-351-6649

Hardwood, Jack O., 1191 Pendlebury Ln., Blackfoot ID 83221/208-785-5368

Harold's Custom Gun Shop, Inc., Broughton Rifle Barrels, Rt. 1, Box 447, Big Spring, TX 79720/915-394-4430

Harper's Custom Stocks, 928 Lombrano St., San Antonio, TX 78207/210-732-5780

Harrell's Precision, 5756 Hickory Dr., Salem, VA 24153/703-380-2683

Harrington & Richardson (See H&R 1871, Inc.)

Harrington Cutlery, Inc., Russell, Subs. of Hyde Mfg. Co., 44 River St., Southbridge, MA 01550/617-765-0201

Harris Engineering, Inc., 999 Broadway, Barlow, KY 42024/502-334-3633; FAX: 502-334-3000

Harris Enterprises, P.O. Box 105, Bly, OR 97622/503-353-2625

Harris Hand Engraving, Paul A., 113 Rusty Lane, Boerne, TX 78006-5746/512-391-5121

Harris Gunworks, 12001 N. cave Creek Rd., Phoenix, AZ 85020-4733/602-997-5370; FAX: 602-997-5335

Harris Publications, 1115 Broadway, New York, NY 10010/212-807-7100; FAX: 212-627-4678

Harrison Bullets, 6437 E. Hobart St., Mesa, AZ 85205

Hart & Son, Inc., Robert W., 401 Montgomery St., Nescopeck, PA 18635/717-752-3655, 800-368-3656; FAX: 717-752-1088

Hart Rifle Barrels, Inc., P.O. Box 182, 1690 Apulia Rd., Lafayette, NY 13084/315-677-9841; FAX: 315-677-9610

Hartford (See U.S. importer— EMF Co., Inc.)

Hartmann & Weiss GmbH, Rahlstedter Bahnhofstr. 47, 22143 Hamburg, GERMANY/(40) 677 55 85; FAX: (40) 677 55 92

Harvey, Frank, 218 Nightfall, Terrace, NV 89015/702-558-6998

Harwood, Jack O., 1191 S. Pendlebury Lane, Blackfoot, ID 83221/208-785-5368

Haselbauer Products, Jerry, P.O. Box 27629, Tucson, AZ 85726/602-792-1075

Hastings Barrels, 320 Court St., Clay Center, KS 67432/913-632-3169; FAX: 913-632-6554

Hawk, Inc., 849 Hawks Bridge Rd., Salem, NJ 08079/609-299-2700; FAX: 609-299-2800

Hawk Laboratories, Inc. (See Hawk, Inc.)

Hawken Shop, The (See Dayton Traister)

Haydel's Game Calls, Inc., 5018 Hazel Jones Rd., Bossier City, LA 71111/318-746-3586, 800-HAYDELS; FAX: 318-746-3711

Haydon Shooters' Supply, Russ, 15018 Goodrich Dr. NW, Gig Harbor, WA 98329-9738/253-857-7557; FAX: 253-857-7884

Heatbath Corp., P.O. Box 2978, Springfield, MA 01101/413-543-3381

Hebard Guns, Gil, 125-129 Public Square, Knoxville, IL 61448

HEBB Resources, P.O. Box 999, Mead, WA 99021-09996/509-466-1292

Hecht, Hubert J., Waffen-Hecht, P.O. Box 2635, Fair Oaks, CA 95628/916-966-1020

Heckler & Koch GmbH, P.O. Box 1329, 78722 Oberndorf, Neckar, GERMANY/49-7423179-0; FAX: 49-7423179-2406 (U.S. importer—Heckler & Koch, Inc.)

Heckler & Koch, Inc., 21480 Pacific Blvd., Sterling, VA 20166-8903/703-450-1900; FAX: 703-450-8160

Hege Jagd-u. Sporthandels, GmbH, P.O. Box 101461, W-7770 Ueberlingen a. Bodensee, GERMANY

Heidenstrom Bullets, Urds GT 1 Heroya, 3900 Porsgrunn, NORWAY

Heilmann, Stephen, P.O. Box 657, Grass Valley, CA 95945/916-272-8758

Heinie Specialty Products, 301 Oak St., Quincy, IL 62301-2500/309-543-4535; FAX: 309-543-2521

Heintz, David, 800 N. Hwy. 17, Moffat, CO 81143/719-256-4194

Hellweg Ltd., 40356 Oak Park Way, Suite H, Oakhurst, CA 93644/209-683-3030; FAX: 209-683-3422

Helwan (See U.S. importer—Interarms)

Henckels Zwillingswerk, J.A., Inc., 9 Skyline Dr., Hawthorne, NY 10532/914-592-7370

Hendricks, Frank E., Inc., Master Engravers, HC03, Box 434, Dripping Springs, TX 78620/512-858-7828

Henigson & Associates, Steve, P.O. Box 2726, Culver City, CA 90231/310-305-8288; FAX: 310-305-1905

Henriksen Tool Co., Inc., 8515 Wagner Creek Rd., Talent, OR 97540/541-535-2309

Henry Repeating Arms Co., 110 8th St., Brooklyn, NY 11215/718-499-5600

Hensler, Jerry, 6614 Country Field, San Antonio, TX 78240/210-690-7491

Hensley & Gibbs, Box 10, Murphy, OR 97533/541-862-2341

Hensley, Gunmaker, Darwin, P.O. Box 329, Brightwood, OR 97011/503-622-5411

Heppler, Keith M., Keith's Custom Gunstocks, 540 Banyan Circle, Walnut Creek, CA 94598/510-934-3509; FAX: 510-934-3143

Heppler's Machining, 2240 Calle Del Mundo, Santa Clara, CA 95054/408-748-9166; FAX: 408-988-7711

Hercules, Inc. (See Alliant Techsystems, Smokeless Powder Group)

Heritage Firearms (See Heritage Manufacturing, Inc.)

Heritage Manufacturing, Inc., 4600 NW 135th St., Opa Locka, FL 33054/305-685-5966; FAX: 305-687-6721

Heritage/VSP Gun Books, P.O. Box 887, McCall, ID 83638/208-634-4104; FAX: 208-634-3101

Heritage Wildlife Carvings, 2145 Wagner Hollow Rd., Fort Plain, NY 13339/518-993-3983

Herrett's Stocks, Inc., P.O. Box 741, Twin Falls, ID 83303/208-733-1498

Hertel & Reuss, Werk f r Optik und Feinmechanik GmbH, Quellhofstrasse, 67/34 127 Kassel, GERMANY 0561-83006; FAX: 0561-893308

Herter's Manufacturing, Inc., 111 E. Burnett St., P.O. Box 518, Beaver Dam, WI 53916/414-887-1765; FAX: 414-887-8444

Hesco-Meprolight, 2139 Greenville Rd., LaGrange, GA 30241/706-884-7967; FAX: 706-882-4683

Heydenberk, Warren R., 1059 W. Sawmill Rd., Quakertown, PA 18951/215-538-2682

Hickman, Jaclyn, Box 1900, Glenrock, WY 82637

Hidalgo, Tony, 12701 SW 9th Pl., Davie, FL 33325/954-476-7645

High Bridge Arms, Inc., 3185 Mission St., San Francisco, CA 94110/415-282-8358

High North Products, Inc., P.O. Box 2, Antigo, WI 54409/715-627-2331

High Performance International, 5734 W. Florist Ave., Milwaukee, WI 53218/414-466-9040

High Standard Mfg. Co., Inc., 4601 S. Pinemont, Suite 144, Houston, TX 77041/713-462-4200; FAX: 713-462-6437

High Tech Specialties, Inc., P.O. Box 387R, Adamstown, PA 19501/215-484-0405, 800-231-9385

Highline Machine Co.,Randall Thompson, 654 Lela Place, Grand Junction, CO 81504/970-434-4971

Hill, Loring F., 304 Cedar Rd., Elkins Park, PA 19117

Hill Speed Leather, Ernie, 4507 N. 195th Ave., Litchfield Park, AZ 85340/602-853-9222; FAX: 602-853-9235

Hillmer Custom Gunstocks, Paul D., 7251 Hudson Heights, Hudson, IA 50643/319-988-3941

Hines, S.C., P.O. Box 423, Tijeras, NM 87059/505-281-3783

Hinman Outfitters, Bob, 1217 W. Glen, Peoria, IL 61614/309-691-8132

Hi-Grade Imports, 8655 Monterey Rd., Gilroy, CA 95021/408-842-9301; FAX: 408-842-2374

Hi-Point Firearms, 5990 Philadelphia Dr., Dayton, OH 45415/513-275-4991; FAX: 513-522-8330

Hi-Performance Ammunition Company, 484 State Route 366, Apollo, PA 15613/412-327-8100

Hiptmayer, Armurier, RR 112 750, P.O. Box 136, Eastman, Quebec J0E 1P0, CANADA/514-297-2492

Hiptmayer, Heidemarie, RR 112 750, P.O. Box 136, Eastman, Quebec J0E 1P0, CANADA/514-297-2492

Hiptmayer, Klaus, RR 112 750, P.O. Box 136, Eastman, Quebec J0E 1P0, CANADA/514-297-2492

Hirtenberger Aktiengesellschaft, Leobersdorferstrasse 31, A-2552 Hirtenberg, AUSTRIA/43(0)2256 81184; FAX: 43(0)2256 81807

HiTek International, 484 El Camino Real, Redwood City, CA 94063/415-363-1404, 800-54-NIGHT; FAX: 415-363-1408

Hiti-Schuch, Atelier Wilma, A-8863 Predlitz, Pirming Y1 AUSTRIA/0353418278

HJS Arms, Inc., P.O. Box 3711, Brownsville, TX 78523-3711/800-453-2767, 210-542-2767

H.K.S. Products, 7841 Founion Dr., Florence, KY 41042/606-342-7841, 800-354-9814; FAX: 606-342-5865

Hoag, James W., 8523 Canoga Ave., Suite C, Canoga Park, CA 91304/818-998-1510

Hobbie Gunsmithing, Duane A., 2412 Pattie Ave., Wichita, KS 67216/316-264-8266

Hobson Precision Mfg. Co., Rt. 1, Box 220-C, Brent, AL 35034/205-926-4662

Hoch Custom Bullet Moulds (See Colorado Shooter's Supply)

Hodgdon Powder Co., 6231 Robinson, Shawnee Mission, KS 66202/913-362-9455; FAX: 913-362-1307; WEB: http://www.hodgdon.com

Hodgman, Inc., 1750 Orchard Rd., Montgomery, IL 60538/708-897-7555; FAX: 708-897-7558

Hodgson, Richard, 9081 Tahoe Lane, Boulder, CO 80301

Hoehn Sales, Inc., 2045 Kohn Road, Wright City, MO 63390/314-745-8144; FAX: 314-745-8144

Hoelscher, Virgil, 11047 Pope Ave., Lynwood, CA 90262/310-631-8545

Hoenig & Rodman, 6521 Morton Dr., Boise, ID 83704/208-375-1116

Hofer Jagdwaffen, P., Buchsenmachermeister, Kirchgasse 24, A-9170 Ferlach, AUSTRIA/04227-3683

Hoffman New Ideas, 821 Northmoor Rd., Lake Forest, IL 60045/312-234-4075

Hogue Grips, P.O. Box 1138, Paso Robles, CA 93447/800-438-4747, 805-239-1440; FAX: 805-239-2553

Holland & Holland Ltd., 33 Bruton St., London, ENGLAND 1W1/44-171-499-4411; FAX: 44-171-408-7962

Holland, Dick, 422 NE 6th St., Newport, OR 97365/503-265-7556

Holland's Gunsmithing, P.O. Box 69, Powers, OR 97466/541-439-5155; FAX: 541-439-5155

Hollis Gun Shop, 917 Rex St., Carlsbad, NM 88220/505-885-3782

Hollywood Engineering, 10642 Arminta St., Sun Valley, CA 91352/818-842-8376

Holster Shop, The, 720 N. Flagler Dr., Ft. Lauderdale, FL 33304/305-463-7910; FAX: 305-761-1483

Homak, 5151 W. 73rd St., Chicago, IL 60638-6613/312-523-3100, FAX: 312-523-9455

Home Shop Machinist, The, Village Press Publications, P.O. Box 1810, Traverse City, MI 49685/800-447-7367; FAX: 616-946-3289

Hondo Ind., 510 S. 52nd St.,I04, Tempe, AZ 85281

Hoover, Harvey, 5750 Pearl Dr., Paradise, CA 95969-4829

Hoppe's Div., Penguin Industries, Inc., Airport Industrial Mall, Coatesville, PA 19320/610-384-6000

Horizons Unlimited, P.O. Box 426, Warm Springs, GA 31830/706-655-3603; FAX: 706-655-3603

Hornady Mfg. Co., P.O. Box 1848, Grand Island, NE 68802/800-338-3220, 308-382-1390; FAX: 308-382-5761

Horseshoe Leather Products, Andy Arratoonian, The Cottage Sharow, Ripon HG4 5BP ENGLAND/44-1765-605858

Horton Dist. Co., Inc., Lew, 15 Walkup Dr., Westboro, MA 01581/508-366-7400; FAX: 508-366-5332

House of Muskets, Inc., The, P.O. Box 4640, Pagosa Springs, CO 81157/970-731-2295

Houtz & Barwick, P.O. Box 435, W. Church St., Elizabeth City, NC 27909/800-775-0337, 919-335-4191; FAX: 919-335-1152

Howa Machinery, Ltd., Sukaguchi, Shinkawa-cho, Nishikasugai-gun, Aichi 452, JAPAN (U.S. importer—Interarms)

Howell Machine, 8151/2 D St., Lewiston, ID 83501/208-743-7418

Hoyt Holster Co., Inc., P.O. Box 69, Coupeville, WA 98239-0069/360-678-6640; FAX: 360-678-6549

H-S Precision, Inc., 1301 Turbine Dr., Rapid City, SD 57703/605-341-3006; FAX: 605-342-8964

HT Bullets, 244 Belleville Rd., New Bedford, MA 02745/508-999-3338

Hubertus Schneidwarenfabrik, P.O. Box 180 106, D-42626 Solingen, GERMANY/01149-212-59-19-94: FAX: 01149-212-59-19-92

Huebner, Corey O., P.O. Box 2074, Missoula, MT 59806-2074/406-721-7168

Huey Gun Cases, P.O. Box 22456, Kansas City, MO 64113/816-444-1637; FAX: 816-444-1637

Hugger Hooks Co., 3900 Easley Way, Golden, CO 80403/303-279-0600

Hughes, Steven Dodd, P.O. Box 545, Livingston, MT 59047/406-222-9377; FAX: 406-222-9377

Hume, Don, P.O. Box 351, Miami, OK 74355/918-542-6604; FAX: 918-542-4340

Hungry Horse Books, 4605 Hwy. 93 South, Whitefish, MT 59937/406-862-7997

Hunkeler, 'A. (See Buckskin Machine Works)

Hunter Co., Inc., 3300 W. 71st Ave., Westminster, CO 80030/303-427-4626; FAX: 303-428-3980

Hunters Supply, Rt. 1, P.O. Box 313, Tioga, TX 76271/800-868-6612; FAX: 817-437-2228

Hunter's Specialties, Inc., 6000 Huntington Ct. NE, Cedar Rapids, IA 52402-1268/319-395-0321; FAX: 319-395-0326

Hunterjohn, P.O. Box 771457, St. Louis, MO 63177/314-531-7250

Hunting Classics Ltd., P.O. Box 2089, Gastonia, NC 28053/704-867-1307; FAX: 704-867-0491

Huntington Die Specialties, 601 Oro Dam Blvd., Oroville, CA 95965/916-534-1210; FAX: 916-534-1212

Hutton Rifle Ranch, P.O. Box 45236, Boise, ID 83711/208-345-8781

Hydrosorbent Products, P.O. Box 437, Ashley Falls, MA 01222/413-229-2967; FAX: 413-229-8743

Hyper-Single, Inc., 520 E. Beaver, Jenks, OK 74037/918-299-2391

I

I.A.B. (See U.S. importer—Taylor's & Co., Inc.)

IAI (See A.M.T.)

IAR, Inc., 33171 Camino Capistrano, San Juan Capistrano, CA 92675/714-443-3642; FAX: 714-443-3647

Ibberson (Sheffield) Ltd., George, 25-31 Allen St., Sheffield, S3 7AW ENGLAND/0114-2766123; FAX: 0114-2738465

ICI-America, P.O. Box 751, Wilmington, DE 19897/302-575-3000

I.D.S.A. Books, 1324 Stratford Drive, Piqua, OH 45356/937-773-4203; FAX: 937-778-1922.

IGA (See U.S. importer—Stoeger Industries)

Illinois Lead Shop, 7742 W. 61st Place, Summit, IL 60501

Image Ind. Inc., 864 Lively, Wood Dale, IL 60191/630-616-1340; FAX: 630-616-1341

Image Ind. Inc., 382 Balm Court, Wood Dale, IL 60191/630-766-2402; FAX: 630-766-7373

IMI, P.O. Box 1044, Ramat Hasharon 47100, ISRAEL/972-3-5485617;FAX: 972-3-5406908

IMI Services USA, Inc., 2 Wisconsin Circle, Suite 420, Chevy Chase, MD 20815/301-215-4800; FAX: 301-657-1446

Impact Case Co., P.O. Box 9912, Spokane, WA 99209-0912/800-262-3322, 509-467-3303; FAX: 509-326-5436

Imperial (See E-Z-Way Systems)

Imperial Magnum Corp., P.O. Box 249, Oroville, WA 98844/604-495-3131; FAX: 604-495-2816

Imperial Russian Armory, 10547 S. Post Oak, Houston, TX 77035/1-800-MINIATURE

Imperial Schrade Corp., 7 Schrade Ct., Box 7000, Ellenville, NY 12428/914-647-7601; FAX: 914-647-8701

Import Sports Inc., 1750 Brielle Ave., Unit B1, Wanamassa, NJ 07712/908-493-0302; FAX: 908-493-0301

IMR Powder Co., 1080 Military Turnpike, Suite 2, Plattsburgh, NY 12901/518-563-2253; FAX: 518-563-6916

I.N.C., Inc. (See Kick Eez)

Independent Machine & Gun Shop, 1416 N. Hayes, Pocatello, ID 83201

Info-Arm, P.O. Box 1262, Champlain, NY 12919/514-955-0355; FAX: 514-955-0357

Ingle, Engraver, Ralph W., 112 Manchester Ct., Centerville, GA 31028/912-953-5824

Innovative Weaponry, Inc., 337 Eubank NE, Albuquerque, NM 87123/800-334-3573, 505-296-4645; FAX: 505-271-2633

Innovision Enterprises, 728 Skinner Dr., Kalamazoo, MI 49001/616-382-1681; FAX: 616-382-1830

INTEC International, Inc., P.O. Box 5708, Scottsdale, AZ 85261/602-483-1708

Inter Ordnance of America LP, 3904-B Sardis Church Rd., Monroe, NC 28110/704-821-8337; FAX: 704-821-8523

Interarms, 10 Prince St., Alexandria, VA 22314/703-548-1400; FAX: 703-549-7826

Intercontinental Munitions Distributors, Ltd., P.O. Box 815, Beulah, ND 58523/701-948-2260; FAX: 701-948-2282

International Shooters Service (See I.S.S.)

Intratec, 12405 SW 130th St., Miami, FL 33186-6224/305-232-1821; FAX: 305-253-7207

Ion Industries, Inc., 3508 E. Allerton Ave., Cudahy, WI 53110/414-486-2007; FAX: 414-486-2017

Iosso Products, 1485 Lively Blvd., Elk Grove Village, IL 60007/847-437-8400; FAX: 847-437-8478

Iron Bench, 12619 Bailey Rd., Redding, CA 96003/916-241-4623

Ironside International Publishers, Inc., P.O. Box 55, 800 Slaters Lane, Alexandria, VA 22313/703-684-6111; FAX: 703-683-5486

Ironsighter Co., P.O. Box 85070, Westland, MI 48185/313-326-8731; FAX: 313-326-3378

Irwin, Campbell H., 140 Hartland Blvd., East Hartland, CT 06027/203-653-3901

Island Pond Gun Shop, P.O. Box 428, Cross St., Island Pond, VT 05846/802-723-4546

Israel Arms International, Inc., 5709 Hartsdale, Houston, TX 77036/713-789-0745; FAX: 713-789-7513

Israel Military Industries Ltd. (See IMI)

I.S.S., P.O. Box 185234, Ft. Worth, TX 76181/817-595-2090

I.S.W., 106 E. Cairo Dr., Tempe, AZ 85282

Ithaca Gun Co., LLC, 891 Route 34-B, King Ferry, NY 13081/315-364-7171, 888-9ITHACA; FAX: 315-364-5134

Ivanoff, Thomas G. (See Tom's Gun Repair)

J

J-4, Inc., 1700 Via Burton, Anaheim, CA 92806/714-254-8315; FAX: 714-956-4421

J&D Components, 75 East 350 North, Orem, UT 84057-4719/801-225-7007

J&J Products, Inc., 9240 Whitmore, El Monte, CA 91731/818-571-5228, 800-927-8361; FAX: 818-571-8704

J&J Sales, 1501 21st Ave. S., Great Falls, MT 59405/406-453-7549

J&L Superior Bullets (See Huntington Die Specialties)

J&R Engineering, P.O. Box 77, 200 Lyons Hill Rd., Athol, MA 01331/508-249-9241

J&R Enterprises, 4550 Scotts Valley Rd., Lakeport, CA 95453

J&S Heat Treat, 803 S. 16th St., Blue Springs, MO 64015/816-229-2149; FAX: 816-228-1135

J.A. Blades, Inc. (See Christopher Firearms Co., Inc., E.)

Jackalope Gun Shop, 1048 S. 5th St., Douglas, WY 82633/307-358-3441

Jaeger, Inc./Dunn's, Paul, P.O. Box 449, 1 Madison Ave., Grand Junction, TN 38039/901-764-6909; FAX: 901-764-6503

J‰gerSport, Ltd., One Wholesale Way, Cranston, RI 02920/800-962-4867, 401-944-9682; FAX: 401-946-2587

Jamison's Forge Works, 4527 Rd. 6.5 NE, Moses Lake, WA 98837/509-762-2659

Jantz Supply, P.O. Box 584-GD, Davis, OK 73030-0584/405-369-2316; FAX: 405-369-3082; WEB: http//www.jantzsupply.com; E-MAIL: jantz@brightok.net

Jarrett Rifles, Inc., 383 Brown Rd., Jackson, SC 29831/803-471-3616

Jarvis, Inc., 1123 Cherry Orchard Lane, Hamilton, MT 59840/406-961-4392

JAS, Inc., P.O. Box 0, Rosemount, MN 55068/612-890-7631

Javelina Lube Products, P.O. Box 337, San Bernardino, CA 92402/714-882-5847; FAX: 714-434-6937

J/B Adventures & Safaris, Inc., 2275 E. Arapahoe Rd. Ste. 109, Littleton, CO 80122-1521/303-771-0977

JB Custom, P.O. Box 6912, Leawood, KS 66206/913-381-2329

Jedediah Starr Trading Co., P.O. Box 2007, Farmington Hill, MI 48333-2007

Jeffredo Gunsight, P.O. Box 669, San Marcos, CA 92079-2695

Jenco Sales, Inc., P.O. Box 1000, Manchaca, TX 78652/800-531-5301; FAX: 800-266-2373

Jenkins Recoil Pads, Inc., 5438 E. Frontage Ln., Olney, IL 62450/618-395-3416

Jensen Bullets, 86 North, 400 West, Blackfoot, ID 83221/208-785-5590

Jensen's Custom Ammunition, 5146 E. Pima, Tucson, AZ 85712/602-325-3346; FAX: 602-322-5704

Jensen's Firearms Academy, 1280 W. Prince, Tucson, AZ 85705/602-293-8516

Jericho Tool & Die Co. Inc., RD 3 Box 70, Route 7, Bainbridge, NY 13733-9494/607-563-8222; FAX: 607-563-8560

Jester Bullets, Rt. 1 Box 27, Orienta, OK 73737

Jewell Triggers, Inc., 3620 Hwy. 123, San Marcos, TX 78666/512-353-2999

J-Gar Co., 183 Turnpike Rd., Dept. 3, Petersham, MA 01366-9604

JGS Precision Tool Mfg., 1141 S. Summer Rd., Coos Bay, OR 97420/541-267-4331; FAX: 541-267-5996

Jim's Gun Shop (See Spradlin's)

Jim's Precision, Jim Ketchum, 1725 Moclips Dr., Petaluma, CA 94952/707-762-3014

J.I.T., Ltd., P.O. Box 230, Freedom, WY 83120/708-494-0937

JLK Bullets, 414 Turner Rd., Dover, AR 72837/501-331-4194

Johanssons Vapentillbehor, Bert, S-430 20 Veddige, SWEDEN

John's Custom Leather, 523 S. Liberty St., Blairsville, PA 15717/412-459-6802

Johns Master Engraver, Bill, 7927 Ranch Roach 965, Fredericksburg, TX 78624-9545/210-997-6795

Johnson's Gunsmithing, Inc., Neal, 208 W. Buchanan St., Suite B, Colorado Springs, CO 80907/800-284-8671 (orders), 719-632-3795; FAX: 719-632-3493

Johnson Wood Products, 34968 Crystal Road, Strawberry Point, IA 52076/319-933-4930

Johnston Bros. (See C&T Corp. TA Johnson Brothers)

Johnston, James (See North Fork Custom Gunsmithing)

Jonad Corp., 2091 Lakeland Ave., Lakewood, OH 44107/216-226-3161

Jonas Appraisals & Taxidermy, Jack, 1675 S. Birch, Suite 506, Denver, CO 80222/303-757-7347: FAX: 303-639-9655

Jones Co., Dale, 680 Hoffman Draw, Kila, MT 59920/406-755-4684

Jones Custom Products, Neil A., 17217 Brookhouser Road, Saegertown, PA 16433/814-763-2769; FAX: 814-763-4228

Jones Moulds, Paul, 4901 Telegraph Rd., Los Angeles, CA 90022/213-262-1510

Jones, J.D. (See SSK Industries)

J.P. Enterprises, Inc., P.O. Box 26324, Shoreview, MN 55126/612-486-9064; FAX: 612-482-0970

J.P. Gunstocks, Inc., 4508 San Miguel Ave., North Las Vegas, NV 89030/702-645-0718

JP Sales, Box 307, Anderson, TX 77830

J.R. Distributing, 2976 E. Los Angeles Ave., Simi Valley, CA 93065/805-527-1090; FAX: 805-529-2368

JRP Custom Bullets, RR2 2233 Carlton Rd., Whitehall, NY 12887/518-282-0084 (a.m.), 802-438-5548 (p.m.)

JRW, 2425 Taffy Ct., Nampa, ID 83687

JS Worldwide DBA (See Coonan Arms)

JSL Ltd. (See U.S. importer—Specialty Shooters Supply, Inc.)

Juenke, Vern, 25 Bitterbush Rd., Reno, NV 89523/702-345-0225

Jumbo Sports Products (See Bucheimer, J.M.)

Jungkind, Reeves C., 5001 Buckskin Pass, Austin, TX 78745-2841/512-442-1094

Jurras, L.E., P.O. Box 680, Washington, IN 47501/812-254-7698

K

K&M Industries, Inc., Box 66, 510 S. Main, Troy, ID 83871/208-835-2281; FAX: 208-835-5211

K&M Services, 5430 Salmon Run Rd., Dover, PA 17315/717-292-3175; FAX: 717-292-3175

K&T Co., Div. of T&S Industries, Inc., 1027 Skyview Dr., W. Carrollton, OH 45449/513-859-8414

KA-BAR Knives, 1116 E. State St., Olean, NY 14760/800-282-0130; FAX: 716-373-6245

Kabar Arms, Inc., P.O. Box 718, Tualatin, OR 97062/503-256-0144; FAX: 503-253-7810

Ka Pu Kapili, P.O. Box 745, Honokaa, HI 96727/808-776-1644; FAX: 808-776-1731

Kahles, A Swarovski Company, 1 Wholesale Way, Cranston, RI 02920-5540/800-426-3089; FAX: 401-946-2587

Kahr Arms, P.O. Box 220, 630 Route 303, Blauvelt, NY 10913/914-353-5996; FAX: 914-353-7833

Kalispel Case Line, P.O. Box 267, Cusick, WA 99119/509-445-1121

Kamik Outdoor Footwear, 554 Montee de Liesse, Montreal, Quebec, H4T 1P1 CANADA/514-341-3950; FAX: 514-341-1861

Kamyk Engraving Co., Steve, 9 Grandview Dr., Westfield, MA 01085-1810/413-568-0457

Kane, Edward, P.O. Box 385, Ukiah, CA 95482/707-462-2937

Kane Products, Inc., 5572 Brecksville Rd., Cleveland, OH 44131/216-524-9962

Kapro Mfg. Co., Inc. (See R.E.I.)

Kasenit Co., Inc., 13 Park Ave., Highland Mills, NY 10930/914-928-9595; FAX: 914-928-7292

Kasmarsik Bullets, 4016 7th Ave. SW, Puyallup, WA 98373

Kaswer Custom, Inc., 13 Surrey Drive, Brookfield, CT 06804/203-775-0564; FAX: 203-775-6872

K.B.I., Inc., P.O. Box 6625, Harrisburg, PA 17112/717-540-8518; FAX: 717-540-8567

K-D, Inc., Box 459, 585 N. Hwy. 155, Cleveland, UT 84518/801-653-2530

KDF, Inc., 2485 Hwy. 46 N., Seguin, TX 78155/210-379-8141; FAX: 210-379-5420

KeeCo Impressions, Inc., 346 Wood Ave., North Brunswick, NJ 08902/800-468-0546

Keeler, R.H., 817 "N" St., Port Angeles, WA 98362/206-457-4702

Kehr, Roger, 2131 Agate Ct. SE, Lacy, WA 98503/360-456-0831

Keith's Bullets, 942 Twisted Oak, Algonquin, IL 60102/708-658-3520

Keith's Custom Gunstocks (See Heppler, Keith M.)

Kelbly's, Inc., 7222 Dalton Fox Lake Rd., North Lawrence, OH 44666/216-683-4674; FAX: 216-683-7349

Keller Co., The, 4215 McEwen Rd., Dallas, TX 75244/214-770-8585

Kelley's, P.O. Box 125, Woburn, MA 01801/617-935-3389

Kellogg's Professional Products, 325 Pearl St., Sandusky, OH 44870/419-625-6551; FAX: 419-625-6167

Kelly, Lance, 1723 Willow Oak Dr., Edgewater, FL 32132/904-423-4933

Kel-Tec CNC Industries, Inc., P.O. Box 3427, Cocoa, FL 32924/407-631-0068; FAX: 407-631-1169

Kemen America, 2550 Hwy. 23, Wrenshall, MN 55797

Ken's Kustom Kartridges, 331 Jacobs Rd., Hubbard, OH 44425/216-534-4595

Ken's Gun Specialties, Rt. 1, Box 147, Lakeview, AR 72642/501-431-5606

Ken's Rifle Blanks, Ken McCullough, Rt. 2, P.O. Box 85B, Weston, OR 97886/503-566-3879

Keng's Firearms Specialty, Inc., 875 Wharton Dr., P.O. Box 44405, Atlanta, GA 30336-1405/404-691-7611; FAX: 404-505-8445

Kennebec Journal, 274 Western Ave., Augusta, ME 04330/207-622-6288

Kennedy Firearms, 10 N. Market St., Muncy, PA 17756/717-546-6695

KenPatable Ent., Inc., P.O. Box 19422, Louisville, KY 40259/502-239-5447

Kent Cartridge Mfg. Co. Ltd., Unit 16, Branbridges Industrial Estate, East, Peckham/Tonbridge, Kent, TN12 5HF ENGLAND 622-872255/; FAX: 622-872645

Keowee Game Calls, 608 Hwy. 25 North, Travelers Rest, SC 29690/864-834-7204; FAX: 864-834-7831

Kershaw Knives, 25300 SW Parkway Ave., Wilsonville, OR 97070/503-682-1966, 800-325-2891; FAX: 503-682-7168

Kesselring Gun Shop, 400 Hwy. 99 North, Burlington, WA 98233/206-724-3113; FAX: 206-724-7003

Ketchum, Jim (See Jim's Precision)

Kick Eez, P.O. Box 12767, Wichita, KS 67277/316-721-9570; FAX: 316-721-5260

Kilham & Co., Main St., P.O. Box 37, Lyme, NH 03768/603-795-4112

Kimar (See U.S. importer—IAR, Inc.)

Kimball, Gary, 1526 N. Circle Dr., Colorado Springs, CO 80909/719-634-1274

Kimber of America, Inc., 1 Lawton St., Yonkers, NY 10705/800-880-2418, 914-964-0771; FAX: 914-964-9340; WEB: www.kimberamerica.com

King & Co., P.O. Box 1242, Bloomington, IL 61702/FAX: 309-473-2161

King's Gun Works, 1837 W. Glenoaks Blvd., Glendale, CA 91201/818-956-6010; FAX: 818-548-8606

Kingyon, Paul L. (See Custom Calls)

Kirkpatrick Leather Co., P.O. Box 677, Laredo, TX 78040/956-723-6631; FAX: 956-725-0672

KJM Fabritek, Inc., P.O. Box 162, Marietta, GA 30061/770-426-8251; FAX: 770-426-8252

KK Air International (See Impact Case Co.)

K.K. Arms Co., Star Route Box 671, Kerrville, TX 78028/210-257-4718; FAX: 210-257-4891

Kleen-Bore, Inc., 16 Industrial Pkwy., Easthampton, MA 01027/413-527-0300; FAX: 413-527-2522

Klein Custom Guns, Don, 433 Murray Park Dr., Ripon, WI 54971/414-748-2931

Kleinendorst, K.W., RR 1, Box 1500, Hop Bottom, PA 18824/717-289-4687

Klingler Woodcarving, P.O. Box 141, Thistle Hill, Cabot, VT 05647/802-426-3811

Kmount, P.O. Box 19422, Louisville, KY 40259/502-239-5447

Kneiper, James, P.O. Box 1516, Basalt, CO 81621-1516/303-963-9880

Knife Importers, Inc., P.O. Box 1000, Manchaca, TX 78652/512-282-6860

Knight & Hale Game Calls, Box 468 Industrial Park, Cadiz, KY 42211/502-924-1755; FAX: 502-924-1763

Knight Rifles (See Modern MuzzleLoading, Inc.)

Knight's Mfg. Co., 7750 9th St. SW, Vero Beach, FL 32968/561-562-5697; FAX: 561-569-2955

Knippel, Richard, 1455 Jubal Ct., Oakdale, CA 95361-9669/209-869-1469

Knock on Wood Antiques, 355 Post Rd., Darien, CT 06820/203-655-9031

Knoell, Doug, 9737 McCardle Way, Santee, CA 92071

Koevenig's Engraving Service, Box 55 Rabbit Gulch, Hill City, SD 57745

KOGOT, 410 College, Trinidad, CO 81082/719-846-9406

Kokolus, Michael M. (See Custom Riflestocks, Inc.)

Kolpin Mfg., Inc., P.O. Box 107, 205 Depot St., Fox Lake, WI 53933/414-928-3118; FAX: 414-928-3687

Kongsberg America L.L.C., P.O. Box 252, Fairfield, CT 06430/203-259-0938; FAX: 203-259-2566

Kopec Enterprises, John (See Peacemaker Specialists)

Kopp Professional Gunsmithing, Terry K., Route 1, Box 224F, Lexington, MO 64067/816-259-2636

Korth, Robert-Bosch-Str. 4, P.O. Box 1320, 23909 Ratzeburg, GERMANY/451-4991497; FAX: 451-4993230 (U.S. importer—Interarms; Mandall Shooting Supplies, Inc.)

Korzinek Riflesmith, J., RD 2, Box 73D, Canton, PA 17724/717-673-8512

Koval Knives, 5819 Zarley St., Suite A, New Albany, OH 43054/614-855-0777; FAX: 614-855-0945

Kowa Optimed, Inc., 20001 S. Vermont Ave., Torrance, CA 90502/310-327-1913; FAX: 310-327-4177

Kramer Designs, P.O. Box 129, Clancy, MT 59634/406-933-8658; FAX: 406-933-8658; WEB: www.snipepod.com

Kramer Handgun Leather, P.O. Box 112154, Tacoma, WA 98411/206-564-6652; FAX: 206-564-1214

Krause Publications, Inc., 700 E. State St., Iola, WI 54990/715-445-2214; FAX: 715-445-4087; Consumer orders only 800-258-0929

Krico Jagd-und Sportwaffen GmbH, Nurnbergerstrasse 6, D-90602 Pyrbaum GERMANY/09180-2780; FAX: 09180-2661 (U.S. importer—Mandall Shooting Supplies, Inc.)

Krieger Barrels, Inc., N114 W18697 Clinton Dr., Germantown, WI 53022/414-255-9593; FAX: 414-255-9586

Krieghoff Gun Co., H., Boschstrasse 22, D-89079 Ulm, GERMANY/731-401820; FAX: 731-4018270 (U.S. importer—Krieghoff International, Inc.)

Krieghoff International, Inc., 7528 Easton Rd., Ottsville, PA 18942/610-847-5173; FAX: 610-847-8691

Kris Mounts, 108 Lehigh St., Johnstown, PA 15905/814-539-9751

KSN Industries, Ltd. (See U.S. importer—Israel Arms International, Inc.)

Kudlas, John M., 622 14th St. SE, Rochester, MN 55904/507-288-5579

Kulis Freeze Dry Taxidermy, 725 Broadway Ave., Bedford, OH 44146/216-232-8352; FAX: 216-232-7305; WEB: http://www.kastaway.com; E-Mail: jkulis@kastaway.com

KVH Industries, Inc., 110 Enterprise Center, Middletown, RI 02842/401-847-3327; FAX: 401-849-0045

Kwik Mount Corp., P.O. Box 19422, Louisville, KY 40259/502-239-5447

Kwik-Site Co., 5555 Treadwell, Wayne, MI 48184/313-326-1500; FAX: 313-326-4120

L

L&R Lock Co., 1137 Pocalla Rd., Sumter, SC 29150/803-775-6127; FAX: 803-775-5171

L&S Technologies, Inc. (See Aimtech Mount Systems)

La Clinique du .45, 1432 Rougemont, Chambly, Quebec, J3L 2L8 CANADA/514-658-1144

Labanu, Inc., 2201-F Fifth Ave., Ronkonkoma, NY 11779/516-467-6197; FAX: 516-981-4112

LaBounty Precision Reboring, P.O. Box 186, 7968 Silver Lk. Rd., Maple Falls, WA 98266/360-599-2047

LaCrosse Footwear, Inc., P.O. Box 1328, La Crosse, WI 54602/608-782-3020, 800-323-2668; FAX: 800-658-9444

LaFrance Specialties, P.O. Box 178211, San Diego, CA 92177-8211/619-293-3373

Lage Uniwad, P.O. Box 2302, Davenport, IA 52809/319-388-LAGE; FAX: 319-388-LAGE

Lair, Sam, 520 E. Beaver, Jenks, OK 74037/918-299-2391

Lake Center, P.O. Box 38, St. Charles, MO 63302/314-946-7500

Lakefield Arms Ltd. (See Savage Arms, Inc.)

Lakelander USA, Inc., Bldg. 9313, Suite 103, Stennis Space Center, MS 39529/800-894-8464; FAX 601-255-7595

Lakewood Products, LLC, 275 June St., Berlin, WI 54923/800-US-BUILT; FAX: 414-361-7719

Lampert, Ron, Rt. 1, Box 177, Guthrie, MN 56461/218-854-7345

Lamson & Goodnow Mfg. Co., 45 Conway St., Shelburne Falls, MA 03170/413-625-6331; FAX: 413-625-9816

Lanber Armas, S.A., Zubiaurre 5, Zaldibar, SPAIN 48250/34-4-6827702; FAX: 34-4-6827999

Langenberg Hat Co., P.O. Box 1860, Washington, MO 63090/800-428-1860; FAX: 314-239-3151

Lanphert, Paul, P.O. Box 1985, Wenatchee, WA 98807

Lapua Ltd., P.O. Box 5, Lapua, FINLAND SF-62101/6-310111; FAX: 6-4388991 (U.S. importer—Keng's Firearms Specialty, Inc.)

L.A.R. Mfg., Inc., 4133 W. Farm Rd., West Jordan, UT 84088/801-280-3505; FAX: 801-280-1972

LaRocca Gun Works, Inc., 51 Union Place, Worcester, MA 01608/508-754-2887; FAX: 508-754-2887

Laseraim Technologies, Inc., P.O. Box 3548, Little Rock, AR 72203/501-375-2227; FAX: 501-372-1445

Laser Devices, Inc., 2 Harris Ct. A-4, Monterey, CA 93940/408-373-0701; FAX: 408-373-0903

Laserlyte, 3015 Main St., #300, Santa Monica, CA 90405/800-255-9133; FAX: 310-392-1754

LaserMax, Inc., 3495 Winton Place, Bldg. B, Rochester, NY 14623-2807/716-272-5420; FAX: 716-272-5427

Lassen Community College, Gunsmithing Dept., P.O. Box 3000, Hwy. 139, Susanville, CA 96130/916-251-8800; FAX: 916-251-8838

Lathrop's, Inc., 5146 E. Pima, Tucson, AZ 85712/520-881-0266, 800-875-4867; FAX: 520-322-5704

Laughridge, William R. (See Cylinder & Slide, Inc.)

Laurel Mountain Forge, P.O. Box 224C, Romeo, MI 48065/810-749-5742

Laurona Armas Eibar, S.A.L., Avenida de Otaola 25, P.O. Box 260, 20600 Eibar, SPAIN/34-43-700600; FAX: 34-43-700616 (U.S. importer—Galaxy Imports Ltd., Inc.)

Law Concealment Systems, Inc., P.O. Box 3952, Wilmington, NC 28406/919-791-6656, 800-373-0116 orders; FAX: 910-791-8388

Lawrence Brand Shot (See Precision Reloading, Inc.)

Lawrence Leather Co., P.O. Box 1479, Lillington, NC 27546/910-893-2071; FAX: 910-893-4742

Lawson Co., Harry, 3328 N. Richey Blvd., Tucson, AZ 85716/520-326-1117

Lawson, John G. (See Sight Shop, The)

Lazzeroni Arms Co., P.O. Box 26696, Tucson, AZ 85726/888-492-7247; FAX: 520-624-4250

LBT, HCR 62, Box 145, Moyie Springs, ID 83845/208-267-3588

Le Clear Industries (See E-Z-Way Systems)

Lea Mfg. Co., 237 E. Aurora St., Waterbury, CT 06720/203-753-5116

Lead Bullets Technology (See LBT)

Leapers, Inc., 7675 Five Mile Rd., Northville, MI 48167/810-486-1231; FAX: 810-486-1430

Leather Arsenal, 27549 Middleton Rd., Middleton, ID 83644/208-585-6212

Leatherman Tool Group, Inc., 12106 NE Ainsworth Dr., P.O. Box 20595, Portland, OR 97294/503-253-7826; FAX: 503-253-7830

Lebeau-Courally, Rue St. Gilles, 386, 4000 Liege, BELGIUM/042-52-48-43; FAX: 32-042-52-20-08 (U.S. importer—New England Arms Co.)

Leckie Professional Gunsmithing, 546 Quarry Rd., Ottsville, PA 18942/215-847-8594

Lectro Science, Inc., 6410 W. Ridge Rd., Erie, PA 16506/814-833-6487; FAX: 814-833-0447

Ledbetter Airguns, Riley, 1804 E. Sprague St., Winston Salem, NC 27107-3521/919-784-0676

Lee Precision, Inc., 4275 Hwy. U, Hartford, WI 53027/414-673-3075; FAX: 414-673-9273; Web: www.leeprecision.co

Lee Supplies, Mark, 9901 France Ct., Lakeville, MN 55044/612-461-2114

Lee's Red Ramps, 4 Kristine Ln., Silver City, NM 88061/505-538-8529

Lee Co., T.K., 1282 Branchwater Lane, Birmingham, AL 35216/205-913-5222

LeFever Arms Co., Inc., 6234 Stokes, Lee Center Rd., Lee Center, NY 13363/315-337-6722; FAX: 315-337-1543

Legend Products Corp., 21218 Saint Andrews Blvd., Boca Raton, FL 33433-2435

Leibowitz, Leonard, 1205 Murrayhill Ave., Pittsburgh, PA 15217/412-361-5455

Leica USA, Inc., 156 Ludlow Ave., Northvale, NJ 07647/201-767-7500; FAX: 201-767-8666

LEM Gun Specialties, Inc., The Lewis Lead Remover, P.O. Box 2855, Peachtree City, GA 30269-2024

Lestrom Laboratories, Inc., P.O. Box 628, Mexico, NY 13114-0628/315-343-3076; FAX: 315-592-3370

Lethal Force Institute (See Police Bookshelf)

Lett Custom Grips, 672 Currier Rd., Hopkinton, NH 03229-2652

Leupold & Stevens, Inc., P.O. Box 688, Beaverton, OR 97075/503-646-9171; FAX: 503-526-1455

Lever Arms Service Ltd., 2131 Burrard St., Vancouver, B.C. V6J 3H7 CANADA/604-736-0004; FAX: 604-738-3503

Lewis Lead Remover, The (See LEM Gun Specialties, Inc.)

Liberty Antique Gunworks, 19 Key St., P.O. Box 183, Eastport, ME 04631/207-853-4116

Liberty Metals, 2233 East 16th St., Los Angeles, CA 90021/213-581-9171; FAX: 213-581-9351

Liberty Safe, 1060 N. Spring Creek Pl., Springville, UT 84663/800-247-5625; FAX: 801-489-6409

Liberty Shooting Supplies, P.O. Box 357, Hillsboro, OR 97123/503-640-5518; FAX 503-640-5518

Liberty Trouser Co., 3500 6 Ave S., Birmingham, AL 35222-2406/205-251-9143

Light Optronics (See TacStar Industries, Inc.)

Lightfield Ammunition Corp. (See Slug Group, Inc.)

Lightforce U.S.A. Inc., 19226 66th Ave. So., L-103, Kent, WA 98032/206-656-1577; FAX:206-656-1578

Lightning Performance Innovations, Inc., RD1 Box 555, Mohawk, NY 13407/315-866-8819, 800-242-5873; FAX: 315-866-8819

Lilja Precision Rifle Barrels, P.O. Box 372, Plains, MT 59859/406-826-3084; FAX: 406-826-3083

Lincoln, Dean, Box 1886, Farmington, NM 87401

Lind Custom Guns, Al, 7821 76th Ave. SW, Tacoma, WA 98498/253-584-6361

Linder Solingen Knives, 4401 Sentry Dr., Tucker, GA 30084/770-939-6915; FAX: 770-939-6738

Lindsay, Steve, RR 2 Cedar Hills, Kearney, NE 68847/308-236-7885

Lindsley Arms Cartridge Co., P.O. Box 757, 20 College Hill Rd., Henniker, NH 03242/603-428-3127

Linebaugh Custom Sixguns, Route 2, Box 100, Maryville, MO 64468/816-562-3031

Lion Country Supply, P.O. Box 480, Port Matilda, PA 16870

List Precision Engineering, Unit 1, Ingley Works, 13 River Road, Barking, Essex 1G11 0HE ENGLAND/011-081-594-1686

Lithi Bee Bullet Lube, 1728 Carr Rd., Muskegon, MI 49442/616-788-4479

"Little John's" Antique Arms, 1740 W. Laveta, Orange, CA 92668

Little Trees Ramble (See Scott Pilkington, Little Trees Ramble)

Littler Sales Co., 20815 W. Chicago, Detroit, MI 48228/313-273-6888; FAX: 313-273-1099

Littleton, J.F., 275 Pinedale Ave., Oroville, CA 95966/916-533-6084

Ljutic Industries, Inc., 732 N. 16th Ave., Suite 22, Yakima, WA 98902/509-248-0476; FAX: 509-576-8233

Llama Gabilondo Y Cia, Apartado 290, E-01080, Victoria, SPAIN (U.S. importer—Import Sports, Inc.)

L.L. Bean, Inc., Freeport, ME 04032, 207-865-4761; FAX: 207-552-2802

Loch Leven Industries/Convert-a-pell, P.O. Box 2751, Santa Rosa, CA 95405/707-573-8735; FAX: 707-573-0369

Lock's Philadelphia Gun Exchange, 6700 Rowland Ave., Philadelphia, PA 19149/215-332-6225; FAX: 215-332-4800

Lodewick, Walter H., 2816 NE Halsey St., Portland, OR 97232/503-284-2554

Log Cabin Sport Shop, 8010 Lafayette Rd., Lodi, OH 44254/330-948-1082; FAX: 330-948-4307

Logan, Harry M., Box 745, Honokaa, HI 96727/808-776-1644

Lohman Mfg. Co., Inc., 4500 Doniphan Dr., P.O. Box 220, Neosho, MO 64850/417-451-4438; FAX: 417-451-2576

Lomont Precision Bullets, RR 1, Box 34, Salmon, ID 83467/208-756-6819; FAX: 208-756-6824

London Guns Ltd., Box 3750, Santa Barbara, CA 93130/805-683-4141; FAX: 805-683-1712

Lone Star Gunleather, 1301 Brushy Bend Dr., Round Rock, TX 78681/512-255-1805

Lone Star Rifle Company, 11231 Rose Road, Conroe, Texas 77303/409-856-3363

Long, George F., 1500 Rogue River Hwy., Ste. F, Grants Pass, OR 97527/541-476-7552

Lorcin Engineering Co., Inc., 10427 San Sevaine Way, Ste. A, Mira Loma, CA 91752

Lortone, Inc., 2856 NW Market St., Seattle, WA 98107/206-789-3100

Lothar Walther Precision Tool, Inc., 3425 Hutchinson Rd., Cumming, GA 30040/770-889-9998; Fax: 770-889-4918

Lovestrand, Erik, 206 Bent Oak Circle, Harvest, AL 35749-9334

Loweth (Firearms), Richard H.R., 29 Hedgegrow Lane, Kirby Muxloe, Leics. LE9 2BN ENGLAND/(0)116 238 6295

L.P.A. Snc, Via Alfieri 26, Gardone V.T., Brescia, ITALY 25063/30-891-14-81; FAX: 30-891-09-51

LPS Laboratories, Inc., 4647 Hugh Howell Rd., P.O. Box 3050, Tucker, GA 30084/404-934-7800

Lucas, Edward E., 32 Garfield Ave., East Brunswick, NJ 08816/201-251-5526

Lucas, Mike, 1631 Jessamine Rd., Lexington, SC 29073/803-356-0282

Luch Metal Merchants, Barbara, 48861 West Rd., Wixon, MI 48393/800-876-5337

Lutz Engraving, Ron, E. 1998 Smokey Valley Rd., Scandinavia, WI 54977/715-467-2674

Lyman Instant Targets, Inc. (See Lyman Products Corp.)

Lyman Products Corp., 475 Smith Street, Middletown, CT 06457-1541/860-632-2020, 800-22-LYMAN; FAX: 860-632-1699

Lynn's Custom Gunstocks, RR 1, Brandon, IA 52210/319-474-2453

Lyons Gunworks, Larry, 110 Hamilton St., Dowagiac, MI 49047/616-782-9478

Lyte Optronics (See TracStar Industries, Inc.,)

M

M&D Munitions Ltd., 127 Verdi St., Farmingdale, NY 11735/800-878-2788, 516-752-1038; FAX: 516-752-1905

M&M Engineering (See Hollywood Engineering)

M&N Bullet Lube, P.O. Box 495, 151 NE Jefferson St., Madras, OR 97741/503-255-3750

MA Systems, P.O. Box 1143, Chouteau, OK 74337/918-479-6378

Mac-1 Airgun Distributors, 13974 Van Ness Ave., Gardena, CA 90249/310-327-3581; FAX: 310-327-0238

Mac's .45 Shop, P.O. Box 2028, Seal Beach, CA 90740/310-438-5046

Macbean, Stan, 754 North 1200 West, Orem, UT 84057/801-224-6446

Madis Books, 2453 West Five Mile Pkwy., Dallas, TX 75233/214-330-7168

Madis, George, P.O. Box 545, Brownsboro, TX 75756/903-852-6480

MAG Instrument, Inc., 1635 S. Sacramento Ave., Ontario, CA 91761/909-947-1006; FAX: 909-947-3116

Mag-Na-Port International, Inc., 41302 Executive Dr., Harrison Twp., MI 48045-1306/810-469-6727; FAX: 810-469-0425

Mag-Pack Corp., P.O. Box 846, Chesterland, OH 44026

Magma Engineering Co., P.O. Box 161, 20955 E. Ocotillo Rd., Queen Creek, AZ 85242/602-987-9008; FAX: 602-987-0148

Magnolia Sports, Inc., 211 W. Main, Magnolia, AR 71753/501-234-8410, 800-530-7816; FAX: 501-234-8117

Magnum Grips, Box 801G, Payson, AZ 85547

Magnum Power Products, Inc., P.O. Box 17768, Fountain Hills, AZ 85268

Magnum Research, Inc., 7110 University Ave. NE, Minneapolis, MN 55432/800-772-6168, 612-574-1868; FAX: 612-574-0109; WEB:http://www.magnumresearch.com

Magnus Bullets, P.O. Box 239, Toney, AL 35773/256-420-8359; FAX: 256-420-8360; Email: magnusinc@juno.com

MagSafe Ammo Co., 2725 Friendly Grove Rd NE, Olympia, WA 98506/360-357-6383; FAX: 360-705-4715

MagTech Recreational Products, Inc., 5030 Paradise Rd., Suite A104, Las Vegas, NV 89119/702-736-2043; FAX: 702-736-2140

Mahony, Philip Bruce, 67 White Hollow Rd., Lime Rock, CT 06039-2418/203-435-9341

Mahovsky's Metalife, R.D. 1, Box 149a Eureka Road, Grand Valley, PA 16420/814-436-7747

Maine Custom Bullets, RFD 1, Box 1755, Brooks, ME 04921

Maionchi-L.M.I., Via Di Coselli-Zona Industriale Di Guamo, Lucca, ITALY 55060/011 39-583 94291

Makinson, Nicholas, RR 3, Komoka, Ont. N0L 1R0 CANADA/519-471-5462

Malcolm Enterprises, 1023 E. Prien Lake Rd., Lake Charles, LA 70601

Mallardtone Game Calls, 2901 16th St., Moline, IL 61265/309-762-8089

M.A.M. Products, Inc., 153 B Cross Slope Court, Englishtown, NJ 07726/908-536-3604; FAX:908-972-1004

Mandell Shooting Supplies, Inc., 3616 N. Scottsdale Rd., Scottsdale, AZ 85252/602-945-2553; FAX: 602-949-0734

Manufacture D'Armes Des Pyrenees Francaises (See Unique/M.A.P.F.)

Mar Knives, Inc., Al, 5755 SW Jean Rd., Suite 101, Lake Oswego, OR 97035/503-635-9229; FAX: 503-223-0467

Marathon Rubber Prods. Co., Inc., 510 Sherman St., Wausau, WI 54401/715-845-6255

Marble Arms (See CRR, Inc.,/Marble's Inc.)

Marchmon Bullets, 8191 Woodland Shore Dr., Brighton, MI 48116

Marent, Rudolf, 9711 Tiltree St., Houston, TX 77075/713-946-7028

Markell, Inc., 422 Larkfield Center 235, Santa Rosa, CA 95403/707-573-0792; FAX: 707-573-9867

Markesbery Muzzle Loaders, Inc., 7785 Foundation Dr., Ste. 6, Florence, KY 41042/606-342-5553; 606-342-2380

Marksman Products, 5482 Argosy Dr., Huntington Beach, CA 92649/714-898-7535, 800-822-8005; FAX: 714-891-0782

Marlin Firearms Co., 100 Kenna Dr., North Haven, CT 06473/203-239-5621; FAX: 203-234-7991

MarMik, Inc., 2116 S. Woodland Ave., Michigan City, IN 46360/219-872-7231; FAX: 219-872-7231

Marocchi F.Ili S.p.A, Via Galileo Galilei 8, I-25068 Zanano di Sarezzo, ITALY/ (U.S. importers—Precision Sales International, Inc.)

Marple & Associates, Dick, 21 Dartmouth St., Hooksett, NH 03106/603-627-1837; FAX: 603-627-1837

Marquart Precision Co., P.O. Box 1740, Prescott, AZ 86302/520-445-5646

Marsh, Johnny, 1007 Drummond Dr., Nashville, TN 37211/615-833-3259

Marsh, Mike, Croft Cottage, Main St., Elton, Derbyshire DE4 2BY, ENGLAND/01629 650 669

Marshall Enterprises, 792 Canyon Rd., Redwood City, CA 94062

Martin Bookseller, J., P.O. Drawer AP, Beckley, WV 25802/304-255-4073; FAX: 304-255-4077

Martin's Gun Shop, 937 S. Sheridan Blvd., Lakewood, CO 80226/303-922-2184

Martz, John V., 8060 Lakeview Lane, Lincoln, CA 95648/FAX:916-645-3815

Marvel, Alan, 3922 Madonna Rd., Jarrettsville, MD 21084/301-557-6545

Marx, Harry (U.S. importer for FERLIB)

Maryland Paintball Supply, 8507 Harford Rd., Parkville, MD 21234/410-882-5607

Masen Co., Inc., John, 1305 Jelmak, Grand Prairie, TX 75050/817-430-8732; FAX: 817-430-1715

MAST Technology, 4350 S. Arville, Suite 3, Las Vegas, NV 89103/702-362-5043; FAX: 702-362-9554

Master Engravers, Inc. (See Hendricks, Frank E.)

Master Lock Co., 2600 N. 32nd St., Milwaukee, WI 53245/414-444-2800

Master Products, Inc. (See Gun-Alert/Master Products, Inc.)

Match Prep—Doyle Gracey, P.O. Box 155, Tehachapi, CA 93581/805-822-5383

Matco, Inc., 1003-2nd St., N. Manchester, IN 46962/219-982-8282

Mathews & Son, George E., Inc., 10224 S. Paramount Blvd., Downey, CA 90241/562-862-6719; FAX: 562-862-6719

Matthews Cutlery, 4401 Sentry Dr., Tucker, GA 30084/770-939-6915

Mauser Werke Oberndorf Waffensysteme GmbH, Postfach 1349, 78722 Oberndorf/N. GERMANY/ (U.S. importer—GSI, Inc.)

Maverick Arms, Inc., 7 Grasso Ave., P.O. Box 497, North Haven, CT 06473/203-230-5300; FAX: 203-230-5420

Maxi-Mount, P.O. Box 291, Willoughby Hills, OH 44094-0291/216-944-9456; FAX: 216-944-9456

Maximum Security Corp., 32841 Calle Perfecto, San Juan Capistrano, CA 92675/714-493-3684; FAX: 714-496-7733

Mayville Engineering Co. (See MEC, Inc.)

Mazur Restoration, Pete, 13083 Drummer Way, Grass Valley, CA 95949/530-268-2412

MCA Sports, P.O. Box 8868, Palm Springs, CA 92263/619-770-2005

McBros Rifle Co., P.O. Box 86549, Phoenix, AZ 85080/602-582-3713; FAX: 602-581-3825

McCament, Jay, 1730-134th St. Ct. S., Tacoma, WA 98444/206-531-8832

McCann Industries, P.O. Box 641, Spanaway, WA 98387/253-537-6919; FAX: 253-537-6919

McCann's Muzzle-Gun Works, 14 Walton Dr., New Hope, PA 18938/215-862-2728

McCluskey Precision Rifles, 10502 14th Ave. NW, Seattle, WA 98177/206-781-2776

McCombs, Leo, 1862 White Cemetery Rd., Patriot, OH 45658/614-256-1714

McCormick Corp., Chip, 1825 Fortview Rd., Ste. 115, Austin, TX 78704/800-328-CHIP, 512-462-0004; FAX: 512-462-0009

McCullough, Ken (See Ken's Rifle Blanks)

McDonald, Dennis, 8359 Brady St., Peosta, IA 52068/319-556-7940
McFarland, Stan, 2221 Idella Ct., Grand Junction, CO 81505/970-243-4704
McGowen Rifle Barrels, 5961 Spruce Lane, St. Anne, IL 60964/815-937-9816; FAX: 815-937-4024
McGuire, Bill, 1600 N. Eastmont Ave., East Wenatchee, WA 98802/509-884-6021
McKee Publications, 121 Eatons Neck Rd., Northport, NY 11768/516-575-8850
McKenzie, Lynton, 6940 N. Alvernon Way, Tucson, AZ 85718/520-299-5090
McKillen & Heyer, Inc., 35535 Euclid Ave. Suite 11, Willoughby, OH 44094/216-942-2044
McKinney, R.P. (See Schuetzen Gun Co.)
McMillan Fiberglass Stocks, Inc., 21421 N. 14th Ave., Suite B, Phoenix, AZ 85027/602-582-9635; FAX: 602-581-3825
McMillan Optical Gunsight Co., 28638 N. 42nd St., Cave Creek, AZ 85331/602-585-7868; FAX: 602-585-7872
McMillan Rifle Barrels, P.O. Box 3427, Bryan, TX 77805/409-690-3456; FAX: 409-690-0156
McMurdo, Lynn (See Specialty Gunsmithing)
MCRW Associates Shooting Supplies, R.R. 1 Box 1425, Sweet Valley, PA 18656/717-864-3967; FAX: 717-864-2669
MCS, Inc., 34 Delmar Dr., Brookfield, CT 06804/203-775-1013; FAX: 203-775-9462
McWelco Products, 6730 Santa Fe Ave., Hesperia, CA 92345/619-244-8876; FAX: 619-244-9398
McWhorter Custom Rifles, 4460 SW 35th Terrace, Suite 310, Gainesville, FL 32608/352-373-9057; FAX: 352-377-3816
MDS, P.O. Box 1441, Brandon, FL 33509-1441/813-653-1180; FAX: 813-684-5953
Meadow Industries, 24 Club Lane, Palmyra, VA 22963/804-589-7672; FAX: 804-589-7672
Measurement Group, Inc., Box 27777, Raleigh, NC 27611
MEC, Inc., 715 South St., Mayville, WI 53050/414-387-4500; FAX: 414-387-5802
MEC-Gar S.r.l., Via Madonnina 64, Gardone V.T., Brescia, ITALY 25063/39-30-8912687; FAX: 39-30-8910065 (U.S. importer—MEC-Gar U.S.A., Inc.)
MEC-Gar U.S.A., Inc., Box 112, 500B Monroe Turnpike, Monroe, CT 06468/203-635-8662; FAX: 203-635-8662
Mech-Tech Systems Inc., 1602 Foothill Rd., Kalispell, MT 59901/406-755-8055
Meister Bullets (See Gander Mountain)
Mele, Frank, 201 S. Wellow Ave., Cookeville, TN 38501/615-526-4860
Melton Shirt Co., Inc., 56 Harvester Ave., Batavia, NY 14020/716-343-8750; FAX: 716-343-6887
Men-Metallwerk Elisenhuette, GmbH, P.O. Box 1263, D-56372 Nassau/Lahn, GERMANY/2604-7819
Menck, Gunsmith Inc., T.W., 5703 S. 77th St., Ralston, NE 68127
Mendez, John A., P.O. Box 620984, Orlando, FL 32862/407-344-2791
Meprolight (See Hesco-Meprolight)
Mercer Custom Stocks, R.M., 216 S. Whitewater Ave., Jefferson, WI 53549/414-674-5130
Merit Corp., Box 9044, Schenectady, NY 12309/518-346-1420
Merkel Freres, Strasse 7 October, 10, Suhl, GERMANY/ (U.S. importer—GSI, Inc.)
Merkuria Ltd., Argentinska 38, 17005 Praha 7, CZECH REPUBLIC/422-875117; FAX: 422-809152
Metal Merchants, 48861 West Rd., Wixom, MI 48393
Metal Products Co. (See MPC)
Metalife Industries (See Mahovsky's Metalife)
Metaloy Inc., Rt. 5, Box 595, Berryville, AR 72616/501-545-3611
Metals Hand Engraver/European Hand Engraving, Ste. 216, 12 South First St., San Jose, CA 95113/408-293-6559
Michael's Antiques, Box 591, Waldoboro, ME 04572
Michaels of Oregon Co., P.O. Box 1690, Portland, OR 97045/503-557-0536; FAX: 503-655-7546
Micro Sight Co., 242 Harbor Blvd., Belmont, CA 94002/415-591-0769; FAX: 415-591-7531
Microfusion Alfa S.A., Paseo San Andres N8, P.O. Box 271, Eibar, SPAIN 20600/34-43-11-89-16; FAX: 34-43-11-40-38
Mid-America Guns and Ammo, 1205 W. Jefferson, Suite E, Effingham, IL 62401/800-820-5177
Mid-America Recreation, Inc., 1328 5th Ave., Moline, IL 61265/309-764-5089; FAX: 309-764-2722
Middlebrooks Custom Shop, 7366 Colonial Trail East, Surry, VA 23883/757-357-0881; FAX: 757-365-0442
Midway Arms, Inc., 5875 W. Van Horn Tavern Rd., Columbia, MO 65203/800-243-3220, 573-445-6363; FAX: 573-446-1018
Midwest Gun Sport, 1108 Herbert Dr., Zebulon, NC 27597/919-269-5570
Midwest Sport Distributors, Box 129, Fayette, MO 65248
Military Armament Corp., P.O. Box 120, Mt. Zion Rd., Lingleville, TX 76461/817-965-3253
Miller Arms, Inc., P.O. Box 260 Purl St., St. Onge, SD 57779/605-642-5160; FAX: 605-642-5160
Miller Custom, 210 E. Julia, Clinton, IL 61727/217-935-9362
Miller Co., David, 3131 E. Greenlee Rd., Tucson, AZ 85716-1267/520-326-3117
Miller Single Trigger Mfg. Co., Rt. 209 Box 1275, Millersburg, PA 17061/717-692-3704
Millett Sights, 7275 Murdy Circle, Adm. Office, Huntington Beach, CA 92647/714-842-5575, 800-645-5388; FAX: 714-843-5707
Mills Jr., Hugh B., 3615 Canterbury Rd., New Bern, NC 28560/919-637-4631
Milstor Corp., 80-975 Indio Blvd. C-7, Indio, CA 92201/760-775-9998; FAX: 760-772-4990
Miltex, Inc., 2225 Pinefield Station, Waldorf, MD 20601/888-642-9123
Miniature Machine Co. (See MMC)

Minute Man High Tech Industries, 10611 Canyon Rd. E., Suite 151, Puyallup, WA 98373/800-233-2734
Mirador Optical Corp., P.O. Box 11614, Marina Del Rey, CA 90295-7614/310-821-5587; FAX: 310-305-0386
Miroku, B.C./Daly, Charles (See U.S. importer—Bell's Legendary Country Wear; K.B.I., Inc.; U.S. distributor—Outdoor Sports Headquarters, Inc.)
Mitchell Bullets, R.F., 430 Walnut St., Westernport, MD 21562
Mitchell Optics Inc., 2072 CR 1100 N, Sidney, IL 61877/217-688-2219, 217-621-3018; FAX: 217-688-2505
Mitchell's Accuracy Shop, 68 Greenridge Dr., Stafford, VA 22554/703-659-0165
MI-TE Bullets, 1396 Ave. K, Ellsworth, KS 67439/785-472-4575; FAX: 785-472-5579
Mittermeier, Inc., Frank, P.O. Box 2G, 3577 E. Tremont Ave., Bronx, NY 10465/718-828-3843
MJK Gunsmithing, Inc., 417 N. Huber Ct., E. Wenatchee, WA 98802/509-884-7683
MJM Mfg., 3283 Rocky Water Ln. Suite B, San Jose, CA 95148/408-270-4207
MKS Supply, Inc. (See Hi-Point Firearms)
MMC, 2513 East Loop 820 North, Ft. Worth, TX 76118/817-595-0404; FAX: 817-595-3074
MMP, Rt. 6, Box 384, Harrison, AR 72601/501-741-5019; FAX: 501-741-3104
M.O.A. Corp., 2451 Old Camden Pike, Eaton, OH 45320/513-456-3669
Modern Gun Repair School, P.O. Box 92577, Southlake, TX 76092/800-493-4114; FAX: 800-556-5112
Modern MuzzleLoading, Inc., 234 Airport Rd., P.O. Box 130, Centerville, IA 52544/515-856-2626; FAX: 515-856-2628
Moeller, Steve, 1213 4th St., Fulton, IL 61252/815-589-2300
Molin Industries, Tru-Nord Division, P.O. Box 365, 204 North 9th St., Brainerd, MN 56401/218-829-2870
Mo's Competitor Supplies (See MCS, Inc.)
MoLoc Bullets, P.O. Box 2810, Turlock, CA 95381-2810/209-632-1644
Monell Custom Guns, 228 Red Mills Rd., Pine Bush, NY 12566/914-744-3021
Moneymaker Guncraft Corp., 1420 Military Ave., Omaha, NE 68131/402-556-0226
Montana Armory, Inc. (See C. Sharps Arms Co. Inc.)
Montana Outfitters, Lewis E. Yearout, 308 Riverview Dr. E., Great Falls, MT 59404/406-761-0859
Montana Precision Swaging, P.O. Box 4746, Butte, MT 59702/406-782-7502
Montana Vintage Arms, 2354 Bear Canyon Rd., Bozeman, MT 59715
Montgomery Community College, P.O. Box 787-GD, Troy, NC 27371/910-576-6222, 800-839-6222; FAX: 910-576-2176
Moore & Co., Wm. Larkin, 8727 E. Via de Commencio, Suite A, Scottsdale, AZ 85258/602-951-8913; FAX: 602-951-8913
Morini (See U.S. importers—Mandall Shooting Supplies, Inc.; Nygord Precision Products)
Morrison Custom Rifles, J.W., 4015 W. Sharon, Phoenix, AZ 85029/602-978-3754
Morrow, Bud, 11 Hillside Lane, Sheridan, WY 82801-9729/307-674-8360
Morton Booth Co., P.O. Box 123, Joplin, MO 64802/417-673-1962; FAX: 417-673-3642
Moss Double Tone, Inc., P.O. Box 1112, 2101 S. Kentucky, Sedalia, MO 65301/816-827-0827
Mossberg & Sons, Inc., O.F., 7 Grasso Ave., North Haven, CT 06473/203-230-5300; FAX: 203-230-5420
Mountain Hollow Game Calls, Box 121, Cascade, MD 21719/301-241-3282
Mountain Plains, Inc., 244 Glass Hollow Rd., Alton, VA 22920/800-687-3000
Mountain Rifles Inc., P.O. Box 2789, Palmer, AK 99645/907-373-4194; FAX: 907-373-4195
Mountain South, P.O. Box 381, Barnwell, SC 29812/FAX: 803-259-3227
Mountain State Muzzleloading Supplies, Inc., Box 154-1, Rt. 2, Williamstown, WV 26187/304-375-7842; FAX: 304-375-3737
Mountain States Engraving, Kenneth W. Warren, P.O. Box 2842, Wenatchee, WA 98802/509-663-6123
Mountain View Sports, Inc., Box 188, Troy, NH 03465/603-357-9690; FAX: 603-357-9691
Mowrey Gun Works, P.O. Box 246, Waldron, IN 46182/317-525-6181; FAX: 317-525-9595
Mowrey's Guns & Gunsmithing, 119 Fredericks St., Canajoharie, NY 13317/518-673-3483
MPC, P.O. Box 450, McMinnville, TN 37110-0450/615-473-5513; FAX: 615-473-5516
MPI Stocks, P.O. Box 83266, Portland, OR 97283/503-226-1215; FAX: 503-226-2661
MSC Industrial Supply Co., 151 Sunnyside Blvd., Plainview, NY 11803-9915/516-349-0330
MSR Targets, P.O. Box 1042, West Covina, CA 91793/818-331-7840
Mt. Alto Outdoor Products, Rt. 735, Howardsville, VA 24562
Mt. Baldy Bullet Co., 12981 Old Hill City Rd., Keystone, SD 57751-6623/605-666-4725
M.Thys (See U.S. importer—Champlin Firearms, Inc.)
MTM Molded Products Co., Inc., 3370 Obco Ct., Dayton, OH 45414/513-890-7461; FAX: 513-890-1747
Milberry House Publishing, P.O. Box 575, Corydon, IN 47112/888-738-1567; FAX: 888-738-1567
Mulhern, Rick, Rt. 5, Box 152, Rayville, LA 71269/318-728-2688
Mullins Ammunition, Rt. 2, Box 304K, Clintwood, VA 24228/540-926-6772; FAX: 540-926-6092
Mullis Guncraft, 3523 Lawyers Road E., Monroe, NC 28110/704-283-6683
Multi-Caliber Adapters (See MCA Sports)
Multiplex International, 26 S. Main St., Concord, NH 03301/FAX: 603-796-2223

Multipropulseurs, La Bertrandiere, 42580 L'Etrat, FRANCE/77 74 01 30; FAX: 77 93 19 34

Multi-Scale Charge Ltd., 3269 Niagara Falls Blvd., N. Tonawanda, NY 14120/905-566-1255; FAX: 905-276-6295

Mundy, Thomas A., 69 Robbins Road, Somerville, NJ 08876/201-722-2199

Munsch Gunsmithing, Tommy, Rt. 2, P.O. Box 248, Little Falls, MN 56345/612-632-6695

Murmur Corp., 2823 N. Westmoreland Ave., Dallas, TX 75222/214-630-5400

Murphy Co., Inc., R., 13 Groton-Harvard Rd., P.O. Box 376, Ayer, MA 01432/617-772-3481

Murray State College, 1 Murray Campus St., Tishomingo, OK 73460/580-371-2371 ext. 238

Muscle Products Corp., 112 Fennell Dr., Butler, PA 16001/800-227-7049, 412-283-0567; FAX: 412-283-8310

Museum of Historical Arms Inc., 2750 Coral Way, Suite 204, Miami, FL 33145/305-444-9199

Mushroom Express Bullet Co., 601 W. 6th St., Greenfield, IN 46140-1728/317-462-6332

Muzzleload Magnum Products (See MMP)

Muzzleloaders Etcetera, Inc., 9901 Lyndale Ave. S., Bloomington, MN 55420/612-884-1161

MWG Co., P.O. Box 971202, Miami, FL 33197/800-428-9394, 305-253-8393; FAX: 305-232-1247

N

N&J Sales, Lime Kiln Rd., Northford, CT 06472/203-484-0247

Nagel's Custom Bullets, 100 Scott St., Baytown, TX 77520-2849

Nalpak, 1937-C Friendship Drive, El Cajon, CA 92020/619-258-1200

Napoleon Bonaparte, Inc. (See Metals Hand Engraver)

Nastoff's 45 Shop, Inc., Steve, 12288 Mahoning Ave., P.O. Box 446, North Jackson, OH 44451/330-538-2977

National Bullet Co., 1585 E. 361 St., Eastlake, OH 44095/216-951-1854; FAX: 216-951-7761

National Security Safe Co., Inc., P.O. Box 39, 620 S. 380 E., American Fork, UT 84003/801-756-7706, 800-544-3829; FAX: 801-756-8043

National Target Co., 4690 Wyaconda Rd., Rockville, MD 20852/800-827-7060, 301-770-7060; FAX: 301-770-7892

Nationwide Airgun Repairs (See Airgun Repair Centre)

Nationwide Sports Distributors, Inc., 70 James Way, Southampton, PA 18966/215-322-2050, 800-355-3006; FAX: 702-358-2093

Naval Ordnance Works, Rt. 2, Box 919, Sheperdstown, WV 25443/304-876-0998

Navy Arms Co., 689 Bergen Blvd., Ridgefield, NJ 07657/201-945-2500; FAX: 201-945-6859

N.B.B., Inc., 24 Elliot Rd., Sterling, MA 01564/508-422-7538, 800-942-9444

N.C. Ordnance Co., P.O. Box 3254, Wilson, NC 27895/919-237-2440; FAX: 919-243-9845

NCP Products, Inc., 3500 12th St. N.W., Canton, OH 44708/330-456-5130: FAX: 330-456-5234

Necessary Concepts, Inc., P.O. Box 571, Deer Park, NY 11729/516-667-8509; FAX 516-667-8588

NECO, 1316-67th St., Emeryville, CA 94608/510-450-0420

Necromancer Industries, Inc., 14 Communications Way, West Newton, PA 15089/412-872-8722

NEI Handtools, Inc., 51583 Columbia River Hwy., Scappoose, OR 97056/503-543-6776; FAX: 503-543-6799; E-MAIL: neiht@mcimail.com

Nelson, Gary K., 975 Terrace Dr., Oakdale, CA 95361/209-847-4590

Nelson, Stephen, 7365 NW Spring Creek Dr., Corvallis, OR 97330/541-745-5232

Nelson/Weather-Rite, Inc., 14760 Santa Fe Trail Dr., Lenexa, KS 66215/913-492-3200; FAX: 913-492-8749

Nesci Enterprises, Inc., P.O. Box 119, Summit St., East Hampton, CT 06424/203-267-2588

Nesika Bay Precision, 22239 Big Valley Rd., Poulsbo, WA 98370/206-697-3830

Nettestad Gun Works, RR 1, Box 160, Pelican Rapids, MN 56572/218-863-4301

Neumann GmbH, Am Galgenberg 6, 90575 Langenzenn, GERMANY/09101/8258; FAX: 09101/6356

Nevada Pistol Academy Inc., 4610 Blue Diamond Rd., Las Vegas, NV 89139/702-897-1100

New England Ammunition Co., 1771 Post Rd. East, Suite 223, Westport, CT 06880/203-254-8048

New England Arms Co., Box 278, Lawrence Lane, Kittery Point, ME 03905/207-439-0593; FAX: 207-439-6726

New England Custom Gun Service, 438 Willow Brook Rd., RR2, Box 122W, W. Lebanon, NH 03784/603-469-3450; FAX: 603-469-3471

New England Firearms, 60 Industrial Rowe, Gardner, MA 01440/508-632-9393; FAX: 508-632-2300

New Orleans Jewelers Supply Co., 206 Charters St., New Orleans, LA 70130/504-523-3839; FAX: 504-523-3836

New SKB Arms Co., C.P.O. Box 1401, Tokyo, JAPAN/81-3-3943-9550; FAX: 81-3-3943-0695

New Win Publishing, Inc., 186 Center St., Clinton, NJ 08809/908-735-9701; FAX: 908-735-9703

Newark Electronics, 4801 N. Ravenswood Ave., Chicago, IL 60640

Newell, Robert H., 55 Coyote, Los Alamos, NM 87544/505-662-7135

Newman Gunshop, 119 Miller Rd., Agency, IA 52530/515-937-5775

NgraveR Co., The, 67 Wawecus Hill Rd., Bozrah, CT 06334/860-823-1533

Nicholson Custom, 17285 Thornlay Road, Hughesville, MO 65334/816-826-8746

Nickels, Paul R., 4789 Summerhill Rd., Las Vegas, NV 89121-5638/702-435-5318

Nicklas, Ted, 5504 Hegel Rd., Goodrich, MI 48438/810-797-4493

Nic Max, Inc., 535 Midland Ave., Garfield, NJ 07026/201-546-7191; FAX: 201-546-7419

Niemi Engineering, W.B., Box 126 Center Road, Greensboro, VT 05841/802-533-7180 days, 802-533-7141 evenings

Nightforce (See Lightforce U.S.A. Inc.)

Nikon, Inc., 1300 Walt Whitman Rd., Melville, NY 11747/516-547-8623; FAX: 516-547-0309

Nitex, Inc., P.O. Box 1706, Uvalde, TX 78801/210-278-8843

Noble Co., Jim, 1305 Columbia St., Vancouver, WA 98660/360-695-1309; FAX: 360-695-6835

Noreen, Peter H., 5075 Buena Vista Dr., Belgrade, MT 59714/406-586-7383

Norica, Avnda Otaola, 16, Apartado 68, 20600 Eibar, SPAIN

Norin, Dave, Schrank's Smoke & Gun, 2010 Washington St., Waukegan, IL 60085/708-662-4034

Norinco, 7A, Yun Tan N Beijing, CHINA/ (U.S. importers—Century International Arms, Inc.; Interarms)

Norincoptics (See BEC, Inc.)

Norma Precision AB (See U.S. importers—Dynamit Nobel-RWS Inc.; Paul Co. Inc., The)

Norman Custom Gunstocks, Jim, 14281 Cane Rd., Valley Center, CA 92082/619-749-6252

Normark Corp., 10395 Yellow Circle Dr., Minnetonka, MN 55343-9101/612-933-7060; FAX: 612-933-0046

Norrell Arms, John, 2608 Grist Mill Rd., Little Rock, AR 72207/501-225-7864

North American Arms, Inc., 2150 South 950 East, Provo, UT 84606-6285/800-821-5783, 801-374-9990; FAX: 801-374-9998

North American Correspondence Schools, The Gun Pro School, Oak & Pawney St., Scranton, PA 18515/717-342-7701

North American Munitions, P.O. Box 815, Beulah, ND 58523/701-948-2260; FAX: 701-948-2282

North American Shooting Systems, P.O. Box 306, Osoyoos, B.C. V0H 1V0 CANADA/604-495-3131; FAX: 604-495-2816

North Devon Firearms Services, 3 North St., Braunton, EX33 1AJ ENGLAND/01271 813624; FAX: 01271 813624

North Fork Custom Gunsmithing, James Johnston, 428 Del Rio Rd., Roseburg, OR 97470/503-673-4467

North Mountain Pine Training Center (See Executive Protection Institute)

North Pass, 425 South Bowen St., Ste. 6, Longmount, CO 80501/303-682-4315/ FAX: 303-678-7109

North Specialty Products, 2664-B Saturn St., Brea, CA 92621/714-524-1665

North Star West, P.O. Box 488, Glencoe, CA 95232/209-293-7010

North Wind Decoy Co., 1005 N. Tower Rd., Fergus Falls, MN 56537/218-736-4378; FAX: 218-736-7060

Northern Precision Custom Swaged Bullets, 329 S. James St., Carthage, NY 13619/315-493-1711

Northlake Outdoor Footwear, P.O. Box 10, Franklin, TN 37065-0010/615-794-1556; FAX: 615-790-8005

Northside Gun Shop, 2725 NW 109th, Oklahoma City, OK 73120/405-840-2353

No-Sho Mfg. Co., 10727 Glenfield Ct., Houston, TX 77096/713-723-5332

Nosler, Inc., P.O. Box 671, Bend, OR 97709/800-285-3701, 541-382-3921; FAX: 541-388-4667

Novak's, Inc., 12061/2 30th St., P.O. Box 4045, Parkersburg, WV 26101/304-485-9295; FAX: 304-428-6722

Now Products, Inc., P.O. Box 27608, Tempe, AZ 85285/800-662-6063; FAX: 602-966-0890

Nowlin Mfg. Co., Rt. 1, Box 308, Claremore, OK 74017/918-342-0689; FAX: 918-342-0624

NRI Gunsmith School, 4401 Connecticut Ave. NW, Washington, D.C. 20008

Nu-Line Guns, Inc., 1053 Caulks Hill Rd., Harvester, MO 63304/314-441-4500, 314-447-4501; FAX: 314-447-5018

Null Holsters Ltd., K.L., 161 School St. NW, Hill City Station, Resaca, GA 30735/706-625-5643; FAX: 706-625-9392

Numrich Arms Corp., 203 Broadway, W. Hurley, NY 12491

Nu-Teck, 30 Industrial Park Rd., Box 37, Centerbrook, CT 06409/203-767-3573; FAX: 203-767-9137

NW Sinker and Tackle, 380 Valley Dr., Myrtle Creek, OR 97457-9717

Nygord Precision Products, P.O. Box 12578, Prescott, AZ 86304/520-717-2315; FAX: 520-717-2198

O

Oakland Custom Arms, Inc., 4690 W. Walton Blvd., Waterford, MI 48329/810-674-8261

Oakman Turkey Calls, RD 1, Box 825, Harrisonville, PA 17228/717-485-4620

Oakshore Electronic Sights, Inc., P.O. Box 4470, Ocala, FL 32678-4470/904-629-7112; FAX: 904-629-1433

Obermeyer Rifled Barrels, 23122 60th St., Bristol, WI 53104/414-843-3537; FAX: 414-843-2129

October Country Muzzleloading, P.O. Box 969, Dept. GD, Hayden, ID 83835/208-772-2068; FAX: 208-772-9230

Oehler Research, Inc., P.O. Box 9135, Austin, TX 78766/512-327-6900

Oglesby & Oglesby Gunmakers, Inc., RR 5, Springfield, IL 62707/217-487-7100

Oil Rod and Gun Shop, 69 Oak St., East Douglas, MA 01516/508-476-3687

Ojala Holsters, Arvo, P.O. Box 98, N. Hollywood, CA 91603/503-669-1404

Oker's Engraving, 365 Bell Rd., P.O. Box 126, Shawnee, CO 80475/303-838-6042

Oklahoma Ammunition Co., 3701A S. Harvard Ave., No. 367, Tulsa, OK 74135-2265/918-396-3187; FAX: 918-396-4270

Oklahoma Leather Products, Inc., 500 26th NW, Miami, OK 74354/918-542-6651; FAX: 918-542-6653

OK Weber, Inc., P.O. Box 7485, Eugene, OR 97401/541-747-0458; FAX: 541-747-5927

Old Wagon Bullets, 32 Old Wagon Rd., Wilton, CT 06897

Old West Bullet Moulds, P.O. Box 519, Flora Vista, NM 87415/505-334-6970

Old West Reproductions, Inc., R.M. Bachman, 446 Florence S. Loop, Florence, MT 59833/406-273-2615; FAX: 406-273-2615

Old Western Scrounger, Inc., 12924 Hwy. A-I2, Montague, CA 96064/916-459-5445; FAX: 916-459-3944

Old World Gunsmithing, 2901 SE 122nd St., Portland, OR 97236/503-760-7681

Old World Oil Products, 3827 Queen Ave. N., Minneapolis, MN 55412/612-522-5037

Ole Frontier Gunsmith Shop, 2617 Hwy. 29 S., Cantonment, FL 32533/904-477-8074

Olson, Myron, 989 W. Kemp, Watertown, SD 57201/605-886-9787

Olson, Vic, 5002 Countryside Dr., Imperial, MO 63052/314-296-8086

Olt Co., Philip S., P.O. Box 550, 12662 Fifth St., Pekin, IL 61554/309-348-3633; FAX: 309-348-3300

Olympic Optical Co., P.O. Box 752377, Memphis, TN 38175-2377/901-794-3890, 800-238-7120; FAX: 901-794-0676, 800-748-1669

Omark Industries, Div. of Blount, Inc., 2299 Snake River Ave., P.O. Box 856, Lewiston, ID 83501/800-627-3640, 208-746-2351

Omega Sales, P.O. Box 1066, Mt. Clemens, MI 48043/810-469-7323; FAX: 810-469-0425

One Of A Kind, 15610 Purple Sage, San Antonio, TX 78255/512-695-3364

Op-Tec, P.O. Box L632, Langhorn, PA 19047/215-757-5037

Optical Services Co., P.O. Box 1174, Santa Teresa, NM 88008-1174/505-589-3833

Orchard Park Enterprise, P.O. Box 563, Orchard Park, NY 14227/616-656-0356

Ordnance Works, The, 2969 Pidgeon Point Road, Eureka, CA 95501/707-443-3252

Oregon Arms, Inc. (See Rogue Rifle Co., Inc.)

Oregon Trail Bullet Company, P.O. Box 529, Dept. P, Baker City, OR 97814/800-811-0548; FAX: 514-523-1803

Original Box, Inc., 700 Linden Ave., York, PA 17404/717-854-2897; FAX: 717-845-4276

Original Mink Oil, Inc., 10652 NE Holman, Portland, OR 97220/503-255-2814, 800-547-5895; FAX: 503-255-2487

Orion Rifle Barrel Co., RR2, 137 Cobler Village, Kalispell, MT 59901/406-257-5649

Or-Un, Tahtakale Menekse Han 18, Istanbul, TURKEY 34460/90212-522-5912; FAX: 90212-522-7973

Orvis Co., The, Rt. 7, Manchester, VT 05254/802-362-3622 ext. 283; FAX: 802-362-3525

Ottmar, Maurice, Box 657, 113 E. Fir, Coulee City, WA 99115/509-632-5717

Outa-Site Gun Carriers, 219 Market St., Laredo, TX 78040/956-722-4678, 800-880-9715; FAX: 956-726-4858

Outdoor Connection, Inc., The, 201 Cotton Dr., P.O. Box 7751, Waco, TX 76714-7751/800-533-6076; 817-772-5575; FAX: 817-776-3553

Outdoor Edge Cutlery Corp., 2888 Bluff St., Suite 130, Boulder, CO 80301/303-652-8212; FAX: 303-652-8238

Outdoor Enthusiast, 3784 W. Woodland, Springfield, MO 65807/417-883-9841

Outdoor Sports Headquarters, Inc., 967 Watertower Ln., West Carrollton, OH 45449/513-865-5855; FAX: 513-865-5962

Outdoorsman's Bookstore, The, Llangorse, Brecon, Powys LD3 7UE, U.K./44-1874-658-660; FAX: 44-1874-658-650

Outers Laboratories, Div. of Blount, Inc., Sporting Equipment Div., Route 2,, P.O. Box 39/Onalaska, WI 54650

608-781-5800; FAX: 608-781-0368

Ox-Yoke Originals, Inc., 34 Main St., Milo, ME 04463/800-231-8313, 207-943-7351; FAX: 207-943-2416

Ozark Gun Works, 11830 Cemetery Rd., Rogers, AR 72756/501-631-6944; FAX: 501-631-6944

P

P&M Sales and Service, 5724 Gainsborough Pl., Oak Forest, IL 60452/708-687-7149

P&S Gun Service, 2138 Old Shepardsville Rd., Louisville, KY 40218/502-456-9346

Pac-Nor Barreling, 99299 Overlook Rd., P.O. Box 6188, Brookings, OR 97415/503-469-7330; FAX: 503-469-7331

Pace Marketing, Inc., P.O. Box 2039, Stuart, FL 34995/561-871-9682; FAX: 561-871-6552

Pachmayr Div. Lyman Products, 1875 S. Mountain Ave., Monrovia, CA 91016/626-357-7771

Pacific Cartridge, Inc., 2425 Salashan Loop Road, Ferndale, WA 98248/360-366-4444; FAX: 360-366-4445

Rimrock Rifle Stocks, P.O. Box 589, Vashon Island, WA 98070/206-463-5551; FAX: 206-463-2526

Pacific Research Laboratories, Inc. (See Rimrock Rifle Stocks)

Pacific Rifle Co., P.O. Box 11, Newberg, OR 97132/503-538-7437

Paco's (See Small Custom Mould & Bullet Co.)

P.A.C.T., Inc., P.O. Box 531525, Grand Prairie, TX 75053/214-641-0049

Page Custom Bullets, P.O. Box 25, Port Moresby Papua, NEW GUINEA

Pagel Gun Works, Inc., 1407 4th St. NW, Grand Rapids, MN 55744/218-326-3003

Paintball Games International Magazine (Aceville Publications), Castle House, 97 High St./Colchester, Essex, CO1 1TH ENGLAND

011-44-206-564840

Palmer Manufacturing Co., Inc., C., P.O. Box 220, West Newton, PA 15089/412-872-8200; FAX: 412-872-8302

Palmer Security Products, 2930 N. Campbell Ave., Chicago, IL 60618/800-788-7725; FAX: 773-267-8080

Palsa Outdoor Products, P.O. Box 81336, Lincoln, NE 68501/402-488-5288; FAX: 402-488-2321

PanaVise Products, Inc., 7540 Colbert Drive, Sparks, NV 89431/702-850-2900; FAX: 702-850-2929

Para-Ordnance Mfg., Inc., 980 Tapscott Rd., Scarborough, Ont. M1X 1E7, CANADA/416-297-7855; FAX: 416-297-1289 (U.S. importer—Para-Ordnance, Inc.)

Para-Ordnance, Inc., 1919 NE 45th St., Ft. Lauderdale, FL 33308

Paragon Sales & Services, Inc., P.O. Box 2022, Joliet, IL 60434/815-725-9212; FAX: 815-725-8974

Pardini Armi Srl, Via Italica 154, 55043 Lido Di Camaiore Lu, ITALY/584-90121; FAX: 584-90122 (U.S. importers—Nygord Precision Products;MCS, Inc.)

Paris, Frank J., 17417 Pershing St., Livonia, MI 48152-3822

Park Rifle Co., Ltd., The, Unit 6a, Dartford Trade Park, Power Mill Lane, Dartford, Kent, ENGLAND DA7 7NX/011-0322-222512

Parker & Sons Shooters Supply, 9337 Smoky Row Rd., Straw Plains, TN 97871-1257;

Parker Div. Reageant Chemical (See Parker Reproductions)

Parker Gun Finishes, 9337 Smokey Row Rd., Strawberry Plains, TN 37871/423-933-3286

Parker Reproductions, 124 River Rd., Middlesex, NJ 08846/908-469-0100; FAX: 908-469-9692

Parsons Optical Mfg. Co., P.O. Box 192, Ross, OH 45061/513-867-0820; FAX: 513-867-8380

Parts & Surplus, P.O. Box 22074, Memphis, TN 38122/901-683-4007

Partridge Sales Ltd., John, Trent Meadows, Rugeley, Staffordshire, WS15 2HS ENGLAND/0889-584438

Pasadena Gun Center, 206 E. Shaw, Pasadena, TX 77506/713-472-0417; FAX: 713-472-1322

Paser Pal, 200 W. Pleasantview, Hurst, TX 76054/817-285-9888, 800-501-1603; FAX: 817-285-8769

Passive Bullet Traps, Inc. (See Savage Range Systems, Inc.)

PAST Sporting Goods, Inc., P.O. Box 1035, Columbia, MO 65205/314-445-9200; FAX: 314-446-6606

Paterson Gunsmithing, 438 Main St., Paterson, NJ 07502/201-345-4100

Pathfinder Sports Leather, 2920 E. Chambers St., Phoenix, AZ 85040/602-276-0016

Patrick Bullets, P.O. Box 172, Warwick QSLD 4370 AUSTRALIA

Paul Co., The, 27385 Pressonville Rd., Wellsville, KS 66092/785-883-4444; FAX: 785-883-2525

Paulsen Gunstocks, Rt. 71, Box 11, Chinook, MT 59523/406-357-3403

Payne Photography, Robert, P.O. Box 141471, Austin, TX 78714/512-272-4554

PC Bullet, 52700 NE First, Scappoose, OR 97056-3212/503-543-5088; FAX: 503-543-5990

PC Co., 5942 Secor Rd., Toledo, OH 43623/419-472-6222

PCE, Ltd., Little Tree Ramble,P.O. Box 97, Monteagle, TN 37356/931-924-3475; FAX: 931-924-3489

Peacemaker Specialists, P.O. Box 157, Whitmore, CA 96096/916-472-3438

Pearce Grip, Inc., P.O. Box 187, Bothell, WA 98041-0187/206-485-5488; FAX:206-488-9497

Pease Accuracy, Bob, P.O. Box 310787, New Braunfels, TX 78131/210-625-1342

Pease International, 53 Durham St., Portsmouth, NH 03801/603-431-1331; FAX: 603-431-1221

PECAR Herbert Schwarz, GmbH, Kreuzbergstrasse 6, 10965 Berlin, GERMANY/004930-785-7383; FAX: 004930-785-1934

Pecatonica River Longrifle, 5205 Nottingham Dr., Rockford, IL 61111/815-968-1995; FAX: 815-968-1996

Pedersen, C.R., 2717 S. Pere Marquette Hwy., Ludington, MI 49431/616-843-2061

Pedersen, Rex C., 2717 S. Pere Marquette Hwy., Ludington, MI 49431/616-843-2061

Pedersoli and Co., Davide, Via Artigiani 57, Gardone V.T., Brescia, ITALY 25063/030-8912402; FAX: 030-8911019 (U.S. importers—Beauchamp & Son, Inc.; Cabela's; Cape Outfitters; Cimarron Arms; Dixie Gun Works; EMF Co., Inc.; Navy Arms Co.; Track of the Wolf, Inc.)

Peerless Alloy, Inc., 1445 Osage St., Denver, CO 80204-2439/303-825-6394, 800-253-1278

Peet Shoe Dryer, Inc., 130 S. 5th St., P.O. Box 618, St. Maries, ID 83861/208-245-2095, 800-222-PEET; FAX: 208-245-5441

Peifer Rifle Co., P.O. Box 192, Nokomis, IL 62075-0192/217-563-7050; FAX: 217-563-7060

Pejsa Ballistics, 2120 Kenwood Pkwy., Minneapolis, MN 55405/612-374-3337; FAX: 612-374-5383

Pelaire Products, 5346 Bonky Ct., W. Palm Beach, FL 33415/561-439-0691; FAX: 561-967-0052

Pell, John T. (See KOGOT)

Peltor, Inc. (See Aero Peltor)

PEM's Mfg. Co., 5063 Waterloo Rd., Atwater, OH 44201/216-947-3721

Pence Precision Barrels, 7567 E. 900 S., S. Whitley, IN 46787/219-839-4745

Pendleton Royal, c/o Swingler Buckland Ltd., 4/7 Highgate St., Birmingham, ENGLAND B12 0XS/44 121 440 3060, 44 121 446 5898; FAX: 44 121 446 4165

Pendleton Woolen Mills, P.O. Box 3030, 220 N.W. Broadway, Portland, OR 97208/503-226-4801

Penguin Industries, Inc., Airport Industrial Mall, Coatesville, PA 19320/610-384-6000; FAX: 610-857-5980

Penn Bullets, P.O. Box 756, Indianola, PA 15051

Penna Gunsmith School, 812 Ohio River Blvd., Pittsburgh, PA 15202-2699

Penna Gun Parts, 1701 Mud Run Rd., York Springs, PA 17372-8826/717-259-8010; FAX: 717-259-0057

Penn's Woods Products, Inc., 19 W. Pittsburgh St., Delmont, PA 15626/412-468-8311; FAX: 412-468-8975

Pennsylvania Gun Parts, 1701 Mud Run Rd., York Springs, PA 17372/717-259-8010; FAX: 717-259-0057

Pennsylvania Gunsmith School, 812 Ohio River Blvd., Avalon, Pittsburgh, PA 15202/412-766-1812

Penrod Precision, 312 College Ave., P.O. Box 307, N. Manchester, IN 46962/219-982-8385

Pentax Corp., 35 Inverness Dr. E., Englewood, CO 80112/800-709-2020; FAX: 303-643-0393

Pentheny de Pentheny, 2352 Baggett Ct., Santa Rosa, CA 95401/707-573-1390; FAX: 707-573-1390

Perazone-Gunsmith, Brian, Cold Spring Rd., Roxbury, NY 12474/607-326-4088; FAX: 607-326-3140

Perazzi m.a.p. S.p.A. (See Armi Perazzi S.p.A.)

Perazzi USA, Inc., 1207 S. Shamrock Ave., Monrovia, CA 91016/818-303-0068; FAX: 818-303-2081

Performance Specialists, 308 Eanes School Rd., Austin, TX 78746/512-327-0119

Peripheral Data Systems (See Arms Software)

Perugini Visini & Co. S.r.l., Via Camprelle, 126, 25080 Nuvolera (Bs.), ITALY

Peters Stahl GmbH, Stettiner Strasse 42, D-33106 Paderborn, GERMANY/05251-750025; FAX: 05251-755611 (U.S. importer—Franzen International, Inc.)

Petersen Publishing Co., 6420 Wilshire Blvd., Los Angeles, CA 90048/213-782-2000; FAX: 213-782-2867

Peterson Gun Shop, Inc., A.W., 4255 W. Old U.S. 441, Mt. Dora, FL 32757-3299/352-383-4258; FAX: 352-735-1001

Petro-Explo, Inc., 7650 U.S. Hwy. 287, Suite 100, Arlington, TX 76017/817-478-8888

Pettinger Books, Gerald, Rt. 2, Box 125, Russell, IA 50238/515-535-2239

Pflumm Mfg. Co., 10662 Widmer Rd., Lenexa, KS 66215/800-888-4867; FAX: 913-451-7857

PFRB Co., P.O. Box 1242, Bloomington, IL 61702/309-473-3964; FAX: 309-473-2161

Phil-Chem, Inc. (See George & Roy's)

Phillippi Custom Bullets, Justin, P.O. Box 773, Ligonier, PA 15658/412-238-9671

Phillips, Jerry, P.O. Box L632, Langhorne, PA 19047/215-757-5037

Phillips & Rodgers, Inc., 100 Hilbig, Suite C, Conroe, TX 77301/409-756-1001, 800-682-2247; FAX: 409-756-0976

Phoenix Arms, 1420 S. Archibald Ave., Ontario, CA 91761/909-947-4843; FAX: 909-947-6798

Photronic Systems Engineering Company, 6731 Via De La Reina, Bonsall, CA 92003/619-758-8000

Piedmont Community College, P.O. Box 1197, Roxboro, NC 27573/910-599-1181

Pierce Pistols, 55 Sorrellwood Lane, Sharpsburg, GA 30277-9523/404-253-8192

Pietta (See U.S. importers—Navy Arms Co.; Taylor's & Co., Inc.)

Pilgrim Pewter, Inc. (See Bell Originals Inc., Sid)

Pine Technical College, 1100 4th St., Pine City, MN 55063/800-521-7463; FAX: 612-629-6766

Pinetree Bullets, 133 Skeena St., Kitimat BC, CANADA V8C 1Z1/604-632-3768; FAX: 604-632-3768

Pioneer Arms Co., 355 Lawrence Rd., Broomall, PA 19008/215-356-5203

Pioneer Research, Inc., 216 Haddon Ave., Suite 102, Westmont, NJ 08108/800-257-7742; FAX: 609-858-8695

Piotti (See U.S. importer—Moore & Co., Wm. Larkin)

Piquette, Paul R., 80 Bradford Dr., Feeding Hills, MA 01030/413-781-8300, Ext. 682

Plaxco, J. Michael, Rt. 1, P.O. Box 203, Roland, AR 72135/501-868-9787

Plaza Cutlery, Inc., 3333 Bristol, 161, South Coast Plaza, Costa Mesa, CA 92626/714-549-3932

Plum City Ballistic Range, N2162 80th St., Plum City, WI 54761-8622/715-647-2539

PlumFire Press, Inc., 30-A Grove Ave., Patchogue, NY 11772-4112/800-695-7246; FAX:516-758-4071

PMC/Eldorado Cartridge Corp., P.O. Box 62508, 12801 U.S. Hwy. 95 S., Boulder City, NV 89005/702-294-0025; FAX: 702-294-0121

P.M. Enterprises, Inc., 146 Curtis Hill Rd., Chehalis, WA 98532/360-748-3743; FAX: 360-748-1802

Poburka, Philip (See Bison Studios)

Pohl, Henry A. (See Great American Gun Co.)

Pointing Dog Journal, Village Press Publications, P.O. Box 968, Dept. PGD, Traverse City, MI 49685/800-272-3246; FAX: 616-946-3289

Police Bookshelf, P.O. Box 122, Concord, NH 03301/603-224-6814; FAX: 603-226-3554

Polywad, Inc., P.O. Box 7916, Macon, GA 31209/912-477-0669

Pomeroy, Robert, RR1, Box 50, E. Corinth, ME 04427/207-285-7721

Ponsness/Warren, P.O. Box 8, Rathdrum, ID 83858-0008/208-687-2231; FAX: 208-687-2233

Pony Express Reloaders, 608 E. Co. Rd. D, Suite 3, St. Paul, MN 55117/612-483-9406; FAX: 612-483-9884

Pony Express Sport Shop, Inc., 16606 Schoenborn St., North Hills, CA 91343/818-895-1231

Potts, Wayne E., 912 Poplar St., Denver, CO 80220/303-355-5462

Powder Horn Antiques, P.O. Box 4196, Ft. Lauderdale, FL 33338/305-565-6060

Powder Horn, Inc., The, P.O. Box 114 Patty Drive, Cusseta, GA 31805/404-989-3257

Powell & Son (Gunmakers) Ltd., William, 35-37 Carrs Lane, Birmingham B4 7SX ENGLAND/121-643-0689; FAX: 121-631-3504 (U.S. importer—The William Powell Agency)

Powell Agency, William, The, 22 Circle Dr., Bellmore, NY 11710/516-679-1158

Power Custom, Inc., 29739 Hwy. J, Gravois Mills, MO 65037/513-372-5684; FAX: 573-372-5799

Powley Computer (See Hutton Rifle Ranch)

Practical Tools, Inc., Div. Behlert Precision, 7067 Easton Rd., P.O. Box 133, Pipersville, PA 18947/215-766-7301; FAX: 215-766-8681

Pragotrade, 307 Humberline Dr., Rexdale, Ontario, CANADA M9W 5V1/416-675-1322

Prairie River Arms, 1220 N. Sixth St., Princeton, IL 61356/815-875-1616, 800-445-1541; FAX: 815-875-1402

Pranger, Ed G., 1414 7th St., Anacortes, WA 98221/206-293-3488

Precise International, 15 Corporate Dr., Orangeburg, NY 10962/914-365-3500; FAX: 914-425-4700

Precise Metalsmithing Enterprises, 146 Curtis Hill Rd., Chehalis, WA 98532/206-748-3743; FAX: 206-748-8102

Precision Airgun Sales, Inc., 5139 Warrensville Center Rd., Maple Hts., OH 44137-1906/216-587-5005

Precision Cartridge, 176 Eastside Rd., Deer Lodge, MT 59722/800-397-3901, 406-846-3900

Precision Cast Bullets, 101 Mud Creek Lane, Ronan, MT 59864/406-676-5135

Precision Castings & Equipment, Inc., P.O. Box 326, Jasper, IN 47547-0135/812-634-9167

Precision Components, 3177 Sunrise Lake, Milford, PA 18337/717-686-4414

Precision Components and Guns, Rt. 55, P.O. Box 337, Pawling, NY 12564/914-855-3040

Precision Delta Corp., P.O. Box 128, Ruleville, MS 38771/601-756-2810; FAX: 601-756-2590

Precision Metal Finishing, John Westrom, P.O. Box 3186, Des Moines, IA 50316/515-288-8680; FAX: 515-244-3925

Precision Munitions, Inc., P.O. Box 326, Jasper, IN 47547

Precision Reloading, Inc., P.O. Box 122, Stafford Springs, CT 06076/860-684-7979; FAX: 860-684-6788

Precision Sales International, Inc., P.O. Box 1776, Westfield, MA 01086/413-562-5055; FAX: 413-562-5056

Precision Shooting, Inc., 222 McKee St., Manchester, CT 06040/860-645-8776; FAX: 860-643-8215

Precision Specialties, 131 Hendom Dr., Feeding Hills, MA 01030/413-786-3365; FAX: 413-786-3365

Precision Sport Optics, 15571 Producer Lane, Unit G, Huntington Beach, CA 92649/714-891-1309; FAX: 714-892-6920

Premier Reticles, 920 Breckinridge Lane, Winchester, VA 22601-6707/540-722-0601; FAX: 540-722-3522

Prescott Projectile Co., 1808 Meadowbrook Road, Prescott, AZ 86303

Preslik's Gunstocks, 4245 Keith Ln., Chico, CA 95926/916-891-8236

Pre-Winchester 92-90-62 Parts Co., P.O. Box 8125, W. Palm Beach, FL 33407

Price Bullets, Patrick W., 16520 Worthley Drive, San Lorenzo, CA 94580/510-278-1547

Prime Reloading, 30 Chiswick End, Meldreth, Royston SG8 6LZ UK/0763-260636

Primos, Inc., P.O. Box 12785, Jackson, MS 39236-2785/601-366-1288; FAX: 601-362-3274

PRL Bullets, c/o Blackburn Enterprises, 114 Stuart Rd., Ste. 110, Cleveland, TN 37312/423-559-0340

Pro Load Ammunition, Inc., 5180 E. Seltice Way, Post Falls, ID 83854/208-773-9444; FAX: 208-773-9441

Pro-Mark, Div. of Wells Lamont, 6640 W. Touhy, Chicago, IL 60648/312-647-8200

Pro-Port Ltd., 41302 Executive Dr., Harrison Twp., MI 48045-1306/810-469-7323; FAX: 810-469-0425

Pro-Shot Products, Inc., P.O. Box 763, Taylorville, IL 62568/217-824-9133; FAX: 217-824-8861

Professional Firearms Record Book Co. (See PFRB Co.)

Professional Gunsmiths of America, Inc., Route 1, Box 224F, Lexington, MO 64067/816-259-2636

Professional Hunter Supplies (See Star Custom Bullets)

Professional Ordnance, Inc., 1215 E. Airport Dr., Box 182, Ontario, CA 91761/909-923-5559; FAX: 909-923-0899

ProlixÆ Lubricants, P.O. Box 1348, Victorville, CA 92393/800-248-LUBE, 760-243-3129; FAX: 760-241-0148

Proofmark Corp., PO Box 610, Burgess, VA 22432-0610

Protecto Plastics, Div. of Penguin Ind., Airport Industrial Mall, Coatesville, PA 19320/215-384-6000

Protector Mfg. Co., Inc., The, 443 Ashwood Place, Boca Raton, FL 33431/407-394-6011

Protektor Model, 1-11 Bridge St., Galeton, PA 16922/814-435-2442

Prototech Industries, Inc., Rt. 1, Box 81, Delia, KS 66418/913-771-3571; FAX: 913-771-2531

P.S.M.G. Gun Co., 10 Park Ave., Arlington, MA 02174/617-646-8845; FAX: 617-646-2133

PWL Gunleather, P.O. Box 450432, Atlanta, GA 31145/770-822-1640; FAX: 770-822-1704

Pyramid, Inc., 3292 S. Highway 97, Redmond, OR 97756/503-548-1041; FAX: 503-923-1004

Q

Quack Decoy & Sporting Clays, 4 Ann & Hope Way, P.O. Box 98, Cumberland, RI 02864/401-723-8202; FAX: 401-722-5910

Quaker Boy, Inc., 5455 Webster Rd., Orchard Parks, NY 14127/716-662-3979; FAX: 716-662-9426

Quality Arms, Inc., Box 19477, Dept. GD, Houston, TX 77224/713-870-8377; FAX: 713-870-8524

Quality Firearms of Idaho, Inc., 659 Harmon Way, Middleton, ID 83644-3065/208-466-1631

Quality Parts Co./Bushmaster Firearms, 999 Roosevelt Trail, Bldg. 3, Windham, ME 04062/800-998-7928, 207-892-2005; FAX: 207-892-8068

Quarton USA, Co. Ltd., 7042 Alamo Downs Pkwy., Suite 370, San Antonio, TX 78238-4518/800-520-8435, 210-520-8430; FAX: 210-520-8433

Que Industries, Inc., P.O. Box 2471, Everett, WA 98203/800-769-6930, 206-347-9843; FAX: 206-514-3266

Queen Cutlery Co., P.O. Box 500, Franklinville, NY 14737/800-222-5233; FAX: 716-676-5535

Quigley's Personal Protection Strategies, Paxton, 9903 Santa Monica Blvd.,, 300/Beverly Hills, CA 90212/310-281-1762

R

R&C Knives & Such, P.O. Box 1047, Manteca, CA 95336/209-239-3722; FAX: 209-825-6947

R&J Gun Shop, 133 W. Main St., John Day, OR 97845/503-575-2130

R&S Industries Corp., 8255 Brentwood Industrial Dr., St. Louis, MO 63144/314-781-5400

Rabeno, Martin, 92 Spook Hole Rd., Ellenville, NY 12428/914-647-4567; FAX: 914-647-2129

Radack Photography, Lauren, 21140 Jib Court L-12, Aventura, FL 33180/305-931-3110

Radiator Specialty Co., 1900 Wilkinson Blvd., P.O. Box 34689, Charlotte, NC 28234/800-438-6947; FAX: 800-421-9525

Radical Concepts, P.O. Box 1473, Lake Grove, OR 97035/503-538-7437

Rainier Ballistics Corp., 4500 15th St. East, Tacoma, WA 98424/800-638-8722, 206-922-7589; FAX: 206-922-7854

Ram-Line Blount, Inc., P.O. Box 39, Onalaska, WI 54650-0039

Rampart International, 2781 W. MacArthur Blvd., #B-283, Santa Ana, CA 92704/800-976-7240, 714-557-6405

Ranch Products, P.O. Box 145, Malinta, OH 43535/313-277-3118; FAX: 313-565-8536

Randall-Made Knives, P.O. Box 1988, Orlando, FL 32802/407-855-8075

Randco UK, 286 Gipsy Rd., Welling, Kent DA16 1JJ, ENGLAND/44 81 303 4118

Randolph Engineering, Inc., 26 Thomas Patten Dr., Randolph, MA 02368/800-541-1405; FAX: 800-875-4200

Range Brass Products Company, P.O. Box 218, Rockport, TX 78381

Ranger Mfg. Co., Inc., 1536 Crescent Dr., P.O. Box 14069, Augusta, GA 30919-0069/706-738-2023; FAX: 404-738-3608

Ranger Products, 2623 Grand Blvd., Suite 209, Holiday, FL 34609/813-942-4652, 800-407-7007; FAX: 813-942-6221

Ranger Shooting Glasses, 26 Thomas Patten Dr., Randolph, MA 02368/800-541-1405; FAX: 617-986-0337

Ranging, Inc., Routes 5 & 20, East Bloomfield, NY 14443/716-657-6161; FAX: 716-657-5405

Ransom International Corp., P.O. Box 3845, 1040-A Sandretto Dr., Prescott, AZ 86302/520-778-7899; FAX: 520-778-7993; E-MAIL: ransom@primenet.com; WEB: http://www.primenet.com/òransom

Rapine Bullet Mould Mfg. Co., 9503 Landis Lane, East Greenville, PA 18041/215-679-5413; FAX: 215-679-9795

Raptor Arms Co., Inc., 115 S. Union St., Suite 308, Alexandria, VA 22314/703-683-0018; FAX: 703-683-5592

Rattlers Brand, P.O. Box 311, 115 E. Main St., Thomaston, GA 30286/706-647-7131, 800-825-7131; FAX: 706-646-5090

Ravell Ltd., 289 Diputacion St., 08009, Barcelona SPAIN/34(3) 4874486; FAX: 34(3) 4881394

Ray's Gunsmith Shop, 3199 Elm Ave., Grand Junction, CO 81504/970-434-6162; FAX: 970-434-6162

Raytech, Div. of Lyman Products Corp., 475 Smith Street, Middletown, CT 06457-1541/860-632-2020; FAX: 860-632-1699

RCBS, Div. of Blount, Inc., Sporting Equipment Div., 605 Oro Dam Blvd., Oroville, CA 95965/800-533-5000, 916-533-5191; FAX: 916-533-1647

Reagent Chemical & Research, Inc. (See Calico Hardwoods, Inc.)

Reardon Products, P.O. Box 126, Morrison, IL 61270/815-772-3155

Recoilless Technologies, Inc., 3432 W. Wilshire Dr., Suite 11, Phoenix, AZ 85009/602-278-8903; FAX: 602-272-5946

Red Ball, 100 Factory St., Nashua, NH 03060/603-881-4420

Red Cedar Precision Mfg., W. 485 Spruce Dr., Brodhead, WI 53520/608-897-8416

Red Diamond Dist. Co., 1304 Snowdon Dr., Knoxville, TN 37912

Redding Reloading Equipment, 1089 Starr Rd., Cortland, NY 13045/607-753-3331; FAX: 607-756-8445

Redfield, Inc., 5800 E. Jewell Ave., Denver, CO 80224/303-757-6411; FAX: 303-756-2338

Redman's Rifling & Reboring, 189 Nichols Rd., Omak, WA 98841/509-826-5512

Redwood Bullet Works, 3559 Bay Rd., Redwood City, CA 94063/415-367-6741

Reed, Dave, Rt. 1, Box 374, Minnesota City, MN 55959/507-689-2944

Refrigiwear, Inc., 71 Inip Dr., Inwood, Long Island, NY 11696

R.E.I., P.O. Box 88, Tallevast, FL 34270/813-755-0085

Reiswig, Wallace E. (See Claro Walnut Gunstock Co.)

Reloaders Equipment Co., 4680 High St., Ecorse, MI 48229

Reloading Specialties, Inc., Box 1130, Pine Island, MN 55463/507-356-8500; FAX: 507-356-8800

Remington Arms Co., Inc., 870 Remington Drive, P.O. Box 700, Madison, NC 27025-0700/800-243-9700; 910-548-8700

Remington Double Shotguns, 7885 Cyd Dr., Denver, CO 80221/303-429-6947

Renegade, P.O. Box 31546, Phoenix, AZ 85046/602-482-6777; FAX: 602-482-1952

Renfrew Guns & Supplies, R.R. 4, Renfrew, Ontario K7V 3Z7 CANADA/613-432-7080

Reno, Wayne, 2808 Stagestop Rd., Jefferson, CO 80456/719-836-3452

Republic Arms, Inc., 15167 Sierra Bonita Lane, Chino, CA 91710/909-597-3873; FAX:909-393-9771

R.E.T. Enterprises, 2608 S. Chestnut, Broken Arrow, OK 74012/918-251-GUNS; FAX: 918-251-0587

Retting, Inc., Martin B., 11029 Washington, Culver City, CA 90232/213-837-2412

R.F.D. Rifles, 8230 Wilson Dr., Ralston, NE 68127/402-331-9529

R.G.-G., Inc., P.O. Box 1261, Conifer, CO 80433-1261/303-697-4154; FAX: 303-697-4154

Rhino, P.O. Box 787, Locust, NC 28097/704-753-2198

Rhodeside, Inc., 1704 Commerce Dr., Piqua, OH 45356/513-773-5781

Rice, Keith (See White Rock Tool & Die)

Richards, John, Richards Classic Oil Finish, Rt. 2, Box 325, Bedford, KY 40006/502-255-7222

Richards Micro-Fit Stocks, 8331 N. San Fernando Ave., Sun Valley, CA 91352/818-767-6097; FAX: 818-767-7121

Rickard, Inc., Pete, RD 1, Box 292, Cobleskill, NY 12043/800-282-5663; FAX: 518-234-2454

Ridgetop Sporting Goods, P.O. Box 306, 42907 Hilligoss Ln. East, Eatonville, WA 98328/360-832-6422; FAX: 360-832-6422

Riebe Co., W.J., 3434 Tucker Rd., Boise, ID 83703

Ries, Chuck, 415 Ridgecrest Dr., Grants Pass, OR 97527/503-476-5623

Rifle Works & Armory, 707 12th St., Cody, WY 82414/307-587-4919

Rifles Inc., 873 W. 5400 N., Cedar City, UT 84720/801-586-5996; FAX: 801-586-5996

RIG Products, 87 Coney Island Dr., Sparks, NV 89431-6334/702-331-5666; FAX: 702-331-5669

Rigby & Co., John, 66 Great Suffolk St., London SE1 0BU, ENGLAND/0171-620-0690; FAX: 0171-928-9205

Riggs, Jim, 206 Azalea, Boerne, TX 78006/210-249-8567

Riling Arms Books Co., Ray, 6844 Gorsten St., P.O. Box 18925, Philadelphia, PA 19119/215-438-2456; FAX: 215-438-5395

Rim Pac Sports, Inc., 1034 N. Soldano Ave., Azusa, CA 91702-2135

Ringler Custom Leather Co., 31 Shining Mtn. Rd., Powell, WY 82435/307-645-3255

Ripley Rifles, 42 Fletcher Street, Ripley, Derbyshire, DE5 3LP ENGLAND/011-0773-748353

R.I.S. Co., Inc., 718 Timberlake Circle, Richardson, TX 75080/214-235-0933

River Road Sporting Clays, Bruce Barsotti, P.O. Box 3016, Gonzales, CA 93926/408-675-2473

Rizzini, Battista, Via 2 Giugno, 7/7Bis-25060 Marcheno (Brescia), ITALY/ (U.S. importers—Wm. Larkin Moore & Co.; New England Arms Co.)

Rizzini F.lli (See U.S. importers—Moore & CEngland Arms Co.)

RLCM Enterprises, 110 Hill Crest Drive, Burleson, TX 76028\

R.M. Precision, Inc., Attn. Greg F. Smith Marketing, P.O. Box 210, LaVerkin, UT 84745/801-635-4656; FAX: 801-635-4430

RMS Custom Gunsmithing, 4120 N. Bitterwell, Prescott Valley, AZ 86314/520-772-7626

Robar Co.'s, Inc., The, 21438 N. 7th Ave., Suite B, Phoenix, AZ 85027/602-581-2648; FAX: 602-582-0059

Roberts/Engraver, J.J., 7808 Lake Dr., Manassas, VA 22111/703-330-0448

Roberts Products, 25328 SE Iss. Beaver Lk. Rd., Issaquah, WA 98029/206-392-8172

Robinett, R.G., P.O. Box 72, Madrid, IA 50156/515-795-2906

Robinson, Don, Pennsylvania Hse., 36 Fairfax Crescent, Southowram, Halifax, W. Yorkshire HX3 9SQ, ENGLAND/0422-364458

Robinson Firearms Mfg. Ltd., 1699 Blondeaux Crescent, Kelowna, B.C. CANADA V1Y 4J8/604-868-9596

Robinson H.V. Bullets, 3145 Church St., Zachary, LA 70791/504-654-4029

Rochester Lead Works, 76 Anderson Ave., Rochester, NY 14607/716-442-8500; FAX: 716-442-4712

Rockwood Corp., Speedwell Division, 136 Lincoln Blvd., Middlesex, NJ 08846/908-560-7171, 800-243-8274; FAX: 980-560-7475

Rocky Mountain Arms, Inc., 1813 Sunset Place, Unit D, Longmont, CO 80501/800-375-0846; FAX: 303-678-8766

Rocky Mountain High Sports Glasses, 8121 N. Central Park Ave., Skokie, IL 60076/847-679-1012, 800-323-1418; FAX: 847-679-0184

Rocky Mountain Rifle Works Ltd., 1707 14th St., Boulder, CO 80302/303-443-9189

Rocky Mountain Target Co., 3 Aloe Way, Leesburg, FL 34788/352-365-9598

Rocky Mountain Wildlife Products, P.O. Box 999, La Porte, CO 80535/970-484-2768; FAX: 970-484-0807

Rocky Shoes & Boots, 294 Harper St., Nelsonville, OH 45764/800-848-9452, 614-753-1951; FAX: 614-753-4024

Rodgers & Sons Ltd., Joseph (See George Ibberson (Sheffield) Ltd.)

Rogers Gunsmithing, Bob, P.O. Box 305, 344 S. Walnut St., Franklin Grove, IL 61031/815-456-2685; FAX: 815-288-7142

Rogue Rifle Co., Inc., P.O. Box 20, Prospect, OR 97536/541-560-4040; FAX: 541-560-4041

Rogue River Rifleworks, 1317 Spring St., Paso Robles, CA 93446/805-227-4706; FAX: 805-227-4723

Rohner, Hans, 1148 Twin Sisters Ranch Rd., Nederland, CO 80466-9600

Rohner, John, 710 Sunshine Canyon, Boulder, CO 80302/303-444-3841

Rolston, Fred W., Inc., 210 E. Cummins St., Tecumseh, MI 49286/517-423-6002, 800-314-9061 (orders only); FAX: 517-423-6002

Romain's Custom Guns, Inc., RD 1, Whetstone Rd., Brockport, PA 15823/814-265-1948

Rooster Laboratories, P.O. Box 412514, Kansas City, MO 64141/816-474-1622; FAX: 816-474-1307

Rorschach Precision Products, P.O. Box 151613, Irving, TX 75015/214-790-3487

Rosenberg & Sons, Jack A., 12229 Cox Ln., Dallas, TX 75234/214-241-6302

Rosenthal, Brad and Sallie, 19303 Ossenfort Ct., St. Louis, MO 63038/314-273-5159; FAX: 314-273-5149

Ross & Webb (See Ross, Don)

Ross, Don, 12813 West 83 Terrace, Lenexa, KS 66215/913-492-6982

Rosser, Bob, 1824 29th Ave., Suite 214, Birmingham, AL 35209/205-870-4422; FAX: 205-870-4421

Rossi S.A., Amadeo, Rua: Amadeo Rossi, 143, Sao Leopoldo, RS, BRAZIL 93030-220/051-592-5566 (U.S. importer—Interarms)

Roto Carve, 2754 Garden Ave., Janesville, IA 50647

Round Edge, Inc., P.O. Box 723, Lansdale, PA 19446/215-361-0859

Rowe Engineering, Inc. (See R.E.I.)

Royal Arms Gunstocks, 919 8th Ave. NW, Great Falls, MT 59404/406-453-1149

Roy's Custom Grips, Rt. 3, Box 174-E, Lynchburg, VA 24504/804-993-3470

RPM, 15481 N. Twin Lakes Dr., Tucson, AZ 85739/520-825-1233; FAX: 520-825-3333

Rubright Bullets, 1008 S. Quince Rd., Walnutport, PA 18088/215-767-1339

Rucker Dist. Inc., P.O. Box 479, Terrell, TX 75160/214-563-2094

Rudnicky, Susan, 9 Water St., Arcade, NY 14009/716-492-2450

Ruger (See Sturm, Ruger & Co., Inc.)

Rundell's Gun Shop, 6198 Frances Rd., Clio, MI 48420/313-687-0559

Robert P. Runge, 94 Grove St., Ilion, NY 13357/315-894-3036

Rumanya, Inc., 4994-D Hwy. 6N, Ste. 101, Houston, TX 77084/281-345-2077; FAX: 281-345-2005

Rupert's Gun Shop, 2202 Dick Rd., Suite B, Fenwick, MI 48834/517-248-3252

Russ Trading Post, 23 William St., Addison, NY 14801-1326/607-359-3896

Russell Knives, Inc., A.G., 1705 Hwy. 71B North, Springdale, AR 72764/501-751-7341

Rusteprufe Laboratories, 1319 Jefferson Ave., Sparta, WI 54656/608-269-4144

Rusty Duck Premium Gun Care Products, 7785 Foundation Dr., Suite 6, Florence, KY 41042/606-342-5553; FAX: 606-342-5556

Rutgers Book Center, 127 Raritan Ave., Highland Park, NJ 08904/908-545-4344; FAX: 908-545-6686

Rutten (See U.S. importer—Labanu, Inc.)

Ruvel & Co., Inc., 4128-30 W. Belmont Ave., Chicago, IL 60641/773-286-9494; FAX: 773-286-9323

RWS (See U.S. importer—Dynamit Nobel-RWS, Inc.)

Ryan, Chad L., RR 3, Box 72, Cresco, IA 52136/319-547-4384

Rybka Custom Leather Equipment, Thad, 134 Havilah Hill, Odenville, AL 35120

S

S&B Industries, 11238 McKinley Rd., Montrose, MI 48457/810-639-5491

S&K Mfg. Co., P.O. Box 247, Pittsfield, PA 16340/814-563-7808; FAX: 814-563-4067

S&S Firearms, 74-11 Myrtle Ave., Glendale, NY 11385/718-497-1100; FAX: 718-497-1105

Sabatti S.r.l., via Alessandro Volta 90, 25063 Gardone V.T., Brescia, ITALY/030-8912207-831312; FAX: 030-8912059 (U.S. importer—E.A.A. Corp.)

SAECO (See Redding Reloading Equipment)

Saf-T-Lok, 5713 Corporate Way, Suite 100, W. Palm Beach, FL 33407

Safari Outfitters Ltd., 71 Ethan Allan Hwy., Ridgefield, CT 06877/203-544-9505

Safari Press, Inc., 15621 Chemical Lane B, Huntington Beach, CA 92649/714-894-9080; FAX: 714-894-4949

Safariland Ltd., Inc., 3120 E. Mission Blvd., P.O. Box 51478, Ontario, CA 91761/909-923-7300; FAX: 909-923-7400

SAFE, P.O. Box 864, Post Falls, ID 83854/208-773-3624

Safeguard Ordnance Systems Inc., P.O. Box 2028, Eaton Park, FL 33840/941-682-2829; FAX: 941-682-2829

Safety Speed Holster, Inc., 910 S. Vail Ave., Montebello, CA 90640/213-723-4140; FAX: 213-726-6973

Sako Ltd. (See U.S. importer—Stoeger Industries)

Salter Calls, Inc., Eddie, Hwy. 31 South-Brewton Industrial Park, Brewton, AL 36426/205-867-2584; FAX: 206-867-9005

Samco Global Arms, Inc., 6995 NW 43rd St., Miami, FL 33166/305-593-9782

Sampson, Roger, 2316 Mahogany St., Mora, MN 55051/320-679-4868

San Francisco Gun Exchange, 124 Second St., San Francisco, CA 94105/415-982-6097

San Marco (See U.S. importers—Cape Outfitters; EMF Co., Inc.)

Sanders Custom Gun Service, 2358 Tyler Lane, Louisville, KY 40205/502-454-3338; FAX: 502-451-8857

Sanders Gun and Machine Shop, 145 Delhi Road, Manchester, IA 52057

Sandia Die & Cartridge Co., 37 Atancacio Rd. NE, Albuquerque, NM 87123/505-298-5729

Sarco, Inc., 323 Union St., Stirling, NJ, Stirling, NJ 07980/908-647-3800; FAX: 908-647-9413

S.A.R.L. G. Granger, 66 cours Fauriel, 42100 Saint Etienne, FRANCE/04 77 25 14 73; FAX: 04 77 38 66 99

Sauer (See U.S. importers—Paul Co., The; Sigarms, Inc.)

Saunders Gun & Machine Shop, R.R. 2, Delhi Road, Manchester, IA 52057

Savage Arms, Inc., 100 Springdale Rd., Westfield, MA 01085/413-568-7001; FAX: 413-562-7764

Savage Arms (Canada), Inc., 248 Water St., P.O. Box 1240, Lakefield, Ont. K0L 2H0, CANADA/705-652-8000; FAX: 705-652-8431

Savage Range Systems, Inc., 100 Springdale RD., Westfield, MA 01085/413-568-7001; FAX: 413-562-1152

Saville Iron Co. (See Greenwood Precision)

Savino, Barbara J., P.O. Box 1104, Hardwick, VT 05843-1104

Scanco Environmental Systems, 5000 Highlands Parkway, Suite 180, Atlanta, GA 30082/770-431-0025; FAX: 770-431-0028

Scansport, Inc., P.O. Box 700, Enfield, NH 03748/603-632-7654

Scattergun Technologies, Inc., 620 8th Ave. S., Nashville, TN 37203/615-254-1441; FAX: 615-254-1449

Sceery Game Calls, P.O. Box 6520, Sante Fe, NM 87502/505-471-9110; FAX: 505-471-3476

Schaefer Shooting Sports, P.O. Box 1515, Melville, NY 11747-0515/516-379-4900; FAX: 516-379-6701

Scharch Mfg., Inc., 10325 CR 120, Salida, CO 81201/719-539-7242, 800-836-4683; FAX: 719-539-3021

Scherer, Box 250, Ewing, VA 24240/615-733-2615; FAX: 615-733-2073

Schiffman, Curt, 3017 Kevin Cr., Idaho Falls, ID 83402/208-524-4684

Schiffman, Mike, 8233 S. Crystal Springs, McCammon, ID 83250/208-254-9114

Schiffman, Norman, 3017 Kevin Cr., Idaho Falls, ID 83402/208-524-4684

Schmidtke Group, 17050 W. Salentine Dr., New Berlin, WI 53151-7349

Schmidt & Bender, Inc., Brook Rd., P.O. Box 134, Meriden, NH 03770/603-469-3565, 800-468-3450; FAX: 603-469-3471

Schmidtman Custom Ammunition, 6 Gilbert Court, Cotati, CA 94931

Schneider Bullets, 3655 West 214th St., Fairview Park, OH 44126

Schneider Rifle Barrels, Inc., Gary, 12202 N. 62nd Pl., Scottsdale, AZ 85254/602-948-2525

School of Gunsmithing, The, 6065 Roswell Rd., Atlanta, GA 30328/800-223-4542

Schrimsher's Custom Knifemaker's Supply, Bob, P.O. Box 308, Emory, TX 75440/903-473-3330; FAX: 903-473-2235

Schroeder Bullets, 1421 Thermal Ave., San Diego, CA 92154/619-423-3523; FAX: 619-423-8124

Schuetzen Pistol Works, 620-626 Old Pacific Hwy. SE, Olympia, WA 98513/360-459-3471; FAX: 360-491-3447

Schulz Industries, 16247 Minnesota Ave., Paramount, CA 90723/213-439-5903

Schumakers Gun Shop, 512 Prouty Corner Lp. A, Colville, WA 99114/509-684-4848

Schwartz Custom Guns, David W., 2505 Waller St., Eau Claire, WI 54703/715-832-1735

Schwartz Custom Guns, Wayne E., 970 E. Britton Rd., Morrice, MI 48857/517-625-4079

Scobey Duck & Goose Calls, Glynn, Rt. 3, Box 37, Newbern, TN 38059/901-643-6241

Scope Control, Inc., 5775 Co. Rd. 23 SE, Alexandria, MN 56308/612-762-7295

ScopLevel, 151 Lindbergh Ave., Suite C, Livermore, CA 94550/925-449-5052; FAX: 925-373-0861

Score High Gunsmithing, 9812-A, Cochiti SE, Albuquerque, NM 87123/800-326-5632, 505-292-5532; FAX: 505-292-2592; E-MAIL: scorehi@rt66.com; WEB: http://rt66.com/òscorehi/home.htm

Scot Powder, Rt.1 Box 167, McEwen, TN 37101/800-416-3006; FAX: 615-729-4211

Scot Powder Co. of Ohio, Inc., Box GD96, Only, TN 37140/615-729-4207, 800-416-3006; FAX: 615-729-4217

Scott Fine Guns, Inc., Thad, P.O. Box 412, Indianola, MS 38751/601-887-5929

Scott, McDougall & Associates, 7950 Redwood Dr., Cotati, CA 94931/707-546-2264; FAX: 707-795-1911

Scott, Dwight, 23089 Englehardt St., Clair Shores, MI 48080/313-779-4735

S.C.R.C., P.O. Box 660, Katy, TX 77492-0660/FAX: 713-578-2124

Scruggs' Game Calls, Stanley, Rt. 1, Hwy. 661, Cullen, VA 23934/804-542-4241, 800-323-4828

Second Chance Body Armor, P.O. Box 578, Central Lake, MI 49622/616-544-5721; FAX: 616-544-9824

Security Awareness & Firearms Education (See SAFE)

Seebeck Assoc., R.E., P.O. Box 59752, Dallas, TX 75229

Seecamp Co., Inc., L.W., P.O. Box 255, New Haven, CT 06502/203-877-3429

Segway Industries, P.O. Box 783, Suffern, NY 10901-0783/914-357-5510

Seligman Shooting Products, Box 133, Seligman, AZ 86337/602-422-3607

Selsi Co., Inc., P.O. Box 10, Midland Park, NJ 07432-0010/201-935-0388; FAX: 201-935-5851

Semmer, Charles (See Remington Double Shotguns)

Sentinel Arms, P.O. Box 57, Detroit, MI 48231/313-331-1951; FAX: 313-331-1456

Serva Arms Co., Inc., RD 1, Box 483A, Greene, NY 13778/607-656-4764

Service Armament, 689 Bergen Blvd., Ridgefield, NJ 07657

Servus Footwear Co., 1136 2nd St., Rock Island, IL 61204-3610/309-786-7741; FAX: 309-786-9808

S.G.S. Sporting Guns Srl., Via Della Resistenza, 37, 20090 Buccinasco (MI) ITALY/2-45702446; FAX: 2-45702464

Shanghai Airguns, Ltd. (U.S. importer—Sportsman Airguns, Inc.)

Shappy Bullets, 76 Milldale Ave., Plantsville, CT 06479/203-621-3704

Shaw, Inc., E.R. (See Small Arms Mfg. Co.)

Sharp Shooter Supply, 4970 Lehman Road, Delphos, OH 45833/419-695-3179

C. Sharps Arms Co. Inc., 100 Centennial, Box 885, Big Timber, MT 59011/406-932-4353

Shay's Gunsmithing, 931 Marvin Ave., Lebanon, PA 17042

Sheffield Knifemakers Supply, Inc., P.O. Box 741107, Orange City, FL 32774-1107/904-775-6453; FAX: 904-774-5754

Shell Shack, 113 E. Main, Laurel, MT 59044/406-628-8986

Shepherd & Turpin Distributing Co., P.O. Box 40, Washington, UT 84780/801-635-2001

Shepherd Scope Ltd., Box 189, Waterloo, NE 68069/402-779-2424; FAX: 402-779-4010

Sheridan USA, Inc., Austin, P.O. Box 577, 36 Haddam Quarter Rd., Durham, CT 06422/203-349-1772; FAX: 203-349-1771

Sherwood, George, 46 N. River Dr., Roseburg, OR 97470/541-672-3159

Shilen, Inc., 205 Metro Park Blvd., Ennis, TX 75119/972-875-5318; FAX: 972-875-5402

Shiloh Creek, Box 357, Cottleville, MO 63338/314-925-1842; FAX: 314-925-1842

Shiloh Rifle Mfg., 201 Centennial Dr., Big Timber, MT 59011/406-932-4454; FAX: 406-932-5627

Shockley, Harold H., 204 E. Farmington Rd., Hanna City, IL 61536/309-565-4524

Shoemaker & Sons, Inc., Tex, 714 W. Cienega Ave., San Dimas, CA 91773/909-592-2071; FAX: 909-592-2378

Shooten' Haus, The, 102 W. 13th, Kearney, NE 68847/308-236-7929

Shooter's Choice, 16770 Hilltop Park Place, Chagrin Falls, OH 44023/216-543-8808; FAX: 216-543-8811

Shooter's Edge, Inc., P.O.Box 769, Trinidad, CO 81082

Shooter's World, 3828 N. 28th Ave., Phoenix, AZ 85017/602-266-0170

Shooters Supply, 1120 Tieton Dr., Yakima, WA 98902/509-452-1181

Shootin' Accessories, Ltd., P.O. Box 6810, Auburn, CA 95604/916-889-2220

Shootin' Shack, Inc., 1065 Silver Beach Rd., Riviera Beach, FL 33403/561-842-0990

Shooting Chrony, Inc., 3269 Niagara Falls Blvd., N. Tonawanda, NY 14120/905-276-6292; FAX: 416-276-6295

Shooting Gallery, The, 8070 Southern Blvd., Boardman, OH 44512/216-726-7788

Shooting Specialties (See Titus, Daniel)

Shooting Star, 1825 Fortview Rd., Ste. 115, Austin, TX 78747/512-462-0009

Shoot-N-C Targets (See Birchwood Casey)

Shotguns Unlimited, 2307 Fon Du Lac Rd., Richmond, VA 23229/804-752-7115

ShurKatch Corporation, 50 Elm St., Richfield Springs, NY 13439/315-858-1470; FAX: 315-858-2969

S.I.A.C.E. (See U.S. importer—IAR, Inc.)

Siegrist Gun Shop, 8754 Turtle Road, Whittemore, MI 48770

Sierra Bullets, 1400 W. Henry St., Sedalia, MO 65301/816-827-6300; FAX: 816-827-6300; WEB: http://www.sierrabullets.com

Sierra Specialty Prod. Co., 1344 Oakhurst Ave., Los Altos, CA 94024/FAX: 415-965-1536

SIG, CH-8212 Neuhausen, SWITZERLAND/ (U.S. importer—Mandall Shooting Supplies, Inc.)

Sigarms, Inc., Corporate Park, Exeter, NH 03833/603-772-2302; FAX: 603-772-9082

SIG-Sauer (See U.S. importer—Sigarms, Inc.)

Sight Shop, The, John G. Lawson, 1802 E. Columbia Ave., Tacoma, WA 98404/206-474-5465

Sightron, Inc., 1672B Hwy. 96, Franklinton, NC 27525/919-528-8783; FAX: 919-528-0995

Signet Metal Corp., 551 Stewart Ave., Brooklyn, NY 11222/718-384-5400; FAX: 718-388-7488

Sile Distributors, Inc., 7 Centre Market Pl., New York, NY 10013/212-925-4111; FAX: 212-925-3149

Silencio/Safety Direct, 56 Coney Island Dr., Sparks, NV 89431/800-648-1812, 702-354-4451; FAX: 702-359-1074

Silent Hunter, 1100 Newton Ave., W. Collingswood, NJ 08107/609-854-3276

Silhouette Leathers, P.O. Box 1161, Gunnison, CO 81230/303-641-6639

Silver Eagle Machining, 18007 N. 69th Ave., Glendale, AZ 85308

Silver Ridge Gun Shop (See Goodwin, Fred)

Simmons, Jerry, 715 Middlebury St., Goshen, IN 46526/219-533-8546

Simmons Enterprises, Ernie, 709 East Elizabethtown Rd., Manheim, PA 17545/717-664-4040

Simmons Gun Repair, Inc., 700 S. Rogers Rd., Olathe, KS 66062/913-782-3131; FAX: 913-782-4189

Simmons Outdoor Corp., 201 Plantation Oak Parkway, Thomasville, GA 31792/912-227-9053; FAX: 912-227-9054

Sinclair International, Inc., 2330 Wayne Haven St., Fort Wayne, IN 46803/219-493-1858; FAX: 219-493-2530

Singletary, Kent, 2915 W. Ross, Phoenix, AZ 85027/602-582-4900

Sipes Gun Shop, 7415 Asher Ave., Little Rock, AR 72204/501-565-8480

Siskiyou Gun Works (See Donnelly, C.P.)

Six Enterprises, 320-D Turtle Creek Ct., San Jose, CA 95125/408-999-0201; FAX: 408-999-0216

SKAN A.R., 4 St. Catherines Road, Long Melford, Suffolk, CO10 9JU ENGLAND/011-0787-312942

SKB Arms Co. (See New SKB Arms Co.)

SKB Shotguns, 4325 S. 120th St., P.O. Box 37669, Omaha, NE 68137/800-752-2767; FAX: 402-330-8029

Skeoch Gunmaker, Brian R., P.O. Box 279, Glenrock, WY 82637/307-436-9655

Skip's Machine, 364 29 Road, Grand Junction, CO 81501/303-245-5417

Sklany's Machine Shop, 566 Birch Grove Dr., Kalispell, MT 59901/406-755-4257

S.L.A.P. Industries, P.O. Box 1121, Parklands 2121, SOUTH AFRICA/27-11-788-0030; FAX: 27-11-788-0030

Slezak, Jerome F., 1290 Marlowe, Lakewood (Cleveland), OH 44107/216-221-1668

Slings 'N Things, Inc., 8909 Bedford Circle, Suite 11, Omaha, NE 68134/402-571-6954; FAX: 402-571-7082

Slug Group, Inc., P.O. Box 376, New Paris, PA 15554/814-839-4517; FAX: 814-839-2601

Slug Site, Ozark Wilds, 21300 Hwy 5, Versailles, MO 65084/573-378-6430

Small Arms Mfg. Co., 5312 Thoms Run Rd., Bridgeville, PA 15017/412-221-4343; FAX: 412-221-4303

Small Arms Review, 223 Sugar Hill Rd., Harmony, ME 04942

Small Arms Specialties, 29 Bernice Ave., Leominster, MA 01453/800-635-9290

Small Custom Mould & Bullet Co., Box 17211, Tucson, AZ 85731

Smart Parts, 1203 Spring St., Latrobe, PA 15650/412-539-2660; FAX: 412-539-2298

Smires, C.L., 5222 Windmill Lane, Columbia, MD 21044-1328

Smith & Wesson, 2100 Roosevelt Ave., Springfield, MA 01102/413-781-8300; FAX: 413-731-8980

Smith, Art, 230 Main St. S., Hector, MN 55342/320-848-2760; FAX: 320-848-2760

Smith, Mark A., P.O. Box 182, Sinclair, WY 82334/307-324-7929

Smith, Michael, 620 Nye Circle, Chattanooga, TN 37405/615-267-8341

Smith, Ron, 5869 Straley, Ft. Worth, TX 76114/817-732-6768

Smith, Sharmon, 4545 Speas Rd., Fruitland, ID 83619/208-452-6329

Smith Abrasives, Inc., 1700 Sleepy Valley Rd., P.O. Box 5095, Hot Springs, AR 71902-5095/501-321-2244; FAX: 501-321-9232

Smith Saddlery, Jesse W., 16909 E. Jackson Road, Elk, WA 99009-9600/509-325-0622

Smokey Valley Rifles (See Lutz Engraving, Ron E.)

Snapp's Gunshop, 6911 E. Washington Rd., Clare, MI 48617/517-386-9226

Sno-Seal (See Atsko/Sno-Seal)

Societa Armi Bresciane Srl. (See U.S. importer—Cape Outfitters; Gamba, USA)

Soque River Knives, P.O. Box 880, Clarkesville, GA 30523/706-754-8500; FAX: 706-754-7263

SOS Products Co. (See Buck Stix—SOS Products Co.)

Sotheby's, 1334 York Ave. at 72nd St., New York, NY 10021/212-606-7260

Sound Technology, Box 391, Pelham, AL 35124/205-664-5860; Summer phone: 907-486-2825

South Bend Replicas, Inc., 61650 Oak Rd., South Bend, IN 46614/219-289-4500

Southeastern Community College, 1015 S. Gear Ave., West Burlington, IA 52655/319-752-2731

Southern Ammunition Co., Inc., 4232 Meadow St., Loris, SC 29569-3124/803-756-3262; FAX: 803-756-3583

Southern Armory, The, 25 Millstone Road, Woodlawn, VA 24381/703-238-1343; FAX: 703-238-1453

Southern Bloomer Mfg. Co., P.O. Box 1621, Bristol, TN 37620/615-878-6660; FAX: 615-878-8761

Southern Security, 1700 Oak Hills Dr., Kingston, TN 37763/800-251-9992

Southwind Sanctions, P.O. Box 445, Aledo, TX 76008/817-441-8917

Sparks, Milt, 605 E. 44th St. No. 2, Boise, ID 83714-4800

Spartan-Realtree Products, Inc., 1390 Box Circle, Columbus, GA 31907/706-569-9101; FAX: 706-569-0042

Specialty Gunsmithing, Lynn McMurdo, P.O. Box 404, Afton, WY 83110/307-886-5535

Specialty Shooters Supply, Inc., 3325 Griffin Rd., Suite 9mm, Fort Lauderdale, FL 33317

Speer Products, Div. of Blount, Inc., Sporting Equipment Div., P.O. Box 856, Lewiston, ID 83501/208-746-2351; FAX: 208-746-2915

Spegel, Craig, P.O. Box 3108, Bay City, OR 97107/503-377-2697

Speiser, Fred D., 2229 Dearborn, Missoula, MT 59801/406-549-8133

Spence, George W., 115 Locust St., Steele, MO 63877/314-695-4926

Spencer Reblue Service, 1820 Tupelo Trail, Holt, MI 48842/517-694-7474

Spencer's Custom Guns, Rt. 1, Box 546, Scottsville, VA 24590/804-293-6836

Spezial Waffen (See U.S. importer—American Bullets)

SPG, Inc., P.O. Box 1625, Cody, WY 82414/307-587-7621; FAX: 307-587-7695

Sphinx Engineering SA, Ch. des Grandes-Vies 2, CH-2900 Porrentruy, SWITZERLAND/41 66 66 73 81; FAX: 41 66 66 30 90 (U.S. importer—Sphinx USA Inc.)

Sphinx USA Inc., 998 N. Colony, Meriden, CT 06450/203-238-1399; FAX: 203-238-1375

Spokhandguns, Inc., 1206 Fig St., Benton City, WA 99320/509-588-5255

Sport Flite Manufacturing Co., P.O. Box 1082, Bloomfield Hills, MI 48303-1082/248-647-3747

Sporting Arms Mfg., Inc., 801 Hall Ave., Littlefield, TX 79339/806-385-5665; FAX: 806-385-3394

Sports Innovations, Inc., P.O. Box 5181, 8505 Jacksboro Hwy., Wichita Falls, TX 76307/817-723-6015

Sportsman Safe Mfg. Co., 6309-6311 Paramount Blvd., Long Beach, CA 90805/800-266-7150, 310-984-5445

Sportsman Supply Co., 714 East Eastwood, P.O. Box 650, Marshall, MO 65340/816-886-9393

Sportsman's Communicators, 588 Radcliffe Ave., Pacific Palisades, CA 90272/800-538-3752

Sportsmatch U.K. Ltd., 16 Summer St., Leighton Buzzard, Bedfordshire, LU7 8HT ENGLAND/01525-381638; FAX: 01525-851236

Sportsmen's Exchange & Western Gun Traders, Inc., 560 S. "C" St., Oxnard, CA 93030/805-483-1917

Spradlin's, 113 Arthur St., Pueblo, CO 81004/719-543-9462; FAX: 719-543-9465

Springfield, Inc., 420 W. Main St., Geneseo, IL 61254/309-944-5631; FAX: 309-944-3676

Springfield Sporters, Inc., RD 1, Penn Run, PA 15765/412-254-2626; FAX: 412-254-9173

Spyderco, 4565 N. Hwy. 93, P.O. Box 800, Golden, CO 80403/303-279-8383, 800-525-7770; FAX: 303-278-2229

SSK Industries, 590 Woodvue Lane, Wintersville, OH 43953/740-264-0176; FAX: 740-264-2257

Stackpole Books, 5067 Ritter Rd., Mechanicsburg, PA 17055-6921/717-796-0411; FAX: 717-796-0412

Stalker, Inc., P.O. Box 21, Fishermans Wharf Rd., Malakoff, TX 75148/903-489-1010

Stalwart Corporation, 76 Imperial, Unit A, Evanston, WY 82930/307-789-7687; FAX: 307-789-7688

Stanley Bullets, 2085 Heatheridge Ln., Reno, NV 89509

Star Ammunition, Inc., 5520 Rock Hampton Ct., Indianapolis, IN 46268/317-872-5840, 800-221-5927; FAX: 317-872-5847

Star Bonifacio Echeverria S.A., Torrekva 3, Eibar, SPAIN 20600/43-107340; FAX: 43-101524 (U.S. importer—E.A.A. Corp.; Interarms; P.S.M.G. Gun Co.)

Star Custom Bullets, P.O. Box 608, 468 Main St., Ferndale, CA 95536/707-786-9140; FAX: 707-786-9117

Star Machine Works, 418 10th Ave., San Diego, CA 92101/619-232-3216

Star Master-Match Bullets (See Star Ammunition, Inc.)

Star Reloading Co., Inc. (See Star Ammunition, Inc.)

Starke Bullet Company, P.O. Box 400, 605 6th St. NW, Cooperstown, ND 58425/888-797-3431

Starkey Labs, 6700 Washington Ave. S., Eden Prairie, MN 55344

Starkey's Gun Shop, 9430 McCombs, El Paso, TX 79924/915-751-3030

Stark's Bullet Mfg., 2580 Monroe St., Eugene, OR 97405

Starline, 1300 W. Henry St., Sedalia, MO 65301/816-827-6640; FAX: 816-827-6650

Starlight Training Center, Inc., Rt. 1, P.O. Box 88, Bronaugh, MO 64728/417-843-3555

Starnes Gunmaker, Ken, 32900 SW Laurelview Rd., Hillsboro, OR 97123/503-628-0705; FAX: 503-628-6005

Starr Trading Co., Jedediah, P.O. Box 2007, Farmington Hills, MI 48333/810-683-4343; FAX: 810-683-3282

Starrett Co., L.S., 121 Crescent St., Athol, MA 01331/617-249-3551

State Arms Gun Co., 815 S. Division St., Waunakee, WI 53597/608-849-5800

Steelman's Gun Shop, 10465 Beers Rd., Swartz Creek, MI 48473/810-735-4884

Steiner (See Pioneer Research, Inc.)

Steffens, Ron, 18396 Mariposa Creek Rd., Willits, CA 95490/707-485-0873

Stegall, James B., 26 Forest Rd., Wallkill, NY 12589

Steger, James R., 1131 Dorsey Pl., Plainfield, NJ 07062

Steves House of Guns, Rt. 1, Minnesota City, MN 55959/507-689-2573

Stewart Game Calls, Inc., Johnny, P.O. Box 7954, 5100 Fort Ave., Waco, TX 76714/817-772-3261; FAX: 817-772-3670

Stewart's Gunsmithing, P.O. Box 5854, Pietersburg North 0750, Transvaal, SOUTH AFRICA/01521-89401

Steyr Mannlicher AG & CO KG, Mannlicherstrasse 1, A-4400 Steyr, AUSTRIA /0043-7252-78621; FAX: 0043-7252-68621 (U.S. importer—GSI, Inc.; Nygord Precision Products)

STI International, 114 Halmar Cove, Georgetown, TX 78628/800-959-8201; FAX: 512-819-0465

Stiles Custom Guns, RD3, Box 1605, Homer City, PA 15748/724-479-9945

Stillwell, Robert, 421 Judith Ann Dr., Schertz, TX 78154

Stoeger Industries, 5 Mansard Ct., Wayne, NJ 07470/201-872-9500, 800-631-0722; FAX: 201-872-2230

Stoeger Publishing Co. (See Stoeger Industries)

Stone Enterprises Ltd., Rt. 609, P.O. Box 335, Wicomico Church, VA 22579/804-580-5114; FAX: 804-580-8421

Stone Mountain Arms, 5988 Peachtree Corners E., Norcross, GA 30071/800-251-9412

Stoney Baroque Shooters Supply, John Richards, Rt. 2, Box 325, Bedford, KY 40006/502-255-7222

Stoney Point Products, Inc., P.O. Box 234, 1815 North Spring Street, New Ulm, MN 56073-0234/507-354-3360; FAX: 507-354-7236

Storage Tech, 1254 Morris Ave., N. Huntingdon, PA 15642/800-437-9393

Storey, Dale A. (See DGS, Inc.)

Storm, Gary, P.O. Box 5211, Richardson, TX 75083/214-385-0862

Stott's Creek Armory, Inc., 2526 S. 475W, Morgantown, IN 46160/317-878-5489; FAX: 317-878-9489

Stott's Creek Printers, 2526 S. 475W, Morgantown, IN 46160/317-878-5489

Stratco, Inc., P.O. Box 2270, Kalispell, MT 59901/406-755-1221; FAX: 406-755-1226

Strawbridge, Victor W., 6 Pineview Dr., Dover, NH 03820/603-742-0013

Streamlight, Inc., 1030 W. Germantown Pike, Norristown, PA 19403/215-631-0600; FAX: 610-631-0712

Strong Holster Co., 39 Grove St., Gloucester, MA 01930/508-281-3300; FAX: 508-281-6321

Strutz Rifle Barrels, Inc., W.C., P.O. Box 611, Eagle River, WI 54521/715-479-4766

Stuart, V. Pat, Rt.1, Box 447-S, Greenville, VA 24440/804-556-3845

Sturgeon Valley Sporters, K. Ide, P.O. Box 283, Vanderbilt, MI 49795/517-983-4338

Sturm, Ruger & Co., Inc., 200 Ruger Rd., Prescott, AZ 86301/520-541-8820; FAX: 520-541-8850

"Su-Press-On," Inc., P.O. Box 09161, Detroit, MI 48209/313-842-4222 7:30-11p.m. Mon-Thurs.

Sullivan, David S. (See Westwind Rifles, Inc.)

Summit Specialties, Inc., P.O. Box 786, Decatur, AL 35602/205-353-0634; FAX: 205-353-9818

Sundance Industries, Inc., 25163 W. Avenue Stanford, Valencia, CA 91355/805-257-4807

Sunny Hill Enterprizes, Inc., W1790 Cty. HHH, Malone, WI 53049/414-795-4822

Sun Welding Safe Co., 290 Easy St. No.3, Simi Valley, CA 93065/805-584-6678, 800-729-SAFE; FAX: 805-584-6169

Surecase Co., The, 233 Wilshire Blvd., Ste. 900, Santa Monica, CA 90401/800-92ARMLOC

Sure-Shot Game Calls, Inc., P.O. Box 816, 6835 Capitol, Groves, TX 77619/409-962-1636; FAX: 409-962-5465

Survival Arms, Inc., P.O. Box 965, Orange, CT 06477/203-924-6533; FAX: 203-924-2581

Svon Corp., 280 Eliot St., Ashland, MA 01721/508-881-8852

Swampfire Shop, The (See Peterson Gun Shop, Inc., A.W.)

Swann, D.J., 5 Orsova Close, Eltham North, Vic. 3095, AUSTRALIA/03-431-0323

Swanndri New Zealand, 152 Elm Ave., Burlingame, CA 94010/415-347-6158

SwaroSports, Inc. (See J‰gerSport, Ltd.)

Swarovski Optik North America Ltd., One Wholesale Way, Cranston, RI 02920/401-946-2220, 800-426-3089; FAX: 401-946-2587

Sweet Home, Inc., P.O. Box 900, Orrville, OH 44667-0900

Swenson's 45 Shop, A.D., P.O. Box 606, Fallbrook, CA 92028

Swift Bullet Co., P.O. Box 27, 201 Main St., Quinter, KS 67752/913-754-3959; FAX: 913-754-2359

Swift Instruments, Inc., 952 Dorchester Ave., Boston, MA 02125/617-436-2960; FAX: 617-436-3232

Swift River Gunworks, 450 State St., Belchertown, MA 01007/413-323-4052

Swiss Army Knives, Inc., 151 Long Hill Crossroads, 37 Canal St., Shelton, CT 06484/800-243-4032

Swivel Machine Works, Inc., 11 Monitor Hill Rd., Newtown, CT 06470/203-270-6343

Szweda, Robert (See RMS Custom Gunsmithing)

T

Tabler Marketing, 2554 Lincoln Blvd., Suite 555, Marina Del Rey, CA 90291/818-755-4565; FAX: 818-755-0972

TacStar Industries, Inc., 218 Justin Drive, P.O. Box 70, Cottonwood, AZ 86326/602-639-0072; FAX: 602-634-8781

TacTell, Inc., P.O. Box 5654, Maryville, TN 37802/615-982-7855; FAX: 615-558-8294

Taconic Firearms Ltd., Perry Lane, PO Box 553, Cambridge, NY 12816/518-677-2704; FAX: 518-677-5974

Tactical Defense Institute, 574 Miami Bluff Ct., Loveland, OH 45140/513-677-8229

Talbot QD Mounts, 2210 E. Grand Blanc Rd., Grand Blanc, MI 48439-8113/810-695-2497

Talley, Dave, P.O. Box 821, Glenrock, WY 82637/307-436-8724, 307-436-9315

Talmage, William G., 10208 N. County Rd. 425 W., Brazil, IN 47834/812-442-0804

Talon Mfg. Co., Inc., 621 W. King St., Martinsburg, WV 25401/304-264-9714; FAX: 304-264-9725

Tamarack Products, Inc., P.O. Box 625, Wauconda, IL 60084/708-526-9333; FAX: 708-526-9353

Tanfoglio Fratelli S.r.l., via Valtrompia 39, 41, 25068 Gardone V.T., Brescia, ITALY/30-8910361; FAX: 30-8910183 (U.S. importer—E.A.A. Corp.)

Tanglefree Industries, 1261 Heavenly Dr., Martinez, CA 94553/800-982-4868; FAX: 510-825-3874

Tank's Rifle Shop, P.O. Box 474, Fremont, NE 68026-0474/402-727-1317; FAX: 402-721-2573

Tanner (See U.S. importer—Mandall Shooting Supplies, Inc.)

Taracorp Industries, Inc., 1200 Sixteenth St., Granite City, IL 62040/618-451-4400

Tar-Hunt Custom Rifles, Inc., RR3, P.O. Box 572, Bloomsburg, PA 17815-9351/717-784-6368; FAX: 717-784-6368

Tarnhelm Supply Co., Inc., 431 High St., Boscawen, NH 03303/603-796-2551; FAX: 603-796-2918

Tasco Sales, Inc., 7600 NW 26th St., Miami, FL 33122-1494/305-591-3670; FAX: 305-592-5895

Taurus Firearms, Inc., 16175 NW 49th Ave., Miami, FL 33014/305-624-1115; FAX: 305-623-7506

Taurus International Firearms (See U.S. importer—Taurus Firearms, Inc.)

Taurus S.A., Forjas, Avenida Do Forte 511, Porto Alegre, RS BRAZIL 91360/55-51-347-4050; FAX: 55-51-347-3065

Taylor & Robbins, P.O. Box 164, Rixford, PA 16745/814-966-3233

Taylor's & Co., Inc., 304 Lenoir Dr., Winchester, VA 22603/540-722-2017; FAX: 540-722-2018

TCCI, P.O. Box 302, Phoenix, AZ 85001/602-237-3823; FAX: 602-237-3858

TCSR, 3998 Hoffman Rd., White Bear Lake, MN 55110-4626/800-328-5323; FAX: 612-429-0526

TDP Industries, Inc., 606 Airport Blvd., Doylestown, PA 18901/215-345-8687; FAX: 215-345-6057

Techni-Mec (See F.A.I.R. Techni-Mec s.n.c. di Isidoro Rizzini & C.)

Techno Arms (See U.S. importer—Auto-Ordnance Corp.)

Tecnolegno S.p.A., Via A. Locatelli, 6, 10, 24019 Zogno, ITALY/0345-55111; FAX: 0345-55155

Tele-Optics, 630 E. Rockland Rd., P.O. Box 6313, Libertyville, IL 60048/847-362-7757

Ten-Ring Precision, Inc., Alex B. Hamilton, 1449 Blue Crest Lane, San Antonio, TX 78232/210-494-3063; FAX: 210-494-3066

10-X Products Group, 2915 Lyndon B. Johnson Freeway, Suite 133, Dallas, TX 75234/972-243-4016, 800-433-2225; FAX: 972-243-4112

Tennessee Valley Mfg., P.O. Box 1175, Corinth, MS 38834/601-286-5014

Tepeco, P.O. Box 342, Friendswood, TX 77546/713-482-2702

Testing Systems, Inc., 220 Pegasus Ave., Northvale, NJ 07647

Teton Arms, Inc., P.O. Box 411, Wilson, WY 83014/307-733-3395

Tetra Gun Lubricants (See FTI, Inc.)

Texas Armory (See Bond Arms, Inc.)

Texas Longhorn Arms, Inc., 5959 W. Loop South, Suite 424, Bellaire, TX 77401/713-660-6323; FAX: 713-660-0493

Texas Platers Supply Co., 2453 W. Five Mile Parkway, Dallas, TX 75233/214-330-7168

T.F.C. S.p.A., Via G. Marconi 118, B, Villa Carcina, Brescia 25069, ITALY/030-881271; FAX: 030-881826

Theis, Terry, HC 63 Box 213, Harper, TX 78631/830-864-4438

Theoben Engineering, Stephenson Road, St. Ives, Huntingdon, Cambs., PE17 4WJ ENGLAND/011-0480-461718

Thiewes, George W., 14329 W. Parada Dr., Sun City West, AZ 85375

Things Unlimited, 235 N. Kimbau, Casper, WY 82601/307-234-5277

Thirion Gun Engraving, Denise, P.O. Box 408, Graton, CA 95444/707-829-1876

Thomas, Charles C., 2600 S. First St., Springfield, IL 62794/217-789-8980; FAX: 217-789-9130

Thompson, Norm, 18905 NW Thurman St., Portland, OR 97209

Thompson, Randall (See Highline Machine Co.)

Thompson Bullet Lube Co., P.O. Box 472343, Garland, TX 75047-2343/972-271-8063; FAX: 972-840-6743

Thompson/Center Arms, P.O. Box 5002, Rochester, NH 03866/603-332-2394; FAX: 603-332-5133

Thompson Precision, 110 Mary St., P.O. Box 251, Warren, IL 61087/815-745-3625

Thompson Target Technology, 618 Roslyn Ave., SW, Canton, OH 44710/216-453-7707; FAX: 216-478-4723

Thompson Tool Mount (See TTM)

3-D Ammunition & Bullets, 112 W. Plum St., P.O. Box J, Doniphan, NE 68832/402-845-2285, 800-255-6712; FAX: 402-845-6546

300 Below Services (See Cryo-Accurizing)

300 Gunsmith Service, Inc., at Cherry Creek State Park Shooting Center, 12500 E. Belleview Ave./Englewood, CO 80111 303-690-3300

3-Ten Corp., P.O. Box 269, Feeding Hills, MA 01030/413-789-2086; FAX: 413-789-1549

T.H.U. Enterprises, Inc., P.O. Box 418, Lederach, PA 19450/215-256-1665; FAX: 215-256-9718

Thunden Ranch, HCR1, Box 53, Mt. Home, TX 78058/830-640-3138

Thunder Mountain Arms, P.O. Box 593, Oak Harbor, WA 98277/206-679-4657; FAX: 206-675-1114

Thunderbird Cartridge Co., Inc. (See TCCI)

Thurston Sports, Inc., RD 3 Donovan Rd., Auburn, NY 13021/315-253-0966

Tiger-Hunt Gunstocks, Box 379, Beaverdale, PA 15921/814-472-5161

Tikka (See U.S. importer—Stoeger Industries)

Timber Heirloom Products, 618 Roslyn Ave. SW, Canton, OH 44710/216-453-7707; FAX: 216-478-4723

Time Precision, Inc., 640 Federal Rd., Brookfield, CT 06804/203-775-8343

Timney Mfg., Inc., 3065 W. Fairmont Ave., Phoenix, AZ 85017/602-274-2999; FAX: 602-241-0361

Tink's Safariland Hunting Corp., P.O. Box 244, 1140 Monticello Rd., Madison, GA 30650/706-342-4915; FAX: 706-342-7568

Tinks & Ben Lee Hunting Products (See Wellington Outdoors)

Tioga Engineering Co., Inc., P.O. Box 913, 13 Cone St., Wellsboro, PA 16901/717-724-3533, 717-662-3347

Tippman Pneumatics, Inc., 3518 Adams Center Rd., Fort Wayne, IN 46806/219-749-6022; FAX: 219-749-6619

Tirelli, Snc Di Tirelli Primo E.C., Via Matteotti No. 359, Gardone V.T., Brescia, ITALY 25063/030-8912819; FAX: 030-832240

Titus, Daniel, Shooting Specialties, 119 Morlyn Ave., Bryn Mawr, PA 19010-3737/215-525-8829

TMI Products (See Haselbauer Products, Jerry)

TM Stockworks, 6355 Maplecrest Rd., Fort Wayne, IN 46835/219-485-5389

Tom's Gun Repair, Thomas G. Ivanoff, 76-6 Rt. Southfork Rd., Cody, WY 82414/307-587-6949

Tom's Gunshop, 3601 Central Ave., Hot Springs, AR 71913/501-624-3856

Tombstone Smoke`n'Deals, 3218 East Bell Road, Phoenix, AZ 85032/602-905-7013; Fax: 602-443-1998

Tonoloway Tack Drives, HCR 81, Box 100, Needmore, PA 17238

Tooley Custom Rifles, 516 Creek Meadow Dr., Gastonia, NC 28054/704-864-7525

Top-Line USA, Inc., 7920-28 Hamilton Ave., Cincinnati, OH 45231/513-522-2992, 800-346-6699; FAX: 513-522-0916

Torel, Inc., 1708 N. South St., P.O. Box 592, Yoakum, TX 77995/512-293-2341; FAX: 512-293-3413

Totally Dependable Products (See TDP Industries, Inc.)

TOZ (See U.S. importer—Nygord Precision Products)

TR Metals Corp., 1 Pavilion Ave., Riverside, NJ 08075/609-461-9000; FAX: 609-764-6340

Track of the Wolf, Inc., P.O. Box 6, Osseo, MN 55369-0006/612-424-2500; FAX: 612-424-9860

TracStar Industries, Inc., 218 Justin Dr., Cottonwood, AZ 86326/520-639-0072; FAX: 520-634-8781

Tradewinds, Inc., P.O. Box 1191, 2339-41 Tacoma Ave. S., Tacoma, WA 98401/206-272-4887

Traditions, Inc., P.O. Box 776, 1375 Boston Post Rd., Old Saybrook, CT 06475/860-388-4656; FAX: 860-388-4657

Trafalgar Square, P.O. Box 257, N. Pomfret, VT 05053/802-457-1911

Traft Gunshop, P.O. Box 1078, Buena Vista, CO 81211

TrailTimer Co., 1992-A Suburban Ave., P.O. Box 19722, St. Paul, MN 55119/612-738-0925

Trail Visions, 5800 N. Ames Terrace, Glendale, WI 53209/414-228-1328

Trammco, 839 Gold Run Rd., Boulder, CO 80302

Trappers Trading, P.O. Box 26946, Austin, TX 78755/800-788-9334

Trax America, Inc., P.O. Box 898, 1150 Eldridge, Forrest City, AR 72335/501-633-0410, 800-232-2327; FAX: 501-633-4788

Treadlok Gun Safe, Inc., 1764 Granby St. NE, Roanoke, VA 24012/800-729-8732, 703-982-6881; FAX: 703-982-1059

Treemaster, P.O. Box 247, Guntersville, AL 35976/205-878-3597

Treso, Inc., P.O. Box 4640, Pagosa Springs, CO 81157/303-731-2295

Trevallion Gunstocks, 9 Old Mountain Rd., Cape Neddick, ME 03902/207-361-1130

de Treville & Co., Stan, 4129 Normal St., San Diego, CA 92103/619-298-3393

Trico Plastics, 590 S. Vincent Ave., Azusa, CA 91702

Trigger Lock Division/Central Specialties Ltd., 1122 Silver Lake Road, Cary, IL 60013/847-639-3900; FAX: 847-639-3972

Trijicon, Inc., 49385 Shafer Ave., P.O. Box 930059, Wixom, MI 48393-0059/810-960-7700; FAX: 810-960-7725

Trilux Inc., P.O. Box 24608, Winston-Salem, NC 27114/910-659-9438; FAX: 910-768-7720

Trinidad State Junior College, Gunsmithing Dept., 600 Prospect St., Trinidad, CO 81082/719-846-5631; FAX: 719-846-5667

Triple-K Mfg. Co., Inc., 2222 Commercial St., San Diego, CA 92113/619-232-2066; FAX: 619-232-7675

Tristar Sporting Arms, Ltd., 1814-16 Linn St., P.O. Box 7496, N. Kansas City, MO 64116/816-421-1400; FAX: 816-421-4182

Trius Products, Inc., P.O. Box 25, 221 S. Miami Ave., Cleves, OH 45002/513-941-5682; FAX: 513-941-7970

Trooper Walsh, 2393 N. Edgewood St., Arlington, VA 22207

Trophy Bonded Bullets, Inc., 900 S. Loop W., Suite 190, Houston, TX 77054/713-645-4499, 888-308-3006; FAX: 713-741-6393

Trotman, Ken, 135 Ditton Walk, Unit 11, Cambridge CB5 8PY, ENGLAND/01223-211030; FAX: 01223-212317

Tru-Balance Knife Co., P.O. Box 140555, Grand Rapids, MI 49514/616-453-3679

Tru-Square Metal Prods., Inc., 640 First St. SW, P.O. Box 585, Auburn, WA 98071/206-833-2310; FAX: 206-833-2349

True Flight Bullet Co., 5581 Roosevelt St., Whitehall, PA 18052/610-262-7630; FAX: 610-262-7806

Trulock Tool, Broad St., Whigham, GA 31797/912-762-4678

TTM, 1550 Solomon Rd., Santa Maria, CA 93455/805-934-1281

Tucker, James C., P.O. Box 575, Raymond, NH 03077

Tucson Mold, Inc., 930 S. Plumer Ave., Tucson, AZ 85719/520-792-1075; FAX: 520-792-1075

Turkish Firearms Corp., 522 W. Maple St., Allentown, PA 18101/610-821-8660; FAX: 610-821-9049

Turnbull Restoration, Doug, 6426 County Rd. 30, P.O. Box 471, Bloomfield, NY 14469/716-657-6338; WEB: http://gunshop.com/dougt.htm

Tuttle, Dale, 4046 Russell Rd., Muskegon, MI 49445/616-766-2250

Twin Pine Armory, P.O. Box 58, Hwy. 6, Adna, WA 98522/360-748-4590; FAX: 360-748-1802

Tyler Manufacturing & Distributing, 3804 S. Eastern, Oklahoma City, OK 73129/405-677-1487, 800-654-8415

U

Uberti USA, Inc., P.O. Box 469, Lakeville, CT 06039/860-435-8068; FAX: 860-435-8146

Uberti, Aldo, Casella Postale 43, I-25063 Gardone V.T., ITALY/ (U.S. importers—American Arms, Inc.; Cabela's; Cimarron Arms; Dixie Gun Works; EMF Co., Inc.; Forgett Jr., Valmore J.; IAR, Inc.; Navy Arms Co; Taylor's & Co., Inc.; Uberti USA, Inc.)

UFA, Inc., 6927 E. Grandview Dr., Scottsdale, AZ 85254/800-616-2776

Ugartechea S.A., Ignacio, Chonta 26, Eibar, SPAIN 20600/43-121257; FAX: 43-121669 (U.S. importer—Aspen Outfitting Co.; The Gun Shop; Bill Hanus Birdguns; Lion Country Supply)

Ultimate Accuracy, 121 John Shelton Rd., Jacksonville, AR 72076/501-985-2530

Ultra Dot Distribution, 2316 N.E. 8th Rd., Ocala, FL 34470

Ultra Light Arms, Inc., P.O. Box 1270, 214 Price St., Granville, WV 26505/304-599-5687; FAX: 304-599-5687

Ultralux (See U.S. importer—Keng's Firearms Specialty, Inc.)

UltraSport Arms, Inc., 1955 Norwood Ct., Racine, WI 53403/414-554-3237; FAX: 414-554-9731

Uncle Bud's, HCR 81, Box 100, Needmore, PA 17238/717-294-6000; FAX: 717-294-6005

Uncle Mike's (See Michaels of Oregon Co.)

Unertl Optical Co., Inc., John, 308 Clay Ave., P.O. Box 818, Mars, PA 16046-0818/412-625-3810

Unique/M.A.P.F., 10, Les Allees, 64700 Hendaye, FRANCE 64700/33-59 20 71 93 (U.S. importer—Nygord Precision Products)

UniTec, 1250 Bedford SW, Canton, OH 44710/216-452-4017

United Binocular Co., 9043 S. Western Ave., Chicago, IL 60620

United Cutlery Corp., 1425 United Blvd., Sevierville, TN 37876-1549/423-428-2532, 800-548-0835; FAX: 423-428-2267

United States Ammunition Co. (See USAC)

United States Optics Technologies, Inc., 5900 Dale St., Buena Park, CA 90621/714-994-4901; FAX: 714-994-4904

United States Products Co., 518 Melwood Ave., Pittsburgh, PA 15213-1136/412-621-2130; FAX: 412-621-8740

Unmussig Bullets, D.L., 7862 Brentford Drive, Richmond, VA 23225/804-320-1165

Upper Missouri Trading Co., 304 Harold St., Crofton, NE 68730/402-388-4844

USAC, 4500-15th St. East, Tacoma, WA 98424/206-922-7589

U.S.A. Magazines, Inc., P.O. Box 39115, Downey, CA 90241/800-872-2577

USA Sporting Inc., 1330 N. Glassell, Unit M, Orange, CA 92667/714-538-3109, 800-538-3109; FAX: 714-538-1334

U.S. Patent Fire Arms, No. 25-55 Van Dyke Ave., Hartford, CT 06106/800-877-2832; FAX: 800-644-7265

U.S. Repeating Arms Co., Inc., 275 Winchester Ave., Morgan, UT 84050-9333/801-876-3440; FAX: 801-876-3737

Utica Cutlery Co., 820 Noyes St., Utica, NY 13503/315-733-4663; FAX: 315-733-6602

Uvalde Machine & Tool, P.O. Box 1604, Uvalde, TX 78802

V

Valade Engraving, Robert, 931 3rd Ave., Seaside, OR 97138/503-738-7672

Valmet (See Tikka/U.S. importer—Stoeger Industries)

Valor Corp., 5555 NW 36th Ave., Miami, FL 33142/305-633-0127; FAX: 305-634-4536

Valtro USA Inc., 1281 Andersen Dr., San Rafael, CA 94901/415-256-2575; FAX: 415-256-2576

Van Epps, Milton (See Van's Gunsmith Service)

Van's Gunsmith Service, 224 Route 69-A, Parish, NY 13131/315-625-7251

Van Gorden & Son, Inc., C.S., 1815 Main St., Bloomer, WI 54724/715-568-2612

Van Horn, Gil, P.O. Box 207, Llano, CA 93544

Van Patten, J.W., P.O. Box 145, Foster Hill, Milford, PA 18337/717-296-7069

Vancini, Carl (See Bestload, Inc.)

Vann Custom Bullets, 330 Grandview Ave., Novato, CA 94947

Varner's Service, 102 Shaffer Rd., Antwerp, OH 45813/419-258-8631

Vega Tool Co., c/o T.R. Ross, 4865 Tanglewood Ct., Boulder, CO 80301/303-530-0174

Venco Industries, Inc. (See Shooter's Choice)

Venus Industries, P.O. Box 246, Sialkot-1, PAKISTAN/FAX: 92 432 85579

Verney-Carron, B.P. 72, 54 Boulevard Thiers, 42002 St. Etienne Cedex 1, FRANCE/33-477791500; FAX: 33-477790702; E-MAIL: Verney-Carron@mail.com

Versa-Pod (See Keng's Firearms Specialty, Inc.

Vest, John, P.O. Box 1552, Susanville, CA 96130/916-257-7228

VibraShine, Inc., P.O. Box 577, Taylorsville, MS 39168/601-785-9854; FAX: 601-785-9874

Vibra-Tek Co., 1844 Arroya Rd., Colorado Springs, CO 80906/719-634-8611; FAX: 719-634-6886

Vic's Gun Refinishing, 6 Pineview Dr., Dover, NH 03820-6422/603-742-0013

Victory USA, P.O. Box 1021, Pine Bush, NY 12566/914-744-2060; FAX: 914-744-5181

Vihtavuori Oy, FIN-41330 Vihtavuori, FINLAND/358-41-3779211; FAX: 358-41-3771643

Vihtavuori Oy/Kaltron-Pettibone, 1241 Ellis St., Bensenville, IL 60106/708-350-1116; FAX: 708-350-1606

Viking Leathercraft, Inc., 1579A Jayken Way, Chula Vista, CA 91911/800-262-6666; FAX: 619-429-8268

Viking Video Productions, P.O. Box 251, Roseburg, OR 97470

Vincent's Shop, 210 Antoinette, Fairbanks, AK 99701

Vintage Arms, Inc., 6003 Saddle Horse, Fairfax, VA 22030/703-968-0779; FAX: 703-968-0780

Vintage Industries, Inc., 781 Big Tree Dr., Longwood, FL 32750/407-831-8949; FAX: 407-831-5346

Viper Bullet and Brass Works, 11 Brock St., Box 582, Norwich, Ontario, CANADA N0J 1P0

Viramontez, Ray, 601 Springfield Dr., Albany, GA 31707/912-432-9683

Visible Impact Targets, Rts. 5 & 20, E. Bloomfield, NY 14443/716-657-6161; FAX: 716-657-5405

Vitt/Boos, 2178 Nichols Ave., Stratford, CT 06497/203-375-6859

Voere-KGH m.b.H., P.O. Box 416, A-6333 Kufstein, Tirol, AUSTRIA/0043-5372-62547; FAX: 0043-5372-65752 (U.S. importers— J‰agerSport, Ltd.)

Volquartsen Custom Ltd., 24276 240th Street, P.O. Box 271, Carroll, IA 51401/712-792-4238; FAX: 712-792-2542

Vom Hoffe (See Old Western Scrounger, Inc., The)

Von Minden Gunsmithing Services, 2403 SW 39 Terrace, Cape Coral, FL 33914/813-542-8946

Vorhes, David, 3042 Beecham St., Napa, CA 94558/707-226-9116

Vortek Products, Inc., P.O. Box 871181, Canton, MI 48187-6181/313-397-5656; FAX:313-397-5656

VSP Publishers (See Heritage/VSP Gun Books)

Vulpes Ventures, Inc., Fox Cartridge Division, P.O. Box 1363, Bolingbrook, IL 60440-7363/708-759-1229

W

W. Square Enterprises, 9826 Sagedale, Houston, TX 77089/713-484-0935; FAX: 281-484-0935

Wagoner, Vernon G., 2325 E. Encanto, Mesa, AZ 85213/602-835-1307

Wakina by Pic, 24813 Alderbrook Dr., Santa Clarita, CA 91321/800-295-8194

Waldron, Herman, Box 475, 80 N. 17th St., Pomeroy, WA 99347/509-843-1404

Walker Arms Co., Inc., 499 County Rd. 820, Selma, AL 36701/334-872-6231; FAX: 334-872-6262

Walker Mfg., Inc., 8296 S. Channel, Harsen's Island, MI 48028

Walker Co., B.B., P.O. Box 1167, 414 E. Dixie Dr., Asheboro, NC 27203/910-625-1380; FAX: 910-625-8125

Wallace, Terry, 385 San Marino, Vallejo, CA 94589/707-642-7041

Waller & Son, Inc., W., 2221 Stoney Brook Road, Grantham, NH 03753-7706/603-863-4177

Walls Industries, Inc., P.O. Box 98, 1905 N. Main, Cleburne, TX 76031/817-645-4366; FAX: 817-645-7946

Walnut Factory, The, 235 West Rd. No. 1, Portsmouth, NH 03801/603-436-2225; FAX: 603-433-7003

Walt's Custom Leather, Walt Whinnery, 1947 Meadow Creek Dr., Louisville, KY 40218/502-458-4361

Walters Industries, 6226 Park Lane, Dallas, TX 75225/214-691-6973

Walters, John, 500 N. Avery Dr., Moore, OK 73160/405-799-0376

Walther GmbH, Carl, B.P. 4325, D-89033 Ulm, GERMANY/ (U.S. importer— Champion's Choice; Interarms; P.S.M.G. Gun Co.)

WAMCO, Inc., Mingo Loop, P.O. Box 337, Oquossoc, ME 04964-0337/207-864-3344

WAMCO—New Mexico, P.O. Box 205, Peralta, NM 87042-0205/505-869-0826

Ward & Van Valkenburg, 114 32nd Ave. N., Fargo, ND 58102/701-232-2351

Ward Machine, 5620 Lexington Rd., Corpus Christi, TX 78412/512-992-1221

Wardell Precision Handguns Ltd., 48851 N. Fig Springs Rd., New River, AZ 85027-8513/602-465-7995

Warenski, Julie, 590 E. 500 N., Richfield, UT 84701/801-896-5319; FAX: 801-896-5319

Warne Manufacturing Co., 9039 SE Jannsen Rd., Clackamas, OR 97015/503-657-5590; FAX: 503-657-5695

Warren & Sweat Mfg. Co., P.O. Box 350440, Grand Island, FL 32784/904-669-3166; FAX: 904-669-7272

Warren Muzzleloading Co., Inc., Hwy. 21 North, P.O. Box 100, Ozone, AR 72854/501-292-3268

Warren, Kenneth W. (See Mountain States Engraving)

Washita Mountain Whetstone Co., P.O. Box 378, Lake Hamilton, AR 71951/501-525-3914

Wasmundt's Gun Shop, 680 Main St., Fossil, OR 97830-0551/541-763-3041

WASP Shooting Systems, Rt. 1, Box 147, Lakeview, AR 72642/501-431-5606

Waterfield Sports, Inc., 13611 Country Lane, Burnsville, MN 55337/612-435-8339

Watson Bros., 39 Redcross Way, London Bridge, London, United Kingdom, SE1 1HG/FAX: 44-171-403-3367

Watson Trophy Match Bullets, 2404 Wade Hampton Blvd., Greenville, SC 29615/864-244-7948; 941-635-7948 (Florida)

Wayne Firearms for Collectors and Investors, James, 2608 N. Laurent, Victoria, TX 77901/512-578-1258; FAX: 512-578-3559

Wayne Specialty Services, 260 Waterford Drive, Florissant, MO 63033/413-831-7083

WD-40 Co., 1061 Cudahy Pl., San Diego, CA 92110/619-275-1400; FAX: 619-275-5823

Weatherby, Inc., 3100 El Camino Real, Atascadero, CA 93422/805-466-1767; FAX: 805-466-2527

Weaver Arms Corp. Gun Shop, RR 3, P.O. Box 266, Bloomfield, MO 63825-9528

Weaver Products, P.O. Box 39, Onalaska, WI 54650/800-648-9624, 608-781-5800; FAX: 608-781-0368

Weaver Scope Repair Service, 1121 Larry Mahan Dr., Suite B, El Paso, TX 79925/915-593-1005

Webb, Bill, 6504 North Bellefontaine, Kansas City, MO 64119/816-453-7431

Weber & Markin Custom Gunsmiths, 4-1691 Powick Rd., Kelowna, B.C. CANADA V1X 4L1/250-762-7575; FAX: 250-861-3655

Weber Jr., Rudolf, P.O. Box 160106, D-5650 Solingen, GERMANY/0212-592136

Webley and Scott Ltd., Frankley Industrial Park, Tay Rd., Rubery, Rednal, Birmingham B45 0PA, ENGLAND/011-021-453-1864; FAX: 021-457-7846 (U.S. importer—Beeman Precision Airguns; Groenewold, John)

Webster Scale Mfg. Co., P.O. Box 188, Sebring, FL 33870/813-385-6362

Weems, Cecil, P.O. Box 657, Mineral Wells, TX 76067/817-325-1462

Weigand Combat Handguns, Inc., 685 South Main St., Mountain Top, PA 18707/717-868-8358; FAX: 717-868-5218

Weihrauch KG, Hermann, Industriestrasse 11, 8744 Mellrichstadt, GERMANY/ 09776-497-498 (U.S. importers—Beeman Precision Airguns; E.A.A. Corp.)

Weisz Parts, P.O. Box 20038, Columbus, OH 43220-0038/614-45-70-500; FAX: 614-846-8585

Welch, Sam, CVSR 2110, Moab, UT 84532/801-259-8131

Wellington Outdoors, P.O. Box 244, 1140 Monticello Rd., Madison, GA 30650/706-342-4915; FAX: 706-342-7568

Wells Creek Knife & Gun Works, 32956 State Hwy. 38, Scottsburg, OR 97473/541-587-4202; FAX: 541-587-4223

Wells Custom Gunsmith, R.A., 3452 1st Ave., Racine, WI 53402/414-639-5223

Wells, Fred F., Wells Sport Store, 110 N. Summit St., Prescott, AZ 86301/520-445-3655

Wells, Rachel, 110 N. Summit St., Prescott, AZ 86301/520-445-3655

Welsh, Bud, 80 New Road, E. Amherst, NY 14051/716-688-6344

Wenig Custom Gunstocks, Inc., 103 N. Market St., P.O. Box 249, Lincoln, MO 65338/816-547-3334; FAX: 816-547-2881

Werner, Carl, P.O. Box 492, Littleton, CO 80160

Werth, T.W., 1203 Woodlawn Rd., Lincoln, IL 62656/217-732-1300

Wescombe, Bill (See North Star West)

Wessinger Custom Guns & Engraving, 268 Limestone Rd., Chapin, SC 29036/803-345-5677

Wesson Firearms, Dan, 119 Kemper Lane, Norwich, NY 13815/607-336-1174; FAX: 607-336-2730

West, Jack L., 1220 W. Fifth, P.O. Box 427, Arlington, OR 97812

Western Cutlery (See Camillus Cutlery Co.)

Western Design (See Alpha Gunsmith Division)

Western Gunstock Mfg. Co., 550 Valencia School Rd., Aptos, CA 95003/408-688-5884

Western Missouri Shooters Alliance, P.O. Box 11144, Kansas City, MO 64119/816-597-3950; FAX: 816-229-7350

Western Munitions (See North American Munitions)

Western Nevada West Coast Bullets, 2307 W. Washington St., Carson City, NV 89703/702-246-3941; FAX: 702-246-0836

Westley Richards Agency USA (U.S. importer for Westley Richards & Co.)

Westley Richards & Co., 40 Grange Rd., Birmingham, ENGLAND B29 6AR/010-214722953 (U.S. importer—Westley Richards Agency USA)

Westrom, John (See Precision Metal Finishing)

Westwind Rifles, Inc., David S. Sullivan, P.O. Box 261, 640 Briggs St., Erie, CO 80516/303-828-3823

Weyer International, 2740 Nebraska Ave., Toledo, OH 43607/419-534-2020; FAX: 419-534-2697

Whildin & Sons Ltd., E.H., RR2, Box 119, Tamaqua, PA 18252/717-668-6743; FAX: 717-668-6745

Whinnery, Walt (See Walt's Custom Leather)

Whiscombe (See U.S. importer—Pelaire Products)

White Flyer Targets, 124 River Road, Middlesex, NJ 08846/908-469-0100, 602-972-7528 (Export); FAX: 908-469-9692, 602-530-3360 (Export)

White Laboratory, Inc., H.P., 3114 Scarboro Rd., Street, MD 21154/410-838-6550; FAX: 410-838-2802

White Owl Enterprises, 2583 Flag Rd., Abilene, KS 67410/913-263-2613; FAX: 913-263-2613

White Pine Photographic Services, Hwy. 60, General Delivery, Wilno, Ontario K0J 2N0 CANADA/613-756-3452

White Rock Tool & Die, 6400 N. Brighton Ave., Kansas City, MO 64119/816-454-0478

White Muzzleloading Systems, 25 E. Hwy. 40, Suite 330-12, Roosevelt, UT 84066/801-722-5996; FAX: 801-722-5909

White Shooting Systems (See White Muzzleloading Systems)

Whitestone Lumber Corp., 148-02 14th Ave., Whitestone, NY 11357/718-746-4400; FAX: 718-767-1748

Whitetail Design & Engineering Ltd., 9421 E. Mannsiding Rd., Clare, MI 48617/517-386-3932

Wichita Arms, Inc., 923 E. Gilbert, P.O. Box 11371, Wichita, KS 67211/316-265-0661; FAX: 316-265-0760

Wick, David E., 1504 Michigan Ave., Columbus, IN 47201/812-376-6960

Widener's Reloading & Shooting Supply, Inc., P.O. Box 3009 CRS, Johnson City, TN 37602/615-282-6786; FAX: 615-282-6651

Wideview Scope Mount Corp., 13535 S. Hwy. 16, Rapid City, SD 57702/605-341-3220; FAX: 605-341-9142

Wiebe, Duane, 33604 Palm Dr., Burlington, WI 53105-9260

Wiest, M.C., 10737 Dutchtown Rd., Knoxville, TN 37932/423-966-4545

Wilcox All-Pro Tools & Supply, 4880 147th St., Montezuma, IA 50171/515-623-3138; FAX: 515-623-3104

Wild Bill's Originals, P.O. Box 13037, Burton, WA 98013/206-463-5738; FAX: 206-465-5925

Wild West Guns, 7521 Old Seward Hwy, Unit A, Anchorage, AK 99518/800-992-4570, 907-344-4500; FAX: 907-344-4005

Wilderness Sound Products Ltd., 4015 Main St. A, Springfield, OR 97478/503-741-0263, 800-437-0006; FAX: 503-741-7648

Wildey, Inc., P.O. Box 475, Brookfield, CT 06804/203-355-9000; FAX: 203-354-7759

Wildlife Research Center, Inc., 1050 McKinley St., Anoka, MN 55303/612-427-3350, 800-USE-LURE; FAX: 612-427-8354

Wilkinson Arms, 26884 Pearl Rd., Parma, ID 83660/208-722-6771; FAX: 208-722-5197

Will-Burt Co., 169 S. Main, Orrville, OH 44667

William's Gun Shop, Ben, 1151 S. Cedar Ridge, Duncanville, TX 75137/214-780-1807

Williams Bullet Co., J.R., 2008 Tucker Rd., Perry, GA 31069/912-987-0274

Williams Gun Sight Co., 7389 Lapeer Rd., Box 329, Davison, MI 48423/810-653-2131, 800-530-9028; FAX: 810-658-2140

Williams Mfg. of Oregon, 110 East B St., Drain, OR 97435/503-836-7461; FAX: 503-836-7245

Williams Shootin' Iron Service, The Lynx-Line, 8857 Bennett Hill Rd., Central Lake, MI 49622/616-544-6615

Williamson Precision Gunsmithing, 117 W. Pipeline, Hurst, TX 76053/817-285-0064; FAX: 817-280-0044

Willow Bend, P.O. Box 203, Chelmsford, MA 01824/508-256-8508; FAX: 508-256-8508

Willson Safety Prods. Div., P.O. Box 622, Reading, PA 19603-0622/610-376-6161; FAX: 610-371-7725

Wilson Arms Co., The, 63 Leetes Island Rd., Branford, CT 06405/203-488-7297; FAX: 203-488-0135

Wilson Case, Inc., P.O. Box 1106, Hastings, NE 68902-1106/800-322-5493; FAX: 402-463-5276

Wilson, Inc., L.E., Box 324, 404 Pioneer Ave., Cashmere, WA 98815/509-782-1328; FAX: 509-782-7200

Wilson's Gun Shop, Box 578, Rt. 3, Berryville, AR 72616/870-545-3618; FAX: 870-545-3310

Winchester (See U.S. Repeating Arms Co., Inc.)

Winchester Div., Olin Corp., 427 N. Shamrock, E. Alton, IL 62024/618-258-3566; FAX: 618-258-3599

Winchester Press (See New Win Publishing, Inc.)

Winchester Sutler, Inc., The, 270 Shadow Brook Lane, Winchester, VA 22603/540-888-3595; FAX: 540-888-4632

Windish, Jim, 2510 Dawn Dr., Alexandria, VA 22306/703-765-1994

Windjammer Tournament Wads, Inc., 750 W. Hampden Ave. Suite 170, Englewood, CO 80110/303-781-6329

Wingshooting Adventures, 0-1845 W. Leonard, Grand Rapids, MI 49544/616-677-1980; FAX: 616-677-1986

Winkle Bullets, R.R. 1 Box 316, Heyworth, IL 61745

Winter, Robert M., P.O. Box 484, 42975-287th St., Menno, SD 57045/605-387-5322

Wise Guns, Dale, 333 W. Olmos Dr., San Antonio, TX 78212/210-828-3388

Wiseman and Co., Bill, P.O. Box 3427, Bryan, TX 77805/409-690-3456; FAX: 409-690-0156

Wolf's Western Traders, 40 E. Works, No. 3F, Sheridan, WY 82801/307-674-5352

Wolfe Publishing Co., 6471 Airpark Dr., Prescott, AZ 86301/520-445-7810, 800-899-7810; FAX: 520-778-5124

W.C. Wolff Co., P.O. Box 458, Newtown Square, PA 19073/610-359-9600, 800-545-0077; FAX: 610-359-9496; WEB: www.gunsprings.com

Wolverine Footwear Group, 9341 Courtland Dr. NE, Rockford, MI 49351/616-866-5500; FAX: 616-866-5658

Wood, Frank (See Classic Guns, Inc.)

Wood, Mel, P.O. Box 1255, Sierra Vista, AZ 85636/602-455-5541

Woodleigh (See Huntington Die Specialties)

Woods Wise Products, P.O. Box 681552, 2200 Bowman Rd., Franklin, TN 37068/800-735-8182; FAX: 615-726-2637

Woodstream, P.O. Box 327, Lititz, PA 17543/717-626-2125; FAX: 717-626-1912

Woodworker's Supply, 1108 North Glenn Rd., Casper, WY 82601/307-237-5354

Woolrich Inc., Mill St., Woolrich, PA 17701/800-995-1299; FAX: 717-769-6234/6259

Working Guns, 250 NW Country Club Lane, Albany, OR 97321/541-928-4391

World of Targets (See Birchwood Casey)

World Class Airguns, 2736 Morningstar Dr., Indianapolis, IN 46229/317-897-5548

World Trek, Inc., 7170 Turkey Creek Rd., Pueblo, CO 81007-1046/719-546-2121; FAX: 719-543-6886

Worthy Products, Inc., RR 1, P.O. Box 213, Martville, NY 13111/315-324-5298

Wosenitz VHP, Inc., Box 741, Dania, FL 33004/305-923-3748; FAX: 305-925-2217

Wostenholm (See Ibberson [Sheffield] Ltd., George)

Wright's Hardwood Gunstock Blanks, 8540 SE Kane Rd., Gresham, OR 97080/503-666-1705

W. Square Enterprises (See Load From A Disk)

WTA Manufacturing, Bill Wood, P.O. Box 164, Kit Carson, CO 80825/800-700-3054, 719-962-3570

Wyant Bullets, Gen. Del., Swan Lake, MT 59911

Wyant's Outdoor Products, Inc., P.O. Box B, Broadway, VA 22815

Wyoming Bonded Bullets, Box 91, Sheridan, WY 82801/307-674-8091

Wyoming Custom Bullets, 1626 21st St., Cody, WY 82414

Wyoming Knife Corp., 101 Commerce Dr., Ft. Collins, CO 80524/303-224-3454

X, Y

X-Spand Target Systems, 26-10th St. SE, Medicine Hat, AB T1A 1P7 CANADA/ 403-526-7997; FAX: 403-528-2362

Yankee Gunsmith, 2901 Deer Flat Dr., Copperas Cove, TX 76522/817-547-8433

Yavapai College, 1100 E. Sheldon St., Prescott, AZ 86301/602-776-2359; FAX: 602-776-2193

Yavapai Firearms Academy Ltd., P.O. Box 27290, Prescott Valley, AZ 86312/520-772-8262

Yearout, Lewis E. (See Montana Outfitters)

Yee, Mike, 29927 56 Pl. S., Auburn, WA 98001/206-839-3991

Yellowstone Wilderness Supply, P.O. Box 129, W. Yellowstone, MT 59758/406-646-7613

Yesteryear Armory & Supply, P.O. Box 408, Carthage, TN 37030

York M-1 Conversions, 803 Mill Creek Run, Plantersville, TX 77363/800-527-2881, 713-477-8442

Young, Paul A., RR 1 Box 694, Blowing Rock, NC 28605-9746

Young Country Arms, P.O. Box 3615, Simi Valley, CA 93093

Yukon Arms Classic Ammunition, 1916 Brooks, P.O. Box 223, Missoula, MT 59801/406-543-9614

Z

Z's Metal Targets & Frames, P.O. Box 78, South Newbury, NH 03255/603-938-2826

Zabala Hermanos S.A., P.O. Box 97, Eibar, SPAIN 20600/43-768085, 43-768076; FAX: 34-43-768201 (U.S. importer—American Arms, Inc.)

Zander's Sporting Goods, 7525 Hwy 154 West, Baldwin, IL 62217-9706/800-851-4373 ext. 200; FAX: 618-785-2320

Zanoletti, Pietro, Via Monte Gugielpo, 4, I-25063 Gardone V.T., ITALY/ (U.S. importer—Mandall Shooting Supplies, Inc.)

Zanotti Armor, Inc., 123 W. Lone Tree Rd., Cedar Falls, IA 50613/319-232-9650

Z-Coat Industrial Coatings, Inc., 3375 U.S. Hwy. 98 S. No. A, Lakeland, FL 33803-8365/813-665-1734

ZDF Import Export Inc., 2975 South 300 West, Salt Lake City, UT 84115/801-485-1012; FAX: 801-484-4363

Zeeryp, Russ, 1601 Foard Dr., Lynn Ross Manor, Morristown, TN 37814/615-586-2357

Zeiss Optical, Carl, 1015 Commerce St., Petersburg, VA 23803/800-388-2984; FAX: 804-733-4024

Zero Ammunition Co., Inc., 1601 22nd St. SE, P.O. Box 1188, Cullman, AL 35056-1188/800-545-9376; FAX: 205-739-4683

Ziegel Engineering, 2108 Lomina Ave., Long Beach, CA 90815/562-596-9481; FAX: 562-598-4734; Email: ZIEGEL@aol.com

Zim's Inc., 4370 S. 3rd West, Salt Lake City, UT 84107/801-268-2505

Z-M Weapons, 203 South St., Bernardston, MA 01337

Zoli, Antonio, Via Zanardelli 39, Casier Postal 21, I-25063 Gardone V.T., ITALY

Zriny's Metal Targets (See Z's Metal Targets & Frames)

Zufall, Joseph F., P.O. Box 304, Golden, CO 80402-0304

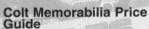

HUNTERS AND SHOOTING ENTHUSIASTS MUST HAVE THESE GUIDES

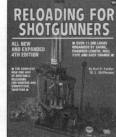